"In American Samoa, where I live, South Pacific [...] inventive island travelers. The best guidebook this [...]
—Robert Brock, THE COEVOLUTI[...]

"Stanley provides the reader with solid and up-[...] traditional and modern history, and contemporary *trends of every p[...]* islands in which even the most avid travel buff is likely to find himself."
—Norman Douglas, PACIFIC ISLANDS MONTHLY, Fiji

"The book is worth reading for its historical perspective alone, for the author is unafraid to approach such 'delicate issues' as nuclear testing and 'culture clash'—topics one would not normally find in Fielding's or Birnbaum's."
—Georgia Lee, RAPA NUI JOURNAL, California

". . . the information source most often recommended by young budget travelers . . . the cheapest and most interesting means to visit over 500 South Sea islands . . . for the adventurous there are suggested mountain climbs, jungle walks, cave explorations, river trips, camping, bicycle routes, skin diving and snorkeling locations. Among the most valuable points are ideas on how to get around the islands on your own, from money-saving freighter travel to island transportation systems. The South Pacific Handbook by David Stanley is well worth the investment."
—Lucy Izon, TORONTO STAR

"Frankly, we at Pacific Magazine have to say we couldn't get along without this book as a principal reference source . . . travelers and adventurers going to the South Pacific will find this is the only book they really need."
—Bud Bendix, PACIFIC MAGAZINE, Honolulu

"If you want to visit off-beat destinations and you only have a shoestring budget this soft-cover bible belongs in your backpack. The advice is specific and invaluable, the kind that takes the average traveler weeks to acquire."
—Ronn Ronck, STAR-BULLETIN & ADVERTISER, Honolulu

"This is not your usual travel guide . . . it is simply 'packed with information.' The compilers lace all the practical details (how to get there, where to stay, how much) with doses of well-reasoned opinion so that the book stands ahead of many travel guides in giving you a down-to-earth feeling for the places described."
—Phil Hanson, VANCOUVER SUN

SOUTH PACIFIC
HANDBOOK

I saw that island first when it was neither night nor morning. The moon was to the west, setting but still broad and bright. To the east, and right amid ships of the dawn, which was all pink, the daystar sparkled like a diamond. The land breeze blew in our faces, and smelt strong of wild lime and vanilla. . . . Here was a fresh experience . . . and the look of these woods and mountains, and the rare smell of them, renewed my blood.

—ROBERT LOUIS STEVENSON,
ISLAND NIGHTS

SOUTH PACIFIC

PACIFIC HANDBOOK

SIXTH EDITION

DAVID STANLEY

MOON
PUBLICATIONS INC.

SOUTH PACIFIC HANDBOOK
6TH EDITION

Published by
Moon Publications, Inc.
P.O. Box 3040
Chico, California 95927-3040, USA
tel. (916) 345-5473
fax (916) 345-6751

Printed by
Colorcraft Ltd., Hong Kong

ISBN: 1-56691-040-4

ISSN: 1085-2700

Editor: Valerie Sellers Blanton
Copy Editor: Nicole Revere
Production & Design: Karen McKinley
Line Drawings: Louise Foote and Diana Lasich Harper
Cartographer: Bob Race
Index: Deana Corbitt Shields

Front cover photo: Cloudbreak near Tavarua Island, Fiji, by Tom Servais
All photos by David Stanley unless otherwise noted.

Distributed in the U.S.A. and Canada by Publishers Group West
Printed in Hong Kong

Please send all comments,
corrections, additions,
amendments, and critiques to:

**SOUTH PACIFIC HANDBOOK
MOON PUBLICATIONS, INC.
P.O. BOX 3040
CHICO, CA 95927-3040, USA
e-mail: travel@moon.com**

Printing History
  1st edition — July, 1979
  2nd edition — January, 1982
    Reprinted — April, 1983
    Reprinted — April, 1984
  3rd edition — November, 1985
    Reprinted — July, 1986
    Reprinted — January, 1988
  4th edition — November, 1989
    Reprinted — January, 1992
  5th edition — July, 1993
    Reprinted — September, 1994
  6th edition — May, 1996

CONTENTS

CHARTS

MAPS

(continues on next page)

MAPS
(continued)

MAP SYMBOLS

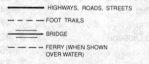

HIGHWAYS, ROADS, STREETS

FOOT TRAILS

BRIDGE

FERRY (WHEN SHOWN OVER WATER)

MOUNTAIN

WATERFALL

WATER

REEF

O ■ SIGHTS, POINTS OF INTEREST

O TOWNS, CITIES

O VILLAGES

● ACCOMMODATIONS

SPECIAL TOPICS

ABBREVIATIONS

A$—Australian dollars
a/c—air-conditioned
B.P.—*boîte postale*
C—Centigrade
C$—Canadian dollars
CDW—collision damage waiver
CFP—French Pacific Franc
EEZ—Exclusive Economic Zone
E.U.—European Union
F$—Fiji dollars
4WD—four-wheel drive
km—kilometer
kph—kilometers per hour
LDS—Latter-day Saints (Mormons)
LMS—London Missionary Society
MV—motor vessel
No.—number
N.Z.—New Zealand
NZ$—New Zealand dollars
PK—*point kilométrique*

P.N.G.—Papua New Guinea
pp—per person
P.W.D.—Public Works Department
SDA—Seventh-Day Adventist
SI$—Solomon Islands dollars
SPARTECA
SPC—South Pacific Commission
SPF—South Pacific Forum
STD—sexually transmitted disease
tel.—telephone
T$—Tongan *pa'anga*
U.S.—United States
US$—U.S. dollars
Vt—Vanuatu *vatu*
WS$—Western Samoan *tala*
WW II—World War Two
YHA—Youth Hostel Association
YWCA—Young Women's Christian
    Association

ACKNOWLEDGMENTS

The nationalities of those listed below are identified by the following signs which follow their names: A (Austria), AUS (Australia), B (Belgium), C (Chile), CDN (Canada), CH (Switzerland), CI (Cook Islands), D (Germany), DK (Denmark), F (France), FI (Fiji), GB (Great Britain), IL (Israel), J (Japan), N (Norway), NC (New Caledonia), NL (Netherlands), NZ (New Zealand), P (Philippines), S (Sweden), SI (Solomon Islands), T (Thailand), TO (Tonga), TP (Tahiti-Polynesia), USA (United States), V (Vanuatu), and WS (Western Samoa).

The antique engravings by M.G.L. Domeny de Rienzi are from the classic three-volume work *Oceanie ou Cinquième Partie du Monde* (Paris: Firmin Didot Frères, 1836).

Chico artist Gordon Ohliger (USA) used the drawings at the beginning of each chapter to set the theme: the rugged majesty of Fatu Hiva's Hanavave Bay, Marquesas Islands (Tahiti-Polynesia); the forbidding remoteness of Bounty Bay (Pitcairn Islands); lonely Ahu Akivi (Easter Island); Rarotonga's famous Betela Dance Troupe (Cook Islands); a tailed Niuean boy picking passion fruit (Niue); imposing Rainmaker Mountain, Tutuila Island (American Samoa); relaxed Samoan *fale* (Western Samoa); men unloading supplies at Nukunonu (Tokelau); haunting Lake Lalololo, Wallis Island (Wallis and Futuna); boys playing in the Nanumea lagoon (Tuvalu); a Fijian village (Fiji); the pine-fringed beauty of Anse de Kanumera, Isle of Pines (New Caledonia); Vanuatu's proverbial cattle beneath coconuts (Vanuatu); headhunters setting out (in times gone by) from New Georgia's Roviana Lagoon (Solomon Islands). When Gordy heard we weren't going to include his photo in the book, he decided to have the last word: that's him on the Tonga banner.

Special thanks to Dr. Peter Bellwood (AUS) of the Australian National University, Canberra, for taking the trouble to go through the entire book pointing out inaccuracies in the sections relating to population origins, racial affinities, languages, and traditional cultures; to David Fanshawe (GB), Ad Linkels (NL), and Musiques du Monde in Amsterdam (NL) for information on Pacific music; to Colin Hinchcliffe (GB) for identifying some of the old prints used as illustrations; to Jos Poelman (NL) of the Dutch STD Foundation, Box 9074, 3506 GB Utrecht, and Steven Vete (FI), editor of *Pacific AIDS Alert,* for information on AIDS; to Tjalling Terpstra (NL) for help in updating Pacific air routes; to Anselm Zänkert (D) for a fascinating report on his trip to Mangareva; to Norm Buske (USA) for information on the leakage of nuclear materials at Moruroa; to Georgia Lee (USA) for updating the Easter Island chapter; to Howard R. Conant (USA) for information on yachting facilities at Easter Island; to Andrew Hempstead (AUS) for helping update the Cook Islands chapter and checking Australian phone numbers; to Roger Malcolm (NZ) for revising the Atiu section; to Peter P. Goldstern (TO) for last-minute information on Tonga; to Joshua Craig (CDN) for verifying that the guns rumored to be at Poloa, Tutuila, do not exist; to James M. Conway (USA), Jack D. Haden (AUS), Rolf Koepke (D), and Alexandra Scherer-Papamau (D) for researching the Tuvalu chapter; to Stacey M. King (AUS) for information on Rambi and the Banabans; to Dianne Bain (FI) for information on Taveuni and yachting facilities around Fiji; to John Connell (AUS) for sending valuable materials about New Caledonia; to David Legard (AUS) for his impressions of New Caledonia; to Peter McQuarrie (FI) for setting the author straight on the subject of pine trees; to David Sharland (NZ) for detailed information on village resorts around Vanuatu; to Robert Kennington (NZ) for several reports on the Solomons (Robert has been contributing to this book for many years); to Hanne Finholt (N) for a fascinating account of her travels through six Pacific countries; to Udo Schwark (D) for arranging my latest research trip; to Asha Johnson (USA) for pulling the production process together; to Valerie "Hurricane Val" Sellers Blanton (USA) for ably whirling the bits and pieces together; and to Ria de Vos (NL) for her continuing assistance, suggestions, and support.

Thanks too to the following readers who took the trouble to write us letters about their trips: D.J. Adler (GB), Ian Anderson (USA), Dr. Jean-François Baré (F), Dr. Ross Barnard (AUS), Eric Beauchemin (NL), David Beattie (NZ), Joy Bloom (USA), Maja Björklöv (S), Hartwig Bohne

(D), Beth Boyer (USA), Alexander K. Braden (GB), Jonathan Bray (GB), André Brugiroux (F), Alston Callahan (USA), Emma Campbell (USA), Derek Cheeserough (GB), Dietmar Clauss (D), Teri A. Cleeland (USA), John and Mavis Dixon (GB), Dieter Dorn (D), Juergen Eckstein (D), K.L. Eiden (USA), Bernard Fernandez (CDN), Hans F. Fletcher (USA), Frances Forbes (USA), Sherry Freeman (USA), Bruce French (USA), Lynn Fritchman (USA), Marcus F. Fuchs (USA), Heinz Geiser (CH), Shibolet Gilat (IL), Kathleen Gilligan (USA), Gerhard Gloor (CH), Diane Goodwillie (CDN), Vera Graf (USA), Mary Graham (USA), Lorraine Guthrie (USA), Evelyn Götte-Huhn (D), Lady Hermione Grimston (GB), Anne and Marcus Hackel (D), Jackie Halter (USA), Adam Hall (GB), Sandy Harford (USA), Claus-Walter Herbertz (D), Jason Hershey (USA), Bev and Frank Higgens (AUS), L. Himmelmann (D), Ms. B. Hiscock (CDN), Boudry Hjalmar (B), Herbert Hans Hoppe (D), Anita Jackson (GB), Jon Jennings (GB), Arthur Jones (GB), Jeffrey Jones (CDN), Prof. Dr. Ruprecht Keller (D), Daniel Klause (D), Marguerite Lake (AUS), Larry Leach (USA), Ward and Judy LeHardy (USA), Chris Letsinger (USA), Frank Lewin (USA), Mike Long (AUS), Dieter Marmet (CH), Allegra E. Marshall (AUS), Philip R. Marshall (USA), Gerhard Martin (D), Jennewein Martin (A), Pat Mathews (USA), Kevin McAuliffe (USA), Steve McCarthy (USA), James K. McIntyre (USA), Douglas McKenna (USA), Peter McQuarrie (FI), Tim and Clair Newton (GB), Randy Niblett (USA), Ewa Ochimowski (CDN), Susan and Charles Paclat (USA), Will Paine (GB), Thomas Passow (D), Jeff Perk (USA), Lea A. Pierce (USA), William J. Plumley (USA), Jackie Plusch (USA), Marlene Rain (USA), John Ray (GB), Almut Reichardt (D), Jörg Reisser (D), Gary Roberts (USA), Toru Sasaki (J), Greg Sawyer (USA), Wolfgang Schaar (D), Steve Schlein (USA), Werner Scholz (D), Ursula Schüssler (D), Bevan Sharp (AUS), Elliot Smith (USA), Maggie Smith (GB), Heinz Stelte (D), Andrea C. Stephenson (USA), Douglas P. Stives (USA), Sarah Thompson-Copsly (GB), Christine Tuttle (USA), Thomas Uhlemann (DK), Nancy Vander Velde (USA), Kik Velt (TO), Thom A. Votaw (USA), N.C. Webb (USA), Elizabeth D. Whitbeck (USA), Brendan R. Whyte (NZ), and Steve Williams (GB).

All their comments have been incorporated into the volume you're now holding. To have your own name included here next edition, write: David Stanley, c/o Moon Publications Inc., P.O. Box 3040, Chico, CA 95927-3040, U.S.A.

Attention Hotel Keepers, Tour Operators, and Divemasters
The best way to keep your listing in South Pacific Handbook up to date is to send us current information about your business. If you don't agree with what we've written, please tell us why—there's never any charge or obligation for a listing. Thanks to the following island tourism workers and government officials who did write in:

Raywadee Archjananun (T), Edwina Arnold (USA), Al Bakker (AUS), Donny Barnhardt (USA), Joanne Batty (USA), Leo Berkelouw (AUS), Elsie Blake (TO), Ron Blake (NZ), René Boehm (D), Ratu Kini Boko (FI), Louise Bonno (TP), Sherrill L. Bounnell (USA), Christa Brantsch-Harness (USA), Gordon Burrow (NZ), John Carter (AUS), Marie Isabelle Chan (TP), Gavin Clarke (FI), Terry Coe (NZ), Anne and Michel Condesse (TP), Mary Ann Cook (USA), Yan Constans (NC), D.B. Costello (FI), Mary T. Crowley (USA), Catherine Cuny (USA), Simone Daulaca (FI), Wendy Dell (CDN), Ingrid Denk (FI), Michael Dennis (FI), William Dobbie (NZ), Sylvia Dobry (FI), Carol Douglas (FI), Mrs. Akanisi Dreunimisimisi (FI), Alain G. Druet (TP), Professor Francis Dubus (TP), Gordon Edris (FI), Joanna Edwards (FI), Dennis P. Eichhorn (USA), Andrea Eimke (CI), Paul Ellerby (GB), Rick Elms (FI), Victor Emanuel (USA), Anne Fairlie (CDN), Manon Fala (NZ), Taina Fehr (D), Agatha Ferei (FI), Rena Forster (FI), Paul Fritz (WS), Valerie Gadway (USA), Val Gavriloff (AUS), Bruno Gendron (TP), Ingeborg Gillegot (B), Bob Goddess (USA), Ronna Goldstein (FI), Michael Graves-Johnston (GB), Kevin Green (V), Michael Ann Harvey (USA), G.D. Harraway (NZ), Billy Hawkins (GB), Peter Heays (CI), Mary J. Heffron (USA), Nicholas Henry (CI), Diana Hepworth (SI), Mary-Lou Hewett (AUS), Stanley W. Hosie (USA), Anne Hughes (USA), Judith Huntsman (NZ), R.G. Ingram (CI), Simon Jackson (NZ), Karen Jeffery (USA), Richard Johnson (USA), Sally Johnson (FI), Loraini V. Jones (FI), Walter Kamm (CH), Evelynn M. Kern

(USA), Rehnuma Khan (FI), Stephen J. Kelly (AUS), Debora Kimitete (TP), Fred Kleckham (V), M. Kulikovi (F), Ellison Kyere (SI), Carolyne Kyle (USA), Elisabeth Lajtonyi (D), Brij Lal (FI), Evelyn League (USA), Jennifer Lee (NC), Yves Lefèvre (TP), Geneviève Lemaire (TP), Peni and Gail Lesuma (FI), April Lief (USA), Neil Lidstrom (USA), Martin Livingston (FI), Hector Macdonald (FI), Max Macdonald (FI), Iain MacDougall (NZ), Stephanie Malach (TP), Ms. J. Mamtora (FI), Sione A. Manu (TO), Jokapeci Maopa (FI), Jimmy Matthews (TO), Toni Matthias (GB), James F. McCann (FI), Brenda McCroskey (USA), Dorothy McIntosh (GB), Lee McLauchlan (FI), Jose Antonio Mendizabal (C), Lynette Mercer (FI), Robert Miller (FI), Joan and Tom Moody (USA), Peter Moore (GB), Irene Morrell (SI), Anthony J. Morris (FI), Merle J. Murray (FI), Caroline Nalo (NC), Agnes Nateba (FI), Petra F. Netzorg (USA), Donna Oakley (USA), Noel Omeri (SI), Brendan O'Shea (SI), Nicola Owers (NZ), Jill Palise (FI), Jennifer Patterson (CDN), Nicholas Panza (USA), Rob Pearce (SI), J.C. Perelli (TP), Ms. A. Perraud (NC), Michelene Petaia (WS), Sandra Peterson (TO), Andria Piekarz (USA), Denis Pierce (AUS), Varney Pierrette (TP), Karine Plouhinec (TP), Vijen Prasad (USA), Gerry Van Pypen (AUS), Waltraud Quick (D), Linda Rabidue (USA), Fred Radewagen (USA), Bill William Reece (FI), Susan Reed (USA), Wendy Reeve (USA), Robert F. Reynolds (USA), Nicolas de Riviere (F), Philippe Robard (TP), David Robie (NZ), Yves Roche (TP), Carl Roessler (USA), Barry Rose (WS), Jon Roseman (FI), Paola et Christian Ruotolo (F), Brian Rutherford (AUS), Dr. R.M. Sarda (P), Hans Schmeiser (D), Tom Sheehan (USA), Diana Sikora (USA), Pascale Siu-Chow (USA), Jona Siva (FI), Mary Slaney (CI), Virginia Smith (FI), Pam Soderberg (USA), Lynne Solomon (CI), Jürgen Stavenov (D), Christopher Stein (USA), Brooke Stevens (USA), Max Storck (FI), Mark P. Striker (V), Mosie Su'a (WS), Alex Sword (CI), Bernard Tairea (CI), Verna Takashima (USA), Jennifer Terrell (AUS), Margaret Thaggard (FI), Chris Thompson (FI), Esther Turaga (SI), Niumaia Turaganicolo (FI), Andy Turpin (USA), Dr. Jeffrey P. Vadheim (USA), John R. Van't Slot (USA), Piet van Zyl (F), Damien Vincent (B), Sandy Wand (USA), Alex Wang (SI), Wesley Ward (NZ), Katrina Wards (NZ), Lindsay J. Watt (NZ), Tom Wells (V), Ric West (FI), Roy West (USA), Viti Whippy (FI), C.C. Wilson (WS), Christine Wilson (AUS), Jerry Wittert (USA), Roy F. Whitton (FI), Jules C. Wong (USA), Patrick Wong (FI), Kay T. Yogi (USA), Wanda Young (USA), Angélian Zéna (TP), Keith Zoing (FI), and Kettily Zongahite (SI).

From the Author

On my latest field research trip I was able to personally visit and inspect facilities on these islands: Bora Bora, Efate, Foa, Gizo, Guadalcanal, Huahine, Lifuka, Malaita, Manono, Moorea, Nananu-i-Ra, New Georgia, Norfolk, Ovalau, Raiatea, Rarotonga, Savai'i, Tahiti, Tanna, Taveuni, Tongatapu, Tutuila, Upolu, Vanua Levu, Vava'u, and Viti Levu. Other islands had to be updated through secondary sources (including direct reports from the correspondents listed above), and that information should be used with a bit more care. However, over the past 19 years I've visited almost every area included herein. This edition was actually written in Amsterdam, The Netherlands.

While out researching my books I find it cheaper to pay my own way, and you can rest assured that nothing in this book is designed to repay freebies from hotels, restaurants, tour operators, or airlines. I prefer to arrive unexpected and uninvited, and to experience things as they really are. On the road I seldom identify myself to anyone. The essential difference between this book and the myriad travel brochures free for the taking in airports and tourist offices all across the region is that this book represents you, the traveler, while the brochures represent the travel industry. The companies and organizations included herein are there for information purposes only, and a mention in no way implies an endorsement.

EXCHANGE RATES

(approximate figures for orientation only)

US$1 = CFP 87 (French Pacific francs)
US$1 = NZ$1.49 (New Zealand dollars)
US$1 = A$1.35 (Australian dollars)
US$1 = T$1.25 (Tongan *pa'anga*)
US$1 = WS$2.46 (Western Samoan *tala*)
US$1 = F$1.39 (Fiji dollars)
US$1 = Vt111 (Vanuatu *vatu*)
US$1 = SI$2.99 (Solomon Islands dollars)

IS THIS BOOK OUT OF DATE?

Travel writing is like trying to take a picture out the side of a bus: time frustrates the best of intentions. Because it takes over a year to research and write a new edition, some things are bound to have changed. A strong hurricane can blow away half the tourist facilities on an island overnight! So if something in this book doesn't sound quite right, please let us hear about it. Did anything lead you astray or inconvenience you? In retrospect, what sort of information would have made your trip easier?

Unlike many other travel writers, the author doesn't solicit "freebies" or announce who he is to one and all, and at times that makes it difficult to audit the expensive resorts. Thus we especially welcome comments from readers who stayed at the upmarket places, particularly when the facilities didn't match the rates. Rest assured that legitimate complaints will most certainly influence future coverage in this book, and no hotel or restaurant is exempt from fair criticism.

When writing, please be as precise and accurate as you can. Notes made on the scene are far better than later recollections. Write comments in your copy of *South Pacific Handbook* as you go along, then send us a summary when you get home. You can recycle used travel brochures by sending them to us when you're done with them. If this book helped you, please help us make it even better. Address your letters to:

David Stanley
c/o Moon Publications Inc.
P.O. Box 3040
Chico, CA 95927-3040, U.S.A.

INTRODUCTION

$t$he Pacific, greatest of oceans, has an area exceeding that of all dry land on the planet. Covering more than a third of earth's surface—as much as the Atlantic, Indian, and Arctic oceans combined—it's the largest geographical feature in the world. Its awesome 165,384,000 square km (up to 16,000 km wide and 11,000 km long) have an average depth of around 4,000 meters. The greatest depths in any ocean are encountered in the western Pacific, reaching 10,924 meters in the Marianas Trench, the deepest point on earth. One theory claims the moon may have been flung from the Pacific while the world was still young.

The liquid continent of Oceania is divided between Melanesia, several chains of relatively large, mountainous landmasses, and Polynesia, scattered groups of volcanic and coral islands. North of the equator are the coral and volcanic islands of Micronesia. It's believed that, in all, some 30,000 islands dot the Pacific basin—more than are found in all other oceans and seas combined. There's something about these islands that has always fascinated humans and made them want to learn what's there. Each one is a cosmos with a character of its own. This book is about some of those islands.

GORDON OHLIGER

INTRODUCTION
THE LAND

Plate Tectonics
Much of the western Pacific is shaken by the clash of tectonic plates (a phenomenon once referred to as continental drift), when one section of earth's drifting surface collides head-on with another. The northern and central Pacific rest on the Pacific Plate, while New Guinea, Australia, Fiji, New Caledonia, and part of New Zealand sit on the Indo-Australian Plate. The west edge of the Pacific Plate runs northeast from New Zealand up the eastern side of Tonga to Samoa, where it swings west and continues up the southwestern side of Vanuatu and the Solomons to New Britain. North of New Guinea the Pacific Plate faces the Eurasian Plate, with a series of ocean trenches defining the boundary.

The dividing line between the Pacific Plate and the plates to the west is known as the Andesite Line, part of the circumpacific "Ring of Fire." In the South Pacific much of the land west of this line remains from the submerged Australasian continent of 100 million B.C. East of the line, only volcanic and coraline islands exist.

About 85% of the world's annual release of seismic energy occurs around the edge of the Pacific Plate. As the thinner Pacific Plate pushes under the thicker Indo-Australian Plate at the Tonga Trench it melts; under tremendous pressure, some of the molten material escapes upward through fissures, causing volcanoes to erupt and atolls to tilt. Farther west the Indo-Australian Plate dives below the Pacific Plate, causing New Caledonia to slowly sink as parts of Vanuatu and the Solomons belch, quake, and heave. Fiji, between these two active areas, is strangely stable.

Darwin's Theory of Atoll Formation
The famous formulator of the theory of evolution surmised that atolls form as high volcanic islands subside into lagoons. The original island's fringing reef grows into a barrier reef as the volcanic portion sinks. When the last volcanic material finally disappears below sea level, the coral rim of the reef/atoll remains to indicate how big the island once was.

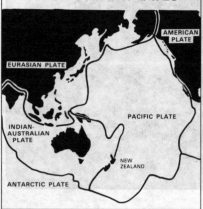

PACIFIC AND INDIAN-AUSTRALIAN PLATES

EURASIAN PLATE

AMERICAN PLATE

PACIFIC PLATE

INDIAN-AUSTRALIAN PLATE

NEW ZEALAND

ANTARCTIC PLATE

© DAVID STANLEY

Of course, all this takes place over millions of years, but deep down below every atoll is the old volcanic core. Darwin's theory is well-illustrated at Bora Bora, where a high volcanic island remains inside the rim of Bora Bora's barrier reef; this island's volcanic core is still sinking imperceptibly at the rate of one centimeter a century. Return to Bora Bora in 25 million years and all you'll find will be a coral atoll like Rangiroa or Manihi.

Hot Spots

High or low, all of the islands have a volcanic origin best explained by the "Conveyor Belt Theory." A crack opens in the earth's mantle and vol-

canic magma escapes upward. A submarine volcano builds up slowly until the lava finally breaks the surface, becoming a volcanic island. The Pacific Plate moves northwest approximately 10 centimeters a year; thus, over geologic eons the volcano disconnects from the hot spot or crack from which it emerged. As the old volcanoes disconnect from the crack, new ones appear to the southeast, and the older islands are carried away from the cleft in earth's crust from which they were born.

The island then begins to sink under its own weight and erosion also cuts into the now-extinct volcano. In the warm, clear waters a living coral reef begins to grow along the shore. As the island subsides, the reef continues to grow upward. In this way a lagoon forms between the reef and the shoreline of the slowly sinking island. This barrier reef marks the old margin of the original island.

As the hot spot shifts southeast in an opposite direction from the sliding Pacific Plate (and shifting magnetic pole of the earth), the process is repeated, time and again, until whole chains of islands ride the blue Pacific. Weathering is most advanced on the composite islands and atolls at the northwest ends of the Society, Austral, Tuamotu, and Marquesas chains. Maupiti and Bora Bora, with their exposed volcanic cores, are the oldest of the larger Society Islands. The Tuamotus have eroded almost to sea level; the Gambier Islands originated out of the same hot spot and their volcanic peaks remain inside a giant atoll reef. In every case, the islands at the southeast end of the chains are the youngest.

By drilling into the Tuamotu atolls, scientists have proven their point conclusively: the coral

The theory of atoll formation according to Darwin: As the volcanic portion of the island subsides, the fringing reef is converted into a barrier reef. After the volcanic core has disappeared completely into the lagoon, the remaining reef island is called an atoll.

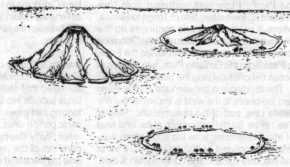

LOUISE FOOTE

formations are about 350 meters thick at the southeast end of the chain, 600 meters thick at Hao near the center, and 1,000 meters thick at Rangiroa near the northwest end of the Tuamotu Group. Clearly, Rangiroa, where the volcanic rock is now a kilometer below the surface, is many millions of years older than the Gambiers, where a volcanic peak still stands 482 meters above sea level.

Equally fascinating is the way ancient atolls have been uplifted by adjacent volcanoes. The upper crust of earth is an elastic envelope enclosing an incompressible fluid. When this envelope is stretched taut, the tremendous weight of a volcano is spread over a great area, deforming the seabed. In the Cook Islands, for example, Atiu, Mauke, Mitiaro, and Mangaia were uplifted by the weight of Aitutaki and Rarotonga.

Island-building continues at an active undersea volcano called MacDonald, 50 meters below sea level at the southeast end of the Australs. The crack spews forth about a cubic mile of lava every century and someday MacDonald too will poke its smoky head above the waves. The theories of plate tectonics, or the sliding crust of the earth, seem proven in the Pacific.

Life of an Atoll

A circular or horseshoe-shaped coral reef bearing a necklace of sandy, slender islets *(motus)* of debris thrown up by storms, surf, and wind is known as an atoll. Atolls can be up to 100 km across, but the width of dry land is usually only 200-400 meters from inner to outer beach. The central lagoon can measure anywhere from one km to 50 km in diameter; huge Rangiroa Atoll is 77 km long. Entirely landlocked lagoons are rare; passages through the barrier reef are usually found on the leeward side. Most atolls are no higher than four to six meters.

A raised or elevated atoll is one that has been pushed up by some trauma of nature to become a platform of coral rock rising up to 20 meters above sea level. Raised atolls are often known for their huge sea caves and steep oceanside cliffs. The largest coral platform of this kind in the South Pacific is 692-square-km Rennell in the Solomons.

Where the volcanic island remains there's often a deep passage between the barrier reef and shore; the reef forms a natural breakwater,

which shelters good anchorages. Australia's Great Barrier Reef is 1,600 km long and 25 to 44 km offshore. Soil derived from coral is extremely poor in nutrients, while volcanic soil is known for its fertility. Dark-colored beaches are formed from volcanic material; the white beaches of travel brochures are entirely coral-based. The black beaches are cooler and easier on the eyes, enabling plantlife to grow closer and providing patches of shade; the white beaches are generally safer for swimming, as visibility is better.

The Greenhouse Effect

The gravest danger facing the atolls of Oceania is the greenhouse effect, a gradual warming of Earth's environment due to fossil fuel combustion and the widespread clearing of forests. By the year 2030 the concentration of carbon dioxide in the atmosphere will have doubled from preindustrial levels. As infrared radiation from the sun is absorbed by the gas, the trapped heat melts mountain glaciers and the polar ice caps. In addition, seawater expands as it warms up, so water levels could rise almost a meter by the year 2100, destroying shorelines created 5,000 years ago.

A 1982 study demonstrated that sea levels had already risen 12 centimeters in the previous century; in 1993 the United Nations Environment Program predicted a further rise of 20 centimeters by the year 2030 and 65 centimeters by the end of the next century. Not only will this reduce the growing area for food crops, but rising sea levels will mean salt water intrusion into groundwater supplies—a horrifying prospect if accompanied by the droughts that have been predicted. Coastal erosion will force governments to spend millions of dollars on road repairs and coastline stabilization.

Increasing temperatures may already be contributing to the dramatic jump in the number of hurricanes in the South Pacific. For example, Fiji experienced only 12 tropical hurricanes from 1941 to 1980 but 10 from 1981 to 1989. After a series of devastating hurricanes in Western Samoa, insurance companies announced in 1992 that they were withdrawing coverage from the country. Widespread instances of coral bleaching and reefs being killed by rising sea temperatures have been confirmed. (Coral

LARGEST ISLANDS IN THE SOUTH PACIFIC

New Guinea	820,033 square km
South Island, New Zealand	149,861 square km
Tasmania, Australia	67,800 square km
New Britain, P.N.G.	37,736 square km
Grande Terre, New Caledonia	16,192 square km
North Island, New Zealand	14,682 square km
Big Island, Hawaii	10,458 square km
Viti Levu, Fiji Islands	10,429 square km
Bougainville, P.N.G.	10,000 square km
New Ireland, P.N.G.	8,650 square km
Vanua Levu, Fiji Islands	5,556 square km
Guadalcanal, Solomon Islands	5,302 square km
Isabela, Galapagos Islands	4,588 square km
Isabel, Solomon Islands	4,014 square km
Espiritu Santo, Vanuatu	4,010 square km
Malaita, Solomon Islands	3,885 square km
New Georgia, Solomon Islands	3,365 square km
Makira, Solomon Islands	3,188 square km
Choiseul, Solomon Islands	2,538 square km
Malekula, Vanuatu	2,053 square km
Manus, P.N.G.	1,943 square km
Maui, Hawaii	1,885 square km
Stewart, New Zealand	1,746 square km
Savai'i, Western Samoa	1,709 square km
Oahu, Hawaii	1,572 square km
New Hanover, P.N.G.	1,544 square km
Kauai, Hawaii	1,432 square km
Fergusson, P.N.G.	1,345 square km
Lifou, New Caledonia	1,196 square km
Upolu, Western Samoa	1,114 square km
Tahiti, Society Islands	1,045 square km

bleaching occurs when an organism's symbiotic algae are expelled in response to environmental stresses, such as changes in water temperature.) Reef destruction will reduce coastal fish stocks and impact tourism.

As storm waves wash across the low-lying atolls, eating away the precious land, the entire populations of archipelagos such as Tokelau and Tuvalu may be forced to evacuate long before they're actually flooded. The construction of seawalls to keep out the rising seas would be prohibitively expensive, so instead Australia and New Zealand will be asked to take in these hapless victims of first-world affluence when the time comes.

Unfortunately, those most responsible for the problem, the industrialized countries led by the United States, have strongly resisted taking any action to significantly cut greenhouse gas emissions. And as if that weren't bad enough, the hydrofluorocarbons (HFCs) presently being developed by corporate giants like Du Pont to replace the ozone-destructive chlorofluorocarbons (CFCs) presently used in cooling systems are far more potent greenhouse gases than carbon dioxide. This is only one of many similar consumption-related problems, and it seems as if one section of humanity is hurtling down a suicidal slope, unable to resist the momentum, as the rest of our race watches the catastrophe approach in helpless horror. It will cost a lot to rewrite our collective ticket but there may not be any choice.

CORAL REEFS

To understand how a basalt volcano becomes a limestone atoll, it's necessary to know a little about the growth of coral. Coral reefs cover some 200,000 square km worldwide, between 35 degrees north and 32 degrees south latitude. A reef is created by the accumulation of millions of tiny calcareous skeletons left by myriad generations of tiny coral polyps, some no bigger than a pinhead. Though the skeleton is usually white, the living polyps are of many different colors.

They thrive in clear salty water where the temperature never drops below 18° C. They must also have a base not over 50 meters below the water's surface on which to form. The coral colony grows slowly upward on the consolidated skeletons of its ancestors until it reaches the low-tide mark, after which development extends outward on the edges of the reef. Sunlight is critical for coral growth. Colonies grow quickly on the ocean side due to clearer water and a greater abundance of food. A strong, healthy reef can grow four to five centimeters a year. Fresh or cloudy water inhibits coral growth, which is why villages and ports all across the Pacific are located at the reef-free mouths of rivers.

Polyps extract calcium carbonate from the water and deposit it in their skeletons. All reef-building corals also contain limy encrustations of microscopic algae within their cells. The algae, like all green plants, obtain their energy from the sun and contribute this energy to the growth of the reef's skeleton. As a result, corals behave (and look) more like plants than animals, competing for sunlight just as terrestrial plants do. Many polyps are also carnivorous; with minute stinging tentacles they supplement their energy by capturing tiny planktonic animals and organic particles at night. A small piece of coral is a colony composed of large numbers of polyps.

Coral Types

Corals belong to a broad group of stinging creatures, which includes polyps, soft corals, stony corals, sea anemones, sea fans, and jellyfish. Only those types with hard skeletons and a single hollow cavity within the body are considered true corals. Stony corals such as brain, table, staghorn, and mushroom corals have external skeletons and are important reef builders. Soft corals, black corals, and sea fans have internal skeletons. The fire corals are recognized by their smooth, velvety surface and yellowish brown color. The stinging toxins of this last group can easily penetrate human skin and cause swelling and painful burning that can last up to an hour. The many varieties of soft, colorful anemones gently waving in the current might seem inviting to touch, but beware: many are also poisonous.

The corals, like most other forms of life in the Pacific, colonized the ocean from the fertile seas of Southeast Asia. Thus the number of species declines as you move east. Over 600 species of coral make their home in the Pacific, compared to only 48 in the Caribbean. The diversity of coral colors and forms is endlessly amazing. This is our most unspoiled environment, a world of almost indescribable beauty.

Exploring a Reef

Until you've explored a good coral reef, you haven't experienced one of the greatest joys of nature. While one cannot walk through pristine forests due to the lack of paths, it's quite possible to swim over untouched reefs—the most densely populated living space on earth. Dive shops throughout the region rent or sell snorkeling gear, so do get into the clear, warm waters around you. Be careful, however, and know the dangers. Practice snorkeling in the shallow water; don't head into deep water until you're sure you've got the hang of it. Breathe easily; don't hyperventilate.

When snorkeling on a fringing reef, beware of deadly currents and undertows in channels that drain tidal flows. Observe the direction the water is flowing before you swim into it. If you feel yourself being dragged out to sea through a reef passage, try swimming across the current rather than against it. If you can't resist the pull at all, it may be better to let yourself be carried out. Wait till the current diminishes, then swim along the outer reef face until you find somewhere to come back in. Or use your energy to attract the attention of someone onshore.

Snorkeling on the outer edge or drop-off of a reef is thrilling for the variety of fish and corals, but attempt it only on a very calm day. Even then it's best to have someone stand onshore or paddle behind you in a canoe to watch for occasional big waves, which can take you by sur-

LONGEST REEFS IN THE WORLD

Great Barrier Reef, Australia	1,600 km
Southwest Barrier Reef, New Caledonia	600 km
Northeast Barrier Reef, New Caledonia	540 km
Great Sea Reef, Fiji Islands	260 km
Belize Reef, Central America	250 km
South Louisiade Archipelago Reef, P.N.G.	200 km

staghorn fire coral
(Millepora alcicornis)

acropora

CORALS OF THE PACIFIC

table coral

mushroom coral
(Fungia fungites)

elkhorn fire coral
(Millepora
platyphylla)

honeycomb coral
(Favia matthaii)

brain coral
(Meandrina)

DIANA LASICH HARPER

prise and smash you into the rocks. Also, beware of unperceived currents outside the reef—you may not get a second chance.

A far better idea is to limit your snorkeling to the protected inner reef and leave the open waters to the scuba diver. Commercial scuba operators know their waters and will be able to show you the most amazing things in perfect safety. Dive centers at all the main resorts operate year-round, with marinelife most profuse July to November. If you wish to scuba dive you'll have to show your scuba certification card, and occasionally divers are also asked to show a medical report from their doctor indicating that they are in good physical condition. Serious divers will bring along their own mask, buoyancy compensator, and regulator. Many of the scuba operators listed in this book offer introductory "resort courses" for those who only want a taste of scuba diving, and full CMAS, NAUI, or PADI open-water certification courses for those wishing to dive more than once or twice. The main constraint is financial: snorkeling is free, while scuba diving can get expensive.

Conservation

Coral reefs are one of the most fragile and complex ecosystems on earth, providing food and shelter for countless species of fish, crustaceans (shrimps, crabs, and lobsters), mollusks (shells), and other animals. The coral reefs of the South Pacific protect shorelines during storms, supply sand to maintain the islands, furnish food for the local population, form a living laboratory for science, and are major tourist attractions. Without coral, the South Pacific would be immeasurably poorer.

Hard corals grow only about 10 to 25 millimeters a year and it can take 7,000 to 10,000 years for a coral reef to form. Though corals look solid they're easily broken; by standing on them, breaking off pieces, or carelessly dropping anchor you can destroy in a few minutes what took so long to form. Once a piece of coral breaks off it dies, and it may be years before the coral reestablishes itself and even longer before the broken piece is replaced. The "wound" may become infected by algae, which can multiply and kill the entire coral colony. When this happens over a wide area, the diversity of marinelife declines dramatically.

We recommend that you not remove seashells, coral, plantlife, or marine animals from the sea. Doing so upsets the delicate balance of nature, and coral is much more beautiful underwater anyway! This is a particular problem along shorelines frequented by large numbers of tourists, who can completely strip a reef in very little time. The triton shell, for example, keeps in check the reef-destroying crown-of-thorns starfish. If you'd like a souvenir, content yourself with what you find on the beach (although even a seemingly empty shell may be inhabited by a hermit crab). Also think twice about purchasing jewelry or souvenirs made from coral or seashells. Genuine traditional handicrafts that incorporate shells are one thing, but by purchasing unmounted seashells or mass-produced coral curios you are contributing to the destruction of the marine environment.

The anchors and anchor chains of private yachts can do serious damage to coral reefs. Pronged anchors are more environmentally friendly than larger, heavier anchors, and plastic tubing over the end of the anchor chain helps minimize damage. If at all possible, anchor in sand. A longer anchor chain makes this easier, and a good windlass is essential for larger boats. A recording depth sounder will help locate sandy areas when none are available in shallow water. If you don't have a depth sounder and can't see the bottom, lower the anchor until it just touches the bottom and feel the anchor line as the boat drifts. If it "grumbles" lift it up, drift a little, and try again. Later, if you notice your chain grumbling, motor over the anchor, lift it out of the coral and move. Not only do sand and mud hold better, but your anchor will be less likely to become fouled. Try to arrive before 1500 to be able to see clearly where you're anchoring—Polaroid sunglasses make it easier to distinguish corals.

There's an urgent need for stricter government regulation of the marine environment, and in some places coral reefs are already protected. Exhortations such as the one above have only limited impact—legislators must write stricter laws and impose fines. Resort developers can minimize damage to their valuable reefs by providing public mooring buoys so yachts don't have to drop anchor and pontoons so snorkelers aren't tempted to stand on coral. Licensing authorities can make such amenities mandatory whenever appropriate, and in extreme cases, especially endangered coral gardens should be declared off limits to private boats. As consumerism spreads, once-remote areas become subject to the problems of pollution and overexploitation: the garbage is visibly piling up on many shores. As a visitor, don't hesitate to practice your conservationist attitudes, and leave a clean wake.

CLIMATE

The Pacific Ocean has a greater impact on the world's climate than any other geographical feature on earth. By taking heat away from the equator toward the poles, it stretches the bounds of the area in which life can exist. Broad circular ocean currents flow from east to west across the tropical Pacific, clockwise in the North Pacific, counterclockwise in the South Pacific. North and south of the "horse latitudes" just outside the tropics the currents cool and swing east. The prevailing winds move the same way: the southeast trades south of the equator, the northeast trades north of the equator, and the low-pressure "doldrums" in between. Westerlies blow east above the cool currents north and south of the tropics. This natural air-conditioning system brings warm water to Australia and Japan, cooler water to Peru and California.

The climate of the high islands is closely related to these winds. As air is heated near the equator it rises and flows at high altitudes toward the poles. By the time it reaches about 30° south latitude it will have cooled enough to cause it to fall and flow back toward the equator near sea level. In the Southern Hemisphere the rotation of the earth deflects the winds to the left to become the southeast trades. When these cool moist tradewinds hit a high island, they are warmed by the sun and forced up. Above 500 meters elevation they begin to cool again and their moisture condenses into clouds. At night the winds do not capture much warmth and are more likely to discharge their moisture as rain. The windward slopes of the high islands catch the trades head-on and are usually wet, while those on the leeward side may be dry.

Rain falls abundantly and frequently in the islands during the southern summer months (December to March). This is also the hurricane season south of the equator, a dangerous time for cruising yachts. However, New Zealand and southern Australia, outside the tropics, get their best weather at this time; many boats head south to sit it out. The southeast tradewinds sweep the South Pacific from April to November, the cruising season. Cooler and drier, these are the ideal months for travel in insular Oceania, though the rainy season is only a slight inconvenience. Over the past five years climatic changes have turned weather patterns upside down, so don't be surprised if you get prolonged periods of rain and wind during the official "dry season."

Temperatures range from warm to hot year-round; however, the ever-present sea moderates the humidity by bringing continual cooling breezes. Countries nearer the equator (Samoa, Solomon Islands) are hotter than those farther south (Cook Islands, Tonga, New Caledonia). There's almost no twilight in the tropics, which makes Pacific sunsets brief. When the sun begins to go down, you have less than half an hour before darkness.

FLORA AND FAUNA

FLORA

The flora and fauna of Oceania originated in the Malaysian region; in the two regions, ecological niches are filled by similar plants. Yet one sees a steady decline in the variety of genera as one moves east: even in distant Hawaii very few native plants have an American origin. Some species such as casuarinas and coconuts spread by means of floating seeds or fruit, and wind and birds were also effective in colonization. The microscopic spores of ferns can be carried vast distances by the wind. Yet how creatures like Fiji's crested iguana or the flightless megapode bird of Niuafo'ou and Savo could have reached the Pacific islands remains a mystery. Later, humans became the vehicle: the Polynesians introduced taro, yams, breadfruit, plantains, coconuts, sugarcane, kava, paper mulberry, and much more to the islands.

The high islands of the South Pacific support a great variety of plantlife, while the low islands are restricted to a few hardy, drought-resistant species such as coconuts and pandanus. Rainforests fill the valleys and damp windward slopes of the high islands, while brush and thickets grow in more exposed locations. Hillsides in the

drier areas are covered with coarse grasses. Yet even large islands such as Viti Levu are extremely limited when compared to Indonesia. The absence of leaf-eating animals allowed the vegetation to develop largely without the protective spines and thorns found elsewhere.

Distance, drought, and poor soil have made atoll vegetation among the most unvaried on earth. Though a tropical atoll might seem "lush," no more than 15 native species may be present! On the atolls, taro, a root vegetable with broad heart-shaped leaves, must be cultivated in deep organic pits. The vegetation of a raised atoll is apt to be far denser, with many more species, yet it's likely that less than half are native.

Mangroves can occasionally be found along some high island coastal lagoons. The cable roots of the saltwater-tolerant red mangrove anchor in the shallow upper layer of oxygenated mud, avoiding the layers of hydrogen sulfide below. The tree provides shade for tiny organisms dwelling in the tidal mudflats—a place for birds to nest and for fish or shellfish to feed and spawn. The mangroves also perform the same task as land-building coral colonies along the reefs. As sediments are trapped between the roots, the trees extend farther into the lagoon,

pandanus (fara) *growing at Tahiti*

The cassava bush (Manihot esculenta) *can grow over two meters high. The tuberous root, though less prized than yams, sweet potatoes, and breadfruit, is a common source of island food. A native of Brazil, cassava was transported to the Pacific in post-Columbian times. Other names for this plant include yuca, manioc, and tapioca.*

creating a unique natural environment. The past decade has seen widespread destruction of the mangroves.

Sugarcane probably originated in the South Pacific. On New Guinea the islanders have cultivated the plant for thousands of years, selecting vigorous varieties with the most colorful stems. The story goes that two Melanesian fishermen, To-Kabwana and To-Karavuvu, found a piece of sugarcane in their net one day. They threw it away, but after twice catching it again they decided to keep it and painted the stalk a bright color. Eventually the cane burst and a woman came forth. She cooked food for the men but hid herself at night. Finally she was captured and became the wife of one of the men. From their union sprang the whole human race.

Rainforests at Risk

In our day man has greatly altered the original vegetation by cutting the primary forests and introducing exotic species. For example, most of the plants now seen in the coastal areas of the main islands are introduced. The virgin rainforests of the world continue to disappear at the rate of 40 hectares a minute, causing erosion, silting, flooding, drought, climatic changes, and the extinction of countless life forms. The Solomon Islands and New Caledonia have been the hardest hit by commercial logging, but the forests of Vanuatu, Fiji, and Western Samoa are also suffering.

Locally operated portable sawmills have been promoted in Melanesia as an alternative to large-

scale exploitation by foreign corporations. These low-tech sawmills can be operated by a couple of persons, and there's a ready market for the cut lumber. Logging roads and heavy equipment are not required, and nearly 100% of the income remains in the community. By providing villagers with a steady income from their forests, the *wokabout somils* make customary landowners far less ready to sign away timber rights to large companies that devastate the environment. The need for sustainable development rather than short-term exploitation, the creation of forest reserves, and better management across the board is becoming recognized.

FAUNA

As with the flora, the variety of animal and bird species encountered in Oceania declines as you move away from the Asian mainland. The Wallace Line between Indonesia's Bali and Lombok was once believed to separate the terrestrial fauna of Southeast Asia from that of Australia. Although it's now apparent that there's no such clear-cut division, it still provides a frame of reference. Many of the marsupials and monotremes of Australia are also native to Papua New Guinea. Sea cows (dugongs) are found in New Guinea, the Solomons, and Vanuatu. The fauna to the east of New Guinea is much sparser, with flying foxes and insect-eating bats the only mammals that spread to all of Oceania (except Eastern Polynesia) without the aid of man.

Island birdlife is far more abundant than land-based fauna but still reflects the decline in variety from west to east. Birdwatching is a highly recommended pursuit for the serious Pacific traveler; you'll find it opens unexpected doors. Good field guides are few (ask at local bookstores, museums, and cultural centers), but a determined interest will bring you into contact with fascinating people and lead to great adventures. The best time to observe forest birds is in the very early morning—they move around a lot less in the heat of the day.

Introduced Fauna
Ancient Polynesian navigators introduced wild pigs, dogs, and chickens; they also brought along rats (a few species of mice are native to Australia and New Guinea). Captain Cook contributed cattle, horses, and goats; Captain Wallis left behind cats. The mongoose was introduced to the region over a century ago to combat rats. Giant African snails *(Achatina fulica)* were brought to the islands by gourmets fond of fancy French food. Some of the snails escaped, multiplied, and now crawl wild, destroying the vegetation.

Perhaps the most unfortunate newcomer of all is the hopping Indian mynah bird *(Acridotheres tristis)*, introduced to many islands from Indonesia at the turn of the century to control insects, which were damaging the citrus and coconut plantations. The mynahs multiplied profusely and have become major pests, inflicting great harm on the very trees they were brought in to protect. Worse still, many indigenous birds are forced out of their habitat by these noisy, aggressive birds with yellow beaks and feet. This and rapid deforestation by man have made the South Pacific the region with the highest proportion of endangered endemic bird species on earth.

MARINELIFE

The South Pacific's richest store of life is found in the silent underwater world of the pelagic and lagoon fishes. Coral pinnacles on the lagoon floor provide a safe haven for angelfish, butterfly fish, damselfish, groupers, soldierfish, surgeonfish, triggerfish, trumpet fish, and countless more. These fish seldom venture more than a few meters away from the protective coral, but larger fish such as barracuda, jackfish, parrot fish, pike, stingrays, and small sharks range across lagoon waters that are seldom deeper than 30 meters. The external side of the reef is also home to many of the above, but the open ocean is reserved for bonito, mahimahi, swordfish, tuna, wrasses, and the larger sharks. Passes between ocean and lagoon can be crowded

with fish in transit, offering a favorite hunting ground for predators.

In the open sea the food chain begins with phytoplankton, which flourish wherever ocean upswellings bring nutrients such as nitrates and phosphates to the surface. In the western Pacific this occurs near the equator, where massive currents draw water away toward Japan and Australia. Large schools of fast-moving tuna ply these waters feeding on smaller fish, which consume tiny phytoplankton drifting near the sunlit surface. The phytoplankton also exist in tropical lagoons where mangrove leaves, sea grasses, and other plant material are consumed by far more varied populations of reef fish, mollusks, and crustaceans.

It's believed that most Pacific marine organisms evolved in the triangular area bounded by New Guinea, the Philippines, and the Malay Peninsula. This "Cradle of Indo-Pacific Marinelife" includes a wide variety of habitats and has remained stable through several geological ages. From this cradle the rest of the Pacific was colonized.

Dolphins
While most people use the terms dolphin and porpoise interchangeably, a porpoise lacks the dolphin's beak (although many dolphins are also beakless). There are 62 species of dolphins, and only six species of porpoises. Dolphins leap from the water and many legends tell of their saving humans, especially children, from drowning (the most famous concerns Telemachus, son of Odysseus). Dolphins often try to race in front of ferries and large ships.

Because herds of dolphins in the Eastern Pacific tend to swim above schools of yellowfin tuna, tens of thousands a year drown in purse seine nets deliberately set around the marine mammals, crushing or suffocating them. In 1990, after a worldwide tuna boycott spearheaded by San Francisco's Earth Island Institute, H.J. Heinz (StarKist) and many other American tuna packers announced that they would only can tuna caught using dolphin-safe fishing methods. Unfortunately, some canneries in Italy, Japan, and other countries continue to accept tuna without reservations from dolphin-killing Mexican and South American vessels. If you care about marine mammals, look for the distinctive "dolphin-safe" label before buying any tuna at all. (No dolphins are killed by purse seiners in the South Pacific, and all fish canned in the region are caught using dolphin-safe methods.)

Sharks

The danger from sharks has been greatly exaggerated. Of some 300 different species, only 28 are known to have attacked humans. Most dangerous are the white, tiger, hammerhead, and blue sharks. Fortunately, all of these inhabit deep water far from the coasts. An average of only 50 shark attacks a year occur worldwide, so considering the number of people who swim in the sea, your chances of being involved are about one in a million. In the South Pacific shark attacks on snorkelers or scuba divers are extremely rare and the tiny mosquito is a far more dangerous predator.

Sharks are not aggressive where food is abundant, but they can be very nasty far offshore. You're always safer if you keep your head underwater (with a mask and snorkel), and don't panic if you see a shark—you might attract it. Even if you do, they're usually only curious, so keep your eye on the shark and slowly back off. The swimming techniques of humans must seem very clumsy to fish, so it's not surprising if they want a closer look.

Sharks are attracted by shiny objects (a knife or jewelry), bright colors (especially yellow and red), urine, blood, spearfishing, and splashing (divers should ease themselves into the water). Sharks normally stay outside the reef, but get local advice. White beaches are safer than dark, and clear water safer than murky. Avoid swimming in places where sewage or edible wastes enter the water, or where fish have just been cleaned. You should also exercise care in places where local residents have been fishing with spears or even hook and line that day.

Never swim alone if you suspect the presence of sharks. If you see one, even a supposedly harmless nurse shark lying on the bottom, get out of the water calmly and quickly, and go elsewhere. Recent studies indicate that sharks, like most other creatures, have a "personal space" around them that they will defend. Thus an attack could be a shark's way of warning someone to keep his distance, and it's a fact

that over half the victims of these incidents are not eaten but merely wounded. Sharks are much less of a problem in the South Pacific than in colder waters because marine mammals (commonly hunted by sharks) are rare here, so you won't be mistaken for a seal or an otter.

Let common sense be your guide, not irrational fear or carelessness. Many scuba divers come actually *looking* for sharks, and local divemasters seem able to swim among them with impunity. If you're in the market for some shark action, most dive shops can provide it. Just be aware that getting into the water with feeding sharks always entails some danger, and the divemaster who admits this and lays down some basic safety guidelines (such as keeping your hands clasped or arms folded) is probably a safer bet than the macho man who says he's been doing it for years without incident. Like all other wild animals, sharks deserve to be approached with respect.

Sea Urchins

Sea urchins (living pincushions) are common in tropical waters. The black variety is the most dangerous: their long, sharp quills can go right through a snorkeler's fins. Even the small ones, which you can easily pick up in your hand, can pinch you if you're careless. They're found on rocky shores and reefs, never on clear, sandy beaches where the surf rolls in.

Most sea urchins are not poisonous, though quill punctures are painful and can become infected if not treated. The pain is caused by an injected protein, which you can eliminate by holding the injured area in a pail of very hot water for about 15 minutes. This will coagulate the protein, eliminating the pain for good. If you can't heat water, soak the area in vinegar or urine for a quarter hour. Remove the quills if possible, but being made of calcium, they'll decompose in a couple of weeks anyway—not much of a consolation as you limp along in the meantime. In some places sea urchins are considered a delicacy: the orange or yellow urchin gonads are delicious with lemon and salt.

Others

Although jellyfish, stonefish, crown-of-thorns starfish, cone shells, eels, and poisonous sea snakes are hazardous, injuries resulting from

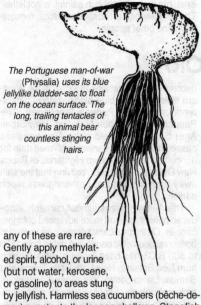

The Portuguese man-of-war (Physalia) uses its blue jellylike bladder-sac to float on the ocean surface. The long, trailing tentacles of this animal bear countless stinging hairs.

any of these are rare. Gently apply methylated spirit, alcohol, or urine (but not water, kerosene, or gasoline) to areas stung by jellyfish. Harmless sea cucumbers (bêche-de-mer) punctuate the lagoon shallows. Stonefish also rest on the bottom and are hard to see due to camouflaging; if you happen to step on one, its dorsal fins inject a painful poison, which burns like fire in the blood. Fortunately, stonefish are not common.

It's worth knowing that the venom produced by most marine animals is destroyed by heat, so your first move should be to soak the injured part in very hot water for 30 minutes. (Also hold an opposite foot or hand in the same water to prevent scalding due to numbness.) Other authorities claim the best first aid is to squeeze blood from a sea cucumber scraped raw on coral directly onto the wound. If a hospital or clinic is nearby, go there immediately.

Never pick up a live cone shell; some varieties have a deadly stinger dart coming out from the pointed end. The tiny blue-ring octopus is only five centimeters long but packs a poison that can kill a human. Eels hide in reef crevices by day; most are dangerous only if you inadvertently poke your hand or foot in at them. Of course, never tempt fate by approaching them (fun-loving divemasters sometimes feed the big ones by hand and stroke their backs).

REPTILES

Six of the seven species of sea turtles are present in the South Pacific (the flatback, green, hawksbill, leatherback, loggerhead, and olive ridley turtles). These magnificent creatures are sometimes erroneously referred to as "tortoises," which are land turtles. All species of sea turtles now face extinction due to overhunting and egg harvesting. Sea turtles come ashore from November to February to lay their eggs on the beach from which they themselves originally hatched, but female turtles don't commence this activity until they are twenty years old. Thus a drop in numbers today has irreversible consequences a generation later, and it's estimated that breeding females already number in the hundreds or low thousands. Turtles are often choked by floating plastic bags they mistake for food, or they drown in fishing nets. Importing any sea turtle product is prohibited in most developed countries, but protection is often inadequate in the South Pacific countries themselves.

Geckos and skinks are small lizards often seen on the islands. The skink hunts insects by day; its tail breaks off if you catch it, but a new one quickly grows. The gecko is nocturnal and has no eyelids. Adhesive toe pads enable it to pass along vertical surfaces, and it changes color to avoid detection. Unlike the skink, which avoids humans, geckos often live in people's homes, where they eat insects attracted by electric lights. Its loud clicking call may be a territorial warning to other geckos. Two species of geckos are asexual: in these, males do not exist and the unfertilized eggs hatch into females identical to the mother. Geckos are the highest members of the animal world where this phenomenon takes place. During the 1970s a sexual species of house gecko was introduced to Samoa and Vanuatu, and in 1988 it arrived on Tahiti. These larger, more aggressive geckos have drastically reduced the population of the endemic asexual species.

Saltwater crocodiles, an endangered species, are present from the Western Caroline Islands down through the Solomons to Australia. There are very few land snakes in Oceania and the more common sea snakes are shy and inoffensive. This, and the lack of leeches, poisonous plants, and dangerous wild animals, makes the South Pacific a paradise for hikers. Centipedes exist, but their bite, though painful, is not lethal. The main terrestrial hazards are dogs, mosquitoes, and other people.

HISTORY

THE ERA OF DISCOVERY AND SETTLEMENT

Prehistory

Oceania is the site of many "lasts." It was the last area on earth to be settled by humans, the last to be discovered by Europeans, and the last to be both colonized and decolonized. It all began over 50,000 years ago when Papuan-speaking Australoid migrants from Southeast Asia arrived in New Guinea and Australia, at a time when the two formed a single landmass. Buka Island in the North Solomons had already been settled by Papuans 30,000 years ago. During the Pleistocene (Ice Age), sea level was 150 meters lower and people could cross the narrow channels from Indonesia on primitive rafts more easily. Cut off by rising waters 10,000 years ago, the Australian Aboriginals maintained their Paleolithic (Old Stone Age) culture undisturbed until modern times.

Little is known about the prehistory of the Papuan peoples of New Guinea as their first coastal settlements are now covered by the sea, but they spoke non-Austronesian languages and were characterized by convex noses. Similar short, black peoples are found in various parts of Asia (the Philippine Negritos, for example). Some of the Dravidian peoples of southern India are also very short and dark, indicating the direction from which these migrations came. These pre-Austronesian societies were egalitarian, religious rites were performed communally, and a preference was shown for the curvilinear style in art.

The Austronesians

Next to arrive, after about 1600 B.C., were the broad-nosed, lighter-skinned Austronesians from Indonesia or the Philippines. They settled in enclaves along the coast of New Guinea and gradually populated the islands of Melanesia as far as Fiji. They mixed with the Papuans to become the Melanesians of today; in the Western Solomons the blue-black-skinned inhabitants still speak Papuan languages. The Papuans evolved their Neolithic (New Stone Age) culture long before the Austronesians passed this way: the earliest confirmed date for agriculture in the Western Highlands of Papua New Guinea is 4000 B.C., proving that the shift away from hunting and gathering was much earlier.

The Austronesians almost certainly introduced pottery and had more advanced outrigger canoes. Distinctive *Lapita* pottery, decorated in horizontal geometric bands and dated from 1500 to 500 B.C., has been found at sites ranging from New Britain to New Caledonia, Tonga, and Samoa. *Lapita* pottery has allowed archaeologists not only to study Melanesian prehistory, but also to trace the migrations of an Austronesian-speaking race, the Polynesians, with some precision. These *Lapita* people were great traders: obsidian from New Britain Island in Papua New Guinea was exported to Santa Cruz in the Solomons—some 1,700 km away. By A.D. 300 at the latest the Polynesians had ceased to make pottery.

It's interesting to note that the third to second millenniums B.C. saw continuous movement of peoples from Southeast Asia and southern China into Indonesia. All insular Southeast Asian peoples are Austronesian-speaking, and the Polynesians were the advance guard of this migration. These population movements continue today with contemporary Javanese colonization of West Papua and Polynesian migration to New Zealand, Hawaii, and the American continent.

The colorful theory that Oceania was colonized from the Americas is no longer seriously entertained. The Austronesian languages are today spoken from Madagascar through Indonesia all the way to Easter Island and Hawaii, half the circumference of the world! All of the introduced plants of old Polynesia, except the

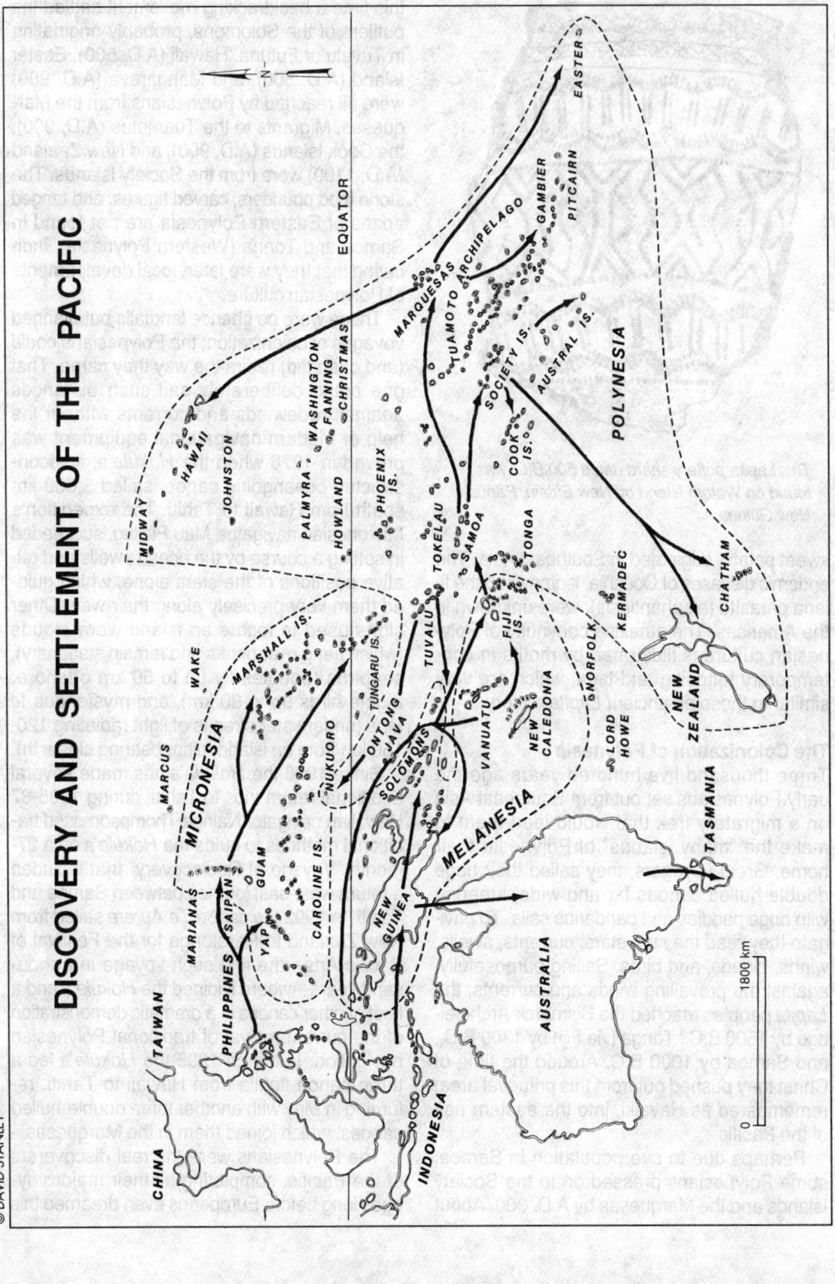

DISCOVERY AND SETTLEMENT OF THE PACIFIC

© DAVID STANLEY

CHINA

TAIWAN

PHILIPPINES

INDONESIA

AUSTRALIA

NEW GUINEA

MELANESIA

MICRONESIA

POLYNESIA

MARIANAS
SAIPAN
GUAM
YAP
CAROLINE IS.
MARSHALL IS.
WAKE
MARCUS
MIDWAY
HAWAII
JOHNSTON
PALMYRA
WASHINGTON
FANNING
CHRISTMAS
HOWLAND
PHOENIX IS.
TOKELAU
SAMOA
TUVALU
FIJI IS.
TONGA
KERMADEC
NEW CALEDONIA
VANUATU
SOLOMONS
ONTONG JAVA
NUKUORO
TUNGARU IS.
NORFOLK
LORD HOWE
NEW ZEALAND
CHATHAM
TASMANIA
COOK IS.
SOCIETY IS.
AUSTRAL IS.
TUAMOTU ARCHIPELAGO
MARQUESAS
GAMBIER
PITCAIRN
EASTER

EQUATOR

1800 km

0

This Lapita pottery shard dated 500 B.C. was found on Watom Island off New Britain, Papua New Guinea.

sweet potato, originated in Southeast Asia. The endemic diseases of Oceania, leprosy and the filaria parasite (elephantiasis), were unknown in the Americas. The amazing continuity of Polynesian culture is illustrated by motifs in contemporary tattooing and tapa, which are very similar to those on ancient *Lapita* pottery.

The Colonization of Polynesia
Three thousand five hundred years ago the early Polynesians set out from Southeast Asia on a migratory trek that would lead them to make the "many islands" of Polynesia their home. Great voyagers, they sailed their huge double-hulled canoes far and wide, steering with huge paddles and pandanus sails. To navigate they read the sun, stars, currents, swells, winds, clouds, and birds. Sailing purposefully, against the prevailing winds and currents, the *Lapita* peoples reached the Bismarck Archipelago by 1500 B.C., Tonga (via Fiji) by 1300 B.C., and Samoa by 1000 B.C. Around the time of Christ they pushed out from this primeval area, remembered as Havaiki, into the eastern half of the Pacific.

Perhaps due to overpopulation in Samoa, some Polynesians pressed on to the Society Islands and the Marquesas by A.D. 300. About

this time a backtracking movement settled the outliers of the Solomons, probably originating in Tuvalu or Futuna. Hawaii (A.D. 500), Easter Island (A.D. 500), and Mangareva (A.D. 900) were all reached by Polynesians from the Marquesas. Migrants to the Tuamotus (A.D. 900), the Cook Islands (A.D. 900), and New Zealand (A.D. 1100) were from the Society Islands. The stone food pounders, carved figures, and tanged adzes of Eastern Polynesia are not found in Samoa and Tonga (Western Polynesia), indicating that they were later, local developments of Polynesian culture.

These were no chance landfalls but planned voyages of colonization: the Polynesians could (and often did) return the way they came. That one could deliberately sail such distances against tradewinds and currents without the help of modern navigational equipment was proved in 1976 when the *Hokule'a,* a reconstructed oceangoing canoe, sailed 5,000 km south from Hawaii to Tahiti. The expedition's Micronesian navigator, Mau Piailug, succeeded in setting a course by the ocean swells and relative positions of the stars alone, which guided them very precisely along their way. Other signs used to locate an island were clouds (which hang over peaks and remain stationary), seabirds (boobies fly up to 50 km offshore, frigate birds up to 80 km), and mysterious *te lapa* (underwater streaks of light radiating 120-150 km from an island, disappearing closer in).

Since 1976 the *Hokule'a* has made several additional return trips to Tahiti; during 1985-87 Hawaiian navigator Nainoa Thompson used traditional methods to guide the *Hokule'a* on a 27-month "Voyage of Rediscovery" that included a return west-east journey between Samoa and Tahiti. In 1992 the canoe *Te Aurere* sailed from New Zealand to Rarotonga for the Festival of Pacific Arts—the first such voyage in a thousand years—where it joined the *Hokule'a* and a fleet of other canoes in a dramatic demonstration of the current revival of traditional Polynesian navigation. In March 1995 the *Hokule'a* led a three-canoe flotilla from Hawaii to Tahiti, returning in May with another three double-hulled canoes, which joined them in the Marquesas.

The Polynesians were the real discoverers of the Pacific, completing all their major voyages long before Europeans even dreamed this ocean existed. In double canoes lashed together to form rafts, carrying their plants and animals with them, they penetrated as close to Antarctica as the South Island of New Zealand, as far north as Hawaii, and as far east as Easter Island—a full 13,000 km from where it's presumed they first entered the Pacific!

Neolithic Society

To some extent, the peoples of Polynesia, Micronesia, and Melanesia all kept gardens and a few domestic animals. Taro was cultivated on ingenious terraces or in organic pits; breadfruit was preserved by fermentation through burial (still a rare delicacy). Stone fishponds and fish traps were built in the lagoons. Pandanus and coconut fronds were woven into handicrafts. On the larger Polynesian islands these practices produced a surplus, which allowed the emergence of a powerful ruling class. The common people lived in fear of their gods and chiefs.

The Polynesians and Melanesians were cannibals, although the intensity of the practice varied from group to group: cannibalism was rife in the Marquesas but relatively rare on Tahiti. Early European explorers were occasionally met by natives who would kneel beside them on the shore, squeezing their legs and pinching their posteriors to ascertain how tasty and substantial these white people would be to eat. It was believed that the mana or spiritual power of an enemy would be transferred to the consumer;

to eat the body of one who was greatly despised was the ultimate revenge. Some Melanesians perceived the pale-skinned newcomers with "odd heads and removable skin" (hats and clothes) as evil spirits, perhaps ancestors intent on punishing the tribe for some violation of custom.

Jean-Jacques Rousseau and the 18th-century French rationalists created the romantic image of the "noble savage." Their vision of an ideal state of existence in harmony with nature disregarded the inequalities, cannibalism, and warfare that were a central part of island life, just as much of today's travel literature ignores the poverty and political/economic exploitation many Pacific peoples now face. Still, the legend of the South Pacific maintains its magic hold.

EUROPEAN CONTACT AND EXPLORATION

Hispanic Exploration

The first Europeans on the scene were Spaniards and Portuguese. The former were interested in gold and silver, new territories and colonies, and conversion of the heathen, while the latter were concerned with finding passages from Europe to the Moluccas, fabled Spice Islands of the East. Vasco Núñez de Balboa be-

---

THE TU'I TONGAS

The Tu'i Tongas (hereditary kings of Tonga) were considered to be of divine origin. The creator god Tanaloa descended from the sky and had a son, 'Aho'eitu, by a beautiful Tongan girl named Va'epopua, The child became the first of the line, perhaps about A.D. 950. These absolute monarchs were the only Tongan males who were not tattooed or circumcised; there was an elaborate etiquette to be observed in all contacts with their subjects.

Fatafehi Paulaho, the 36th Tu'i Tonga, who hosted Captain Cook at Tongatapu in 1777

JOHN WEBBER

EUROPEAN CONTACT COUNTDOWN

DATE	EXPLORER AND NATIONALITY	DESTINATION
1513	Balboa, Spanish	Pacific Ocean
1521	Magellan, Spanish	Mariana Islands, Philippines
1526	Meneses, Portuguese	Irian Jaya
1527	Saavedra, Spanish	Marshall Islands
1543	Villalobos, Spanish	Caroline Islands
1545	Ortiz de Retes, Spanish	New Guinea
1568	Mendaña, Spanish	Tuvalu, Solomon Islands
1595	Mendaña, Spanish	Marquesas Islands
1606	Quirós, Spanish	Tuamotu Islands, Vanuatu
1606	Torres, Spanish	Australia
1615	Schouten/Le Maire, Dutch	Futuna
1642	Tasman, Dutch	Tasmania, New Zealand
1643	Tasman, Dutch	Tonga, Fiji
1722	Roggeveen, Dutch	Easter Island, Samoa
1765	Byron, English	Tokelau Islands
1767	Wallis, English	Tahiti, Wallis
1767	Carteret, English	Pitcairn
1769	Cook, English	Leeward Islands, Australs
1773	Cook, English	Cook Islands
1774	Cook, English	Niue, New Caledonia, Norfolk
1777	Cook, English	Christmas Island
1778	Cook, English	Hawaiian Islands
1781	Mourelle, Spanish	Vava'u
1791	Vancouver, English	Chatham Islands, Rapa
1798	Fearn, English	Nauru

Ocean. He did it by making a wide sweep to almost 40° north latitude, where he picked up the westerlies. This enabled a ship, if it left Manila in June, to sail to Acapulco in five or six months, a navigational discovery that turned the Pacific into a settled highway. Previously it had been easy to enter the Pacific, but another matter to return the same way.

In 1568 Álvaro de Mendaña sailed from Peru to the Solomon Islands in search of gold. On his second trip to the Solomons in 1595 Mendaña discovered the southern Marquesas Islands. The voyage of Mendaña's pilot, Pedro Fernandez de Quirós, from Espiritu Santo in what is now Vanuatu to Mexico in 1606, against contrary winds in rotten ships with a starving, dying company, must rank as one of the greatest feats of Pacific journeying. The 16th-century Spaniards defined the bounds of the Pacific and added whole clusters of islands to geographic knowledge.

came the first to set eyes on this great ocean when he crossed the Isthmus of Panama in 1513 to discover the Mar del Sur, or South Seas (as opposed to the Mar del Norte, or North Seas, the Caribbean). On 28 November 1520 Ferdinand Magellan's three ships entered the Pacific around the bottom of South America. Pointing the vessels northwest, their next landfall was Guam, two months later. Though Magellan himself was killed in the Philippines, his surviving crew made it back to Spain in September 1522. The first circumnavigation in history had taken three years!

In 1565 a Spanish friar-seaman, Fray Andres de Urdaneta, succeeded in returning eastward to Mexico after a voyage deep into the Pacific

Terra Australis Incognita

The systematic European exploration of the Pacific was actually a search for *terra australis incognita,* a great southern continent believed to balance the continents of the north. There were many daring voyages during this period. The 17th century was the age of the Dutch explorations in search of new markets and trade routes. The first Dutch ships followed the routes pioneered by the Spanish and made few discoveries of significance. However, Van Diemen, the Dutch governor-general of Batavia (present-day Jakarta) and a man of vision and great purpose, provided the backing for Abel Tasman's noteworthy voyage of 1642, which entered the Pacific from the west, rather than the east.

Tasman was instructed to find "the remaining unknown part of the terrestrial globe"—your basic Herculean task. Because of his meticulous and painstaking daily journals, Tasman is known as the historian of Pacific explorers. His observations proved invaluable to geography, adding Tasmania, New Zealand, Tonga, and parts of Fiji to Western knowledge. Tasman was the first to sail right around Australia. Jacob Roggeveen's voyage in 1722 also failed to discover the unknown continent, but he narrowed down the area of conjecture considerably.

The exploratory success of the 18th-century English was due to this 17th-century scientific labor. Although using 17th-century equipment, William Dampier explored with an 18th-century attitude. In 1745, the British Parliament passed an act promising £20,000 to the first British subject who could, in a British ship, discover and sail through a strait between Hudson's Bay and the South Seas. Thus many explorers were spurred to investigate the region. This route would have proven infinitely shorter than the one around Cape Horn, where the weather was often foul and the ships in perpetual danger; on Samuel Wallis's voyage of 1766-67, his two ships took four months to round the chaotic Straits of Magellan. Captain John Byron (grandfather of the poet) ignored his orders to find a passage between the South Seas and Hudson's Bay and instead sought the Solomons, discovered initially by Mendaña. His circumnavigation took only two years. The great ocean was becoming an explorer's lake.

Captain Cook

The extraordinary achievements of James Cook on his three voyages in the ships *Endeavor, Resolution, Adventure,* and *Discovery* left his successors with little to do but marvel over them. A product of the Age of Enlightenment, Cook was a mathematician, astronomer, practical physician, and master navigator. Son of a Yorkshire laborer, he learned seamanship on small coastal traders plying England's east coast. Chosen to command the *Endeavor* in 1768 though only a warrant officer, Cook was the first captain to eliminate scurvy from his crew (with sauerkraut).

The scientists of his time needed accurate observations of the transit of Venus, for if the passage of Venus across the face of the sun were measured from points on opposite sides of the earth, then the size of the solar system could be determined for the first time. In turn, this would make possible accurate predictions of the movements of the planets, vital for navigation at sea. Thus Cook was dispatched to Tahiti, and Father Hell (a Viennese astronomer of Hungarian origin) to Vardo, Norway.

So as not to alarm the French and Spanish, the British admiralty claimed Cook's first voyage (1768-71) was primarily to take these measurements. His real purpose, however, was to further explore the region, in particular to find *terra australis incognita.* After three months on Tahiti, he sailed west and spent six months exploring and mapping New Zealand and the whole east coast of Australia, nearly tearing the bottom off his ship, the *Endeavor,* on the Great

WILLIAM HODGES

Omai, a Polynesian from Huahine, accompanied Captain Cook to England and returned.

Barrier Reef in the process. Nine months after returning to England, Cook embarked on his second expedition (1772-75), resolving to settle the matter of *terra australis incognita* conclusively. In the *Resolution* and *Adventure*, he sailed entirely around the bottom of the world, becoming the first to cross the Antarctic Circle and return to tell about it.

In 1773 John Harrison won the greater part of a £20,000 reward offered by Queen Anne in 1714 "for such Person or Persons as shall discover the Longitude at Sea." Harrison won it with the first marine chronometer (1759), which accompanied Cook on his second and third voyages. Also on these voyages was Omai, a native of Tahiti who sailed to England with Cook in 1774. Omai immediately became the talk of London, the epitome of the "noble savage," but to those who knew him he was simply a sophisticated man with a culture of his own.

In 1776 Cook set forth from England for a third voyage, supposedly to repatriate Omai but really to find a Northwest Passage from the Pacific to the Atlantic. He rounded Cape Horn and headed due north, discovering Kauai in what we know as the Hawaiian Islands on 18 January 1778. After two weeks in Hawaii, Cook continued north via the west coast of North America but was forced back by ice in the Bering Strait. With winter coming, he returned to Hawaiian waters and located the two biggest islands of the group, Maui and Hawaii. On 14 February 1779, in a short, unexpected, petty skirmish with the Hawaiians, Cook was killed. Today he remains the giant of Pacific exploration. He'd dispelled the compelling, centuries-old hypothesis of an unknown continent, and his explorations ushered in the British era in the South Seas.

The Fatal Impact

Most early contacts with Europeans had a hugely disintegrating effect on native cultures. When introduced into the South Pacific, European sicknesses—mere discomforts to the white man—devastated whole populations. Measles, influenza, tuberculosis, dysentery, smallpox, typhus, typhoid, and whooping cough were deadly because the islanders had never developed resistance to them. The white man's alcohol, weapons, and venereal disease further accelerated the process.

CONVERSION, COLONIALISM, AND WAR

Conversion

The systematic exploration of the South Pacific began in the 18th century as the Industrial Revolution in Europe stimulated the need for raw materials and markets. After the American Revolution, much of Britain's colonizing energy was deflected toward Africa, India, and the Pacific. This gave them an early lead, but France and the U.S. weren't far behind.

As trade with China developed in the late 18th and early 19th centuries, Europeans combed the Pacific for products to sell to the Chinese. A very profitable triangular pattern of trade developed, in which European ships traded the natives cheap whiskey, muskets, and glass beads for sandalwood, bêche-de-mer (sea cucumbers), pearls, and turtle shell, which were then sold to the Chinese for silk, tea, and porcelain. Ruffian whalers, sealers, and individual beachcombers flooded in. Most were unsavory characters who acted as mercenaries or advisors to local chiefs, but two, William Mariner and Herman Melville, left valuable accounts of early Polynesia.

After the easily exploited resources were depleted, white traders and planters arrived to establish posts and to create copra and cotton plantations on the best land. Missionaries came to "civilize" the natives by teaching that all their customs—cannibalism, warring with their neighbors, having more than one wife, wearing leaves instead of clothes, dancing, drinking kava, chewing betel nut, etc.—were wrong. They taught hard work, shame, thrift, abstention, and obedience. Tribes now had to wear sweaty, rain-soaked, germ-carrying garments of European design. Men dressed in singlets and trousers, and the women in Mother Hubbards, one-piece smocks trailing along the ground. To clothe themselves and build churches required money, obtained only by working as laborers on European plantations or producing a surplus of goods to sell to European traders. In many instances this austere, harsh Christianity was grafted onto the numerous taboo systems of the Pacific.

Members of the London Missionary Society arrived at Tahiti in 1797, though it was not until 1815 that they succeeded in converting the

Tahitians. One famous LMS missionary, Rev. John Williams, spread Protestantism to the Cook Islands (1823) and Samoa (1830). The children of some of the European missionaries who "came to do good, stayed to do well" as merchants. Later, many islanders themselves became missionaries: some 1,200 of them left

their homes to carry the word of God to other islands. The first Catholic priests arrived in Polynesia in 1834. They competed with the Protestants for influence and divided whole islands on religious grounds.

Due to the inhospitable environment and absence of a chiefly class, the conversion and

A PACIFIC CHRONOLOGY

50,000 B.C.	Papuans enter the Pacific	1893	Solomon Islands becomes a British protectorate
8000 B.C.	Papuans reach the Solomons	1893	American-led military coup in Hawaii
1600 B.C.	Polynesians enter the Pacific		
1300 B.C.	Polynesians reach Tonga	1906	Britain and France assume joint control of Vanuatu
1000 B.C.	Polynesians reach Samoa		
A.D. 300	Polynesians reach Tahiti and the Marquesas	1914	New Zealand takes Western Samoa from Germany
A.D. 500	Polynesians reach Hawaii and Easter Island	1942	Japanese invade Solomon Islands
		1962	Western Samoa achieves independence
A.D. 900	Polynesians reach Cook Islands		
A.D. 1100	Polynesians reach New Zealand	1965	Cook Islands becomes self-governing
1768	Captain Cook's first Pacific voyage		
1779	Captain Cook killed by the Hawaiians	1966	France begins nuclear testing at Moruroa
1788	Australia becomes a British colony	1970	Fiji and Tonga achieve independence
1789	the mutiny on the *Bount*		
1797	Protestant missionaries reach Tahiti	1971	South Pacific Forum established
1836	Catholic missionaries reach Tahiti	1974	Niue becomes internally self-governing
1840	New Zealand becomes a British colony	1975	Papua New Guinea achieves independence
1842	Tahiti becomes a French protectorate	1978	Solomon Islands and Tuvalu achieve independence
1845	George Tupou I becomes king of Tonga	1980	Vanuatu achieves independence
1847	Tongans invade eastern Fiji	1985	French agents sink the *Rainbow Warrior*
1852	New Caledonia becomes a French colony	1985	South Pacific Nuclear-free Zone Treaty signed
1874	Fiji becomes a British colony	1987	two military coups in Fiji
1879	the first Indians arrive in Fiji	1988	French troops massacre Kanak independence fighters
1880	Tahiti-Polynesia becomes a full French colony		
1888	Cook Islands becomes a British protectorate	1992	France suspends nuclear testing in Polynesia
1888	Chile annexes Easter Island	1994	Law of the Sea comes into force
1889	Germany and the U.S. partition Samoa	1995	Chirac restarts French nuclear testing

Sea slug, sea cucumber, trepang, or bêche-de-mer: The rows of feet along the length of this echinoderm show its close relationship to the sea urchin and starfish. Food particles caught on the long sticky tentacles are licked off in the mouth. These creatures, obtained in the South Pacific by early traders, are eaten in China as an aphrodisiac.

commercialization of Melanesia was not carried out until several decades later. After the 1840s, islanders were kidnapped by "blackbirders," who sold them as slaves to planters in Fiji and Queensland. Worst were the Peruvians, who took 3,634 islanders to Peru in 1862 and 1863, of whom only 148 were returned.

Colonialism

The first European colonies in Oceania were Australia (1788) and New Zealand (1840). Soon after, the French seized Tahiti-Polynesia (1842) and New Caledonia (1853). A canal across Central America had already been proposed and Tahiti was seen as a potential port of call on the sea routes to Australia and New Zealand. New Caledonia was used first as a penal colony; nickel mining only began in the 1870s. The French annexed several other island groups near Tahiti in the 1880s.

Not wishing to be burdened with the expense of administering insignificant, far-flung colonies, Britain at first resisted pressure to officially annex other scattered South Pacific island groups, though Fiji was reluctantly taken in 1874 to establish law and order. In 1877 the Western Pacific High Commission was set up to protect British interests in the unclaimed islands.

Then the emergence of imperialist Germany and construction of the Panama Canal led to a sudden rush of annexations by Britain, France, Germany, and the U.S. between 1884 and 1900. In 1899 Samoa was partitioned between Germany and the U.S., with Tonga and the Solomon Islands added to the British sphere of influence as compensation. The last island group to be taken over was New Hebrides (Vanuatu), declared a "condominium" by Britain and France in 1906 to forestall German advances.

Around the time of WW I Britain transferred responsibility for many island groups to Australia and New Zealand. The struggle for hegemony in imperialist Europe in 1914-18 prompted Germany's colonies (New Guinea, Western Samoa, and Micronesia) to be taken by the British and Japanese empires. The South Pacific had become a British lake, economically dependent on Australia and New Zealand, a situation largely unchanged today.

By the late 19th century, the colonies' tropical produce (copra, sugar, vanilla, cacao, and fruits) had become more valuable and accessible; minerals, such as nickel and phosphates, and guano were also exploited. Total control of these resources passed to large European trading companies, which owned the plantations, ships, and retail stores.

This colonial economy stimulated the immigration of Indian laborers to Fiji, the alienation of major tracts of native land in New Caledonia, and a drop in the indigenous populations in general by a third, not to mention the destruction of their cultures. Between the world wars, Japan developed Micronesia militarily and economically by bringing in thousands of Koreans, Okinawans, and Japanese, who supplanted the native populations. Although the U.S. had gained a toehold in the Pacific by annexing Hawaii and the Spanish colonies (Guam and the Philippines) in 1898, further expansion was frustrated by the British and Japanese.

War

World War II provided the U.S. with unparalleled opportunities to project power across the Pacific and grab territory. Japan had hoped to become the dominant force in Asia and the Pacific by establishing a "Greater East Asia Co-Prosperity Sphere." After the Japanese occupation of French Indochina in July 1941, an economic embargo on iron from the U.S. and oil from the Dutch East Indies presented the Japanese with a choice: strangulation, retreat, or war.

The history of the Pacific War can be found in many books. Half a million Japanese soldiers and civilians died far from their native shores. The only area covered in this handbook actually occupied by Japanese troops was the Solomon Islands; an account of the fighting there is included in that chapter's introduction. Large American staging and supply bases were created on Grande Terre, Espiritu Santo, Guadalcanal, and Bora Bora. The Americans built airfields on islands right across the South Pacific, while their ships controlled the southern supply routes to Australia and New Zealand.

DECOLONIZATION

World War II gave the U.S. almost the whole of Micronesia, which became the Trust Territory of the Pacific Islands, a "strategic trust" in which military bases and nuclear testing were allowed. During the late 1980s the U.S. restructured its colonial empire north of the equator through a series of "compacts of free association" establishing three quasi-independent client states, the Republic of the Marshall Islands, the Federated States of Micronesia, and the Republic of Palau, all completely dependent on U.S. monetary handouts in exchange for continuing American military domination of the region. A fourth area, the Commonwealth of the Northern Mariana Islands, had already been annexed by the U.S. in 1976.

NAVAL HISTORY CENTER, WASHINGTON, D.C.

As a Korean scout interpreter of the 2nd Marine Raider Battalion savors his rice-mash-and-tea breakfast, Solomon Islanders prepare to move. The U.S. forces on Guadalcanal enjoyed the islanders' full cooperation during WW II.

South of the equator, a more straightforward decolonization process took place. In 1960 the United Nations issued a Declaration of Granting of Independence to Colonial Countries and Peoples, which encouraged the trend toward self-government, yet it was not until the independence of Western Samoa from New Zealand in 1962 that a worldwide wave of decolonization reached the region. During the 1960s and 1970s seven South Pacific countries (Fiji, Papua New Guinea, Solomon Islands, Tonga, Tuvalu, Vanuatu, and Western Samoa) became independent as Britain, Australia, and New Zealand dismantled their colonial systems.

Cook Islands and Niue have achieved de facto independence in association with New Zealand. The French territories, Tahiti-Polynesia, New Caledonia, and Wallis and Futuna, have varying degrees of internal autonomy, although great power continues to be wielded by appointed French officials who are not responsible to the local assemblies. Decolonization is a hot issue in these French colonies, where the South Pacific's only active independence movements are found. American Samoa remains firmly tied to Washington by the subsidies it receives. Pitcairn is still a British colony, and New Zealand administers Tokelau, but this is at the request of the inhabitants. Easter Island is an old-fashioned colony of Chile.

The postwar period also witnessed the growth of regionalism. In 1947 the South Pacific Commission was established by Australia, Britain, France, the Netherlands, New Zealand, and the U.S. to maintain the status quo through coordination among the colonial powers, yet conferences organized by the SPC brought the islanders together for the first time. In 1971 the newly independent states formed the South Pacific Forum, a more vigorous regional body able to tackle political as well as social problems. In 1988 Papua New Guinea, the Solomon Islands, and Vanuatu formed the Melanesian Spearhead regional grouping, though relations between P.N.G. and the Solomons became strained after P.N.G. military incursions from Bougainville in 1992 in pursuit of rebels opposed to the Port Moresby government.

French Colonialism .
New Caledonia, Tahiti-Polynesia, and Wallis and Futuna are part of a worldwide chain of French colonies also including Kerguelen, Guyana, Martinique, Guadeloupe, Mayotte, Reunion, and St. Pierre and Miquelon, under the DOM-TOM (Ministry of Overseas Departments and Territories). France spends FF16 billion a year to maintain this system, a clear indicator that it's something totally different from colonial empires of the past, which were based on economic exploitation, not investment. A closer analogy is the American network of military bases around the world, which serves the same purpose—projecting power. What is at stake is French national prestige.

These conditions contradict what has happened elsewhere in the South Pacific. Over the past 20 years, as Britain voluntarily withdrew from its Pacific colonies, French pretensions to global medium-sized nuclear power status grew stronger. This digging in has created the anachronism of a few highly visible bastions of white colonialism in the midst of a sea of English-speaking independent nations. When French officials summarily rejected all protests against their nuclear testing and suppression of independence movements, even going to the extreme of employing state terrorism to stop the Greenpeace protest vessel *Rainbow Warrior* from leaving New Zealand in 1985, most Pacific islanders were outraged. By continuing its uncontrolled immigration and military buildups, France destabilizes the region.

Nuclear Testing
No other area on earth has been more directly affected by the nuclear arms race than the Pacific. From 6 August 1945 until the present with only a short break from 1992 to 1995, not a year passed without one nuclear power or another testing their weapons here. The U.S., Britain, and France have exploded over 250 nuclear bombs at Bikini, Enewetak, Christmas Island, Moruroa, and Fangataufa, an average of over six a year for 40 years, more than half of them by France. The U.S. and British testing was only halted by the 1963 Partial Nuclear Test Ban Treaty with the Soviets, while the French tests continued until President Mitterrand decided to freeze testing in April 1992 in light of the collapse of the Cold War. Soon after being elected president of France in May 1995, Jacques Chirac decided to spit in the face of world opinion and ordered that the testing start again.

VOYAGES OF THE *RAINBOW WARRIOR*

Beginning in 1978 the *Rainbow Warrior* confronted whalers, sealers, and nuclear waste dumpers in the North Atlantic. In 1980 the ship was seized in international waters by the Spanish navy while interfering with the Spanish whale kill. After five months under arrest in Spain the ship made a dramatic escape. In 1981-82 *Rainbow Warrior* led the struggle against the Canadian harp seal slaughter, bringing about a European Economic Community ban on the import of all seal products. The next year the ship battled Soviet whalers in Siberia, finally

escaping to Alaska with naval units in hot pursuit. A confrontation with Peruvian whalers led to the termination of that whale hunt. In 1985, fresh from being fitted with sails in Florida, the *Rainbow Warrior* reentered the Pacific to rescue nuclear victims from Rongelap in the Marshalls. In July, 1985, as the valiant little ship lay at anchor in Auckland Harbor, New Zealand, externally attached terrorist bombs tore through the hull in the dead of night to prevent a voyage to Moruroa to protest French nuclear testing in the Pacific.

Rainbow Warrior, *onetime flagship of the Greenpeace fleet*

The issue of nuclear testing is bound up with decolonization. American and British testing is no longer possible now that their test sites in Micronesia have achieved self-government; an independent Tahiti-Polynesia would never allow French testing. The Marshallese still suffer radiation sickness from U.S. testing in the 1940s and 1950s (some of it deliberately inflicted by the use of islanders as human guinea pigs), and the French are still covering up the consequences of their tests. The end result of nuclear testing in Micronesia and Polynesia is ticking away in the genes of thousands of servicemen and residents present in those areas during the tests, and at the fragile underground test site used by the French.

The fact that the nuclear age began in their backyard at Hiroshima and Nagasaki has not been lost on the islanders. They see few benefits coming from nuclear power, only deadly dangers. On 6 August 1985 eight member states of the South Pacific Forum signed the South Pacific Nuclear-Free Zone Treaty, also known as the Treaty of Rarotonga, which bans nuclear testing, land-based nuclear weapon storage, and nuclear waste dumping on their territories. Each country may decide for itself if nuclear-armed warships and aircraft are to be allowed entry. In effect, the treaty merely formalized the existing status quo, and Vanuatu refused to sign because it felt all nuclear weapons should have

been banned from the region. Of the five nuclear powers, China and the USSR promptly signed the treaty, while to date the U.S., France, and Britain have steadfastly refused, demonstrating that these three have no arms control policies for the South Pacific, only military policies. (American Samoa's congressional delegate, Eni Faleomavaega, has tried without success to get Washington's signature on the treaty.)

Moruroa

In July 1985, French General Directorate for Foreign Security (DGSE) agents attached terrorist bombs to the Greenpeace ship *Rainbow Warrior* as it lay anchored at Auckland, New Zealand, and Greenpeace photographer Fernando Pereira drowned in the sinking. Top officials in the French government who ordered the bombing and the agents who carried out the attack have never been brought to trial.

The bombing was intended to prevent the ship from sailing to Moruroa in the Tuamotu Islands of Tahiti-Polynesia to commemorate the 40th anniversary of Hiroshima. The French also feared that the Greenpeace environmentalists intended to carry doctors to Mangareva in the Gambiers for a survey that might have uncovered serious health problems the French have successfully covered up. The French attack couldn't stop a five-boat "peace flotilla," which formed a floating picket line off Moruroa in October 1985. The ketch *Vega,* which deliberately breached the 12-nautical-mile limit, was seized by a French warship.

In December 1990 Greenpeace's *Rainbow Warrior II* attempted to visit Moruroa. Although forbidden to enter the lagoon or tie up to the dock, radiation expert Norm Buske managed to take plankton samples from the ship's position just outside the atoll's 12-mile exclusion zone while surrounded by French helicopters and destroyers. The samples were found to contain cobalt 60 and cesium 134, proof that radiation is leaking into the sea from Moruroa. Buske and four others then embarked in an inflatable craft and attempted to enter the lagoon to take further samples, but were immediately arrested by the French naval armada and deported to Los Angeles. Tahitian political leaders have asked the World Health Organization to intervene and properly investigate the radiation leaking from Moruroa, but the French government continues to prevent this. Turn to "The Nuclear Test Zone" in the Tahiti-Polynesia chapter for more information about these matters.

THE PACIFIC TODAY

The modern world is transforming the Pacific more and more. Outboards replace outriggers; Coca-Cola substitutes for coconuts. Consumerism has caught on in the towns. As money becomes more important, the islanders learn the full meaning of urban unemployment, poverty, homelessness, inequality, and acculturation. Television is still absent from many Pacific homes; instead attitudes are molded by the tens of thousands of VCRs that play pirated videotapes available at hundreds of corner stores. Villagers are trapped by material desires.

The diet is changing as imported processed foods take the place of fiber-rich fresh foods such as breadfruit, taro, and plantain. The ocean would seem a bountiful resource, but on many islands the reef waters are already overharvested, and the inhabitants often lack the ability to fish the open sea. Thus the bitter irony of Japanese canned mackerel.

Noncommunicable nutrition-related ailments such as heart disease, diabetes, and cancer now account for three-quarters of all deaths in urban Polynesia, but less than a quarter in predominantly rural Vanuatu and Solomon Islands, where infectious and parasitic diseases such as malaria, dengue fever, pneumonia, diarrhea, hepatitis, and tuberculosis prevail. Cigarette smoking is a major health problem, with over 50% of Pacific men habitual smokers. Rural islanders tend to smoke more than those in the towns, and 88% of rural indigenous Fijian men are smokers.

Salaried employment leads inevitably to the replacement of the extended family by the nuclear family, and in Melanesia there's a growing gap between new middle classes with government jobs and the village-based populace. Western education has aroused expectations the island economies are unable to fulfill, and the influx to the capitals has strained social services to the breaking point, creating serious housing and employment problems, especially among the young. Melanesian women are victimized by domestic violence, economic burdens, and cultural change.

Subsistence agriculture continues to play an important role in the South Pacific, and most land is still held communally by extended families or clans; however, pressure is mounting from outside agencies such as the World Bank and the International Monetary Fund (IMF) to convert communal land into individual ownership under the guise of "economic development." Western economic models only give importance to commodity crops useful to industrialized countries as raw materials, discounting the stabilizing effect of subsistence. When the tiller of the soil is no longer able to eat his own produce, he becomes a consumer of processed foods marketed by food-exporting countries such as Australia and New Zealand, and the country loses a measure of its independence.

Individually registered land can be taxed and sold on the open market, and throughout the third world the privatization of land has inevitably led to control of the best tracts passing into the hands of transnational corporations, banks, and the government. Pressure from agencies such as the IMF to force local governments to register land and allow it to be used as loan collateral is part of a stratagem to dispossess the islanders of their land. Once their communal land is gone, people are no longer able to fall back on their own produce when economies deteriorate, and they find themselves forced to take any job they are offered. Acutely aware of the fate of the Hawaiians and the New Zealand Maoris, the islanders are highly sensitive about land rights, yet these instincts are coming under increasing pressure as tottering governments have "land mobilizations" forced upon them by foreign capital.

All across the South Pacific, regional stability is eroded by class differences, government corruption, uneven development, industrial exploitation, and the declining terms of trade. By making the economies dependent on external markets, much current "economic development" destabilizes societies once secure in "primitive affluence," and virtually every Pacific entity is now subservient to some degree of neocolonial control. Local interests are sacrificed for the benefit of transnational corporations and industrialized states far across the sea.

GOVERNMENT

Generally, the South Pacific is governed on the basis of constitutional law, an independent judiciary, and regular elections, with some regional idiosyncrasies. In Western Samoa only *matai* (Samoan chiefs) may stand as candidates for 47 of the 49 parliamentary seats, although since 1991 all adults can vote. Fiji has a constitution that stipulates that the president and prime minister must be indigenous Fijians and segregates voting along racial lines, while in Tonga only nine of the 30 members of parliament are elected directly by the people.

The two-party system is a relatively recent legacy of the last years of colonial rule. Traditionally, Melanesians governed themselves by consensus: those involved would sit down and discuss a problem until a compromise was reached, which everyone then accepted, and this bottom-up democracy still governs life throughout Melanesia. Governments in Melanesia today are typically weak coalitions of small parties dependent on skillful leaders to hold them together. There were no regional leaders or powerful chiefs in Melanesia before the arrival of Europeans. Polynesia, on the other hand, was governed by powerful hereditary chiefs and kings; the Fijian political system was strongly influenced by the Polynesians.

Although only six of the 15 political entities covered in this book are fully independent, most of the others are internally self-governing. Tokelau, a dependency of New Zealand, has resisted self-government out of fear that it might lead to a reduction in subsidies. The appointed French high commissioners in Tahiti-Polynesia, Wallis and Futuna, and New Caledonia run the administrations of those territories, though locally elected assemblies have some control over economic matters.

Regional Organizations

The **South Pacific Commission** (B.P. D5, 98848 Nouméa Cédex, New Caledonia; tel. 687/26-20-00, fax 687/26-38-18) is a regional technical assistance organization established in 1947 to promote the economic and social well-being of the peoples of the South Pacific. Fields of activity include agriculture, plant protection, fisheries, community health, rural development, community education training, women's development, and statistical services. Twenty-two Pacific island countries and territories are members, together with Australia, France, New Zealand, and the United States. Each October delegates from all 26 member governments meet at the **South Pacific Conference** to discuss the Commission's program and budget for the coming year. About 90% of the SPC's US$20-million budget comes out of grants from the colonial or ex-colonial members; the island governments contribute only token amounts. The Netherlands withdrew from the SPC in 1962 after Indonesia annexed eastern New Guinea, and in 1995 Britain also pulled out.

A higher-profile regional organization is the **South Pacific Forum** with 16 self-governing members (Australia, Cook Islands, Federated

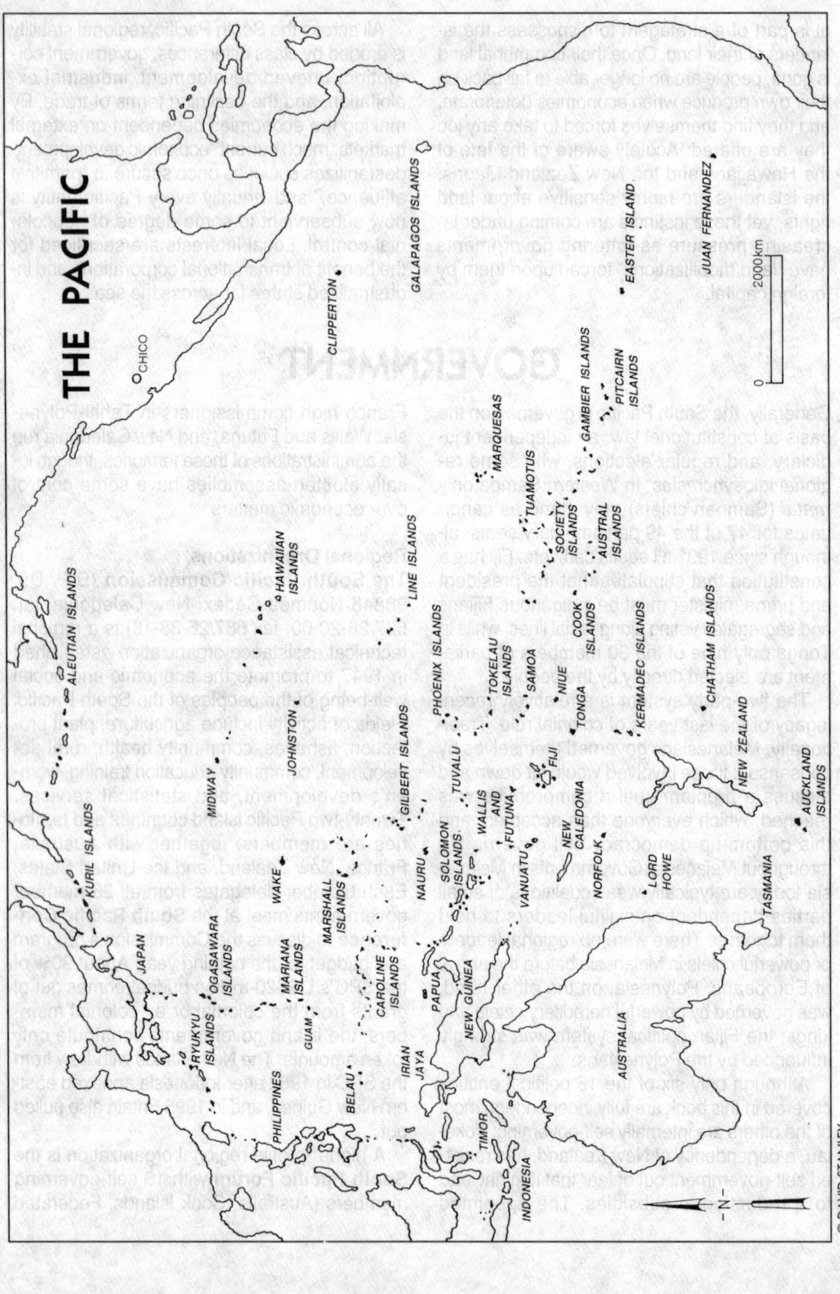

THE PACIFIC

CHICO

ALEUTIAN ISLANDS

KURIL ISLANDS

JAPAN

RYUKYU ISLANDS

OGASAWARA ISLANDS

MARIANA ISLANDS

GUAM

BELAU

PHILIPPINES

TIMOR

INDONESIA

IRIAN JAYA

PAPUA NEW GUINEA

CAROLINE ISLANDS

MARSHALL ISLANDS

WAKE

MIDWAY

JOHNSTON

HAWAIIAN ISLANDS

LINE ISLANDS

PHOENIX ISLANDS

GILBERT ISLANDS

NAURU

TUVALU

SOLOMON ISLANDS

WALLIS AND FUTUNA

TOKELAU ISLANDS

SAMOA

NIUE

TONGA

FIJI

VANUATU

NEW CALEDONIA

NORFOLK

LORD HOWE

AUSTRALIA

TASMANIA

NEW ZEALAND

AUCKLAND ISLANDS

CHATHAM ISLANDS

KERMADEC ISLANDS

COOK ISLANDS

AUSTRAL ISLANDS

SOCIETY ISLANDS

TUAMOTUS

MARQUESAS

GAMBIER ISLANDS

PITCAIRN ISLANDS

EASTER ISLAND

JUAN FERNANDEZ

GALAPAGOS ISLANDS

CLIPPERTON

0   2000km

N

© DAVID STANLEY

OCEANIA AT A GLANCE

Land areas and sea areas (the ocean area included within the 200-nautical mile Exclusive Economic Zone, or EEZ, of each country) are expressed in square kilometers. The Political Status category denotes the year in which the country became independent, or in which the territory or province fell under colonial rule by the power named. The sea areas (and various other figures) were taken from South Pacific Economies: Statistical Summary, published by the South Pacific Commission, Noumea.

COUNTRY	POPULATION	LAND AREA	SEA AREA	CAPITAL	POLITICAL STATUS	CURRENCY	AIRPORT TAX
Tahiti-Polynesia	188,814	3,543	5,030,000	Papeete	France 1842	CFP	none
Pitcairn Islands	65	47	800,000	Adamstown	Britain 1838	NZ$	none
Easter Island	2,770	171	355,000	Hanga Roa	Chile 1888	peso	US$5
Cook Islands	18,543	240	1,830,000	Avarua	N.Z. 1901	NZ$	NZ$25
Niue	2,300	259	390,000	Alofi	N.Z. 1900	NZ$	NZ$20
Kingdom of Tonga	94,649	691	700,000	Nuku'alofa	ind. 1970	pa'anga	T$15
American Samoa	46,773	201	390,000	Utulei	U.S. 1900	US$	none
Western Samoa	161,298	2,842	120,000	Apia	ind. 1962	tala	WS$20
Tokelau	1,577	12	290,000	Fakaofo	N.Z. 1925	tala	none
Wallis and Futuna	14,000	274	300,000	Mata Utu	France 1887	CFP	none
Tuvalu	9,061	25	900,000	Funafuti	ind. 1978	A$	A$30
TOTAL POLYNESIA	**539,850**	**8,305**	**11,105,000**				
Fiji	758,275	18,272	1,290,000	Suva	ind. 1970	F$	F$20
New Caledonia	164,173	18,576	1,740,000	Noumea	France 1853	CFP	none
Vanuatu	149,739	12,189	680,000	Vila	ind. 1980	vatu	Vt2000
Solomon Islands	285,796	27,556	1,340,000	Honiara	ind. 1978	SI$	SI$30
Papua New Guinea	3,963,000	462,243	3,120,000	Moresby	ind. 1975	kina	K15
TOTAL MELANESIA	**5,320,983**	**538,836**	**8,170,000**				
Nauru	8,902	21	320,000	Yaren	ind. 1968	A$	none
Kiribati	72,298	810	3,550,000	Bairiki	ind. 1979	A$	A$10
Marshall Islands	43,380	181	2,131,000	Majuro	ind. 1986	US$	US$10
Federated States of Micronesia	98,071	701	2,978,000	Pohnpei	ind. 1986	US$	US$10
Palau	15,122	488	629,000	Koror	ind. 1994	US$	US$10
Guam	133,152	541	218,000	Agana	U.S. 1898	US$	none
Northern Marianas	43,345	478	777,000	Saipan	U.S. 1976	US$	none
TOTAL MICRONESIA	**414,270**	**3,220**	**10,603,000**				
TOTAL OCEANIA	**6,275,103**	**550,361**	**29,878,000**				

States of Micronesia, Fiji, Kiribati, Marshall Islands, Nauru, New Zealand, Niue, Palau, Papua New Guinea, Solomon Islands, Tonga, Tuvalu, Vanuatu, and Western Samoa). The three French colonies have been refused membership on the basis that they are not self-governing entities. Founded in 1971, the Forum grew out of dissatisfaction with the apolitical SPC, which was seen as a vestige of colonialism. Two-thirds of the Forum's budget is provided by Australia and New Zealand. Each year the heads of government of the Forum countries meet for informal political discussions. The South Pacific Nuclear-Free Zone treaty was signed at the Forum's meeting on Rarotonga in 1985, and the 1992 meeting at Honiara identified global warming and sea-level rise as the most serious threats to the region. The 1994 Brisbane Forum strongly condemned "environmental piracy" by Asian logging and fishing companies operating in the region. In October 1994 the Forum's international influence was enhanced when the SPF was granted observer status at the United Nations (Fiji, Solomon Islands, Vanuatu, and Western Samoa were already U.N. members).

In 1972 the SPF established the **Forum Secretariat** (G.P.O. Box 856, Suva, Fiji Islands; tel. 679/312-600, fax 679/302-204), called the South Pacific Bureau for Economic Cooperation until 1988, as its executive body. The SPC has set up a regional shipping line (the Pacific Forum Line), an association of airlines, a relief fund, and a trade agreement known as SPARTECA. The **Forum Fisheries Agency** (Box 629, Honiara, Solomon Islands; tel. 677/21124, fax 677/ 23995), formed in 1979, coordinates the fisheries policies of the 16 member states, negotiates licensing agreements with foreign countries and 2,600 foreign fishing boats, assists in surveillance and enforcement, carries out scientific and commercial studies of marine resources, and provides technical assistance to local fishing industries.

The **South Pacific Regional Environment Program** (Box 240, Apia, Western Samoa; fax 685/20-231), established in 1982 by the SPC, the SPF, and the United Nations, promotes sustainable development by creating programs in fields such as environmental management, global change, species conservation, nature reserves, and pollution management, and through

education and international coordination. Their list of mail-order "Technical Publications" is worth requesting. In early 1992 the SPREP's offices were moved from Nouméa to Apia, Western Samoa, and in 1993 it became an autonomous regional organization with 26 member countries.

Other Regional Institutions

The **University of the South Pacific** (Box 1168, Suva, Fiji Islands; tel. 679/313-900, fax 679/301-305) was organized in 1967 to serve the Cook Islands, Fiji, Kiribati, Marshall Islands, Nauru, Niue, Solomon Islands, Tokelau, Tonga, Tuvalu, Vanuatu, and Western Samoa. The initial campus was at Lauthala, near Suva, and in 1977 the USP's School of Agriculture was established at Alafua, outside Apia, Western Samoa. The USP has six action-oriented institutes, such as the Institute of Marine Resources at Honiara. The major USP complex at Port Vila houses the Pacific Languages Unit and Law Department. The original aim of the USP was to facilitate the localization of posts held by expatriates until independence, but in recent years the emphasis has shifted from teacher training to business studies and technology. In 1994 the USP had almost 3,000 students studying at the two main campuses, plus 5,000 taking degree courses at USP extension centers in all 12 member countries except Tokelau. Another 1,600 persons were enrolled in Continuing Education courses. The USP extension centers are well worth visiting to purchase the excellent, inexpensive books published by the university's Institute of Pacific Studies. Recently, however, the university's image as an agent of regional cooperation and integration has been tarnished by an increase in racial tension on the Suva USP campus, with ugly brawls between Fijian, Samoan, ni-Vanuatu, and Solomon Island students, often leading to serious injuries and the expulsion of those involved. The university administration has attempted to sweep this situation under the carpet, and the exploration of racial subjects in the classroom is unofficially taboo. Student associations and sporting teams on campus are organized along racial lines, greatly contributing to the problem.

In 1987 the **Université Française du Pacifique** (B.P. 4635, Papeete; tel. 689/42-16-80, fax 689/41-01-31) was established, with university centers at Tahiti and Nouméa specializing in law, humanities, social sciences, languages, and science. In 1994 this university had about 2,400 students.

One of the few regional grass roots coalitions is the **Nuclear-Free and Independent Pacific** (NFIP) movement, which organizes conferences periodically (Fiji 1975, Pohnpei 1978, Hawaii 1980, Vanuatu 1983, Manila 1987, New Zealand 1990) to allow activists from groups from all around the Pacific to get together and map out strategy and solidarity in the struggle against militarism and colonialism. The directing body of the NFIP movement is the **Pacific Concerns Resource Center** (Private Mail Bag, Suva, Fiji Islands; tel. 679/304-649, fax 679/304-755).

Other institutions fostering a feeling of regional unity include the **Festival of Pacific Arts** and the **South Pacific Games** (see "Holidays and Festivals" later in this introduction).

ECONOMY

Trade

Australia and New Zealand have huge trade surpluses with the Pacific islands. In 1990, for example, Australia sold them A$1483 million in goods while only purchasing A$661 million worth. New Zealand sells four times more than it buys. New Zealand meat exporters routinely ship low-quality "Pacific cuts" of fatty, frozen mutton flaps unsalable on world markets to Pacific countries like Tonga and Samoa. American companies dump junk foods such as "turkey tails" on the islands, and tinned mystery meats arrive from afar.

The only country consistently recording a trade surplus is phosphate-rich Nauru in Micronesia, though Nauru's phosphate reserves will be completely exhausted before the end of the decade. The trade deficits make the industrialized, exporting nations the main beneficiaries of the island economies. For Australia and New Zealand the South Pacific market is not very important, but for every island nation this trade is vital to their interests.

The main products exported by the South Pacific countries are minerals (Papua New Guinea, New Caledonia, Nauru, Fiji); fish and seafood

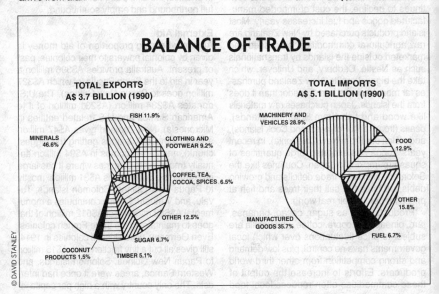

BALANCE OF TRADE

TOTAL EXPORTS
A$ 3.7 BILLION (1990)

- MINERALS 46.6%
- FISH 11.9%
- CLOTHING AND FOOTWEAR 9.2%
- COFFEE, TEA, COCOA, SPICES 6.5%
- OTHER 12.5%
- SUGAR 6.7%
- TIMBER 5.1%
- COCONUT PRODUCTS 1.5%

TOTAL IMPORTS
A$ 5.1 BILLION (1990)

- MACHINERY AND VEHICLES 28.9%
- FOOD 12.9%
- OTHER 15.8%
- FUEL 6.7%
- MANUFACTURED GOODS 35.7%

© DAVID STANLEY

TRADING PARTNERS

(1990—A$ MILLION)	IMPORTS FROM	EXPORTS TO
Australia	1,483	661
New Zealand	405	104
South Pacific	73	125
France	1,120	238
United Kingdom	248	272
Other Europe	447	574
U.S.A.	826	540
Japan	668	788
Other Asia	803	503
Other countries	1,020	451
TOTAL	**7,093**	**4,256**

(American Samoa, Solomon Islands, Fiji, Papua New Guinea); coffee, tea, and cocoa (Papua New Guinea, Solomon Islands); sugar (Fiji); and timber (Papua New Guinea, Solomon Islands, Vanuatu, Fiji). Compared to these, palm oil, animal feed, coconut oil, copra, fruits, and vegetables are regionally insignificant. Most of the countries are large importers of processed food.

While the value of agricultural exports continues to decline, the cost of imported manufactured goods and fuel increases yearly. Most island products purchased by New Zealand are raw agricultural commodities, processed and marketed outside the islands by transnationals such as Nestlé, Cadbury, and Unilever, which take the biggest profits. New Zealand purchases far more bananas from Ecuador than it does from the islands. Japan purchases raw materials like wood and fish (from Solomon Islands), pearls (from Tahiti-Polynesia and Cook Islands), and nickel ore (from New Caledonia). In recent years Tonga has exported large quantities of squash (pumpkin) to Japan. Countries like the Solomons with large trade deficits and growing debts are forced to sell their trees and fish at prices far below their real worth.

Products such as sugar, cacao, bananas, taro, pineapples, copra, coffee, and vanilla are subject to price fluctuations over which local governments have no control, plus low demand and strong competition from other third world producers. Efforts to increase the output of these commodities often reduces local food production, leading to expensive food imports.

The Lomé Convention provides for the entry of set quotas of agricultural commodities from the coastal countries of Africa, the Caribbean, and the Pacific into the European Union at fixed prices. This arrangement is crucial to countries that rely on a single export for much of their foreign exchange, but Lomé IV is due to expire in the year 2000 and it's possible it will not be renewed, with disastrous consequences for Fiji and Solomon Islands.

Aid, investment, and tourism help offset the trade imbalance, but this also fosters dependence. Trade between the various South Pacific countries is limited by a basic similarity of their products and shipping tariffs that encourage bulk trade with Australia and New Zealand rather than local interisland trade. Ten countries participate in the Pacific Forum Line set up by the South Pacific Forum to facilitate trade with Australia and New Zealand. In practice, the Line's large container ships run full northbound and empty southbound.

External Aid

An overwhelming proportion of aid money is given by colonial powers to their colonies, past or present. Australia provides A$396 million a year in aid to the South Pacific (of which A$327 million goes to Papua New Guinea). The U.S. donates A$234 million (A$231 million of it to American Samoa and U.S.-related entities in Micronesia), New Zealand gives A$47 million a year (with Cook Islands getting the biggest chunk), and Japan pumps in A$94 million annually (most of it to countries where it has large investments). Britain gives A$31 million, mostly to Papua New Guinea, Solomon Islands, Tuvalu, and Vanuatu. France contributes a monumental A$632 million, but A$612 million of that goes to maintaining the three French colonies. Even Germany, which lost its colonies in 1914, still gives all but a tiny fraction of its A$15 million to Papua New Guinea, Solomon Islands, and Western Samoa, areas were it once had interests. The only country with a high per capita income that is not greatly dependent on aid is Fiji. (All figures above are from 1990.)

With the collapse of the Cold War, American checkbook diplomats are reducing the amount of influence they buy. In 1994 the U.S. closed its two regional aid offices, citing higher American priorities in Eastern Europe. The U.S. did pay for the new parliament building in Honiara, and the Chinese government has bankrolled huge government complexes in Vanuatu and Western Samoa. British aid is being replaced by the growing influence of the European Union, providing soft loans, import quotas and subsidies, technical assistance, etc. Japanese aid is intended primarily to ensure easy access to rich fishing waters or to support Japanese business activities in the islands.

The current rhetoric calls for the substitution of trade for aid, but the terms of this trade are certainly not to the islands' advantage. The World Bank and other international banks aggressively market "project loans" to facilitate the production of goods for sale on world markets. Of course, the main beneficiaries of these projects are the contractors who carry them out, while transnational corporations obtain the ability to exploit the region's natural resources more easily. The recipient state is left with a debt burden it can only service through exports. Should the golden carriage turn into a pumpkin, as happened in the 1980s when tropical commodity prices collapsed, the International Monetary Fund steps in with emergency loans to make sure the foreign banks don't lose their money. Local governments are forced to accept "structural adjustment programs" dictated from Washington, and the well-paid Western bankers always insist that social spending be cut first. Tottering governments are forced to clearcut their rainforests and sell their soil to meet financial obligations. This kind of chicanery has caused untold misery in Africa, Asia, and Latin America, often with the connivance of corrupt officials. Today, countries like Western Samoa and Solomon Islands seem on the brink of falling into the clutches of the IMF.

Although the South Pacific absorbs the highest rate of aid per capita in the world, much aid is wasted on doing things for people instead of helping them do things for themselves. Aid that empowers people by increasing their capacity to

identify, understand, and resolve problems is the exception, while prestige projects like huge airports, sophisticated communications networks, and fancy government buildings, which foster dependence on outsiders, are the rule. Aid spent in the capitals prompts unproductive migrations to the towns. Virtually all Japanese aid is "tied," with most of the benefit going to Japanese companies. In contrast, Australia, Canada, and New Zealand are to be commended for taking the trouble to develop low-profile microprojects to assist individual communities. There's a growing imbalance between the cost of government in relation to locally generated revenues. Salaries for officials, consultants, and various other "experts" eat up much aid.

Aid to local communities is often provided more effectively by nongovernment organizations such as the Foundation for the Peoples of the South Pacific, a branch of **Counterpart** (Farragut Square, 910 17th St. N.W., #328, Washington, D.C. 20006, U.S.A.; tel. 202/296-9676, fax 202/296-9679), a nonprofit voluntary organization 85% funded by the U.S. Agency for International Development as part of the privatization of U.S. foreign policy. The FPSP has projects in Fiji, Solomon Islands, Tonga, Vanuatu, and Western Samoa that emphasize sustainable development, health and nutrition, income generation, and family food production. Other groups of this kind include the **South Pacific Peoples Foundation of Canada** (1921 Fernwood Road, Victoria, BC V8T 2Y6, Canada; tel. 604/381-4131, fax 604/388-5258) and the **United Kingdom Foundation for the South Pacific** (32 Howe Park, Edinburgh EH10 7HF, Scotland; tel. 44-131/445-5010, fax 44-131/445-5255). Each May the Canadian group organizes a "Pacific Networking Conference" on Vancouver Island that brings together North Americans and representatives from Pacific development groups to discuss themes of regional interest. This conference is open to the public and well worth attending.

Business
Foreign investment in tourism, commerce, banking, construction, transportation, and mining is heavy. Foreign logging operations and local slash-and-burn agriculture threaten the rain-

forests of the high islands, and many governments lack the political will to enforce conservation. In Solomon Islands, Malaysian logging companies are cutting the forests at far beyond the sustainable rate while paying landowners a royalty of *less than one percent* of the value of the timber. An Australian study has shown how Vanuatu and Solomon Islands lost A$350 million in 1993 due to overcutting and underpaying by the Asian loggers. Payoffs to local officials allow this practice to continue.

One hopeful sign as far as industrial employment goes is the **Pacific Islands Industrial Development Scheme** (PIIDS), which assists in establishing new factories and encouraging exports. Since 1980 the **South Pacific Regional Trade and Economic Cooperation Agreement** (SPARTECA) has allowed most products of the South Pacific Forum countries unrestricted duty-free entry to New Zealand and Australia on a nonreciprocal basis, provided they have 50% local content. The only exceptions are sugar, steel, motor vehicles, and clothing, which are subject to quotas in Australia. Tonga and Western Samoa have set up Small Industries Centers (SIC) as a result of PIIDS and SPARTECA.

Garments are now Fiji's second-largest export, with US$90.4 million sold in 1991. Tonga and Cook Islands export much smaller quantities of locally made clothing. Low wages, inadequate labor legislation, and weak unions combine with tax concessions, exemption from customs duties, government subsidies in the form of infrastructure and training, and an open market in Australia and New Zealand to make Fiji attractive to foreign garment manufacturers. Women make up the vast majority of the workforce, earning less than a tenth as much as their counterparts in New Zealand, where working conditions are far better. Similarly a large Japanese factory in Western Samoa exports automotive electrical parts.

Critics of SPARTECA say the 50% local content rule discourages companies from operating efficiently by reducing local costs and relegates them to the bottom end of the market since the raw materials required for upmarket products are not available in the islands. Now with universal trade barriers falling in the wake of the 1994 signing of the GATT, the value of selective trade agreements such as SPARTECA and the Lomé Convention is decreasing, and in the future it will be much more difficult for the Pacific island industries to compete with cheap-labor areas in Asia.

Various Moneymaking Scams

In 1971 the New Hebrides (now Vanuatu) became the first Pacific entity to offer offshore banking facilities to foreign corporations attempting to avoid taxation in their home countries. In 1982 Cook Islands also set up a tax haven, followed by Tonga in 1985 and Western Samoa in 1989. Tonga and Niue have also entered the field. Almost a hundred brass-plate banks and over a thousand dummy corporations now operate in Vanuatu with little or no staff, fixed assets, or capital.

In 1990 Australia plugged the loopholes, which had been costing it millions of dollars a year in lost taxation, and most of the clients of the "financial centers" are now companies based in Asia. In September 1993 *Pacific Magazine* reported that Thomas J. Baker of the American FBI had told a crime conference in Sydney that illegal offshore banking seemed to be moving into the South Pacific as British and U.S. pressure closed similar operations in the Caribbean islands. Baker expressed concern that the Pacific tax havens had not ratified the United Nations convention on controlling drug transactions.

Vanuatu also runs a "Flag of Convenience" shipping register that allows first world shipping companies to evade Western safety, environmental, and labor regulations, while employing cheap third world crews on their ships. Tonga sells its sovereignty to affluent foreigners in the form of dummy Tongan passports intended to be used to slip into other countries.

In recent years representatives of American corporations seeking to dodge U.S. safety standards have appeared in a number of countries looking for alternate disposal sites for U.S. toxic wastes. The real danger of leaks, spills, and emissions from the land-based incinerators of chemical detoxification plants, and the problem of what to do with the toxic ash, indicate why third world countries are being offered large sums of money to get involved in this dirty business. Luckily all offers of this kind of "economic development" have thus far been refused, and Fiji, Solomon Islands, Tonga, Tuvalu, Western Samoa, and Vanuatu have passed legislation banning the import of wastes. The only country actively trying to sell itself as a garbage dump is U.S.-associated Marshall Islands (in Micronesia).

Minerals

The most important minerals are nickel in New Caledonia and gold in Fiji. Extensive mineral exploration is being conducted in Solomon Islands, and there are potential oil basins around Tonga, Fiji, New Caledonia, Vanuatu, and the Solomons, though as yet no oil has been discovered.

More important are the undersea mineral nodules within the Exclusive Economic Zones of Tahiti-Polynesia, Cook Islands, and Kiribati. Three known nodule deposits sit in over 6,000 meters of water in the Pacific: one stretches from Mexico to a point southeast of Hawaii; another is between Hawaii and the Marshall Islands; a third is in Tahiti-Polynesia. The potato-sized nodules contain manganese, cobalt, nickel, and copper; total deposits are valued at US$3 trillion, enough to supply the world for thousands of years. The **South Pacific Applied Geoscience Commission** (Mead Road, Nambua, Suva, Fiji Islands; tel. 679/381-377, fax 679/370-040) or SOPAC, a regional body set up by the United Nations in 1972, is in charge of assessing the development of mineral resources in the EEZs of the Pacific countries.

This undersea wealth has made France unwilling to consider independence for its Pacific colonies and made industrialized countries such as the U.S. and Britain reluctant to sign the Law of the Sea. The original text of this treaty required transnational corporations to share the benefits of undersea mining with developing nations, but a compromise adopted by the U.N. General Assembly on 28 July 1994 watered down those provisions considerably and four months later the treaty came into force. The ocean bed in international waters has been divided among the U.S., Britain, France, Germany, South Korea, China, Japan, and others by the United Nations' International Seabed Authority.

Law of the Sea

This treaty has changed the face of the Pacific. States traditionally exercised sovereignty over a three-mile belt of territorial sea along their shores; the high seas beyond those limits could be freely used by anyone. Then on 28 September 1945, President Harry Truman declared U.S. sovereignty over the natural resources of the adjacent continental shelf. U.S. fishing boats soon became involved in an acrimonious dispute with several South American countries over their rich anchovy fishing grounds, and in 1952 Chile, Ecuador, and Peru declared a 200-nautical-mile Exclusive Economic Zone along their shores. In 1958 the United Nations convened a Conference on the Law of the Sea at Geneva, which accepted national control over shelves up to 200 meters deep. Agreement could not be reached on extended territorial sea limits.

The nickel smelter just north of Nouméa, New Caledonia, is one of the largest industrial installations in the South Pacific.

AIR NEW ZEALAND

EXCLUSIVE ECONOMIC ZONES

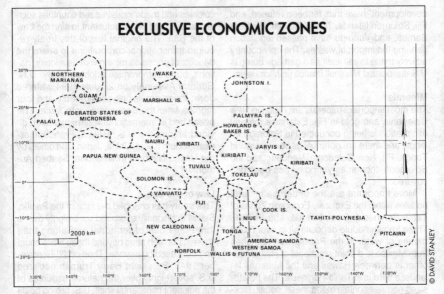

© DAVID STANLEY

National claims multiplied so much that in 1974 another U.N. conference was convened, leading to the signing of the Law of the Sea convention at Jamaica in 1982 by 159 states and other entities. This complex agreement—200 pages, nine annexes, and 320 articles—extended national control over 40% of the world's oceans. The territorial sea was increased to 12 nautical miles and the continental shelf was ambiguously defined as extending 200 nautical miles offshore. States were given full control over all resources, living or nonliving, within this belt. Fiji was the first country to ratify the convention, and by November 1994 a total of 60 countries had signed up, allowing the treaty to come into force for them.

Even before it became international law, many aspects of the Law of the Sea were accepted in practice. The EEZs mainly affect fisheries and seabed mineral exploitation; freedom of navigation within the zones is guaranteed. In 1976 the South Pacific Forum declared an EEZ for each member and decided to set up a fisheries agency soon after. The Law of the Sea increased immensely the territory of independent oceanic states, giving them real political weight for the first time. The land area of the 23 separate entities in Micronesia, Melanesia, and Polynesia (excluding Hawaii and New Zealand) total only 550,361 square km, while their EEZs total 29,878,000 square km! It's known that vast mineral deposits are scattered across this seabed, though the cost of extraction (estimated at US$1.5 billion) has prevented their exploitation to date.

Fisheries

Tuna is the second-largest commercial fishing industry in the world (after shrimp and prawns), and 55% of the world's catch is taken in the central and western Pacific. Most of the 1.5 million metric tonnes of tuna (worth US$1.5 billion) fished from the region each year is taken by about 1,300 foreign fishing boats, which pay a mere US$50 million in annual fees to work the EEZs of the island nations. Catches doubled in the 1980s and there seems to be scope to increase the take even more, yet to collect fair compensation the islanders have been forced to sail a stormy course.

For many years the U.S. tuna fleet refused to pay licensing fees because the fish were deemed migratory, but unlicensed American tuna fishing was viewed by the South Pacific states as systematic poaching, raising the specter of citizens of one of the richest nations on earth stealing from some of the poorest. Then, after the U.S. purse seiner *Jeanette Diana* was confiscated in the Solomons in 1984 and Kiribati signed a fishing agreement with the Soviets in 1985, the U.S. government finally got the message.

In 1987 the U.S. agreed to a US$60-million aid package, which included five-year licensing fees for American tuna boats to work the EEZs of the 16 member states of the South Pacific Forum Fisheries Agency. In 1990 the whole matter seemed settled when the U.S. Congress imposed management on tuna stocks in the U.S. EEZ. The "migratory" fish had finally found owners. In 1992 the U.S. agreed to pay another US$180 million to allow 55 American purse seiners access to FFA waters for 10 years. The money is divided up according to the quantity of fish caught in the waters of each member country.

The Forum Fisheries Agency, which negotiated the Tuna Treaty, now handles all fisheries agreements between the FFA member states and the U.S., Korea, Japan, and Taiwan. In past the Koreans and Taiwanese have massively under-reported their catches to avoid paying proper access fees, so in June 1993 regulations were introduced requiring purse seiners to transfer their catches to carrier ships at island ports. Port visits have the corollary benefit of bringing in about US$10,000 per ship in shore spending. This requirement reduces fishing time about 30%, which helps conserve fish stocks. Australia has donated 20 patrol boats worth A$4 million each to the island states to help police their fisheries zones.

The Japanese report their catches more honestly than the other Asians, but Japan has steadfastly refused to sign a multilateral fisheries agreement with the FFA. Instead the Japanese prefer to drive a hard bargain with each Pacific country individually, using aid money as bait. When Fiji refused to sign a bilateral fisheries agreement with Japan, Japanese fisheries aid to Fiji was slashed. Smaller Pacific countries are often unable to stand up to this bullying, and Japanese fishing companies are not above paying bribes to island officials to dissuade them from uniting to defend their only renewable resource.

Some Pacific countries have established small pole-and-line fishing industries, but the capital-intensive, high-tech purse seiner operations carried out by the Americans and Japanese are beyond their means. A workable fishing fleet requires at least 10 boats plus large amounts of fresh water and electricity for processing. Also, U.S. customs regulations tax tuna heavily unless it's processed in an American territory, which is why the two canneries at Pago Pago and three in Puerto Rico receive most of the fish. Low-wage canneries in Thailand and Indonesia also claim much of the South Pacific catch. Longline vessels are used to supply the Japanese sashimi market with the fish being transshipped by air. Very little of the catch is canned in the countries in which it's caught, although shore processing facilities exist at Levuka (Fiji) and Noro (Solomon Islands).

TOURISM

Tourism is the world's largest and fastest-growing industry, growing 260% between 1970 and 1990. A half billion people traveled abroad in 1993 compared to only 25 million in 1950, and each year over 20 million first-world tourists visit third-world countries, transferring an estimated US$25 billion from North to South. Tourism is the only industry that allows a net flow of wealth from richer to poorer countries, and in the islands it's one of the few avenues open for economic development, providing much-needed foreign exchange required to pay for imports. Unlike every other export, purchasers of tourism products pay their own transportation costs to the market.

Australia provides the greatest number of South Pacific tourists, followed by the U.S., New Zealand, Japan, and France in that order. Australia is the main source of visitors to Fiji, Solomon Islands, and Vanuatu, while New Zealanders are the biggest group in Cook Islands, Niue, Tonga, and Western Samoa. Americans are the largest single group in Tahiti-Polynesia, while the Japanese lead in New Caledonia. On a per-capita basis, Cook Islands gets the most tourists and Solomon Islands the least. Yet tourism is relatively low key: overcrowded Hawaii gets ten times as many annual visitors as the entire South Pacific combined.

Arrival levels from Australia and New Zealand are expected to remain stable and Japan, Europe, and North America are seen as the main growth markets for South Pacific tourism. Japanese interest in the region increased dramatically in the late 1980s, and Japanese companies now own top hotels in Fiji, Tahiti-Polynesia, Vanuatu, Western Samoa, and the Solomon Islands. Yet the Japanese tend to go on short holidays and only those countries with direct flights from Japan (Fiji, New Caledonia, and Tahiti-Polynesia) receive sizable numbers of Japanese tourists. Increasing numbers of European and North American visitors can be expected if airfares remain low and the region's many advantages over competing Mediterranean and Caribbean destinations can be properly marketed.

Transnational corporations promote travel only to areas where they have sizable investments, and on several islands foreign companies have gained such a death grip over the industry that they can shut off the flow of visitors overnight by simply canceling tours, bookings, and flights. To encourage hotel construction, local governments must commit themselves to crippling tax concessions and large infrastructure investments for the benefit of foreign companies. The cost of airports, roads, communications networks, power lines, and sewers can exceed the profits from tourism.

Only about 40% of the net earnings from transnational tourism actually stays in the host country. The rest is "leaked" in repatriated profits, salaries for expatriates, commissions, imported goods, food, fuel, etc. Top management positions usually go to foreigners, with local residents offered only a few low-paying service jobs.

Mass tourism plays a role in undermining the social fabric by establishing enclaves of affluence which in turn create local dissatisfaction and desires impossible to satisfy. Tourism spreads foreign values and often sets a bad example. Traditional ways of making a living are disrupted as agricultural land is converted to resort and recreational use. Major beauty spots are purchased, commercialized, and rendered inaccessible to the locals. Access to the ocean can be blocked by wall-to-wall hotels. Resort sewage causes lagoon pollution, while the reefs are blasted to provide passes for tourist craft

TOURIST ARRIVALS (1992)

Fiji Islands	278,534
Tahiti-Polynesia	123,619
New Caledonia	80,840
Cook Islands	50,009
American Samoa	45,574
Western Samoa	43,744
Vanuatu	42,653
Papua New Guinea	40,553
Tonga	19,053
Solomon Islands	10,114
Easter Island	8,000
Niue	1,668
Tuvalu	862

and stripped of corals or shells by visitors. Tourism-related construction can cause unsightly beach erosion due to the clearing of vegetation and the extraction of sand. Locally scarce water supplies are diverted to hotels, and foods such as fruit and fish can be priced out of reach of many local residents.

Although tourism is often seen as a way of experiencing other cultures, it can undermine those same cultures. Traditional dances and ceremonies are shortened or changed to fit into tourist schedules and mock celebrations are held out of season and context, and their significance is lost. Cheap mass-produced handicrafts are made to satisfy the expectations of visitors; thus, the New Guinea-style masks of Fiji and the mock-Hawaiian tikis of Tonga. Authenticity is sacrificed for immediate profits. While travel cannot help but improve international understanding, the aura of glamour and prosperity surrounding tourist resorts can present a totally false image of a country's social and economic realities.

To date most attention has focused on luxury resorts and all-inclusive tours—the exotic rather than the authentic. Packaged holidays create the illusion of adventure while avoiding all risks and individualized variables, and on many tours the only islanders seen are maids and bartenders. This elitist tourism perpetuates the colonial master-servant relationship as condescending foreigners instill a feeling of inferiority in local residents and workers. Many island governments are publicly on record as favoring development based on local resources and island technology, yet inexplicably this concept is rarely applied to tourism. Without proper planning, tourism can be the proverbial wolf in sheep's clothing.

Ecotourism

Recently "ecotourism" has become fashionable, and with increasing concern in Western countries over the damaging effects of sunlight, more and more people are looking for land-based activities as an alternative to lying on the beach. In the South Pacific the most widespread manifestation of ecotourism is the current scuba diving boom, and adventure tours by chartered yacht, ocean kayak, bicycle, or on foot are increasing in number.

This presents both a danger and an opportunity. Income from visitors wishing to experience nature gives local residents and governments an economic incentive for preserving the environment, although tourism can quickly degrade that environment through littering, the collection of coral and shells, and encouraging the development of roads, docks, camps, etc. in natural areas. Perhaps the strongest argument in favor of the creation of national parks and reserves in the South Pacific is the ability of such parks to attract visitors from industrialized countries while at the same time creating a framework for preserving nature. For in the final analysis, it is government which must enact regulations that protect the environment—market forces usually do the opposite.

Too often what is called ecotourism is actually packaged consumer tourism with a green coating. A genuine ecotourism resort will be built of local materials using natural ventilation. This means no air conditioning and only limited use of fans. The buildings should fit into the natural landscape and not restrict access to customary lands. Imported meats should not be served at the expense of local fish and vegetables, and wastes should be minimized. The use of motorized transport should be kept to an absolute minimum. Cultural sensitivity is enhanced by local ownership, and bank loans should be avoided if at all possible, as debts create pressures to cater to ecoterrorism rather than ecotourism.

Through this handbook we've tried to encourage this type of people-oriented tourism which we feel is more directly beneficial to the islanders themselves. Whenever possible we've featured smaller, family-operated, locally owned businesses. By patronizing these you'll not only get to meet the inhabitants on a person-to-person basis, but also contribute to local development. Guesthouse tourism offers excellent employment opportunities for island women as proprietors, *and* it's exactly what most visitors want. Appropriate tourism requires little investment, there's less disruption, and full control remains with the people themselves. The luxury hotels are monotonously uniform around the world—the South Pacific's the place for something different.

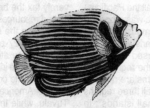

emperor angelfish
(Pomacanthus imperator)

DAVID STANL

THE PEOPLE

The aquatic continent of Oceania is divided into three great cultural areas: Polynesia and Melanesia lie mostly below the equator while Micronesia is above it. The name Polynesia comes from the Greek words *poly* (many) and *nesos* (islands). The Polynesian Triangle has Hawaii at its north apex, New Zealand 8,000 km to the southwest, and Easter Island an equal distance to the southeast. Melanesia gets its name from the Greek word *melas* (black), probably for the dark appearance of its inhabitants as seen by the early European navigators. Micronesia comes from the Greek word *mikros* (small), thus, the "small islands."

The term Polynesia was coined by Charles de Brosses in 1756 and applied to all the Pacific islands. The present restricted use was proposed by Dumont d'Urville during a famous lecture at the Geographical Society in Paris in 1831. At the same time he also proposed the terms Melanesia and Micronesia for the regions that still bear those names. The terms are not particularly good, considering that all three regions have "many islands" and "small islands"; in Melanesia it is not the islands, but the people, that are black.

The notion that the Pacific islands and their peoples are all similar—if you've seen one

you've seen 'em all—is a total fallacy. No other group of six million people anywhere on earth comes from such a variety of cultures. The population is divided between Melanesians (80%), Polynesians (seven percent), Asians (six percent), Micronesians (five percent), and Europeans (two percent). Ninety percent of the people live on high islands, the rest on low islands and atolls. About one million reside in urban areas. The region's charming, gentle, graceful peoples are among its main attractions.

Population

The high birth rate (over three percent a year in parts of Melanesia) and rapid urbanization severely tax the best efforts of governments with limited resources. The average population density across the region (excluding Papua New Guinea) is 27 persons per square kilometer, though some atolls can have over 1,000 people per square kilometer. The most densely populated Pacific countries are the Polynesian islands of American Samoa, Tokelau, Tonga, and Tuvalu, while the larger Melanesian countries have far fewer people per square kilometer. Due to the absence of family planning, populations in Melanesia are doubling every 20 years and half the total population is under 18 years of age.

More developed countries like American Samoa, Fiji, New Caledonia, and Tahiti-Polynesia are highly urbanized, with around half the population living in the towns. Solomon Islands and Vanuatu are the least urbanized, with about 85% still living in villages. The rapid growth of cities like Apia, Honiara, Nuku'alofa, Papeete, Port Vila, and Suva has led to high levels of unemployment and social problems such as alcoholism, crime, and domestic violence.

Emigration relieves the pressure a little and provides income in the form of remittances sent back. However, absenteeism also creates the problem of idled land and abandoned homes. Cook Islanders, Niueans, Tongans, and Western Samoans emigrate to New Zealand; American Samoans and Micronesians to the U.S.; Fiji Indians to Canada and Australia; and Tahitians and Wallis Islanders to New Caledonia. In American Samoa, Cook Islands, Niue, Tokelau, and Wallis and Futuna, more islanders now live off their home islands than on them. About 125,000 insular Polynesians now live in New Zealand, another 65,000 in the United States. Some 25,000 Fiji Indians are in Canada. In 1987 New Zealand withdrew visa-free entry facilities for Fijians, Tongans, and Western Samoans to limit the flow.

Many Pacific countries conduct a census only once every 10 years, and the populations statistics provided in the "At a Glance" charts in the chapter introductions of this book were the most up-to-date available at the time we went to press. Rather than publish estimates or projections, we prefer to provide hard facts. Actual population growth rates vary from 1.5% per annum in Niue to 3.5% in Solomon Islands.

Pacific Women

Traditionally Pacific women were confined to the home, while the men would handle most matters outside the immediate family. The clear-cut roles of the woman as homemaker and the man as defender and decision-maker gave stability to village life. In Melanesia the woman was responsible for working the land and doing most of the housework, thereby increasing the status of the man as head of the family; life was similar for Polynesian women, though they had greater influence.

Western education has caused many Pacific women to question their subordinate position and the changing lifestyle has made the old relationship between the sexes outmoded. As paid employment expands and women are able to hold their jobs thanks to family planning, they demand equal treatment from society. Polynesian women are more emancipated than their sisters in Melanesia, though men continue to dominate public life throughout the region. Tradition is often manipulated to deny women the right to express themselves publicly on community matters.

There are cultural barriers hindering women's access to education and employment, and the proportion of girls in school falls rapidly as the grade level increases. Female students are nudged into low-paying fields such as nursing or secretarial services; in Fiji and elsewhere, export-oriented garment factories exploit women workers with low wages and poor working conditions. Levels of domestic violence vary greatly. In Fiji, for example, it's far less accepted among indigenous Fijians than it is among Fiji Indians, and in Fiji's Mathuata Province women have a suicide rate seven times above the world average, with most of the victims being Indians.

Traditional Customs

Although the South Pacific is a region of great variety, there are a number of rituals and ceremonies which many islands have in common. The most important of these is the kava ceremony found in Fiji, Samoa, Tonga, and Vanuatu. Kava (called *yanggona* in Fiji) is a drink made from the crushed root of the pepper plant. The powder or pulp is strained or mixed with water in a large wooden bowl and drink from a coconut-shell cup. Elaborate protocols accompany formal kava ceremonies although kava is also a social drink consumed by ordinary people when they get together to relax and chat. See the introductions to the Fiji Islands and Vanuatu chapters for more information.

Another widespread feature of Pacific culture is the making of bark cloth called tapa *(masi* in Fijian) used for clothing or decoration. This felt-like cloth with stenciled or printed designs is described under "Arts and Crafts" in this introduction.

Other customs include firewalking (see under "Customs" in Fiji Islands chapter), stone fishing (see under "On the Road" in the Tahiti-Poly-

moai *on the slopes of Rano Raraku, Easter Island*

AUCKLAND INSTITUTE AND MUSEUM

nesia chapter), the use of an earth oven called an *umu* in Polynesia or a *lovo* in Fiji (see "Food and Drink" in this introduction), tattooing (see "Kava and Tattoos" under "People" in the Western Samoa chapter), land diving (see "Pentecost" under "Other Islands" in the Vanuatu chapter), shell money (see the Solomon Islands chapter), and the presentation of a whale's tooth called a *tambua* (see under "Customs" in the Fiji Islands chapter). These unique traditions are a thread uniting the diverse peoples of the Pacific.

THE POLYNESIANS

The Polynesians, whom Robert Louis Stevenson called "God's best, at least God's sweetest work," are a tall, golden-skinned people with straight or wavy, but rarely fuzzy, hair. They have fine features, almost intimidating physiques, and a soft, flowing language. One theory holds that the Polynesians evolved their great bodily stature through a selective process on their long ocean voyages, as the larger individuals with more body fat were better able to resist the chill of evaporating sea spray on their bodies. Others ascribe their huge body size to their high-carbohydrate vegetable diet.

The ancient Polynesians developed a rigid social system with hereditary chiefs; descent

was usually through the father. In most of Polynesia there were only two classes, chiefs and commoners, but in Hawaii, Tahiti, and Tonga an intermediate class existed. Slaves were outside the class system entirely, but there were slaves only in New Zealand, the Cook Islands, and Mangareva. People lived in scattered dwellings rather than villages, although there were groupings around the major temples and chiefs' residences.

They lived from fishing and agriculture, using tools made from stone, bone, shell, and wood. The men were responsible for planting, harvesting, fishing, cooking, house and canoe building; the women tended the fields and animals, gathered food and fuel, prepared food, and made clothes and household items. Both males and females worked together in family or community groups, not as individuals.

The Polynesians lost the art of pottery making during their long stay in Havaiki and had to cook their food in underground ovens *(umu)*. Breadfruit, taro, yams, sweet potatoes, bananas, and coconuts were cultivated (the Polynesians had no cereals). Pigs, chickens, and dogs were also kept for food, but the surrounding sea yielded the most important source of protein.

Numerous taboos regulated Polynesian life, such as prohibitions against taking certain plants or fish that were reserved for exploitation by the chiefs. Land was collectively owned by families and tribes, and there were nobles and commoners. Though the land was worked collectively by commoners, the chiefly families controlled and distributed its produce by well-defined customs. Large numbers of people could be mobilized for public works or war.

Two related forces governed Polynesian life: mana and *tapu*. Mana was a spiritual power of which the gods and high chiefs had the most and the commoners the least. In this rigid hierarchical system, marriage or even physical contact between persons of unequal mana was forbidden, and children resulting from sexual relations between the classes were killed. Our word "taboo" originated from the Polynesian *tapu*. Early missionaries would often publicly violate the taboos and smash the images of the gods to show that their mana had vanished.

Gods

The Polynesians worshiped a pantheon of gods, who had more mana than any human. The most important were Tangaroa (the creator and god of the oceans), and Oro, or Tu (the god of war), who demanded human sacrifices. The most fascinating figure in Polynesian mythology was Maui, a Krishna- or Prometheus-like figure who caught the sun with a cord to give its fire to the world. He lifted the firmament to prevent it from crushing mankind, fished the islands out of the ocean with a hook, and was killed trying to gain the prize of immortality for humanity. Also worth noting is Hina, the heroine who fled to the moon to avoid incest with her brother, and so the sound of her tapa beater wouldn't bother anyone. Tane (the god of light) and Rongo (the god of agriculture and peace) were other important gods. This polytheism, which may have disseminated from Raiatea in the Society Islands, was most important in Eastern Polynesia. The *Arioi* confraternity, centered

in Raiatea and thought to be possessed by the gods, traveled about putting on dramatic representations of the myths.

The Eastern Polynesians were enthusiastic temple builders, evidenced today by widespread ruins. Known by the Polynesian name *marae,* these platform and courtyard structures of coral and basalt blocks often had low surrounding walls and internal arrangements of upright wooden slabs. Once temples for religious cults, they were used for seating the gods and for presenting fruits and other foods to them at ritual feasts. Sometimes, but rarely, human sacrifices took place on the *marae.* Religion in Western Polynesia was very low-key, with few priests or cult images. No temples have been found in Tonga and very few in Samoa. The gods of Eastern Polynesia were represented in human form. There was an undercurrent of ancestor worship, but this was nowhere as strong as in Melanesia. The ancestors were more important as a source of descent for social ranking, and genealogies were carefully preserved. Surviving elements of the old religion are the still-widespread belief in spirits *(aitu),* the continuing use of traditional medicine, and the influence of myth. More than 150 years after conversion by early missionaries, most Polynesians maintain their early Christian piety and fervid devotion.

Art

The Polynesians used no masks and few colors, usually leaving their works unpainted. Art forms were very traditional, and there was a defined class of artists producing works of remarkable delicacy and deftness. Three of the five great archaeological sites of Oceania are in Polynesia: Easter Island, Huahine, and Tongatapu (the other two are Pohnpei and Kosrae in Micronesia).

This carving of a bonito from Santa Ana, Solomon Islands, was used to preserve the skull of an individual totemically related to the fish. The bones were stored in a model canoe.

THE MELANESIANS

The Melanesians have features which resemble those of the Australian Aborigines and have tightly curled hair. Their color ranges from chocolate brown to deep blue-black, with the inhabitants of the Western Solomons the most heavily pigmented people in the world. Most Melanesians live on high, volcanic islands and great differences exist between the bush people of the interiors and the saltwater people of the coasts. There's also great variety among the tribes of the interior because of the terrain; for centuries they waged wars with each other. Some clans were matrilineal, others patrilineal.

man blong Vanuatu

Art and Society

The Melanesians have developed a startling variety of customs, traditions, and cultures. The tremendous array of art objects and styles was due to the vast number of microsocieties; there was little variation within a single clan. Art among the Melanesians was a rigidly traditional medium of expression. If an object didn't correspond precisely to an accepted form, it couldn't capture the magic and the spirits, and thus would be meaningless and useless.

Melanesian society was based on consensus, gift giving, exchange, and obligation. Although there was a headman and a few sorcerers in each village, these were either elected at village councils or they "bought" their way up in society by giving feasts and pigs. Unlike Polynesian life, there were no hereditary classes of rulers or priests and no political unions outside the clan unit (the social structures in Fiji were influenced by Polynesia).

Secret societies existed and needed objects for initiation ceremonies and feasts to mark a man's passage to a higher grade. Some objects ensured fertility for man and the soil; others celebrated the harvest. Totemic figures (animals believed to be related to the clan by blood) were common. Everyday objects were artistically made, and almost everything was brightly painted. Many figures and masks were made specifically for a single ceremony, then discarded or destroyed.

More important than the social function of art was the religious function, especially in the cult of the dead. Ancestors were believed to remain in this world, and their advice and protection were often sought. The skull, considered the dwelling place of the soul, was often decorated and kept in the men's house. Sometimes carvings were made to provide a home for the spirits of the ancestors, or they were represented by posts or images. Masks were used to invoke the spirits in dance. The beauty of the objects was secondary; what the Melanesian artist sought was to create an embodied symbolism of the ancestors. In this rigid, ritual world the spirits of the dead possessed greater power than the living, and this power could be both harmful and beneficial.

Today we know little about the precise meaning of many Melanesian art objects, largely due

MUSEUMS

The most important South Pacific history or anthropology museums are at Punaauia (Tahiti), Rarotonga, Nuku'alofa, Pago Pago, Suva, Nouméa, Port Vila, and Honiara, but most of the objects in their collections are of relatively recent origin. To see Pacific artifacts dating from the period of first European contact you must visit museums outside the region. The Museum of Man (or British Museum) in London, for example, has a huge collection covering the entire region, gathered by British officials and missionaries, but most of it is locked in storage for lack of display space and funding. The warehouses of many other European museums are also bulging with Pacific art objects inaccessible to the public for the same reason, yet very few are willing to return their treasures to the islands where they originated.

Some of the 2,000 objects brought back from the Pacific by Captain Cook can be seen in the Institut für Volkskunde, Göttingen, Germany, the Hunterian Museum, Glasgow, Scotland, and the Museo Borbonico, Naples, Italy. Many British universities, such as those of Cambridge, Oxford, and Aberdeen, have impressive Pacific collections. The ethnographical museums of Budapest, St. Petersburg, and Vienna have Oceanic artifacts from former imperial collections. The vast collections of the ethnographical museums of Germany were gathered by scientific expeditions during the German colonial period before 1914. The collection of Berlin's Dahlem Museum is perhaps the best displayed, but those of Bremen, Cologne, Dresden, and Hamburg are also outstanding.

Many objects in New England museums were brought back by whalers, including the rich array of objects from Fiji and Tonga in the Peabody Museum, Salem, Massachusetts. The collections of the American Museum of Natural History, New York, and the University Museum of Philadelphia were gathered by systematic collectors at the turn of the century. The Field Museum of Natural History, Chicago, has the best collection of Melanesian art in the world, and its "Traveling the Pacific" exhibit gives you the sensation of undertaking an ocean voyage. The Bernice Bishop Museum, Honolulu, has been adding to its Polynesian collection for over a century.

Mention must also be made of the Melanesian art at Basel, plus the fine collections of the Royal Museum of Art and History, Brussels, the Museum of Man, Paris, the Musée Barbier-Muller, Geneva, the Asia and Pacific Museum, Warsaw, the Exeter City Museum, the Metropolitan Museum of Art, New York, the St. Louis Art Museum, the de Young Memorial Museum, San Francisco, and the Australian Museum, Sydney. The museums of New Zealand, especially those of Auckland, Christchurch, Dunedin, and Wellington, hold a rich store of Pacific art, and a few have recently loaned objects for display at South Pacific museums such as the Museum of the Cook Islands on Rarotonga.

to the haphazard, unscientific way in which they were collected many years ago. Yet we can appreciate and enjoy their beauty and power nonetheless, just as we may enjoy a song sung in a language we don't know.

RELIGION

Religion plays an important role in the lives of the Pacific islanders, holding communities together and defending moral values. No other non-European region of the world is as solidly Christian as the South Pacific. The first missionaries to arrive were Protestants, and the Catholic fathers who landed almost forty years later had to rely on French military backing to establish missions in Tahiti, the Marquesas, and New Caledonia. In Fiji 45% of the population is Hindu or Muslim due to the large Indian population.

Since the 1960s, the old rivalry between Protestant and Catholic has been largely replaced by an avalanche of well-financed American fundamentalist missionary groups that divide families and spread confusion in an area already strongly Christian. While the indigenous churches have long been localized, the new evangelical sects are dominated by foreign personnel, ideas, and money. American televangelists proselytize from TV screens clear across the South Pacific Bible Belt from Rarotonga to Fiji. The ultraconservative outlook of the new religious imperialists continues the tradition of allying Christianity with colonialism or neocolonialism.

The fundamentalists tend to portray God as a white man and discourage self-sufficiency by telling the islanders to await their reward in heaven. They stress passages in the Bible calling for obedience to authority and resignation, often providing the ideological justification for the repression of dissent, as happened after the military coups in Fiji. "Liberation theologists," on the other hand, whether Catholic or Protestant, try to apply the spirit of the Bible to everyday life by discussing social problems and protecting the human rights of all. The late Roman Catholic Bishop of Tonga, Patelisio Finau, was a good example of a church leader with the courage to identify social injustices and take an active role in correcting them.

The established Protestant denominations are the Evangelicals of Tahiti-Polynesia and New Caledonia, the Methodists of Tonga and Fiji, the Congregationalists of Samoa, the Presbyterians of Vanuatu, and the Anglicans of Solomon Islands. Catholics are present in every country. The ecumenical **Pacific Conference of Churches** (G.P.O. Box 208, Suva, Fiji Islands; tel. 679/311-277, fax 679/303-205) began in 1961 as an association of the mainstream Protestant churches, but since 1976 many Catholic dioceses have been included as well. The publishing arm of the PCC, Lotu Pasifika Productions, produces many fascinating books on regional social issues. Both the Pacific Theological College (founded in 1966) and the Pacific Regional Seminary (opened in 1972) are in southern Suva, and the South Pacific is one of the few areas of the world with a large surplus of ministers of religion.

The Mormons

Mormon missionaries arrived on Tubuai in the Austral Islands as early as 1844, and today "Mormonia" covers much of the South Pacific. It all dates back to 1827 when a 22-year-old upstate New Yorker named Joseph Smith claimed to have discovered inscribed gold plates in an Indian burial mound near his home. These he translated with help of a "seer stone" and in 1830 the resulting *Book of Mormon* was used to launch his Church of Jesus Christ of Latter-day Saints. After Smith's assassination in 1844, Brigham Young led a group of followers west to Salt Lake City, Utah, where the group is headquartered today.

Smith's book purports to be a history of the American Indians, who are portrayed as descendants of the ten lost tribes of Israel that migrated to the Western Hemisphere around A.D. 600. According to the book, the skin color of these people turned red due to their abandonment of the faith, and to hasten the second coming of Christ, they must be reconverted. Like Thor Heyerdahl, Mormons believe American Indians settled Polynesia, so the present church is willing to spend a lot of time and money spreading the word. The pairs of clean-cut young Mormon "elders" seen on the outliers, each in shirt and tie, riding a bicycle or driving a minibus, are sent down from the States for two-year stays.

You don't have to travel far in the South Pacific to find the assembly-line Mormon chapels, schools, and sporting facilities, paid for by church members, who must contribute 10% of their incomes. The Mormon church spends over US$500 million a year on foreign missions and sends out almost 50,000 missionaries, more than any other American church by far. The Mormons are especially successful in countries like Tonga and Western Samoa, which are too poor to provide public education for all. There's a strong link to Hawaii's Brigham Young University, and many island students help pay for their schooling by representing their home country at the Mormon-owned Polynesian Cultural Center on Oahu. In Melanesia, Mormon missionary activity is a recent phenomenon, as prior to a "revelation" in 1978 the church considered blacks spiritually inferior.

Other Religious Groups

More numerous than the Mormons are adherents of the **Seventh-Day Adventist Church,** a politically ultra-conservative group which grew out of the 19th century American Baptist movement. This is the largest non-historical religious group in the South Pacific, holding the allegiance of 10% of the population of Solomon Islands, and with large followings in Tahiti-Polynesia, Tonga, Samoa, Fiji, and Vanuatu. The SDA Church teaches the imminent return of Christ, and Saturday (rather than Sunday) is observed as the Sabbath. SDAs regard the human body as the temple of the Holy Spirit, thus much attention is paid to health matters. Members are forbidden to partake of certain foods, alcohol, drugs, and tobacco, and the church expends considerable energy on the provision of medical and dental services. They're also active in education and local economic development. Like many of the other fundamentalist sects, the SDAs tend to completely obliterate traditional cultures.

The **Assemblies of God** (AOG) is a Pentecostal sect founded in Arkansas in 1914 and presently headquartered in Springfield, Missouri. Although the AOG carries out some relief work, it opposes social reform in the belief that only God can solve humanity's problems. The sect is strongest in Fiji, where their numbers increased twelvefold between 1966 and 1992. A large AOG Bible College operates in Suva, and from Fiji the group has spread to other Pacific countries. Disgraced American tele-evangelists Jimmy Swaggart and Jim Bakker were both former AOG ministers.

The **Jehovah's Witnesses** originated in 19th century America and since 1909 their headquarters has been in Brooklyn, from whence their worldwide operations are financed. Jehovah's Witnesses' teachings against military service and blood transfusions have often brought them into conflict with governments, and they in turn regard other churches, especially the Catholic Church, as instruments of the Devil. Members must spread the word by canvassing their neighborhood door-to-door, or by standing on streetcorners offering copies of *The Watchtower.* This group focuses mostly on Christ's return, and since "the end of time" is fast approaching, it has little interest in relief work. They're most numerous in Tahiti-Polynesia, Fiji, New Caledonia, and Solomon Islands, but you'll find them in virtually every Pacific country.

Another 40 new religious groups of various shades and hues are active in the South Pacific, far too many to include here. Anyone interested in the subject, however, should consult Manfred Ernst's trailblazing study, *Winds of Change,* which can be purchased at the office of Lotu Pasifika Productions in Suva.

Sunday
A good thing to do on Sunday is to go to church. Of course, try to look as clean as you can, and be aware the services can last one and a half hours and will often be in the local language. If you decide to go, don't get up and walk out in the middle—see it through. You'll be rewarded by the joyous singing and fellowship, and you'll encounter the islanders on a different level. After church, people gather for a family meal or picnic and spend the rest of the day relaxing and socializing. If you're a guest in an island home you'll be invited to accompany them to church.

In the South Pacific Bible Belt, extending through the Cook Islands, Tonga, Samoa, and Fiji, almost everything outside the churches grinds to a halt on Sunday. Only hotel restaurants will be open, most buses and taxis will have vanished, and even sports may be banned. Secular travelers may choose to clear out of town on Saturday and spend Sunday swimming, snorkeling, or hiking in the boonies.

LANGUAGE

Some 1,200 languages, a quarter of the world's total, are spoken in the Pacific islands, though most have very few speakers. The Austronesian language family includes over 900 distinct languages spoken in an area stretching from Madagascar to Easter Island. Of all the Oceanic languages, only the Papuan languages spoken in New Guinea and the Solomons do not belong to this group. In all some 720 languages are spoken in Papua New Guinea, 105 in Vanuatu, and 65 in the Solomon Islands (the 250 languages spoken by the Australian Aborigines are unrelated to these). Many islanders are trilingual, equally fluent in the national lingua franca (pidgin), a local tribal tongue (or two), and an international language (either English or French). English is the predominant language of business and government in all but the French colonies.

Pidgin
Pidgin developed in Fiji and Queensland during the labor trade of the late 19th century. Because many separate local languages might be spoken on a single Melanesian island, often in villages only a few kilometers apart, the need for a common language arose when it became possible for people to travel beyond tribal boundaries. The three Pacific pidgins are Tok Pisin (P.N.G.), Pijin (Solomon Islands), and Bislama (Vanuatu). The Solomons' Pidgin is the

THE PACIFIC IN LITERATURE

Over the years a succession of European writers has traveled to the South Pacific in search of Bougainville's Nouvelle Cythère or Rousseau's noble savage. Brought to the stage and silver screen, their stories entered the popular imagination alongside Gauguin's rich images, creating the romantic myth of the South Seas paradise presently cultivated by the travel industry. Only since independence have indigenous writers such as Epeli Hau'ofa, Julian Maka'a, Fata Sano Malifa, Raymond Pillai, John Saunana, Subramani, and Albert Wendt come to the fore.

Herman Melville, author of the whaling classic *Moby Dick* (1851), deserted his New Bedford whaler at Nuku Hiva in 1842 and *Typee* (1846) describes his experiences there. An Australian whaling ship carried Melville on to Tahiti, but he joined a mutiny

HAWAII STATE ARCHIVES

Scottish author Robert Louis Stevenson spent his last years in Samoa.

on board, which landed him in the Papeete *calabooza* (prison). His second Polynesian book, *Omoo* (1847), was a result. In both, Melville decries the ruin of Polynesian culture by Western influence.

Pierre Loti's *The Marriage of Loti* (1880) is a sentimental tale of the love of a young French midshipman for a Polynesian girl named Rarahu. Loti's naiveté is rather absurd, but his friendship with Queen Pomare IV and his fine imagery make the book worth reading. Loti's writings influenced Paul Gauguin to come to Tahiti.

In 1888-90 Robert Louis Stevenson, famous author of *Treasure Island* and *Kidnapped,* cruised the Pacific in his schooner, the *Casco*. His book *In the South Seas* describes his visits to the Marquesas and Tuamotus. In 1890 Stevenson and his family bought a large tract of land just outside Apia, Western Samoa, and built a large, framed house he called Vailima. In 1894 he was buried on Mt. Vaea, just above his home.

Jack London and his wife Charmian cruised the Pacific aboard their yacht, the *Snark*, in 1907-09. A longtime admirer of Melville, London found only a wretched swamp at Taipivae in the Marquesas. His *South Sea Tales* (1911) was the first of the 10 books that he wrote on the Pacific. London's story "The House of Mapuhi," about a Jewish pearl buyer, earned him a costly lawsuit. London was a product of his time, and the modern reader is often shocked by his insensitive portrayal of the islanders.

In 1913-14 the youthful poet Rupert Brooke visited Tahiti, where he fell in love with Mamua, a girl from Mataiea whom he immortalized in his poem "Tiare Tahiti." Later Brooke fought in WW I and wrote five famous war sonnets. He died of blood poisoning on a French hospital ship in the Mediterranean in 1915.

W. Somerset Maugham toured Polynesia in 1916-17 to research his novel, *The Moon and Sixpence* (1919), a fictional life of Paul Gauguin. Of the six short stories in *The Trembling of a Leaf* (1921), "Rain" casts strumpet Sadie Thompson against the

more Anglicized; the other two are surprisingly similar.

Pacific Pidgin, although less sophisticated than West African or China Coast Pidgin, is quite ingenious within its scope. Its vocabulary is limited, however, and pronouns, adverbs, and prepositions are lacking, but it has a bona fide Melanesian syntax. A very roundabout speech method is used to express things: "mine" and

"yours" are *blong mifela* and *blong yufela,* and "we" becomes *yumi tufela*. Frenchman is *man wewi* (oui-oui), *meri* is woman, while *bulamakau* (bull and cow) means beef or cattle. Pidgin's internal logic is delightful.

Polynesian

The Polynesians speak about 21 closely related languages with local variations and consonantal

Rev. Mr. Davidson during an enforced stay at Pago Pago, "marooned in a dilapidated lodging house, upon whose corrugated roof the heavy tropical rain beat incessantly." Three film versions of the story have appeared. Maugham's *A Writer's Notebook,* published in 1984, 19 years after his death, describes his travels in the Pacific.

American writers Charles Nordhoff and James Norman Hall came to Tahiti after WW I, married Tahitian women, and collaborated on 11 books. Their most famous was the *Bounty* trilogy (1934), which tells of Fletcher Christian's *Mutiny on the Bounty,* the escape to Dutch Timor of Captain Bligh and his crew in *Men Against the Sea,* and the mutineer's fate in *Pitcairn's Island.* Three generations of filmmakers have selected this saga as their way of presenting paradise.

Hall remained on Tahiti until his death in 1951 and his house at Arue still stands. His last book, *The Forgotten One,* is a collection of true stories about expatriate intellectuals and writers lost in the South Seas. Hall's account of the 28-year correspondence with his American friend Robert Dean Frisbie, who settled on Pukapuka in the Cook Islands, is touching.

James A. Michener joined the U.S. Navy in 1942 and ended up visiting around 50 South Sea islands, among them Bora Bora. His *Tales of the South Pacific* (1947) tells of the impact of WW II on the South Pacific and the Pacific's impact on those who served. It was later made into the long-running Broadway musical, *South Pacific.* Michener's *Return to Paradise* (1951) is a readable collection of essays and short stories.

Eugene Burdick is best known for his best sellers *The Ugly American* (1958) and *Fail-Safe* (1962). Like Michener, Burdick served in the Pacific during WW II. His 1961 book *The Blue of Capricorn* is a collection of essays and short stories on the area.

The literary traditions of the Pacific islanders themselves were largely oral until 1967 when the University of the South Pacific was established at Suva, Fiji. The student newspaper *Unispac* began

carrying fiction by Pacific writers in 1968, but it was the formation of the South Pacific Creative Arts Society and its magazine *Mana* in 1973 which really stimulated the creation of a Pacific literature distinct from the expatriate writings which had prevailed up until that time. The first Festival of Pacific Arts held at Suva in 1972 greatly encouraged the development of a unique South Pacific culture.

Whereas the main characters in the expatriate writings are Europeans with the islands and islanders treated only as background, the local writers deal with the real problems and concerns of the island people. The writings of outsiders such as Maugham and Michener often tell us more about the writers themselves than about the islands where their stories are set. In contrast to the Pacific paradise approach, island authors decry the impact of European colonialism and materialism on their traditional cultures.

The Pacific's most famous contemporary writer is Western Samoan novelist Albert Wendt. His novels, such as *Sons for the Return Home* (1973), *Flying Fox in a Freedom Tree* (1974), *Pouliuli* (1977), and *Leaves of the Banyan Tree* (1979) portray the manipulative nature and complex social organization of Samoan society. Wendt studied in New Zealand for 12 years before returning to teach in Samoa in 1965, and he is now a professor of English literature at Auckland University.

Tongan poet and short-story writer Epeli Hau'ofa satirizes the foreign aid business and other aspects of island life in his humorous book *Tales of the Tikongs.* His 1977 essay *Our Crowded Islands* deals with overpopulation in Tonga and the westernization of Tongan life. *Kisses in the Nederends* and *Corned Beef and Tapioca* are among his other books. Other Pacific writers of note include Western Samoa's Fata Sano Malifa *(Alms for Oblivion),* Fiji's Sudesh Mishra *(Tandava)* and Raymond Pillai *(The Celebration),* and Solomon Island's John Saunana *(The Alternative).* See "Resources" at the end of this book for more detailed reviews of some of these titles and a list of booksellers and publishers.

changes. They're mutually unintelligible to those who haven't learned them, although they have many words common. For instance, the word for land varies between *whenua, fenua, fanua, fonua, honua, vanua,* and *henua.* In the Polynesian languages the words are softened by the removal of certain consonants. Thus the Tagalog word for coconut, *niog,* became *niu, ni,* or *nu.* They're musical languages whose ac-

cent lies mostly on the vowels. Polynesian is rhetorical and poetical but not scientific, and to adapt to modern life many words have been borrowed from European languages; these too are infused with vowels to make them more melodious to the Polynesian ear. Thus in Tahitian governor becomes *tavana* and frying pan *faraipani.* Special vocabularies used to refer to or address royalty or the aristocracy also exist.

CONDUCT AND CUSTOMS

Foreign travel is an exceptional experience enjoyed mostly by privileged Westerners. Too often, affluent visitors from developed countries try to transfer their lifestyles to tropical islands, thereby missing out on what is unique to the region. Travel can be a learning experience if approached openly and with a positive attitude, so read up on the local culture before you arrive and become aware of the social and environmental problems of the area. A wise traveler soon graduates from hearing and seeing to listening and observing. Speaking is good for the ego and listening is good for the soul.

The path is primed with packaged pleasures, but pierce the bubble of tourism and you'll encounter something far from the schedules and organized efficiency: time to learn how other people live. Walk gently, for human qualities are as fragile and responsive to abuse as the brilliant reefs. The islanders are by nature soft-spoken and reserved. Often they won't show open disapproval if their social codes are broken, but don't underestimate them: they understand far more than you think. Consider that you're only one of thousands of visitors to their country, so don't expect to be treated better than anyone else. Respect is one of the most important things in life and humility is also greatly appreciated.

Don't try for a bargain if it means someone will be exploited. What enriches you may violate others. Be sensitive to the feelings of those you wish to "shoot" with your camera and ask their permission first. Don't promise things you can't or won't deliver. Keep your time values to yourself; the islanders lead an unstressful lifestyle and assume you are there to share it.

If you're alone you're lucky, for the single traveler is everyone's friend. Get away from other tourists and meet the people. There aren't many places on earth where you can still do this meaningfully, but the South Pacific is one. If you do meet people with similar interests keep in touch by writing. This is no tourist's paradise, though, and local residents are not exhibits or paid performers. They have just as many problems as you, and if you see them as real people you're less likely to be viewed as

a stereotypical tourist. You may have come to escape civilization, but keep in mind that you're just a guest.

Visitors may think they have come to the South Pacific to travel around, seeing and experiencing the islands, when in fact they're ambassadors for their cultures overseas. On an isolated island, if you're English you represent England; if you're American you represent America. On the outer islands especially, you may think you're spending your time going around studying everything, without realizing that you're the one who is being studied and examined. The islanders are very observant, and visitors should be on their best behavior.

Most important of all, try to see things their way. Take an interest in local customs, values, languages, challenges, and successes. If things work differently than they do back home, give thanks—that's why you've come. Reflect on what you've experienced and return home with a better understanding of how much we all have in common, outwardly different as we may seem. Do that and your trip won't have been wasted.

The Pacific Way

A smile costs nothing but is priceless. Islanders smile at one another; tourists look the other way. In Western societies wealth is based on the accumulation of goods; in Pacific societies it's based on how much you can give away. Obligations define an individual's position in society, while sharing provides the security that holds a community together. If people are hospitable, look for some way of repaying their kindness and never exploit their goodwill. It's an island custom that a gift must be reciprocated, which is why tipping has never caught on.

Questions

The islanders are eager to please, so phrase your questions carefully. They'll answer yes or no according to what they think you want to hear—don't suggest the answer in your question. Test this by asking your informant to confirm something you know to be incorrect. Also don't ask negative questions, such as "you're not going to Suva, are you?" Invariably the answer will be "yes," meaning "yes, I'm not going to Suva." It also could work like this: "Don't you have anything cheaper?" "Yes." "What do you have that is cheaper?" "Nothing." Yes, he doesn't have anything cheaper. If you want to be sure of something, ask several people the same question in different ways.

Dress

It's important to know that the dress code in the islands is strict. Short shorts, halter tops, and bathing costumes in public are considered offensive: a *sulu* or pareu wrapped around you solves this one. Women should wear dresses that adequately cover their legs while seated. Nothing will mark you so quickly as a tourist nor make you more popular with street vendors than scanty dress. There *is* a place for it, of course: that's on the beach in front of a resort hotel. In a society where even bathing suits are considered extremely risqué for local women, public nudity is unthinkable. Exceptions are Tahiti, Bora Bora, and Nouméa, where the French influence has led to topless beaches.

Women

In many traditional island cultures a woman seen wandering aimlessly along a remote beach was thought to be in search of male companionship, and "no" meant "yes." Single women hiking, camping, sunbathing, and simply traveling alone may be seen in the same light, an impression strongly reinforced by the type of videos available in the islands. In some cultures local women rarely travel without men, and some day hikes and inter-island ship journeys mentioned in this book may be uncomfortable or even dangerous for women who are unprepared. Two women together will have little to worry about in most cases, especially if they're well covered and look purposeful.

Women traveling alone should avoid staying in isolated tourist bungalows by themselves—it's best to team up with other travelers before heading to the outer islands. In many Polynesian cultures there's a custom known as "sleep crawling" in which a boy silently enters a girl's home at night and lies beside her to prove his bravery, and visiting women sometimes become objects of this type of unwanted attention even in well-known resorts like Bora Bora.

Annette Nyberg of Sweden sent us this:

The South Pacific is an easy place for a single woman, as long as she's not stupid. I'm talking about shorts, minitops, bikinis, etc., which place an unnecessary barrier between you and the local women. In the handbook a lot of traditional ceremonies are described, and

island-style dress at Ngau Island, Fiji

DAVID STANLEY

I think it's important to point out that some of them (such as a traditional kava party) are open to men only. On the other hand, as a woman I could sit down with the local women when they were weaving, cooking, etc. and get plenty of contact, something a man couldn't do. There's nothing like weaving a mat to make a Tongan woman more talkative! I've had "complicated" discussions I believe wouldn't have taken place if both of us hadn't been so occupied with those pandanus leaves! Don't attempt to be an "independent modern woman" trying to get a close look at every aspect of village life, but take advantage of those opportunities which come naturally from your being a woman.

Children

Karen Addison of Sussex, England, sent us the following:

Traveling with children can have its ups and downs, but in the Pacific it's definitely an up. Pacific islanders are warm, friendly people, but with children you see them at their best. Your children are automatically accepted, and you, as an extension of them, are as well. As the majority of the islands are free of any deadly bugs or diseases, acclimatizing to the water, food, and climate would be your paramount concern. Self-contained units, where you can do your own cooking, are easy to find and cheap; having set meals every day gives children a sense of security. Not having television as a distraction, I've attempted to teach my son the rudiments of reading and writing. As a single mother with a little boy, traveling with him opened my eyes to things I'd normally overlook and has been an education to us both.

parrotfish (Scarus frenatus)

ON THE ROAD

HIGHLIGHTS

Few parts of the world are as rewarding to visit as the South Pacific. Life is relaxed, and the tremendous variety of cultures and choice of things to see and do make this the sort of area you keep coming back to. When you tire of beachlife you can go to the mountains; city and town visits can alternate with stays in rural areas. There's no overcrowding, and you don't have to hassle with vendors or be constantly on guard against thieves. Public transportation of all kinds is well developed, and almost everywhere you can easily sidestep the tourist track and go native.

The South Pacific's distance from Europe and North America has saved it from becoming overrun, as Spain and the main Caribbean resorts are overrun. Only tiny New Zealand has the South Pacific in its backyard (Australians are more attracted to Bali and Thailand). Part of the higher amount you'll spend on airfare will come back to you in the form of lower everyday prices. The islanders themselves are the region's greatest attraction: you'll seldom make friends as fast as you do here.

Each Pacific country is unique. In Tahiti-Polynesia the spectacular scenery of Tahiti, Moorea, and Bora Bora compensates for the higher cost of living. Cook Islands has easygoing resort life on Rarotonga and unspoiled outer-island life everywhere else. Each of the three main island groups of Tonga has its own distinct character and Vava'u is an undiscovered pearl of the South Seas. Samoa is notable for its intact traditional life. Everyone likes Fiji, both for its excellent facilities and the fascinating variety of cultures. New Caledonia is also a land of stirring contrasts. In Vanuatu you alternate between polished main towns and unspoiled outer islands. Solomon Islands is perhaps the South Pacific's biggest surprise: friendly welcoming people, satisfactory transportation, reasonable prices, and lots of things to do.

In the "Highlights" sections of each chapter introduction we list a few sights you won't want to miss. Give yourself as much time in the islands as you can, and try to get to at least three different countries to be able to see things in perspective. No matter how hard you travel, there will always be lots left over to see next time.

SPORTS AND RECREATION

Scuba diving is offered in resort areas throughout the South Pacific, with certification courses usually available. It's a great way to see the islands at their best, while meeting some interesting people and having a lot of fun. The waters are warm, varying less than one degree centigrade between the surface and 100 meters, so a wetsuit is not essential (although it will protect you from coral cuts). Prices differ slightly across the region: a one-tank dive with equipment will cost about US$30-35 in Cook Islands, Fiji, and Vanuatu, US$45 in the Solomons, and US$50 and up in New Caledonia, Western Samoa, Tahiti-Polynesia, and Tonga. Precise information on scuba diving is provided throughout this handbook, immediately after the sightseeing sections and before "Accommodations."

Scuba diving can become expensive if you get addicted, but snorkeling is free—all you need is a mask and pipe. Many scuba operators will take snorkelers out on their regular trips for a third to a quarter the cost of diving. This is an easy way to reach some good snorkeling spots, just don't expect to be chaperoned for that price. For a few tips, see "Exploring a Reef" under "Coral Reefs" in the Introduction.

Ocean kayaking is a viable sport best practiced in sheltered lagoons, such as those of Raiatea/Tahaa, Bora Bora, Aitutaki, Vava'u, and New Georgia, or among Fiji's Yasawa Islands. You can rent kayaks in some places, but it's much better to bring a folding kayak of your own if you're serious. See "Other Travel Options" under "Getting Around," later in this chapter, for more information on kayaking.

Cruising the South Pacific by yacht is also covered in "Getting Around," and for those with less time there are several established yacht charter operations, the most important of which are based at Raiatea (Tahiti-Polynesia), Vava'u (Tonga), Malololailai (Fiji), Savusavu (Fiji), and Nouméa (New Caledonia). Turn to "Yacht Tours and Charters" in "Getting There," which follows, and check the introductions to the chapters mentioned above.

Hiking is an excellent, inexpensive way to see the islands. These are a few of the outstanding treks covered in this handbook: Mt. Aorai on Tahiti, Vaiare to Paopao on Moorea, the Cross-island Track on Rarotonga, Mt. Matafao on Tutuila, Lake Lanoto'o on Upolu, the Singatoka River Trek on Viti Levu, White Sands to Port Resolution on Tanna, and the Mataniko River on Guadalcanal. There are many others.

The South Pacific's most renowned surfer's camps are Club Masa (Kulukulu), Frigate Surfriders (Yanutha Island), Seashell Cove (Momi Bay), and Tavarua Island (Mamanutha Group), all in Fiji, and the Ha'atafu Beach Resort on Tongatapu. Other famous surfing spots include Tahiti's Papara Beach, Huahine's Fare Reef, Laulii and Solosolo on Upolu, Salailua and Lano on Savai'i, Suva's Sandspit Lighthouse, Grande Terre's Po'e Beach, and Malu'u (Malaita). The best surfing season is generally July to September when the tradewinds push the Antarctic swells north. During the hurricane season from January to March tropical storms can generate some spectacular waves. Prime locales for windsurfing include Tahiti's Hiti Mahana Beach Club, Rarotonga's Muri Lagoon, Fiji's Club Masa, and many others. Pago Pago Harbor would be the windsurfing locale par excellence if the quality of the water weren't so bad.

There isn't much to hunt in the islands, and the wretches who shoot flying foxes and birds are only worthy of contempt. Sportfishing is also a questionable activity—especially spearfishing, which is sort of like shooting a cow with a handgun. An islander who spearfishes to feed his family is one thing, but the tourist who does it for fun is perhaps worthy of the attention of sharks. Deep-sea game fishing from gas-guzzling powerboats isn't much better, and it's painful to see noble fish slaughtered and strung up just to inflate someone's ego. That said,

big-game fishing is a viable sport, and we do cover it throughout this book.

The former British and New Zealand administrators left behind an abundance of golf courses in the islands, and virtually all are open to visitors. Major international competitions are held at Fiji's Pacific Harbor Golf Course and Tahiti's Olivier Breaud Golf Course. Green fees vary considerably: Olivier Breaud Golf Course, US$30; Rarotonga Golf Club, US$7; Tonga Golf Club, US$4; Tutuila's 'Ili'ili Golf Course, US$7; Apia's Royal Samoa Country Club, US$9; Nandi Airport Golf Course, US$10; Pacific Harbor Golf Course, US$35; Suva Golf Club, US$9; Port Vila's White Sands Country Club, US$23; Port Vila Golf and Country Club, US$14; Honiara Golf Club, US$3. Club and cart rentals are usually available for a bit less than the green fees and most of the courses have clubhouses with pleasant colonial-style bars.

Package tours incorporating the activities just mentioned are described under "Getting There" in this introduction. For information on bicycling, see "Other Travel Options" under "Getting There," which follows.

ENTERTAINMENT

Considering the strong Aussie presence and the temperature, it's not surprising that the South Seas has its fair share of colorful bars where canned or bottled beer is consumed cold in amazing quantities. These are good places to meet local characters at happy hour around 1700, and many bars become discos after 2200. Respectably attired visitors are welcome at the ex-colonial "clubs," where the beer prices are generally lower and the clientele more sedate. Barefoot (or flip-flop-shod) beachcombers in T-shirts and shorts may be refused entry, and take off your hat as you come in. Don't overlook the resort bars, where the swank surroundings cost only slightly more. Unlike in Australia and New Zealand, it's not customary to bring your own (BYO) booze into restaurants.

Many big hotels run "island nights," or feasts where you taste the local food and see traditional dancing. If you don't wish to splurge on the meal it's often possible to witness the spectacle from the bar for the price of a drink. These events are held weekly on certain days, so ask. On most islands Friday night is the time to let it all hang out; on Saturday many people are preparing for a family get-together or church on Sunday. Except in the French territories, everything grinds to a halt Saturday at midnight and Sunday is *very quiet*—a good day to go hiking or to the beach.

In the English-speaking countries it's cheap to go to the movies. Unfortunately it's usually romance, horror, or adventure and, as everywhere, good psychological films are the exception. In the French territories the films are just as bad, plus they're dubbed into French and admission is three times as high. Video fever is the latest island craze, and you often see throngs of locals crowded into someone's living room watching a violent and/or sexy tape rented from one of the ubiquitous video rental shops. Some guesthouses have video too, so make sure your room is well away from it.

Music and Dance

Traditional music and dance is alive and well in the South Pacific, be it the exciting *tamure*

dancing of Tahiti-Polynesia and Cook Islands, the graceful *siva* of Samoa, the formalized *meke* of Fiji, or the *kastom* dances of Vanuatu. British ethnomusicologist David Fanshawe (see "Discography" under "Resources" at the end of this volume) has suggested that the sitting dances common in Tonga, Fiji, and elsewhere may be related to the movements of the upper part of the body while paddling a canoe.

The slit-log gong (or *lali* in Fiji) beaten with a wooden stick is a common instrument throughout Polynesia. Melanesia has always excelled in the use of the flute, especially the panpipes of Solomon Islands. Flutes were known in Polynesia too, for example the nose flutes of Tonga and Tahiti. In the early 19th century, missionaries replaced the old chants of Polynesia with the harmonious gospel singing heard in the islands today, yet even the hymns were transformed into an original Oceanic medium. Contemporary Pacific music includes bamboo bands, brass bands, and localized Anglo-American pop. String bands have made European instruments such as the guitar and ukulele an integral part of Pacific music.

HOLIDAYS AND FESTIVALS

The special events of each island group are described in the respective chapters. Their dates often vary from year to year, so it's best to contact the local tourist information office soon after your arrival to learn just what will be happening during your stay.

The most important annual festivals are the Tapati Rapa Nui festival on Easter Island (late January or early February), American Samoa's Flag Day (17 April), the Independence Celebrations at Apia (first week of June), Nuku'alofa's Heilala Festival (first week in July), the Heiva i Tahiti at Papeete and Bora Bora (first two weeks of July), Solomon Islands Independence Day (7 July), Independence Day at Port Vila (30 July), the Constitution Celebrations on Rarotonga (early August), and Suva's Hibiscus Festival (August). Catch as many as you can and try to participate in what's happening, rather than merely watching like a tourist.

Nuclear-Free Pacific Day is 1 March, in commemoration of the 1954 atmospheric hydrogen

bomb test (code-named Bravo) on Bikini Atoll in the Marshall Islands, which contaminated hundreds of islanders. On the Sunday closest to 1 March member churches of the Pacific Conference of Churches have special services and show films or videos on nuclear issues. Marches, rallies, street theater, and information seminars are often held at this time. Hiroshima Day (6 August) and Nagasaki Day (9 August) are also widely observed and present the opportunity for you to join the local people in expressing your awareness of disarmament issues.

Regional Events

The most important cultural event of the region is the **Festival of Pacific Arts,** held every four years (Suva, Fiji, 1972; Rotorua, N.Z., 1976; Port Moresby, P.N.G., 1980; Tahiti, 1985; Townsville, Australia, 1988; Rarotonga, 1992; Western Samoa, 1996). The festival gathers in one place the cultures and folklores of all of Oceania. The coordination of each festival is in the hands of the Council of Pacific Arts, founded at Nouméa in 1977 under the auspices of the South Pacific Commission. In August 1995 heads of government at the annual summit of Melanesian Spearhead Grouping decided to create a **Melanesian Arts Festival,** the first of which will take place in Solomon Islands in 1998.

The **South Pacific Games,** the region's major sporting event, was created at the 1961 South Pacific Conference to promote friendship among the peoples of the Pacific and encourage the development of amateur sports. Since then the

games have been held in Fiji (1963), New Caledonia (1966), P.N.G. (1969), Tahiti-Polynesia (1971), Guam (1975), Fiji (1979), Western Samoa (1983), New Caledonia (1987), P.N.G. (1991), and Tahiti-Polynesia (1995), with the larger Pacific countries (New Caledonia, Fiji, P.N.G., and Tahiti-Polynesia) dominating. The 1999 games will take place on Guam. Some 2,000 athletes from 20 countries gather for the games and, to give the smaller countries a better chance, Australia, Hawaii, and New Zealand don't participate. The Mini South Pacific Games take place two years after the main games.

ARTS AND CRAFTS

Not surprisingly, the traditional handicrafts that have survived best are the practical arts done by women (weaving, basketmaking, tapa). In cases where the items still perform their original function (such as the astoundingly intricate fine mats of Samoa—not for sale to tourists), they remain as vital as ever. A tourist will purchase whatever corresponds to his image of the producing community and is small enough to be accepted as airline luggage. Thus a visitor to Fiji may be looking for masks, figures with large penises, or carvings of pigs, even though none of these has any place in Fijian tradition. The mock-Hawaiian "tikis" of Tonga have no precedents in traditional Tongan art.

Buy handicrafts from local women's committee shops, church groups, local markets, or from the craftspeople themselves, but avoid objects

made from turtle shell/leather, clam shell, or marine mammal ivory, which are prohibited entry into many countries under endangered species acts. Failure to declare such items to customs officers can lead to heavy fines. Also resist the temptation to purchase jewelry or other items made from seashells and coral, the collection of which damages the reefs. Souvenirs made from straw or seeds may be held for fumigation or confiscated upon arrival.

Weaving
Woven articles are the most widespread handicrafts, with examples in almost every South Seas country. Pandanus fiber is the most common, but coconut leaf and husk, vine tendril, banana stem, tree and shrub bark, the stems and leaves of water weeds, and the skin of the

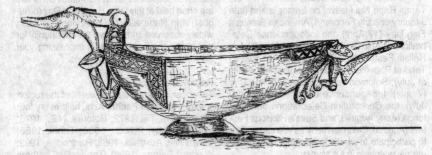

a food bowl from the eastern Solomons, carved in the form of a frigate bird holding a fish, used for ritual offerings to ancestral spirits

sago palm leaf are all used. On some islands the fibers are passed through a fire, boiled, then bleached in the sun. Vegetable dyes of very lovely mellow tones are sometimes used, but gaudier store dyes are much more prevalent. Shells are occasionally utilized to cut, curl, or make the fibers pliable. Polynesian woven arts are characterized by colorful, skillful patterns.

Tapa

To make tapa, the white inner bark of the tall, thin paper mulberry tree (Broussonetia papyrifera) is stripped and scraped with shells, rolled into a ball, and soaked in water. The sodden strips are then pounded with wooden mallets until they reach four or five times their original length and width. Next, several pieces are placed one on top of another, pressed and pounded, and joined together with a manioc juice paste. Sheets of tapa feel like felt when finished.

In Tonga, tapa (ngatu) is decorated by stitching coconut fiber designs onto a woven pandanus base that is placed under the tapa, and the stain is rubbed on in the same manner one makes temple rubbings from a stone inscription. The artisan then fills in the patterns freehand. In Fiji, stencils are used to decorate tapa (masi). Sunlight deepens and sets the copper brown colors.

Each island group has its characteristic colors and patterns, ranging from plantlike paintings to geometric designs. On some islands tapa is still used for clothing, bedding, and room dividers, and as ceremonial red carpets. Tablecloths, bedcovers, place mats, and wall hangings of tapa make handsome souvenirs.

Woodcarving

Melanesia is especially well known for its woodcarvings, with designs passed down from generation to generation. Though shells are sometimes used for polishing the finest artifacts, steel tools are employed for the most part these days. Melanesian woodcarvings often suggest the mystic feelings of their former religious beliefs, the somber spirits of the rainforests and swampy plains of Melanesia. Polynesia also produces fine woodcarvings (especially kava bowls and war clubs), and those of the Marquesas Group are outstanding in detail.

Other Products

Other handicrafts include polished shell, inlays of shell in ebony, spears with barbs of splintered bone, thorn spines or caudal spines, "bride money," shell necklaces, and anklets. Among the European-derived items are the patchwork quilts (tifaifai) of Tahiti and the Cooks, and the hand-painted and silk-screened dress fabrics of Fiji, Western Samoa, Cook Islands, and Tahiti.

ACCOMMODATIONS

Hotels

With South Pacific Handbook in hand you're guaranteed a good, inexpensive place to stay on every island. Each and every hotel in the region is included herein, not just a selection. We consistently do this to give you a solid second reference in case your travel agent or someone else recommends a certain place. To allow you the widest possible choice, all price categories are included, and throughout we've tried to point out which properties offer the best value for your money. If you think we are wrong or you were badly treated, be sure to send a written complaint to the author of this book. Equally important, let us know when you agree with what's here or if you think a place deserves a better rave. Your letter will have an impact!

We don't solicit freebies from the hotel chains; our only income derives from the price you paid for this book. So we don't mind telling you that, as usual, most of the luxury hotels are just not worth the exorbitant prices they charge. Many simply re-create Hawaii at twice the cost, offering far more luxury than you need. Even worse, they tend to isolate you in a French/American/Australian environment, away from the South Pacific you came to experience. Most are worth visiting as sightseeing attractions, watering holes, or sources of entertainment, but unless you're a millionaire sleep elsewhere.

One of the golden rules of independent travel is the more you spend, the less you experience. If you're on a budget, avoid prepaying hotel accommodations booked from home, as you can always do better locally upon arrival. If, however, you really do intend to spend most of your time at a specific first-class hotel, you'll benefit from bulk rates by taking a package tour instead of paying the higher "rack rate" the hotels charge individuals who just walk in off the street. Call Air New Zealand's toll-free number and ask them to mail you their *Hotpac* brochure, which lists deluxe hotel rooms in Fiji, Cook Islands, Tahiti, Tonga, and Western Samoa that can be booked on an individual basis at slightly reduced rates. Bear in mind, however, that on all the islands there are middle-level hotels that charge half what these top-end places ask, while providing adequate comfort. And if you really *can* afford US$250 a night and up, you'd do better chartering a skippered or bareboat yacht.

When picking a hotel, keep in mind that although a thatched bungalow is cooler and infinitely more attractive than a concrete box, it's also more likely to have insect problems. If in doubt check the window screens and carry mosquito coils and/or repellent. Hopefully there'll be a resident lizard or two to feed on the bugs.

A room with cooking facilities can save you a lot on restaurant meals, and some moderately priced establishments have weekly rates. If you have to choose a meal plan, take only breakfast and dinner (Modified American Plan or "half pension") and have fruit for lunch. As you check into your room, note the nearest fire exits. And don't automatically take the first room offered; if you're paying good money look at several, then choose.

Dormitory or "bunkroom" accommodations are available on all of the main islands except American Samoa, with communal cooking facilities usually provided. These are excellent if you're traveling alone, since they're just the place to meet other travelers. Couples can usually get a double room for a price only slightly above two dorm beds. For the most part, the dormitories are safe and congenial for those who don't mind sacrificing their privacy to save money.

Throughout the South Pacific, double rooms with shared bath at budget guesthouses average US$20-25, dorm beds US$6-12 pp. Tonga and Western Samoa have double rooms beginning as low as US$12, but in American Samoa accommodation prices are much higher. The cheapest dormitory beds are found in Fiji, Tonga, and Western Samoa.

Be aware that some of the low-budget places included in this book are a lot more basic than what is sometimes referred to as "budget" accommodations in the States. The standards of cleanliness in the common bathrooms may be lower than you expected, the furnishings "early attic," the beds uncomfortable, linens and towels skimpy, housekeeping nonexistent, and window screens lacking, but ask yourself, where in the U.S. are you going to find a room for a similar price? Luckily, good medium-priced accommodations are usually available for those of us unwilling to put up with spartan conditions, and we include all of them in this book too.

Homestays

In some countries such as Tahiti-Polynesia there are bed and breakfast *(logement chez l'habitant)* programs, where you pay a set fee to stay with a local family in their own home. Meals may not be included in the price, but they're often available, tending toward your host family's fare of seafood and native vegetables. Ask about homestays at tourist information offices once you're in the islands.

A new development in Western Samoa is the appearance of basic beach resorts run by local families who supply meals, bedding, and *fale* (hut) accommodations at set rates. See the Western Samoa chapter for details. This is genuine ecotourism for you, and we hope people on some of the other islands catch on and start doing the same sort of thing.

Staying in Villages

If you're in the islands long and get off the beaten track, you'll eventually be invited to spend the night with a local family. There's a certain etiquette to follow and you'll be a lot more welcome if you observe the customs. For example, in Fiji the guest is expected to present a bundle of kava roots to the host. Although payment is rarely the islander's objective in inviting you, it's sort of expected that you'll somehow pay them back.

The peoples of the Pacific are so naturally hospitable that it sometimes works to their disadvantage. We recommend that you repay their kindness with either cash (US$10 pp a day is standard) or gifts. In places that obviously receive a regular flow of visitors, such as villages on hiking trails or surfing beaches, the villagers are probably used to receiving money. We're not suggesting that hospitality is a commodity to be bought and sold, but it's easy to see how the unscrupulous can and have taken advantage of the situation. The offer of a little money to show your appreciation may not be accepted, but it won't cause offense when done properly and with sincerity.

Things to take with you as gifts include T-shirts, flashlights and batteries, a big jar of instant coffee, and marbles and balloons for the kids (not candy, which rots their teeth and attracts ants). You may also be able to buy a few things at village trade stores to leave as gifts, but don't count on it.

If you're headed to a really remote atoll for an extended stay, take with you all the food you'll need, plus gifts. Be friendly, patient, and courteous, and don't seem afraid. Respect the property and customs of your hosts, and do your best to leave a good impression. Once you get home, don't forget to mail prints of any photos you've taken. If you do make friends on one island, ask them to write you a letter of introduction to their relatives on another.

If you're embarking on a trip that involves staying in villages, make sure everyone who's going agrees in advance on what you're going to do to compensate the islanders for their trouble. Of course, don't go to the opposite extreme and overpay. But if you really can't afford to contribute anything to your hosts, it's better to camp or sleep on the beach. Staying in villages is a way to meet and communicate with the people, an act of good will with great reward. It's *not* a cheap way to travel.

Camping

Your best home away from home is a tent. There are now organized campgrounds in Tahiti-Polynesia, Western Samoa, Fiji, New Caledonia, and Vanuatu, and the only place where camping is totally forbidden is Cook Islands. Always get permission of the landowner; you'll rarely be refused in places off the beaten track. Set a good precedent by not leaving a mess or violating custom. If you pitch your tent near a village or on private property without asking permission, you're asking for problems. Otherwise, camp out in the bush well away from gardens and trails.

Make sure your tent is water- and mosquito-proof, and try to find a spot swept by the trades. Never camp under a coconut tree, as falling coconuts hurt (actually, coconuts have two eyes so they only strike the wicked). If you hear a hurricane warning, pack up your tent and take immediate cover with the locals.

FOOD AND DRINK

The traditional diet of the Pacific islanders consists of root crops and fruit, plus lagoon fish and the occasional pig. The vegetables include taro, yams, cassava (manioc), breadfruit, and sweet potatoes. The sweet potato *(kumara)* is something of an anomaly—it's the only Pacific food plant with a South American origin. How it got to the islands is not known, but it and tobacco seem to have been introduced into New Guinea about 1600, suggesting the possibility of an Hispanic connection.

Taro is an elephant-eared plant cultivated in freshwater swamps. Although yams are considered a prestige food, they're not as nutritious as breadfruit and taro. Yams can grow up to three meters long and weigh hundreds of kilos. Papaya (pawpaw) is nourishing: a third of a cup contains as much vitamin C as 18 apples. To ripen a green papaya overnight, puncture it a few times with a knife. Don't overeat papaya—unless you *need* an effective laxative.

Raw fish *(poisson cru)* is an appetizing dish enjoyed in many Pacific countries. To prepare it, clean and skin the fish, then dice the fillet. Squeeze lemon or lime juice over it, and store in a cool place about 10 hours. When it's ready to serve, add chopped onions, garlic, green peppers, tomatoes, and coconut cream to taste. Local fishmongers know which species make the best raw fish, but know what you're doing before you join them—island stomachs are probably stronger than yours. It's sometimes safer to eat well-cooked food and to peel your own fruit.

Lobsters have become almost an endangered species on some islands due to the high prices they fetch on restaurant tables. Countless more are airfreighted to Hawaii. Before deciding to have one of these creatures sacrificed to provide your dinner, consider that the world will be poorer for it. Coconut crabs are even more threatened and it's almost scandalous that local governments should allow them to be fed to tourists. Sea turtles and flying foxes other delicacies to avoid, although these are seldom offered to visitors.

Islanders in the towns now eat mostly imported foods, just as we Westerners often opt for fast foods instead of meals made from basic ingredients. The Seventh-Day Adventists don't smoke, chew betel nut, dance, eat pork or rabbit, or drink tea, coffee, or alcohol. If you're going to the outer islands, take as many edibles with you as you can; they're always more expensive there. And keep in mind that virtually every food plant you see growing on the islands is cultivated by someone. Even sea shells washed up on a beach, or fish in the lagoon near someone's home, may be considered private property.

Restaurants
Eating out is an adventure, and first-rate restaurants are found in all the main towns, so whenever your travels start to get to you and it's time for a lift, splurge on a good meal and then see how the world looks. Tahiti-Polynesia and New Caledonia have some of the finest restaurants in the region, with prices to match. Fiji is outstanding for the variety of cuisines you can sample, and prices are very reasonable. Nuku'alofa and Apia also offer an increasing number of good inexpensive places to eat. In all of the islands except Tahiti-Polynesia and New Caledonia, you should be able to get a filling meal at a local restaurant for US$4 or less, at a tourist restaurant for US$7-14. Drink prices vary but in the French territories expect them to be about double what they are elsewhere. Beer drinkers will find some of the cheapest and best brew in Western Samoa, followed closely by Tonga, Fiji, and the Solomons.

Cooking
The ancient Polynesians stopped making pottery over a millennium ago and instead developed an ingenious way of cooking in an underground earth oven known as an *umu* or *lovo*. First a stack of dry coconut husks is burned in a pit. Once the fire is going well, coral stones are heaped on top, and when most of the husks have burnt away the food is wrapped in banana leaves and placed on the hot stones—fish and meat below, vegetables above. A whole pig may be cleaned, then stuffed with banana leaves and hot stones. This cooks the beast from inside out as well as outside in, and the leaves create steam. The food is then covered with more leaves and stones, and after about two and a half hours everything is cooked. Water can be boiled in a coconut shell placed on the hot stones of the *umu;* so long as the shell doesn't come into contact with a flame it won't catch fire. If you decide to give the *umu* a try, be sure to break open any sections of bamboo you plan to burn in the fire. Otherwise, get ready for a series of devastating explosions.

Breadfruit
The breadfruit *(uru)* is the plant most often associated with the South Pacific. The theme of a man turning himself into such a tree to save his family during famine often recurs in Polynesian legends. Ancient voyagers brought breadfruit shoots or seeds from Southeast Asia. When baked in an underground oven or roasted over flames, the now-seedless Polynesian variety resembles bread. Joseph Banks, botanist on Captain Cook's first voyage, wrote:

> *If a man should in the course of his lifetime plant 10 trees, which if well done might take the labor of an hour or thereabouts, he would completely fulfill his duty to his own as well as future generations.*

The French naturalist Sonnerat transplanted breadfruit to Reunion in the Indian Ocean as early as 1772, but it's Captain William Bligh who shall always be remembered when the plant is mentioned. In 1787 Bligh set out to collect young shoots in Tahiti for transfer to the West Indies, where they were to be planted to feed slaves. On the way back, his crew mutinied in Tongan waters and cast off both breadfruit and Bligh. The indomitable captain managed to reach

FOOD PLANTS OF THE PACIFIC

cacao (Theobroma cacao)

avocado
(Persea americana)

breadfruit (Artocarpus communis)

cashew nut
(Anacardium occidentale)

sasalapa (Annona muricata)

bananas (Musa cavendishii)

star fruit (Averrhoa carambola)

mangosteen
(Garcinia mangostana)

mangos (Mangifera indica)

guava (Psidium guajava)

LOUISE FOOTE

Dutch Timor in a rowboat and in 1792 returned to Tahiti with another ship to complete his task.

The breadfruit *(Artocarpus altilis),* a tall tree with broad green leaves, provides shade as well as food. A well-watered tree can produce as many as 1,000 pale green breadfruits a year. Robert Lee Eskridge described a breadfruit thus:

Its outer rind or skin, very hard, is covered with a golf-ball-like surface of small irregular pits or tiny hollows. An inner rind about a half-inch thick surrounds the fruit itself, which when baked tastes not unlike a doughy potato. Perhaps fresh bread, rolled up until it becomes a semifirm mass, best describes the breadfruit when cooked.

The starchy, easily digested fruit is rich in vitamin B. When consumed with a protein such as fish or meat it serves as an energy food. The Polynesians learned to preserve breadfruit by pounding it into a paste, which was kept in leaf-lined pits to ferment into *mahi.* Like the coconut, the breadfruit tree itself had many uses, including the provision of wood for outrigger canoes.

The Coconut Palm
Human life would not be possible on most of the Pacific's far-flung atolls without this all-purpose tree. It reaches maturity in eight years, then produces about 50 nuts a year for 60 years. Aside from the tree's aesthetic value and usefulness in providing shade, the water of the green coconut provides a refreshing drink, and the white meat of the young nut is a delicious food. The harder meat of more mature nuts is grated and squeezed, giving rise to a coconut cream eaten alone or used in cooking. The oldest nuts are cracked open, the hard meat removed, then dried to be sold as copra. It takes about 6,000 coconuts to make a ton of copra.

Copra is pressed to extract the oil, which in turn is made into candles, cosmetics, and soap.

The juice or sap from the cut flower spathes of the palm provides toddy, a popular drink; the toddy is distilled into a spirit called arrack, the whiskey of the Pacific. Millionaire's salad is made by shredding the growth cut from the heart of the tree. For each salad, a fully mature tree must be sacrificed.

The nut's hard inner shell can be used as a cup and makes excellent firewood. Rope, cordage, brushes, and heavy matting are produced from the coir fiber of the husk. The smoke from burning husks is a most effective mosquito repellent. The leaves of the coconut tree are used to thatch the roofs of the islanders' cottages or are woven into baskets, mats, and fans. The trunk provides timber for building and furniture. Actually, these are only the common uses: there are many others as well.

Others
Betel chewing is a widespread practice among men, women, and children in the Western Pacific, as far southeast as Santa Cruz in the Solomons. First the unripe nut of the Areca palm is chewed, then the leaves of the fruit of the betel pepper. Lime from a gourd (made by burning coral or shells, or grinding limestone) is inserted into the mouth with a spatula, and the chewer's saliva turns bright red. It's said to relieve hunger and fatigue—give it a try and the locals will love you.

Kava drinking is easier to get into (see under "Customs" in the Fiji chapter for a full description). While kava is extremely popular in Fiji and Tonga, extremely potent in Vanuatu, and extremely dignified in Samoa, it's unknown in Tahiti, Hawaii, and New Zealand. Recently German pharmaceutical firms have discovered kava's usefulness in the manufacture of nonaddictive painkillers and anti-depressants.

SERVICES AND INFORMATION

VISAS AND OFFICIALDOM

If you're from an English-speaking country or Western Europe you won't need a visa to visit most of the South Pacific countries. Exceptions are the French territories, where Australians still require a visa, and Easter Island, where New Zealanders may need one. If you fall into one of those categories check the latest requirements with your airline well ahead, as consulates are few and far between. Unlike the U.S., which is very sticky about visas, American Samoa does not require a visa of most tourists. Australia requires a visa (free) of everyone except New Zealanders. Ironically, the Pacific islanders themselves are confronted with a complicated series of requirements when they attempt to travel.

Other Requirements

Everyone must have a passport, sufficient funds, and a ticket to leave. Your passport should be valid six months beyond your departure date. Some officials object to tourists who intend to camp or stay with friends, so write the name of a likely hotel on your arrival card.

Immigration officials will often insist on seeing an air ticket back to your home country, no matter how much money you're able to show them. The easy way to get around this if you're on an open-ended holiday or traveling by yacht is to purchase a regular OW ticket to Hawaii or Los Angeles from Air New Zealand. This will be accepted without question, and Air New Zealand offices throughout the Pacific will reissue the ticket, so you'll always have a ticket to leave from the next country on your itinerary. When you finally get home, you can turn in the unused coupons for a full refund. (See also "Onward Tickets" under "Getting There" later in this chapter.)

Diplomatic Missions

The country with the best representation in the South Pacific is New Zealand, which has high commissions in Apia, Honiara, Nuku'alofa, Port Vila, and Rarotonga, an embassy in Suva, a consulate in Nouméa, and an honorary consul in Papeete. Australia has exactly the same level of diplomatic representation as New Zealand except that they lack an office on Rarotonga. Britain has high commissions in Honiara, Nuku'alofa, and Port Vila, an embassy in Suva, and an honorary consul in Papeete. Canada has only an honorary consul in Suva, but in 1986 Canada and Australia signed a reciprocal agreement extending full consular service to Canadians at Australian missions throughout the region. The United States is very poorly represented with only an embassy in Suva and a consulate in Apia (it's rumored that the Apia consulate is soon to close due to budgetary cutbacks).

France has embassies in Port Vila and Suva, high commissions in Nouméa and Papeete, and honorary consuls in Nuku'alofa and Rarotonga. China has embassies in Apia, Port Vila, and Suva, while Taiwan has embassies in Honiara and Nuku'alofa. Japan has embassies in Honiara and Suva and a consulate in Nouméa. South Korea has an embassy in Suva, a consulate in Pago Pago, and honorary consuls in Nuku'alofa and Papeete. Papua New Guinea has an embassy in Suva, a high commission in Honiara, and an honorary consul in Port Vila.

Numerous member countries of the European Union have consulates or honorary consuls in Nouméa and Papeete, and these are listed in the respective chapters. Other honorary consuls include those of Germany in Apia, Nuku'alofa, and Papeete; of Sweden in Nuku'alofa, Papeete, and Port Vila; of Switzerland in Nouméa and Papeete; of Spain in Nuku'alofa; of Chile in Papeete; and of Indonesia and Vanuatu in Nouméa. Israel has an embassy in Suva.

Customs

Agricultural regulations in most Pacific countries prohibit the import of fresh fruit, flowers, meat (including sausage), live animals and plants, as well as any old artifacts that might harbor pests. If in doubt, ask about having your souvenirs fumigated by the local agricultural authorities and a certificate issued prior to departure. Canned food, dried flowers, mounted insects, mats, baskets, and tapa cloth are usually okay. If you've been on a farm, wash your clothes and shoes before going to the airport. If you've been camping, make sure your tent is clean.

Yacht owners should think twice before taking their pet dog along, as regulations in the rabies-free South Pacific are strict. Most countries require the animal to be held in quarantine on board for four to nine months. A bond of US$250 may be required, and it will be a hassle to get the money back come time to leave. You may be denied permission to dock and get a shorter visa if you have a dog. Pets found ashore illegally can be confiscated and destroyed. Cats and birds may be happy spending a year aboard, but it's no life for a dog.

Moving to the South Pacific

No country or territory in the South Pacific is accepting immigrants, unless you happen to be a Frenchman bound for Tahiti or Nouméa or an investor intending to put a lot of money into a local economy. Population densities in the Pacific islands are among the highest in the world, and Europeans who do settle there take the best jobs away from the islanders. Local immigration officials are wary of Europeans attempting to escape the dreary wastelands of the industrial world, hence the "ticket to leave" requirement.

Marriage to a local woman is no passport for a European man to spend the rest of his days in the islands; in fact, in the Solomons a tourist who attempts to marry a local person is subject to deportation. A foreign woman, on the other hand, may be allowed to stay if she's married to an islander.

Though virtually every Pacific island is claimed by one country or another, not all are effectively controlled by governments. In his book *Uninhabited Ocean Islands* (available from Loompanics Unlimited, Box 1197, Port Townsend, WA 98368, U.S.A.), Jon Fisher describes numerous South Seas islands on which you could "get lost" (until found by the authorities).

If you want to buy an island try René Boehm Private Islands (Box 891, Forest Hills, NY 11375, U.S.A.; tel. 718/520-8428) or René Boehm Privatinseln (Neuer Wall 2, D-20354 Hamburg, Germany; tel. 49-40/342-222, fax 49-40/340-568). Herr Boehm has been in the business of selling private islands for 20 years.

Pacific Island Investments (Box 383970, Waikoloa, HI 96738, U.S.A.; tel. 808/883-8000, fax 808/883-8838) specializes in the sale of estates, resorts, islands, and businesses throughout the Pacific. PII's president, Karen Jeffery, has considerable real estate experience in Hawaii and the South Pacific.

MONEY

All prices quoted herein are in the local currency unless otherwise stated. Each Monday the *Wall Street Journal* runs a "World Value of the Dollar" column which lists the current exchange rates of all Pacific currencies.

Most South Pacific airports have banks changing money at normal rates (check the "Airport" listing at the end of each chapter introduction) and the most convenient currencies to carry are Australian, N.Z., and U.S. dollars. If you'll be visiting American Samoa or the U.S., be sure to have enough U.S. dollar traveler's checks to see you through, as foreign currencies are little known in the States and whopping commissions are charged. French francs are the best currency by far to carry to Tahiti-Polynesia and New Caledonia as they're exchanged at a fixed rate without any commission.

The bulk of your travel funds should be in traveler's checks, preferably American Express, although that company's representation in the region is dwindling. American Express has travel service offices in Papeete, Rarotonga, Suva, Nandi, and Nouméa, but the American Express agencies in Pago Pago and Apia have closed and the company has no representation in Tonga, Vanuatu, and Solomon Islands. Thomas Cook has a large office in Suva, Fiji. To claim a refund for lost or stolen American Express traveler's checks call the local office (listed in the respective chapter) or their Sydney office collect (tel. 61-2/9886-0689). They'll also cancel lost credit cards, provided you know the numbers. The banks best represented in this part of the world are the ANZ Bank, the Bank of Hawaii, and the Westpac Bank, so if you need to have money sent, you'd do best working through one of them.

If you want to use a credit card, always ask beforehand, even if a business has a sign or brochure that says it's possible. Visa and MasterCard can be used to obtain cash advances at banks in most countries, but remember that cash advances accrue interest from the moment you receive the money—ask your bank if they have a debit card which allows charges to be deducted from your checking account automatically. The use of bank cards such as Visa and MasterCard is expensive in Western Samoa and Solomon Islands because those currencies aren't recognized internationally. Thus the charge must first be converted into N.Z. or Australian dollars, then into your own currency, and you'll lose on the exchange several times. American Express is probably the best card to use as they don't go through third currencies (this could vary—ask).

Cost-wise, you'll find Fiji, Cook Islands, Tonga, and Western Samoa to be the least expensive South Pacific countries, with Tahiti-Polynesia and New Caledonia consistently dearer. The lack of budget accommodations makes the price of a visit to American Samoa stiff, while in Vanuatu it's the cost of transportation that breaks your budget. Solomon Islands is very reasonable if you avoid facilities intended mainly for up-market tourists. Inflation is consistently low in New Caledonia and Tahiti-Polynesia but high in Solomon Islands, Tonga and Western Samoa, something to keep in mind when looking at the prices in this book.

Upon departure avoid getting stuck with local banknotes, as currencies such as the Fiji dollar, Pacific franc, Solomon Islands dollar, Vanuatu *vatu,* and Tongan *pa'anga* are difficult to change and heavily discounted even in neighboring countries; Western Samoan *tala,* Cook Islands dollars, and Chilean pesos are worthless outside the country of origin. Change whatever you have left over into the currency of the next country on your itinerary.

Don't show everyone how much money you have in your wallet, as this causes resentment and invites theft. Bargaining is not common: the first price you're quoted is usually it. Tipping is *not* customary in the South Pacific and often generates more embarrassment than gratitude.

POST AND TELECOMMUNICATIONS

Postal Services

Always use airmail when posting letters from the South Pacific. Airmail takes two weeks to reach North America and Europe, surface mail takes up to six months. Postage rates to the U.S. are very low from Fiji, Solomon Islands,

PHILATELY

Postage stamps of the South Pacific are highly valued by collectors around the world, and many smaller Commonwealth countries such as the Cook Islands, Kiribati, Niue, Norfolk Island, Pitcairn, Western Samoa, Tokelau, Tonga, and Tuvalu earn a substantial portion of government revenue from the sale of stamps. In order to generate more revenue, the Cook Islands issues separate stamps for Penrhyn and Aitutaki, and Tonga has Niuafo'ou stamps. Some countries also try to boost income by increasing the number of annual issues, a practice that can cost them collectors. The worst offender in this regard is Tuvalu. Most of the stamps are printed in Britain, where the highest technical standards are employed.

Popular themes include birds, seashells, coral, maps, atoll scenes, fishing, dancing, musical instru-

ments, and headdresses. As the bicentenaries of his voyages of discovery rolled around during the 1970s, Captain Cook was the subject of stamp issues by many of the islands he discovered. Easily obtained, inexpensive postage stamps and first-day covers make memorable souvenirs. Local post offices usually have a few colorful ones, or write for information in advance. The only address you need is Philatelic Bureau, the name of the country, and South Pacific Ocean. A dealer specializing in the region is Pacific Stamps (Box 816, Tewantin, QLD 4565, Australia; tel. 61-7/5474-0799, fax 61-7/5474-0757). *Pacifica,* the quarterly journal of the Pacific Islands Study Circle of Great Britain (c/o John Ray, 24 Woodvale Ave., London SE25 4AE, England), contains a wealth of useful information on collecting Pacific stamps.

and American Samoa, medium-priced from Tonga and Western Samoa, and considerably higher from Tahiti-Polynesia, Cook Islands, Vanuatu, and New Caledonia.

When writing to South Pacific individuals or businesses, include the post office box number (or *Boîte Postale* in the French territories), as mail delivery is rare. If it's a remote island or small village you're writing to, the person's name will be sufficient. Sending a picture postcard to an islander is a very nice way of saying thank you.

When collecting mail at poste restante (general delivery), be sure to check for the initials of your first and second names, plus any initial that is similar. Have your correspondents print and underline your last name.

Telephone Services

The telephone service varies, but international calls placed from hotel rooms are always much more expensive than the same calls made at post offices or telephone company offices. Telephone booths for local calls are usually found only at post offices. Cook Islands, Fiji, New Caledonia, Tahiti-Polynesia, and Vanuatu recently introduced card telephones and these are very handy. By using a telephone card to call long distance you limit the amount the call can possibly cost and won't end up overspending should you forget to keep track of the time. On short calls you avoid three-minute minimum charges. If you'll be staying in a country more than a few days and intend to make your own arrangements, it's wise to purchase a phone card at a post office right away. In this book we provide all the numbers you'll need to make local hotel reservations, check restaurant hours, find out about cultural shows, and compare car rental rates, saving you a lot of time and inconvenience.

A three-minute station-to-station call to the U.S. will cost under US$7 from Fiji and both Samoas, under US$8 from Tonga, under US$10 from Tuvalu or Solomon Islands, under US$12 from Cook Islands, around US$14.50 from Vanuatu, and US$18 from Tahiti-Polynesia or New Caledonia. These differences make it well worth waiting to call home from a cheaper country.

Calling from the U.S. to the South Pacific is cheaper than going in the other direction, so if you want to talk to someone periodically, leave

a list of your travel dates and hotel telephone numbers (provided in this book) where friends and relatives can try to get hold of you. All the main islands have direct dialing via satellite. One reader on a wide-ranging trip said he found it very effective to leave an extra copy of this book with his family. Not only were they able to follow his travels around the Pacific, but they had all the telephone and fax numbers needed to contact him.

To place a call to a Pacific island from outside the region, first dial the international access code (check your phone book), then the country code, then the number. The country codes are: 108 (Easter Island), 675 (Papua New Guinea), 676 (Tonga), 677 (Solomon Islands), 678 (Vanuatu), 679 (Fiji), 681 (Wallis), 682 (Cook Islands), 683 (Niue), 684 (American Samoa), 685 (Western Samoa), 687 (New Caledonia), 688 (Tuvalu), 689 (Tahiti-Polynesia), and 872 (Pitcairn Islands).

None of the Pacific countries have local area codes, but local telephone numbers have varying numbers of digits: four digits in Niue; five digits in Tonga, Western Samoa, Vanuatu, and Solomon Islands; six digits in Tahiti-Polynesia, Easter Island, Fiji, and New Caledonia; and seven digits in American Samoa.

If a fax you are trying to send to the South Pacific doesn't go through smoothly on the first or second try, wait and try again at another time of day. If it doesn't work then, stop trying as the fax machine at the other end may not be able to read your signal, and your telephone company will levy a hefty minimum charge for each attempt. Call the international operator to ask what is going wrong.

TIME

The international date line generally follows 180 degrees longitude and creates a difference of 24 hours in time between the two sides. It swings east at Tuvalu to avoid slicing Fiji in two. This can be confusing, as Tonga, which chooses to observe the same day as neighboring Fiji and New Zealand, has the same clock time as Samoa but is a day ahead! Everything in the Eastern Hemisphere west of the date line is a day later, everything in the Western Hemisphere east of the line is a day earlier (or behind). Air travelers lose a day when they fly west across the date line and gain it back when they return. Keep track of things by repeating to yourself, "If it's Sunday in Samoa, it's Monday in Melbourne."

In this book all clock times are rendered according to the 24-hour airline timetable system, i.e. 0100 is 1:00 a.m., 1300 is 1:00 p.m., 2330 is 11:30 p.m. The islanders operate on "coconut time"—the nut will fall when it is ripe. In the languid air of the South Seas punctuality takes on a new meaning. Appointments are approximate

---

PACIFIC TIME

	Hours from GMT	Standard Time at 1200 GMT
Easter Island	-6	0600
California	-8	0400
Hawaii, Tahiti	-10	0200
Cook Islands	-10	0200
Niue, Samoa	-11	0100

(International Date Line)
yesterday

↑↓

today

Tonga	+13	0100
Fiji Islands	+12	2400
Tuvalu, Tarawa	+12	2400
Majuro, Nauru	+12	2400
New Zealand	+12	2400
New Caledonia	+11	2300
Vanuatu	+11	2300
Solomon Islands	+11	2300
Ponape	+11	2300
Queensland	+10	2200
Papua New Guinea	+10	2200
Truk, Guam	+10	2200
Japan, Koror	+9	2100

note: Easter Island and New Zealand adopt daylight saving time from October to February, while California does so from April to October. The others do not. GMT is Greenwich mean time, the time at London, England.

---

and service relaxed. Even the seasons are fuzzy: sometimes wetter, sometimes drier, but almost always hot. Slow down to the island pace and get in step with where you are. You may not get as much done, but you'll enjoy life a lot more. Daylight hours in the tropics run 0600-1800 with few seasonal variations.

WEIGHTS AND MEASURES

The metric system is now used everywhere except in American Samoa. Study the conversion table in the back of this handbook if you're not used to thinking metric. Most distances herein are quoted in kilometers—they become easy to comprehend when you know than one km is the distance a normal person walks in 10 minutes. A meter is slightly more than a yard and a liter is just over a quart.

Unless otherwise indicated, north is at the top of all maps in this handbook. When using official topographical maps you can determine the scale by taking the representative fraction (RF) and dividing by 100. This will give the number of meters represented by one centimeter. For example, a map with an RF of 1:10,000 would represent 100 meters for every centimeter on the map.

Electric Currents
If you're taking along a plug-in razor, radio, or other electrical appliance, be aware that two different voltages are used in the South Pacific. American Samoa uses 110 volts AC, while the rest of the region uses 220-240 volts AC. Most appliances require a converter to change from one voltage to another. You'll also need an adapter to cope with different socket types, which vary between flat two-pronged plugs in American Samoa, round two-pronged plugs in the French territories, and three-pronged plugs with the two on top at angles almost everywhere else. Pick up both items before you leave home, as they're hard to find in the islands. Keep voltages in mind if you buy duty-free appliances: dual voltage (110/220 V) items are best.

Videos
Commercial travel video tapes make nice souvenirs, but always keep in mind that there are

three incompatible video formats loose in the world: NTSC (used in North America), PAL (used in Britain, Germany, Japan, and Australia), and SECAM (used in France and Russia). Don't buy prerecorded tapes abroad unless they're of the system used in your country.

MEDIA AND INFORMATION

Daily newspapers are published in Tahiti-Polynesia (La Dépêche de Tahiti and Les Nouvelles de Tahiti), Cook Islands (Cook Islands News), American Samoa (Samoa Daily News), Fiji (The Fiji Times and The Daily Post), and New Caledonia (Les Nouvelles Calédoniennes). Weekly or twice-weekly papers of note include the Tahiti Beach Press, Tonga Chronicle, Samoa Journal & Advertiser, The Samoa Observer, and The Solomon Star.

The leading regional news magazines are Islands Business Pacific and Pacific Islands Monthly, both published in Fiji, and Pacific Magazine from Honolulu. Copies of these are well worth picking up during your trip, and a subscription will help you keep in touch. Turn to

"Resources" at the end of this book for more Pacific-oriented publications.

The **Pacific Islands News Association** (46 Gordon St., Suva, Fiji Islands; fax 679/303-943) holds an annual conference of regional editors to discuss media issues. PINA is usually seen as representing management interests, while the **Pacific Journalists' Association** is comprised of working journalists. The regional news service **PacNews** (Box 116, Port Vila; tel. 678/26300, fax 678/26301) was founded in 1987 with the assistance of the Friedrich Ebert Stiftung of Germany. In 1990 PacNews was forced to evacuate its premises in Fiji due to government harassment.

Information Offices

All the main countries have official tourist information offices. Their main branches in the capitals open during normal business hours but information desks at the airports only open for the arrival of international flights, if then. Always visit the local tourist office to pick up brochures and ask questions. Their overseas offices, listed in this handbook's Appendix, often mail out useful information on their country.

HEALTH

For a tropical area, the South Pacific's a healthy place. The sea and air are clear and usually pollution-free. The humidity nourishes the skin and the local fruit is brimming with vitamins. If you take a few precautions, you'll never have a sick day. The information provided below is intended to make you knowledgeable, not fearful.

Some medical facilities are listed in this book; otherwise go to the nearest hospital or government clinic, or ask a local pharmacist to recommend a private doctor. The facilities may not be up to American standards but the fee will be infinitely lower.

The sale of travel insurance is big business in the U.S., but the value of the policies themselves is often questionable. If your regular group health insurance also covers you while you're traveling abroad it's probably enough. If you do opt for the security of travel insurance, insist on a policy that also covers theft or loss of luggage and emergency medical evacuations. If

you'll be involved in any "dangerous activities," such as scuba diving or surfing, read the fine print to make sure your policy is valid.

American-made medications may by unobtainable in the islands, so bring a supply of whatever you think you'll need. Otherwise go to any Chinese general store and ask the owner to recommend a good Chinese patent medicine for what ails you. The cost will be a third of what European medicines or herbs cost, and the Chinese medicine is often as effective or more so. Antibiotics should only be used to treat serious wounds, and only after medical advice.

Acclimatizing

Don't go from winter weather into the steaming tropics without a rest before and after. Minimize jet lag by setting your watch to local time at your destination as soon as you board the flight. Westbound flights into the South Pacific from North America or Europe are less jolting since you follow the sun and your body gets a few hours extra sleep. On the way home you're moving against the sun and the hours of sleep your body loses cause jet lag. Airplane cabins have low humidity, so drink lots of juice or water instead of carbonated drinks, and don't overeat in-flight. It's also best to forgo coffee, as it will only keep you awake, and alcohol, which will dehydrate you.

Scuba diving on departure day can give you a severe case of the bends. Before flying there should be a minimum of 12 hours surface interval after a non-decompression dive and a minimum of 24 hours after a decompression dive. Factors contributing to decompression sickness include a lack of sleep and/or the excessive consumption of alcohol before diving.

If you start feeling seasick onboard a ship, stare at the horizon, which is always steady, and stop thinking about it. Anti-motion-sickness pills are useful to have along; otherwise, ginger helps alleviate seasickness.

Frequently the feeling of thirst is false and only due to mucous membrane dryness. Gargling or taking two or three gulps of warm water should be enough. Keep moisture in your body by having a hot drink like tea or black coffee, or any kind of slightly salted or sour drink in small quantities. Salt in fresh lime juice is remarkably refreshing.

The tap water is safe to drink in the main towns, but ask first elsewhere. If in doubt, boil it or use purification pills. Tap water that is uncomfortably hot to touch is usually safe. Allow it to cool in a clean container. Don't forget that if the tap water is contaminated, the local ice will be too. Avoid brushing your teeth with water unfit to drink, and wash or peel fruit and vegetables if you can. Cooked food is less subject to contamination than raw.

Sunburn

The Tahitian name for us white folks, *papa'a*, literally means "sunburned skin." Though you may think a tan will make you *look* healthier and more attractive, it's very damaging to the skin, which becomes dry, rigid, and prematurely old and wrinkled, especially on the face. And a burn from the sun greatly increases your risk of getting skin cancer. Begin with short exposures to the sun, perhaps half an hour at a time, followed by an equal time in the shade. Drink plenty of liquids to keep your pores open and avoid the sun from 1000 to 1400. Clouds and beach umbrellas will not protect you fully. Wear a T-shirt while snorkeling to protect your back. Sunbathing is the main cause of cataracts to the eyes, so wear sunglasses and a wide-brimmed hat and beware of reflected sunlight.

Use a sunscreen lotion containing PABA rather than oil, and don't forget to apply it to your nose, lips, forehead, neck, hands, and feet. Sunscreens protect you from ultraviolet rays (a leading cause of cancer), while oils magnify the sun's effect. A 15-factor sunscreen provides 93% protection (a more expensive 30-factor sunscreen is only slightly better at 97% protection). Apply the lotion *before* going to the beach to avoid being burned on the way, and reapply periodically to replace sunscreen washed away by perspiration. After sunbathing take a tepid shower rather than a hot one, which would wash away your natural skin oils. Stay moist and use a vitamin E evening cream to preserve the youth of your skin. Calamine ointment soothes skin already burned, as does coconut oil. Pharmacists recommend Solarcaine to soothe burned skin. Rinsing off with a vinegar solution reduces peeling, and aspirin relieves some of the pain and irritation. Vitamin A and calcium counteract overdoses of vitamin D received from the sun. The fairer your skin, the more essential it is to take care.

As earth's ozone layer is depleted due to the commercial use of chlorofluorocarbons (CFCs) and other factors, the need to protect oneself from ultraviolet radiation is becoming more urgent. In 1990 the U.S. Centers for Disease Control in Atlanta reported that deaths from skin cancer increased 26% between 1973 and 1985. Previously the cancers didn't develop until age 50 or 60, but now much younger people are affected.

Ailments

Cuts and scratches infect easily in the tropics and take a long time to heal. Prevent infection from coral cuts by immediately washing wounds with soap and fresh water, then rubbing in vinegar or alcohol (whiskey will do)—painful but effective. Use a good antiseptic, if you have one. Islanders usually dab coral cuts with lime juice.

All cuts turn septic quickly in the tropics, so try to keep them clean and covered.

For bites, burns, and cuts, an antiseptic such as Solarcaine speeds healing and helps prevent infection. Pure aloe vera is good for sunburn, scratches, and even coral cuts. Bites by *nono* flies itch for days and can become infected. Not everyone is affected by insect bites in the same way. Some people are practically immune to insects, while traveling companions experiencing exactly the same conditions are soon covered with bites. You'll soon know which type you are.

Prickly heat, an intensely irritating rash, is caused by wearing heavy clothing that is inappropriate for the climate. When the glands are blocked and the sweat is unable to evaporate, the skin becomes soggy and small red blisters appear. Synthetic fabrics like nylon are especially bad in this regard. Take a cold shower, apply calamine lotion, dust with talcum powder, and take off those clothes! Until things improve, avoid alcohol, tea, coffee, and any physical activity that makes you sweat. If you're sweating profusely, increase your intake of salt slightly to avoid fatigue, but not without concurrently drinking more water.

Use antidiarrheal medications sparingly. Rather than take drugs to plug yourself up, drink plenty of unsweetened liquids like green coconut or fresh fruit juice to help flush yourself out. Egg yolk mixed with nutmeg helps diarrhea, or have a rice and tea day. Avoid dairy products. Most cases of diarrhea are self-limiting and require only simple replacement of fluids and salts lost in diarrheal stools. If the diarrhea is persistent or you experience high fever, drowsiness, or blood in the stool, stop traveling, rest, and consider attending a clinic. For constipation eat pineapple or any peeled fruit.

If you're sleeping in villages or with the locals you may pick up head or body lice. Pharmacists and general stores usually have a remedy that will eliminate the problem in minutes (pack a bottle with you if you're uptight). You'll know you're lousy when you start to scratch: pick out the little varmints and snap them between your thumbnails for fun. The locals pluck the creatures out of each other's hair one by one, a way of confirming friendships and showing affection. Intestinal parasites (worms) are

also widespread. The hookworm bores its way through the soles of your feet, and if you go barefoot through gardens and plantations you're sure to pick up something.

Malaria

Malaria is the most serious regional health hazard, but it's restricted to Vanuatu, Solomon Islands, and Papua New Guinea *only*. Guadalcanal now ranks as one of the most malarial areas in the world, and chloroquine-resistant *falciparum* malaria is widespread in all three countries. Read the relevant references in the introductions to the "Vanuatu" and "Solomon Islands" chapters a couple of weeks before you embark for those islands.

Malaria *can* be avoided, and even if you're unlucky, it won't kill you so long as you're taking prophylactics. So don't become alarmed or let fear of malaria prevent you from visiting Melanesia. If you're only going to Fiji or the Polynesian countries, forget it entirely as it's unknown there. Symptoms of malaria are chills, aches in the back, head, and joints, plus a high periodic fever. Doctors outside the area often misdiagnose these symptoms (which may not begin until months after you leave the area) as common flu. Yet once identified through a blood test, malaria can usually be cured.

The *Anopheles* carrier mosquitoes are most active from dusk to dawn, so try to avoid getting bitten at this time. Wear long shirts and pants, sleep in a screened room, burn a mosquito coil, and use an insect repellent containing a high concentration of N,N diethylmetatoluamide (deet). For some reason people taking vitamin B-1 aren't as attractive to mosquitoes. On the other hand perfumes, colognes, and scented soaps do attract them. *Anopheles* mosquitoes don't hum, so you won't be able to hear them.

Begin taking an antimalarial drug a week before you arrive in Vanuatu or the Solomons and continue for four weeks after you leave. Malaria pills are much cheaper in the South Pacific than in North America or Australia, so only buy the minimum number required to get you started.

The U.S. Peace Corps in the Solomons recommends taking two 100-mg Paludrine tablets a day, plus chloroquine (brand name Nivaquine) twice a week. Some people also carry a three-tablet dose of the drug Fansidar to be used for self-treatment in case of fever. If you choose to take Fansidar in combination with chloroquine, discontinue taking the drug if you experience adverse skin reactions. Fansidar must not be taken by pregnant women or anyone allergic to sulfa drugs. Paludrine can cause nausea if taken on an empty stomach, so take it after dinner. Chloroquine can affect the eyes, but only if you take it continuously for eight years! Other oft-mentioned antimalarial drugs are Maloprim, Lariam, and Daraprim. It's always useful to ask a local pharmacist what he/she recommends after you arrive in the area.

There's still no successful vaccination against malaria and none of the various pills are 100% effective. It's something of a scandal in the medical profession that while hundreds of millions of dollars are spent annually on research into the lifestyle diseases of the affluent, such as cancer and heart disease, comparatively little is allocated to the tropical and parasitic diseases of the third world. Vaccines only account for one percent of the profits of the big pharmaceutical companies, and just three percent of their research budgets are devoted to tropical diseases, largely because there's little money to be made from them.

AIDS

In 1981 scientists in the United States and France first recognized the Acquired Immune Deficiency Syndrome (AIDS), which was later discovered to be caused by a virus called the Human Immuno-deficiency Virus (HIV). HIV breaks down the body's immunity to infections leading to AIDS. The virus can lie hidden in the body for many years without producing any obvious symptoms or before developing into the AIDS disease.

HIV lives in white blood cells and is present in the sexual fluids of humans. It's difficult to catch and is spread mostly through sexual intercourse, by needle or syringe sharing among intravenous drug users, in blood transfusions, and during pregnancy and birth (if the mother is infected). Using another person's razor blade or having your body pierced or tattooed are also risky, but the HIV virus cannot be transmitted by shaking hands, kissing, cuddling, fondling, sneezing, cooking food, or sharing eating or drinking utensils. One cannot be infected by saliva,

sweat, tears, urine, or feces; toilet seats, telephones, swimming pools, or mosquito bites do not cause AIDS. Ostracizing a known AIDS victim is not only immoral but also absurd.

Most blood banks now screen their products for HIV, and you can protect yourself against dirty needles by only allowing an injection if you see the syringe taken out of a fresh unopened pack. The simplest safeguard during sex is the proper use of a condom. Unroll the condom onto the erect penis; while withdrawing after ejaculation, hold onto the condom as you come out. Never try to recycle a condom, and pack a supply with you as it's a nuisance trying to buy them locally.

HIV is spread more often through anal than vaginal sex because the lining of the rectum is much weaker than that of the vagina, and ordinary condoms sometimes tear when used in anal sex. If you have anal sex, only use extra-strong condoms and special water-based lubricants since oil, Vaseline, and cream weaken the rubber. During oral sex you must make sure you don't get any semen or menstrual blood in your mouth. A woman runs 10 times the risk of contracting AIDS from a man than the other way around, and the threat is always greater

when another sexually transmitted disease (STD) is present.

The very existence of AIDS calls for a basic change in human behavior. No vaccine or drug exists that can prevent or cure AIDS, and because the virus mutates frequently, no remedy may ever be totally effective. Other STDs such as syphilis, gonorrhea, chlamydia, hepatitis B, and herpes are far more common than AIDS and can lead to serious complications such as infertility, but at least they can usually be cured.

The euphoria of travel can make it easier to fall in love or have sex with a stranger, so travelers must be informed of these dangers. As a tourist you should always practice safe sex to prevent AIDS and other STDs. You never know who is infected or even if you yourself have become infected. It's important to bring the subject up *before* you start to make love. Make a joke out of it by pulling out a condom and asking your new partner, "Say, do you know what this is?" Or perhaps, "Your condom or mine?" Far from being unromantic or embarrassing, you'll both feel more relaxed with the subject off your minds and it's much better than worrying afterwards if you might have been infected. The golden rule is safe sex or no sex.

By mid-1994 an estimated 16 million people worldwide were HIV carriers, and hundreds of thousands had died of AIDS. Statistics released by the South Pacific Commission in February 1995 acknowledge 611 HIV infections and 220 cases of AIDS in the Pacific islands. Most affected were Tahiti-Polynesia (HIV 144, AIDS 43), New Caledonia (HIV 115, AIDS 37), Papua New Guinea (HIV 236, AIDS 87), and Guam (HIV 64, AIDS 24). In Tahiti-Polynesia and New Caledonia over two-thirds of those affected are males, but in Papua New Guinea men and women are affected in equal numbers. Although these figures are negligible compared to the 401,789 confirmed AIDS cases in the U.S., the real number could be 50 times higher, and other STDs have already reached epidemic proportions in the islands. Thus it's essential that everyone do their utmost to combat this killer disease.

An HIV infection can be detected through a blood test because the antibodies created by the body to fight off the virus can be seen under a microscope. It takes at least three weeks for the antibodies to be produced and in some cases as long as six months before they can be picked up during a screening test. If you think you may have run a risk, you should discuss the appropriateness of a test with your doctor. It's always better to know if you are infected so as to be able to avoid infecting others, to obtain early treatment of symptoms, and to make realistic plans. If you know someone with AIDS you should give them all the support you can (there's no danger in such contact unless blood is present).

Toxic Fish

Over 400 species of tropical reef fish, including wrasses, snappers, groupers, barracudas, jacks, moray eels, surgeonfish, and shellfish, are known to cause seafood poisoning (ciguatera). There's no way to tell if a fish will cause ciguatera: a species can be poisonous on one side of the island, but not on the other.

Over a decade ago scientists on Tahiti determined that a one-celled dinoflagellate called *Gambierdiscus toxicus* was the cause. Normally these microalgae are found only in the ocean depths, but when a reef is disturbed by natural or human causes they can multiply dramatically in a lagoon. The dinoflagellates are consumed by tiny herbivorous fish and the toxin passes up through the food chain to larger fish where it becomes concentrated in the head and guts. The toxins have no effect on the fish that feed on them.

Tahiti-Polynesia's 700-800 cases of ciguatera a year are more than in the rest of the South Pacific combined, leading to suspicions that the French nuclear testing program is responsible. Ciguatera didn't exist on Hao atoll in the Tuamotus until military dredging for a 3,500-meter runway began in 1965. By mid-1968 43% of the population had been affected. Between 1971 and 1980 over 30% of the population of Mangareva near the Moruroa nuclear test site suffered from seafood poisoning.

The symptoms (tingling, prickling, itching, nausea, vomiting, erratic heartbeat, joint and muscle pains) usually subside in a few days. Induce vomiting and take castor oil as a laxative if you're unlucky. Symptoms can recur for up to a year, and victims may become allergic to all seafoods. In the Marshall Islands, a drug called

Mannitol has been effective in treating ciguatera, but as yet little is known about it. Avoid biointoxication by cleaning fish as soon as they're caught, discarding the head and organs, and taking special care with oversized fish. Whether the fish is consumed cooked or raw has no bearing on this problem. Local residents often know from experience which species may be eaten.

Other Diseases

Infectious hepatitis A (jaundice) is a liver ailment transmitted person to person or through unboiled water, uncooked vegetables, or other foods contaminated during handling. The risk of infection is highest for those who eat village food, so if you'll be spending much time in rural areas an immune globulin shot is recommended. In 1995 a hepatitis A vaccine called Havrix was approved by the U.S. Food and Drug Administration. You'll know you've got the hep when your eyeballs and urine turn yellow. Time and rest are the only cure. Viral hepatitis B is spread through sexual or blood contact.

There have been sporadic outbreaks of cholera in the Gilbert and Caroline islands (in Micronesia). Cholera is acquired via contaminated food or water, so avoid uncooked foods, peel your own fruit, and drink bottled drinks if you happen to arrive in an infected area. Typhoid fever is also caused by contaminated food or water, while tetanus (lockjaw) occurs when cuts or bites become infected. Horrible disfiguring diseases such as leprosy and elephantiasis are hard to catch, so it's unlikely you'll be visited by one of these nightmares of the flesh.

Dengue fever is a mosquito-transmitted disease endemic in the South Pacific. Signs are headaches, sore throat, pain in the joints, fever, chills, nausea, and rash. The illness can last anywhere from five to 15 days; although you can relieve the symptoms somewhat, the only real cure is to stay in bed, drink lots of water, take aspirin for the headaches, and wait it out. It's painful, but dengue fever usually only kills infants. No vaccine exists, so just avoid getting bitten.

Vaccinations

Officially, most visitors are not required to get any vaccinations at all before coming to the South Pacific. Tetanus, diphtheria, typhoid fever, and polio shots are not required, but they're a good idea if you're going off the beaten track. Tetanus and diphtheria shots are given together, and a booster is required every 10 years. The typhoid fever shot is every three years, polio every five years.

The cholera vaccine is only 50% effective and valid just six months, and bad reactions are common, but get it if you know you're headed for an infected area (such as Micronesia). All passengers arriving in Fiji from Funafuti, Tarawa, or Majuro must show proof of a cholera vaccination. A yellow-fever vaccination is required if you've been in an infected area (such as the jungles of South America and Africa) within six days prior to arrival. Since the vaccination is valid 10 years, get one if you're an inveterate globe-trotter.

Immune globulin (IG) and the Havrix vaccine aren't 100% effective against hepatitis A, but they do increase your general resistance to infections. IG prophylaxis must be repeated every five months. Hepatitis B vaccination involves three doses over a six-month period (duration of protection unknown) and is recommended mostly for people planning extended stays in the region.

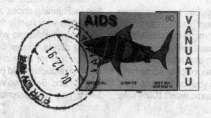

WHAT TO TAKE

Packing

Assemble everything you simply must take and cannot live without—then cut the pile in half. If you're still left with more than will fit into a medium-size suitcase or backpack, continue eliminating. You have to be tough on yourself and just limit what you take. Now put it all into your bag. If the total (bag and contents) weighs over 16 kg, you'll sacrifice much of your mobility. If you can keep it down to 10 kg, you're traveling *light*. Categorize, separate, and pack all your things into plastic bags or stuff sacks for convenience and protection from moisture. In addition to your principal bag, you'll want a day pack or flight bag. When checking in for flights, carry anything that cannot be replaced in your hand luggage.

Your Luggage

A soft medium-size backpack with a lightweight internal frame is best. Big external-frame packs are fine for mountain climbing but get caught in airport conveyor belts and are very inconvenient on public transport. The best packs have a zippered compartment in back where you can tuck in the straps and hip belt before turning your pack over to an airline or bus. This type of pack has the flexibility of allowing you to simply walk when motorized transport is unavailable or unacceptable; and with the straps zipped in it looks like a regular suitcase, should you wish to go upmarket for a while.

Make sure your pack allows you to carry the weight on your hips, has a cushion for spine support, and doesn't pull backwards. The pack should strap snugly to your body but also allow ventilation to your back. It should be made of a water-resistant material such as nylon and have a Fastex buckle.

Look for a pack with double, two-way zipper compartments and pockets you can lock with miniature padlocks. They might not *stop* a thief, but they will deter the casual pilferer. A 60-cm length of lightweight chain and another padlock will allow you to fasten your pack to something. Keep valuables locked in your bag, out of sight, as even upmarket hotel rooms aren't 100% safe.

Camping Equipment and Clothing

A small nylon tent guarantees you a place to sleep every night, but it *must* be mosquito- and waterproof. Get one with a tent fly, then waterproof both tent and fly with a can of waterproofing spray. You'll seldom need a sleeping bag in the tropics, so that's one item you can easily cut. A Youth Hostel sleeping sheet is ideal—all YHA handbooks give instructions on how to make your own or buy one at your local hostel. You don't really need to carry a bulky foam pad, as the ground is seldom cold.

For clothes take loose-fitting cotton washables, light in color and weight. Synthetic fabrics are hot and sticky, and most of the things you wear at home are too heavy for the tropics—be prepared for the humidity. Dress is casual, with slacks and a sports shirt okay for men even at dinner parties. Local women often wear long colorful dresses in the evening, but shorts are okay in daytime. If in doubt, bring the minimum with you and buy tropical garb upon arrival. Stick to clothes you can rinse in your room sink. In midwinter (July, August) it can be cool at night in the Cooks, Tonga, and New Caledonia, so a warm piece of clothing may come in handy.

The *lavalava, sulu,* or pareu (pronounced "par-RAY-o") is a bright two-meter piece of cloth both men and women wrap about themselves as an all-purpose garment. Any islander can show you how to wear it. Missionaries taught the South Sea island women to drape their attributes in long, flowing gowns, called muumuus in Hawaii. In the South Pacific, the dress is better known as a Mother Hubbard for the muumuu-attired nursery rhyme character who "went to the cupboard to fetch her poor dog a bone."

Take comfortable shoes that have been broken in. Running shoes and rubber thongs (flip-flops) are very handy for day use but will bar you from nightspots with strict dress codes. Scuba divers' rubber booties are lightweight and perfect for both crossing rivers and reef walking, though an old pair of sneakers may be just as good. Below we've provided a few checklists to help you assemble your gear. The listed items combined weigh well over 16 kg, so eliminate what doesn't suit you:

- pack with internal frame
- day pack or airline bag
- nylon tent and fly
- tent-patching tape
- mosquito net
- sleeping sheet
- sun hat or visor
- essential clothing only
- bathing suit
- sturdy walking shoes
- rubber thongs
- rubber booties
- mask and snorkel

Accessories

Bring some reading material, as good books can be hard to find in some countries. A clip-on book light with extra batteries allows campers to read at night. Serious scuba divers bring their own regulator, buoyancy compensator, and gauges, and perhaps a lightweight three-mm Lycra wetsuit for protection against marine stings and coral. A mask and snorkel are essential equipment—you'll be missing half of the Pacific's beauty without them.

Also take along postcards of your hometown and snapshots of your house, family, workplace, etc; islanders love to see these. Always keep a promise to mail islanders the photos you take of them. Think of some small souvenir of your country (such as a lapel pin bearing a kangaroo or maple leaf, or Kennedy half dollars), which you can take along as gifts. Miniature compasses sold in camping stores also make good gifts.

Neutral gray eyeglasses protect your eyes from the sun and give the least color distortion. Take an extra pair (if you wear them). Keep the laundry soap inside a couple of layers of plastic bags. To cook at campsites you'll often need a small stove: trying to keep rainforest wood burning will drive you to tears from smoke and frustration. Camping fuel cannot be carried on commercial airliners, however, so choose a stove that uses a common fuel like kerosene or gasoline.

- camera and 10 rolls of film
- compass
- pocket flashlight
- extra batteries
- candle
- pocket alarm calculator
- pocket watch
- extra pair of glasses
- sunglasses
- padlock and lightweight chain
- collapsible umbrella
- string for a clothesline
- powdered laundry soap
- universal sink plug
- minitowel
- silicon glue
- sewing kit
- miniscissors
- nail clippers
- fishing line for sewing gear
- plastic cup and plate
- can and bottle opener
- corkscrew
- penknife
- spoon
- water bottle
- matches
- tea bags

Toiletries and Medical Kit

Since everyone has his/her own medical requirements and brand names vary from country to country, there's no point going into detail here. Note, however, that even the basics (such as aspirin) are unavailable on some outer islands, so be prepared. Bring medicated powder for prickly heat rash. Charcoal tablets are useful for diarrhea and poisoning (they absorb the irritants). Bring an adequate supply of any personal medications, plus your prescriptions (in generic terminology).

High humidity causes curly hair to swell and bush, straight hair to droop. If it's curly have it cut short or keep it long in a ponytail or bun. A good cut is essential with straight hair. Water-based makeup is best, as the heat and humidity cause oil glands to work overtime. High-quality locally made shampoo, body oils, and insect repellent are sold on all the islands, and the bottles are conveniently smaller than those sold in Western countries. See "Health," above, for more ideas.

- wax earplugs
- soap in plastic container
- soft toothbrush
- toothpaste
- roll-on deodorant
- shampoo
- comb and brush
- skin creams
- makeup
- tampons or napkins
- white toilet paper
- vitamin/mineral supplement
- Cutter's insect repellent
- PABA sunscreen
- Chap Stick
- a motion-sickness remedy
- contraceptives
- iodine
- water-purification pills
- delousing powder
- a diarrhea remedy
- Tiger Balm
- a cold remedy
- Alka-Seltzer
- aspirin
- antihistamine
- antifungal
- Calmitol ointment
- antibiotic ointment
- painkiller
- antiseptic cream
- disinfectant
- simple dressings
- adhesive bandages (like Band-Aids)
- prescription medicines

Money and Documents

All post offices have passport applications. If you lose your passport you should report the matter to the local police at once, obtain a certificate or receipt, then proceed to your consulate (if any!) for a replacement. If you have your birth certificate with you it expedites things considerably. By official agreement, Canadian citizens can turn to any of the numerous Australian diplomatic offices throughout the region for assistance.

Traveler's checks in U.S. dollars are recommended, and in the South Pacific, American Express is the most efficient company when it comes to providing refunds for lost checks. Bring along a small supply of US$1 and US$5 bills to use if you don't manage to change money immediately upon arrival or if you run out of local currency and can't get to a bank. In the French territories French francs are best currency to have by far as they're exchanged at a fixed rate without commission.

If you have a car at home, bring along the insurance receipt so you don't have to pay for insurance every time you rent a car. Ask your agent about this.

Carry your valuables in a money belt worn around your waist or neck under your clothing; most camping stores have these. Make several photocopies of the information page of your passport, personal identification, driver's license, scuba certification card, credit cards, airline tickets, receipts for purchase of traveler's checks, etc.—you should be able to get them all on one page. A brief medical history with your blood type, allergies, chronic or special health problems, eyeglass and medical prescriptions, etc., might also come in handy. Put these inside plastic bags to protect them from moisture, then carry the lists in different places, and leave one at home.

How much money you'll need depends on your lifestyle, but time is also a factor. The longer you stay, the cheaper it gets. Suppose you have to lay out US$1000 on airfare and have (for example) US$40 a day left over for expenses. If you stay 15 days, you'll average US$107 a day ($40 times 15 plus $1000, divided by 15). If you stay 30 days, you'll average US$74 a day. If you stay 90 days, the per-day cost drops to US$52. If you stay a year it'll cost only US$43 a day. Some countries are more expensive than others: while you'll certainly want to experience the spectacular scenery of Tahiti, spend those extra days lounging in the sun in Fiji, Tonga, Western Samoa, or the Solomons.

- passport
- vaccination certificates
- airline tickets
- scuba certification card
- driver's license
- traveler's checks
- some U.S. cash
- photocopies of documents
- money belt

- address book
- notebook
- envelopes
- extra ballpoints

FILM AND PHOTOGRAPHY

Look at the ads in photographic magazines for the best deals on mail-order cameras and film, or buy at a discount shop in any large city. Run a roll of film through your camera to be sure it's in good working order; clean the lens with lens-cleaning tissue and check the batteries. Remove the batteries from your camera when storing it at home for long periods. Register valuable cameras or electronic equipment with customs before you leave home so there won't be any argument over where you bought the items when you return, or at least carry the original bill of sale.

The type of camera you choose could depend on the way you travel. If you'll be staying mostly in one place, a heavy single-lens reflex (SLR) camera with spare lenses and other equipment won't trouble you. If you'll be moving around a lot for a considerable length of time, a 35-mm automatic compact camera may be better. The compacts are mostly useful for close-up shots; landscapes will seem spread out and far away. A wide-angle lens gives excellent depth of field, but hold the camera upright to avoid converging verticals. A polarizing filter prevents reflections from glass windows.

Take double the amount of film and mailers you think you'll need: only in American Samoa, Fiji, and Vanuatu is film cheap and readily available, and even then you never know if it's been spoiled by an airport X-ray on the way there. In the U.S. film can be purchased at big discounts through mail-order companies, which advertise in photography magazines. Choose 36-exposure film over 24-exposure to save on the number of rolls you have to carry. In Tahiti-Polynesia and New Caledonia camera film costs over double what you'd pay in the U.S., but you can import 10 rolls duty free. When purchasing film in the islands take care to check the expiration date.

Films are rated by their speed and sensitivity to light, using ISO numbers from 25 to 1600.

The higher the number, the greater the film's sensitivity to light. Slower films with lower ISOs (like 100-200) produce sharp images in bright sunlight. Faster films with higher ISOs (like 400) stop action and work well in low-light situations, such as in dark rainforests or at sunset. If you have a manual SLR you can avoid overexposure at midday by reducing the exposure half a stop, but *do* overexpose when photographing dark-skinned Melanesians. From 1000 to 1600 the light is often too bright to take good photos, and panoramas usually come out best early or late in the day.

Keep your photos simple with one main subject and an uncomplicated background. Get as close to your subjects as you can and lower or raise the camera to their level. Include people in the foreground of scenic shots to add interest and perspective. Outdoors a flash can fill in unflattering facial shadows caused by high sun or backlit conditions. Most of all, be creative. Look for interesting details and compose the photo before you push the trigger. Instead of taking a head-on photo of a group of people, step to one side and ask them to face you. The angle improves the photo. Photograph subjects coming toward you rather than passing by. Ask permission before photographing people. If you're asked for money (rare) you can always walk away—give your subjects the same choice.

When packing, protect your camera against vibration. Checked baggage is scanned by powerful airport X-ray monitors, so carry both camera and film aboard the plane in a clear plastic bag and ask security for a visual inspection. Some airports (such as Nouméa) will refuse to do this, however. Otherwise, use a lead-laminated pouch. The old high-dose X-ray units are the worst, but even low-dose inspection units can ruin fast film (400 ASA and above). Beware of the cumulative effect of X-ray machines.

Keep your camera in a plastic bag during rain and while traveling in motorized canoes, etc. In the tropics the humidity can cause film to stick to itself; silica-gel crystals in the bag will protect film from humidity and mold growth. Protect camera and film from direct sunlight and load the film in the shade. When loading, check that the takeup spool revolves. Never leave camera or film in a hot place like a car floor, glove compartment, or trunk.

GETTING THERE

Preparations

First decide where you're going and how long you wish to stay. Some routes are more available or practical than others. The major transit points for visitors are Auckland, Honolulu, Nandi, Nauru, Nouméa, Papeete, and Sydney; you'll notice how feeder flights radiate from these hubs. Most North Americans and Europeans will pass through Los Angeles International Airport (code-named LAX) on their way to Polynesia or Fiji, and Fiji's Nandi Airport (NAN) is the gateway to the Melanesian countries.

Your plane ticket will be your biggest single expense, so spend some time considering the possibilities. Start by calling the airlines directly over their toll-free 800 numbers to get current information on fares. In the U.S., the ones to call are Air France (tel. 800/237-2747), Air New Zealand (tel. 800/262-1234), Air Pacific (tel. 800/227-4500), AOM French Airlines (tel. 800/892-9136), Corsair (tel. 800/677-0720), Hawaiian Airlines (tel. 800/367-5320), Lan Chile Airlines (tel. 800/735-5526), and Qantas Airways (tel. 800/227-4500), all with flights to the South Pacific. Sometimes Canada and the various parts of the U.S. have different toll-free numbers, so if the number given above doesn't work, dial 800 information at 800/555-1212 (all 800 numbers are free). In Canada, Air New Zealand's toll-free number is 800/663-5494.

Call all of these carriers and say you want the *lowest possible fare*. Ask about fare seasons and restrictions. If you're not happy with the answers you get, call the number back later and try again. Many different agents take calls on these lines, and some are more knowledgeable than others. The numbers are often busy during business hours, so call at night or on the weekend. *Be persistent.*

Discount Fares

The cheapest way to get to the South Pacific is on an excursion fare from one of the major airlines. These fares often have limitations and restrictions, however—be sure to ask. Some have an advance-purchase deadline, so it's best to begin shopping early. See "The Coral Route"

under "Air Services," following, for specific information.

The month of outbound travel from the U.S. determines which seasonal fare you pay, and inquiring far in advance could allow you to reschedule your vacation slightly to take advantage of a noticeably lower fare. Most carriers from the U.S. to the South Pacific have their **low season** from April to August, **shoulder season** from September to mid-November and in March, and **high season** from mid-November to February. The airlines have made April to mid-November, the best months in the South Pacific, their off-season because that's winter in Australia and New Zealand. If you're only going to the islands and can make it at that time, it certainly works to your advantage.

Cheap Flights

Check the Sunday travel section in a newspaper like the *San Francisco Examiner* or the *Toronto Star,* or a major entertainment weekly. They often carry ads for bucket shops, agencies that deal in bulk and sell seats for less than airline offices will. Many airlines have more seats than they can market through normal channels, so they sell their unused long-haul capacity on this gray market at discounts of 40-50% off the official IATA tariffs.

There are well-known centers around the world where globetrotters regularly pick up such tickets (Amsterdam, Athens, Bangkok, Hong Kong, London, Penang, San Francisco, and Singapore are only a few—unfortunately none are in the South Pacific itself). Rates are com-

PACIFIC AIR ROUTES

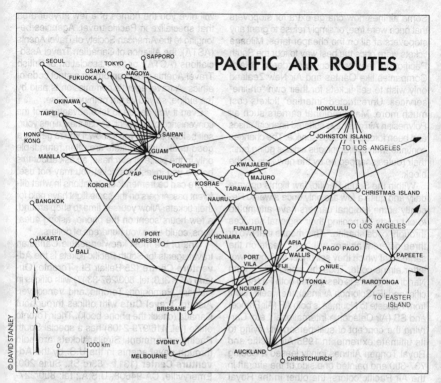

© DAVID STANLEY

0   1000 km

petitive, so check a few agencies before deciding. In Thailand, for example, **J. Travel & Trading** (21/33 Soi Ngam Dupli, Near Malaysia Hotel, Rama 4 Road, Bangkok 10120; fax 66-2/287-1468) offers Singapore-Auckland-Nandi-Rarotonga-Papeete-Los Angeles for US$965. Despite their occasionally shady appearance, most bucket shops are perfectly legitimate, and your ticket will probably be issued by the airline itself. Most discounted tickets look and are exactly the same as regular full-fare tickets but they're usually nonrefundable.

Mileage Tickets

With a mileage ticket you pay the full fare from A to B, plus a mileage surcharge up to 25%, and are permitted to stop anywhere along the way on any reasonable routing, provided you don't exceed the maximum allowable mileage. Study the "Pacific Air Routes" map in this section and

work out a transpacific routing that hits as many islands as possible. Try to plan a circular route; avoid backtracking and zigzagging. These tickets are good for up to a year, and you can fly any day there's a flight. With a little creativity you can get as many as 14 stops each way. Once you're in the area you might even be able to add additional stopovers to the ticket, perhaps for a small extra charge. For example, add Vava'u-Ha'apai between Pago Pago and Tongatapu, and Lamap-Norsup-Espiritu Santo between Port Vila and Honiara. See what your travel agent can come up with.

Current Trends

Soaring fuel costs have caused the larger airlines to switch to wide-bodied aircraft and long-haul routes with less frequent service and fewer stops. In the South Pacific this works to your disadvantage, as many islands get bypassed.

Some airlines now charge extra for stopovers that once were free, or simply refuse to grant any stopovers at all on the cheaper fares. Mileage tickets were once the best way to tour the South Pacific, but they've become harder to obtain. Companies like Qantas and Air New Zealand only wish to sell tickets for their own "on-line" services. Unrestricted "interline" tickets cost much more. Many regional carriers such as Polynesian Airlines have suffered financial crises and been forced to reduce service. The changes continue, with overambitious airlines going bust, their routes snapped up by the new kids on the block.

Within the South Pacific, few flights operate daily and quite a few are only once a week. Recently some regional carriers have attempted to cut costs by pooling their regional services through "code sharing." This means that two or three different airlines will "own" seats on the same flight which they sell under their own two-letter airline code. Thus the weekly flight from Nandi to Honiara is designated both FJ (Air Pacific) and IE (Solomon Airlines), the weekly flight from Papeete to Nouméa is both AF (Air France) and SB (Air Calédonie International), etc. Carrying the concept of split-personality flying to its ultimate extreme, in 1995 Air Pacific and Royal Tongan Airlines jointly leased a Boeing 737-300 and painted one side of the aircraft in the Air Pacific colors, the other in the Royal Tongan livery! It's all part of a drive to reverse losses of A$100 million the region's carriers suffered in 1994.

Travel Agents

Use your local travel agent, but be aware that any agent worth his/her commission will probably want to sell you a package tour, and it's a fact that some vacation packages actually cost less than regular roundtrip airfare! If they'll let you extend your stay to give you some time to yourself this could be a good deal, especially with the hotel thrown in for "free." But check the restrictions.

Pick your agent carefully as many are pitifully ignorant about the South Pacific. Many don't want to hear about discounts, cheap flights, or alternative routes. With alarming frequency, they give wrong or misleading information in an off-hand manner. Ask an airline to suggest a travel agent. They won't *recommend* any, but they

will give you the names of a few in your area that specialize in Pacific travel. Agencies belonging to the American Society of Travel Agents (ASTA), the Alliance of Canadian Travel Associations (ACTA), or the Association of British Travel Agents must conform to a strict code of ethics. A travel agent's commission is paid by the airline, so you've got nothing to lose.

Even if you decide to take advantage of the convenience of an agent, do call the airlines yourself beforehand so you'll know if you're getting a good deal. Airline tickets are often refundable only in the place of purchase, so ask about this before you invest in a ticket you may not use. There can be tremendous variations in what different passengers on the same flight have paid for their tickets. Allow yourself time to shop around; a few hours spent on the phone, asking questions, could save you hundreds of dollars.

One of the most knowledgeable Canadian travel agents for South Pacific tickets is the **Adventure Centre** (25 Bellair St., Toronto, Ontario M5R 3L3; tel. 800/267-3347) with offices in Calgary, Edmonton, Toronto, and Vancouver. Also try **Travel Cuts** with offices throughout Canada (check the phone book). Their Toronto office (tel. 416/979-2406) has a special South Pacific department. Similar tickets are sold through travel agents in the U.S. by the **Adventure Center** (1311 - 63rd St., Suite 200, Emeryville, CA 94608, U.S.A.; tel. 800/227-8747). The Emeryville office doesn't accept direct consumer sales, but ask your travel agent to check with them. One agent who can help you is Rob Jenneve of **Island Adventures** (574 Mills Way, Goleta, CA 93117, U.S.A.; tel. 800/289-4957, fax 805/685-0960).

Discover Wholesale Travel (2192 Dupont Dr., Suite 105, Irvine, CA 92715, U.S.A.; tel. 800/576-7770 in California, tel. 800/759-7330 elsewhere in the U.S., fax 714/833-1176) is one of the few large tour operators willing to sell discounted air tickets alone directly to the public. President Mary Anne Cook claims everyone on her staff has 10 years experience selling the South Pacific and "most importantly, we all love the area!"

Onward Tickets

All of the South Pacific countries require an onward ticket as a condition for entry. If you're planning a long trip including locally arranged sea travel between countries, this can be a nuisance. One way to satisfy the ticket-to-leave requirement is to purchase a full-fare one-way economy ticket out of the area from Air New Zealand (valid one year). As you're about to depart for the next country on your route have the airline reissue the ticket, so it's a ticket to leave from there. Otherwise buy a ticket across the Pacific with stops in all the countries you'll visit, then use it *only* to satisfy immigration. When you finally complete your trip return the ticket to the issuing office for a full refund. Keep in mind that the sort of deals and discount air fares available elsewhere are not available in the South Pacific. Have your *real* means of departure planned.

Airport Taxes

When planning your route, keep airport departure taxes in mind, as they can add up fast on a trip with lots of stops. You needn't worry in Tahiti-Polynesia and New Caledonia, where no tax is collected, but in places like Cook Islands, Fiji, Niue, Tonga, Tuvalu, and Vanuatu increasingly high airport taxes are charged. New Zealand and Australia also have very high airport taxes (as does the U.S., though it's usually included in the ticket price). You can usually avoid paying the tax if you're in transit for less than 24 hours, although in some countries such as Vanuatu everyone clearing customs and immigration must pay. All such taxes are listed in local currency in this book's "Oceania at a Glance" chart.

AIR SERVICES

From North America

Air France, Air New Zealand, Air Pacific, AOM French Airlines, Corsair, and Qantas are the major carriers serving the South Pacific out of Los Angeles, although **Air France, AOM French Airlines,** and **Corsair** only go as far as Tahiti. The Australian carrier **Qantas** stops at Tahiti and Nandi on the way to Australia.

In July 1994 Fiji's **Air Pacific** launched a weekly nonstop Boeing 747 service from Los Angeles to Nandi. They offer very competitive fares, so check. By flying a regional carrier like Air Pacific you become absorbed in an island atmosphere from the moment you enter the plane.

The only American airline serving the South Pacific is **Hawaiian Airlines,** which offers flights to Pago Pago and Tahiti via its base in Honolulu, with connections to and from Las Vegas, Los Angeles, San Francisco, and Seattle. (In 1993 Hawaiian canceled their services to Apia, Nuku'alofa, and Rarotonga.) In the past Hawaiian has had a reputation for poor service, lost luggage, late flights, and overbooking, but things are said to have improved. Unfortunately there are no direct flights from Canada to the South Pacific and all passengers must change planes at Honolulu or Los Angeles, although there are immediate connections from **Canadian Airlines International** flights. Several other North American carriers, including Continental and United, pulled out of the South Pacific after losing money on their routes.

The Coral Route

In the 1950s **Air New Zealand** pioneered its "Coral Route" across the South Pacific using Solent flying boats, and today the carrier has achieved a death grip over long-haul air routes into the region by allowing stopovers in Tahiti-Polynesia, Cook Islands, Fiji, Western Samoa, and Tonga as part of their through services between North America and New Zealand. Smaller island-based carriers have difficulty competing due to Air New Zealand's lower operating costs and high capacity (they're one of the few regional carriers that makes a profit). Air New Zealand's near monopoly does have the big advantage of allowing you to include a number of countries in a single ticket.

For a wide-ranging trip, ask for Air New Zealand's "Coral Explorer Airpass," which costs US$1858/1958/2158 low/shoulder/high season (see "Discount Fares" above for season definitions). This worthwhile ticket allows you to fly Los Angeles-Tahiti-Rarotonga-Fiji-Auckland-Tongatapu-Apia-Honolulu-Los Angeles or vice versa. To throw in Australia, add US$100 more and drop one of your other stopovers. You can stay up to six months but rerouting costs US$75 and there's a 35% cancellation penalty.

If you plan a shorter trip with fewer stops, their "Coral Adventure Airpass" allows you to fly Los Angeles-Tahiti-Rarotonga-Fiji-Honolulu-Los Angeles, or Los Angeles-Honolulu-Apia-Tonga-Honolulu-Los Angeles, for US$1369/

1469/1669. This ticket is valid only three months, must be purchased 14 days in advance, and there's a US$75 penalty to change your flight dates less than 14 days in advance. The 35% cancellation fee also applies.

Return tickets from Los Angeles to a single island are cheaper and here even the day on which you begin matters, with Monday, Tuesday, and Wednesday US$60 cheaper than starting your trip toward the end of the week. The "Coral Experience" is US$998/1098/1298 at the beginning of the week to either Rarotonga, Fiji, Apia, or Tongatapu, with a US$150 surcharge if you want an extra stop. The ticketing conditions are similar to those of the Coral Adventure Airpass. If you only want to stay one month and buy your ticket 21 days in advance, a "Coral Direct" ticket is US$100 cheaper, but no stopovers or date charges are allowed and there's a 50% cancellation fee.

If you're only flying to Tahiti the fares and seasons are slightly different. Here the high season runs from July to mid-August and in mid-December; the rest of the year is low season. The cheapest fare is the "Economy APEX" at US$838/995 low/high return between Los Angeles and Tahiti. You must purchase this at least 14 days in advance, there's a 35% cancellation penalty, and the maximum stay is one month. Tickets bought on shorter notice are about 50% more expensive.

Special "add-on" fares to Los Angeles are available from cities right across the U.S. and Canada. For travel originating in the U.S., Air New Zealand guarantees your fare against subsequent price increases once you've been ticketed (provided you don't change your outbound reservation). One problem with Air New Zealand is its schedules, which are built around Auckland and California: they'll drop you off in the middle of the night if you stop almost anywhere else. If you fly with them a lot, you'll soon tire of watching their insipid *Blue Pacific* videos or reading their boring *Pacific Way* inflight magazine. Alternative reading material is usually unavailable, so bring along some of your own.

Circle-Pacific Fares
Thanks to agreements between the carriers mentioned above and Asian or American companies, you can get a Circle-Pacific fare, which combines the South Pacific with Jakarta, Singapore, Bangkok, Hong Kong, Manila, Taipei, Tokyo, and many other cities. These tickets must be purchased 21 days in advance, but they're valid up to six months and only the initial flight out of North America has to be booked 21 days ahead. The rest of the ticket can be left open-dated.

Air New Zealand has the most to offer in the South Pacific, but the different carriers offer differing routes in Asia, so ask your travel agent to explain the alternatives to you. The Circle-Pacific fares are excellent value if you have enough time for a wide-ranging trip. Also ask about round-the-world tickets via the South Pacific.

From Australia
Since the Australian government sold Qantas and deregulated airfares, the cost of flying out of Australia has dropped dramatically. Now you can often find deals much better than the published APEX fares, especially during off months. Air New Zealand is competing fiercely in the Australian market, and they offer competitive fares to many South Pacific points via Auckland. Occasionally you can buy such tickets for a lower price by working through an agent specializing in bargain airfares than you'd pay at the airline office itself. Check the classified ads in the daily papers and shop around.

The Circle-Pacific fares described above are also available here, and from Brisbane/Melbourne/Sydney these tickets cost A$2310-2899 depending on the season. For information on slightly reduced fares available from STA Travel, see "Student Fares," below.

Qantas flies to Honiara, Nandi, Nouméa, Papeete, and Port Vila. From Brisbane, Melbourne, and Sydney there are nonstop flights to Fiji on **Air Pacific,** to Nouméa on **Air Calédonie International,** and to Port Vila on **Air Vanuatu. Polynesian Airlines** has direct flights to Apia from Melbourne and Sydney. **Air France** services Nouméa and Papeete from Sydney. **Royal Tongan Airlines** flies to Nuku'alofa from Sydney and **Solomon Airlines** flies to Honiara from Brisbane.

From New Zealand
Unrestricted low air fares to the South Pacific are surprisingly hard to come by in New Zealand.

Some tickets have advance purchase requirements, so start shopping well ahead. Ask around at a number of different travel agencies for special unadvertised or under-the-counter fares. Air New Zealand has advance-purchase EPIC fares to Cook Islands. Again, see your travel agent. Fares to Tahiti often allow a stop in the Cook Islands, but it's hard to get a seat on these fully booked planes.

Air New Zealand offers reduced excursion fares from Auckland to all the main South Pacific islands with a minimum stay of seven days and a maximum stay depending on the destination: Fiji 60 days, Tahiti 45 days, Tonga and Samoa 90 days. These fares typically cost NZ$831-996 return to Fiji depending on the season, and it's possible to change flight dates. "Epic" fares are available to some destinations (for example, NZ$1025-1258 to Rarotonga, one-year return), but a change of dates involves being upgraded to full fare. It's actually cheaper to buy a package tour to the islands with airfare, accommodations, and transfers all included, but these are usually limited to seven nights on one island and you're stuck in a boring touristic environment.

Other airlines with flights from Auckland include **Air Calédonie International** to Nouméa, **Air Nauru** to Nauru, **Air Pacific** to Nandi (also from Christchurch), **Air Vanuatu** to Port Vila, **Polynesian Airlines** to Nuku'alofa and Apia, **Royal Tongan Airlines** to Nuku'alofa, and **Solomon Airlines** to Honiara.

From South America
Lan Chile Airlines flies from Santiago to Tahiti via Easter Island twice a week, with two additional weekly flights between Chile and Easter Island only during the high southern summer season. The regular one-way fare Santiago-Easter-Papeete is US$1100 economy class. Santiago-Easter Island is US$426 each way.

Lan Chile's 30-day roundtrip excursion fare between Tahiti and Santiago, with a stopover on Easter Island, costs US$1433/1809 low/high season. If you only want to visit Easter Island, 30-day excursion tickets Papeete-Easter Island-Papeete are available in Papeete for US$819/998 low/high.

Lan Chile's special 21-day **Visit Chile Pass** costs US$812 for a return trip to Easter Island from Santiago, or US$1080 for Easter Island plus a number of cities in southern Chile including Punta Arenas. The pass is not valid for travel to/from Tahiti. This ticket must be purchased outside Chile in conjunction with an intercontinental Lan Chile ticket, and advance bookings are required (valid all year).

In conjunction with other airlines, Lan Chile offers several "Circle-Pacific" fares, including Los Angeles-Papeete-Easter Island-Santiago-Miami (US$1694), Los Angeles-Papeete-Easter Island-Santiago-New York (US$1828), and Los Angeles-Santiago-Easter Island-Papeete-Los Angeles (US$1828), all valid one year.

Fares to Easter Island can vary spectacularly: during a spot check one week, Air New Zealand in Vancouver quoted a fare almost double that given by Lan Chile over its U.S. tollfree number (tel. 800/735-5526)! Lan Chile must rate as one of the most unreliable carriers flying to the South Pacific, and schedule irregularities are routine. The Santiago-Easter Island portion of their Tahiti service is often heavily booked, so try to reserve far in advance, though this can be hard to do.

From Europe
Since few European carriers reach the South Pacific, you may have to use a gateway city such as Singapore, Hong Kong, Tokyo, Honolulu, or Los Angeles. Air New Zealand offers nonstop flights London-Los Angeles three times a week, Frankfurt-Los Angeles twice a week, with connections in L.A. to their Coral Route. Air France, AOM French Airlines, and Corsair fly to Tahiti from Paris via Los Angeles. AOM also flies from Paris to Nouméa via Bangkok and round-the-world tickets Paris-Los Angeles-Papeete-Nouméa-Bangkok-Paris begin as low as FF13,475 (French francs).

Air New Zealand reservations numbers around Europe are tel. 32-3/202-1355 (Belgium), tel. 33/0590-7712 (France), tel. 49-1/3081-7778 (Germany), tel. 39/1678-76126 (Italy), tel. 41/0800-2527 (Luxemburg), tel. 31-06/0221016 (Netherlands), tel. 34-900/993241 (Spain), tel. 020-910-150 (Sweden), tel. 41/155-7778 (Switzerland), and tel. 44-181/741-2299 (United Kingdom). Call them up and ask about their Coral Route fares.

The British specialist in South Pacific itineraries is **Trailfinders** (42-50 Earls Court Rd.,

Kensington, London W8 6FT, England; tel. 44-171/938-3366), in business since 1970. They offer a variety of discounted round-the-world tickets through Tahiti, which are often much cheaper than the published fares. All rates are seasonal and depend on the airlines actually giving them deals, plus exchange rates play a part. Call or write for a free copy of their magazine, *Trailfinder,* which appears in April, July, and December. Also check the ads in *Time Out* for other such companies.

In Holland **Pacific Island Travel** (Dam 3, 1012 JS Amsterdam, the Netherlands; tel. 31-20/626-1325, fax 31-20/623-0008) sells most of the air passes and long-distance tickets mentioned in this section, plus package tours. Manager Rob Kusters is quite knowledgeable about the Pacific. **Barron & De Keijzer Travel** (Herengracht 340, 1016 CG Amsterdam, the Netherlands; tel. 31-20/625-8600, fax 31-20/622-7559) sells Air New Zealand's Coral Route with travel via London. **Malibu Travel** (Damrak 30, 1012 LJ Amsterdam, the Netherlands; fax 31-20/638-2271) offers a variety of routes, but verify the prices on their printed list. Also in Amsterdam, **Reisbureau Amber** (Da Costastraat 77, 1053 ZG Amsterdam, the Netherlands; tel. 31-20/685-1155) is one of the best places in Europe to pick up books on the South Pacific.

In Switzerland try **Globetrotter Travel Service** (Rennweg 35, CH-8023 Zürich, Switzerland; tel. 41-1/211-7780, fax 41-1/211-2035), with offices in Baden, Basel, Bern, Luzern, St. Gallen, Winterthur, and Zürich. Their quarterly newsletter, *Ticket-Info,* lists hundreds of cheap flights, including many through the South Pacific. Just for example, Frankfurt-Los Angeles-Tahiti-Rarotonga-Fiji-Auckland-Los Angeles-Frankfurt costs 2350 Swiss francs from Globetrotter (2100 Swiss francs for those under 30 years). Most Europeans, however, go right around the world, and according to Globetrotter a favorite routing is Zürich-Rome-Bangkok-Singapore-Bali-Sydney-Auckland-Fiji-Tahiti-Los Angeles-Frankfurt, which costs 2500 Swiss francs. Globetrotter also has slightly more expensive round-the-world tickets via South America and South Africa that hit Fiji, Tonga, and Samoa. Highly recommended.

Bucket shops in Germany sell a "Pacific Airpass" on Air New Zealand from Frankfurt to the South Pacific for around DM 2500 low season, DM 3000 high season. You may stop at a choice of any six of Tahiti, Rarotonga, Fiji, Auckland, Tonga, Apia, and Honolulu, and the ticket is valid six months. All flights must be booked prior to leaving Europe, and there's a US$50 charge to change the dates once the ticket has been issued. One agency selling such tickets is **Walther-Weltreisen** (Hirschberger Strasse 30, D-53119 Bonn, Germany; tel. 49-228/661-239, fax 49-228/661-181).

French Charter Flights

Nouvelles Frontières Inc. (87 boulevard de Grenelle, Paris Cedex 75015, France; tel. 33-1/4141-5858) handles weekly charter flights from Paris and Los Angeles to Papeete and Nouméa on the French charter company **Corsair.** Fares to Papeete are broken down into four seasons, beginning at US$725/1150 single/return from Paris or US$475/780 from Los Angeles in the low season (mid-September to mid-June), and going up to US$1150/1850 from Paris or US$700/1150 from Los Angeles in the peak season. Penalties must be paid to change your flight dates, and in Papeete changes of date can only be made 15 days in advance. Refunds (minus a US$75 penalty) are only possible if the agency manages to resell your ticket, but you're forbidden to sell your own ticket to a third party. Corsair reserves the right to alter flight times up to 48 hours without compensation, but if you miss your flight you lose your money. Still, if you're sure when you'll be traveling, these prices are a couple of hundred dollars lower than anything offered by the scheduled airlines.

Nouvelles Frontières has 200 offices in France and 40 others around the world, including these: 12 East 33rd St., 11th Floor, New York, NY 10016, U.S.A. (tel. 212/779-0600); APS, Inc., 5757 West Century Blvd., Suite 660, Los Angeles, CA 90045-6407, U.S.A. (tel. 310/670-7302; fax 310/338-0708); and 11 Blenheim St., London W1, England (tel. 44-171/629-7772).

Air Nauru

Air Nauru (Level 49, 80 Collins St., Melbourne, Victoria 3000, Australia; tel. 61-3/9653-5602; fax 61-3/9654-7376), flag carrier of the tiny phosphate-rich Republic of Nauru, links the North and South Pacific. Air Nauru takes you across the very heart of this great ocean instead of skirting it as most other carriers do. In Micronesia it connects with Continental Air Micronesia, which flies Manila-Koror-Yap-Guam-Chuuk-Pohnpei-Kosrae-Majuro-Honolulu four times a week. (See Moon Publication's *Micronesia Handbook* for information on this area.)

Most Air Nauru fares are calculated point to point via Nauru, so to work out a routing, combine any two of these one-way economy fares out of Nauru itself: Auckland (A$503), Guam (A$339), Honiara (A$183), Manila (A$546), Melbourne (A$486), Nandi (A$271), Pohnpei (A$289), Suva (A$282), Sydney (A$432), Tarawa (A$144). Although the exchange rate is currently about US$1 = A$1.33, if you buy your ticket in a U.S.-dollar area you'll probably be charged the same figure, but in U.S. currency rather than Australian! All the above services operate at least once a week. North of the equator, Air Nauru also flies Nauru-Tarawa-Christmas Island-Honolulu (A$727) once a week.

In the past Air Nauru has had a reputation for canceling flights on a moment's notice and bumping confirmed passengers to make room for local VIPs, but they fly modern Boeing 737-400 aircraft and have a good safety record. In recent years Air Nauru's prices have increased 50% as their routes contracted, so they're no longer the big bargain they once were.

In the South Pacific, Air Nauru has offices at Suite 502, 17 Castlereagh St., Sydney, NSW 2001, Australia (tel. 61-2/221-8622, fax 61-2/221-7032); Sheraton Mall, 105 Symonds St., Auckland, New Zealand (tel. 64-9/379-8113, fax 64-9/379-3763); and Ratu Sakuna House, Macarthur St., Suva, Fiji Islands (tel. 679/312-377). Their general sales agent in the U.S. is Air Nauru, 1221 Kapiolani Blvd., PH60, Honolulu, HI 96814, U.S.A. (tel. 808/591-2163, fax 808/593-8433). You can call them toll-free from Canada and the U.S. at 800/998-6287.

Regional Airlines

Aside from the big international airlines described above, a number of island-based carriers fly around the South Pacific. These include the Fijian carrier **Air Pacific,** with flights from Fiji to Apia, Auckland, Brisbane, Christchurch, Honiara, Los Angeles, Melbourne, Osaka, Port

---

STUDENT TRAVEL OFFICES

STA Travel, 297 Newbury St., Boston, MA 02115, U.S.A. (tel. 617/266-6014)

STA Travel, 7202 Melrose Ave., Los Angeles, CA 90046, U.S.A. (tel. 213/934-8722)

STA Travel, 10 Downing St. (6th Ave. and Bleecker), New York, NY 10014, U.S.A. (tel. 212/477-7166, fax 212/477-7348)

STA Travel, 3730 Walnut St., Philadelphia, PA 19104, U.S.A. (tel. 215/382-2928)

STA Travel, 51 Grant Ave., San Francisco, CA 94108, U.S.A. (tel. 415/391-8407)

STA Travel, 120 Broadway #108, Santa Monica, CA 90401, U.S.A. (tel. 310/394-5126, fax 310/394-8640)

STA Travel, 2401 Pennsylvania Ave. #G, Washington, D.C. 20037, U.S.A. (tel. 202/887-0912)

STA Travel, 222 Faraday St., Carlton, Melbourne 3053, Australia (tel. 61-3/9349-2411, fax 61-3/9347-8070)

STA Travel, 1st Floor, 732 Harris St., Ultimo, Sydney, NSW 2007, Australia (tel. 61-2/9212-1255, fax 61-2/9281-4183)

STA Travel, 10 High St., Auckland, New Zealand (tel. 64-9/366-6673, fax 64-9/309-9723)

STA Travel, #02-17 Orchard Parade Hotel, 1 Tanglin Road, Singapore 1024 (tel. 65/734-5681, fax 65/737-2591)

STA Travel, Wall Street Tower, Suite 1405, 33 Surawong Road Bangrak, Bangkok 10500, Thailand (tel. 66-2/233-2582)

SRID Reisen, Bockenheimer Landstrasse 133, D-60325 Frankfurt, Germany (tel. 49-69/703-035, fax 49-69/777-014)

STA Travel, Priory House, 6 Wright's Lane, London W8 6TA, England (tel. 44-171/937-9962)

Vila, Sydney, Tokyo, and Tonga. Western Samoa's **Polynesian Airlines** serves Auckland, Melbourne, Pago Pago, Rarotonga, Sydney, Tonga, and Wellington from Apia. **Air Calédonie International** flies to Auckland, Brisbane, Futuna, Melbourne, Nandi, Papeete, Port Vila, Sydney, and Wallis from Nouméa. From Fiji **Air**

COUNCIL TRAVEL OFFICES

Council Travel, 2000 Guadalupe St., Austin, TX 78705, U.S.A. (tel. 512/472-4931)

Council Travel, 2486 Channing Way, Berkeley, CA 94704, U.S.A. (tel. 510/848-8604)

Council Travel, 729 Boylston St., Suite 201, Boston, MA 02116, U.S.A. (tel. 617/266-1926)

Council Travel, 1153 N. Dearborn St., 2nd Floor, Chicago, IL 60610, U.S.A. (tel. 312/951-0585)

Council Travel, 1138 13th St., Boulder, CO 80302, U.S.A. (tel. 303/447-8101)

Council Travel, 1093 Broxton Ave., Suite 220, Los Angeles, CA 90024, U.S.A. (tel. 310/208-3551)

Council Travel, One Datran Center, Suite 320, 9100 South Dadeland Blvd., Miami, FL 33156, U.S.A. (tel. 305/670-9261)

Council Travel, 205 East 42nd St., New York, NY 10017-5706, U.S.A. (tel. 212/661-1450)

Council Travel, 715 S.W. Morrison, Suite 600, Portland, OR 97205, U.S.A. (tel. 503/228-1900)

Council Travel, 953 Garnet Ave., San Diego, CA 92109, U.S.A. (tel. 619/270-6401)

Council Travel, 919 Irving St., Suite 102, San Francisco, CA 94122, U.S.A. (tel. 415/566-6222, fax 415/566-6730)

Council Travel, 1314 N.E. 43rd St., Suite 210, Seattle, WA 98105, U.S.A. (tel. 206/632-2448)

Travel Cuts, 187 College St., Toronto, Ont. M5T 1P7, Canada (tel. 416/979-2406, fax 416/979-8167)

110D Killiney Road, Tah Wah Building, Singapore 0923 (tel. 65/738-7066)

Council Travel, 108/12-13 Kosan Road, Banglumpoo, Bangkok 10200, Thailand (tel. 66-2/282-7705)

Council Travel, Sanno Grand Building, Room 102, 14-2 Nagata-cho 2-chome, Chiyoda-ku, Tokyo 100, Japan (tel. 81-3/3581-5517)

Council Travel, 18 Graf Adolph Strasse, D-40212 Düsseldorf 1, Germany (tel. 49-211/329-088, fax 49-211/327-469)

Council Travel, 22 rue des Pyramides, 75001 Paris, France (tel. 33-1/4455-5565)

Council Travel, 28A Poland St., near Oxford Circus, London W1V 3DB, England (tel. 44-171/437-7767)

Marshall Islands flies north to Funafuti, Tarawa, and Majuro (turn to the Tuvalu chapter for details). Pago Pago-based **Samoa Air** services only Apia and Vava'u. **Royal Tongan Airlines** has flights from Nuku'alofa to Auckland, Nandi, and Sydney. **Air Vanuatu** flies from Port Vila to Auckland, Brisbane, Melbourne, Nandi, and Sydney. **Solomon Airlines** links Honiara to Auckland, Brisbane, Fiji, Port Moresby, and Port Vila. Details of these services are included in the relevant destination chapters of this book.

Student Fares

If you're a student, recent graduate, or teacher, you can sometimes benefit from lower student fares by booking through a student travel office. There are two rival organizations of this kind: Council Travel Services, with offices in college towns across the U.S. and a sister organization in Canada known as Travel Cuts; and STA Travel (Student Travel Australia), formerly called the Student Travel Network in the United States. Both organizations require you to pay a nominal fee for an official student card, and to get the cheapest fares you have to prove you're really a student. Slightly higher fares on the same routes are available to nonstudents, so they're always worth checking out.

STA Travel has been flying students across the Pacific for years. They offer special airfares for students and young people under 26 years with minimal restrictions. A one-year return ticket Los Angeles-Honolulu-Fiji-Rarotonga-Los Angeles will cost US$1380/1471/1654 low/shoulder/high. One-way tickets run about half the roundtrip price and cheaper fares are available for shorter stays. Call their toll-free number, 800/777-0112, for the latest information.

Slightly different student fares are available from **Council Travel Services,** a division of the nonprofit Council on International Educational Exchange (CIEE). Both they and **Travel Cuts** in Canada are much stricter about making sure you're a "real" student: you must first obtain the widely recognized International Student Identity Card (US$16) to get a ticket at the student rate. Some fares are limited to students and youths under 26 years of age, but part-time students and teachers also qualify. Seasonal pricing applies, so plan ahead. Get hold of a copy of their free *Student Travel Catalog,* which, although mostly oriented toward travel to Europe, contains useful information for students. Circle-Pacific and round-the-world routings are also available from Council Travel Services and there are special connecting flights to Los Angeles from other U.S. points.

Important Note

Airfares, rules, and regulations tend to fluctuate a lot, so some of the above may have changed. This is only a guide; we've included precise fares to give you a rough idea how much things might cost. Your travel agent will know best what's available at the time you're ready to travel, but if you're not satisfied with his/her advice, keep shopping around. The biggest step is deciding to go—once you've done that, the rest is easy!

PROBLEMS

When planning your trip allow a minimum two-hour stopover between connecting flights at U.S. airports, although with airport delays on the increase even this may not be enough. In the islands allow at least a day between flights. In some airports flights are not called over the public address system, so keep your eyes open. Whenever traveling, always have a paperback or two, some toiletries, and a change of underwear in your hand luggage.

If your flight is canceled due to a mechanical problem with the aircraft, the airline will cover your hotel bill and meals. If they reschedule the flight on short notice for reasons of their own or you're bumped off an overbooked flight, they should also pay. They may not feel obligated to pay, however, if the delay is due to weather conditions, a strike by another company, national emergencies, etc., although the best airlines still pick up the tab in these cases. Just don't expect much from local, "third-level" airlines on remote islands where such difficulties are routine.

It's an established practice among airlines to provide light refreshments to passengers delayed two hours after the scheduled departure time and a meal after four hours. Don't expect to get this on an outer island, but politely request it if you're at a gateway airport. If you are unexpectedly forced to spend the night somewhere, the airline may give you a form offering to telephone a friend or relative to inform them of the delay. Don't trust them to do this, however. Call your party yourself if you want to be sure they get the message. (Air New Zealand is notorious for not conveying messages of this kind.)

Overbooking

To compensate for no-shows, most airlines overbook their flights. To avoid being bumped, ask for your seat assignment when booking, check in early, and go to the departure area well before flight time. Of course, if you *are* bumped by a reputable airline at a major airport you'll be regaled with free meals and lodging and sometimes even free flight vouchers (don't expect anything like this from a domestic carrier on a remote Pacific island).

Whenever you break your journey for more than 72 hours, always reconfirm your onward reservations and check your seat assignment at the same time. Get the name of the person who takes your reconfirmation so they cannot later deny it. Failure to reconfirm could result in the cancellation of your complete remaining itinerary. This could also happen if you miss a flight for any reason. If you want special vegetarian or kosher food in-flight, request it when buying your ticket, booking, and reconfirming.

When you try to reconfirm your Air New Zealand flight the agent will probably tell you that this formality is no longer required. Theoretically this may be true, but unless you request your seat assignment in advance, either at an Air New Zealand office or over the phone, you could be "bumped" from a full flight, reservation or no reservation. Air New Zealand's ticket cover bears this surprising message:

. . . no guarantee of a seat is indicated by the terms "reservation," "booking," "O.K." status, or the times associated therewith.

They do admit in the same notice that confirmed passengers denied seats may be eligible for compensation, so if you're not in a hurry, a night or two at an upmarket hotel with all meals courtesy of Air New Zealand may not be a hardship. Your best bet if you don't want to get "bumped" is to request seat assignments for your entire itinerary before you leave home, or at least at the first Air New Zealand office you pass during your travels. Any good travel agent selling tickets on Air New Zealand should know enough to automatically request your seat assignments as they make your bookings. Check Air New Zealand's reconfirmation policy at one of their offices as it could change.

Baggage

International airlines allow economy-class passengers either 20 kilos of baggage or two pieces not over 32 kilos each (ask which applies to you). Under the piece system, neither bag must have a combined length, width, and height of over 158 centimeters (62 inches) and the two pieces together must not exceed 272 centimeters (107 inches). On most long-haul tickets to/from North America or Europe, the piece system applies to all sectors, but check this with the airline. The frequent flier programs of some major airlines allow participants to carry up to 10 kilos of excess baggage free of charge. Small commuter carriers often restrict you to as little as 10 kilos, so it's better to pack according to the lowest common denominator.

Bicycles, folding kayaks, and surfboards can usually be checked as baggage (sometimes for an additional US$50-100 charge), but sailboards may have to be shipped airfreight. If you do travel with a sailboard, be sure to call it a surfboard at check-in.

Tag your bag with name, address, and phone number inside and out. Stow anything that could conceivably be considered a weapon (scissors, penknife, toy gun, mace, etc.) in your checked luggage. Incidentally, it can be considered a criminal offense to make jokes about bombings or hijackings in airports or aboard aircraft.

One reason for lost baggage is that some people fail to remove used baggage tags after they claim their luggage. Get into the habit of tearing off old baggage tags, unless you want

your luggage to travel in the opposite direction! As you're checking in, look to see if the three-letter city codes on your baggage tag receipt and boarding pass are the same.

If your baggage is damaged or doesn't arrive at your destination, inform the airline officials immediately and have them fill out a written report; otherwise future claims for compensation will be compromised. Airlines usually reimburse out-of-pocket expenses if your baggage is lost or delayed over 24 hours. The amount varies from US$25 to US$50. Your chances of getting it are better if you're polite but firm. Keep receipts for any money you're forced to spend to replace missing articles.

Claims for lost luggage can take weeks to process. Keep in touch with the airline to show your concern and hang on to your baggage tag until the matter is resolved. If you feel you did not receive the attention you deserved, write the airline an objective letter outlining the case. Get the names of the employees you're dealing with so you can mention them in the letter. Of course, don't expect any pocket money or compensation on a remote outer island. Report the loss, then wait till you get back to their main office. Whatever happens, try to avoid getting angry. The people you're dealing with don't want the problem any more than you do.

BY BOAT

Even as much Pacific shipping was being sunk during WW II, airstrips were springing up on all the main islands. This hastened the inevitable replacement of the old steamships with modern aircraft, and it's now extremely rare to arrive in the South Pacific by boat (private yachts excepted). Most islands export similar products and there's little interregional trade; large container ships headed for Australia, New Zealand, and Japan don't usually accept passengers.

Those bitten by nostalgia for the slower prewar ways may like to know that a couple of passenger-carrying freighters do still call at the islands, though their fares are much higher than those charged by the airlines. A specialized agency booking such passages is **TravLtips**

(Box 188, Flushing, NY 11358, U.S.A.; tel. 800/872-8584 in the U.S. and 800/548-7823 in Canada). They can place you aboard a British-registered **Banks Line** container ship on its way around the world from England via the Panama Canal, Papeete, Apia, Suva, Lautoka, Nouméa, Port Vila, Honiara, and Papua New Guinea. A round-the-world ticket for the four-month journey is US$12,125, but segments are sold if space is available 30 days before sailing. Similarly, TravLtips books German-registered **Columbus Line** vessels, which make 45-day roundtrips between Los Angeles and Australia via Suva (US$4500 roundtrip double occupancy). One-way segments (when available) are half price. These ships can accommodate only about a dozen passengers, so inquire well in advance. Also ask about passenger accommodation on cargo vessels of the **Blue Star Line,** which call at Suva and Nouméa between the U.S. and New Zealand.

Several times a year **Saga Holidays** (222 Berkeley St., Boston, MA 02116, U.S.A.; tel. 800/343-0273, fax 617/375-5950) offers luxury cruises from Los Angeles or Honolulu to Tahiti via Christmas Island aboard Princess Cruises' vessels.

Adventure cruises to the Marquesas Islands aboard the freighter *Aranui* are described in the Tahiti-Polynesia chapter. **Windstar Cruises** offers tourist trips around Tahiti-Polynesia on the huge four-masted cruise ship *Wind Song.* The 392-passenger cruiseship *Club Med 2* is similar (details of both in the introduction to the Tahiti-Polynesia chapter). In Fiji, **Blue Lagoon Cruises Ltd.** (Box 130, Lautoka, Fiji Islands; tel. 679/661-622, fax 679/664-098) runs very popular deluxe cruises to the Yasawa Islands from Lautoka. Turn to the Fiji chapter for details.

Work-a-Way Passages

You can sometimes arrange free passage on ships of the Columbus, Pacific Forum, or Sofrana lines if you're willing to work in the deck, engine room, or catering departments as unpaid crew. Arrival and departure times of vessels appear in the daily newspapers, or phone the harbormaster of the port concerned. Since these ships are only in port four or five hours, you must be prepared to jump right on. The only real way to get on a ship is to see the captain, so

try to see him/her as soon as they've cleared customs.

Most of the ships make regular trips around the Pacific on fixed schedules, so if you work hard and gain a captain's favor, you might be able to jump off, then rejoin the same ship when they return a few weeks later. All valuables will be held by the captain, and you must work the same hours as the regular crew. You'll be asked to put up a cash bond of US$300 or more, and money will be deducted from the bond for days you don't work. Unless you're a citizen of the country of disembarkation, you'll have to present a return air ticket. German passport holders are given preference on Columbus Line ships. This is an excellent opportunity to experience life on a freighter.

ORGANIZED TOURS

Packaged Holidays

While this book is written for independent travelers rather than packaged tourists, reduced group airfares and hotel rates make some tours worth considering. For two people with limited time and a desire to stay at a first-class hotel, this may be the cheapest way to go. The "wholesalers" who put these packages together get their rooms at rates far lower than individuals pay. Special-interest tours are very popular among sportspeople who want to be sure they'll get to participate in the various activities they enjoy. The main drawback to the tours is that you're on a fixed itinerary among other tourists, out of touch with local life. Singles pay a healthy supplement. Some of the companies mentioned below do not accept consumer inquiries and require you to work through a travel agent.

Specialists in tours (and all travel arrangements) to Tahiti-Polynesia include **Manuia Tours** (74 New Montgomery St., San Francisco, CA 94105, U.S.A.; tel. 415/495-4500, fax 415/495-2000), **Tahiti Vacations** (9841 Airport Blvd., Suite 1124, Los Angeles, CA 90045, U.S.A.; tel. 800/553-3477), **Tahiti Nui's Island Dreams** (Box 9170, Seattle, WA 98109, U.S.A.; tel. 800/359-4359), **Islands in the Sun** (2381 Rosecrans Ave. #325, El Segundo, CA 90245-4913, U.S.A.; tel. 800/828-6877 in the U.S., tel. 800/667-4648 in Canada, fax 310/536-6266),

Island Vacations (2042 Business Center Dr., Irvine, CA 92715, U.S.A.; tel. 800/745-8545), and **Discover Wholesale Travel** (2192 Dupont Dr., Suite 105, Irvine, CA 92715, U.S.A.; tel. 800/576-7770 in California, tel. 800/759-7330 elsewhere in the U.S., fax 714/833-1176). Check all of these companies for specials before booking a tour to Tahiti.

A company dealing with all aspects of travel to Fiji is **Fiji Holidays** (3790 Dunn Dr., Suite A, Los Angeles, CA 90034, U.S.A.; tel. 800/500-FIJI, fax 310/202-8233). **Islands in the Sun** (address above) has a useful brochure describing many package tours to Fiji. **Sunmakers** (Box 9170, Seattle, WA 98109, U.S.A.) books customized itineraries in Cook Islands, Fiji, Tahiti-Polynesia, and Western Samoa. **Destinations Pacific** (100 W. Harrison, So. Tower, Suite 350, Seattle, WA 98119, U.S.A.; fax 206/216-2990) offers all-inclusive packages to Cook Islands.

Club Méditerranée (40 W. 57th St., New York, NY 10019, U.S.A.; tel. 800/CLUB-MED, fax 212/315-5392) offers one-week packages to their resort villages on Bora Bora, Moorea, and Nouméa. Package prices include room (double occupancy), food, land and water sports, evening entertainment, and transfers, but airfare and bicycle rentals are extra. Due to all the activities, Club Med's a good choice for single travelers; families with small children should look elsewhere. Book a couple of months in advance, especially if you want to travel in July, August, or December. For more information on *le Club,* see the Tahiti-Polynesia and New Caledonia chapters in this handbook.

Qantas Holidays (141 Walker St., North Sydney, NSW 2060, Australia; tel. 800/427-399) offers a variety of standard package tours to Fiji, Vanuatu, and Tahiti. In Europe these trips can be booked through Jetabout Holidays, Sovereign House, 361 King St., Hammersmith, London W6 9NJ, England (tel. 44-181/748-8676, fax 44-181/748-7236).

Swingaway Holidays (Level 5, 22 York St., Sydney, NSW 2000, Australia; tel. 61-2/9237-0300, fax 61-2/9262-6024) runs package tours to Fiji and books Blue Lagoon Cruises. They also book most tourist facilities in the Solomon Islands. The **Pacific Island Travel Center** (Level 7, 39-41 York St., Sydney, NSW 2000,

Australia; tel. 61-2/9262-6011, fax 61-2/9262-6318) is similar. **Hideaway Holidays** (994 Victoria Rd., West Ryde, NSW 2114, Australia; tel. 61-2/9807-4222, fax 61-2/9808-2260) specializes in off-the-beaten-track packages to every part of the South Pacific and can organize complicated itineraries.

From New Zealand **ASPAC Vacations Ltd.** (Box 4330, Auckland; tel. 64-9/623-0259, fax 64-9/623-0257) has the same sort of packaged tours and cruises as Swingaway to Cook Islands, Fiji, New Caledonia, Niue, Tonga, Western Samoa, and Vanuatu. ASPAC can book services in remote areas upon request. **Islands International Travel** (Ground Floor, 8-10 Whitaker Place, Auckland, New Zealand; tel. 0800/108-004, fax 64-9/309-4332) offers standard tourist packages to Tonga and Samoa on Polynesian Airlines.

Tours for Children

About the only packages to the South Pacific especially designed for families traveling with children are the "Rascals in Paradise" programs offered by **Adventure Express** (650 5th St., Suite 505, San Francisco, CA 94107, U.S.A.; tel. 800/U-RASCAL, fax 415/442-0289). Special "family week" group tours to Fiji's Vatulele Island Resort are operated between July and September. The US$7180 price is based on two adults with one or two children aged two to 11, and international airfares and transfers to Vatulele are additional. Less expensive independent one-week family trips are available year-round to places like Plantation Island, Fiji (US$1005 per adult with two kids under 16 free, airfare additional). A single parent with child would have to pay two adult fares. Adventure Express also books regular scuba diving tours and upmarket hotel rooms throughout the Pacific.

Scuba Tours

The South Pacific is one of the world's prime scuba locales, and most islands have good facilities for divers. Although it's not difficult to do it on your own, if you have limited time and want to get in as much diving as possible, you should consider joining an organized scuba tour. To stay in business, dive travel specialists are forced to charge prices similar to what you'd pay if you just walked in off the street, and the convenience of having all your arrangements made for you by a company able to pull weight with island suppliers is often worth it. Request the brochures of the companies listed below, and before booking, find out exactly where you'll be staying and ask if daily transfers and meals are provided. Of course, diver certification is mandatory.

Tropical Adventures Travel (111 2nd Ave. N, Seattle, WA 98109, U.S.A.; tel. 800/247-3483, fax 206/441-5431) sends divers to Fiji and the Solomon Islands for seven nights from US$1799 including airfare from the U.S., accommodations, diving, taxes, and more. They can also book a week on the Solomons live-aboard dive boat *Bilikiki* for US$2072, airfare extra. Tropical's president, Bob Goddess, claims he's always accessible by phone. Over 6,000 divers a year book through this company, which has been in business since 1973.

Founded in 1966, **See & Sea Travel Service** (50 Francisco St., Suite 205, San Francisco, CA 94133, U.S.A.; tel. 800/DIV-XPRT, fax 415/434-3409) is *the* authority on live-aboard dive experiences. This is a bit more expensive than land-based diving, but you're offered up to five dives each day and a total experience. See & Sea represents the selected cream of Pacific dive boats, such as the *Nai'a* in Fiji (US$2080 a week), and the *Bilikiki* in the Solomons (US$2980 for 10 days). All meals are included, but airfare is extra. If you have access to the Internet you can browse their 20-megabyte treasure trove of photos and text at **http://www.divxprt.com/see&sea.** Thanks to this new resource, divers wishing to know about conditions in Fiji, the Solomons, or any other world-class destination can merely point and click. See & Sea's president is the noted underwater photographer and author, Carl Roessler.

The Fiji specialist is **Aqua-Trek** (110 Sutter St., Suite 811, San Francisco, CA 94104, U.S.A.; tel. 800/541-4334). Ocean Voyages mentioned under "Yacht Tours and Charters" below offers live-aboard scuba diving from chartered yachts in Polynesian waters—an option well worth checking.

Poseidon Ventures Tours (359 San Miguel Dr., Newport Beach, CA 92660, U.S.A.; tel. 800/854-9334; or 505 North Belt, Suite 675, Houston, TX 77060, U.S.A.; tel. 713/820-3483) offers seven-night diving tours to Fiji beginning at US$1775 including five days of two-tank diving, airfare from Los Angeles, double-occupancy hotel accommodations, meals, taxes, and transfers. They also sell live-aboard diving in Solomon Islands.

New Zealanders requiring information about scuba diving facilities in and around the Pacific should call up Ed Meili of **The Diving Network** (Box 38-023, Howick, Auckland, New Zealand; tel. 64-9/367-5066). Ed has first-hand knowledge of diving facilities in the islands and can provide valuable tips.

Dive 'N Fishing Travel (15E Vega Place, Mairangi Bay, Auckland 10, New Zealand; tel. 64-9/479-2210, fax 64-9/479-2214) arranges scuba and game fishing tours to Fiji, Solomon Islands, Tonga, and Vanuatu at competitive rates. They can book you on the 24-meter, six-cabin live-aboard *Kiwi Diver*, which cruises Tongan waters from June to October on humpback whalewatching expeditions, with cave, reef, and wreck diving thrown in! ("We have always seen humpbacks but only 70-80% of the time have the whales shown interest in us and allowed us to join them.")

One of the leading experts on scuba diving around Tahiti-Polynesia is marine biologist and dive instructor Richard Johnson, director of **Paradise Dive Travel** (B.P. 6008, Faa'a, Tahiti; tel./fax 689/41-08-54). Dick sells "prepaid diving vouchers" for customized scuba diving at Tahiti, Moorea, Huahine, Raiatea, Bora Bora, Rangiroa, and Manihi at discounts of five to 20 percent. Write or fax for his free leaflet, *Why Dive Tahiti?* which outlines the advantages and disadvantages of each island in refreshingly straightforward language. Dick's U.S. agent is Islands in the Sun (tel. 800/828-6877).

Jean-Michel Cousteau's **Ocean Search Project** offers all-inclusive two-week programs based at the Cousteau Fiji Islands Resort near Savusavu for serious scuba divers. For information contact Cousteau Productions (tel. 805/899-8899, fax 805/899-8898) in Santa Barbara, California.

Alternatively, you can make your own arrangements directly with island dive shops. Information about these operators is included under the heading "Sports and Recreation" in the respective destination chapters of this book.

Tours for Naturalists

Perhaps the most rewarding way to visit the South Seas is with **Earthwatch** (Box 403, Watertown, MA 02272, U.S.A.; tel. 800/776-0188, fax 617/926-8532), a nonprofit organization founded in 1971 to serve as a bridge between the public and the scientific community. The programs vary from year to year, but in the past they've sent teams to survey spinner dolphins at Moorea, examine the coral reefs of Fiji and Tonga, study the rainforests of Fiji, restore *marae* at Rarotonga, assist archaeologists on Easter Island, or save the giant clams of Tonga. These are not study tours but opportunities for amateurs to help out with serious work, kind of like a short-term scientific Peace Corps. As a research volunteer, a team member's share of project costs is tax-deductible in the U.S. and some other countries. For more information contact Earthwatch at the address above, or 1st Floor, 453-457 Elizabeth St., Melbourne, Victoria 3000, Australia (tel. 61-3/9600-9100, fax 61-3/9600-9066), or Belsyre Court, 57 Woodstock Rd., Oxford OX2 6HU, England (tel. 44-1865/311-600, fax 44-865/311-383), or Technova Inc., 13th Floor, Fukoku Building, 2-2 Uchisaiwai-Cho, 2-Chome, Chiyoda-Ku, Tokyo 100, Japan (tel. 81-3/3508-2280, fax 81-3/3508-7578).

Victor Emanuel Nature Tours (Box 33008, Austin, Texas 78764, U.S.A.; tel. 800/328-VENT, fax 512/328-2919) often arranges first-class birdwatching tours to remote islands. Noted ornithologists escort the groups in their search for rare species of doves, finches, flycatchers, fruitdoves, honeyeaters, lorikeets, parakeets, parrots, parrotfinches, pigeons, sandpipers, silktails, and even New Caledonia's endangered *cagou*. These two-week tours begin around US$4000 (double occupancy), airfare extra.

Kayak Tours

Among the most exciting tours to the South Pacific are the 10- to 16-day kayaking expeditions to Fiji offered from April to November by **Southern Sea Ventures** (51 Fishermans Dr., Emerald Beach, NSW 2456, Australia; tel. 61-2/6656-1907, fax 61-2/6656-2109). Their groups of 10 persons maximum paddle stable two-person sea kayaks through the sheltered tropical waters of the Yasawa chain. Accommodations are tents on the beach, and participants must be in reasonable physical shape, as three or four hours a day are spent on the water. The price varies from US$1073-1850 and doesn't include airfare. In April 1992 Southern Sea Ventures launched 10-day kayak trips to remote Santa Isabel in the Solomon Islands. In the U.S. book through **Journeys** (1536 NW 23rd Ave., Portland, OR 97210-2618, U.S.A.; tel. 503/226-7200, fax 503/226-4940), in New Zealand through **Suntravel** (Box 12-424, Auckland; tel. 64-9/525-3074, fax 64-9/525-3065).

Mountain Travel/Sobek Expeditions (6420 Fairmount Ave., El Cerrito, CA 94530, U.S.A.; tel. 800/227-2384, fax 510/525-7710) runs a 16-day combination hiking/sea kayaking tour to Fiji four times a year at US$1850 plus airfare. Participants spend four days trekking through central Viti Levu, then eight days kayaking the Yasawas.

Fiji By Kayak (Box 43, Savusavu, Fiji; tel. 679/850-372, fax 679/850-344) offers kayak/camping tours in Vanua Levu's Natewa Bay monthly from July to October at US$945 for six nights, plus 10% Fijian tax (US$50 single supplement). Groups are restricted to eight participants, and the staff of four does all the chores. The first and last nights are spent at Kontiki Resort and transfers to/from Savusavu Airport are included. Bookings can be made through Adventure Express (650 5th St., Suite 505, San Francisco, CA 94107, U.S.A.; tel. 800/443-0799, fax 415/442-0289). Kayaking tours of this kind are highly recommended for the adventurous, active traveler.

The **Friendly Islands Kayak Company** operates ocean kayaking tours through Tonga's Vava'u Group. A typical nine-day package costs T$515 pp and includes transfers from Vava'u airport, four nights at the Tongan Beach Resort (double occupancy), seven days kayak rental, a Tongan guide for the first day, and two feasts on outer islands. After the initial orientation, participants do their own thing and arrange meals for themselves (although a guide can be hired for the duration). This approach keeps prices low and gives you the flexibility to plan your own trip, while benefiting from the presence of a local support team. From May to November the Canadian managers, Doug and Sharon Spence, will be in Tonga (Box 104, Neiafu, Vava'ua, Tonga; tel./fax 676/70-380), but from December to April they should be contacted at their New Zealand address (Box 142, Waitati, Otago; tel./fax 64-3/482-1202). In North America, kayaking tours to Tonga can be booked through **Ecosummer Expeditions** (1516 Duranleau St., Vancouver, BC V6H 3S4, Canada; fax 604/669-3244). Call them toll-free at 800/465-8884 in Canada or 800/688-8605 in the United States.

In New Caledonia, **Terra Incognita** (B.P. 18, Dumbea; tel. 687/41-61-19) offers kayak trips on a diffrent river, lake, or bay every weekend, and they also rent canoes and kayaks. Special kayak expeditions can be organized for groups of eight or more. Their specialty is whitewater kayaking on wild and scenic rivers, one of the few places in the South Pacific where this is offered.

Bicycle Tours

About the only North American company offering tours especially designed for cyclists is **Journeys Beyond** (Box 7511, Jackson, WY 83001, U.S.A.; tel. 307/733-9615). Three times a year there are 10-day cycle tours of the Leeward Islands of Tahiti-Polynesia (US$2620, double occupancy). Interisland travel between the four islands visited is by chartered yacht. Prices include food, a shared cabin on the yacht, and bicycles, but airfare is extra. This trip offers an excellent combination of sailing and cycling.

Hiking Tours

From May to October **Adventure Fiji,** a division of Rosie The Travel Service (Box 9268, Nandi Airport, Fiji Islands; tel. 679/722-755, fax 679/722-607), runs adventuresome five-night hiking trips in the upper Wainimbuka River area of central Viti Levu south of Rakiraki. Horses carry trekkers' backpacks, so the trips are feasible for almost anyone in good condition. The F$570 pp price includes transport to the trailhead, food and accommodations at a few of the 11 Fijian villages along the way, guides, and a bamboo raft ride on the Wainimbuka River. Trekkers only hike about five hours a day, allowing lots of time to get to know the village people. These tours begin from Nandi every Monday. In Australia bookings can be made through Rosie The Travel Service (Level 5, Ste.

505, 9 Bronte Rd., Bondi Junction, Sydney, NSW 2022; tel. 61-2/9389-3666, fax 61-2/9369-1129), in North America through **Goway Travel** (3284 Yonge St., Suite 300, Toronto, Ontario M4N 3M7, Canada; tel. 800/387-8850). Highly recommended.

Surfing Tours

The largest operator of surfing tours to the South Pacific is **The Surf Travel Company** (Box 446, Cronulla, NSW 2230, Australia; tel. 61-2/9527-4722, fax 61-2/9527-4522) with packages to Ha'atafu Beach (Tonga), Frigates Pass (Fiji), Seashell Cove (Fiji), and Savai'i (Western Samoa). At Raiatea/Huahine (Tahiti-Polynesia) they offer surfing from a chartered Beneteau yacht (A$1699 pp for seven nights, including accommodations, meals, transfers (but not airfare). Their groups are never bigger than 12. In New Zealand book through Mark Thompson (7 Danbury Dr., Torbay, Auckland; tel./fax 09-473-8388).

Tours for Veterans

Every August **Valor Tours Ltd.** (Box 1617, Sausalito, CA 94966, U.S.A.; tel. 415/332-7850, fax 415/332-4807) organizes a tour of WW II battlefields in the Solomons by chartered ship. The prices varies from US$3800-5000 depending on cabin selection and includes airfare and all meals. Most tours are personally led by Valor's president, Robert F. Reynolds, who was the moving force behind construction of the U.S. war memorial in Honiara.

Yacht Tours and Charters

If you were planning on spending a substantial amount to stay at a luxury resort, consider chartering a yacht instead! Divided up among the members of your party the per-person charter price will be about the same, but you'll experience much more of the Pacific's beauty on a boat than you would staying in a hotel room. All charterers visit remote islands accessible only by small boat and thus receive special insights into island life unspoiled by normal tourist trappings. Of course, activities such as sailing, snorkeling, and general exploring by sea and land are included in the price.

Yacht charters are available either "bareboat" (for those with the skill to sail on their own) or "crewed" (in which case charterers pay a daily fee for a skipper plus his/her provisions). On a "flotilla" charter a group of bareboats follow an experienced lead yacht.

One of the finest companies arranging such charters is **Ocean Voyages Inc.** (1709 Bridgeway, Sausalito, CA 94965, U.S.A.; tel. 415/332-4681, fax 415/332-7460). Unlike their competitors, Ocean Voyages organizes "shareboat" charters in which singles and couples book a single cabin on a chartered yacht sailing to the remotest corners of the South Pacific. Ask about shareboat yacht cruises on fixed one- and two-week itineraries, usually between Huahine and Bora Bora. Individuals are welcome and there are about 10 departures a year from April to November. Prices average a little over US$150 pp a day, and scuba diving is possible at extra cost on some boats (ask). This is perfect if you're alone or in a party of two and can't afford to charter an entire bareboat yacht. The groups are limited to a maximum of 15 participants, often less.

Other outstanding Ocean Voyages offerings include the annual voyages from Tahiti to Pitcairn, charter programs out of Port Vila, Raiatea, Vava'u, and Taveuni, and extended tours of the entire South Pacific by classic square-rigger sailing boats such as the brigantine *Soren Larsen* or the schooner *Old Glory.* They've also developed one-week catamaran cruises especially designed for individual scuba divers to the remote islands of the Tuamotus (US$2350) and Marquesas (US$2150 pp)—the *crème de la crème* of Polynesian dive experiences. These prices are all-inclusive, covering everything but air transportation and liquor. All trips should be booked and paid for at least 60 days in advance. Ocean Voyages caters to a very select, professional clientele, and their crews are carefully chosen. Over 35% of the participants are repeaters—the best recommendation there is.

The Moorings (4th Floor, 19345 U.S. 19 North, Clearwater, FL 34624, U.S.A.; tel. 800/535-7289) offers bareboat and crewed yacht charters from their own bases at Raiatea, Vava'u, Fiji, and Vanuatu. At Raiatea (Tahiti-Polynesia), prices range from US$2800 a week for a four-berth boat to US$10,780 weekly for an six-berth air-conditioned yacht. Charters out of

Vava'u (Tonga) and Fiji are a bit less expensive. Prices are for the entire boat, but extras are airfare, food (US$32 pp daily), skipper (US$65-140 daily, if required), and cook (US$60-120, if desired). They check you out to make sure you're really capable of handling their vessels. Other obligatory extras are security insurance (US$18 a day), cancellation insurance (US$60 pp), and local tax (three percent in Tahiti-Polynesia, 7.5% in Tonga, and 10% in Fiji). Their New Zealand office, **Moorings Rainbow Yacht Charters** (Box 8327, Symonds St., Auckland, New Zealand; tel. 64-9/377-4840, fax 64-9/377-4820), specializes in charters in Fiji's Mamanutha and Yasawa groups. In Europe contact **Adventure Holidays** (Box 920113, 90266 Nürnberg, Germany; fax 49-911/979-9588).

The Moorings' Raiatea competitor, ATM Yacht Charters, is represented by **Tahiti Vacations** (9841 Airport Blvd., Suite 1124, Los Angeles, CA 90045, U.S.A.; tel. 800/553-3477), so call to compare prices. There are many yacht charter opportunities in Fiji and these are detailed in the introduction to the Fiji chapter.

A few private brokers arranging bareboat or crewed yacht charters at Raiatea, Vava'u, and Nouméa are **Sun Yacht Charters** (Box 737, Camden, ME 04843, U.S.A.; tel. 800/772-3500, fax 207/236-3972), **Charter World Pty. Ltd.** (579 Hampton St., Hampton, Melbourne 3188, Australia; tel. 61-3/9521-0033, fax 61-3/9521-0081), **Sail Connections Ltd.** (Freepost 4545, Box 3234, Auckland, New Zealand; tel. 64-9/358-0556, fax 64-9/358-4341), and **Yachting Partners International** (28/29 Richmond Place, Brighton, BN2 2NA, East Sussex, England; tel. 44-1273/571722, fax 44-1273/571720). As they don't own their own boats (as the Moorings does), they'll be more inclined to fit you to the particular boat that suits your individual needs.

GETTING AROUND

BY AIR

In 1995 the Association of South Pacific Airlines introduced a "Visit South Pacific Pass" to coincide with "Visit South Pacific Year." This allows travelers to include the services of nine regional carriers in a single ticket at US$150, US$200, or US$300 per leg. The initial two-leg air pass has to be purchased in conjunction with an international ticket into the region, but additional legs up to eight maximum can be purchased after arrival. Only the first sector has to be booked ahead. The pass has been so successful that the Association decided to extend it to March 1997. It's a great way of getting around the South Pacific, so be sure to ask Air New Zealand, Air Pacific or Qantas about it.

Air Pacific

Air Pacific has two different "triangle fares," good ways to get around and experience the region's variety of cultures: Fiji-Apia-Tonga-Fiji (F$667) and Fiji-Nouméa-Port Vila-Fiji (F$785), plus F$15 tax if purchased in Fiji. Both are valid for one year and can be purchased at any travel agency in Fiji or direct from the airline. Usually they're only good for journeys commencing in Fiji. Flight dates can be changed at no charge. When booking these circular tickets, be aware that it's much better to go Fiji-Apia-Tonga-Fiji than vice versa, because the flights between Apia and Tonga leave Apia in the late morning but return from Tonga to Apia late at night. In addition, the flights between Apia and Fiji are often fully booked while it's easy to get on between Tonga and Fiji. Also obtainable locally are Air Pacific's special 28-day roundtrip excursion fares from Fiji to Apia (F$659), Tonga (F$569), Port Vila (F$560), and Honiara (F$1015).

A "Pacific Air Pass" allows 30 days travel (on Air Pacific flights only) from Fiji to Apia, Tonga, and Port Vila (US$449). Extended to Honiara, the pass costs US$599. This pass can only be purchased from Qantas Airways offices in North America and Europe, from Mr. Karl Philipp,

Guiollett Strasse 30, D-60325 Frankfurt/Main, Germany (tel. 49-69/172260; fax 49-69/729314), or from Air Pacific's U.S. office, 6151 West Century Blvd., Suite 524, Los Angeles, CA 90045 (tel. 800/227-4500, fax 310/337-1380). The inflight service on Air Pacific is good.

Polynesian Airlines

For Australians and New Zealanders with a month to see the islands, Polynesian Airlines offers the **Polypass**, which allows 30 days unlimited travel on their limited network (including one roundtrip from Sydney, Melbourne, Auckland, or Wellington) for US$999. One flight on Air Pacific through Nandi is also included. Restrictions are that your itinerary must be worked out in advance and can only be changed once. Thus it's important to book all flights well ahead. A 20% penalty is charged to refund an unused ticket (no refund after one year), and travel cannot begin in December or January.

In recent years Polynesian's network has shrunk drastically, and they now only fly to Apia, Pago Pago, Nuku'alofa, Rarotonga, Sydney, Melbourne, Wellington, and Auckland. The Polypass may be marginally interesting to Aussies and Kiwis, but North Americans and Europeans beginning their trip in the islands will prefer Polynesian's Pacific Triangle Fare (US$450), which allows one a full year to complete the Apia-Nuku'alofa-Nandi loop. Also ask about the "Two Coupon Plus Pass," which costs only US$100 per flight.

Solomon Airlines

Solomon Airlines offers a 30-day "Discover Pacific Pass," which includes two international flights for US$399, three flights for US$499, or four flights for US$599. To include Australia or New Zealand is US$100 extra. A typical three-coupon routing is Nandi-Port Vila-Honiara-Nandi. All flights must be booked in advance and there's a US$50 fee to make changes.

There's also a 30-day "Discovery Solomons Fare," which allows four domestic flights within the Solomons for US$199 (additional coupons US$50). On this one you only book your first flight at the time of ticketing; the other flights can only be booked the day before, so it's sort of like going standby. To reissue the ticket costs US$50, and since Solomon Airline's domestic flights are heavily booked, this pass is not recommended.

These tickets must be purchased prior to arrival in the South Pacific, in North America through Air Promotions Systems, 5757 West Century Blvd., Suite 660, Los Angeles, CA 90045-6407, U.S.A. (tel. 310/670-7302; fax 310/338-0708), and in Europe through Mr. Karl Philipp, Guiollett Strasse 30, D-60325 Frankfurt/Main, Germany (tel. 49-69/172260; fax 49-69/729314).

Domestic Air Services

Nearly every Pacific country has its local airline servicing the outer islands. These flights, described in the destination chapters of this guide, can be booked on arrival. The most important local carriers are Air Calédonie (New Caledonia), Air Fiji (Fiji), Air Tahiti (Tahiti-Polynesia), Air Rarotonga (Cook Islands), Polynesian Airlines (Western Samoa), Royal Tongan Airlines (Tonga), Samoa Air (American Samoa), Solomon Airlines (Solomon Islands), Sunflower Airlines (Fiji), Vanair (Vanuatu), and Western Pacific Air Services (Solomon Islands). Most fly small aircraft, so only 10 kilograms free baggage may be allowed.

BY SEA

Ninety-nine percent of travel around the South Pacific is by air. With few exceptions travel by boat is a thing of the past, and about the only regular international service is Pago Pago to Apia. Local boats to the outer islands within a single country are available everywhere, however. Among the local trips you can easily do by regularly scheduled boat are Tahiti-Moorea, Tahiti-Bora Bora, Nuku'alofa-Vava'u, Nuku'alofa-'Eua, Pago Pago-Apia, Upolu-Savai'i, Suva-Kandavu, Suva-Taveuni, Nambouwalu-Natovi, Natovi-Ovalau, Honiara-Malaita, and Honiara-Gizo. Details of these and other shipping possibilities are explored in the different destination chapters of this book.

BY SAILING YACHT

Getting Aboard

Hitch rides into the Pacific on yachts from California, New Zealand, and Australia, or around the yachting triangle Papeete-Suva-Honolulu. At home, scrutinize the classified listings of yachts seeking crews, yachts to be delivered, etc., in magazines like *Yachting, Cruising World, Sail,* and *Latitude 38*. You can even advertise yourself for about US$25 (plan to have the ad appear three months before the beginning of the season). Check the bulletin boards at yacht clubs. The **Seven Seas Cruising Association** (1525 South Andrews Ave., Suite 217, Fort Lauderdale, FL 33316, U.S.A.; tel. 305/463-2431, fax 305/463-7183) is in touch with yachties all around the Pacific, and the classified section "Crew Exchange" in their monthly *Commodores' Bulletin* (US$53 a year) contains ads from captains in search of crew.

Cruising yachts are recognizable by their foreign flags, wind-vane steering gear, sturdy appearance, and laundry hung out to dry. Put up notices on yacht club and marine bulletin boards, and meet people in bars. When a boat is hauled out, you can find work scraping and repainting the bottom, varnishing, and doing minor repairs. It's much easier, however, to crew on yachts already in the islands. In Tahiti, for example, after a month on the open sea, some of the original crew may have flown home or onward, opening a place for you. Pago Pago, Vava'u, Suva, Malololailai, and Port Vila are other places to look for a boat.

If you've never crewed before, it's better to try for a short passage the first time. Once at sea on the way to Tahiti, there's no way they'll turn around to take a seasick crew member back to Hawaii. Good captains evaluate crew on personality and attitude more than experience, so don't lie. Be honest and open when interviewing with a skipper—a deception will soon become apparent. It's also good to know what a captain's *really* like before you commit yourself to an isolated month with her/him. To determine what might happen should the electronic gadgetry break down, find out if there's a sextant aboard and whether he/she knows how to use it. A run-down-looking boat may often be mechanically unsound too. Once you're on a boat and part of the yachtie community, things are easy. (P.S. from veteran yachtie Peter Moree: "We do need more ladies out here—adventurous types naturally.")

Time of Year

The weather and seasons play a deciding role in any South Pacific trip by sailboat and you'll have to pull out of many beautiful places, or be unable to stop there, because of bad weather. The best season for rides in the South Pacific is May to October; sometimes you'll even have to turn one down. Around August or September start looking for a ride from the South Pacific to Hawaii or New Zealand.

Be aware of the hurricane season: November to March in the South Pacific, July to December in the northwest Pacific (near Guam), and June to October in the area between Mexico and Hawaii. Few yachts will be cruising these areas at these times. A few yachts spend the winter at Pago Pago and Vava'u (the main "hurricane holes"), but most South Pacific cruisers will have left for hurricane-free New Zealand by October.

Also, know which way the winds are blowing; the prevailing trade winds in the tropics are from the northeast north of the equator, from the southeast south of the equator. North of the tropic of Cancer and south of the tropic of Capricorn the winds are out of the west. Due to the action of prevailing southeast tradewinds boat trips are smoother from east to west than west to east throughout the South Pacific, so that's the way to go.

Yachting Routes

The South Pacific is good for sailing; there's not too much traffic and no piracy like you'd find in the Mediterranean or in Indonesian waters. The common yachting route across the Pacific utilizes the northeast and southeast trades: from California to Tahiti via the Marquesas or Hawaii, then Rarotonga, Vava'u, Suva, and New Zealand. Some yachts continue west from Fiji to Port Vila. In the other direction, you'll sail on the westerlies from New Zealand to a point south of the Australs, then north on the trades to Tahiti.

Some 300 yachts leave the U.S. West Coast for Tahiti every year, almost always crewed by couples or men only. Most stay in the South Seas about a year before returning to North America, while a few continue around the world. About 60-80 cross the Indian Ocean every year (look for rides from Sydney in May, Cairns or Darwin from June to August, Bali from August to October, Singapore from October to December); around 700 yachts sail from Europe to the Caribbean (from Gibraltar and Gran Canaria from October to December).

Cruising yachts average about 150 km a day, so it takes about a month to get from the U.S. west coast to Hawaii, then another month from Hawaii to Papeete. To enjoy the best weather conditions many yachts clear the Panama Canal or depart California in February to arrive in the Marquesas in March. Many yachts stay on for the *Heiva i Tahiti* festival, which ends on 14 July, at which time they sail west to Vava'u or Suva, where you'll find them in July and August. In mid-September the yachting season culminates with a race by about 40 boats from Fiji's Malololailai Island to Port Vila (it's very easy to hitch a ride at this time). By late October the bulk of the yachting community is sailing south via New Caledonia to New Zealand or Australia to spend the southern summer there. In April or May on alternate years (1995, 1997, etc.) there's a yacht race from Auckland and Sydney to Suva, timed to coincide with the cruisers' return after the hurricane season.

A law enacted in New Zealand in February 1995 requires foreign yachts departing New Zealand to obtain a "Certificate of Inspection" from the New Zealand Yachting Federation prior to customs clearance. Before heading into a situation where thousands of dollars may have to be spent upgrading safety standards on their boats, yachties should query others who have left New Zealand recently about the impact of this law. It's shameful that New Zealand should burden the yachting community with this unwanted regulation merely to force them to spend money on refits in that country.

Life Aboard

To crew on a yacht you must be willing to wash and iron clothes, cook, steer, keep watch at night, and help with engine work. Other jobs might include changing and resetting sails, cleaning the boat, scraping the bottom, pulling up the anchor, and climbing the main mast to watch for reefs. Do more than is expected of you. A safety harness must be worn in rough weather. As a guest in someone else's home you'll want to wash your dishes promptly after use and put them, and all other gear, back where you found them. Tampons must not be thrown in the toilet bowl. Smoking is usually prohibited as a safety hazard.

You'll be a lot more useful if you know how to use a sextant—the U.S. Coast Guard Auxiliary holds periodic courses in its use. Also learn how to tie knots like the clove hitch, rolling hitch, sheet bend, double sheet bend, reef knot, square knot, figure eight, and bowline. Check your local library for books on sailing or write away for the comprehensive free catalog of nautical books available from International Marine/TAB Books, Blue Ridge Summit, PA 17294-0840, U.S.A.

Anybody who wants to get on well under sail must be flexible and tolerant, both physically and emotionally. Expense-sharing crew members pay US$50 a week or more per person. After 30 days you'll be happy to hit land for a freshwater shower. Give adequate notice when you're ready to leave the boat, but do disembark when your journey's up. Boat people have few enough opportunities for privacy as it is. If you've had a good trip, ask the captain to write you a letter of recommendation; it'll help you hitch another ride.

Food for Thought

When you consider the big investment, depreciation, cost of maintenance, operating expenses, and considerable risk (most cruising yachts are not insured), travel by sailing yacht is quite a luxury. The huge cost can be surmised from charter fees (US$400 a day and up for a 10-meter yacht). International law makes a clear distinction between passengers and crew. Crew members paying only for their own food, cooking gas, and part of the diesel are very different from charterers who do nothing and pay full costs. The crew is there to help operate the boat, adding safety, but like passengers, they're very much under the control of the captain. Crew has no say in where the yacht will go.

The skipper is personally responsible for crew coming into foreign ports: he's entitled to hold their passports and to see that they have onward tickets and sufficient funds for further traveling. Otherwise the skipper might have to pay their hotel bills and even return airfares to the crew's country of origin. Crew may be asked to pay a share of third-party liability insurance. Possession of dope can result in seizure of the yacht. Because of such considerations, skippers often hesitate to accept crew. Crew members should remember that at no cost to themselves they can learn a bit of sailing and see places nearly inaccessible by other means.

OTHER TRAVEL OPTIONS

By Bus

Almost all of the islands have highly developed bus systems serving mostly local people. In this handbook, we cover them all. Bus services are especially good in Fiji with all of the main centers connected by frequent services at very reasonable prices. Buses are also a good and inexpensive way to get around Tahiti, Rarotonga, Tongatapu, Tutuila, Upolu, and Guadalcanal. There's a good city bus service in Port Vila but other than that, buses are few and far between in Vanuatu. A 20-km bus ride will cost under a dollar in Fiji, Tonga, and both Samoas, about US$1.25 in Cook Islands and Solomon Islands, and over US$2 in Tahiti-Polynesia, New Caledonia, and Vanuatu.

By Car

A rental car will generally cost US$40-60 a day with unlimited mileage. The field is competitive and it's usually best to shop around for a good deal upon arrival instead of booking ahead. A 1994 South Pacific Commission report gave the following average 1993 prices in Australian dollars for one liter of gasoline: American Samoa A$0.45, Western Samoa A$0.48, Tonga A$0.66, Cook Islands A$0.84, Vanuatu A$1.10, New Caledonia A$1.32, Tahiti-Polynesia A$1.48.

Due to the alternative means of travel available, the only places where you really need to consider renting a car are in New Caledonia (Grande Terre), Tahiti-Polynesia, and Vanuatu (Efate), and perhaps also on Upolu in Western Samoa and Guadalcanal in the Solomons. Renting a car is an optional luxury in American Samoa, Fiji, and the Solomon Islands due to the excellent public transportation in those countries. In Cook Islands and Tonga one must pay a stiff fee for a local driver's license (international driver's license not recognized) and it's better to tour those countries by rented bicycle anyway. Bicycle is also the way to see Bora Bora.

Driving is on the right (as in continental Europe and North America) in American Samoa, New Caledonia, Tahiti-Polynesia, Vanuatu, and Western Samoa, and on the left (as in Britain, New Zealand, and Japan) in Cook Islands, Fiji, Solomon Islands, and Tonga. If you do rent a car, remember those sudden tropical downpours and don't leave the windows open. Also avoid parking under coconut trees (a falling nut might break the window), and never go off and leave the keys in the ignition.

By Bicycle

Bicycling in the South Pacific? Sure, why not? It's cheap, convenient, healthy, quick, environmentally sound, safe, and above all, *fun.* You'll be able to go where and when you please, stop easily and often to meet people and take photos, save money on taxi fares—really *see* the countries. Cycling every day can be fatiguing, however, so it's best to have bicycle-touring experience beforehand. Most roads are flat along the coast, but be careful on coral roads, especially inclines: if you slip and fall you could hurt yourself badly. On the high islands interior roads tend to be very steep. Never ride your bike through mud.

A sturdy, single-speed mountain bike with wide wheels, safety chain, and good brakes might be best. Thick tires and a plastic liner between tube and tire will reduce punctures. Know how to fix your own bike. Take along a good repair kit (pump, puncture kit, freewheel tool, spare spokes, cables, chain links, assorted nuts and bolts, etc.) and a repair manual; bicycle shops are poor to nonexistent in the islands. Don't try riding with a backpack: sturdy, waterproof panniers (bike bags) are required; you'll also want a good lock. Refuse to lend your bike to *anyone.*

Many international airlines will carry a bicycle as checked luggage, either free, at the standard overweight charge, or for a flat US$50 fee. Take off the pedals and panniers, turn the handlebars sideways, and clean off the dirt before checking in (or use a special bike-carrying bag). The commuter airlines won't usually accept bikes on their small planes. Interisland boats sometimes charge a token amount to carry a bike; other times it's free. Have plenty of time if you're going this way.

By Ocean Kayak

Ocean kayaking is experiencing a boom in Hawaii, but the South Pacific is still largely virgin territory. Virtually every island has a sheltered lagoon ready-made for the excitement of kayak touring, but this effortless new transportation mode hasn't yet arrived, so you can be a real independent 20th-century explorer! Many airlines accept folding kayaks as checked baggage at no charge.

Companies like **Long Beach Water Sports** (730 E. 4th St., Long Beach, CA 90802, U.S.A.; tel. 310/432-0187, fax 310/436-6812) sell inflatable one- or two-person sea kayaks for around US$1800, fully equipped. If you're new to the game, take a LBWS four-hour introductory sea kayaking class (US$55), held every Saturday. They also run all-day intermediate classes (US$70) monthly—a must for L.A. residents. They also rent kayaks by the day or week. Write for a free copy of their newsletter, *Paddle Strokes.*

For a better introduction to ocean kayaking than is possible here, check at your local public library for *Sea Kayaking, A Manual for Long-Distance Touring* by John Dowd (Seattle: University of Washington Press, 1981) or *Derek C. Hutchinson's Guide to Sea Kayaking* (Seattle: Basic Search Press, 1985). Noted author Paul Theroux toured the entire South Pacific by kayak, and his experiences are recounted in *The Happy Isles of Oceania: Paddling the Pacific* (London: Hamish Hamilton, 1992).

By Canoe

If you get off the beaten track, it's more than likely that a local friend will offer to take you out in his canoe. Never attempt to take a dugout canoe through even light surf: you'll be swamped. Don't try to pull or lift a canoe by its outrigger—it will break. Drag the canoe by holding the solid main body. A bailer is *essential* equipment.

POLYNESIA

TAHITI-POLYNESIA, PITCAIRN ISLANDS, EASTER ISLAND, COOK ISLANDS, NIUE, KINGDOM OF TONGA, AMERICAN SAMOA, WESTERN SAMOA, TOKELAU, WALLIS AND FUTUNA, TUVALU

JOHN WEBBER

*T*he Polynesian triangle between Hawaii, New Zealand, and Easter Island stretches 8,000 km across the central Pacific Ocean—a fifth of the earth's surface. Since the late 18th century, when Captain Cook first revealed Polynesia to European eyes, artists and writers have sung the praises of the graceful golden-skinned peoples of the "many islands." While there's certainly homogeneity in Polynesia, there are also striking contrasts resulting from a history of American, French, and New Zealand rule. Hawaii and New Zealand are parts of Polynesia not covered herein because most visitors carry separate guidebooks to them.

Polynesia consists of boundless ocean and little land. This vast region is divided into two cultural areas, Western Polynesia (Tonga and Samoa) and Eastern Polynesia (Hawaii, Tahiti-Polynesia, Cook Islands, and New Zealand). Of the three countries and eight territories included in this section, only Tahiti-Polynesia and Western Samoa are larger than 1,000 square km, though both Cook Islands and Tahiti-Polynesia control sea areas well above a million square km.

Only Tahiti-Polynesia, Tonga, and Western Samoa have populations over 100,000; seven of the 11 have less than 20,000 inhabitants. The mainly subsistence economies have forced many Polynesians to emigrate to the Pacific rim: there are now more Samoans in the U.S. than in American Samoa itself and more Cook Islanders in New Zealand than in their homeland. Only three Polynesian states are completely independent: Tonga, Western Samoa, and Tuvalu. All the rest still have ties to some outside power.

GORDON OHLIGER

TAHITI-POLYNESIA

INTRODUCTION

Legendary Tahiti, isle of love, has long been the vision of "la Nouvelle Cythère," the earthly paradise. Explorers Wallis, Bougainville, and Cook all told of a land of spellbinding beauty and enchantment, where the climate was delightful, hazardous insects and diseases unknown, and the islanders, especially the women, among the handsomest ever seen. Rousseau's "noble savage" had been found! A few years later, Fletcher Christian and Captain Bligh acted out their drama of sin and retribution here.

The list of famous authors who came and wrote about these islands reads like a high-school literature course: Herman Melville, Robert Louis Stevenson, Pierre Loti, Rupert Brooke, Jack London, W. Somerset Maugham, Charles Nordhoff and James Norman Hall (the Americans who wrote *Mutiny on the Bounty*), among others. Exotic images of uninhibited dancers, fragrant flowers, and pagan gods fill the pages. Here, at least, life was meant to be enjoyed.

The most unlikely PR man of them all was a once-obscure French painter named Paul Gau-

guin, who transformed the primitive color of Tahiti and the Marquesas into powerful visual images seen around the world. When WW II shook the Pacific from Pearl Harbor to Guadalcanal, rather than bloodcurdling banzais and saturation bombings, Polynesia got a U.S. serviceman named James A. Michener, who added Bora Bora to the legend. Marlon Brando arrived in 1961 on one of the first jets to land in Polynesia and, along with thousands of tourists and adventurers, has been coming back ever since.

The friendly, easygoing manner of the people of Tahiti-Polynesia isn't only a cliché! Tahiti gets just 140,000 tourists a year (compared to the seven million that visit Hawaii) and many are French nationals visiting friends, so you won't be facing a tourist glut! Despite over a century and a half of French colonialism, the Tahitians retain many of their old ways, be it in personal dress, Polynesian dancing, or outrigger canoe racing. Relax, smile, and say hello to strangers—you'll almost always get a warm response. Welcome to paradise!

POLYNESIA AT A GLANCE

	POPULATION (1988)	AREA (hectares)
WINDWARD ISLANDS	140,341	118,580
Tahiti	131,309	104,510
Moorea	8,801	12,510
LEEWARD ISLANDS	22,232	38,750
Huahine	4,479	7,480
Raiatea	8,560	17,140
Tahaa	4,005	9,020
Bora Bora	4,225	1,830
Maupiti	963	1,140
AUSTRAL ISLANDS	6,509	14,784
Rurutu	1,953	3,235
Tubuai	1,846	4,500
TUAMOTU ISLANDS	11,754	72,646
Rangiroa	1,305	7,900
Manihi	429	1,300
GAMBIER ISLANDS	620	4,597
MARQUESAS ISLANDS	7,358	104,930
Nuku Hiva	2,100	33,950
Hiva Oa	1,671	31,550
TAHITI-POLYNESIA	188,814	354,287

TAHITI-POLYNESIA

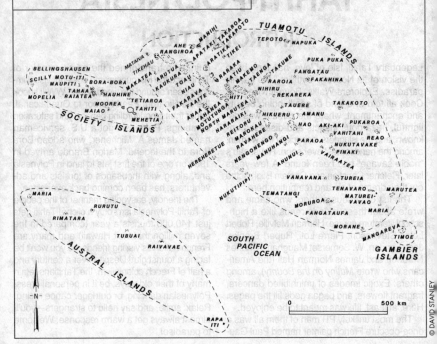

© DAVID STANLEY

Trouble in Paradise

In the early 1960s, President Charles de Gaulle transferred France's atomic testing program from Algeria to Moruroa Atoll in the Tuamotu Islands, 1,200 km southeast of Tahiti. Since then over 175 nuclear explosions, 44 of them in the atmosphere, have rocked the Tuamotus, spreading contamination as far as Peru and New Zealand.

The official French attitude to its Pacific colonies has changed little since 1842 when Admiral Du Petit-Thouars sailed into Papeete harbor and forced young Queen Pomare IV to sign a request for a French protectorate. In the 1960s-70s, as independence blossomed across the South Pacific, France tightened its strategic grip on Tahiti-Polynesia.

In April 1992, President Mitterrand halted the French nuclear testing program at Moruroa, but in June 1995, newly elected President Jacques Chirac ordered a resumption of underground nuclear testing in Polynesia. Deadly radiation could already be leaking into the sea from dumps and cracks at the French facilities on Moruroa, and the leakage of radioactive materials up through the atoll's coral cap could eventually contaminate the Pacific Ocean.

The release of this book may coincide with the actual nuclear testing itself, and we leave it up to the individual reader to decide whether he or she cares to visit Tahiti at that time. If you do go, take the opportunity to ask the Tahitians what they think about all of this.

THE LAND

Tahiti-Polynesia consists of five great archipelagos, the Society, Austral, Tuamotu, Gambier, and Marquesas islands. The Society Islands are subdivided into the Windwards, or *Îles du Vent* (Tahiti, Moorea, Maiao, Tetiaroa, and Mehetia), and the Leewards, or *Îles Sous le Vent* (Huahine, Raiatea, Tahaa, Bora Bora, Maupiti, Tupai, Maupihaa/Mopelia, Manuae/Scilly, and Motu One/Bellingshausen).

Together the 35 islands and 83 atolls of Tahiti-Polynesia total only 3,543 square km in land area, yet they're scattered over 5,030,000 square km of the southeastern Pacific Ocean, between 7° and 29° south latitude and 131° and 156° west longi-

tude. Though Tahiti-Polynesia is only half the size of Corsica in land area, if Papeete were Paris then the Gambiers would be in Romania and the Marquesas near Stockholm.

There's a wonderful geological diversity to these islands midway between Australia and South America—from the dramatic, jagged volcanic outlines of the Society and Marquesas islands, to the 400-meter-high hills of the Australs and Gambiers, to the low coral atolls of the Tuamotus. All of the Marquesas are volcanic islands, while the Tuamotus are all coral islands or atolls. The Societies and Gambiers include both volcanic and coral types.

Tahiti, just over 4,000 km from both Auckland and Honolulu, is not only the best known and most populous of the islands, but also the largest (1,045 square km) and highest (2,241 meters). Bora Bora and Maupiti are noted for their combination of high volcanic peaks within low coral rings. Rangiroa is one of the world's largest coral atolls while Makatea is an uplifted atoll. In the Marquesas, precipitous and sharply crenelated mountains rise hundreds of meters, with craggy peaks, razorback ridges, plummeting waterfalls, deep, fertile valleys, and dark broken coastlines pounded by surf. Compare them to the pencil-thin strips of yellow reefs, green vegetation, and white beaches enclosing the transparent Tuamotu lagoons. In all, Tahiti-Polynesia offers some of the most varied and spectacular scenery in the entire South Pacific.

Climate

The hot and humid summer season runs from November to April. The rest of the year the climate is somewhat cooler and drier. The refreshing southeast trade winds blow consistently from May to August, varying to easterlies from September to December. The northeast trades from January to April coincide with the hurricane season.

The trade winds are caused by hot air rising near the equator, which then flows toward the poles at high altitude. Cooler air drawn toward the vacuum is deflected to the west by the rotation of the earth. Tahiti-Polynesia's proximity to the intertropical convergence zone (5° north and south of the equator), or "doldrum zone"—where the most heated air is rising—explains

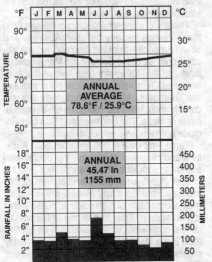

ATUONA'S CLIMATE

ANNUAL AVERAGE
78.6°F / 25.9°C

ANNUAL
45.47 in
1155 mm

PAPEETE'S CLIMATE

ANNUAL AVERAGE
77.7°F / 25.4°C

ANNUAL
73.74 in
1873 mm

the seasonal shift in the winds from northeast to southeast. The trade winds cool the islands and offer clear sailing for mariners, making May to October the most favorable season to visit.

Hurricanes are relatively rare, although they do hit the Tuamotus and occasionally Tahiti. From November 1980 to May 1983 an unusual wave of eight hurricanes and two tropical storms battered the islands. A hurricane would merely inconvenience a visitor staying at a hotel, though campers and yachties might get blown into oblivion. The days immediately following a hurricane are clear and dry. Tahiti-Polynesia enjoys some of the cleanest air on earth—air that hasn't blown over a continent for weeks.

Rainfall is greatest in the mountains and along the windward shores of the high islands. The Societies are far damper than the Marquesas. In fact, the climate of the Marquesas is erratic: some years the group experiences serious drought, other years it could rain the whole time you're there. The low-lying Tuamotus get the least rainfall of all. Tahiti-Polynesia encompasses such a vast area that latitude is an important factor: at 27° south latitude Rapa Iti is far cooler than Nuku Hiva (9° south).

Winds from the southeast *(maramu)* are generally drier than those from the northeast or north. The northeast winds often bring rain: Papenoo on the northeast side of Tahiti is twice as wet as rain-shadowed Punaauia. The annual rainfall is extremely variable, but the humidity is generally high, reaching 98%. In the evening the heat of the Tahiti afternoons is replaced by soft, fragrant mountain breezes called *hupe*, which drift down to the sea.

HISTORY

Discovery and Settlement

The eastern Polynesian islands, including those of Tahiti-Polynesia, were colonized at uncertain dates during the 1st millennium A.D. It's thought that about A.D. 300 the Polynesians reached the Marquesas from Samoa, and sometime around A.D. 500 they sailed on from the Marquesas to Hawaii and Easter Island. They were on the Society Islands by 800 and sailed from there to the Cooks and New Zealand around 1000, completing the occupation of the Polynesian triangle. These were planned voyages of colonization carrying all the plants and animals needed to continue their way of life.

Prior to European contact three hereditary classes structured the Society Islands: high chiefs *(ari'i)*, lesser chiefs *(raatira)*, and commoners *(manahune)*. A small slave class *(titi)* also existed. The various *ari'i* tribes controlled wedge-shaped valleys, and their authority was balanced. None managed to gain permanent supremacy over the rest.

Religion centered around an open-air temple, called a *marae*, with a stone altar. Here priests prayed to the ancestors or gods and conducted all the significant ceremonies of Polynesian life. An individual's social position was determined by his or her family connections, and the recitation of one's genealogy confirmed it. Human sacrifices took place on important occasions on a high chief's *marae*. Cannibalism was rife in the Marquesas and was also practiced in the Tuamotus.

The museums of the world possess many fine stone and wood tikis in human form from the Marquesas Islands, where the decorative sense was highly developed. Sculpture in the Australs was more naturalistic, and only here were female tikis common. The Tahitians showed less interest in the plastic arts but excelled in the social arts of poetry, oratory, theater, music, song, and dance. Life on the Tuamotus was a struggle for existence, and objects had utilitarian functions. Countless Polynesian cult objects were destroyed in the early 19th century by overzealous missionaries.

European Exploration

While the Polynesian history of the islands goes back at least 1,700 years, the European period only began in the 16th century when the Magellan expedition sailed past the Tuamotus and Mendaña visited the Marquesas. Quirós saw the Tuamotus in 1606, as did the Dutchmen Le Maire and Schouten in 1616 and Roggeveen in 1722. But it was not until 18 June 1767 that Capt. Samuel Wallis on the HMS *Dolphin* happened upon Tahiti. He and most of his contemporary explorers were in search of *terra australis incognita,* a mythical southern landmass thought to balance the Northern Hemisphere.

At first the Tahitians attacked the ship, but after experiencing European gunfire they decided to be friendly. Eager to trade, they loaded the Englishmen down with pigs, fowl, and fruit. Iron was in the highest demand, and Tahitian women lured the sailors to exchange nails for love. Consequently, to prevent the ship's timbers from being torn asunder for the nails, no man was allowed onshore except in parties strictly for food and water. Wallis sent ashore a landing party, which named Tahiti "King George III Island," turned some sod, and hoisted the Union Jack. A year later the French explorer Louis-Antoine de Bougainville arrived on the east coast, unaware of Wallis's discovery, and claimed Tahiti for the king of France.

Wallis and Bougainville only visited briefly, leaving it to Capt. James Cook to really describe Polynesia to Europeans. Cook visited "Otaheite" four times, in 1769, 1773, 1774, and 1777. His first three-month visit was to observe the transit of the planet Venus across the face of the sun. The second and third were in search of the southern continent, while the fourth was to locate a northwest passage between the Pacific and Atlantic oceans. Some of the finest artists and scientists of the day accompanied Captain Cook. Their explorations added the Leeward Islands, two Austral islands, and a dozen Tuamotu islands to European knowledge. On Tahiti Cook met a high priest from Raiatea named Tupaia, who had an astonishing knowledge of the Pacific and could name dozens of islands. He drew Cook a map that included the Cook Islands, the Marquesas, and perhaps also some Samoan islands!

In 1788 Tahiti was visited for five months by HMS *Bounty* commanded by Lt. William Bligh with orders to collect young breadfruit plants for transportation to the West Indies. However, the famous mutiny did not take place at Tahiti but in Tongan waters, and from there Bligh managed to escape by navigating an open boat 6,500 km to Dutch Timor. Thus in 1791, the HMS *Pandora* came to Tahiti in search of the *Bounty* mutineers, intending to take them to England for trial. They captured 14 survivors of the 16 who had elected to stay on Tahiti when Fletcher Christian and eight others left for Pitcairn. Although glamorized by Hollywood, the mutineers helped destroy traditional Tahitian society by acting as mercenaries for rival chiefs.

By the early 19th century, ruffian British and American whalers were fanning out over the

ARCHAEOLOGY

The first archaeological survey of Tahiti-Polynesia was undertaken in 1925 by Professor Kenneth P. Emory of Honolulu's Bernice P. Bishop Museum. Emory's successor, Professor Yoshihiko Sinoto of the same museum, has carried out extensive excavations and restorations in the area since 1960. In 1962, at a 9th-century graveyard on Maupiti's Motu Paeao, Emory and Sinoto uncovered artifacts perfectly matching those of the first New Zealand Maoris. A few years later, at Ua Huka in the Marquesas, Sinoto discovered a coastal village site dating from A.D. 300, the oldest yet found in Eastern Polynesia. Sinoto was responsible for the restoration of the Maeva *marae* on Huahine and many historical *marae* on Tahiti, Moorea, Raiatea, and Bora Bora. During construction of the Bali Hai Hôtel on Huahine in 1973-77 Sinoto's student diggers located 10 flat hand clubs of the *patu* model, previously thought to exist only in New Zealand, plus some planks of a 1,000-year-old sewn double canoe.

Pacific. Other ships traded with the islanders for sandalwood, bêche-de-mer, and mother-of-pearl, as well as the usual supplies. They brought with them smallpox, measles, influenza, tuberculosis, scarlet fever, and venereal diseases, which devastated the unprepared Polynesians. Slave raids, alcohol, and European firearms did the rest.

Kings and Missionaries

In 1797 the ship *Duff* dropped off on Tahiti 18 English missionaries and their wives. By this time Pomare, chief of the area adjoining Matavai Bay, had become powerful through the use of European tools, firearms, and mercenaries. He welcomed the missionaries but would not be converted; infanticide, sexual freedom, and human sacrifices continued. By 1800 all but five of the original 18 had left Tahiti disappointed.

In 1803 Pomare I died and his despotic son, Pomare II, attempted to conquer the entire island. After initial success he was forced to flee to Moorea in 1808. Missionary Henry Nott went with him, and in 1812 Pomare II turned to him for help in regaining his lost power. Though the missionaries refused to baptize Pomare II himself because of his heathen and drunken habits, his subjects on Moorea became nominal Christians. In 1815 this "Christian king" managed to regain Tahiti and overthrow paganism. The eager missionaries then enforced the Ten Commandments and dressed the Tahitian women in "Mother Hubbard" costumes—dresses that covered their bodies from head to toe. Henceforth singing anything but hymns was banned, dancing proscribed, and all customs that offended puritanical sensibilities wiped away. Morality police terrorized the confused Tahitians in an eternal crusade against sin. Even the wearing of flowers in the hair was prohibited.

The Rape of Polynesia

Upon Pomare II's death from drink at age 40 in 1821, the crown passed to his infant son, Pomare III, but he passed away in 1827. At this junction the most remarkable Tahitian of the 19th century, Aimata, half-sister of Pomare II, became Queen Pomare IV. She was to rule Tahiti, Moorea, and part of the Austral and Tuamotu groups for half a century until her death in 1877, a barefoot Tahitian Queen Victoria. She allied herself closely with the London Missionary Society (LMS), and when two French-Catholic priests, Honoré Laval and François Caret, arrived on Tahiti in 1836 from their stronghold at Mangareva (Gambier Islands), she expelled them promptly.

This affront brought a French frigate to Papeete in 1838, demanding $2000 compensation and a salute to the French flag. Although the conditions were met, the queen and her chiefs wrote to England appealing for help, but none came. A second French gunboat returned and threatened to bombard Tahiti unless its missionaries were given free entry. Back in Mangareva, Laval pushed forward a grandiose building program, which wiped out 80% of the population of the Gambiers from overwork.

A French consul named Moerenhout was appointed to Queen Pomare in 1838. In September 1842, while the queen and George Pritchard, the English consul, were away, he tricked a few local chiefs into signing a petition asking to be brought under French "protection." This demand was immediately accepted by French Admiral

Dupetit-Thouars, who was in league with Moerenhout, and on 9 September 1842 they forced Queen Pomare to accept a French protectorate. When the queen tried to maintain her power and kept her red-and-white royal flag, Dupetit-Thouars deposed the queen on 8 November 1843 and occupied her kingdom, an arbitrary act that was rejected by the French king who reestablished the protectorate in 1844. Queen Pomare fled to Raiatea and Pritchard was deported to England in March 1844, bringing Britain and France to the brink of war. The Tahitians resisted for three years: old French forts and war memorials recall the struggle.

A French Protectorate

At the beginning of 1847, when Queen Pomare realized that no British assistance was forthcoming, she and her people reluctantly accepted the French protectorate. As a compromise, the British elicited a promise from the French not to annex the Leeward Islands, so Huahine, Raiatea, and Bora Bora remained independent. The French had taken possession of the Marquesas in 1842, even before imposing a pro-

Queen Pomare IV

tectorate on Tahiti. French missionaries then attempted to convert the Tahitians to Catholicism, but only in the Marquesas were they successful.

Queen Pomare tried to defend the interests of her people as best she could, but much of her nation was dying: between the 18th century and 1926 the population of the Marquesas fell from 80,000 to only 2,000. In April 1774 Captain Cook had tried to estimate the population of Tahiti by counting the number of men he saw in a fleet of war canoes and ascribing three members to each one's family. Cook's figure was 204,000, but according to Bengt Danielsson, the correct number at the time of discovery was about 150,000. By 1829 it had dropped to 8,568, and a low of 7,169 was reached in 1865. The name "Pomare" means "night cough," from *po,* night, plus *mare,* cough, because Pomare I's infant daughter died of tuberculosis in 1792.

Pomare V, the final, degenerate member of the line, was more interested in earthly pleasures than the traditions upheld by his mother. In 1880, with French interests at work on the Panama Canal, a smart colonial governor convinced him to sign away his kingdom for a 5000-franc-a-month pension. Thus, on 29 June 1880 the protectorate became the full French colony it is today, the "Etablissements français de l'Océánie." In 1957 the name was changed to "Polynésie Française."

The most earthshaking event between 1880 and 1960 was a visit by two German cruisers, the *Scharnhorst* and *Gneisenau,* which shelled Papeete on 22 September 1914. (Both were subsequently sunk by the British at the Battle of the Falkland Islands.) On 2 September 1940 the colony declared its support for the Free French, and the Americans arrived to establish a base on Bora Bora soon after Pearl Harbor. Polynesia remained cut off from occupied metropolitan France until the end of the war, although Tahitians served with the Pacific battalion in North Africa and Italy.

Recent History

The early 1960s were momentous times for Polynesia. Within a few years, MGM filmed *Mutiny on the Bounty,* an international airport opened on Tahiti, and the French began testing

Then as now the French show off their military muscle in Polynesia. The cruiser Duquesne, *flagship of the French Pacific Squadron, and escorts were photographed in Papeete harbor during the mid-1880s.*

NAVAL HISTORY CENTER, WASHINGTON, D.C.

their atomic bombs. After Algeria became independent in July 1962 the French decided to move their Sahara nuclear testing facilities to the Tuamotus. In 1963, when all local political parties protested the invasion of Polynesia by thousands of French troops and technicians sent to establish a nuclear testing center, Pres. Charles de Gaulle simply outlawed political parties. The French set off their first atmospheric nuclear explosion at Moruroa on 2 July 1966. In 1974, 44 bombs later, international protests forced the French to switch to the underground tests that continue today.

The spirit of the time is best summed up in the life of one man, Pouvanaa a Oopa, an outspoken WW I hero from Huahine. In 1949 he became the first Polynesian to occupy a seat in the French Chamber of Deputies. In 1957 he was elected vice-president of the Government Council. A dedicated proponent of independence, Pouvanaa was arrested in 1958 on trumped-up charges of arson, eventually sentenced to an eight-year prison term, and exiled by the French government. De Gaulle wanted Pouvanaa out of the way until French nuclear testing facilities could be established in Poly-

nesia, and he was not freed until 1968. In 1971 he won the "French" Polynesian seat in the French Senate, a post he held until his death in early 1977. Tahitians refer to the man as *metua* (father), and his statue stands in front of Papeete's Territorial Assembly.

Pouvanaa's successors, John Teariki (now deceased) and Francis Sanford (since retired), were also defenders of Polynesian autonomy and opponents of nuclear testing. Their combined efforts convinced the French government to grant Polynesia a new statute with a slightly increased autonomy in 1977.

GOVERNMENT

In 1885 an organic decree created the colonial system of government, which remained in effect until the proclamation of a new statute in 1958, making Tahiti-Polynesia an overseas territory. In 1977 the French granted the territory partial internal self-government, and Francis Sanford was elected premier of "autonomous" Polynesia. A new local-government statute, passed by the French parliament and promulgated on 6 September 1984, gave only slightly more powers to the Polynesians; the constitution of the Republic of France remains the supreme law of the land.

A Territorial Assembly elects the president of the government, who chooses 10 ministers. The Territorial Assembly is responsible for public works, sports, health, social services, and primary education. The 41 assembly members are elected from separate districts, with 22 seats from Tahiti/Moorea, eight from the Leeward Islands, five from the Tuamotus and Gambiers, three from the Australs, and three from the Marquesas. One vote in the Tuamotus has the weight of three on Tahiti, and many constituencies have been gerrymandered. French soldiers and civil servants can vote in local elections the day they arrive in the territory, and there are thousands of them, including many in the Tuamotus.

The territory is represented in Paris by two elected deputies, a senator, and a social and economic counselor. The French government, through its high commissioner, assisted by a secretary-general of his choice, retains control over defense, foreign affairs, money, justice, immigration, the police, the civil service, foreign trade, TV and radio broadcasting, international communications, secondary education, and the municipal councils. As may be seen, the high commissioner has considerable power. He can also dissolve the Territorial Assembly, refer its decisions to an administrative tribunal, or take personal control of the territorial budget (as happened in 1992).

Tahiti-Polynesia is divided into 48 communes, each with an elected Municipal Council, which chooses a mayor from its ranks. These elected bodies, however, are controlled by appointed French civil servants, who run the five administrative subdivisions. The administrators of the Windward, Tuamotu-Gambier, and Austral subdivisions are based at Papeete, while the headquarters of the Leeward Islands administration is at Uturoa, and that of the Marquesas Islands is at Taiohae.

Politics

In 1982 the neo-Gaullist Tahoeraa Huiraatira (Popular Union) won the territorial elections, and the pronuclear, anti-independence mayor of Pirae, Gaston Flosse, became premier of the local government. In the 1986 territorial elections Flosse's party won a majority of assembly seats, but a year later Flosse resigned as president to devote his full time to the post of French secretary of state for the South Pacific. Flosse's reputation for fixing government contracts while in office earned him the title "Mr. Ten Percent" from the Paris newspaper *Libération*.

After rioting in Papeete and allegations of corruption, Tahoeraa deputy leader Alexandre Léontieff broke with Flosse in December 1987 and formed a coalition government with other Tahoeraa defectors and several smaller parties. Léontieff's 1987-91 administration was marked by financial mismanagement and political fence-sitting on the nuclear and independence issues, and the 17 March 1991 Territorial Assembly elections returned Flosse's Tahoeraa Huiraatira to power. Half of those voting for Flosse's party were French expatriates, civil servants, and military personnel.

The antinuclear, pro-independence Tavini Huiraatira No Te Ao Maohi (Polynesian Liberation Front), formed in 1978 by Faa'a mayor Oscar Temaru, doubled its assembly representation from two to four in the 1991 election. The *indépendentistes* are strongest in Papeete, weakest in the Tuamotus and Marquesas—areas heavily dependent on French aid.

ECONOMY

Government Spending

The inflow of people and money since the early 1960s has substituted consumerism for subsistence, and except for tourism and cultured pearls, the economy of Tahiti-Polynesia is now totally dominated by French government spending. Paris contributes very little to the territorial budget, but it finances the many departments and services under the direct control of the high commissioner, spending an average of US$300 million a year in the territory, two-thirds of it on the military. Much of the rest goes into salaries 1.84 times higher than those in France for 2,200 expatriate French civil servants.

Just a third of the population receives any direct benefit from French spending. The rest feel only the effects of inequalities and foreign interference. The nuclear testing program provoked an influx of 30,000 French settlers, plus a massive infusion of capital, which distorted the formerly self-supporting economy into one totally dependent on France.

In the early 1960s, many Polynesians left their homes for construction jobs with the *Centre d'Expérimentations du Pacifique* (CEP), the government, and the hotel chains. Now that the volume of this work is decreasing, most of them subsist in precarious circumstances on Tahiti, dependent on government spending. Some 2,000 locals are employed by the shameful testing program (compared to 10,000 in 1968). The CEP is headquartered at Pirae, just east of Papeete, with a major support base opposite the yacht club at Arue.

Tahiti-Polynesia has the highest gross domestic product per capita in the South Pacific (A$19,745 in 1990). The suspension of nuclear testing from 1992 to 1995 caused a recession as local workers were laid off and tax revenues on military imports suddenly dropped, so in 1993 the French government agreed to provide Tahiti-Polynesia with additional subsidies totaling US$118 million a year over five years as part of a "Pacte de Progrès" development plan. A condition was that new revenue had to be raised locally, so the territorial government introduced an income tax of three percent on earnings over CFP 150,000 a month where none had previously existed, plus new taxes on gasoline, wine, telecommunications, and unearned income.

Trade

Prior to the start of nuclear testing, trade was balanced. Only 29 years later, 1991 imports stood at A$1117 million while exports amounted to only A$156 million, one of the highest disparities in the world. Much of the imbalance is consumed by the French administration itself, and a quarter of imports are related to military activities. Foreign currency spent by tourists on imported goods and services also helps explain the situation.

Half the imports come from France, which has imposed a series of self-favoring restrictions. Imports include food, fuel, building material, consumer goods, and automobiles. The main agricultural export from the outer islands is copra which is heavily subsidized by the government. The copra is crushed into coconut oil and animal feed at the Papeete mill, while cultured pearls from farms in the Tuamotus are the biggest export by far. Perfume and vanilla are also exported.

Indirect taxes, such as customs duties of 20-200% and licensing fees, have long accounted for half of territorial government revenue, and the price of many imported goods is more than doubled by taxation. There's also a flat 35% levy on businesses, which is simply passed along to consumers.

Agriculture

Labor recruiting for the nuclear testing program caused local agriculture to collapse in the mid-'60s. Between 1962 and 1988 the percentage of the workforce employed in agriculture dropped from 50% to nine percent. Exports of coffee and vanilla had ceased completely by 1965 and coconut products dropped 40% despite massive subsidies. Today about 80% of all food consumed locally is imported. Tahiti-Polynesia does manage, however, to cover three-quarters of its own fruit requirements, and most of the local pineapple and grapefruit crop goes to the fruit-juice factory on Moorea. In the 1880s-90s four million oranges a year were exported to Australia, New Zealand, and California. The industry was wiped out by a blight at the turn of the century, and now only a few trees grow wild.

Local vegetables supply half of local needs, while Tahitian coffee only covers 20% of consumption. Considerable livestock is kept in the Marquesas. Large areas have been planted in Caribbean pine to provide for future timber needs. Aquaculture, with tanks for freshwater shrimp, prawns, live bait, and green mussels, is being developed. Most industry is related to food processing (fruit-juice factory, brewery, soft drinks, etc.) or coconut products. It's rumored that marijuana *(pakalolo)* is now the leading cash crop, though you won't be aware of it.

Cultured Pearls

Tahiti-Polynesia's cultured-pearl industry, now second only to tourism as a money earner, originated in 1963 when an experimental farm was established on Hikueru atoll in the Tuamotus. Today cooperative and private pearl farms operate on 26 atolls in Tahiti-Polynesia, employing thousands of people. Pearl farming is ecologically benign, relieving pressure on natural stocks and creating a need to protect marine environments. Pollution from fertilizer runoff or sewage can make a lagoon unsuitable for pearl farming, which is why the farms are concentrated on lightly populated atolls where other forms of agriculture are scarcely practiced.

Unlike the Japanese cultured white pearl, the Polynesian black pearl is created only by the giant blacklipped oyster *(Pinctada margaritifera)*, which thrives in the Tuamotu lagoons. Beginning in the 19th century the oysters were collected by Polynesian divers who could dive up to 40 meters. The shell was made into mother-of-pearl buttons; finding a pearl this way was pure chance. By the middle of this century overharvesting had depleted the slow-growing oyster beds and today live oysters are collected only to supply cultured-pearl farms. The shell is a mere by-product, made into decorative items or exported. The strings of oysters must be monitored constantly and lowered or raised if there are variations in water temperature.

It takes around three years for a pearl to form in a seeded oyster. A spherical pearl is formed when a Mississippi River mussel graft is introduced inside the coat; the oyster only creates a hemispherical half pearl if the graft goes between the coat and the shell. Half pearls are much cheaper than real pearls and make outstanding rings and pendants. Some of the grafts used are surprisingly large and the layer of nacre around such pearls may be relatively thin, but only an X-ray can tell.

The cooperatives sell their production at an auction in Papeete organized by the chamber of commerce each October. The pearls are offered to bidders in lots of about 400 which can attract bids as high as US$170,000. Local jewelers vie with Japanese buyers at these events, with some 50,000 black pearls changing hands for about US$5 million. Private producers sell their pearls through independent dealers or plush retail outlets in Papeete. In 1991 black pearl exports were worth A$54 million, with 60% going to Japan. The next largest agricultural export, coconut oil, brought in only A$3.3 million that year.

The relative newness of this gemstone is reflected in wildly varying prices. A brilliant, perfectly round, smooth, and flawless pearl with a good depth of metallic green-gray/blue-gray color can sell for 100 times more than a similar pearl with only one or two defects. Unless you really know your pearls it's intelligent to stick to the cheaper, even "baroque" ones, which, mounted in gold and platinum, still make exquisite jewelry. These pearls are now in fashion in Paris, so don't expect any bargains. Quality pearls cost US$1000 and up, but slightly flawed pearls are much cheaper (US$50 is average). Half the fun is in the shopping, so be in no hurry to decide. A reputable dealer will give you an invoice or certificate verifying the authenticity of your pearl.

Tourism

Two kinds of people visit Tahiti-Polynesia: packaged tourists on two-week trips from the States, who book all their accommodations in advance, stay at the best hotels, and travel interisland by air; and independent budget travelers (often young Europeans), who have more time, find a place to stay upon arrival, and travel by boat as much as possible. Tahiti, Moorea, Huahine, Raiatea, and Bora Bora are popular among visitors for their combination of beaches, mountain scenery, easy access, and the wealth of budget accommodations. The Society group is closely linked by sea and air, an island-hopper's playground.

Tourism only got underway with the opening of Faa'a Airport in 1961 and today Tahiti-Polynesia is second only to Fiji as a South Pacific tourist center, with 123,619 visitors in 1992, a third of them from the United States and another third from Europe. Yet tourism is far less developed than in Hawaii. A single Waikiki hotel could have more rooms than the entire island of Tahiti; Hawaii gets more visitors in 10 days than Tahiti-Polynesia gets in a year. In Tahiti-Polynesia only one tourist is present for every 100 inhabitants at any given time, while overcrowded Hawaii has 11.

Distance and reports of high prices have kept Tahiti out of the American mass market, and high local labor costs have hampered development. Now tourism by high-budget Japanese (especially honeymooners) is being vigorously promoted and the number of European visitors is growing quickly. The US$200 million a year generated by tourism covers 18% of Tahiti-Polynesia's import bill and provides 4,000 jobs, but 80% of the things tourists buy are also imported.

Transnational corporations, either hotel chains, tour companies, or airlines, dominate the tourist industry. Top management of the big hotels is invariably French or foreign, as ownership rests with Japanese (Beachcomber Parkroyal, Hyatt Regency, Moana Beach, Bora Bora Lagoon, Kia Ora Village), French (Sofitel, Club Med), and American (Bali Hai) corporations. Carriers such as Air New Zealand and Qantas only promote Tahiti as a stopover on the way Down Under, limiting many tourists to a few nights in Papeete.

In September 1989 the Japanese corporation Electronic and Industrial Enterprises (EIE) purchased four major hotels, in 1990 a Tokyo company bought Rangiroa's Kia Ora Village, and in 1993 the Bora Bora Lagoon Resort opened, as the Japanese scramble to recycle their massive foreign-exchange surpluses. Many Polynesians are rather nervous about this Japanese-driven development, and in June 1991 voters on Moorea decided against a US$93.4 million Sheraton hotel and Arnold Palmer championship golf course Japanese investors had wanted to build on their island. In May 1990 the 200 traditional owners of Tupai, just north of Bora Bora, blocked the atoll's sale to a Japanese corporation that had intended to build a major resort there. On Tahiti, a 1993 protest occupation by 600 Tahitians halted construction of a 330-room Méridien Hôtel complex near the Museum of Tahiti in Punaauia. As a result, planned Méridien developments on Moorea, Bora Bora, and Rangiroa have been put on hold.

THE PEOPLE

The criteria used for defining the racial groups making up the 1988 population of 188,814 are so unsatisfactory that only an approximate breakdown can be made: 70% Polynesian, 12% European, 10% Polynesian/European, five percent Chinese, and three percent Polynesian/Chinese. All are French citizens. About 70% of the total population lives on Tahiti (compared to only 25% before the nuclear-testing boom began in the 1960s), but a total of 65 far-flung islands are inhabited.

The indigenous people of Tahiti-Polynesia are the Maohi or Eastern Polynesians (as opposed to the Western Polynesians in Samoa and Tonga), and some local nationalists refer to their country as Maohinui. The word *colon* formerly applied to Frenchmen who arrived long before the bomb and made a living as planters or traders, and practically all of them married Polynesian women. Most of these *colons* have already passed away and their descendants are termed *demis,* or *afa.* The present Europeans are mostly recently arrived metropolitan French *(faranis).* Most *faranis* live in urban areas or are involved in the administration or military. Their numbers increased dramatically in the 1960s and 1970s.

Local Chinese *(tinito)* dominate the retail trade throughout the territory. In Papeete and Uturoa entire streets are lined with Chinese stores, and individual Chinese merchants are found on almost every island. During the American Civil War, when the supply of cotton to Europe was disrupted, Scotsman William Stewart decided to set up a cotton plantation on the south side of Tahiti. Unable to convince Tahitians to accept the heavy work, Stewart brought in a contingent of 1,010 Chinese laborers from Canton in 1865-66. When the war ended the enterprise

a Polynesian woman

went bankrupt, but many of the Chinese managed to stay on as market gardeners or shopkeepers.

From 1976 to 1983 some 18,000 people migrated to the territory, 77% of them from France and another 13% from New Caledonia. Nearly 1,000 new settlers a year continue to arrive. Some 40,000 Europeans are now present in the territory, plus 8,000 soldiers, policemen, and transient officials. Most Tahitians would like to see this immigration restricted, as it is in virtually every other Pacific state. Yet with the integration of the European Union, all 300 million E.U. citizens may soon gain the right to live in Polynesia. To protest this threatened "second invasion" (the first, related to nuclear testing, began in 1963), all local political parties boycotted the 1989 elections to the European Parliament.

There's an undercurrent of anti-French sentiment; English speakers are better liked by the Tahitians. Yet inevitably the newcomers get caught up in the Polynesian openness and friendliness—even the surliest Parisian. In fact, the Gallic charm you'll experience even in government offices is a delight. Tahiti-Polynesia really is a friendly place.

Big Bad Mama proves she can pull a paddle as well as the rest.

Tahitian Life

For the French, lunch is the main meal of the day, followed by a siesta. Dinner may consist of leftovers from lunch. Tahitians traditionally eat their main meal of fish and native vegetables in the evening, when the day's work is over. People at home often take a shower before or after a meal and put flowers in their hair. If they're in a good mood a guitar or ukulele might appear.

Tahitians often observe with amusement or disdain the efforts of individuals to rise above the group. In a society where sharing and reciprocal generosity have traditionally been important qualities, the deliberate accumulation of personal wealth was always viewed as a vice. Now with the influx of government and tourist money, Tahitian life is changing, quickly in Papeete, more slowly in the outer islands. To prevent the Polynesians from being made paupers in their own country, foreigners other than French are not usually permitted to purchase land here and 85% of the land is still owned by the Polynesians. A new impoverished class is forming among those who have sold their ancestral lands to recent French immigrants.

The educational curriculum is entirely French. Children enter school at age three and for 12 years study the French language, literature, culture, history, and geography, but not much about Polynesia. The failure rate ranges 40-60%, and most of the rest of the children are behind schedule. The best students are given scholarships to continue studying, while many of the dropouts become delinquents. About half the schools are privately run by the churches, but these must teach exactly the same curriculum or lose their subsidies. The whole aim is to transform the Polynesians into Pacific French. In 1987 the Université française du Pacifique (B.P. 4635, Papeete; tel. 42-16-80, fax 41-01-31) opened on Tahiti, specializing in law, humanities, social sciences, languages, and science.

Most Tahitians live along the coast because the interior is too rugged and possibly inhabited by *tupapau* (ghosts). Some people leave a light on all night in their home for the latter reason. A traditional Tahitian residence consists of several separate buildings: the *fare tutu* (kitchen), the *fare tamaa* (dining area), the *fare taoto* (bedrooms), plus bathing and sanitary outhouses. Often several generations live together, and young children are sent to live with their grandparents. Adoption is commonplace and family relationships complex. Young Tahitians generally go out as groups, rather than on individual "dates."

The lifestyle may be summed up in the words *aita e peapea* (no problem) and *fiu* (fed up, bored). About the only time the normally languid Tahitians go really wild is when they're dancing or behind the wheel of a car.

Sex

Since the days of Wallis and Bougainville, Tahitian women have had a reputation for promiscuity. Well, for better or worse, this is largely a thing of the past, if it ever existed at all. As a short-term visitor your liaisons with Tahitians are likely to remain polite. Westerners' obsession with the sexuality of Polynesians usually reflects their own frustrations, and the view that Tahitian morality is loose is rather ironic considering that Polynesians have always shared whatever they have, cared for their old and young, and refrained from ostracizing unwed mothers or attaching stigma to their offspring. The good Christian Tahitians of today are highly moral and compassionate.

Polynesia's *mahus* or "third sex" bear little of the stigma attached to female impersonators in the West. A young boy may adopt the female role by his own choice or that of his parents, performing female tasks at home and eventually finding a job usually performed by women, such as serving in a restaurant or hotel. Usually only one *mahu* exists in each village or community, proof that this type of individual serves a certain sociological function. George Mortimer of the British ship *Mercury* recorded an encounter with a *mahu* in 1789. Though Tahitians may poke fun at a *mahu,* they're fully accepted in society, seen teaching Sunday school, etc. Many, but not all, *mahus* are also homosexuals. Today, with money all-important, some transvestites have involved themselves in male prostitution and the term *raerae* has been coined for this category. Now there are even Miss Tane (Miss Male) beauty contests! All this may be seen as the degradation of a phenomenon that has always been part of Polynesian life.

Religion

Though the old Polynesian religion died out in the early 19th century, the Tahitians are still a strongly religious people. Protestant missionaries arrived on Tahiti 39 years before the Catholics and 47 years before the Mormons, so over half of the Polynesians now belong to the Evangelical Church, which is strongest in the Austral and Leeward Islands. Of the 34% of the total population who are Catholic, half are Polynesians from the Tuamotus and Marquesas, and the other half are French. Another six percent are Mormons. Seventh-Day Adventists and Jehovah's Witnesses are also represented, and some Chinese are Buddhists. It's not unusual to see two or three different churches in a village of 100 people. All the main denominations operate their own schools. Local ministers and priests are powerful figures in the outer-island communities. One vestige of the pre-Christian religion is a widespread belief in ghosts *(tupapau).*

Protestant church services are conducted mostly in Tahitian, Catholic services are in French. Sitting through one (one to two hours) is often worthwhile just to hear the singing and to observe the women's hats. Never wear a pareu to church—you'll be asked to leave. Young missionaries from the Church of Latter-day Saints (Mormons) continue to flock to Polynesia from the U.S. for two-year stays. They wear short-sleeved white shirts with ties and travel in pairs—you may spot a couple.

Language

Tahitian and French are both official languages, but official documents and speeches as a rule are in French and are rarely translated. French is spoken throughout the territory, and visitors will sometimes have difficulty making themselves understood in English, although everyone involved in the tourist industry speaks English. It's useful to brush up on your high school French a little by checking out some French language records/tapes from your local public library before you arrive. The "Capsule French Vocabulary" at the end of the New Caledonia chapter may also help you get by. Large Chinese stores often have someone who speaks English, though members of the Chinese community use "Hakka" among themselves. Young Polynesians often become curious and friendly when they hear you speaking English.

Tahitian or Maohi is one of a family of Austronesian languages spoken from Madagascar through Indonesia, all the way to Easter Island and Hawaii. The related languages of Eastern Polynesia (Hawaiian, Tahitian, Tuamotuan, Mangarevan, Marquesan, Maori) are quite different from those of Western Polynesia (Samoan, Tongan). Today, as communications improve, the outer-island dialects are becoming mingled with the predominant Tahitian. Among the Polynesian languages the consonants did the changing rather than the vowels. The *k* and *l* in Hawaiian are generally rendered as a *t* and *r* in Tahitian.

Instead of attempting to speak French to the Tahitians—a foreign language for you both—turn to the Tahitian vocabulary at the end of this chapter and give it a try. Remember to pronounce each vowel separately, *a* as the *ah* in "far," *e* as the *ai* in "day," *i* as the *ee* in "see," *o* as the *oh* in "go," and *u* as the *oo* in "lulu"—same as in Latin or Spanish. Written Tahitian has only eight consonants: *f, h, m, n, p, r, t, v.* Two consonants never follow one another, and all words end in a vowel. No silent letters exist in Tahitian, but there is a glottal stop, often marked with an apostrophe. A slight variation in pronunciation or vowel length can change the meaning of a word completely, so don't be surprised if your efforts produce some unexpected results!

CONDUCT AND CUSTOMS

The dress code in Tahiti-Polynesia is very casual—you can even go around barefoot.

Cleanliness *is* important, however. Formal wear or jacket and tie are unnecessary (unless you're to be received by the high commissioner!). One exception is downtown Papeete, where scanty dress would be out of place. For clothing tips, see "What to Take" in the On the Road chapter.

People usually shake hands when meeting; visitors are expected to shake hands with everyone present. If a Polynesian man's hand is dirty he'll extend his wrist or elbow. Women kiss each other on the cheeks. When entering a private residence it's polite to remove your shoes. It's okay to show interest in the possessions of a host, but don't lavish too much praise on any single object or he/she may feel obligated to give it to you. It's rude to refuse food offered by a Tahitian, but don't eat everything on your plate just to be polite, as this will be a signal to your host that you want another helping. Often guests in a private home are expected to eat while the family watches.

All the beaches of Tahiti-Polynesia are public to one meter above the high-tide mark, although some watchdogs don't recognize this. Topless sunbathing is completely legal in Tahiti-Polynesia, though total nudity is only practiced on offshore *motus* and floating pontoons.

Despite the apparent laissez-faire attitude promoted in the travel brochures and this book, female travelers should take care: there have been sexual assaults by Polynesian men on foreign women who seemed to project an image of promiscuity by sunbathing topless on a remote beach or even by traveling alone! Women should avoid staying in isolated tourist bungalows or camping outside organized campgrounds. We've also heard of cases of laundry being stolen from the line, hotel and car break-ins, park muggings, and even mass holdups at knifepoint, but luckily such things are still the exception here.

ON THE ROAD

Highlights

Tahiti-Polynesia abounds in things to see and do, including many in the "not to be missed" category. Papeete's colorful morning market and captivating waterfront welcome you to Polynesia. No visitor should miss the ferry ride to Moorea and the island's stunning Opunohu Valley, replete with splendid scenery, lush vegetation, and fascinating archaeological sites. Farther afield, an even greater concentration of old Polynesian *marae* (temples) awaits visitors to Maeva on the enchanting island of Huahine. The natural wonders of Bora Bora have been applauded many times but neighboring Maupiti has more of the same, though its pleasures are far less known. Polynesia's most spectacular atoll may be Rangiroa, where the Avatoru and Tiputa passes offer exciting snorkel rides on the incoming tide.

Sports and Recreation

As elsewhere in the South Pacific, scuba diving is the most popular sport among visitors, and well-established dive shops exist on Tahiti, Moorea, Huahine, Raiatea, Bora Bora, Rangiroa, and Tikehau. Prices are highest on Bora Bora, so you may want to schedule your diving elsewhere. Instead, take one of the highly recommended boat trips (with shark feeding) on the Bora Bora lagoon. At Rangiroa, divers get to float through the pass for their money. In these warm waters wetsuits are not required. Golfers will certainly want to complete the 18 holes at the International Golf Course Olivier Breaud on Tahiti, the territory's only major course. Horseback riding is available on Moorea, Huahine, and Raiatea, with the Huahine operation especially recommended. Virtually all of Tahiti-Polynesia's charter yacht operations are concentrated on Raiatea.

Entertainment

The big hotels on Tahiti and Bora Bora offer exciting dance shows several nights a week. They're usually accompanied by a barbecue or traditional feast, but if the price asked for the meal is too steep, settle for a drink at the bar and enjoy the show (no cover charge). Many of the regular performances are listed in this book, but be sure to call the hotel to confirm the time and date as these do change to accommodate tour groups.

On Friday and Saturday nights discos crank up in most towns and these are good places to meet the locals. The nonhotel bar scene is limited mostly to Papeete. The drinking age in Tahiti-Polynesia is officially 18, but it's not strictly enforced.

Music and Dance

Though the missionaries banned dancing completely in the 1820s and the 19th-century French colonial administration only allowed performances that didn't disturb Victorian decorum, traditional Tahitian dancing experienced a revival in the 1950s with the formation of Madeleine Moua's Pupu Heiva dance troupe, followed in the 1960s by Coco Hotahota's Temaeva and Gilles Hollande's Ora Tahiti. These groups rediscovered the near-forgotten myths of old Polynesia and popularized them

TAHITI TOURISME

with exciting music, dance, song, and costumes. Now during major festivals several dozen troupes of 20-50 dancers and six to 10 musicians participate in thrilling competitions.

The Tahitian *tamure* or *'ori Tahiti* is a fast, provocative, erotic dance done by rapidly shifting the weight from one foot to the other. The rubber-legged men are almost acrobatic, though their movements tend to follow those of the women closely. The tossing, shell-decorated bast or fiber skirts *(mores),* the pandanus wands in the hands, and the tall headdresses add to the drama.

Dances such as the *aparima,* *'ote'a,* and *hivinau* reenact Polynesian legends, and each movement tells part of a story. The *aparima* is a dance resembling the Hawaiian hula or Samoan siva executed mainly with the hands in a standing or sitting position. The hand movements repeat the story told in the accompanying song. The *'ote'a* is a theme dance executed to the accompaniment of drums with great precision and admirable timing by a group of men and/or women arrayed in two lines. The *ute* is a restrained dance based on ancient refrains.

Listen to the staccato beat of the *to'ere,* a slit rosewood-wood drum, each slightly different in size and pitch, hit with a stick. A split-bamboo drum *(ofe)* hit against the ground often provides a contrasting sound. The *pahu* is a more conventional bass drum made from a hollowed coconut tree trunk with a sharkskin cover. Another traditional Polynesian musical instrument is the bamboo nose flute *(vivo),* though today guitars and ukuleles are more often seen. The ukulele was originally the *braguinha,* brought to Hawaii by Portuguese immigrants a century ago. Homemade ukuleles with the half-shells of coconuts as sound boxes emit pleasant tones, while those sporting empty tins give a more metallic sound.

Traditional Tahitian vocal music was limited to nonharmonious chants conveying oral history and customs, and the *himene* or "hymn" sung by large choirs today is based on these ancient chants. The spiritual quality of the *himene* can be electrifying, so for the musical experience of a lifetime, attend church any Sunday.

Stone Fishing

This traditional method of fishing is now practiced only on very special occasions in the Lee-

The race of the banana bearers is part of July's Tiurai Festival.

ward Islands. Coconut fronds are tied end to end until a line a half-km long is ready. Several dozen outrigger canoes form a semicircle. Advancing slowly together, men in the canoes beat the water with stones tied to ropes. The frightened fish are thus driven toward a beach. When the water is shallow enough, the men leap from their canoes, push the leaf line before them, yell, and beat the water with their hands. In this way the fish are literally forced ashore into an open bamboo fence, where they are caught. See "Tahaa" under "Raiatea and Tahaa" in this chapter for more information.

Public Holidays and Festivals

Public holidays in Tahiti-Polynesia include New Year's Day (1 January), Gospel Day (5 March), Good Friday and Easter Monday (March/April), Labor Day (1 May), Ascension Day (May), Whitsunday and Whitmonday (May/June), Bastille Day (14 July), Assumption Day (15 August), Internal Autonomy Day (29 June), All Saints' Day (1 November), Armistice Day (11 November), and Christmas Day (25 December). Ironically, Internal Autonomy Day actually commemorates 29 June

1880 when Tahiti-Polynesia became a full French colony, not 6 September 1984 when the territory achieved a small degree of internal autonomy. *Everything* will be closed on these holidays (and maybe also the days before and after—ask).

The big event of the year is the two-week-long **Heiva i Tahiti,** which runs from the end of June to Bastille Day (14 July). Formerly known as La Fête du Juillet or the Tiurai Festival (the Tahitian word *tiurai* comes from the English July), it brings contestants and participants to Tahiti from all over the territory to take part in elaborate processions, competitive dancing and singing, feasting, and partying. There are bicycle, car, horse, and outrigger-canoe races, petanque, archery, and javelin-throwing contests, sidewalk bazaars, arts and crafts exhibitions, tattooing, games, and joyous carnivals. **Bastille Day** itself, which marks the fall of the Bastille in Paris on 14 July 1789 at the height of the French Revolution, features a military parade in the capital. Ask at the Papeete tourist office about when to see the historical reenactments at Marae Arahurahu, the canoe race along Papeete waterfront, horse racing at the Pirae track, and the traditional dance competitions at the Moorea ferry landing. Tickets to most Heiva events are sold at the Cultural Center in Papeete or at the door. As happens during carnival in Rio de Janeiro, you must pay to sit in the stands and watch the best performances, but acceptable seats begin at just CFP 500 and you get four hours or more of unforgettable non-stop entertainment.

The July celebrations on Bora Bora are as good as those on Tahiti, and not as commercial. Note that all ships, planes, and hotels are fully booked around 14 July, so be in the right place beforehand or get firm reservations, especially if you want to be on Bora Bora that day.

Chinese New Year in January or February is celebrated with dances and fireworks. On Nuclear-Free and Independent Pacific Day (1 March), a protest march proceeds from Faa'a to Papeete, to commemorate a disastrous nuclear test on Bikini atoll in Micronesia that day in 1954. On **All Saints' Day** (1 November) the locals illuminate the cemeteries at Papeete, Arue, Punaauia, and elsewhere with candles. On **New Year's Eve** the Papeete waterfront is beautifully illuminated and there's a seven-km footrace.

Ask at the Departement Fêtes et Manifestations in Papeete's Cultural Center (B.P. 1709, Papeete; tel. 42-88-50) about special events, and check the daily papers.

Shopping

Most local souvenir shops sell Marquesas-style wooden "tikis" carved from wood or stone. The original Tiki was a god of fertility, and really old tikis are still shrouded in superstition. Today they're viewed mainly as good luck charms and often come decorated with mother-of-pearl. Other items carved from wood include mallets (to beat tapa cloth), *umete* bowls, and slit *to'ere* drums. Carefully woven pandanus hats and mats come from the Australs. Other curios to buy include hand-carved mother-of-pearl shell, sharks'-tooth pendants, hematite (black stone) carvings, and bamboo fishhooks.

Black-pearl jewelry is widely available throughout Tahiti-Polynesia. The color, shape, weight, and size of the pearl are important. The darkest pearls are the most valuable. Prices vary considerably, so shop around before purchasing pearls. For more information on Polynesia's fabulous black pearls, see "Economy" earlier in this chapter.

As this is a French colony, it's not surprising that many of the best buys are related to fashion. A tropical shirt, sundress, or T-shirt is a purchase of immediate usefulness. The pareu is a typically Tahitian leisure garment consisting of a brightly colored hand-blocked or painted local fabric about two meters long and a meter wide. There are dozens of ways both men and women can wear a pareu and it's the most common apparel for local women throughout the territory, including Papeete, so pick one up! Local cosmetics like Monoi Tiare Tahiti, a fragrant coconut-oil skin moisturizer, and coconut-oil soap will put you in form. Jasmine shampoo, cologne, and perfume are also made locally from the tiare Tahiti flower. Vanilla is used to flavor coffee.

Early missionaries introduced the Tahitians to quilting, and two-layer patchwork *tifaifai* have now taken the place of tapa (bark cloth). Used as bed covers and pillows by tourists, *tifaifai* is still used by Tahitians to cloak newlyweds and to cover coffins. To be wrapped in a *tifaifai* is the highest honor. Each woman has individual quilt patterns that are her trademarks and bold floral designs are popular, with contrasting colors drawn from nature. A good *tifaifai* can take up to six months to complete and cost US$1000. The French artist Henri Matisse, who in 1930 spent several weeks at the now-demolished Stuart Hôtel on Papeete's boulevard Pomare, was so impressed by the Tahitian *tifaifai* that he applied the same technique and adopted many designs for his *"gouaches découpees."*

Those who have been thrilled by hypnotic Tahitian music and dance will want to take some Polynesian music home with them on cassette (CFP 2000) or compact disc (CFP 3000), available at hotels and souvenir shops throughout the islands. The largest local company producing these CDs is Editions Manuiti or Tamure Records (B.P. 755, Papeete; tel. 42-82-39, fax 43-27-24). Among the well-known local singers and musicians appearing on Manuiti are Bimbo, Charley Mauu, Guy Roche, Yves Roche, Emma Terangi, Andy Tupaia, and Henriette Winkler. Small Tahitian groups like the Moorea Lagon Kaina Boys, the Barefoot Boys, and Tamarii Punaruu, and large folkloric ensembles such as Maeva Tahiti, Tiare Tahiti, and Coco's Temaeva (often recorded at major festivals) are also well represented. Turn to "Resources" at the end of this book for specific CD listings.

Hustling and bargaining are not practiced in Tahiti-Polynesia: it's expensive for everyone. Haggling may even be considered insulting, so just pay the price asked or keep looking. Many local food prices are subsidized by the government. Avoid whopping markups and taxes; instead, purchase food and handicrafts from the producers themselves at markets or roadside stalls. Luckily, there's no sales tax in Tahiti!

ACCOMMODATIONS AND FOOD

Accommodations

A wise government regulation prohibiting buildings higher than a coconut tree outside Papeete means that most of the hotels are low-rise or consist of small Tahitian *fares.* As the lagoon waters off the northwest corner of Tahiti become increasingly polluted with raw sewage, hotels like the Beachcomber and Maeva Beach fall back on their swimming pools. On all of the outer islands open to foreign tourists, the water is so clear it makes pools superfluous.

Hotel prices range from CFP 800 for a dormitory bed all the way up to CFP 58,000 single or double without meals, plus tax. Price wars often erupt between rival hotels, and at times you're charged less than the prices quoted herein! When things are really slow even the luxury hotels sometimes discount their rooms. If your hotel can't provide running water, electricity, air-conditioning, or something similar because of a hurricane or otherwise, ask for a price reduction. You'll often get 10% off. The budget places often provide cooking facilities, which allow you to save a lot on food. An eight percent room tax is added to the room rates at the hotels, but it doesn't apply to pensions and family-operated accommodations (the tax is used to finance tourism promotion). Many small hotels add a surcharge to your bill if you stay only one night and some charge a supplement during the high season (July, August, and at Christmas).

A tent saves the budget traveler a lot of money and proves very convenient to fall back on. The Polynesians don't usually mind if you camp, and quite a few French locals also have tents. Regular campgrounds exist on Tahiti, Moorea, Raiatea, and Bora Bora, catering to the growing number of camper-tourists. On Huahine and Rangiroa it's possible to camp at certain small hotels (listed herein). On the outer islands camping should be no problem, but ask permission of the landowner, or pitch your tent well out of sight of the road. Ensure this same hospitality for the next traveler by not leaving a mess. Make sure your tent is water- and mosquito-proof and never pitch a tent directly below coconuts hanging from a tree or a precariously leaning trunk.

Paying Guests

A unique accommodations option worth looking into is the well-organized homestay program, in which you get a private room or bungalow with a local family. *Logement chez l'habitant* is available on all the outer islands, and even in Papeete itself; the tourist office supplies printed lists. Travel agents abroad won't book the cheaper hotels or lodgings with the inhabitants because no commissions are paid, so you must make reservations directly with the owners themselves by either mail or phone. Letters are usually not answered, so calling ahead from Papeete is best; things change fast and printed listings are often out of date. Most pensions don't accept credit cards, and English may not be spoken.

These private guesthouses can be hard to locate. There's usually no sign outside, and some don't cater to walk-in clients who show up unexpectedly. Also, the limited number of beds in each may all be taken. Sometimes you'll get airport transfers at no additional charge if you book ahead. Don't expect hot water in the bath or a lot of privacy. Often cooking facilities or meals are included (often seafood); the provision of blankets and towels may depend on the price. The family may loan you a bicycle and can be generally helpful in arranging tours, etc. It's a great way to meet the people while finding a place to stay.

Food and Drink

Restaurants are expensive, but you can bring the price way down by ordering only a single main dish. Fresh bread and cold water come with the meal. Avoid appetizers, alcohol, and desserts. No taxes or service charges are tacked on, and tipping is unnecessary. So it's really not as expensive as it looks! US$15 will usually see you through an excellent no-frills lunch of fried fish at a small French restaurant. The same thing in a hotel dining room will be about 50% more. Even the finest places are affordable if you order this way.

Most restaurants post their menu in the window. If not, have a look at it before sitting down. Check the main plates, as that's all you'll need to take. If the price is right, the ambience is congenial, and local French are at the tables, sit right down. Sure, food at a snack bar would be half as much, but your Coke will be extra, and in the end it's smart to pay a little more to enjoy excellent cuisine once in a while. Steer clear of restaurants where you see a big plastic bottle of mineral water on every table, as this will add a couple of hundred francs to your bill. Also beware of set meals designed for tourists as these usually cost double the average entree. If you can't order a la carte walk back out the door.

Local restaurants offer French, Chinese, Vietnamese, Italian, and, of course, Tahitian dishes. The nouvelle cuisine Tahitienne is a combination of European and Asian recipes, with local seafoods and vegetables, plus the classic maa Tahiti (Tahitian food). The French are famous for their sauces, so try something exotic. Lunch is the main meal of the day in Tahiti-Polynesia, and many restaurants offer a plat du jour designed for regular customers. This is often displayed on a blackboard near the entrance and is usually good value. Most restaurants stop serving lunch at 1400, dinner at 2200. Don't expect snappy service: what's the rush, anyway?

If it's all too expensive, groceries are a good alternative. There are lots of nice places to picnic, and at CFP 35 a loaf, that crisp French white bread is incredibly cheap and good. French baguettes are subsidized by the government, unlike that awful sliced white bread in a plastic package that's CFP 240 a loaf! Cheap red wines like Selection Faragui are imported from France in bulk and bottled locally in plastic bottles. Add a nice piece of French cheese to the above and you're ready for a budget traveler's banquet. Casse-croûtes, big healthy sandwiches made with those long French baguettes, are CFP 250.

There's also Martinique rum and Hinano beer (CFP 130 in grocery stores), brewed locally by Heineken. Remember the CFP 60 deposit on Hinano beer bottles, which makes beer cheap to buy cold and carry out. Moorea's famous Rotui fruit drinks are sold in tall liter containers in a variety of types. The best is perhaps pamplemousse (grapefruit), produced from local Moorea fruit, but the pineapple juice is also outstanding. At about CFP 210 a carton, they're excellent value.

Tahitian Food

If you can spare the cash, attend a Tahitian tamaaraa (feast) at a big hotel and try some Polynesian dishes roasted in an ahimaa (underground oven). Basalt stones are preheated with a wood fire in a meter-deep pit, then covered with leaves. Each type of food is wrapped separately in banana leaves to retain its own flavor and lowered in. The oven is covered with more banana leaves, wet sacking, and sand, and left one to three hours to bake: suckling pig, mahimahi, taro, umara (sweet potato), uru (breadfruit), and fafa, a spinachlike cooked vegetable made from taro tops.

Also sample the gamy flavor of *fei,* the red cooking banana that flourishes in Tahiti's uninhabited interior. The Tahitian chestnut tree *(mape)* grows near streams and the delicious cooked nuts can often be purchased at markets. *Miti hue* is a coconut-milk sauce fermented with the juice of river shrimp. Traditionally *maa Tahiti* is eaten with the fingers.

Poisson cru (ia ota), small pieces of raw bonito (skipjack) or yellowfin marinated with lime juice and soaked in coconut milk, is enjoyable, as is *fafaru* ("smelly fish"), prepared by marinating pieces of fish in seawater in an airtight coconut-shell container. Like with the durian, although the smell is repugnant, the first bite can be addicting. Other typical Tahitian plates are chicken and pork casserole with *fafa,* pork and cabbage casserole *(pua'a chou),* and kid cooked in ginger.

Poe is a sweet pudding made of starch flour flavored with either banana, vanilla, papaya, taro, or pumpkin and topped with salted coconut-milk sauce. Many varieties of this treat are made throughout Polynesia. *Faraoa ipo* is Tuamotu coconut bread. The local coffee is flavored with vanilla bean and served with sugar and coconut cream.

SERVICES AND INFORMATION

Visas and Officialdom

Everyone needs a passport. French citizens are admitted freely for an unlimited stay, and citizens of the European Union (E.U.) countries, Norway, and Switzerland, get three months without a visa. Citizens of the United States, Canada, New Zealand, and Japan can obtain a one-month "visa" free upon arrival at Papeete (no different than any other passport stamp). Most others (Australians included) must apply to a French diplomatic mission for a three-month visa (US$50), but it's usually issued without delay. Make sure the words "French Polynesia" are endorsed on the visa, otherwise you could have problems.

Extensions of stay are possible after you arrive, but they cost CFP 3000 and you'll have to go to the post office to buy a stamp. You'll also need to show "sufficient funds" and your ticket to leave Tahiti-Polynesia and provide one photo.

North Americans are limited to three months total; it's better to ask for a three-month stay upon arrival, making this formality unnecessary.

Tahiti-Polynesia requires a ticket to leave of everyone (including nonresident French citizens). If you arrive without one, you'll be refused entry or required to post a cash bond equivalent to the value of a ticket back to your home country. If you're on an open-ended holiday, you can easily get around this requirement by purchasing a refundable Air New Zealand ticket back to the U.S. or wherever before leaving home. If you catch a boat headed to Fiji, for example, simply have the airline reissue the ticket so it's a ticket to leave from your next destination—and on you go.

Yacht Entry

The main port of entry for cruising yachts is Papeete. Upon application to the local gendarme, entry may also be allowed at Moorea, Huahine, Raiatea, Bora Bora, Rurutu, Tubuai, Raivavae, Rangiroa, Nuku Hiva, Hiva Oa, or Ua Pou. The gendarmes are usually friendly and courteous, if you are. Boats arriving from Tonga, Fiji, and the Samoas must be fumigated.

Anyone arriving by yacht without an onward ticket must post a bond at a local bank equivalent to the airfare back to their country of origin. In Taiohae the bond is US$1200 pp, but in Papeete it's only US$600 (for Americans). This is refundable upon departure at any branch of the same bank, less a three percent administrative fee. Make sure the receipt shows the currency in which the original deposit was made and get an assurance that it will be refunded in kind. To reclaim the bond you'll also need a letter from Immigration verifying that you've officially checked out. If any individual on the yacht doesn't have the bond money, the captain is responsible. Once the bond is posted, a "temporary" three-month visa (CFP 3000) is issued, which means you have three months to get to Papeete where an additional three months (another CFP 3000) may be granted. Actually, the rules are not hard-and-fast, and everyone has a different experience. Crew changes should be made at Papeete.

After clearing Customs in Papeete, outbound yachts may spend the duration of their period of stay cruising the outer islands. Make sure every island where you *might* stop is listed on your clearance. The officials want all transient boats out of the country by 31 October, the onset of the hurricane season. Yachts staying longer than one year are charged full Customs duty on the vessel.

Money

The French Pacific franc or *Cour de Franc Pacifique* (CFP) is legal tender in both Tahiti-Polynesia and New Caledonia. There are beautifully colored big banknotes of CFP 500, 1000, 5000, and 10,000, coins of CFP 1, 2, 5, 10, 20, 50, and 100.

The CFP is fixed at one French franc (FF) to 18.18 Pacific francs, so you can determine how many CFP you'll get for your dollar or pound by finding out how many FF you get, then multiplying by 18.18. Or to put it another way, 5.5 FF equals CFP 100, so divide the number of FF you get by 5.5 and multiply by 100. At last report US$1 = CFP 87, but a rough way to convert CFP into U.S. dollars would be simply to divide by 100, so CFP 1000 is US$10, etc.

All banks levy a stiff commission on foreign currency transactions. The Banque Socredo and Banque de Tahiti both deduct CFP 350 commission, the Banque de Polynésie CFP 400, and the Westpac Bank CFP 450. Traveler's checks bring a rate of exchange about 1.5% higher than cash, but a passport is required for identification (photocopy sometimes accepted). The best currency to have with you by far is French francs in cash or traveler's checks as these are converted back and forth at the fixed rate of CFP 18.18 to one FF without any commission charge. If you're from the States, you might also bring a few U.S. dollars in small bills to cover emergency expenses.

Credit cards are accepted in many places, but Pacific francs in cash are easier to use at restaurants, shops, etc. To avoid wasting time hassling at banks for cash advances, it's best to bring enough traveler's checks to cover all your out-of-pocket expenses and then some. If you do wish to use a credit card at a restaurant, ask first. Visa and MasterCard credit cards are universally accepted in the Society Islands, but American Express is not. The **American Express** representative on Tahiti is Tahiti Tours (B.P. 627, Papeete, tel. 54-02-50) at 15 rue Jeanne d'Arc near the Vaima Center in Papeete.

On some outer islands credit cards, traveler's checks, and foreign banknotes won't be accepted, so it's essential to change enough money before leaving Papeete. Apart from Tahiti, there are banks on Bora Bora, Huahine, Hiva Oa, Moorea, Nuku Hiva, Raiatea, Rangiroa, Rurutu, Tahaa, Tubuai, and Ua Pou. All of these islands have Banque Socredo branches, and the Banque de Tahiti (38% of which is owned by the Bank of Hawaii) is represented on six of them. Bora Bora, Moorea, and Raiatea each have four different banks. If you're headed for any island other than these, take along enough CFP in cash to see you through.

Although Tahiti is easily the most expensive corner of the South Pacific, it also has the lowest inflation rate in the region (never over three percent between 1986 and 1990, compared to 10% in many neighboring countries). In 1991 the retail price index rose only 0.1%. Fortunately facilities for budget travelers are now highly developed throughout the Society Islands, often with cooking facilities, which allow you to save a lot on meals. Cheap transportation is available by interisland boat and local *truck,* and bicycles can be hired in many places. What you need the most of to see Tahiti-Polynesia on a low budget is time, and the wisdom to avoid trying to see and do too much. There are countless organized tours and activities designed to separate you from your money, but none are really essential and the beautiful scenery, spectacular beaches, challenging hikes, and exotic atmosphere are free. Bargaining is not common in Tahiti-Polynesia, and no one will try to cheat you. There's *no tipping,* and they *mean* it.

Post

The 34 regular post offices and 58 authorized agencies throughout Tahiti-Polynesia are open weekdays 0700-1500. Main branches sell readymade padded envelopes and boxes. Parcels with an aggregate length, width, and height of over 90 cm or weighing more than 20 kg cannot be mailed. Rolls (posters, calendars, etc.) longer than 90 cm are also not accepted. Letters cannot weigh over two kg. Registration *(recommandation)* and insurance *(envois avec valeur déclarée)* are possible. Always use airmail *(poste aérienne)* when posting a letter; surface mail takes months to arrive. Postcards can still take up to two weeks to reach the United States.

To pick up poste restante (general delivery) mail, you must show your passport and pay CFP 40 per piece. If you're going to an outer island and are worried about your letters being returned to sender after 30 days (at Nuku Hiva after 15 days), pay CFP 1500 per month for a *garde de courrier,* which obliges the post office to hold all letters for at least two months. If one of your letters has "please hold" marked on it, the local postmaster may decide to hold all your mail for two months, but you'll have to pay the CFP 1500 to collect it. Packages may be returned after one month in any case. For a flat fee of CFP 1600 you can have your mail forwarded for one year. Ask for an *"Ordre de Réexpédition Temporaire."*

In this chapter all post office box numbers are rendered B.P. *(Boîte Postale).* Since there are usually no street addresses, always include the B.P. when writing to a local address, plus the name of the commune or village and the island. The postal authorities recognize "French Polynesia" as the official name of this country, and it's best to add "South Pacific Ocean" to that for good measure. Tahiti-Polynesia issues its own colorful postage stamps—available at local post offices. They make excellent souvenirs.

Telecommunications

Local telephone calls are CFP 50, and the pay phones usually work! A flashing light means you're about to be cut off, so have another coin ready. All calls within a single island are considered local calls, except on Tahiti, which is divided into two zones. Long-distance calls are best placed at post offices, which also handle fax *(télécopier)* services. Calls made from hotel rooms are charged double or triple. Collect calls overseas are possible to Canada, the U.S., Australia, and New Zealand (but not to the U.K.): dial 19 and say you want a *conversation payable a l'arrive.* For information (in French), dial 12; to get the operator, dial 19.

Anyone planning on making a lot of calls should pick up a telephone card *(télécarte),* sold at all post offices. They're valid for both local and overseas calls, and are available in denominations of 30 units (CFP 1000), 60 units (CFP 2000), and 150 units (CFP 5000). It's

cheaper than paying cash and you don't get hit with three-minute minimum charges for operator-assisted calls (CFP 1824 to the U.S.). North American AT&T telephone cards can be used in Tahiti-Polynesia.

To dial overseas direct from Tahiti, listen for the dial tone, then push 00 (Tahiti's international access code). When you hear another dial tone, press the country code of your party (Canada and the U.S. are both 1), the city or area code, and the number. The procedure is clearly explained in notices in English in the phone booths.

With a card, the cost per minute is CFP 250 to Australia and New Zealand, CFP 375 to Hawaii, CFP 490 to the U.S., CFP 576 to Britain, and CFP 600 to Canada. That's still very expensive, so wait to call from another country if you can. If you're calling North America, it's cheaper to quickly leave your number and have your party call you back. Otherwise fax them your hotel's phone and fax numbers. To call Tahiti-Polynesia direct from the U.S., one must dial 011-689 and the six-digit telephone number. International access codes do vary, so always check in the front of your local telephone book. If you need to consult the Tahiti-Polynesia phone book, ask to see the *annuaire* at any post office.

Throughout this chapter we've tried to supply the local telephone numbers you'll need. Any tourist-oriented business is sure to have someone handy who speaks English, so don't hesitate to call ahead. You'll get current information, be able to check prices and perhaps make a reservation, and often save yourself a lot of time and worry.

Tahiti-Polynesia's telephone code is 689.

Business Hours and Time

Businesses open early in Tahiti-Polynesia and often close for a two-hour siesta at midday. Normal office hours are weekdays 0730-1130/1330-1630. Many shops keep the same schedule but remain open until 1730 and Saturday 0730-1200. A few shops remain open at lunchtime and small convenience stores are often open Saturday afternoon until 1800 and Sunday 0600-0800. Banking hours are variable, either 0800-1530 or 0800-1100/1400-1700 weekdays. A few banks in Papeete open Saturday morning (check the sign on the door).

Tahiti-Polynesia operates on the same time as Hawaii, 10 hours behind Greenwich mean time or two hours behind California (except May to September, when it's three hours). The Marquesas are 30 minutes behind the rest of Tahiti-Polynesia. Tahiti-Polynesia is east of the international date line, so the day is the same as that of the Cook Islands, Hawaii, and the U.S., but a day behind Fiji, New Zealand, and Australia.

Media

There are two French-owned morning papers, *La Dépêche de Tahiti* (B.P. 50, Papeete; tel. 42-43-43) and *Les Nouvelles de Tahiti* (B.P. 1757, Papeete; tel. 43-44-45). *La Dépêche* is the larger, with more international news, but both papers provide the daily exchange rate. In 1989 the previously locally owned *Les Nouvelles* was purchased by French publishing magnate Robert Hersant, who also owns *La Dépêche*.

The free weekly *Tahiti Beach Press* (B.P. 887, Papeete; tel. 42-68-50), edited by Al Prince, was called the *Tahiti Sun Press* from 1980 till the end of 1990, when the paper was forced to drop all news coverage unrelated to tourism due to economic pressure from the big hotel chains and government tourism officials. The present "sanitized" newspaper is still well worth perusing to find out which local companies are interested in your business; just don't expect to find Al's excellent articles on social or political conditions in Tahiti-Polynesia in it anymore.

The French government attempts to control what happens in the territory through the state-owned TV and radio. Television was introduced to Tahiti in the mid-1960s and Radio France Outre-Mer (RFO) broadcasts on two channels in French and (occasionally) Tahitian. Nine private radio stations also operate and it's fun to listen to the Tahitian-language stations, which play more local music than the French stations. The Tahitian call-in shows with messages to families on outer islands are a delightful slice of real life. Pro-independence Radio Te Reo o Tefana (tel. 81-97-97) broadcasts from Faa'a on Tahiti.

Information

Tahiti-Polynesia has one of the best-equipped tourist offices in the South Pacific, Tahiti Tourisme (B.P. 65, Papeete; tel. 50-57-00, fax 43-66-19). For a list of their overseas offices, turn to the Information Offices appendix at the back of this book. Within Tahiti-Polynesia the same organization calls itself Tahiti Animation and operates tourist information offices on Tahiti, Moorea, Huahine, Raiatea, Bora Bora, and Hiva Oa. These offices can provide free brochures and answer questions, but they're not travel agencies, so you must make your own hotel and transportation bookings. Ask for their current information sheets on the islands you intend to visit.

TRANSPORTATION

Getting There

Air Calédonie International, Air France, Air New Zealand, AOM French Airlines, Corsair, Hawaiian Airlines, Lan Chile Airlines, and Qantas Airways all have flights to Papeete. For more information on these, turn to the Introduction to this book.

In 1990 France's state-owned national airline, **Air France,** bought out privately owned UTA French Airlines to become *the* international carrier to the French colonies in the South Pacific. Both Air France and **AOM French Airlines** (9841 Airport Blvd., Suite 1104, Los Angeles, CA 90045, U.S.A.) fly three times a week from Paris to Papeete via Los Angeles. In October 1992 Air France discontinued direct flights from San Francisco to Tahiti, but they still fly nonstop between Tokyo and Papeete once a week. AOM (Air Outre-Mer), owned by the French bank Crédit Lyonnais, has a policy of consistently setting their fares slightly below those of Air France while offering comparable service.

The charter airline **Corsair,** owned by the French tour operator Nouvelles Frontières (APS, Inc., 5757 West Century Blvd., Suite 660, Los Angeles, CA 90045-6407, U.S.A.), also has weekly scheduled Paris-Los Angeles-Papeete flights. Corsair prices their tickets differently than the other carriers: you pay according to the season in which each leg is actually flown, whereas all of the other airlines base their fares on the season when the journey begins. Thus while Corsair may be cheaper, it's also more complicated, and requires more careful planning. The seating on Corsair planes is reported to be rather cramped.

Both **Air New Zealand** and **Qantas** have flights from Los Angeles to Papeete twice a week, with connections to/from many points in North America and Western Europe. Both carriers continue southwest to Auckland with one of the Air New Zealand flights calling at Rarotonga on the way. Qantas carries on to Sydney and Melbourne. **Hawaiian Airlines** offers weekly nonstop service to Papeete from Honolulu with connections from Los Angeles, San Francisco, and Seattle. North Americans planning a trip should always use the toll-free 800 numbers of Air France, Air New Zealand, AOM French Airlines (Tahiti Vacations), Corsair (Nouvelles Frontières), Hawaiian Airlines, and Qantas to compare airfares to Tahiti.

Lan Chile Airlines runs their Boeing 767 service from Santiago to Tahiti via Easter Island twice a week.

An interesting way to arrive is on the weekly **Air Calédonie International** flight from Nouméa to Papeete via Wallis Island. This flight is combined with Air France's service to/from Sydney via Nouméa.

Getting Around by Air

The domestic carrier, **Air Tahiti** (B.P. 314, Papeete; tel. 86-42-42, fax 86-40-69), flies to 35 airstrips in every corner of Tahiti-Polynesia, with important hubs at Papeete (Windward Islands), Bora Bora (Leeward Islands), Rangiroa (western Tuamotus), Hao (eastern Tuamotus), and Nuku Hiva (Marquesas). Their fleet consists of two 66-seat ATR 72s, four 46-seat ATR 42s, and one 19-seat Dornier 228. The Italian-made ATRs are economical in fuel consumption and maintenance requirements, and perform well under island conditions.

Air Tahiti doesn't allow stopovers on their tickets, so if you're flying roundtrip from Tahiti to Bora Bora and want to stop at Raiatea on the way out and Huahine on the way back, you'll have to purchase four separate tickets (total CFP 29,800). Ask about their "Pass Bleu," which allows you to visit these islands plus Moorea for CFP 20,000 (certain restrictions apply).

No student discounts are available, but persons under 25 and over 60 can get discounts of up to 50% on certain flights by paying CFP 1000 for a discount card *(carte de réduction)*. Family reduction cards (CFP 2000) provide a 50% reduction for the parents and 75% off for children 16 and under. Identification and one photo are required.

Slightly better than point-to-point fares are the Air Tahiti **Air Passes**. These are valid 28 days, but only one stopover can be made on each island included in the package. For example, you can go Papeete-Moorea-Huahine-Raiatea-Bora Bora-Papeete for CFP 30,500. Otherwise pay CFP 45,500 for Papeete-Moorea-Huahine-Raiatea-Bora Bora-Rangiroa-Manihi-Papeete. This compares with an individual ticket price of CFP 33,200 to do the first circuit, CFP 67,500 for the second, which makes an air pass good value if you want to get to Rangiroa and Manihi as well as Bora Bora, but hardly worth considering if you're only going as far as Bora Bora. Air Passes that include the Austral Islands are CFP 50,500 (compared to CFP 78,800 on an individual basis); with the Tuamotu and Marquesas islands they're CFP 87,000 (compared to CFP 113,200). All flights must be booked in advance but date changes are possible. Tahiti Tourisme and Air France offices around the world act as Air Tahiti agents, so inquire at any of them about Air Passes. The passes are nonrefundable once travel has begun.

Air Tahiti tickets are refundable at the place of purchase, but you must cancel your reservations at least two hours before flight time to avoid a CFP 1000 penalty. Do this in person and have your flight coupon amended as no-shows are charged CFP 2000 to make a new reservation. It's not necessary to reconfirm confirmed reservations for flights between Tahiti, Moorea, Huahine, Raiatea, Bora Bora, Rangiroa, and Manihi, but elsewhere it's essential to reconfirm. Beware of planes leaving 20 minutes early.

The main Air Tahiti office in Papeete is upstairs in Fare Tony, the commercial center off boulevard Pomare just west of rue Georges Lagarde. They're closed on weekends. Check carefully to make sure all the flights listed in their published timetable are actually operating! Any travel agency in Papeete can book Air Tahiti flights for the same price as the Air Tahiti office, and the service tends to be better.

If you buy your ticket locally, the baggage allowance on domestic flights is 10 kg, but if your flight tickets were purchased prior to your arrival in Tahiti-Polynesia, the allowance is 20 kg. Excess baggage is charged at the rate of the full fare for that sector divided by 80 per kilogram. Fresh fruit and vegetables cannot be carried from Tahiti to the Austral, Tuamotu, Gambier, or Marquesas islands.

On Bora Bora, Maupiti, and Nuku Hiva passengers are transferred from the airport to town by boat. This ride is included in the airfare at Bora Bora but costs extra at Maupiti (CFP 400). Smoking aboard the aircraft is prohibited on flights under one hour.

An Air Tahiti subsidiary, **Air Moorea** (B.P. 6019, Papeete; tel. 86-41-41, fax 86-42-69), has hourly flights between Tahiti and Moorea (CFP 2700 one-way) during daylight hours only. Reservations are not necessary on this commuter service: just show up 15 minutes before the flight you wish to take. The Air Moorea terminal is in a separate building at the east end of Faa'a Airport. However, flying between Tahiti and Moorea is not recommended because going over by ferry is a big part of the experience and there's no bus service to/from Moorea Airport. A cramped, stuffy plane ride at three times the cost of the relaxing 30-minute ferry is to be avoided.

Air Tahiti Services

Air Tahiti flies from Papeete to Huahine (CFP 8600), Raiatea (CFP 9900), and Bora Bora (CFP 12,100) several times a day. Three times a week there's a direct connection from Moorea to Huahine (CFP 9100); Raiatea to Maupiti (CFP 5500) is also three times a week. The two weekly transversal flights between Bora Bora and Rangiroa (CFP 20,700) eliminate the need to backtrack to Papeete.

Flights between Papeete and Rangiroa (CFP 13,300) operate daily, continuing on from Rangiroa to Manihi (CFP 8600) three times a week. Air Tahiti has numerous flights to the East Tuamotu atolls and Mangareva, but these are usually closed to non-French tourists due to French military activity in the area. Check with Air Tahiti or Tahiti Tourism for the current situation. Many flights between outer islands of the Tuamotus operate in one direction only.

Flights bound for the Marquesas are the longest, most expensive, and most heavily booked of Air Tahiti's services. Four times a week there's an ATR 42 service from Papeete to Nuku Hiva (CFP 37,800). Twice a week these flights call at Hiva Oa on their way to Nuku Hiva, and one weekly ATR 42 flight calls at Rangiroa. In addition, there's a heavily booked Dornier 228 flight from Rangiroa to Hiva Oa via Napuka once a week. At Nuku Hiva one of the Papeete flights connects for Ua Pou (CFP 5000), Hiva Oa (CFP 8600), and Ua Huka (CFP 5000). If you know you'll be going on to Hiva Oa, Ua Huka, or Ua Pou, get a through ticket there from Papeete; the fare is the same as a ticket only as far as Nuku Hiva.

The Austral group is better connected to Papeete, with flights to Rurutu (CFP 17,700) and Tubuai (CFP 19,800) three days a week. These operate Papeete-Rurutu-Tubuai-Papeete twice a week and Papeete-Tubuai-Rurutu-Papeete weekly, with the leg Tubuai-Rurutu costing CFP 8100.

During July and August, the peak holiday season, extra flights are scheduled. Air Tahiti is fairly reliable; still, you should never schedule a flight back to Papeete on the same day that your international flight leaves Tahiti. It's always best to allow a couple of days' leeway in case there's a problem with the air service. Maybe save your travels to Moorea or around Tahiti until the end.

Getting Around by Sea

Most budget travelers tour Tahiti-Polynesia by boat as the planes are far more expensive. There's a certain romance and adventure to taking an interisland freighter and you can go anywhere by copra boat, including islands without airstrips and popular resorts. Ships leave Papeete regularly for the different island groups. You'll meet local people and fellow travelers, and receive a gentle introduction to the island of your choice. Problems about overweight baggage, tight reservations, and airport transport are eliminated, and travel by ferry or passenger-carrying freighter is four times cheaper than the plane. Seasickness, cockroaches, diesel fumes, and the heavy scent of copra are all part of the experience.

Below you'll find specific information on the main interisland boats. The tourist office in Papeete also has lists. Prices and schedules have been fairly stable over the past few years, and new services are being added all the time. Lots of visitors travel this way to Moorea and Bora Bora, so don't feel intimidated if you've never done it before.

For the cheapest ride and the most local color, travel deck class. There's usually an awning in case of rain, and you'll be surrounded by Tahitians, but don't count on getting a lot of sleep if you go this way—probably no problem for one night, right? Lay your mat pointed to one side of the boat because if you lie parallel to the length of the boat you'll roll from side to side. Don't step over other peoples' mats, but if you must, first remove your shoes and excuse yourself. Otherwise take a cabin, which you'll share with three or four other passengers, still cheaper than an airplane seat. Food is only included on really long trips (ask), but snacks may be sold on board. On a long trip you're better off taking all your own food than buying a meal plan.

For any boat trip farther than Moorea check the schedule and pick up tickets the day before at the company office listed below. If you're headed for a remote island outside the Societies or want cabin class, visit the office as far in advance as possible. Except on the *Aranui,* it's not possible (nor recommended) to book your passage before arriving on Tahiti. If you really want to go, there'll be something leaving around the date you want. On an outer island, be wary when someone, even a member of the crew, tells you the departure time of a ship: they're as apt to leave early as late.

Boat trips are always smoother northwest-bound than southeast-bound because you go with the prevailing winds. Take this into consideration if you plan to fly one way, in which case it would be better to come back by air. *Bon voyage.*

Ferry to Moorea

There are two types of ferries to Moorea: two fast 320-passenger catamarans carrying walk-on commuters only (30 minutes), and two large car ferries with a capacity for 400 foot-passengers and 80 vehicles (one hour). Departure times are posted at the ferry landing on the Papeete waterfront (punctual) and reservations are not required: you buy your ticket just before you board. Stroll around the open upper deck and enjoy the scenic one-hour crossing. The crossing can be rather rough on a stormy day, so if you're prone to seasickness, try to cross in good weather.

The high-speed catamarans *Aremiti II* (B.P. 9254, Papeete; tel. 42-88-88, fax 42-06-15) and *Tamahine Moorea II* (tel. 43-76-50) make five trips a day between Tahiti and Moorea at CFP 800 pp. Unlike the airport catamaran at Bora Bora where you're forced to stay in a stuffy enclosed room, on the Moorea cats you're allowed to sit outside on the roof, which makes them fun and well worth taking one way.

The two car ferries, both named *Tamarii Moorea* (B.P. 3917, Papeete; tel. 43-76-50, fax 42-10-49), shuttle five or six times a day between Papeete and Vaiare Wharf on Moorea (CFP 700 one-way, students and children under 13 CFP 350, car CFP 2000, scooter CFP 500, bicycle CFP 200).

Le truck meets all ferries on the Moorea side and will take you anywhere on that island for CFP 200. Just don't be too slow getting on or it could be full.

Cargo Ships to the Leeward Islands

You have a variety of choices if you're headed for the Leeward Islands. The cargo ship MV *Taporo VI* departs Papeete's Motu Uta wharf every Monday, Wednesday, and Friday afternoon around 1600. *Taporo VI* calls at Huahine at 0200, Raiatea at 0530, and Tahaa at 0700, reaching Bora Bora at 1000 Tuesday, Thursday, and Saturday. It departs Bora Bora for Papeete once again Tuesday, Thursday, and Saturday at 1130, calling at Raiatea at 1500 and Huahine at 1730, reaching Papeete early Wednesday, Friday, and Sunday morning (you can stay on board till dawn).

Northbound the MV *Vaeanu* leaves Papeete Monday, Wednesday, and Friday at 1700;

*horseplay at Huahine
as an interisland ship
arrives at Fare*

DAVID STANLEY

southbound it leaves Bora Bora Tuesday at noon, Thursday at 0830, and Sunday at 0930. On both ships, the timings are more civilized if you go direct from Papeete to Bora Bora, then work your way back via Raiatea and Huahine. However, travelers on extremely low budgets who don't mind discomfort can save on accommodations by visiting Huahine and Raiatea first and sleeping on the dock those nights. There's a good shelter for this purpose at Huahine.

Although the ships do make an effort to stick to their timetables, the times are approximate—ask at the company offices. Expect variations if there's a public holiday that week. Also beware of voyages marked "carburant" on the schedules because when fuel *(combustible)* is being carried, only cabin passengers are allowed aboard (this often happens on the Wednesday departures from Papeete). Northbound you won't get much sleep due to noise and commotion during the early-morning stops. No mattresses or bedding are provided for deck passengers. In Papeete board the ship two hours prior to departure to be sure of a reasonable place on deck to sleep (mark your place with a beach mat). If you've got some time to kill before your ship leaves Papeete, have a look around the coconut-oil mill next to the wharf.

On *Taporo VI* the deck fare from Papeete to any of the Leeward Islands is CFP 1656. However, they only accept 12 deck passengers (who sleep in a large open container on the rear deck), so it's important to book ahead at the

Compagnie Française Maritime de Tahiti (B.P. 368, Papeete; tel. 42-63-93, fax 42-06-17) in Fare Ute (open weekdays 0730-1100/1330-1700, Saturday 0730-1100). The two four-bed cabins are CFP 20,000 each. If you're only traveling between the islands of Huahine, Raiatea, Tahaa, and Bora Bora, the interisland deck fares are under CFP 1000 each trip. If you jump off for a quick look around while the ship is in port, you may be asked to buy another ticket when you reboard. A bicycle is about CFP 600 extra. No meals are included, so take food and water with you.

The *Vaeanu* carries a much larger number of deck and cabin passengers, and you can usually buy a ticket at their office (B.P. 9062, Motu Uta; tel. 41-25-35, fax 41-24-34) facing the wharf at Motu Uta a few hours prior to departure (except on holidays). Do buy your ticket before boarding, however, as there can be problems for non-Tahitians trying to pay once the ship is underway. In the Leeward Islands buy a ticket from the agent on the wharf as soon as the boat arrives.

The Compagnie Française Maritime de Tahiti also runs a supply ship from Papeete to Maiao occasionally, so ask. (The CFMT itself has a place in local history, having been founded around 1890 by Sir James Donald, who had the contract to supply limes to the British Pacific fleet. At the turn of the century Donald's schooner, the *Tiare Taporo*, was the fastest in Polynesia, and the CFMT is still the Lloyd's of London agent.)

Ferry to the Leeward Islands

The **Compagnie Maritime des Îles Sous-Le-Vent** (B.P. 50712, Pirae; tel. 43-19-88, fax 43-19-99), with an office in a red-and-white kiosk at the Moorea ferry wharf in Papeete, handles the car-carrying, 400-passenger *Raromatai Ferry,* which departs Papeete to Huahine, Raiatea, Tahaa, and Bora Bora on Tuesday and Friday afternoons. This ship uses a landing behind the tourist office in downtown Papeete, not the wharf at Motu Uta where *Taporo VI* and the *Vaeanu* dock. Tickets for walk-on passengers are usually available just prior to departure. Prices from Papeete to Bora Bora are CFP 3800 for a seat in the salon, CFP 6000 in a four-berth cabin, CFP 10,000 for a car, CFP 500 for a bicycle. A double "cruise cabin" is CFP 17,000 for two people. There are discounts for students and those 18 and under.

The *Raromatai Ferry* salon is a spacious sitting room with aircraft-style Pullman seats, but French TV shows blast at you nonstop and the powerful air-conditioning means you freeze at night unless you have a sleeping bag. The *Raromatai Ferry* rolls a lot in rough weather. Between the Leeward Islands the *Raromatai Ferry* is a good deal (CFP 1000 salon interisland) for these daylight crossings (southbound), with an excellent open promenade deck on top.

Jet Cruiser to the Leeward Islands

The big news in sea travel from Papeete to Huahine, Raiatea, and Bora Bora is the high-speed monohull *Ono-Ono* (Sociéte Polynesienne d'Investissement Maritime, B.P. 16, Papeete; tel. 45-35-35, fax 43-83-45), which began service in 1994. This Australian-built, 48-meter jet boat carries 450 passengers at speeds of up to 35 knots, cutting traveling times from Papeete to Huahine to just three hours (CFP 4300), to Raiatea four and a half hours (CFP 4800), and to Bora Bora six hours (CFP 5800). Children under 12 years of age pay half price on tickets to/from Papeete.

The *Ono-Ono* departs Papeete's Moorea ferry wharf Monday and Wednesday at 0900, Friday at 1630, departing Bora Bora for the return trip on Tuesday and Thursday at 1200, Sunday at 1400. On Saturday there's an shorter interisland run within the Leeward Islands only (about CFP 1600 a hop). Tickets should be purchased in advance (for insurance purposes,

the booking agent will need to know the middle name and age of each passenger). Seating is 10 or 12 abreast on two enclosed decks. Though twice as expensive as the cargo boats or ferry, it's half the price of going by air and certainly makes getting around these enchanting islands a lot easier.

Government Ships
To Maupiti and Beyond

The government supply ship *Meherio III* leaves Papeete for Maupiti about twice a month via Raiatea, usually on a Wednesday. Tickets to Maupiti are available from the **Direction de l'Equipment** (weekdays 0730-1500; B.P. 85, Papeete; tel. 42-44-92, fax 42-13-41) at Motu Uta, costing CFP 1374 from Papeete or CFP 1035 from Raiatea. This office also sells tickets on government boats to the Tuamotus and Marquesas, and only deck passage is available.

Ships to the Austral Islands

The **Service de Navigacion des Australes** (B.P. 1890, Papeete; tel. 43-15-88, fax 42-06-09), at the Motu Uta interisland wharf on the west side of the copra sheds in Papeete, runs the *Tuhaa Pae II* to the Austral Islands twice a month: CFP 31,518 cabin, CFP 18,010 deck for the 10-day RT. No meals are included, but food can be ordered at CFP 2300 pp a day extra (take your own). Some of the cabins are below the waterline and very hot. The rear deck has a diesely romantic feel, for a day or two. For sanitary reasons the seats have been removed from the ship's toilets (squat). The *Tuhaa Pae II* calls at Rimatara, Rurutu, Tubuai, Raivavae, and very occasionally Rapa Iti. Maria Atoll is visited annually. Their schedule changes at a moment's notice, so actually being able to go with them is pure luck.

Ships to the Tuamotus and Gambiers

The 26-meter motor vessel *Dory* (B.P. 9274, Papeete; tel./fax 42-88-88) leaves every Monday at 1300 from the Moorea ferry wharf in Papeete for Tikehau (Tuesday 0600), Rangiroa (Tuesday 1200), Arutua (Wednesday 0600), and Kaukura (Wednesday 1400), arriving back in Papeete Thursday at 0800 (CFP 3000 one-way). This routing means it takes only 23 hours to go from Papeete to Rangiroa but 44 hours to return.

There are no cabins and meals are not included. The *Dory* visits the islands to pick up fish and deliver frozen bread, chicken, and ice cream. The same company runs the *Cobia II* to the Tuamotus, departing Monday at 1200 for Kaukura (Tuesday 0800), Arutua (Tuesday 1300), Apataki (Tuesday 1630), Aratika (Wednesday 0700), and Toau (Wednesday 1330), returning to Papeete Friday at 1000 (also CFP 3000 one-way). Foreign visitors use these boats regularly, so they're probably your best bet.

The *Kauaroa Nui* (B.P. 9266, Papeete; tel./fax 41-07-11), with an office next to the *Vaeanu* office at the Motu Uta interisland wharf, has three departures a month for the middle Tuamotus (Fakarava, Faaite, Raraka, Katiu, and Makemo), leaving Thursday afternoons. Roundtrip fares are CFP 10,200 deck, CFP 17,000 in a basic four-bed cabin; no meals are included.

The 48-meter cargo boat *Manava II* (B.P. 1816, Papeete; tel. 43-83-84, fax 42-25-53) runs to the northern Tuamotus (Rangiroa, Tikehau, Mataiva, Ahe, Manihi, Takaroa, Takapoto, Aratika, Kauehi, Fakarava, Toau, Apataki, Arutua, and Kaukura) once or twice a month. There are no cabins: the deck passage to Rangiroa is CFP 3000.

Many smaller copra boats, such as the *Kura Ora, Rairoa Nui, Ruahatu,* and *Saint Xavier Maris Stella,* also service the Tuamotu and Gambier groups. Ask around the large workshops west of Papeete's Motu Uta interisland wharf. The *Saint Xavier Maris Stella* (B.P. 11366, Papeete; tel. 42-23-58) charges CFP 25,000 including meals for a one-week trip Tahiti-Mataiva-Tikihau-Rangiroa-Ahe-Manihi-Takaroa-Kauehi-Fakarava-Tahiti. Some of the ships serving the forbidden military zone in the Tuamotus won't accept non-French tourists as passengers, and others accept only men due to a lack of facilities for women.

Ships to the Marquesas

The 57-meter cargo ship *Taporo V* departs Papeete Thursday at 1400 every two weeks for Tahuata, Hiva Oa, Nuku Hiva, and Ua Pou, charging CFP 17,000 deck or CFP 24,000 cabin one-way from Papeete to Hiva Oa. It takes three and a half days on the open sea to reach the first Marquesan island, so you should certainly try for a cabin. Otherwise you can do the whole eight-day roundtrip for CFP 36,000 deck or CFP 50,000 cabin, but only three to eight hours are spent at each port. Food is included but it's marginal, so take extras and bring your own bowl. Meals are served at 0600, 1100, and 1800. No pillows or towels are supplied in the cabins and the shower is only open three hours a day. The agent is **Compagnie Française Maritime de Tahiti** (B.P. 368, Papeete; tel. 42-63-93, fax 42-06-17) at Fare Ute.

The *Tamarii Tuamotu II* departs every five weeks to the Marquesas with only deck passage available (no cabins). This ship runs from Papeete direct to the Marquesas, but visits several of the Tuamotu atolls on the way back. It calls at every inhabited bay in the Marquesas (this alone takes 12 days). Check at their city office (Vonken et Cie., B.P. 2606, Papeete; tel. 42-95-07), corner of rue des Remparts and Ave. du Prince Hinoi. Since the *Tamarii Tuamotu II* calls at certain restricted islands in the Tuamotus a permit from the Subdivision Administrative des Tuamotu-Gambier in Papeete may be required (see "Permission" in "The Tuamotu Islands" in this chapter for more information).

The *Aranui*, a passenger-carrying freighter, cruises 15 times a year between Papeete and the Marquesas. The ship calls at most of the inhabited Marquesas Islands, plus a couple of the Tuamotus. The routing might be Papeete-Takapoto-Ua Pou-Nuku Hiva-Hiva Oa-Fatu Hiva-Hiva Oa-Ua Huka-Nuku Hiva-Ua Pou-Rangiroa-Papeete. A vigorous daily program with fairly strenuous but optional hikes is included in the tour price. The only docks in the Marquesas are at Taiohae, Vaipaee, Hakahau, and Atuona; elsewhere everyone goes ashore in whale boats, a potential problem for elderly passengers. Still, the *Aranui* is fine for the adventuresome visitor who wants to see a lot in a short time.

This modern freighter had its inaugural sailing in 1990, replacing a smaller German-built boat that had served the Marquesas since 1981. It's clean and pleasant compared to the other schooners, but far more expensive. A hundred passengers are accommodated in 30 a/c cabins or given mattresses on the bridge deck. Deck passage for a 15-day, eight-island cruise to the Tuamotus and Marquesas costs CFP 153,800 roundtrip; the cheapest cabin is CFP 280,500 roundtrip (double occupancy), all meals included. An additional US$75 port tax is charged. Single occupancy costs 50% more. Cheaper one-way deck fares on the *Aranui* are for local residents, not available to tourists. In any case, deck passage can be hot, noisy, and tiring on such a long trip.

Despite the fares charged, don't expect cruise-ship comforts on the *Aranui*. Accommodations are spartan (but adequate), and meals are served in two shifts due to lack of space in the dining area. Aside from three classes of cabins (the cheaper ones are cramped), there's a large covered area where the deck passengers sleep. The roster of American/French/German passengers is congenial.

The *Aranui's* Papeete office (**Compagnie Polynésienne de Transport Maritime,** B.P. 220, Papeete; tel. 42-62-40, fax 43-48-89) is at the interisland wharf at Motu Uta. In the U.S. advance bookings should be made through the CPTM office at 595 Market St., Suite 2880, San Francisco, CA 94105, U.S.A. (tel. 415/541-0677, fax 415/541-0766). One Australian reader wrote: "The trip is fantastic and I hope to do it again soon." (The *Aranui* recently costarred with Warren Beatty and Annette Bening in the Warner Brothers film *Love Affair*.)

Luxury Cruises out of Papeete

Windstar Cruises (300 Elliott Ave. W, Seattle, WA 98119, U.S.A.; tel. 206/281-3535, fax 206/286-3229) offers cruises around the Society Islands year-round in their gigantic, four-masted *Wind Song*. Participants join the boat at Papeete on a Saturday. The pp price for one of 74 double, classless cabins for an eight-day cruise varies according to season: US$2695 (low), US$2795 (base), US$2895 (peak), plus US$125 port charges. Single occupancy is 50% more, and airfare to Tahiti is extra. Bookings can be made through **Tahiti Vacations** (9841 Airport Blvd., Suite 1124, Los Angeles, CA 90045, U.S.A.; tel. 800/553-3477, fax 310/337-1126).

Although the 134-meter-long, 62-meter-high Bahamas-registered *Wind Song* could hardly be classed a yacht, it is a step up from the impersonal pretentiousness of a love boat. The food is superb and you can dine with whoever you like, whenever you want. One of three identical high-tech vessels that also ply the Mediter-

ranean and Caribbean, the *Wind Song's* sails are fully computer-controlled, saving on both fuel and crew! Though the ship can heel up to six degrees, ballast tanks and stabilizers ensure a smooth ride and nights are often spent in port, so you don't have to struggle to get to sleep on a rolling ship. The Windstar fleet, commissioned at Le Havre, France, during 1986-88, deserves credit for experimenting with an alternative energy source (the wind!).

Very similar but bigger, and with five masts instead of four, is the 188-meter, US$125-million *Club Med 2,* which moved here from New Caledonia in 1995. Four-night cruises from Papeete to Moorea, Huahine, and Bora Bora begin at US$1150, plus US$80 port charges. A three-day cruise from Bora Bora to Rangiroa and back to Papeete begins at US$850, plus US$60. The complete seven-night Saturday-to-Saturday circuit begins at US$1980, plus US$140. These can be combined with stays at the Club Med villages on Moorea and Bora Bora. The 392 passengers enjoy many luxuries, and like the *Wind Song,* the *Club Med 2* is environmentally correct: computerized sails, ozone-friendly high-grade fuel, proper waste disposal, and vegetarian food (upon request). Information is available from **Club Méditerranée** (40 W. 57th St., New York, NY 10019, U.S.A.; tel. 800/4-LE-SHIP, fax 212/315-5392) or at the Club Med office in the Vaima Center, Papeete.

Yacht Charters

Bareboat and shareboat yacht charters in the Leeward Islands are offered by **The Moorings Ltd.** (19345 US 19 North, Ste. 402, Clearwater, FL 34624, U.S.A.; tel. 800/535-7289). Bareboat prices begin at US$500 a day for a small yacht accommodating five and go up to US$1000 daily for a large 10-person sailing boat. Prices are higher during the April to October high season. Provisioning is US$32 pp a day (plus US$120 a day for a cook, if required). If you're new to sailing a skipper must be hired at US$140 a day and the charterer is responsible for the skipper/cook's provisions. Security insurance costs US$18 a day and local tax is three percent. All charters are from noon to noon.

For more information on this and other yacht charter companies, see "Bareboating" in the "Raiatea" section of this chapter.

By Bus

Polynesia's folkloric *le truck* provides an entertaining unscheduled passenger service on Tahiti and some outer islands. Passengers sit on long wooden benches in back and there's no problem with luggage. Fares are fairly low and often posted on the side of the vehicle. You pay through the window on the right side of the cab. Drivers are generally friendly and will stop to pick you up anywhere if you wave—they're all privately owned, so there's no way they'd miss a fare! On Tahiti the larger *trucks* leave Papeete for the outlying districts periodically throughout the day until 1700; they continue running to Faa'a Airport and the Maeva Beach Hôtel until around 2200. On Huahine and Raiatea service is usually limited to a trip into the main town in the morning and a return to the villages in the afternoon. On Moorea and Bora Bora they meet the boats from Papeete.

Car Rentals

Car rentals are available at most of the airports served by Air Tahiti, but they ain't cheap. On Tahiti there's sometimes a mileage charge, whereas on Moorea, Huahine, Raiatea, and Bora Bora all rentals come with unlimited mileage. Public liability insurance is included by law, but collision damage waiver (CDW) insurance is extra. If you can get a small group together, consider renting a minibus for a do-it-yourself island tour. Unless you have a major credit card you'll have to put down a cash deposit on the car. Your home driver's license will be accepted, although you must have had your driver's license for at least a year. Visitors under the age of 25 are usually refused service unless they show a major credit card, and those under 21 cannot rent a car at all. Rental scooters are usually available. On Tahiti a strictly enforced local regulation requires you to wear a helmet *(casque)* at all times (CFP 5000 fine for failure to comply).

One major hassle with renting cars on the outer islands is that they usually give you a car with the fuel tank only a quarter full, so immediately after renting you must go to a gas station and tank up. Try to avoid putting in more gas than you can use by calculating how many km you might drive, then dividing that by 10 for the number of liters of gasoline you might use. Don't put in over CFP 2000 (about 20 liters) in any case or you'll be giving a nice gift to the rental agency (which, of course, is their hope in giving you a car that's not full). Gas stations are usually only in the main towns and open only during business hours on weekdays, plus perhaps a couple of hours on weekend mornings. Expect to pay around CFP 100 a liter for gas, which works out to just under US$4 per American gallon.

Two traffic signs to know: a white line across a red background indicates a one-way street, while a slanting blue line on a white background means no parking. At unmarked intersections in Papeete, the driver on the right has priority. As in continental Europe and North America, driving is on the right-hand side of the road. The seldom-observed speed limit is 40 kph in Papeete, 60 kph around the island. Drive with extreme care in congested areas—traffic accidents are frequent.

Others

Taxis are a rip-off throughout Tahiti-Polynesia and are best avoided. If you must take one, always verify the fare before getting in. The hitching is still fairly good in Polynesia, although local residents along the north side of Moorea are getting tired of it. Hitching around Tahiti is only a matter of time.

Bicycling on the island of Tahiti is risky due to wild devil-may-care motorists, but most of the outer islands (Moorea included) have excellent, uncrowded roads. It's best to use *le truck* on Tahiti, though a bike would come in handy on the other islands where *le truck* is rare. The distances are just made for cycling!

International Airport

Faa'a Airport (PPT), 5.5 km southwest of Papeete, handles around 32,000 domestic, 2,300 international, and 1,000 military flights a year. The runway was created in 1959-61, using material dredged from the lagoon or trucked in from the Punaruu Valley. A taxi into town is CFP 1000 (CFP 1200 on Sunday), double that after 2000. *Le truck* up on the main highway will take you to the same place for only CFP 140 (CFP 200 at night) and starts running around 0530.

Many flights to Tahiti arrive in the middle of the night, but you can stretch out on the benches inside the terminal. Representatives of the low-budget hostels are often on hand looking for prospective guests off the international flights, so ask the tourist information counter if there's anyone around from the place you've picked and, if there is, you'll probably get a free ride. If it's already early morning, you may be allowed to occupy your room for the balance of the night at no additional charge, provided you agree to stay at least two nights.

The Westpac Bank (tel. 82-44-24) in the terminal opens weekdays 0745-1530, and one hour before and after the arrival and departure of all international flights. They give the same rate as the banks in town and take the usual CFP 450 commission on all currencies other than French francs. The post office in the airport is open weekdays 0500-0900 and 1830-2230, weekends 0600-1000. Public toilets are located near the domestic check-in counter and upstairs from the bank.

The airport luggage-storage counter is open 0700-1700 and two hours before and after international departures. They charge CFP 180 per day for a small bag, CFP 360 for a large bag, CFP 600 for surfboards, etc. If they're closed when you arrive, ask at the nearby bar. The left-luggage counter is poorly marked; it's to the right as you come out of customs and just outside the main terminal in an adjacent building.

You can spend your leftover Pacific francs at the duty-free shops in the departure lounge, but don't expect any bargains. The Fare Hei, just outside the terminal, sells shell and flower leis for presentation to arriving or departing passengers.

All passengers arriving from Samoa or Fiji must have their baggage fumigated upon arrival, a process that takes about two hours (don't laugh if you're told this is to prevent the introduction of the "rhinoceros" into Polynesia—they mean the rhinoceros *beetle*). Fresh fruits, vegetables, and flowers are prohibited entry. There's no airport tax.

One nice touch is the welcoming committee Tahiti Tourisme sends out to meet every incoming international flight. As pareu-clad musicians strum their guitars or ukuleles, a smiling *vahine* puts a white *tiare Tahiti* blossom behind your ear. There's no catch: it's their way of saying *maeva*.

mole cowries (Cypraea talpa)

TAHITI

Tahiti, largest of the Societies, is an island of legend and song lying in the eye of Polynesia. Though only one of 118, this lush island of around 135,000 inhabitants is paradise itself to most people. Here you'll find an exciting city, big hotels, restaurants, nightclubs, things to see and do, valleys, mountains, reefs, trails, and history, plus transportation to everywhere. Since the days of Wallis, Bougainville, Cook, and Bligh, Tahiti has been the eastern gateway to the South Pacific.

In 1891 Paul Gauguin arrived at Papeete after a 63-day sea voyage from France. He immediately felt that Papeete "was Europe—the Europe which I had thought to shake off . . . it was the Tahiti of former times which I loved. That of the present filled me with horror." So Gauguin left the town and rented a native-style bamboo hut in Mataiea on the south coast, where he found happiness in the company of a 14-year-old Tahitian *vahine* whose "face flooded the interior of our hut and the landscape round about with joy and light." Somerset Maugham's *The Moon and Sixpence* is a fictional tale of Gauguin's life on the island.

Legends created by the early explorers, amplified in Jean-Jacques Rousseau's "noble savage" and taken up by the travel industry, make it difficult to write objectively about Tahiti. Though the Lafayette Nightclub is gone from Arue and Quinn's Tahitian Hut no longer graces Papeete's waterfront, Tahiti remains a delightful, enchanting place. In the late afternoon, as Tahitian crews practice canoe racing in the lagoon and Moorea gains a pink hue, the romance resurfaces. If you steer clear of the traffic jams and congestion in commercial Papeete and avoid the tourist ghettos west of the city, you can get a taste of the magic Gauguin encountered. But in fact, it's only on the outer islands of Polynesia, away from the motorists and the military complexes, that the full flavor lingers.

The Land

The island of Tahiti accounts for almost a quarter of the land area of Tahiti-Polynesia. Like Hawaii's Maui, Tahiti was formed by two ancient volcanoes joined at the isthmus of Taravao. The rounded, verdant summits of Orohena (2,241

Vahine no te Tiare

P. Gauguin

CARLSBERG GLYPTOTEK, COPENHAGEN

PAUL GAUGUIN

Paul Gauguin's "Girl with a Flower," pictured here, is now in the Carlsberg Glyptotek, Copenhagen. Gauguin was one of the first patrons of the French impressionists. Before he turned professional painter, Gauguin was a successful broker who worked at the Paris exchange. He went further than most of his contemporaries to search out the exotic, to paint in strong flat color, and to employ broad, bold decorative patterns made popular in France by the widespread distribution of Japanese wood block prints. Whereas later painters borrowed from African masks and carvings, Gauguin himself traveled directly to the source of his inspiration, arriving in Tahiti on 9 June 1891.

meters) and Aorai (2,066 meters) rise in the center of Tahiti Nui and deep valleys radiate in all directions from these central peaks. Steep slopes drop abruptly from the high plateaus to coastal plains. The northeast coast is rugged and rocky, without a barrier reef, and thus exposed to intense, pounding surf; villages lie on a narrow strip between mountains and ocean. The south coast is broad and gentle with large gardens and coconut groves; a barrier reef shields it from the sea's fury.

Tahiti Iti (also called Taiarapu) is a peninsula with no road around it. Mount Rooniu (1,323 meters) is its heart. The populations of big *(nui)* and small *(iti)* Tahiti are concentrated in Papeete and along the coast; the interior of both Tahitis is almost uninhabited. Contrary to the popular stereotype, mostly brown/black beaches of volcanic sand fringe this turtle-shaped island. To find the white/golden sands of the travel brochures, you must cross over to Moorea.

Orientation

Almost everyone arrives at Faa'a International Airport five km west of Papeete, the capital and main tourist center of Tahiti-Polynesia. East of Papeete are Pirae, Arue, and Mahina, with a smattering of hotels and things to see, while south of Faa'a lie the commuter communities Punaauia, Paea, and Papara. On the narrow neck of Tahiti is Taravao, a refueling stop on your 117-km way around Tahiti Nui. Tahiti Iti is a backwater, with dead-end roads on both sides. Boulevard Pomare curves around Papeete's harbor to the tourist office near the market—that's where to begin. Moorea is clearly visible to the northwest.

PAPEETE

Papeete (pa-pay-EH-tay) means "Water Basket." The most likely explanation for this name is that islanders originally used calabashes enclosed in baskets to fetch water at a spring behind the present Territorial Assembly. In the 1820s whalers began frequenting its port, which offered better shelter than Matavai Bay. It became the seat of government when young Queen Pomare settled here in 1827. The French governors who "protected" the island from 1842 also used Papeete as their headquarters.

Today Papeete is the political, cultural, economic, and communications hub of Tahiti-Polynesia. A hundred thousand people live in this cosmopolitan city and its satellite towns, Faa'a, Pirae, and Arue—over half the people on the island. "Greater Papeete" extends for 32 km from Paea to Mahina. In addition, some 4,000 French soldiers are stationed here, mostly hardened foreign legionnaires and police. The French Navy maintains facilities in the harbor area to support its bases in the Tuamotus.

Since the opening of Faa'a International Airport in 1961 Papeete has blossomed with new hotels, expensive restaurants, bars with wild dancing, radio towers, skyscrapers, and electric rock bands pulsing their jet-age beat. Where a nail or red feather may once have satisfied a Tahitian, VCRs and Renaults are now in demand. Over 50,000 registered vehicles jam Tahiti's 200 km of roads. Noisy automobiles, motorcycles, and mopeds clog Papeete's downtown and roar along the boulevards buffeting pedestrians with pollution and noise. Crossing the street you can literally take your life in your hands.

Yet along the waterfront the yachts of many countries rock luxuriously in their Mediterranean moorings (anchor out and stern lines ashore). Many of the boats are permanent homes for expatriate French working in the city. "Bonitiers" moored opposite the Vaima Center fish for *auhopu* (bonito) for the local market. You should not really "tour" Papeete, just wander about without any set goal. Visit the highly specialized French boutiques, Chinese stores trying to sell everything, and Tahitians clustered in the market. Avoid the capital on weekends when life washes out into the countryside; on Sunday afternoons it's a ghost town. Explore Papeete, but make it your starting point—not a final destination.

Orientation

Thanks to airline schedules you'll probably arrive at the crack of dawn. Change money at the airport bank or use a couple of US$1 bills to take *le truck* to Papeete market. The helpful tourist office on the waterfront opens early, as do the banks nearby. You'll probably want a hotel in town for the first couple of nights to attend to "business": reconfirm your flights, check out the boats or planes, then take off for the outer islands.

A trip around the island will fill a day if you're waiting for connections, and Papeete itself can be fun. Fare Ute, north of French naval headquarters, was reclaimed with material dredged from the harbor in 1963. West across a bridge, past more military muscle, is Motu Uta, where you can jump aboard a passenger-carrying freighter. The high-speed boats and all of the Moorea ferries leave from the landing behind the tourist office downtown. For a day at the beach take a *truck* to Point Venus (see below).

SIGHTS

Papeete

Begin your visit at teeming **Papeete market** where you'll see Tahitians selling fish, fruit, root crops, and breadfruit; Chinese gardeners with their tomatoes, lettuce, and other vegetables; and French or Chinese offering meat and bakery products. The colorful throng is especially picturesque 1600-1700 when the fishmongers spring to life. Fish and vegetables are sold downstairs on the main floor, handicrafts and pareus upstairs on the balcony. The biggest market of the week begins around 0500 Sunday morning and is over by 0730.

The streets to the north of the market are lined with two-story Chinese stores built after the great fire of 1884. The US$14.5-million **Town Hall** on rue Paul Gauguin was inaugurated in 1990 on the site of a smaller colonial building demolished to make way. The architect designed the three-story building to resemble the palace of Queen Pomare that once stood on Place Tarahoi near the present post office.

Notre Dame Catholic Cathedral (1875) is on rue du Général de Gaulle, a block and a half southeast of the market. Notice the Polynesian faces and the melange of Tahitian and Roman dress on the striking series of paintings of the crucifixion inside. Diagonally across the street is the **Vaima Center,** Papeete's finest window shopping venue.

Farther down on rue de Gaulle is Place Tarahoi. The **Territorial Assembly** on the left occupies the site of the former royal palace, demolished in 1966. The adjacent residence of the French high commissioner is private, but

the assembly building and its lovely gardens are worth a brief visit. In front of the entrance gate is a monument to **Pouvanaa a Oopa** (1895-1977), a Tahitian WW I hero who struggled all his life for the independence of his country (see "Recent History" in the introduction to this chapter). The plaque on the monument says nothing about Pouvanaa's fight for independence and against the bomb! In July 1995 nearly a third of the adult population of Tahiti gathered here to protest French nuclear testing in the Tuamotus.

Beside the post office across the busy avenue from Place Tarahoi is **Bougainville Park.** A monument to Bougainville himself, who sailed around the world in 1766-69, is flanked by two old naval guns. One, stamped "Fried Krupp 1899," is from Count Felix von Luckner's famous raider *Seeadler,* which ended up on the Maupihaa reef in 1917; the other is off the French gunboat *Zélée,* sunk in Papeete harbor by German cruisers in 1914.

Much of the bureaucracy works along Ave. Bruat just west, a gracious tree-lined French provincial avenue. You may observe French justice in action at the **Palais de Justice** (weekdays 0800-1100). The public gallery is up the stairway and straight ahead. Farther up Ave. Bruat, beyond the War Memorial, are the colonial-style French army barracks, **Quartier Broche.**

Back on the waterfront just before the Protestant church is the **Tahiti Perles Center** (B.P. 850, Papeete; tel. 50-53-10). A black pearl museum (weekdays 0800-1200 and 1400-1730, Saturday 0900-1200; admission free) and aquarium are the main attractions, but look around the showroom where the famous black pearls are sold. A 20-minute video presentation shown on request explains how cultured black pearls are "farmed" in the Gambier Islands.

Next to the pearl museum is Paofai, the headquarters of the **Evangelical Church** in Tahiti-Polynesia, with a church (rebuilt 1980), public cafeteria, girls' hostel, and health clinic. This church is descended from the London Missionary Society; the British consulate occupied the hostel site from 1837 to 1958. George Pritchard (see this chapter's "History" section) had his office here.

Continue west along the bay past the outrigger racing canoes to the "neo-Polynesian" **Cultural Center** (1973), which houses a public library, notice boards, and auditoriums set among pleasant grounds. This complex is run by the Office Territorial d'Action Culturelle (OTAC), which organizes the annual Heiva Festival and many other events. The municipal swimming pool is beyond (go upstairs to the snack bar for a view). Return to the center of town along the waterfront.

Another walk takes you east from downtown to the Catholic **Archbishop's Palace** (1869), a lonely remnant of the Papeete that Gauguin saw. To get there, take the road behind the Catholic cathedral, keep straight, and ask for the *archevêché catholique*. Without doubt, this is the finest extant piece of colonial architecture in a territory of fast-disappearing historic buildings. The park grounds planted in citrus and the modern open-air church nearby (to the right) also merit a look.

Fautaua Valley

If you'd like to make a short trip out of the city, go to the Hôtel de Ville and take a Mamao-Titioro *truck* to the **Bain Loti,** three km up the Fautaua Valley from the Mormon Temple. A bust of writer Pierre Loti marks the spot where he had the love affair described in *The Marriage of Loti,* but the area has been spoiled by tasteless construction.

A dirt road continues three km farther up the Fautaua Valley but because it's part of a water catchment, private cars are prohibited, so you must walk. From the end of the road, a trail straight ahead leads directly to **Fautaua Falls** (30 minutes) with several river crossings. Back a bit on the left, just before the end of the road, is a wooden footbridge across the river. Here begins a steep one-hour trail up to a 19th-century French fort at the top of the falls. The fort controlled the main trail into Tahiti's interior, and it's still an excellent hiking area. There's occasionally a CFP 500 pp charge to go up the valley, and officially you're supposed to go on a weekday. Go early and make a day of it.

Back on Ave. Georges Clemenceau near the Mormon Temple is the impressive **Kanti Chinese Temple,** built in 1986.

East of Papeete

Arue (a-roo-AY) and Point Venus can be done easily as a half-day side trip from Papeete by *le truck* (12 km each way). Begin by taking a Mahina *truck* from near the tourist office to the **tomb of King Pomare V** at PK 4.7 Arue, five km outside the city. The mausoleum was built in 1879 for Queen Pomare IV, but her remains were subsequently removed to make room for her son, Pomare V, who died of drink in 1891 (Paul Gauguin witnessed the funeral). A century earlier, on 13 February 1791, his grandfather, Pomare II, then nine, was made first king of Tahiti on the great *marae* that once stood on this spot. Pomare II became the first Christian convert and built a 215-meter-long version of King Solomon's Temple here, but nothing remains of either temple.

At PK 5.4, Arue, next to the École Maternelle Ahutoru, stand the tombs of Pomare I, II, III, and IV in the **Cimetière Pomare.** This lesser-known site is not signposted, but a building across the street is marked Artisanat. A board next to the cemetery clearly identifies the many Pomare graves here.

The **Hyatt Regency Hôtel** (PK 8.1) on One Tree Hill, a couple of km east of the Pomare graves, was built in 1968 on a spectacular series of terraces down the hillside to conform to a local regulation that no building should be more than two-thirds the height of a coconut tree. There's a superb view of Point Venus, Tahiti, and Moorea from the Governor's Bench on the knoll just beyond the hotel entrance. In Matavai Bay below the Hyatt Regency, Capt. Samuel Wallis anchored in 1767, after having "discovered" Tahiti. There's good swimming off the black beach below the hotel.

Catch another *truck* or walk on to **Point Venus** (PK 10). Captain Cook camped on this point between the river and the lagoon during his visit to observe the transit of the planet Venus across the sun on 3 June 1769. Captain Bligh also occupied Point Venus for two months in 1788 while collecting breadfruit shoots for transportation to the West Indies. On 5 March 1797, the first members of the London Missionary Society landed here, as a monument recalls. From Tahiti, Protestantism spread throughout Polynesia and as far as Vanuatu.

Today there's a park on the point, with a 25-meter-high lighthouse (1867) among the palms and ironwood trees. The view of Tahiti across Matavai Bay is superb, and twin-humped Orohena, highest peak on the island, is in view (you can't see it from Papeete itself). Topless sunbathing is common on the wide dark sands along the bay and you can see pareus being made in the handicraft center in the park. Weekdays, Point Venus is a peaceful place, the perfect choice if you'd like to get away from the rat race in Papeete and spend some time at the beach (weekends it gets crowded).

AROUND THE ISLAND

A 117-km Route de Ceinture (Belt Road) runs right around Tahiti Nui, the larger part of this hourglass-shaped island. Construction began in the 1820s as a form of punishment. For orientation you'll see red-and-white kilometer stones, called PK (point kilométrique), along the inland side of the road. These are numbered in each direction from the Catholic cathedral in Papeete, meeting at Taravao.

Go clockwise to get over the most difficult stretch first; also, you'll be riding on the inside lane of traffic and less likely to go off a cliff in case of an accident (an average of 55 people a year are killed and 700 injured in accidents on this island). Southern Tahiti is much quieter than the northwest, whereas from Paea to Mahina it's hard to slow down as tailgating motorists roar behind you.

If you're a bit adventurous it's quite possible to do a circle-island tour on le truck, provided you get an early start and go clockwise with no stop until Taravao. Ask for the Tautira truck, but if it looks like they won't be going for quite a while, take any truck headed for Papenoo and wait there. Once at Taravao, walk across the peninsula (15 minutes) and look for another truck coming from Teahupoo to take you back to Papeete along the south coast. If you get stuck, it's comforting to know that hitchhiking (l'autostop) is fairly easy and relatively safe on Tahiti. The local people are very receptive to foreign visitors, so you'll improve your chances if it's obvious you're not French. For instance, try using a destination sign (never used by locals). There's lots of traffic along the straight south coast highway

all day and it's almost certain you'll get a ride eventually. For more information on le truck, see "Getting Around" under "Practicalities" later in this section.

However you travel around Tahiti, it's customary to smile and wave to the Tahitians you see (outside Papeete). And if you want an excellent second resource, pick up Bengt Danielsson's Tahiti, Circle Island Tour Guide at a Papeete bookstore before you set out.

The Northeast Coast

The coast is very rugged all along the northeast side of the island. The **leper colony** at Orofara (PK 13.2) was founded in 1914. Previously the colony was on Reao atoll in the Tuamotus, but this proved too remote to service. Some 50 patients are housed at Orofara today.

Surfers ride the waves at Chinaman's Bay, Papenoo (PK 16). The bridge over the broad **Papenoo River** (PK 17.1) allows a view up the largest valley on Tahiti.

At the **Arahoho Blowhole** (PK 22), jets of water shoot up through holes in the lava rock beside the highway at high tide. It's dangerous to get too close to the blowhole as a sudden surge could toss you out to sea! Just a little beyond it, a road to the right leads one km up to the three **Tefa'aurumai Waterfalls** (admission free), also known as the Faarumai Falls. Vaimahuta Falls is accessible on foot in five minutes along the easy path to the right across the bridge. The 30-minute trail to the left leads to two more waterfalls, Haamaremare Iti and Haamaremare Rahi, but it's more difficult and even impassible if the river is high. The farthest falls has a pool deep enough for swimming. Bring insect repellent and beware of theft if you park a rental car at these falls.

At **Mahaena** (PK 32.5) is the battleground where 441 well-armed French troops defeated a dug-in Tahitian force twice their size on 17 April 1844 in the last fixed confrontation of the French-Tahitian War. The Tahitians carried on a guerrilla campaign another two years until the French captured their main mountain stronghold.

The French ships La Boudeuse and L'Étoile, carrying explorer Louis-Antoine de Bougainville, anchored by the southernmost of two islets off **Hitiaa** (PK 37.6) on 6 April 1768. Unaware that an Englishman had visited Tahiti a year before, Bougainville christened the island "New Cythera,"

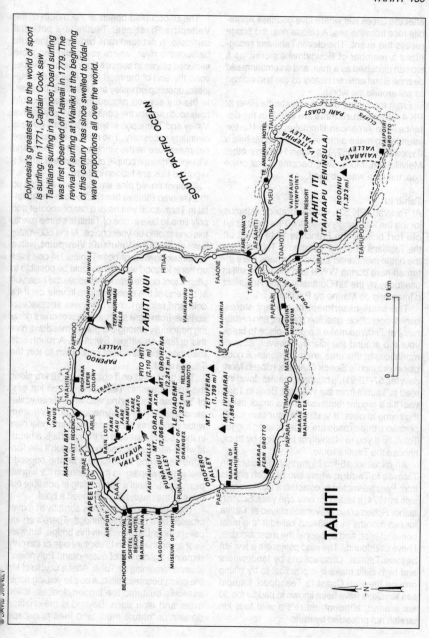

Polynesia's greatest gift to the world of sport is surfing. In 1771, Captain Cook saw Tahitians surfing in a canoe; board surfing was first observed off Hawaii in 1779. The revival of surfing at Waikiki at the beginning of this century has since swelled to tidal-wave proportions all over the world.

SOUTH PACIFIC OCEAN

TAHITI

TAHITI NUI

POINT VENUS
MATAVAI BAY
Hyatt Regency
PIRAE
ARUE
BAIN LOTI
FARE RAU APE
FARE HAMUTA
FARE MATO
Fautaua Falls
FAUTAUA VALLEY
PUNARUU VALLEY
PUNARUU MT. AORAI (2,066 m)
ORANGES
PUNAAUIA PLATEAU DE LA MAROTO
OROFERO VALLEY

PAPEETE
AIRPORT
FAAA
BEACHCOMBER PARKROYAL
SOFITEL MAEVA BEACH HOTEL
MARINA TAINA
LAGOONARIUM
MUSEUM OF TAHITI

MAHINA
OROFARA LEPER COLONY
PAPENOO TRAIL
PAPENOO VALLEY
PITO HITI (2,110 m)
LE DIADEME (1,321 m)
MT. OROHENA (2,241 m)
RELAIS DE LA MAROTO
MT. OROHENA ATA

ARAHOHO BLOWHOLE
TIAREI
TEFA'AURUMAI
TEFA'AURUMAI FALLS
MAHAENA
HITIAA
FAAONE

MT. TETUFERA (1,799 m)
MT. IVIRAIRAI (1,696 m)
MARAE OF ARAHURAHU
PAEA
MARAA FERN GROTTO
PAPARA
MARAE OF MAHAIATEA
MATAIEA
ATIMAONO
GAUGUIN MUSEUM
PAPEARI
Lake Vaihiria
VAIHARURU FALLS

TARAVAO
TARAVAO JUNCTION
PORT PHAETON
VAIRAO
TEAHUPOO
MARINA
PUUNUI RESORT
VAIUFAUFA VIEWPOINT
PUEU
AFAAHITI
TOAHOTU
FARE NANA'O

TAHITI ITI (TAIARAPU PENINSULA)
MT. ROONIU (1,323 m)

TAUTIRA
TE ANUANUA HOTEL
VAITEPIHA VALLEY
VAIARAVA VALLEY
TAIPORO GROTTO
PARI COAST
CLIFFS

0   10 km

N

after the Greek isle where love goddess Aphrodite rose from the sea. A plaque near the bridge recalls the event. The clever Tahitians recognized a member of Bougainville's crew as a woman disguised as a man, and an embarrassed Jeanne Baret entered history as the first woman to sail around the world.

From the bridge over the Faatautia River at PK 41.8 **Vaiharuru Falls** are visible in the distance. The American filmmaker John Huston intended to make a movie of Herman Melville's *Typee* here in 1957, but when Huston's other Melville film, *Moby Dick,* became a box-office flop, the idea was dropped.

Tahiti Iti

At Taravao (PK 53), on the strategic isthmus joining the two Tahitis where the PKs meet, is an **old fort** built by the French in 1844 to cut off the Tahitians who had retreated to Tahiti Iti after the battle mentioned above. Germans were interned here during WW II and the fort is still in use today by the 1st Company of the Régiment d'Infanterie de Marine du Pacifique.

The small assortment of grocery stores, banks, post office, gasoline stations, and restaurants at Taravao make it a good place to break your trip around the island; however, accommodations in this area are inadequate. A good place for lunch is **Snack Guilloux** (closed Monday; tel. 57-12-91), a hundred meters down the road to Tautira from the Westpac Bank in Taravao. It's a regular restaurant, not a snack bar as the name implies. If you have your own transportation, three roads are explorable on rugged Tahiti Iti. If you're hitching or traveling by *truck,* choose the Tautira route.

An excellent 18-km highway runs east from Taravao to Tautira, where two Spanish priests from Peru attempted to establish a Catholic mission in 1774; it lasted for only one year. Scottish author Robert Louis Stevenson stayed at Tautira for two months in 1888 and called it "the most beautiful spot, and its people the most amiable, I have ever found." The road peters out a few km beyond Tautira. Obstructions by landowners and high cliffs make it impractical to try hiking around the Pari Coast to Teahupoo. Intrepid sea kayakers have been known to paddle the 30 km around, although there's a wild four-km stretch not protected by reefs.

The unoccupied beach at the mouth of the **Vaitepiha River** near Tautira is a potential campsite. A dirt road runs two km up the right bank of the river, where you could find more secluded places to camp. If you're keen, hike beyond the end of the road for a look at this majestic, unoccupied valley and a swim in the river. In the dry season rugged backpackers could hike south across the peninsula to the Vaiarava Valley and Teahupoo in two days, but a guide is definitely necessary. The ruins of at least three old *marae* are at the junction of the Vaitia and Vaitepiha rivers a couple of hours inland, and it's reported tikis are hidden in there.

Another paved nine-km road runs straight up the Taravao Plateau from just before the hospital in Taravao. If you have a car or scooter and only time to take in one of Tahiti Iti's three roads, this one should be your choice. At the 600-meter level on top is the **Vaiufaufa Viewpoint,** with a breathtaking view of both Tahitis. No one lives up here: in good weather it would be possible to pitch a tent on the grassy hill above the reservoir at the end of the road (or sleep in your car if it's cold and raining). You'll witness spectacular sunsets from here and the herds of cows grazing peacefully among the grassy meadows give this upland an almost Swiss air. A rough side road near the viewpoint cuts down to join the Tautira road.

The third road on Tahiti Iti runs 18 km along the south coast to Teahupoo. Seven km east of Taravao is a **marina** with an artificial white-sand beach (PK 7). American pulp Western writer Zane Grey had his fishing camp near here in the 1930s. Just east of the marina is a natural white-sand public beach where you'll see fishermen spearing by torchlight on the opposite reef in the evening. In the afternoon it's a great picnic spot. Tahiti's best surfing is possible out there in the pass, but you'll need a boat.

The **Teahupoo** road ends abruptly at a river crossed by a narrow footbridge. There's an excellent mountain view from this bridge, but walk east along the beach to capture one of the only remaining glimpses of outer-island Polynesian lifestyle remaining on Tahiti. After a couple of km the going becomes difficult due to yelping dogs, seawalls built into the lagoon, fences, fallen trees, and *tapu* signs. Beyond is the onetime domain of "nature men" who tried to escape civilization by living alone with nature over half a century ago.

Three hours on foot from the end of the road is **Vaipoiri Grotto,** a large water-filled cave best reached by boat. Try hiring a motorized canoe or hitch a ride with someone at the end of the road. Beyond this the high cliffs of Te Pari terminate all foot traffic along the shore; the only way to pass is by boat. All the land east of Teahupoo is well fenced off, so finding a campsite would involve getting someone's permission. It's probably easier to look elsewhere.

Gauguin Museum

Port Phaeton on the southwest side of the Taravao Isthmus is an excellent harbor. Timeless oral traditions tell that the first Polynesians to reach Tahiti settled at Papeari (PK 52—measured now from the west). In precontact times the chiefly family of this district was among the most prestigious on the island.

The Gauguin Museum (B.P. 7029, Taravao; tel. 57-10-58; open daily 0900-1700, CFP 450 admission) is at PK 51.7 in Papeari District. The museum, opened in 1965, tells the painter's tormented life story and shows the present locations of his works throughout the world. Strangely, Gauguin's Tahitian mistresses get little attention in the museum. A couple of his minor woodcarvings and prints are exhibited (but no Gauguin paintings). Most of the photos are numbered and you may be able to borrow a catalog.

Ex-Paris stockbroker Paul Gauguin arrived at Papeete in 1891 at age 43 in search of the roots of "primitive" art. He lived at Mataiea with his 14-year-old mistress Teha'amana for a year and a half, joyfully painting. In 1893 he returned to France with 66 paintings and about a dozen woodcarvings, which were to establish his reputation. Unfortunately, his exhibition flopped and Gauguin returned to Tahiti a second time, infected with VD and poor, settling at Punaauia. After an unsuccessful suicide attempt he recovered somewhat, and in 1901 a Paris art dealer named Vollard signed a contract with Gauguin, assuring him a monthly payment of 350 francs and a purchase price of 250 francs per picture. His financial problems alleviated, the painter left for Hiva Oa, Marquesas Islands, to find an environment uncontaminated by Western influences. During the last two years of his life at Atuona Gauguin's eccentricities put him on the wrong side of the ecclesiastical and official hierarchies. He died in 1903 at age 53, a near outcast among his countrymen in the islands, yet today a Papeete street and school are named after him!

The two-meterish, two-ton stone tiki on the museum grounds is said to be imbued with a sacred *tapu* spell. Tahitians believe this tiki, carved on the island of Raivavae hundreds of years ago, still lives. The three Tahitians who moved the statue here from Papeete in 1965 all died mysterious deaths within a few weeks. A curse is still said to befall all who touch the tiki.

A **botanical garden** rich in exotic species is part of the Gauguin Museum complex (CFP 400 additional admission). This 137-hectare garden was created in 1919-21 by the American botanist Harrison Smith (1872-1947), who introduced over 200 new species to the island, among them the sweet grapefruit (pomelo), mangosteen, rambutan, and durian. Actually, if you have to choose between the garden or the museum (due to the high admission fees), it's probably better to see the garden and give the superficial museum a miss.

The attractive **Gauguin Museum Restaurant** (tel. 57-13-80), a km west of the museum, hosts circle-island tour groups for lunch, and you can join them for CFP 2100 for the buffet (daily noon-1430). Even if you're not hungry, it's still worth a stop to see the fish swimming in the enclosure around the wharf and to take in the view.

At PK 49 is the **Jardin Vaipahi** with a lovely waterfall minutes from the road (admission free).

Lake Vaihiria

The unmarked road to Lake Vaihiria begins at PK 47.6 between a housing settlement and a Mormon church (Église de Jesus-Christ des Saints des Derniers Jours), just before the bridge over the Vairaharaha River as you travel west. The rough track leads 12 km up to Lake Vaihiria, Tahiti's only lake, following the Vaihiria River, which has been harnessed for hydroelectricity. Two km up the road you'll encounter a white hydro substation and the first of a series of Piste Privée signs advising motorists that the road is closed to nonresidents, though open to pedestrians. This regulation is not enforced, and in dry weather a rental car could continue another five km to a dam and the lower power station, provided the chain across the road isn't locked.

A km beyond is an archaeological site with restored *marae*. Three km beyond this (11 km from the main road) is a second dam and an upper (larger) power station. Beyond this point only a 4WD vehicle could proceed, passing prominent Danger signs, another km up a steep concrete track to Lake Vaihiria itself.

Sheer cliffs and spectacular waterfalls squeeze in around the spring-fed lake, and the shore would make a fine campsite (though overrun by mosquitoes). Native floppy-eared eels known as *puhi taria*, up to 1.8 meters long, live in these cold waters. With its luxuriant vegetation this rain-drenched 473-meter-high spot is one of the most evocative on the island. The track proceeds up and through a 200-meter tunnel and over to the Papenoo Valley, a four-hour trip by 4WD jeep or two days on foot. You must wade through the rivers about 20 times.

The easiest way to do this trip is seated in a chauffeur-driven 4WD jeep booked through **Tahiti Mer et Loisirs** (B.P. 3488, Papeete; tel. 43-97-99, fax 43-33-68), in a houseboat on the Papeete waterfront opposite the post office. It's CFP 9500 pp including lunch and drinks (four-person minimum participation).

The 24-room **Relais de la Maroto** (B.P. 20687, Papeete; tel. 41-48-60 or 58-26-12, fax 57-90-30) is a cluster of large concrete buildings at the junction of the Vaituoru and Vainave-

nave rivers in the upper Papenoo Valley. The accommodations here are upmarket at CFP 6000 pp, plus CFP 4500 extra for breakfast and dinner in the sharp modern restaurant. The only access is by 4WD, helicopter, or foot. Local French often come here for the weekend. If you can afford it, the Relais provides a good base for exploring the many waterfalls and archaeological remains in this area.

The South Coast

Tahiti-Polynesia's only golf course, the **International Golf Course Olivier Breaud** (B.P. 12008, Papara; tel. 57-40-32) at PK 41, Atimaono, stretches up to the mountainside on the site of Terre Eugenie, a cotton and sugar plantation established by Scotsman William Stewart at the time of the U.S. Civil War (1863). Many of today's Tahitian Chinese are descended from Chinese laborers imported to do the work, and a novel by A. T'Serstevens, *The Great Plantation,* was set here. The present 6,355-meter, 18-hole course (run by Tahiti Tourisme) was laid out in 1970 with a par 72 for men, par 73 for women. If you'd like to do a round, the green fees are CFP 3000, and clubs and cart rent for another CFP 2500 (open daily 0800-1700). The Tahiti Open in June or July attracts professionals from around the Pacific. The golf course restaurant is said to be good.

Behind the golf course is the **Parc d'Atimaono,** a favorite hiking area. A road closed to cars, which begins next to the golf course parking lot, leads several kilometers up into this

Mahaiatea Marae at Papara on the south coast of Tahiti: This 11-step pyramid was once the largest pagan temple on the island, but time, nature, and the depredations of man have taken their toll.

M.G.L. DOMENY DE RIENZI

area, though you may be charged CFP 500 as a "day visitor" to the golf course.

The **Marae of Mahaiatea** (PK 39.2) at Papara was once the most hallowed temple on Tahiti. Captain Cook's botanist Joseph Banks wrote, "It is almost beyond belief that Indians could raise so large a structure without the assistance of iron tools." Less than a century later planter William Stewart raided the *marae* for building materials, and storms did the rest. Today it's only a rough heap of stones, but still worth visiting for its aura and setting. You could swim and snorkel off the beach next to the *marae,* but watch the currents. The unmarked turnoff to the *marae* is a hundred meters west of Beach Burger, then straight down to the beach.

Surfers take the waves at Papara Beach (PK 38), one of the best sites on Tahiti. By the church at **Papara** (PK 36) is the grave of Dorence Atwater (1845-1910), U.S. consul to Tahiti from 1871-88. Atwater's claim to fame dates back to the American Civil War, when he recorded the names of 13,000 dead Union prisoners at Andersonville Prison, Georgia, from lists the Confederates had been withholding. Himself a Union prisoner, Atwater escaped with his list in March 1865. When you consider how the present U.S. government continues to use troops allegedly missing in Indochina as pawns in its dealings with Vietnam, the political value of Atwater's contribution to the Union officials of his day is clear. Atwater's tombstone provides details. Across the street from the church is a Centre Artisanal selling handicrafts, and a Sea Shell Museum.

Maraa Fern Grotto (PK 28.5) is by the road just across the Paea border. An optical illusion, the grotto at first appears small but is quite deep and some Tahitians believe *varua ino* (evil spirits) lurk in the shadowy depths. Others say that if you follow an underground river back from the grotto you'll emerge at a wonderful valley in the spirit world. Paul Gauguin wrote of a swim he took across the small lake in the cave; you're also welcome to jump in the blue-gray water. You can fill your water bottle with fresh mineral water from eight spouts next to the parking lot.

On the mountain side of the road at PK 26.5 is the small **Ava Tea Distillery** (B.P. 10398, Paea; tel. 53-32-43), which can be visited daily 0900-1200 and 1400-1700.

The Southwest Coast

The **Marae Arahurahu** at PK 22.5, Paea, is up the road from Magasin Laut—take care, the sign faces Papeete, so it's not visible if you're traveling clockwise. This temple, lying in a tranquil, verdant spot under high cliffs, is perhaps Tahiti's only remaining pagan mystery. The ancient open altars built from thousands of cut stones were completely restored in 1954 (open daily, admission free). Historical pageants (CFP 1500 admission) recreating pagan rites are performed here during the July festivities.

For some hiking, Paea's **Orofero Valley** is recommended and camping might be possible up beyond the end of the road (six km). From the main highway take the first road inland south of the large Catholic church by the Vaiatu River at PK 21.5 (look for the sign reading Prefabriques Piccolini). You can drive a car three km up. When you get to the *tapu* sign, park, cross the river, and continue up the other side on foot. A jeep track runs another three km up the valley (half-hour walk), through half a dozen river crossings (wear rubber booties or zories). At the end of the road a tall waterfall is to the left and the trail continues ahead. Orofero is one of the few Tahitian valleys free of trash!

The West Coast

On Fishermen's Point, Punaauia, is the **Museum of Tahiti and the Islands** (B.P. 6272, Faa'a; tel. 58-22-09; open Tuesday to Sunday 0930-1700; admission CFP 500). Located in a large, modern complex on the lagoon, about a km down a narrow road from PK 15.1, this worthwhile museum has four halls devoted to the natural environment, the origins of the Polynesians, Polynesian culture, and the history of Polynesia. What isn't covered is the history of France's nuclear testing program in Polynesia and how the Polynesians feel about it. Outside is a huge double-hulled canoe and Captain Cook's anchor from Tautira. Most of the captions are in French, Tahitian, and English (photography allowed).

When the waves are right, you can sit on the seawall behind the museum and watch the Tahitian surfers bob and ride, with the outline of Moorea beyond. On your way back to the main highway from the museum, look up to the top of the hill at an **old fort** used by the French to sub-

Early tourists ride in style in this 1910 photo taken at Punaauia.

jugate the Tahitians in the 1840s. The crown-shaped pinnacles of **Le Diadème** (1,321 meters) are also visible from this road.

If you want to see pollution on a massive scale, follow the route up the once-beautiful **Punaruu Valley** behind the Punaauia industrial zone (PK 14.8). You can drive a normal car five km up a valley incredibly trashed out with garbage dumps all the way. At the end of the valley is a water catchment and, although the way leads on to the fantastic Plateau of Oranges, entry is forbidden. Tahitian enterprises dump their refuse in valleys all around the island, but this has got to be the ugliest! Here paradise ends.

From 1896 to 1901 Gauguin had his studio at PK 12.6 Punaauia, but nothing remains of it; his *Two Tahitian Women* was painted here. The **Lagoonarium** (B.P. 2381, Papeete; tel. 43-62-90), below the lagoon behind Captain Bligh Restaurant at PK 11.4, Punaauia, provides a vision of the underwater marinelife of Polynesia safely behind glass. The big tank full of black-tip sharks is a feature. Entry is CFP 500 pp, open daily, half price for restaurant customers, and CFP 300 for children under 12. The shark feeding takes place around noon.

Punaauia and Paea are Tahiti's "Gold Coast," with old colonial homes hidden behind trees along the lagoonside and *nouveau riche* villas dotting the hillside above. At PK 8, Outumaoro, is the turnoff for the RDO bypass to Papeete, Tahiti's only superhighway! Follow the Université signs from here up to the ultramodern campus of the **French University of the Pacific** with its fantastic hilltop view of Moorea and excellent library (tel. 45-01-65).

On the old airport road just north are Tahiti's biggest hotels: the **Sofitel Maeva Beach** (PK 7.5) and **Beachcomber Parkroyal** (PK 7), each worth a stop—though their beaches are polluted. From the point where the Beachcomber Parkroyal is today, the souls of deceased Tahitians once leapt on their journey to the spirit world. A sunset behind Moorea's jagged peaks, across the Sea of the Moon from either of these hotels, is a spectacular finale to a circle-island tour. As you reenter Papeete, **Uranie Cemetery** (PK 1.5) is on your right.

The west coast of Tahiti can also be visited as a day-trip from Papeete; start by taking a *truck* to the Fern Grotto at Paea, then work your way back. *Trucks* back to Papeete from the vicinity of the Maeva Beach Hôtel run late into the night, but the last one from the Museum of Tahiti is around 1630.

MOUNTAIN CLIMBING

Tahiti's finest climb is to the summit of **Aorai** (2,066 meters), third-highest peak on the island. A beaten 10-km track all the way to the top makes a guide unnecessary, but food, water, flashlight, and long pants *are* required, plus a sleeping bag and warm sweater if you plan to spend the night up there. At last report the refuges at Fare Mato (1,400 meters) and Fare Ata (1,800 meters) were in good shape with drinking water available and splendid sunset views.

The trailhead is at Fare Rau Ape (600 meters) near **Le Belvédère** (tel. 42-73-44), an overpriced tourist restaurant seven km up a rough, potholed road from Pirae. The restaurant provides a free *truck* from Papeete at 1130 and 1700 for those willing to spend CFP 4200 on a mediocre meal (the *truck* is the easiest way to get there if you're going). Parking near the restaurant is limited. Taxis want CFP 5000 for the trip and few people live up there, so hitching would be a case of finding tourists headed for the restaurant, and weekends are best for this. A large signboard outside the restaurant maps out the hike.

Just above the restaurant is the French Army's Centre d'Instruction de Montagne, where you must sign the register. From Fare Rau Ape to the summit takes seven hours: an hour and a half to Hamuta, another two to Fare Mato (good view of Le Diadème, not visible from Papeete), then two and a half hours to Fare Ata, where most hikers spend the first night in order to cover the last 40 minutes to the summit the following morning. The hut at Fare Ata is in a low depression 100 meters beyond an open shelter.

The view from Aorai is magnificent, with Papeete and many of the empty interior valleys in full view. To the north is Tetiaroa atoll, while Moorea's jagged outline fills the west. Even on a cloudy day the massive green hulk of neighboring Orohena (2,241 meters) often towers above the clouds like Mt. Olympus. A bonus is the chance to see some of the original native vegetation of Tahiti, which survives better at high altitudes and in isolated gullies. In good weather Aorai is exhausting but superb; in the rain it's a disaster.

When the author of this book climbed Aorai some years ago, the trip could be done by any-

one in reasonable physical shape. Later we heard that the trail had deteriorated, with sheer slopes and slippery, crumbling ridges to be negotiated. In the past we've asked readers to write in with current information on Aorai, and we're grateful to Charlie Appleton of Nottingham, England, for sending us this report:

The trail has been restored and is now well maintained. The chalets at Fare Mato and Fare Ata were in excellent order, the former sitting on a recently reconstructed platform. They'll sleep 12-15 without difficulty, though only the hut at Fare Ata has drinking water. Just above Fare Mato cables have been fixed along the section of trail with the steepest drops on both sides, allowing some fairly inexperienced hikers I met to traverse it with confidence. Very few people do the climb, and if you go in the middle of the week you can expect to have the mountain to yourself. It might be worth mentioning that the compelling reason for spending the night on top (apart from sunset and sunrise) is that those who make the roundtrip in a day are likely to find that by the time they near the summit the mountain will have put on its midday hat of clouds, limiting their views.

The track to the top of Aorai runs along this razor-back ridge.

DAVID STANLEY

More recently, Will Paine of Maidstone, England, sent us this:

Thanks to clear weather, Aorai was one of the most satisfying "officially endorsed" hikes I've ever done. It's not for the faint-hearted, but otherwise thoroughly recommended. The dangerous part is from 1,400 meters onwards and constant awareness is necessary on the knife-edge ridges (walking roped together is an idea). Some early sections have cables for hanging on, but the irons are shaky as they've only been installed "after the fact," as it were.

Neighboring **Orohena** is seldom climbed, since the way involves considerable risks. The route up Orohena begins at the office of the Sheriff de Mahina, opposite the military laboratories. Follow the road five km straight up through Mahinarama subdivision. At about 600 meters elevation, where the paved road becomes a dirt track, there's a chain across the road. Park here and hike up the track past two large water tanks. A jeep track built into the slope in 1975 follows the contour six km up the Tuauru River valley to the **Thousand Springs** at 900 meters elevation. Anyone at Mahinarama will be able to direct you to the "Route des Mille Sources." The actual Orohena trail begins at the Thousand Springs and climbs steeply to Pito Iti where hikers spend the night before ascending Orohena the following morning. To climb Orohena a guide is most certainly required, but anyone can do the Thousand Springs hike of their own, enjoying good views of the rounded peaks of Orohena to the left and Aorai's long ridge to the right. There's nothing special to see at the Thousand Springs, so turn back whenever you like.

Guides

These and other hikes on Tahiti are led on weekends and holidays by **Pierre Florentin** (B.P. 5323, Pirae; tel./fax 43-72-01), a professional mountain guide with 20 years of experience. Pierre charges a fixed rate of CFP 16,000 a day for groups of up to eight persons maximum—well worth considering if there are a few of you.

The trips offered include climbs up Orohena (three days) and Aorai (two days), the hike across Tahiti Iti (two days), and day-trips to Fautaua Falls, Papenoo Falls, Mt. Marau, a lava tube, etc. Pierre also organizes hang gliding from Mt. Marau. Transport to the trailheads is included, but backpacks and tents are extra (if required), and participants must bring their own food. Pierre's services are highly recommended for small groups of serious hikers/climbers concerned about both safety and success.

Another professional guide, **Angélien Zéna** (B.P. 7426, Taravao; tel. 57-22-67), specializes in hikes around the Pari Coast at the east end of Tahiti Iti, the "Circuit Vert." Angélien's three-day trip costs CFP 110,000 for up to 10 persons, meals and transport from/to Taravao included. Time off is allowed for swimming and fishing. A boat from Vairao to Vaipoiri Grotto is used on the two-day hikes, and day-trips can also be arranged. Even if there are only a few of you, it's worth calling both Pierre and Angélien to learn if they have any trips scheduled that you might join.

The **Club Te Fenua O Te Mau Mato** (Pierre Wrobel, B.P. 9304, Papeete; tel. 43-04-64) organizes weekend hikes on Tahiti and Moorea several times a month. Also call the president of the **Tahitian Alpine Club,** Marc Allain (B.P. 11553, Mahina; tel. 48-10-59).

SPORTS AND RECREATION

For information on the International Golf Course Olivier Breaud at Atimaono, see "The South Coast" under "Around the Island," above.

Tahiti Plongée (B.P. 2192, Papeete; tel. 41-00-62, fax 42-26-06), also known as "Club Corail Sub," offers scuba diving several times daily from its base at the Hôtel Te Puna Bel Air, Punaauia. The charge is CFP 3800 per dive all-inclusive, or CFP 18,000 for a five-dive card, CFP 28,000 for 10 dives. You can ocean dive Tuesday to Sunday at 0800 and on Wednesday and Saturday at 1400; lagoon diving is daily at 1000 and weekdays at 1400 (no diving on Monday).

Divemaster Henri Pouliquen was one of the first to teach scuba diving to children. The youngest person Henri has taken down was aged two years, six months—the oldest was a woman of 72 on her first dive. Since 1979 Tahiti Plongée has arranged over 10,000 dives with children, certainly a unique accomplishment. Handicapped diving is also a specialty. Most diving is on the Punaauia reef. Other favorite scuba locales include a scuttled Pan Am Catalina PBY seaplane near the airport, its upper wing 12 meters down; and a schooner wreck, 10 meters down, about 45 meters from the breakwater at the entrance to the harbor.

Tahiti Aquatique (B.P. 6008, Faa'a; tel. 42-80-42, fax 41-08-54) beside the wharf at the Maeva Beach Hôtel also offers professional scuba-diving services. Their prices are higher than those of Tahiti Plongée (CFP 5000 for scuba diving). For CFP 700 pp roundtrip they'll shuttle you out to their offshore sunbathing pontoon anchored above a snorkeling locale (no lifeguard or shade). Rental of mask, snorkel, and fins is extra. Underwater photography equipment and PADI certification courses are available. This company is run by American marine biologist Dick Johnson who came to Tahiti to research a book on sharks, and never left.

Scuba diving can also be arranged with Pascal Le Cointre at the **Yacht Club of Tahiti** (B.P. 1456, Papeete; tel. 42-23-55, fax 42-37-07) at PK 4, Arue. Outings are offered at 0900 and 1400 daily except Sunday afternoon and Monday with reduced rates for five-dive packages. They also do certification courses.

If you want to set out on your own, **Nauti-Sport** (B.P. 62, Papeete; tel. 42-09-94, fax 42-17-75) sells every type of scuba gear and also rents tanks (CFP 2500). They sometimes offer scuba trips at very competitive prices and have information on diving all around Polynesia. For serious divers, this is an excellent place to come for information.

Deep-sea fishing can be arranged by **Tahiti Mer et Loisirs** (B.P. 3488, Papeete; tel. 43-97-99, fax 43-33-68), in a houseboat on the Papeete waterfront opposite the post office. Their charter boats begin at CFP 60,000 a day (0800-1600) and up to six anglers can go for that. Bring your own snacks and drinks.

Papeete's **municipal swimming pool** (tel. 42-89-24) is open to the public Tuesday to Friday 1145-1600, Saturday and Sunday 0730-1700 (CFP 350). Most evenings after 1800 soc-

cer is practiced in the sports field opposite the municipal swimming pool.

ACCOMMODATIONS

Almost all of the places to stay are in the congested Punaauia-to-Mahina strip engulfing Faa'a International Airport and Papeete. Representatives of the various hotels often meet incoming flights, and most provide free transport to their establishments. If not, call them up and ask. The hotels below are listed clockwise in each category, beginning in Punaauia.

Budget Accommodations near the Airport

Chez Armelle (B.P. 13291, Punaauia; tel. 58-42-43, fax 58-42-81) at PK 15.5 in Punaauia (almost opposite a large Mobil service station), has 10 rooms at CFP 3500/6000 single/double including breakfast. Some of the rooms have private bath, and communal cooking facilities are provided. Dinner is available at CFP 1000 pp. It's right on the beach (though the rooms are not), but this place caters more to people planning long stays: you get seven nights for the price of five and one month is CFP 100,000 double.

In a pinch, **Chez Sorensen** (Joséphine Dahl, tel. 82-63-30), directly across the street from the airport terminal (the second house on the left up the hill beside Blanchisserie Pressing Mea Ma), has three rooms with bath at CFP 3500/6000 single/double, breakfast included. Communal cooking facilities are available, but the location is noisy due to the nearby industrial laundry and airport.

The **Heitiare Inn** (B.P. 6830, Papeete; tel. 83-33-52 or 82-77-53) at PK 4.3, Faa'a, a km east of the airport, has six rooms at CFP 3500/4500 single/double with shared bath, CFP 5000/5500 with a/c, and CFP 6000 double with a/c and private bath. Communal cooking facilities are provided. The snack bar at the inn is inexpensive and you'll meet the locals here, but otherwise it's overpriced for what it is and the location isn't great.

Budget Accommodations in Papeete

Chez Myrna (Myrna Dahmeyer, B.P. 790, Papeete; tel. 42-64-11), Chemin vicinal de Tipaerui

VICINITY OF PAPEETE

Map labels:

HITI MAHANA BEACH CLUB · MILITARY LABS · THOUSAND SPRINGS TRAIL · SHERIFF DE MAHINA · MAHINA · TUAURU VALLEY · MAHINA TOWN HALL · MATAVAI BAY · HYATT REGENCY · POINT VENUS · TAHITI ISLAND · TOMB OF POMARE V · ROYAL TAHITIEN YACHT CLUB · NUCLEAR TESTING SUPPORT BASE · CHINESE CEMETERY · ARUE · RACETRACK · PIRAE VALLEY · FARE RAU APE (600 m) · AORAI TRAIL · OLD FRENCH FORT · HAMUTA VALLEY · TITIORO · HAMUTA · BAIN LOTI · FAUTAUA VALLEY · FAUTAUA FALLS · MT. PAPAIONA (696 m) · TAUNOA PASSAGE · PIRAE · CENTRE D'EXPERIMENTATION DU PACIFIQUE · PAPEETE · MORMON TEMPLE · ARCHBISHOPS PALACE · HOSPITAL · SAINTE AMELIE VALLEY · PIC ROUGE (299 m) · PAOFAI · TIPAERUI VALLEY · MOTU UTA · PAPEETE PASSAGE · PAMATAI · NUUTANIA PRISON · HOTEL TAHITI · HEITIARE INN · FAAA · AIRPORT · FAAA CHANNEL · TERMINAL · FRENCH UNIVERSITY · OUTUMAORO · BEACHCOMBER PARKROYAL · SOFITEL MAEVA BEACH HOTEL

0 — 2 km

© DAVID STANLEY

106, half a km up the road from the Hôtel Matavai, offers two shared-bath rooms at CFP 3500/4500 single/double with breakfast (minimum stay two nights). Dinner is CFP 1000 pp extra. Myrna's husband, Walter, is a German expat who has been on Tahiti for 30 years.

The **Hôtel Shogun** (Bruno Gato, B.P. 2880, Papeete; tel. 43-13-93), 10 rue du Commandant Destremeau, Papeete, has seven a/c rooms facing the noisy road at CFP 6000 single or double, or CFP 6500 single or double on the back side. A monthly rate of CFP 90,000 double is available.

The **Hôtel Mahina Tea** (B.P. 17, Papeete; tel. 42-00-97), up rue Sainte-Amélie from Ave. Bruat, is about the only regular budget hotel in the city. The 16 rooms with private bath are CFP 3800 single or double (CFP 3500 with a single bed), discounted 15% if you stay three or more nights. There are also six small studios with cooking facilities at CFP 90,000 a month double. Dishes are not provided, electricity is extra, and the availability of hot water is irregular. The Mahina Tea could be cleaner, friendlier, and quieter—at night, the rooster noise here can be annoying. This place has been around for many years.

Women can stay at the five-story **Foyer de Jeunes Filles de Paofai** (B.P. 1719, Papeete; tel. 42-87-80) near the Protestant church on boulevard Pomare. This Evangelical Church-operated women's residence provides 125 beds in rooms of two, three, four, or six beds at CFP 2000 a day, CFP 30,000 a month, breakfast included. There's a 2200 curfew daily, except Wednesday, Friday, and Saturday when it's midnight. This hostel is officially open to travelers in July and August only (although you can always try other months—they may have beds available). The bulk of the guests are outer-island Polynesian women aged 16-23, so it's a good opportunity for female travelers to meet local women.

Many backpackers head straight for **Hostel Teamo** (Kay Teriierooiterai, B.P. 2407, Papeete; tel. 42-47-26, fax 43-56-95), 8 rue du pont Neuf, Quartier Mission, a characterful century-old house in an attractive neighborhood near the Archbishop's Palace, just a short walk east of downtown. To get there from the market walk straight inland on rue François Cardella. It's a lit-

tle hard to find the first time, but very convenient once you know it. Shared dormitory-style accommodations (four to eight beds) with satisfactory cooking facilities are CFP 1200-1500 pp, private rooms CFP 3000 double with shared bath, CFP 4000 double with private bath (bring your own towel). The place is clean, there's a nice veranda with French TV, and English is spoken, but beware of mosquitoes. They'll hold luggage at CFP 100 a day. Checkout time is 1000, but you can stay until 1900 for an additional CFP 700 pp fee. Assistant manager Philippe does seven-hour tours around the island with 10 stops for CFP 2500 pp, provided enough people sign up. He also meets most international flights at the airport and provides free transfers to the hostel. Recommended.

Nearby on rue du Frère Alain is the **Tahiti Budget Lodge** (B.P. 237, Papeete; tel. 42-66-82, fax 43-06-79), a quiet white wooden house with green trim, straight back on rue Edouard Ahnne from the market. The 11 four-bed rooms are CFP 1800 pp, CFP 3800 double with shared bath, CFP 4800 double with private bath. Communal cooking facilities are provided, but use of the washing machine is extra. It's better kept and less crowded than Teamo for only a little more money.

Camping

The only regular campsite on Tahiti is **Hiti Mahana Beach Club** (Coco Pautu, B.P. 11580, Mahina; tel. 48-16-13) near Point Venus, 12 km east of Papeete. It's CFP 1000 pp to camp under the fruit trees on the spacious fenced grounds. Otherwise pay CFP 1500 pp to sleep on a mattress in the dormitory of the white colonial mansion adjacent to the club. Rooms here run CFP 3500/4500 single/double (usually full), and there's a communal kitchen, toilet, showers, and dining/lounge area. A special Blue Room with king-size bed is CFP 5000/6000. If you stay a week the seventh night is free. If you pay by the week you don't need to stay seven nights in a row but can split it up, and baggage storage is free between stays. Otherwise luggage storage is CFP 100 a day.

A reasonable breakfast is included in all rates. Cooking facilities and a shared fridge come with the above. Campers have simpler facilities of their own, and there's a lighted area for reading until 2200 in the evening. Only cold showers are available at Hiti Mahana, except in the Blue Room, which has hot water. It costs CFP 500 to use the washing machine and CFP 500 to dry, up to eight kg, or you can wash clothes free by hand. The resort has a number of posted rules and regulations with which you should familiarize yourself, and there's lots of useful tourist information at the reception.

A nice thing about Hiti Mahana is its location right on a black-sand beach. The resort has a tiny offshore island of its own within swimming distance, where you could sunbathe nude or surf off the *motu*'s east end. There's good snorkeling and plenty of fish (a limited selection of snorkeling gear is loaned free). Windsurfers churn the waters, especially on windy weekends. Cold beer and rum punch are on tap daily and happy hour runs 1700-1900 (except Monday), but the resort snack bar is only open weekends. Video films are shown on rainy days at 2030. On Sunday the resort offers excursions to Tefa'aurumai Falls in the back of a pickup truck (CFP 500 pp) and on Tuesday there's a circle-island tour (CFP 2500). They also act as an agent for Pacificar, renting cars and bicycles (though they're often all taken). Hiti Mahana is also a good place to begin a circle-island tour (clockwise).

To get to Hiti Mahana at PK 10.5, Mahina, take the Mahina *truck* (CFP 160, no service after 1715) from near the Papeete tourist office. If you ask, the driver will often bring you directly to the campsite. You pass the Point Venus turnoff, cross a bridge, then turn left at a school and follow the road straight to the beach (one km). The Hiti Mahana *truck* is often at the airport in search of arriving clients, even in the middle of the night, so ask (transfers free). The office is closed 1200-1500.

Upmarket Hotels near the Airport

The French-owned **Sofitel Maeva Beach** (B.P. 6008, Faa'a; tel. 42-80-42, tel. 43-84-70) at PK 7.5, Punaauia, built by UTA French Airlines in the late 1960s, is the least expensive of the three big international hotels on Tahiti (the others are the Beachcomber Parkroyal and the Hyatt Regency). The 224 a/c rooms in this pyramidal high-rise cost CFP 18,500 single or double garden view, CFP 21,500 lagoon view, CFP 25,000 panoramic view (children under 12 free). The seven-story Maeva Beach faces a man-made white beach. With pollution on the increase in the adjacent lagoon, most swimmers stick to the hotel pool, however.

The **Hôtel Te Puna Bel Air** (B.P. 6634, Faa'a; tel. 42-09-00, fax 41-31-84) at PK 7.2, Punaauia, also known as the Belair Hôtel, is one of the few large hotels owned and operated by a Tahitian family. The way in is rather confusing: around the corner and down a side road to an unmarked entrance opposite the scuba diving office. Rates are CFP 8000/9000/11,500 single/double/triple for the 24 garden bungalows and 48 standard rooms. The beach is poor, and watch out for eels if you decide to swim in their lovely pond. At night gays cruise the hotel's access road and the beach south of the Sofitel.

The **Tahiti Country Club** (B.P. 13019, Punaauia; tel. 42-60-40, fax 41-09-28) is up on the hillside above the Te Puna Bel Air. The 40 a/c rooms with TV in a neat two-story building are CFP 10,400 single, CFP 14,400 double or triple (children under 12 free), plus CFP 3800 pp extra for breakfast and dinner (if desired). Prices have almost doubled here in recent years. Swimming pool, volleyball, and tennis courts are on the premises (free). The hike up to this hotel from the main road is also quite a workout! One reader wrote in complaining about bugs in the rooms and poor food in the hotel restaurant.

The **Tahiti Beachcomber Parkroyal** (B.P. 6014, Faa'a; tel. 86-51-10, fax 86-51-30), PK 7 Faa'a, a former TraveLodge (1974), was purchased by a Japanese corporation in September 1989 for US$35 million. It's the first place west of the airport, and a smart international hotel. The 212 rooms in the main building begin at CFP 24,500/28,500 single/double; for one of the 15 overwater bungalows add 50% again. Children and teens (to age 16) sharing the room with their parents stay for free. A breakfast and dinner meal plan is CFP 6000 pp extra. Tahitian dancing and crafts demonstrations are regular features. The hotel pool is reserved for guests and the beach is artificial, but the attendants in the water sports kiosk on the beach will gladly ferry you out to the nudist pontoons anchored in mid-lagoon for CFP 700 roundtrip. Every afternoon at 1645 there's a one-and-a-half-hour sunset cruise along the coast from the Beachcomber Parkroyal (CFP 2000 including one drink).

The tastefully decorated **Hôtel Tahiti Noa Noa** (B.P. 416, Papeete; tel. 82-95-50, fax 81-31-51), at PK 2.6 between Papeete and the airport, is the most charming of the higher-priced hotels, with a gracious South Seas atmosphere. There are 86 spacious a/c rooms with bath beginning at CFP 8000/9000 single/double, and 18 thatched lagoonfront bungalows with fan at CFP 12,000 single or double, CFP 14,000 triple—good value for Tahiti. This colonial-style hotel opened in 1960 with a freshwater pool, overwater restaurant (great salads), and bar, plus a lovely lagoonside setting on the grounds of what was the residence of Princess Pomare, daughter of the last king of Tahiti. It's very easy to jump on *le truck* to downtown, yet the hotel is a world away when you tire of the hustle and bustle of Papeete. In previous editions we've recommended this place as your best choice in the middle-to-upper price range, but reader Georgia Lee of Los Osos, California, recently sent us this:

Hôtel Tahiti has gone from gentle decay to just plain run-down. The air conditioner blew out hot air, the phone didn't work, the bathroom floor was grimy, I had to go looking for a dry towel, and it was noisy. We had reservations and a single woman traveling with us also had one. Upon arrival they had no record of hers despite a receipt, so they moved us all into a three-bed room at 0300. This immediately made us suspicious. If they had an extra room with three beds, why not give her that room? Our original reserved room had a queen bed. All in all, I would not stay there again.

Upmarket Hotels in Papeete

The 138-room **Hôtel Matavai** (B.P. 32, Papeete; tel. 42-67-67, fax 42-36-90) has little going for it at CFP 12,000/16,000/20,000 single/double/ triple with bath, TV, and two double beds. You can almost tell this four-floor concrete edifice was once a Holiday Inn, but it is the closest luxury hotel to the center. Tennis and squash courts are on the premises.

Business travelers often stay at the high-rise **Hôtel Prince Hinoi** (B.P. 4545, Papeete; tel. 42-32-77, fax 42-33-66), Ave. du Prince Hinoi at boulevard Pomare, formerly known as the Hôtel Ibis Papeete. The 72 small a/c rooms are CFP 8000/9000 single/double, plus CFP 3500 for breakfast and dinner (if desired).

The **Hôtel Le Mandarin Noa Noa** (B.P. 302, Papeete; tel. 42-16-33, fax 42-16-32), 51 rue Colette, is a clean, modern hotel with an Asian flair. Unfortunately, the 37 rooms are somewhat overpriced at CFP 12,000/13,500/15,500 single/double/triple (children under 12 free).

The elegant old **Hôtel Royal Papeete** (B.P. 919, Papeete; tel. 42-01-29, fax 43-79-09), downtown on boulevard Pomare opposite the Moorea ferry landing, has 78 rooms beginning at CFP 9000/10,500/12,000 single/double/triple. The Royal Papeete should be your choice if you don't mind spending a fair bit of money to stay right in the heart of Papeete's nightlife quarter. The hotel's two lively nightclubs downstairs offer free admission to guests. Just make sure you don't get a room directly above the clubs unless you enjoy being rocked to sleep by a disco beat.

Hôtel Kon Tiki Pacific (B.P. 111, Papeete; tel. 43-72-82, fax 42-11-66) is the cheapest high-rise hotel in the city center. The 44 spacious rooms begin at CFP 8000/9700/11,700 single/double/triple. Don't accept one of the noisy rooms near the elevator, which are always offered first. This hotel is popular with French military personnel and secret agents in transit. Immerse yourself in the intrigue (and get an eyeful of Papeete) by having a meal in the 7th-floor restaurant (closed Sunday).

Upmarket Hotels East of Papeete

The **Royal Tahitien Hôtel** (B.P. 5001, Papeete; tel. 42-81-13, fax 41-05-35), at PK 3.5, directly behind the Mairie de Pirae, is a peaceful two-story building with 40 rooms facing beautifully kept grounds on a black-sand beach. The windsurfing offshore is good. For CFP 15,000 single or double, CFP 18,000 triple, you may just find the Tahiti you imagined here. Breakfast and dinner served on the terrace overlooking the lagoon are CFP 4400 pp extra.

The **Hyatt Regency Tahiti** (B.P. 14700, Arue; tel. 48-12-34, fax 48-25-44) at PK 8, Mahina, takes the award for charging the highest prices on the island. The 190 spacious rooms begin at CFP 27,000 single or double, CFP 32,000 triple (children under 18 free). For breakfast and dinner, add CFP 4300 pp. Happy hour at the hotel bar is 1730-1830. Formerly known as the Tahara'a Hôtel, the Hyatt was built by Pan American Airways in 1968 and purchased for US$30 million in September 1989 by the Japanese group Electronic and Industrial Enterprises, which also has big investments in Fiji. Built on a hillside overlooking Matavai Bay, this is one of the few hotels in the world where you take an elevator *down* to your room. The views from the balconies are superb and a black-sand beach is at the foot of the hill. The Hyatt provides a shuttle service to and from Papeete for guests. Reader Andrea C. Stephenson of Houston, Texas, sent us this comment about the Hyatt:

The service at the Hyatt was poor. Whether we were at the "Beach Club," or at one of their indoor restaurants or bars, the staff was rude, inattentive, and unmotivated. During dinner, I went practically the whole meal with no water, and when I asked for it, it seemed like a big hassle for the waitress to get it for me. We saw a guest at a table next to us spill a full drink on the table and on himself. Two servers also clearly saw this occur, and they both actually ignored this and left the area so they wouldn't be faced with cleaning it up. All my husband and I could think was that we were sooooo happy that we weren't staying there all week.

Accommodations near Taravao

The only reasonably inexpensive place to stay on the far side of the island is **Fare Nana'o** (B.P. 7193, Taravao; tel. 57-18-14, fax 57-76-10), operated by sculptor Jean-Claude Michel and his wife Monique. It's on the lagoon side in a colorful compound overflowing with vegetation and fragments of sculpture, very near the PK 52 marker a km north of the old French fort at Taravao. The seven thatched bungalows vary in price, from CFP 5000 double for the treehouse (you climb up a pole), CFP 5500 double for an overwater *fare* on stilts (you must wade through the lagoon), CFP 6000 double for one of the three units with cooking facilities, to CFP 7500 double for the only room with private bath. A third person is CFP 500 at all these, and the weekly discount is 10% (no credit cards). Although unique and wonderful, Fare Nana'o is not for everyone: the walls are constructed of tree trunks and branches left partially open, there's no hot water, flashlights are required to reach the shared toilet and shower at night, and you may be visited in the night by crabs, spiders, lizards, and a marauding cat. This Robinson Crusoe-style place has had TV exposure in Los Angeles, so advance reservations are necessary, especially on weekends. Recommended.

At the four-unit **Te Anuanua Hôtel** (B.P. 1553, Papeete; tel. 57-12-54, fax 45-14-39), just west of the church in Pueu at PK 10, Tahiti Iti, the garden bungalows are CFP 8000 single, double, or triple. Lagoonfront bungalows are CFP 1000 more. Check the rooms before checking in, as some lack window screens, fans, or functioning plumbing. A nice seafood restaurant faces the lagoon, making the Te Anuanua worth a stop as you travel around the island, and every Sunday at noon there's a buffet of authentic Tahitian food (CFP 3800 pp). This hotel doesn't have a beach, but the water off their wharf is crystal clear and inviting to jump in.

A more distant choice would be the **Puunui Resort** (B.P. 7016, Taravao; tel. 57-19-20, fax 57-27-43), four km up a steep paved road off the Teahupoo road, seven km from Taravao. You'll have to rent a car if you stay here. At CFP 12,000 for one of the 54 four-bed bungalows or CFP 18,000 for each of the 23 six-bed villas, the Puunui is overpriced unless you're in a small group. A breakfast and dinner meal plan is CFP 4000 pp extra, though the units have kitchenettes. They do offer horseback riding (tel. 57-19-20; for reservations call 48 hours in advance), so it may be worth dropping by for a ride and the view. Roundtrip airport transfers are CFP 4500 pp. Be sure to call ahead to check availability if you wish to stay here.

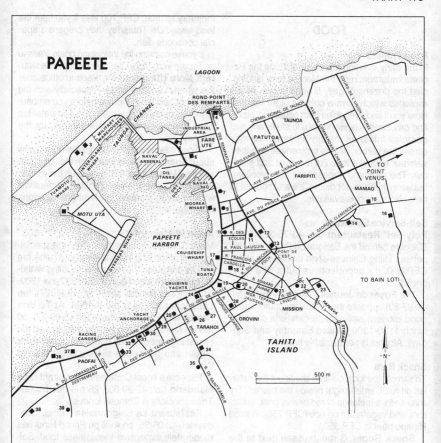

PAPEETE

LAGOON

ROND-POINT
DES REMPARTS

MILITARY
WAREHOUSES

INTERISLAND
WHARF

TUAMOTU
WHARF

TAUNOA
CHANNEL

INDUSTRIAL
AREA

FARE
UTE

CHEMIN VICINAL DE TAUNOA

TAUNOA

PATUTOA

BOULEVARD POMARE

COURS DE L'UNION SACRÉE

AVE. DU COMMANDANT CHESSE

TO
POINT
VENUS

NAVAL
ARSENAL

OIL
TANKS

DRY
DOCK

NAVAL
HQ

MOOREA
WHARF

MOTU UTA

R. DES REMPARTS

AVE. DU CHEF VAIRAATOA

FARIIPITI

AVE. DU PRINCE HINOI

MAMAO

AVE. GEORGES CLEMENCEAU

PAPEETE
HARBOR

CRUISESHIP
WHARF

TUNA
BOATS

OVERSEAS WHARF

R. DES
ECOLES

R. PAUL GAUGUIN

R. FRANCOIS
CARDELLA

R. DU MARECHAL FOCH

PONT DE
L'EST

TO BAIN LOTI

CRUISING
YACHTS

YACHT
ANCHORAGE

RACING
CANOES

BOULEVARD POMARE

AVE. DU GEN. DE GAULLE

GEORGES LAGARDE

R. EDWARD
AHNNE

R. DE
L'EVECHE

PAEAVA

MGR. TEPANO
JAUSSEN

OROVINI

MISSION

TAHITI
ISLAND

PAOFAI

R. DU COMMANDANT
DESTREMEAU

R. COOK

R. DES POILUS TAHITIENS

AVE. BRUAT

TARAHOI

R. DE SAINTE-AMELIE

STREAM

N

0   500 m

1. Direction de l'Equipment
2. Coconut Oil Mill
3. Bureau *Aranui*
4. Mobil Oil/Budget
   Rent-a-Car
5. Nauti-Sport
6. Bureau *Taporo*
7. Hôtel Kon Tiki Pacific
8. Moorea ferries
9. Hôtel Royal Papeete
10. Hôtel Prince Hinoi
11. New Town Hall
12. Archipels Bookstore
13. Pacificar

14. Mamao Hospital
15. Kanti Chinese Temple
16. Mormon Temple
17. Tahiti Tourisme
18. Market
19. Vaima Center
20. Catholic Cathedral
21. Tahiti Budget Lodge
22. Hostel Teamo
23. Archbishop's Palace
24. Post Office
25. Hôtel Shogun
26. High Commissioner's
    Office

27. Territorial Assembly
28. Pizzeria Lou Pescadou
29. Robert Rent-a-Car
30. Tahiti Perles Center
31. Protestant Church
32. Foyer de Jeunes Filles
33. Intermarket Supermarket
34. Quartier Broche Army
    Barracks
35. Hôtel Mahina Tea
36. Municipal Swimming Pool
37. Cultural Center (OTAC)
38. Uranie Cemetery
39. Hôtel Matavai

FOOD

Food Trailers

In the early evening take a stroll along the Papeete waterfront near the Moorea ferry landing, past the dozens of gaily lit vans known as *les roulettes* which form a colorful night market. Here you'll find everything from couscous, pizza, and *brouchettes* (shish kebab) to steak with real *pommes frites*. As the city lights wink gently across the harbor, sailors promenade with their *vahines,* adding a touch of romance and glamour. The food and atmosphere are excellent, but even if you're not dining, it's a scene not to miss. No alcohol is available.

Self-Service Cafeterias

Poly-Self Restaurant (tel. 43-75-32), 8 rue Gauguin behind the Banque de Polynésie, dispenses filling Chinese-style lunches at about CFP 800. It's unpretentious but a little overpriced.

The **Foyer de Jeunes Filles de Paofai** (tel. 42-87-80) opposite the Protestant church has a good modern self-service cafeteria open for lunch 1130-1300 (closed Saturday and Sunday). Alcohol is not available here.

Snack Bars

To sample the local cuisine, check out the eateries on rue Cardella right beside the market. Try *maa tinito,* a mélange of red beans, pork, macaroni, and vegetables on rice (CFP 750). A large Hinano beer is CFP 350.

Snack Roger, 3 rue Jaussen next to the Catholic cathedral, offers good plate lunches, *plats du jour,* cheap salads, real espresso coffee, and ice cream. It's a good place to catch your breath, so locate it early in your visit!

The *plat du jour* at **Big Burger** (tel. 43-01-98), beside Aline, is often big value´(CFP 1400), and it's not fast food as the name implies (closed Sunday).

Salvani's Café (tel. 45-17-45) below Hôtel Shogun serves reasonably priced meals in a bright, attractive locale.

Inexpensive grilled meat and fish dishes are the specialty at **Snack Paofai** (tel. 42-95-76) near Clinique Paofai (daily 1730-2130). A complete meal here will run CFP 700 if you dine on

their airy terrace, CFP 100 less if you take the food away. On Thursday they prepare a special couscous dish.

If you're catching the interisland boats *Vaeanu* or *Taporo* from Motu Uta, check out the **Restaurant Motu Uta** behind the *Vaeanu* office near the wharf. Lunch is good—especially with big bottles of cold beer. Indulge before you embark (if they're open). There's also a public water tap here where you can fill your canteen for the journey.

Those staying at Hôtel Tahiti will want to know about **Snack Nu'utere Faa'a,** on the left opposite the Mobil station, 300 meters up the road to the airport. The friendly Tahitian owners will welcome you warmly and feed you delicious local fare.

Asian Restaurants

Many Chinese restaurants in Papeete specialize in chicken and Hinano beer, but none are special bargains. The most popular is the **Waikiki Restaurant** (open daily 1100-1300 and 1800-2100, closed Sunday lunch; tel. 42-95-27), rue Leboucher 20, near the market. At **Te Hoa Restaurant** (closed Sunday; tel. 43-99-27), 30 rue du Maréchal Foch behind the market, the furnishings aren't as neat, but the portions are bigger and the prices slightly lower than at Waikiki.

Papeete's finest Cantonese restaurant is **Le Mandarin** (tel. 42-99-03), 26 rue des Écoles. Their specialty is Chinese fondue.

Restaurant La Saigonnaise (closed Sunday; tel. 42-05-35) on Ave. du Prince Hinoi has moderately expensive Vietnamese food. Saigonese soup makes a good lunch.

Italian Restaurants

For a taste of the Mediterranean, **La Pizzeria** (closed Sunday and holidays; tel. 42-98-30), on boulevard Pomare near the Tahiti Pearl Center, prepares real pizza in a brick oven. The prices are reasonable for the waterfront location—they're all spelled out in a big blackboard menu.

Pizzeria Lou Pescadou (open daily 1130-1400 and 1830-2230; tel. 43-74-26) on rue Anne-Marie Javouhey behind the cathedral is friendly, unpretentious, breezy, and inexpensive. Their pizza pescatore makes a good lunch, and a big pitcher of ice water is included in the price. Owner Mario Vitulli may be from Marseilles, but you won't complain about his spaghetti—a huge meal for about CFP 700. Drinks are on the house while you stand and wait for a table. The service is lively, and Lou Pescadou is very popular among local French, a high recommendation.

A block toward the mountains on rue Georges Lagarde is **Pizzeria Caesario** with a home delivery service at tel. 42-21-21. More good pizza is baked at **Don Camillo** (tel. 42-80-96), 14 rue des Écoles, next to the Piano Bar.

Other Restaurants

Papeete's most famous restaurant is **Acajou** (closed Sunday; tel. 42-87-58), corner of rue Georges Lagarde and boulevard Pomare near the Vaima Center. House specialties include slices of mahimahi *au gratin,* coconut-curry shrimp, and filet mignon with mustard sauce. The plates are individually prepared, so allow some time. One reader complained about the surly waitress and overcooked food at Acajou.

A cheaper branch of Acajou (open Monday to Saturday 0400-1700, Sunday 0300-1100; tel. 43-19-22) is at 7 rue Cardella by the market, half a block from the tourist office. The coffee with fresh buttered bread offered here makes an excellent breakfast or mid-morning snack.

For a change of pace have lunch at the restaurant of the **Lycée Hôtelier** (tel. 45-23-71), a bit east of Pirae Municipal Market (open October to June from Tuesday to Friday noon-1400, except during the Christmas holidays). The food is prepared and served by students.

Cafes

Le Retro (tel. 42-40-01) on the boulevard Pomare side of the Vaima Center is *the* place to sit and sip a drink while watching the passing parade. The atmosphere here is really Côte d'Azur.

The Papeete equivalent of a Hard Rock Cafe is **Morrison's Café** (tel. 42-78-61), upstairs in the Vaima Center, which offers a full bar, a short pub menu (not cheap), and a swimming pool. Here MTV-deprived local youths mix with island-hopping yachties on an airy terrace with a view of Tahiti (weekdays 1100-0100, Saturday 1600-0100).

On boulevard Pomare across the park from the Moorea ferry landing is a row of sidewalk cafes frequented by French servicemen, happy hookers, gays, and assorted groupies. Some establishments even have a happy hour. This is a good place to sit and take in the local color of every shade and hue.

When the heat gets to you, **Pâtisserie La Marquisienne** (tel. 42-83-52), 29 rue Colette, offers coffee and pastries in a/c comfort. It's popular among French expats.

Groceries

The supermarket in the **Fare Tony Commercial Center** next to the Vaima Center in central Papeete is open weekdays 0730-1830, Saturday 0730-1800. **Intermarket** is a large supermarket on rue du Commandant Destremeau (open Monday to Friday 0730-1845, Saturday 0730-1200 and 1500-1830, Sunday 0730-1130). Get whole barbecued chickens and chow mein in the deli section.

At PK 8 Punuuai, just south of the junction of the autoroute to Papeete, is the **Centre Commercial Moana Nui,** Tahiti's first enclosed shopping mall, with a large adjoining supermarket, **Continent.** A barbecued chicken from the deli section in the supermarket makes for a good meal, and there's also a snack bar on the mall.

ENTERTAINMENT AND EVENTS

Five Papeete cinemas show B-grade films dubbed into French (admission CFP 700). The Concorde is in the Vaima Center; Hollywood I and II are on rue Lagarde beside the Vaima Center; Liberty Cinema is on rue du Maréchal Foch near the market; and the Mamao Palace is near Mamao Hospital.

Ask for the monthly program of activities at the departement Fêtes et Manifestations in the **Cultural Center** (B.P. 1709, Papeete; tel. 42-88-50) at Te Fare Tahiti Nui on the waterfront.

Nightlife

Papeete after dark is not just for the tourists! Lots of little bars crowding the streets around rue des Écoles are full of locals. The places with live music or a show generally impose a CFP 1000 cover charge, which includes one

fire dancers at a Papeete resort

drink. Nothing much gets going before 2200 and by 0100 everything is very informal for the last hour before closing.

The **Piano Bar** (tel. 42-88-24), beside Hôtel Prince Hinoi on rue des Écoles, is the most notorious of Papeete's *mahu* (transvestite) discos; **Le Lido Nightclub** (tel. 42-95-84) next door offers unisex striptease. **Le Club 5** nearby features female stripping. Young French servicemen are in their element in these places.

Café des Sports on the corner across the street from the Piano Bar has beer on tap and usually no cover. More locals than tourists patronize this pleasant, inexpensive establishment, where a good Tahitian band plays on weekends.

Another local drinking place is the **Royal Kikiriri** (no cover; tel. 43-58-64), rue Colette 66, where you can get a beer without paying a cover.

French soldiers and sailors out of uniform patronize the bars along boulevard Pomare opposite the Moorea ferry landing, such as **La Cave** (tel. 42-01-29) inside the Hôtel Royal Papeete (entry through the lobby), which has live Tahitian music for dancing on Friday and Saturday 2200-0300 (CFP 1500 cover charge, free for Royal Papeete guests). **Le Tamure Hut** (tel. 42-01-29), also at the Royal Papeete, is one of the few

downtown Papeete clubs that caters for visitors. Through the music and decor they've attempted to recapture the nightlife milieu of a decade or more ago, before Quinn's Tahitian Hut closed in 1973. It's open Friday 1600-0300, Saturday 2100-0300, and Sunday 1600-2200. There's no cover charge for guests of the Royal Papeete, otherwise it's CFP 1500 (includes one drink).

The **Tiki d'Or Bar Américain** (no cover; tel. 42-07-37), 26 rue Georges Lagarde near the Vaima Center, gets lively around happy hour. You'll locate it by the ukuleles and impromptu singing.

The **Pitate Bar,** on the corner of Ave. Bruat beside the Air France office, is loud and dark, but there's often Tahitian-style music you can dance to and lots of local atmosphere. Check out the Pitate on Sunday afternoon.

Discos
Papeete's top disco is **Galaxy Night-Club Discotheque** (tel. 43-15-36) on rue Jaussen directly back from the Catholic cathedral (open Wednesday to Saturday 2200-0300). There's no cover charge on Wednesday and Thursday, otherwise it's CFP 1500 on Friday and Saturday, but they often let foreign tourists in free. Galaxy mostly caters to people in their teens and twenties, and smart dress is required. A slightly older crowd patronizes the **New Orleans Jazz Club** (tel. 43-15-36) next door, which is open the same hours.

Le Rolls Club Discotheque (tel. 43-41-42) in the Vaima Center (opposite Big Burger) is open Wednesday to Saturday, with *karaoke* singing 2100-2300 and disco dancing 2300-0300. Friday and Sunday they're also open from 1600-2100. It's also popular with teenagers.

Cultural Shows for Visitors
A Tahitian dance show takes place in the Bougainville Restaurant, downstairs at the **Maeva Beach Hôtel** (tel. 42-80-42), Friday and Saturday at 2000. If you're not interested in having dinner, a drink at the Bar Moorea by the pool will put you in position to see the action (no cover charge). Sunday this hotel puts on a full Tahitian feast at 1200, complete with earth oven *(ahimaa)* and show (CFP 4900).

The **Beachcomber Parkroyal Hôtel** (tel. 86-51-10) presents one of the best Tahitian dance shows on the island; attend for the price of a drink at the bar near the pool (no cover charge). Tahiti's top dance troupe, Coco's Temaeva, often performs here (check). The dancers' starting time tends to vary (officially Wednesday, Friday, Saturday, and Sunday at 2000), so arrive early and be prepared to wait. For something special try the barbecue (on Wednesday) and the Tahitian feast (on Sunday)—CFP 4500 each. The seafood dinner show on Friday is CFP 5950.

At the **Hyatt Regency** (tel. 48-11-22) the Tahitian dancing is Friday and Saturday at 2015.

Sometimes there's Tahitian dancing in the **Captain Bligh Restaurant** (tel. 43-62-90) at the Punaauia Lagoonarium on Friday and Saturday nights at 2100 (call ahead to check).

SHOPPING

Normal shopping hours in Papeete are weekdays 0730-1130 and 1330-1730, Saturday 0730-1200. Papeete's largest shopping complex is the **Vaima Center,** where numerous shops sell black pearls, designer clothes, souvenirs, and books. It's certainly worth a look; then branch out into the surrounding streets. **Galerie Winkler** (tel. 42-81-77), 17 rue Jeanne d'Arc beside American Express, sells contemporary paintings of Polynesia.

For reproductions of authentic Marquesan woodcarvings, have a look in **Manuia Curios** on the east side of the cathedral. Also try **Manuia Junior,** corner of rues Albert Leboucher and des Écoles opposite the Café des Sports. Upstairs in the market is another good place to buy handicrafts, or just a pareu.

Don't overlook the local fashions. **Marie Ah You** on the waterfront between the Vaima Center and the tourist office sells very chic island clothing—at prices to match.

Magasin Côte d'Azur, rue Paul Gauguin 26, has cheap pareus; several other shops along this street also flog inexpensive tropical garb.

If you're a surfer, check **Shop Tahiti Surf and Skate,** 10 rue Édouard Ahnne near the market, for boards, plus all attendant gear. **Caroline,** 41 rue Colette, and **Waikiki Beach,** 9 rue Jeanne d'Arc, also sell surfing gear.

Photo Lux (tel. 42-84-31) on rue du Maréchal Foch near the market has some of the cheapest color print film you'll find, and they repair Minolta cameras.

The **Philatelic Bureau** (tel. 41-43-35) at the main post office sells the stamps and first-day covers of all the French Pacific territories. Some are quite beautiful and inexpensive.

SERVICES

Money and Banks

The Banque de Tahiti in the Vaima Center (weekdays 0800-1145 and 1330-1630, Saturday 0800-1130) charges CFP 350 commission to change traveler's checks. The Banque Socredo also deducts CFP 350, but the Banque de Polynésie and Westpac Bank are a bit more expensive. There's no commission at all if you're changing French francs, and the buying and selling rates are identical! Several banks around town have automatic tellers where you can get cash advances on credit cards.

Post and Telecommunications

The main post office is on boulevard Pomare across from the yacht anchorage. Aerograms and large mailing envelopes/boxes are sold at the counters up the escalators (closes at 1500). Pick up poste restante (general delivery) mail at window No. 15 downstairs (CFP 40 per piece). The post office is also the place to make a long-distance telephone call, but there's a CFP 1824 three-minute minimum for an operator-assisted call to the States. It's cheaper to use a telephone card for such calls.

Around Tahiti, small branch post offices with public telephones are found in Arue, Faa'a Airport, Mahina, Mataiea, Paea, Papara, Papeari, Pirae, Punaauia, and Taravao.

If you have an American Express card you can have your mail sent c/o Tahiti Tours, B.P. 627, Papeete. Their office (tel. 54-02-50) is at 15 rue Jeanne d'Arc next to the Vaima Center.

Immigration Office

If you arrived by air, visa extensions are handled by the **Police de l'Air et des Frontières** (open weekdays 0800-1200 and 1400-1700; B.P.

6362, Faa'a; tel. 82-67-99) at the airport (up the stairs beside the snack bar). Yachties are handled by the immigration office next to a small Banque Socredo branch on the waterfront behind Tahiti Tourisme in the center of town (Monday to Thursday 0730-1100 and 1330-1530, Friday 0730-1100 and 1330-1500; tel. 42-40-74). Be patient and courteous with the officials if you want good service.

For those uninitiated into the French administrative system, the **police station** (in emergencies tel. 17) opposite the War Memorial on Ave. Bruat deals with Papeete matters, while the *gendarmerie* (tel. 46-73-73) at the head of Ave. Bruat is concerned with the rest of the island. The locally recruited Papeete police wear blue uniforms, while the paramilitary French-import gendarmes are dressed in khaki.

Consulates

The honorary consul of Australia is Brian Banston (B.P. 1695, Papeete; tel. 43-88-38) at the Qantas office in the Vaima Center. The honorary consul of New Zealand is Richard Hall (B.P. 73, Papeete; tel. 43-88-29). The honorary British consul is Robert Withers (B.P. 1064, Papeete; tel. 42-84-57) at Avis Rent A Car, 35 rue Charles Viénot. The honorary consul of Germany is Claude-Eliane Weinmann (B.P. 452, Papeete; tel. 42-99-94), rue Tihoni Te Faatau off Ave. du Prince Hinoi in Afareru on the far east side of the city. Other countries with honorary consuls at Papeete are Austria, Belgium, Chile, Denmark, Finland, Holland, Italy, Monaco, Norway, South Korea, Sweden, and Switzerland. There's no U.S. diplomatic post in Tahiti-Polynesia. All visa applications and requests for replacement of lost passports must be sent to Suva, Fiji, where the paperwork can take up to five weeks. Canada and Japan are also *not* represented.

Laundromats

Central Pressing, 72 rue Albert Leboucher (the street behind the Royal Papeete Hôtel), offers a special service to visitors: for CFP 600 they'll wash, dry, and fold one kg of laundry.

Laverie Gauguin Pressing Lavomatic, rue Gauguin 64 (weekdays 0630-1730, Saturday 0630-1200), charges CFP 600 to wash six kg, another CFP 600 to dry, and CFP 100 for soap.

Public Toilets

Public toilets are found next to the immigration office near the small Banque Socredo behind Tahiti Tourisme, at the bus stop opposite Hôtel Le Mandarin beside the Hôtel de Ville, and on the waterfront opposite Air France. The ones near immigration are the most likely to be open regularly, so locate them early in your stay.

Yachting Facilities

Yachts pay CFP 900 a day to moor Mediterranean-style (stern-to, bow anchor out) along the quay on boulevard Pomare. For half the price you can anchor farther west along the boulevard. A one-time entry fee and optional daily electricity hookup are charged. The port captain, customs, and immigration are all in the building next to Banque Socredo behind Tahiti Tourisme. Visiting boats can also use one of the anchor buoys at the **Yacht Club of Tahiti** (B.P. 1456, Papeete; tel. 42-78-03) at PK 4, Arue, for a monthly charge.

INFORMATION

Tahiti Tourisme (B.P. 65, Papeete; tel. 50-57-00) at Fare Manihini, a neo-Polynesian building on the waterfront not far from the market, can answer questions and supply maps. Ask for *Le Guide de la Petite Hôtellerie et du Logement Chez l'Habitant,* which lists "small hotel" accommodations on virtually all of the islands. Ask here about special events and boats to the outer islands. The office is open weekdays 0730-1700, Saturday 0800-1200.

The **Institute Territorial de la Statistique** (B.P. 395, Papeete; tel. 43-71-96), 2nd floor, Bloc Donald (behind Voyagence Tahiti, opposite the Vaima Center), puts out a quarterly *Statistical Bulletin.*

Bookstores and Maps

You'll find Papeete's best selection of English books at **Libraire Archipels** (B.P. 20676, Papeete; tel. 42-47-30), 68 rue des Remparts. Archipels is about the only place you can find books and guides to the Pacific.

Vaima Libraire (B.P. 2399, Papeete; tel. 45-57-44), in the Vaima Center, and **Polygraph** (B.P. 707, Papeete; tel. 42-80-47), 12 Ave.

Bruat, are Papeete's largest French bookstores. **Libraire Le Petit Prince** (B.P. 13080, Papeete; tel. 43-26-24) in the Centre Commercial Moana Nui, Punaauia, is also good.

La Boutique Klima (B.P. 31, Papeete; tel. 42-00-63), behind the cathedral, sells old topographical maps, nautical charts, and many interesting books on Polynesia.

Newer topographical maps (CFP 1500) of some islands are available from the **Service de l'Aménagement** (B.P. 866, Papeete), 4th floor, Administrative Building, 11 rue du Commandant Destremeau.

For the best selection of French nautical charts, visit **Ouvrages Cartes et Instruments** in the white Marine Nationale building next to the Air France office on the waterfront (open Monday, Tuesday, Thursday, and Friday 1330-1600).

There's a **newsstand** with magazines in English in front of the Vaima Center by the taxi stand on boulevard Pomare.

Public Library

A public library (open Monday to Thursday 0800-1700, Friday 0800-1600; tel. 42-88-50) is located in the Cultural Center. To take books out you must buy an annual card for CFP 4000.

Travel Agencies

One of Papeete's most reliable regular travel agencies is **Tahiti Tours** (B.P. 627, Papeete; tel. 54-02-50), 15 rue Jeanne d'Arc next to the Vaima Center. **Tahiti Nui Travel** (B.P. 718, Papeete; tel. 42-68-03, fax 43-53-00) in the Vaima Center often has cheap package tours to Easter Island.

Yacht cruises around the Society Islands, Tuamotus, and Marquesas can be arranged by **Tahiti Mer et Loisirs** (B.P. 3488, Papeete; tel. 43-97-99, fax 43-33-68), in a houseboat on the Papeete waterfront opposite the post office. For example, a seven-night cruise around the Marquesas from Nuku Hiva will run CFP 180,000 pp.

Airline Offices

Reconfirm your international flight at your airline's Papeete office. Most of the airline offices are in the Vaima Center: Air New Zealand (tel. 43-01-70), Hawaiian Airlines (tel. 42-15-00), Lan Chile (tel. 42-64-55), and Qantas (tel. 43-06-

65). AOM French Airlines (tel. 43-25-25) is at 90 rue des Remparts; Corsair (tel. 42-28-28) is at 9 rue Jaussen next to the Catholic cathedral. Air France (tel. 43-63-33), which also represents Air Calédonie International, is on boulevard Pomare near Ave. Bruat.

HEALTH

Mamao Hospital is always crowded with locals awaiting free treatment, so you're better off attending a private clinic. The **Clinique Paofai** (B.P. 545, Papeete; tel. 43-02-02) on boulevard Pomare accepts outpatients weekdays 0700-1900, Saturday 0700-1200, emergencies anytime. The facilities and attention are excellent, but be prepared for fees of around CFP 2900. The **Clinique Cardella** (tel. 42-81-90) on rue Anne-Marie Javouhey is also open day and night.

Dr. Vincent Joncker and Dr. J.-M. P. Rosenstein, in the building above the pharmacy opposite the Catholic cathedral, operate a **Cabinet Médical** (tel. 43-10-43) where you'll pay around CFP 3000 for a consultation during business hours. Otherwise, their **S.O.S. Médecins** (tel. 42-34-56) are on call 24 hours a day, but home visits begin at CFP 6000.

To call an ambulance dial 15.

TRANSPORTATION

For information on air and sea services from Tahiti to other Polynesian islands, see "Transportation" in the introduction to this chapter.

Le Truck

You can go almost anywhere on Tahiti by *les trucks,* converted cargo vehicles with long benches in back. *Trucks* marked Outumaoro run from Papeete to Faa'a International Airport and the Maeva Beach Hôtel every few minutes during the day, with sporadic service after dark until 2000 daily, then again in the morning from 0500 on. On Sunday long-distance *trucks* run only in the very early morning and evening; weekdays the last trip to Mahina, Paea, and points beyond is around 1700.

Trucks don't run right around the island. Although a couple go as far as Tautira and

Not many public transport systems are as much fun as Tahiti's le truck.

Teahupoo on Tahiti Iti, you could have difficulty getting a *truck* back to Papeete from those remote villages in the afternoon. To go around the island by *truck,* start early and travel clockwise. Get out at Taravao and walk down to the Gauguin Museum (three km). With lots of traffic along the south coast, it'll be easy to hitch a ride back this way, though the last Papeete-bound *truck* leaves around 1300. Luckily, so far, hitching is usually no problem.

Trucks to Arue, Mahina, and Papenoo leave from boulevard Pomare across the street from Tahiti Tourisme. Those to the airport, Outumaoro, Punaauia, Paea, and Papara are found on rue du Maréchal Foch near the market. Local services to Motu Uta, Mission, Mamao, Titioro, and Tipaeriu depart from rue Colette near the Hôtel de Ville.

Destinations and fares are posted on the side of the vehicle: CFP 140 to Punaauia, CFP 160 to Mahina, CFP 170 to Paea, CFP 200 to Papara, CFP 240 to Mataiea or Papeari, CFP 300 to Taravao, CFP 350 to Teahupoo or Tautira. After dark all *truck* fares increase. Outside Papeete you don't have to be at a stop: *trucks* stop anywhere if you wave. Luggage rides for free.

Taxis

Taxis in Papeete are expensive, and it's important not to get in unless there's a meter that works or you've agreed to a flat fare beforehand. Expect to pay at least CFP 800 for a trip within Papeete, CFP 1000 to the airport, or CFP 1500 to the Hyatt Regency or Maeva Beach. Fares are 25% more on Sunday and holidays;

from 2000 to 0600 daily they're 50% higher. The taxis also charge extra for luggage at these times. Taxi stands are found at the Vaima Center (tel. 42-33-60), the market (tel. 43-19-62), the Hôtel de Ville, and the airport (tel. 43-30-07). If you feel cheated by a taxi driver, take down the license number and complain to the tourist office.

Car Rentals

To rent a car you must be 21 (or 18 with Pacificar, 25 with Avis) and have held a driver's license for at least a year. Check the car as carefully as they check you; be sure to comment on dents, scratches, flat tires, etc. All the car rental agencies include third-party public liability insurance in the basic price, but collision damage waiver (CDW) varies from CFP 700 to CFP 1300 extra per day. Most agencies charge the client for damage to the tires, insurance or no insurance, and Tahiti insurance isn't valid if you take the car across to Moorea. On Tahiti the car comes full of gas, and you'll see Mobil and Total gas stations all around the island.

If you want to whiz the island and pack in as many side trips as you can in one day, an unlimited-mileage rental is for you, and with four people sharing it's not a bad deal. You should only consider renting on a per-kilometer basis if you plan to keep the car for at least three days and intend to use it only for short hops. Most agencies impose a 50-km daily minimum on their per-km rentals to prevent you from traveling *too* slowly; most rentals are for a minimum of 24 hours. Many car rental companies have kiosks inside Faa'a Airport, and most offer clients a free pickup and drop-off service to the hotels and airport.

The best rates are usually offered by **Pacificar** (B.P. 1121, Papeete; tel. 41-93-93, fax 42-19-11), 56 rue des Remparts at pont de l'Est, at the east end of rue Paul Gauguin. They also have a counter in the large wooden building facing the Moorea ferry wharf and a desk at the airport. Their smallest car is CFP 1500 a day, plus CFP 28 a km, plus CFP 800 insurance. They also offer a flat three-day rental price of CFP 12,000, mileage and insurance included (additional days CFP 4000). They're open 24 hours a day—if the main office is closed, the guard in the parking lot can give you a car.

Budget (B.P. 306, Papeete; tel. 43-80-79, fax 45-01-01), in the flashy Mobil Oil Australia building north of downtown, charges CFP 6600 a day with unlimited mileage plus CFP 1100 insurance. With their weekend rate you pay only two days' rental to keep the car from Friday to Monday, but you're charged three days' insurance.

Avis (B.P. 1683, Papeete; tel. 42-96-49, 41-08-47), 35 rue Charles Viénot, offers cars with unlimited mileage (CFP 7400 (minimum two-day rental) and their insurance charges are also among the highest (CFP 1300). They're expensive because most of their business is through desks at the big hotels.

Hertz (tel. 42-04-71, fax 42-48-62), at Paradise Tours, on Vicinal de Tipaerui opposite Hôtel Matavai, is also overpriced (from CFP 2500 a day, plus CFP 35 a km, or CFP 7300 with unlimited mileage). Their CDW insurance is CFP 1300.

A good place to try for a per-km rental is **Robert Rent-a-Car** (B.P. 1047, Papeete; tel. 42-97-20, fax 42-63-00), rue du Commandant Destremeau (from CFP 1200 daily, plus CFP 35 a km, plus CFP 700 insurance). More expensive is **Garage Daniel** (B.P. 1445, Papeete; tel. 82-30-04), at PK 5.5 across the highway from the airport terminal. They charge CFP 1600 a day, plus CFP 33 a km, plus CFP 1000 insurance, or CFP 14,000 for three days with unlimited mileage.

Scooter and Cycle Rentals

Pacificar (tel. 41-93-93) on pont de l'Est rents one-person motor scooters at CFP 1000 a day, plus CFP 23 a km (50-km daily minimum). Compulsory helmets are provided, but no insurance is available for the scooters. They will let you take the scooter to Moorea (ferry charges are CFP 1000 return), but an authorization must be obtained from Pacificar in advance. They'll warn you that if you have any problems with the scooter while on Moorea, it's up to you to get it back to Tahiti. (On Moorea scooters are more expensive at CFP 3000 a day with unlimited kilometers.)

Cycles Evasion (tel. 45-11-82), boulevard Pomare 483 (directly behind the Moana Iti Restaurant), rents quality mountain bikes at CFP 1000 daily (CFP 20,000 deposit). The fast and furious traffic on Tahiti's main highways makes cycling dangerous and unpleasant, but you might consider getting a bicycle here to take over to Moorea. They're open weekdays 0830-1200 and 1400-1700, Saturday 0800-1200.

Garage Bambou (B.P. 5592, Papeete; tel. 42-80-09), on Ave. Georges Clemenceau near the Chinese temple, sells new bicycles from CFP 24,000 and does repairs.

Local Tours

Twice a day William Leeteg of **Adventure Eagle Tours** (B.P. 6719, Faa'a; tel. 41-37-63) takes visitors on four-hour trips to the top of Mt. Marau (1,372 meters) by 4WD vehicle for CFP 5000 pp. A visit to Vaimahuta Falls is included, but the tour is canceled on rainy days. There's also a full-day tour around the island at CFP 3800 (admissions and lunch not included). William speaks good English and can arrange special guided tours for groups of up to seven.

Patrice Bordes of **Tahiti Safari Expedition** (B.P. 14445, Arue; tel. 42-14-15, evenings only) offers 4WD jeep tours to Mt. Marau, the Papenoo Valley, and Lake Vaihiria.

Getting Away

The **Air Tahiti** booking office (tel. 42-24-44) is upstairs in Fare Tony, the building behind Acajou off boulevard Pomare. **Air Moorea** (tel. 86-41-41) is at Faa'a International Airport. Interisland services by air and sea are covered in "Getting Around" in the "Transportation" section of the introduction to this chapter.

The ferries to Moorea depart from the landing just behind the tourist office downtown. The *Raromatai Ferry* and *Ono-Ono* to the Leeward Islands also leave from there, as do cruise ships and a few other small boats. All other interisland ships, including the cargo vessels *Taporo VI* and *Vaeanu,* leave from the Tuamotu wharf or Quai des Caboteurs in Motu Uta, across the harbor from downtown Papeete. You can catch a *truck* directly to Motu Uta from the Hôtel de Ville. The ticket offices of some of the vessels are in Fare Ute just north of downtown, while others are at Motu Uta (addresses given in the "Transportation" section in the introduction to this chapter).

OTHER WINDWARD ISLANDS

Mehetia is an uninhabited high island (435 meters) about 100 km east of Tahiti. It's less than two km across, with no lagoon, and landing is difficult. Anglers from the south coast of Tahiti visit occasionally.

Maiao, or Tapuaemanu, 70 km southwest of Moorea, is a low coral island with an elongated, 154-meter-high hill at the center. On each side of this hill is a large greenish blue lake. Around Maiao is a barrier reef with a pass on the south side accessible only to small boats. Some 250 people live on 8.3-square-km Maiao, all Polynesians. Europeans and Chinese are not allowed to reside on the island as a result of problems with an Englishman, Eric Trower, who attempted to gain control of Maiao for phosphate mining in the 1930s.

There are no tourist accommodations on Maiao and an invitation from a resident is required to stay. There's no airstrip. For information on the monthly supply ship from Papeete, contact the **Compagnie Française Maritime de Tahiti** (B.P. 368, Papeete; tel. 42-63-93) at Fare Ute. A roundtrip voyage on this ship would at least give you a glimpse of Maiao.

TETIAROA

AUROA

TAUINI HIRA ANAE

TIARAUNU OROATERA

MOTU AIE

HONUEA LAGOON

AIRSTRIP HOTEL ONETAHI RIMATUU

TAHUNA ITI

TAHUNA RAHI

REIONO

0   2 km

N

© DAVID STANLEY

Tetiaroa

Tetiaroa, 42 km north of Tahiti, is a low coral atoll with a turquoise lagoon and 13 deep-green coconut-covered islets totaling 490 hectares. Only small boats can enter the lagoon. Tahuna Iti has been designated a seabird refuge (fenced off), the lagoon a marine reserve. On three-km-long Rimatuu islet may be seen the remains of Polynesian *marae* and giant *tuu* trees.

In 1904 the Pomare family gave Tetiaroa, once a Tahitian royal retreat, to a British dentist named Walter Williams to pay their bills. Dr. Williams, who was also the British consul from 1923 to 1935, had a daughter who sold Tetiaroa to actor Marlon Brando in 1962. Brando came to Tahiti in 1960 to play Fletcher Christian in the MGM film *Mutiny on the Bounty* and ended up marrying his leading lady, Tarita Teriipaia. She and her family still run the small tourist resort on Motu Onetahi. Tarita and Marlon had two children, son Teihotu, born in 1965, and daughter Cheyenne, born in 1970.

The gunshot death of Dag Drollet, Cheyenne's ex-boyfriend and father of her son Tuki, at the Brando residence in Los Angeles in 1990 resulted in a 10-year prison sentence for Cheyenne's half-brother, Christian Brando, on a plea bargain. On Easter Sunday 1995 Cheyenne committed suicide and was buried next to Dag in the Drollet family crypt on Tahiti. These tragedies continue to haunt the Brando family, and the resort on Tetiaroa has been seriously neglected as a result. Marlon is seldom present on Tetiaroa these days, and when he is the atoll is closed to tourists.

Getting There

A reservation office (B.P. 2418, Papeete; tel. 82-63-03, fax 85-00-51) in the Air Moorea terminal at Faa'a International Airport arranges flights to Tetiaroa. A seven-hour day-trip including airfare, bird island tour, and lunch is CFP 22,500 pp. If you arrange this trip through your hotel, their commission will boot the price up a bit. To spend the night in a rustic bungalow at the **Tetiaroa Village Hôtel** you'll pay CFP 35,000/64,000/84,000 single/double/triple for a one-night package, or CFP 40,000/74,000/102,000 for a two-night package including air ticket, bungalow, meals, and excursion. But to be frank, this hotel is in need of major renovations and you'll be shocked to see traces of past glory slowly being eaten away by termites. So—though the price may suggest it—don't expect anything resembling a luxury resort, and come prepared to rough it.

Less expensive visits to Tetiaroa can be arranged at **Tahiti Mer et Loisirs** (B.P. 3488, Papeete; tel. 43-97-99, fax 43-33-68), in a houseboat on the Papeete waterfront opposite the post office. Their yacht cruises to the atoll are CFP 16,000 pp for one day (CFP 9500 without lunch or drinks), CFP 26,400 pp for two days, including snorkeling gear, trips ashore, and all meals. Longer stays are possible at CFP 10,000 pp for each additional day, all-inclusive. (In mid-1995 Marlon Brando won a lawsuit to prohibit "floating hotels" in the Tetiaroa lagoon, so overnight trips many now only be possible for those staying at the Tetiaroa Village Hôtel.)

Other yachts moored near Mer et Loisirs offer day-trips to Tetiaroa for as little as CFP 7000 (meals not included), but they don't depart according to any set schedule, so you just have to look around and ask. On all boat trips to Tetiaroa, be aware that up to three hours will be spent traveling each way and on a day-trip you'll only have about four hours on the atoll. The boat trip tends to be rough and many people throw up their fancy lunch on the way back to Papeete.

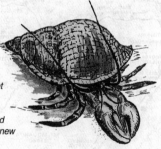

The hermit crab (Pagurus) uses empty snail shells to protect its soft abdomen from predators. The crab hooks himself into the shell and would sooner be torn in half than let go. As these nocturnal scavengers grow, they must find larger shells to live in. Contrary to the name, the hermits are quite sociable and are often seen in groups searching for food or new shells.

MOOREA

Moorea, Tahiti's heart-shaped sister island, is clearly visible across the Sea of the Moon, just 16 km northwest of Papeete. This enticing island offers the white-sand beaches rare on Tahiti, plus long, deep bays, lush volcanic peaks, and a broad blue-green lagoon. Dino de Laurentiis filmed *The Bounty* here in 1983. Much more than Tahiti, Moorea is the laid-back South Sea isle of the travel brochures. And while Bora Bora has a reputation as Polynesia's most beautiful island, easily accessible Moorea seems to merit the distinction more.

With a population of just 9,000, Moorea lives a quiet, relaxed lifestyle; coconut, pineapple, and vanilla plantations alternate with pleasant resorts and the vegetation-draped dwellings of the inhabitants. Tourism is concentrated along the north coast around Paopao and Club Med; most of the locals live in the south. The accommodations are good and plentiful, while weekly and monthly apartment rentals make even extended stays possible. Don't try to see it as a day-trip from Tahiti: this is a place to relax!

The Land

This triangular island is actually the surviving south rim of a volcano once 3,000 meters high. Moorea is twice as old as its Windward partner, Tahiti, and weathering is noticeably advanced. The two spectacular bays cutting into the north coast flank Mt. Rotui (899 meters), once Moorea's core. The crescent of jagged peaks facing these long northern bays is scenically superb.

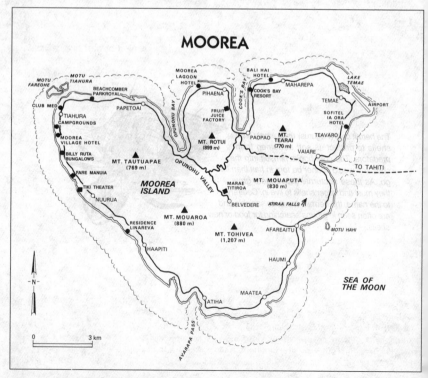

MOOREA

Shark-tooth-shaped Mouaroa (880 meters) is a visual triumph, but Mt. Tohivea (1,207 meters) is higher. Polynesian chiefs were once buried in caves along the cliffs. Moorea's peaks protect the north and northwest coasts from the rain-bearing southeast trades; the drier climate and scenic beauty explain the profusion of hotels along this side of the island. Moorea is surrounded by a coral ring with several passes into the lagoon. Three *motus* enhance the lagoon, one off Afareaitu and two off Club Med.

Moorea's interior valley slopes are unusually rich, with large fruit and vegetable plantations and human habitation. At one time or another, coconuts, sugarcane, cotton, vanilla, coffee, rice, and pineapples have all been grown in the rich soil of Moorea's plantations. Stock farming and fishing are other occupations. Vegetables like taro, cucumbers, pumpkins, and lettuce, and fruit such as bananas, oranges, grapefruit, papaya, star apples, rambutans, avocados, tomatoes, mangoes, limes, tangerines, and breadfruit make Moorea a veritable Garden of Eden.

History

Legend claims that Aimeho (or "Eimeo," as Captain Cook spelled it) was formed from the second dorsal fin of the fish that became Tahiti. The present name, Moorea, means "offshoot." A hole right through the summit of Mt. Mouaputa (830 meters) is said to have been made by the spear of the demigod Pai, who tossed it across from Tahiti to prevent Mt. Rotui (899 meters) from being carried off to Raiatea by Hiro, the god of thieves.

Captain Samuel Wallis was the European discoverer of the Windward Islands in 1767. After leaving Tahiti, he passed along the north coast of Moorea without landing. He named it Duke of York's Island. The first European visitors were botanist Joseph Banks, Lieutenant Gore, the surgeon William Monkhouse, Herman Sporing, and half a dozen sailors sent over by Captain Cook on 1 June 1769 to observe the transit of Venus. (The main observatory was, of course, on Point Venus, but the transit was also observed by officers on Moorea and on a small islet off the east coast of Tahiti.) The telescope was set up on the small Motu Irioa, halfway between Club Med and Opunohu Bay, and the observation was duly made on 3 June.

Banks landed several times on the north coast at Papetoai. The party returned to Tahiti on 4 June. Captain Cook anchored in Opunohu Bay for one week in 1777, but he never visited the bay that today bears his name! His visit was uncharacteristically brutal, as he smashed the islanders' canoes and burned their homes when they refused to return a stolen goat.

In 1792 Pomare I conquered Moorea using arms obtained from the *Bounty* mutineers. Moorea had long been a traditional place of refuge for defeated Tahitian warriors, thus in 1808 Pomare II fled into exile here with a party of English missionaries after his bid to bring all Tahiti under his control failed. Moorea has a special place in the history of Christianity: here in 1812 the missionaries finally managed to convert Pomare II after 15 years of trying. On 14 February 1815, Patii, high priest of Oro, publicly accepted Protestantism and burned the old heathen idols at Papetoai, where the octagonal church is today. Shortly afterward the whole population followed Patii's example. The *marae* of Moorea were then abandoned and the Opunohu Valley depopulated. The first Tahitian translation of part of the Bible was printed on Moorea in 1817. From this island Protestantism spread throughout the South Pacific.

After Pomare II finally managed to reconquer Tahiti in 1815 with missionary help (the main reason for his "conversion"), Moorea again became a backwater. American novelist Herman Melville visited Moorea in 1842 and worked with other beachcombers on a sweet-potato farm in Maatea. His book *Omoo* contains a marvelous description of his tour of the island. Cotton and coconut plantations were created on Moorea in the 19th century, followed by vanilla and coffee in the 20th, but only with the advent of the travel industry has Moorea become more than a beautiful backdrop for Tahiti.

Orientation

If you arrive by ferry you'll get off at Vaiare, four km south of Temae Airport. Your hotel may be at Maharepa (Hôtel Bali Hai), Paopao (Bali Hai Club, Motel Albert), Pihaena (Moorea Lagoon Hôtel), or Tiahura (Club Med, the campgrounds, Moorea Village Hôtel), all on the north coast. The Paopao hotels enjoy better scenery, but the beach is far superior at Tiahura.

The PKs (kilometer stones) on Moorea are measured in both directions from PK 0 at the access road to Temae Airport. They're numbered up to PK 35 along the north coast via Club Med and up to PK 24 along the south coast via Afareaitu, meeting at Haapiti halfway around the island. Our circle-island tour and the accommodations and restaurant listings below begin at Vaiare Wharf and go counterclockwise around the island in each category.

SIGHTS

Northeast Moorea

You'll probably arrive on Moorea at **Vaiare Wharf,** which is officially PK 4 on the 59-km road around the island. To the north is the **Sofitel Ia Ora** (PK 1.5), Moorea's most sophisticated resort. If you have your own transport, stop here for a look around and to see the colorful fish swimming below the Ia Ora's wharf. It's also enjoyable to walk north along the beach from this hotel or even to go snorkeling. At PK 1 on the main road, high above the Ia Ora, is a fine **lookout** over the deep passage, romantically named the Sea of the Moon, between Tahiti and Moorea.

One of the few good public beaches on Moorea is at **Temae,** about a km down a gravel road to the right a bit before you reach the airport access road. Watch out for black spiny sea urchins here. There's good snorkeling opposite Lilishop Boutique at **Maharepa** (look for the gaudy pareus hanging outside).

Around Cook's Bay

On the grounds of the American-owned **Hôtel Bali Hai** at PK 5 are replicas of historic anchors lost by Captains Bougainville and Cook in the 18th century. Just past the Bali Hai on the mountain side of the road is the "White House," the stately mansion of a former vanilla plantation, now used as a pareu salesroom.

At the entrance to Cook's Bay (PK 7) is the **Galerie Aad Van der Heyde** (tel. 56-14-22), as much a museum as a gallery. Aad's paintings hang outside in the flower-filled courtyard; inside are his black-pearl jewelry, a large collection of Marquesan sculpture, and artifacts from around the Pacific.

Paopao boasts a *gendarmerie,* pharmacy,

Cook's Bay, Moorea

three banks, gas station, municipal market, hotels, and restaurants. At the **Moorea Pearl Center** (admission free; tel. 56-13-13), opposite Club Bali Hai in Paopao (PK 8.5), are exquisite black pearls and more Polynesian woodcarvings.

A rough dirt road up to the Belvédère begins just west of the bridge at Paopao (PK 9) and it's nice to hike up it past the pineapple plantations. On the west side of Cook's Bay, a km farther along the north-coast highway, is a **Catholic church** (PK 10); an interesting altar painting with Polynesian angels was done by the Swedish artist Peter Heyman in 1948.

It's possible to visit the Distillerie de Moorea **fruit-juice factory** (B.P. 23, Moorea; tel. 56-11-33, fax 56-21-52), up off the main road at PK 12, Monday to Thursday 0800-1130. Monday to Wednesday they'll show you the pineapple processing; Thursday is grapefruit or papaya day. Aside from the excellent papaya, grapefruit, and pineapple juices made from local fruits, the factory produces apple, orange, and passion fruit juices from imported concentrate, with no preservatives added. They also make 40-proof brandies (carambola or "star fruit," ginger, grapefruit, mango, orange, and pineapple flavors) and 25-proof liqueurs (coconut, ginger, and pineapple varieties). These are sold to the public at the Accueil counter, and if they think you might buy a bottle, they'll invite you to sample the brews.

Opunohu Bay to Le Belvédère

The **Moorea Lagoon Hôtel** at PK 14 is the only large hotel between Paopao and Tiahura. An overgrown trail up **Mt. Rotui** begins opposite the "Faimano Village" accommodations nearby. Ask a local to point out the way.

Shrimp are bred in large basins at the head of Opunohu Bay (PK 18). A paved road up the pineapple-filled **Opunohu Valley** to the Belvédère begins here: one and a half km to the connecting road from Cook's Bay, another two km to Marae Titiroa, then one more steep km up to the lookout. On the way, you'll pass Moorea's agricultural high school. This worthy institution, with students from all the islands of Tahiti-Polynesia, has hundreds of hectares planted in pineapples, vanilla, coffee, fruit trees, decorative flowers, and native vegetables.

Marae Titiroa, high up near the geographical center of Moorea, is the largest of a group of Polynesian temples restored in 1969 by Prof. Y.H. Sinoto of Honolulu. The small platform or

ahu at the end of this *marae* (and the others) was a sacred area reserved for the gods. Stone backrests for chiefs and priests are other features of the *marae*. Here the people offered gifts of tubers, fish, dogs, and pigs, and prayed to their gods, many of whom were deified ancestors. Just 50 meters northwest of Marae Titiroa near the water tanks is a long council platform, and 50 meters farther are two smaller *marae* surrounded by towering Tahitian chestnut trees *(mape)*. The most evocative of the group is four-tiered **Marae Ahu o Mahine,** about 250 meters down the trail.

Some 500 ancient structures have been identified in this area, and if you're very keen, you should be able to find a few in the forest across the stream, evidence of a large population with a highly developed social system. With the acceptance of Christianity in the early 19th century, the Opunohu Valley's importance declined sharply. Naturalists may enjoy the natural vegetation in there (you must bushwhack).

Continue up the main road from Marae Titiroa about 200 meters and watch for some stone **archery platforms** on the left. Here kneeling nobles once competed to see who could shoot an arrow the farthest. The bows and arrows

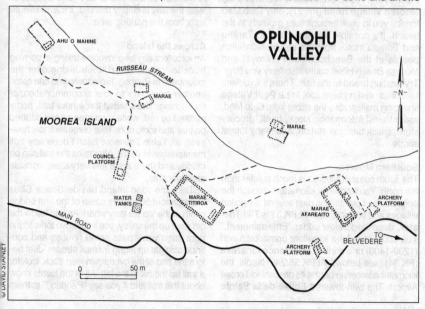

employed in these contests were never used in warfare. Just up on the left is access to another archery platform and **Marae Afareaito.** The stone slabs you see sticking up in the middle of the *marae* were backrests for participants of honor.

Above is the **Belvédère,** or Roto Nui, a viewpoint from which much of northern Moorea is visible. From here it's easy to visualize the great volcano that was Moorea. Mt. Rotui (899 meters) in front of you was once the central core of an island more than three times as high as the present. The north part is now missing, but the semicircular arch of the southern half is plain to see.

Papetoai to Club Med

Return to the main circuminsular highway and continue west. The octagonal **Protestant church,** behind the post office at Papetoai (PK 22), was built on the site of the temple of the god Oro in 1822. Despite having been rebuilt several times, the church is known as "the oldest European building still in use in the South Pacific."

As the road begins to curve around the northwest corner of Moorea, you pass a number of large resort hotels, including the **Beachcomber Parkroyal** (PK 24), **Club Med** (PK 26), and the **Moorea Village Hôtel** (PK 27); only Club Med forbids you to walk through their grounds to the beach. It's possible to snorkel out to Tarahu and Tiahuru *motus* from this beach; recreation people at the Beachcomber Parkroyal and Moorea Beach Hôtel could also ferry you over. Try feeding bread to the fish. There's excellent reef break surfing here, too. In **Le Petit Village** shopping mall, across the street from Club Med, are a tourist information kiosk, bank, grocery store, snack bar, gas station, and many tourist shops.

Southern Moorea

The south coast of Moorea is much quieter than the north. You'll drive for kilometers through the open coconut plantations past several unspoiled villages and scenic vistas. At PK 31 is **Tiki Theater,** described below under "Entertainment." You could stop for a excellent upmarket lunch (1200-1400) or a drink at **Résidence Linareva** (PK 34) (see below). At PK 35/24, Haapiti, the kilometer numbering begins its descent to Temae Airport. The twin-towered **Église de la Sainte Famille** (1891) at Haapiti was once the head church of the Catholic mission on the island.

Tiny Motu Hahi lies just off **Afareaitu** (PK 9), the administrative center of Moorea. The London Missionary Society originally had its Academy of the South Seas here. On 30 June 1817, at the missionary printing works at Afareaitu, King Pomare II ceremonially printed the first page of the first book ever published on a South Pacific island, a Tahitian translation of the Gospel of St. Luke. Before the press was moved to Huahine a year later, over 9,000 books totaling more than half a million pages were printed at Afareaitu!

Hike an hour up the **Afareaitu Valley** from the old Protestant church (1912) to a high waterfall, which cascades down a sheer cliff into a pool. You can drive a car two-thirds of the way up the valley. Park at the point where a normal car would have problems and hike up the road to the right. When this road begins to climb steeply, look for a well-beaten footpath on the right which will take you directly to the falls. You'll need a bit of intuition to find the unmarked way on your own.

The access road to a different waterfall, **Atiraa Falls,** is a little beyond the hospital at Afareaitu. Admission to this one is CFP 200 pp, but at least the way is clearly marked. It's a 30-minute walk from the parking area.

Across the Island

An excellent day hike involves taking a morning *truck* to Vaiare Wharf, then hiking over the mountains to Paopao. From there you can catch another *truck* back to your accommodation, or try hitching. The shaded three-hour trail, partly marked by red, white, and green paint dabbed on tree and rock, does take perseverance, however, as Tahiti Tourisme hasn't done any trail maintenance in years. After rains the trail can be muddy and there are a few very steep ascents and descents.

Take the road inland beside Snack Chez Meno, about 50 meters south of the first bridge south of the Vaiare ferry wharf. As you follow the dirt road up the valley, you'll take two forks to the right, then you'll pass some houses and continue straight up along a small stream. Just before the end of the overgrown jeep track, look for a trail up the hill to the left. All of the locals know about this trail and if you say "Paopao?" to them in a questioning way, they'll point you in the right direction.

When you reach the divide, go a short distance south along the ridge past some barbed wire to a super viewpoint over the pineapple plantations behind Paopao. On a clear day the rounded double peak of Orohena, Tahiti's highest, is visible, plus the whole interior of Moorea. This rigorous hike is also worth doing simply to see a good cross section of the vegetation. Don't miss it, but do take water and wear sturdy shoes.

Sports and Recreation

The waters of northern Moorea are the realm of **M.U.S.T. Plongée Scuba Diving**, or Moorea Underwater Scuba-diving Tahiti (B.P. 336, Moorea; tel. 56-17-32, fax 56-29-18), on the dock behind the Cook's Bay Resort Hotel. They offer diving daily except Monday at 0900 and 1400 for CFP 5000 for one dive, CFP 22,500 for five dives. Divemaster Philippe Molle, author of a well-known French book on scuba diving, knows 20 different spots in and outside the reef. Philippe's slogan is: "Diving with M.U.S.T. is a must!"

Bernard and Collette Begliomini's **Bathy's Club** (B.P. 1019, Papetoai; tel. 56-21-07), at the Beachcomber Parkroyal, offers scuba diving for CFP 5000, plus PADI certification courses. Both the M.U.S.T. and Bathy's Club dive shops specialize in underwater fish, eel, and shark feeding. Sometimes the swarm of fish becomes so thick the guide is lost from sight, yet as the resident shark scatters the mass of fish to steal the bait, the divemaster is seen again patting *le requin* as it passes!

Marc Quattrini's **Scubapiti** (B.P. 58H, Haapiti, Moorea; tel. 56-20-38 or 56-29-25), at Résidence Les Tipaniers, offers scuba diving daily at 0900 and 1430 (CFP 4000). Instead of putting on a show, Marc keeps things natural on his cave dives, canyon dives, and drift dives. There's something for everyone, and he also offers PADI or CMAS scuba certification courses.

The "Activities Nautiques" kiosk on the wharf at the **Beachcomber Parkroyal** (tel. 56-19-19) has a one-hour glass-bottom boat ride (CFP 1200 pp), which leaves at 1000 and 1400. A two-hour lagoon cruise is CFP 2600. For more excitement hire a lagoon jet ski (CFP 6500 for half an hour, CFP 10,000 for one hour) or try your hand at parasailing.

For horseback riding try **Rupe-Rupe Ranch** (tel. 56-17-93), on the mountain side just south of the Hôtel Hibiscus. To take one of their 12 horses along the beach for an hour is CFP 2000. Group rides commence at 0830, 1400, and 1600, but it's best to call ahead. **Tiahura Ranch** (tel. 56-28-55) across the highway offers more of the same.

ACCOMMODATIONS

Camping

One of the nicest campgrounds in the South Pacific is **Backpackers' Beach Club** (tel. 56-15-18), beside the Hôtel Hibiscus, just south of Club Med (PK 26). Also known as "Chez Nelson et Josiane" and "Tumoana Village," it's beautifully set in a coconut grove right on the beach. The camping charge is CFP 700 pp, with toilets, showers, refrigerator, and good communal cooking facilities provided. No tents are for rent, but the 10 two-bed "dormitory" rooms go for CFP 1000 pp (CFP 1200 for one night). The five beach cabins with shared bath are CFP 2200 single or double (CFP 2500 for one night); four larger *fares* near the office are CFP 2500 single or double (CFP 3000 for one night). They also have three larger bungalows with kitchen and private bath at CFP 6000 double. For CFP 300 pp (minimum of seven) they'll ferry you across to a *motu* for snorkeling. Josiane is a little eccentric and can be rather reserved at first, but she has a heart of gold. The place is clean, quiet, breezy, spacious, and well equipped, but unfortunately, however, there have been reports of theft here, so don't leave valuables unattended or within reach of an open window at night.

A second, smaller campground (CFP 500 pp) is just a little south of Backpackers' Beach Club, near the Moorea Village Hôtel. **Backpackers' Paradise** (tel. 56-14-47), also known as "Moorea Camping" and "Chez Viri et Claude," faces the same white-sand beach and has nine four-bed dorms at CFP 800 pp (CFP 1000 for one night), plus another nine double rooms in a long building at CFP 2000 single or double (CFP 2500 for one night). The five beachfront bungalows with fridge are CFP 4000 single or double. Communal kitchen and washing facilities are provided, and they'll loan you snorkeling gear and perhaps even a canoe. Bus trips around the island are CFP 1000 pp if at least six people sign up and they can also take you to a *motu*. Several readers wrote in recommending this place. Both campgrounds are simple, but great for young low-budget travelers and other adventurers. A large grocery store (with cold beer) is between the two camping grounds.

Budget Accommodations

Motel Albert (Albert Haring, tel./fax 56-12-76), up on the hill opposite Club Bali Hai at Paopao (PK 8.5), catches splendid views across Cook's Bay. The eight older units with double beds are CFP 3000 single or double, CFP 4000 triple (two-night minimum stay). The 10 larger houses, accommodating up to four persons each, are CFP 6000. Monthly rates are CFP 70,000 double. Each unit has cooking facilities, and several stores are nearby. Despite an oversupply of mosquitoes and undersupply of hot water, it's excellent value and often full (try to make reservations).

The three bungalows behind **Boutique Dina** (Dina Dhieux, tel. 56-10-39) at Pihaena, a km east of the Moorea Lagoon Hôtel, are CFP 4500 triple, CFP 5000 for up to five; subtract CFP 500 a day for the weekly rate. Cooking facilities are provided, and the bathroom is communal. It's easy to drive past this place, so watch for the pareu display.

Several small places near the Moorea Lagoon Hôtel (PK 14) rent more expensive bungalows. **Chez Nani** (Maeva Bougues, B.P. 117, Papeete; tel. 56-19-99) on the west side of the hotel has three thatched bungalows with kitchenettes for CFP 7000 single or double. The signposted **Faimano Village** (Hinano Feidel, B.P. 1676, Papeete; tel. 56-10-20, fax 56-36-47) next to Chez Nani has six bungalows with cooking facilities at CFP 10,500 for up to six persons with private bath, CFP 7500/8000 double/triple with shared bath (two-night minimum stay). **Chez Francine** (Francine Lumen, tel. 56-13-24), 400 meters farther west (no sign), has a two-room house at CFP 6000 double with kitchenette or CFP 5000 double without. There's no grocery store near the Moorea Lagoon—the nearest is by the bridge in Paopao.

Hôtel Résidence Tiahura (William Estall, B.P. 1068, Papetoai; tel. 56-15-45, fax 56-37-67), at PK 25 Tiahura on the mountain side just east of Club Med, is a five-minute walk from the beach. One of the six bungalows without kitchenette is CFP 4500 single or double, one of the six with kitchenette CFP 5500 double. All units have fridge and private bath. It's friendly but has an abandoned feel.

Billy Ruta Bungalows (tel. 56-12-54) is right on the beach at PK 28, Tiahura. The 12 thatched A-frame bungalows begin at CFP 4000 double without kitchenette, CFP 5000 double with kitchenette. There's disco dancing here on Friday and Saturday nights from 2230. Billy drives the local school and church *truck* and is a very friendly guy.

Fare Mato Tea (Ronald Cabral, B.P. 1111, Papetoai; tel. 56-14-36), on the beach just south of Billy Ruta (PK 29), is okay if you're in a group: CFP 8000 for four, CFP 10,000 for six (minimum stay two nights). All eight large thatched bungalows on the spacious grounds have full cooking facilities and private bath.

At the south end of the west coast strip (PK 30) is **Fare Manuia** (Jeanne Salmon, tel. 56-26-17) with five thatched bungalows with cooking facilities at CFP 7000 for up to four people, CFP 8500 for up to six people.

Chez Pauline (Pauline Teariki, tel. 56-11-26) at PK 9, Afareaitu, is between the two stores near the church (no sign). The seven rooms with double beds and shared bath in this lovely old colonial house run CFP 2500 single or double, CFP 4000 triple. A picturesque restaurant (closed Sunday), with Pauline's tikis on display, rounds out this establishment, which would have great atmosphere if it weren't for the eccentric manner of the proprietors. Dinner here is around CFP 2000 (fish and Tahitian vegetables).

Medium-Priced Accommodations

The locally owned **Cook's Bay Resort Hotel** (B.P. 30, Paopao; tel. 56-10-50, fax 56-29-18) is by the highway at the entrance to Cook's Bay. You can't miss this mock-colonial edifice constructed in 1985, with its false-front Waikiki feel (even the manager is Hawaiian). The 76 rooms begin at CFP 8400 single or double, CFP 9900 triple with fan, though the rates seem to fluctuate according to what the market will bear, so you might call ahead to find out if they have a special going. Though it isn't on the beach, you can swim off the pier in front of the restaurant and there's a swimming pool. Moorea's top dive shop is on the premises, and all the usual resort

(top) sunset over Moorea (Paul Bohler)
(bottom) rainbow over Rarotonga, Cook Islands (David Stanley)

(top left) painting tapa, Savai'i, Western Samoa (Dieter Dorn); (top right) police band tuba player, Apia, Western Samoa (Richard Eastwood); (bottom) treasure hunter, Pinaki, Tuamotu Islands, Tahiti-Polynesia (Anselm Zänkert)

activities are available. A sunset cruise aboard the *Fat Cat* is offered every other afternoon at 1630 (CFP 500).

Right next door to the Cook's Bay Resort (and under the same ownership) is the **Kaveka Beach Club** (B.P. 13, Temae, Moorea; tel. 56-18-30), at PK 7.5, Paopao. The 24 thatched bungalows run CFP 9500/11,000/12,000 single/double/triple plus tax; the breakfast and dinner meal plan is CFP 3200 pp extra.

The **Moorea Lagoon Hôtel** (B.P. 11, Moorea; tel. 56-11-55, fax 56-26-25) at PK 14, Pihaena, is CFP 7000 single or double garden view, CFP 9000 ocean view, CFP 11,000 beachfront for 40 thatched bungalows. A small gambling casino is on the premises (Tuesday to Saturday 2000-0100; passport required). This hotel, along with the Te Puna Bel Air Hôtel on Tahiti, is owned by the local Rey family. The beach is fine—have fun if your tour company drops you here.

The **Moorea Beach Club** (B.P. 1017, Papetoai; tel. 56-15-48, fax 56-25-70), formerly the Climate de France, is the first hotel on the white sandy shores of the Tiahura tourist strip. The 40 a/c rooms with fridge begin at CFP 10,000 single, CFP 12,000 double or triple, plus CFP 3500 pp extra for breakfast and dinner (if desired). The more expensive bungalows have cooking facilities. The less expensive units are on two floors, so you will have someone above or below. Outrigger canoes, tennis, snorkeling, and fishing gear are free.

Résidence Les Tipaniers (B.P. 1002, Moorea; tel. 56-12-67, fax 56-29-25) is cramped around the reception, but better as you approach the beach. The 22 rooms are CFP 7800/10,000 single/double, while the 11 thatched bungalows with kitchen capable of accommodating up to five are a few thousand francs extra. They'll shuttle you over to a *motu* for snorkeling at no charge. This hotel has a good reputation and a resident divemaster.

The **Hôtel Hibiscus** (B.P. 1009, Papetoai; tel. 56-12-20, fax 56-20-69), beside Club Med (PK 26), offers 29 thatched garden bungalows beneath the coconut palms at CFP 10,000 for up to two adults and two children (CFP 12,000 with kitchenette). There's a two-night minimum stay and weekly rates are available. Late-night party noise from Club Med can be a nuisance.

The 48-unit **Moorea Village Noa Noa** (B.P. 1008, Moorea; tel. 56-10-02, fax 56-22-11), also

called "Fare Gendron," at PK 27 has fan-cooled thatched bungalows beginning at CFP 7000/8000 single/double, or CFP 10,500 for up to four people. For a kitchen in your unit add CFP 3500 to the price; all units have fridges. To be on the beach is another CFP 2500. The breakfast and dinner plan costs CFP 3500 pp. Saturday at 1900 there's a barbecue; the Tahitian feast with Polynesian dancing is Sunday at 1230. There are lots of free activities, such as the canoe trip to the *motu,* outrigger canoes, tennis, snorkeling, swimming pool, and bicycles. This place is somewhat of a hangout for local Tahitians, and the management leaves a lot to be desired.

Résidence Linareva (B.P. 1, Haapiti; tel. 56-15-35, fax 56-25-25) sits amid splendid mountain scenery at PK 34 on the wild side of the island. Prices begin at CFP 7200/8200/9800 single/double/triple, with 20% weekly discounts. Each of the seven units is unique, but there are no cooking facilities. Linareva's floating seafood restaurant, the *Tamarii Moorea I,* is an old ferryboat that once plied between Moorea and Tahiti. Colorful reef fish swim around the dock.

Upmarket Accommodations

The easygoing **Sofitel Ia Ora** (B. P. 28, Temae; tel. 56-12-90, fax 56-12-91), at PK 1.5 between Vaiare and the airport, is *the* place if you want luxury and don't give a damn about the price. The 80 deluxe thatched bungalows begin at CFP 21,500 single or double (children under 12 free). Breakfast and dinner are CFP 5000 pp extra together. Unfortunately, the service deteriorates when large groups are present. On the shore is a restaurant with its own open-air aquarium (free), and the adjacent beach is one of the best on the island, with a splendid view of Tahiti.

The 63-room **Hôtel Bali Hai** (B.P. 26, Moorea; tel. 56-13-59, fax 56-19-22) at PK 5, Maharepa, caters mainly to American tour groups staying three, four, or seven nights. The cheapest rooms are CFP 9500/14,000/16,000 single/double/triple (children under 12 free), bungalows 50% more and up. For breakfast and dinner add CFP 3900 pp extra. Rides on the Bali Hai's new thatched catamaran *Liki Tiki* are free for guests. The Bali Hai was founded by the so-called Bali Hai Boys, Hugh, Jay, and Muk. The happy-go-lucky tale of this gang of three's arrival on Moorea in 1959 is posted in the lobby, if you're interested.

Club Bali Hai (B.P. 8, Temae; tel. 56-13-68, fax 56-13-27) at PK 8.5, Paopao, has 20 rooms in the main two-story building start at CFP 7500 single or double, and 19 beachfront or over-water bungalows at CFP 18,000 or 22,500 for up to four persons. Only the bungalows include cooking facilities, but all rooms have a spectacular view of Cook's Bay. Many units have been sold to affluent Americans on a time-share basis, with each owner getting two weeks a year at the Club. It's homey, clean, and not at all pretentious. Enjoy half-price drinks during happy hour at the lagoonside bar Tuesday and Friday 1800-1900. We've heard Club Bali Hai welcomes visiting yachties warmly.

The 150-room **Moorea Beachcomber Park-royal** (B.P. 1019, Papetoai; tel. 56-19-19, fax 56-18-88) at PK 24, takes the cake as the most expensive hotel on Moorea. Rooms in the main building start at CFP 28,000 single or double—much too much. For an overwater bungalow, tack on an additional 50%. The breakfast and dinner plan is CFP 6100 pp. The Beachcomber Parkroyal, built in 1987, was purchased for US$13.5 million in 1989 by Japanese interests that have since spent further millions of dollars upgrading the place.

Club Méditerranée (B.P. 1010, Moorea; tel. 56-17-51, fax 56-19-51) at PK 26 has 350 simple fan-cooled bungalows. You can reserve one by paying CFP 14,000 pp a day (double occupancy) at the Club Med office in the Vaima Center, Papeete (B.P. 575, Papeete; tel. 42-96-99). The price includes breakfast, lunch, and dinner, and a wide range of regimented activities (including one scuba dive a day), but no airport transfers. Unlimited beer and wine come with lunch and dinner, but other drinks are expensive and laundry charges will knock your socks off! The full PADI scuba diving center here is for guests only. Sunbathing in the raw is permitted on the small *motu* just offshore. Club Med's for you if nonstop activity is a high priority, otherwise all the canned entertainment can be to the detriment of peace at night, and occasional helicopter landings beside the restaurant often interrupt afternoon naps. Clocks inside the village are set ahead to give guests an extra hour in the sun. Club Med's G.O.s *(gentils organisateurs)* tend to resist the unusual or nonroutine (such as requesting a specific room), so try to "go with the flow" (i.e., conform). It's not a "swinging singles club" anymore, but rather a haven for couples where singles can also be found. No visitors are allowed.

FOOD

Aside from the hotel restaurants, table hoppers are catered to by a mixed bag of eateries along the east side of Cook's Bay. **Le Cocotier Restaurant** (closed Sunday; tel. 56-12-10) at PK 4, Maharepa, offers a number of reasonably priced fish dishes on a blackboard menu at the entrance.

The upscale **Restaurant Chez Michel et Jackie** (tel. 56-11-08), at PK 5, on the main road just east of the Hôtel Bali Hai, features French cooking and big two-person pizzas (from CFP 1850).

Le Pécheur Restaurant (tel. 56-36-12), also at Maharepa, near the pharmacy at the east entrance to Cook's Bay, has an excellent reputation for its seafood dishes which begin around CFP 1500. If you lack transport, they'll come and pick you up. The overwater **Fisherman's Wharf Restaurant** at the Kaveka Beach Club also serves excellent seafood.

Snack Te Honu Iti (closed Tuesday; tel. 56-19-84), at PK 9 near the municipal market at the head of Cook's Bay, lists a good selection of dishes on their blackboard, such as hamburgers, tuna burgers, and a *plat du jour,* all of which you consume on their airy terrace. The papaya, coconut, and banana milkshakes are served warm! A food *truck* parks in front of the market at Paopao in the evening.

The restaurant at **Club Bali Hai** (tel. 56-16-25) at Paopao is surprisingly reasonable, so wander in and peruse the posted menu. The snack bar down by the dock serves a wicked hot dog! Happy hour at the bar is 1830-1930 (half-price drinks).

Alfredo's Restaurante Italiano (open daily; tel. 56-17-71) on the inland side of the road by Cook's Bay, a few hundred meters south of Club Bali Hai, has some of the island's best pizza and pasta, plus a few fish and meat dishes. It's owned by an American named Syd Pollock who has been running hotels and restaurants around Polynesia for years. He's an interesting guy to chat with and he does hotel pickups on request.

Restaurant Fare Manava (closed Wednesday; tel. 56-14-24), also known as "Chez Monique et Conny," at the inland end of Paopao Bay, has a pleasant dining room overlooking Cook's Bay. Prices are reasonable (superb mahimahi steamed with ginger at CFP 1400), and there's excellent Chinese food too. It's probably Moorea's best restaurant for the money.

Restaurants near Club Med
Tropical Iceberg (tel. 56-29-53) in Le Petit Village shopping mall opposite Club Med has ice cream sundaes (CFP 650), and it's also a good place for breakfast with bacon and eggs for CFP 350 (served 0900-1100 only). **Le Dauphin Restaurant,** attached to Tropical Iceberg, has pizza from CFP 950 and fish dishes from CFP 1600 (Tuesday to Sunday 1130-1430 and 1830-2130). Good reports.

Better pizza, reasonable fish dishes, and ocean views are available at beachfront **Caesario Pizzeria** (closed Monday) at the Hôtel Hibiscus. **Pâtisserie Le Sylesie II** (tel. 56-20-45) is next door.

Groceries
If you've got access to cooking facilities, there are lots of grocery stores spread all around Moorea. The largest and cheapest is **Toa Moorea,** a km south of the Vaiare ferry wharf (Monday to Saturday 0800-2000, Sunday 0700-1300).

Don't make a special trip to the **municipal market** at Paopao, however, as all you're likely to find there is some sliced fish and a few pineapples, limes, papaya, and grapefruit. Fresh produce is much harder to obtain on Moorea than it is on Tahiti, so buy things when you see them and plan your grocery shopping carefully. Ask the stores what time the bread arrives, then be there promptly. The hybrid lime-grapefruit being developed on Moorea has a thick green skin and a really unique taste.

ENTERTAINMENT

Moorea's top nonhotel disco with live music is **Le Tabou** (tel. 45-02-62), directly across the street from the Moorea Lagoon Hôtel (PK 14). It all happens on Friday and Saturday nights from around 2200 (admission CFP 500-1000).

The disco at **Billy Ruta Bungalows** (tel. 56-12-54), at PK 28, Tiahura, is a nice, very Polynesian scene with a good music mix of Tahitian, French, American, reggae, etc. It's a fun place that gets very busy with some very talented dancers (Friday and Saturday from 2230).

See **Tahitian dancing** in the Sofitel Ia Ora's La Pérouse Restaurant (tel. 56-17-61) on Tuesday, Thursday, and Saturday at 2000. The Tahitian show at the Moorea Beachcomber Parkroyal (tel. 56-19-19) is on Wednesday and Saturday nights. Both Hôtel Bali Hai (tel. 56-13-59) and the Moorea Village Hôtel (tel. 56-10-02) present Polynesian dancing Sunday at lunchtime. The Tahitian feasts that come with the shows cost CFP 4000 and up, but you can often observe the action from the bar for the price of a drink.

Moorea has its own instant culture village, the **Tiki Theater** (B.P. 1016, Moorea; tel. 56-18-97, fax 43-20-06) at PK 31, Haapiti. The doors are open Tuesday to Saturday 1100-1500, with a charge of CFP 1000 to visit the village and see the small dance show at 1300. The guided tour of the village is informative and the staff enthusiastic, but sometimes they're a little disorganized so you might obtain some details about the show time before parting with your francs. Lunch is available in the a la carte restaurant. Line fishing from a *pirogue* is CFP 1500 extra. Tuesday, Thursday, Friday and Saturday nights at 1800 there's a big sunset show with a *tamaaraa* buffet and open bar (CFP 5800, reservations advised). If you're not hungry it's possible to pay CFP 2000 for the show alone at 2000. If you've got CFP 110,000 to blow, a "royal" Tahitian wedding can be arranged at the village (bring your own husband/wife). The ceremony lasts two hours, from 1600 to sunset, and is a private party, with the village closed to the public. The bridegroom arrives by canoe and the newlyweds are carried around in procession by four "warriors." Otherwise there's the less extravagant "princely" wedding for CFP 80,000, photos included. Yes, it's kinda tacky, but that's show biz! (Such weddings are not legally binding.)

SERVICES AND INFORMATION

Services
The Banque Socredo, Banque de Polynésie, and Banque de Tahiti are near the Hôtel Bali

Hai at Maharepa. The Westpac Bank is in Le Petit Village shopping mall opposite Club Med. None of these banks are open on Saturday.

The main **post office** (Monday to Thursday 0700-1500, Friday 0700-1400) is near the banks at Maharepa. Branch post offices are found at Afareaitu and Papetoai.

The **Tahiti Parfum** shop (tel. 56-34-61) in Le Petit Village will wash and dry six kg of laundry for CFP 1400 (same-day service if you get your wash in early). Look for the Lav'matic sign.

Information

The **Moorea Visitors Bureau** (B.P. 1019, Papetoai; tel. 56-29-09) has a poorly marked but helpful kiosk next to the gas station in front of Le Petit Village (Monday to Saturday 0900-1700). Activities and tours can be booked here, including day-trips to Tetiaroa.

The boutique at the Hôtel Bali Hai offers a book-exchange service.

Health

The island's main hospital (tel. 56-11-97) is at Afareaitu.

Dr. Hervé Paulus (tel. 56-10-09) is at Le Petit Village near Club Med. Dr. Christian Jonville (tel. 56-32-32), who has his office behind the Banque de Polynésie at Maharepa, not far from the Hôtel Bali Hai, is fluent in English. In the same complex is a private dentist, Dr. Jean-Marc Thurillet (tel. 56-32-44). The island's pharmacy (tel. 56-10-51) is nearby.

TRANSPORTATION

Air Moorea and **Air Tahiti** (both tel. 56-10-34) are based at Moorea Temae Airport. Details of the air and ferry services from Tahiti are given in the "Transportation" section of the introduction to this chapter.

Trucks meet the ferries at Vaiare Wharf five times a day, charging CFP 200 to anywhere on the island. Although they don't go right around the island, the northern and southern routes meet at Club Med, so you could theoretically effect a circumnavigation by changing there, provided you caught the last *truck* back to Vaiare at 1545 from Club Med.

In mid-1994 an eight-seater minibus service along Moorea's north coast was launched by **Moorea Nui** (tel. 56-12-54). Minibuses depart the Sofitel Ia Ora and Résidence Linareva about every two hours Monday to Saturday (CFP 200 one-way, children CFP 100, baggage CFP 50).

A taxi on Moorea is actually a minibus with a white letter **T** inside a red circle. In past, the taxi drivers have occasionally employed heavy-handed tactics to discourage visitors from using other forms of transportation such as rental cars and *le truck.* Some hotel staff will claim not to know about *le truck,* and we've even heard of rental car tires being slashed! You should have no problem catching *le truck* when you arrive from Tahiti by ferry (be quick to jump aboard), and it's a good idea to ask the driver at what times he goes back to the wharf as information may be hard to obtain later. Hitching is wearing thin with Moorea motorists, although it's still quite possible. If you need the ride you'll probably get it; just be prepared to do some walking.

Car Rentals and Tours

If you're staying at one of the luxury hotels, you'll do better dealing with a kiosk on the highway for rental cars and circle-island tours, as reservations desks inside the hotels tack on commissions.

There are four gasoline stations around Moorea: Mobil near Vaiare Wharf, Total at the airport access road, another Mobil near Motel Albert at Paopao, and another Total opposite Club Med. The maximum speed limit is 60 kph.

Pacificar (tel. 56-16-02) at Vaiare Wharf, the airport, and seven other locations on Moorea has cars at CFP 5800 for 24 hours, unlimited mileage and insurance included. Pacificar also rents scooters at CFP 3500 and bicycles for CFP 1000.

Europcar (tel. 56-34-00) at various locations has unlimited-mileage cars beginning at CFP 3800/4800/5300 for four/eight/24 hours. A weekend rate of CFP 9600 is also offered. Scooters are CFP 2100/2700/3000, bicycles CFP 500/800/900.

Good rates for rental cars and bicycles are also obtained at **Albert Activities Center** (B.P. 77, Moorea; tel. 56-13-53, fax 56-10-42), with locations opposite the Hôtel Bali Hai, Club Bali Hai, and Club Med. Unlimited-mileage cars begin at CFP 6000 for 24 hours, CFP 11,000 for 48 hours, including insurance. Bicycles cost about CFP 500 for four hours.

Pierre Rent-A-Car (Pierre Danloue, tel. 56-12-58), which represents Avis on Moorea, has an office at the Total service station on the airport access road (and elsewhere). At CFP 7800 for 24 hours with unlimited mileage, plus CFP 1300 insurance, they're extremely expensive.

Local Tours
Albert Activities (tel. 56-13-53) runs a five-hour motorized aluminum canoe ride right around Moorea with a stop for snorkeling (gear provided), departing the Hôtel Bali Hai dock every Monday, Wednesday, and Friday at 0930 (CFP 4000 pp, minimum of four). For a free pickup inquire at one of the three Albert Activities centers around Moorea, or call the hotel at tel. 56-13-59.

Albert Activities does a three-hour circle-island bus tour daily at 0900 (CFP 1500) and a two-hour interior-island tour to the Belvédère at 1330 (CFP 1500). If you take both tours on the same day it will be just CFP 2000 (lunch not included).
Ron's Tours (B.P. 1097, Papetoai; tel. 56-35-80) specializes in hiking tours and mountain climbing, such as an ascent of Mt. Mouaputa

(CFP 3500 pp, minimum of eight participants). Contact them through the Moorea Visitors Bureau kiosk in front of Le Petit Village.

Moorea Airport
Moorea Temae Airport (MOZ) is at the northeast corner of the island. No *trucks* service the airport, so unless you rent a car you'll be stuck with a rip-off taxi fare in addition to the airfare: CFP 1150 to the Hôtel Bali Hai or Vaiare Wharf, CFP 2100 to the Moorea Lagoon Hôtel, CFP 3500 to Club Med. You could also walk out to the main highway and wait for the boat *truck* (CFP 200), or just hitch. Thanks to intimidation from the taxi drivers, none of the hotels are allowed to offer airport pickups. This considered, we suggest you give Air Moorea a miss and take the ferry to/from Moorea. At a third the price of the plane, the scenic 30-minute catamaran ride to/from Tahiti may end up being one of the highlights of your visit. If you do fly, be sure to sit on the left side of the aircraft on the way to Moorea and on the right on the way to Papeete.

HUAHINE

Huahine, the first Leeward island encountered on the ferry ride from Tahiti, is a friendly, inviting island, 170 km northwest of Papeete. In many ways lush, mountainous Huahine has more to offer than overcrowded Bora Bora. The variety of scenery, splendid beaches, archaeological remains, and charming main town all call on you to visit. Huahine is a well-known surfing locale, with excellent lefts and rights in the passes off Fare. (Don't leave valuables unattended on the beaches here.)

It's claimed the island got its name because, when viewed from the sea, Huahine has the shape of a reclining woman—very appropriate for such a fertile, enchanting place. *Hua* means "phallus" (from a rock on Huahine Iti) while *hine* comes from *vahine* (woman). The almost entirely Polynesian population numbers under 5,000, yet some of the greatest leaders in the struggle for the independence of Polynesia, Pouvanaa a Oopa among them, have come from this idyllic spot.

In recent years Huahine has been discovered by international tourism, with several deluxe hotels and bungalow-style developments now

operating on the island. Luckily Huahine is able to absorb these new properties fairly painlessly, as it's a much larger island than Bora Bora and the resorts are well scattered and tastefully constructed in the traditional Tahitian style. The island has also become a major port of call for locally chartered or cruising yachts that anchor just off the Hôtel Bali Hai. Backpackers pioneered Huahine in the mid-1980s, and there are still good facilities for them.

Archaeology
Archaeologists have found that human habitation goes back 1,300 years on Huahine; Maeva village was occupied as early as A.D. 850. In 1925 Dr. K.P. Emory of Hawaii's Bishop Museum recorded 54 *marae* on Huahine, most of them built after the 16th century. In 1968 Prof. Yosihiko H. Sinoto found another 40. Huahine Nui was divided into 10 districts, with Huahine Iti as a dependency. As a centralized government complex for a whole island, Maeva, on the south shore of Lake Fauna Nui, is unique in Tahiti-Polynesia. Both of the great communal *marae*

HUAHINE

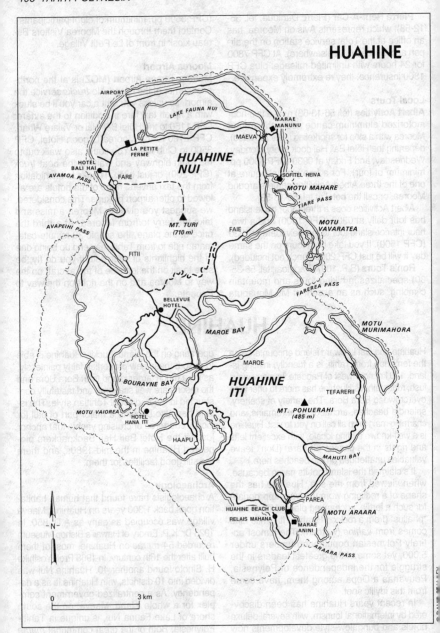

AIRPORT

LAKE FAUNA NUI

MARAE
MANUNU

MAEVA

LA PETITE
FERME

CREPUSCULE POINT

SOFITEL HEIVA

HOTEL
BALI HAI

FARE

AVAMOAMA
PASS

HUAHINE
NUI

MOTU MAHARE

AVAPEIHI PASS

TIARE PASS

MT. TURI
(710 m)

MOTU
VAVARATEA

FAIE

FITII

FAREREA PASS

BELLEVUE
HOTEL

MAROE BAY

MOTU
MURIMAHORA

MAROE

HUAHINE
ITI

BOURAYNE BAY

TEFARERII

MOTU VAIOREA

HOTEL
HANA ITI

MT. POHUERAHI
(485 m)

HAAPU

MAHUTI BAY

PAREA

HUAHINE BEACH CLUB

MOTU ARAARA

RELAIS MAHANA

MARAE
ANINI

ARAARA PASS

N

0   3 km

at Maeva and Parea have two-stepped platforms *(ahu)* that served as raised seats for the gods. Since 1967 about 16 *marae* have been restored, and they can easily be visited today. During construction of the Hôtel Bali Hai just north of Fare in 1972 a *patu* hand club was uncovered, proving that New Zealand's Maoris originated in this area.

History of the Leeward Islands
Roggeveen, coming from Makatea in the Tuamotus, discovered (but did not land on) Bora Bora and Maupiti on 6 June 1722. Captain Cook discovered the other Leeward Islands in July 1769, which was quite easy since the Tahitians knew them well. Cook had the Raiatean priest Tupaia on board the *Endeavour* as a pilot. Cook wrote: "To these six islands, as they lie contiguous to each other, I gave the names of Society Islands." Later the name was extended to the Windward Islands. In 1773 a man named Omai from Huahine sailed to England with Cook's colleague, Captain Furneaux, aboard the *Adventure;* he returned to Fare in 1777.

During the 19th century American whalers spent their winters away from the Antarctic in places like Huahine, refurbishing their supplies with local products such as sugar, vegetables, oranges, salted pork, and *aito,* or ironwood. These visits enriched the island economy, and the New England sailors presented the islanders with foreign plants as tokens of appreciation for the hospitality received.

Though Tahiti and Moorea came under French control in 1842, the Leeward Islands remained a British protectorate until 1887 when these islands were traded for fishing rights off Newfoundland and a British interest in what was then New Hebrides (today Vanuatu). Armed resistance to France, especially on Raiatea, was only overcome in 1897, and the English missionary group that had been there 88 years was asked to leave. Today 80% of the population of the Leewards remains Protestant.

Orientation
The unsophisticated little town of Fare, with its tree-lined boulevard along the quay, is joyfully peaceful after the roar of Papeete. A beach runs right along the west side of the main street and local life unfolds without being overwhelmed by tourism. The seven other villages on Huahine are joined by winding, picturesque roads, which are fairly flat and easily managed by bicycle riders. A narrow channel crossed by a bridge slices Huahine into Huahine Nui and Huahine Iti (Great and Little Huahine, respectively). The story goes that the demigod Hiro's canoe cut this strait. The airstrip sits on an elevated barrier reef north of Lake Fauna Nui. White beaches line this cantaloupe- and watermelon-rich north shore.

SIGHTS

Near Fare
After you've had a look around Fare, walk inland on the road that begins near the house marked "Oliveti" near the Total service station to see the beautiful *mape* (chestnut) forest up the valley. After the road becomes a trail, follow the small stream into a forest laced with vanilla vines. By the stream is a long bedlike rock known as Ofaitere, or "Traveling Rock." With a guide you could continue right to the summit of Mt. Turi (710 meters) in about three hours, but it's rough going.

Maeva
At Maeva, six km east of Fare, you encounter that rare combination of an easily accessible archaeological site in a spectacular setting. Here each of the 10 district chiefs of Huahine Nui had his own *marae,* and huge stone walls were erected to defend Maeva against invaders from Bora Bora (and later France). The plentiful small fish in Lake Fauna Nui supported large chiefly and priestly classes (ancient stone fish traps can still be seen under the bridge at the east end of the village). In the 1970s Prof. Y.H. Sinoto of Hawaii restored many of the structures strewn along the lakeshore and in the nearby hills.

On the shores of the lake is round-ended **Fare Potee** (1974), a replica of an old communal meeting house that now contains an historical exposition. In front of the building is a large map of the area.

From Fare Potee, walk back along the road toward Fare about 100 meters, to a **fortification wall** on the left. Follow this inland to an ancient well at the foot of the hill, then turn right and continue around the base of the hill until you

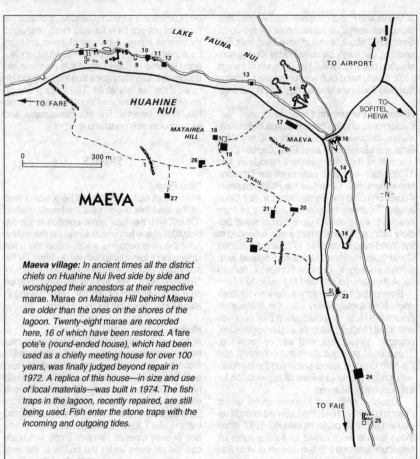

LAKE FAUNA NUI

TO AIRPORT

TO FARE

HUAHINE NUI

TO SOFITEL HEIVA

MATAIREA HILL

MAEVA

0 300 m

TRAIL

N

TO FAIE

Maeva village: In ancient times all the district chiefs on Huahine Nui lived side by side and worshipped their ancestors at their respective marae. Marae on Matairea Hill behind Maeva are older than the ones on the shores of the lagoon. Twenty-eight marae are recorded here, 16 of which have been restored. A fare pote'e (round-ended house), which had been used as a chiefly meeting house for over 100 years, was finally judged beyond repair in 1972. A replica of this house—in size and use of local materials—was built in 1974. The fish traps in the lagoon, recently repaired, are still being used. Fish enter the stone traps with the incoming and outgoing tides.

1. fortification walls
2. Marae Fare Roi
3. Marae Fare Tai
4. Marae Vaitotaha
5. Fare Potee
6. Marae Haumaru
7. Marae Rauhuru
8. Marae Fare Ie
9. *truck* drivers' house
10. Marae Oavauru
11. Marae Faretou
12. Marae Avaroa
13. Protestant church
14. fish traps
15. Marae Manunu
16. monument with cannon
17. grocery stores
18. Marae Matairea
19. Marae Matairea Rahi
20. Marae Paepae Ofata
21. Marae Ofata
22. Marae Tamata Uporu
23. Marae Te Ava
24. Marae Fare Miro
25. Marae Tahaa
26. Marae Tefano
27. Marae Te Ana

© DAVID STANLEY

find the trail up onto Matairea Hill. Just beyond a second fortification wall along the hillside is the access to **Marae Te Ana** on the right. The terraces of this monumental *marae* excavated in 1986 climb back up the hillside.

Return to the main trail and continue up to the ruins of **Marae Tefano,** which are engulfed by an immense banyan tree. **Marae Matairea Rahi,** to the left, was the most sacred place on Huahine, dedicated to Tane, god of light. The backrests of Huahine's eight principal chiefs are in the southernmost compound of the *marae,* where the most important religious ceremonies took place. Backtrack a bit and keep straight, then head up the fern-covered hill to the right to **Marae Ofata,** which gives a magnificent view over the whole northeast coast of Huahine.

Continue southeast on the main trail past several more *marae* and you'll eventually cross another fortification wall and meet a dirt road down to the main highway near **Marae Te Ava.** Throughout this easy two-hour hike, watch for stakes planted with vanilla.

When you get back down to the main road, walk south a bit to see photogenic **Marae Fare Miro,** then backtrack to the bridge, across which is a **monument** guarded by seven cannon. Underneath are buried the French soldiers killed in the Battle of Maeva (1846), when the islanders successfully defended their independence against French marines sent to annex the island.

A few hundred meters farther along toward the ocean and to the left is two-tiered **Marae Manunu,** the community *marae* of Huahine Nui. In its base is the grave of Raiti, the last great priest of Huahine. When he died in 1915 a huge stone fell from the *marae.*

Maeva is accessible by infrequent *truck* from Fare (CFP 150), and there are two small stores in the village where you can get cold drinks. From **Faie,** south of Maeva, a very steep track crosses the mountains to Maroe Bay, making a complete circuit of Huahine Nui possible on foot (not feasible by rental car and dangerous even by bicycle). If you're driving, you can return to Fare via the airport road for a change of scenery.

Huahine Iti

Though the "July Bridge" joins the two islands, Huahine Iti is far less accessible than Huahine

Nui. *Trucks* to **Parea** village (CFP 250) run only once a day, so you'll have to stay the night unless you rent a bicycle, scooter, or car. The hotels are very expensive, so you may want to bring a tent. Bourayne Bay, to the west of the interisland bridge, is one of the loveliest spots on the island.

On a golden beach on Point Tiva, one km south of Parea, is **Marae Anini,** the community *marae* of Huahine Iti. Look for petroglyphs on this two-tiered structure, dedicated to the god Oro, where human sacrifices once took place. (If you decide to camp near the *marae,* don't leave a mess. Search for the water tap by the road at the end of the path. Be aware of theft by dogs at night and small boys by day.) Surfing is possible in Araara Pass, beside the *motu* just off Marae Anini. Another nice beach with better swimming is a couple of km west.

Haapu village was originally built entirely over the water, for lack of sufficient shoreline to house it. The only grocery store on Huahine Iti is at Haapu, but three grocery trucks circle the island several times daily; the locals can tell you when to expect them.

Sports and Recreation

Pacific Blue Adventure (B.P. 193, Fare; tel. 68-87-21, fax 68-80-71) at Fare offers scuba diving at CFP 5000 a dive (night diving CFP 6500) and CMAS certification courses (CFP 30,000 including four dives, texts, and documentation). Trips leave at 0915 and 1415, depending on demand.

La Petite Ferme (B.P. 12, Huahine; tel. 68-82-98), between Fare and the airport, offers riding with Pascale, Yvan, and their 10 small, robust Marquesan horses. A two-hour ride along the beach is CFP 3500 pp, and they also offer a two-day ride and campout in the mountains or on the beach for CFP 13,500 pp, meals included. Call the day before to let them know you're coming. If riding is your main interest, it's possible to stay in their onsite guesthouse at CFP 3600 double or CFP 1500 pp dormitory, breakfast included. They also have a self-catering bungalow at CFP 5000/7500/9500 single/double/triple. This is the best horseback-riding operation in Tahiti-Polynesia.

PRACTICALITIES

Budget Accommodations

Several inexpensive lodgings await you in and around Fare (most of them levying a CFP 500 surcharge if you stay only one night). **Guynette's Lodging** (Alain and Hélène Guerineau, B.P. 87, Fare; tel. 68-83-75), also known as "Club Bed," on the waterfront to the left as you get off the boat, has an eight-bed CFP 1200 dorm and three rooms at CFP 3000/3500/4500 single/double/triple, minimum stay two nights, maximum one month. Mosquito nets are provided in the fan-cooled rooms. You can cook your own meals in the communal kitchen here, and the meals prepared by the friendly staff are good value (order before 1400). It's a very clean place; no shoes or radios are allowed in the house. Upon arrival peruse the list of rules and rates—applied rigorously (for example, it's lights out at 2200). Most readers say they liked the efficiency. Thankfully, the management doesn't allow overcrowding and will turn people away rather than pack them in for short-term gain. Recommended.

Nearby on the waterfront is decrepit three-story **Hôtel Huahine** (B.P. 220, Fare; tel. 68-82-69), at CFP 2500/3500/4500 single/double/triple, or CFP 1000 in a dorm. There's no surcharge for a one-night stay. It's not possible to lock the rooms, and they have water problems. Don't order any meals here as the food is lousy and far too expensive, but they will let you sit in the restaurant and watch TV for the price of a beer. (Reader Rowland Burley reports that "this pleasant hotel as been refurbished. The rooms are large with their own toilet and shower, all doors can now be locked, and there are no water problems. I feel your piece on this place is quite unfair!" Any comments from other readers?)

Pension Martial et Enite (Enite Temaiana, B.P. 37, Fare; tel./fax 68-82-37) is an eight-room boardinghouse at the west end of the waterfront beyond the snack bar. Rooms with shared bath are CFP 5200 pp with half board, CFP 6300 pp with full board (two-night minimum stay, no room rentals without meals). In the event of a shortened stay, the pension will bill for the number of nights originally reserved. Middle-of-the-night arrivals mustn't knock on the door before 0700. French expats often stay here. Martial and Enite also serve meals to outsiders in their thatched cookhouse on the beach for CFP 2200, or CFP 3000 if shellfish is on the menu. Advance notice must be given, but the food is good (closed on Sunday).

Three good places to stay are between Fare and the airport, about 800 meters north of the wharf. Look for a signposted dirt road leading west from the main highway, just north of the Bali Hai. Chez Richard is on the left, and almost opposite it are the high thatched roofs of Chez Lovina. About a hundred meters farther along on the same road is Chez Marie Louise (see below). A reasonable beach for snorkeling is nearby at the end of this road.

Chez Richard (B.P. 121, Fare; tel. 68-87-86) caters to budget travelers with four pleasant shared-bath rooms at CFP 3000 single or double, and a four-bed dorm at CFP 1000 pp. Cooking is possible and their two bicycles are loaned free. Owner Richard Bowens will pick you up free at the airport if you call ahead, and he's usually on the wharf in search of guests when the interisland ships arrive.

Chez Lovina (Lovina Richmond, B.P. 173, Fare; tel. 68-88-06, fax 68-82-64) has five small *fares* with TV and shared bath at CFP 2500/4000 single/double. For families and groups, Chez Lovina has four oversized bungalows with cooking and bathing facilities at CFP 5000/6000/7000 single/double/triple, CFP 10,000 for up to five persons, CFP 15,000 for eight people. Dormitory accommodations are CFP 1200 pp and camping is CFP 1000 pp. The layout of the communal toilets and showers can lead to exasperating situations. All guests have access to cramped cooking facilities (and mosquitoes). The minimum stay is two nights, and discounts may be negotiable. Airport pickups cost CFP 1000 pp; from the harbor it's CFP 400 pp.

One of the best budget places on Huahine is **Chez Marie Louise** (B.P. 5, Fare; tel. 68-81-10), with three neat little bungalows at CFP 2500/3500 double/triple. A larger bungalow with private bath, kitchen, and TV is CFP 5000/6000 double/triple. Camping is CFP 1000 per tent. There's a large open communal kitchen. This place is run by a friendly German/Tahitian couple: Hans (a former

French foreign legionnaire) scouts for guests at the harbor and airport and provides free transfers in his rickety old car, while Marie Louise greets newcomers with a large bowl of tropical fruit. This easygoing resort, just 100 meters from the beach, is perfect for a long, restful stay. Recommended.

The **Hôtel Bellevue** (B.P. 21, Huahine; tel. 68-82-76, fax 68-85-35), six km south of Fare, offers eight rooms in the main building at CFP 3500/4500/5000 single/double/triple and 15 bungalows for CFP 6000/7000/8000. The rooms are stuffy due to the lack of fans, and the poor lighting makes it hard to read in the evening. There's an expensive restaurant (meals CFP 3000 each) with a lovely view of Maroe Bay. Roundtrip airport transfers are CFP 1000. Considering the expense, isolation, and absence of a beach (there is a swimming pool), the Bellevue has little going for it.

Upmarket Hotels

In recent years the American-owned **Hôtel Bali Hai** (B.P. 2, Fare; tel. 68-84-77, fax 68-82-77), just north of Fare, has faced closure due to labor disputes, but it's now operating again under lease from the Moorea Bali Hai company. This was always the nicest of the Bali Hai chain, tastefully placed between a lake and the beach. The 10 rooms in the main building begin at CFP 9500 single or double; the 34 bungalows cost 25% more in the garden, 50% more facing the beach. Cooking facilities are not provided, but the restaurant serves excellent food and the largely French crowd is chic. The breakfast and dinner plan is CFP 3900 pp, airport transfers CFP 800 pp. Visit the lobby to see the showcase displaying artifacts found here by Dr. Yoshihiko H. Sinoto of the Bishop Museum, Hawaii, who excavated the site during construction of the hotel in 1973-75. Marae Tahuea has been reconstructed on the grounds.

In October 1989 the exclusive **Sofitel Heiva Huahine** (B.P. 38, Huahine; tel. 68-86-86, fax 68-85-25) opened in a coconut grove on a *motu* just east of Maeva along a rough road. Striking neo-Polynesian paintings by the late artist/singer Bobby Holcomb highlight the decor in public areas, and ancient *marae* are preserved in the gardens. Unspoiled white beaches are all along

this section of lagoon, and the Maeva archaeological area is only a 30-minute walk away. The 58 tastefully decorated rooms are CFP 21,000 single or double, the nine thatched beach bungalows 50% more. The breakfast and dinner plan is CFP 5000 pp, airport transfers CFP 1600 pp. One of the best Polynesian cultural shows you'll ever see usually takes place here on Monday, Thursday, and Saturday nights at 2000, complete with fire dancing, acrobatics, and coconut tree climbing. Pacificar has a desk at this hotel.

The US$12-million **Hôtel Hana Iti** (B.P. 185, Fare; tel. 68-87-41, fax 68-85-04) opened in 1992 on a verdant ridge high above Bourayne Bay. A three-room thatched bungalow complete with whirlpool spa will set you back CFP 53,000/58,000 double/triple or more. Breakfast and dinner are another CFP 7200 pp, return airport transfers CFP 2400 pp. Yes, this is the most expensive hotel in Tahiti-Polynesia, but each of the 26 traditional *fare* units is unique. Some perch on rocks, more stand on stilts, and a few are built into huge trees. The Hana Iti is owned by American meat-packing millionaire Thomas C. Kurth, who bought the property from Spanish singer Julio Iglesias. If you're a Hollywood star in search of an exotic hideaway, this is it.

The 22-unit **Relais Mahana** (B.P. 30, Huahine; tel. 68-81-54, fax 68-85-08), on a wide white beach near Parea, charges CFP 15,800 single or double, CFP 18,800 triple for a garden bungalow, CFP 2000 more for a beach bungalow. For breakfast and dinner add another CFP 3900 pp; roundtrip airport transfers are an extra CFP 1800 pp. This French-operated hotel has a certain snob appeal.

The 17-unit **Huahine Beach Club** (B.P. 39, Huahine; tel. 68-81-46, fax 68-85-86) at Parea is overpriced at CFP 19,000 for a large garden bungalow, CFP 4000 more for a beach bungalow. Breakfast and dinner are CFP 3800 pp, airport transfers CFP 1800 pp. Saturday night there's a Tahitian buffet with traditional dancing (CFP 3200). This well-constructed resort sits on a small beach between Parea village and Marae Anini, and there's also a swimming pool. Windsurfing, snorkeling, and fishing gear are loaned free. The Club can arrange cars through Kake Rent-A-Car, a necessity due to the lack of public transport.

Food

Food trailers congregate at Fare Wharf when a ship is due in. One trailer has a good selection of sandwiches and pastries. The numerous Chinese stores along the waterfront sell groceries and cold beer. The tap water on Huahine can be clouded after heavy rains.

Restaurant Te Manu (tel. 68-86-61), facing the boat landing in Fare, has basic Chinese fare and cheap beer. There's no sign outside, so ask.

Snack Temarara (closed Sunday) at the west end of the waterfront charges prices similar to those of the deluxe hotel restaurants, which is a little ridiculous. Temarara does have an unpretentious terrace built over the lagoon, so drop in for a sunset beer. On Friday evening the place is crowded with Polynesians enjoying *kaina* (folkloric) music.

The **Restaurant Bar Orio** (closed Monday; tel. 68-83-03) at the east end of the waterfront is similar to Snack Temarara.

Noticeably cheaper than either of these is the **Tiare Tipanier Restaurant** (closed Monday; tel. 68-80-52), next to the Mairie (town hall) at the north entrance to Fare from the Bali Hai. They serve mahimahi with pepper sauce (CFP 1000), omelettes (CFP 350), shrimp (CFP 1250), and hamburgers (CFP 350), and a large Hinano beer here is CFP 350.

Also check **Restaurant Te Moana** (tel. 68-88-63) on the beach next to Hôtel Bali Hai; they also have a few thatched bungalows for rent.

Cultural Shows for Visitors

If you're staying in budget accommodations around Fare, you'll be able to witness the Polynesian dancing at the **Hôtel Bali Hai** (tel. 68-84-77) on Friday evening for the price of a drink or a meal. Drop by beforehand to check the program. There's also traditional dancing at the **Sofitel Heiva Huahine** and **Huahine Beach Club** certain nights, but you'll need motorized transportation to get there unless you're a guest.

Services

The Banque de Tahiti facing the waterfront is open weekdays 0745-1145/1330-1630. Banque Socredo, on the first street back from the Fare waterfront, opens Monday to Thursday 0730-1130/1330-1600, Friday 0730-1130/1330-1500.

The **post office** is opposite the access road to the Hôtel Bali Hai. The *gendarmerie* is op-

posite the hospital over the bridge at the south end of town.

The **laundromat** opposite Kake Rent-A-Car charges CFP 750 to wash and CFP 750 to dry (Monday to Thursday 0700-1600, Friday 0730-1500).

Public toilets and washbasins are in one of the yellow buildings on the waterfront (if open).

The useless **Comité du Tourisme** information office (weekdays 0800-1500, Saturday 0800-1000: B.P. 54, Fare; tel. 68-86-34, fax 68-87-34) shares a pavilion on the waterfront with Pacificar, Kake Rent-A-Car, and Pacific Blue Adventure.

TRANSPORTATION

Getting There

The **Air Tahiti** agent (tel. 68-82-65) is at the airport. For information on flights to Huahine from Papeete, Moorea, Raiatea, and Bora Bora see the "Transportation" section in the introduction to this chapter.

The Papeete cargo ships tie up to the wharf in the middle of town, where there's a large open pavilion on the wharf at which you can sleep until dawn. *Taporo VI* arrives from Papeete bound for Raiatea, Tahaa, and Bora Bora around 0200 on Tuesday, Thursday, and Saturday, returning from Raiatea on its way to Papeete Tuesday, Thursday, and Friday afternoons. Northbound, the *Vaeanu* calls at Huahine on Tuesday and Saturday at 0230; southbound on Tuesday at 1830, and Thursday and Sunday at 1700. The *Raromatai Ferry* arrives from Papeete Wednesday and Saturday at 0030 or 0230, departing for Papeete again on Thursday at 1300 and Sunday at 2030 (nine hours, CFP 3800 deck). You can also take this ship to Raiatea, Tahaa, and Bora Bora (all CFP 1000) Wednesday and Saturday in the middle of the night.

Tickets for *Taporo VI* and *Vaeanu* go on sale at their offices four hours before sailing and you can buy one as the ship is loading. Tickets for the *Raromatai Ferry* are sold on board upon arrival. The *Vaeanu* office adjoins the yellow warehouse on the wharf. *Taporo VI* has an office next to Pacificar on the waterfront.

The high-speed monohull *Ono-Ono* (tel. 68-85-85) departs Huahine for Raiatea (one hour, CFP 1600) and Bora Bora (three hours, CFP 2800) Monday and Wednesday at 1230, Friday at 2000, Saturday at 1130. To Papeete (three hours, CFP 4300) it leaves Huahine Tuesday and Thursday at 1500, Sunday at 1700.

Getting Around

Getting around Huahine is not easy. You'll find *trucks* to anywhere on Huahine when a ship arrives; otherwise, they're irregular. Only one *truck* a day runs to Maeva, leaving Fare at 0900 (CFP 150). It's fairly easy to hitch back to Fare from Maeva. The bus to Parea leaves Fare on Monday, Tuesday, Thursday, and Friday at 1100, returning from Parea to Fare at 1400 (CFP 250 one-way).

Car Rentals

Pacificar (tel. 68-81-81), on the Fare waterfront, rents small cars (from CFP 5200, plus CFP 1000 for insurance), scooters (CFP 3000),

and bicycles (CFP 1000). **Kake Rent-A-Car** (B.P. 34, Fare; tel. 68-82-59, fax 68-80-59), beside the entrance to the Hôtel Bali Hai, is similar. Pacificar will rent to persons aged 18 and over, Kake 21 and over. Both companies charge identical rates and never give you the car with a full tank of gas, which means you have to take the time to fill it up as soon as you get it. There are only two gas stations on Huahine, both in Fare: Mobil is open weekdays 0630-1700, Saturday 0700-1100, Sunday 0700-0900, while Total is open somewhat shorter hours.

Airport

The airport (HUH) is four km north of Fare. Make arrangements for the regular airport minibus (CFP 400 pp) at Pension Martial et Enite. Both Kake and Pacificar have counters at the airport.

RAIATEA

Raiatea is the second largest high island of Tahiti-Polynesia. Its main town and port, Uturoa, is the business and administrative center of the Leeward Islands; the balance of the island's population of about 9,000 lives in eight flower-filled villages around the island: Avera, Opoa, Puohine, Fetuna, Vaiaau, Tehurui, Tevaitoa, and Tuu Fenua. The west coast of Raiatea south of Tevaitoa is old Polynesia through and through. Raiatea is traditionally the ancient Havai'i, the sacred isle from which all of eastern Polynesia was colonized. Today it's mostly worth visiting if you want to get off the beaten tourist track, though public transportation and budget accommodations are scarce. The island does offer good possibilities for scuba diving, charter yachting, and hiking, and the varied scenery is worth a stop.

The Land

Raiatea, 220 km northwest of Tahiti, shares a protected lagoon with Tahaa three km away. Legends tell how the two islands were cut apart by a mythical eel. About 30 km of steel-blue sea separates Raiatea from both Huahine and Bora Bora. Mount Temehani on mountainous Raiatea rises to 772 meters, and some of the coastlines are rugged and narrow. The highest mountain is Toomaru (1,017 meters). All of the people live on a coastal plain planted in coconuts, where cattle also graze.

No beaches are found on big, hulking Raiatea itself. Instead, picnickers are taken to picture-postcard *motus* in the lagoon. Surfing is possible at the eight passes that open onto the Raiatea/Tahaa lagoon, and sailboarders are active. The Leeward Islands (Îles Sous le Vent) are the most popular sailing area in Tahiti-Polynesia, and most of the charter boats are based at Raiatea.

History

Before European encroachment, Raiatea was the religious, cultural, and political center of Tahiti-Polynesia. Tradition holds that the great Polynesian voyagers to Hawaii and New Zealand departed from these shores.

Raiatea was Captain Cook's favorite island; he visited three times. During his first voyage in 1769 he called first at Opoa from 20 to 24 July. After having surveyed Bora Bora from the sea, he anchored for a week in the Rautoanui Pass on the northwest coast of Raiatea, near the village of Tuu Fenua. During his second voyage Cook lay at anchor twice, first from 8 to 17 September 1773 and again from 25 May to 4 June 1774, both times at Rautoanui. His third visit was from 3 November to 7 December 1777, again at Rautoanui. It can therefore be said that Rautoanui (which he calls "Haamanino Harbour" in his journals) was one of Cook's favorite anchorages.

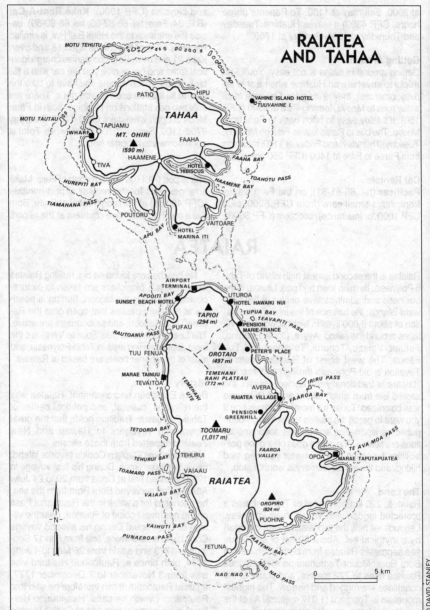

**RAIATEA
AND TAHAA**

MOTU TEHUTU

PATIO

HIPU

TAPUAMU

TAHAA

VAHINE ISLAND HOTEL
TUUVAHINE I.

MOTU TAUTAU

WHARF

MT. OHIRI
(590 m)

FAAHA

TIVA

HAAMENE

FAAHA BAY

HUREPITI BAY

HOTEL
L'HIBISCUS

HAAMENE BAY

TOAHOTU PASS

TIAMAHANA PASS

POUTORU

APU BAY

VAITOARE

HOTEL
MARINA ITI

RAIATEA

AIRPORT
TERMINAL

APOOITI BAY

UTUROA

SUNSET BEACH MOTEL

HOTEL HAWAIKI NUI

TUPUA BAY

TAPIOI
(294 m)

TEAVAPITI PASS

PUFAU

PENSION
MARIE-FRANCE

RAUTOANUI PASS

PETER'S PLACE

TUU FENUA

OROTAIO
(497 m)

MARAE TAINUU

IRIRU PASS

TEVAITOA

TEMEHANI
RAHI PLATEAU
(772 m)

AVERA

RAIATEA VILLAGE

FAAROA BAY

TEMEHANI
UTE

PENSION
GREENHILL

TE AVA MOA PASS

TETOOROA BAY

TOOMARU
(1,017 m)

FAAROA
VALLEY

OPOA

MARAE TAPUTAPUATEA

TEHURUI BAY

TEHURUI

TOAMARO PASS

VAIAAU

RAIATEA

VAIAAU BAY

VAIHUTI BAY

OROPIRO
(824 m)

PUNAEROA PASS

PUHOINE

FETUNA

FAATEMU BAY

-N-

NAO NAO I.

NAO NAO PASS

0   5 km

© DAVID STANLEY

The last resistance to the French takeover on Raiatea lasted until 1897, when French troops and warships used arms to conquer the island. The native leader of the resistance, Teraupoo, was deported to New Caledonia.

SIGHTS

Everything is easy to find in Uturoa (pop. 3,200). The double row of Chinese stores along the main drag opens onto a colorful **market,** which is most crowded on Wednesday and Friday mornings when the Tahaa people arrive by motorized canoe to sell their products here. The Sunday market is over by 0700. Beyond the market is the harbor, with a pleasant park alongside. All of the stores in Uturoa close for lunch 1200-1300.

For a view of four islands, climb **Tapioi Hill** (294 meters), the peak topped by a TV antenna behind Uturoa—one of the easiest and best climbs in Tahiti-Polynesia. Take the road beside the Gendarmerie Nationale up past the Propriété Privé sign (don't worry, visitors are allowed). The fastest time on record for climbing Tapioi is 17 minutes, but it's best to allow two or three hours to hike up and down.

Around the Island

It takes five to 10 hours to ride a bicycle around Raiatea (97 km), depending on how fast you go. The road down the east coast is paved to the

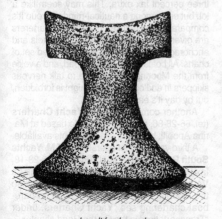

a basalt food pounder

head of Faaroa Bay, then the paved road cuts directly across the island to the south coast. Down the west coast, the road is paved as far as Tehurui. The bottom half of the circuminsular road is unpaved, but no problem for a car.

The road down the east coast circles fjordlike **Faaroa Bay,** associated with the legends of Polynesian migration. From the popular yacht anchorage in the middle of the bay there's a fine view of Toomaru, highest peak in the Leeward Islands. The Apoomau River drains the Faaroa Valley. (The boat trips occasionally offered up this river are not recommended, as the boat can only proceed a couple of hundred meters.)

Instead of crossing the island on the paved road, keep left and follow the coast around to a point of land just beyond Opoa, 32 km from Uturoa. Here stands **Marae Taputapuatea,** one of the largest and best preserved in Polynesia, its mighty *ahu* measuring 43 meters long, 7.3 meters wide, and between two and three meters high. Before it is a rectangular courtyard paved with black volcanic rocks. A small platform in the middle of the *ahu* once bore the image of Oro, god of fertility and war (now represented by a reproduction); backrests still mark the seats of high chiefs on the courtyard. Marae Taputapuatea is directly opposite Te Ava Moa Pass, and fires on the *marae* may have been beacons to ancient navigators. Human sacrifices and firewalking once took place on the *marae.*

The only places to buy food in the southern part of Raiatea are the two Chinese grocery stores at **Fetuna** and another at **Vaiaau.** Behind Tevaitoa church, on the west side of Raiatea, is **Marae Tainuu,** dedicated to the ancient god Taaroa. Petroglyphs on a broken stone by the road at the entrance to the church show a turtle and some other indistinguishable figure.

Hiking

According to Polynesian mythology the god Oro was born from the molten rage of **Mt. Temehani** (772 meters), the cloud-covered plateau that dominates the northern end of the island. *Tiare apetahi,* a sacred white flower that exists nowhere else on earth and resists transplantation, grows on the slopes around the summit. The fragile blossom represents the five fingers of a beautiful Polynesian girl who fell in love with the handsome son of a high chief, but was unable to marry him due to her lowly birth. These flowers are now rare, so don't pick any! Small pink orchids also grow by the way.

Temehani can be climbed from Pufau, the second bay south of Marina Apooiti. Note a series of old concrete benches by the road as you come around the north side of the bay. The track inland begins at a locked gate, 700 meters south of the bridge, beyond the concrete benches. It's private property, so ask permission to proceed of anyone you meet. You hike straight up through pine reforestation till you have a clear view of Temehani Rahi and Temehani Ute, divided by a deep gorge. Descend to the right and continue up the track you see on the hillside opposite. It takes about three hours to go from the main road to the Temehani Rahi Plateau. Friday and Saturday are the best days to go, and long pants and sturdy shoes are required. A guide up Temehani should charge about CFP 5000 for the group.

Reader Will Paine of Maidstone, England, sent us this:

The through hike from Pufau to Uturoa takes five or six hours on foot with beautiful views from high vantage points where the difficultly manageable jeep track becomes a path. The same trail is shared by the Temehani route until it splits up shortly after the ford/bathing pool on the higher reaches. Here take the left branch. Follow it down across a water catchment and up to a ridge. The Orotaio cone will come into view to the east and the path drops to a better four-wheel-drive track. From here it's just under two hours down to a gas station on the coastal road a few km south of Uturoa.

Sports and Recreation

Raiatea Plongée (B.P. 272, Uturoa; tel. 66-37-10, fax 66-26-25) is run by Patrice Philip, husband of the Marie-France mentioned under "Accommodations" below. He'll take you to the century-old wreck of a 100-meter Dutch coal boat, the top of which is 18 meters down. The coral life is rather poor, but there's ample marinelife, including sharks, moray eels, barracudas, manta rays, and countless tropical fish. Patrice charges CFP 5000 for a one-tank dive. A trip right around Tahaa by motorized canoe with visits to two *motus* is CFP 4500 (eight-person minimum), snorkeling in a pass is CFP 3500, or you can just be dropped off on a nearby *motu* for CFP 800. PADI scuba certification (four dives) is CFP 35,000. A swimming pool on the premises is used for the lessons. We've had varying reports about Patrice's operation.

Hémisphere Sub (B.P. 492, Raiatea; tel. 66-11-66, fax 66-11-67), at the Marina Apooiti, offers scuba diving at CFP 4500 per dive. A five-dive CMAS certification course is CFP 24,000. There's diving daily at 0830 and 1430.

There's good swimming in a large pool open to the sea at the **Centre Nautique** *("la piscine")* on the coast just north of Uturoa.

The **Kaoha Nui Ranch** (Patrick Marinthe, B.P. 568, Uturoa; tel. 66-25-46) at PK 6, Avera, a few hundred meters north of Pension Manava, charges CFP 3000 for horseback riding (an hour and a half). You must reserve 24 hours in advance (closed Wednesday), and there's a two-person minimum.

Bareboating

The Moorings (B.P. 165, Uturoa; tel. 66-35-93, fax 66-20-94), a bareboat charter operation with 19 yachts, is based at Marina Apooiti, one km west of the airport. Leeward island charter rates begin at US$500 a day, with food, drink, and three percent tax extra. This may seem like a lot, but split among a nautical-minded group it's comparable to a deluxe hotel room. Charterers are given a complete briefing on channels and anchorages, and provided with a detailed set of charts. All boats are radio-equipped, and a voice from the Moorings is available to talk nervous skippers in and out. Travel by night is forbidden, but by day it's easy sailing.

Another company, **Tahiti Yacht Charters** (tel. 66-28-86, fax 66-28-85), also based at Marina Apooiti, has eight charter yachts available.

A third yacht charter operation, **A.T.M. Yachts South Pacific** (B.P. 705, Uturoa; tel. 66-23-18, fax 66-23-19), based at Faaroa Bay next to La Veranda Restaurant, is slightly cheaper than the Moorings. For more information on bareboat chartering see "Yacht Charters" under "Transportation" in the On the Road chapter.

PRACTICALITIES

Accommodations

All of the places to stay are on the northeast side of Raiatea and we've arranged them below from north to south. The proprietors often pick up guests at the airport or harbor if they call ahead for reservations. Transfers are usually free, but ask.

The friendly **Sunset Beach Motel Apooiti** (Jean and Elianne Boubée, B.P. 397, Uturoa; tel. 66-33-47, fax 66-33-08) is in a coconut grove by the beach, five km west of Uturoa. Look on the point across the bay from Marina Apooiti, about 2.5 km west of the airport. The 16 comfortable, well-spaced bungalows with cooking facilities and private bath (hot water) are CFP 6000/7000/8000 single/double/triple—good value for families. Camping is CFP 1000 pp here, and there's a large communal kitchen. Discounts of 10% a fortnight and 20% a month are available, but there's a CFP 2000 surcharge if you stay only one night. Bicycles are for rent and hitching into Uturoa is easy.

The **Hôtel Hinano** (B.P. 196, Uturoa; tel. 66-13-13; fax 66-14-14), conveniently located on the main street in the center of Uturoa, has 10 rooms at CFP 4000/5000 single/double (CFP 1000 extra for a/c). Cooking facilities are not available.

Pension Marie-France (Patrice and Marie-France Philip, B.P. 272, Uturoa; tel. 66-37-10, fax 66-26-25), by the lagoon just beyond Magasin Andre Chinese store, 2.5 km south of Uturoa (yellow sign), caters to misplaced backpackers and scuba divers. The four rooms with shared bath are CFP 4000 single or double in back, or CFP 4500 single or double facing the lagoon. Five bungalows with kitchen and TV facing the lagoon are CFP 6000/7000/8000 single/double/triple. There's also a six-bed dormitory with cooking facilities at CFP 1000 pp (sheets provided on request). There's a supplement of up to CFP 1000 if you stay only one night. Bicycles (CFP 1000 daily) and a washing machine are for rent, and there's even hot water (sometimes). The lagoon off Pension Marie-France is good for windsurfing, but they're a little pushy in the way they try to convince you to sign up for the half-day minibus tour of the island (CFP 3500), so don't come expecting to rest. As soon as Marie-France senses that you're not interested in taking any of her trips, she becomes rather abrupt. The meals served here are poor value. Airport transfers are CFP 500 pp each way (nothing is free here).

Pension Manava (B.P. 559, Uturoa; tel. 66-28-26), at PK 6, Avera, is run by Andrew and Roselyne Brotherson. This warm, sympathetic couple rents a Polynesian-style bungalow at CFP 4000 pp with breakfast, CFP 6000 pp with half board, CFP 7000 pp with full board. A separate two-room building is CFP 3000 pp, and the four-bed dormitory with cooking facilities CFP 1000 pp. The meals served here are good. Excursions are free for bungalow guests; dormitory residents pay extra, for example, CFP 3500 pp (five-person minimum) for a boat trip around Tahaa.

Peter's Place (Peter Brotherson, tel. 66-20-01) at Hamoa, six km south of Uturoa and just beyond Pension Manava, is the backpacker's best choice on Raiatea. The eight neat double rooms in a long block are CFP 1100 pp and you can pitch a tent in the large grassy area facing the rooms at CFP 700 pp. A large open pavilion is used for communal cooking but there are no grocery stores nearby, so bring food. Bicycles are for rent at CFP 1000 a day. Peter or his son Frame take guests on a hike up the valley to a picturesque waterfall with a tour of a vanilla plantation, swimming in the river, and fish feeding included at CFP 3000 per group. They can also guide you directly to the Temehani Plateau, taking about three hours up and two hours down (CFP 5000 per group). Highly recommended.

Pension Yolande Roopinia (B.P. 298, Uturoa; tel. 66-35-28) is in an attractive location facing the lagoon at PK 10, Avera. The four rooms are CFP 5000 single or double (private bath). Cooking facilities are provided, but you may be asked to take half pension (CFP 7000/13,000 single/double). You'll like the family atmosphere.

A hundred meters beyond Chez Yolande is the 12-unit **Raiatea Village Hôtel** (B.P. 282, Uturoa; tel. 66-31-62, fax 66-10-65), at the mouth of Faaroa Bay (PK 10). A garden bungalow with kitchenette and terrace is CFP 5000/7000/8000/10,000 single/double/triple/quad. Airport transfers are CFP 1000 pp extra.

Pension Greenhill (Marie-Isabelle Chan, B.P. 598, Raiatea; tel./fax 66-37-64), at PK 12, is on the hillside directly above La Veranda Restaurant overlooking lovely Faaroa Bay. The six rooms with private bath are CFP 6500/8000 single/double, including breakfast and dinner at the host's table (minimum stay two nights). Children under 10 pay half price. The walls are rather thin, so peace and quiet depends on your neighbors. Sightseeing trips and occasional boat rides are included, though a minimum of four persons is required before they'll go. Getting into town is no problem—the pension minibus makes several trips a day and will arrange to pick you up later. Bicycles and the jacuzzi are also at your disposal. Gourmet chef Jason makes dining a delight, while hostess Marie-Isabelle loves to sit and chat with guests. They'll pick you up at no charge at the airport or wharf if you call ahead.

The new **Hôtel Te Moana Iti** (Irmine Ariitai, B.P. 724, Uturoa; tel. 66-21-82, fax 66-28-60), on the beach just beyond Marae Taputapuatea, 35 km from Uturoa, has seven tastefully decorated bungalows from CFP 8500/9500 double/triple, plus CFP 3000 for half board. The managers organize excursions to a *motu* and around the island, and they serve excellent if expensive food. There's good snorkeling off their wharf. The hotel's biggest drawback is its isolation, but they'll pick you up at the port or airport if you call ahead (CFP 2000 pp roundtrip). It's good for a couple of days of relaxation.

Upmarket Hotel

The 32-room **Hôtel Hawaiki Nui Noa Noa** (B.P. 43, Uturoa; tel. 66-20-23, fax 66-20-20), 1.5 km south of Uturoa, is Raiatea's only luxury hotel. This is the former Raiatea Bali Hai, destroyed by a kitchen fire in 1992 and completely rebuilt in 1994. It's CFP 10,500 single or double for a garden bungalow, CFP 18,500 for a lagoonside bungalow, or CFP 26,000 for an overwater bungalow. The breakfast and dinner plan is CFP 4500 pp, airport transfers CFP 1200 pp. There's Polynesian dancing once or twice a week. Fire-walking, once commonly practiced on Raiatea, is now a dying art. The pit is just across the street from the Hawaiki Nui, so ask there if they'll be lighting anyone's fire.

Food

To escape the tourist scene, try **Bar Restaurant Maraamu**, also known as Chez Remy, in what appears to be an old Chinese store between the market and the wharf. The few minutes it takes to locate will net you the lowest prices in town. Coffee and omelettes are served in the morning, while the lunch menu tilts toward Chinese food. There's also *poisson cru* and a good selection of other dishes.

Snack Moemoea (closed Sunday; tel. 66-39-84), on the harbor, has hamburgers. **Le Quai des Pêcheurs** (closed Monday; tel. 66-36-83), closer to the wharf, offers a view of the port.

Le Gourmet Restaurant (closed Sunday; tel. 66-21-51), next to the Westpac Bank in Uturoa, serves reasonable meals, which are listed on the blackboard outside. It's a good choice for lunch (come early).

A more upmarket choice would be the **Jade Garden Restaurant** (open Wednesday to Saturday; tel. 66-34-40) on the main street, offering some of the best Chinese dishes this side of Papeete.

Entertainment

Friday, Saturday, and Sunday at 2200 the Moana Chinese Restaurant (tel. 66-27-49) opposite Uturoa Market becomes **Discotheque Le Zénith**.

The nicest place for a drink is Le Quai des Pêcheurs, which transforms itself into **Disco Quaidep** on Friday and Saturday from 2200.

Services

Of Uturoa's four banks, the Banque de Tahiti and Banque Socredo charge a slightly lower commission for currency exchange than the Banque de Polynésie and the Westpac Bank.

The large modern **post office** (Monday to Thursday 0700-1500, Friday 0700-1400, Saturday 0800-1000) is opposite the new hospital just north of town, with the *gendarmerie* about 50 meters beyond on the left.

There are free **public toilets** *(sanitaires publics)* on the wharf behind Le Quai des Pêcheurs.

A km west of the Sunset Beach Motel is **Raiatea Carenage Services** (tel. 66-22-96), a repair facility often used by cruising yachts. The only easily accessible slip facilities in Tahiti-Polynesia are here.

Beside the souvenir stalls opposite the wharf is a **tourist information** stand (B.P. 707, Raiatea; tel. 66-23-18), open Monday and Friday 0800-1100, Tuesday and Thursday 0730-1100 and 1400-1600, Wednesday 0800-1200.

TRANSPORTATION

Getting There and Away

The **Air Tahiti** office (tel. 66-32-50) is at the airport. Flights operate from Raiatea to Maupiti (CFP 5500) three times a week. For information on flights from Papeete, Huahine, and Bora Bora see the "Transportation" section in the introduction to this chapter, Tahiti-Polynesia.

You can catch the *Vaeanu, Taporo VI,* and *Raromatai Ferry* to Tahaa, Bora Bora, Huahine or Papeete twice weekly. Consult the schedule in the "Transportation" section in the introduction to the Tahiti-Polynesia chapter. The agent for the *Taporo VI* is Les Mutuelles du Mans in the same block as Snack Moemoea. Tickets for the *Vaeanu* and *Raromatai Ferry* ferry are sold when the ship arrives.

The high-speed cruiser *Ono-Ono* (tel. 66-35-35) departs Raiatea for Bora Bora (1.5 hours, CFP 1600) Monday and Wednesday at 1345, Friday at 2115, Saturday at 1330. To Huahine (one hour, CFP 1600) and Papeete (4.5 hours, CFP 4800) it leaves Tuesday and Thursday at 1345, Sunday at 1545. Saturday at 1015 there's an extra trip only to Huahine.

A government supply ship, the *Meherio III,* shuttles twice a month between Raiatea and Maupiti, usually departing Raiatea on Thursday (CFP 1035 deck). The exact time varies, so check with the Capitainerie Port d'Uturoa (tel. 66-31-52) on the wharf.

Several village boats run between Raiatea and Tahaa on Wednesday and Friday mornings (CFP 500). The shuttle boat *Uporu* (tel. 65-61-01) departs Uturoa for Tahaa weekdays at 0930, 1400, and 1700, weekends at 0930 and 1700 (CFP 750 one-way).

Getting Around

Getting around Raiatea is a problem as the only *trucks* leaving Uturoa go to Fetuna (CFP 250) and Opoa in the afternoon, but never on Sunday. Bicycle rentals are offered only by the hotels, and scooters are generally unavailable.

Pacificar (tel. 66-11-66, fax 66-11-67), at the Apooiti Marina, and **Raiatea Location** (tel. 66-34-06), between the airport and Uturoa, have cars beginning around CFP 5500, including mileage and insurance. Prices are often higher at peak periods. Apart from cars, Raiatea Location rents a four-meter boat with a six-horsepower motor at CFP 500 a half day, CFP 8000 a full day.

Garage Motu Tapu (Guirouard Rent-a-Car, B.P. 139, Uturoa; tel. 66-33-09), in a poorly marked building a few hundred meters east of the airport, has cars at CFP 6600 for 24 hours, insurance and mileage included.

Airport

The airport (RFP) is three km northwest of Uturoa. A taxi from the Uturoa market taxi stand to the airport is CFP 600 (double tariff late at night). Most of the hotels pick up clients at the airport free upon request. Pacificar and Raiatea Location both have car rental desks inside the terminal. The Air Tahiti reservations office is in a separate building adjacent to the main terminal. The friendly but unknowledgeable Tourist Board information kiosk at the airport is only open at flight times.

TAHAA

Raiatea's lagoonmate Tahaa is shaped like a hibiscus flower. It's a quiet island, with little traffic and few tourists. Mount Ohiri (590 meters), highest point on the island, gets its name from the demigod Hiro, who was born here. There aren't many specific attractions other than a chance to escape the crowds and hurried life on the other Society Islands. Notice the vanilla plantations. Beaches are scarce on the main island, so the pension owners arrange picnics on *motus* such as Tautau off Tapuamu. The *motus* off the northeast side of Tahaa have the finest white-sand beaches. The Tahaa Festival in late October includes stone fishing, with a line of canoes herding the fish into a cove by beating stones on the surface of the lagoon. The 4,000 Tahaa islanders are a little wary of outsiders as it's well off the beaten track.

Orientation

The administrative center is at Patio on the north coast, where the post office, Mairie (town hall), and police station share one compound. The ship from Papeete ties up to the wharf at Tapuamu. There's a large covered area at the terminal where you could spread a sleeping bag in a pinch. The Banque Socredo branch is also at Tapuamu. A new road crosses the mountains from Patio direct to Haamene where a second post office is found.

Sights

Several large sea turtles are held captive in a tank by the lagoon behind the community hall near the church in Tiva. You could walk right around the main part of Tahaa in about eight hours with stops, passing villages every couple of km. Haamene Bay, the longest of Tahaa's four fjords, catches the full force of the southeast trades.

PRACTICALITIES

Accommodations

The most convenient place to stay is **Chez Pascal** (Pascal Tamaehu, tel. 65-60-42). From the Tapuamu ferry wharf you'll see a small bridge at the head of the bay. Turn left as you leave the dock and head for this. Chez Pascal is the first house north of the bridge on the inland side. The rate is CFP 4000 for bed, breakfast, and dinner, or CFP 2000 pp without meals. Boat trips to a *motu* (CFP 4000 pp) and the loan of the family bicycle are possible.

The **Hôtel L'Hibiscus** (B.P. 184, Haamene; tel. 65-61-06, fax 65-65-65), or "Tahaa Lagoon," is run by Leo and Lolita on the northeast side of windy Haamene Bay. L'Hibiscus has two classes of accommodations: three small bungalows with private bath at CFP 7850 double, or a small house nearby called Le Moana, accommodating four persons at CFP 1500 pp. Transfers from Raiatea are CFP 2500 pp return. You could also get there from Raiatea on the Haamene launch (Wednesday and Friday mornings) and ask to be dropped near the hotel.

Although the accommodations are satisfactory, the trick is that virtually everything you consume—even the water you drink—is charged extra at resort prices. Common drinking water is not available at L'Hibiscus; bottled water is CFP 350. The prices of the meals are fixed at CFP 3500 pp half pension, CFP 5000 full pension (not possible to order a la carte). Don't accept a "free welcome drink" from Leo or Lolita unless you don't mind having it added to your bill (which could be breathtaking). There are no cooking facilities, and the nearest store is three km away in Haamene (bring food and bottled water). The running water in the house may be turned off, although you can usually use the communal shower behind the restaurant. Lighting in the house could consist of a kerosene lamp.

The **Hôtel Marina Iti** (Philippe Robin, B.P. 888, Uturoa, Raiatea; tel. 65-61-01, fax 65-63-87) sits at the isolated south tip of Tahaa, opposite Raiatea on Tahaa's only sandy beach. The four clean, pleasant bungalows accommodating three persons are CFP 18,000 by the lagoon or CFP 12,000 in the garden. Meals are CFP 7000 extra for all three. Use of bicycles, canoe, and snorkeling gear is included, and scuba diving is available. Airport transfers are

CFP 3000 pp. As you'll have guessed, the Marina Iti caters to an upmarket crowd here in connection with yacht cruises from Raiatea, and numerous cruising yachts anchor in the calm waters offshore.

It's also possible to stay at the **Hôtel Vahine Island** (B.P. 510, Uturoa; tel. 65-67-38, fax 65-67-70) on lovely Motu Tuuvahine off the northeast side of Tahaa. The 11 bungalows are overpriced at CFP 30,000 single or double on the beach, CFP 45,000 overwater. For three meals add CFP 8800 pp, for airport transfers CFP 2200 pp. Outrigger canoes, windsurfing, snorkeling, and fishing gear are free. Moorings are provided for yachts.

Food
The only nonhotel restaurant on Tahaa is **Snack Melanie** (tel. 65-63-06) in Patio. A grocery truck passes L'Hibiscus around 1000 on Monday, Tuesday, Thursday, and Saturday; the same truck calls at the Marina Iti about noon daily except Sunday.

Transportation
There's no airport on Tahaa. Seven of the eight villages have small passenger launches, which leave for Raiatea at 0500 on Wednesday and Friday only, returning to Tahaa at 1000 these same days (CFP 500 one-way). Make sure your boat is going exactly where you want to go.

The **Tahaa Transport Service** (tel. 65-61-01) runs the shuttle boat *Uporu* from Tapuamu Wharf and the Hôtel Marina Iti to Uturoa twice a day on weekdays and daily on weekends (CFP 750 one-way), connecting with sailings of the high-speed cruiser *Ono-Ono*.

Taporo VI from Papeete, Huahine, and Raiatea calls at Tahaa on Tuesday, Thursday, and Saturday at 0700 and continues on to Bora Bora (southbound it doesn't stop at Tahaa). The *Vaeanu* departs Tahaa for Raiatea, Huahine, and Papeete Thursday and Sunday at noon; Saturday at 0830 it goes to Bora Bora. The *Raromatai Ferry* visits Tahaa on Wednesday and Saturday morning northbound, and Thursday morning and Sunday afternoon southbound. There's a telephone booth at Tapuamu Wharf where you could call your hotel to have them pick you up.

Trucks on Tahaa are for transporting schoolchildren only, so you may have to hitch to get around. It's not that hard to hitch a ride down the west coast from Patio to Haamene, but there's almost no traffic along the east coast. Even car rentals are difficult on Tahaa (try the Marina Iti).

BORA BORA

Bora Bora, 260 km northwest of Papeete, is everyone's idea of a South Pacific island. Dramatic basalt peaks soar 700 meters above a gorgeous, multicolored lagoon. Slopes and valleys blossom with hibiscus. Some of the most perfect beaches you'll ever see are here, complete with topless sunbathers. Not only are the beaches good but there's plenty to see and do. The local population of 4,500 includes many skilled dancers. To see them practicing in the evening, follow the beat of village drums to their source.

Bora Bora is the only island of Tahiti-Polynesia which can be said to have reached a tourist glut. The relentless stream of cars, pickups, hotel *trucks,* and scooters up and down the main road from Vaitape to Matira approaches Tahitian intensity at times. The uncontrolled expansion of tourism continues as luxury resorts are thrown up around the island, creating the illusion of being in Hawaii or some West Indies hot spot. Yet many of the US$250-a-night hotels stand almost empty. Construction of a huge Hyatt Regency on a swampy shore at the far north end of the island was halted by a land dispute. Today the crumbling Hyatt ruins stand as a monument to bad planning and the perils of high-impact development.

The Land
Seven-million-year-old Bora Bora is made up of a 10-km-long main island, a few smaller high islands in the lagoon, and a long ring of *motus* on the barrier reef. Pofai Bay marks the center of the island's collapsed crater with Toopua and Toopuaiti as its eroded west wall. Mount Pahia's gray basalt mass rises 649 meters behind Vaitape and above it soar the sheer cliffs of Otemanu's mighty volcanic plug (727 meters).

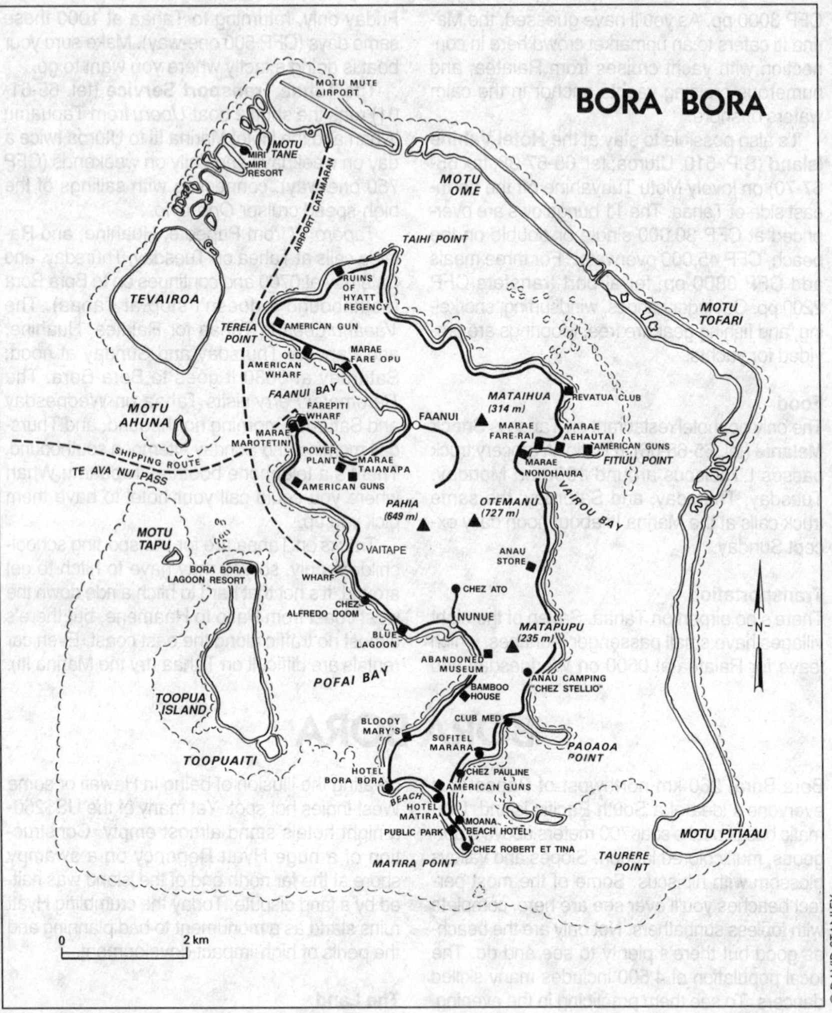

BORA BORA

© DAVID STANLEY

0   2 km

The wide-angle scenery of the main island is complemented by the surrounding coral reef and numerous *motus,* one of which bears the airport. Tiny Motu Tapu of the travel brochures was popularized in Murnau's 1928 film *Tabou.* Te Ava Nui Pass is the only entry through the barrier reef. Watch for dolphins near this channel as your ship enters Bora Bora's lagoon; whole colonies sometimes race the boats.

History

The letter *b* doesn't exist in Tahitian, so Bora Bora is actually Pora Pora (First Born). Bora Borans of yesteryear were indomitable warriors who often raided Maupiti, Tahaa, and Raiatea. "Discovered" by Roggeveen in 1722, Bora Bora was visited by Capt. James Cook in 1777. In 1895 the island was annexed by France.

In February 1942 the Americans hastily set up a refueling and regrouping base code-named "Bobcat" on the island to serve shipping between the U.S. west coast or Panama Canal and Australia/New Zealand. You can still see remains from this time, including eight huge naval guns placed here to defend the island against a surprise Japanese attack that never materialized. The big lagoon with only one pass offered secure anchorage for as many as 100 U.S. Navy transports at a time. A road was built around the island and an airfield constructed. The 4,400 American army troops also left behind 130 half-caste babies, 40% of whom died when the base closed in 1946 and the abandoned infants were forced to switch from their accustomed American baby formulas to island food. The survivors are now approaching ripe middle age. Novelist James A. Michener, a young naval officer at the time, left perhaps the most enduring legacy by modeling his Bali Hai on this "enchanted island," Bora Bora.

Orientation

You can arrive at Motu Mute airport and be carried to Vaitape Wharf by a fully enclosed catamaran, or disembark from a ship at Farepiti Wharf, three km north of Vaitape. Most of the stores, banks, and offices are near Vaitape Wharf. The best beaches are at Matira at the island's southern tip.

SIGHTS

Vaitape

Behind the Banque de Tahiti at Vaitape Wharf is the **monument to Alain Gerbault,** who sailed his yacht, the *Firecrest,* around the world solo from 1925 to 1929—the first Frenchman to do so. Gerbault's first visit to Bora Bora was from 25 May to 12 June 1926. He returned to Polynesia in 1933 and stayed until 1940.

To get an idea of how the Bora Borans live, take a stroll through Vaitape village: go up the road that begins beside the Banque Socredo.

Around the Island

The largely paved and level 32-km road around the island makes it easy to see Bora Bora by rented bicycle (it's unnecessary to rent a car). At

the head of **Pofai Bay** notice the odd assortment of looted war wreckage across the road from Boutique Alain Linda, remnants of an abandoned museum. The seven-inch American gun dragged here from Tereia Point in 1982 is hard to miss. The locations of the other seven MK II naval guns remaining in situ on Bora Bora are given below. The forlorn, violated gun lying on its side at Pofai demonstrates the stupidity of those who would despoil historical monuments.

Stop at **Bloody Mary's Restaurant** to scan the goofy displays outside their gate, but more importantly to get the classic view of the island's soaring peaks across Pofai Bay as it appears in countless brochures. At photographer Erwin Christian's **Moana Art Boutique** just before Hôtel Bora Bora you can buy a postcard of the scene.

The finest beach on the island stretches east from **Hôtel Bora Bora** to Matira Point. Some of the best snorkeling on the island, with a varied multitude of colorful tropical fish, is off the small point at Hôtel Bora Bora, but you may want to enter from beyond the hotel grounds (near Hôtel Matira) and walk or swim back, as the hotel staff don't appreciate strangers who stroll through their lobby to get to the beach. Beware of getting run over by a glass-bottom boat! **Martine's Créations** (tel. 67-70-79) just east of Hôtel Bora Bora has finely crafted black-pearl jewelry and designer beachwear.

Two **naval guns** sit on the ridge above Hôtel Matira. Take the overgrown trail on the mountain side of the road that winds around behind the bungalows from the east end of the property and keep straight ahead to the top of the ridge for good views of the lagoon and neighboring islands (10 minutes).

Bora Bora's most popular public beach is **Matira Beach Park** directly across the street from the Moana Beach Hôtel on Matira Point. At low tide you can wade from the end of Matira Point right out to the reef. Proceed north to the **Sofitel Marara,** a good place for a leisurely beer. Visitors are unwelcome at the new Club Med, which the road climbs over a hill to avoid. The two general stores at **Anau** can supply a cold drink or a snack.

On the north side of Vairou Bay the road begins to climb over a ridge. Halfway up the slope, look down to the right and by the shore you'll see the *ahu* of **Marae Aehautai,** the best of the three *marae* in this area. From the *marae* there's a stupendous view of Otemanu and you should be able to pick out Te Ana Opea cave far up on the side of the mountain. The steep unpaved slope on the other side of this ridge can be dangerous if you're unaware, so slow down. At the bottom of the hill is a rough track along the north shore of Fitiuu Point. Follow it east till you find a jeep track up onto the ridge to two more of the American **seven-inch guns.** Unfortunately the municipality often uses this area for burning refuse, and the stench can make a visit to the guns almost unbearable.

From between Taihi Point and the Hyatt Regency ruins, a steep jeep track climbs to **Popoti Ridge** (249 meters), where the Americans had a radar installation during WW II.

One American **naval gun** remains on the hillside above the rectangular water tank at Tereia Point. The housing of a second gun, vandalized in 1982, is nearby. The remains of several American concrete wharves can be seen along the north shore of **Faanui Bay.** Most of the wartime American occupation force was billeted at Faanui, and a few Quonset huts linger in the bush. **Marae Fare Opu,** just east of a small boat harbor, is notable for petroglyphs of turtles carved into the stones of the *ahu.* Turtles, a favorite food of the gods, were often offered to them on the *marae.* (Mindless guides sometimes highlight the turtles in chalk for the benefit of tourist cameras.)

Between Faanui and Farepiti Wharf, just east of the electricity-generating plant, is **Marae Taianapa;** its long *ahu* is clearly visible on the hillside from the road. The most important *marae* on Bora Bora was **Marae Marotetini,** on the point near Farepiti Wharf—west of the wharf beyond a huge banyan tree. The great stone *ahu,* 25 meters long and up to 1.5 meters high, was restored by Professor Sinoto in 1968 and is visible from approaching ships.

The last two **American guns** are a 10-minute scramble up the ridge from the main road between Farepiti Wharf and Vaitape. Go straight up the concrete road signposted Garderie Creche d'Enfants. If you reach Otemanu Tours (where you see several *trucks* parked), you've passed the road. At the end of the ridge there's a good

view of Te Ava Nui Pass, which the guns were meant to defend. Maupiti is farther out on the horizon. The old Club Med near here was knocked out of service by a hurricane in December 1991.

Hiking

If you're experienced and determined, it's possible to climb **Mt. Pahia** in about four hours of rough going. Take the road inland beside the Banque Socredo at Vaitape and go up the depression past a series of mango trees, veering slightly left. Circle the cliffs near the top on the left side, and come up the back of Snoopy's head and along his toes. (These directions will take on meaning when you study Pahia from the end of Vaitape's Wharf.) The trail is unmaintained and a local guide would be a big help (to hire one inquire at CETAD at the Collège de Bora Bora in Vaitape). Avoid rainy weather, when the way will be muddy and slippery.

Despite what some tourist publications claim, **Otemanu,** the high rectangular peak next to pointed Pahia, has *never* been climbed. It's possible to climb up to the shoulders of the mountain, but the sheer cliffs of the main peak are inaccessible because clamps pull right out of the vertical, crumbly cliff face. Helicopters can land on the summit, but that doesn't count. Otemanu's name means "It's a bird."

Sports and Recreation

The **Bora Diving Center** (Anne and Michel Condesse, B.P. 182, Nanue; tel. 67-71-84, fax 67-74-83), on Pofai Bay opposite Bloody Mary's Restaurant, does open-water scuba diving every day at CFP 6000 and night dives for CFP 7500. Prices are negotiable if you book direct at their office (closed while they're out diving)—don't book through your hotel reception (there's a CFP 500-1000 surcharge if you're staying at Hôtel Bora Bora, Club Med, or the Bora Bora Lagoon Resort). Hotel pickups are at 0830 and 1330.

Scuba diving can also be arranged through Claude Sibani's **Bora Bora Calypso Club** (B.P. 259, Bora Bora; tel. 67-74-64, fax 67-70-34) at the Bora Bora Beach Club. They charge CFP 6000 for a lagoon dive, CFP 6500 for an ocean dive, and go out daily at 0900 and 1400 from the Beach Club dock. Their specialty is diving with manta rays (worth doing to see the mantas, though you won't see much else in that area as the coral is all dead and the waters fished out). Most scuba diving at Bora Bora is within the lagoon and visibility is sometimes limited.

Like Aitutaki in the Cook Islands, Bora Bora is famous for its lagoon trips. Prices vary depending on whether lunch is included, the length of the trip, the luxury of boat, etc., so check around. A seafood picnic lunch on a *motu,* reef walking, and snorkeling gear are usually included, and you get a chance to see giant clams, manta rays, and the hand-feeding of small lagoon sharks. For example, the **Blue Lagoon Bar** (tel. 67-70-54, fax 67-79-10) on the north side of Pofai Bay offers a six-hour reef tour with shark feeding and lunch on a *motu* for CFP 4900 pp—it's said to be quite good. Their three-hour lagoon excursion without lunch is CFP 3000, hotel transfers included. Also see the Chez Nono listing that follows. Motorized canoe trips right around Bora Bora are also offered. An excursion of this kind is an essential part of the Bora Bora experience, so splurge on this one. (Several readers have written in to say they agree completely.)

Three-hour tours to the so-called **Bora Lagoonarium** (B.P. 56, Vaitape; tel. 67-71-34) on a *motu* off the main island occur daily except Saturday at 1400 (CFP 3000); you'll see more colorful fish than you ever thought existed. Call for a free hotel pickup.

Stellio (tel. 67-71-32) of the Anau camping ground mentioned below does an island tour by boat for CFP 3000, which includes shark feeding, clam viewing, snorkeling, reef walking, and picnic on a *motu* (bring your own lunch). For CFP 1000 return Stellio will drop you off on a *motu* where you can do your own thing. Chez Pauline also offers this service.

ACCOMMODATIONS

There's an abundance of accommodations on Bora Bora and, except at holiday times (especially during the July festivities), it's not necessary to book a room in advance. When things are slow, the hotel owners meet the interisland boats in search of guests. If someone from the hotel of your choice isn't at the dock when you arrive, get on the blue *truck* marked Vaitape-

Anau and ask to be taken there. This should cost CFP 500 pp from Farepiti Wharf, CFP 300 pp from Vaitape Wharf, plus CFP 100 for luggage. However, if you're staying at a luxury resort you could be charged CFP 1800 pp return for airport transfers.

The luxury hotels add a seven percent tax to their room rates (often not included in the quoted price) but most of the budget places include the tax in their price. Be aware that the large hotels frequently tack a CFP 1000 commission onto rental cars, lagoon excursions, and scuba diving booked through their front desks. The campgrounds and pensions don't usually take such commissions. Bora Bora suffers from serious water shortages, so use it sparingly.

Camping and Dormitories

Backpackers often stay at **Chez Stellio** (B.P. 267, Bora Bora; tel. 67-71-32) at Anau on the east side of the island. Camping is CFP 1000 pp and there's a 10-bed guesthouse next to the lagoon at CFP 1500 pp. Double rooms are CFP 4000. Cooking facilities are provided (shortage of utensils). Stellio often hangs up big bunches of free bananas for guests, and his grandchildren do their part to keep the grassy camping area clean. This place is not on a beach, but Stellio owns land on idyllic Motu Vaivahia and for CFP 1000 pp he'll drop you off there for a day or two of Robinson Crusoe-style camping (take sufficient food and water). If you know how to swim, ask him about renting an outrigger canoe *(pirogue).* Look for Stellio's blue Vaitape-Anau *truck* with "Vaiho" on the door at the wharf and you'll get a free ride to the camping ground when you first arrive, although upon departure everyone must pay CFP 300-500 pp, plus CFP 100 for luggage, for transfers back to the wharf. Stellio's a helpful, laid-back sort of guy and he'll probably offer you additional free rides in his school bus if he's going anyway and you're staying at his place. The trail up the hill across the street is a shortcut into town. Bora Bora is overrun by land crabs, funny little creatures that make camping exciting.

Despite fast-rising prices, many backpackers make the adjustment and stay at **Chez Pauline** (Pauline Youssef, B.P. 215, Vaitape; tel. 67-72-16, fax 67-78-14), on a white-sand beach between the Moana Beach and Sofitel

Marara hotels, eight km from Vaitape. Pauline charges CFP 1600 pp to camp (own tent), CFP 2000 in the 10-bed dormitory, or CFP 5000 double in one of her eight small, closely packed beach cabins. The six thatched bungalows with kitchens are CFP 9000/11,500 double/triple. There are communal cooking facilities for campers but they become cramped when many guests are present. It's quite a hike to the grocery store at Anau, but the food truck circling the island passes daily except Sunday around 1100 (check with the receptionist). Due to rave reviews in the Australian guidebooks it can get crowded, and unlike Stellio's, which is in the middle of a local village, Pauline's is strictly a tourist scene. An American reader's report: "We couldn't sleep the first night because the mattress was wet and had to move to another bungalow the next day. We were very upset after returning from dinner the second night to find that our bungalow had been broken into and all of my clothes were taken. We'd planned to spend 12 days on Bora Bora but left after four."

Budget Accommodations near Vaitape

Most of the budget places to stay in Vaitape village have closed in recent years, but you can still stay at **Chez Alfredo Doom** (tel. 67-70-31) at Tiipoto, a km south of Vaitape Wharf (just past the Jehovah's Witnesses church, across the street from the garage where you see several *trucks* parked—no sign). Their large thatched house with full cooking facilities, private bath, and plenty of space is fair value at CFP 5000/6000 double/triple for the whole building, but it's a little dark due to the low eaves. Still, if you'd rather stay near town and avoid the tourist ghetto at Matira Point, it's a good choice. The main drawbacks are the steady roar of traffic and a neighbor's radio. Bookings must be made through Madame Doom at the hamburger stand next to the Banque de Polynésie in Vaitape.

CETAD (B.P. 151, Bora Bora; tel. 67-71-47, fax 67-78-20), at the Collège de Bora Bora on the lagoon just north of Magasin Chin Lee in the center of Vaitape, rents a small five-bed bungalow with kitchenette and private bath at CFP 3000 for the first person, plus CFP 1000 for each additional person. It's often full.

At Nunue, right up below Otemanu's soaring peak is **Pension Chez Ato** (tel. 67-77-27), a se-

cluded little hideaway with six rooms at CFP 2000 pp. Cooking facilities are provided and Ato can arrange guides for mountain hikes. Ato is a member of the environmental group *atu atu te natura* and he takes the concept of ecotourism seriously. It's a good way to experience a slice of Tahitian life, so long as you don't mind being away from the beach. Look for a paved road running inland from opposite a large stone engraved Bora 2000 at the head of Pofai Bay and follow it right up to the end (there's no sign). Recommended.

Budget Accommodations at Matira Point

On the Matira peninsula are two excellent alternatives to the upmarket hotels. **Chez Nono** (Noël Leverd, B.P. 282, Vaitape; tel. 67-71-38, fax 67-74-27) faces the beach across from the Moana Beach Hôtel. They have one large bungalow with cooking facilities (CFP 14,000), two smaller bungalows with private bath (CFP 7000), and a six-bedroom thatched guesthouse with shared kitchen at CFP 4000/5000 single/double per room. Ventilation spaces between the ceilings and walls mean you hear *everything* in the other rooms, but the atmosphere is amiable and all guests soon become good friends. Their garden is a pleasant place to sit, but the bungalows occasionally experience a lot of noise from beach parties. The solar hot water heating only works when the sun is shining. Their boat tour around the island includes shark feeding and an excellent fish lunch.

Also good is **Chez Robert et Tina** (tel. 67-72-92), two European-style houses with cooking facilities down the road from Chez Nono at the tip of Matira Point (CFP 3000/6000 single/double). Robert offers excellent lagoon trips at CFP 3000 pp without lunch.

Medium-Priced Hotels

Hôtel Matira (B.P. 31, Vaitape; tel. 67-70-51, fax 67-77-02) is one of the few medium-priced places offering cooking facilities. Their nine thatched bungalows with kitchenettes on the mountain side of the road are CFP 15,200/19,200 double/triple. The units without kitchens are CFP 3000 cheaper. The 16 thatched bungalows with kitchenettes in the annex right on the lagoon at the neck of Matira peninsula are better value at CFP 17,000/21,000. The Matira's Chinese restaurant (closed Monday) is reasonable, and the beach is excellent. Airport transfers are CFP 1000 pp return.

The **Bora Bora Motel** (B.P. 180, Vaitape; tel. 67-78-21, fax 67-77-57) shares a white beach with the Sofitel Marara (see below). Their four studios with bedroom, living room, dining room, and kitchen are CFP 13,000 double; the three slightly larger apartments are CFP 17,000 double, extra persons are CFP 3000 each. These units built in 1991 are comfortable and spacious, a good compromise if you want to go upmarket while keeping to a budget.

Next door to the Bora Bora Motel is the **Bora Bora Beach Club** (B.P. 252, Nunue; tel. 67-71-16, fax 67-71-30), part of the Tahiti Resort Hotels chain. The nine four-unit, single-roof blocks total 36 rooms beginning at CFP 23,000 single, double, or triple (garden) or CFP 25,000 (beach)—highly overpriced for what you get, and air conditioning is CFP 4000 extra! Not all rooms have a fridge (check), and if your room is without a/c make sure your neighbors are in the same predicament, otherwise you could get the noise without the chill. There are no cooking facilities. Jackie Halter of Jackson, Wyoming, sent us this comment: "The bathroom was filthy, an active wasp nest was in our ceiling, the refrigerator was big enough to put a piece of fruit in, and the restaurant which we went to upon arrival because we were starving left a lot to be desired. The beach was so dirty we couldn't even walk along it in bare feet." Windsurfing, fishing, and snorkeling gear are loaned free to guests (that's why they call it a "club"). They also claim to provide free outrigger canoes but most have holes in them. Airport transfers are CFP 1800 pp return. Not recommended.

The 16-room **Revatua Club** (B.P. 159, Vaitape; tel. 67-71-67, fax 67-76-59) on the northeast side of the island is isolated, beachless, and CFP 8900/10,400/11,700 single/double/triple, plus CFP 3800 pp for breakfast and dinner and CFP 800 pp for airport transfers. Its only draws are the excellent overwater French restaurant **Chez Christian**, which offers free transport for diners, and the bar. The mock-Victorian architecture is right out of Hollywood.

Cruising yachties are catered to by the **Yacht Club de Bora Bora** (B.P. 17, Vaitape; tel. 67-70-69) near Farepiti Wharf. They allow boats free use of their 17 moorings, and provide fresh water and showers. In turn, yachties are expected to splash out occasionally in their seafood restaurant. The club has three stuffy garden bungalows at CFP 10,000 double, but no beach (or cooking). During the night you could be visited by both mosquitoes and burglars. Their three floating bungalows with cooking facilities and solar electricity (CFP 20,000 for four persons) can be towed out and moored off a *motu*.

Upmarket Hotels

Hôtel Bora Bora (B.P. 1, Bora Bora; tel. 67-44-60, fax 60-44-66), which opened in June 1961, was the island's first large hotel. At CFP 70,000 single or double without meals for an overwater bungalow, it's one of the most exclusive millionaire's playgrounds in the South Pacific. Standard rooms in this 55-unit resort begin at CFP 39,500 single or double, CFP 46,500 triple. Breakfast and dinner are CFP 7800 pp extra. Their beach is superb and the hotel restaurant's cuisine exceptional. The hotel's scuba diving concession is run by noted photographer Erwin Christian.

Japanese-owned **Hôtel Moana Beach Parkroyal** (B.P. 156, Bora Bora; tel. 67-73-73, fax 67-71-41) on a white-sand beach at Matira Point is also absurdly expensive. One of the 10 beachfront bungalows here will set you back CFP 43,300 single or double; the 30 overwater bungalows are CFP 59,700 (children under 19 free). It's CFP 6400 pp extra for breakfast and dinner.

A less pretentious top-end resort is the **Hôtel Sofitel Marara** (B.P. 6, Bora Bora; tel. 67-74-01, fax 67-74-03). The Sofitel Marara (the name means "Flying Fish") was built in 1978 to house the crew filming Dino de Laurentiis's *Hurricane;* the film flopped but the hotel has been going strong ever since. The 64 bungalows begin at CFP 27,000 single or double, CFP 31,000 triple. It's open and informal, and instead of the Americans you hear at Hôtel Bora Bora and the Japanese you see at the Moana Beach, the Marara caters to an international mix of tourists. The beach doesn't have the policed feel of the Bora Bora's, and this is the only hotel on the main island with a swimming pool. The Marara's bar is fairly reasonable for such a swank place (happy hour is daily 1700-1800), but the restaurant isn't highly rated (and the service is incredibly slow).

In late 1993 a new 150-bungalow **Club Méditerranée** (B.P. 34, Bora Bora; tel. 60-46-04, fax 60-46-11) opened on Bora Bora. The circuminsular road had to be rerouted around this US$30-million enclave just north of the Sofitel, and as usual, security is tight. You don't just stroll in and rent a room at Club Med, as only guests are allowed to set foot on these hallowed grounds, so book in advance at the Club Med office in Papeete's Vaima Center (tel. 42-96-99). The Bora Bora Club Med is more luxurious than Club Med Moorea, and as usual, all meals and nonmotorized nautical activities are included in the basic price (from CFP 22,000 pp, double occupancy). The gaudy orange and yellow bungalows face the beach.

The 80-unit, Japanese-owned **Hôtel Bora Bora Lagoon Resort** (B.P. 175, Vaitape; tel. 60-40-00, fax 60-40-01) on Toopua Island opposite Vaitape offers five-star facilities with prices to match. Beach bungalows start at an amazing CFP 52,000/60,500 double/triple (50% more for an overwater bungalow), plus another CFP 12,000 pp for all meals. A large sign at the landing announces that it's forbidden to bring your own food and drink into the resort. (French expatriates point to this resort, which opened in June 1993, as a good example of Japanese financial lunacy: the investors have sunk countless millions of dollars into the place, though it will revert to the local landowner in 30 years.)

FOOD

Budget Places

Pâtisserie-Bar Le Vaitape, across the street from the Banque de Polynésie in Vaitape, has reasonable beer prices and the *poisson cru* (CFP 700) is excellent but they don't have it every day (ask). They also serve ice cream, but their coffee is terrible.

Snack Matira (tel. 67-77-32), opposite the college just north of Magasin Chin Lee, serves filling meals for CFP 700. Try the *maa tinito*.

The **Restaurant Manuia** at the Collège de Bora Bora (tel. 67-71-47) just north of Magasin Chin Lee in Vaitape is used to train students for employment at the large hotels. Since their aim is not profit, you can get a three-course meal with coffee and a carafe of wine for CFP 1200 here, but only on Wednesday and Friday 1130-1330 during the school year (mid-January to June and August to mid-December). It's a nice change of pace and excellent value.

Facing the beach just east of Hôtel Bora Bora are two reasonable places to eat. **Ben's Snack** (tel. 67-74-54) manages to turn out surprisingly good home-cooked pizza, lasagna, pasta, and omelettes, and the colorful American-Tahitian owners, Robin and Ben, add a Bohemian air to the place. Another snack bar (closed Monday), across the street and along a bit, offers hamburgers and *poisson cru* for noticeably lower prices.

Snack Chez Hinavai (tel. 67-79-26) near Chez Pauline has a few Chinese dishes and fairly reasonable meat and fish. **Snack La Bounty** (tel. 67-70-43) between Chez Pauline and the Sofitel is a simple open-air restaurant with good-quality food at medium prices.

The **Pofai Shoppe** on the road near Hôtel Bora Bora sells cold fruit drinks at normal prices (open daily).

Better Restaurants

Basically, there are two choices if you want to "eat out." **Bloody Mary's Restaurant** (closed Sunday; tel. 67-72-86) is the larger and better established with a tradition dating back to 1979. A board outside lists "famous guests," including Jane Fonda and Baron George Von Dangel. It remains good, with inexpensive pizza for lunch (1100-1500) and upmarket seafood for dinner (1830-2100). Beer is on tap all day (a pitcher of Hinano is CFP 750), so it's worth a stop on your way around the island at any time. Free hotel pickups for diners are available at 1830 or 1930 if you call ahead. Bloody Mary's offers free moorings to yachties who dine with them.

At dinner the newer **Bamboo House Restaurant** (tel. 67-76-24), also on Pofai Bay, does its best to challenge Bloody Mary's famous seafood, and if you call, they'll also pick you up at your hotel. Both places are good, but pick Bloody Mary's if you only have time for one.

In 1995 **Restaurant Le Tiare** opened across the street from the Bora Bora Beach Club. In the evening the tables are all taken, which perhaps says something about the restaurants in the Beach Club and nearby Sofitel Marara.

Groceries

Bora Bora's largest supermarket is **Magasin Chin Lee,** north of Vaitape Wharf (just north of the large church) and opposite the island's Mobil gas station. It and another well-stocked grocery store in Vaitape are open Monday to Saturday 0600-1800. The Total service station is north again. The only other places to buy groceries are the two general stores at Anau, halfway around the island (closed Sunday). No grocery store is found at Matira, although a grocery truck passes this way around 1100 daily (except Sunday).

ENTERTAINMENT AND EVENTS

Entertainment

Le Récife Bar (B.P. 278, Vaitape; tel. 67-73-87), between Vaitape and Farepiti Wharf, is Bora Bora's after-hours club, open Friday and Saturday from 2230. Disco dancing continues almost until dawn, but expect loud, heavy-on-the-beat music with few patrons. Steer clear of the local drunks hanging around outside who can't afford the CFP 1000 cover charge.

Witness Polynesian dancing on the beach at **Hôtel Bora Bora** (tel. 67-44-60) by grabbing a barside seat before it starts at 2030 on Wednesday and Sunday nights.

Additional traditional dancing occurs after dinner Tuesday, Thursday, and Saturday nights at 2030 at the **Moana Beach Hôtel** (tel. 67-73-73).

You may feel more at home watching the Tahitian dance show at the **Hôtel Sofitel Marara** (tel. 67-74-01) every Tuesday, Friday, and Saturday night at 2030; see it all for the price of a draft beer. On Saturday at 1830 they open the earth oven and a Tahitian feast begins. The floor show is good but the food is mediocre.

Events

The **Fêtes de Juillet** are celebrated at Bora Bora with special fervor. The canoe and bicycle races, javelin throwing, flower cars, singing, and dancing competitions run until 0300 nightly. A public ball goes till dawn on the Saturday closest to 14 July. Try to participate in the 10-km foot race to prove that all tourists aren't lazy, but don't take the prizes away from the locals. If you win, be sure to give the money back to them for partying. You'll make good friends that way

and have more fun dancing in the evening. The stands are beautiful because the best decorations win prizes, too.

SHOPPING AND SERVICES

Shopping

There are plenty of small boutiques around Vaitape selling black coral jewelry, pearls, pareus, T-shirts, designer beachwear, etc. The **Centre Artisanal** near Vaitape Wharf is a good place to buy a shell necklace or a pareu directly from the locals.

Services and Information

The four main banks all have offices near Vaitape Wharf but none are open on Saturday. The post office, *gendarmerie,* and health clinic *(Santé Publique)* are within a stone's throw of the wharf. **Pharmacie Fare Ra'au** is farther north.

Dr. Marie-Joseph Juen's private **Cabinet Médical** (tel. 67-70-62) behind the Banque de Polynésie is open weekdays 0700-1200 and 1500-1800, Saturday 0700-1200, Sunday 0900-1000. Dr. François Macouin has his private **dental clinic** (tel. 67-70-55) in the same building.

The helpful **tourist information office** (B.P. 144, Bora Bora; tel./fax 67-76-36) and public toilets are in the Centre Artisanal next to Vaitape Wharf. The unmarked **Air Tahiti** office (tel. 67-70-35) is beside the Banque de Tahiti on the wharf at Vaitape.

TRANSPORTATION

Getting There

Air Tahiti has a useful transversal flight direct from Bora Bora to Rangiroa (CFP 20,700) twice a week. For information on flights to Bora Bora from Papeete, Huahine, and Raiatea, see the "Transportation" section in the introduction to this chapter.

Ships from Raiatea and Papeete tie up at Farepiti Wharf, three km north of Vaitape. The shipping companies have no representatives on Bora Bora, so for departure times just keep asking. Drivers of the *trucks* are the most likely to know. You buy your ticket when the ship arrives. Officially the *Taporo VI* leaves for Raiatea, Huahine, and Papeete on Tuesday, Thursday, and Saturday at 1130. The *Vaeanu* departs Bora Bora for Raiatea, Huahine, and Papeete Tuesday at noon, Thursday at 0830, and Sunday at 0930. The *Raromatai Ferry* leaves for Tahaa, Raiatea, Huahine, and Papeete Thursday at 0700 and Sunday at 1430. Beware of ships leaving early.

The high-speed cruiser *Ono-Ono* (tel. 67-78-00) departs Bora Bora for Raiatea (1.5 hours, CFP 1600), Huahine (three hours, CFP 2800), and Papeete (six hours, CFP 5800) on Tuesday and Thursday at 1200, Sunday at 1400. On Saturday there's a trip to Raiatea and Huahine alone at 0830.

Getting Around

Getting around is a bit of a headache, as *truck* service is irregular and at lunchtime everything stops. Public *trucks* usually meet the boats, but many of the *trucks* you see around town are strictly for guests of the luxury hotels. If you do find one willing to take you, fares between Vaitape and Matira vary from CFP 300-500, plus CFP 100 for luggage. Taxi fares are high, so check before getting in.

Mataura Rent-A-Bike (tel. 67-73-16) just south of Vaitape rents bicycles at CFP 500 a day or CFP 800 for two days. At Chez Pauline bicycles are CFP 900 half day, CFP 1300 full day. Bora Bora is perfect for cycling as there's an excellent paved road right around the island (with only one unpaved stretch on the incline at Fitiuu Point), almost no hills, and lots of scenic bays to shelter you from the wind.

If you must rent a car, **Bora Rent-a-Car** (B.P. 246, Vaitape; tel. 67-70-03) opposite Vaitape Wharf has Renaults at CFP 6500 for a 0800-1700 day, CFP 7500 for 24 hours. The price includes insurance and unlimited km, valid driver's license required. They also have motor scooters for CFP 4500 0800-1700 or CFP 5500 for 24 hours. For service and price they're the best on the island. If driving at night, watch out for scooters and bicycles without lights. However, to better enjoy the scenery and avoid disturbing the environment, we suggest you dispense with motorized transport on little Bora Bora.

The **Yacht Club de Bora Bora** (tel. 67-70-69) rents small, two-person dinghies with six-horsepower outboard motors for CFP 3500 half day, CFP 6000 whole day (gas extra). With an early start you could circumnavigate the island.

The **Blue Lagoon Bar** (tel. 67-70-54) also rents four-person motorboats at CFP 5000 a half day, CFP 8000 a full day, gasoline and insurance included.

Otemanu Tours (tel. 67-70-49), just north of Vaitape, offers a two-and-a-half-hour minibus tour around Bora Bora daily except Sunday at 1400 (CFP 2000). **Jeep Safaris** (tel. 67-70-34) offers Land Rover tours up a steep ridge opposite Otemanu at CFP 4000.

Airport

Bora Bora's vast airfield (BOB) on Motu Mute north of the main island was built by the Americans during WW II. The first commercial flight from Paris to Tahiti-Polynesia landed here in October 1958, and until March 1961 all international flights used this airstrip; passengers were then transferred to Papeete by Catalina amphibious or Bermuda flying boat seaplanes.

Today, a 25-minute catamaran ride brings arriving air passengers to Vaitape Wharf (included in the plane ticket). The boat ride isn't as much fun as it sounds because you have to sit in a stuffy a/c cabin peeping at Bora Bora through salt-encrusted windows and are not allowed to stand on the upper deck. (Why doesn't Air Tahiti get smart and scrap their flash cat? It's hard to imagine a more anticlimactic way to arrive!)

When the catamaran from the airport arrives at Vaitape Wharf, all of the luxury hotels will have guest transportation waiting, but the budget places don't always meet the flights (the deluxe places don't bother meeting the interisland boats). As you arrive at the wharf, shout out the name of your hotel and you'll be directed to the right *truck* (they don't have destination signs).

The airport cafe serves a very good cup of coffee.

If you're flying to Bora Bora from Papeete go early in the morning and sit on the left side of the aircraft for spectacular views—it's only from the air that Bora Bora is the most beautiful island in the world!

MAUPITI

Majestic Maupiti (Maurua), 44 km west of Bora Bora, is the least known of the accessible Society Islands. Maupiti's mighty volcanic plug soars from a sapphire lagoon, and the vegetation-draped cliffs complement the magnificent *motu* beaches. Almost every bit of level land on the main island is taken up by fruit trees, while watermelons thrive on the surrounding *motus*. Maupiti abounds in native seabirds, including frigate birds, terns, and others. The absence of Indian mynahs allows you to see native land birds almost extinct elsewhere.

The 1,000 people live in the adjacent villages of Vai'ea, Farauru, and Pauma. Tourism is not promoted because there aren't any regular hotels, which can be an advantage! Maupiti was

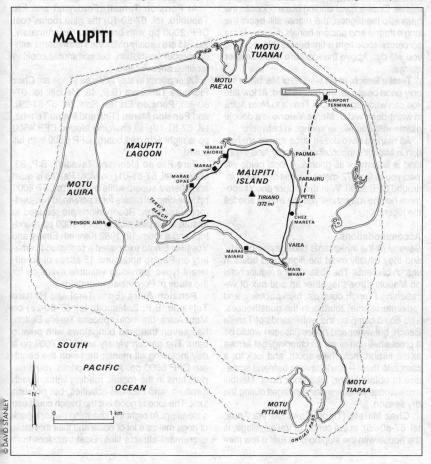

once famous for its black basalt stone pounders and fishhooks made from the seven local varieties of mother-of-pearl shell.

Sights

It takes only three hours to walk right around the island. The nine-km crushed-coral road, lined with breadfruit, mango, banana, and hibiscus, passes crumbling *marae,* freshwater springs, and a beach.

Marae Vaiahu, by the shore a few hundred meters beyond Hotuparaoa Massif, is the largest *marae.* Once a royal landing place opposite the pass into the lagoon, the *marae* still bears the king's throne and ancient burials. Nearby is the sorcerers' rock: light a fire beside this rock and you will die. Above the road are a few smaller *marae.*

Terei'a Beach, at the west tip of Maupiti, is the only good beach on the main island. At low tide you can wade across from Terei'a to Motu Auira in waist-deep water. **Marae Vaiorie** is a double *marae* with freshwater springs in between.

As many as two dozen large *marae* are hidden in Maupiti's mountainous interior, and the island is known for its ghosts. A local guide will lead you to the 372-meter summit of Maupiti for around CFP 2500. With the proper encouragement he/she may show you the *marae* and tell the legends.

Accommodations

Several of the inhabitants take paying guests, and they usually meet the flights and boats in search of clients. The absence of a regular hotel on Maupiti throws together an odd mix of vacationing French couples, backpackers, and "adventuresome" tourists in the guesthouses. You could camp on the white sands of Terei'a Beach, but water and *nonos* (insects) would be a problem. If you're set on camping, get across to the airport *motu,* hike south, and look for a campsite there—you'll have to befriend someone to obtain water. Like Bora Bora, Maupiti experiences serious water shortages during the dry season.

Chez Mareta (Tinorua and Mareta Anua, tel. 67-80-25), in the center of Vai'ea village, is the house with the sloping blue roof a few minutes' walk from the Mairie (town hall). They offer mattresses on the floor in the upstairs double rooms for CFP 1000 pp, or CFP 3000 pp including breakfast and dinner. A pleasant sitting room faces the lagoon downstairs. Upon request, they'll drop you on a *motu* for the day (beware of sunburn). Chez Mareta is okay for a couple of days, but not an extended stay. Agree on the price beforehand and check your bill when you leave. The church choir in the next building practices their singing quite loudly each night.

At **Pension Tamati** (Ferdinand and Etu Tapuhiro, tel. 67-80-10) the nine rooms cost CFP 2000 pp with breakfast. Unfortunately, tourists are usually given the inside rooms without proper ventilation, but communal cooking facilities are available.

Other places to stay in Vai'ea village are **Chez Floriette Tuheiava** (B.P. 43, Maupiti; tel. 67-80-85), **Pension Eri** (Eri Nohi, tel. 67-81-29), and **Pension Marau** (Tino and Marau Tehahe, tel. 67-81-19), all charging around CFP 4500 pp a night with half board, CFP 5500 with full board.

Fare Pae'ao (Jeannine Tavaearii, B.P. 33, Maupiti; tel. 67-81-01) on Motu Pae'ao is quiet and offers a superb white beach. It's CFP 6000 pp including all meals for a screened two-bedroom bungalow. Reservations are required to ensure a airport pickup (CFP 1000 pp roundtrip) and a room. (In 1962 Kenneth Emory and Yoshiko Sinoto excavated a prehistoric cemetery on Pae'ao and found 15 adzes of six different types, providing valuable evidence for the study of Polynesian migrations.)

Pension Auira (Edna Terai and Richard Tefaatau, B.P. 2, Maupiti; tel. 67-80-26) on Motu Auira, the *motu* opposite Terei'a Beach, has seven thatched bungalows with private bath. The garden variety are CFP 7000 pp a day including all meals; those on the beach are CFP 8000 pp. At those prices you'd expect fans in the rooms, reading lights, beach furniture, and nautical activities, but no such luck. The food is good but the beach could use a cleaning. At night the charming owner's pack of dogs makes a lot of noise and their inevitable excrement attracts flies. Boat transfers from

(top) Bahai'i Temple, Apia, Western Samoa (David Stanley); (bottom) pearl altar in the Church of St. Michael, Rikitea, Mangareva, Gambier Islands, Tahiti-Polynesia (Anselm Zänkert)

(top) Champagne Beach, Espiritu Santo, Vanuatu (David Bowden);
(bottom) Rainmaker Mountain, Tutuila, American Samoa (David Stanley)

the airport are CFP 2000 pp. In sum, Pension Auira is a wonderful experience, but not for everyone.

In addition, there are two small resorts on Motu Tiapa'a. **Pension Papahani** (Vilna Tuheiava, B.P. 1, Maupiti; tel. 67-81-58) has two four-room thatched bungalows at CFP 5000 pp with half board. The three individual bungalows with shared bath at the **Kuriri Village** (Gérard Bede, B.P. 23, Maupiti; tel. 67-82-00) are more expensive at CFP 10,000 pp with full board.

Services

No bank exists on Maupiti, so bring money. The **post office** is at the Mairie. The bakery is in the power plant on the edge of town and baguettes are baked and sold around 1100 and 1500. The island youths hang out here from 1000 on. There's a village disco in Fararuru village Friday and Saturday nights with no cover charge, and canned beer is sold.

Getting There

Air Tahiti has flights to Maupiti from Raiatea (CFP 5500 one-way) and Papeete (CFP 12,400) three times a week. Reconfirm with the Air Tahiti agent (tel. 67-80-20) at the Mairie. Here you board the launch to the airport (CFP 400 pp one-way).

For information on the twice-monthly government supply ship *Meherio III* from Papeete and Raiatea to Maupiti, see "Transportation" in the chapter introduction. The boat returns to Raiatea from Maupiti on the afternoon of the arrival day. The pass into Maupiti is narrow, and when there's a southeast wind it can be dangerous—boats have had to turn back. Ships must enter the channel during daylight, thus the compulsory morning arrival and afternoon (or morning) departure. The coming and going of this ship is a major event in the otherwise unperturbed life of the Maupitians. If you arrive by boat you'll be treated with more respect than if you arrive by plane.

Airport

Like that of Bora Bora, Maupiti's airport (MAU) is on a small *motu*. You must take a launch to the main island (CFP 400).

OTHER LEEWARD ISLANDS

Tupai

Tupai or Motu Iti ("Small Island"), 13 km north of Bora Bora, is a tiny, privately owned coral atoll measuring 1,100 hectares. The facing horseshoe-shaped *motus* enclose a lagoon. Ships must anchor offshore. The few dozen people who live here make copra from coconuts off the 155,000 trees. In 1990 opposition from traditional landowners blocked resort development here by a Japanese corporation and now the entire atoll is up for sale at US$50,000,000 (contact René Boehm, Neuer Wall 2-6, D-20354 Hamburg, Germany; fax 49-40-340568).

Maupihaa

To approach 360-hectare Maupihaa (Mopelia) in stormy weather is dangerous. The unmarked pass into the atoll's lagoon is a mere 10 meters wide and can only be found by searching for the strong outflow of lagoon water at low tide. Cruising yachts often anchor in the lagoon (no fresh water available here).

The notorious German raider *Seeadler* was wrecked on Maupihaa in 1917. Eventually Count Felix von Luckner was able to carry on to Fiji, where he was captured at Wakaya Island. Count von Luckner's journal, *The Sea Devil*, became a best-seller after the war.

In 1983 the pro-independence Pomare Party filed claim to Maupihaa on the ancestral rights of their leader, Joinville Pomare, a descendent of Queen Pomare IV. Party members occupied the atoll, and declared it and neighboring Manuae and Motu One to be an independent state. On Maupihaa they established a successful pearl farm, which attracted the interest of villagers on Maupiti who had claims of their own to the atoll. In 1991 the French colonial government took advantage of the opportunity to play one group of Polynesians against another by granting land concessions on Maupihaa to the Maupiti people, and on 5 September 1992 the eight Pomare pearl farmers were evicted from the atoll by 40 French gendarmes backed by a helicopter and a frigate. A day later settlers from Maupiti arrived on Maupihaa with the blessing of the deceitful French and took over the Pomare's pearl farm.

Manuae

Manuae (Scilly) is the westernmost of the Society Islands. This atoll is 15 km in diameter but totals only 400 hectares. Pearl divers once visited Manuae. In 1855 the three-masted schooner *Julia Ann* sank on the Manuae reef. It took the survivors two months to build a small boat, which carried them to safety at Raiatea.

Motu One

Motu One (Bellingshausen) got its second name from a 19th-century Russian explorer. Tiny 280-hectare Motu One is circled by a guano-bearing reef, with no pass into the lagoon.

THE AUSTRAL ISLANDS

The inhabited volcanic islands of Rimatara, Rurutu, Tubuai, Raivavae, and Rapa, plus uninhabited Maria (or Hull) atoll, make up the Austral group. This southernmost island chain is a 1,280-km extension of the same submerged mountain range as the southern Cook Islands, 900 km northwest. The islands of the Australs seldom exceed 300 meters, except Rapa, which soars to 650 meters. The southerly location makes these islands notably cooler than Tahiti. Collectively the Australs are known as Tuhaa Pae, the "Fifth Part" or fifth administrative subdivision of Tahiti-Polynesia. It's still a world apart from tourism.

History

Excavations carried out on the northwest coast of Rurutu uncovered 60 round-ended houses arrayed in parallel rows, with 14 *marae* scattered among them, demonstrating the presence of humans here as early as A.D. 900. Ruins of *marae* can also be seen on Rimatara, Tubuai, and Raivavae. Huge stone tikis once graced Raivavae, but most have since been destroyed or removed. The terraced mountain fortifications, or *pa,* on Rapa are unique.

The Australs were one of the great art areas of the Pacific, represented today in many museums. The best-known artifacts are sculptured sharkskin drums, wooden bowls, fly whisks, and tapa cloth. Offerings that could not be touched by human hands were placed on the sacred altars with intricately incised ceremonial ladles. European contact effaced most of these traditions and the carving done today is crude by comparison.

Rurutu was spotted by Capt. James Cook in 1769; he found Tubuai in 1777. In 1789 Fletcher Christian and the *Bounty* mutineers attempted to establish a settlement at the northeast corner of Tubuai. They left after only three months, following battles with the islanders in which 66 Polynesians died. The European discoverer of Rapa was Capt. George Vancouver in 1791. Rimatara wasn't discovered until 1813, by the Australian captain Michael Fodger.

English missionaries converted most of the people to Protestantism in the early 19th century. Whalers and sandalwood ships introduced diseases and firearms, which decimated the Austral islanders. The French didn't complete their annexation of the group until 1900. Since then the Australs have gone their sleepy way.

The People

The 6,500 mostly Polynesian inhabitants are fishermen and farmers who live in attractive villages with homes and churches built of coral limestone. The rich soil and temperate climate stimulate agriculture with staple crops such as taro, manioc, Irish potatoes, sweet potatoes, leeks, cabbage, carrots, corn, and coffee. The coconut palm also thrives, except on Rapa. Today many Austral people live in Papeete.

Getting There

Air Tahiti has three flights a week to Rurutu and Tubuai, the only islands with airports. One flight operates Papeete-Tubuai-Rurutu-Papeete, the other two Papeete-Rurutu-Tubuai-Papeete. One-way fares from Tahiti are CFP 17,700 to Rurutu and CFP 19,800 to Tubuai. Rurutu-Tubuai is CFP 8100.

All the other Austral Islands are accessible only by boat. For information on the twice-monthly sailings of the *Tuhaa Pae II* from Papeete, see the "Transportation" section in the "Introduction" to Tahiti-Polynesia.

RURUTU

This island, 572 km south of Tahiti, is shaped like a miniature replica of the African continent. For the hiker, mountainous, 32-square-km Rurutu is a more varied island to visit than Tubuai. Taatioe (389 meters) and Manureva (384 meters) are the highest peaks. A narrow fringing reef surrounds Rurutu, but there's no lagoon. The climate of this northernmost Austral island is temperate and dry. The history of Rurutu revolves around three important dates: 1821, when the gospel arrived on the island; 1970, when Cyclone Emma devastated the three villages; and 1975, when the airport opened.

In January and July Rurutuans practice the ancient art of stone lifting or *amoraa ofai.* Men get three tries to hoist a 130-kg boulder coated with *monoi* (coconut oil) up onto their shoulders, while women attempt a 60-kg stone. Dancing and feasting follow the event. The women of Rurutu weave fine pandanus hats, bags, baskets, fans, lamp shades, and mats. Rurutu's famous Manureva ("Soaring Bird") Dance Group has performed around the world. The main evening entertainment is watching dancers practice in the villages.

Sights

The pleasant main village, Moerai, boasts a post office, four small stores, two bakeries, and two banks. Two other villages, Avera and Hauti, bring the total island population to about 2,000. Electricity functions 24 hours a day. Neat fences and flower gardens surround the coral limestone houses. This is the Polynesia of 50 years ago: though snack bars have appeared, *trucks* have yet to cover the 30-km coastal road. Beaches, waterfalls, valleys, and limestone caves beckon the explorer.

At **Moerai** village lies the tomb of French navigator Eric de Bisschop, whose exploits equaled, but are not as well known as, those of Thor Heyerdahl. Before WW II de Bisschop sailed a catamaran, the *Kaimiloa,* from Hawaii to the Mediterranean via the Indian Ocean and the tip of Africa. His greatest voyage was aboard the *Tahiti Nui,* a series of three rafts, each of which eventually broke up and sank. In 1956 the *Tahiti Nui* set out from Tahiti to Chile to demonstrate the now-accepted theory that the Polynesians had visited South America in prehistoric times. There, two of his four crewmembers abandoned ship, but Eric doggedly set out to return. After a total of 13 months at sea the expedition's final raft foundered on a reef in the Cook Islands and its courageous leader, one of the giants of Pacific exploration, was killed.

RURUTU

Accommodations
The **Hôtel Rurutu Village** (B.P. 6, Moerai; tel. 94-03-92), on a beach just west of the airport, is Rurutu's only regular hotel. The seven tin-roofed bungalows go for CFP 3500 pp, plus CFP 1000 for breakfast and CFP 2500 each for lunch and dinner (if required). Facilities encompass a restaurant, bar, and swimming pool. The hotel owner, Iareta Moeau, is a dance leader and a very nice fellow. He'll rent you his jeep for a spin around the island at CFP 3000, gasoline included.

Some of the inhabitants of Moerai also rent rooms, so ask around. Talk to Metu Teinaore (tel. 94-04-07) in the large white house across the street from Moerai's Protestant church, or Catherine (tel. 94-02-43) in a concrete building behind the same church. At Avera village, ask for Maurice. In a pinch, you could always find somewhere to camp.

Services and Transportation
Banque Socredo is at Moerai.

Scuba diving is offered by the **Te Ava Ma'o Club** (Jacques Duval, B.P. 31, Moerai; tel. 94-02-29).

Unaa Airport (RUR) is at the north tip of Rurutu, four km from Moerai. **Air Tahiti** can be reached at tel. 94-03-57. The supply ship from Papeete ties up at Moerai.

TUBUAI

Ten-km-long by five-km-wide Tubuai, largest of the Australs, is 670 km south of Tahiti. Hills on the east and west sides of this oval 45-square-km island are joined by lowland in the middle; when seen from the sea Tubuai looks like two islands. Mount Taitaa (422 meters) is its highest point. Tubuai is surrounded by a barrier reef; a pass on the north side gives access to a wide turquoise lagoon bordered by brilliant white-sand beaches. Picnics are often arranged on the small reef *motus,* amid superb snorkeling grounds.

The brisk climate permits the cultivation of potatoes, carrots, oranges, and coffee, but other vegetation is sparse. Several *marae* are on Tubuai, but they're in extremely bad condition, with potatoes growing on the sites. The *Bounty* mutineers attempted unsuccessfully to settle on Tubuai in 1789. Mormon missionaries arrived as early as 1844, and today there are active branches of the Church of Latter-day Saints in all the villages. The islanders weave fine pandanus hats, and some woodcarving is done at Mahu.

Most of the 1,900 inhabitants live in Mataura and Taahuaia villages on the north coast, though

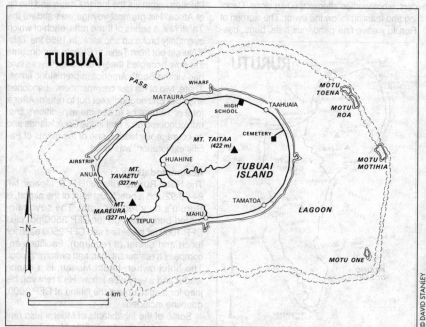

© DAVID STANLEY

houses and hamlets are found all along the 24-km road around the island. A red dirt road cuts right across the middle of Tubuai to Mahu village on the south coast. Mataura is the administrative center of the Austral Islands, and the post office and Banque de Tahiti and Banque Socredo branches are here. *Trucks* haven't reached this island yet.

Accommodations and Food

Chez Taro Tanepau (tel. 95-03-82), by the lagoon near a small beach between Mataura and the wharf, has a two-bedroom house with cooking facilities at CFP 3000 single or double including breakfast (monthly rates available).

In past, **Caroline Chung Tien** (B.P. 94, Mataura; tel. 95-03-46) has rented rooms in her house next to Chung Tien store in Mataura.

In Taahuaia village, two km east of Mataura, **Chez Karine et Tale** (Karine Tahuhuterani, B.P. 34, Mataura; tel. 95-04-52) offers a complete house with cooking facilities at CFP 5000/7000/8500 single/double/triple. Other potential places to stay in Taahuaia include Chez Ah Sing (Fabienne Nibel), Chez Victor Turina (B.P. 7, Mataura; tel. 95-03-27), and Chez Terii Turina (tel. 95-04-98), behind Chez Victor Turina (some of these may no longer be operating).

The **Ermitage Sainte Hélène** (Tihinarii Ilari, B.P. 79, Mataura; tel. 95-04-79) is at Mahu, eight km south of Mataura. There are three quiet houses with cooking facilities, and bicycles are for rent. The Ermitage, named for Napoleon's isle of exile, is a nice place to stay if you don't mind preparing your own meals.

The **Manu Patia Restaurant** at the east end of Mataura has a nice veranda and reasonable prices. The two stores at Mataura bake bread.

Getting There

Tubuai Airport (TUB), in the northwest corner of the island, opened in 1972. **Air Tahiti** (tel. 95-04-76) arrives from Rurutu and Papeete several times a week. Ships enter the lagoon through a passage in the barrier reef on the north side and proceed to the wharf at Mataura. Otherwise, the lagoon is too shallow for navigation.

OTHER AUSTRAL ISLANDS

Rimatara

Without airport, harbor, wharf, hotels, restaurants, bars, and taxis, Rimatara is a place to escape the world. Only a narrow fringing reef hugs Rimatara's lagoonless shore; arriving passengers are landed at Amaru or Mutuaura by whaleboat. It's customary for newcomers to pass through a cloud of purifying smoke from beachside fires. The women of Rimatara make fine pandanus hats, mats, and bags, and shell necklaces. *Monoi* (skin oil) is prepared from gardenias and coconut oil.

This smallest (eight square km) and lowest (83 meters) of the Australs is home to about 1,000 people. Dirt roads lead from Amaru, the main village, to Anapoto and Mutuaura. Several of the inhabitants rent houses to visitors, including Paulette Tematahotoa (tel. 94-42-27) and Rita Hutia (tel. 94-43-09) at Mutuaura, and William Tematahotoa (tel. 94-43-06) at Amaru (all about CFP 2000 a day or CFP 70,000 a month). Water is short in the dry season. Bring food and drink to Rimatara.

Uninhabited Maria (or Hull) is a four-islet atoll 192 km northwest of Rimatara, visited once or twice a year by men from Rimatara or Rurutu for fishing and copra making. They stay on the atoll two or three months, among seabirds and giant lobsters.

Raivavae

This appealing, nine-km-long and two-km-wide island is just south of the tropic of Capricorn, and thus outside the tropics. For archaeology and natural beauty, this is one of the finest islands in Polynesia. Fern-covered Mt. Hiro (437 meters) is the highest point on 16-square-km Raivavae. A barrier reef encloses an emerald lagoon, but the 20 small coral *motus* are all located on the southern and eastern portions of the reef. The tropical vegetation is rich: rose and sandalwood are used to make perfumes for local use.

A malignant fever epidemic in 1826 reduced the people of Raivavae from 3,000 to 120. The present population of around 1,250 lives in four coastal villages, Rairua, Mahanatoa, Anatonu,

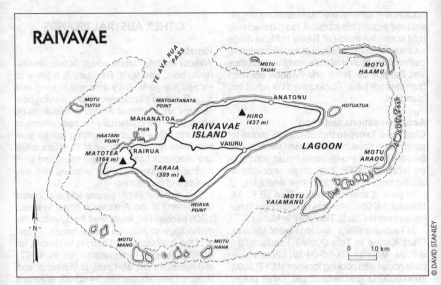

RAIVAVAE

MOTU TAUAI
MOTU HAAMU
TE AVA RUA PASS
MOTU TUITUI
MATOAITANATA POINT
ANATONU
HOTUATUA
MAHANATOA
HIRO (437 m)
HAATANI POINT
PIER
RAIVAVAE ISLAND
LAGOON
MATOTEA (164 m)
RAIRUA
VAIURU
MOTU ARAOO
TARAIA (309 m)
HEIAVA POINT
MOTU VAIAMANU
MOTU MANO
MOTU HAHA
0   10 km
N
© DAVID STANLEY

and Vaiuru, linked by a dirt road. A shortcut route direct from Rairua to Vaiuru crosses a 119-meter saddle, with splendid views of the island. The post office is in Rairua.

Different teams led by Frank Stimson, Don Marshall, and Thor Heyerdahl have explored the ancient temples and taro terraces of Raivavae. Many two- to three-meter-high stone statues once stood on the island, but most have since been destroyed, and two were removed to Tahiti where they can be seen on the grounds of the Gauguin Museum. One big tiki is still standing by the road between Rairua and Mahanatoa villages.

Annie Flores (tel. 95-43-28) runs a two-bedroom guesthouse with cooking facilities next to the *gendarmerie* in Rairua, the main village. The charge is CFP 2000 a day or CFP 35,000 a month for the house. A Chinese shop is nearby, but bring your own bread.

The inhabitants of Raivavae have decided they don't want an airport. If you'll be taking a boat to the Australs anyway, you may as well go to Raivavae, where airborne tourists can't follow! Ships enter the lagoon through a pass on the north side and tie up to the pier at Rairua. A boat calls at the island about every 10-14 days.

Rapa

Rapa, the southernmost point in Tahiti-Polynesia, is one of the most isolated and spectacular islands in the Pacific. Its nearest neighbor is Raivavae, 600 km away. It's sometimes called Rapa Iti (Little Rapa) to distinguish it from Rapa Nui (Easter Island). Soaring peaks reaching 650 meters surround magnificent Haurei Bay, Rapa's crater harbor, the western portion of a drowned volcano. This is only one of 12 deeply indented bays around the island; the absence of reefs allows the sea to cut into the 40-square-km island's outer coasts. Offshore are several sugarloaf-shaped islets. The east slopes of the mountains are bare, while large fern forests are found on the west. Coconut trees cannot grow in the foggy, temperate climate. Instead coffee and taro are the main crops.

A timeworn **Polynesian fortress** with terraces is situated on the crest of a ridge at Morongo Uta, commanding a wide outlook over the steep, rugged hills. Morongo Uta was cleared of vegetation by a party of archaeologists led by William Mulloy in 1956 and is still easily visitable. About a dozen of these *pa* (fortresses) are found above the bay, built to defend the territories of the different tribes of overpopulated ancient Rapa. Today the young men of Rapa organize eight-day bivouacs to hunt wild goats, which range across the island.

During the two decades following the arrival of missionaries in 1826, Rapa's population dropped from 2,000 to 300 due to the introduction of European diseases. By 1851 it was down to just 70, and after smallpox arrived on a Peruvian ship in 1863 it was a miracle that anyone survived at all. The present population of about 550 lives at Area and Haurei villages on the north and south sides of Rapa's great open bay, connected only by boat.

To arrange a stay on Rapa is difficult. Write to Le Maire, Rapa, Îles Australes, four or five months in advance, stating your name, nationality, age, and profession. If you're granted a certificat d'hébergement it means the mayor is willing to arrange room and board for you with a local family, the price to be decided upon your arrival. For example, Tinirau Faraire in Area village rents a house at CFP 3500 a day. Then contact the Subdivision Administrative des Îles Australes, B.P. 82, Mataura, Tubuai (tel. 95-02-26), which may actually grant you a permit to go. The Tuhaa Pae II calls at Rapa every four to six weeks, so that's how long you'll be there.

Marotiri, or the "Bass Rocks," are 10 uninhabited islets 74 km southeast of Rapa. Amazingly enough, some of these pinnacles are crowned with man-made stone platforms and round "towers." One 105-meter-high pinnacle is visible from Rapa in very clear weather. Landing is difficult.

THE TUAMOTU ISLANDS

Arrayed in two parallel northwest-southeast chains scattered across an area of ocean 600 km wide and 1,200 km long, the Tuamotus are the largest group of coral atolls in the world. Of the 78 atolls in the group, 21 have one entrance (pass), 10 have two passes, and 47 have no pass at all. A total of around 12,500 people live on the 45 inhabited islands. Although the land area of the Tuamotus is only 726 square km, the lagoons of the atolls total some 6,000 square km of sheltered water. All are atolls: some have an unbroken ring of reef around the lagoon, while others appear as a necklace of islets separated by channels.

Variable currents, sudden storms, and poor charts make cruising this group by yacht extremely hazardous—in fact, the Tuamotus are popularly known as the Dangerous Archipelago, or the Labyrinth. Wrecks litter the reefs of many atolls. Winds are generally from the east, varying to northeast from November to May and southeast from June to October. A series of hurricanes devastated these islands between 1980 and 1983.

The resourceful Tuamotu people have always lived from seafood, pandanus nuts, and coconuts. They once dove to depths of 30 meters and more, wearing only tiny goggles, to collect mother-of-pearl shells. This activity has largely ceased as overharvesting has made the oysters rare. Today, cultured-pearl farms operate on Ahe, Aratika, Hikueru, Katiu, Kaukura, Manihi, Raroia, South Marutea, Takapoto, Takaroa, Takume, and Taenga. Cultured black pearls (Pinctada margaritifera) from the Tuamotus and Gambiers are world famous.

The scarcity of land and fresh water have always been major problems. Many of these dry, coconut-covered atolls have only a few hundred inhabitants. Though airstrips exist on 12 islands, the isolation has led many Tuamotuans to migrate to Papeete. The only regular hotels are on Rangiroa and Manihi. French military activity has largely closed the eastern Tuamotus to non-French tourism. Beware of eating poisonous fish all across this archipelago.

History
The Tuamotus were originally settled around A.D. 1000 from the Society and Marquesas Islands, perhaps by political refugees. The inhabitants of the atolls frequently warred among themselves or against those of a Society island, and even King Pomare II was unable to conquer the group despite the help of the missionaries and European firearms. After Tahiti came under French "protection" in 1842 the Tuamotus remained independent, and it was not until the

tattooed Tuamotu woman

transformation of the protectorate into a French colony in 1880 that the Tuamotu Islands gradually submitted to French rule. Since 1923 the group has been administered from Papeete. Two-thirds of the people are Catholic, the rest Mormon.

Magellan sighted Pukapuka on the northeast fringe of the Tuamotus in 1521, but it was not until 1835 that all of the islands had been "discovered." On 2 June 1722 a landing was made on Makatea by Roggeveen's men. To clear the beach beforehand, the crew opened fire on a crowd of islanders. The survivors pretended to be pacified by gifts, but the next day the explorers were lured into an ambush by women and stoned, leaving 10 Dutchmen dead and many wounded. Fourteen European expeditions passed the Tuamotus between 1606 and 1816, but only eight bothered to go ashore. Of these, all but the first (Quirós) were involved in skirmishes with the islanders.

Centuries later, a group of Scandinavians under the leadership of Thor Heyerdahl ran aground on Raroia atoll on 7 August 1947, after having sailed 7,000 km from South America in 101 days on the raft *Kon Tiki* to prove that Peruvian Indians could have done the same thing centuries before.

Permission
Due to French military activities connected with nuclear testing in the area, foreigners require special permission to stay on any of the islands south and east of Anaa, especially Hao, Nukutavake, Reao, and Tureia. It's okay to go ashore as a passenger on a through ship, but you must leave again with the ship. Since the *Rainbow Warrior* sinking in 1985 it has been forbidden for non-French to even be aboard a ship when it stops at the military bases at Hao, Moruroa, and Fangataufa. This creates a problem, as Hao is central to the Tuamotus and most ships do call there. Foreigners trying to leave a remote atoll might be sent to Hao! There aren't any ships from Rangiroa, Tikehau, or Manihi to Hao, so those atolls are "safe" for foreigners.

If you do wish to spend time on one of the central or southern Tuamotus, apply at a French embassy a year in advance. Once in Papeete, if you find your ship (to the Marquesas or otherwise) will pass through the forbidden zone, you may require an "Autorisation d'Accès et de Séjour aux Tuamotu-Gambier," available from the Subdivision Administrative des Tuamotu-Gambier (B.P. 34, Papeete; tel. 41-94-14), behind the police station on Ave. Bruat. Take your boat ticket with you. They may send you back to the Police de l'Air et des Frontières, near the tourist office on the harbor or at the airport, and you'll need to know a little French—otherwise forget it. On departure day, get to the boat early enough to allow time for last-minute return visits to the above offices—you never know.

Getting There
Information on the various cargo boats from Papeete is given in the "Transportation" section in the "Introduction" to Tahiti-Polynesia.

RANGIROA

Rangiroa, 200 km northeast of Papeete, is the Tuamotus' most populous atoll and the largest in Polynesia. Its 1,020-square-km aquamarine lagoon is 78 km long, 24 km wide (too far to see), and 225 km around—the island of Tahiti would fit inside its reef. The name Rangiroa means "extended sky." Some 240 *motus* sit on this reef.

What draws people to Rangi (as everyone calls it) is the marinelife in the lagoon. You've never seen so many fish! Deep passages through the atoll's coral ring allow a constant exchange of water between the open sea and the lagoon, creating a most fertile habitat. While lagoons in the Society Islands are often murky due to runoff from the main volcanic islands and pollution from coastal communities, the waters of the Tuamotus are clean and fresh, with some of the best swimming and snorkeling in the South Pacific.

Orientation

Rangiroa's twin villages, each facing a pass 500 meters wide into the lagoon, house 1,400 people. Avatoru village on Avatoru Pass is at the west end of the airport island, about nine km from the airport itself. A paved 20-km road runs east from Avatoru past the airport and the Kia Ora Village Hôtel to Tiputa Pass. Tiputa village is just across the water.

Both villages have small stores; the town hall and *gendarmerie* are at Tiputa, and the health clinic and marine research center at Avatoru. Avatoru has better facilities, but Tiputa is less touristed and offers the chance to escape by simply walking and wading southeast. For yachts, the sheltered Tiputa anchorage by the Kia Ora Village Hôtel is recommended (as opposed to the Avatoru anchorage, which is exposed to swells and chop). Far less English is spoken on Rangiroa than in the Society Islands.

Sports and Recreation

The strong tidal currents *(opape)* through Avatoru and Tiputa passes generate flows of three to six knots. It's exciting to shoot these 30-meter-deep passes on an incoming tide wearing a mask and snorkel, and the hotels offer this activity (CFP 2000-3000) using a small motorboat. The marinelife is fantastic, and sharks are seen in abundance. They're *usually* harmless blacktip or white-tip reef sharks (don't risk touching them even if you see other divers doing so).

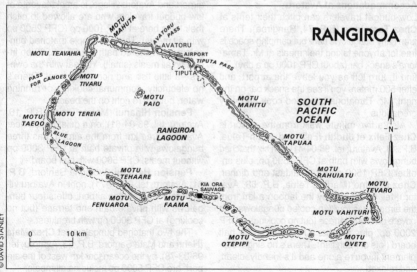

© DAVID STANLEY

Other popular excursions include a picnic to the Blue Lagoon at **Motu Taeoo** (CFP 5000 pp), and tiny mid-lagoon **Motu Paio,** a bird sanctuary (CFP 3500 pp).

Scuba diving is arranged by the friendly **Raie Manta Club** (Yves and Brigette Lefèvre, B.P. 55, Avatoru; tel. 96-04-80, fax 96-05-60), with three branches at Rangiroa: near Rangiroa Lodge in Avatoru village, at Pension Teina et Marie at Tiputa Pass, and at the Kia Ora Village. Diving costs CFP 5000 pp for one tank, including a float through the pass. For regular customers the 11th dive is free. Every dive is different (falling, pass, undulating bottom, hollow, and night), and humphead wrasses, manta rays, barracudas, and lots of sharks are seen. A full-day trip to the Blue Lagoon is CFP 8000 for the boat, diving charges extra. PADI certification courses are offered. Divers come from all parts of the world to dive with Yves and his highly professional team.

The **Centre de Plongée Sous-Marine** (Bernard Blanc, B.P. 75, Rangiroa; tel. 96-05-55, fax 96-05-50), also known as "Rangiroa Paradive," is next to Chez Glorine at Tiputa Pass. Bernard charges CFP 4500 a dive, and he's very obliging and hospitable.

Accommodations at Avatoru

Low-budget travelers can pitch their tents at **Chez Tamatona** (B.P. 74, Rangiroa). There aren't any bungalows here but camping space is free for anyone taking their meals at Mr. Tamatona's snack bar (about CFP 1000 pp a day). To find it, turn left as you leave the airport, and after 500 meters you'll see the snack bar on the right. Mr. Tamatona is a good cook and very gregarious.

Also a five-minute walk from the airport is **Chez Felix et Judith** (Felix and Judith Tetua, B.P. 18, Avatoru; tel. 96-04-41) with six thatched bungalows with bath at CFP 2500 pp, plus another CFP 1500 pp for breakfast and dinner. **Chez Martine** (Martine Tetua, B.P. 68, Avatoru; tel. 96-02-53), by the lagoon a km from the airport, has four fan-cooled bungalows with private bath and terrace (but no cooking) at CFP 2000 pp, plus another CFP 2000 pp for half board (lots of fresh fish). There's no single supplement if you're alone and it's friendly, clean, and relaxed.

The **Raira Lagon** (Bruno and Hinano Chardon, B.P. 87, Avatoru; tel. 96-04-23, fax 96-05-86) near the Rangiroa Beach Club, a km west of the airport, offers five thatched bungalows with private bath and fridge (but no cooking facilities) at CFP 4500 pp with breakfast, CFP 6000 with half board. Nonguests are welcome to order meals here.

About two km from the airport is **Pension Cécile** (Alban and Cécile Sun, B.P. 98, Avatoru; tel. 96-05-06) where the four thatched bungalows with half board are CFP 5000 pp or CFP 3000 for the room only (no cooking). (Reader Rowland Burley writes that "this was the friendliest accommodation I found in Tahiti-Polynesia. Cécile speaks excellent English, the units are spotlessly clean, and dinner is superb.)

In 1994 a new place opened beside the lagoon, two km west of the airport. **Pension Tuanake** (Roger and Iris Terorotua, B.P. 21, Avatoru; tel. 96-04-45) has two thatched bungalows with bath at CFP 6000/8000 pp half/full board. The meals are large enough to make lunch redundant, and camping is possible on the front of the property near the road (separate facilities from the bungalows).

Chez Nanua (Nanua and Marie Tamaehu, B.P. 54, Avatoru; tel. 96-03-88), between the airport and Avatoru village, is an old favorite of low-budget travelers who are allowed to pitch their tents here at CFP 1000 pp (CFP 2500 pp with all meals). The four simple thatched bungalows with shared bath are CFP 3500 pp including all meals (small). You eat with the owners—a little fish and rice every meal. There's no electricity, communal cooking, or running water, but you're right on the beach.

Pension Hinanui (Mareta Bizien, B.P. 16, Avatoru; tel. 96-04-61), on a quiet beach near Avatoru, three km from the airport, has three bungalows with private bath at CFP 3000 pp without meals, CFP 5000 with half board.

Pension Herenui (Victorine Sanford, B.P. 31, Avatoru; tel. 96-04-71), right in Avatoru village, four km from the airport, offers four bungalows with private bath and terrace (but no cooking) at CFP 3000 pp with breakfast.

The two thatched bungalows at **Chez Mata** (Henri and Mata Sanford, B.P. 33, Avatoru; tel. 96-03-78), by the ocean four km west of the airport, are CFP 5000 pp including all meals.

The son of the Nanua mentioned previously operates **Chez Punua et Moana** (Punua and Moana Tamaehu, B.P. 54, Avatoru; tel. 96-04-73) in Avatoru village. The four thatched bungalows with shared bath are CFP 2000 pp, or CFP 3500 pp including all meals. It can be a little noisy due to the activities of the surrounding village. Punua also has eight small huts on Motu Teavahia where you can stay for CFP 3500 pp including all meals, plus CFP 3500 pp for boat transfers. This is the solution for those who really want to get away.

Chez Henriette (Henriette Tamaehu, tel. 96-04-68) by the lagoon in Avatoru village is a four-bungalow place charging CFP 2500 pp for a bed, CFP 5000 with half pension, CFP 6000 full pension. The food is excellent (especially the banana crepes) but it can be a little noisy.

Rangiroa Lodge (Jacques and Rofina Ly, tel. 96-02-13), near the wharf in Avatoru village, has six rooms with shared bath in a main building at CFP 2000 pp (plus CFP 200 for a fan, if desired). This is one of the few places with communal cooking facilities, though the proprietors also prepare meals upon request. The snorkeling just off the lodge is outstanding and they'll loan you gear if you need it. If you book ahead they'll provide free airport transfers.

The **Tuamotel** (Anna Lucas, B.P. 29, Avatoru; tel. 96-02-88), on the airport island back toward Tiputa Pass, has a large bungalow with cooking facilities at CFP 4000 pp.

Pension Teina et Marie (Tahuhu Maraeura, B.P. 36, Avatoru; tel. 96-03-94, fax 96-04-44) at Tiputa Pass has rooms with shared bath upstairs in a concrete house and seven bungalows with private bath at CFP 2000 pp. There are no communal cooking facilities but meals can be ordered. Both Marie and Glorine (see below) prepare meals for nonguests who reserve.

A sister of the Henriette mentioned previously runs the popular **Chez Glorine** (Glorine To'i, tel. 96-04-05), also at Tiputa Pass, five km from the airport. The six thatched bungalows with private bath (cold water) are CFP 5500 pp including all meals (specialty fresh lagoon fish). Bicycle rentals are available.

Accommodations at Tiputa

Chez Lucien (Lucien and Esther Pe'a, B.P. 69, Tiputa; tel. 96-03-55) in Tiputa village offers three traditional bungalows with private bath at CFP 2000 pp for a bed only, or CFP 4000 with half board.

Pension Estall (Ronald Estall, B.P. 13, Tiputa; tel. 96-03-16) also in Tiputa village has four Polynesian-style bungalows with private bath, CFP 5000 pp complete pension.

The **Mihiroa Village** (Maurice Guitteny, no phone), in a coconut grove on Tiputa Island, has four large bungalows with bath at CFP 4500 pp to sleep, or CFP 6000 pp with half board. Boat transfers from the airport are CFP 1000 pp during the day or CFP 2000 pp at night.

Upmarket Hotels

Just west of the airport is the friendly 20-unit **Rangiroa Beach Club** (B.P. 17, Avatoru; tel. 96-03-34), formerly known as "La Bouteille à la Mer." A thatched garden bungalow will set you back CFP 18,000 single, double, or triple, and for CFP 2000 more you can have a beach bungalow. Children under 12 sharing a room with their parents are free. The restaurant serves excellent food (CFP 4500 pp for breakfast and dinner) and the bar functions daily 1200-1400 and 1800-2000 (try one of Lionel's Mai-Tais). The beach here is poor, so protective footwear should be used. Snorkeling and fishing gear are loaned free, and all land and water tours are arranged.

The **Miki Miki Village** (B.P. 5, Avatoru; tel./fax 96-03-83), also known as the Rangiroa Village, is an 11-bungalow resort near Avatoru village: CFP 9200/15,000/19,550 single/double/triple, including breakfast and dinner. Extras are a small "bungalow tax" and CFP 600 pp for airport transfers.

Rangiroa's top resort is the snobbish **Kia Ora Village** (B.P. 1, Tiputa; tel. 96-03-84, fax 96-04-93), established in 1973 near Tiputa Pass, about two km east of the airport by road. The 30 thatched beach bungalows are CFP 32,000/35,000 double/triple with breakfast and dinner CFP 5300 pp extra. Yachties are not especially welcome here. In 1991 the Kia Ora Village began offering accommodation in five A-frame bungalows at "Kia Ora Sauvage" on Motu Avaerahi on the far south side of the lagoon. It's CFP 24,000 a night including all meals, plus CFP 7500 pp for return boat transfers.

The **Village Sans Souci** (Sara Nantz, B.P. 22, Avatoru; tel. 96-03-72) is an escapist's retreat on Motu Mahuta, an islet to the west of Avatoru Pass. The package rates are CFP 7500 pp per night including all meals, with a minimum stay of three nights. The breakfast and desserts offered here are meager and they make you wait until 1930 for dinner. Add CFP 16,000 for return boat transfers from the airport. Despite the price, the 14 thatched bungalows are very simple, with communal shower and toilet stalls (cold water). Scuba diving is possible. It's remarkably overpriced and not recommended.

Services

The Banque de Tahiti has a branch at Avatoru. Banque Socredo has branches in both villages, but the one at the Mairie (town hall) in Tiputa is only open on Monday and Thursday afternoons. **Post offices** are found in Avatoru, Tiputa, and the airport.

Getting There

Air Tahiti (tel. 96-03-41) flies Tahiti-Rangiroa daily (CFP 13,300 one-way). Wednesday and Sunday a flight arrives direct from Bora Bora (CFP 20,700); on Friday it goes back. There's service three times a week from Rangiroa to Manihi (CFP 8600). From Rangiroa to the Marquesas (CFP 25,000), on Saturday there's an ATR 42 flight to Nuku Hiva (46 passengers); the Wednesday flight from Rangiroa to Hiva Oa via Napuka is on a 19-passenger Dornier 228. Seats on flights to the Marquesas should be booked well in advance.

Schooners *(goelettes)* from Papeete (CFP 3000 one-way) take 23 hours to get there from Tahiti, but 72 hours to return (not direct). One cargo boat, the *Dory,* departs Papeete for Rangiroa every Monday at 1300, the most regular connection. To return, ask about the copra boat *Rairoa Nui,* which is supposed to leave Rangiroa Wednesday at 0230 and arrive at Papeete Thursday at 0500 (CFP 3000 including meals and a bunk—men only). For more information on transport to the Tuamotus, see the "Transportation" section in the "Introduction" to Tahiti-Polynesia.

Airport

The airstrip (RGI) is about five km from Avatoru village by road, accessible to Tiputa village by boat. Some of the pensions offer free transfers; others charge CFP 500-1000.

MANIHI

Manihi is the other Tuamotu atoll commonly visited by tourists lured by its white-sand beaches and cultured black pearls. You can see right around the 10-by-22-km Manihi lagoon; Tairapa Pass is at the west end of the atoll. Many of the *motus* are inhabited. The 50,000 resident oysters outnumber the 500 local inhabitants a hundred to one. Due to the pearl industry the people of Manihi are better off than those on the other Tuamotu Islands. The 50 houses of Turipaoa village, shaded by trees and flowers, share a sandy strip across the lagoon from the airstrip.

Accommodations

The **Hôtel Kaina Village Noa Noa** (B.P. 2460, Papeete; tel. 96-42-73, fax 96-42-72), located on the airport *motu* and owned by Air Tahiti, was completely rebuilt in 1995. The 30 overwater bungalows here begin at CFP 23,000 single or double, plus CFP 5600 pp for breakfast and dinner. There's a beachfront swimming pool, floodlit tennis courts, and scuba diving at the Kaina Village.

Pension Le Keshi (Robert and Christine Meurisse, tel. 96-43-13), on Motu Taugaraufara, has seven thatched bungalows with private bath (cold water) at CFP 8000 pp with all meals. Airport transfers are CFP 500 return. Reservations are recommended.

Less expensive lodging may be available with some of the 400 inhabitants of Turipaoa village, but this is uncertain, and Tahitiantourist relations on Manihi have been rather spoiled by upmarket tourism. Unless you're willing to pay the sort of prices just mentioned, it's strongly suggested you pick another atoll.

Getting There

You'll need a boat to go from Manihi airport (XMH) to Turipaoa, which can be expensive unless you've arranged to be picked up. Most Air Tahiti (tel. 96-43-34) flights from Papeete or Bora Bora are via Rangiroa. Boats from Papeete also call here.

OTHER ISLANDS AND ATOLLS

The Japanese-owned Beachcomber Parkroyal hotel chain is building a 40-bungalow resort called Eden Beach on Rangiroa's neighbor, **Tikehau,** so expect to hear a lot more about that almost circular atoll in future. Local residents of Tuterahera village, two km from the airstrip, provide less opulent accommodations with shared cooking facilities at around CFP 2000 pp without meals or CFP 5000 full board. Contact Nini Hoiore (tel. 96-22-70), Colette Huri (tel. 96-22-47), Maxime Metua (tel. 96-22-38), or Habanita Teriiatetoofa (tel. 96-22-48). Scuba diving is available on Tikehau with the **Raie Manta Club** (B.P. 9, Tikehau; tel. 96-22-53).

Makatea is an uplifted atoll with a lunar surface eight km long and 110 meters high. Gray cliffs plunge to the sea. Phosphate was dug up here by workers with shovels from 1917 to 1966 and exported to Japan and New Zealand by a transnational corporation that pocketed the profits. At one time 2,500 workers were present. The mining was abandoned in 1966 but many buildings and a railway remain. Numerous archaeological remains were found during the mining.

Ahe, 13 km west of Manihi, is often visited by cruising yachts, which are able to enter the 16-km-long lagoon. The village is on the southeast side of the atoll. Facilities include two tiny stores, a post office, and a community center where everyone meets at night. Despite the steady stream of sailing boats, the people are very friendly. All of the houses have solar generating panels supplied after a hurricane in the early 1980s. Only a handful of small children are seen in the village; most are away at school on Rangiroa or Tahiti. Many families follow their children to the main islands while they're at school, so you may even be able to rent a whole house. As well as producing pearls, Ahe supplies oysters to the pearl farms on Manihi. A local government boat runs between Ahe and Manihi on an irregular schedule.

In 1972 the private owner of **Taiaro,** Mr. W.A. Robinson, declared the atoll a nature reserve and in 1977 it was accepted by the United Nations as a biosphere reserve. Scientific missions studying atoll ecology sometimes visit Taiaro, the only permanent inhabitants of which are a caretaker family.

The shark-free lagoon at **Niau** is enclosed by an unbroken circle of land. Yachts can enter the lagoon at **Toau,** though the pass is on the windward side. A leper colony once on **Reao** is now closed.

Takapoto and **Takaroa** atolls are separated by only eight km of open sea, and on both the airstrip is within walking distance of the village. On the outer reef near Takaroa's airstrip are two wrecks, one a four-masted sailing ship here since 1906. Due to the fact that all 400 inhabitants of Teavaroa village on Takaroa belong to the Mormon church, their village is often called "little America." Pearl farming is carried out in the Takaroa lagoon, which offers good anchorage. The yachtie log at Takaroa's town hall is a testimony to the splendid character of the atoll's inhabitants. The snorkeling 30 meters across the pass is second to none.

For information on lodging with the inhabitants on Anaa, Arutua, Fakarava, Kaukura, Mataiva, Takapoto, Takaroa, and Tikehau, ask at Tahiti Tourisme in Papeete. Prices average CFP 2000 pp for a room only, or CFP 5000 pp including all meals. All these atolls receive regular Air Tahiti flights from Tahiti and offer a less commercialized environment than heavily promoted Rangiroa and Manihi.

Interisland boats call about once a week, bringing imported foods and other goods and returning to Papeete with fish. If you come by boat, bring along a good supply of fresh produce from the bountiful Papeete market, as such things are in short supply here. It's very difficult to change money on the atolls, so bring enough cash. All the Tuamotu atolls offer the same splendid snorkeling possibilities (take snorkeling gear), though scuba diving is only developed on Rangiroa and Manihi. The advantage of the outer atolls is that the people will be far less impacted by packaged tourism. On these it should be easy to hitch rides with the locals across to *le secteur* (uninhabited *motus*) as they go to cut copra or tend the pearl farms. You don't really need maps or guides to these outer atolls—you'll soon know all you need to know.

THE NUCLEAR TEST ZONE

The nuclear test zone (Centre d'Expérimentations du Pacifique) is at the southeastern end of the Tuamotu group, 1,200 km from Tahiti. The main site is 30-km-long Moruroa atoll, but Fangataufa atoll 37 km south of Moruroa is also being used. In 1962 the French nuclear testing sites in the Algerian Sahara had to be abandoned after that country won its independence, so in 1963 French president Charles de Gaulle announced officially that France was shifting the program to Moruroa and Fangataufa. Between 1966 and 1992 a confirmed 175 nuclear bombs, reaching up to 200 kilotons, were set off in the Tuamotus at the rate of six a year and a cost to French taxpayers of millions of dollars each. By 1974 the French had conducted 44 *atmospheric* tests, 39 over Moruroa and five over Fangataufa.

Way back in 1963, the U.S., Britain, and the USSR agreed in the Partial Test Ban Treaty to halt nuclear tests in the atmosphere. France chose not to sign. On 23 June 1973, the World Court urged France to discontinue the nuclear tests, which might drop radioactive material on surrounding territories. When the French government refused to recognize the court's jurisdiction in this matter, New Zealand Prime Minister Norman Kirk ordered the New Zealand frigate *Otago* to enter the danger zone off Moruroa, and on 23 July Peru broke diplomatic relations with France. On 15 August French commandos boarded the protest vessels *Fri* and *Greenpeace III,* attacking and arresting the crews.

In 1974, with opposition mounting in the Territorial Assembly and growing world indignation, French President Giscard D'Estaing ordered a switch to the *underground* tests. The French forward support base on Hao atoll (population 1,200), 500 km north of Moruroa, allowed the French military to fly materials directly into the area without passing through Faa'a Airport.

On 8 April 1992, as the Greenpeace *Rainbow Warrior II* confronted French commandos off Moruroa, French prime minister Pierre Bérégovoy suddenly announced that nuclear testing was being suspended. President Boris Yeltsin had already halted Russian nuclear testing in October 1991, and in October 1992 U.S. president George Bush followed suit by halting underground testing in Nevada. Despite the French moratorium, the testing facilities were maintained at great expense, and in June 1995 newly elected President Jacques Chirac ordered the testing to resume without bothering to consult the Polynesians.

Chirac is a unpredictable opportunist with a long history of using Pacific islanders as pawns in personal power games. While serving as prime minister in May 1988 he sent French troops to free a group of hostages held by independence activists on the island of Ouvéa in New Caledonia, resulting in a massacre of 19 islanders, several of whom were murdered in cold blood after their capture (see the "The Ouvéa Massacre" under "History" in the New Caledonia chapter introduction for more details). This arrogant man declared that the tests would go ahead despite widespread objections.

On 9 July 1995 the Greenpeace vessel *Rainbow Warrior II* reached Moruroa almost 10 years to the day since its predecessor was sunk by French terrorists at Auckland, New Zealand. Despite opposition from 60% of the French public, on 5 September the French military exploded the first of eight bombs under Moruroa, and during protests at the atoll French commandos seized both the *Rainbow Warrior II* and the MV *Greenpeace,* even though the latter was in international waters. In Papeete thousands of enraged Tahitians ran amok, burning down Faa'a Airport and much of Papeete in the worst rioting ever seen in Polynesia. By declaring that his decision to resume nuclear testing was irreversible and arrogantly disregarding public opinion, Chirac bears personal responsibility for the Papeete disorders and all the unknown future consequences of his dirty little tests.

Moruroa

Obviously, an atoll, with its porous coral cap sitting on a narrow basalt base, is the unsafest place in the world to stage underground nuclear explosions. It's unlikely this was ever considered. Moruroa was chosen for its isolated location, far from major population centers that might be affected by fallout. By 1974, when atmospheric testing had to cease, the French military had a huge investment there. So rather than move to a more secure location in France or elsewhere, they decided to take a chance. Underground testing was to be carried out in Moruroa's basalt core, 500-1,200 meters below the surface of the atoll.

On 10 September 1966 President de Gaulle was present at Moruroa to witness an atmospheric test of a bomb suspended from a balloon. Weather conditions caused the test to be postponed, and the following day conditions were still unsuitable, as the wind was blowing in the direction of inhabited islands to the west instead of toward uninhabited Antarctica to the south. De Gaulle complained that he was a busy man and could afford to wait no longer, so the test went ahead, spreading radioactive fallout across the Cook Islands, Niue, Tonga, Samoa, Fiji, and Tuvalu. Tahiti itself was the most directly affected island, but the French authorities have never acknowledged this fact.

Two serious accidents occurred within weeks of each other in 1979. On 6 July, an explosion and fire in a laboratory bunker on Moruroa killed two people and injured four others. For two weeks after the accident, workers in protective suits tried to clean up the area contaminated with plutonium by the explosion. On 25 July, a nuclear device became stuck halfway down an 800-meter shaft. When the army engineers were unable to move the device, they exploded it where it was, causing a massive chunk of the outer slope of the atoll to break loose. This generated a huge tidal wave, which hit Moruroa, overturning cars and injuring seven people. After the blast, a crack 40 cm wide and two km long appeared on the surface of the island. As a precaution against further tidal waves and hurricanes, refuge platforms were built at intervals around the atoll. For an hour before and after each test all personnel must climb up on these platforms.

Right from the beginning, contaminated debris including scrap metal, wood, plastic, and clothing had carelessly been stored in plastic bags on the north side of the atoll. On 11 March 1981, a hurricane washed large quantities of this nuclear waste into the lagoon and surrounding sea, and that August another storm spread more material from the same dump. Enough radioactive debris to fill 200,000 44-gallon drums is still lying on the north side of the atoll.

By 1981 Moruroa was as punctured as a Swiss cheese and sinking two centimeters after every test, or a meter and a half between 1976 and 1981. With the atoll's 60-km coral rim dangerously fractured by drilling shafts, the French switched to underwater testing in the Moruroa lagoon in 1981, in order to be closer to the center of the island's core. By 1988 the 108 underground blasts had weakened the geological formations beneath Moruroa so severely that French officials announced that henceforth the largest underground tests would take place on nearby Fangataufa atoll, despite the additional cost involved. The military base remained on Moruroa, and small groups of workers and technicians were sent over to Fangataufa every time a test was made there.

The French government claims it owns Moruroa and Fangataufa because in 1964 a standing committee of the Territorial Assembly voted three to two to cede the atolls to France for an indefinite period. This was never ratified by the full assembly, and French troops had occupied the islands before the vote was taken anyway.

Impact

In 1983 the French government invited a delegation of scientists from Australia, New Zealand, and Papua New Guinea to visit Moruroa. Significantly, they were not permitted to take samples from the northern or western areas of the atoll, nor of lagoon sediments. The scientists reported that "if fracturing of the volcanics accompanied a test and allowed a vertical release of radioactivity to the limestones, specific contaminants would, in this worst case, enter the biosphere within five years."

On 21 June 1987 the famous French underwater explorer Jacques Cousteau was present for a test at Moruroa and the next day he took water samples in the lagoon, the first time such independent tests had been allowed. Two samples collected by Cousteau nine km apart contained traces of cesium-134, an isotope with a half-life of two years. Though French officials claimed the cesium-134 remained from atmospheric testing before 1975, a September 1990 *Review of the Calypso Water Samples* by Norm Buske of Search Technical Services (HCR Box 17, Davenport, WA 99122, U.S.A.) has proven that this is not scientifically feasible, and leakage from underground testing is the only possible explanation. In 1990 a computer model of Moruroa developed by New Zealand scientists indicated that radioactive groundwater with a half-life of several thousand years may be seeping through fractures in the atoll at the rate of 100 meters a year and, according to Prof. Manfred Hochstein, head of Auckland University's Geothermal Institute, "in about 30 years the disaster will hit us." In December 1990 Buske found traces of cesium-134 in plankton collected in the open ocean, outside the 12-mile exclusion zone. Buske's findings indicate that the release of contamination into the Pacific from the numerous cracks and fissures has already started, yet despite the 1992 pause in testing, the French government continues its cover-up operations and no independent studies are allowed.

Unlike the U.S., which has paid millions of dollars in compensation money to the Marshallese victims of its nuclear testing program, the French government has refused to even acknowledge the already-apparent effects of its 44 atmospheric tests. From 1963 to 1983, no public health statistics were published. Now the rates of thyroid cancer, leukemia, brain tumors, and stillbirths are on the upswing in Tahiti-Polynesia, and the problem of seafood poisoning (ciguatera) in the nearby Gambier Islands is clearly related. French nonresponse to these first side effects demonstrates vividly how they plan to deal with the more serious environmental consequences yet to come.

The Issue

France is the only nuclear state to have conducted tests *under* a Pacific island. France has not limited itself to testing atomic and hydrogen devices: numerous neutron bombs have also been exploded. The French have always maintained that their tests are harmless and that every precaution has been taken. And yet, such underground tests could be carried out much more effectively, safely, and cheaply in France itself! The claim that the tests are "safe" is disproved by the very choice of the test site, on the opposite side of the globe from their homeland.

French radioactivity will remain in the Tuamotus for thousands of years, and the unknown future consequences of this program are the most frightening part of it. Virtually every South Pacific country has strongly condemned the tests on numerous occasions, and the island people have protested, yet it remains official U.S. government policy not to condemn French nuclear testing in the region. Thus the U.S. must share responsibility with France for this shameful practice. And even with the Cold War over and the need for this type of weaponry gone, little has been done to convert the Partial Test Ban Treaty into a Comprehensive Test Ban Treaty and permanently end all nuclear testing worldwide.

By ordering the resumption of nuclear testing, Jacques Chirac has demonstrated his total disregard for public opinion in the South Pacific and around the world. For him, the islands and their inhabitants are expendable. Thanks to several years of waffling by presidents Mitterrand and Clinton, who failed to irreversibly break the insane chain of nuclear testing when they had the chance, Polynesia is presently being subjected to a new and catastrophic round of environmental terrorism for the glory of France.

THE GAMBIER ISLANDS

The Gambier (or Mangareva) Islands are just north of the tropic of Capricorn, 1,650 km southeast of Tahiti. The archipelago, contrasting sharply with the atolls of the Tuamotus, consists of 10 rocky islands enclosed on three sides by a semicircular barrier reef 65 km long. In all, there are 22 square km of dry land. The Polynesian inhabitants named the main and largest island Mangareva, or "Floating Mountain." Unlike the Marquesas, where the mountains are entirely jungle-clad, the Gambiers have hilltops covered with tall *aeho* grass.

Aside from Mangareva, small groups of people live only on Taravai and Kamaka islands.

Makaroa is a barren, rugged 136-meter-high island. In a cliffside cave on the island of Agakauitai the mummies of 35 generations of cannibal kings are interred. A local seabird, the *karako,* crows at dawn like a rooster.

A dramatic intensification of the ciguatera problem in the Gambiers is believed to be linked to reef damage or pollution originating at the nuclear-testing facilities on Moruroa, 400 km east. During the atmospheric testing series (until 1974), Mangarevans had to take refuge in French-constructed fallout shelters whenever advised by the military. Before each of the 41 atmospheric tests, French warships would evac-

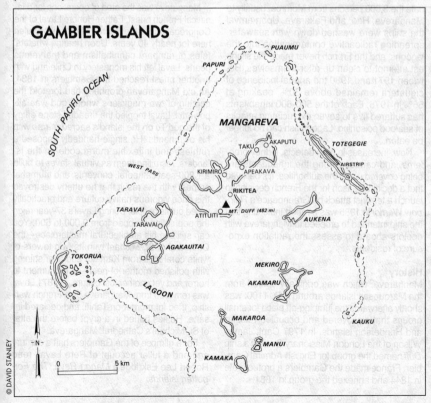

GAMBIER ISLANDS

SOUTH PACIFIC OCEAN

PUAUMU

PAPURI

MANGAREVA

TAKU
AKAPUTU

TOTEGEGIE

AIRSTRIP

WEST PASS

KIRIMIRO
APEAKAVA

RIKITEA

TARAVAI

ATITUITI
MT. DUFF (482 m)

TARAVAI

AUKENA

AGAKAUITAI

TOKORUA

MEKIRO

AKAMARU

LAGOON

MAKAROA

KAUKU

MANUI

KAMAKA

N

0   5 km

© DAVID STANLEY

19th-century sailors
being attacked by
islanders at Mangareva,
Gambier Islands

M.G.L. DOMENY DE RIENZI

uate the 3,000 persons from Moruroa, usually to Mangareva, Hao, and Fakarava. Upon arrival the ships were washed down with seawater, spreading radioactive contamination into the lagoons, and the French never made the slightest attempt to clean up after themselves. Between 1971 and 1980 the annual incidence of ciguatera remained above 30%, peaking at 56% in 1975. Each of the 500-600 inhabitants has suffered five to seven excruciating attacks of seafood poisoning. Lagoon fish can no longer be eaten.

Now, increases in birth defects, kidney problems, and cancer among the inhabitants are being covered up by the authorities. It's believed that a deciding reason for the French decision to launch a terrorist attack on Greenpeace's *Rainbow Warrior* in 1985 was a report indicating that the ship intended to proceed to Mangareva with doctors aboard to assess the radiation exposure of residents.

History

Mangareva, which was originally settled from the Marquesas Islands around A.D. 1100, was shortly afterwards the jumping-off place for small groups that discovered and occupied Pitcairn and Henderson islands. In 1797 Capt. James Wilson of the London Missionary Society's ship *Duff* named the group for English Admiral Gambier. France made the Gambiers a protectorate in 1844 and annexed the group in 1881.

Mangareva was the area of operations for a fanatical French priest, Father Honoré Laval of the Congregation for the Sacred Hearts, who ruled here for nearly 40 years. Upon hearing whalers' tales of rampant cannibalism and marvelous pearls, Laval left his monastery in Chile and with another priest reached the Gambiers in 1834. An old Mangarevan prophecy had foretold the coming of two magicians whose god was all-powerful. Laval toppled the dreaded stone effigy of the god Tu on the island's sacred *marae* with his own hands. He single-handedly imposed a ruthless and inflexible moral code on the islanders, recruiting them as virtual slaves to build a 1,200-seat cathedral, convents, and triumphal arches, with the result that he utterly destroyed this once vigorous native culture and practically wiped out its people. During Laval's 37-year reign the population dropped from 9,000 to 500. You can still see his architectural masterpiece—the Cathedral of St. Michael with its twin towers of white coral rock from Kamaka and altar shining with polished mother-of-pearl—a monument to horror and yet another lost culture. In 1871 Laval was removed from Mangareva by a French warship, tried for murder on Tahiti, and declared insane. He lies buried in a crypt before the altar of St. Michael's Cathedral, Mangareva.

For a glimpse of the Gambiers half a century ago and a fuller account of Père Laval, read Robert Lee Eskridge's *Manga Reva, The Forgotten Islands*.

Orientation

The population of the Gambiers is around 650. Rikitea, on 6.5-by-1.5-km Mangareva, is the main village. A post office, seven small shops, a *gendarmerie,* an infirmary, schools, and a cathedral three times as big as the one in Papeete make up the infrastructure of this administrative backwater.

The tomb of Gregorio Maputeoa, the 35th and last king of Mangareva (died 1868), is in a small chapel behind the church (below the school). On the opposite side of Rikitea is a huge nuclear-fallout shelter built during the French atmospheric testing at Moruroa. Black pearls are cultured on a half dozen platforms on both sides of the Mangareva lagoon. The south coast of Mangareva is one of the most beautiful in Polynesia, with a tremendous variety of landscapes, plants, trees, smells, and colors.

Practicalities

Due to the nearby French nuclear-testing facilities, the entry of foreigners to the Gambier Islands is restricted. For information write: Subdivision Administrative des Tuamotu-Gambiers, B.P. 34, Papeete (tel. 41-94-14). Of course, this is unnecessary if you're French.

There are no hotels, restaurants, or bars at Rikitea, but you can always arrange accommodations with the village people. Madame Duval (tel. 97-82-64) at one of the shops near the wharf can provide a room with hot showers and all meals at CFP 6000 pp. Mr. Jean Anania (nicknamed "Siki") offers speedboat charters and fishing trips.

The airstrip (GMR) is on Totegegie, a long coral island eight km northeast of Rikitea. The expensive, twice-monthly Air Tahiti flight from Papeete (CFP 41,500) is via the huge French military base at Hao, closed to non-French. The monthly supply ship from Papeete, the *Ruahutu,* also travels via Hao. The flights are scheduled in such a way that you can stay either one week or three weeks in the Gambiers.

THE MARQUESAS ISLANDS

The Marquesas Islands are the farthest north of the high islands of the South Pacific, on the same latitude as the Solomons. Though the group was known as Te Fenua Enata ("The Land of Men") by the Polynesian inhabitants, depopulation during the 19th and 20th centuries has left many of the valleys empty. Ten main islands form a line 300 km long, roughly 1,400 km northeast of Tahiti, but only six are inhabited today: Nuku Hiva, Ua Pou, and Ua Huka in a cluster to the northwest, and Hiva Oa, Tahuata, and Fatu Hiva to the southeast. The administrative centers, Atuona (Hiva Oa), Hakahau (Ua Pou), and Taiohae (Nuku Hiva), are the only places with post offices, banks, gendarmes, etc. The total population is just 7,500.

The expense and difficulty in getting there has kept most potential visitors away. Budget accommodations are scarce and public transport is nonexistent, which makes getting around a major expense unless you're really prepared to rough it. Of the main islands, Hiva Oa is appreciably cheaper than Nuku Hiva, and getting to town from Hiva Oa airport is much easier. Cruising yachts from California often call at the Marquesas on their way to Papeete, even though ocean swells reaching the shorelines make the anchorages rough. This is paradise, however, for surfers and hikers. Multitudes of waterfalls tumble down the slopes, and eerie overgrown archaeological remains tell of a golden era long gone. If you enjoy quiet, unspoiled places, you'll like the Marquesas, but one month should be enough. The Marquesas have been left behind by their remoteness.

The Land

These wild, rugged islands feature steep cliffs and valleys leading up to high central ridges, sectioning the islands off into a cartwheel of segments, which creates major transportation difficulties. Reefs don't form due to the cold south equatorial current. The absence of protective reefs has prevented the creation of coastal plains, so no roads go around any of the islands. Most of the people live in the narrow, fertile river valleys. The interiors are inhabited only by hundreds of wild horses, cattle, and goats, which have destroyed much of the original vegetation. A Catholic bishop introduced

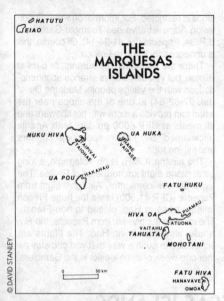

THE
MARQUESAS
ISLANDS

NUKU HIVA *UA HUKA*

UA POU *FATU HUKU*

HIVA OA *PUAMAU*
VAITAHU *ATUONA*
TAHUATA
MOHOTANI

© DAVID STANLEY

0   50 km

FATU HIVA
HANAVAVE
OMOA

the horses from Chile in 1856, and today they're almost a symbol of the Marquesas. The islands are abundant with lemons, tangerines, oranges, grapefruit, bananas, mangoes, and papayas. Taro and especially breadfruit are the main staples. Birdlife is rich, and the waters around the Marquesas teem with lobster, fish, and sharks.

The subtropical climate is hotter and drier than that of Tahiti. July and August are the coolest months. The deep bays on the west sides of the islands are better sheltered for shipping, and the humidity is lower there than on the east sides, which catch the trade winds. The precipitation is uneven, with drought some years, heavy rainfall the others. The southern islands of the Marquesas (Hiva Oa, Tahuata, Fatu Hiva) are green and humid; the northern islands (Nuku Hiva, Ua Huka, Ua Pou) are brown and dry.

Pre-European Society

Marquesan houses were built on high platforms *(paepae)* scattered through the valleys (still fairly easy to find). Each valley had a ceremonial area *(tohua)* where important festivals took place. Archaeologists have been able to trace stone temples *(meae,* called *marae* elsewhere in

Tahiti-Polynesia), agricultural terraces, and earthen fortifications *(akaua)* half hidden in the jungle, evocative reminders of a vanished civilization. Then as now, the valleys were isolated from one another by high ridges and turbulent seas, yet warfare was vicious and cannibalism an important incentive. An able warrior could attain great power. Local hereditary chiefs exercised authority over commoners.

The Marquesans' artistic style was one of the most powerful and refined in the Pacific. The ironwood war club was their most distinctive symbol, but there were also finely carved wooden bowls, fan handles, and tikis of stone and wood, both miniature and massive. The carvings are noted for the faces: the mouth with lips parted and the bespectacled eyes. Both men and women wore carved ivory earplugs. Men's entire bodies were covered by bold and striking tattoos, a practice banned by the Catholic missionaries. Stilts were used by boys for racing and mock fighting. This was about the only part of Polynesia where polyandry was common. There was a strong cult of the dead: the bodies or skulls of ancestors were carefully preserved. Both Easter Island (around A.D. 500) and Hawaii (around A.D. 700) were colonized from here.

European Contact

The existence of these islands was long concealed from the world by the Spanish, to prevent the English from taking possession of them. The southern group was found by Álvaro de Mendaña in July 1595 during his second voyage of exploration from Peru. He named them Las Marquesas de Mendoza after his benefactor, the Spanish viceroy. The first island sighted (Fatu Hiva) seemed uninhabited, but as Mendaña's *San Jerónimo* sailed nearer, scores of outriggers appeared, paddled by about 400 robust, light-skinned islanders. Their hair was long and loose, and they were naked and tattooed in blue patterns. The natives boarded the ship, but when they became overly curious and bold, Mendaña ordered a gun fired, and they jumped over the side.

Then began one of the most murderous and shameful of all the white explorers' entries into the South Pacific region. As a matter of caution, Mendaña's men began shooting natives on sight, in one instance hanging three bodies in the shore camp on Santa Cristina (Tahuata) as a warning. They left behind three large crosses, the date cut in a tree, and over 200 dead Polynesians.

The northern Marquesas Islands were "discovered" by Joseph Ingraham of the American trading vessel *Hope* on 19 April 1791. After that, blackbirders, firearms, disease, and alcohol reduced the population. American whalers called frequently from 1800 onwards. Although France took possession of the group in 1842, Peruvian slavers kidnapped some Marquesans to South America in 1863 to work the plantations and mines. Those few who returned brought a catastrophic smallpox epidemic. The Marquesans clung to their warlike, cannibalistic ways until 95% of their number had died—the remainder adopted Catholicism. (The Marquesas today is the only island group of Tahiti-Polynesia with a Catholic majority.) From 80,000 at the beginning of the 19th century, the population fell to about 15,000 by 1842, when the French "protectors" arrived, and to a devastated 2,000 by 1926.

Getting There

A visit to the Marquesas requires either lots of money or lots of time, or both. An **Air Tahiti** 46-seat ATR 42 flies from Papeete to Nuku Hiva four times a week (four hours, CFP 37,800). Two of the ATR 42 flights are via Hiva Oa, another via Rangiroa. There are also weekly Dornier 228 flights from Rangiroa to Hiva Oa via Napuka in the Tuamotus (CFP 25,000), but the plane is always full. Stopovers on Napuka cost CFP 19,000 extra!

Dornier flights between Nuku Hiva and Ua Huka and Ua Pou operate weekly, connecting with one of the ATR 42 flights from Papeete. Fares from Nuku Hiva are CFP 5000 to Ua Pou, CFP 5000 to Ua Huka, and CFP 8600 to Atuona. No flight goes straight from Ua Pou to Ua Huka—you must backtrack to Nuku Hiva. (Ua Huka airport was closed in 1994, so check.) Get a through ticket to your final destination, as flights to Nuku Hiva, Hiva Oa, Ua Pou, and Ua Huka are all the same price from Papeete. Tahu-

ata and Fatu Hiva are without air service. All flights are heavily booked.

Three ships, the *Aranui, Tamarii Tuamotu,* and *Taporo V,* sail monthly from Papeete, calling at all six inhabited Marquesas Islands. The *Aranui* and *Taporo V* are the easiest to use, as they follow a regular schedule and no special permission is required. To come on the *Tamarii Tuamotu* you may have to go through the procedure described under "Permission" in the introductory pages of the Tuamotu section above.

The freighter *Aranui* is the more convenient and comfortable, if you can afford it. The roundtrip voyages designed for tourists flown in from Europe and the U.S. cost cruise-ship prices (from US$1560 return on deck). See the "Transportation" section in the "Introduction" to Tahiti-Polynesia for details. The other main interisland boat, *Taporo V,* is cheaper at CFP 17,000 deck one-way to Hiva Oa, but it's basic. Food is included in the passages and it's not necessary to reserve deck passage on these boats. The ships tie up to the wharves at Taiohae, Atuona, Vaipaee, and Hakahau; at Tahauta and Fatu Hiva, passengers must go ashore by whaleboat. In stormy weather, the landings can be dangerous.

NUKU HIVA

Nuku Hiva is the largest (339 square km) and most populous (2,250 inhabitants) of the Marquesas. In 1813 Capt. David Porter of the American raider *Essex* annexed Nuku Hiva for the United States, though the act was never ratified by Congress. Porter built a fort at the present site of Taiohae, which he named Madisonville for the U.S. president of his day. Nothing remains of this or another fort erected by the French in 1842. Sandalwood traders followed Porter, then whalers. Herman Melville's *Typee,* written after a one-month stay in the Taipivai Valley in 1842, is still the classic narrative of Marquesan life during the 19th century.

the priest Taawattaa as seen by American explorer Capt. David Porter at Nuku Hiva in 1812

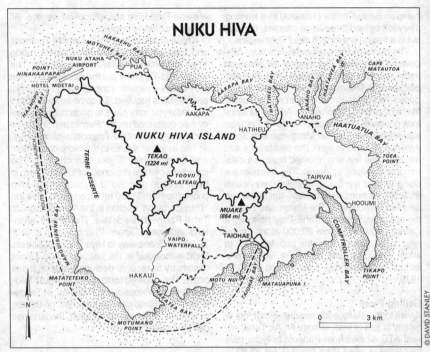

NUKU HIVA

© DAVID STANLEY

Taiohae (population 1,500) on the south coast is the administrative and economic center of the Marquesas. It's a modern little town with a post office, a hospital, a town hall, a bank, five grocery stores, and street lighting. Winding mountain roads lead northeast from Taiohae to Taipivai and Hatiheu villages, where a few dozen families reside. In the center of the island Mt. Tekao (1,224 meters) rises above the vast, empty Toovii Plateau.

Though open to the south, Taiohae's deep harbor offers excellent anchorage, and cruising yachts are often seen here. A nominal "water fee" is charged (don't take on water if it's been raining). Take care with the drinking water at Taiohae. (One reader suggested that yachts should take on clean spring water at Hakatea Bay, although an extension tube would be necessary.)

Sights

Vestiges of an **old prison** can still be seen in Taiohae. Many stone- and woodcarvers continue to work on Nuku Hiva, making wooden tikis, bowls, ukuleles, ceremonial war clubs, etc. Some items are on display at the Banque Socredo. Other woodcarvings may be viewed in the **Catholic cathedral** (1974) at Taiohae. Ask to see the small collection of artifacts at the bishop's residence.

For a good view of Taiohae Bay, hike up to **Muake** (864 meters) on the Taipivai road. From there lifts are possible with market gardeners headed for the agricultural station on the **Toovii Plateau** to the west.

Taipivai is a five-hour, 17-km walk from Taiohae. Herman Melville spent a month here, with his tattooed sweetheart Fayaway, in 1842. In his novel, *Typee* (his spelling for Taipi), he gives a delightful account of the life of the great-grandparents of the present forlorn and decultured inhabitants. The huge *tohua* of Vahangekua at Taipivai is a whopping 170 by 25 meters. Great stone tikis watch over the *meae* of Paeke, also near Taipivai. Vanilla grows wild. At **Hooumi,** a fine protected bay near Taipivai, is a truly magical little church.

Above **Hatiheu** on the north coast, 29 km from Taiohae, are two more tikis and a reconstructed *meae*. **Anaho,** 45 minutes east of Hatiheu on foot, is one of the most beautiful of Nuku Hiva's bays, with a fine white beach and good snorkeling. Unfortunately, it's infested with *nono* and midge sand flies that give nasty bites (a common problem on this island). Even better white-sand beaches face Haatuatua and Haataivea bays beyond Anaho. No one lives there, though wild horses are seen.

At Hakaui, west of Taiohae, a river runs down a steep-sided valley. Fantastic 350-meter **Vaipo Waterfall,** highest in the territory, drops from the plateau at the far end of the valley, four km from the coast. It's a two-hour walk from Hakaui to the waterfall with a few thigh-high river crossings after rains (guide not required). The trail passes many crumbling platforms, indicating that the valley was once well populated. If you swim in the pool at the falls beware of falling pebbles. A boat from Taiohae to Hakaui would cost CFP 12,500 and up return, but an overgrown switchback trail also crosses the 535-meter ridge from Taiohae to Hakaui. You'll need to be adventurous and good at finding your own way to follow it (allow eight hours each way).

Sports and Recreation

Scuba diving is offered by Xavier Curvat's **Centre Plongée Marquises** (B.P. 100, Taiohae; tel. 92-00-88). Xavier has explored the archipelago thoroughly during his 15 years in the Marquesas and his local knowledge is unequaled. One-week catamaran tours with him can be booked through Ocean Voyages in California (see "Getting There" in the main Introduction). Though there's no coral to be seen here, the underwater caves and spectacular schools of hammerhead sharks compensate.

Horseback riding is offered by Sabine and Louis Teikiteetini (B.P. 171, Taiohae), who can be contacted locally through Nuku Hiva Town Hall. Rides from Taiohae to Taipivai are possible.

Accommodations in Taiohae

The least expensive place is **Chez Fetu** (Cyprien Peterano, B.P. 22, Taiohae; tel. 92-03-66), on a hill behind Kamake Store, a five-minute walk from the wharf in Taiohae. The three bungalows with private bath, kitchen, and terrace cost CFP 2000/4000/5000 single/double/triple, or CFP 50,000 a month.

The **Hôtel Moana Nui** (Charles Nombaerts, B.P. 9, Taiohae; tel. 92-03-30, fax 92-00-02), in the middle of Taiohae, has seven rooms with private bath above their restaurant/bar. Bed and breakfast is CFP 3000/3500 single/double, other meals CFP 2500 each. Cars, scooters, and bicycles are for rent.

In 1993 the **Nuku Hiva Village Noa Noa** (Bruno Gendron, B.P. 82, Taiohae; tel. 92-01-94, fax 92-05-97) opened in Taiohae village with 15 thatched *fares* with private bath arrayed along the west side of Taiohae Bay opposite the yacht anchorage. The rates are CFP 6500/7500/8500 single/double/triple, plus CFP 3500 pp a day for breakfast and dinner. Excursions by 4WD, horseback riding, and scuba diving can be arranged.

The **Keikahanui Inn** (B.P. 21, Taiohae; tel. 92-03-82, fax 92-00-74), just beyond the Nuku Hiva Village, is owned by American yachties Rose and Frank Corser (ask to see Maurice's logbooks). They have five screened Polynesian bungalows with private bath: CFP 8500/12,000/14,000 single/double/triple. For breakfast and dinner, add CFP 3500 pp. You can buy Fatu Hiva tapa at the inn.

Accommodations around the Island

The **Hôtel Moetai Village** (Guy Millon, tel. 92-04-91) near Nuku Ataha Airport has five bungalows with private bath (cold water): CFP 2500/3500/4500 single/double/triple for bed and breakfast, other meals CFP 2500.

At Taipivai village, **Chez Martine Haiti** (B.P. 60, Taiohae; tel. 92-01-19) has two bungalows with private bath at CFP 2000 pp, or CFP 4000 pp with half board. You could also camp on Taipivai's football field (ask).

In Hatiheu village, **Chez Yvonne Katupa** (B.P. 199, Taiohae; tel. 92-02-97) offers five bungalows without cooking facilities or hot water at CFP 1800 pp, breakfast included. A small restaurant nearby serves fried fish for CFP 1500, lobster for CFP 2500. Also at Hatiheu, ask if Clarisse Omitai still provides accommodations.

You can also stay on the white-sand beach at Anaho Bay, two km east of Hatiheu on horse or foot. **Pension Anaho** (Léopold and Louise Vaianui, B.P. 202, Taiohae; tel./fax 92-04-25) consists of a three-room house with cooking facilities and two bungalows at CFP 2000 pp, meals available. Or ask if Marie Foucaud at Anaho still rents bungalows.

An English reader wrote in recommending **Daniel's Place** on a white beach in Hakatea Bay near the trail to Vaipo Falls: "basic facilities but a stunning setting."

Buying and Selling
Get bread at Ropa's Bakery and supplies from Maurice McKitrick's store. Yachties who figure they'll need fuel when they get to the Marquesas should write a letter to Maurice c/o the Keikahanui Inn and ask him to order an extra drum or two from Papeete. Things to bring to trade with the locals include perfume, earrings, reggae tapes, T-shirts, and surfing magazines, for which you'll receive tapas, tie-dyed pareus, and all the fruit you can carry. A small crafts center is on the ocean side near Maurice's store. War clubs, wooden bowls, and ukuleles are the most popular items.

Services and Information
Taiohae has a Banque Socredo branch. Tourist information is mailed out by the **Syndicat d'Initiative** (Debora Kimitete, B.P. 23, Taiohae).

Don't have your mail sent c/o poste restante at the local post office as it will be returned via surface after 15 days. Instead have it addressed c/o the Keikahanui Inn, B.P. 21, Taiohae, Nuku Hiva. From 1600-1800 you can also receive telephone calls and faxes through the inn (tel. 92-03-82, fax 92-00-74), but remember that the Corsers are running a restaurant and your patronage will be appreciated.

Getting Around
There are no *trucks* from Taiohae to other parts of the island, though you can hitch fairly easily. Island tours by Land Rover or speedboat can be arranged, but get ready for some astronomical charges (for example, CFP 15,000 for a visit to Hatiheu). Most car rentals are with driver only and thus cost taxi prices. To rent a car without driver for something approaching normal prices, ask at the **Hôtel Moana Nui** (tel. 92-03-30) or check with Alain Bigot (tel. 92-04-34).

Airport
Nuku Ataha Airport (NHV) is in the Terre-Déserte at the northwest corner of Nuku Hiva, 53 km from Taiohae along a twisting dirt road over the Toovii Plateau (two hours). A restaurant and hotel are near the terminal. The main drawback to flying into Nuku Hiva is the cost of airport transfers, which run CFP 3000 each way by 4WD vehicle by day (CFP 5000 pp by night), or CFP 6900 pp each way by helicopter (10 minutes). At last report, the boat service between Taiohae and the airport wasn't operating. The **Air Tahiti** number is tel. 92-03-41.

HIVA OA

Measuring 40 by 19 km, 315-square-km Hiva Oa (population 1,750) is the second largest of the Marquesas. Mount Temetiu (1,276 meters) towers above Atuona to the west. The administrative headquarters for the Marquesas group has switched back and forth several times: Taiohae was the center until 1904, then it was Atuona until 1944, when Taiohae once more took over. The town may be the center of the southern cluster of the Marquesas, but it's quieter still than Taiohae. The Marquesas Festival of Arts takes place in Atuona every December.

Atuona was made forever famous when Paul Gauguin came to live here in 1901. Despite the attentions of his 14-year-old mistress, Vaeoho, he died of syphilis a year later at age 55 and is buried in the cemetery above the town. When Tioka, Gauguin's neighbor, found him stretched out with one leg hanging over the side of his bed, he bit him on the head as the Marquesans do to see if he really was dead. No, there was no doubt. *"Ua mate Koke!"* he cried, and disappeared. Gauguin was constantly in conflict with the colonial authorities, who disapproved of his heavy drinking sessions with the locals. Just a week before his death, Gauguin was summarily convicted of "libel of a gendarme in the course of his official duties," fined, and sentenced to three months in prison.

The famous Belgian *chanson* singer Jacques Brel and his companion Maddly Bamy came to the Marquesas aboard his 18-meter yacht, the *Askoy II,* in 1975. Jacques decided to settle at Atuona and sold his boat to an American couple. Maddly, who had been a dancer on her native Guadeloupe, gave dancing lessons to the local girls, while Jacques ran an open-air cinema. His plane, nicknamed *Jojo,* was kept at Hiva Oa airport for trips to Papeete, 1,500 km south-

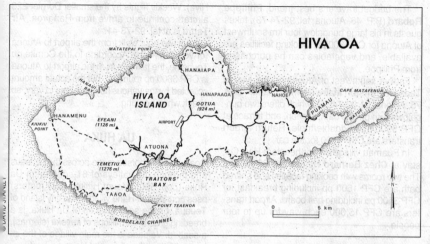

west. The album *Brel 1977* on the Barclay label includes one of his last songs, "Les Marquises." In 1978, chain-smoker Brel died of lung cancer and was buried in Atuona cemetery near Gauguin.

Sights

Gauguin's thatched "Maison du Jouir" (House of Pleasure) has been reconstructed next to the museum in central Atuona. The view of Atuona from the **graveyard** is good (take the first left fork in the road as you climb the hill from the *gendarmerie),* but the beach at Atuona is poor. A **lighthouse** on the point looks across Taaoa, or "Traitors'," Bay. Polynesian ruins may be found up the Vaioa River, just west of Atuona.

For better swimming, take the road five km south along the bay to **Taaoa**. A big *meae* (temple) is found a kilometer up the river from there.

A second village, **Puamau,** is on the northeast coast, 40 km from Atuona over a winding road. It's a good eight-hour walk from Atuona to Puamau, up and down all the way. Five huge stone tikis and Meae Takaii can be seen in the valley behind Puamau, a 10-minute walk from Chez Bernard. One stands over two meters high.

At **Hanaiapa**, ask for William, who keeps a yachties' log. He's happy to have his infrequent visitors sign and is generous with fresh fruit and vegetables. **Hanamenu** in the northwest corner of Hiva Oa is now uninhabited, but dozens of old stone platforms can still be seen. If you'd like to spend some time here as a hermit, ask for Ozanne in Atuona, who has a house at Hanamenu he might be willing to rent. To the right of Ozanne's house is a small, crystal-clear pool.

Accommodations

Pension Gauguin (André Teissier, B.P. 34, Atuona; tel. 92-73-51) in central Atuona consists of a two-story house with four rooms downstairs, a common room and kitchen upstairs (CFP 5000/9000 single/double with half board).

The **Temetiu Village** (Gabriel Heitaa, B.P. 52, Atuona; tel. 92-73-02) overlooking Takauku Bay, near of Atuona on the way to the airport, has three bungalows with bath (cold water) at CFP 5000/9000 single/double with half pension. Airport transfers at both of the above are CFP 2000 pp return.

Atuona's upmarket place, the **Motel Hanakee Noa Noa** (Serge Lecordier, B.P. 57, Hiva Oa; tel. 92-71-62, fax 92-72-51), has five stylish A-frame bungalows on the hillside toward the airport at CFP 12,000/18,000/20,000 single/double/triple. Breakfast and dinner are CFP 3200 pp extra, airport transfers CFP 3600 pp return. Each bungalow contains a TV, VCR, washing machine, kitchen, and bathtub.

Also ask if Jean Saucourt (tel. 92-73-33) at Atuona is still renting his bungalow with cooking facilities.

The budget traveler's best friend, **Philippe Robard** (B.P. 46, Atuona; tel. 92-74-73), takes guests in his large bungalow four km southwest of Atuona for CFP 800 pp. Cooking facilities are available, and vegetables can be purchased from Philippe.

Farther southwest of Atuona on the way to Taaoa is **Pension Maire** (Roméo Ciantar, B.P. 75, Atuona; tel. 92-74-55), which offers two bungalows with private bath, kitchen, and terrace at CFP 5500/6500 double/triple. Return airport transfers are CFP 4500 for the car.

In Puamau village on northeastern Hiva Oa, stay at **Chez Bernard Heitaa** (tel. 92-72-27). The two rooms with cooking facilities and shared bath are CFP 1500 pp including breakfast, or CFP 3500 pp including half board. Airport transfers are CFP 15,000 each way for up to four people.

Services and Information
Banque Socredo is next to the post office and town hall at Atuona. The *gendarmerie* is diagonally opposite.

The Hiva Oa Visitors Bureau (B.P. 62, Hiva Oa; tel./fax 92-75-10) is at the local museum.

Yachting Facilities
Yachts anchor behind the breakwater in Tahauku Bay, two km east of the center of town. The copra boats also tie up here. A shower stall and laundry tub are provided on the wharf, and there's plenty of good water. Of the five small stores in Atuona, only Duncan's (the blue one) sells propane; diagonally across the street from Duncan's is a hardware store. Yachties should stock up on fresh vegetables at Atuona.

Getting Around
Renting a four-passenger Land Rover from Atuona to Puamau will run you CFP 20,000. Inquire at Atuona Town Hall. Roméo Ciantar (tel. 92-74-55) and Location David (Augustine Kaimuko, tel. 92-72-87) also rent cars.

Airport
The airstrip (AUQ) is on a 441-meter-high plateau, 13 km northeast of Atuona. In 1991 the runway was upgraded to allow it to receive direct ATR 42 flights from Papeete (via Nuku

Hiva). Weekly flights by the smaller Dornier 228 aircraft continue to arrive from Rangiroa. **Air Tahiti** is at tel. 92-73-41.

It's a two-hour walk from the airport to Atuona (or you can hitch). According to the Comité du Tourisme, the taxi fare from the airport to Atuona is CFP 3600 pp roundtrip, but the actual amount collected by the various hotels seems to vary, so check when booking.

UA HUKA

Goats and wild horses range across the plateaus and through the valleys of 81-square-km Ua Huka (pop. 550). Mount Hitikau (884 meters) rises northeast of Hane village. The tiny island of Teuaua, off the southwest tip of Ua Huka, is a breeding ground for millions of *kaveka* (sternas), a seabird. Vaipaee is the main village of the island, although the clinic is at Hane.

Archaeological excavations by Prof. Y.H. Sinoto in 1965 dated a coastal site on Ua Huka to A.D. 300, which makes it the oldest in Tahiti-Polynesia; two pottery fragments found here suggest that the island was probably a major dispersal point for the ancient Polynesians. Small tikis may be visited in the valley behind Hane. The botanical garden in Hane is also worth a look. In Vaipaee is a small **museum** of local artifacts and seashells, the only museum in the Marquesas. Woodcarvers are active in the village.

Accommodations
Chez Alexis (Alexis Scallamera, tel. 92-60-19) in Vaipaee village, seven km from the airport, is a four-room house with shared bath at CFP 1500 pp, or CFP 4000 with full board. Return airport transfers are CFP 1500 for the car. Alexis can arrange horseback riding and boat excursions.

Also in Vaipaee, ask if Laura Raioha (tel. 92-60-22), nicknamed "Tati Laura," and Miriama Fournier still rent rooms with cooking facilities.

A more isolated place to stay is **Chez Joseph Lichtle** (tel. 92-60-72) at Haavei Beach, 15 minutes west of Vaipaee by boat (CFP 2500 pp return). It's also possible to hike here along a rough track. There's a white sandy beach with good swimming, and no other families live here.

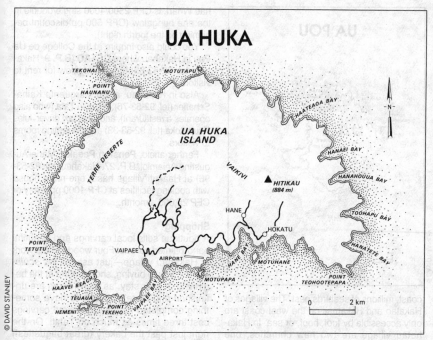

UA HUKA

UA HUKA ISLAND

TEKOHAI
MOTUTAPU
POINT HAUNANU
HAATEAOA BAY
TERRE DESERTE
HANAEI BAY
VAIKIVI
HANAHOUUA BAY
HITIKAU (884 m)
HANE
HOKATU
TOOHAPU BAY
POINT TETUTU
VAIPAEE
AIRPORT
HANE BAY
MOTUHANE
HANATETE BAY
HAAVEI BEACH
MOTUPAPA
POINT TEOHOOTEPAPA
TEUAUA
POINT TEKEHO
HEMENI
VAIPAEE BAY

© DAVID STANLEY

0   2 km

-N-

The pension consists of two bungalows with bath and two houses with two or three rooms at CFP 1500 pp, or CFP 4500 with full board. Communal cooking facilities should also be available. Joseph and Laura are reputedly the best cooks in the Marquesas, and their son Leon, mayor of Ua Huka, is extremely helpful. You can also rent a horse from Joseph.

In Hane village, the **Auberge Hitikau** (Céline Fournier, tel. 92-60-68) offers four rooms with shared bath in a concrete building (no cooking) at CFP 2000/3000 single/double. Food is available at their restaurant.

Ask if Madame Vii Fournier of Hane is still renting rooms in her two-bedroom house with cooking facilities.

Also worth checking is **Chez Maurice et Delphine** (Maurice and Delphine Rootuehine, tel. 92-60-55) at Hokatu village, where rooms in a three-bedroom house with shared bath and kitchen are CFP 1000 pp (CFP 3000 with all meals).

Getting There

The airstrip (UAH) is on a hilltop between Hane and Vaipaee, closer to the latter. (At last report this airport was closed, so check.) Ships tie up to a wharf at Vaipaee.

UA POU

This island lies about 40 km south of Nuku Hiva. Several jagged volcanic plugs loom behind Hakahau, the main village on the northeast coast of 120-square-km Ua Pou. One of these sugarloaf-shaped mountains inspired Jacques Brel's song, "La Cathédrale." Mount Oave (1,203 meters), highest point on Ua Pou, is often cloud-covered. The population of 2,000 is almost the same as Nuku Hiva's. In 1988, 500 French foreign legionnaires rebuilt the breakwater at Hakahau, and yachts can now tie up to the concrete pier.

A track goes right around the island. The road leads south from Hakahau to a beach beyond Hohoi. On 112-meter-high Motu Oa off the south

UA POU

© DAVID STANLEY

0   2 km

coast, millions of seabirds nest. The villages of Hakatao and Hakamaii on the west coast are only accessible by foot, hoof, or sea. In Hakahetau village are two new churches, one Catholic, the other Protestant. The first stone church in the Marquesas was erected at Hakahau in 1859, and the present church has a finely carved pulpit shaped like a boat.

Accommodations

Just a three-minute walk from the wharf at Hakahau is **Chez Marguerite Dordillon** (B.P. 17, Hakahau; tel. 92-53-15), where guests are accommodated in a modern two-room house with cooking facilities at CFP 2000 pp. Airport transfers are CFP 2000 each way for the car.

Chez Samuel et Jeanne Marie (Samuel and Jeanne Teikiehuupoko, B.P. 19, Hakahau; tel. 92-53-16), a km from Hakahau Wharf, has two two-room houses with cooking facilities at CFP 1500 pp. There's a CFP 500 pp surcharge if you want hot water and another CFP 500 is collected if you stay only one night.

Pension Vaikaka (Valja Klima, B.P. 16, Hakahau; tel. 92-53-37), two km south of Haka-

hau Wharf, is CFP 2500/4000 single/double in the one bungalow (CFP 500 pp discount beginning on the fourth night).

You could also inquire at the Collège de Ua Pou in Hakahau where **CETAD** (B.P. 9, Hakahau; tel. 92-53-83) has a bungalow for rent to visitors.

Also in Hakahau, ask if Marguerite Kaiha-Schaffer (tel. 92-53-76), Rosalie Tata (who also operates a restaurant), and local taxi driver Jules Hituputoka (tel. 92-53-33) are still renting rooms to visitors.

Farther afield, **Pension Paeaka** (Marie-Augustine Aniamioi, B.P. 27, Hakahau; tel. 92-53-96) at Haakuti village has a one-room house with cooking facilities at CFP 1000 pp a day or CFP 25,000 a month.

Shopping

A boutique sells local carvings and beautiful hand-painted pareus. Four woodcarvers work in Hakahau village—just ask for *les sculpteurs.* If you're buying, shop around at the beginning of your stay, as many items are unfinished and there'll be time to have something completed for you; the same carvings cost three times as much on Tahiti. On the right just past the bakery (great baguettes!) is the home of Jacob Teikitutoua (tel. 92-51-48), who makes ukuleles.

Services and Information

Banque Socredo, a post office, a *gendarmerie,* and six or seven stores are at Hakahau.

Motu Haka (Georges Teikiehuupoko, B.P. 54, Hakahau; tel. 92-53-21) is a cultural organization that promotes Marquesan language instruction, archaeological projects, and traditional arts while rejecting cultural domination by Tahiti.

Getting There

Ua Pou's Aneou airstrip (UAP) is on the north coast, five km from Hakahau on a very rough road over a ridge. You can reach **Air Tahiti** at tel. 92-53-41.

Friday at 0730 a launch from Nuku Hiva to Ua Pou departs Ua Pou for the return at 1600 (1.5 hours each way, CFP 6000 roundtrip).

TAHUATA

Fifteen km long by nine km wide, 61-square-km Tahuata is the smallest of the six inhabited islands of the Marquesas. The population is about 700.

On the west coast is the main village, Vaitahu, where a new Catholic church was completed in 1988. The anchorage at Hana Moe Noa just north of Vaitahu is protected from the ocean swells. The water here is clear, as no rivers run into this bay. It was here that Mendaña first anchored in 1595, followed by Captain Cook in 1774. Here too, Admiral Dupetit-Thouars took possession of the Marquesas in 1842 and established a fort, provoking armed resistance by the islanders.

Archaeological sites exist in the Vaitahu Valley. Hapatoni village, farther south, is picturesque, with a *tamanu*-bordered road and petroglyphs in the Hanatahau Valley behind. White-sand beaches are found on the north side of the island.

Accommodations

The only official place to stay is **Chez Naani** (François and Lucie Barsinas, tel. 92-92-26) in Vaitahu village. A room in this four-room concrete house with communal cooking facilities is CFP 1500 pp (or CFP 3350 pp with half board).

Getting There

There's no airport on Tahuata, which is only six km south of Hiva Oa across Bordelais Channel. To charter a six-passenger boat between the islands is CFP 15,000 (one hour). Small boats leave Hiva Oa for Tahuata almost daily, so ask around at the harbor on Takauku Bay near Atuona. The launch *Te Pua Omioi,* belonging to the Commune of Tahautu, leaves Atuona on Thursday and Friday at 1230. Take supplies with you.

FATU HIVA

Fatu Hiva was the first of the Marquesas to be visited by Europeans (Mendaña called in 1595). In 1937-38 Thor Heyerdahl spent one year on this southernmost island with his young bride Liv and wrote a book called *Fatu Hiva,* describing their far from successful attempt "to return to a simple, natural life." Fatu Hiva (80 square km) is far wetter than the northern islands, and the vegetation is lush. Mount Tauaouoho (960 meters) is the highest point.

This is the most remote of the Marquesas, and no French officials are present. With 500 inhabitants, Fatu Hiva has only two villages, Omoa and Hanavave. It takes about five hours to walk the 17-km trail linking the two, up and down over the mountains amid breathtaking scenery. Surfing onto the rocky beach at Omoa can be pretty exciting! Hanavave on the Bay of Virgins offers one of the most fantastic scenic spectacles in all of Polynesia, with tiki-shaped cliffs dotted with goats. Horses and canoes are for hire in both villages.

Today a revival of the old crafts is taking place in Fatu Hiva, and it's again possible to buy not only sculptures but painted tapa cloth. Hats and mats are woven from pandanus. *Monoi* oils are made from coconut oil, gardenia, jasmine, and sandalwood. Fatu Hiva doesn't have any *nonos,* but lots of mosquitoes. If you plan on staying awhile, get some free anti-elephantiasis pills at a clinic.

Yachting Facilities

Yachts usually anchor in the Bay of Virgins (from January to September); the swell can be uncomfortable at times, but the holding is good in about six fathoms. Yachties trade perfume, lipstick, and cosmetics for the huge Fatu Hiva grapefruits.

Cruising yachts often make Fatu Hiva their first landfall in Polynesia, but this is technically illegal, as the island is not a port of entry. If the village chief uses his radio to report your presence to the *gendarme* at Atuona, you'll probably pay a CFP 5000 fine when you check in at Hiva Oa.

Accommodations and Food

Several families in Omoa village take paying guests. **Marie-Claire Ehueinana** (tel. 92-80-16) takes guests in her two-room house at CFP 1500 pp a day or CFP 35,000 a month. **Norma Ropati** (tel. 92-80-13) has four rooms at CFP 2000 pp with breakfast or CFP 5000 with all meals. **Cécile Gilmore** (tel. 92-80-54) has two rooms with shared kitchen at CFP 2500 pp or CFP 4000 with all meals. Other residents of Omoa who have accommodated visitors in past include Jean Bouyer, Kehu Kamia, François Peters, and Joseph Tetuanui (tel. 92-80-09). A bakery and four or five small stores are also in Omoa.

Getting There

There's no airstrip on Fatu Hiva but a speedboat, or *bonitier,* travels once a week from Fatu Hiva to Atuona (CFP 3500 one-way), leaving Atuona at 1500 on Friday. The trip takes just over three hours and the boat carries eight people, mail, and videocassettes.

OTHER ISLANDS

Motane (Mohotani) is an eight-km-long island rising to 520 meters about 18 km southeast of

Hiva Oa. The depredations of wild sheep on Motane turned the island into a treeless desert. When the Spaniards "discovered" it in 1595, Motane was well-wooded and populated, but today it's uninhabited.

Uninhabited **Eiao** and **Hatutu** islands, 85 km northwest of Nuku Hiva, are the remotest of the Marquesas. Eiao is a 40-square-km island, 10 km long and 576 meters high, with landings on the northwest and west sides. The French once used Eiao as a site of deportation for criminals or "rebellious" natives. In 1972 the French Army drilled holes 1,000 meters down into Eiao to check the island's suitability for underground nuclear testing but deemed the basalt rock too fragile for such use. Wild cattle, sheep, pigs, and donkeys forage across Eiao, ravaging the vegetation and suffering from droughts. In contrast, the profusion of fishlife off Eiao is incredible.

Hatutu, the northernmost of the Marquesas, measures 6.4 square km. Thousands of birds nest here.

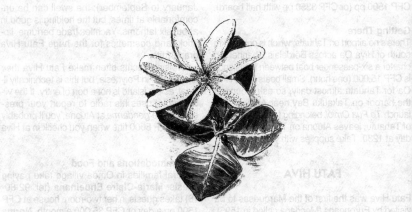

CAPSULE TAHITIAN VOCABULARY

ahiahi—evening
aita—no
aita e peapea—no problem
aita maitai—no good
aito—ironwood
amu—eat
ananahi—tomorrow
arearea—fun, to have fun
atea—far away
atua—god
avae—moon, month
avatea—midday (1000-1500)

e—yes, also *oia*
e aha te huru?—how are you?
e hia?—how much?

faraoa—bread
fare—house
fare iti—toilet
fare moni—bank
fare rata—post office
fenua—land
fetii—parent, family
fiu—fed up, bored

haari—coconut palm
haere mai io nei—come here
haere maru—go easy, take it easy
hauti—play, make love
he haere oe ihea?—where are you going?
hei—flower garland, lei
here hoe—number-one sweetheart
himaa—earth oven
himene—song, from the English "hymn"
hoa—friend

ia orana—good day, may you live, prosper
i nanahi—yesterday
ino—bad
ioa—name
ite—know

maeva—welcome
mahana—sun, light, day

mahanahana—warm
maitai—good, I'm fine; also a cocktail
maitai roa—very good
manava—conscience
manu—bird
manuia—to your health!
mao—shark
mauruuru—thank you
mauruuru roa—thank you very much
miti—salt water
moana—deep ocean
moemoea—dream
moni—money

nana—goodbye
naonao—mosquito
nehenehe—beautiful
niau—coconut-palm frond
niu—coconut tree

oa oa—happy
ora—life, health
ori—dance
oromatua—the spirits of the dead
otaa—bundle, luggage
oti—finished

pahi—boat, ship
pape—water, juice
parahi—goodbye
pareu—sarong
pia—beer
pohe—death
poipoi—morning
popaa—foreigner, European
potii—teenage girl, young woman

raerae—effeminate
roto—lake

taata—human being, man
tahatai—beach
tamaa maitai—bon appetit
tamaaraa—Tahitian feast
tamarii—child
tane—man, husband

taofe—coffee
taote—doctor
taravana—crazy
tiare—flower
toetoe—cold
tupapau—ghost

ua—rain
uaina—wine
uteute—red

vahine—woman, wife
vai—water
veavea—hot

NUMBERS

hoe—1
piti—2
toru—3
maha—four
pae—5
ono—6
hitu—7
vau—8
iva—9
ahuru—10
ahuru ma hoe—11
ahuru ma piti—12
ahuru ma toru—13
ahuru ma maha—14
ahuru ma pae—15
ahuru ma ono—16
ahuru ma hitu—17
ahuru ma vau—18
ahuru ma iva—19
piti ahuru—20
piti ahuru ma hoe—21
piti ahuru ma piti—22
piti ahuru ma toru—23
toru ahuru—30
maha ahuru—40
pae ahuru—50
ono ahuru—60
hitu ahuru—70
vau ahuru—80
iva ahuru—90
hanere—100
tauatini—1,000
ahuru tauatini—10,000
mirioni—1,000,000

GORDON OHLIGER

PITCAIRN ISLANDS
INTRODUCTION

Legendary Pitcairn, last refuge of HMS *Bounty*'s mutinous crew, is the remotest populated place in the Pacific. This tiny colony, founded in 1790 by nine fugitive Englishmen and 19 Polynesians, is presently over two hundred years old. It's one of the ironies of history that Pitcairn, born out of treason to the British crown, was the first Pacific island to become a British colony (in 1838) and remains today the last remnant of that empire in the South Pacific. The very existence of this small community, leading its everyday life as a living piece of history, is an inspiration in this world of mundane consumerism and a delight to those fortunate few able to visit.

The Land
Pitcairn Island, more than 2,200 km southeast of Tahiti, sits alone between Callao (Peru) and New Zealand at 25° south latitude and 130° west longitude. Its nearest inhabited neighbor is Mangareva, a small island in Tahiti-Polynesia 490 km

to the northwest. Easter Island lies 2,100 km to the east. A high volcanic island, Pitcairn reaches 347 meters at the Pawala Ridge and is bounded by rocks and high cliffs on all sides. There's no coral reef, and breakers roll right in to shore. The island is only four and a half square km, almost half of which is fertile ground and well suited for human habitation. The uninhabited islands of Henderson, Ducie, and Oeno, belonging to Pitcairn, are described individually below.

Climate
Pitcairn enjoys an equitable climate, with mean monthly temperatures varying from 19° C in August to 24° C in February. Daily temperatures can vary from 13° C to 33° C. The 2,000 mm of annual rainfall is unevenly distributed, and prolonged rainy periods alternate with droughts. Moderate easterly winds predominate with short east-to-southeast gales occurring between April and September.

HISTORY

The Lost Civilization

Although Pitcairn was uninhabited when the nine *Bounty* mutineers arrived in 1790, the remains of a vanished civilization were clearly evident. The sailors found four platforms with roughly hewn stone statues, somewhat like smaller, simpler versions of those on Easter Island. Being good Christians, the Pitcairners destroyed these platforms and threw the images into the sea. Unfortunately, almost nothing remains of them today. The only surviving piece of sculpture resides in Dunedin's Otago Museum in New Zealand. Sporadic visits by European archaeologists have uncovered traces of ancient burials and stone axes, and 22 petroglyphs are to be seen below "Down Rope." This evidence indicates that Pitcairn was occupied for a considerable period in the past, but where these ancient people came from and where they went are still mysteries.

European Discovery

Pitcairn was discovered in 1767 by Captain Carteret, on the HMS *Swallow*. The island was named for the son of Major Pitcairn of the marines, the first to sight it.

In 1788 the HMS *Bounty* sailed from England for the Pacific to collect breadfruit plants to supplement the diet of slaves in the West Indies. Because the *Bounty* arrived at Tahiti at the wrong time of year, it was necessary to spend a long five months there collecting samples, and during this time, part of the crew became overly attached to that isle of pleasure. On 28 April 1789, in Tongan waters, they mutinied against Lt. William Bligh under 24-year-old Master's Mate Fletcher Christian. Bligh was set adrift in an open boat with the 18 men who chose to go with him. He then performed the amazing feat of sailing 3,618 nautical miles in 41 days, reaching Dutch Timor to give the story to the world.

After the mutiny, the *Bounty* sailed back to Tahiti. An attempt to colonize Tubuai in the Austral Islands failed, and Fletcher Christian set out with eight mutineers, 18 Polynesian men and women, and one small girl, to find a new home where they would be safe from capture. In 1791 the crew members who elected to remain on Tahiti were picked up by the HMS *Pandora* and returned to England for trial. Three were executed. The *Bounty* sailed through the Cook Islands, Tonga, and Fiji, until Christian remembered Carteret's discovery. They changed course for Pitcairn and arrived on 15 January 1790.

Colonizing Pitcairn

After removing everything of value, the mutineers burned the *Bounty* to avoid detection. Right up until the present, each 23 January on the anniversary of the *Bounty*'s demise, a model of the ship is launched and burned at Bounty Bay. For 18 years after the mutiny, the world knew nothing of the fate of the *Bounty,* until the American sealer *Topaz* called at Pitcairn for water in 1808 and solved the mystery.

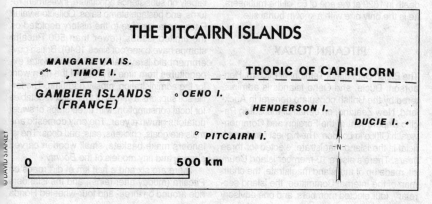

THE PITCAIRN ISLANDS

MANGAREVA IS.

TIMOE I.

TROPIC OF CAPRICORN

GAMBIER ISLANDS
(FRANCE)

OENO I.

HENDERSON I.

DUCIE I.

PITCAIRN I.

N

0   500 km

A LETTER FROM JOHN ADAMS

John Adams was the only mutineer to survive the bloodshed of the first years on Pitcairn. In 1819, 10 years prior to his death, he wrote these words to his brother in England:

I have now lived on this island 30 years, and have a wife and four children, and considering the occasion which brought me here it is not likely I shall ever leave this place. I enjoy good health and except the wound which I received from one of the Otaheiteans when they quarreled with us, I have not had a day's sickness. . . . I can only say that I have done everything in my power in instructing them in the path of Heaven, and thank God we are comfortable and happy, and not a single quarrel has taken place these 18 years.

M.G.L. DOMENY DE RENZI

The first years on Pitcairn were an orgy of jealousy, treachery, and murder, resulting from a lack of sufficient women after the accidental death of one. By 1794, only four mutineers remained alive, and all the Polynesian men had been killed. Three more men had died from a variety of causes by 1800, leaving only John Adams, nine women, and 19 children. Adams brought the children up according to strict Puritanical morality, and later the British Admiralty chose—all things considered—not to take action against him. Adams lived on Pitcairn until his death in 1829 at the age of 65; of the mutineers, he is the only one with a known burial site.

PITCAIRN TODAY

The British Dependent Territory of Pitcairn, Henderson, Ducie, and Oeno Islands is administered by the British consulate general in Auckland, New Zealand, on behalf of the South Pacific Department of the Foreign and Commonwealth Office in London. The highest resident official is the island magistrate, elected for three years. There's also a 10-member Island Council, made up of the island magistrate, the chairman of the Internal Committee, the island secretary, four elected members, and one advisory member appointed by the elected members. One voting and one advisory member are appointed by the governor (the British high commissioner in Wellington). Island Council elections are annual.

The economy is self-sufficient, depending largely on subsistence agriculture, investment returns, and postage stamp sales. Collectors value Pitcairn stamps due to the history depicted on the limited issues (fewer than 500 Pitcairn stamps have come out since 1940). British government aid is available for major capital expenditures from time to time. All the men work for the administration, mostly part-time. The fertile soil supports a variety of fruits and vegetables for local consumption, with three crops of sweet potatoes grown a year. The only domestic animals are goats, chickens, cats, and dogs. The islanders make baskets, small wooden carved sharks, and tiny models of the *Bounty*.

There are six and a half km of dirt roads on Pitcairn (muddy after rains), and the islanders ride around on three- and four-wheeled Honda motorcycles. There are also tractors, microwaves, freezers, and VCRs; electricity is on 0900-1200 and 1600-2200. The quaint Pitcairn wheelbarrows are a thing of the past. The modern conveniences have brightened the lives of the islanders, reduced the number of people required to sustain the community, and convinced more of the young to stay.

The People

Of the 65 permanent inhabitants of Pitcairn, 52 are direct descendants of the mutineers and their Tahitian wives. In 1831, there was an attempt to resettle them on Tahiti, out of fear of drought, but the Pitcairners returned to their island the same year. In 1856, all 194 islanders were forcibly taken by the British to Norfolk Island, between New Zealand and New Caledonia, where many of their descendants still live. Two families returned to Pitcairn in 1858, followed by four more in 1864. The present population is descended from these six families. Nearly half the people bear the surname Christian; all of the others are Warrens, Browns, and Youngs. The population peaked at 233 in 1937.

The Pitcairners speak a local patois of English and Tahitian. There's a primary school with a N.Z. teacher who also assists the post-primary students with their N.Z. correspondence-school lessons. Scholarships are made available by the Island Council for older postprimary students wishing to further their education in New Zealand.

According to David Silverman's 1967 book *Pitcairn Island* there are around 1,500 true Pitcairners: 45 on Pitcairn, 150 in Tahiti-Polynesia, 160 in New Zealand, 400 in Australia, and most of the rest on Norfolk Island.

PRACTICALITIES

Accommodations and Food

There are no hotels or guesthouses on Pitcairn, and the two government hostels are reserved for official use. The island magistrate can organize paying guest accommodation with local families (around NZ$125 pp a week), but such arrangements must be made prior to arrival.

Visiting yachties are welcomed into the Pitcairners' homes in a most hospitable fashion. If you're headed for Pitcairn, take along a good supply of canned foods and butter, plus worthwhile books for the library, to repay the kindness you'll inevitably encounter. They'll feed you mammoth meals. An American Seventh-Day Adventist missionary converted the Pitcairners in 1887, so pork, cigarettes, drugs, and alcohol are banned.

The Cooperative Store opens for a few hours three times a week. Canned foods are usually obtainable, but flour, eggs, meat, and butter must be ordered from New Zealand several months in advance. Since no freight is charged to Pitcairn for foodstuffs, prices are about the same as in New Zealand, with a markup of 20% to cover losses.

Visas

No visa is required of passengers and crew who visit while their vessel is at Pitcairn. Anyone wishing to stay on Pitcairn after the ship has left requires a six-month residence permit issued by the British consulate general, Private Mail Bag 92014, Auckland, New Zealand (fax 64-9/303-1836). Applications must be approved by the Island Council and the governor, and it's unlikely they'll take you seriously unless you have a particular reason for going. A medical certificate and character references must be provided. Apply half a year in advance. Permanent residence is only granted to British subjects, after seven years' continuous residence on the island.

Telecommunications

On 17 April 1992 the island magistrate made the first-ever telephone call from Pitcairn via the new Inmarsat A Satellite Communications System. It's now possible to contact Pitcairn directly at tel. (872) 144-5372 and fax (872) 144-5373. Incoming calls are answered by an operator only at 0900 (1830 GMT), 1200 (2030 GMT), 1600 (0030 GMT), and 2100 (0530 GMT). At other times an answering machine is used, although from 2100-0900 (0530-1730 GMT) the whole system is switched off because the main power supply closes down at night. Outgoing calls are expensive at NZ$20 a minute to the U.S. (faxes NZ$30 per page), and if the number you're trying to call is engaged, you still have to pay the satellite connection time. It's reported the locals aren't very happy with this high-tech replacement of the much cheaper radio telephone link with New Zealand that closed down in September 1993. To keep in touch, a dozen Pitcairners are licensed ham radio operators, the highest proportion of amateur radio operators per capita in the world.

Money

New Zealand currency is used, with local Pitcairn coins. No bank exists on Pitcairn, but the island secretary will change foreign cash and traveler's checks.

Media and Information

The *Pitcairn Miscellany* is a delightful monthly newsletter sponsored by the Pitcairn Island School. One may become a subscriber by sending US$10 cash or an undated check to: *Pitcairn Miscellany, Pitcairn Island, via New Zealand.* Allow several months for your letter to reach Pitcairn.

The British consulate general in Auckland publishes *A Guide to Pitcairn,* a 75-page booklet with background information and photos. To obtain a copy, send US$10 to the British consulate general, Private Mail Bag 92014, Auckland, New Zealand, or include a similar amount with your *Miscellany* subscription money.

The **Pitcairn Islands Study Group** publishes *The Pitcairn Log* quarterly (US$10 a year). It contains much interesting material on the people of Pitcairn, as well as the collecting of Pitcairn postage stamps. For more information write: Mr. William Volk, 2184 - 6th Ave., Yuma, AZ 85364, U.S.A., or Mr. David R. Tomeraasen, Box 178100, San Diego, CA 92177-8100, U.S.A. (fax 619/274-1200).

Getting There

There's no airport or harbor on Pitcairn. All shipping anchors in the lee, moving around when the wind shifts. This is why most passing ships don't drop anchor but only pause an hour or so to pick up and deliver mail. The islanders come out to meet boats anchored in Bounty Bay and ferry visitors ashore.

There are two open anchorages: Bounty Bay when winds are blowing from the southwest, west, and northwest; Western Harbor when there's an east wind. Both have landings, but Bounty Bay is tricky to negotiate through the surf, and Western Harbor is far from the village. A jetty was constructed at Bounty Bay by the Royal Engineers in 1976. The anchorage at Down Rope could be used in case of north or northeast winds, but there's no way up the cliff except the proverbial rope. Dangerous rocks lie off the south coast. The wind is irregular, so yachts must leave someone aboard in case it shifts (on 12 May 1991 the yacht *Wiggy* was wrecked at Pitcairn, with a loss of one life). From 1983 to 1988, an average of only 12 yachts a year called at Pitcairn.

The British consulate general in Auckland will have information on container vessels that call at Pitcairn between New Zealand and the Panama Canal three or four times a year. Other ships occasionally stop at the discretion of the captain. Passage on these ships is fixed at NZ$750 one way. Return passage is usually a matter of chance, and it may be necessary to wait several months for the next ship.

Tours

Unless you own a yacht, the only practical way of visiting Pitcairn is on the annual yacht tour arranged by **Ocean Voyages Inc.** (1709 Bridgeway, Sausalito, CA 94965, U.S.A.; tel. 415/332-4681, fax 415/332-7460). The exact program varies from year to year, but it usually involves a flight from Tahiti to Mangareva in the Gambier group, then a two-day sail to Pitcairn aboard a chartered yacht. Two weeks are spent ashore as guests of the Pitcairners, and rather than lie idle the yacht often does a wood run to Henderson and a fishing trip to Oeno during this period. Group members are invited to participate in the sailing of the yacht, if they wish. The number of people who can go depends on the number of

an early 19th-century view of Adamstown, Pitcairn Island

M.G.L. DUMENY DE RIENZI

berths on the yacht, but it's never over 10, so bookings should be made well ahead. In recent years the trip has taken place between April and June. Expect to pay around US$4000 pp including lodging and all meals, plus US$850 for the return flight from Papeete to Mangareva. These trips are the absolute cream of South Pacific itineraries.

Some years Ocean Voyages also offers several days at Pitcairn as part of a round-the-world cruise on a larger sailing vessel. Typically, the boat picks up passengers in Panama and takes them to Galapagos, Easter Island, Pitcairn, Mangareva, and Tahiti. Trips like this are a once-in-a-lifetime opportunity for most of us, so if you have the time and money, just go. Luxury cruise ships also visit Pitcairn occasionally, but they spend only a few hours ashore and are unable to land at all in bad weather.

If you can organize a small group, Ocean Voyages and the other yacht charter brokers listed in the main Introduction to this book can book crewed Tahiti-based yachts for trips to Pitcairn via Mangareva anytime. The cost will be US$8000 a week for six persons, and three weeks must be allowed for the roundtrip sea journey alone, with the possibility of stops at the Tuamotus.

THE PITCAIRN ISLANDS

Pitcairn Island

Scattered along a plateau 120 meters above the landing at Bounty Bay is Adamstown, the only settlement. At the top of the hill over the bay is The Edge, a restful spot with benches, shady trees, and a great view of everything. The original Bible from the *Bounty* is showcased in the church at Adamstown. The Bible, sold in 1839, was eventually acquired by the Connecticut Historical Society, which returned it to Pitcairn in 1949. The four-meter anchor of the *Bounty,* salvaged in 1957, is now mounted in the square outside the courthouse. Pitcairn postage stamps may be purchased at the post office between the courthouse and church. The library is adjacent. A bell on the square is used to announce church services and the arrival of ships. The graves of John Adams, his wife Teio, and daughter Hannah are also visited.

On the ridge west of Adamstown is a cave in which Fletcher Christian stayed during the period of strife on the island. He was finally killed by two Tahitians.

Oeno and Ducie

Grouped together with Pitcairn under the same administration are the uninhabited islands of Oeno, Henderson, and Ducie, annexed by Britain in 1902. The four islands together total 47.4 square km. Unlike Pitcairn and Henderson, both Ducie and Oeno have central lagoons inaccessible to shipping.

Oeno, a tiny 5.1-square-km atoll 128 km northwest of Pitcairn, is visited by the Pitcairners from time to time to collect shells, coral, and pandanus leaves to use in their handicrafts. Small boats can enter the shallow lagoon through a passage on the north side. In 1969-70 Oeno was used by the U.S. Air Force as a satellite observation post.

Ducie atoll (6.4 square km) is 472 km east of Pitcairn. The poor soil and lack of fresh water account for the sparse vegetation. Large whirlpools in the Ducie lagoon are caused by tunnels that drain the lagoon to the sea. Due to its inaccessibility Ducie is rarely approached, and tens of thousands of petrels and other seabirds nest here.

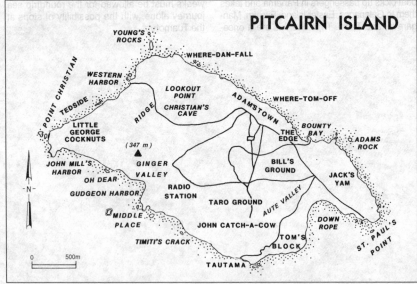

OENO

SANDY I.

BOAT PASSAGE

NORTHEAST POINT

LAGOON

-N-

0   1 km

© DAVID STANLEY

Henderson

Henderson, a 31-square-km elevated atoll 169 km east-northeast of Pitcairn, is the largest of the Pitcairn Islands. The island measures five km by 10 km and is flanked by 15-meter-high coral cliffs on the west, south, and east sides. Henderson is surrounded by a fringing reef with only two narrow passages: one on the north, the other on the northwest coast. The passages lead to a sandy beach on the island's north shore. The interior of the island is a flat coral plateau about 30 meters high, but the dense undergrowth, prickly vines, and sharp coral rock make it almost impenetrable. There's said to be a freshwater spring visible only at low tide at the north end of the island, but this is doubtful, and no other source of water on the island is known.

There are two unique species of land birds on the island: a black flightless rail (Henderson chicken) and a green fruit pigeon. Fish and lobster are numerous, as are Polynesian rats. The Pitcairners visit Henderson to collect *miro* wood, which is excellent for carving. The last human inhabitant was an American, Robert Tomarchin, who was dropped off on Henderson in 1957 with his chimpanzee, Moko. Tomarchin lasted only three weeks before being rescued by a passing ship. In 1983 an American coal-mining millionaire named Smiley Ratliff offered to build airstrips on Pitcairn and Henderson, and to donate three small planes and about a million dollars for development projects if the British gov-

ernment would give him title to the latter. Luckily, he was turned down. There was also talk of constructing an emergency runway on Henderson to support air services between South America and the South Pacific but this was also rejected, and in 1988 the island was declared a UNESCO World Heritage Site to preclude any development. From January 1991 a Cambridge University team studied the flora and fauna of Henderson continuously for a 15-month period.

NORFOLK ISLAND

Norfolk Island, 1120 km northwest of Auckland, 800 km south of Nouméa, and 1400 km east of Brisbane, measures eight km by five km and is 3455 hectares in area. When Captain Cook discovered this uninhabited island in 1774 it was tightly packed with tall straight pine trees which he incorrectly judged would make fine masts for sailing ships. In 1788 the British government set up a penal colony here, but the island was abandoned in 1814. Fears that Norfolk might be occupied by a rival power led the British to reestablish their penal colony in 1825, but this facility gained notoriety through reports of wanton cruelty and in 1855 the remaining prisoners were transferred to Tasmania, Australia.

In 1856 the existing prison infrastructure of staff quarters and farms was used to resettle the Pitcairn Islanders, and today a third of the 1800 inhabitants have Pitcairn names. The Melanesian Mission established its headquarters on Norfolk in 1866, and until 1921 it had a college here used to train Solomon Islanders and others as pastors. The mission church and burial ground remain. Whaling was practiced by the islanders from the 1850s until 1962, but the event that changed Norfolk forever was the building of a wartime airport in 1944.

Today the island is a favorite vacation spot for middle-aged or retired Australians and New Zealanders who come for a quiet holiday. A small national park with hiking trails, the convict settlement, and lovely coastal scenery are the main attractions. The Pitcairn connection is heavily exploited by the local tourist industry, and there are Pitcairn museums, shows, film evenings, tours, and souvenirs.

Norfolk Island is a self-governing territory under Australian authority. Those making a return visit from Auckland or Nouméa do not require a visa for a stay of 30 days, but an Australian tourist visa is required of those continuing on to Australia (obtain beforehand). There are scheduled flights to Norfolk Island from Auckland, Brisbane, Lord Howe Island, and Sydney, and charters from Nouméa. An A$25 airport tax is collected upon departure.

Tourism is tightly controlled by the Norfolk Island Government Tourist Bureau (Box 211, Norfolk Island 2899, Australia; fax 672-3/23109) and only persons with prepaid accommodations are allowed entry. Camping, youth hostels, and most other forms of independent budget travel are strictly prohibited. There are over 40 official

places to stay on the island and prices are reasonable for a couple of nights, just be sure to get something with cooking facilities and perhaps a rental car included.

If your air ticket allows a stopover on Norfolk Island between New Zealand and Australia, contact The Travel Center (Box 172, Norfolk Island 2899, Australia; fax 672-3/23205), which can make direct accommodation bookings. Four or five days on the island should be enough. From New Zealand, package tours are offered by Passport Holidays (Box 2698, Auckland; fax 64-9/309-6895), ASPAC Vacations Ltd. (Box 4330, Auckland; fax 64-9/623-0257), and others. An A$1 pp per night local bed tax must be paid directly to the hotel.

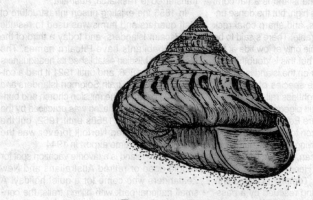

The trochus shell (Entemnotrochus rumphii) is sometimes called the top shell because it looks like an inverted spinning top.

GORDON OHLIGER

EASTER ISLAND
INTRODUCTION

The mystery of Easter Island (Isla de Pascua) and its indigenous inhabitants, the Rapanui, has intrigued travelers and archaeologists for many years. Where did these ancient people come from? How did they transport almost 600 giant statues from the quarry to their platforms? What cataclysmic event caused them to over-throw all they had erected with so much effort? And most importantly, what does it all mean? With the opening of Mataveri airport in 1967, Easter Island became more easily accessible, and many visitors now take the opportunity to pause and ponder the largest and most awe-some collection of prehistoric monuments in the Pacific. This is one of the most evocative places you will ever visit.

The Land
Barren and detached, Easter Island lies mid-way between Tahiti and Chile, 4,000 km from the former and 3,600 km from the latter. Pit-cairn Island, 2,100 km west, is the nearest in-habited land. No other populated island on earth

is as isolated as this. Easter Island is triangular, with an extinct volcano at each corner. It mea-sures 23 by 11 km, totaling 171 square km.

The interior consists of high plateaus and craters surrounded by coastal bluffs. Ancient lava flows from Maunga Terevaka (507 meters), the highest peak, covered the island, creating a rough, broken surface. Pua Katiki and Rano Kau (to the east and south respectively) are nearly 400 meters high. Many parasitic craters exist on the southern and southeast flanks of Maunga Terevaka. Three of these, Rano Aroi, Rano Raraku, and Rano Kau, contain crater lakes, with the largest (in Rano Kau) over a kilo-meter across. Since 1935 the areas around Maunga Terevaka and Rano Kau have been set aside as **Parque Nacional Rapa Nui.**

The forests of Easter Island were wiped out by the indigenous inhabitants long ago, and during the 19th century sheep finished off most of the remaining native vegetation. Grasslands now cover the green, windswept surface, and there are few endemic plants and no native land birds.

The lakes feature thick, floating bogs of peat; *totora* reeds related to South American species surround and completely cover their surfaces. Pollen studies have determined that these reeds have existed here for at least 30,000 years. Large tracts of eucalyptus have been planted in recent years.

Small coral formations occur along the shoreline, but the lack of any continuous reef has allowed the sea to cut cliffs around much of the island. These bluffs are high where the waves encountered ashy material, low where they beat upon lava flows. Lava tubes and volcanic caves are other peculiarities of the coastline. The only sandy beaches are at Ovahe and Anakena, on the northeast coast.

Climate

Temperatures are moderated by the cool Humboldt Current. The southeast trades blow continuously from September to May; the rest of the year north and northwest winds are more common. The climate is moist and some rain falls 200 days a year. March to June are the rainiest months; July to October are generally the driest and coolest, although heavy rains are possible year-round. Drizzles and mist are common, and a heavy dew forms overnight. Snow

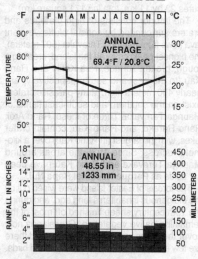

EASTER I. CLIMATE

and frost are unknown, however. The porous volcanic rock dries out quickly, so the dampness need not deter the well-prepared hiker/camper.

HISTORY

Polynesian Genesis

It's believed that Easter Island was colonized around A.D. 500 by Polynesians from the Marquesas Islands, as part of an eastward migratory trend that originated in Southeast Asia around 1500 B.C. Here they developed one of the most remarkable cultures in all of Polynesia.

Long platforms or *ahu* bearing slender statues known as *moai* were built near the coasts, with long retaining walls facing the sea. Each *ahu* carried four to six *moai* towering four to eight meters high. These statues, or *aringa ora* (living faces), looked inland towards the villages, to project the mana (protective power) of the *aku-aku* (ancestral spirits) they represented.

The *moai* were all cut from the same quarry at Rano Raraku, the yellowish volcanic tuff shaped by stone tools. Some writers have theorized that the statues were "walked" to their platforms by a couple of dozen men using ropes to lean the upright figures from side to side while moving forward; others claim they were pulled along on a sledge or log rollers. Some statues bore a large cylindrical topknot *(pukao)* carved from the reddish stone of Punapau. Eyes of cut coral were fitted into the faces.

Other unique features of Easter Island are the strange canoe-shaped house foundations with holes for wall supports, and the still-undeciphered, incised wooden tablets *(rongo rongo)*, the only ancient form of writing known in Oceania. Although there have been several scholarly attempts to read these neat rows of symbols, their meaning remains unknown.

In 1774 Captain Cook reported internecine fighting among the islanders, with statues toppled and their platforms damaged, and by 1840 all of the *moai* had been thrown off their *ahu*.

Fantasy and Fact

The first comprehensive explorations of Easter Island were carried out by Katherine Routledge in 1914-15, Alfred Metraux in 1934, and Thor

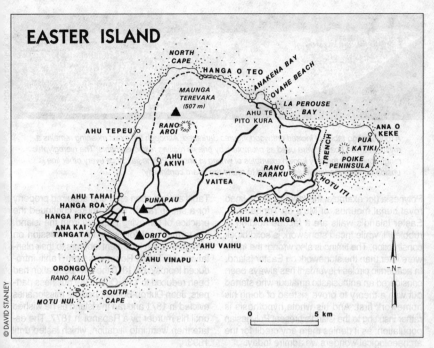

EASTER ISLAND

NORTH CAPE
HANGA O TEO
ANAKENA BAY
OVAHE BEACH
MAUNGA TEREVAKA (507 m)
LA PEROUSE BAY
AHU TE PITO KURA
ANA O KEKE
RANO AROI
PUA KATIKI
AHU TEPEU
POIKE PENINSULA
AHU AKIVI
RANO RARAKU
TRENCH
VAITEA
HOTU ITI
AHU TAHAI
HANGA ROA
PUNAPAU
HANGA PIKO
ANA KAI TANGATA
AHU AKAHANGA
ORITO
AHU VAIHU
AHU VINAPU
ORONGO
RANO KAU
SOUTH CAPE
MOTU NUI

0   5 km

N

© DAVID STANLEY

Heyerdahl in 1955-56. Earlier, in 1947, Heyerdahl had achieved notoriety by sailing some 6,500 km from South America to the Tuamotu Islands in a balsa-raft, the *Kon Tiki*. His 1955 Norwegian Archaeological Expedition was intended to uncover proof that Polynesia was populated from South America, and Heyerdahl developed a romantic legend that still excites the popular imagination today.

Heyerdahl postulated that Easter Island's first inhabitants (the "long ears") arrived from South America around A.D. 380. They dug a three-km-long defensive trench isolating the Poike Peninsula and built elevated platforms of perfectly fitted basalt blocks. Heyerdahl noted a second wave of immigrants, also from South America, who destroyed the structures of the first group and replaced them with the *moai*-bearing *ahu* mentioned above. Heyerdahl sees the toppling of the *moai* as a result of the arrival of Polynesian invaders (the "short ears") who arrived from the Marquesas and conquered the original inhabitants in 1680. According to

Heyerdahl the birdman cult, centering on the sacred village of Orongo, was initiated by the victors.

Modern archaeologists discount the South American theory and see the statues as having developed from the typical backrests of Polynesian *marae*. The civil war would have resulted from over-exploitation of the island's environment, leading to starvation, cannibalism, and the collapse of the old order. Previous destruction of the forests would have deprived the inhabitants of the means of building canoes to sail off in search of other islands. The Poike trench was only a series of discontinuous ditches dug to grow crops, probably taro. Despite decades of study by some of the world's best archaeologists, no South American artifacts have ever been excavated on the island.

Heyerdahl argued that the perfectly fitted, polished stonework of the stone wall of Ahu Vinapu (Ahu Tahira) was analogous to Incan stone structures in Cuzco and Machu Picchu, but fine stonework can be found elsewhere in

A rongo-rongo *tablet of incised driftwood, figures darkened. Although the exact meaning remains a mystery, these boards were used as prompters by priests reciting religious chants. The hieroglyphic* rongo-rongo *are the only known examples of writing in ancient Polynesia. Since every other line is upside down, a reader would have had to rotate the board continually.*

Polynesia (for example, the *langi,* or stone-lined royal burial mounds, of Mu'a on Tongatapu). Easter Island's walls are a facade holding in rubble fill, while Incan stonework is solid block construction. The timing is also wrong: the Incas were later than the stonework on Easter Island. In academic circles Heyerdahl has always been considered an enthusiastic amateur who started out with a theory to prove instead of doing his homework first. And his whole hypothesis is rather insulting to the island's present Polynesian population, as it denies them any credit for the archaeological wonders we admire today.

European Penetration

European impact on Easter Island was among the most dreadful in the history of the Pacific. When Jacob Roggeveen arrived on Easter Sunday, 1722, there were about 4,000 Rapanui (though the population had once been as high as 20,000). Roggeveen's landing party opened fire and killed 12 of the islanders; then the great white explorer sailed off. Contacts with whalers, sealers, and slavers were sporadic until 1862 when a fleet of Peruvian blackbirders kidnapped some 1,400 Rapanui to work in the coastal sugar plantations of Peru and dig guano on the offshore islands. Among those taken were the last king and the entire learned class. Missionaries and diplomats in Lima protested to the Peruvian government, and eventually 15 surviving islanders made it back to their homes, where they sparked a deadly smallpox epidemic.

French Catholic missionaries took up residence on Easter Island in 1865 and succeeded in converting the survivors; businessmen from

Tahiti arrived soon after and acquired property for a sheep ranch. Both groups continued the practice of removing Rapanui from the island: the former sent followers to their mission on Mangareva, the latter sent laborers to their plantations on Tahiti. Returnees from Tahiti introduced leprosy. By 1870 the total population had been reduced to 110. One of the business partners, Jean Dutrou-Bornier, had the missionaries evicted in 1871 and ran the island as he wished until his murder by a Rapanui in 1877. The estate then went into litigation, which lasted until 1893.

The Colonial Period

In 1883 Chile defeated Peru and Bolivia in the War of the Pacific. With their new imperial power, the Chileans annexed Easter Island in 1888, erroneously believing that the island would become a port of call after the opening of the Panama Canal. Their lack of knowledge about the island is illustrated by plans to open a naval base when no potential for harbor construction existed. As this became apparent, they leased most of the island to a British wool operation, which ran it as a company estate until the lease was revoked in 1953. The tens of thousands of sheep devastated the vegetation, causing soil erosion, and stones were torn from the archaeological sites to build walls and piers. During this long period, the Rapanui were forbidden to go beyond the Hanga Roa boundary wall without company permission, to deter them from stealing the sheep. (A local joke tells of a cow that inadvertently wandered into Hanga Roa during this period, only to be arrested and tried under

Chilean naval law as a "ship." Sentenced to 30 days on bread and water, it died of starvation after two weeks.)

In 1953 the Chilean Navy took over and continued the same style of paternal rule. After local protests, the moderate Christian Democratic government of Chile permitted the election of a local mayor and council in 1965. Elections were terminated by Pinochet's 1973 military coup, and Easter Island, along with the rest of Chile, suffered autocratic rule until the restoration of democracy in 1990. In 1984 archaeologist Sergio Rapu became the first Rapanui governor of Easter Island.

GOVERNMENT

Easter Island is part of the Fifth Region of Chile, with Valparaiso (Chile) as capital. The Chilean government names the governor; the appointed mayor and council have little power. The present mayor, Petero Edmunds, wants Easter Island made a separate region of Chile, a change that would greatly increase local autonomy. Chile heavily subsidizes services on the island, and a large military and official staff are present, mostly *continentales* (mainlanders). A five-member Comisión de Desarrollo (development committee) representing the 800 ethnic Rapanui was established under Chile's Indigenous Law in 1994.

After the return to democracy in Chile an indigenous rights group, the Consejo de Ancianos, was formed to represent the island's 36 original families. They called for the creation of a new electoral district giving Easter Island its own representative in the Chilean Congress. In 1994 the Consejo split into two rival factions over the question of land rights, a moderate wing led by former Mayor Alberto Hotus and a more radical camp headed by Juan Chavez.

Most of Easter Island's land is held by the Chilean State. On several occasions Chilean governments have offered to give the Rapanui clear title to certain areas, but these offers have been consistently refused. The islanders fear such titles might eventually pass out of their hands, and besides, they never ceded the land to anyone in the first place, they say. Only about 10% of the island has ever been offered, and the

Rapanui are worried about the fate of the other 90%. Now the government is forcing some islanders to accept land titles by making them a requirement for needed housing subsidies. Protesters from the Chavez group demand that the government return to them much more land than is presently on offer, despite the negative impact this would have on the environment and archaeological sites. At the moment Hanga Roa is the only settlement, and although it's understandable how local residents might wish to colonize other parts of the island, it would not be an entirely positive development.

THE PEOPLE

The original name of Easter Island was Te Pito o Te Henua, "navel of the world." The Rapanui believe they are descended from Hotu Matua, who arrived by canoe at Anakena Beach from Te Hiva, the ancestral homeland. The statues were raised by magic. The original inhabitants wore tapa clothing and were tattooed like Marquesans; in fact, there's little doubt their forefathers arrived from Eastern Polynesia. The language of the Rapanui is Austronesian, closely related to all the other languages of Polynesia, with no South American elements.

The Rapanui have interbred liberally with visitors for over a century, but the Polynesian element is still strong. The 1992 census places 2,770 people on Easter Island, three-quarters of them Rapanui or Rapanui-related. Some 1,000 Rapanui live abroad. Many of the local Rapanui made money during the 1993 filming of Kevin Costner's *Rapa Nui,* and almost all of them bought a car. There's now one car for every two Rapanui and the newly paved streets of Hanga Roa are often jammed! The sweet potato gardens around Hanga Roa were abandoned, and frozen chickens, vegetables, and TV dinners are imported from Santiago in increasing quantities. Many people earn money from tourism as innkeepers, guides, and craftspeople, and lots more are employed by the Chilean government. About a thousand *continentales* also live on Easter Island, most of them government employees and newly arrived small shopkeepers.

Since 1966 the Rapanui have been Chilean citizens, and many have emigrated to the mainland. The locals generally speak Rapanui in private, Spanish in public, French if they've been to Tahiti, and English almost not at all. Spanish is gradually supplanting Rapanui among the young, and it's feared the language will go out of everyday use within a generation or two. In general, the Rapanui are honest and quite friendly.

Conduct

The archaeological sites of Easter Island are fragile and easily damaged by thoughtless actions, such as climbing on the fallen statues or walking on petroglyphs. The volcanic tuff is soft and easily broken off or scuffed. Incredibly, some people have scraped ancient rock carvings with stones to make them easier to photograph! Cruise ships can land hundreds of people a day, and the large groups often spin out of control, swarming over the quarry at Rano Raraku or standing on the stone house tops at Orongo (several of which have collapsed in recent years). Local residents have had to organize voluntary projects to pick up trash discarded in the national park by tourists.

Though it may seem that these places are remote from the world of high-impact consumer tourism, they are in fact endangered by the selfishness of some visitors and those locals who would profit from them. It's strictly prohibited to remove any ancient artifacts (such as spearheads, fishhooks, or basalt chisels) from the island. Warning signs erected in the park are there for a reason, and the human bones often encountered on the *ahu* and in caves deserve to

be left in peace. For most of us these things go without saying, but it can be really upsetting to see the way some tourists behave.

Public Holidays and Festivals

In late January or early February is the carnival-like Tapati Rapa Nui festival, with traditional dancing, sporting events, canoe races, a horse race, art shows, statue-carving contest, shell-necklace-stringing competition, body-painting contest, *kai-kai* (string figure) performances, mock battles, and the election of Queen Rapa Nui (who is dramatically crowned on a spotlit Ahu Tahai). A unique trilithon at Rano Raraku involves male contestants in body paint who paddle tiny reed craft across the lake, pick up bunches of bananas on poles and run around the crater and up the hill, where they grab big bundles of totara reeds to carry down and around the lake before a final swim across. There's also *haka pe'i,* which involves young men sliding down a grassy mountainside on banana-trunk sleds at great speed. Colored lights are strung up along the main street. The 1994 Tapati Rapa Nui parade displayed strong Hollywood influence in the floats and costumes, and for the first time ever, topless young women rode on floats through Hanga Roa, just as they appeared in *Rapa Nui!*

Chilean Independence Day (18 September) is celebrated with parades and a *fonda* (carnival). Everybody takes three days off for this big fiesta. On the day of their patron saint, the main families stage a traditional feast *(curanto),* complete with an earth oven.

ON THE ROAD

SIGHTS

Vicinity of Hanga Roa

The **Catholic church** in the center of town is notable for its woodcarvings. Buried next to the church is Father Sebastian Englert, who founded the one-room **Anthropological Museum** (open every morning except Saturday; US$1 admission) on the north side of Hanga Roa. Inside is kept the white coral and red scoria eye of the *moai* found at Anakena in 1978. A William Mulloy Research Library is scheduled to be built here.

Nearby at **Ahu Tahai,** just outside the town, are three *ahu,* one bearing five restored *moai* and a large restored statue complete with a red 10-ton topknot reerected by the late Dr. William Mulloy in 1967. The statue's "eyes" are crude copies recently cemented in place for the benefit of tourists. The islanders launched their canoes from the ramp leading down to the water between the *ahu.*

ATLAS DU VOYAGE DE LA PÉROUSE (1797)

When La Pérouse visited Easter Island in 1786, the stone statues were still erect on their stepped platforms, topknots still in place. Notice the islander behind the statue attempting to steal an article of clothing from the explorers.

Five km north along the coast is unrestored **Ahu Tepeu,** with the foundations of canoe-shaped and round houses nearby. Inland and 10 km from Hanga Roa via the coast is **Ahu Akivi** (Siete Moai), with seven statues restored in 1960 by Dr. Mulloy. The seven *moai* that once overlooked a village are visible from afar.

On the way back to Hanga Roa climb **Punapau,** where the topknots were quarried. About 25 red topknots are in or near Punapau, the largest weighing 11 tons. **Maunga Orito,** south of Punapau, contains black obsidian, which the islanders used for weapons and tools.

Five km from Hanga Roa via the road along the north side of the airstrip are the fine Inca-like stone walls of the two *ahu* at **Ahu Vinapu** (Ahu Tahira). According to Heyerdahl, the perfectly fitted stonework of one dates from the earliest period and is due to contact with South America. Most authorities dispute this claim and suggest it was a later development by the skilled Polynesian stonemasons.

Rano Kau and Orongo

From Hanga Roa, the brisk six-km uphill hike south to Orongo and the vast crater of Rano Kau (316 meters) is easily done in a morning, but make a day of it if you have time. On the way, just past the west end of the airstrip, at the foot of the cliff near the water, is **Ana Kai Tangata,** the Cannibal Cave. Paintings of birds grace the ceiling of this cave.

The road, which swings around and up the side of Rano Kau to Orongo, offers an exciting panorama of cliffs, crater lake, and offshore islands. An admission of US$10 is charged by the national park ranger, who also sells a few interesting publications about the island and an excellent map. The entry fee may seem stiff, but all the other sites on the island are free, and the National Parks Department (CONAF) is desperately short of funds needed to protect and maintain Easter Island's monuments.

At **Orongo,** the main ceremonial center on the island, are many high-relief carvings of bird-headed men on the rock outcrops. The 40 cave-like dwellings here (restored by Dr. Mulloy in

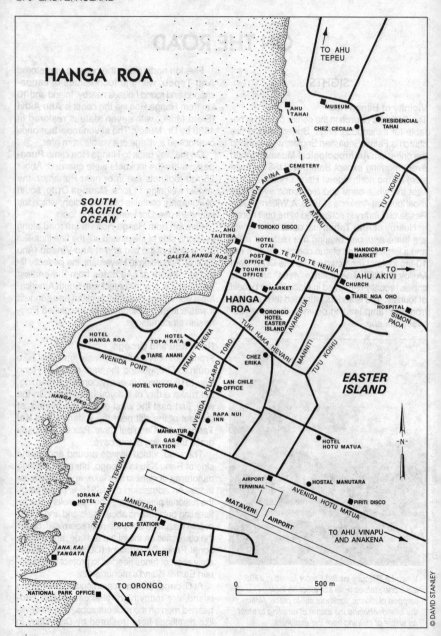

HANGA ROA

SOUTH
PACIFIC
OCEAN

TO AHU
TEPEU

MUSEUM

RESIDENCIAL
TAHAI

AHU
TAHAI

CHEZ CECILIA

CEMETERY

AVENIDA APINA

PETERU ATAMU

TU'U KOIHU

AHU
TAUTIRA

TOROKO DISCO

HOTEL
OTAI

HANDICRAFT
MARKET

CALETA HANGA ROA

TE PITO TE HENUA

POST
OFFICE

TOURIST
OFFICE

TO
AHU
AKIVI

MARKET

CHURCH

HANGA
ROA

TIARE NGA OHO

ORONGO
HOTEL
EASTER
ISLAND

HOSPITAL

AVAREIPUA

SIMON
PAOA

HOTEL
HANGA ROA

HOTEL
TOPA RA'A

TIARE ANANI

AVENIDA PONT

MANNITI

TUKI HAKA HEVARI

ATAMU TEKENA

AVENIDA POLICARPO TORO

TU'U KOIHU

CHEZ
ERIKA

EASTER
ISLAND

HOTEL
VICTORIA

HANGA PIKO

LAN CHILE
OFFICE

RAPA NUI
INN

-N-

MAHINATUR

GAS
STATION

HOTEL
HOTU MATUA

IORANA
HOTEL

AIRPORT
TERMINAL

HOSTAL MANUTARA

MANUTARA

AVENIDA HOTU MATUA

PIRITI DISCO

MATAVERI

AIRPORT

ANA KAI
TANGATA

POLICE STATION

AVENIDA ATAMU TEKENA

MATAVERI

TO AHU VINAPU
AND ANAKENA

NATIONAL PARK OFFICE

TO ORONGO

0   500 m

© DAVID STANLEY

1974) were used by island chiefs and participants during the birdman festival. Each year a race was staged to the farthest offshore island, **Motu Nui,** to find the first egg of a species of migratory sooty tern *(manutara).* The winning swimmer was proclaimed birdman *(tangata manu)* and thought to have supernatural powers. It's possible to hike right around the rim of Rano Kau and cut straight down to Ahu Vinapu from the east side.

Around the Island
Although many of the enigmatic statues *(moai)* are concentrated at Rano Raraku (the statue quarry), they are also found along the coast around the island. The stone walls seen at various places date from the English sheep ranch. Take the road along the south coast toward Rano Raraku, 18 km from Hanga Roa. Eight fallen *moai* lie facedown at **Ahu Vaihu.** The first king of the island, Hotu Matua, is buried at **Ahu Akahanga,** where four toppled statues are seen.

Work on the statues ended suddenly, and many were abandoned en route to their *ahu.* About 200 are still in the quarry at **Rano Raraku** in various stages of completion, allowing one to study the process; one unfinished giant measures 21 meters long. Others, visible from the top of Rano Raraku, lie scattered along the roadway to the coast. Some 70 statues stand on the slopes or inside the volcano; another 30 lie facedown on the ground. The kneeling statue, called Tuturi, on the west side of Rano Raraku is unusual.

After climbing Rano Raraku, circle around to **Ahu Tongariki** at Hotu Iti, destroyed in 1960 by a huge tidal wave that tossed the 15 statues around like cordwood. Between 1992 and 1994 Japanese archaeologists reconstructed the *ahu* and reerected the *moai* using an enormous crane donated by the Japanese crane manufacturer Tadano. There are some extraordinary petroglyphs at Tongariki, very close to the road. This is about the best ocean kayaking site on Easter Island.

Continue up along the ancient trench, which still isolates the **Poike Peninsula.** Legends maintain that the "long ears" filled the trench with wood to create a burning barrier between them and their "short-eared" adversaries, but were annihilated in the end. Heyerdahl claimed to have found a thick layer of red ash in the

trench, but more recent excavations here have found no evidence of any battle.

The tallest *moai* ever to stand on Easter Island is at **Ahu Te Pito Kura** on the north coast by La Pérouse Bay. The toppled 10-meter-long statue lies facedown beside the *ahu,* awaiting restoration.

The inviting white sands of palm-fringed **Anakena Beach** are 20 km northeast of Hanga Roa via the central road or 30 km via Rano Raraku. The National Parks Department has set up picnic tables, barbecue pits, toilets, and a campground here, and many locals come to swim or fish on Sunday (a good time to hitch a ride). Anakena is the traditional disembarkation point of Hotu Matua, the legendary founder of the island. The one *moai* on **Ahu Ature Huki** here was reerected by Thor Heyerdahl in 1955, as is indicated on a bronze plaque—the first statue to be restored on the island. **Ahu Naunau** at Anakena bears seven *moai,* four with topknots. During the restoration of this *ahu* in 1978, archaeologist Sergio Rapu discovered the famous white coral eyes of the statues.

ACCOMMODATIONS

Unless you're very fussy, accommodations are most easily arranged upon arrival, as most of the *residencial* (guesthouse) owners meet the flights. Only members of the Tourist Association representing the more expensive hotels are allowed inside the arrivals area at the airport. Outside the terminal you'll find several people offering less expensive accommodations, and you'll save money by waiting to deal with them. The peak season with the highest visitor levels is December and January; June is the slackest month. Except perhaps during the Tapati Rapa Nui festival, plenty of rooms are always available and advance bookings are not required.

If you do have reservations beware of touts who may come up to you as you're leaving the baggage area claiming that the hotel you booked is full and that your reservation has been transferred to another hotel. If you get this story insist on checking directly with the original hotel, otherwise you could end up with a worse room for a higher price. Japanese tourists who don't speak English or Spanish are often targeted in this way.

The medium price for guesthouse accommodation is US$35/50/75 single/double/triple with private bath and meals—expensive for Chile. The rooms are clean and simple, often facing a garden, but the cheaper places don't always have hot water (ask if it's included). All rates include a light breakfast, but for a full English breakfast you'll have to add US$5-10 pp. If you're asked to choose a meal plan, take only breakfast and dinner as it's a nuisance to have to come back for lunch. Picnic fare can be purchased at local stores. Unfortunately few places offer cooking facilities, and unless you order meals with the room, eating out will be expensive. Room prices do fluctuate according to supply and demand, and when things are slow bargaining is possible everywhere except at the most upmarket places. If you're on a very low budget, ask about camping at a *residencial*. The only organized campsite is the one left by the Norwegian archaeological expedition at Anakena Beach, and you'll need to carry all your own food and water if you go there.

Most of the properties listed below can be faxed at 56-2/690-2674, a central office on the island that will call the hotel and ask them to come and pick up their fax. Unlike other chapters of this book in which all possible accommodations are included, the places that follow are only a selection because almost every family on the island is involved in tourism in some way. The tourist office keeps a complete list.

Budget Accommodations
Martin and Anita Hereveri (tel. 108/223593), opposite the hospital on Simon Paoa just east of the church, offer double rooms at US$20 with shared bath, US$30 with private bath, breakfast included. Another US$10 pp nets you an ample three-course dinner. Camping on their lawn is also possible. Martin picks up guests at the airport and he's very helpful.

Anna Rapu Briones on Avenida Policarpo Toro offers bed and breakfast at US$12 pp with shared bath, US$15 pp with private bath. Dinner is US$7. You can wash clothes here and cook your own food. Ask for Anna at the airport.

Chez Cecilia Casa de Familia (tel. 108/223499), on Avenida Policarpo Toro north of center near Ahu Tahai, charges US$18/30 single/double for bed and breakfast, US$35/50/75 single/double/triple with half board. Camp-

ing is US$7 pp. Cecilia is a good cook and there's hot water. A city tour is also included. Also check **Residencial Tahai** (tel. 108/223395) on Pasaje Reimiro nearby.

Also rumored to be good is **Residencial Tadeo et Lili** (tel. 108/223422), corner of Atamu Tekena and Avenida Apina, run by Lili Frechet (French) and her Polynesian husband Tadeo. They have six bungalows with private bath (hot water).

Martin Rapu's **Rapa Nui Inn** (tel. 108/223228), on Avenida Policarpo Toro near the airport, has 10 rooms with bath beginning at US$30/45 single/double with breakfast. Other budget *residenciales* include the **Tiare Anani** (tel. 108/223580) on Avenida Pont and **Tiare Nga Oho** (tel. 108/223259) near the church. Ask about them at the airport.

The cheapest places on the tourist office's official list are **Residencial Chez Erika** (tel. 108/223474) on Calle Tuki Haka Hevari with accommodations at US$15 pp with breakfast, and **Residencial Ma'ori** (tel. 108/223497), Calle Te Pito o Te Henua, at US$15/25 single/double with breakfast. Expect basic conditions at the cheapest places.

Medium-Priced Accommodations
A good middle-range selection is the **Hotel Orongo Easter Island** (Casilla 19, Isla de Pascua; tel. 108/223294), formerly the Hotel Easter Island International, on Avenida Policarpo Toro in the center of town. The 10 rooms with private bath are US$50/80/100 single/double/triple, breakfast and dinner included.

Also recommended is Rosita Cardinali's **Hotel O'tai** (Casilla 22, Isla de Pascua; tel. 108/223250, fax 108/223482), also known as "Rosita's Pension," on Calle Te Pito o Te Henua across from the post office. It's exceptionally well run, with excellent food—US$60/85/100 single/double/triple, including breakfast. For half pension add US$15-20 pp, for full pension US$30-40 pp. In 1993 the movers and shakers in Kevin Costner's team stayed here during the filming of *Rapa Nui,* and with her profits Rosita has increased the number of rooms to 26 (all with private bath). The new swimming pool and jacuzzi also came out of movie money. It's usually full, so book ahead.

The friendly **Hotel Topa Ra'a** (tel. 108/223225), Calle Hetereki at Atamu Tekena, is conveniently located right in town. It's US$45/65/90 single/double/triple with a good view from the patio. Ask to see the room before accepting. This place belongs to archaeologist and ex-governor Sergio Rapu, who also owns the new Tumu Kai shopping mall and supermarket on Avenida Policarpo Toro.

One reader said he liked **Hostal Manutara** (tel. 108/223297) on Avenida Hotu Matua near the airport (US$50/80/100 single/double/triple with breakfast). **Hotel Victoria** (tel. 108/223272) on Avenida Pont is similar.

Upmarket Hotels

The mainlander-operated **Hotel Hanga Roa** (tel. 108/223299), on Avenida Pont overlooking the bay, has 60 rooms with private bath and continental breakfast at US$133/166/208 single/double/triple. The food is lousy, and you have to scream like a wounded eagle to get hot water. This prefabricated Florida motel simply isn't worth its tariff: transient Hollywood moviemakers occupied the entire building for six months in 1993, and they really tore the place apart. A year later it was announced the hotel had been taken over by the Panamericana hotel chain and would be rebuilt with bungalows replacing the main building.

Top of the line on Easter Island is the owner-operated **Hotel Hotu Matua** (Carlos Paoa, Casilla 17, Isla de Pascua; tel. 108/223242, fax 108/223445), on Avenida Pont near the airport. The 50 motel-style rooms with private bath and fridge are US$95/154/176 single/double/triple with breakfast. Otherwise it's US$147/202 single/double for a suite. Dinner is US$25 pp. A pleasant freshwater swimming pool forms the core of the complex, and there's a bar. If the price doesn't bother you, you'll have few complaints here, and they'll give you a discount if you pay in U.S. dollars (cash) instead of with pesos or by credit card.

The **Iorana Hotel** (tel./fax 108/223312), on Avenida Atamu Tekena outside town, is just below the west end of the runway, and the middle-of-the-night landings and takeoffs can be jarring. Rooms begin at US$84/112/166 single/double/triple with breakfast, but they're rather hot due to the thinness of the walls. At least there's a swimming pool. The tennis court has a *low* wire fence around it.

FOOD AND ENTERTAINMENT

Food

Although three supermarkets sell basic foodstuffs, a limited selection of postcards, Chilean newspapers a week or two old, and expensive recordings of local music, bring with you everything you're likely to need during your stay, especially film, PABA sunscreen, a canteen, and sturdy shoes. Only two supply ships arrive a year, meaning high prices and limited selection, so canned or snack foods might also be a good idea if you can spare the weight. It's prohibited to bring in fresh fruit and vegetables however, so get these at the local *feria* (market) held on Avenida Policarpo Toro near the governor's office (largest early Tuesday and Saturday mornings). The new **Tumu Kai Supermarket** on Avenida Policarpo Toro stays open all day. Fresh fish is available from fishermen who land their catch at the *caleta*. Watch for tasty local pastries called *empanadas*.

The snack bars of Hanga Roa are no bargain, so most visitors arrange to take meals at their lodgings for a fixed price. The **Yarvaika Bar** on Avenida Policarpo Toro is good for hamburgers, pizza, and such. Also try **Copacabana,** on Calle Te Pito o Te Henua just down from the church. The new seafood restaurant down by the *caleta* charges US$15 for dinner. The local lobsters *(langostas)* are becoming very scarce due to overharvesting, and you might like to do your bit for biodiversity by refusing to eat them. The local water has a high magnesium content, but it's safe to drink.

Entertainment

The two discos, **Toroko** in town and **PiRiTi** near the airport, crank up on Thursday, Friday, and Saturday nights: US$6 for a Coke. They open around 2200, but nothing much happens before midnight.

Ask at the tourist office and the Hotel Hanga Roa about Polynesian dancing. Sunday there's church singing at 0900 and soccer in the afternoon. Otherwise it's pretty dead at night, with lots of private *pisco* (brandy) drinking by the locals (no problem). Expect everything except church to start late.

OTHER PRACTICALITIES

Shopping

Aside from shell necklaces, the main things to buy are *moai kavakava* (woodcarvings of emaciated ancestor figures), dance paddles, miniature stone *moai,* and imitation *rongo rongo* tablets. The obsidian jewelry sold locally is imported from mainland Chile. The handicraft market near the church in Hanga Roa sells overpriced woodcarvings, and this is one of the only places in Polynesia where bargaining is expected.

The vendors at the handicraft market are always eager to trade woodcarvings for jeans, windbreakers, T-shirts, sneakers, cosmetics, and rock music cassettes. But don't count on unloading old winter clothes just before leaving for Tahiti. The locals know that trick and will give you next to nothing for them.

Visas and Officialdom

Most visitors require only a passport to visit Chile. Citizens of France and New Zealand may also require a visa (US$50). Check with any Lan Chile Airlines office, the Chilean Consulate on Tahiti, or the Chilean embassies in France (2 Avenue de la Motte Picquet, 75007 Paris; tel. 33-1/4551-8490) or New Zealand (1-3 Willeston St., 7th floor, Wellington; tel. 64-4/725-180). No vaccinations are required, and malaria is not present anywhere in Chile.

Money

The local currency is the Chilean peso (approximately US$1 = 415 pesos). Chilean currency is almost worthless outside Chile itself, so only change what you're sure you'll need, and get rid of the remainder before you leave. The Banco del Estado, beside the tourist office in Hanga Roa, charges a rip-off 15% commission to change traveler's checks, so bring U.S. dollars in cash, which are accepted as payment at all tourist-oriented establishments (though not always at good rates). If coming from Santiago, bring an adequate supply of pesos. The Sunoco gas station gives the best rates for U.S. cash (posted in the office) and the Tumu Kai Supermarket gives a better rate for traveler's checks than the local bank. Currencies other than U.S. dollars can be difficult to exchange, and credit cards are rarely usable.

Except for the most basic things, it's often hard to determine exactly what a service will cost and some islanders have an inflated idea of value. To avoid shocks, it's best to make sure prices are clearly understood beforehand.

Yachting Facilities

Some 40 cruising yachts a year visit Easter Island between Galapagos or South America and Pitcairn/Tahiti. Due to Rapa Nui's remoteness, boats will have been at sea two to four weeks before landfall. As Easter is well outside the South Pacific hurricane zone, they usually call between January and March, so as to time their arrival in Tahiti-Polynesia with the beginning of the best sailing season there. The southeast trades extend south to Easter Island most reliably from December to May, allowing for the easiest entry/exit. The rest or the year, winds are westerly and variable.

Anchorages include Hanga Roa, Vinapu, Hotu Iti, and Anakena/Ovahi, and a watch must be maintained over yachts at anchor at all times as the winds can shift quickly in stormy weather. The anchorages are deep with many rocks to foul the anchor and little sand. Landing can be difficult through the surf. The frequent moves necessitated by changing winds can be quite exhausting, and crews often have only one or two days a week ashore. Luckily the things to see are quite close to these anchorages.

A pilot is required to enter the small boat harbor at Hanga Piko and US$100 is asked. Entry through the breakers and rocks is only possible in calm weather. Mooring to the concrete wharf here is stern to as at Tahiti (no charge), but there's little space and this is only supposed to be done by boats in need of repairs. The harbor has 2.8 meters of water at low tide.

Information

There's a tourist office (tel. 108/223255) a few doors west of the bank in Hanga Roa, open weekday mornings. Their airport branch opens only for flights. In Santiago, the **Servicio Nacional de Turismo** (Avenida Providencia 1550, Santiago de Chile; tel. 56-2/236-1416) can supply maps, brochures, and a complete list of hotels on Easter Island.

A very good 1:30,000 topographical map of Easter Island printed in Spain is published by **Editiones del Pacific Sur,** Hernando de Aguirre 720, Departamento 63, Providencia, Chile. It's sold locally at souvenir shops, such as Hotua Matua's Favorite Shoppe on Avenida Policarpo Toro.

The CONAF office on the road to Orongo sells an even better map coated with rainproof plastic. It's called *Parque Nacional Rapa-Nui/Easter Island Chile, Corporación Nacional Forestal/World Monuments Fund* and is nice enough to frame. The Fund put up the money to print the map and all proceeds from sales go to CONAF's conservation efforts.

No newspapers or magazines are published on Easter Island, so the easiest way to keep in touch with what's happening is to subscribe for Georgia Lee's *Rapa Nui Journal* (Box 6774, Los Osos, CA 93412, U.S.A.; fax 805/534-9301). The *Journal* comes out four times a year, and contains an interesting mix of scientific studies, announcements, and local gossip—well worth the US$25 annual subscription price (US$35 airmail outside Canada and the U.S.).

Two basic books about the island are *The Island at the Center of the World* by Father Sebastian Englert and *Ethnology of Easter Island* by Alfred Metraux. *The Modernization of Easter Island,* by J. Douglas Porteous, concentrates on the postcontact period. Paul Bahn and John Flenley's 1992 book *Easter Island,* *Easter Island* presents the collapse of the island's civilization in environmental terms and warns that mankind is once again headed along that track. The best travel guides to the island are *An Uncommon Guide to Easter Island* by Georgia Lee (available from International Resources, Box 840, Arroyo Grande, CA 93420, U.S.A.) and Alan Drake's *The Ceremonial Center of Orongo.* Both are the sort of books you can pick up and read from cover to cover without getting bored.

If you're arriving in Santiago from the South Pacific and aren't carrying the *South American Handbook,* pick one up at Librería Eduardo Albers, Vitacura 5648, or Librería Inglesa Kuatro, Pedro de Valdivia 47, both in Santiago (see Resources).

TRANSPORTATION AND TOURS

Getting There

Lan Chile Airlines flies a Boeing 767 to Easter Island from Tahiti and Santiago twice a week, with two additional weekly flights between Easter Island and Santiago operating from November to March (summer holiday time for Chilean students). In Santiago, check carefully which terminal you'll be using, as flights that turn around at Easter Island and return to Santiago are classified "domestic" and leave from the old terminal, whereas flights continuing to Tahiti are "international" and use the new terminal. Occasionally you'll be sent to the wrong terminal, so allow a little extra time. The "international" flights are often inconveniently timed, with late-night arrivals common at all three points.

Lan Chile has a history of changing schedules or canceling flights at a moment's notice, and occasionally the Tahiti plane simply doesn't bother to land here at all. Book and reconfirm your onward flight well ahead, as the plane is often overbooked between Easter Island and Santiago—a week is enough time to see everything. You'll occasionally witness heated arguments at Mataveri Airport as people who were careless with their bookings try desperately to get off Easter Island, and there have even been cases when the police had to intervene to restore order! Foreigners pay higher fares than local residents, so it's usually the locals who get bumped. The local Lan Chile office (tel. 108/223279) is on Avenida Policarpo Toro (open mornings). See the main Introduction to this book for sample fares and special deals. In the U.S., call Lan Chile toll-free at 800/735-5526 for information.

A German reader sent us this comment:

Your description of Lan Chile is absolutely correct! One hand doesn't know what the other is doing: very unfriendly personnel at the airport, lengthy flight delays with no information available, no explanation of the delay later on, and no "I'm sorry." I'll never fly Lan Chile again if I can avoid it.

Getting Around

There's no public transport; a daylong minibus tour around the island is US$25-50 pp. One of the most reliable travel agencies on the island is **Mahinatur** (tel. 108/223220) on Avenida Policarpo Toro. They can book hotel accommodations, tours, and rental vehicles, and their services are used by most overseas tour operators. Beware of Anakena Tours—bad reports.

Rental vehicles are available at US$50 a half day, US$100 a full day, or less. An International Driver's License is required. Insurance is not available but gasoline is cheaper than on the mainland. Lots of cars are available and to find one all you need to do is stroll down the main street watching for the signs. Do ask around, as prices vary (bargaining possible), and check to make sure the car has a spare tire *(neumático)* and a jack *(gata)*. Sometimes they'll throw in a driver for "free." Scooters can be hired at US$35 a day, but a motorcycle license is mandatory. The gas tanks on some of the scooters are too small to visit both Rano Raraku and Anakena, and the red cinder roads outside Hanga Roa are pretty bad.

Cheaper and more fun is horseback riding, which runs about US$15 a half day, US$25 a full day. Guys on the street rent horses for as little as US$10 a day, but both animal and saddle may be, sadly, the worse for wear. Anakena is a little far to go by horse and return in a day. Ask for Alejo Rapu, who meets the flights at the airport, as he has horses at US$15 a day, bicycles US$15 a day, and scooters at US$25 a day. Fishing boats are available to visit the *motus* off the southwestern tip of the island for around US$50 a half day (up to six persons).

You can walk 60 km clockwise right around the island in three or four days, but take all the food and water you'll need. Camping is allowed at the national park attendant's post at Rano Raraku, and there's a regular campsite at Anakena. The park rangers may deign to replenish your water supply, but on very dry years no water is available for campers, so ask. If you camp elsewhere, try to stay out of sight of motorized transport. This is not an easy trip, so only consider it if you're in top physical shape. Good boots and a wide-brimmed hat are musts, as the terrain is rough and there's absolutely no shade.

Airport

Mataveri Airport (IPC) is walking distance (with backpack) from the places to stay in Hanga Roa. Ask for the free map and hotel list at the tourist office to the right past customs. The departure tax is US$5. If you're headed for Tahiti, don't bother taking any fresh fruit as it will be confiscated at Papeete.

A rough airstrip was begun here in the early 1950s and improved by the U.S. Air Force as an "ionospheric observation center" in the 1960s. In fact, the Americans used the base to spy on French nuclear testing in the Tuamotus. It closed with the election of Salvador Allende in 1970, but in 1986 the Americans were back with permission from Pinochet to extend both ends of the airstrip for use as an emergency landing strip by NASA space shuttles. In late 1995 the older part of the runway was repaired.

Tours

Nature Expeditions International (Box 11496, Eugene, OR 97440, U.S.A.; tel. 800/869-0639, fax 503/484-6531) runs a comprehensive archaeology tour of Easter Island about once a month (US$2290 double occupancy, airfare extra). The groups spend seven of the tour's 14 days exploring Easter Island under the guidance of local archaeologists.

Far Horizons Trips (Box 91900, Albuquerque, NM 87199, U.S.A.; tel. 800/552-4575, fax 505/343-8076) organizes a 10-day tour to coincide with the Tapati Rapa Nui festival in early February (US$2990 double occupancy, airfare extra). Noted archaeologist and author Dr. Georgia Lee escorts the group.

GORDON OHLIGER

COOK ISLANDS
INTRODUCTION

About 4,500 km south of Hawaii, the Cook Islands range from towering Rarotonga, the country's largest, to the low oval islands of the south and the lonely atolls of the north. Visitors are rewarded with natural beauty and colorful attractions at every turn. There is motion and excitement on Rarotonga and Aitutaki, peaceful village life on the rest. The local tourist industry is efficient and competitive, which has its up sides and its down sides. Hotel and motel development is proceeding apace and visitor/resident ratios have already reached Hawaiian densities on Rarotonga. You can still find an unspoiled paradise here, though every year you must go farther away from the center to reach the "last heaven on earth." Nevertheless, it's still packaged Polynesia at its best.

The local greeting is *kia orana* (may you live on). Other words to know are *meitaki* (thank you), *aere ra* (goodbye), and *kia manuia!* (cheers!).

The Land

These 15 islands, with a land area of only 240 square km, are scattered over 1.83 million square km of the Pacific, leaving a lot of empty ocean in between. It's 1,400 km from Penrhyn to Mangaia. The nine islands in the Southern Group are a continuation of the Austral Islands of Tahiti-Polynesia, formed as volcanic material escaped from a southeast/northwest fracture in the earth's crust. The rich, fertile southern islands account for 89% of the Cooks' land area and population.

Practically every different type of oceanic island can be found in the Cooks. Rarotonga is the only high volcanic island of the Tahiti type. Aitutaki, like Bora Bora, consists of a middle-aged volcanic island surrounded by an atoll-like barrier reef, with many tiny islets defining its lagoon. Atiu, Mangaia, Mauke, and Mitiaro are uplifted atolls with a high cave-studded outer coral ring *(makatea)* enclosing volcanic soil at the center. There are low rolling hills in the interiors of both

Atiu and Mangaia, while Mauke and Mitiaro are flat. The swimming and snorkeling possibilities at Atiu, Mangaia, Mauke, and Mitiaro are limited, as there's only a fringing reef with small tidal pools. Aitutaki and Rarotonga have protected lagoons where snorkeling is relatively safe. Manihiki, Manuae, Palmerston, Penrhyn, Pukapuka, Rakahanga, and Suwarrow are typical lagoon atolls, while tiny Takutea and Nassau are sand cays without lagoons. All of the northern atolls are so low that waves roll right across them during hurricanes, and you have to be within 20 km to see them. This great variety makes the country a geologist's paradise.

Climate

The main Cook Islands are about the same distance from the equator as Hawaii and have a similarly pleasant tropical climate. Rain clouds hang over Rarotonga's interior much of the year, but the coast is often sunny. The rain often comes in brief, heavy downpours. The other islands are drier and can even experience severe water shortages. Winter evenings from June to August can be cool. From May to October the trade winds blow from the southeast in

THE ISLANDS OF THE COOKS

	AREA IN HECTARES	POPULATION (1991)
Rarotonga	6,718	10,918
Mangaia	5,180	1,105
Atiu	2,693	1,003
Mitiaro	2,228	249
Mauke	1,842	639
Aitutaki	1,805	2,366
Penrhyn	984	503
Manuae	617	0
Manihiki	544	666
Pukapuka	506	670
Rakahanga	405	262
Palmerston	202	49
Takutea	122	0
Nassau	121	103
Suwarrow	40	10
COOK ISLANDS	**24,007**	**18,543**

the Southern Cooks and from the east in the more humid Northern Cooks; the rest of the year winds are generally from the southwest or west. November to April is the summer hurricane season, with an average of one every other year, coming from the direction of Samoa. If you happen to coincide with one, you're in for a unique experience!

The Hurricane Coordination Center number is tel. 22-261. For weather information call the Meteorological Office (tel. 20-603) near Rarotonga Airport.

Flora and Fauna

The *au* is a native yellow-flowered hibiscus. The all-purpose plant's flower is used for medicine, the leaves to cover the *umu* (earth oven), the fiber for skirts, reef sandals, and rope, and the branches for walling native cottages. The lush vegetation of the high islands includes creepers, ferns, and tall trees in the interior, while coconuts, bananas, grapefruit, and oranges grow on the coast. Avocados and papayas are so abundant that the locals feed them to their pigs. Taro and yams are subsistence crops. On the elevated atolls the vegetation in the fertile volcanic center contrasts brusquely with that of the infertile limestone *makatea*. From November to February, the flamboyant trees bloom red.

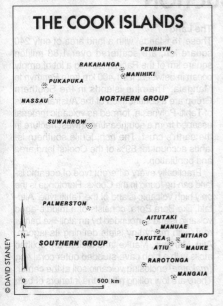

THE COOK ISLANDS

PENRHYN

RAKAHANGA

MANIHIKI

PUKAPUKA

NASSAU

NORTHERN GROUP

SUWARROW

PALMERSTON

AITUTAKI

MANUAE

TAKUTEA MITIARO

SOUTHERN GROUP

ATIU MAUKE

RAROTONGA

MANGAIA

-N-

0   500 km

© DAVID STANLEY

RAROTONGA'S CLIMATE

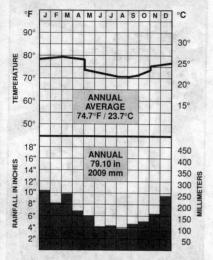

The only native mammals are bats and rats. The mynah is the bird most often seen, an aggressive introduced species that drives native birds up into the mountains and damages fruit trees. Only about 50 examples of the Rarotonga Flycatcher or *Kakerori* remain, due to attacks on the birds' nests by ship rats. The most interesting aspect of the natural environment is found among the fish and corals of the lagoons and reefs. Reef walks on Rarotonga and lagoon trips on Aitutaki display this colorful world to visitors. Whales can sometimes be seen cruising along the shorelines. Sharks are not a problem in the Cook lagoons.

HISTORY AND GOVERNMENT

Discovery

Though peppered across a vast empty expanse of ocean, the Polynesians knew all these islands by heart long before the first Europeans happened on the scene. One of several legends holds that Rarotonga was settled about A.D. 1200 by two great warriors, Karika from Samoa and Tangiia-nui from Tahiti. The story goes that Karika and Tangiia-nui met on the high seas but decided not to fight because there would be no one to proclaim the victor. Instead they carried on to Rarotonga together and divided the island among themselves by sailing their canoes around it in opposite directions, with a line between their starting and meeting points becoming the boundary. Even today, tribes in the Cooks refer to themselves as *vaka* (canoes), and many can trace their ancestry back to these chiefs.

Archaeologists believe Rarotonga was reached much earlier, probably around A.D. 800 from Raiatea or the Marquesas. The mythical chief Toi who built the Ara Metua on Rarotonga is associated with this earlier migration. Atiu was a chiefly island that dominated Mauke, Mitiaro, Takutea, and sometimes Manuae.

The Spanish explorer Mendaña sighted Pukapuka in 1595, and his pilot, Quirós, visited Rakahanga in 1606. Some 500 inhabitants gathered on the beach to gaze at the strange ships. Quirós wrote, "They were the most beautiful white and elegant people that were met during the voyage—especially the women, who, if properly dressed, would have advantages over our Spanish women."

Then the islands were lost again to Europeans until the 1770s when Captain Cook contacted Atiu, Mangaia, Manuae, Palmerston, and Takutea—"detached parts of the earth." *He* named Manuae the Hervey Islands, a name others applied to the whole group; it was not until 1824 that the Russian cartographer, Johann von Krusenstern, labeled the Southern Group the Cook Islands. Cook never saw Rarotonga, and the Pitcairn-bound *Bounty* is thought to be its first European visitor (in 1789). The mutineers gave the inhabitants the seeds for their first orange trees. Mauke and Mitiaro were reached in 1823 by John Williams of the London Missionary Society.

European Penetration

Williams stopped at Aitutaki in 1821 and dropped off two Tahitian teachers. Returning two years later, he found that one, Papeiha, had done particularly well. Williams took him to Rarotonga and left him there for four years. When he returned in 1827, Williams was welcomed by Papeiha's many converts. The missionaries taught an austere, puritanical morality and believed the white man's diseases such as dysentery, measles, smallpox, and influenza, which killed two-thirds of the population, were the punishment of God descending on the sinful islanders. The missionaries became a law unto themselves; today, ubiquitous churches still full on Sunday are their legacy. (The missionaries weren't aware of the idea of an international date line and held Sunday service on the wrong day for the first 60 years of their presence!) About 63% of the population now belongs to the Cook Islands Christian Church (CICC), founded by the London Missionary Society. Takamoa College, the Bible school they established at Avarua in 1837, still exists.

Reports that the French were about to annex the Cooks led the British to declare a protectorate in 1888. The French warship approaching Manihiki to claim the islands turned back when it saw a hastily sewn Union Jack flying. Both the Northern and Southern groups were annexed under the British Crown and included in the boundaries of New Zealand on 8 October 1900 in what was probably the most ornate European ceremony ever held on a South Pacific island. New Zealand law took effect in the Cooks

daughter of the ex-queen of Manikiki, turn of the century, Cook Islands

in 1901. During WW II, the U.S. built air bases on Aitutaki and Penrhyn.

After decolonizing pressure from the United Nations, the Cook Islands were allowed to become an internally self-governing state in free association with New Zealand on 4 August 1965. There is no New Zealand veto over local laws; the Cook Islands operate as an independent country. The paper connection with New Zealand deprives the country of a seat at the U.N. but brings in millions of dollars in financial and technical assistance from Wellington that might otherwise be withheld. New Zealand citizenship, which the Cook Islanders hold, is greatly valued (New Zealanders are not Cook Islands citizens, however). The arrangement has been very successful and is looked upon as a model by many Tahitian leaders. In recent years Cook Islands has sought closer economic and cultural ties with Tahiti-Polynesia to balance their relationship with New Zealand.

Reader Robert Bisordi of New York had this comment:

Sir Nathaniel Dance's 1776 portrait of Captain Cook

Over the years we've spent more time on Rarotonga than on any other island, visiting it five times. We've seen rapid development that can only be described as culturally destructive: huge banks in Avarua, disfiguring coastal and inland quarries, access to American video tapes which induce profanity and materialism, etc. A tremendous Sheraton complex is under construction, defacing the geography, creating artificial beaches and islets, detouring the road . . . surely the end. These islanders just don't know where they're going, and there is a blind excitement over the novelty of this materialistic path they're on. But we westerners know where they are heading and that it holds much dismay. After all, why do we go to the South Seas, we disenchanted westerners?

Government

Cook Islands' 24-member Parliament operates on the Westminster system, with a prime minister at the head of government. The cabinet consists of seven members. The 15-member House of Ariki (chiefs) advises on custom and land issues.

On all the outer islands there's an appointed chief administrative officer (CAO), formerly known as the Resident Agent. Although each island also has an elected Island Council, the CAO runs the local administration on behalf of the local and central governments. Government control is more pervasive in the Cooks than in any of the large Western democracies.

Politics

Party politics, often based on personalities, is vicious. The most dramatic event in recent years was the removal of Premier Albert Henry and the Cook Islands Party from office in 1978 when it was proven that Henry had misused government funds to fly in his voters from New Zealand during the preceding election. Then, Queen Elizabeth stripped Sir Albert of his knighthood. This

was the first time in Commonwealth history that a court ruling had changed a government: the shock waves are still being felt in Rarotonga. Albert Henry died in 1981, it's said of a broken heart.

Albert Henry's successor, Sir Tom Davis of the Democratic Party, served as prime minister from 1978 until July 1987, when he was ousted by a vote of no confidence. The Cook Islands Party, led by Sir Geoffrey Henry, a cousin of Albert, won the 1989 and 1994 elections. The Democratic and Alliance parties are in opposition.

ECONOMY AND PEOPLE

Economy

Cook Islanders live beyond their means. Imports outweigh exports by eight times, and food imports alone are nearly double all exports. Tourism makes up for some of this, but without N.Z. aid (about NZ$10 million a year), which totals a fifth of government revenue, the Cooks would be bankrupt (in 1992 and 1993 the Cook Islands government ran NZ$3 million budget deficits). New Zealand has announced that it plans to phase out budgetary aid over the next 20 years. Meanwhile there have been reports of tax evasion by local companies using fraudulent tax certificates.

AIR NEW ZEALAND

The largest exports are cultured pearls, tropical produce (papaya, bananas, beans, taro), pearl shells, and preserved fish, in that order. Fresh fruit production is hindered by the small volume, uneven quality, inadequate shipping, poor marketing, and the unreliability of island producers.

In 1982 a cultured-pearl industry modeled on that of Tahiti-Polynesia was established on Manihiki. With some 400,000 oysters already held at the 50 farms that are now operating on Manihiki, the atoll's lagoon is approaching its maximum sustainable holding capacity, and Penrhyn, Rakahanga, and Suwarrow are being developed as new pearl-farming areas. Fluctuations in water temperature and overstocking can affect the amount of plankton available to the oysters and reduce the quality of the pearls. Rising temperatures can have an immediate impact. To establish a farm, an investment of NZ$5000 is required, and no return will be forthcoming for five years. The oysters are seeded once or twice a year by Japanese experts contracted by the Ministry of Marine Resources, and some 40,000 pearls are sold in lots of over 500 at an annual auction in June, with Japanese and Chinese dealers the big buyers. Black pearls are now Cook Islands' largest export industry, bringing in US$4.5 million a year and employing 600 people.

The economy's small size is illustrated by the importance of the post office's Philatelic Bureau. Money remitted by Cook Islanders resident in N.Z. contributes about NZ$3 million a year to the local economy, and licensing fees from South Korean and other foreign fishing companies to exploit the Exclusive Economic Zone bring in additional income. The export of clothing has declined in recent years, but a number of small clothing factories in Avarua continue to supply the local and tourist markets. Of 2,600 individual taxpayers in the Cooks, some 1,800 are employed by the government!

Despite the strident Christianity displayed on Sunday, since 1982 Cook Islands has operated as an International Finance Center by providing offshore banking facilities to foreign corporations and individuals attempting to avoid legitimate taxation in their home countries. In contrast to local businesses, which are heavily taxed, some 2,000 Asian (mostly Hong Kong) companies that don't operate in the Cooks now are registered in the Rarotonga "tax haven," bringing in over NZ$1 million a year in banking and licensing fees. Australian and New Zealand corporations were formerly active participants, but in 1991 those countries revised their tax laws to restrict the use of tax havens by their citizens (penalties of up to 125% of the tax due and five years in prison). Offshore "banks" can be owned by a single person and there have been persistent rumors of illicit money laundering through Rarotonga. In early 1995 *Islands Business Pacific* reported that the Cook Islands Government had guaranteed 12 letters of credit worth a total of US$1.2 billion in a scam that Prime Minister Geoffrey Henry hoped would earn US$10 million in commissions. The worthless guarantees were quickly withdrawn when they came under scrutiny by the Reserve Bank of New Zealand. That an outspokenly Christian country such as Cook Islands should go out of its way to profit from the scheming of sharp operators is rather ironic.

Cook Islands also runs a low-cost "flag of convenience" ship registry that allows foreign shipping companies to avoid the more stringent safety and labor regulations of industrialized countries. Ominously, one of the first ships to sign up, the freighter *Celtic Kiwi,* sank off New Zealand in October 1991. After further sinkings and reports of gun running, many insurance companies won't touch ships registered in the Cooks.

The country has a NZ$250 million national debt, much of it incurred by tourism-related developments such as the Sheraton Hotel project, the National Cultural Center, power generation, and telecommunications since 1987 when the administration of Sir Geoffrey Henry took over. In mid-1994 local branches of the ANZ and Westpac banks began to severely restrict private credit after the government proved unable to service its heavy debt load. A few months later the banks stopped clearing checks drawn in Cook Islands dollars through the New Zealand banking system and announced that these would have to be collected locally. Local businesses began moving their money offshore, and in late 1994 the Reserve Bank of New Zealand confirmed that it no longer guaranteed the convertibility of the Cook Islands dollar. The threat of imminent financial collapse forced the government to withdraw the currency from circulation in 1995.

Tourism

Since the opening of the international airport in 1973, tourism has been important, and directly or indirectly, it employs a quarter of the workforce and accounts for over half the gross national product. Cook Islands has the highest tourist density in the South Pacific by far with three tourists a year for every local resident, compared to three Fijians, four Western Samoans, and five Tongans for every tourist visiting those countries. At times Rarotonga (with five tourists a year per Cook islander) really has the feel of a little Hawaii.

About a third of the 50,000-odd arriving tourists are New Zealanders who spend all their time at resorts on Rarotonga and Aitutaki on prepaid packaged holidays. The rest are fairly evenly divided between Americans, Australians, Canadians, and Europeans. With improved air service from Los Angeles the number of arrivals from North America is rapidly increasing and overdevelopment has led to serious sewage disposal and water supply problems on Rarotonga.

The 151-room Rarotongan Resort Hotel was built in 1977 by the Cook Islands government, the Tourist Hotel Corporation of N.Z., and Air New Zealand, with each owning a third. In 1982, after the hotel proved to be a consistent money-loser, the Cook Islands government had to buy out its two partners to prevent closure. When the poorly planned Aitutaki Lagoon Hotel tottered on bankruptcy in 1989, the government was forced to take it over too.

In 1984 "experts" from the United Nations Development Program advised that the way to make tourism more "profitable" was to allow more large hotels and stop construction of the smaller, family-owned motels. Finding itself unable to attract the required foreign investment, the government itself decided to bankroll construction of a new four-star luxury hotel, and in 1987 NZ$51 million was borrowed from an Italian bank. A year later the Democratic Party was defeated and Sir Geoffrey Henry's Cook Islands Party was voted in after promising to stop the project. Once in office, however, Sir Geoffrey did an about-face and announced that he now backed the hotel. A management contract was signed with the Sheraton chain and in May 1990, despite many objections from local residents, construction began on the south side of Rarotonga using Italian building materials and contractors.

The 204-room Cook Islands Sheraton Resort was conceived as a cluster of two-story buildings, similar to the Fiji Sheraton, with the inevitable 18-hole golf course. The project suffered repeated delays, and then it was announced that the Italian construction company had gone broke after spending NZ$30 million of the government's loan money without getting much done. A second Italian construction company was brought in, and the government borrowed another NZ$20 million so work could resume. In mid-1993 the Italian government began its "clean hands" crackdown on mafia activities, and several people involved in the Sheraton project were arrested in Italy, causing the Italian insurers to freeze coverage on the loans, and work on the Sheraton stopped again. In November, 1994, the former manager of the first Italian construction company, Mr. Franco Pichi, was murdered at Port Vila, Vanuatu, in a mysterious mafia-style killing.

The empty structure of the unfinished Sheraton now faces an uncertain future, and the full story of what went on behind the scenes has yet to be told. It's estimated that at least another NZ$18 million (US$12 million) is required to finish the hotel, plus about NZ$4.5 million (US$3 million) for the golf course. Anyone interested in putting up the money should contact ECIL Ltd., Box 431, Rarotonga (tel. 21-705, fax 22-520). Incredibly, a monument bestowing full credit on Sir Geoffrey for inaugurating the project still stands in front of the ruins! Meanwhile there are NZ$81 million in accumulated bad debts to pay, and Cook Islands is facing financial ruin. (Sheraton has had nothing to do with the construction scandal and will only take over if and when the resort is ever finished.)

The People

Almost all of the people are Polynesian Cook Island Maoris, most of whom also have some other ancestry. The Pukapukans are unique in that they are closer to the Samoans. Cook Islands Maoris are related to the Maoris of New

Zealand and the Tahitians. Over half the population resides on Rarotonga; only 12% live in the Northern Group. Until self-government, Cook Islanders were only allowed to consume alcohol if they had a permit; now it's a serious social problem. Cook Islanders live near the seashore, except on Atiu and Mauke, where they are interior dwellers. The old-style thatched *kikau* houses have almost disappeared from the Cook Islands, even though they're cooler, more aesthetic, and much cheaper to build than modern housing. A thatched pandanus roof can last 15 years.

While 18,543 (1991) Cook Islanders live in their home islands, some 35,000 reside in New Zealand and another 10,000 in Australia. Emigration to N.Z. increased greatly after the airport opened in 1973, but New Zealanders do not have the right to reside permanently in Cook Islands. Recently the migratory patterns have reversed with many ex-islanders returning from New Zealand to set up tourism-related businesses. There are almost no Chinese in the Cooks due to a deliberate policy of discrimination initiated in 1901 by N.Z. Prime Minister Richard Seddon, although many islanders have some Chinese blood resulting from the presence of Chinese traders in the 19th century. Under the British and N.Z. regimes, the right of the Maori

people to their land was protected, and no land was sold to outsiders. These policies continue today, although foreigners can lease land subject to strict limitations. The fragmentation of inherited landholdings into scattered miniholdings hampers agriculture.

The powerful *ariki,* or chiefly class, that ruled in pre-European times is still influential today. The *ariki* were the first to adopt Christianity, instructing their subjects to follow suit and filling leadership posts in the church. British and N.Z. colonial rule was established with the approval of the *ariki.* Now materialism, party politics, and emigration to N.Z. are eroding the authority of the *ariki.*

Dangers and Annoyances

There's been an increase in rape cases lately. It's okay to have fun, but women should keep this in mind when stepping out at night and when choosing a place to stay. There's safety in numbers. Scanty dress outside the resorts will cause offense and maybe trouble. Be aware of petty theft, particularly if you're staying somewhere with young children running loose. Don't go off and leave things on the clothesline. Try to avoid being bitten by mosquitoes, as these are sometimes carriers of dengue fever (see "Health" in the main Introduction).

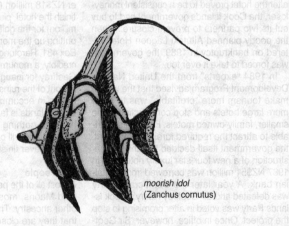

moorish idol
(Zanchus cornutus)

ON THE ROAD

Sports and Recreation

Most organized sporting activities are on Rarotonga and Aitutaki. Several professional scuba diving operators are based on these islands, and there are many snorkeling possibilities. Both islands offer lagoon tours by boat, with those at Aitutaki among the best in the South Pacific.

Several companies based on Rarotonga's Muri Beach rent water-sports equipment, including sailboards, sailboats, and kayaks, with training in their use available. The surfing possibilities are limited in Cook Islands—windsurfing's the thing to do. Horseback riding and deep-sea fishing are other popular activities.

Most of the hiking possibilities are on mountainous Rarotonga, but uplifted islands such as Atiu, Mauke, and Mangaia are also fascinating to wander around, with many interesting, hidden features. The nine-hole golf courses on Aitutaki and Rarotonga aren't too challenging, but green fees are low and the atmospheres amicable. Tournaments are held at both in September.

The Round Raro Run (32 km) is in early October or November: Kevin Ryan set a record (98.14 minutes) in 1979. The spectator sports are cricket from December to March, with matches every Saturday afternoon, and rugby from June to August. On Rarotonga, ask about rugby matches at Tereora National Stadium (built for the 1985 South Pacific Mini Games), on the inland side of the airport, and in the sports ground opposite the National Cultural Center in Avarua.

Public Holidays and Festivals

Public holidays include New Year's Days (1 and 2 January), ANZAC Day (25 April), Good Friday, Easter Monday (March/April), Queen Elizabeth's Birthday (first Monday in June), Constitution Days (4 and 5 August), Gospel Day (26 October), Christmas Day (25 December), and Boxing Day (26 December). On Rarotonga Gospel Day is celebrated on 26 July; elsewhere it's 26 October.

Cultural Festival Week, with arts and crafts displays, is in mid-February. The Dancer of the Year Competition is in late April. The 10-day Constitution Celebrations, beginning on the Fri-

day before 4 August, are the big event of the year. There are parades, dancing and singing contests, sporting events, and an agricultural fair. Gospel Day (26 October) recalls 26 October 1821, when Rev. John Williams landed on Aitutaki. Ask about religious plays *(nuku)* on this day. On All Souls' Day (November 1st), Catholics visit the cemeteries to place candles and flowers on the graves of family members. The third or fourth week in November is Tiare Festival Week, with flower shows and floral parades. A food festival is also held in November. On Takitumu Day (3 December), visits are made to historic *marae*.

Accommodations

There's an abundance of accommodations in all price categories on Rarotonga and Aitutaki, and many outer islands also have one or two official places to stay. Local regulations prohibit visitors from staying in private homes, camping, living in rental cars, or sleeping on the beach, so have the name of a licensed hotel ready upon arrival. The government has refused to license public camping grounds and banned camping in general in an effort to force visitors to spend more money. It's also official policy to impose unrealistic standards on the low-budget hostels, to prevent the existing hostels from expanding, and to discourage backpackers. Yet the same officials responsible for these petty policies think nothing of squandering their country's limited resources subsidizing loss-making luxury hotels!

As you come out of the airport terminal, someone may ask you which hotel you plan to stay at, and will direct you to the representative of that establishment (if he/she happens to be present). This person is an employee of the government-run Cook Islands Tourist Authority, and problems can arise if you're suspected of being a covert camper, so play the game as best you can. Repeat the name of the licensed accommodations you wrote on your arrival card, then go over and talk to the representative of that establishment if he/she is pointed out to you. Sometimes a uniformed immigration officer will ask those waiting in line to have their passports stamped if they have prearranged hotel reservations. Those who admit they don't are taken aside, given a brief lecture of the rules and regulations of Cook Islands, and introduced to a representative from one of the low-budget hostels. If this happens to you, act innocent and cooperate.

It used to be necessary to make a hotel booking before you were allowed entry to Cook Islands, but this regulation has since been modified and you're now only required to stay at a licensed hotel, motel, or hostel. However, if you happened to arrive without a reservation on a day when all of the budget places were full, you could be presented with the choice of taking a expensive room at a luxury hotel or leaving on the same flight. In practice, this is unlikely to happen as there are lots of places to stay, and someone will almost always be happy to earn a few extra dollars by picking up an unexpected guest. Keep in mind too that when everything's full on Rarotonga, rooms are often still available on Aitutaki, and a connecting flight to that outer island will extricate you from this confusing situation.

In order to have the best choice of places to stay and maximum flexibility in your plans, it's best not to prepay any hotel accommodations at all. However, with Rarotonga's growing popularity among North Americans and increasing flight frequencies, accommodation is sometimes tight, especially in the medium-price range. If you're sure you want to stay at a particular place and wish to play it safe, you can make an advance hotel booking through Air New Zealand or Polynesian Airlines offices in the South Pacific (but not overseas), the Cook Islands Tourist Authority in Avarua (fax 21-435), or directly to the hostel or hotel. This service costs nothing extra and you can pay upon arrival. If you end up with something you don't like, it's always possible to move somewhere else after a day or two. If you do have a reservation, a representative of your hotel will be at the airport to take you to your assigned room for a fee of about NZ$20 roundtrip.

You'll save money and get closer to the people by staying at the smaller, locally owned "self-catering" motels and guesthouses. The fewer

the rooms the motel has, the better. A "motel" in the Cooks is styled on the New Zealand type of motel, which means a fully equipped kitchen is built into each unit. Some of them are quite attractive, nothing like the dreary roadside motels of the United States. The motels generally offer rooms with private bath and hot water, but some guesthouses and hostels do not, although communal cooking facilities are usually available. At the big resorts you not only pay a much higher price, but you're forced to eat in fancy dining rooms and restaurants.

All of the officially approved accommodations are listed herein. Prices are more or less fixed, and haggling at the airport is *not* the thing to do! One local hostel owner sent us this:

In order to hang onto the cheap accommodation on Rarotonga it's important that our budget visitors behave well and give a good impression while they're here. Often they cause problems at the airport with their "Fiji" bargaining techniques. They can be thoroughly unpleasant and give the locals the impression that we'd be better off without them. It's a delicate situation here—bargaining has never been a part of the local culture and the locals find it really offensive when tourists start trying to beat prices down. The reality is that we walk away from them. Costs like electricity, motor vehicle parts, and insurance are high here, there's a 10% turnover tax, and we're socked with all kinds of license fees— at last count I had to pay eight! The climate is hell on maintenance and I don't know of a budget property that has made a profit in the last three years. Tourists don't realize that in a small airport like ours the person standing next to you may be a member of parliament who is already prejudiced against budget travelers. Now they're after us to put in all sorts of "improvements" such as landscaping and 24-hour security which will force us to raise prices to make ends meet.

On many Pacific Islands taro (below) is an important subsistence crop, while papaya (above) is exported.

DAVID STANLEY

Outer islands without licensed accommodations, or where such accommodations are full, may be effectively closed to visitors. Ask Air Rarotonga about this before heading too far off the beaten track. Three times a week **Stars Travel** (Box 75, Rarotonga; tel. 23-669; fax 21-569), near Foodland in Avarua, has a seven-night package tour from Rarotonga to Atiu, Mitiaro, and Mauke for NZ$701 for one person, NZ$598 pp for two, NZ$567 pp for three, including airfare, accommodations (double occupancy), meals on Mitiaro, transfers, and tax. Other Stars Travel packages offer two nights on Aitutaki, Atiu, or Mauke. These individualized tours are recommended, and Stars Travel can also reserve rooms alone at any hotel or guesthouse in the Cook Islands. **Island Hopper Vacations** (Box 240, Rarotonga; tel. 22-026, fax 22-036), next to Foodland in Avarua, offers similar deals and arranges airport transfers to outer island flights. Another agency specialized in booking rooms from overseas is **Hugh Henry & Associates** (Box 440, Rarotonga; tel. 25-320, fax 25-420). It's sometimes (but not always) cheaper to make your own arrangements.

Food and Drink

The Rarotonga restaurant scene has improved in recent years and you now have an adequate choice, despite unexplained arson attacks that have eliminated a few good places. A few restaurants are found on Aitutaki, but none exist on the outer islands. When ordering, keep in mind that an "entree" is actually an appetizer and not a main dish. On Sunday almost everything outside the hotels closes down, which makes Sunday a good day to be on an outer island.

By law all bars are required to close at midnight, except Friday night when they can stay open until 0200. On Sunday alcohol may only be ordered with a meal, although this rule is not always followed. Wine is expensive at restaurants, due to high import duties, and drinking alcoholic beverages in the street is prohibited. Most of the motels and guesthouses offer cooking facilities and you'll save a lot on meals if you stay at one of them.

Rukau is Cook Islands *palusami*, made from spinachlike young taro leaves cooked in coconut cream. *Ika mata* is marinated raw fish with coconut sauce. Locals insist that slippery foods such as bananas lead to forgetfulness, while gluey foods like taro help one to remember. Dogs are sometimes eaten by young men on drinking sprees. Turn to "Entertainment and Refreshment" in the "Atiu" section for information on "bush beer" (called "home-brewed" on Rarotonga and Aitutaki).

SERVICES AND INFORMATION

Visas and Officialdom

No visa is required for a stay of up to 31 days, but you must show an onward ticket. You can get a maximum of five extensions, one month at a time, at NZ$30 for each extension. Proof that you're staying in licensed accommodations is required. After the initial one-month stay in licensed accommodations, tourists are allowed to live in unlicensed places for the balance of their permitted six months in the Cooks. Actually, one week is plenty of time to see Rarotonga and 31 days is quite sufficient to visit all of the Cook Islands accessible to tourists.

If you're thinking of taking a boat trip to the Northern Group, be sure to get a visa extension before you leave Rarotonga. Otherwise you could have problems with immigration if your entry permit has expired by the time you get back. A letter from the immigration office on Rarotonga is required to stay on an island in the Northern Group.

For a foreigner to obtain permanent residency in Cook Islands is difficult and only allowed in exceptional circumstances (such as if you're willing to invest money). Cook Islands citizenship has never been extended to Europeans. For more information write: Principal Immigration Officer, Department of Immigration, Box 473, Rarotonga, Cook Islands (tel. 682/29-363, fax 682/29-364).

Anyone interested in obtaining permanent residence through investment should contact Karen Jeffery of Pacific Island Investments (Box 383970, Waikoloa, HI 96738, U.S.A., fax 808/883-8838), who knows of many tourism-related business opportunities in the Cooks.

Rarotonga, Aitutaki, and Penrhyn are ports of entry for cruising yachts; the only harbors for yachts are at Aitutaki, Penrhyn, Suwarrow, and Rarotonga.

Money

The currency is the New Zealand dollar, which was valued at US$1 = NZ$1.49 at press time. After a financial crisis in 1995 the Cook Islands dollar, which had circulated at par with the New Zealand dollar, was withdrawn. Cook Islands coins and the CI$3 banknote are still in use, however, although these are worthless

outside Cook Islands. A further hitch is that N.Z. one- and two-dollar coins are not accepted in the Cook Islands. The Cook Islands dollar coin, bearing an image of the god Tangaroa, and the three-dollar banknote, depicting Ina and the shark, make excellent souvenirs—great gifts for friends elsewhere in the Pacific.

Traveler's checks are worth about three percent more than cash at the banks. Changing money on an outer island is difficult or impossible—do it before you leave Rarotonga. The up-market hotels and restaurants accept the main credit cards, and the banks will give cash advances. The local American Express representative is Stars Travel (tel. 23-669). Unless otherwise indicated, all prices this chapter are in N.Z. dollars, currently worth about two-thirds as much as U.S. dollars, which makes the Cook Islands inexpensive.

A 10% gross sales or "turnover tax" is added to all sales, services, activities, and rentals. Most places include it in the price, but some charge it extra, so ask. Do not try to bargain, but tipping is optional.

Telecommunications

Telecom Cook Islands (Box 106, Avarua; tel. 29-680, fax 20-990) charges a flat rate for international telephone calls with no off-hours discounts. Three-minute operator-assisted calls cost NZ$7.60 to New Zealand, NZ$10.90 to Australia, and NZ$18.50 a minute to most other countries (three-minute minimum). Person-to-person calls attract an additional two-minute charge. It's a bit cheaper to use a local telephone card for these calls, and there's no three-minute minimum with a card (dial the international access code 00, the country code, the

area code, and the number). More importantly, with a card you can't lose track of the time and end up being presented with a tremendous bill. The cards come in denominations of NZ$10 and NZ$20 and are good for all domestic and international calls. Calls to outer islands within Cook Islands cost NZ$1 a minute with a card.

Collect calls can be placed to Australia, Canada, Fiji, Japan, Malaysia, New Zealand, Niue, Sweden, Switzerland, Tahiti-Polynesia, Tonga, the United Kingdom, and the U.S.A. only. To call collect, dial the international/outer island operator at tel. 015. Directory assistance numbers within Cook Islands are tel. 010, international tel. 017.

For calls to the U.S., AT&T's "USADirect" service is more expensive than using a local telephone card, but perhaps useful in emergencies. To be connected to this service dial 09111 from any phone in the Cook Islands.

The country code of Cook Islands is 682.

Measurements and Time

The electric voltage is 240 volts DC, 50 cycles, the same as in New Zealand and Australia. American appliances will require a converter. The type of plug varies, but bring a three-pin adaptor. On outer islands other than Aitutaki electricity is only provided a few hours a day.

The time is the same as in Hawaii and Tahiti, two hours behind California and 22 hours behind New Zealand. "Cook Islands time" also runs a bit behind "Western tourist's time," so relax and let things happen. All travel agencies, banks, and offices are closed on Saturday, although most shops and restaurants are open until noon. Almost everything outside the churches and hotels is closed from noon Saturday to Monday morning.

Media

Be sure to pick up a copy of the *Cook Islands News* (Box 15, Rarotonga; tel. 22-999, fax 25-303), published daily except Sunday (50 cents). Its reporting on island affairs really gives you a feel for where you are, and local events are listed. In 1993 the *News* was threatened with closure after it published a mild cartoon showing the hand of parliament holding a gun to the head of free speech. The paper was forced to print a retraction on the front page. The *Cook Islands Sun* (Box 608, Rarotonga) is a free tourist newspaper.

Information

For advance information about the country, write to one of the branches of the government-operated **Cook Islands Tourist Authority** listed in the appendix, or to their head office at Box 14, Rarotonga (fax 21-435). Ask for their free magazine, *What's On In The Cook Islands.*

Elliot Smith's *Cook Islands Companion* (Pacific Publishing, 735 San Carlos Ave., Albany, CA 94706, U.S.A.) is recommended for those who want more detailed information on the country than can be included here. Smith's book has much more of a "hands-on" feel than other guides to the Cooks.

TRANSPORTATION

Getting There

Air New Zealand (tel. 26-300) has direct services to Rarotonga from Auckland, Honolulu, Nandi, Papeete, and Los Angeles, and the Cooks can be included in its Coral Route and Circle-Pacific fares. Epic excursion fares to Rarotonga from Australia and New Zealand are seasonal, and some have to be purchased 21 days in advance.

All air services into Rarotonga are heavily booked, so reserve your inward and outward flights as far ahead as possible. If you try to change your outbound flight after arrival you'll probably be put on standby. Check in for your outgoing international flight at least one hour before the scheduled departure time, as the airlines are short of staff: if everyone is needed to attend to a flight arrival, they may simply close the check-in counter and you'll be out of luck.

Polynesian Airlines (tel. 20-845) has a flight between Apia and Rarotonga twice a week, and it can be included in their Polypass (see "Getting Around" in this book's main introduction). In the Cooks, their agent is Air Rarotonga.

If you have to buy any sort of international air ticket in Cook Islands, check with **Stars Travel** (tel. 23-669), which offers the best deals.

Getting Around by Air

All of the main islands of the Southern Cooks and a few of the Northern Group have regular air service from Rarotonga, although no flights operate on Sunday. **Air Rarotonga** (Box 79,

Rarotonga; tel. 22-888, fax 23-288) services Aitutaki (NZ$246 roundtrip) three times a day except Sunday; Atiu (NZ$222 roundtrip), Mangaia (NZ$222 roundtrip), and Mauke (NZ$246 roundtrip) every weekday; Mitiaro (NZ$246 roundtrip) three times a week; Manihiki (NZ$1000 roundtrip) twice a week; and Penrhyn (NZ$1100 roundtrip) weekly. The interisland connection Atiu-Mitiaro-Mauke only works once a week. Sitting in one of their 18-seat Bandierantes for four hours to Manihiki or Penrhyn is quite an experience!

Children under 15 pay half price. Ask about seven day advance-purchase "Early Bird" or "Super Saver" roundtrip excursion fares (not available in December and January). Another special fare allows you to fly Rarotonga-Aitutaki-Rarotonga for NZ$198 (instead of NZ$246) provided you depart Rarotonga on the last flight of the day and return on the first. Air Rarotonga also has a "Paradise Island Pass" costing NZ$96 per sector but you must visit at least two islands (four sectors). Of course, it's only valid in the Southern Group.

The baggage allowance is 16 kilos, though you can sometimes get by with more. On flights to Manihiki and Penrhyn the limit is 10 kilos. Overweight is not expensive, but if the plane is full and too heavy for the short outer-island runways they'll refuse excess baggage from all passengers. Thus it pays to stay below the limit.

Advance reservations are required, as space is limited. Your best bet is to leave Rarotonga on Friday or Saturday, as everything shuts down on Sunday—not such a problem on an outer island. Always reconfirm your return flight, and beware of planes leaving early! Never schedule your flight back to Rarotonga for the same day you're supposed to catch your international flight.

Air Rarotonga offers 20-minute scenic flights (NZ$49 pp) around Rarotonga out of their hangar (tel. 29-888), 500 meters west of the main terminal. You can often arrange this on the spur of the moment if a pilot and plane are available. Tandem skydiving is NZ$220 pp.

Getting Around by Ship

Outer Island Shipping (Box 378, Rarotonga; tel. 27-651) runs the freighter MV *Marthalina* to the Northern Group about once a month

(NZ$400 return for the three-week trip), and to the Southern Group every two months (NZ$100 return for a six-day tour or NZ$38 one-way to an individual island such as Aitutaki or Atiu). Only deck class is available and conditions are basic. There's no set schedule, and the only way to find out if they're going is to ask at their office at Avatiu Harbor. (The *Marthalina* has a colorful history, including a 1991 seizure by Sri Lankan customs officials after an undeclared cargo of 11,000 Belgian rocket launchers was discovered aboard.)

The smaller interisland boat *Avatapu* is captained by an American named Nancy Griffith (Box 131, Rarotonga; tel. 22-369, fax 24-369), who has circumnavigated the globe by yacht three times and is very knowledgeable about both the islands and sailing. The *Avatapu* only goes when there is sufficient cargo (ask in the green shed at the wharf). A one-week trip around the southern islands might cost NZ$100, a two-week trip to the northern group NZ$200, a bunk in the 10-bed dorm included, but meals are extra (package price available).

Be forewarned that accommodations on this sort of ship are usually next to noisy, hot engine rooms and are often cluttered with crates. Deck passengers sleep under a canvas awning, and although it may be a little crowded, the islanders are friendly and easy to get along with. The interisland ships leave from Avatiu Harbor, so ask the captains of those you see tied up along the quay. On the outer islands, check with the radio operator in the post office to find out when a ship from Rarotonga might be in. Delays of a few days are routine.

In practice, however, interisland travel by boat within the Cook Islands is highly infrequent and irregular, so it's best to save your interisland freighter adventures for Tahiti or Fiji, where such things are far more easily arranged.

Airport

Rarotonga International Airport (RAR) is 2.4 km west of Avarua. The terminal is functional and businesslike after the relaxed elegance of Tahiti's airport. Immigration will stamp a 31-day entry permit onto your passport. As you come out of the customs area someone from the Tourist Authority will ask you the name of your hotel. If you haven't prebooked, just give the name of any of the establishments listed herein, and their representative will inform you whether they have vacant rooms.

The Westpac Bank at the airport charges NZ$2.50 commission per transaction (no commission to change New Zealand dollars either way). Cook Islands Tours & Travel (tel. 27-270) at the airport will store excess luggage at NZ$2 per piece per day. Clarify their hours to make sure they'll be there when you want to collect your bags. Several duty-free shops open for international arrivals and departures, and arriving passengers are allowed to duck into the duty-free liquor shop (tel. 29-322) to the right before clearing customs. Duty-free prices here are lower than in Tahiti and New Zealand but a bit higher than Fiji. A NZ$25 departure tax is charged for international flights (children aged two to 11 pay NZ$10, and transit passengers staying fewer than 24 hours are exempt).

RAROTONGA

The name Rarotonga means "in the direction of the prevailing wind, south," the place where the chief of Atiu promised early explorers they would find an island. It's fairly small, just 32 km around. Twisting valleys lead up to steep ridges and towering mountains covered with luxuriant green vegetation and crowned in clouds. Yet, Te Manga (653 meters) is only a fraction of the height Rarotonga reached before the last volcanic eruption took place, over two million years ago.

Though Rarotonga is younger than the other Cook islands, continuous erosion has cut into the island, washing away the softer material and leaving the hard volcanic cones naked. The mountains are arrayed in a U-shaped arch, starting at the airport and then swinging south around to Club Raro, with Maungatea plopped down in the middle. Together they form the surviving southern half of the great broken volcanic caldera that became Rarotonga.

The reef circling the island defines a lagoon that is broad and sandy to the south, and narrow and rocky on the north and east. The best beaches are on the southeast side near the Muri Lagoon, with crystal-clear water and a sandy bottom, but the best snorkeling is at Titikaveka. Elsewhere the water can be cloudy, with a lot of coral and shells that make wading difficult. Take care everywhere, as several snorkelers have drowned after being sucked out through the passes where a lot of water moves due to surf and tidal swings. All beaches on the island are public.

In recent years Rarotonga has become New Zealand's answer to Hawaii with 50,000 visitors to an island of 10,000 inhabitants, the same five-to-one ratio experienced in Hawaii. Unlike Tahiti where many women wear the pareu, almost everyone on Rarotonga wears Western dress, and their demeanor toward visitors is about as laid-back as their attitude to life. To find the wild, romantic Polynesia of the travel books you have to get beyond Rarotonga. Yet Raro remains one of the most beautiful islands in Polynesia, somewhat reminiscent of Moorea (although only half as big). If you enjoy the excitement of big tourist resorts with plenty of opportunities for shopping and eating out, you'll like Rarotonga.

SIGHTS

Avarua

This attractive town of around 5,000 inhabitants is strung along the north coast beneath the green, misty slopes of Maungatea. Somehow Avarua still retains the air of a 19th-century South Seas trading post, and offshore in Avarua Harbor lies the boiler of the Union Steam Ship SS *Maitai,* wrecked in 1916. Across the street from the new post office is the **Seven-in-One Coconut Tree** (planted 1906). In May 1992 a devastating fire swept through old colonial buildings of the government complex here, badly damaging the post office, telephone exchange, and courthouse, all of which have since been demolished. Two local men convicted of lighting the fire allegedly did so to avoid being put on trial in the courthouse on a charge of stealing a pair of running shoes (although rumor has it that the fire may have had more to do with the destruction of the Company Register at a time when

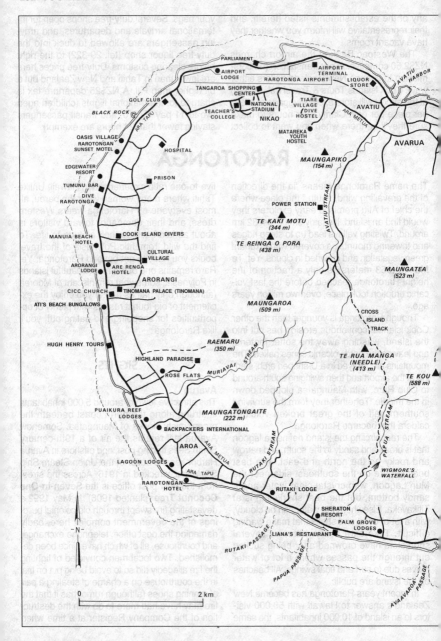

PARLIAMENT

AIRPORT
LODGE

AIRPORT
TERMINAL

RAROTONGA AIRPORT

LIQUOR
STORE

AVATIU
HARBOR

TANGAROA SHOPPING
CENTER

TIARE
VILLAGE
DIVE HOSTEL

AVATIU

GOLF CLUB

TEACHER'S
COLLEGE

NATIONAL
STADIUM

NIKAO

AVARUA

BLACK ROCK

MATAREKA
YOUTH HOSTEL

ARA TAPU

OASIS VILLAGE
RAROTONGAN
SUNSET MOTEL

RAROTONGA

MAUNGAPIKO
(154 m)

HOSPITAL

EDGEWATER
RESORT

ARA METUA

POWER STATION

AVATIU STREAM

TUMUNU BAR
DIVE
RAROTONGA

PRISON

TE KAKI MOTU
(344 m)

MANUIA BEACH
HOTEL

COOK ISLAND DIVERS

TE REINGA O PORA
(438 m)

ARORANGI
LODGE

ARE RENGA
HOTEL

CULTURAL
VILLAGE

MAUNGATEA
(523 m)

CICC CHURCH

ARORANGI

TINOMANA PALACE (TINOMANA)

MAUNGAROA
(509 m)

ATI'S BEACH BUNGALOWS

CROSS
ISLAND
TRACK

RAEMARU
(350 m)

HUGH HENRY TOURS

MURIAVAI STREAM

TE RUA MANGA
(NEEDLE)
(413 m)

HIGHLAND PARADISE

TE KOU
(588 m)

ROSE FLATS

PUAIKURA REEF
LODGES

MAUNGATONGAITE
(222 m)

BACKPACKERS INTERNATIONAL

AROA

ARA METUA

LAGOON LODGES

ARA TAPU

RUTAKI STREAM

PAPUA STREAM

WIGMORE'S
WATERFALL

RAROTONGAN
HOTEL

RUTAKI LODGE

SHERATON
RESORT

PALM GROVE
LODGES

LIANA'S RESTAURANT

N

RUTAKI PASSAGE

0   2 km

PAPUA PASSAGE

AVAAVAROA PASSAGE

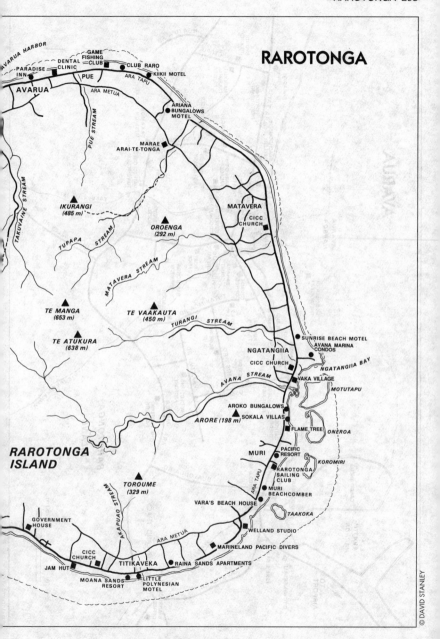

RAROTONGA

AVARUA HARBOR

PARADISE INN

DENTAL CLINIC

GAME FISHING CLUB

CLUB RARO

KIIKII MOTEL

PUE

ARA TAPU

AVARUA

ARA METUA

ARIANA BUNGALOWS MOTEL

PUE STREAM

MARAE ARAI-TE-TONGA

TAKUVAINE STREAM

IKURANGI (485 m)

MATAVERA

CICC CHURCH

OROENGA (292 m)

TUPAPA STREAM

MATAVERA STREAM

TE MANGA (653 m)

TE VAAKAUTA (450 m)

TURANGI STREAM

TE ATUKURA (638 m)

SUNRISE BEACH MOTEL

AVANA MARINA CONDOS

NGATANGIIA

CICC CHURCH

NGATANGIIA BAY

AVANA STREAM

VAKA VILLAGE

MOTUTAPU

AROKO BUNGALOWS

ARORE (198 m)

SOKALA VILLAS

FLAME TREE

ONEROA

RAROTONGA ISLAND

MURI

PACIFIC RESORT

KOROMIRI

RAROTONGA SAILING CLUB

MURI BEACHCOMBER

TOROUME (329 m)

AKAPUAO STREAM

ARA TAPU

VARA'S BEACH HOUSE

TAAKOKA

GOVERNMENT HOUSE

ARA METUA

WELLAND STUDIO

MARINELAND PACIFIC DIVERS

CICC CHURCH

TITIKAVEKA

RAINA SANDS APARTMENTS

JAM HUT

MOANA SANDS RESORT

LITTLE POLYNESIAN MOTEL

© DAVID STANLEY

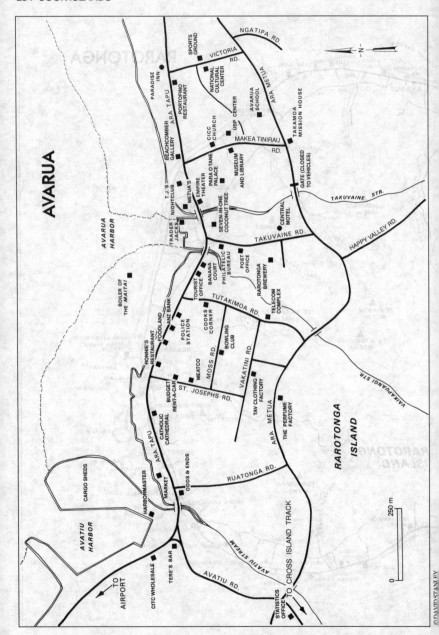

AVARUA

© DAVID STANLEY

DAVID STANLEY

The Museum and Library at Avarua is well worth a visit.

the Cook Islands "tax haven" was coming under intense scrutiny in New Zealand).

Just inland from the post office is the privately owned **Rarotonga Brewery** (Box 814, Rarotonga; tel. 21-083, fax 21-089), which offers a free guided tour weekdays at 1400, during which participants get to taste the four-and-a-half-percent-alcohol draft beer (bottled beer is six percent alcohol). The Cooks Lager T-shirts sold at the brewery souvenir counter are hot items.

The **Beachcomber Gallery** (tel. 21-939), at the corner of the Ara Tapu and Makea Tinirau Roads, is housed in a former London Missionary Society school building (1843). It's well worth entering this museum-like gallery to peruse the lovely pearl jewelry and other art works on sale.

Check out the massive wooden balcony inside the **Cook Islands Christian Church** (1853). It's worth being here Sunday morning at 1000, if only to see the women arrive in their Sunday best and to stand outside and listen to the wonderful singing (only go inside and sit down if you're prepared to stay for the whole service). Near the front of the church is the tomb of Albert Henry (1907-81), topped by a lifelike statue of the man (see "Politics" in the introduction to this chapter). Writer Robert Dean Frisbie (1895-1948), author of *The Book of Pukapuka,* is buried in the southwest corner of the graveyard.

Across the road, beyond some old graves, is the **Para O Tane Palace** of Queen Makea Takau Ariki, onetime high chief of this area.

Marae Taputaputea and a basalt investiture pillar are on the palace grounds.

Farther inland is the **Museum and Library of the Cook Islands** (Box 71, Rarotonga; tel. 20-748; open Monday to Saturday 0900-1300, donation)—well worth a visit to see the assorted artifacts, many of them on loan from museums in New Zealand. At the end of the road is the two-story **Takamoa Mission House** (1837) with mementos of the early missionaries.

Farther east is the NZ$11.6-million **National Cultural Center,** erected for the 6th Festival of Pacific Arts in 1992. Highlights are a museum (weekdays 0800-1600) with a collection of model canoes and modern replicas of South Pacific artifacts, a library (tel. 20-725; Monday and Wednesday 0900-2000, Tuesday, Thursday, and Friday 0900-1600), and a 2000-seat auditorium.

The Ara Metua

Two roads circle Rarotonga: the new coastal road (the Ara Tapu) and an old inner road (the Ara Metua). As many of the hotels are on the southwest side of Rarotonga, the main sights are arranged below for a counterclockwise tour of the island on the Ara Tapu. The distances in parentheses are from Avarua. On a scooter you should be able to do it in four hours with stops; by bicycle give yourself a leisurely day.

On your second time around try using the Ara Metua, passable much of the way (see the Avarua map). You'll encounter lush gardens, orchards, and good viewpoints. This inner road is said to be the oldest in Polynesia, the coral-block foundation laid some 1,000 years ago by chief Toi. Up until the mid-19th century, when the missionaries concentrated the population around their churches on the coast, most of the people lived on the inland side of this road. During WW II the road was resurfaced and much of it is now paved.

Around the Island

Just under a km west of Rarotonga airport is the **Parliament of the Cook Islands** (1973), which meets from February to March and July to September. If you're properly dressed (no shorts or jeans), you can observe the proceedings from the public gallery (Monday, Tuesday, and Thursday 1300-1700, Wednesday and Friday 0900-1300). Call 26-500 for information.

West of Avarua, beyond the airport and golf course (see "Sports and Recreation" below), is **Black Rock** (6 km), standing alone in a coral lagoon (good swimming). This rock marks the spot where the spirits of deceased Rarotongan Polynesians pass on their way back to the legendary homeland, Avaiki. The Tahitian missionary Papeiha is said to have swum ashore here, holding a Bible above his head (in fact he landed in a small boat).

Arorangi (8.5 km) was established by the early missionaries as a model village, and Papeiha is buried in the historic white cemetery at the old CICC church (1849). The restored **Tinomana Palace** of the last native ruler of this district stands nearby. The flattened top of **Mt. Raemaru** (350 meters) rises up behind Arorangi. Legends tell how Aitutaki warriors carried off Raemaru's missing upper part. To climb Raemaru, take the steep jeep track off the Ara Metua at Sam Rere Panelbeaters (a large green auto repair shop—no sign), then up the fern-covered ridge to Raemaru's western cliffs. When you get close to the forest at the base of the cliffs, take the right fork of the trail up to the cliff itself. The final climb to the mountain's flat summit can be dangerous if the rocks on the cliff are wet and slippery, but once on top, you can see the whole western side of Rarotonga. There's an easier track down the back of Raemaru that you can use to return, but you'd probably get lost if you tried to climb it. Along this route you circle down a taro-filled valley back to the Ara Metua.

Takitumu

The southeast side of Rarotonga is known as Takitumu. East of the skeletal Sheraton Resort with its ironic monument to Sir Geoffrey Henry is **Government House,** residence of the governor general (tel. 29-311). Another fine coral-block CICC church (1841) stands beside the road at **Titikaveka** (19 km from Avarua counterclockwise, 14 km clockwise). Some of the best **snorkeling** on Rarotonga is off the beach opposite Raina Sands Apartments, behind the cemetery with the radio mast next to TM Motors. There's not a lot of coral but plenty of fish. All of the scuba operators bring their clients here.

Turn in at the Rarotonga Sailing Club, four km northeast, to see the lovely **Muri Lagoon,** with the best swimming and windsurfing area on the island. At low tide you can wade across to uninhabited Koromiri Island, where hermit crabs forage as bathers enjoy the oceanside beach. Full nautical gear is for rent at the club (open daily) and the restaurant serves a good lunch.

The road up the **Avana Valley** begins near the bridge over Avana Stream and runs along the south bank. You can cycle halfway up, then continue on foot.

On the right just beyond the Avana Stream bridge is **Vaka Village** with a monument marking the historic gathering of ocean voyaging and war canoes here during the 1992 Festival of Pacific Arts. Local fishing boats anchor on the spot today. A little beyond is another old white CICC church on the left and across the street is a small park with a good view of the islands in the Muri Lagoon and **Ngatangiia Harbor.** Legend claims seven canoes departed from here in A.D. 1350 on a daring voyage to N.Z., and the names of the canoes are inscribed on a monument. Cruising yachts sometimes anchor here, though it's rather exposed to the southeast trades.

Back near the bridge is a road in to the **Ara Metua.** On the right a short distance along this road is an old burial ground with a Polynesian *marae* among the trees on a hillock behind. Many other similar *marae* are in the vicinity.

Continue along the Ara Metua and turn left up the road alongside Turangi Stream, just on the far side of a small bridge. The **Turangi Valley** is larger and more impressive than Avana, and swamp taro is grown in irrigated paddies. Once again, you cycle halfway up and continue on foot.

Toward Ikurangi

At **Matavera** there's yet another lovely CICC church (1865) beside the road. Farther along, just a few km before Avarua, watch for a signboard on Maotangi Road pointing the way in to **Marae Arai-te-tonga,** on the Ara Metua. Marae Arai-te-tonga, the most sacred on the island, was a *koutu,* or place where the *ta'unga* (priest) invested and anointed the high chiefs *(ariki)* of the island. The site is still considered sacred, so don't walk on the *marae.* The route of the ancient Ara Metua is quite evident here, and there are other stone constructions 100 meters along it to the east.

Take the road inland between these ruins as far as Tupapa Stream, where two rather difficult climbs begin. Just a km up the trail is a fork in the path: the right fork leads to the top of **Ikurangi** (485 meters), while the one up the stream continues to **Te Manga** (653 meters). Neither climb is easy, so a local guide would be a good idea. From the top of Ikurangi ("Tail of the Sky") you can see the whole wave-washed reef, tomato patches, and plantations of grapefruit, orange, tangerine, and lemon trees. This climb is best done in the cool hours of the early morning.

The Cross-Island Track

From Avarua walk three km up the Avatiu Valley. Just beyond the power station you get your first view of Te Rua Manga, **the Needle** (413 meters). In another 10 minutes the road ends at a concrete water intake; you continue up a footpath for 15 minutes until you reach a huge boulder. Pass it and head up the steep forested incline. This climb is the hardest part of the trip, but when you reach the top, the Needle towers majestically above you (the hike from the end of the road to the top takes less than an hour).

There's a fork at the top of the ridge: the Needle up on your right, the trail down to the south coast on the left. After scrambling around the Needle (you can't scale the top without climbing gear), start down the trail to the south coast, past the giant ferns along the side of the stream. The road out begins at **Wigmore's Waterfall** at the bottom of the hill. The stream above Wig-

more's is a drinking water source, so save your swimming for the pool below the falls. The hapless Sheraton Resort is in this vicinity.

Though sometimes slippery, the cross-island track can be covered in all weather and even if it has been raining, you can still do the trip the next day. Parts of the track are badly eroded, so it might not be a good idea to go alone. The crossing takes two to five hours depending on how fast you walk, but there's a slightly easier roundtrip to the Needle from the end of the road on the Avatiu side, allowing a return to a parked vehicle. Several companies offer guided cross-island treks Monday to Saturday at 0930, but lots of visitors do this hike on their own every day, so you don't really need a guide. The Tourist Authority may tell you the track is "closed" on Sunday, but if you keep a low profile it's unlikely anyone will take it upon themselves to try to stop you.

Commercial Visitor Attractions

Weekdays at 1000 the **Cultural Village** (Box 320, tel. 21-314, fax 25-557; admission NZ$30), on the back road in Arorangi, enthusiastically demonstrates Cook Islands history, medicine, cooking, arts, crafts, dances, and traditions during an informative three-hour program, which includes a lunch of local foods. Advance reservations through a hotel, travel agency, or direct by phone are required. Several readers have written in strongly endorsing the Cultural Village.

Another attraction accessible weekdays at 1000 is **Highland Paradise** (tel. 20-610; admission NZ$20), a private botanical garden where old *marae* and other historic sites are scattered among the vegetation. The steep access road begins next to Rose Flats, a km south of the Cultural Village.

Sports and Recreation

Most of the organized sporting activities mentioned below are canceled on Sunday, a good day for fasting and meditation as most restaurants and bars are shut too. Even swimming and hiking are officially discouraged on that day.

Try your swing at the nine-hole **Rarotonga Golf Club** (tel. 27-360; closed Sunday), under the radio towers near the end of the airstrip. Green fees and club rentals are NZ$10 each. If you hit a mast, wire, or stay during your round, there's a compulsory replay; balls have been known to bounce back at players. There's an annual tournament here in late September and the club has a very pleasant colonial-style bar perfect for a cold beer (visitors are always most welcome).

Dive Rarotonga (Barry and Shirley Hill, Box 38, Rarotonga; tel. 21-873) offers scuba trips every afternoon at 1300 (NZ$50 with one tank); snorkelers can go along for NZ$20 pp (rental of snorkeling gear extra). It's open on Sunday!

Scuba diving is also offered by Greg Wilson's **Cook Island Divers** (Box 1002, Rarotonga; tel. 22-483, fax 22-484), just up the road. It's NZ$10 more expensive, but Greg goes out twice a day, at 0800 and 1300, and he runs a highly professional show. His four-day NAUI scuba certification course is NZ$425—what better place to learn?

Marineland Pacific Divers (Box 811, Rarotonga; tel. 22-450, fax 23-616) at the Pacific Resort on Muri Beach offers scuba diving on the nearby Titikaveka Reef at 0900 and 1400 (NZ$55). All three scuba operators offer discounts for three or more dives.

The **Aqua Sports Centre** (Box 67, Rarotonga; tel. 27-350, fax 20-932) at the Rarotonga Sailing Club on Muri Beach rents kayaks (NZ$10 an hour), windsurfers (NZ$30 an hour), sailboats (NZ$40 an hour), and snorkeling gear (NZ$15 a day). Lessons in windsurfing (NZ$40) and sailing (NZ$50) are given, and daily except Sunday at 1100 Aqua Sports runs a two-hour glass-bottom snorkeling trip at NZ$25 pp, hotel transfers and lunch included. They'll also ferry you over to an uninhabited offshore island for NZ$5 return. Equipment rental is possible every day. **Captain Tama's Water Sportz World** (Box 45, Rarotonga; tel. 20-427) at the Pacific Resort, Muri, rents out the same sort of gear and also does lagoon cruises in a boat with a thatched sunroof.

Pacific Marine Charters (Box 770, Rarotonga; tel. 21-237, fax 27-464) at Avatiu Harbor offers deep-sea fishing from its yellow cruiser. Also at Avatiu is the MV *Seafari* of **Seafari Charters** (Box 148, Rarotonga; tel./fax 20-328). Four hours of fishing costs about NZ$95 pp (NZ$60 pp for non-fishing passengers), a light lunch included. Both boats depart weekdays at

0900 and the fishing takes place right off Rarotonga, so you don't waste time commuting and you get very good views of the island. The captain gets to keep the fish.

For horseback riding it's **Aroa Pony Treks** (tel. 20-048), up the road from Kaena Restaurant near the Rarotongan Resort Hotel. They offer two-hour rides to Wigmore's Waterfall, returning along the beach, weekdays at 1000 (NZ$28 pp). Both the Edgewater Resort and Rarotongan Hotel have tennis courts open to the public, and the Edgewater also has squash courts.

Monday at 1730 you can jog with the Hash House Harriers. For the venue, call David Lobb at tel. 22-000 during business hours, check the notice outside the Westpac Bank, or scrutinize the back page (bottom) of the Monday edition of the *Cook Islands News*. It's good fun and a nice way of meeting people.

ACCOMMODATIONS

Accommodations in every price category are plentiful on Rarotonga, just insist on a place with cooking facilities as restaurant meals can add up. All of the budget and medium-priced hotels are self-catering, but many of the up-market resorts are not. Some places include the 10% turnover tax in the quoted rate, while others charge it extra. Check out time at the motels is 1000. When choosing, keep in mind that the west coast is drier and gets beautiful sunsets, while the finest snorkeling is at windy Titikaveka in the south. The places near Avarua are best for those more into shopping and nightlife than beachlife. In past all of the budget hotels have provided free or inexpensive airport transfers to those who booked direct, but the Tourist Authority is attempting to prevent them from doing this, so check. The listings below are arranged counter-clockwise around the island in each price category.

Budget Accommodations

There's such an abundance of budget accommodation on Rarotonga that you'd have to be very unlucky to arrive on a day when everything was full (such as at Christmas). The closest Rarotonga comes to a youth hostel is Hugh

Baker's **Matareka Youth Hostel** (Box 587, Rarotonga; tel. 23-670, fax 23-672), on the hillside facing the far side of the airport. There are three four-bed dormitories at NZ$15 pp, plus three single or double rooms (NZ$25/40 single/double). A communal kitchen, laundry, and lounge area are available, and bicycles/scooters are for rent. In season, Hugh will give you all the free fruit you want. It's quiet, breezy, and has some of the best views on the island (ask for the upper dormitory).

At the bottom of the hill below Hugh Baker's are the three A-frame chalets and guesthouse of the **Tiare Village Dive Hostel** (Box 719, Rarotonga; tel. 23-466). This establishment functions as a backpackers' hostel with 13 rooms at NZ$16/32/48 single/double/triple (no big dormitories). The 23 guests share the communal cooking facilities, lounge, and hot water showers in a family-style environment, and the tropical garden is bursting with fruit free for the picking. It's only a 30-minute walk from town (and provides a convenient base for hiking to the Needle), though the Island Bus passes here only once or twice a day.

The **Are Renga Motel** (Box 223, Rarotonga; tel. 20-050, fax 26-174) at Arorangi has 20 simple thin-walled units with well-equipped kitchens at NZ$25/40/45 single/double/triple. The quality varies, so ask to see another room if the first one you're shown isn't to your liking. Beware of rooms with open ventilation spaces near the ceiling, as these let in every sound from adjacent rooms. The Are Renga offers a reduced "backpacker's rate" of NZ$15 per bed in a couple of shared double rooms. The location is great with a store and other facilities nearby, and a lending library is available in the office. Use of their washing machine costs NZ$5, but there's no dryer. When the motel is full, the Are Renga folk may offer you a room at **Airport Lodge** (tel. 27-395), near the Meteorological Station at the end of the airport runway. There are six self-catering duplex units, four of them facing the runway and two facing a coconut tree. It's rather isolated with no store nearby and only worth accepting as a last resort.

Arorangi Lodge (Box 584, Rarotonga; tel. 21-687, fax 26-174), about 200 meters south of the Are Renga, has eight rooms at NZ$30/40/50 single/double/triple, four of them upstairs in the main building and another four in a long block facing the garden. Several have been converted into three- or four-bed dormitories (NZ$14 pp). Communal cooking facilities are provided. This property has direct access to the beach, one of the only low-budget properties on Rarotonga where this is so. Low-season rates are available. If their representative doesn't happen to be at the airport when you arrive, call 21-773 for pickup.

Backpackers International Hostel (Bill Bates, Box 878, Rarotonga; tel./fax 21-847) is in the southwest corner of the island, only 150 meters from a grocery store, the Island Bus, and the beach. Ten twin-bed rooms are available at NZ$25/30/45 single/double/triple in a two-story building, five downstairs and five upstairs. A bed in a shared room is NZ$14. The common TV lounge and cooking area are downstairs (Bill will probably give you some free fruit). It's convivial, and on Saturday night the managers prepare a special buffet dinner for guests at NZ$10 pp.

Under the same management is **Rutaki Lodge** (Box 878, Rarotonga; tel./fax 21-847), a single-story building adjacent to Rutaki Store on the south side of the island. There are seven rooms: one single, three doubles (double beds), and three triples (three single beds). Communal cooking is available and prices are identical to Backpackers International.

In August 1994 the **Aremango Guesthouse** (Box 714, Rarotonga; tel. 24-362, fax 24-363) opened 50 meters from Muri Beach between the Muri Beachcomber Motel and the Taakoka Island Villas. The 10 fan-cooled rooms with shared bath are NZ$15 pp plus tax (airport transfers NZ$10 pp). Singles must be prepared to share or pay for both beds. Communal cooking facilities are available, and lockable cupboards for groceries are provided. Upon request, a traditional dinner is prepared on Sunday night at NZ$10 pp (nonguests NZ$20 pp). Mountain bikes are for hire.

Vara's Beach House (Vara Hunter; tel. 22-619), on the south side of the Muri Beachcomber Motel, rents rooms in several houses with their own kitchenettes at NZ$15 pp. The rooms near the lagoon have only communal cooking facilities, but on the mountain side you could have your own kitchen.

The **Ariana Bungalows Motel** (Box 925, Rarotonga; tel. 20-521, fax 26-174), also known as Ariana Backpackers Accommodation or the Ariana Hostel, a couple of km east of Avarua, offers quite a range of accommodation. The seven individual self-catering bungalows are NZ$48 single, double, or triple, whereas the six shared doubles are NZ$17 pp. The two dormitories are NZ$15 pp (11 beds for men, four beds for women). The pleasant grounds are peaceful and spacious, but it's 500 meters in off the main road and quite a distance from town or the beach (their swimming pool is a substitute). They rent bicycles and scooters, and a few basic groceries are sold at the office for normal prices.

Medium-Priced Accommodations
Ati's Beach Bungalows (Box 693, Rarotonga; tel. 21-546, fax 25-546), on the beach a little south of the church in Arorangi, offers nine nicely appointed self-contained units with cooking facilities and hot water showers at NZ$70 single, double, or triple. There's a communal TV lounge/bar. Outside they fly the flags of all nationalities of people currently staying there.

An inexpensive place to stay at Ngatangiia is Daniel Roro's **Aroko Bungalows** (Box 850, Rarotonga; tel. 21-625) facing Muri Beach. The four individual bungalows with basic cooking facilities are NZ$65 single or double, and Daniel also has a larger two-bedroom house for rent at NZ$50 a day.

The **Sunrise Beach Motel** (Depot 8, Rarotonga; tel. 20-417, fax 22-991) at Ngatangiia has six self-catering bungalows at NZ$85 single or double, NZ$100 triple. It's right on a poor beach and the swimming pool is small, but it's peaceful and a store is nearby. There are some lovely nature walks in the nearby valleys, and it's an easy walk to the Muri Lagoon.

The clean, pleasant **Kiikii Motel** (Box 68, Rarotonga; tel. 21-937, fax 22-937) has an attractive swimming pool overlooking a rocky beach. Rooms in this solid two-story motel begin at NZ$54/67/113 single/double/triple, and even the four older "budget rooms" are quite adequate. The eight standard rooms in the west wing are 20% more expensive but they're large enough to accommodate a family of five. The six deluxe and six premier rooms (overlooking the sea) are 20% higher again. All 24 rooms have

good cooking facilities, and the efficient staff is helpful in assisting with any special arrangements. Club Raro and its nightlife is only a stroll away (although you won't be bothered by the noise when you want to sleep). It's probably the closest you'll come to a U.S.-style motel, although much nicer. Airport transfers are NZ$7 each way.

Your best bet near town is the **Paradise Inn** (Box 674, Rarotonga; tel. 20-544, fax 22-544), just east of Portofino Restaurant. In a former existence "the Paradise" was the Maruaiai Dancehall, but it's now fully renovated into a cozy little 16-room motel. The fan-cooled split-level rooms are NZ$60/66/77 single/double/triple, and there are two smaller budget singles that are 50% cheaper. Cooking facilities are available, and there's a nice terrace out back overlooking the lagoon where you can sit and have a drink. Children under 12 are not accommodated.

Expensive Accommodations
The **Central Motel** (Box 183, Rarotonga; tel. 25-735, fax 25-740), in Avarua opposite the entrance to Rarotonga Breweries, might be okay if you were there on business and had to be right in town. The 14 units in this two-story concrete block edifice are overpriced at NZ$100/120 single/double (no cooking facilities).

Ronnie and Janice Siulepa of Ronnie's Restaurant operate **Wild Palms** (tel. 20-823) on the inland road near the end of the airstrip. The six self-catering bungalows are NZ$100 single or double, NZ$125 triple (children under 12 not accommodated). A swimming pool is on the premises.

The **Oasis Village** (Box 2093, Rarotonga; tel. 28-213, fax 28-214), on the beach a bit south of Black Rock, has four a/c units at NZ$150 single or double. Cooking facilities are not provided and everyone eating in the adjacent steakhouse has an excellent view into your room.

Next door is the **Rarotongan Sunset Motel** (Box 377, Rarotonga; tel. 28-028, fax 28-026) with 20 self-catering units from NZ$150 single, double, or triple. There's a swimming pool.

If your flight is delayed the airline may accommodate you at the snobbish **Edgewater Resort** (Box 121, Rarotonga; tel. 25-435, fax 25-475), a crowded cluster of two-story blocks, service buildings, and tennis courts facing a mediocre beach. This is Raro's largest hotel, with 182 a/c rooms beginning at NZ$165 single, double, or triple (no cooking facilities). There's traditional dancing here twice a week. The original Edgewater was built in the early 1970s by controversial Czech "cancer specialist" Milan Brych to house his patients, most of whom ended up in the cemetery near the airport. Brych himself departed for greener pastures in the U.S. in 1978.

The **Manuia Beach Hotel** (Box 700, Rarotonga; tel. 22-461, fax 22-464) at Arorangi has 20 fan-cooled thatched duplex bungalows at NZ$375 single or double, NZ$445 triple with fridge (no cooking facilities). Children under 12 are not admitted. It's all very pleasant with a nice beach, pool, and free nautical activities (sailing, windsurfing, canoeing). The drinks and snacks at their "sand on the floor" beach bar are reasonable, and there's traditional dancing weekly.

Puaikura Reef Lodges (Box 397, Rarotonga; tel. 23-537, fax 21-537) on the southwest side of the island offers 12 neat, orderly self-catering rooms in three single-story wings attractively arranged around a swimming pool at NZ$106 single or double, NZ$150 triple. A grocery store is adjacent, and the beach is just across the road with no houses blocking access to the sea.

Lagoon Lodges (Box 45, Rarotonga; tel. 22-020, fax 22-021), on spacious grounds near the Rarotongan Resort Hotel, has 15 self-catering units of varying descriptions beginning at NZ$130 single, double, or triple. There's a swimming pool, and like the Puaikura, it's a good choice for families.

The government-owned **Rarotongan Resort Hotel** (Box 103, Rarotonga; tel. 25-800, fax 25-799), in the southwest corner of Rarotonga, has been the island's premier hotel since its opening in 1977. The 151 rooms in nine one- and two-story blocks begin at NZ$160 single or double, NZ$220 triple (no cooking facilities). Some water sports are free. The beach and swimming pool are fine, and island nights with traditional dancing are held twice a week.

Palm Grove Lodges (Box 23, Rarotonga; tel. 20-002, fax 21-998) on the south side of the island has 13 self-catering units beginning at NZ$140 single or double, NZ$155 triple. It's similar to Lagoon Lodges.

At Titikaveka is the **Moana Sands Resort** (Box 1007, Rarotonga; tel. 26-189, fax 22-189) with 12 units in a two-story building at NZ$170 single, double, or triple. The beach is good and some water sports are offered, but only very limited cooking facilities are available.

The **Little Polynesian Motel** (Box 366, Rarotonga; tel. 24-280, fax 21-585), also at Titikaveka, has eight well-spaced self-catering duplex units at NZ$147 single or double, NZ$177 triple, plus a "honeymoon bungalow," which is in high demand. The motel faces one of the best snorkeling beaches on the island (a swimming pool is also provided), and it has long been one of the most popular top-end places to stay on Rarotonga, too long in fact because the management has become rather complacent. Don't trust them to take telephoned messages, send your faxes, respond promptly to maintenance complaints, or provide advice. Inquiries outside of office hours (weekdays 0830-1700, Saturday 0830-1200) are unwelcome.

Raina Sands Apartments (Box 1047, Rarotonga; tel. 26-189, fax 23-602) nearby has four self-catering rooms in a three-story main building at NZ$170 single or double, NZ$200 triple. Its only advantages are proximity to a good snorkeling area and the view from the roof.

At the south end of Muri Beach is the **Muri Beachcomber Motel** (Box 379, Rarotonga; tel. 21-022, fax 21-323) with 10 self-catering units in five duplex blocks at NZ$135/160/200 single/double/triple. Facing the pool are two larger family units (the only rooms where children are allowed). In mid-1995 a further six units were added.

The **Pacific Resort** (Box 790, Rarotonga; tel. 20-427, fax 21-427) at Muri offers 54 self-catering rooms at NZ$230 single or double, NZ$265 triple. The sandy beach is okay for swimming but not for snorkeling. A swimming pool, water-sports facility, and evening entertainment are part of this well-rounded resort. Their Barefoot Bar is fine for a hamburger and beer lunch.

. Packed together amid luxuriant vegetation next to the Flame Tree Restaurant is **Sokala Villas** (Box 82, Rarotonga; tel. 29-200, fax 21-222) with seven self-catering bungalows at NZ$160 single, double, or triple. Children under 12 are not admitted.

The six two-story condos at **Avana Marina Condominiums** (Box 869, Rarotonga; tel. 20-836, fax 22-991) are NZ$350 for up to five people (two or three bedrooms). Full cooking facilities are in each unit and they even throw in a small boat. This area seems to be perpetually under construction, and you can do better elsewhere for that kind of money.

Club Raro Inclusive (Box 483, Rarotonga; tel. 22-415, fax 24-415), formerly known as the Tamure Resort, is just two km east of Avarua. The 39 recently renovated rooms are NZ$158/226/324 single/double/triple standard or NZ$188/256/369 superior, which includes all meals, drinks, and daily island tours. Twice a week the evening meal is off-site at a local restaurant. In 1995 an artificial beach was constructed, and there's also a swimming pool. It's walking distance from town and might be a good choice for those interested in activities and having fun. Traditional dancing is staged twice a week in their adjacent entertainment center (the Club itself is closed to nonguests).

House Rentals

For house rentals for periods of five weeks and up try **Cook Islands Commercial Realty Brokers** (Box 869, Rarotonga; tel. 23-840, fax 23-843) next to BECO Hardware Store (upstairs).

Nan Noovao of **Cook Islands Tours & Travel** (Box 611, Rarotonga; tel. 20-270, fax 27-270) rents two-bedroom houses at Titikaveka for NZ$300 a week—a good option for families and small groups. Write ahead for reservations or just ask for Nan upon arrival as she meets most international flights.

Mary and Malcolm MacQuarie (tel. 22-792) have three houses for rent on the beach near the Little Polynesian Motel at NZ$500 a week. Lots of other places are available and advertisements for house rentals are often published in the *Cook Islands News*.

FOOD

Budget Places to Eat

The outdoor lunch counter at the **Cooks Corner Cafe** (tel. 22-345; open weekdays 0700-1500, Saturday 0630-1215) beside the Island Bus stop is popular, and specials are posted on blackboards.

Mama's Cafe (tel. 23-379; open weekdays 0800-1630, Saturday 0800-1230), beside Foodland in Avarua, offers an interesting combination of healthy sandwiches and fattening desserts. The ice cream cones here are great! It's always crowded with locals.

Opposite Empire Theater is **Metua's Cafe** (tel. 20-850; open 0730-2200, closed Sunday) with inexpensive lunches (large portions). It's good for a coffee anytime.

Better Restaurants

Ronnie's Bar and Restaurant (tel. 20-823; closed Sunday), on the Avarua waterfront, serves lunch and dinner, and beside the restaurant bar is a pleasant, shady patio for cool drinks and conversation. It's okay to bring your own bottle of wine to dinner.

Priscilla's Restaurant (tel. 23-530; closed Sunday), just east of the Beachcomber Gallery, serves good Indian curry dishes, and their prices are a bit lower than other similar places.

The slightly upmarket **Portofino Restaurant** (tel. 26-480), on the east side of town, specializes in Italian dishes such as pizza, pasta, and seafood. It opens for dinner at 1830 but is closed Sunday. It gets good reviews from readers ("good food, lots of it, and well prepared") and could be crowded, so try to reserve.

Under the same management and with an equally good reputation is the **Flame Tree Restaurant** (tel. 25-123), near the Pacific Resort at Muri, which has a special three-course set menu from a different part of the world every day for NZ$22. This is one of the few restaurants on Rarotonga with a no-smoking section! It opens at 1830 (closed Sunday) and reservations are recommended.

Sails Restaurant (tel. 27-349; open Sunday), above the Rarotonga Sailing Club, serves good lunches, though dinner is more expensive. The downstairs section on the beach can be rather windy.

Liana's Restaurant (tel. 26-123), on the south side of the island, offers an upmarket combination of Chinese dishes and steaks (open daily except Friday from 1830).

The **Tumunu Tropical Garden Bar and Restaurant** (tel. 20-501) near the Edgewater Resort at Arorangi has a spacious bar, and seafood, steaks, and chicken are available daily

1800-2130. The bartender, Eric, offers sight-seers a popular guided tour of the picturesque establishment for a NZ$1 tip. Ask the waitress if you can see Erik's scrapbooks of life on Raro in the early 1970s.

Weekly Barbecues

Tere's Bar (tel. 20-352), across the street from Avarua Harbor, is a breezy local hangout with mugs of cold beer, and on Monday and Wednesday at 1800 there's a steak barbecue here for NZ$12. It's the sort of place where you might expect to meet a former prime minister and other colorful characters.

Every Friday afternoon at 1630 a bargain barbecue dinner (NZ$5 a large plate) is served beside the road in front of St. Mary's Catholic Church, across the street from the Are Renga Motel in Arorangi.

Several hotels such as the Edgewater and Rarotongan Sunset prepare a special Sunday barbecue dinner. The Rarotongan Resort Hotel has a good buffet Sunday brunch (NZ$27 pp) 1200-1400. Call ahead for information.

Groceries and Alcohol

Every budget hotel provides kitchen facilities, so Rarotonga is perfect for those who like to do their own cooking. At supermarkets newcomers to the South Pacific will be surprised to find the milk and juice in boxes on the shelves and long loaves of unwrapped bread in barrels near the check-out. CITC Wholesale, Foodland Su-

permarket, and Meatco Ltd. have the cheapest canned goods. Meatco usually has the least expensive vegetables and the best meat (except pork). For pork go to Charlie Bros. Home Market next to the Paradise Inn. The Mad Butcher opposite Metua's Cafe also sells quality meats. About the only place to get fresh fish is the public market on the waterfront in Avarua.

Fresh milk and fruit juices are sold at **Frangi Dairy** (tel. 22-153), beside Parliament. You can also buy imported frozen meat and vegetables here at good prices. Great ice cream cones are available too.

For beer or liquor, go to the government-operated **Liquor Supply Store** (tel. 28-382; weekdays 1000-1630, Saturday 0900-1200) at Avatiu on the way to the airport. The water on Rarotonga is heavily chlorinated and safe to drink.

ENTERTAINMENT AND EVENTS

The **Empire Theater** (tel. 25-429) in Avarua projects features nightly except Sunday at 1930 and 2130 (NZ$4) in two separate halls. It's almost worth going just to experience the enthusiasm of the local audience!

T.J.'s Maruaiai Club (tel. 24-722), next to BECO Hardware Store just east of Metua's Cafe, opens Wednesday to Saturday around 1930. There's karaoke singing Wednesday to Friday from 2100, a disco on Saturday. It's popular with the local teenagers, and dress regulations are in force to maintain standards.

musicians at island night

DAVID STANLEY

The **Reefcomber Nightclub** (tel. 20-823), behind Ronnie's Bar and Restaurant in Avarua, is open Wednesday to Saturday after 2000. Friday is the big night.

The most popular watering hole on the island used to be the historic **Banana Court** in what was the first hotel in the Cooks. In mid-1994 the government closed the place down claiming it wasn't profitable. Check to see if they've reopened (or what massive development has gone up on this prime piece of real estate facing Avarua Harbor).

The bar at the **Rarotonga Bowling Club** (tel. 26-277) on Moss Road, Avarua, opens at 1600 weekdays, at noon on Saturday. If you've never tried lawn bowling, do so—it's only NZ$1 green fees plus NZ$1 bowls hire.

Another good drinking place is the **Cook Islands Game Fishing Club** (tel. 21-419; weekdays 1600-midnight, Saturday 1400-midnight) near Club Raro. Try the local beer, Cooks Lager.

The **Returned Services Association Club** or "RSA" (tel. 20-590; closed Sunday), directly across the street from the airport terminal, is a good place for a beer while you're waiting for a flight. They also have two pool tables, but food service is erratic.

The **Arorangi Clubhouse** on a side street near the church in Arorangi has a good bar, and on Friday and Saturday nights there's often live music. A predominantly local crowd comes here and it can get rough, but it's a good place to mix.

Cultural Shows for Visitors

Rarotonga is one place where the dance shows put on for tourists are worth seeing. Cook Islands dancers are renowned. "Island night" performances are staged regularly at hotels and restaurants, and you can usually get in for a cover charge (around NZ$5-10) and the price of a drink. A buffet of traditional Cook Islands food (*umukai*) is also laid out (around NZ$30) and those ordering the meal can watch the show for free. Things change, so call the hotels to check times, prices, transport, and

fisherman's god, Tangaroa

the necessity of reservations. Best of all, try to attend a show related to some special local event when the islanders themselves participate (look in the newspaper for listings).

Island night at the **Manuia Beach Hotel** (tel. 22-461) begins Wednesday at 2030 with a traditional dinner. The floor show put on by the local kids is lots of fun. **Club Raro** (tel. 22-415) also does its island nights on Wednesday and Friday at 2130. The **Edgewater Resort** (tel. 25-435) has island nights on Tuesday and Saturday at 2100 (stuffy, pretentious atmosphere), while the **Rarotongan Resort Hotel** (tel. 25-800) offers shows Wednesday and Saturday at 2030. The **Pacific Resort** (tel. 20-427) at Muri has an island night with children dancing Friday at 1930.

SHOPPING

Shopping hours in Avarua are weekdays 0800-1600, Saturday 0800-1200. Supermarkets in Avarua stay open about an hour longer, and small general stores around the island are open as late as 2000 weekdays and also on Saturday afternoon.

As usually, the duty-free outlets are unlikely to have much of interest to North Americans and, as usual, local handicrafts are better value than imported Japanese electrical goods. Check out government-sponsored **Women's Handicraft Center** (tel. 28-033) at the Avatiu Market, which carries grass skirts, baskets, dancing shakers, pandanus *rito* hats, and hat bands. *Tivaevae* quilts are available on request, NZ$200 and up for a medium-size one. This is the only shop where you can be sure that anything you buy is a genuine locally made handicraft. Also peruse the other handicraft stands in the market.

More commercial but also recommended is **Island Craft** (Box 28, Rarotonga; tel. 22-010), selling teak or *tamanu* (mahogany) carvings of Tangaroa, the fisherman's god (a fertility symbol), white woven hats from Penrhyn, mother-of-pearl jewelry, and good, strong bags. Other popular items include handbags, fans, tapa cloth from Atiu, replicas of staff gods, wooden bowls, food pounders, pearl jewelry, seats *(no'oanga),* headrests, slit gongs *(tokere),* and fishhooks. They've also got a branch at the airport that opens for international departures, but the selection in town is much better.

Get into style with some bright tropical apparel from **Joyce Peyroux Garments** (tel. 20-201) with four locations around the island. Joyce Peyroux and other retailers carry beautiful selections of hand-printed dresses, pareus, tie-dyed T-shirts, bikinis, etc.—all locally made.

Also visit the **TAV Clothing Factory** on Vakatini Road with attractive lightweight tropical clothing and swimsuits produced on the premises. Special-size items can be made to measure.

The black pearls of Manihiki may be inspected at the **Pearl Shop** (tel. 21-902, fax 21-903) at Cooks Corner. They provide certificates of authenticity, essential when you're spending hundreds of dollars for a single one! Cheaper, slightly imperfect gold-set pearls (with imperfections only obvious to an expert) are also available. Unfortunately, prices are not marked. See also the Beachcomber Gallery mentioned under "Sights," above.

The **Philatelic Bureau** (Box 142, Rarotonga; tel. 29-336, fax 22-428) next to the post office has colorful stamps, first-day covers, and mint sets of local coins, which make good souvenirs. In addition to the Cook Islands issues, they also sell stamps of Aitutaki and Penrhyn (only valid for postage on those islands). A crisp, new Cook Islands $3 bill costs NZ$6 here (at the banks they're NZ$3).

SERVICES AND INFORMATION

Services

Two banks serve Rarotonga, the **Westpac Bank** and the **ANZ Bank,** both open Monday to Friday 0900-1500. Both change traveler's checks. The Westpac branch at the airport charges NZ$2.50 commission on traveler's checks, while the branch of the same bank in Avarua charges no commission. The ANZ Bank in Avarua charges NZ$2 commission on traveler's checks but gives a significantly better rate than the Westpac. If you're changing over US$100 it's probably better to pay the NZ$2 and change at the ANZ Bank, otherwise the

commission-free Westpac Bank in town is best. Cash advances on Visa and MasterCard are possible.

Postal rates are reasonable in Cook Islands and even surface mail is reliable. The post office holds general delivery mail 28 days and there's no charge to pick up letters.

Telecom Cook Islands (tel. 29-680, fax 20-990) at the Earth Station Complex on Tutakimoa Road, Avarua, is open 24 hours a day for overseas telephone calls and telegrams. For information on rates see "Telecommunications" in the chapter introduction.

For an extension of stay (NZ$30) go to the Immigration office (tel. 29-363) next to the airport. Visa requirements for Tahiti-Polynesia can be checked by calling the Honorary Consul of France; Mrs. Diane McKegg (tel. 22-000). At last report, Australians still needed a visa to visit Tahiti. The New Zealand High Commission (tel. 22-201; weekdays 0800-1200/1300-1600) is next to the Philatelic Bureau.

Snowbird Laundromat (tel. 20-952) next to the Tumunu Restaurant in Arorangi will do your wash for NZ$3.50 a load, plus NZ$5.50 for drying.

There are public toilets at Cooks Corner and at the Avatiu Market.

Yachting Facilities

Yachts pay a nominal fee to tie up at Avatiu Harbor and are subject to the NZ$25 pp departure tax. The harbor is overcrowded and the harbormaster is not overjoyed when he sees it filling up with private boats, so you might not be given permission to stay as long as you want. Check with the harbormaster for the arrival times of freighters, which might necessitate a move. There's a freshwater tap on the wharf, plus cold showers accessible 24 hours a day near the harbormaster's office. Weather reports are sometimes posted outside the Waterfront Commission office. During occasional northerly winds from November to March, this harbor becomes dangerous.

Information

The government-run **Tourist Authority Visitor Center** (Box 14, Rarotonga; tel. 29-435, fax 21-435; open weekdays 0800-1600), has brochures and information sheets giving current times and prices. Ask for a free copy of *What's On In The Cook Islands,* which contains a wealth of useful information.

The **Department of Statistics** (Box 125, Rarotonga; tel. 29-390, fax 21-590) on Avatiu Road sells the informative *Quarterly Statistic Bulletin* (NZ$3).

The **Bounty Bookshop** (tel. 26-660), next to the ANZ Bank in Avarua, carries books on the Cook Islands, the latest regional news-magazines, and the *Cook Islands News.* Good cultural books can also be purchased at the **Cook Islands Museum** and the **University of the South Pacific Extension Center.** Ask for *Atiu Nui Maruarua: E au tua ta'ito,* a collection of legends of Atiu.

Stars Travel (tel. 23-669) is Rarotonga's most efficient and reliable travel agency. This agency and **Island Hopper Vacations** (tel. 22-026) both have offices in Avarua and arrange package tours to the outer islands with flights and accommodations included.

Health

The **Outpatients Medical Clinic** (tel. 20-066) at Tupapa, a km east of town, is open weekdays 0800-1600, Saturday 0800-1100. In the same building is the **Central Dental Clinic** (tel. 29-312), open weekdays 0800-1200 and 1300-1600.

You'll save time and get more personal attention by visiting **Dr. Robert Woonton** (tel. 23-680; weekdays 0900-1430, Saturday 0900-1100, consultations NZ$20), upstairs in Ingram House opposite Avatiu Harbor. To call an ambulance dial 998.

TRANSPORTATION

For information on air and sea service from Rarotonga to other Cook islands turn to "Transportation" in the introduction to this chapter.

By Road

The **Cooks Island Bus Passenger Transport Ltd.** (Box 613, Rarotonga; tel./fax 25-512) operates a round-the-island bus service leaving Cooks Corner every half hour 0700-1600 weekdays, 0800-1200 Saturday. These yellow, 32-seat buses alternate in traveling clockwise and

counterclockwise, stopping anywhere (no counterclockwise service on Saturday). The night bus runs at 1800, 1900, 2100, and 2200 Monday to Thursday, plus midnight and 0130 Friday and midnight Saturday. The current schedule is published in *What's On In The Cook Islands.* Fares are NZ$2 one-way, NZ$3 return, NZ$4 return at night, or NZ$5 for an all-day pass (NZ$12 for families). There's also a NZ$15 10-ride ticket that can be shared. Tourists are the main users of this excellent service, and the drivers make a point of being helpful.

Taxi rates are NZ$1 a km (NZ$2 minimum), but the service is slightly erratic. Ask the fare before getting in and clarify whether it's per person or for the whole car. Some drivers will drive you the long way around the island to your destination. Beware of prebooking taxis to the airport over the phone, as they often don't turn up, especially at odd hours. Service is generally from 0600 to 2200 only. Hitchhiking is officially discouraged.

One reader wrote in recommending the four-hour, NZ$24 circle-island tour offered by **Hugh Henry** (Box 440, Rarotonga; tel. 25-320) in Arorangi. Call ahead and they'll pick you up at your hotel. The **Cultural Village** (tel. 21-314) offers a full-day combined circle-island tour and cultural show for NZ$45 including lunch.

Pa's Nature Walk (tel. 21-079) is a good way to get acquainted with the natural history of the island. The four-hour hike through the bush behind Matavera includes a light lunch; both it and Pa's guided cross-island hike are NZ$30 pp with hotel transfers included. With his blond Rastafarian good looks, Pa's a bit of a character, and it's worth signing up just to hear his spiel.

Rentals

A Cook Islands Driver's License (NZ$10 and one photo) is required to operate motorized rental vehicles (the International Driver's License is not accepted). This can be obtained in a few minutes at the police station (tel. 22-499) in the center of Avarua any day 0800-1530 upon presentation of your home driver's license (minimum age 21 years). They may require you to show something that states explicitly that you're licensed to drive a motorcycle, otherwise you may have to pass a test (NZ$2 extra) that involves riding one up and down the street without falling off. Bring your own scooter and keep in mind that if you fail the test you won't be allowed to ride any further and that day's scooter rental must still be paid. (In theory the person giving the driving tests takes lunch 1200-1300 and knocks off at 1500.) Without a license the insurance on the vehicle is not valid and you'll be liable for a stiff fine if caught. No license is required to ride a bicycle.

Greg Sawyer of Lafayette, Indiana, sent us this:

I rented a scooter and went to get my required Cook Islands Drivers License and because my U.S. license had no motorcycle status, it was necessary to take a "practical driving test" first. The officer at the police station said, however, that the person doing the tests would return in 30 minutes. So off I scootered to run errands, returning half an hour later. No test person again, come back in one hour. Off I go, return in an hour, and still no tester. I returned in another hour: come back after lunch. Well, my patience gone and wishing to use my hard-won vacation time more vacation-like, I never went back. That's the hassle I got at the police station, but it's only half the story.

Late one night returning to my room, I was flagged down on my scooter by a man I thought was in distress. I was quickly surrounded on each side by one small and one very large man. The large one claimed to be a policeman, charged me with drunken driving, and demanded to see my license (which, remember, I had not). I responded by charging that he was no policeman (which he obviously wasn't), that he was drunk (which he obviously was), and that my license was none of his business. To shorten the story, he became more nasty, more demanding of the license (claiming I had none), and seemed much larger. I asked what he wanted and he said NZ$20. So I gave it to him, preferring extortion to

a doctor or dentist visit. Then he became very friendly and sent me on my way. As his expense to me was nearly the same as my untendered driver's license expense, I figure that I basically broke even. I feared to go to the police with my tale and let it slide. It's very possible these ruffians will keep this scam going.

You're supposed to wear a helmet while operating a motorbike. Although it's unlikely you'll ever see anybody with one on, an anti-tourist cop can always bring it up. Drive slowly, as local children tend to run onto the road unexpectedly, and beware of free-roaming dogs. Take special care on Friday and Saturday nights, when there are more drunks on the road than sober drivers. The speed limit is 40 km per hour in Avarua, 50 km per hour on the open road, and driving is on the left.

The prices listed below are for the cheapest car. Rates include unlimited km, and the seventh consecutive day is usually free. Some places quote prices including the 10% government tax, others without tax. Check all the agencies for special deals—most are open on Sunday. Most cars and scooters rent for 24 hours, so you can use them for a sober evening on the town.

In past, readers of this book have often dealt with Raymond Pirangi at **T.P.A. Rental Cars** (Box 327, Rarotonga; tel. 20-611) opposite the Rarotongan Sunset Motel in Arorangi. His cars are NZ$38 daily, insurance and tax additional. Since Raymond offers the cheapest car rentals on the island, don't expect to receive a new car.

Tipani Rentals (Box 751, Rarotonga; tel. 22-328, fax 25-611), in Avarua opposite the Edgewater Resort, charges NZ$60 a day for cars, tax and insurance included, scooters NZ$20 daily, bicycles NZ$8.

Two of the international chains are represented on Rarotonga. **Budget/Polynesian** (Box 607, Rarotonga; tel. 20-895, fax 20-888), at the Edgewater Resort and Rarotongan Hotel and in Avarua, has cars for NZ$60 a day, jeeps NZ$75 a day, scooters NZ$20 a day, bicycles NZ$10 a day, tax and insurance included. Budget has the best quality cars and bicycles.

Avis (Box 317, Rarotonga; tel. 22-833, 21-702), next to the Tourist Authority in Avarua, charges NZ$55 for cars or jeeps, but tax and insurance are additional. Avis also has scooters at NZ$20 a day and bicycles at NZ$7, tax additional.

Many smaller companies rent motor scooters for NZ$15-20 a day, NZ$100 a week, and bicycles at NZ$8-10 daily. **Odds 'n Ends** (Box 401, Rarotonga; tel. 20-942, fax 27-595), opposite the market at Avatiu Harbor, rents scooters at NZ$15 a day, NZ$90 a week. **Hogan Rentals** (Box 100, Rarotonga; tel./fax 22-632), a little north of the Are Renga Motel in Arorangi, rents cars at NZ$55 a day, tax, insurance, and kms included. Hogan's 12-speed mountain bikes

are NZ$8 daily or NZ$48 weekly (NZ$20 deposit). The bicycles have baskets on the front and are fairly sturdy, but there are no lamps for night riding.

There aren't enough women's bicycles to go around, but men's cycles are easy to rent. The main advantage to renting a bicycle for the week is that you have it when you want it. Many other places around the island also rent bicycles—ask your hotel for the nearest. Rarotonga is small enough to be easily seen by bicycle, which makes renting a car or scooter an unnecessary expense—you also avoid the compulsory local driver's license rip-off. Bicycles are also quiet, easy on the environment, healthy, and great fun.

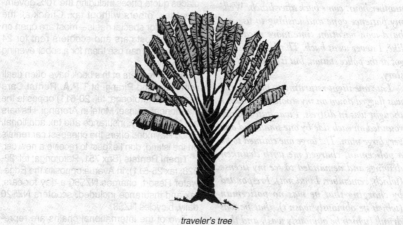

traveler's tree

AITUTAKI

Aitutaki, 259 km north of Rarotonga, is the second-most-visited Cook Island. The main island is volcanic: its highest hill, Maungapu (124 meters), is said to be the top of Rarotonga's Raemaru, chopped off and brought back by victorious Aitutaki warriors. The low rolling hills are flanked by banana plantations and coconut groves. A triangular barrier reef 45 km around catches Aitutaki's turquoise lagoon like a fishhook. Fifteen small *motus* on the eastern barrier reef all have picture-postcard white sands, aquamarine water, and occasional sand flies and mosquitoes. Like Bora Bora, this beauty is best appreciated from the air.

A Polynesian myth tells that Aitutaki is a giant fish tethered to the seabed by a vine. After a perilous journey from Tubuai in the canoe *Little Flowers,* the legendary hero Ru landed here with four wives, four younger brothers, and 20 virgins to colonize the island. Ru named the atoll Utataki-enua-o-Ru-ki-te-moana, meaning "A Land Sought and Found in the Sea by Ru," which the first Europeans corrupted to Aitutaki. Ru named various parts of the island for the head, stomach, and tail of a fish, but more places he named for himself. His brothers became angry when most of the land was divided among the 20 virgins, and they left for New Zealand where they won great honor. Ru himself suffered the consequences of his arrogance as higher chiefs eventually arrived and relegated him to the subordinate position held by his descendants today.

Captain Bligh "discovered" Aitutaki in 1789, only 17 days before the notorious mutiny. In 1821, when the Tahitian pastors Papeiha and Vahapata were put ashore, it became the first of the Cook islands to receive Christian missionaries. Americans built the island's huge airfield during WW II. Tasman Empire Airways (now Air New Zealand) used Akaiami Island as a refueling stop for its four-engined Solent flying boats during the 1950s. The Coral Route, from Auckland to Tahiti via Suva and Apia, became obsolete when Faa'a Airport opened near Papeete in 1961.

Today, the people live in villages strung out along the roads on both sides of the main island and generally travel about on motor scooters. The roads are red-brown in the center of the island, coral white around the edge. The administration and most of the businesses are clustered near the wharf at Arutanga. All the villages have huge community halls built mostly with money sent from New Zealand. There's tremendous rivalry among the villages to have the biggest and best one, although they're unused most of the time. The *motus* are uninhabited, and there aren't any dogs at all on Aitutaki.

Dangerous coral heads and currents make passage through Aitutaki's barrier reef hazardous, so passengers and cargo on interisland ships must be transferred ashore by lighters. The Americans built Arutanga Wharf during WW II. They had planned to dredge the anchorage and widen the pass, but the war ended before they got around to it. Blasting by the N.Z. military in July 1986 improved Arutanga Passage somewhat, but it's still narrow, with a

AITUTAKI

GOLF CLUB
AIRSTRIP
MAUNGAPU
(124 m)
OOTU
AKITUA
VAIPEKA
AMURI
UREIA
ANGAREI
NIURA
ARUTANGA
MANGERE
REUREU
NIKAUPARA
VAIPAE
TAUTU
JETTY
PAPAU
TAVAERUA ITI
TAVAERUA NUI
TE KOUTU
AKAIAMI
LAGOON
MAINA
MURITAPUA
MOTURAKAU
RAPOTA
TEKAPUA
TAPUAETAI
MOTUKITIU
0   2   4 km

© DAVID STANLEY

This is how they looked on Aitutaki in 1903.

AUCKLAND INSTITUTE AND MUSEUM

six-knot current draining water blown into the lagoon from the south. The depth in the pass is limited to two meters and the anchorage off Arutanga can accommodate six boats at most.

Aitutaki is the only Cook island other than Rarotonga where there's a good choice of places to stay, entertainment, and organized activities, yet it's still very unspoiled. The best way to go is to catch a Friday flight up from Rarotonga so as to be on hand for "island night" at the Rapae Hotel that evening. Book a lagoon trip for Saturday and you'll still have Sunday to scooter around the island or laze on the beach. Fly back on Monday or Tuesday, having sidestepped Rarotonga's dull Sunday.

Sights

The oldest **CICC church** in the country, erected in 1828, is just south of the post office at Arutanga. In front is a monument to missionaries John Williams and Papeiha. An old *marae* is near Te Koutu Point at the south end of the main island, and east of the *marae* is an eerie chestnut forest. When the tide is low you can easily hike along the beach at the south end of the island, right around to Tautu jetty, built during WW II by the Americans.

Also at low tide you can walk along a sandbar from the Rapae Hotel right out to the reef; wear something on your feet to protect yourself from the coral, sea urchins, eels, stonefish, algae, etc. To reach the summit of **Maungapu,** start from opposite Paradise Cove on the main road

up the west side of the island; it's a leisurely half-hour jaunt and from the top you get a sweeping view of Aitutaki. The **water tanks** on a hill in the middle of the island, directly east of the Rapae Hotel, also allow good views.

The best beach on the main island is at the northwest end of the airstrip. Beware of dangerous currents in the passes near the edge of the reef here. A deluxe resort hotel is on Akitua Island near Ootu Beach at the southeast end of the airstrip, connected by a pedestrian causeway.

Sports and Recreation

The various boat trips to a *motu* in the Aitutaki Lagoon are highly recommended. If you go to Akaiami or Tapuaetai ("One Foot Island"), you'll have an unforgettable swim in the clear deep-green water. No one should leave Aitutaki without experiencing it. Other great attractions are Maina, or "Bird Island," at the southwest corner of the lagoon, and snorkeling on the south barrier reef during the southeast tradewinds. **Bishop's Lagoon Cruises** (Teina Bishop, Box 53, Aitutaki; tel. 31-009, fax 31-493), inland from the wharf, and **Viking's Cruises** (Tereapii Viking, tel. 31-180, fax 31-407), near the Rapae, both offer a variety of catamaran trips daily except Sunday (from NZ$40 including lunch). Unfortunately the very popularity of these trips may be their undoing as some of the "desert islands" can get a little crowded when all of the tourist boats arrive! Take insect repellent.

Neil Mitchell's **Aitutaki Scuba** (Box 40, Aitutaki; tel. 31-103, fax 31-310) offers diving at the drop-off once or twice a day (except Sunday) for NZ$76. No reservations are required, but bring your own mask; wetsuits are recommended from June to December. You'll find Neil about a hundred meters down the side road that branches off the main road at the bakery. Aitutaki is great place to learn to dive and Neil does four-day NAUI certification courses for NZ$490 (minimum of two persons). He also rents the best-quality motorcycles and bicycles on the island. Several other Aitutaki "dive operators" charge about NZ$10 less than Neil, but check their credentials before doing business with them. The best diving here is from March to November.

The bottom of the Aitutaki lagoon is dotted with harmless bêche-de-mer (sea cucumbers). Stonefish are not common, but they're almost impossible to spot until it's too late, so wear shoes. Sand flies, a nuisance on the north side of the main island, are far less so on the *motus*. Snorkelers and paddlers must keep at least 200 meters inside the main reef entrance at Arutanga, due to the strong outgoing current.

The **Aitutaki Golf Club** (Box 98, Aitutaki; tel. 31-405) beside the airport welcomes visitors. If your ball falls on the airstrip, it's considered out of bounds. The Aitutaki Open Golf Tournament is in mid-September.

PRACTICALITIES

Budget Accommodations

A number of small guesthouses offer rooms with shared bath, and discounts are possible if you stay a week or more. The cooking facilities aren't as good as on Rarotonga—often you have to share with the family and pay NZ$2 per day extra. Air Rarotonga or Stars Travel can book you into any of the places mentioned below.

The pleasant **Tiare Maori Guest House** (Box 16, Aitutaki; tel. 31-119), formerly known as Mama Tunui's, at Ureia just north of the wharf, has seven rooms at NZ$28/38 single/double. Mama serves an all-you-can-eat dinner (NZ$15) including clams, chicken, and all the island vegetables. She may also allow you to use her stove, and you can watch the family television.

She'll even give you a flower *ai* to wear to island night at the Rapae.

Josie's Lodge (Josie and David Sadaraka, tel. 31-111), next door to Tiare Maori, has four double and two single rooms with shared bath at NZ$28/38 single/double. The rooms are screened for insects, and communal cooking facilities are provided.

On the beach opposite Josie's is **Rino's Beach Apartments** (Box 140, Aitutaki; tel. 31-197, fax 31-329) with four self-catering units in a two-story block at NZ$85 each. Rino also has an older three-bedroom house across the street that he rents out at NZ$200 a week.

Tom's Beach Cottage (Box 51, Aitutaki; tel. 31-051, fax 31-409), just up from Rino's, charges NZ$32/42/54 single/double/triple for the nine

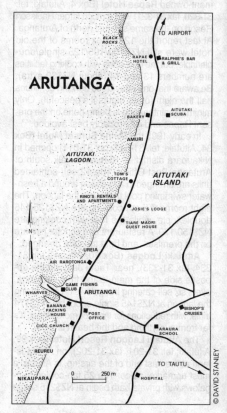

ARUTANGA

rooms. It's run by Mormons, so smoking, tea, coffee, and alcohol are discouraged in the rooms. This place is clean and good.

Junior Maoate's **Paradise Cove** guesthouse (Box 64, Aitutaki; tel. 31-218, fax 31-456) is on a good beach at Anaunga, between the airstrip and the Rapae Hotel. The five rooms in the main house are NZ$30/40 single/double, while the six thatched Polynesian huts with fridge and shared bath beside the beach are NZ$40/60. Junior offers the best cooking facilities, if you don't mind being away from the action. It's quiet, and this is the only guesthouse that allows smoking and drinking on the premises.

Upmarket Accommodations

Plans call for the replacement of the government-owned **Rapae Hotel** (Box 4, Aitutaki; tel. 31-320, fax 31-321) with a much larger Radisson Resort on the same site just north of Arutanga. At last report the 12 duplex rooms of the old hotel were still NZ$100/105/125 single/double/triple, but the only ones with cooking facilities are numbers 13 and 14 (about NZ$30 extra). Be aware that on Friday disco dancing continues half the night (other nights it's peaceful). Only minimal maintenance is being done on the present Rapae and it's probably best avoided.

In early 1995 the **Maina Sunset Motel** (Box 34, Aitutaki; tel. 31-511, fax 31-611) opened in Nikaupara district, a 10-minute walk south of Arutanga Post Office. The 12 self-contained units are arranged in a U-shape around a freshwater swimming pool that faces the lagoon. The eight rooms without cooking are NZ$125/145 double/triple, while the four with cooking are NZ$150/170. A restaurant and scooter hire are on the premises, and boat trips are arranged.

Aitutaki Lodges (Box 70, Aitutaki; tel. 31-334, fax 31-333), near Tautu Jetty on the opposite side of the main island from Arutanga, offers six self-catering bungalows on stilts facing the lagoon at NZ$145 single or double, NZ$174 triple, with reductions for three or more nights. It's far from everything and the beach is lousy.

The **Aitutaki Lagoon Resort Hotel** (Box 99, Aitutaki; tel. 31-201, fax 31-202), on Akitua Island at the east end of the airstrip, is Aitutaki's most upmarket place. The 25 fan-cooled bungalows with private bath begin at NZ$215 single

or double, NZ$265 triple, but cooking facilities are not provided and meals in the restaurant are extra. The breakfast is good here. It's a little isolated but the beach is great and there's also a swimming pool.

Food

The restaurant at the **Rapae Hotel** is open daily 0700-2200, but reservations are required. Sunday 1900-2100 there's a beachside barbecue at the hotel.

Ralphie's Bar & Grill (tel. 31-418), across the street from the Rapae, offers takeaway cheeseburgers (NZ$4.50) and fish and chips (NZ$7.50) for lunch, which you can eat at the picnic tables places outside. Dinner (F$15) is served in an a/c room and the food is good. They're open daily, but on Sunday only dinner is served.

The **Crusher Bar & Restaurant** (tel. 31-283), near Paradise Cove on the way to the airport, serves a grilled steak or fish dinner with salad bar for NZ$9.50 from Monday to Thursday from 1800 (closed Friday). Saturday and Sunday nights there's a special menu (about NZ$15 pp). Call ahead for bookings.

Ask the people where you're staying if the water is safe to drink. It's always best to boil it and store it in your fridge, if you can. A small vegetable market operates during the week at the banana packing house. Ice cream is available at Tip Top between Rino's and the bakery, and many other shops. The wavy-shelled clams (pahua) abundant in the lagoon make good eating.

Entertainment

Aitutaki dancers are famous, and the big event of the week is Friday's "island night" at the **Rapae Hotel** (tel. 31-320). It's NZ$27 for dinner (at 1930) and the show (at 2130). Excellent atmosphere—don't miss it.

The **Aitutaki Game Fishing Club** (tel. 31-077; daily except Sunday from 1600), behind the petrol station on the way to the harbor, has cheap beer and is a good place to meet people at happy hour.

Services

Traveler's checks can be cashed at the hotels but it's smarter to change your money on Rarotonga beforehand as the rates here are lousy.

Trying to use one of the small banking agencies on Aitutaki can be a real pain.

In 1995 the **Orongo Center** opened with a farmers' market, handicraft shop, tourist office, restaurant, and bar. It's worth checking out.

Outpatients are accepted at the hospital (tel. 31-002) Monday to Saturday 0800-1000. The hospital also has a dentist.

Transportation and Tours

Air Rarotonga (tel. 31-888) has an office at Ureia. Airport transfers are NZ$5 pp. Air Rarotonga runs day trips to Aitutaki from Rarotonga, but these are prohibitively expensive at NZ$289 including air tickets, transfers, a lagoon tour, lunch, and drinks.

The shipping companies have no local agent, but the people at the Waterfront Commission near the wharf will know when a ship's due in. Both cargo and passengers have to be brought in to the wharf by lighter. Because Aitutaki doesn't have a regular ferry service from Rarotonga, getting here is much more expensive than visiting similar outer islands in Tahiti-Polynesia, Tonga, or Fiji, usually involving an expensive plane ticket. For flight and boat information see "Transportation" in the chapter introduction.

Rino's Rentals (tel. 31-197), in front of Josie's Lodge, **Swiss Rentals** (tel. 31-372, fax 31-329), near the wharf, and **Aitutaki Rentals** (tel. 31-127), on the way to the airport, all have cars (from NZ$65 daily), motor scooters (from NZ$30 daily), and pushbikes. Rino has a NZ$100 weekly rate for Honda 50's. Some of the guesthouses and hotels also rent bicycles—all you really need.

ATIU

The old name of Atiu, third largest of the Cook Islands, was originally Enuamanu, which means "land of birds," and native birds still abound on the island. While neighboring Mauke and Mitiaro are flat, Atiu has a high central plateau (71 meters) surrounded by low swamps and an old raised coral reef known as a *makatea,* which is 20 meters high and covered with dense tropical jungle. The poor volcanic soil on the central plateau was once planted with pineapple to supply fresh fruit to New Zealand, but this led to massive erosion and proved uneconomical, and pineapples are now grown only on a small scale for local consumption. Taro is now the main cash crop, and taro patches occupy the swamps along the inner edge of the *makatea.* The slopes up to the central plateau have been reforested to check erosion. Arabica coffee is grown, processed, roasted, packaged, and marketed as "Kaope Atiu."

Atiu is one of the only islands in Polynesia where the people prefer the center to the shore. Once fierce warriors who made cannibal raids on Mauke and Mitiaro, the islanders became Christians after missionary John Williams converted high chief Rongomatane in 1823. Today the Atiuans live peacefully in five villages on the high central plain. The villages radiate out from an administrative center where the post office, hospital, PWD workshops, stores, and government offices are all found. The women of Atiu meet throughout the week to work on handicrafts in their community halls. Cooling ocean breezes blow across Atiu's plain.

On Atiu good beaches, fine scenery, fascinating walks, varied historic sites, and geological curiosities combine with satisfactory accommodations and enjoyable activities to make a visit well worthwhile. Atiu beckons the active, adventuresome traveler who wants to experience a slice of real outer island life without sacrificing creature comforts.

SIGHTS

The **library and museum** at Atiu College opens at 1300 weekdays only. **Teapiripiri Marae,** where John Williams preached in 1823, is just across the field from the post office. This large rectangle, with its dramatic stalactite and stalagmite boundaries and crushed-coral floor, is easy to spot.

Just off the road down to Matai Landing is **Arangirea Marae** (to the right behind the citrus plantation). There are a few large stones in the shape of a seat here, and places where pigs were killed for festival celebrations, but not much else.

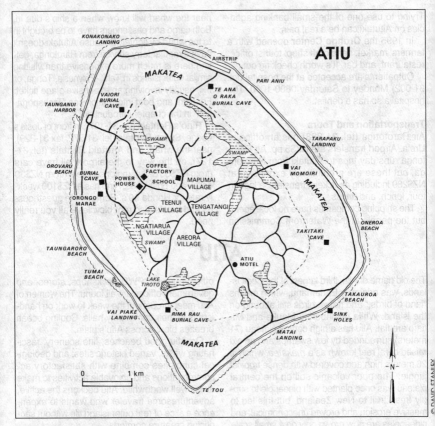

The most important *marae* on Atiu was **Orongo Marae** at Mokoero—obtain permission from Mr. Tearai Mokoroa (tel. 33-011) of Teenui village or Mr. Teura Kea (tel. 33-003) of Ngatiarua village to visit. Those who go without permission or who behave badly will be cursed and stricken by a terrible disease (and resented by the Atiuans).

The best beach on Atiu, and one of the finest in the Cooks, is **Taungaroro.** The white sand descends far into the quiet blue-green lagoon, protected from ocean breakers by the surrounding reef. The cliffs of the *makatea* frame this scenic masterpiece. A short footpath from the road leads to the spot at **Orovaru Beach** where Captain Cook arrived on 3 April 1777. On the inland side of the road there still exists

the path through the *makatea* that Captain Cook's crew followed to the settlement of that time around Orongo Marae. Dense *puka* forests fill the shore along Atiu's west coast, with low bird's-nest ferns making a dense green cover. These leaves are used to wrap fish for cooking in the *umu.*

Farther north is **Taunganui Harbor,** with a striking zigzag configuration, constructed in 1973. Barges can dock here in all weather but large ships must anchor offshore. The swimming and snorkeling in the deep, clear harbor water are good. If you're here at 1500 you may be able to purchase fresh fish from returning fishermen. Stick to ocean fish, however, as since 1987 the ciguatera toxin has appeared in reef fish.

Oneroa Beach, near the end of the road northwest of Matai Landing, is the largest on Atiu, but you must scramble down a cliff to get to it. A good place to snorkel on Atiu is **Takauroa Beach,** about 500 meters up the Oneroa road from Matai. Look for an old pig fence, then go down to the beach, where there are two sinkholes draining the reef. At low tide when the sea is calm many varieties of fish may be seen in the holes and among the coral nearby. A stretch of reefless shoreline on the northeast coast lets breakers roll right in to the cliffs.

A path off the road from Tarapaku Landing to Tengatangi village leads through the *makatea* to **Vai Momoiri,** a large water-filled cave that tunnels under the path then opens up on both sides. The road crosses a swamp passing **Vairakai Marae** and a pool where Rongomatone's 12 wives used to bathe. The remains of the original *tamanu* stump seats can still be seen. (Rongomatane later adopted Christianity and forsook all of his wives except the youngest.)

Lake Tiroto

Many scenic viewpoints from the roads of Atiu look down across the *makatea* to the blue ocean beyond. Lake Tiroto is clearly visible from a number of these points. According to legend, the eel Rauou dug this lake and, when he was finished, traveled to Mitiaro to dig the lakes there. A tunnel runs under the *makatea* from the lake through to the shore. You can enter it with a lamp and guide if you're willing to wade

through the muddy water. Wear old shoes and clothes, plus an old hat to protect your head from bumping against the cave's sharp roof. Retired schoolteacher Vaine Moeroa (tel. 33-046) takes advantage of visits to catch eels by organizing teams that herd the creatures up dead-end tunnels—a rare experience. Be sure to sign his Cave of Lake Tiroto visitors book.

Rima Rau Burial Cave

This cave near Lake Tiroto is said to contain the bones of those who died in a battle involving 1,000 Atiu warriors. Ask someone to tell you the legend of this cave's dead. Kiikii Tatuaua (tel. 33-063) of Areora village can guide you to the cave, with side trips to the lake, taro fields, Katara Marae, and Vaitapoto Sinkhole.

Takitaki Cave

This cave is one of the few in the Cooks inhabited by birds: little *kopekas,* a type of swallow, nest in the roof. Their huge saucerlike eyes help them catch insects on the wing. They never land nor make a sound while outside the cave; inside, they make a cackling, clicking sound, the echoes of which help them find their way through the dank dark. Visitors to the cave should try not to disturb the birds, nor should they allow their guide to catch any.

Takitaki is in the middle of the *makatea,* east of the old airstrip, a taxing 40-minute hike in from the road. A guide (NZ$10 plus NZ$5 pp) is required. The main part of the cave is large and

A fragment from one of Atiu's caves marks the spot adjoining Marae Teapiripiri where John Williams preached in 1823.

DAVID STANLEY

dry, and you can walk in for quite a distance. Many stalactites, broken off by previous visitors, lie scattered about the floor. The story goes that Ake, wife of the hero Rangi, lived many years alone in this cave before being found by her husband, led to the spot by a *ngotare* (kingfisher) bird.

Keep an eye out for *unga* (coconut crabs) while exploring the *makatea,* and wear boots or sturdy shoes as the coral is razor-sharp. Go slowly and take care, as a fall could lead to a very nasty wound.

PRACTICALITIES

Accommodations and Food

The **Atiu Motel** (Roger and Kura Malcolm, Box 7, Atiu; tel. 33-777, fax 33-775), near the old airstrip, offers three comfortable self-catering chalets, each capable of accommodating four persons, at NZ$80/90/100 single/double/triple. There's also a family unit capable of accommodating up to six at NZ$100 single, plus NZ$10 per additional guest. These A-frame units are constructed of native materials with beams of coconut-palm trunks and cupboard fronts of hibiscus. The pantries are fully provisioned with everything required for preparing basic meals; you mark what you've used on a stock list and settle up when you leave (normal prices). Yamaha 50 motor scooters are available (NZ$25), but sadly, no bicycles. An entertainment evening is staged every Saturday night in the pavilion overlooking the grass tennis court. Roger is a very attentive host and will arrange everything for you, if you wish. Otherwise you can have all the privacy you like. The minimum stay is two nights.

Andrea Eimke's **Tivaivai Café** (Box 13, Atiu; tel. 33-031, fax 33-032; closed Sunday) in Areora village serves Atiu coffee with homemade cakes. Local handicrafts such as *tivaivai* quilts are available at Andrea's **Atiu Fiber Arts Studio.**

There are five shops on Atiu and two bakers make bread weekdays and Sunday. Kura Malcolm runs the **Center Store** (closed Saturday afternoon and Sunday), which dispenses liquor and cold drinks, as well as basic foodstuffs. Public toilets are opposite the CICC church. The electricity runs about 19 hours a day on Atiu.

An eel trap. Eels are found in the swamps and lakes of Atiu, Mitiaro, and Mangaia; the locals catch them in traps or with hooks. The eel traps (inaki) are made of bush vines woven in long, basketlike form, which the eel can easily enter but cannot get out of. Pieces of chicken, crab, or bee's wax are used as bait.

Entertainment and Refreshment

Friday or Saturday night at 2200 there's a dance in the community hall near the CICC church or in a building opposite the Catholic church. Check the notice board outside the Administration Building for times.

Tennis is popular on Atiu and village rivalry has produced no less than nine tennis courts. As each village constructed its tennis court it was made a little bigger than the last. The first village had a single netball court; the fourth built two tennis courts, two netball courts, and erected floodlights. The fifth village said it was "all too hard" and gave up.

Atiu won the Constitution Day dancing competitions on Rarotonga in 1982, 1983, 1984, 1985, 1988, 1992, and 1993, so ask where you can see them practicing. Special performances are held on Gospel Day and Christmas Day.

Venerable institutions of note are the **bush beer schools,** of which there are nine on Atiu. Bush beer is a moonshine made locally from imported yeast, malt, hops, and sugar. The concoction is fermented in a *tumunu,* a hollowed-out coconut tree stump about a meter high. Orange-flavored "jungle juice" is also made. The mixing usually begins on Wednesday, and the resulting brew ferments for two days and is ready to drink on the weekend. A single batch will last three or four nights; the longer it's kept, the stronger it gets.

Gatherings at a school resemble the kava ceremonies of Fiji and other islands. Only the barman is permitted to ladle bush beer out of the *tumunu* in a half-coconut-shell cup. The potent contents of the cup must be swallowed in one hearty gulp. Those who developed a taste for the stuff usually refer to regular beer as "lemonade." The village men come together at dusk, and after a few rounds, the barman calls them to order by tapping a cup on the side of the *tumunu.* A hymn is sung and a prayer said. Announcements are made by various members, and work details assigned to earn money to buy the ingredients for the next brew. After the announcements, guitars and ukuleles appear, and the group resumes drinking, dancing, and singing for as long as they can. The barman, responsible for maintaining order, controls how much brew each participant gets.

Nonmembers visiting a school are expected to bring along a kilo of sugar, or to put NZ$5 pp on the table, as their contribution. Guests may also be asked to work in the taro patches the next day. This is no place for casual sightseeing: you either join in wholeheartedly or stay away.

Airport

A new airstrip (AIU) was built on Atiu's north side in 1983, after the old airstrip on the plateau, built only in 1977, was found to be too small. Roger Malcolm from the Atiu Motel is often there to meet flights (transfers NZ$7.50 pp each way).

MITIARO

Mitiaro is a low island with two lakes and vast areas of swampland. Of the lakes, Rotonui is much longer and broader than Rotoiti. This surprisingly large lake is surrounded by an unlikely combination of pine trees and coconut palms. The lake bed is covered by a thick layer of black and brown peat, and the eastern shore is firmer than the western. On one side of the lake is the small, coconut-studded island of Motu. Large banana plantations grow in the interior of Mitiaro and old tin cans are planted below young coconut trees to provide the trees with minerals to absorb as the cans rust away. Like its neighboring islands, Mitiaro has a chronic water shortage.

The People

Before the arrival of Europeans, the people occupied the center of the island near their gardens. Today they all live in one long village on the west coast. The village is neat and clean, with white sandy roads between the Norfolk pines and houses. European-style dwellings predominate, though thatched cottages are still common on the back roads. Four different sections of the village maintain the names of the four original villages, and each has a garden area inland bearing the same name. Because the *makatea* cannot support crops, it's used for keeping pigs or growing coconuts. The fine outrigger canoes of Mitiaro are made of hollowed-out *puka* logs, held together with coconut-husk rope. These are used for longline tuna and *paara* fishing outside the reef.

Sights

The small church is quite exquisitely decorated; you might find it worth a look and a quiet moment of reflection on the European influence that still pervades island life. Cut over to the beach when you reach the graveyard and football field south of the village. This long stretch of white sand is the best beach close to the village and has many small pools in the reef where you can relax when the tide is out. The restless rhythm and flow of the waves beating against the reef at low tide is almost hypnotic. If you're looking for secluded coves, you'll find many farther south along the coast. Walking along the reef at low tide all around Mitiaro is an incomparable experience.

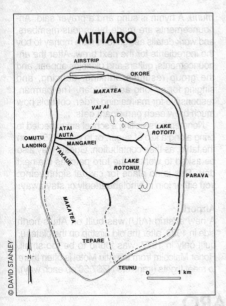

MITIARO

AIRSTRIP
OKORE
MAKATEA
VAI AI
ATAI AUTA
OMUTU LANDING
MANGAREI
TAKAUE
LAKE ROTOITI
LAKE ROTONUI
PARAVA
MAKATEA
TEPARE
TEUNU
0   1 km

© DAVID STANLEY

Inland

Vai Marere, on the road to Takaue, is an easy 10-minute walk inland from the village. The locals enjoy swimming in the green, sulfur-laden waters of this cave *(vai)*. Take the road to the end, then carry on down the trail to Teunu. To the west of the trail is an old Polynesian fort *(tepare)*, but you'll probably need a guide to find it. The Mitiaroans once used this fort to defend themselves against raids from Atiu. On a high crest in the *makatea* on the coast just northeast of Teunu are several stone *marae* platforms with slabs of coral propped upright at the ends. At Parava there's a road in to the east side of Lake Rotonui, and Vai Naure and Vai Tamaroa are off the east coast road between Parava and the airport.

Inland again on the northernmost road is **Vai Ai,** the Sandalwood Cave, a 40-minute walk from the road along a twisting, winding track through the bush. This cave is a large open hole in the *makatea* filled with clear water, good for swimming and diving—refresh yourself. Back on the road, continue on to the west side of **Lake Rotonui.** The dry upper mud on the west bank will spring up and settle down on the deeper layer below as you walk on it. These mudflats stretch so far out into the water that it's hard to launch a canoe.

Lake Rotoiti is harder to reach than Lake Rotonui. You'll need a guide to lead you through the swamp. Small, edible black tilapia (fish introduced from New Caledonia) are abundant; each has a red streak along its back fins, and they average 15 centimeters long. Black eels can also be seen undulating by the shore. The lake water is fresh and clear, although the bottom is muddy. The low-lying surroundings are peaceful and serene, but the mud will make you forget about swimming.

Practicalities

The **Nane Pokoati Guest House** (tel. 36-107), run by the Air Rarotonga agent, offers one of the few legal opportunities to stay with a local family. The three rooms with shared bath are NZ$51/82 single/double, and that includes three meals with local fruit and vegetables featured. If that's not enough, two small stores sell canned foods, but no bread is made on the island. This guesthouse is often closed for family reasons, so check ahead, and ask Air Rarotonga about Tearoa's Guest House. When these places are out of action, Mitiaro is effectively closed to tourists.

There's often a volleyball game near the church in the afternoons, which you're welcome to join. It's easy to make friends among the local anglers and go out with them in their outriggers. At low tide many people fish from the edge of the reef with long bamboo poles.

(top) coconut crabs, Suwarrow, Cook Island (Roland E. Hopkins); (bottom left) islander, Mitiaro, Cook Islands (David Stanley); (bottom right) dancer from Rurutu, Tahiti-Polynesia (Tahiti Tourisme)

(top left) saltwater girl, Takwa market, Malaita, Solomon Islands (Rod Buchko); (top right) dancer, Western Samoa (Western Samoa Visitors Bureau); (bottom) children at Funafuti, Tuvalu (Peter McQuarrie)

MAUKE

Mauke, the easternmost of the Cooks, is a flat raised atoll. It and neighboring Mitiaro and Atiu are collectively known as Nga Pu Toru, "The Three Roots." As on its neighbors, the crops grow in the center of Mauke; the *makatea* ringing the island is infertile and rocky. Both the *makatea* and the central area are low; you barely notice the transition as you walk along the road inland from the coast to the taro swamps and manioc plantations. In addition to citrus trees, the government is experimenting with beef cattle. Some ginger is still grown, but production has largely ceased due to marketing difficulties. Pigs and chickens run wild across the island, and occasional goats can be seen, but dogs are banned from the island.

The men fish for tuna in small outrigger canoes just offshore and the women weave fine pandanus mats with brilliant borders of blue, red, yellow, and orange along one end. There are also wide-rimmed pandanus hats and *kete* baskets of sturdy pandanus with colorful geometric designs. The men carve the attractive white-and-black *tou* or red-and-brown *miro* wood into large bowls shaped like breadfruit leaves. They also carve large spoons and forks, miniature models of chiefs' seats, and small replicas of Uke's canoe. Uke, the legendary founder of Mauke, gave the island its name. It's a very friendly island to poke around for a few days.

Sights

The **CICC Church** (1882) has an almost Islamic flavor, with its long rectangular courtyard, tall gateways, perpendicular alignment, and interior decoration of crescents and interlocking arches. Due to an old dispute between Areora and Ngatiarua villages, the church was divided across the center and each side decorated differently. The dividing partition has been removed, but dual gateways lead to dual doors, one for each village. The soft pastels (green, pink, yellow, and white) harmonize the contrasting designs, and the pulpit in the middle unifies the two. Inset into the railing in front of the pulpit are nine old Chilean pesos. Look carefully at the different aspects of this building; it's one of the most fascinating in the Cook Islands.

Inland

Vaitaongo Cave, a 10-minute walk from Ngatiarua, is fairly easy to find. A large circular depression with banyan trees growing inside, it has a clear freshwater pool under overhanging stalactites. The locals swim and bathe here. To reach this cave, follow the road to the right along a row of hibiscus and across the citrus plots. Beyond Vaitaongo there are other caves for swimming (Vai Ou, Vai Tunamea, and Vai Moraro), but a guide is necessary to find them.

Moti Cave is a large, open cave beyond the airstrip, and farther into the *makatea* is **Motuanga Cave,** the "Cave of 100 Rooms," with freshwater pools. Limestone growth has made all but the first three rooms inaccessible. A powerful lamp and willing guide are necessary to explore this one.

Just behind the queen's palace at Makatea village is **Koenga Well,** a source of fresh drinking water. The area behind the government residency is known as **Te Marae O Rongo,** a sacred place to the people of Mauke. All that re-

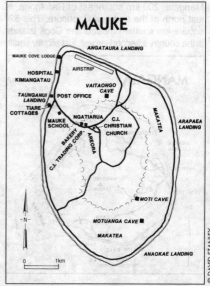

MAUKE

MAUKE COVE LODGE
HOSPITAL
KIMIANGATAU
POST OFFICE
TAUNGANUI LANDING
TIARE COTTAGES
MAUKE SCHOOL
ANGATAURA LANDING
AIRSTRIP
VAITAONGO CAVE
NGATIARUA
C.I. CHRISTIAN CHURCH
AREORA
C.I. TRADING CORP
BAKERY
MAKATEA
ARAPAEA LANDING
MOTI CAVE
MOTUANGA CAVE
MAKATEA
ANAOKAE LANDING

0   1km

-N-

© DAVID STANLEY

mains is the large stone once used as a seat by the chief.

Around the Island

It's only 18 km around Mauke. There's a good beach on the east side at Arapaea landing, but the best beaches are on the south side of the island. Especially inviting is the beach at Anaokae, where a long stretch of clean white sand rings a green lagoon. This piece of paradise is flanked by rugged limestone cliffs and backed by palm, pine, and pandanus. A short track leads down to the beach. No one lives on the south or east sides of Mauke, so these fine secluded beaches are ideal for those who want to be completely alone. There's good reef walking at low tide on the west side of Mauke, but ocean swimming is difficult everywhere.

Accommodations and Food

Tiare Holiday Cottages (tel. 35-077) offers three simple thatched cottages *(are rau),* some with fridge, at NZ$35/45 single/double. These have shared bath, and a newer unit with pri-

vate bath is NZ$10 more expensive. There's no hot water. Filling meals are served at reasonable prices, and discounts are given for long stays. Scooters and bicycles are for rent. Your hosts Tautara and Kura Purea are very helpful and make you feel like one of the family.

Archie and Kura Guinea run **Mauke Cove Lodge** (tel. 35-664), near the sea on the northwest side of the island. Archie's a semiretired Scottish doctor who resettled here in 1983; Kura is a Maukean. The three rooms with private bath in a main house are NZ$28/44/60 single/double/triple. No food is provided, but you may share the kitchen and lounge.

Bread is made on the island, and fresh tuna can be purchased directly from the fishermen at the landing. Try the meat along the top of the backbone near the fin—raw, with ginger, onions, and salt—for a tastebud orgasm. The brown insides of sea urchins, collected along the reef, are also eaten raw (the egg cases are the most delicious part—the texture of raw liver and a strong taste of the sea). For bush beer, ask for the local *tumunu.*

MANGAIA

Mangaia, 200 km southeast of Rarotonga, is just north of the tropic of Capricorn. This 52-square-km southernmost of the Cook Islands is the country's second largest, just slightly small-

MANGAIA

AIRSTRIP
MAKATEA
TERUARERE CAVE
AVARUA LANDING
IVIRUA
ONEROA
RANGIMOTIA (169 m)
MAKATEA
MAKATEA
LAKE TIRIARA
TAMARUA
TUATINI CAVE
-N-
0 1 2 3 km

© DAVID STANLEY

er than Rarotonga. One of the major geological curiosities of the South Pacific, Mangaia is similar to Atiu and Mauke but much more dramatic. A *makatea* or raised coral reef forms a 60-meter-high ring around the island with sheer cliffs towering as high as 80 meters on the inland side. The volcanic earth inside the *makatea* is the only fertile soil on the island; this rises in rolling hills to slopes once planted with pineapples. Near the inner edge of the *makatea,* where water is caught between the coral cliffs and the hills, low taro swamps are flanked by banana fields and miscellaneous crops. Nothing but bush and coconut palms grow on the *makatea* itself, and pigs are kept there in makeshift pens.

Legend tells how Rongo rose from the deep with his three sons to colonize the island. Captain Cook "discovered" Mangaia in 1777 and Polynesian missionaries followed in 1826. The people live in three scattered coastal villages, Oneroa, Tamarua, and Ivirua. The population is static, with some continuing to migrate to New Zealand as others return. A 30-km road rings most of the island, along the coastal strip. It's 10 km from the airstrip to Oneroa, the main village. Traditionally, the Mangaians have a reputation for being a cautious lot, but you'll probably find them quite friendly when you get to know them. Mangaia was the last island to accept Christianity in the Cook Islands.

Crafts

Mangaia is represented in museum collections around the world by large ceremonial adzes, which were used to decapitate prisoners taken in battles. The head, right arm, and right leg were regarded as prized possessions because of the mana they possessed. Later the missionaries had the adzes changed to incorporate "steeple stands," reproducing church steeples. This was used to symbolize church authority over the *ariki.*

The yellow *pupu* shell necklaces *(ei)* of Mangaia are also unique. The tiny black *pupu* shells are found on the *makatea* only after rainfall. The yellow color comes from boiling them in caustic soda, though they can also be bleached white or dyed other colors. The shells are pierced one by one with a needle and threaded to make the *ei.*

Sights

A monument in front of the church at **Oneroa** recalls Mangaian church ministers and missionaries. In a large stone near Avarua landing are the footprints of the legendary giant, Mokea, and his son; both jumped across the island in a race to this spot. The huge stones on the reef to the north were thrown there by Mokea, to prevent a hostile canoe from landing. The queen of Mangaia still has a large flag given to her grandfather by Queen Victoria.

George Tuara (tel. 34-105) of Tavaenga village will guide you through **Teruarere Cave.** Used as a burial ground in the distant past, the cave has old skeletons that add a skin-crawling touch of reality. The opening is small and you have to crawl in, but the cave goes on for a great distance. A lamp is necessary. Below Teruarere on the cliff is **Touri Cave.** Use indicators to find your way back out—be careful not to get lost inside! There are two streams in this cave: one fresh water, the other salty.

An impressive cut leads up through the *makatea* from Oneroa. Follow a jeep track up to

a decorated adze from Mangaia

FIELD MUSEUM OF NATURAL HISTORY, CHICAGO

the flat summit of **Rangimotia** (169 meters), the highest point on the island, for varied views. From the plateau follow a footpath back down to **Ivirua** and you can return to Oneroa via **Tamarua,** a rather longish day hike. The church at Tamarua also has a sennit-bound roof.

A water-filled cave at **Lake Tiriara** is the legendary hiding place of the island hero Tangiia. Water from the lake runs through the cave under the *makatea* to the sea, and rises and falls with the tide. **Tuatini Cave** near Tamarua village has a huge gaping entrance, but gets narrower toward the back. There's really nowhere safe to swim on the island.

Accommodations

The government-operated **Mangaia Lodge** (Nga Ruatoe, tel. 34-042), on a cliff in Oneroa, has three rooms and a kitchen, but the toilet/shower block is in a separate building 25 meters away. It's NZ$44 pp with all meals included, served by managers Nga and Metu, but there's no hot water. Armchairs are provided on the porch of this pleasant colonial-style building.

The entire lodge is sometimes booked for extended periods by people on official business, but a few of the residents of Oneroa, including Norma Atariki (tel. 34-206), Tuaine Papatua (tel. 34-164), and Peiaa Teinangaro (tel. 34-168), take in paying guests or even rent whole houses. Call them up, or ask Air Rarotonga to arrange something. Also try **Tere's Guest House** (tel. 34-066) in Ivarua, and **Babe's Place** (tel. 34-092) in Oneroa, which is noisy on Friday and Saturday nights due to dances in a nearby bar.

OTHER SMALL ISLANDS

Manuae

This small island consists of two islets, Manuae and Te Au O Tu, inside a barrier reef. The unspoiled wealth of marinelife in this lagoon has prompted the government to offer the atoll as an international marine park. There's no permanent habitation. Copra-cutting parties from Aitutaki used to use an abandoned airstrip to come and go, though they haven't done so for years. In 1990 the 1,600 traditional Aitutaki-origin owners of Manuae rejected a government proposal to lease the island to an Australian company for tourism development. Captain Cook gave Manuae its other, fortunately rarely used, name, Hervey Island.

Takutea

Clearly visible 16 km off the northwest side of Atiu, to whose people it belongs, Takutea is in no place over six meters high. The island's other name, Enuaiti, means "Small Island." Until 1959 the people of Atiu called here to collect copra, but Takutea gets few visitors now. There are a few abandoned shelters and a freshwater collection tank. The waters along the reef abound with fish; many red-tailed tropic birds and red-footed boobies nest on the land. Permission of the Atiu Island Council is required for visits.

Palmerston

Palmerston, 366 km northwest of Aitutaki, is an atoll 11 km across at its widest point. Some 35 tiny islands dot its pear-shaped barrier reef, which encloses the lagoon completely at low tide. Palmerston was uninhabited when Captain Cook discovered it in 1774.

William Marsters, legendary prolific settler, arrived here to set up a coconut plantation in 1862. He brought with him his Polynesian wife and her sister, who were soon joined by a third sister. Marsters married all three, and by the time he died in 1899 at the ripe age of 78 he had begotten 20 children. Thousands of his descendants are scattered around the Cook Islands, throughout New Zealand, and beyond, but the three Marsters branches on Palmerston are down to about 60, and as in any small, isolated community there's some tension between the families. Marsters's grave may be seen near the remains of his original homestead. Palmerston is the only island in the Cooks where English is the first language.

Ships visit Palmerston three or four times a year to bring ordered supplies and to take away copra and parrot fish. Although unable to enter the lagoon, they can anchor offshore. The copra is packed in bags that hold close to 70 pounds each, 30 bags to the ton, so there's no need for weighing, only counting.

MANUAE

LANDING
SETTLEMENT
MANUAE
LAGOON
TE AU O TU
-N-
0   2 km

© DAVID STANLEY

THE NORTHERN GROUP

The Northern Cooks are far more traditional than the Southern Cooks. All of the northern atolls except Penrhyn sit on the 3,000-meter-deep Manihiki Plateau; the sea around Penrhyn is 5,000 meters deep. These low-lying coral rings are the very image of the romantic South Seas, but life for the inhabitants can be hard. Many have left for New Zealand. Reef fish and coconuts are abundant, but fresh water and everything else is limited. Now a commercial cultured pearl industry is developing on several of the atolls.

All of the scattered atolls of the Northern Cooks except Nassau have central lagoons. Only the Penrhyn lagoon is easily accessible to shipping, although yachts can anchor in the pass at Suwarrow. Until recently these isolated islands were served only by infrequent ships from Rarotonga, and tourists could only visit during the ship's brief stop, as to get off would have meant a stay of several weeks or even months. Now Air Rarotonga has flights to Mani-

hiki and Penrhyn, taking four and a half hours each way.

Anyone desiring a fuller picture of life of the northern atolls should read Robert Dean Frisbie's *The Book of Pukapuka*, serialized in the *Atlantic Monthly* in 1928. Though interesting, Frisbie's book seems distorted to contemporary eyes, catering to European stereotypes.

Suwarrow

In 1814 the Russian explorer Mikhail Lazarev discovered an uninhabited atoll, which he named for his ship, the *Suvarov*. A mysterious box containing US$15,000 was dug up in 1855; remains of ancient occupation have also been unearthed. Early this century, Lever Bros. unsuccessfully attempted to introduce to the lagoon gold-lipped pearl oysters from Australia's Torres Straits. In the 1920s and 1930s A.B. Donald Ltd. ran Suwarrow as a copra estate, until the island became infested with termites and the export of copra was prohibited. During WW II New

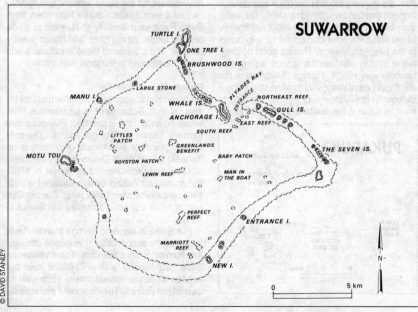

Zealand coastwatchers were stationed here—the few decrepit buildings on Anchorage Island date from that time.

At various times from 1952 onward, New Zealander Tom Neale lived alone on Suwarrow and wrote a book about his experiences titled, not surprisingly, *An Island to Oneself.* Tom never found the buried treasure he was searching for on Suwarrow, and in 1977 he died of cancer. His few possessions are as he left them, although someone has stolen his visitor's book. An entry in the new logbook at Tom's house places a lifelong curse on anyone who removes any of his things from the island, and encourages visitors to leave unneeded supplies on Suwarrow for the use of those who become shipwrecked.

Today coconut-watchers serve on Suwarrow to ensure that none of the termite-infested nuts are removed. Officially Suwarrow is a Marine Park, and the caretakers now live in Tom Neale's house. A government meteorologist may also be present, and there's even talk of an airstrip! Pearl divers from Manihiki and Penrhyn visit occasionally.

Yachts often call on their way from Rarotonga or Bora Bora to Samoa: Suwarrow and Penrhyn are the only atolls in the Cook Islands with lagoons that can be entered by ships. The wide, easy lagoon entrance is just east of Anchorage Island and a 40-meter-long coral rock jetty points to the deep anchorage. There's good holding, but in stormy weather the lagoon waters can become very rough. Though Suwarrow is not an official port of entry, yachts often stop without clearing in at Rarotonga or Aitutaki. Passports must be taken to the caretakers in Tom's house,

who also accept outgoing mail. If you haven't been officially cleared in the Cooks, your stay may be limited to three days. The table and chairs outside the caretaker family's home provide welcome neutral ground for whiling away the time. Scuba diving is not allowed.

Of the 25 *motus,* only five are sizable. The snorkeling in the lagoon is fantastic, with lots of shark action—they won't bother you unless you're spearfishing. In the past, hurricanes have washed four-meter waves across the island; during one in 1942 those present survived by tying themselves to a large tree (see *The Island of Desire,* by Robert Dean Frisbie). Thousands of seabirds nest on this historically strange and still mysterious island.

Nassau

Egg-shaped Nassau has no inner lagoon; instead, taro grows in gardens at the center of the island. The American whaler *Nassau* called in 1835. Europeans ran a coconut plantation here until l945, when the government bought the island for £2000 in order to get it back for the Pukapukans. In 1951, the chiefs of Pukapuka, 88 km to the northwest, purchased it from the government for the same amount and they've owned it ever since. Korean fishermen from Pago Pago stop illegally at Nassau to trade canned foods, fishing gear, and cheap jewelry for love. The children of these encounters add an exotic element to the local population.

Pukapuka

An island sits at each corner of this unusual triangular atoll. Because of its treacherous reef, where no anchorage is possible, Pukapuka was formerly known as "Danger Island." The only landing place for small boats or canoes is on the west side of Wale. Discovered by Mendaña in 1595 and rediscovered by Byron in 1765, Pukapuka was outrageously victimized in mid-19th-century Peruvian slaver raids. Captain Gibson of HMS *Curacao* annexed the island in 1892.

Pukapuka is closer to Samoa than to Rarotonga, so the people differ in language and custom from other Cook Islanders. Three villages on Wale (pronounced "wah-lay") island have coexisted since precontact times, each with its own island council. They compete enthusiasti-

PUKAPUKA

WALE ISLAND

YATO — ROTO — NGAKE

TOKA SAND BANK — LAGOON

KOTAWA ISLAND

KO ISLAND

0   5 km

© DAVID STANLEY

cally with each other in singing, dancing, contests, and cricket. The people make copra collectively, each receiving an equal share in the proceeds. Bananas and papaya also grow here in limited quantities; their harvesting is controlled by the councils. Each village owns one of the three main islands. The best swimming and snorkeling are off Kotawa Island, also known as Frigate Bird Island for the thousands of seabirds that nest there. Pukapuka's Catholic church is beautifully decorated with cowry shells.

Manihiki

One of the Pacific's most beautiful atolls, Manihiki's reef bears 39 coral islets, enclosing a closed lagoon four km wide that's thick with sharks. The dark green *motus* are clearly visible across the blue waters. Until 1852, Manihiki was owned by the people of Rakahanga, who commuted the 42 km between the two islands in outrigger canoes, with great loss of life. In that year the missionaries convinced the islanders to divide themselves between the two islands and give up the hazardous voyages. In 1889 some disenchanted Manihiki islanders invited the French to annex their island. When a French warship arrived to consummate the act, anxious missionaries speedily hoisted the Union Jack, so the French sailed off. A few years later, Britain officially took over the island.

Mother-of-pearl shell was once taken from the lagoon by island divers who plunged effortlessly to depths of 25-30 meters. Today some 50 farms on Manihiki produce cultured pearls; the largest of these farms (250,000 oysters) is owned by the Tahitian Chinese Yves Tchen Pan, who operates joint ventures with many of the others. Tekake Williams, a Manihiki local, has the oldest and second-largest (50,000 oysters) farm. It's believed that with the growth in pearl farming over the past decade the Manihiki lagoon has already reached its maximum carrying capacity of oysters, and further development here would be disastrous. The Island Council has been involved in an acrimonious dispute with the Ministry of Marine Resources over who should control this multi-million-dollar industry. All this activity caused the atoll's population to increase 31% between 1986 and 1991, and the money has eroded the authority of the *ariki* and led to drinking problems.

© DAVID STANLEY

The administrative center is Tauhunu, and there is a second village at Tukao. Permission of the chief of Tauhunu is required to dive in the lagoon. There's no safe anchorage for visiting ships but with the pearl boom in full swing, Air Rarotonga now flies here twice a week from Rarotonga. Accommodations are now available at Danny's Bungalow. Manihiki is famous for its handsome people.

Reader Robert Bisordi of New York sent us this:

We spent nine days on Manihiki and were told by the locals that we were the first tourists ever to stay overnight. Could that be true in this day and age? The difficulty in getting there was considerable. It cost about US$600 each from Rarotonga, and we had to provide Air Rarotonga with the name of the family we would be staying with, otherwise no plane reservations would be given.

Let me say that I have never seen such a happy group of people. We have been to all of the Southern Cooks, Samoa, Fiji, and Tahiti, but here we encountered a warmth and happiness the source of which remains a mystery to us here in New York. In extremely tight clusters of homes they live, inescapably sharing each other's noises, emotions, and actions with a tolerance perhaps only possible in a homogeneous society in which so much is tacitly understood and accepted, to the point of resembling a genetic disposition. And the laughter, the giggling—it never ceased! It caused me anguish because it was the affirmation of an achievement that has always been beyond our reach: to be truly happy with so very, very little.

Our host was gracious and tender beyond justification. Of course, not only did we provide some monetary relief for putting us up, we took along pounds of meat, vegetables, and gifts for each member of the family. But I was convinced that none of this was the impetus for our most tender treatment.

Now for the downside. As soon as the aspiring snorkeler descends below the Manihiki lagoon, sharks come at you with the utmost curiosity. I saw at least three species, not to mention the black ones that attack you between the motus *(the* motus *themselves were absolutely gorgeous). Another problem was the water situation. Clearly visible in a random glass of water from the cement tanks were little tadpolelike creatures swimming merrily about. This stuff shot through our systems like lightning, and to make matters worse, I contracted dengue fever. I was dehydrating and unable to drink the water, having to get up three or four times in the middle of the night and walk about 300 meters to the reef toilets with a flashlight, under a downpour.*

Then, as if matters could not get any worse, there came the news that there may not be enough fuel on the island for our plane to make the return trip. It was all like a surreal nightmare—take the squatting, half-naked, 400-pound islander with torn shorts, bare feet, and a dried ring of taro around his lips telling me that the "contractual stipulations" of the ticket we bought meant the carrier was not obligated

to make a special flight for us. I truly thought a squid would be more apt to speak those words than that guy—stereotypers beware!

The prospect of staying on Manihiki, dehydrating to a shrivel, was on the horizon as we waited for the next boat shipment of petrol. And, in typical island torture, I received so much misinformation about the flight that was or was not to be that I became numb until the day of our scheduled departure. Then that day, as if no one had ever said anything at all, it came and took us away, that bird of salvation, right on schedule.

Rakahanga

Two opposing horseshoe-shaped islands almost completely encircle the lagoon of this rectangular atoll. Lacking the pearl wealth of Manihiki, this is a quieter island. There are several small *motus* that can be reached on foot at low tide. Breadfruit and *puraka* (a tarolike vegetable) are the staples here, and copra is made for export. So that not too many coconuts are taken at one time, the island councils regulate visits to the *motus*. These usually take place only two or three times a year, to give nature a chance to regenerate. Coconut crabs, a delicacy in Rakahanga, are mostly caught on the small uninhabited *motus*. Nivano village is at the southwest corner of the atoll. Although unable to enter the lagoon, ships can anchor offshore. An airstrip in the middle of the west side of the atoll was destroyed by Hurricane Wasa in December 1991 and has not been repaired.

An old Polynesian legend explains the origin of Rakahanga and Manihiki. The mythological fisherman Huku caught an island he considered too small to take, so he tied it up to give it time to grow. After Huku left, the demigod Maui happened along and, with the help of a mermaid, finished Huku's work by fishing the island from the sea. When Huku returned, a great struggle ensued, and Maui leapt straight into the sky to escape, leaving his footprints embedded in the reef. His fishhook became the stars, and such was the force of his jump that the island was split in two, forming these neighbor-

© DAVID STANLEY

ing atolls, which were later colonized by Huku's sister and her husband Toa, a warrior banished from Rarotonga.

Penrhyn

Penrhyn's turquoise 280-square-km lagoon is so wide that you can just see the roof of the church at Tautua from Omoka, the administrative center. The *motus* at the far end of the lagoon are too far away to be seen. The lagoon is thick with sharks, mostly innocuous black-tips; only the black shark is dangerous. Islanders ignore them as they dive for pearls.

Penrhyn was named for the British ship *Lady Penrhyn,* which arrived in 1788, although one of the native names is Tongareva. The legendary hero Vatea fished Penrhyn up from the sea using a hook baited with a piece of flesh from his own thigh. In 1863 four native missionaries

on Penrhyn were tricked into recruiting their congregation for Peruvian slavers for $5 a head and sailed with them to Callao as overseers at $100 a month in the hope of obtaining enough money to build a new church! The blackbirders dubbed Penrhyn the "Island of the Four Evangelists" in gratitude. Remnants of old graves and villages abandoned after the raid can still be seen on the *motus,* and the ruins of an unfinished church crumble away at Akasusu.

The island has a good natural harbor, one of the few in the Cook Islands, and vessels can enter the lagoon through Taruia Passage, just above Omoka, to tie up at Omoka wharf. American forces occupied Penrhyn during 1942-46 and built a giant airfield at the south end of Omoka. The islanders use aluminum from the wreck of a four-engine WW II bomber, named *Go-Gettin' Gal,* by the airfield to make combs and other items. Fine pandanus *rito* hats and mother-of-pearl shell jewelry are also made. Visiting yachties trade kitchen- and tableware, dry cell batteries, rope, and small anchors for crafts and pearls. Development plans by the Rarotonga government have been resisted as various local factions vie for influence.

Air Rarotonga flies once a week from Rarotonga (1,364 km) to this most northerly Cook island. The airfare (NZ$1100 return from Rarotonga) is high due in part to exorbitant landing fees levied by the island council. **Soa's Guest House** (tel. 42-015) at Omoka accommodates visitors. The waters around the atoll are a rich fishing ground, and Penrhyn is used as a base for patrol boats and planes monitoring the activities of foreign fishing fleets.

GORDON OHLIGER

NIUE
INTRODUCTION

A single 259-square-km island 386 km east of Vava'u, Tonga, Niue is one of the world's smallest self-governing states (in association with New Zealand). The name comes from *niu* (coconut tree) and *e* (behold). This little-known island boasts the finest coastal limestone crevices and chasms in the South Pacific, all open to visitors and freely accessible. Each is unique—you'll need a week to do them justice.

Niue is for the explorer who likes to get out and make discoveries on his or her own, for the skin diver in search of clean clear water, colorful coral, fish, and sea snakes, and for those who want to relax in a peaceful, uncommercialized environment among charming, friendly people, yet still have the conveniences of modern life at their disposal. Niue is *not* for tourists who require long sandy beaches, resorts, nightlife, and shopping centers. Niue is perhaps the most unspoiled island in the Pacific—it's still an island of adventure.

The Land
Niue is an elevated atoll shaped like a two-tiered wedding cake with two terraces. It's one of the largest coral islands in the world (though 692-square-km Rennell Island in the Solomons is much bigger). The lower terrace rises sharply from the sea, creating 20-meter cliffs that virtually surround the island. Inland, the second terrace rises abruptly from this coastal belt to a central plateau some 60 meters above the ocean. A fringing reef borders much of the coast, but at places the ocean breakers smash directly into the precipitous cliffs. Faulting during the island's uplifting has created the chasms and crevices that are Niue's greatest attractions. Water dripping from their ceilings has added a touch of the surreal in the form of stalactites and stalagmites.

Climate
December to March are the hurricane months, with average temperatures of 27° C. The southeast trades blow from April to November and temperature average 24° C. The 2,047 mm of annual rainfall is fairly well distributed throughout the year, with a slight peak during the hot southern summer. There is good anchorage at Alofi, except during strong westerly winds.

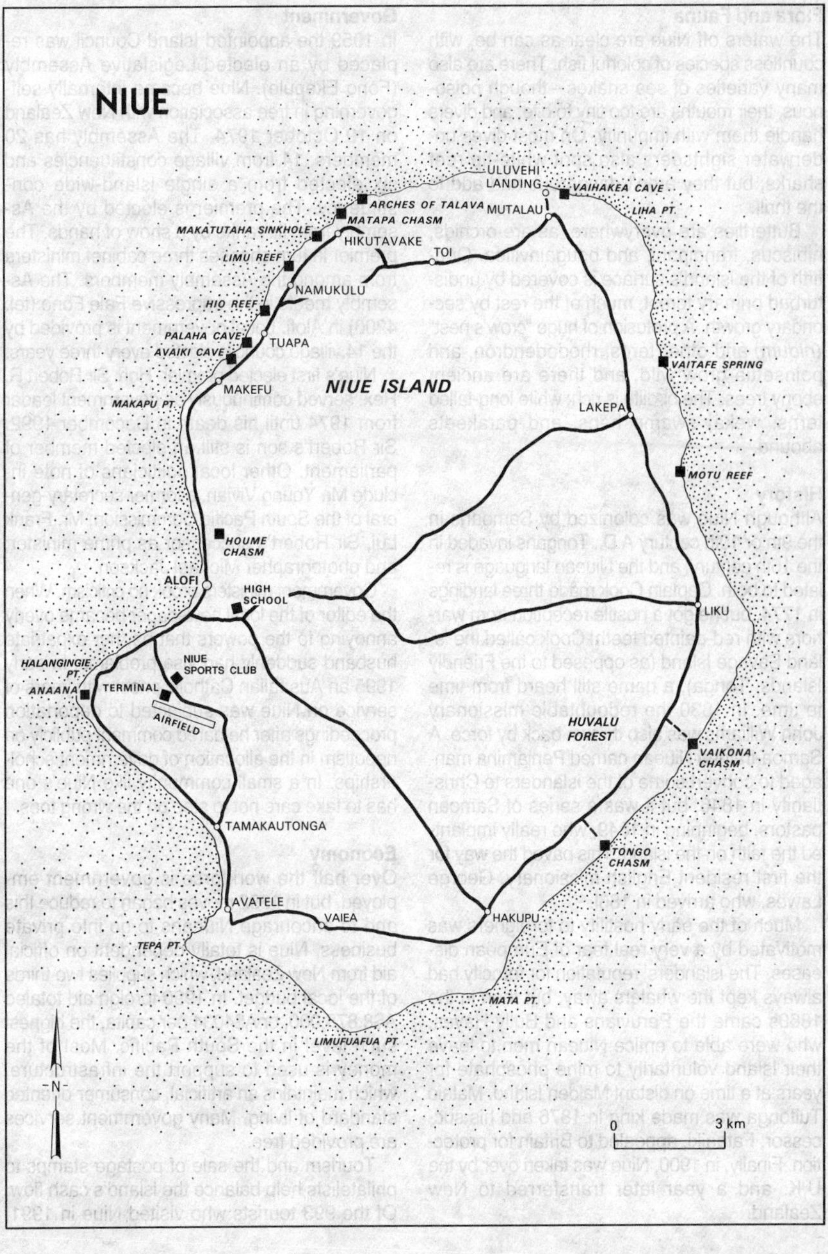

NIUE

NIUE ISLAND

ULUVEHI LANDING
VAIHAKEA CAVE
MUTALAU
LIHA PT.
ARCHES OF TALAVA
MATAPA CHASM
MAKATUTAHA SINKHOLE
HIKUTAVAKE
TOI
LIMU REEF
NAMUKULU
HIO REEF
PALAHA CAVE
AVAIKI CAVE
TUAPA
MAKEFU
VAITAFE SPRING
MAKAPU PT.
LAKEPA
MOTU REEF
HOUME CHASM
ALOFI
HIGH SCHOOL
LIKU
HALANGINGIE PT.
ANAANA
NIUE SPORTS CLUB
TERMINAL
AIRFIELD
HUVALU FOREST
VAIKONA CHASM
TAMAKAUTONGA
TONGO CHASM
AVATELE
HAKUPU
VAIEA
TEPA PT.
MATA PT.
LIMUFUAFUA PT.

0   3 km

-N-

© DAVID STANLEY

Flora and Fauna

The waters off Niue are clear as can be, with countless species of colorful fish. There are also many varieties of sea snakes—though poisonous, their mouths are too tiny to bite, and divers handle them with impunity. On most dives underwater sightseers also spot white-tip reef sharks, but they aren't dangerous and add to the thrill.

Butterflies are everywhere, as are orchids, hibiscus, frangipani, and bougainvillea. One-fifth of the island's surface is covered by undisturbed primary forest, much of the rest by secondary growth. A profusion of huge "crow's nest" *(nidum)* and other ferns, rhododendron, and poinsettia grow wild, and there are ancient ebony trees. The birdlife is rich; white long-tailed terns, weka, swamp hens, and parakeets abound.

History

Although Niue was colonized by Samoans in the 9th or 10th century A.D., Tongans invaded in the 16th century, and the Niuean language is related to both. Captain Cook made three landings in 1774, but he got a hostile reception from warriors with red-painted teeth! Cook called the island Savage Island (as opposed to the Friendly Islands, Tonga), a name still heard from time to time. In 1830 the redoubtable missionary John Williams was also thrown back by force. A Samoa-trained Niuean named Peniamina managed to convert some of the islanders to Christianity in 1846, but it was a series of Samoan pastors, beginning in 1849, who really implanted the faith on the island. This paved the way for the first resident English missionary, George Lawes, who arrived in 186l.

Much of the early hostility to foreigners was motivated by a very real fear of European diseases. The islanders' reputation for ferocity had always kept the whalers away, but then in the 1860s came the Peruvians and Bully Hayes, who were able to entice Niuean men to leave their island voluntarily to mine phosphate for years at a time on distant Malden Island. Mataio Tuitonga was made king in 1876 and his successor, Fataaiki, appealed to Britain for protection. Finally, in 1900, Niue was taken over by the U.K. and a year later transferred to New Zealand.

Government

In 1959 the appointed Island Council was replaced by an elected Legislative Assembly (Fono Ekepule). Niue became internally self-governing in free association with New Zealand on 19 October 1974. The Assembly has 20 members, 14 from village constituencies and six elected from a single island-wide constituency. The premier is elected by the Assembly from its ranks by a show of hands. The premier in turn chooses three cabinet ministers from among the Assembly members. The Assembly meets in the impressive Fale Fono (tel. 4200) in Alofi. Local government is provided by the 14 village councils elected every three years.

Niue's first elected premier, Hon. Sir Robert R. Rex, served continuously as government leader from 1974 until his death in December 1992. Sir Robert's son is still an elected member of parliament. Other local politicians of note include Mr. Young Vivian, a former secretary-general of the South Pacific Commission; Mr. Frank Lui, Sir Robert's successor as prime minister; and photographer Michael Jackson.

Government ministers brook no criticism. When the editor of the local newspaper became overly annoying to the powers that be, her expatriate husband suddenly had visa problems. In early 1995 an Australian Catholic priest with years of service on Niue was subjected to deportation proceedings after he dared comment publicly on nepotism in the allocation of government scholarships. In a small community like Niue's one has to take care not to step on the wrong toes.

Economy

Over half the workforce is government employed, but in 1992 moves began to reduce this and to encourage Niueans to go into private business. Niue is totally dependent on official aid from New Zealand, which supplies two-thirds of the local budget. In 1990 foreign aid totaled A$8,875,000, or A$4034 per capita, the highest such level in the South Pacific. Most of the money is used to support the infrastructure, which maintains an artificial, consumer-oriented standard of living. Many government services are provided free.

Tourism and the sale of postage stamps to philatelists help balance the island's cash flow. Of the 993 tourists who visited Niue in 1991,

This impressive stairway at Motu is used to lower dugouts to the reef.

DAVID STANLEY

81% were from New Zealand. In fact, due to the limited air service there are so few tourists that many of the facilities mentioned in this chapter are perennially closed and the managers off island. Plans are underway to extend the airport runway to allow in larger planes, so this could change. In the past hand-sewn footballs sent to N.Z. were the biggest export, but recent transportation difficulties have halted this and virtually all other exports. In 1993 Niue announced it was setting up a "tax haven" for overseas companies, similar to those of Vanuatu and Cook Islands.

Although the Niue Development Board and other agencies have attempted to stimulate agriculture, the economy is continually undermined by emigration of working-age Niueans to New Zealand (to which Niueans have unhindered entry). In the past, small quantities of passion fruit, lime juice, canned coconut cream, and honey have been exported. The coconut cream factory closed in 1989 after a hurricane wiped out the island's coconut plantations; in 1990 Hurricane Ofa destroyed the lime and passion fruit crops. Periodic droughts have also taken a heavy toll. Taro, yams, cassava, sweet potatoes, papaya, and bananas are actively cultivated in bush gardens for personal consumption by the grower. Some farmers also grow vanilla, and some pigs, poultry, and beef cattle are kept. Saturday is bush day when people go inland to clear, plant, and weed their gardens.

The People

Niueans are related to Tongans and Samoans rather than Tahitians. There are about 2,300 people on Niue (down from 4,000 at self-government in 1974). Another 14,400 Niueans reside in New Zealand (all Niueans are N.Z. citizens), and every year more people leave "the Rock" (Niue) to seek employment and opportunity abroad. Many of the landowners have left—you'll never see as many empty houses and near-ghost towns as you see here. The villages on the east coast give an idea of how Europe must have looked in the Middle Ages after a plague, as direct flights to Auckland have drained the population. Remittances from Niueans in New Zealand are important sources of income.

The inhabitants live in small villages scattered along the coast, with a slight concentration near the administrative center, Alofi, on the west coast. After disastrous hurricanes in 1959 and 1960, the New Zealand government replaced the traditional lime-plastered, thatched-roofed houses of the people with tin-roofed "hurricane-resistant" concrete-block dwellings. Half the population was touched by a dengue fever epidemic in 1980, and five died. Two Polynesian dialects are spoken: motu in the north and tafiti in the south.

All land is held by families. Three-quarters belong to the Ekalesia Nieue, founded by the London Missionary Society. Other churches such as the Catholics and Mormons have only a few hundred members. There are no longer any chiefs, and lineage means little. Everyone on the island knows one another.

A major event for a teenage boy is his hair-cutting ceremony, when the long tail of hair he has kept since childhood is removed. Guests invited to the concurrent feast each contribute hundreds of dollars to a fund that goes to the boy after celebration expenses are paid. For girls there's a similar ear-piercing ceremony. These gatherings are usually held on a Saturday in private homes; you may be allowed to observe if you know someone.

Public Holidays and Festivals

Public holidays include New Year's Day, Commission Day (2 January), Good Friday, Easter Monday (March/April), ANZAC Day (25 April), Queen Elizabeth's Birthday (a Monday in early June), Constitution Day (19 October), Peniamina Day (fourth Monday in October), and Christmas Days (25 and 26 December).

Player Week and Takai Week are both the first week of January. The main event of the year is the Constitution Celebrations, which last three days around 19 October. There are traditional dancing and singing, parades, sports, and a display of produce and handicrafts at the high school grounds two km inland from Alofi. A highlight is the exciting outrigger canoe race off Alofi wharf. Peniamina Day falls on the Monday during the Constitution Celebrations.

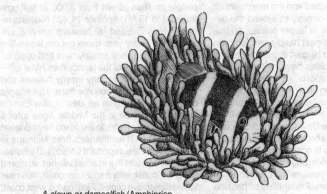

A clown or damselfish (Amphiprion clarkii) *nestles among the venomous tentacles of an anemone. A mucous secretion protects the fish from the creature's stinging cells, providing it with a safe refuge. Anemones gather plankton from the water, but also feed on mussels, snails, or barnacles that fall their way.*

ON THE ROAD

SIGHTS

Exploring Niue

Virtually all of Niue's scenic attractions are within earshot of the ocean, but while sites on the west coast are easily accessible in a few minutes from the road, those on the east coast are only reached over slippery rough trails requiring hikes of up to 40 minutes. Some of these trails, such as those through fantastic petrified coral forests at Vaikona and Tongo, are not well marked. Sturdy shoes are required to go almost anywhere off the road on Niue.

If you're a good walker, you could visit the sites south of Alofi on foot in less than a day. Those to the north can be covered by a combination of walking, hitching, and good luck, but to get to the places on the northeast and southeast coasts and return to Alofi the same day, you'll need your own transport. Alternatively, camp in one of the east coast villages and visit the area more at your leisure. Take your own food with you, as little is available in the villages.

Photographers should note that conditions on the east coast are best in the morning, on the west coast in the afternoon. Vaikona and Tongo are definitely not afternoon trips, as the declining light in the forest makes the trails hard to discern. Also, limestone makes for slow walking.

Near Alofi

The **Huanaki Museum and Cultural Center** (open weekdays 0800-1500, free) is next to the hospital near the junction of the airport and coastal roads in Alofi. According to popular tradition, Captain Cook landed at **Opaahi Reef** opposite the Mormon church in Alofi. It's a scenic spot, well worth the short detour.

Two kings of Niue, Mataio Tuitonga (reigned 1876-87) and Fataaiki (reigned 1888-96), are buried in front of the **LMS Church** opposite Alofi's post office. Nearby, adjoining the war memorial, are two stone slabs against which these kings rested their backs. The last king of Niue, Togia (died 1917), ceded his kingdom to Britain on 21 April 1900, just four days after the

Americans annexed Eastern Samoa. He's buried in front of the church at Tuapa.

It's fascinating to walk on the reef southwest of Alofi wharf at low tide. Crevices, cliffs, and coral abound, and there are natural pools on the reef where you can swim safely. Beware of waves heralding the incoming tide, however.

South of Alofi

A couple of small government-run food processing plants and experimental farms are in the area around the airport. Passion fruit, limes, and papaya are grown here, and honey is produced. It's interesting to poke around a bit and people you meet will probably be only too happy to explain what's what.

The road drops to **Tamakautonga,** where you'll find a couple of small beaches behind the church. Farther south at **Avatele** (pronounced Avasele), there's another poor excuse for a beach at the canoe landing. Return to Alofi along the coastal road with a stop at **Anaana** near Halangingie Point, where you can sit atop a cliff by the road and watch as tons of water are thrown at your feet.

North of Alofi

Houme Chasm at Alofi North, about four km from the hotel, is behind the house across the street and slightly north of the Catholic Mission. A flashlight is required to reach the pool.

Avaiki Sea Cave is another six km north and an easy five minutes from the road. The pool in the main cave just north of the landing contains a variety of marinelife and is a great place to swim, but this is often prohibited. The limestone formations are outstanding. Just 200 meters north of the Avaiki sign is the trail down to **Palaha Cave,** with stalagmites and stalactites. **Hio Reef,** a little over a km farther north, just before the point where the road divides, is a nice secluded sandy beach best for swimming at high tide.

Farther north again, just beyond Namukulu, is the trail to **Limu Reef,** a perfect snorkeling locale with colorful coral and fish. A natural stone bridge over the lagoon is just a little north of here across the rocks. The trail to **Makalea Cave** is 200 meters north of the Limu signboard. Near the road just opposite the southernmost house in Hikutavake is **Makatutaha,** a large pothole containing a pool connected to the sea.

Two of Niue's highlights are **Matapa Chasm** and the **Arches of Talava,** reached along an extension of the coastal road just north of Hikutavake. Follow the road straight down to Matapa, a wide, sunken chasm that was once the bathing place of Niuean royalty—very good swimming and snorkeling. The Arches of Talava are harder to find. The trail branches off the Matapa track to the right just before the beginning of the descent. Keep straight on the trail about 15 minutes, then watch for yellow marks on the trees, which indicate the branch trail on the left to Talava. The site itself is entered through a cave. A great series of stone arches above the sea complement side caves with red and green stalactites and stalagmites in fantastic flowing formations. Behind the outermost arch is a large cave best entered at low tide with a flashlight. The constant roar of the surf adds to the overwhelming impression the place makes.

The Southeast Coast

Niue's wild east coast has some of the most fantastic limestone features in the entire South Pacific, though finding your way around without a guide requires intuition and caution. About four km northeast of Hakupu, second-largest village on the island, is the unmarked trail to **Tongo Chasm.** After a 20-minute walk you reach a wasteland of coral pinnacles much like the interior of Nauru Island. The path leads down to a wide chasm with coconut trees growing on the sandy bottom. Climb down the ladder to the sand, and swim in the pools at each end of the chasm. The green of the coconut trees combined with the golden sand contrasts sharply with the rocky wasteland, creating an almost North African effect—until you hear the ocean crashing into the cliffs just meters away: one of the scenic wonders of the Pacific.

From the Tongo trailhead, travel northeast another four km through the **Huvalu Forest,** with its many species of banyan, Tahitian chestnut, and *kafika* trees, to the Vaikona trailhead. The trail to **Vaikona Chasm** is partially marked with red paint, but careful attention is required, as

there is a good chance of getting lost. This trip is for experienced hikers only, unless you come with a guide. As you approach the coast through pandanus brush covering the jagged limestone, you pass a sudden opening straight down into the chasm. Wind your way around the back of the opening and drop into a deep cave, grasping the stout orange rope provided for the purpose. You enter the chasm over huge rocks from the cave. There are two crystal clear pools to swim in, one at each end of Vaikona; tiny freshwater crayfish and black carp live here.

It would take a major expedition to explore all this chasm has to offer. Resembling a ruined Gothic cathedral, the walls soar 30 meters to a canopy of vegetation, and huge blocks of the collapsed roof litter the floor. The stalagmites and stalactites of the entrance cave are like images on a broken medieval portal; by plunging into the cool, clear water of the pools, one has communion with the bowels of the earth. The crashing of the breakers into the coast nearby is like the expurgation of sin—a spectacular visual experience. This awe-inspiring chasm is outstanding even for Niue. Hopefully Vaikona, Tongo, and the Huvalu Forest will someday be set aside as a national park.

The Northeast Coast

The trail to **Motu Reef** is about a kilometer south of Lakepa. There's a wide wooden stairway down to the reef from the cave where canoes are stored. It's a 25-minute walk along an easy-to-follow trail from the trailhead to **Vaitafe Spring,** a couple of km north of Lakepa. Fresh water from a crevice at the foot of a sheer cliff bubbles into a pool where you can swim, but the area is only accessible at low tide. You can reef walk here.

At the north end of the island, opposite the church in **Mutalau** village, is a monument commemorating the arrival of the first Christian missionaries; the first Niuean convert, Peniamina (1846); and Paulo (1849), the first Samoan teacher. A jeep track across from the monument leads down to Uluvehi Landing, an easy five-minute walk. This was the main landing on the island in the early days; the islanders' sleek outrigger canoes are still stored in caves in the cliffs. To reach **Vaihakea Cave,** look for an overgrown trail just 100 meters inland from the streetlight at Uluvehi on the east side of the track. Once you get on the trail, it's only a five-minute walk to this fantastic submerged cave full of fish and coral, but you must climb down a sharp limestone cliff near the trail end. There's excellent swimming and snorkeling at low tide.

The sites mentioned above are only the *highlights* of Niue; there are many other caves for the avid spelunker to explore.

Sports and Recreation

Niue Adventures (Box 141, Alofi; tel. 4276, fax 4010) offers scuba diving at NZ$55 for one dive, or NZ$410 for a six-dive package with two boat dives. The price includes all gear and transportation (certification card required). They will also rent tanks and other equipment if you just want to go off on your own. Featured are dives through caves to drop-offs, and Niue's small, timid sea snakes. If you're very lucky, you may be able to dive with dolphins or migrating whales (June to November). Due to the absence of rivers, the water is unbelievably clear (25-meter visibility).

Kevin Fawcett runs the diving side of Niue Adventures, while Terry Coe takes care of fishing and/or coastal sightseeing trips aboard their two 10-meter *alia* catamarans. Groups of up to six persons can go fishing with Terry for three hours at NZ$200 for the boat, three such trips NZ$500 (their gear or yours). All fish caught belong to Terry and he prefers to tag and release marlin and sailfish. Fishing on Sunday is taboo. A three-hour scenic boat trip that offers the chance to see turtles and whales in season costs NZ$40 pp. A special scuba diving trip to the eastern side of the island by *alia* is NZ$300 for the boat only. (In 1993 Mr. Coe, a former principal of Niue High School, became the first *palagi* ever elected to the Niue Assembly.)

Sporting events such as soccer (March to June), rugby (June to August), and netball (June to August) take place on the high school grounds. Cricket (December to February) and softball matches are usually held in the villages on alternating Saturdays. The locals will know what is happening.

Visitors are welcome at the nine-hole **golf course** (tel. 4292) near the airport.

PRACTICALITIES

Accommodations

The two-story **Niue Hotel** (Reg and Annette Newcombe, Box 80, Alofi; tel. 4092, fax 4310), on the coast between the airport and Alofi, was built in 1975 and completely refurbished after the destruction wrought by Hurricane Ofa in February 1990. It charges NZ$109/125/155 single/double/triple for one of the 32 fan-cooled rooms with fridge and private bath. An oceanview executive suite is NZ$132/160 single/double. Children under 12 are free. Cooking facilities are not available but the hotel has a 100-seat dining room, plus bar, gift shop, and swimming pool.

Peleni's Guest House (Siona Talagi, Box 11, Alofi; tel. 4135, fax 4010) is in a former family house near the Handicraft Center in central Alofi. The three very homey bedrooms with shared bath and cooking facilities are NZ$42 single or double. A three-bed family room costs NZ$54. Prepared meals are available at reasonable cost. The helpful owner, Siona, keeps everything clean and well maintained. He's happy to have his guests tag along as he goes to tend his bush garden, do his weekly mail run, or attend church on Sunday. Ask for Siona at the airport.

Kololi's Guest House near the Commercial Center in central in Alofi charges NZ$35 single or double for the three standard rooms and NZ$48 for the family room upstairs. Your hosts Neal and Rupina Morrisey provide communal cooking and laundry facilities in this newly built guesthouse.

The **Coral Gardens Motel** (Box 91, Alofi; tel. 4235, fax 4222), at Makapu Point four km north of Alofi, has five wooden clifftop bungalows with cooking facilities and excellent views at NZ$120/150 single/double including breakfast. Sails Restaurant is on the premises, and there's an excellent swimming hole at the foot of the cliff. Managers Stafford and Salome Guest are very helpful and can make any arrangements you may require.

Near the Avaiki Caves at Makefu is the **Anaiki Motel** (Moka and Loma Mitihepi, Box 183, Alofi; tel. 4321, fax 4320) with five units in a long block at NZ$75/85/95 single/double/triple,

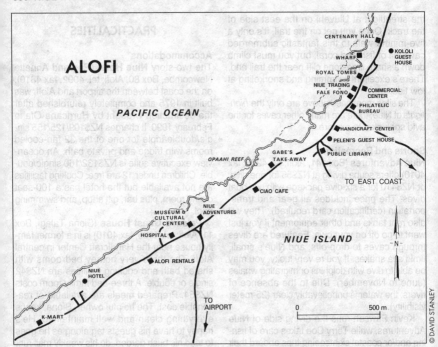

ALOFI

PACIFIC OCEAN

CENTENARY HALL

KOLOLI
GUEST
HOUSE

WHARF

ROYAL TOMBS

NIUE TRADING
FALE FONO

COMMERCIAL
CENTER

PHILATELIC
BUREAU

HANDICRAFT CENTER

PELENI'S GUEST HOUSE

PUBLIC LIBRARY

GABE'S
TAKE-AWAY

OPAAHI REEF

CIAO CAFE

TO EAST COAST

MUSEUM &
CULTURAL
CENTER

NIUE
ADVENTURES

NIUE ISLAND

HOSPITAL

ALOFI RENTALS

-N-

NIUE
HOTEL

K-MART

TO
AIRPORT

0   500 m

© DAVID STANLEY

breakfast included. A hot plate is provided for heating up simple meals.

Esther's Village Motel (Sifa and Kuso Pavihi, Box 107, Alofi; fax 4010) in Avatele has three double units with private bath and full kitchens at NZ$42/52 single/double, and one four-bed family unit at NZ$62 triple (children under 12 are free). The large veranda is a great place for an evening meal while watching the sunset. A village store and beach are nearby—families will like it here. There's a small shop on the premises, but the distance from Alofi (seven km) is a drawback.

Damiana's Holiday Motel (Mono and Stencil Kingi, Box 119, Alofi; fax 4010), also at Avatele, is very similar to Esther's with two duplex units with good cooking facilities and private bath, NZ$42/52/62 single/double/triple (children under 12 free). Their tropical garden is really lovely.

The German-owned **Kokosnuss Motel** (Karl and Petra Hofmann, Box 3, Alofi; tel./fax 4262), at Talamaitonga between Avatele and Vaiea,

has one wooden self-catering cabin at NZ$52/62 single/double. Airport transfers are free and they rent motor scooters.

In 1995 it was announced that a 24-room upmarket resort was to be erected on a cliff between Tamakautonga and Avatele. The **Matavai Resort** will include a restaurant, bar, swimming pool, tennis, and lawn bowls, but precise details were unavailable at press time.

For a longer stay, ask around about renting a house by the week or month. There are usually plenty available. Unexpected complications can arise, however, as the house may have hundreds of owners, and visiting relatives might throw you out! **Camping** would be possible on the east coast, but get permission or keep out of sight. For indoor camping, unfurnished houses without hot water in Hakupu village are about NZ$50 a week.

Food and Entertainment
The dining room at the **Niue Hotel** (tel. 4092) serves lunch 1200-1300 sharp (open daily).

Check to see if they're still feeding endangered species like the *unga* (coconut crab), fruit bat, and native pigeon to tourists. Thursday or Sunday at 1900 (check to find out which day) the hotel has a tropical smorgasbord, sometimes followed by disco dancing to recorded music. The hotel bar picks up in the afternoon as people get off work, but they close early if nobody's around, even on Friday night.

Light snacks are served at **Gabe's Take-Away** on the seaside south of Alofi, at the **Huanaki Snack Bar** (tel. 4071) at the Cultural Center, and at **Tavana Cafeteria** (tel. 4334) in the Commercial Center in Alofi. Also try **Jenna's de la Cuisine** (closed Sunday) between Peleni's Guest House and the Handicraft Center in Alofi. **Island Style Restaurant** is at Talamaitonga near Avatele.

Sails Restaurant (tel. 4235) at the Coral Gardens Motel north of town serves good food at prices lower than those asked at the Niue Hotel. Their patio is a great place for a drink around sunset, and a live band plays on Friday night (closed Sunday and Monday). Ask about their weekly barbecue.

The **Niue Sports Club** (tel. 4292), better known as the Top Club, at the nine-hole golf course near the airport, is nominally private, but visitors are welcome and bar prices low. Drop by for happy hour and a meal on Friday night. Village dances take place on Friday and Saturday nights.

Liquor is sold by the Treasury Department near the post office. On paydays the Department's hours are restricted; alcoholism is a problem here and drunks can suddenly turn aggressive, so be careful what you say in such situations. Drinking alcohol in the street is prohibited. Tap water is safe to drink on Niue.

Shopping

Imported goods are fairly cheap due to low customs duties. Rex and Sons and Kmart are the largest stores, but both close at 1500 weekdays and don't open at all weekends. This presents a serious problem as the flight from Auckland arrives on Friday afternoon and there's no chance to do any grocery shopping until Monday. Thus one should bring along some instant noodles and canned foods to avoid being dependent on the rather expensive restaurants all weekend (don't bring fresh fruits or vegetables, which could cause quarantine complications).

There's only a market once a week, held early Friday morning beside Rex and Sons Store in Alofi. This is pretty useless to visitors staying only one week as the weekly flight to Auckland departs Friday afternoon. Buy a bottle of Niue honey, if you can.

The people produce very fine, firmly woven baskets of pandanus wound over a coconut-fiber core—among the best in Polynesia. Fine pandanus and coconut leaf bud hats are also made. Visit the **Niue Handicraft Shop** (tel.

The Handicraft Center in Alofi is the place to pick up a distinctive souvenir.

MICHAEL JACKSON

4144) in Alofi and **Hinapoto Handicrafts** at the Cultural Center. Coral and valuable shells cannot be exported from Niue.

The **Philatelic Bureau** (tel. 4152, fax 4033) sells beautiful stamps, which make excellent souvenirs.

Services

The administration buildings in Alofi contain the post office, Treasury Department, and Telecommunications Office. Change money at the Westpac Bank branch (weekdays 0900-1400). New Zealand currency is used. The Niue Hotel is the only place on the island accepting credit cards.

The Telecommunications Office (tel. 4000) handles overseas calls and wires. Niue's telephone code is 683.

Doctors are available at the hospital (tel. 4100) weekdays 0730-1500.

Information

The **Tourism Office** (Box 42, Alofi; tel. 4224, fax 4225) in Alofi's Commercial Center can answer most questions about the island. The public library (weekdays 0730-1500) at the Dept. of Education has a good Pacific section. Farther back in the same complex is the USP Extension Center (tel. 4049, fax 4315), which sells a few books on Niue.

The excellent "Map of Niue" can be purchased at the hotel or the Handicraft Center. The booklets *Camera on Niue* and *Niue In Focus* make excellent souvenirs.

The *Niue Star* (Box 84, Alofi; tel. 4207) is an independent weekly newspaper. Cable TV is available throughout Niue 1730-2300 and "Radio Sunshine" broadcasts on AM594/FM91 0600-0900/1130-1330/1800-2130, but both are off the air on Sunday. Most TV programs are supplied by Television New Zealand.

TRANSPORTATION

Getting There

With only 2,300 people on the island, running an air service into Niue isn't a very profitable proposition. In mid-1994 Polynesian Airlines stopped calling here between Apia and Rarotonga, and Samoa Air dropped their service from Pago Pago about the same time. In fact, the situation seems to change from month to month, so check with these carriers to find out if they've decided to return to Niue.

In 1992 **Air Nauru** (tel. 4286, fax 4131) commenced a weekly service between Auckland and Niue (NZ$698 one-way, NZ$1117 roundtrip, valid one month) but in August 1995 this airline announced it was terminating the service, leaving Niue without any scheduled flights at all! At last report the Niue Government was negotiating with Royal Tongan Airlines for a flight to/from Nuku'alofa; the tour companies mentioned below should have details. (Flying from Auckland or Nuku'alofa to Niue, keep in mind that you'll arrive a day earlier because you cross the international date line.)

Go Pacific Holidays (Box 68-440, Auckland, New Zealand; tel. 64-9/379-5520, fax 64-9/377-0111), **ASPAC Vacations Ltd.** (Box 4330, Auckland, New Zealand; tel. 64-9/623-0259, fax 64-9/623-0257), **Passport Holidays** (tel. 64-9/357-2500, fax 64-9/309-6895), and **Islands International Travel** (8-10 Whitaker Place, Auckland, New Zealand; tel. 64-9/309-4233, fax 64-9/309-4332) offer well-planned package tours to Niue from Auckland. These trips are less expensive than a regular roundtrip ticket, and airfare, seven nights lodging, transfers, and a circle-island tour are included!

Reconfirm your flight reservations at the Rex's Travel (tel. 67001) in Alofi. This office might also have information about the irregular supply ship from Niue to Rarotonga. Large ships must anchor offshore; their cargo is transferred by lighters.

Yachts anchor in about 15 meters (good holding) in an open roadstead off Alofi and are well protected except for winds from the west. A NZ$5-a-day port charge is levied. Water is available at the wharf. Customs and immigration for clearing in are closed on weekends.

Getting Around

There's no bus service. Hitching is possible along the west coast, but you could get stranded on the east. Don't underestimate the size of the island: it's a long, long way to walk. The road around the island is 64 km and the pavement doesn't extend beyond the west coast.

Budget Rent-a-Car (Box 81, Alofi; tel. 4307, fax 4308), at Helens Tours next to the Niue

Hotel, rents Suzuki vehicles with unlimited mileage at NZ$70 a day. Ama's Rentals, part of the same operation, rents 125-cc motorcycles (NZ$35 daily, NZ$175 weekly), 80-cc scooters (NZ$30 daily, NZ$150 weekly) and 10-speed mountain bikes (NZ$12 daily, NZ$75 weekly).

Alofi Rentals (tel. 4316, fax 4262), near the Niue Hotel, offers a/c cars (NZ$50 daily, NZ$300 weekly), pick-up trucks (NZ$40 daily, NZ$250 weekly), motorbikes (NZ$23 daily, NZ$110 weekly), scooters (NZ$18 daily, NZ$110 weekly), and mountain bikes (NZ$5 daily, NZ$30 weekly).

Also try **Maile Rentals** (Box 29, Alofi; tel. 4027, fax 4131) at Rex and Sons Store in central Alofi. All rental vehicles are in short supply, so don't wait until the last minute. A Niue driver's license (NZ$2 for scooters, NZ$10 for motorcycles, NZ$25 for cars) must be obtained at the police station opposite the Philatelic Bureau. Driving is on the left.

Helens Tours (Helen Sipeli, Box 81, Alofi; tel. 4307, fax 4308) next to the Niue Hotel offers a variety of trips, including a Vaikona Chasm tour on Tuesday morning (NZ$30), a breakfast bush walk on Wednesday morning (NZ$28), a "behind the hedges" tour on Wednesday afternoon (NZ$20), a circle-island tour on Saturday (NZ$20), and a Huvalu Forest and Tongo tour on Sunday afternoon (NZ$20). On Saturday afternoon at 1730 Helen runs a *fia fia* feast tour with *umu* food and Niuean dancing (NZ$35).

Tali Magatogia of **Tali's Tours** can take you to hard-to-reach attractions such as Vaikona Chasm, Ulupaka Cave, and Anatoloa Cave. Ulupaka (near Lakepa) is over a kilometer long and coated with dirty black fungus.

Airport

Hanan International Airport (IUE) is three km southeast of Alofi. Airport transfers are NZ$5 each way, otherwise it's fairly easy to hitch a ride into town. Though you'll need a passport and onward ticket, no visa is required for a stay of up to 30 days. There's no bank or duty-free shop. The airport departure tax is NZ$20.

GORDON OHLIGER

KINGDOM OF TONGA
INTRODUCTION

The ancient Kingdom of Tonga, oldest and last remaining Polynesian monarchy, is the only Pacific nation never brought under foreign rule. Though sprinkled over 700,000 square km of ocean from Niuafo'ou, between Fiji and Samoa, to the Minerva Reef 290 km southwest of Ata, the total land area of the kingdom is only 691 square km.

Tonga is divided into four main parts: the Tongatapu Group in the south, with the capital, Nuku'alofa; the Ha'apai Group, a far-flung archipelago of low coral islands and soaring volcanoes in the center; the Vava'u Group, with its immense landlocked harbor; and in the north, the isolated, volcanic Niuas. The four groups are pleasingly diverse, each with interesting aspects to enjoy: no other Pacific country is made up of components as scenically varied as these.

There's over 100 km of open sea between Tongatapu and Ha'apai, then another 100 between Ha'apai and Vava'u, then *another* 300 km north are the Niuas, including remote Niuafo'ou and Niuatoputapu. In all, Tonga comprises 170 islands, 36 of them inhabited. Even though they're some of the most densely popu-

lated in the Pacific, the Tongan islands are set quite apart from the 20th century.

The Land

Tonga sits on the eastern edge of the Indo-Australian Plate, which is forced up as the Pacific Plate pushes under it at the Tonga Trench. This long oceanic valley running from east of Tonga to New Zealand is one of the lowest parts of the ocean floor, in places over 10 km deep. Tonga is on the circum-Pacific Ring of Fire, which extends from New Zealand to Samoa, then backtracks into Vanuatu and the Solomons. Where Tongatapu (a raised atoll), Lifuka (a low coral island), and Vava'u (another uplifted atoll) are today, towering volcanoes once belched fire and brimstone. When they sank, coral polyps gradually built the islands.

Study the map of Tonga and you'll distinguish four great atolls in a line 350 km long. The two central atolls (Ha'apai) are now largely submerged, with Lifuka and Nomuka the largest remaining islands of each. As Ha'apai sank under the weight of new volcanoes such as Kao and Tofua, the outermost groups, Vava'u and Tongatapu, tilted toward the center, creating cliffs on their outer edges and half-submerged islands facing in. The crack in the earth's crust that originally built Tonga has shifted northwest, and the active volcanoes of today are in a line 50 km west of Ha'apai-Vava'u. Fonuafo'ou, Tofua, Lateiki, Late, Fonualei, and Niuafo'ou have all erupted over the last 200 years.

Climate

The name Tonga means south; it's cooler and less humid here than in islands closer to the equator, such as Samoa. December to April is the hot, rainy season, with especially high humidity from January to March. June to August can be cool enough to make a sweater occasionally necessary.

Tonga gets an average of two tropical hurricanes a year, usually between November and April, although they can occur as late as May. Rainfall, temperatures, and the probability of hurricanes increase the farther north you go. The southeast tradewinds prevail from May to November, and easterlies the rest of the year; in Tonga, west and northwest winds herald bad weather. In February and March north winds bring heat waves and heavy rains.

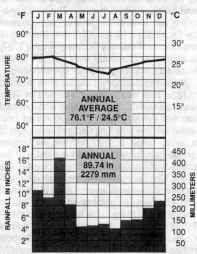

VAVAU'S CLIMATE

For local weather information dial 23-401 in Nuku'alofa during business hours.

HISTORY AND GOVERNMENT

Prehistory

According to myth, the demigod Maui acquired a fishhook from Samoa which he used to yank the Tonga Islands out of the sea. He then stamped on the islands to make them flat and suitable for gardening. The Polynesians reached Tonga from Fiji over 3,000 years ago. These early arrivers made incised *Lapita* pottery, though later the art was lost. Tangaloa, the creator god, descended from the sky and had a son, Aho'eitu, by a beautiful Tongan maiden named Va'epopua. This child became the first hereditary king, or Tu'i Tonga, perhaps around A.D. 950.

Fierce Tongan warriors traveled throughout Western Polynesia in large double-hulled canoes *(kalia),* each capable of carrying up to 200 people. In the 13th century the domain of the Tu'i Tonga extended all the way from Rotuma in the west through part of the Lau Group, Wallis and Futuna, Samoa, and Tokelau, to Niue in the east. The eventual collapse of this empire led to unrest and a series of Tu'i Tonga assassinations, so in 1470 the 24th Tu'i Tonga delegated much of his political power to a brother, the *hau,* or temporal ruler, while retaining the spiritual authority. Later the power of the *hau* was divided between the Tu'i Ha'atakalaua and Tu'i Kanokupolu, resulting in three distinct lines.

European Contact

Although the Dutchmen Schouten and Le Maire sighted the Niuas in 1616, another Dutchman, Abel Tasman, was the first European to visit Tongatapu and Ha'apai. Arriving on 19 January 1643, as Tongans approached his ship in narrow canoes, Tasman fired a gun—terrifying the chief. A trumpet, violin, and flute were then played in succession to this chief's further astonishment. Tasman received sorely needed food and water to carry on with his journey. At one point he escaped disaster by charging full-tilt over the Nanuku Reef, which was luckily covered with sufficient water to be traversed.

When Captain Cook visited Tonga in 1773, 1774, and 1777, he and his men were received with lavish friendliness—pyramids of food were offered them, and dances and boxing matches in which little girls and women took part were staged in their honor. (The skillful Tongan pugilists made short work of Cook's crew in a competition.) Some say the islanders intended to roast and eat Cook and his men as part of the feast, but

TONGA AT A GLANCE

	POPULATION (1986)	AREA (sq. km)
Eua	4,393	87
Tongatapu	63,794	259
Ha'apai Group	8,919	109
Vava'u Group	15,175	119
Niuas *	2,368	72
Tonga	**94,649**	**646 ** **

* Niuafo'ou, Niuatoputapu, Tafahi
** inhabited islands only

KINGDOM OF TONGA

NIUAFO'OU I.
TAFAHI I.
NIUATOPUTAPU I.

FONUALEI I.
TOKU I.

VAVA'U GROUP VAVA'U I.
LATE I. NEIAFU

LATEIKI I.

HA'APAI GROUP
PANGAI
KAO I. HA'ANO I.
TOFUA I. FOA I.
LIFUKA I.
LOFANGA I. UIHA I.
KOTU I. HA'AFEVA I.
FONUAFO'OU I. NOMUKA I.
HUNGA HUNGA KELEFESIA I.
HA'APAI I. TONGA I.

NUKU'ALOFA TONGATAPU GROUP
'EUAIKI I.
TONGATAPU I. EUA I.
KALAU I.

ATA I.

0   100 km

N

© DAVID STANLEY

Cook's profuse thanks at his reception prompted them to change their minds. Cook presented the Tu'i Tonga with a male Galapagos tortoise, which was left to wander blind in the royal garden right up until 1966, when it died at the ripe old age of over 200. Ever since Cook's visit, Tonga has been known as "The Friendly Islands." Cook never visited Vava'u, which was only "discovered" in 1781 by the Spaniard Mourelle.

The Formation of a Nation
European contact led to a decline in population as warring chiefs turned newly acquired muskets and cannons on each other. The new armaments also allowed Tongan warriors to conquer the Lau Group of Fiji about this time. Members of the London Missionary Society arrived in 1797, in the middle of these civil wars, but were unable to attract a following, and by 1804 all had left.

Wesleyan (Methodist) missionaries returned in 1822. Their most noteworthy convert (in 1831) was Taufa'ahau, chief of Ha'apai, who defeated two rival dynasties with the missionaries' help and in 1845 became King George Tupou I, ruler of a united Tonga. In 1862 he freed the Tongan people from forced labor on the estates of the chiefs while making hereditary nobles of the chiefs. King George decreed that each of his subjects be allotted a tax'api consisting of a town lot and 3.34 hectares of farmland for only T$3.20 annual rental. At the same time, the king established constitutional government, with a Privy Council of his choice and representation for both nobles and commoners in a Legislative Assembly.

This system, institutionalized in the Tongan Constitution of 4 November 1875, remains in force today. A year later Germany concluded a Treaty of Friendship, which recognized Tongan independence and the sovereignty of the king. Similar treaties were signed with England (1879) and the U.S. (1888). King George died in 1893 at 97 years of age, the creator of a unified Christian Tonga and one of the most remarkable men of the 19th century.

The Twentieth Century

Tonga (along with Japan, Thailand, Nepal, and a few Middle Eastern states) is one of the few countries in the world that has never been colonized by a European power. Germany had strong influence in Tonga during the late 19th century and wanted to include it in its colonial empire but bowed out to the British in exchange for a free hand in Samoa. In 1900 Tonga signed a new Treaty of Friendship with Britain, which gave the latter control of Tonga's foreign affairs as a means of forestalling encroachments by other colonial powers. British protection remained in effect until 1970, but the rule of the royal family continued unbroken.

The pervasive influence of the missionaries, who dominated Tonga from the early 19th century onward, can still be experienced any Sunday. Magnificent, much-loved Queen Salote ruled Tonga from 1918 until her death in 1965. Her achievements included the reunification of part of the Wesleyan church and the development of public health and education services (Tonga has one of the highest levels of school enrollment in the South Pacific, and 99.6% of Tongans are literate). In 1953, she won the hearts of millions by riding through London in an open coach, despite torrential rain, at Queen Elizabeth's coronation. In fact, she was only observing the Tongan custom of showing respect for royalty by appearing before them unprotected in bad weather.

Although just short of his mother's two-meter height, H.R.H. King Taufa'ahau Tupou IV, the present monarch, is a 1.9-meter, 28-stone giant who looks every bit the Polynesian king he is. As crown prince during WW II, he studied at the University of Sydney, becoming the first Tongan to earn a university degree. He served as prime minister from 1949 until he was crowned

king in 1967. King Tupou initiated a cautious modernization program, and on 4 June 1970 he reestablished Tonga's full sovereignty.

For almost three decades King Tupou has steered Tonga on a conservative course. Unlike Western Samoa, which has established relations with mainland China, Tonga still recognizes the Taiwan-based Republic of China. Yet way back in 1976 Tonga became the first South Pacific country to establish diplomatic relations with the USSR, leading to an absurd panic over alleged Soviet expansionism in the Pacific. This worked to Tonga's advantage as overdue aid from Australia, New Zealand, and the U.S. came pouring in.

Government

Tonga is a constitutional monarchy in which the king rules absolutely. He appoints the 10 members of the Cabinet, who retain their posts until

King George Tupou I. In 1831 this young chief of Ha'apai was baptized by Wesleyan missionaries. With their help he supplanted the Tu'i Tonga on Tongatapu and in 1845 was proclaimed king, taking the name of England's monarch. The present royal line is descended from him. In 1862 George I freed the Tongan slave class and in 1875 he gave his country the Constitution that is in effect today.

TONGA CHRONICLE

This magnificent statue of His Majesty King Taufa'ahau Tupou IV can be seen at Fau'amotu International Airport's old terminal.

retirement (as in the British House of Lords). They and the governors of Ha'apai and Vava'u (both appointed by the king) sit in the 30-seat Legislative Assembly or Parliament, along with nine members who represent the 33 Nobles of the Realm, and another nine elected every three years to represent Tonga's 95,000 commoners. The king appoints one of the nobles as speaker of parliament (the king also decides who will hold the 33 noble titles). The king can dissolve parliament, dismiss ministers, veto legislation, suspend habeas corpus, and proclaim martial law at will.

The king's younger brother, Prince Fatafehi Tu'ipelehake, served as prime minister for 26 years until his retirement in 1991 (the current prime minister, Baron Vaea, is a well-respected moderate). The king's eldest son and heir, H.R.H. Crown Prince Tupouto'a, is minister of foreign affairs and defense. There are no municipal councils; Nuku'alofa is administered directly by the central government. The judiciary is independent, with the highest court of appeal consisting of three judges from other Commonwealth countries. Tonga has a small but efficient 200-person defense force, with facilities behind the royal palace and at the airport. The press and radio are government-owned, and no formal criticism of the king is permitted.

Yet as educational levels increase and Tongan commoners become economically independent, the power of the privileged few is being called into question. There have been accusations of widespread corruption, and church leaders have backed increased democracy. The February 1990 elections gave candidates advocating an increase in the number of people's representatives five of the nine commoner seats, and in August 1992 four of them banded together to form the Tonga Prodemocracy Movement. Constitutional reform was discussed at a landmark November 1992 convention, which foreigners and overseas Tongans with foreign passports were prevented from attending.

In the February 1993 elections the number of pro-democracy members increased from five to six with those from Tongatapu and Ha'apai winning by huge margins. Unfortunately several attempts to create viable political parties have degenerated into factional squabbles.The old guard has attempted to muzzle the elected members through legal action, and as this book went to press Tongatapu representative 'Akilisi Pohiva was facing treason charges for allegedly calling the king a dictator. As yet no one questions the continued existence of the monarchy, and King Tupou is dearly loved by a majority of his subjects, but the intermediate noble class is declining in both economic and political influence.

In a way, Tonga's current political problems are a direct result of the absence of colonization, because a European system of representative government was not instituted in Tonga as part of a normal decolonization process, as happened in virtually every other island state. The world has changed beyond recognition since 1875 yet Tonga's missionary-inspired constitution remains the law of the land. This cannot last forever and the future of the monarchy may well depend on its ability to adapt to the times.

ECONOMY

Agriculture and Land

In Tonga's feudal system, all land is property of the crown but administered by nobles who allot it to the common people. The king and nobles retain 27% of the land for their own use, while the government owns another 18%. Although Tongan commoners still have a right to the 3.34-hectare tax'api granted them by King George, there's no longer enough land to go around. This system has not been altered substantially since 1862, and a 1976 parliamentary law intended to redistribute unused land was vetoed by the king. Frustrations with the system are relieved by migration to New Zealand and the United States. If those avenues were to close, Tonga would face serious unrest. Foreigners cannot purchase land, and even leasing requires Cabinet approval.

Only half the population is involved in the cash economy; the rest live from subsistence agriculture, fishing, and collecting. The production of food, housing, and handicrafts used by the producer is higher than the value of all goods sold for cash, a situation rarely reflected in official statistics. The staples are yams, taro, manioc, and sweet potato. Crops are rotated, and up to two-thirds of a garden is left fallow at any time. In many localities, humans are outnumbered by domestic pigs, which range freely across the islands.

The biggest cash crop is pumpkins (squash) and since the vegetable was first introduced in 1987, it has become Tonga's biggest export by far, shipped mostly to Japan by air and worth US$10 million a year. Tongan pumpkins supply about half Japan's requirements in November and December, a "niche market" producers in other parts of the world can't cover for climatic reasons. Some 2,000 small farmers grow pumpkins from July to December and overproduction has led to soil degradation, groundwater pollution, deforestation, and an increase in pests. Much of the income has gone into cars and there's now bumper-to-bumper traffic on Taufa'ahau Road throughout the day as nouveau riche Tongans drive up and down to show off. Tonga's growing dependence on this monoculture carries with it the risk of economic collapse should the Japanese market dry up due to competition from new producers in Vanuatu and New Caledonia, a fall in yields caused by depleted soils, plant disease, or any other cause.

Trade and Development

From a favorable trade balance prior to 1960, today Tonga imports four times as much as it exports, with food imports alone equivalent to all exports. Australia and New Zealand profit most from the trade imbalance, selling food, machinery, fuels, and manufactured goods to Tonga. In 1993 New Zealand sold Tonga goods worth NZ$34,800,000 yet purchased only NZ$1,300,000 in Tongan products. Australia, the European Union, the Asian Development Bank, New Zealand, Japan, and the Utah-based Church of Latter-day Saints are Tonga's largest aid donors, and total aid compensates for over half of the trade deficit.

Tonga's main exports in order of importance are pumpkins, vanilla, tuna, leather goods, clothing, coconut oil, and taro. In 1980 the government created a Small Industries Center (SIC) in the eastern section of Nuku'alofa for companies producing consumer goods for export to Australia and New Zealand under the regional free-trade agreement, SPARTECA, which was designed to correct the imbalance mentioned above. By the mid-1990s the value of SPARTECA had declined due to "globalization," a worldwide liberalization of trade; Tongan exports of knitwear, leather jackets, and footballs have been pushed off Australasian markets by competitors in Asia. Today companies in the SIC produce mostly for a tariff-sheltered local market. Traditional agricultural exports to New Zealand such as bananas have been wiped out by transnational producers and strict quarantine requirements. The replanting of Tonga's aging coconut plantations has been inadequate and copra exports have dwindled to almost nothing in recent years.

As yet, Tonga has managed to avoid the extreme financial crises that have gripped Samoa in recent years, but both countries are still very much a part of the third world. Money remitted by Tongans living abroad, the country's largest single source of income, is crucial to maintaining the balance of payments. Rural areas are neglected as government facilities and light industry become concentrated in Nuku'alofa. A quarter of all Tongans now live in the capital, and hundreds more commute daily from outlying villages. Shantytowns have sprung up in the suburbs of Nuku'alofa, and there's a growing gap between the haves and have-nots. In 1986 the income tax was slashed from 40% to a flat 10% and company taxes were greatly reduced; the lost revenue was made up by a five percent sales tax, an unprecedented shift in taxation from the rich to the poor. Labor unions are banned.

Tourism

Earnings from tourism are higher than all exports combined, and a larger proportion of the tourist dollar remains in Tonga than is the case in some other Pacific countries because of the high proportion of small, locally owned guesthouses and motels. Tonga remains off the beaten track and is nowhere overrun by tourists (Fiji gets 10 times as many visitors). About 25,000 tourists a year visit Tonga, coming from New Zealand, the U.S., Australia, Germany, and Fiji, in that order. In 1989 the airport runway at Tongatapu was extended with Australian aid, in 1990 Japan paid for the new terminal building, in 1991 Royal Tongan Airlines was formed, and in 1992 Taiwanese interests began building an 86-room luxury hotel (still unfinished) next to the airport.

One of the South Pacific's most important yacht charter operations has been based at Vava'u for years, and now the European Union is to provide funds to upgrade Vava'u's airport to allow the island to be developed into Tonga's main tourist center. Vava'u has the potential to become one of the prime whalewatching destinations in the South Pacific. It's hard to believe but in 1995 a Japanese company called MACA Pacific requested permission to "harvest" 50 humpback and 200 sperm and minke whales a year in Tongan waters. Of course, not wishing to lose one of the country's most unique tourist attractions for a few meager royalties, the Tongan government turned them down, yet the very fact that a Japanese company could propose such a wretched scheme illustrates the utter lack of environmental consciousness in some Japanese business circles.

Satellite Communications

In 1989 Tonga scored a coup by claiming six satellite orbital slots which it registered with the International Telecommunications Union over the objections of most large satellite communications companies. One condition was that the slots had actually to be used within 10 years, so a company called Tongasat was formed with Princess Pilolevu as president to run the operation on behalf of the government. At last report Tongasat had three satellites in orbit launched from Kazakhstan thanks to American telecommunications experts who have arranged the leasing of Tonga's valuable slots. Tongasat and the government split the income from this arrangement, which goes into millions of dollars. Thus Tonga is now the world's second largest commercial satellite power! In response the Telecom conglomerates have organized a boycott of the remaining Tongan slots in the hope they will be forfeited to them in 1999.

Sale of Passports

One of the most bizarre moneymaking schemes in recent years has involved the sale of Tongan passports to Hong Kong Chinese and others in need of an alternative nationality. In 1983 Tonga began issuing "Tongan Protected Persons" passports to all comers at US$10,000 a shot. As the bearers required a visa to enter Tonga, many countries, including Australia and New Zealand, refused to recognize them. Thus in 1984 legislation was passed allowing ordinary Tongan passports and naturalization certificates to be issued to anyone willing to pay US$20,000—among the 426 takers were Imelda Marcos and her children. This was questioned by commoner members of the Tongan parliament, who pointed out that the five-year residency requirement was being ignored, so in 1988 the previous legislation was repealed, but the sales strangely continued.

In 1989 Mr. 'Akilisi Pohiva, the leading people's representative in parliament, filed suit against the ministers of finance and police and the government, claiming that the sale of passports to foreigners was unlawful. It took Pohiva a year to formulate his case, then another year to get a court date, and in February 1991, just as the Supreme Court was about to act, the government called an emergency session of Parliament to alter the constitution to legalize things. When it became obvious that the government intended to use its large majority of appointed members to ram through the amendment, the three people's representatives from Tongatapu walked out. On 7 March 1991, 2,500 people marched through Nuku'alofa to the Royal Palace to present petitions protesting the constitutional changes, the largest popular demonstration of its kind in Tongan history.

A new US$50,000 type of Tongan "National Passport" is still available. This does not grant foreigners permanent residency, nor the right to vote, but does allow the holder to spend 12 months in Tonga for the purpose of obtaining onward visas. These "nationals" are not supposed to engage in business during their year in Tonga, but a recent surge in the number of Chinese-operated hotels and restaurants in Nuku'alofa indicates otherwise. The passport scheme has brought in an estimated US$25 million, which is deposited at the Bank of America in San Francisco. A full accounting of passport income has not been made public. Many countries, including Australia and New Zealand, do not recognize these mail-order passports and even genuine Tongans traveling on bona fide Tongan passports occasionally face unexpected immigration hassles abroad as a result of this scam.

THE PEOPLE

Most of all, Tonga is its culture and people. The Tongans are exceptionally warm, relaxed, impassive toward delays, etc. With the world's lowest death rate, it seems Tongans even pass away slowly. They have a lot of fun and tease each other and sympathetic visitors constantly. The very happy, contented lifestyle is summed up in expressions like *mo'ui fiemalie* (a contented life), *mo'ui nonga* (a peaceful life), *nofo fiefia* (living happily), and *nofo fakalata* (making others feel at home). It's also said that if a Tongan loses his identity, he will slowly become cold and die.

Tonga is typical of developing countries, with its large families and young population. Tongans live in small villages near their bush gardens, and except in the Europeanized areas, isolated houses along the roads are rare. With 147 people per square kilometer, Tonga is one of the most densely populated countries in the Pacific (twice as dense as the Cooks, three times as dense as Fiji). Yet despite a high birth rate, emigration has kept population figures stable since the 1970s. Thousands of Tongans have left, many for good, and some 24,000 now live in New Zealand, 10,500 in the U.S., and 4,500 in Australia.

In Tonga women have traditionally enjoyed a higher social status than in some other parts of Polynesia due to the *fahu* system, which gives Tongan women certain authority over male family members. The eldest sister is the family matriarch, exercising considerable control over younger brothers, nieces, and nephews. Public life in Tonga, however, is almost completely dominated by men due to sexist succession and land ownership laws, as well as cultural norms.

The missionaries increased the importance of the family unit. Each family member has a role, with the older persons commanding the most respect. Children may reside with an aunt or uncle just as easily as with their parents and are taught obedience from an early age, which is why they are so much better behaved than Samoan children. The most important occasions in Tongan life are first and twenty-first birthdays, marriages, and funerals.

Acculturation is proceeding fast in Nuku'alofa, where many families now have a VCR, and the 30 video rental outlets do roaring business. There are few controls on videos, and Tongans can see everything from horror to soft pornography on their screens. The videos have effectively done away with *faka'apa'apa*, or respect between brother and sister, an old taboo that would never have allowed them to sit in the same room and watch a sex scene. (This also explains some of the physical attention lone foreign women receive from Tongan men at discos.)

Tongans have a long traditional history, and many can name up to 39 generations by heart. There is little social mobility: a commoner can never become a noble, though a noble or a member of the royal family can be stripped of his title. Commoners have been appointed Cabinet ministers through education and ability, however, and may be elevated to the rank of *mata-*

pule (talking chief), a spokesperson for the king or a noble. Ordinary Tongans must use a special dialect quite different from everyday Tongan when speaking to a noble or member of the royal family. An equivalent English example for "eating heartily" might go as follows: commoners *gorge,* the nobles *feed,* and the king *dines.*

To a Tongan, great physical size is the measure of beauty—Tongan women begin increasing prodigiously in beauty from age 15 onward.

Traditional Dress

The *ta'ovala* is the distinctive Tongan traditional skirt. The custom may have originated when Tongan mariners used canoe sails to cloak their nakedness. Made of a finely woven pandanus-leaf mat, the *ta'ovala* is worn around the waist. The men secure it with a coconut-fiber cord, while the women wear a *kiekie* waistband. The sight of a group of Tongan women on the road, each with a huge pandanus mat tied around herself, is truly striking. Worn especially on formal occasions, these mats are often prized heirlooms. Tongans dress in black and wear huge *ta'ovalas* when mourning. The king and queen wear European dress to a European function but dress in their plaited *ta'ovala,* tied around the waist over the *vala* (skirt or kilt), and wear sandals or go barefoot to a Tongan ceremony or entertainment.

Religion

Tonga is the most difficult country in the South Pacific as far as Sunday blue laws go. The Tongan Constitution (drafted by Methodist missionary Shirley Baker) declares the Sabbath day forever sacred: it's unlawful to work, hold sporting events, or trade on Sunday. Contracts signed that day are void. Most tours are also canceled, though picnic trips do run to the small islands off Nuku'alofa. All shops and most restaurants are closed on Sunday. The Sabbath is so strong that even the Seventh-Day Adventists here observe Sunday as the Lord's Day (not Saturday). They claim this is permissible because of the "bend" in the international date line, but it would be intolerable to have two Sundays in Tonga!

Tongans are great churchgoers—a third of all Tongans and most of the noble class are members of the mainstream Free Wesleyan

Church. Three other branches of Methodism also have large followings in Tonga: the Free Church of Tonga (9,250 members), the Church of Tonga (6,250 members), and the Tokaikolo Christian Fellowship (2,600 members). In addition, there are 14,200 Mormons, 13,500 Roman Catholics, and 5,000 Seventh-Day Adventists. Smaller groups include the Anglicans, Assemblies of God, and Baha'is. In all, 16 official churches are active in the country, and missionaries from new groups are arriving all the time. Between 1966 and 1992 affiliation in the new religious groups increased from 9.7% to 29.5% of Tongans as all four Methodist churches declined.

Attend the service at Centenary Church (Free Wesleyan) in Nuku'alofa Sunday at 1000 to hear the magnificent church choir and perhaps catch a glimpse of the royal family. Gentlemen are expected to wear coats and ties (although tourists are usually admitted without). After church, the rest of the day is spent relaxing, strolling, and visiting friends—what Tongans like to do anyway, so it wasn't hard for the missionaries to convince them to set aside a whole day for it.

The Mormons

According to Manfred Ernst's *Winds of Change* (see the Resources chapter at the end of the book), Mormons accounted for 15.2% of the 1992 population of Tonga, the highest such ratio in the world. The Church of Latter-day Saints has become the largest private employer in the kingdom, spending more on construction than even the government, and the American church sends far more financial aid to its Tongan flock than the U.S. government provides to Tonga as a whole. Mormon missionary efforts in Tonga are aimed at making this the first country on earth with a Mormon majority.

Assembly line Mormon churches (with their inevitable basketball courts) are popping up in villages all over Tonga as the children of Israel convert in droves to be eligible for the free buildings, schools, sporting facilities, and children's lunches. Many Tongans become "school Mormons," joining as their children approach high school age and dropping out as they complete college in Hawaii. Unlike Cook Islanders and American Samoans, Tongans don't have the free right of entry to a larger country, so church help in gaining a toehold in Honolulu or Salt Lake City is highly valued.

Mormonism still has a lower profile in Nuku'alofa, however, as the king, a Wesleyan, is reputed to be uncomfortable with the new fast-faith religion. A building behind the International Dateline Hotel was a Mormon church until it was judged too close to the palace for comfort. The Mormon Temple, the largest building in Tonga, is beside Mormon-operated Liahona High School near Houma on the opposite side of the island. Yet the Church of Latter-day Saints is a bastion of conservatism and a strong supporter of the political status quo (which is rather ironic in view of American posturing on democracy and human rights in other parts of the world). This could change.

Cemeteries

Tongan cemeteries are unique. Usually set in a grove of frangipani trees, the graves are strange, sandy mounds marked with flags and banners, surrounded by inverted beer bottles, artificial flowers, seashells, and black volcanic stones.

CONDUCT AND CUSTOMS

The key to getting things done in Tonga is knowing how to find the right person to do the thing you want to have done. Tongans hate to say no to requests, and if you ask people to do things that aren't really their responsibility, they may give the impression of agreeing to do it, but in fact nothing will be done.

Tongans in official positions may seem sluggish and could keep you waiting while they finish chatting to friends over the phone. Keep smiling and be patient: they'll certainly notice that and will usually go out of their way to be helpful once they're done. Impatiently demanding service will have the opposite effect.

Both men and women appearing in public topless are punished with a T$20 fine. Of course, this doesn't apply to men at the beach. Like Victorian English, Tongans often go swimming fully dressed—most of them don't even have bathing suits. For a Tongan woman to appear in a halter top and miniskirt is almost unthinkable, and female travelers too will feel more accepted in skirts or long pants than in shorts. It's also considered bad form to kiss or even hold hands in public. (Despite all the strident public morality, in private Tongans are often sexually permissive, and it's commonplace for married men to have affairs.)

In Tonga the possession of dope is a serious offense, and the word soon gets around. Customs watches for yachts with drugs aboard. If you're busted, they'll toss you in a tiny flea-ridden cell and throw away the key. Make no mistake—they mean business.

Be careful too with your gear in Tonga, as there have been reports of thefts—don't tempt people by leaving valuables unattended. Even hotel rooms are unsafe. It's said that a Tongan will never buy anything if he thinks he can borrow or steal it. Thus, *everything* left unattended will be pilfered, especially if it's out where anyone could have taken it. It's safe to invite one or two Tongans to your home or room, but with three or more things will disappear. Items left on the beach while you're swimming may have vanished by the time you come out of the water. Armed robbery, on the other hand, is almost unheard of.

Dogs can be a nuisance in Tonga, chasing cyclists and barking through the night. They can be especially aggressive as you approach a private residence, but pretending to pick up a stone will usually be enough to scare them away. (Looking at it the other way, you'll see some of the most wretched, abused dogs in the world in Tonga and it's not surprising they bite.)

ON THE ROAD

HIGHLIGHTS

Tonga stands out for its living Polynesian culture, which can be traced from the Ha'amonga trilithon on northeastern Tongatapu through the ancient *langi* or royal tombs of Mu'a to the contemporary Royal Palace in downtown Nuku'alofa. Traditional arts and crafts are nurtured and preserved at the Tongan National Center just south of town. The country's most charming town, however, is Neiafu, which faces Vava'u's magnificent Port of Refuge Harbor. In fact, along with Levuka in Fiji and Gizo in the Solomons, Neiafu is one of the three most picturesque towns in the South Pacific.

Tonga's foremost natural feature is probably its coastal cliffs, especially the striking limestone formations at Keleti Beach Resort on Tongatapu, the east coast of 'Eua Island, and the north coast of Vava'u. Lovers of wildlife will not want to miss the flying foxes of Kolovai on Tongatapu. Humpback whales come to Ha'apai and Vava'u to mate and calve from July to October, and there are whalewatching cruises from Neiafu at this time.

SPORTS AND RECREATION

Although Tonga's best hiking areas are on 'Eua and its only golf course is on Tongatapu, it is Vava'u that has the most to offer water sports enthusiasts. Vava'u is a famous sailing locale with one of the South Pacific's largest yacht charter operations, and yacht cruises are available on boats such as the *Melinda* and the *Orion*. Vava'u is also perfect for ocean kayaking with lots of lovely protected waterways; a kayak touring company operates in this area. Deep-sea fishers too will find Tonga's top charter fishing boats based here. There's also undeveloped potential for windsurfing at Vava'u, but the mecca for regular reef-break surfers is Ha'atafu Beach on Tongatapu.

Scuba divers are well catered for by professional dive shops in both Nuku'alofa and Neiafu,

with many outstanding diving possibilities. Snorkelers have even more options, beginning with the island resorts off Nuku'alofa, all of which operate day trips by boat. The best snorkeling off Tongatapu itself is reputed to be at Ha'atafu Beach. At Ha'apai there's excellent snorkeling at the Captain Cook Beach Resort on Uoleva Island, and a scuba diving operation is due to open in late 1995. At Vava'u visitors can get in some excellent snorkeling on any of the day excursions from Neiafu by boat.

MUSIC AND DANCE

Music

Tongan church music is renowned and the singing of choir and congregation is often backed by a Salvation Army-style brass band. Traditionally a *lali* (slit drum) is beaten just before the service to call the faithful to prayer. The Tongans transformed the hymns taught by early missionaries, singing in minor instead of major. They also created hymns of their own, called *hiva usu,* which are closer to traditional chants than the imported hymns. The *hiva usu* are now most commonly sung at services of the Free Church of Tonga and the Church of Tonga, the most conservative of Tonga's four branches of Methodism.

Harmonious Polynesian singing can also be heard at kava-drinking sessions *(faikava),* when groups of men sing popular Tongan songs to entertain themselves. Tonga's traditional string bands (guitar, violin, banjo, bass, and ukulele) have been upstaged by modern electric pop bands, though the former may still be heard at hotels, private parties, or even *faikava.* Public festivities and parades are animated by college brass bands. The traditional *fangufangu* (bamboo nose flute) would probably have died out had not the 'Atenisi Institute in Nuku'alofa begun to teach its use. The *'utete* (jew's harp) is a child's toy formed from a coconut leaf held horizontally across the mouth by a palm leaf midrib, which is twanged. Other Tongan instruments include the *nafa* (skin drum), *kele'a* (conch shell),

(top) Ha'amonga Trilithon, Tongatapu, Tonga
(bottom) Banks Islands dancers, Port Vila, Vanuatu (David Stanley)

(top) a *mbure* at Nathula, Yasawa Island, Fiji (Karl Partridge); (bottom left) church window, Palmerston, Cook Island (David Stanley); (bottom right) a Samoan *fale* (Traugott Goll)

and the *tutua* (tapa-beating mallet). The *mimiha* (panpipes) seen by Captain Cook are no longer used.

Dance

Traditional Tongan dances are stories sung by the singers and acted out by the dancers. The words are represented by movements of the hands and feet, not the hips. The graceful movements of the female dancers contrast with those of the males, who dance with great vigor. A *punake* is a combination poet, composer, and choreographer who writes the songs then trains and leads the dancers.

The *lakalaka* is a standing dance that begins slowly but builds to a rhythmic finish. The male and female dancers stand on opposite sides of the stage, backed by a choir, and everyone sings a song especially composed for the occasion. A major *lakalaka* can involve hundreds of people and last half an hour. The *ma'ulu'ulu* is a sitting dance usually performed by groups of women accompanied by *nafa* on formal occasions. Standing girls perform the *ula*. Unlike these, the *kailao*, or war dance, has no accompanying song. The stamping feet, shouts of the leader, and insistent rhythm of the drums combine to make this dance popular among visitors. Very different is the dignified *tau'olunga*, in which a girl dances alone, knees held closely together, at weddings or village functions.

Your best chance to see real Tongan dancing is a fund-raising event (watch how the Tongans contribute, then give your share), on national holidays or during visits by VIPs. For a listing of compact discs of traditional Tongan music turn to Resources at the end of this volume.

PUBLIC HOLIDAYS AND FESTIVALS

Public holidays include New Year's Day, Good Friday, Easter Monday (March/April), ANZAC Day (25 April), Crown Prince's Birthday (4 May), Emancipation Day (4 June), King's Birthday (4 July), Constitution Day (4 November), King Tupou I Day (4 December), and Christmas Days (25 and 26 December).

The **Vava'u Festival** during the first week of May features all sorts of sporting, cultural, and social events to mark H.R.H. Crown Prince

Tupouto'a's birthday on 4 May. The **Ha'apai Festival** coincides with Emancipation Day in early June. Nuku'alofa's **Heilala Festival,** with brass band and dancing contests, parades, and sporting competitions, occupies the week coinciding with the king's birthday, the first week in July. The Miss Galaxy beauty contest for *fakaleitis* (men dressed as women) at the International Dateline Hotel is great fun and always sold-out. On the night of 4 July, Tongans standing along the beach light palm-leaf torches, illuminating the entire coast.

Agricultural shows are held throughout Tonga during September and October, with the king in attendance at each. The ferry *Olovaha* makes special trips at these times, so ask and book early. Red Cross Week in May is marked by several fund-raising activities, including a grand ball. During the National Music Association Festival in late June and early July you can hear string bands, brass bands, electric bands, and singers. A military parade in Nuku'alofa marks the closing of parliament in late October. The Tonga Visitors Bureau should know what's happening.

ARTS AND CRAFTS

Most of the traditional handicrafts are made by women: woven baskets, mats, and tapa cloth. The weaving is mostly of tan, brown, black, and white pandanus leaves. The large sturdy baskets have pandanus wrapped around coconut-leaf midribs. A big one-meter-high laundry basket makes an excellent container to fill with other smaller purchases for shipment home. (Remember, however, that the post office will not accept articles more than a meter long or weighing over 10 kilograms by airmail or 20 kilograms by surface mail, though this varies according to destination.) The soft, fine white mats from the Niuas, often decorated with colored wool, are outstanding but seldom sold.

Tonga's tapa *(ngatu)* cloth originates mostly on Tongatapu, where the paper mulberry tree *(Broussonetia papyrifera)* grows best. When the tree is about four meters high the bark is stripped and beaten into pieces up to 20 meters long, then hand-painted with natural brown and tan dyes. These big pieces make excellent

Miniature wooden statues of this kind were the only graven images made in Tonga. In 1830 the missionary John Williams witnessed the desecration of five of these at Ha'apai by hanging.

wall hangings or ceiling covers. In the villages, listen for the rhythmic pounding of tapa cloth mallets. The women are always happy to let you watch the process, and you may be able to buy something directly from them for about T$45 for a five-by-two-meter piece. Smaller pieces made for sale to tourists are often sloppily painted in a hurried fashion, and serving trays, fans, and purses made from tapa are often in poor taste.

Unfortunately too, Tongan woodcarving is now oriented toward producing imitation Hawaiian or Maori "tikis" for sale to tourists. Some shops will tell you the figures represent traditional Tongan gods, which is nonsense. Buy them if you wish, but know that they're not traditionally Tongan. The beautiful war clubs one sees in museums are rarely made today, perhaps out of fear they might be used! Tongan kava bowls are also vastly inferior to those made in Western Samoa and Fiji.

Many handicraft shops in Tonga sell items made from turtle shell, whale bone, ivory, black coral, seeds, and other materials that are prohibited entry into the U.S., New Zealand, and many other countries, so be careful. Triton shells, conch shells, giant helmet shells, giant clam shells, winged oyster pearl shells, trochus shells, green snail shells, and other sea shells may also be banned. It's one of the negative aspects of tourism that such a catalog of endangered species should be so widely sold.

ACCOMMODATIONS AND FOOD

All of the middle and upmarket hotels add five percent sales tax and a further two and a half percent room tax to their rates (not usually included in the quoted prices). The room tax covers the salaries of the staff at the Tonga Visitors Bureau. Inexpensive accommodations are easier to find in Tonga than anywhere else in the Pacific. Upmarket places, on the other hand, are less common, and even in the select few, the service is often lacking. This has advantages and disadvantages, but for the adventurous it's mostly advantageous.

There are no real campgrounds, though some of the beach resorts, such as the Good Samaritan Inn at Tongatapu and the Niu'akalo Beach

a stylized turtle on a piece of Tongan tapa

Hotel at Ha'apai, will allow you to pitch your own tent on their grounds. Elsewhere, always ask permission and your wish will usually be granted. Unlike in Fiji and Western Samoa (but as in the Cook Islands), you'll rarely be invited to spend the night in a local home. It's not forbidden to stay with the locals (as it is on Rarotonga), it's just that the Tongans prefer to keep a certain distance between themselves and *palangi* tourists. Fair enough.

Self-catering accommodations are much harder to find than in Cook Islands or Fiji and only a couple of the guesthouses in Nuku'alofa have cooking facilities. At Ha'apai most accommodations do allow cooking, but grudgingly, and they levy a T$1 to T$2 pp charge for gas and electricity. Several places at Vava'u allow you to cook. Fortunately restaurant meals are inexpensive and Tonga is an ice cream lover's paradise with huge, inexpensive cones sold almost everywhere (seldom any choice of flavors, however). Nuku'alofa and Neiafu have good public markets. Some stores sell horrendous fatty New Zealand mutton flaps called *sipi*, which unfortunately constitute the diet of many Tongans. Dogs and horses are also eaten occasionally.

More inviting are Tonga's gargantuan feasts. The most spectacular of these, marking such important events as King Tupou's coronation or Queen Elizabeth's visit, feature a whole roasted suckling pig for *each* of the thousands of guests. Literally tons of food are piled on long platters *(polas)* for these occasions, including taro, yams, cassava, breadfruit, sweet potato, fish, lobster, octopus, chicken, pork, corned beef, cooked taro leaves, and fruit. Cooking is done in an underground oven *(umu),* and coconut cream is added to everything. Less earth-shaking feasts are put on for visitors to Tongatapu and Vava'u. Try to attend at least one.

The tap water is chlorinated and it won't bother you if you have a strong stomach, otherwise boil it or drink something else. Several readers have reported that the water made them sick.

SERVICES AND INFORMATION

Visas and Officialdom

Visitors in possession of a passport and onward ticket do not require a visa for a stay of one month. Extensions of up to six months are possible (though the actual length of the extension is entirely up to the officers). A good indicator of Tonga's Third-World status is the small fee you pay for every form you have to fill out to satisfy civil servants.

Government authorization is required to do any sort of scientific research in Tonga, including archaeological excavations and sociological studies. The application fee of T$1000 is refundable if your project is approved. Clearly, officialdom wants to control just who is poking around. Recently one researcher on alcoholism had his application rejected. No drinking problems in Tonga, was the reply!

Ports of entry for cruising yachts include Niuatoputapu, Vava'u, and Nuku'alofa. Yachts arriving from the east should call at Vava'u before Nuku'alofa, as the prevailing winds make it much easier to sail from Vava'u to Nuku'alofa than vice versa and there are fewer hazardous reefs between Nuku'alofa and Fiji than between Vava'u and Fiji.

Money

The Tongan *pa'anga* (divided into 100 *seniti*) is worth about the same as the Australian dollar (around US$1 = T$1.25), although the actual value fluctuates slightly. From 1976 to 1991 the *pa'anga* was actually tied to the Australian dollar, but it's now based on a basket of the Australian, New Zealand, and U.S. dollars. There are notes of one, two, five, 10, 20, and 50 *pa'anga,* and coins of one, two, five, 10, 20, and 50 *seniti.* Try to keep a supply of small coins in your pocket if you don't want petty expenditures to be rounded up to your disadvantage. Tongan banknotes are difficult to exchange outside Tonga, so get rid of them before you leave.

The Bank of Tonga is 40% government-owned, with the Bank of Hawaii and the Westpac Bank of Australia each holding another 30%. Change money at the bank branches in Nuku'alofa, 'Ononua ('Eua), Pangai (Lifuka), and Neiafu (Vava'u); shopkeepers, market vendors, and the airport exchange counter give a much lower rate. Foreign banknotes are changed at a rate about four percent lower than traveler's checks. The banks are very crowded on Friday. There's no American Express representative in Tonga.

Tipping and bargaining are not customary here, although monetary gifts *(fakapale)* are often given to performers at cultural events (Tongans stick small bills onto the well-oiled arms and shoulders of the dancers during the performance). A five percent sales tax is added to all goods and services. Unlike most other Pacific countries, in Tonga the sales tax is often not included in the sticker price and is added on at the cash register.

In general, Tonga is an inexpensive country offering good value for your money.

Post and Telecommunications

The domestic telephone service within Tonga is run by the government-owned Tonga Telecommunications Commission (Box 46, Nuku'alofa; tel. 24-255, fax 24-800), while international service is operated by the British company Cable & Wireless (Private Mailbag 4, Nuku'alofa; tel. 23-499, fax 22-970).

International calls go through an operator. Three-minute calls cost T$5 to Australia or New Zealand, T$9.60 to Canada, the U.S., or Europe. Person-to-person calls are T$3 extra. Collect calls are possible to Australia, New Zealand, the U.S., and the U.K. (but not to Canada or Germany). Long-distance interisland telephone calls within Tonga cost T$1 for three minutes. Urgent telegrams within Tonga cost only 70 cents for the first seven words, plus 10 cents for each additional word. Internationally, faxing is a good inexpensive alternative to telephoning.

To place a long-distance or international call you should go to the respective telephone exchange listed in the travel sections of this chapter. Calls placed from hotel rooms are much more expensive. Directory assistance is 919, the interisland operator 910, the international operator 913.

In early 1995 it was announced that card phones would be introduced into Tonga, with telephone cards available in denominations of T$5, T$10, and T$20. Inquire about this at a post office as phone cards will make calling much cheaper and easier (no three-minute minimums). All direct-dial telephones in Tonga use 00 as the international access code.

Tonga's telephone code is 676.

Business Hours and Time

Normal business hours are weekdays 0800-1300/1400-1700, Saturday 0800-1200. Government working hours are weekdays 0830-1230 and 1330-1630. Banking hours are weekdays 0900-1530. Post offices are open weekdays 0830-1600. Everything is closed on Sunday.

Due to its position just west of the international date line, Tonga is the first country in the world to usher in each new day.

In fact, the date line seems to have so confused the local roosters that they crow constantly just to be safe. A tremendous bash is planned for New Year's Eve, 1999, when hundreds of world celebrities will usher in the new millennium here in an extravaganza to be televised around the world! Tonga shares its day with Fiji, New Zealand, and Australia, but is one day ahead of Samoa, Tahiti, and Hawaii. The time is the same as in Samoa, but one hour behind Hawaii and one ahead of Fiji and New Zealand.

Tonga's sacred Sunday adds to the fun of the date line confusion. Commercial flights (and most other transport) are banned in the kingdom that day. Don't get worried if you suddenly realize that it's Sunday on a flight to Tonga from Honolulu or Samoa—you'll land on Monday. Just keep repeating: "If it's Sunday for the Samoans, it's Monday for the monarch."

Electricity

The electric voltage is 240 volts, 50 cycles, with a three-pronged plug used, as in Australia and New Zealand.

Media

The *Tonga Chronicle* (Box 197, Nuku'alofa; tel. 23-302, fax 23-336) comes out every Thursday and you can usually pick up a copy at the Friendly Islands Bookshop in Nuku'alofa. This government-owned newspaper is compiled by employees of the prime minister's office.

Also look for the monthly newsletter *Kele'a* (Box 1567, Nuku'alofa), published by 'Akilisi Pohiva, leader of the democratic reform movement in parliament. The newsletter's attempts to expose corruption among the old guard have made it the object of libel suits involving awards of T$80,000 in damages. Three of the cases were heard while Pohiva was out of the country and unable to defend himself.

The worldwide subscription rate to the bimonthly national news magazine *Matangi Tonga* (Box 427, Nuku'alofa; tel. 23-101) is US$30 (airmail)—a practical way to keep in touch. The

same company publishes a free bimonthly tourist newspaper called *'Eva,* available from Royal Tongan Airlines or the Tonga Visitors Bureau.

Information Offices

The Tonga Visitors Bureau (Box 37, Nuku'alofa; tel. 21-733, fax 22-129) has information offices in Nuku'alofa, Lifuka, and Neiafu. Drop in or write for a supply of free brochures, especially the useful booklet *What's On in the Kingdom of Tonga.* These offices are good places to ask about events, but verify their information.

TRANSPORTATION

Getting There

Tonga's flag carrier, **Royal Tongan Airlines** (Private Mail Bag 9, Nuku'alofa; tel. 23-414, fax 24-056), has flights to Nuku'alofa from Sydney and Auckland twice a week, from Nandi three times a week. Development plans call for a weekly flight between Nandi and Vava'u by late 1995. In the U.S., call 800/486-6426 for information about Royal Tongan. Western Samoa's **Polynesian Airlines** (tel. 21-566) arrives from Apia, Auckland, and Sydney twice a week. The Fijian airline, **Air Pacific** (tel. 23-423), has service to Tonga from Nandi and Suva three times a week with connections from Brisbane. Around Christmas all flights are fully booked six months in advance with Tongans returning home.

Air Pacific's triangle fares on the route Suva-Western Samoa-Tonga-Nandi cost F$667 (valid one year) and are available in Fiji. Air Pacific's "Pacific Air Pass" allows 30 days travel between Fiji, Western Samoa, Tonga, and Vanuatu for US$449 (or US$549 with the Solomon Islands included), but this ticket must be purchased prior to arrival in the South Pacific. See "Getting Around" in the main Introduction for details.

Air New Zealand (tel. 21-646) has direct weekly flights from Honolulu and Apia with connections from Los Angeles and London. Their flights between Tonga and Auckland operate twice a week. This Coral Route connection is discussed under "Getting There" in the main Introduction.

Samoa Air (tel. 70-477) has services twice a week from Pago Pago to Vava'u (US$173 one-way, US$315 roundtrip), a useful backdoor route.

The Tonga
Chronicle
Where Time Begins

40 seniti

Volume XXXI No. 39   Nuku'alofa, TONGA   Thursday, September 29, 1994

Getting Around by Air

Royal Tongan Airlines (tel. 23-414), formerly Friendly Islands Airways, has Twin Otter flights from Tongatapu to 'Eua (T$16), Ha'apai (T$55), Vava'u (T$109), Niuatoputapu (T$218), and Niuafo'ou (T$245), but never on Sunday. The flights to 'Eua operate twice a day, to Ha'apai daily, to Vava'u three times a day, to the Niuas weekly or every other week. Book a northbound Friday or Saturday flight from Nuku'alofa to escape a depressing Sunday in the capital. Ask about special packages from Nuku'alofa to Vava'u including airfare, transfers, accommodations, breakfast, and some meals. The baggage allowance is only 10 kilos, but if your Royal Tongan domestic flights were booked from abroad as part of an international ticket the baggage allowance is 20 kilos. Overweight baggage is 45 cents a kilogram.

In "emergencies" Royal Tongan bumps passengers with confirmed reservations for VIPs. This doesn't happen often, but be forewarned and check in early (never less than 30 minutes prior to the flight). Always reconfirm your onward flights a few days in advance. "No shows" are liable for a penalty of 50% of the ticket price if they fail to use confirmed space, but Royal Tongan reserves the right to cancel any flight without compensation. Flights to Vava'u are heavily booked. In fact, the staff is friendly and cooperative, which makes the occasional hiccup easier to take.

Getting Around by Ship

The government-owned **Shipping Corporation of Polynesia** (Box 453, Nuku'alofa; tel. 21-699, fax 22-617), at Queen Salote Wharf, Nuku'alofa, offers safe, reliable boat service among the Tonga Islands. Their large car ferry, the MV *Olovaha,* departs Nuku'alofa every Tuesday at 1730, arriving at Pangai (T$28 deck) very early Wednesday morning and Vava'u (T$42 deck) on Wednesday afternoon. It leaves Vava'u again Thursday afternoon, calling at Pangai in the middle of the night and arriving back in Nuku'alofa Friday afternoon. In Ha'apai the ship calls at both Ha'afeva and Pangai. It's usually punctual.

Deck travel is sometimes very crowded but when the ship isn't too full you can stretch out on the plastic benches or the floor in a clean, protected room. No meals are included. Cabins cost four times the deck fare, as you must book an entire twin room (T$120 double to Ha'apai, T$170 double to Vava'u). There are only four such cabins, and they can be just as noisy as deck, though more comfortable.

The private **Uata Shipping Lines** (Box 100, Nuku'alofa; tel. 23-855), also known as the Walter Shipping Lines, has three red-and-white ships, the MV *Loto Ha'angana,* the MV *Fokololo 'oe Hau,* and the MV *Pulupaki.* The 32-meter *Loto Ha'angana,* an old Chinese ferry, is larger and faster than the *Olovaha,* but it does toss a bit more. The *Loto Ha'angana* leaves Nuku'alofa Monday at 1800, reaching Pangai late the same night and Vava'u Tuesday afternoon. It departs Vava'u for Ha'apai and Nuku'alofa Wednesday at 1600. No cabins are available. Take food, water, and anti-seasickness pills. Every month this boat goes to the Niuas, weather permitting. The *Loto Ha'angana* has lots of long padded benches on which you can stretch out and try to get some sleep if it's not too crowded (as is usually the case between Ha'apai and Vava'u). The loud music broadcast over the ship's public address system all night is a disadvantage. The smaller *Fokololo 'oe Hau* also services Vava'u and the Niuas. Uata Shipping runs a boat from Vava'u to Niuatoputapu (T$50) and Niuafo'ou (T$60) about once a month.

Several boats shuttle back and forth between Nuku'alofa and 'Eua (2.5 hours, T$6). The Shipping Corporation of Polynesia's *Ngaluta'ane* departs Faua Jetty Tuesday to Friday at 1300, returning in the morning. You pay onboard. The *Ngalu Ta'ane* also travels from Faua Jetty to 'Eua Tuesday to Friday at 1300, returning from 'Eua the same days between 0600 and 0700. The smaller, privately owned *Vaomapa* does the same trip daily except Sunday. The 24-meter MV *Pulupaki,* smallest of the Uata Shipping Lines ferries, also travels between Nuku'alofa and 'Eua. However you go, be prepared for an extremely rough four-hour eastbound trip and a smoother, faster westbound voyage.

The **"W" Islands Line** (Box 1166, Nuku'alofa; tel. 22-699, fax 24-099), behind the Fakafanua Center opposite Queen Salote Wharf, Nuku'alofa, has monthly sailings on the *Moana II* to Vava'u and occasional trips to Niue (T$95) and the Niuas. Bring your own food. Most of "W" Islands Line's business revolves around shipping cargo, but you'll probably be allowed on their Tonga-Niue run. The *Moana II* also sails to Norfolk Island and Auckland but they don't usually take passengers on those trips.

Note that all of the above information is only an indication of what might or should happen in ideal weather—the reality is often quite different. Make careful inquiries upon arrival and be prepared for a few delays. It's all part of the fun.

Airport

Fua'amotu International Airport (TBU) is 21 km southeast of Nuku'alofa. The new terminal building was constructed with Japanese aid money in 1990. A large bronze statue of H.R.H. King Tupou IV stands near the old terminal and it's worth asking your taxi driver to make a detour so you can see it. The airport is closed on Sunday.

The airport bus (T$6 pp) operates four times a day. If there are two or more of you, the T$12 taxi fare to town is just as good or better. Be sure to ask the fare before getting into the taxi and don't let the driver steer you to some hotel you never intended to stay at only because the managers pay him a commission that will later be added to your bill. Hope that your flight doesn't arrive in Tonga late at night as the taxis demand as much as T$30 then. Airport-bound, the International Dateline and Pacific Royale hotels have buses directly to the terminal costing T$6 pp, but they're only worth taking if you're alone. If you're on the lowest of budgets you could take the infrequent Fua'amotu bus right to the airport, or any Mu'a bus to the crossroads near Malapo, then walk or hitch the last six km.

The airport exchange counter gives a rate five percent lower than the banks in town. There's a duty-free shop in the departure lounge. The departure tax on international flights is T$15.

TONGATAPU

Tongatapu's 259 square km are just over a third of the kingdom's surface area, yet two-thirds of Tonga's population lives here. Of coral origin, Tongatapu is flat with a slight tilt—from 18.2-meter cliffs south of the airport to partly submerged islands and reefs to the north. Some 20,000 years ago Tongatapu was blanketed with volcanic ash from the explosion of Tofua Island, creating the rich soil that today supports intensive agriculture.

Nuku'alofa, the capital (population 30,000), is just north of the azure Fanga'uta Lagoon, now sterile because sewage from adjacent Vaiola Hospital eliminates the fish and other marinelife. It's a dusty, ramshackle little place, yet quite clean compared to Pago Pago. Tourism, industry, commerce, and government are all concentrated in the town, which retains its slow-paced South Seas atmosphere. Nuku'alofa means "Abode of Love," while Tongatapu is "Sacred Tonga." Famous for its tapa cloth, Tongatapu also contains some of the most compelling archaeological remains in the Pacific. And unlike Western Samoa, no "custom fees" are collected from visitors out to see the island's sights. Captain Cook was enthralled by Tongatapu, and you will be too.

SIGHTS

Nuku'alofa

Begin your visit at **Vuna Wharf,** the main port of entry to Tonga from 1906 until construction of Queen Salote Wharf in 1967. The **Treasury Building** (1928), opposite the wharf, was once Nuku'alofa's main post office. Nearby on Railway Road (named for a former line that once carried copra to the wharf) is the **House of Parliament,** a small wooden building prefabricated in New Zealand and reassembled here in 1894. The 30 members of parliament deliberate from May to October (no visitors). Walk through the park across the street from Parliament, passing the **Tongan war memorial,** and turn left on Taufa'ahau Road to the imposing **prime minister's office,** with its central tower.

Continue west to the Victorian **Royal Palace,** closed to the public but easily viewable from outside the grounds. This gingerbread palace was also prefabricated in New Zealand for reassembly here in 1867. The second-story veranda was added in 1882. The gables and scalloped eaves of this white frame building

TONGATAPU

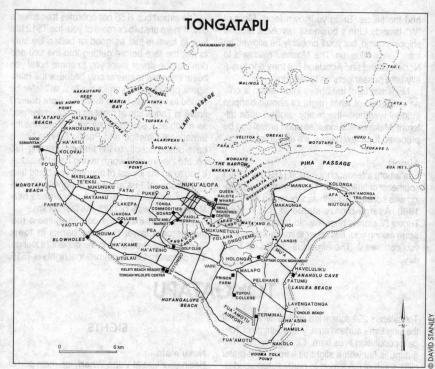

© DAVID STANLEY

are crowned by a red roof and surrounded by stately Norfolk pines. (The king and queen no longer live here but in the Fua'amotu Palace near the airport. The stately villa of the crown prince is at Pea, on the airport road, and across the street from it is the residence of another prince with a pair of white Bengali tigers guarding the gate.)

Many old colonial-style residences line Vuna Road west of the palace, including the **British High Commissioner's residence,** with a flag-pole surrounded by cannon from the privateer *Port-au-Prince,* sacked at Ha'apai in 1806. South of the residence is **Mount Zion,** site of an 18th-century Tongan fortress and, in 1830, the first missionary chapel. This hill is now crowned by several communications towers.

Centenary Church (1952), south of Mount Zion, is the principle house of worship of the Free Wesleyan Church, the largest of Tonga's three Methodist sects. Some 2,000 persons can be seated here, and most Sunday mornings the

king and queen are among them. The church's president lives in the impressive mansion (1871) on the west side of the church, a former residence of 19th century missionary and prime minister Rev. Shirley Baker.

East on the south side of Laifone Road are the **Royal Tombs,** where Tongan royalty has been buried since 1893. Across Laifone Road from the Royal Tombs is the main church of the Free Wesleyans, which was only completed in 1985. The striking **Basilica of St. Anthony of Padua** (1980), back on Taufa'ahau Road, is worth visiting for its soaring interior, and in the basement are a library and well-known restaurant. During an unprecedented four-day convention held at the basilica in November 1992, several hundred Tongans discussed ideas for constitutional reform in their country.

Cultural Center

Don't miss the **Tongan National Center** (Box 2598, Nuku'alofa; tel. 23-022), a complex of

Polynesian-style buildings built in 1988 beside the Fanga'uta Lagoon opposite Vaiola Hospital using Japanese aid money. Here you'll see handicraft demonstrations (tapa and canoe making, woodcarving, basket making, mat weaving), contemporary art, and historical displays. The Center's impressive Exhibition Hall contains historic photos of Tonga, a didactic display, a collection of war clubs and other carvings, and the shell of a Galapagos turtle left in Tonga by Captain Cook (the turtle was allowed to wander through the grounds of the Royal Palace until its death in 1968). The hall is open weekdays 0900-1600, admission T$2.

Weekdays at 1230 the Center prepares a barbecue lunch and traditional fashion show (T$12), and at 1400 the excellent two-hour guided cultural tour begins, featuring a kava ceremony, the telling of ancient legends and myths, and traditional Tongan dancing in the 450-seat amphitheater (T$8). The handicraft workshops will be operating at this time, and craft items may be purchased directly from the artisans. Some of the activities are curtailed or canceled when not enough visitors are on hand, so you might check that there really will be a performance in the amphitheater before signing up. Tuesday and Thursday are the usually the best days to come; otherwise just visit the museum and craft shop and come back for the evening performance another day.

Not to be missed is the dinner show put on every Tuesday and Thursday at 1900 (T$15). The package includes a visit to the exhibition hall, string band entertainment, kava drinking, an all-you-can-eat buffet dinner of authentic Tongan cuisine, and some very good traditional dancing (take small banknotes to give to the dancers). A small additional charge is collected for minibus hotel transfers. Advance reservations are required if you want to take lunch or dinner, but not for the afternoon tour. Reserve the evening shows before 1630 at either the Tonga Visitors Bureau or directly by phone. Admission for children is half price to all of the above events.

Western Tongatapu

Take the Hihifo bus or ride a bicycle to Kolovai to see the **Flying Fox Sanctuary**, where countless thousands of the animals *(Pteropus tonganus)* hang in casuarina trees for about a kilometer along the road. Flying foxes are actually bats (the only mammals that can fly) with foxlike heads and wingspans of up to a meter across. Nocturnal creatures, they cruise after dark in search of food and hang upside down during the day. Legend says the bats were a gift from a Samoan maiden to an ancient Tongan navigator. Considered sacred, they may only be hunted by the royal family.

Just beyond Kolovai is the turnoff for the **Good Samaritan Inn** (see "At the Beach"

the Royal Palace at Nuku'alofa

DAVID STANLEY

under "Accommodations," below). Farther west, behind the primary school at **Kanokupolu**, is the *langi* or stone-lined burial mound of the Tu'i Kanokupolu, an ancestor of the present royal family. The stones to built this tomb were quarried at nearby **Ha'atafu Beach,** and a few partially cut slabs are still anchored to the bedrock at the water's edge, just where the access road meets the beach. The marinelife at Ha'atafu is good because it's a designated "reef reserve" and there's a T$200 fine for fishing. This is a good place to come for a picnic or a swim on Sunday, but don't leave any rubbish or you'll also be liable for the fine. Some of the best reef-break surfing in Tonga is here, and there's excellent snorkeling, especially at high tide—see dozens of species of fish. Be aware of an east to west current. The adjacent Ha'atafu Beach Motel does not serve food or drink to nonguests, so you'll have to bring your own.

Hihifo buses from Ha'atafu head straight back to town (70 cents), but there's no bus from Fo'ui to Fahefa. If you want to go on to the blowholes, you'll find it a pleasant five-km walk (or hitch).

Southern Tongatapu

Surf forced through naturally formed air vents creates spectacular **blowholes** on the rocky, terraced southwest coast near Houma, 15 km from Nuku'alofa. From the end of the road, walk along the path to the right. Waves batter the coral cliffs and spout water up to 30 meters in the air through eroded tunnels. These impressive blowholes number in the hundreds—come at high tide on a windy day! Bus service from Nuku'alofa to Houma is fairly frequent and continues west to Fahefa.

Just east of Utulau a dirt road branches off the paved highway (and bus route) between

Houma and Nuku'alofa via Pea and runs along the south coast. Three km along this dirt road is **Keleti Beach Resort,** with more blowholes and several small but strikingly beautiful beaches and pools protected from the open sea by unusual coral terraces. Keleti is down an unmarked road to the right, distinguishable from other similar roads only by the electricity lines. As previously mentioned, there's no bus service east of the Utulau-Pea road, so you're better off coming by bicycle.

The **Tongan Wildlife Center** (tel. 23-561) is near the coast, a short distance east of Keleti on the south coast road. If you want to come by bus you'll have to walk about two and a half km south from the main highway at Veitongo. The Center is unique in Tonga for its small bird park and botanical garden. Examples of most native Tongan land birds are kept in aviaries brimming with vegetation—take the time to wait for them to appear. The small botanical garden displays all of the common Polynesian food plants, and at the entrance is an informative photo display on Tongan birds and reptiles. The Center is open Monday to Saturday 0900-1700, Sunday and holidays 0900-1800. The Center is run by a nonprofit organization working to save endangered species of Tongan birds, so your T$3 admission fee goes to a good cause.

Also on the south coast is **Hufangalupe** ("Pigeon's Doorway"), a huge natural coral bridge with a sandy cove flanked by towering cliffs, six km east of the bird park and four km from Vaini, the closest bus stop. Make your way down the inside of the fault from the back to see bridge and sea before you. As you return to the main south coast road, watch for a path on the left at the bottom of a slight dip, which leads down to a lovely white beach (beware of theft while you're swimming).

Eastern Tongatapu

Tupou College (tel. 32-240) at Toloa, three km off the airport road (no bus service), has a small museum of local relics, crafts, and artifacts. There are no fixed hours, and if you wish to visit it's best to call ahead to make an appointment. Tupou College is the oldest secondary school in the South Pacific, established by the Free Wesleyan Church in 1866.

Across the lagoon from Nuku'alofa, just outside Mu'a is a monument marking the spot where in 1777 Captain Cook landed from his ship the *Endeavor* and rested under a banyan tree (which has since disappeared). He then continued into Lapaha, the capital of Tonga at the time, to visit Pau, the Tu'i Tonga. Retrace Cook's footsteps into this richest archaeological area in western Polynesia.

For over 600 years beginning around A.D. 1200, **Lapaha** (Mu'a) was the seat of the Tu'i Tonga dynasty. Nothing remains of the royal residence today, but some 28 *langi* (burial

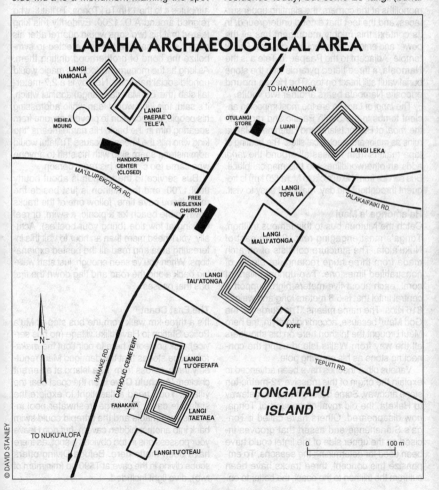

LAPAHA ARCHAEOLOGICAL AREA

LANGI NAMOALA

HEHEA MOUND

LANGI PAEPAE'O TELE'A

OTULANGI STORE

TO HA'AMONGA

LUANI

LANGI LEKA

HANDICRAFT CENTER (CLOSED)

MA'ULUPEKOTOFA RD.

FREE WESLEYAN CHURCH

LANGI TOFA UA

TALAKAIFAIKI RD.

LANGI MALU'ATONGA

LANGI TAU'ATONGA

KOFE

TEPUITI RD.

HAHAKE RD.

CATHOLIC CEMETERY

LANGI TU'OFEFAFA

FANAKAVA

LANGI TAETAEA

TONGATAPU ISLAND

TO NUKU'ALOFA

LANGI TU'OTEAU

0   100 m

© DAVID STANLEY

mounds of ancient royalty) have been located in or near Mu'a. Due to local objections, none has yet been excavated. Several of these great rectangular platforms with recessed tiers of coraline limestone are clearly visible from the main road, including the *langi* of the last Tu'i Tonga (1865), a Catholic, which has a cross on top.

The finest of the terraced tombs, rather hidden down a side road, is the **Paepae 'o Tele'a,** built during the early 17th century for the 28th Tu'i Tonga. Notice in particular the gigantic L-shaped monoliths at the corners, the slanting upper surfaces, and the feet that extend underground. In its context, this mighty monument has all the power and emotional impact of a classical Greek temple. Adjacent to the Paepae 'o Tele'a is the **Namoala,** a three-tiered pyramid with the stone burial vault still intact on top. The **Hehea mound** opposite Namoala bears another two vaults.

The *langi* of Lapaha are the most imposing ancient tombs in the South Pacific and rank with the *moai* of Easter Island and Huahine's Maeva ruins as major archaeological sites. The beating of tapa mallets from houses all around the *langi* adds an otherworldliness to this magical place. Bus service from Nuku'alofa to Mu'a (20 km) is frequent throughout the day, making it easy to visit.

Ha'amonga 'a Maui

Catch the Niutoua bus to this famous trilithon, Tonga's most engaging relic, 32 km east of Nuku'alofa. The structure consists of an arch made from three huge rectangular blocks of nonstratified limestone. Two upright pillars of coral, each about five meters high, support a central lintel that is 5.8 meters long and weighs 816 kilos. The name means "The Burden of the God Maui" because, according to myth, the hero Maui brought the trilithon here on his shoulders all the way from Wallis Island using the connecting stone as his carrying pole.

Various other theories have been advanced to explain the origin of this massive 12-metric-ton stone archway. Some believe it was the gateway to Heketa, the old royal compound of Tonga, now disappeared. Others have called it Tonga's Stonehenge and assert that grooves incised on the upper side of the lintel could have been used for determining the seasons. To emphasize this concept, three tracks have been cut from the trilithon to the coast, the better to observe sunrise on the equinox, as well as the summer and winter solstices. This would have been useful to determine the planting and harvesting periods for yams or the sailing seasons. Most scholars believe, however, that the grooves were cut long after the trilithon was built and discount their utility as an astronomical calendar.

Since few archaeological excavations of ancient monuments have been conducted in Tonga, it's not known for sure when or why the Ha'amonga 'a Maui was built. Local tradition attributes it to the 11th Tu'i Tonga, Tu'itatui, who reigned around A.D. 1200. Evidently this king feared that his two sons would quarrel after his death, so he had the trilithon erected to symbolize the bond of brotherhood uniting them. As long as the monument stood, its magic would uphold social harmony. Nearby is a 2.7-meter-tall slab (the 'Esi Makafakinanga) against which, it's said, this king would lean while addressing his people, a precaution to prevent anyone from spearing him in the back. His name means "the king who hits the knees" because Tu'itatui would administer a sharp slap with his staff to anyone who came too close to his regal person.

Bus service to the trilithon is about hourly until 1700, and the trilithon is just beside the road. If you have time, follow one of the tracks down to the beach for a picnic, a swim, or reef walking at low tide (bring your booties). Actually, you'll need more than an hour to visit this interesting area and read all the posted explanations. When you've seen enough, just start walking back along the road and flag down the first bus that passes.

The East Coast

It's a three-km walk from the bus stop at Mu'a Police Station to Haveluliku village (no bus service). Ask someone here to point out the *makatolo,* huge stones that the demigod Maui reputedly threw across from 'Eua Island at an errant chicken. **'Anahulu Cave** is on the coast near the village. You'll need a flashlight to explore the stalactite cave. The large freshwater pool inside is swimmable and the intrepid could swim back into another hidden cavern, but don't leave your possessions in too obvious a spot, as there have been thefts here. Beluga Diving offers scuba diving in the cave at T$90 pp (minimum of two), dive light included.

At low tide only, you can walk south from the cave to **Laulea Beach**. The beach continues unbroken for several km to **'Oholei Beach** where Tongan feasts are put on for cruise ship passengers. There's a fine view across to 'Eua Island. Sporadic bus service runs from Lavengatonga village near 'Oholei back to town.

Sports and Recreation

The Tonga Golf Club (closed Sunday), opposite the indoor stadium at Alele near Veitongo on the road to the airport, charges green fees of T$15. Inquire about club hire at the International Dateline Hotel.

Since 1983 Bob and Sioa Holcomb of **Coralhead Diving Ltd.** (Box 211, Nuku'alofa; tel. 22-176) have offered scuba diving using the dive boats *African Queen* and *White Knuckles* from their base opposite Faua Jetty. A two-tank boat dive will cost T$65 pp for one to three divers, T$50 pp for four to six, T$40 pp for seven or more. Lunch at Pangaimotu Island is T$6 extra. They depart Monday to Saturday at 1000, and snorkelers are welcome to go along at T$15 pp, plus T$5 for mask, snorkel, and fins. Coralhead also does one-week PADI certification courses (T$400 pp), an excellent opportunity to learn diving. They will rent and repair equipment and fill tanks, and they specialize in underwater photography and night dives. A wetsuit is recommended during the cooler months, April through August. Drop into their office on the backstreet behind the Waterfront Grill near Faua Jetty for information. Bob is a reliable guy who will give you a straight answer to any question you put to him.

The new kid on the block is **Beluga Diving** (Box 2660, Nuku'alofa; tel./fax 23-576) nearby beside the Moana Hotel (open Monday to Wednesday 0900-1500, Thursday to Saturday 0900-1700) They charge T$75 for a one-tank dive, T$88 for a two-tank dive, T$20 pp for a snorkeling trip (minimum of four people), and T$400 for a PADI open-water scuba certification course. Beluga caters almost exclusively to the tourist market, while much of Coralhead's trade comes from government and business contracts.

One of the favorite local dive sites is **Hakaumama'o Reef**, 14 km north of Nuku'alofa, a deep wall populated by large numbers of brilliant parrot fish. **Malinoa Island** to the southeast features a great variety of marinelife on the surrounding reef plus a lighthouse and some old graves on the island itself. Both of the above are marine reserves, and taking fish, clams, or coral is prohibited (T$200 fine). Black coral can be seen at **Kings Reef** just off Nuku'alofa. Visibility ranges from 15 meters within the Tongatapu Lagoon to 50 meters on the barrier reefs.

Catch a game of rugby (April to June) at the Teufaiva Stadium on Friday or Saturday at 1500. During the soccer season (May to July) you can watch them play at the Pangai Soccer Field on

Island athletes play with a passion. Here Tonga meets Samoa at the annual Three-Nations Tournament in Suva, Fiji.

TONGA CHRONICLE

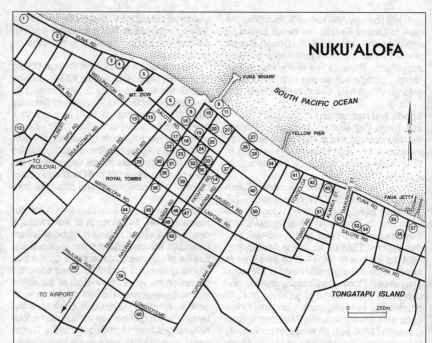

NUKU'ALOFA

SOUTH PACIFIC OCEAN

TONGATAPU ISLAND

0   250m

1. Captain Cook Vacation Apartments
2. Sunrise Taloa Restaurant
3. Breeze Inn
4. Seaview Restaurant
5. British High Commissioner's Residence
6. Royal Palace
7. Pangai Soccer Field
8. Fishermen's Wharf Grill
9. Bank of Tonga
10. Treasury Building
11. Long Distance Bus Station
12. 'Atenisi Institute
13. Centenary Church
14. Angeles Guest House
15. Vilai Army Barracks
16. Post Office
17. Air Pacific
18. Langafonua Handicraft Center
19. Central Police Station
20. Parliament House
21. Ministry Block
22. German Consulate
23. Fakalato Chinese Restaurant/Uata Shipping
24. ANZ Bank
25. Talamahu Market
26. Tonga Visitors Bureau
27. Local Bus Station
28. Fasi-Moe-Afi Guest House
29. Free Wesleyan Church of Tonga
30. Pacific Royale Hotel
31. John's Place Takeaway
32. Loni's Cinema/Teta Tours
33. Royal Tongan Airlines
34. International Dateline Hotel
35. Hotel Nuku'alofa
36. German Clinic
37. Tong Hua Restaurant
38. Catholic Basilica
39. Telecom Telephone Exchange
40. Australian High Commission
41. Beach House
42. Kimiko's Guest House and Restaurant
43. Yacht Club
44. Queen Salote Memorial Hall
45. Toni's Guest House
46. Lotolua Motel
47. Phoenix Hotel
48. Church of Tonga
49. Shels Hotel
50. Tonga Club
51. Joe's Tropicana Top Club
52. Cable & Wireless Office
53. Fred's Restaurant
54. Kinikinilau Shopping Center
55. Moana Hotel/Beluga Diving
56. Coralhead Diving
57. Davina's Restaurant
58. Teufaiva Stadium
59. K's Guest House
60. Sela's Guest House

the waterfront next to the Bank of Tonga Saturday at 1500. Joggers meet in front of the Bank of Tonga every Monday at 1700 for a recreational run. It's a good way to meet local expats.

ACCOMMODATIONS

Budget Accommodations

The accommodations listings below are arranged beginning with those closest to Queen Salote Wharf and Faua Jetty, then south through town. The only budget places with satisfactory communal cooking facilities are Breeze Inn, Lotolua Motel, Toni's Guest House, K's Guest House, and Heilala Guest House. Add five percent sales tax and two and a half percent room tax to all accommodation rates quoted below.

Sika and Kama Guest House (Box 1568, Nuku'alofa; tel. 22-651, fax 24-043), next to the Fakafanua Center opposite Queen Salote Wharf, has four clean rooms with private bath in a three-story building at T$50 single or double. There's a restaurant/bar downstairs.

The **Moana Hotel** (Box 169, Nuku'alofa; tel. 21-440), opposite Faua Jetty, has three bungalows with private facilities at T$14/28 single/double, but it can be noisy due to the adjacent bar, which has a pool table.

Kimiko's Guest House (Box 1323, Nuku'alofa; tel. 22-170) on Vuna Road has nine bare rooms with shared bath at T$10 pp (discounts for long stays). Empty beds in the double rooms are filled up as new guests arrive—singles must share or pay for both beds. There are no cooking facilities. When you first arrive the Chinese manager may tell you that you can use the kitchen in the adjacent restaurant, but don't believe it.

The **Beach House** (Box 33, Nuku'alofa; tel. 21-060) nearby on Vuna Road is one of the last of the old South Seas guesthouses that are fast disappearing in the wake of self-catering flats and motels. Somerset Maugham would have stayed here—the veranda has such an air about it (although the place could use a coat of paint). Bed and breakfast is T$20/35/45 single/double/triple (shared bath). Though the Beach House doesn't advertise, their eight rooms are generally full of young American and Japanese volunteers, so reserve in advance. The bench on the waterfront opposite the Beach House is a good place to make contacts. Rumor has it that the Beach House may soon be demolished to make way for a new Taiwanese Embassy.

The five-room **Fasi-Moe-Afi Guest House** (Box 1392, Nuku'alofa; tel. 22-289, fax 23-313), next to the visitors bureau on Vuna Road, is T$16/26 single/double, including a good breakfast. The lighting in the rooms could be better—ask for one on the outside. The adjacent cafe/pizzeria is great for cappuccino and a sandwich on the terrace, as you watch the world go by.

Kava session at
Toni's Guest House,
Nuku'alofa

M.E. DE VOS

The **Breeze Inn** (Box 2739, Nuku'alofa; tel. 23-947), next to the Seaview Restaurant west of the palace on Vuna Road, has seven spacious rooms with private bath (hot water) at T$43 single or double. Communal cooking facilities are available. This place is spotlessly clean, so make it your choice if you're the fussy type.

Two-story **Angeles Guest House** (Box 1617, Nuku'alofa; tel. 23-930, fax 22-149), on Wellington Road in the center of town, has eight clean rooms with shared bath at T$20/30/45 single/double/triple. The Chinese managers provide guests with a hot plate for warming up food.

The **Phoenix Hotel** (Box 2410, Nuku'alofa; tel. 23-270, fax 21-834) on Fatafehi Road has rooms upstairs in the new building at T$25 single or double, or T$10/15 single/double in the old building at back. Noise from the adjacent night club rocks the whole complex nightly except Sunday, and this place is only of interest to lowlife swingers. The adjacent Chinese restaurant (open Sunday), on the other hand, is good for lunch.

Shels Hotel (Box 1167, Nuku'alofa; tel. 23-037), on Fatafehi Road a block south of the Phoenix, offers 34 fan-cooled rooms with bath at T$35/45/55 single/double/triple. Arrayed around the interior courtyard of this new two-story building, the rooms are comfortable and might be worth considering by business travelers.

The **Lotolua Motel** (Box 1336, Nuku'alofa; no phone) on Unga Road has three small self-catering units at T$20 single or double, with weekly and monthly rates available. Though perhaps a little run-down, it's still a good budget choice, but at last report the owner was thinking of selling out and moving to New Zealand.

Toni's Guest House (Toni, Kesi, and Vili, Box 3084, Nuku'alofa; tel. 21-049), on Mateialona Road around the corner from the Catholic basilica, has six clean rooms at T$10 pp. There's a pleasant lounge where guests swap travelers tales around the kava bowl every evening, but Toni's biggest advantage is the cooking facilities, which are probably the best you'll find in the low-budget range. This and the nice homey atmosphere mean it's usually full, but the proprietors were thinking of opening an annex out in Tofoa with individual *fales*. They do full-day island tours in a pickup truck at T$50 for up to five people—good value. Toni's rents bicycles

(T$5-10 a day) and snorkeling gear (T$3 daily), but take care before accepting the taxi services offered by the staff. For example, don't agree a few days beforehand to use their taxi to go to the airport. Your plans may change, and someone may still try to force you to pay for a ride you no longer want or need. This could apply at other Nuku'alofa guesthouses as well. On the other hand, Toni only charges T$10 to drive five people to the airport.

K's Guest House (Box 1062, Nuku'alofa; tel. 21-185), also known as Kuluni's, farther south on Fatafehi Road, has two rooms in a separate house with shared bath and cooking facilities at T$8/15 single/double. Not many travelers seem to stay here for some reason.

Though it's a bit out of the way, **Sela's Guest House** (Box 24, Nuku'alofa; tel. 21-430, fax 22-755), south of K's, has been a favorite of overseas volunteers working in Tonga since the mid-1970s. There are 18 clean rooms with shared facilities at T$15/20 single/double, or T$8 in the eight-bed dormitory. A room with private bath and hot shower will run T$25/30 single/double. Cooking facilities for guests are not provided, but you can get a full breakfast for T$4 and a large dinner for T$10. Sela serves the best home-cooked meals you'll receive at any guesthouse in Nuku'alofa (which perhaps accounts for the many repeat visitors). If noise bothers you, however, be sure to get a room away from the VCR and dining room, otherwise they'll keep you awake half the night. On the positive side, you can sit and watch videos or CNN to your heart's content. It's a good family-style place to relax and meet people, bicycles are for hire, and it's seldom full.

Frangipani Guest House (Box 1416, Nuku'alofa; tel. 22-026), on Alaivahamamgo Road southeast of town, has one single room at the back of the house for T$25 and a lovely double facing the Fanga'uta Lagoon at T$45. Both have private bath but unfortunately cooking facilities are not available. The family that runs it is very friendly, but watch their dogs.

Waltraud Quick's quiet, two-story **Heilala Guest House** (Box 1698, Nuku'alofa; tel./fax 23-586), at Tofoa three km south of town (off the road to the airport), has four fan-cooled rooms at T$20/25 single/double and four-bed dorm at T$12 pp. Bathrooms are shared (hot water) and communal cooking facilities are provided. Bicycles are for rent. Waltraud (or Maria as the Tongans call her) arranges sightseeing tours with German-speaking guides at T$20 pp and most of her guests are German. If you call ahead and provide your flight number, she'll meet you at the airport.

Medium-Priced Accommodations
The 31-room **Friendly Islander Hotel** (Box 142, Nuku'alofa; tel. 23-810, fax 24-199), on Vuna Road 500 meters beyond the Shell oil storage tanks three km east of town, is T$50/60 single/double for one of the 11 fan-cooled, one-bedroom units with cooking facilities and balcony in a two-story main building. The 14 bungalows without cooking are T$65/75 single/double. There are also six large a/c bungalows at T$75 for up to four persons (no cooking), T$85 for up to five persons (with cooking). A restaurant and the 'Ofa Atu Night Club are also on the premises. The owner, Papiloa Foliaki, is a former member of parliament and an interesting person to meet. Unfortunately, she seems to spend most of her time on matters other than running her hotel, and the staff do whatever they like. The bathrooms are grubby, the swimming pool dirty, and the service variable. It's not bad value for the money, but it could be a lot better.

Captain Cook Vacation Apartments (Box 2329, Nuku'alofa; tel. 23-615, fax 24-138), facing the lagoon a kilometer west of the Royal Palace, offers four two-bedroom apartments accommodating up to four persons at T$70. One apartment has been split in half and has one single at T$45 and one double at T$55. Each apartment has a kitchen, living room, and private bath, but the housekeeping could be better.

The German-owned **Hotel Nuku'alofa** (Box 32, Nuku'alofa; tel. 24-244, fax 23-154), opposite the Tungi Arcade on Taufa'ahua Road, has 14 a/c rooms with private bath at T$60/75/90 single/double/triple. There's a restaurant and bar.

The **Kahana Lagoon Resort** (Box 3097, Nuku'alofa; tel./fax 21-144) is on the Fanga'uta Lagoon about five km southeast of town. The 12 spacious, attractively decorated *fale* units with private bath vary in price from T$65/80 single/double to T$80/100 or T$100/120, depending on size and location. There's a swimming pool (but no beach), and canoes and kayaks are available for use on the lagoon. Cooking facilities are not provided but the resort has a large restaurant/bar. The whole resort is cooled by gentle breezes across the lagoon. The Italian management that took over in 1994 has worked hard to upgrade the place.

Upmarket Hotels
The three-story, government-owned **International Dateline Hotel** (Box 39, Nuku'alofa; tel. 23-411, fax 23-410) on Vuna Road was originally built in 1967 to accommodate guests at the coronation of King Taufa'ahau Tupou IV. The 76 a/c rooms with private bath and fridge begin at T$83/97/108 single/double/triple in the old wing along Vuna Road. The adjacent new wing on Tupoulahi Road is T$109/120/130. Some of the rooms are a little the worse for wear but the Dateline has a pleasant resort atmosphere and the location is excellent. Their reasonably priced restaurant is one of the few open to the public on Sunday, and Polynesian dance shows are staged here Wednesday and Saturday nights at 2030. If you pay T$18 for the buffet (Wednesday) or the set three-course menu (Saturday), there's no cover charge. Otherwise T$5 is collected at the door. Despite the flip-flop-shod waiters, persons dressed in shorts, T-shirts, or sandals are not admitted to the dining room. A cold beer by the Dateline's pool is the perfect way to top off an afternoon, and nonguests are allowed to swim upon payment of a T$2 fee. Excursions to the islands just off Nuku'alofa can be booked at the hotel's tours and information desk, and transportation to the wharf is included.

The **Pacific Royale Hotel** (Box 74, Nuku'alofa; tel. 23-344, fax 23-833) on Taufa'ahau Road is owned by the Ramanlal brothers, sons of a Fiji Indian father and Tongan mother and the real movers and shakers in Tonga's private-sector tourism industry. The 15 economy rooms are T$65/75/85 single/double/triple, the 45 superior rooms T$89/101/111 (tax extra). All 60 rooms have private bath, fridge, and noisy air-conditioners, but they're dimly lit and rather overpriced. Back from the flashy new reception area, just past the restaurant, is a tiny garden and swimming pool. Although the service is good here, the Dateline is a more memorable place to stay.

At the Beach

If you came to Tonga for the sand, tan, and salt, you'll find it at the **Good Samaritan Inn** (Box 306, Nuku'alofa; tel. 41-022, fax 24-102) on Kolovai Beach, 18 km west of Nuku'alofa. The nine older bungalows with shared bath are T$20 single or double, while three newer bungalows with private bath are T$30 single or double, T$40 triple, and one deluxe two-bedroom bungalow with private bath and cooking facilities is T$50 single or double. Weekly rates are available. You can pitch your tent on the grounds for T$6 per tent. There's no hot water and no cooking facilities are provided, but the Inn has a very pleasant if expensive restaurant/bar that overlooks the so-so beach. Friday night there's a buffet dinner accompanied by Polynesian dancing (T$18 pp). The Inn has been around a long time and is getting a little tired, but it's still a good choice (although women traveling on their own should ensure that their room is secure at night). Take the Hihifo bus to Kolovai, then walk one and a half km to the Inn. A taxi from Nuku'alofa will cost T$10.

The **Ha'atafu Beach Motel** (Box 490, Nuku'alofa; tel. 41-088, fax 22-970), near the end of the road, three km north of Kolovai, is a surfers' hideaway run by Australian surfer Steve Burling and his Tongan wife Sesika. The six thatched *fales* with shared facilities are T$75/110 single/double including breakfast, dinner, and nonmotorized sporting equipment, or T$50 pp if you're willing to share a bungalow with others. These prices only apply if you book direct; through a travel agent it's about 20% more. Call ahead if you don't have a booking, as they only take 15 guests at a time and are often full. There's a 10% discount if you stay a month (many do). Dining is by candlelight, and the motel's kerosene lighting adds to the charm. Ha'atafu experiences water shortages, but it's on a better beach than the Good Samaritan with great snorkeling. Steve organizes boat trips for snorkeling, fishing, or surfing on outlying reefs when enough people are interested. (The peak **surfing season** here is June, July, and August with five great lefthanders within a 10-minute walk of the motel, as southern swells generated around New Zealand crash into the Ha'atafu coast. From January to March you have a choice of four righthanders and one left nearby, but at this time it's usually better to take a boat around to the reefs on the northwest side of Tongatapu, which catch waves rolling down from Hawaii.) The Ha'atafu Beach Motel is just a five-minute walk from the Ha'atafu bus stop. Don't bother dropping in if you don't intend to stay, however, as meals and drinks are not served to nonguests.

The secluded **Keleti Beach Resort** (Box 3116, Nuku'alofa; tel. 21-179, fax 21-735), on the south coast 10 km from Nuku'alofa, has four individual *fales* with private bath and cold showers at T$35/40/50 single/double/triple. Four duplex *fales* with shared facilities are T$25 single or double. Families can rent an entire duplex unit for T$50 and comfortably accommodate two adults and two children. Weekly rates with full board are available. No cooking facilities are provided, but moderately priced Tongan cuisine is served Western style in a restaurant overlooking the sea. Traditional dancing takes place at the Tongan feast Friday night (T$15 pp). Tuesday is barbecue night and Sunday dinner is a family affair. The coast here is strikingly beautiful with several small beaches, blowholes, and coral terraces—in fact, this is Keleti's main attraction. One can snorkel in the large tidal pools at the foot of the resort among the brightly colored tropical fish. The nearest public transport is three km away at Veitongo, though almost everyone will stop to offer you a lift up to the main highway. A taxi from Keleti to town is about T$6, to the airport T$8.

All three beach resorts are *palagi* beaches, which means there's no hassle about swimming on Sunday. They fill up on Saturday night, so check to see if any rooms are available before heading out. If you have wheels and only want to spend Sunday at the beach, be sure to call ahead for lunch reservations at the Good Samaritan or Keleti, or buy picnic provisions on Saturday for a picnic at Ha'atafu.

Island Living

Several of the small islands off Nuku'alofa are being developed for tourism. **Pangaimotu Island Resort** (Box 740, Nuku'alofa; tel./fax 23-759), the closest, is owned by the royal family (the name means "Royal Island"), but it's managed by the Embersons, an old South Seas European family. The four simple *fales* are T$55 single or double, transfers and some sporting equipment included. Camping is not allowed. Electricity is lacking and the tap water saline, but there is a seafood restaurant (compulsory T$25 pp meal plan). The reef around the island is good, and there's even a half-sunken ship, the *Marner*, sticking up out of the water for snorkelers to explore. If you're a yachtie you'll want to know that Pangaimotu has an excellent anchorage (all the other offshore islands are surrounded by treacherous reefs). It's a day-trip island and somewhat of a local hangout—on Sunday it can become very crowded.

The American-operated **Sun Island Resort** (Box 44, Nuku'alofa; tel. 23-335), on Makaha'a Island just beyond Pangaimotu, is something of a shoestring operation. The 10- to 20-bed dormitories are T$20 pp, whereas the two bungalows are T$50 single or double. At last report, overnight campers were welcome. There's a restaurant/bar and a full range of water sports is available. The nearby reef features huge coral formations alive with baby fish but the beach isn't as good as at Pangaimotu. Their boat leaves Faua Jetty weekdays at 1000, weekends 0900 and 1100 (T$10 roundtrip).

Fafa Island Resort (Box 1444, Nuku'alofa; tel. 22-800, fax 23-592), quite a distance farther out than Pangaimotu, is very professionally managed by German expats Bernt and Rainer. Their eight "village" *fales* run T$60/70/85 single/double/triple, while one of the four superior beach *fales* will be T$130 single or double, T$170 triple. It's rustic but adequate, although meals and drinks in the pleasant thatched restaurant/bar are expensive (no cooking facilities for guests). The full meal plan is T$55 pp. A full range of nonmotorized sporting activities is offered in the sapphire blue lagoon surrounding this delightful palm-covered, seven-hectare island. The initial 30-minute boat ride is T$15 roundtrip, but once you're staying they'll ferry you into town and back when you want at no extra cost.

The **Royal Sunset Island Resort** (Box 960, Nuku'alofa; tel. 24-923, tel./fax 21-254), on Atata Island 11 km northwest of town, is the most remote of the small island hotels off Tongatapu. It's a purely New Zealand-oriented operation run by New Zealanders for packaged tourists from New Zealand. The 26 units with private bath, fridge, kitchenette, and overhead fan begin at T$99/108/144/168 single/double/triple/quad. The food served in the restaurant is bland New Zealand-style fare and Tongan dishes are the exception (bring groceries). Drinks at the bar are very expensive, so also take along a couple of bottles of duty-free booze if somebody booked you into this place. There's a swimming pool, and free activities for guests include tennis, Hobie Cat sailing, paddleboarding, windsurfing, rowboating, and snorkeling. Scuba diving and equipment rental is available at additional charge, and there's good shore diving from the resort. The resort is right on a broad white-sand beach, and the snorkeling along Egeria Channel is great. Deep-sea fishing can be arranged at T$700 a day plus tax. The resort has a three-cabin yacht, the *Impetuous,* available for overnight charters. Return transfers to the island are T$22 from Nuku'alofa, T$36 from the airport.

Long Stays

To organize a long stay on Tongatapu, talk to Jimmy Matthews at the **House Rental Agency** (Box 134, Nuku'alofa; tel. 23-092, fax 22-970; weekdays 0930-1200) in the Tungi Arcade. There isn't a lot to choose from, but Jimmy can usually get you a fully equipped apartment in a new two-story building near Vaiola Hospital at T$1100 a month for a one-bedroom, T$1500 for a two-bedroom. Included are cooking facilities, gas, electricity, and telephone (local calls free), and a swimming pool is on the premises. Occasionally Jimmy also organizes less luxurious flats at under T$400 a month without phone or hot water, over T$400 a month with hot water. In these you must supply your own linen, cutlery, and crockery.

A more local place to try is the **Olota'ane Motel** (Box 2834, Nuku'alofa; tel. 22-560), beside the lagoon on the road from the airport, four km south of town (and easily accessible on the Vaiola bus). The 10 spacious *fales* with private bath and cooking facilities are rented at T$250 a month, but you must supply your own sheets and cutlery, so it's only practical for a long stay. The units are mixed among the stalls of Olota'ane Fair Market in a garden setting. Some are completely surrounded by the market, while others are pleasantly located on a slope overlooking the lagoon. Down by the water is a miniature golf course and a restaurant/bar called the Lagoon Club. The friendly owners put on a barbecue for the market people Saturday 0900-1400, costing T$3 pp. As you may have gathered, the Olota'ane is only for rather adventurous travelers prepared to adapt to a Tongan lifestyle.

FOOD

Budget Places to Eat

For delicious, exotic food at the right price it's **Akiko's Japanese Restaurant** (open Monday to Friday 1130-1400 and 1830-2000), in the basement of the Catholic basilica on Taufa'ahau Road. The lunch special is cheap but good, and there's a more extensive menu at dinner (but no alcohol). It's so popular there's often a line to get in—come early.

John's Place Takeaway (tel. 21-246) on Taufa'ahau Road dishes out the familiar hamburgers or grilled chicken and chips, or cassava and curry. It's okay for a quick snack but with a little effort you'll do better elsewhere for the same money. They're open until midnight, but closed Sunday. **Angela Restaurant** (closed Sunday) next door is similar but better.

The **Fishermen's Wharf Bar & Grill** (closed Sunday) at the end of Vuna Wharf serves cheeseburgers and fried chicken with cheap beer.

Kimiko Restaurant (tel. 22-170) on Vuna Road is okay for a coffee, but they'd rather you order a full meal, but their food is more expensive and the portions smaller than at other places around town.

Better Restaurants

The **Fakalato Chinese Restaurant** (tel. 24-044), above a supermarket on Wellington Road, serves medium-priced Chinese dishes of the type familiar to North Americans, so there will be no difficulty ordering. (While you're there, check out the Italian ice cream place nearby on the corner of Taufa'ahau Road.)

Another Chinese restaurant of note is at the **Phoenix Hotel** (tel. 23-849) on Fatafehi Road. Weekdays the Phoenix offers good lunch specials advertised outside on a blackboard, and this is one of the few places open on Sunday (dinner daily 1730-2200).

The **Italian Restaurant** (tel. 23-313) at the Fasi-Moe-Afi Guest House on Vuna Road serves pizzas big enough for two or three people, and they're also open for dinner on Sunday. Don't expect fast service here.

Several seafood restaurants are opposite the fish market at Faua Jetty, including Davina's Harborside (tel. 23-385; closed Sunday), the Waterfront Grill, and the Marina Restaurant.

Surprisingly, some of Nuku'alofa's finest restaurants are managed by Germans. For in-

the Basilica of St. Anthony of Padua at Nuku'alofa, popular among travelers for its library and Japanese restaurant in the basement

DAVID STANLEY

ROYAL BEER COMPANY LTD, NUKU´ALOFA, THE KINGDOM OF TONGA

stance, there's **Fred's Restaurant** (tel. 22-100; closed Saturday and Sunday), on Salote Road a few blocks east of Cable and Wireless, which specializes in seafood, steak, and pork. Lunch specials (served 1200-1400) are around T$5, as advertised outside. Dinner prices vary T$10-20, and it's best to call ahead to let Fred know you're coming (open 1900-2200). You'll like the pleasant open atmosphere.

A slightly more upmarket place is the **Seaview Restaurant** (tel. 23-709; closed Saturday and Sunday) in a colonial-style house on Vuna Road west of the palace. The German chefs, Lothar and Martina, ensure that the food and atmosphere are excellent. Try the fillet of pork with banana-curry sauce. Tropical fruit appears in some dishes. They're open for dinner 1800-2200 (reservations recommended), or just coffee and cake in the garden 1430-1800.

Also under German management and specializing in international and Tongan cuisine is the **Sunrise Taloa Restaurant** (tel. 24-711), west on the waterfront beyond the Seaview. They're open for dinner Monday to Saturday 1800-2200, with piano entertainment Friday 1900-2000. Lunch is served Tuesday to Friday 1200-1400. You may bring your own bottle of wine here.

Groceries
Talamahu Market (closed Sunday) is a colorful place for fruit and vegetable shopping. Prices are posted. Donuts are sold in one corner of the market.

Nuku'alofa's largest supermarket is the **Kinikinilau Shopping Center** (Monday to Thursday 0730-1800, Friday 0730-2100, Saturday 0730-1300) on Salote Road toward Faua Jetty. They also have an adjacent bottle shop called the Supa-Kava Market.

ENTERTAINMENT

Nuku'alofa's only surviving movie house is **Loni's Cinema** (tel. 23-621), also known as Finau Theater Twin. Films begin Monday to Saturday at 2000, with additional showings Friday at 1300, Saturday at 1100, and Sunday at midnight. Loni's sound system is very bad.

The upmarket **Space Walker Disco** at the Pacific Royale Hotel (tel. 23-344) is *the* place to be on Thursday and Friday nights, but you'll have to arrive soon after they open at 2000 (T$6 cover). Both here and at all the other places mentioned below, men must wear long pants and a shirt with a collar if they want to be admitted. A $100 silk T-shirt from Gucci won't do if it doesn't have a collar. This place was reported to have closed, so check beforehand.

Joe's Tropicana Top Club (tel. 21-544) on Salote Road offers rock music by Pacific Comets and the Barbarians. Watch your drinks when you get up to dance. Joe's is okay for single males but not recommended for women or couples.

On Friday night try the **'Ofa Atu Night Club** at the Friendly Islander Hotel (tel. 23-810), a couple of km east of town. Foreign women shouldn't go unescorted.

The downmarket disco at the **Phoenix Hotel** (tel. 23-270) has live music from 2000 Monday to Saturday. Occasional fights break out here among local Tongans. There's also **Ambassador Night Club** (tel. 23-338) on the Fanga'uta Lagoon just beyond the Tonga National Center. After being closed all day Sunday, some clubs reopen at midnight and there's dancing until sunrise Monday morning—ask.

Drink with the local elite at the **Tonga Club** (tel. 22-710). You're supposed to be a member, but you'll be admitted if you look all right.

The **Yacht Club** (tel. 21-840) on Vuna Road is a good place for a beer, but sandals and shorts are not acceptable dress (foreign visitors welcome). Despite the name, this club is not involved in any yachting activities.

Cultural Shows for Visitors

Traditional Tongan dancing can be witnessed at Fafa Island Resort on Monday night, at the Tongan National Center on Tuesday and Thursday nights, at the International Dateline Hotel on Wednesday and Saturday nights, and at the Good Samaritan Inn and Keleti Beach Resort on Friday nights. A lunchtime performance takes place at the Tongan National Center weekdays. Package tours with dinner and transfers are available to all of the above.

Intellectual Activities

The privately run **'Atenisi Institute** (Box 90, Nuku'alofa; tel. 21-196), in the western part of the city, began as an evening high school in 1963 but now offers university-level courses right up to Ph.D. If you're an "expert" on anything, Professor-Director Futa Helu may invite you to lecture the students. Write in advance or make an appointment soon after you arrive. There's no pay, but someone might end up buying you lunch. During the school year (February to November) there's a free public lecture at the Institute every Monday at 2000. It's a good opportunity to meet a few of the students over coffee, but you might call ahead or visit beforehand to check the subject and to make sure there really will be a lecture that week.

SHOPPING

Handicraft prices in Tonga have increased sharply in recent years but you can still find bargains if you shop around. Baskets, mats, and occasionally tapa are reasonable buys and the handicraft shop at the Tongan National Center is a good place to start. In the center of town, there's **Langafonua,** the Tongan Women's Association Handicraft Center (tel. 21-014) on Taufa'ahau Road. Also try the **Friendly Islands Marketing Cooperative Handicraft Shop** (Box 523, Nuku'alofa; tel. 23-155), otherwise known as "FIMCO" or "Kalia Handicrafts," next to the Family Christian Bookshop on Fatafehi Road. There's no hard sell and you're welcome to browse at leisure.

Also check **Talamahu Market,** where you buy direct from the craftspeople, but avoid buying anything at the market on a cruise-ship day when prices are jacked up. Tapa is best pur-

chased directly from the producers—just listen for the sound of the beating while you're touring the island.

The **Philatelic Bureau** (tel. 23-066) above the post office sells beautiful stamps and first-day covers from Tonga and Niuafo'ou.

The government maintains a monopoly on the duty-free trade, and the lack of competition is reflected in the limited selection at the International Dateline Hotel's duty-free shop. Bring with you all the film you'll need as it's rather expensive in Tonga.

SERVICES AND INFORMATION

Services

The **Bank of Tonga** (tel. 23-933; open Monday to Friday 0900-1530, Saturday 0830-1130) and the **ANZ Bank** diagonally opposite the police station change traveler's checks without commission. The Malaysian-owned **MBf Bank** below Hotel Nuku'alofa charges T$2 commission to change traveler's checks. Outside banking hours the Dateline Hotel will change money for about two percent less than the banks. You must show your passport to change money.

The Bank of Tonga gives cash advances on MasterCard and Visa, and they'll store valuables for you in their vault at T$8 per sealed envelope. American Express is not represented here.

Postage in Tonga is inexpensive compared to other countries, but if you plan on making any heavy purchases it's a good idea to drop in at the post office (tel. 21-700) beforehand to check the rules and rates. It should be possible to mail parcels up to 20 kilograms by surface mail, though this does vary according to the destination country. Poste restante mail is held "one year," or until they get tired of seeing the letter, at which time it's sent back.

The **Cable and Wireless** office (tel. 23-499) on Salote Road is open for international telephone calls, faxes, and telegrams weekdays 0800-2400, Saturday 0900-1600, Sunday 1600-2400, holidays 0800-1200 and 2000-2400.

To make a domestic long-distance call to 'Eua, Ha'apai, Vava'u, or anywhere else in Tonga you must go to the **Telecom telephone exchange** on Unga Road (open 24 hours daily).

You can get an extension of stay at no charge from the **Immigration Office** (tel. 23-222; Monday to Thursday 0900-1200 and 1330-1600, Friday 0900-1200) at the central police station on Salote Road.

The countries with diplomatic representatives in Nuku'alofa are Britain (tel. 21-020), France (tel. 21-831), Germany (tel. 23-477), Korea (tel. 21-633), Nauru (tel. 21-810), New Zealand (tel. 23-122), Spain (tel. 21-196), Sweden (tel. 22-855), and Taiwan (tel. 21-766). The European Union (tel. 23-820) also has an office. The **Australian High Commission** (tel. 23-244) on the street behind the International Dateline Hotel issues free tourist visas weekdays 0900-1100.

Yachting Facilities

Cruising yachts can tie up to the seawall in the small boat harbor beside Queen Salote Wharf three km east of Nuku'alofa, though the channel is only two and a half meters deep in the center. Customs is on the wharf, but immigration is in town. Keep valuables carefully stowed, as there have been many thefts from boats here.

Information

The **Tonga Visitors Bureau** (open weekdays 0830-1630, Saturday 0900-1300; tel. 21-733) on Vuna Road is usually helpful and has lots of free brochures, but check their information personally. Get good maps from the **Lands and Survey Department** in the backyard of the Ministry Block.

The **Friendly Islands Bookshop** (tel. 23-787) below the Tungi Arcade is great for browsing. Ask for books by local authors 'Epeli Hau'ofa, Pesi Fonua, Konai Helu Thaman, and Tupou Posesi Fanua. They also carry Tongan music cassettes and compact discs. For a mail-order list of books on Tonga write: Friendly Islands Bookshop, Box 644, Nuku'alofa, or Vava'u Press Ltd., Box 427, Nuku'alofa.

Family Christian Bookshop (Box 167, Nuku'alofa; tel. 22-562), opposite the Tonga Development Bank on Fatafehi Road, has postcards and posters bearing marvelous photos of Tongan lifestyle and culture. The **Dateline Bookshop** (Box 1291, Nuku'alofa; tel. 24-049), opposite Loni's Cinema on Wellington Road, also has a branch at the airport.

Ginette, who runs the **Tapa Craft** shop next to the Baha'i Temple on Lavina Road, sells used paperbacks for T$1 apiece and trades two of your books for one of hers. She's open weekdays 1200-1800. (If you love cats, drop in to visit Ginette's big family.)

The **'Utue'a Public Library** (open weekdays 1500-2100, Saturday 1000-1500) below the Catholic basilica on Taufa'ahau Road charges T$5 annual membership. There's also a good library in the **University of the South Pacific, Tonga Campus** (tel. 21-540) near the Golf Club at Ha'ateiho, out on the road to the airport. Ask to see their collection of antique Tongan war clubs.

The **Air New Zealand** office (tel. 21-646) is in the Tungi Arcade. The **Air Pacific** agent is E.M. Jones Ltd. (tel. 23-423) on Taufa'ahau Road. The **Royal Tongan Airlines** office (tel. 23-414) is in the Royco Building on Fatafehi Road. **Polynesian Airlines** (tel. 21-566) is at the corner of Fatafehi and Salote roads.

If you need a travel agent, **Vital Travel** (Box 838, Nuku'alofa; tel. 23-617) next to Loni's Cinema on Wellington Road is recommended.

Health

Medical and dental consultations are available at **Vaiola Hospital** (tel. 23-200), just outside town on the way to the airport.

Unless you have unlimited time and are on the barest of budgets, it's better to attend the **German Clinic** (tel. 22-736, after hours tel. 22-350) on Wellington Road a block east of the cinema. There's also a female doctor here. Clinic hours are Monday, Tuesday, Thursday, and Friday 0900-1230 and 1400-1600, Wednesday 1400-1700, Saturday 1000-1200, but call for an appointment.

A recommended **dentist** is Dr. Sione Kilisimasi (tel 21-380), near the Australian High Commission.

TRANSPORTATION

For information on air and sea services from Tongatapu to the other Tongan islands, see "Transportation" in the chapter introduction.

Ferries to 'Eua leave from Faua Jetty but all ships to Ha'apai and Vava'u depart the adjoining Queen Salote Wharf. The office of **Uata Ship-**

ping is upstairs in the building at the corner of Taufa'ahau and Wellington roads. The **Shipping Corporation of Polynesia** office (tel. 21-699) is at the entrance to Queen Salote Wharf.

By Bus

Buses leave from the long-distance bus station on the waterfront opposite the Ministry Block for Veitongo, Mu'a (60 cents), Ha'amonga (T$1), Niutoua, Liahona, Houma (50 cents), Hofoa, Puke, Kolovai (60 cents), and Hihifo (70 cents). Some local buses also leave from here. Farther east opposite the Tonga Visitors Bureau is a local bus station with buses to Halaleva, Longolongo, Ma'ufanga, Popua, Sopu, and Vaiola. The last bus back to Nuku'alofa from Kolovai and Ha'amonga is at 1500. The buses stop running around 1700 and don't run at all on Sunday. The buses are inexpensive, relatively efficient, and a great way to observe Tongan life.

Taxis

Throughout Tonga, registered taxis have a "T" on their license plate. Meterless taxis at the market are T$1 for a trip in town, T$2 for a longer trip in the vicinity, T$12 to the airport. Always ask the price beforehand. Don't expect to find a taxi on Sunday (if you want one then, arrange it with a driver on Saturday and expect to pay a higher fare). Also, only telephone for a taxi at the exact moment you need it. If you call and ask them to come in 30 minutes they'll probably forget and not come at all.

Some taxi drivers double as tour guides, and an island tour with them will run T$50-60 (check the price beforehand). There have been reports of thefts in taxis as drivers removed objects from handbags left in the car while visitors got out to take photos, so be forewarned.

Car Rentals

Foreign and international driver's licenses are not valid for driving in Tonga, so before renting a car you must visit the Traffic Section at the Central Police Station (tel. 23-222) on Salote Road (weekdays 0830-1230 and 1330-1630) to purchase a Tongan driver's license (T$4 for regular cars, T$8 for rental cars). You must queue up several times—once to get the form, another time to pay, then again to get a stamp—so allow at least an hour.

The speed limit is 40 kph in town and 65 kph on the open road. Speed limits are strictly enforced on Tongatapu by radar-equipped police, and on-the-spot T$50 fines are routine. Avoid hitting a pig, as heavy compensation will have to be paid. Also beware of getting hit from behind when you stop. Driving is on the left.

Avis (Box 74, Nuku'alofa; tel. 23-344, fax 23-833) at the Pacific Royale Hotel rents cars with unlimited mileage beginning at T$47 a day. A 15-seat minibus is T$75 daily if you can get a small group together. Both these rates are for a minimum of two days, the T$8 daily collision insurance only covers damages over the first T$1000, and tax is seven and a half percent extra. Weekend rates are available.

By Bicycle

Rather than going to all the trouble and expense of renting a car, see Tongatapu by bicycle. From Nuku'alofa you can easily see all the main sights in two days, visiting the east and west sides of the island on alternate days. The main roads are excellent without too much traffic, and steep hills don't exist. The open landscape invites you to look around at leisure and there are lots of small villages. Abundant road signs make it very easy to find your own way, but don't trust the indicated distances. Cycling can be tiring and dusty, but the friendly islanders are quick to smile and wave at a pedaling visitor. And if you happen to see a six-door Mercedes with a police escort coming your way, get off your bicycle and remove your hat: you're about to see the king and queen!

Rent bicycles (T$5 per day) at the **Bicycle Hire** next to the Dateline Hotel. They rent for 24 hours but are only there in the morning. Sadly, children's cycles are not available. Many guesthouses also rent bicycles.

Tours

The easy way to see Tongatapu is on a full-day bus tour (T$30 pp without lunch) with **Teta Tours** (Box 215, Nuku'alofa; tel. 21-688, fax 23-238) on Wellington Road. Half-day trips to east or west Tongatapu are also offered. If you're interested, check well ahead, as they need a certain number of people to run a tour and they don't go every day. The friendly, helpful staff can also make any hotel bookings for you around Tonga.

Tisha Magic Tours (Box 2393, Nuku'alofa; tel. 24-506), opposite the Langafonua Handicraft Shop on Taufa'ahau Road, also has tours of eastern and western Tongatapu (T$28 pp for two or three hours or T$35 pp for four or five hours). The Sunday bus tour all around Tongatapu is T$40 pp without lunch.

Island Cruises

Sunday is the day for a leisurely boat trip to one of the island resorts described under "Accommodations," above. The closest is **Pangaimotu Island Resort,** whose boat leaves daily at 1100, with extra trips at 1000 and 1200 on Sunday (T$21 including lunch or T$8 for transfers only). Children under 12 pay half price. **Sun Island**

Resort on Makaha'a Island charges T$10 for return transfers Monday to Saturday at 1000, Sunday at 1000, 1100, and 1200 (T$5 extra charge for boat shuttles to the reef). **Fafa Island Resort** also does excellent day-trips daily at 1100 (T$30 including lunch). On Monday Fafa Island Resort offers a romantic dinner cruise with Polynesian floor show departing Nuku'alofa at 1730 (T$40). **Royal Sunset Island Resort's** day-trip departs Sunday at 0900 (T$30 including a barbecue lunch). All these trips leave from Faua Jetty near the fish market, and bookings can be made at Teta Tours or at the International Dateline Hotel tour desk. Provided the weather cooperates, they're an excellent way to pass Nuku'alofa's pious Sunday.

TONGA
THE FRIENDLY ISLANDS

Protect
the Whales

64s Postage

HUMPBACK WHALE
Megaptera novaeangliae

'EUA ISLAND

A rough 40-km boat ride from Nuku'alofa, 'Eua is a good place to go for the weekend. Since tourist facilities are undeveloped you won't feel as oppressed as you might on a Nuku'alofa Sunday, and you'll have to entertain yourself here anyway. Bony bareback horses can be hired, but all spots on the island are within walking distance.

'Eua's hills are a contrast to flat Tongatapu. The thickly forested spine down the east side of 'Eua drops to perpendicular cliffs, while the west half is largely taken up by plantations and villages.

Facilities on 'Eua are extremely basic; this is a chance to get off the beaten tourist track and see real Tongan life. It's a rather scrubby, depressing place, indicative of why so many Tongans live in Auckland. Three full days are enough to get the feel of the island.

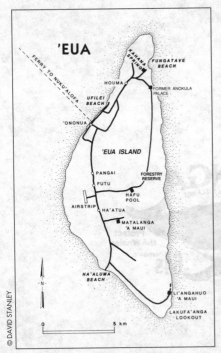

SIGHTS

Matalanga 'a Maui

Legend tells how the demigod Maui thrust his digging stick into 'Eua and pulled it back and forth in anger at his mother, threatening thereby to upset the island. To visit the great pothole that remains from this event, head south of the sawmill and Ha'atua Mormon Church, take the third bush road on the left, and walk inland about 10 minutes. You'll need intuition or a guide to locate the pit hidden in the middle of a plantation on the right, although the lower level of the trees growing in it is an indicator. Holding onto vines, you can get right down into Matalanga 'a Maui itself for an eerie view of jungle-clad walls towering around you.

Southern 'Eua

Most of the families in Pangai and farther south were relocated here from Niuafo'ou Island after a devastating volcanic eruption there in 1946.

The road south from the wharf terminates after 10 km at **Ha'aluma Beach.** The deserted beach is a weathered reef with sandy pools to swim in, but it's only safe as long as you hug the shore. There are some small blowholes and a view of Kalau Island.

Just before the descent to the beach take the road to the left and keep straight one hour almost to the south tip of the island. The good road ends at a prison camp, from whence a track veers left through high grass and starts going north up the east coast. The first cliff you come to across the field from the track is **Lakufa'anga,** where Tongans once called turtles from the sea. So many have been slaughtered that none appear anymore. Look down on the grassy ledges below the cliffs and you'll spot the nesting places of seabirds.

Continue north on the track a short distance, watching on the left for a huge depression partly visible through the trees. This is **Li'angahuo 'a Maui,** a tremendous natural stone bridge by the sea, which you can pass right over without realizing if you're not paying attention. Work your way around the north side of the pothole for a clear view of the bridge. The story goes that after creating Matalanga, Maui threw his digging stick across 'Eua. It pierced the cliffs at this point and dove into the sea to carve out the Tonga Deep. After this impressive sight, continue up the coast a short distance to see more cliffs, which explain why the east side of 'Eua is uninhabited.

Northern 'Eua
The safest place to snorkel on 'Eua is in 'Ononua harbor. **Ufilei Beach,** just two km north of the wharf across the only river bridge in Tonga, is fine for a sunset stroll, but the undertow is deadly.

Tonga's most spectacular scenic viewpoint is just east of Houma village at **Anokula,** where in 1983 the king built himself a palace of which only the concrete foundations now remain. The soaring cliffs drop 120 meters straight into the coastal strip, creating an unsurpassed panorama of power and beauty.

After this visual blast look for a trail north up the coast to another access road that leads down to **Kahana Spring,** now spoiled by a water supply system. Just beyond the spring is a second magnificent viewpoint over the east coast, directly above inaccessible **Fungatave Beach.**

From Anokula the "Takai" or "Lote" road runs south over the mountain ridge with occasionally splendid views to the left and right. It continues to the forest reserve and beyond, passing Topuva'e 'a Maui, the highest point on the island, where there's the simple grave of a New Zealand soldier who died here during WW II.

The Interior
Tonga's finest tropical forest is on the slopes just above Futu. Take the road inland a little south of Haukinima Motel toward the Forestry Experimental Farm. Continue along the main road about 30 minutes till you reach the Forestry Office. **Hafu Pool** is near the office, down a trail that continues straight ahead from the road on the right, but it's hardly worth the effort.

The forest, on the other hand, is well worth exploring for the many exotic species planted by the Forestry Department (pine, red cedar, tree ferns) and the abundant birdlife, especially Pacific pigeons, crimson-crowned fruit doves, white-collared kingfishers, blue-crowned lorikeets, and red-breasted musk parrots. Now both forests and birds of 'Eua are threatened by vil-

Legend tells how Li'angahuo 'a Maui on 'Eua Island was formed when the demigod Maui hurled his spear across the island.

lagers who burn the trees for land on which to plant their sweet potatoes and yams. After a few years the soil is depleted and the farmers move on, while the loss of trees lowers 'Eua's water table, threatening the island with drought. Just as in Brazil and Indonesia, the rainforests of Tonga need better protection.

Ata
Ata Island, 136 km southwest of 'Eua, has been uninhabited since the 1860s, when King George Tupou I ordered the 200 villagers to move to 'Eua, where he could better protect them against the depredations of Peruvian slavers. An extinct volcano, one of its twin peaks reaches 382 meters. Lack of a harbor and the remote location make resettlement unlikely.

PRACTICALITIES

Accommodations
The only place to stay is the 15-room **Haukinima Motel** (Sione Manukia, tel. 50-088) near the airstrip at Futu. It's T$17/22 single/double, with communal cooking facilities (watch your food!). Simple but filling Tongan meals are T$7 and Royal Tongan beer is available. Unfortunately

time for a nap on the rough boat ride from Nuku'alofa to 'Eua

a bar and nightclub are annexed to the building, and unless you're stone deaf, don't expect to get any sleep until 0200 nightly, except on Saturday when it's 2330. If you were looking forward to sleeping peacefully on Sunday night, forget it: a few seconds after midnight when Sunday becomes Monday the music comes on and continues until 0400. After that barking dogs take over. 'Eua certainly could use another place to stay!

Beware of rip-offs if you're camping on the beach on the inhabited west side of the island. A better plan is to trek down to the southeast side and camp wild. Carry all the food and water you'll need.

Entertainment

The best time to come to 'Eua is late August or early September during the 'Eua Agricultural Show. The show grounds are just above the hospital at Futu.

If the nightlife at the Haukinima Motel doesn't satisfy you, there's **Maxi Disco Hall** across the street. A live band plays Saturday at 2000 plus possibly a couple of other nights a week. The hall is run by Taina, who named it after her cat, Maxi. On dance nights the place is packed.

Getting There

From Monday to Saturday **Royal Tongan Airlines** (tel. 50-126) has flights twice a day between Nuku'alofa and 'Eua (T$16 one-way, T$29 roundtrip).

The various boats shuttling between Nuku'alofa and 'Eua are described under "Getting Around by Ship" in the chapter introduction. In general the boats leave 'Eua Tuesday to Saturday at 0630, departing Nuku'alofa's Faua Jetty for the return at 1300 the same days. It's often possible to find a boat on Monday, but none operate on Sunday. All charge T$6 each way. Due to the action of the southeast trades the four-hour boat trip is far less rough westbound than eastbound, so if you're a terrible sailor you might want to fly over from Nuku'alofa and catch the boat back. In fact, so many people have figured that one out that the airline folks have made their roundtrip tickets slightly cheaper!

THE HA'APAI GROUP

This great group of low coral islands between Nuku'alofa and Vava'u is a beachcomber's paradise. Perfect white sandy beaches run right around the mostly uninhabited islands, but treacherous shoals keep cruising yachts away. There are two clusters: Nomuka is the largest of the seldom-visited southern islands, while Lifuka is at the center of a string of islands to the north. Ha'apai is mostly for beach people; if you're not a beach person you'll soon get bored.

Captain Cook made prolonged stops at Nomuka in 1774 and 1777; on a visit to Lifuka in 1773 he coined the term "Friendly Islands," unaware of a plot by the Tongans on Lifuka to murder him. Later, on 28 April 1789 off Tofua, Fletcher Christian and his mutineers lowered Captain William Bligh and 18 loyal members of his crew into a rowboat, beginning one of the longest voyages in an open boat in maritime history, from Tongan waters to Timor in the Dutch East Indies (6,500 km)—a fantastic accomplishment of endurance and seamanship. Bligh's group suffered its only casualty of the trip, John Norton, quartermaster of the *Bounty*, when they landed on the northwest side of Tofua just after the mutiny and clashed with Tongans.

Tofua

Tofua (56 square km) is a flat-topped volcanic island about 500 meters high with a steep and rocky shoreline all the way around the island. The 10 houses and three churches at Hokula near the north coast are used by villagers from Kotu Island, who come to harvest Tofua's potent

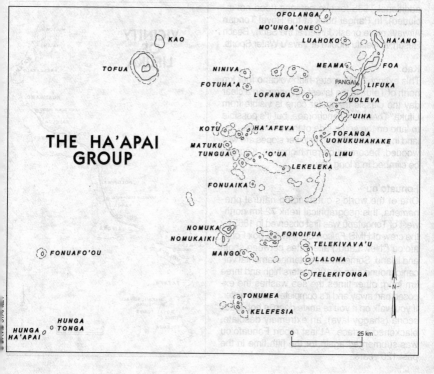

THE HA'APAI
GROUP

OFOLANGA
MO'UNGA'ONE
KAO
LUAHOKO
HA'ANO
TOFUA
NINIVA
MEAMA
FOA
FOTUHA'A
PANGAI
LIFUKA
LOFANGA
UOLEVA
UIHA
KOTU
HA'AFEVA
TOFANGA
UONUKUHAHAKE
MATUKU
TUNGUA
'O'UA
LIMU
LEKELEKA
FONUAIKA
NOMUKA
FONOIFUA
NOMUKAIKI
TELEKIVAVA'U
FONUAFO'OU
MANGO
LALONA
TELEKITONGA
TONUMEA
KELEFESIA
HUNGA
HUNGA   TONGA
HA'APAI

0   25 km

-N-kava. It takes about four hours to climb up to Tofua's rim from Manaka, a tiny settlement on the east coast. The large steep-sided, four-km-wide caldera in the interior is occupied by a freshwater crater lake 30 meters above sea level and 250 meters deep. Tofua is still active: steam and gases issue from a volcanic cone on the north side of the lake, and a hot pool is on the east side. Flames can be seen from passing ships at night.

Peter Goldstern of **Vava'u Amphibian Air** (Box 150, Neiafu, Vava'u; tel./fax 70-193 or fax 24-225) runs charter flights to Tofua from Pangai and Neiafu. The four-person seaplane makes a photo pass over Kao and lands on Tofua's crater lake. Passengers then hike across the caldera for an hour to a smoking crater, and later there's time for a swim in the lake. From Lifuka this memorable excursion costs T$525 for up to three persons, lunch included. It's also possible to spend the night camping on Tofua for an additional T$65 for two persons (food not included). In Pangai book at the Royal Tongan Airways office or ask Jürgen at the Sandy Beach Resort; in Neiafu inquire at Vava'u Water Sports.

Kao
This extinct 1,046-meter-high volcano four km north of Tofua is the tallest in Tonga; on a clear day the classic triangular cone is visible from Lifuka. There is no anchorage, but it's possible to land on the south side of the uninhabited island in good weather. The lower slopes are well wooded, becoming barren higher up. Kao can be climbed in a long day.

Fonuafo'ou
One of the world's outstanding natural phenomena, this geographical freak 72 km northwest of Tongatapu was first observed in 1865 by the crew of HMS *Falcon.* Jack-in-the-box Fonuafo'ou ("New Land") alternates between shoal and island. Sometimes this temperamental volcanic mound stands 100 meters high and three km long; other times the sea washes the exposed part away and it's completely under water. If you walk on it you're ankle deep in hot, black scoria (shaggy lava), an extremely desolate, blackened surface. At last report Fonuafo'ou was submerged again for the fifth time in the past 120 years.

LIFUKA AND ADJACENT ISLANDS

Most visitors to Ha'apai spend their time on Lifuka and its adjacent islands. There are convenient facilities in Pangai, a sleepy big village (1,500 inhabitants) strung along Holopeka Road parallel to the beach. There's even electric lighting! It's only a 10-minute walk out of this "metropolis," however; then you're all alone among the coconut palms or strolling along an endless deserted beach.

Sights
On Holopeka Road at the south end of town is the **King's Palace,** with many fine old trees bordering the compound. The king comes every September for the agricultural fair, which is held in the field across the street.

Just north of the palace and inland a block on Faifekau Road is the Wesleyan Free Church, where a **miraculous cross** appeared in 1975. The spot is now outlined in cement on the grass outside the church. Palasi Road, the next street north, runs right across the island to the long, lonely **beach** of high golden sands extending down the east side of Lifuka, only a 10-minute walk from town. Unfortunately the locals have adversely affected the beauty of this beach by mining it for sand.

Just north of Pangai is the grave and monument of Wesleyan missionary **Reverend Shirley Baker** (1836-1903), an adviser to George Tupou I, who helped frame the Emancipation Edict of 1862 and the 1875 constitution. In 1880 Baker resigned his ministry and governed Tonga in the name of the elderly king. To increase his power he persuaded King George to break with Wesleyan headquarters in Australia and establish the independent Free Wesleyan Church. Baker's persecution of Tongan Wesleyans still loyal to the Australian church and his dictatorial rule prompted the British High Commissioner in Fiji to send a warship to collect him in 1890. Baker was later allowed to retire to Ha'apai.

Foa Island

A causeway links Lifuka and Foa. Weekdays from early morning until around 1600, and also on Saturday morning, buses leave intermittently from in front of 'Ofa Kelepi Toutai Store opposite Pangai Market for **Faleloa,** Foa's northernmost village. Continue 20 minutes on foot to Foa's northern tip to look across to **Nukunamo Island,** owned by the king. The beach is beautiful here and the snorkeling is fine at slack tide.

Outboard motorboats bring villagers from **Ha'ano Island** to the wharf at Faleloa, and you can go back with them most afternoons for about T$1 one-way. Ask permission to camp or stay in the village.

Uoleva and 'Uiha Islands

From the south end of Lifuka, three and a half km from town, you can wade across the reef at low tide to sparsely populated Uoleva Island, which has excellent snorkeling off its southwest end. Check the tides at the visitors bureau in town and wear rubber booties or reef shoes to protect your feet. Sunday is a good day to go as you won't meet any copra cutters.

'Uiha Island, south of Lifuka, is fairly easy to get to on small boats departing the beach at Pangai, but at best the service is only once a day, so you'll have to spend the night. And don't be in a hurry to get back from 'Uiha, or the T$2 regular trip will become a T$40 charter. There aren't any guesthouses on 'Uiha, but you should be able to arrange something. The people at Neo Vaikona's Store on the Pangai waterfront will take a small group over to 'Uiha Island for a few hours sightseeing and bring them back at around T$50 for the boat—worth considering if you can get a small group together.

The burial ground of the Tongan royal family was on 'Uiha until the move to Nuku'alofa. Visit the Makahokovalu, an ancient monument comprised of eight connecting stones about an hour's walk from 'Uiha village. A cannon from the British privateer *Port-au-Prince,* sacked off the northwest end of Lifuka in 1806, can be seen in the middle of the village at 'Uiha.

PRACTICALITIES

Accommodations

All of the guesthouses except the Niu'akalo Beach Hotel and the Captain Cook Resort allow guests to cook their own food, but a small additional charge for cooking gas is levied to use the communal kitchen. Of course, they'd rather do the cooking for you at T$4 for breakfast, T$8 for dinner. Their food is good and the portions are gargantuan (as you'd expect in Tonga) but at those prices it gets expensive. If you really do want to cook for yourself, check out the kitchen as soon as you arrive and ask about extra charges for gas and electricity if you use it. Expect to have to share the facilities with the managers, who will be cooking for other guests.

Fifita's Guest House (Fifita Vi, tel. 60-175), near the market in the center of the village, offers comfortable rooms in a two-story building at T$10/15 single/double. You can cook your own food for a daily T$2 fee (or Fifita will happily do it for you at T$11 for breakfast and dinner). Bicycle rentals are T$5 and boat trips to Uoleva Island can be arranged at T$40 for up to four persons. Airport transfers are free upon request.

Evaloni Guest House (Mrs. Sitali Hu'akau, Box 56, Pangai; tel. 60-029), back behind the

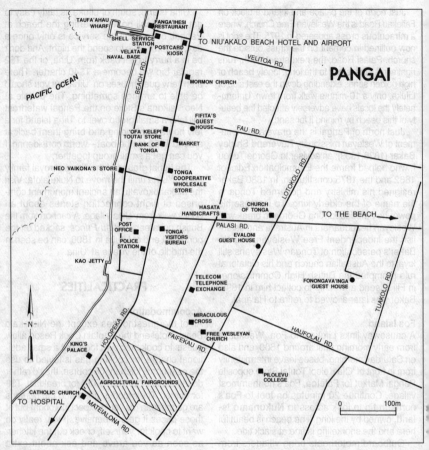

PANGAI

TAUFA'AHAU WHARF
FANGA'IHESI RESTAURANT
SHELL SERVICE STATION
POSTCARD KIOSK
VELATA
NAVAL BASE
PACIFIC OCEAN
BEACH RD.
TO NIU'AKALO BEACH HOTEL AND AIRPORT
VELITOA RD.
MORMON CHURCH
FIFITA'S GUEST HOUSE
FAU RD.
'OFA KELEPI TOUTAI STORE
BANK OF TONGA
MARKET
NEO VAIKONA'S STORE
TONGA COOPERATIVE WHOLESALE STORE
LOTOKOLO RD.
HASATA HANDICRAFTS
CHURCH OF TONGA
TO THE BEACH
POST OFFICE
POLICE STATION
TONGA VISITORS BUREAU
PALASI RD.
EVALONI GUEST HOUSE
KAO JETTY
TELECOM TELEPHONE EXCHANGE
FONONGAVA'INGA GUEST HOUSE
TUAKOLO RD.
MIRACULOUS CROSS
FAIFEKAU RD.
FREE WESLEYAN CHURCH
HAUFOLAU RD.
KING'S PALACE
HOLOPEKA RD.
PILOLEVU COLLEGE
CATHOLIC CHURCH
TO HOSPITAL
AGRICULTURAL FAIRGROUNDS
MATEIALONA RD.
-N-
0   100m

visitors bureau in Pangai, has six basic rooms for T$10/14 single/double. Meals are available at T$4 for breakfast or lunch, T$10 for dinner. It costs T$1 pp a day to use the cooking facilities. They're seldom full.

The friendly, nine-room **Fonongava'inga Guest House** (Mrs. Langilangi Vi, Box 14, Pangai; tel. 60-038) nearby has five small rooms in the main building at T$8/15 single/double and four larger rooms in the new wing at T$15/22/30 single/double/triple. The bathroom facilities are communal in all cases but only the new rooms have access to hot water. You can cook your own food in the owners' house next door at T$2 pp a week, or order excellent meals at T$3 for breakfast or lunch, T$8 for dinner. The atmosphere here is pleasant, with a large living room and front porch available to travelers. Bicycles are for hire at T$7. Langilangi is very kind and helpful.

The quiet **Niu'akalo Beach Hotel** (Box 18, Pangai; tel. 60-028), north of town between Pangai and Holopeka, offers 16 neat little rooms on landscaped grounds facing a long, sandy beach (unfortunately not that good for swimming). A small room with shared bath in a four-room standard unit is T$16.50/22 single/double, while rooms with private bath in the two-room deluxe units are T$27.50/32 single/double, or T$60 for a complete unit (up to six persons). Each cluster has a common living room shared by all guests, but there's only cold water. You can also sleep in a Tongan *fale* for T$6 pp or camp for T$5 pp in your own tent. The biggest drawback is the price of the meals in the restaurant/bar (T$6 for breakfast and T$10 for dinner). To be frank, the food isn't really worth that money, and there are no cooking facilities for guests. Friday at 1900 there's a beach barbecue (T$5) or a full Tongan feast (T$10), depending on how many guests are present. Rental snorkels, boats, and bicycles are available. Your charming hosts, Mrs. Seletute Falevai, her husband, son, and two daughters, are very helpful.

The cheapest place to stay is **Mele Tonga Guest House** (tel. 60-042), on a reasonable beach at Holopeka about 500 meters south of the airstrip. At T$5/8 single/double, there are two double rooms and a single in the main house, plus another double in an adjacent *fale,* and a communal kitchen in a separate building. It's run by a local schoolteacher named Letty, and if she's not around when you arrive, ask at the small store beyond the church next to the guesthouse.

By the beach at the south end of Hihifo village is the **Vaimoana Holiday House** (Mrs. Selai Taufetofua, Box 13, Pangai; tel. 60-105) with four rooms and cooking facilities.

For a real South Seas experience stay at the **Captain Cook Beach Resort** (Soni Kaifoto, Box 49, Pangai; tel. 60-014), on the southwest side of Uoleva Island south of Lifuka. There are four rooms in two basic duplex units at T$18 pp for bed, breakfast, and dinner. The beach here is fabulous (splendid snorkeling), and you'll share this sizable, coconut-covered island with only your fellow guests, the occasional local who comes to work his/her garden, and free-ranging cows, goats, and pigs. Boat transfers from Pangai are T$10 pp return for guests. Ask Fifita at Fifita Guest House in Pangai about the Captain Cook, as it's run by her uncle. Don't expect luxuries like electricity and running water here, in fact, you probably won't get closer to nature anywhere in Tonga than you will here.

In May 1995 Jürgen and Sigrid Stavenow, former managers of the Seaview Restaurant in Nuku'alofa, opened the medium-priced **Sandy Beach Resort** (Box 61, Pangai; tel./fax 60-600) near the north end of Foa Island, one and a half km from Faleloa. The 12 beachfront *fales* with ceiling fan, fridge, 24-hour electricity, porch, and private bath (but no cooking facilities) cost T$130 single or double, plus tax. Of course, the food in the restaurant is geared to an upscale clientele (T$45 for breakfast and dinner), and if that's your price bracket, it's unlikely you'll have any complaints. The German owners add a touch of class to their terrace by broadcasting classical music at sunset, and there's a weekly Tongan cultural show. The swimming and snorkeling are fine, even at low tide, and snorkeling gear, bicycles, and an outrigger canoe are loaned free. Dolphins swim offshore. Paid activities include bareback horse riding, boat trips, amphibian excursions, and ocean kayaking. At Sandy Beach you'll find peace and quiet, interrupted only by the sound of the waves and wind. Airport transfers are free.

There are places to camp freelance at the north and south ends of Lifuka. Ask permission, if you can. Most Tongans don't mind so long as they know you are there and you don't bother their plantations.

Food and Entertainment

The **Fanga'ihesi Restaurant** (tel. 60-125; closed Saturday and Sunday), at the end of Tauta'ahua Wharf in Pangai, serves reasonable, filling lunches (arrive before 1 p.m.), but dinner is much more expensive and must be ordered in advance. Cold beer is available anytime they're open, and there's a dance here Friday and Saturday nights. Ask around for other dances in church halls. You can drink kava all evening at several saloons around Pangai for a flat fee.

Services

Pangai has several adequate stores and a small market opposite the Bank of Tonga, which changes traveler's checks weekdays 0900-1230 and 1330-1530. The **Telecom telephone exchange** (tel. 60-111, fax 60-200), where you can place long-distance calls, is on the small street behind the visitors bureau.

The **Tonga Visitors Bureau** (tel. 60-733) has an office on Holopeka Road in the center of

Pangai that can provide brochures and good local advice.

Niu'ui Hospital (tel. 60-201) is two kilometers south of the wharf.

Getting There

Royal Tongan Airlines (tel. 60-566) next to the post office flies to Ha'apai daily except Sunday from Tongatapu (T$55), and from Ha'apai to Vava'u four times a week (T$54), a useful supplement to the boat service if you only want to spend a couple of days at Pangai. Koulo Airport (HPA) is five km north of Pangai, but transport is easily arranged.

Ferries between Nuku'alofa and Vava'u call regularly at Pangai, northbound early Tuesday and Wednesday morning, southbound in the middle of the night on Wednesday and Thursday. The *Lotoha'angana* runs a day before the *Olovaha* in both directions. The *Olovaha* office (tel. 60-699) is inside the red container on Taufa'ahau Wharf. The office of the *Lotoha'angana* is in the adjacent cream-colored container. Deck fares from Pangai are T$28 to Nuku'alofa and T$21 to Vava'u. Ships tie up to Taufa'ahau Wharf near the center of Pangai; turn right as you disembark. When there are strong westerly winds, the ships may not risk landing at Pangai.

THE VAVA'U GROUP

This elevated limestone cluster tilts up to cliffs in the north and submerges in a myriad of small islands in the south. A labyrinth of waterways wind between plateaus thrust up by some subterranean muscle-flexing. In Vava'u one superb scenic vista succeeds another, all so varied you're continually consulting your map to discover just what you're seeing. Only Port Vila (Vanuatu) is comparable.

The Vava'u Group measures about 21 km east to west and 25 km north to south, and of the 34 elevated, thickly forested islands, 21 are inhabited. Ships approach Vava'u up fjordlike, 11-km Ava Pulepulekai channel, which leads to picturesque, landlocked Port of Refuge Harbor, one of the best in the South Pacific. The appealing main town of Neiafu, 275 km north of Nuku'alofa, looks out onto Puerto de Refugio, christened by Captain Francisco Antonio Mourelle, whose Spanish vessel chanced upon Vava'u in 1781 while en route from Manila to Mexico, one of the last South Pacific islands to be contacted by Europeans.

The many protected anchorages make Vava'u a favorite of cruising yachties, and it's also one of the best places in the Pacific to bring an ocean kayak. Beaches can be hard to find in this uplifted limestone environment, although there are many on the outlying islands.

Vava'u is an economic backwater. There's a giant clam breeding project at Falevai on Kapa Island, and black pearl farming near Utulei in Port of Refuge Harbor. Most of Tonga's vanilla is produced on plantations covering over 500 hectares. Large quantities of taro are exported.

From July to September humpback whales come to Vava'u to bear their young before returning to the colder Antarctic waters for the southern summer. They generally stay on the western side of the group, in the lee of the prevailing trade winds. Most of the tour boats do whalewatching trips upon request, and you'll easily see eight whales on a good day. If you're very lucky, you might even see a spectacular courtship display.

Vava'u is a much more colorful, attractive, appealing, restful, and beautiful place than Nuku'alofa. The longer you stay, the more you'll like it and become more attuned to the relaxed pace of life. You get the impression that this is a place where everyone knows one another and where things can be arranged on short notice. This is one Pacific island group you can't afford to miss.

Sights

Neiafu is a sleepy little town of 4,000 inhabitants, and the points of interest are so obvious you don't really need a guide. The old fig tree in front of Neiafu's red and white colonial-style **post office** is a local meeting place. One of the burials in the **cemetery** on the corner, a block back from the Bank of Tonga, is of the ancient *langi* type. Also buried here is early Methodist missionary David Cargill who rendered the Tongan and Fijian languages into writing. To the southeast, the imposing **Catholic mission** overlooks Neiafu.

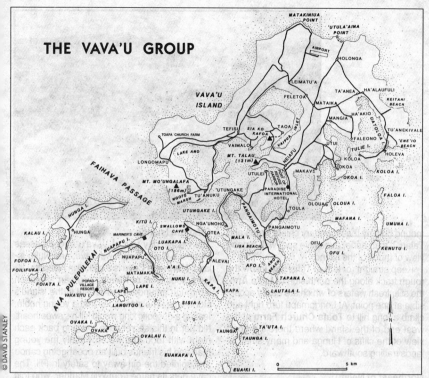

THE VAVA'U GROUP

© DAVID STANLEY

For a splendid view of Port of Refuge and much of the archipelago, climb **Mt. Talau** (131 meters), the flat-top hill that dominates Neiafu to the west. Take the road between the police station and market and follow it high above the shoreline until it begins to descend and you see a trail up the hill on the right just past an isolated house on the left. Turn right at the top of the hill. This is an easy trip from town.

Another excellent walk at low tide is along the shore from the old harbor to **Makave**; you pass a freshwater spring.

South of Neiafu

At **Toula** village, a half-hour walk south of Neiafu beyond the hotel, is a large cave by the shore with a freshwater pool where you can swim. To get there, turn left just beyond the Mormon church and go through the village and up the hill past a cemetery to the cave. At low tide you

can walk back to the old harbor along the beach in about an hour.

The road south from Neiafu crosses two causeways before reaching **Nga'unoho** village (10 km), which has a lovely, clean beach. You can also swim at the Tongan Beach Resort at 'Utungake, and at Lisa and Ano Beaches south of Pangaimotu, although the snorkeling at all four is only fair. By bicycle, you'll find this is the hilliest part of Vava'u.

West of Neiafu

From the Seventh-Day Adventist church on Tui Road in Neiafu a new highway leads west across the Vaipua Inlet causeway to western Vava'u. Beyond the causeway is a long steep incline at the top of which is a hill called **Sia Ko Kafoa** on the left. The track up the hill is on the left near the point where the road begins to descend again. Sia Ko Kafoa is an ancient burial

looking east along Vava'u's wild north coast from 'Utula'aina Point near Holonga

DAVID STANLEY

mound built by the legendary chiefs Kafoa and Talau. It's an eerie, evocative spot with a good view of much of the island.

Keep straight (or left) at Tefisi and follow the rough track along the north side of **Lake Ano**, the still, fresh waters of which are easily accessible at one point. At Longomapu turn right and climb a long hill to **Toafa Church Farm** at the west end of the island where there's a good view of the cliffs of Hunga and many small islands trailing southward.

Northeast of Neiafu

At **Feletoa** village, ask to see the burial place of Finau Ulukalala II behind the house opposite the primary school. The large rectangular *langi* is surrounded by big stone slabs. Finau was the tyrant king of Vava'u who held Will Mariner prisoner and conquered Tongatapu. Two centuries ago Feletoa was the center of power on Vava'u, and a Polynesian fortress was built here in 1808. Little remains today.

For a splendid view of the north coast, travel due north from Neiafu to Holonga. About two km beyond the village, turn left when the trail begins to descend to the beach, then right some 500 meters farther along. With a little luck you'll come out on **'Utula'aina Point,** a sheer cliff a couple of hundred meters above the sea. The quiet beach here is fine for relaxing but the water is too shallow for swimming. You could spend a whole day exploring this area.

Offshore Islands

The classic day tour at Vava'u encompasses Mariner's Cave, Swallows Cave, and Nuku Island. **Mariner's Cave** is a hollow in Nuapapu Island, southwest of Neiafu. You can approach it through an underwater tunnel in the island's stone face. The story goes that a young noble, fearing a despotic king would kill his sweetheart, hid her in this secret cave, coming back each night with food and water. Finally the young man and his friends built an oceangoing canoe and spirited the girl away to safety in Fiji. The cave gets its name from Will Mariner, who told the story to the world.

To find it, go west along the cliff about 300 meters from the northeast tip of Nuapapu, watching for a patch of dark, deep water. White calcium deposits speckle the rocks to the right of the underwater opening; a single coconut tree standing high above also marks the place. Snorkeling gear is recommended for entry, though a strong swimmer could go in without. The opening is about one meter below sea level at low tide, and you have to swim about four meters underwater to get through. The water is illuminated by sunlight, but come up slowly to avoid banging your head on a ledge. Swimming into Mariner's Cave is a bit like doing a bungee jump: it's certainly not for everyone and claustrophobic souls should give it a miss.

Swallows Cave on Kapa Island is far more obvious, and a small boat can motor right inside. Inside Swallows Cave is a rock that rings like a bell when struck, and in front of the entrance to another cave next to Swallows is a huge round coral that looks like an underwater elephant. There are also sea snakes here and an exciting vertical drop-off. All these caves face west, so the best conditions for photography are in the afternoon. This day-trip usually includes a picnic on **Nuku Island.**

Boat trips to the caves cost T$15-35 pp, depending on where you book, how many people are going, and whether lunch is included. **Soki Island Tours** (Sione Katalau) is a good company to go with and all the guesthouse owners know about it. There's also Orion Charters and a few others. Soki Island Tours usually includes snorkeling on the Mala Island reef and along the dropoff at A'a Island in the Mariner's Cave trip. Soki departs from the Bounty Wharf daily except Sunday at 1000 so long as four people book—highly recommended.

If you enjoyed the Mariner's Cave tour and are staying longer, consider going on the eastern islands tour with **Lekeleka Tours** (Siaosi Maeakafa, tel. 70-062). Siaosi takes you from Neiafu's Old Harbor to Umuna Island (interesting cave), Kenutu Island (sea cliffs with huge breakers), and Ofu Island (nice beach), where an island-style lunch is served (T$25 pp all inclusive). It's also possible to spend a few days at Siaosi's house in Ofu village.

The two tourist cafes, the Bounty Bar and Double Dolphin, are good sources of information about all tours and activities around Vava'u and can quickly put you in touch. The guesthouse managers too are very knowledgeable about such things.

Sports and Recreation

Peter Goldstern's **Vava'u Water Sports** (Box 150, Neiafu; tel. 70-541, tel./fax 70-193 or fax 24-225) operates out of a shack beside the water down the hill from The Moorings office. Peter has run his dive shop here since 1982, so he knows all the best spots. Scuba diving with him off his seven-meter Hamilton jet costs T$75 for two tanks. Six-dive packages and rental equipment are available at reasonable prices. A PADI scuba certification course is T$375. Peter often takes his divers to Swallows and Mariner's Caves after the dives, so diving with him could save you an additional trip. Recommended.

Paty Vogan's **Dolphin Pacific Diving** (tel. 70-380) is based at the Tongan Beach Resort (T$80 for a two-tank dive). Her five-day NAUI open-water scuba certification course is T$450. The Dolphin Pacific booking office (Box 131, Neiafu; tel./fax 70-292), opposite Neiafu Police Station, also books most tours and feasts happening around Vava'u. We've heard varying reports about Dolphin Pacific.

Scuba divers frequent the wreck of the 123-meter-long *Clan McWilliam*, a copra steamer that burned and sank in Port of Refuge Harbor in 1917. Huge fish and clams hang around the wreck 20 meters down, marked by a buoy just out past the yacht anchorage. Many other good dive sites are only 30 minutes by speedboat from Neiafu. Most diving is drift diving and there aren't many spots where dive boats can anchor, so it's important to note the current.

From May to November the **Friendly Islands Kayak Company** (Box 104, Neiafu; tel. 70-173, tel./fax 70-380) is based at the Tongan Beach Resort in 'Utungake. The Canadian operators Doug and Sharon Spence run kayaking trips of three to eight days at T$75 a day including meals, tents, and snorkeling gear.

Delray Charters (Box 104, Neiafu; tel./fax 70-380) at the Tongan Beach Resort offers deep-sea game fishing at T$550 a day for up to four anglers. All fishing gear is supplied but you must bring your own lunch. New Zealander John Going and his 14-meter cruiser *Delray* are based here from June to October only. Marlin, mahi-mahi, spearfish, and tuna are caught along the dropoffs below 200-meter cliffs on the northwest side of the island.

Jim McMahon's **Hook-Up Vava'u** (tel. 70-185) offers sportfishing "island style," which means fishing for big game from a small boat. Jim takes clients out in a five-meter, twin-engined fiberglass boat equipped with professional fishing gear, swivel seats, radio, etc. It's T$90/120 a half day (five hours) for one/two anglers, T$160/190 a full day, and you're welcome to bring along a nonfishing child or spouse and still pay the one-angler rate. Jim also charters his boat for sightseeing, snorkeling, and scuba diving at T$14 an hour plus fuel (up to four passengers). Look for him in the same office as Vava'u Water Sports down by the water next to The Moorings.

See rugby Saturday afternoons (April to June) on the Fangatongo Rugby Ground, just off the road to Mt. Talau.

Yacht Charters

Vava'u is one of the top cruising grounds of the Pacific with more than fifty "world class" anchorages. Florida-based **The Moorings** (Box 119, Neiafu; tel. 70-016, fax 70-428), also known as Rainbow Yacht Charters or Rainbow Moorings, has a variety of charter yachts beginning at US$364 a day for a two-couple Moorings 38 and increasing to US$629 daily for a 10-person Moorings 510. Add US$30 pp daily for provisioning, US$18 daily insurance, and 7.5% tax. If you're new to sailing (they check you out) it's another US$95 a day for a skipper. Additional crew might include a cook (US$85 daily) and a guide (US$60 daily). These charges soon add up—a party of four can expect to spend around US$4000 a week to rent an uncrewed bareboat Beneteau yacht, meals included.

A 20% discount and security insurance waiver are possible if you book in person through the Vava'u office, though of course there would be no guarantee they'd have a yacht available for you if you followed that route. The American staff at The Moorings Vava'u office can be a little arrogant and hard to deal with at times, so be prepared. They certainly don't like answering questions over the phone and will just tell you to fax them if you call. More information on The Moorings is provided under "Getting There" in the main introduction.

The Moorings is an expensive, foreign-owned operation geared to the credit-card crowd. If prices matter to you, a much more economical way to go sailing is with Verne Kirk on his 13-meter trimaran *Orion.* Verne does a day cruise to Swallows Cave and other sites daily from 1000-1630 at T$35 pp (T$95 minimum). Book before 1700 the afternoon before at the Paradise International Hotel.

Similar is the 15-meter ketch *Melinda* (Box 153, Neiafu; tel./fax 70-441), which has an office opposite Chanel College between the Paradise International and town. An eight-hour day cruise on the *Melinda* is T$45 pp without lunch (minimum of three), and you can charter the entire boat for overnight trips at T$340 a day for up to six passengers, plus T$20 pp for food. Of course, John, Julia, and their dog Sandwich come with the boat, and you can participate in the sailing if you want. They also do the Mariner's/Swallows Caves tour, and although more expensive than going with Soki, it's well worth the extra cost.

There's also the 17-meter sloop *Jakaranda* (Private Bag, Neiafu; tel. 70-179, fax 70-292), which offers day-trips from the Paradise International Hotel dock (T$50 pp including a picnic lunch). Overnight charters cost T$360 for the boat plus T$20 pp for food—a lot less than The Moorings asks. They prefer groups of four or less and families are most welcome. Skippers Andy and Sandy Peterson have run a sailmaking business at Vava'u since 1989.

If the *Orion, Melinda,* and *Jakaranda* have sailed away by the time you get there, ask around for something similar. Small local operators like these know their waters and will take you on the South Seas adventure of your dreams.

ACCOMMODATIONS

Budget Accommodations

The backpacker's best headquarters at Vava'u is the clean and attractive **Hill-Top Guest House** (tel. 70-209, fax 70-522), which offers spectacular views of Neiafu and the harbor. The 13 rooms vary in price from T$7 pp in the five-bed dorm to T$12/15 single/double for a small, stuffy room with no view, T$17/20 or T$20/24 for a large, airy room with a view, and T$35 for a four-person apartment with kitchen and private bath (7.5% tax additional). They sometimes have water problems and towels are not provided. The excellent communal cooking facilities allow you to save a lot of money on restaurant meals—just don't lose any of your assigned plates or cutlery or you'll be charged for them. Standard precautions against theft should be taken here; for example, don't leave money and valuables in the room when you go out, and make sure nothing is within reach of an open window at night. The German manager rents safety deposit boxes for a flat T$3 fee. The Hill-Top offers bicycle rentals at T$6 a day, an inflatable kayak at T$12 a day, snorkeling gear at T$3 a day, mosquito nets at T$3 for the duration,

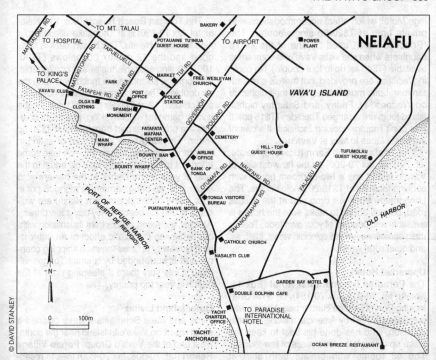

NEIAFU

TO MT. TALAU
BAKERY
TO HOSPITAL
MAFALONA RD.
TAPUELUELU RD.
POTAUAINE TU'INIUA GUEST HOUSE
TO AIRPORT
POWER PLANT
MATEKITONGA RD.
HAAMEA RD.
TO KING'S PALACE
PARK
FATAFEHI RD.
MARKET TUI RD.
FREE WESLEYAN CHURCH
VAVA'U ISLAND
VAVA'U CLUB
OLGA'S CLOTHING
POST OFFICE
POLICE STATION
GOVERNOR RD.
POUONO RD.
SPANISH MONUMENT
FATAFATA MAFANA CENTER
CEMETERY
HILL-TOP GUEST HOUSE
TUFUMOLAU GUEST HOUSE
MAIN WHARF
BOUNTY BAR
AIRLINE OFFICE
BOUNTY WHARF
BANK OF TONGA
NAUFAHU RD.
FALALEU RD.
OTUMAPA RD.
PORT OF REFUGE HARBOR
(PUERTO DE REFUGIO)
PUATAUTANAVE MOTEL
TONGA VISITORS BUREAU
TAKANGAHAAU RD.
OLD HARBOR
CATHOLIC CHURCH
NASALETI CLUB
-N-
0   100m
GARDEN BAY MOTEL
DOUBLE DOLPHIN CAFE
YACHT CHARTER OFFICE
TO PARADISE INTERNATIONAL HOTEL
YACHT ANCHORAGE
OCEAN BREEZE RESTAURANT
© DAVID STANLEY

and a six-hour boat trip at T$20 pp (bring your own lunch). The view from the benches on the hill just above the guesthouse is the best in Neiafu.

The **Potauaine Tu'iniua Guest House** (Box 65, Neiafu; tel. 70-479, fax 70-200), a block west of the market, has six basic rooms in two houses at T$5 pp with communal cooking facilities (T$1 pp extra charge). It's well worth checking out if you're looking for the least expensive accommodation.

The **Hamana Lake Guest House** (tel. 70-507, fax 70-200), just west of the King's Palace, has a great location on the hillside overlooking Port of Refuge, but the smallish rooms are on the expensive side at T$20/30 single/double with shared bath (T$25/35 with the best view). There's a communal kitchen.

The new **Puatautanave Motel** (Box 24, Neiafu; tel. 70-080, fax 70-464) opposite the Tonga Visitors Bureau has six fan-cooled rooms with private bath and balconies overlooking the bay

at T$50/60 single/double. There are no cooking facilities for guests, and it's directly above a noisy disco, so only stay there if you'll be spending a lot of time drinking and dancing. You can always drop in for a drink and the satellite TV.

The nine-room **Vava'u Guest House** (Mr. Mikio Filitonga, Box 148, Neiafu; tel. 70-300, fax 70-441), right across the street from the Paradise International Hotel, has a laid-back atmosphere. Mikio's guests pay T$8/11 single/double for a room with shared bath in the old building, or T$15/20 single/double in one of the four new *fale* units with private facilities and cold showers, breakfast included. At these prices don't expect luxury. It lacks cooking facilities, but the bountiful family-style dinners (T$8) served in the restaurant are quite good, although the service is extremely slow. Nonguests are welcome to eat here.

On the Old Harbor is the 13-room **Garden Bay Motel** (Box 102, Neiafu; tel. 70-025, fax 70-200), formerly known as the Stowaway Village Motel, which offers accommodations with private bath at T$20/30 single/double. The "Princess Fale," used by one of the king's daughters when she visits Vava'u, is sometimes available (T$48 for up to four people). No cooking facilities are provided, but there's a restaurant/bar. Loud music blares from their nightclub on Wednesday, Friday, and Saturday nights. Island tours are arranged Thursday (T$15 pp). If you don't require cooking facilities, it's one of the best places to stay at Vava'u.

The **Toafa Church Farm** (Box 313, Neiafu; tel. 70-269, fax 70-200) on the far west side of Vava'u Island has a two-bedroom house with cooking facilities at T$15/20 single/double. The Longomapu truck will drop you at the access road, but call ahead to make sure the house is available and bring all of your own food. Toafa's main attractions are the splendid views, fresh air, and quiet rural walks.

Upmarket Hotels

The **Paradise International Hotel** (Box 11, Neiafu; tel. 70-211, fax 70-184), on a hill overlooking Port of Refuge Harbor near Neiafu, was purchased in 1981 by American millionaire Carter Johnson, who has done his best to keep the place up through the lean years of few tourists. The 43 rooms with private bath start at T$37/42/50 single/double/triple for a fan-cooled economy room and go up to T$80/90/100 single/double/triple for a deluxe a/c harbor-view room—good value. The economy rooms have older furnishings and cold showers only, but they're clean with lots of towels and satisfactory beds. Unlike some hotels in this category, the Paradise International doesn't mind nonguests wandering in to use the restaurant, bar, and even the swimming pool (T$1 fee), and the atmosphere is friendly, relaxed, and welcoming. The bar at the Paradise International is a good place to meet yachties and other visitors (try the ice cream) but skip the overpriced, poorly served meals in the restaurant. There's dancing to live music at the Paradise International on Wednesday, Friday, and Saturday nights; things pick up after 2200. Video films (T$1.50) are shown nightly at 2030; if you're a hotel guest ask to see the movie list and request a favorite. The hotel's bus tours are good.

The **Tongan Beach Resort** (Box 104, Neiafu; tel./fax 70-380) is at 'Utungake village about nine km from Neiafu. The beach here is fairly good and the 12 duplex bungalows (T$90/100/120 single/double/triple) are comfortable, although the six triples are much nicer than the six doubles. There's a three-day minimum stay, and children 12 and under are half price. Scuba diving, game fishing, kayaking, and yacht charters are offered; airport transfers cost T$20 pp return. One drawback is the cost of eating in their fancy thatched restaurant—it'll take some effort not to run up a daily food bill equal to the cost of your room. Drinks at the bar are also expensive, so bring something along to put in your fridge (day-trippers from Neiafu are welcome to use the beach if they buy a few drinks). Actually, the resort suffers from its isolation without achieving the exotic effect of an outer island hideaway (it faces the main shipping channel and is surrounded by a small Tongan village). Only stay there if sleeping right at the beach is your top priority.

Outer Island Living

Hans and Mele Schmeisser have opened a small resort on Vaka'eitu Island near the southwest end of the Vava'u Group. **Popao Village Resort** (tel. 70-308, fax 70-200) tries to recapture the lifestyle of an old Tongan village with four deluxe *fales* with double beds, private bath, and wooden floors at T$34 double; four traditional *fales* with single beds, shared bath, and mat floors at T$18/28 single/double; and one four-bed dormitory at T$12 pp. Discounts are available for those who stay seven nights or more. There's no camping or electricity. Bucket showers are provided in a central bathhouse. You can buy meals (T$12 for breakfast and dinner) or cook your own. Wooden outrigger canoes are provided free, and fishing trips (T$7 pp) are organized. You'll fish using traditional methods such as the long spear and round throwing net *(kupenga)* and try octopus fishing. Boat trips to the southernmost Vava'u islands not visited by boats from Neiafu are offered at T$20 pp including lunch. Excursions to a kava-drinking club on nearby Hunga Island cost T$8 pp. Boat transfers from Neiafu to Popao are on Wednesday and Saturday, costing T$12 pp each way (free if you stay at least a week). A three-person speedboat is available for transfers anytime at T$35 for the boat. In Nuku'alofa, bookings are handled by Heilala Guest House. Popao is recommended as an authentic Tongan experience, provided you don't mind roughing it a bit.

Ask about camping at **Diana's Beach Retreat** south of Otea on Kapa Island. Diana's main business is serving meals to yachties who anchor offshore and row their dinghies in. The people at the Bounty Bar may have information and should be able to establish contact over their VHF radio. Soki Island Tours provides boat transfers from Neiafu if enough people want to go.

In 1994 two Germans named Leonore and Joanna set up a restaurant and basic resort called the **Berlin Bar** (tel. 70-218) on Kenutu Island off the east side of Vava'u. There's good snorkeling in the turquoise green sea off their beach. Once again, they cater mostly to yachties who come for a fried fish dinner or German curry wurst, but you can also sleep in their treehouse at T$15 pp or rent a hut for T$20 pp. The shuttle boat leaves Neiafu daily at 1000 from May to October. Bookings can be made from the Bounty Bar over VHF channel 16.

Long Stays

Olga Moa at **Olga's Clothing** (Box 84, Neiafu; tel. 70-064) has a few apartments for rent by the month. The flat below her clothing factory just up from the post office is T$250 a month (up to four persons), but it's dark and gets a lot of noise from the adjacent fish freezer. Another house up on the hill has two three-bedroom apartments, T$500 for the one upstairs, T$350 for the one downstairs. Add T$100 to these rates if you require linen.

The **Tufumolau Guest House** on the Old Harbor has gone downhill since the former owners left for New Zealand, but up to three people can still stay there for T$8 a day or T$180 a month. There's a kitchen but you must supply all of your own cooking and eating utensils. The building is now owned by the Tonga Development Bank (tel. 70-031), and you should be able to get information about it at their Vava'u office. It's worth considering only for a long stay.

FOOD

The **Bounty Bar** (tel. 70-576) across from the taxi stand in the center of town serves breakfast, lunch, and dinner on weekdays, dinner only on Saturday (closed Sunday). The menu includes six kinds of burgers, sashimi, fried rice, sandwiches, and cinnamon buns at reasonable prices. On Friday night there's live music. This place is run by veteran yachties John and Phyllis Hickey and it's a real yachting hangout. You get a great view of everything (including sunsets) from the back porch, though it's often hard to get a table.

Hainite McLean at the **Double Dolphin Cafe** (tel. 70-327; closed Sunday), on the main street across from The Moorings, can rustle up a wicked burger or fish-and-chips lunch.

The **Ocean Breeze Restaurant** (tel. 70-582), on the Old Harbor southeast of Neiafu, is probably Neiafu's top place to eat, with large portions, a good wine list, outstanding service, and excellent views. They specialize in seafood such as lobster (T$25), but they also serve steak, lamb, and chicken. It's open daily 1800-2100 with reservations required on Sunday. One reader called it "an immaculate oasis of civilization." (Whenever at least three people want to go, the English restaurant manager, John Dale, runs day tours to outlying islands in his fiberglass speedboat at T$40 pp including lunch. Ask to be shown the flying foxes.)

The Spanish-operated **Restaurant "La Paella"** on Tapana Island off Ano Beach caters to upscale aquatic tourists here on one-week bareboat yacht charters. Pepe and Maria will prepare an excellent meal for you at about T$25 (reservations required).

Groceries

Sailoame Market at Neiafu is crowded with people selling bananas, cabbage, carrots, Chinese lettuce, coconuts, green beans, lettuce, manioc, onions, papaya, tomatoes, taro, yams, zucchini, and oranges. Everything is about T$1 a bunch, and you're only assured a fair selection of fresh vegetables if you arrive early. You can also have lunch here for about T$2. The largest market is on Saturday and, if you come early enough, you'll hear street evangelists preach to the crowd as a policeman directs traffic.

Neiafu's largest supermarket, the **Fatafata Mafana Center,** closes weekdays at 1600, Saturday 1200, so shop early. Bakeries on Neiafu don't bake bread on Saturday but you can buy it (usually through the back door) on Sunday afternoon. Buy fish directly from locals at the harbor.

ENTERTAINMENT

The **Neiafu Club** (tel. 70-566) near the Paradise International Hotel has a nice mix of tourists and locals. Once you sign the guest book for the bartender, he'll remember your name next time you come in.

The **Vava'u Club** (tel. 70-498) has a great view but it's more of a men's drinking place. They have two enormous pool tables where snooker and other such games are played; the bartender keeps sets of balls for eight-ball (hi-lo) and 15-ball pool. Beware of "mosquitoes" who will want you to buy them drinks. These characters are not allowed in the Neiafu Club.

A live dance band plays at the **Puatautanave Motel** (tel. 70-080) on Friday and Saturday nights.

For real earthy interplay, drink watery *kava-tonga* at the **Nasaleti Club** opposite the Catholic church all evening for a T$2 flat fee (open Monday to Saturday 1930-2400).

Sunday morning the singing at the Free Wesleyan Church on Tui Road opposite the market is almost worth the plane fare to Vava'u.

The best time to be in Vava'u is the first week of May for the **Vava'u Festival** marking the crown prince's birthday on 4 May. There will be a display of handicrafts, sporting events, a game fishing tournament, a yacht regatta, boat parades, the Vava'u Marathon, island nights, concerts, dances, feasts, art exhibitions, church choir meetings, traditional Tongan games, a baby show, and a Grand Ball with the crowning of Miss Vava'u. Hotel rooms should be booked ahead at this time, as they should be during the **Agricultural Show** in September when the king will be present.

Cultural Shows for Visitors

Several "feasts" are organized weekly for both land-based and water-bound visitors. For a set fee of around T$20 you get a buffet-style meal of island foods such as roast suckling pig, octopus, fish, clams, lobster, crayfish, and taro, all baked in an *umu* (earth oven). Cooked papaya with coconut cream in the middle is served in half-coconut shells, and lots of watermelon is eaten while sitting on mats on the ground. Have a swim as soon as you arrive, then enjoy a drink (extra charge) to the strains of guitar music. Traditional dancing is performed later, and handicrafts are available for sale.

All of the feasts take place on outlying beaches; clients of The Moorings and other yachties are the biggest customers. Free minibus transfers are provided for visitors staying in Neiafu. Mr. 'Aisea Sikaleti of **Lisa Beach** is said to put on one of the best feasts; Matoto Latavao at **Ano Beach** also does a good job. John Tongia prepares a "gigantic roast" at Rove Hinakauea Beach adjacent to Ano Beach Thursday at 1700. There's always an island feast at one place or another on Saturday afternoon, sometimes Wednesday, Thursday, and Friday as well if demand warrants.

Book your spot for the feasts at the Paradise International Hotel (tel. 70-211) or at the Bounty Bar (tel. 70-576). Often the feasts are canceled if not enough people sign up.

SERVICES AND INFORMATION

Shopping

Handicrafts can be purchased at the **Langafonua Shop** (tel. 70-356) next to the Tonga Visitors Bureau; the **FIMCO Handicraft Shop** (tel. 70-614), next to the Fatafata Mafana Center; and the **Double Dolphin Gift Shop** opposite The Moorings.

Olga's Clothing (tel. 70-064), between the post office and the Vava'u Club, makes clothes to order with enough lead time.

Services

The **Bank of Tonga** (tel. 70-068) at Neiafu changes traveler's checks without commission, while the **MBf Bank** deducts T$2 commission. On the positive side, the MBf is open Saturday 0900-1130, when the Bank of Tonga is not. The Paradise International Hotel will sometimes change money for a small commission when the banks are closed.

Vava'u poste restante holds mail for two months. You can place long-distance telephone calls at the **Telecom telephone exchange** (tel. 70-255, fax 70-200; open 24 hours) behind the post office.

Officially, extensions of stay up to six months are available free at the police station near the market. In practice, however, it's entirely up to the officers how long you get, and your attitude could have a lot to do with it.

Information

The **Tonga Visitors Bureau** (tel. 70-115; closed Saturday and Sunday) has the usual brochures and can answer questions. If possible, verify what they tell you through some other source.

Actually, you'll get better information about what's on around Vava'u by checking the notice boards at the Bounty Bar, Double Dolphin, and the Paradise International. John and Phyllis Hickey at the Bounty Bar have a VHF radio that can be used to contact yachts at Vava'u.

The **Friendly Islands Bookshop** diagonally opposite the Bank of Tonga has postcards and a few good books about the islands.

The **Vava'u Public Library** behind the post office is open weekdays 1330-1700.

Health

Ngu Hospital (tel. 70-201) is on the northwest side of town. You'll get better attention at Dr. Alfredo Carafa's **Italian Clinic** (tel. 70-607 or 70-519; weekdays 0800-1200) at Toula village south of Neiafu.

TRANSPORTATION

By Air

Royal Tongan Airlines (tel. 70-488) flies to Vava'u four times a week from Ha'apai (T$54), weekly from Niuafo'ou (T$137) and Niuatoputapu (T$110). Service from Nuku'alofa (T$110) is three times daily except Sunday. The flights are often heavily booked, and flights canceled without warning or compensation are commonplace, so reconfirm early. In late 1995 Royal Tongan announced that they would soon launch direct weekly flights between Nandi, Fiji, and Vava'u, so check into that service.

Samoa Air (tel. 70-477) at Sanfts Industries opposite the Bank of Tonga sells tickets for the twice-weekly flight from Vava'u to Pago Pago (US$173 one-way). It works out much cheaper to pay for your ticket in U.S. dollars cash rather than Tongan *pa'anga*.

Lupepau'u Airport (VAV) is 11 km north of Neiafu. The Paradise International bus is T$4 pp (free for guests) and a taxi is T$7 for the car. A driver named Stiveni meets most flights, and his transfers cost T$3 pp or less depending on the number of passengers. Local buses (40 cents) run to/from Leimatu'a village a couple of km from the airport sporadically on weekdays and Saturday mornings; otherwise, it's easy to hitch from the airport into town (offer the driver a couple of *pa'anga*).

By Ship

Ships tie up to the wharf. The **Uata Shipping Lines** ferry leaves Neiafu for Ha'apai and Nuku'alofa Wednesday at 1600, whereas the **Shipping Corporation of Polynesia** boat leaves Thursday at 1600. Departures to the Niuas are about once a month. The office of the Shipping Corporation (tel. 70-128) is in the red container in front of the fish market on the main wharf. The Uata Shipping office is in the nearby white kiosk. See "Transportation" in the chapter introduction for more information.

The **"W" Islands Line** has a passenger-carrying freighter, the *Moana II,* to Nuku'alofa and the Niuas monthly. The "W" Islands Line doesn't have an agent at Vava'u, so the only way to find out when their ship is due in is to call the Nuku'alofa office (tel. 22-699) and ask.

By Yacht

To crew on a cruising yacht, put up notices at the Paradise International Hotel, the Bounty Bar, and Double Dolphin, and ask around the bar at the Neiafu Club and at the hotel. The yachting season is March to October. Until September try for a watery ride to Fiji; later most boats will be thinking of a run south to New Zealand.

Getting Around

Passenger trucks and minibuses departing Neiafu market cover most of the roads on an unscheduled basis. Leimatua is fairly well serviced, as is Tu'anekivale. If you want to go to Holonga, you must take a bus as far as Mataika or Ha'alaufuli, then walk. Hitching is easy, but offer

Vava'u's Mt. Talau overlooks Port of Refuge Harbor as a freighter unloads cargo at Neiafu's main wharf.

DAVID STANLEY

to pay if it looks like a passenger truck. They'll never ask more than T$1. Taxis charge about T$1.50 for the first kilometer, 50 cents each additional km. Ask the price beforehand.

Though Vava'u is a lot hillier than Tongatapu, a bicycle is still a good way to get around, and these can be rented at **Chanel Boy Scouts Bike Hire** (Box 40, Neiafu; tel. 70-187), between town and the Paradise International Hotel, for T$5 a half day, T$10 a full day, T$40 a week. They're open weekdays 0900-1000; otherwise ask at the nearby high school office. Several of the guesthouses also rent bicycles, usually for less money.

You can rent a car from **Liviela Taxi** (tel. 70-240) opposite the Fatafata Mafana Center at T$60 a day without insurance. Before you do, you'll have to obtain a Tongan driver's license (T$6) at the police station around the corner (bring your home driver's license).

Minibus tours of Vava'u are offered by **Soane's Scenic Tours** (tel. 70-211) at T$25 pp including lunch (minimum of three persons). Book through the tour desk at the Paradise International Hotel. Also ask for a guy named Tame who does seven-hour minibus tours to the lake, vanilla plantations, scenic viewpoints, and a beach for T$18 pp.

THE NIUAS

The isolated volcanic islands of Niuatoputapu, Tafahi, and Niuafo'ou sit midway between Vava'u and Samoa and often share the devastating hurricanes common to the latter. Two owe their names to their ubiquitous coconut trees *(niu)*. Surprisingly, these were the first Tongan Islands to be seen by Europeans (by Schouten and Le Maire in 1616). The number of visitors to the Niuas today is negligible, but the islands have a lot to offer and are well worth including in your trip if you can afford the extra airfare (and if the air service is operating).

NIUATOPUTAPU

Niuatoputapu Island (18 square km), 300 km north of Vava'u, is a triangular island with a long central ridge 150 meters high. You can climb this ridge from Vaipoa village in the north and explore the many bush trails, which lead to small garden patches on top. A plain surrounds the ridge like the rim of a hat, and lovely white sandy beaches fringe the island, with a sheltered lagoon on the north side and pounding surf on the south. Much of the island is taken up by gardens producing copra and exquisite limes, but some fast-disappearing native forest remains in the south.

NIUATOPUTAPU

Niuatoputapu is a traditional island, where the horse and cart are still widely used and fine pandanus mats are made. All 1,300 inhabitants live in the three villages along the north coast. Hihifo, the administrative center, is about three km north of the airstrip. The wharf at Falehau offers good anchorage for yachties, good swimming for everyone.

The best beaches are on **Hunganga Island,** accessible by wading at low tide. The channel between Hihifo and Hunganga is strikingly beautiful, with clean white sands set against curving palms, the majestic cone of Tafahi Island looming in the distance. The waterways south of the village are not only scenic but also idyllic swimming areas. Within Hihifo itself is **Niutoua Spring,** a long freshwater pool in a crevice—perfect for an afternoon swim. Countless pigs forage on the beach at Hihifo.

Practicalities

The only place to stay is the **Niuatoputapu Guest House** (no phone) in Hihifo, with five rooms at T$18/22 single/double (shared facilities). Meals can be ordered here.

The Produce Board maintains an adequate general store at Hihifo, and traveler's checks can be cashed at the post office. There's a bakery near the Mormon church at Vaipoa.

The best time to come is mid- to late August, when the king arrives for the annual Agricultural Show.

Getting There

Royal Tongan Airlines has weekly flights to Niuatoputapu (NTT) from Nuku'alofa (T$218) and Vava'u (T$110). Interisland flights between the Niuas are T$98 each way every two weeks, and the flight from Niuafo'ou back to Vava'u (T$137) is also every two weeks. Thus a trip to both Niuas by air from Vava'u will cost T$345 return, with a minimum stay of one week on Niuatoputapu and two weeks on Niuafo'ou. That's assuming all goes according to plan and none of the flights are canceled, which is assuming a lot. The Royal Tongan Airlines agent on each island should be able to arrange accommodation, and the airline office in Vava'u will radio ahead to let them know you're coming.

The supply ship from Nuku'alofa and Vava'u arrives about every month. Otherwise there's the *Moana II* of the "W" Islands Line, which sometimes calls here. Niuatoputapu is a port of entry and clearance for cruising yachts, most of which call on their way from Samoa to Vava'u between August and November.

Tafahi Island

Fertile, cone-shaped Tafahi Island, 3.4 square km in size and nine km north of the Niuatoputapu wharf, produces some of the best kava and vanilla in the South Pacific. Only a few hundred people live on the island and the only access is by small boat at high tide from Niuatoputapu (T$5 pp if someone's already going, T$50 each way for a charter). There are 154 concrete steps from the landing to clusters of houses on Tafahi's north slope.

The climb to the summit (555 meters) of extinct Tafahi volcano takes only three hours—get fresh water from bamboo stalks on top. On a clear day Samoa is visible from up here! You can also walk around the island in half a day, using the beach as your trail.

NIUAFO'OU

Niuafo'ou is Tonga's northernmost island, 574 km from Nuku'alofa and equidistant from Savai'i (Western Samoa), Taveuni (Fiji), and Vava'u. Despite the new airstrip, Niuafo'ou remains one of the remotest islands in the world. The supply ship calls about once a month, but there's no wharf on the island. Landings take place at Futu on the west side of the island.

For many years Niuafo'ou received its mail in kerosene tins wrapped in oilcloth thrown overboard from a passing freighter to waiting swimmers or canoeists, giving Tin Can Island its other name. In bad weather, rockets were used to shoot the mail from ship to shore. Early trader Walter George Quensell doubled as postmaster and brought fame to Niuafo'ou by stamping the mail with colorful postmarks. Special Niuafo'ou postage stamps, first issued in 1983, are prized by collectors.

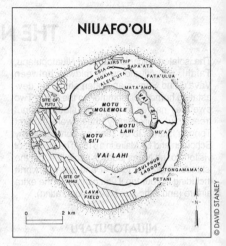

© DAVID STANLEY

The Land

Niuafo'ou (50 square km) is a collapsed volcanic cone once 1,300 meters high. Today the north rim of the caldera reaches 210 meters. The center of the island is occupied by a crater lake, **Vai Lahi,** nearly five km wide and 84 meters deep, lying 21 meters above sea level. From this lake rise small islands with crater lakes of their own—lakes within islands within a lake within an island. Grayish *lapila* fish live in these sulfurous waters.

Presently Niuafo'ou is dormant, but the southern and western sides of the island are covered by bare black **lava fields** from the many eruptions earlier this century. Lava flows emanating from fissures on the outer slopes of the caldera destroyed the villages of 'Ahau in 1853 and Futu in 1929. After Angaha disappeared under lava in 1946, the government evacuated the 1,300 inhabitants to 'Eua Island, where many live today. In 1958 some 200 refugees returned to Niuafo'ou, and by 1976 there were 678 people on the island once more. Signs of the 1946 eruption are apparent in the vicinity of the airstrip.

Apart from the lava fields, the island is well forested. Incubator birds *(Megapodius pritchardis)* or *malau,* lay eggs one-fifth the size of a grown bird in burrows two meters deep in the warm sands of the hot springs by the lake. Natural heating from magma close to the surface incubates the eggs, and the megapode chicks emerge fully feathered and ready to fend for themselves. Many tracks lead to the lake from all directions.

Facilities

Most government offices on Niuafo'ou are at Esia, but the Telecom office and Civil Aviation offices are at Sapa'ata. Unfortunately, there are no official accommodations on Niuafo'ou, though some of the locals will accept paying guests.

Getting There

Niuafo'ou (NFO) is theoretically accessible twice on a month on the **Royal Tongan Airlines** flights from Nuku'alofa (T$245) and Vava'u (T$137). In practice the plane has a 50-50 chance of landing, as Niuafo'ou's airstrip is placed in such a way that dangerously strong winds whip across it. When that happens, the plane has to fly all the way back to Vava'u, and the people on the island see their long-awaited cargo go back where it came from for another two weeks.

CAPSULE TONGAN VOCABULARY

Tongan and Samoan are the main Western Polynesian languages, and although most people speak English, a few words of Tongan will enrich your stay. Listen for the many glottal stops (marked below by apostrophes), which sound something like co'n (for cotton) in American English. In Tongan, "ng" is pronounced as in longing, not as in longer, making it Tong-a, rather than Tong-ga. The vowels sound as they do in Spanish or Italian.

afe to'ohema—turn left
afe to'omata'u—turn right
aha—no
alu—go (singular)
'alu a e—goodbye (to person going)
'alu hangatonu—go straight
amo—yes
baro—maybe
bimi—later
fakaleiti—transvestite
fakamolemole—please
fale—house
fe'unga—that's enough
fefe hake?—how are you?
fefine—woman
ha'u—come (singular)
hena—there (by you)
heni—here (beside you)
'i fe?—where?
ika—fish
'ikai—no
'ikai ha taha—none, nothing
'io—yes
kataki—please
kaukau—bath
kaume'a—friend
koau—I
ko e ha?—what?
ko e me'a 'e fiha?—how many?

ko fe 'a e fale malolo?—where is the toilet?
kohai ia?—who is it?
ko koe—you
ko moutolu—you (plural)
kovi—bad
lahi—big, much
ma'ama'a—cheap
makona—full (of food)
malo 'aupito—thank you very much
malo e lelei—hello
malohi—strong
malo pe—no thank you (at meals)
malo—thank you
mamafa—expensive
mohe—sleep
mou nofo a e—goodbye (to several staying)
mou o a e—goodbye (to several going)
niu mata—drinking nut
niu motu'u—mature coconut
nofo a e—goodbye (to person staying)
o—go (plural)
'ofa—love
'oku fiha?—how much?
'oku mau—we
'oku nau—they

'oku ou fieinua—I'm thirsty
'oku ou fiekaia—I'm hungry
omai—come (plural)
palangi—foreigner
sai—good
sai pe—just fine
si'i—small
ta'ahine—girl
talitali fiefia—welcome
tamasi'i—boy
tangata—man
tulou—excuse me
tu'u—stop

NUMBERS

taha—1
ua—2
tolu—3
fa—4
nima—5
ono—6
fitu—7
valu—8
hiva—9
tahanoa—10
tahataha—11
uanoa—20
uanima—25
teau—100
tahaafe—1,000
tahamano—10,000

GORDON OHLIGER

AMERICAN SAMOA
INTRODUCTION

American, or Eastern, Samoa, 3,700 km southwest of Hawaii, is the only U.S. territory south of the equator. Pago Pago Harbor (pronounced "Pahngo Pahngo"), made famous in Somerset Maugham's *Rain,* is one of the finest in the South Pacific, a natural hurricane shelter for shipping. It was this feature that attracted American attention in the late 19th century, as Germany built a vast commercial empire based around the coconut plantations of neighboring Western Samoa.

Until 1951 American Samoa was run as a naval base, but with advances in U.S. military technology it became obsolete, and control was turned over to civilian colonial administrators who created the welfare state of today. To replace lost income from the base closure, U.S. companies were encouraged to build tuna canneries in the territory. Today traffic constantly winds along Tutuila's narrow south coast highway, and American-style cops prowl in big black-and-white cruisers. Shopping centers and department stores have spread from the head of

Pago Pago Harbor out into suburbia beyond the airport.

American Samoa is a fascinating demonstration of the impact of American materialism on a communal island society. Although the Samoans have eagerly accepted the conveniences of modern life, the *fa'a Samoa,* or Samoan way, remains an important part of their lives. Thus far the Samoans have obtained many advantages from the U.S. connection, without the loss of lands and influx of aliens that have overwhelmed the Hawaiians. While this part of Samoa will always be American, the Samoans are determined to prevent it from going the way of Hawaii.

Don't believe all the negative things you hear about American Samoa, especially from people who have never been there. After you've accepted the high cost of accommodation you'll find American Samoa a friendly, relaxing place to visit with beautiful scenery, easygoing people, inexpensive food and transportation, and a variety of things to see and do. The territory gets few bona fide tourists other than yachties, and once the locals know you're a short-term visitor who has only come to see their islands, you'll usually get a very positive reaction. About the only times the Samoans are a nuisance are if they've been drinking or if they think you're being too active on Sunday. If you can spare the cash it's well worth a side-trip from Apia.

The Land

American Samoa is composed of seven main islands. Tutuila, Aunu'u, and the Manu'a Group (Ofu, Olosega, Ta'u) are high volcanic islands; Rose and Swains are small coral atolls. Tutuila is about midway between the far larger islands of Western Samoa and the smaller Manu'a Group.

Tutuila is by far the largest island, with a steep north coast cut by long ridges and open bays. The entire eastern half of Tutuila is crowded with rugged jungle-clad mountains, continuing west as a high broken plateau pitted with verdant craters of extinct volcanoes. The only substantial flat area is in the wide southern plain between Leone and the airport. Fjordlike Pago Pago Harbor, which almost bisects Tutuila, is a submerged crater, the south wall of which collapsed millions of years ago. Despite the natural beauty, recent studies have shown that the harbor is dying biologically as a result of pollutants dumped by the two tuna canneries and local villagers, and the culminating effect of oil and ammunition spills by the U.S. Navy decades ago. The marinelife of inner Pago Pago harbor is poisonously contaminated by heavy metals and unsafe for human consumption.

In October 1988 the U.S. Congress authorized the creation the **National Park of American Samoa,** comprising 32 square km of tropical rainforest, coastal cliffs, and coral reef on Tutuila, Ofu, and Ta'u, and five years later 50-year leases were signed (this is the only U.S. national park in which the federal government leases the land). On Tutuila the park stretches from Fagasa Bay to Afono Bay, encompassing every-

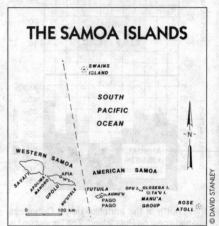

THE SAMOA ISLANDS

© DAVID STANLEY

SAMOA AT A GLANCE

	POPULATION	AREA (SQUARE KM)	HIGHEST POINT (METERS)
Savai'i	45,050 (1991)	1,709	1,858
Apolima	63 (1991)	1	168
Manono	1,064 (1991)	3	107
Upolu	115,121 (1991)	1,114	1,100
Western Samoa	**161,298 (1991)**	**2,842***	
Tutuila	44,643 (1990)	137	652
Aunuu	400 (1990)	2	88
Ofu	353 (1990)	7	494
Olosega	225 (1990)	5	639
Ta'u	1,136 (1990)	46	965
Rose	nil	1	5
Swains	16 (1990)	3	5
American Samoa	**46,773(1990)**	**201**	

*The uninhabited islands of Nu'usafe'e, Nu'utele, Nu'ulua, Namu'a, and Fanuatapu are included in this total.

PAGO PAGO'S CLIMATE

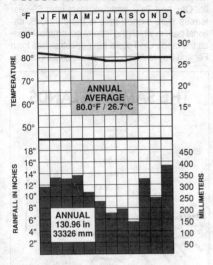

thing north of the knifelike ridge. Countless seabirds nest on Pola Island. The largest unit is on Ta'u with Mt. Lata and the entire southeast corner of the island, including coastal, lowland, montane, and cloud forest communities. Ta'u's soaring cliffs and Laufuti Falls are spectacular. On Ofu the lovely southeastern beach and coral reef are included. Two endangered species of pe'a (flying fox), pollinators of the rainforest, will be protected in the park. This splendid national park, which ranks with Yellowstone and the Grand Canyon in majesty, seems destined to become American Samoa's biggest tourist attraction if an appropriate infrastructure for visitors can be put in place. Current information is available from the park administrative office (tel. 633-7082, fax 633-7085) in Suite 214 of the Pago Shopping Plaza at Pago Pago.

Climate
Although the climate is hot and humid year-round, it's hotter and rainier from November to April (the hurricane season). The frequency of hurricanes has increased dramatically in recent years. The old rule of thumb was one every seven to 10 years, but during the five-year period up to 1991, three major storms hit Tutuila. Many believe this is related to rising ocean tempera-

tures—and things could get worse in the future. Most hurricanes move into the area from the north but they can also come from east or west.

Temperatures are usually steady, but the stronger winds from May to October ventilate the islands. The prevailing tradewinds are from the east or southeast, with west or northwest winds and long periods of calm during the wetter season.

As warm easterlies are forced up and over Tutuila's Rainmaker Mountain, clouds form that drop their moisture on the harbor just to the west. Apia, Western Samoa, receives only half the annual rainfall of Pago Pago. From December to March the rain can continue for days, while the rest of the year it often comes in heavy downpours. The exact amount of rain in any given month varies greatly from year to year, and much of it falls at night. Actually, the weather can change from bright sunshine to heavy rain within five or 10 minutes at any time of year.

You can hear a recorded weather report by calling 699-9333 on Tutuila.

Fauna
Some 61 species of birds are found in American Samoa, including forest birds such as the lupe (Pacific pigeon), manutagi (purple-capped fruit dove), ve'a (banded rail), and 'iao (wattled honeyeater), and seabirds like the fua'o (red-footed booby) and tava'e (white-tailed tropicbird). The rarest of the territory's birds is the manuma (many-colored fruit dove), with only about 50 birds left in the wild. The only food the manuma has ever been observed to eat is the fruit of the aoa (banyan) tree, and the bird is now facing extinction largely due to the disappearance of the aoa, many of which have been cut down by humans or blown over by hurricanes.

Hurricanes have also been blamed for an 85% drop in pe'a (fruit bat) populations between 1987 and 1992. The bats are often seen soaring above the ridgetops around sunset as they leave their roosts to feed at night. Introduced bulbuls and mynahs are now common on Tutuila, but in the Manu'a Group there are only native birds. In an attempt to protect Samoa's endangered wildlife, a ban on hunting birds and bats was enacted in April 1992.

Over 1,000 species of tropical fish dwell along American Samoa's coasts (twice the number found around Hawaii). Only 120 female hawksbill and green turtles still nest here, and there's a US$10,000 fine for killing a sea turtle. From August to October humpback whales visit American Samoa to bear their young in these warm waters before returning to Antarctica, where they pass the southern summer. Sperm whales also call occasionally.

Two land snakes exist, neither poisonous. The blind potted soil snake, which looks rather like a plump earthworm, was introduced to Tutuila accidentally. The two-meter-long Pacific boa of Ta'u is found on islands from Indonesia to Samoa. Both are extremely rare and it's highly unlikely you'll ever see one.

History

The Polynesians emerged in Samoa some 3,000 years ago. By 600 B.C. they'd established a settlement on Tutuila at Tula. This nucleus (or a similar one in the Manu'a Group) may have been the jumping-off point for colonizing Eastern Poly-

JEAN P. HAYDON MUSEUM, PAGO PAGO

The Tu'i Manu'a, highest ranking chief of Eastern Samoa, was the last to sign a cession agreement with the U.S. (in 1904, four years after the chiefs of Tutuila signed). Before he died he willed that his title die with him, and to this day there has not been another Tu'i Manu'a. This photo was taken at Ta'u circa 1904.

nesia (Tahiti and the Marquesas) about A.D. 300. The Samoans maintained regular contact by canoe with the other island groups of Western Polynesia, Tonga, and Fiji. Both Samoas belong to a single cultural area: the chiefs of Tutuila were subordinate to those of Upolu.

The first European in Samoa was the Dutchman Jacob Roggeveen, who visited the Manu'a Group in 1722. In 1786 Antoine de Bougainville, who was French, christened Samoa the "Navigator Islands" for the islanders in canoes he observed chasing schools of tuna far offshore. Another Frenchman, La Pérouse, called in 1787 and had a bloody encounter with the islanders. The Samoans nicknamed these early visitors *papalagi,* or "sky bursters," shortened today to *palagi* and applied to all whites.

Protestant missionary John Williams arrived in 1830 with eight Tahitians and influenza. His son, John Williams, Jr., became one of the first European traders. Nearly 40 years later, American businessmen chose Pago Pago Harbor as an ideal coaling station for their new steamship service from San Francisco to Australia. In 1872 the U.S. Navy sent a ship to negotiate a treaty with local chiefs. Though never ratified by the U.S. Senate, this agreement kept other powers out of Tutuila. By the treaty of 7 November 1899, Germany and the U.S. partitioned Samoa between themselves, with British interests recognized in Tonga. In 1900 the U.S. annexed Tutuila and Aunu'u, adding the Manu'a Group in 1904. This act was not formally ratified by the U.S. Congress until 1929.

From 1900 to 1951 American Samoa was under the Navy Dept.; since then it has been the responsibility of the Department of the Interior. Thousands of U.S. Marines were trained on Tutuila during WW II, and concrete pillboxes built at that time still punctuate much of the island's coastline. The only action experienced, however, was a few shells lobbed from a Japanese sub on 11 January 1942, which ironically damaged the store of one of Tutuila's few Japanese residents, Frank Shimasaki.

The Americanization of Samoa

Outside the war years, little happened to alter the centuries-old lifestyle of the Samoans until the early 1960s, when Western Samoa attained independence and U.S. officials in Washington suddenly realized that unless they moved fast their only South Pacific colony would soon go the same way. In 1961, President Kennedy appointed Governor H. Rex Lee, a Mormon, to dispense a giant infusion of federal funds. A massive public works program financed construction of roads, schools, housing, port facilities, electrification, a new hospital, a tuna cannery, a modern hotel, and an international airport. Lee's most publicized innovation was educational television, introduced in 1964; by the mid-'70s, however, the emphasis of the broadcasts had shifted to the usual commercial programming.

This excessive government spending has created an artificial American standard of living. The Samoans became so dependent that three times they voted down proposals to increase home rule for fear it would mean less subsidies from Uncle Sam. Only in 1976, after a short tenure by unpopular Gov. Earl B. Ruth, did they finally agree in a referendum to elect their own governor.

Government

While Western Samoa received independence from New Zealand in 1962, American Samoa remains an "unincorporated" territory of the United States, meaning the U.S. Constitution and certain other laws don't apply. The territory is also defined as "unorganized," because it doesn't have a constitution sanctioned by the U.S. Congress.

In 1966 federal officials authorized a Samoan constitution that included a bill of rights and gave legislative authority to the Fono, a body composed of 20 representatives (two-year term) elected by the public at large and 18 senators (four-year term) chosen by the customary Samoan *matai* (chiefs), but none of this has yet been made U.S. law by Congress. American Samoa's own colony, Swains Island, has a non-voting representative.

Every four years since 1977, American Samoans have elected their own governor and lieutenant governor. The governor can veto legislation passed by the Fono. Local political parties don't exist, although candidates often identify themselves with the U.S. Democratic or Republican parties.

Local government is conducted by three district governors, 15 county chiefs, and 55 *pulenu'u* (village mayors), all under the Secretary

of Samoan Affairs, a leading *matai* himself. Since 1981 the territory has been represented in Washington by a nonvoting congressman elected every two years. Representative Eni F.H. Faleomavaega, a Democrat, was elected in 1988 (and reelected in 1990, 1992, and 1994) after his predecessor, Fofo Sunia, was disgraced in a scandal involving Sunia relatives being put on the federal payroll.

The powers of the Fono increased during the 1970s; it now exercises considerable control over budget appropriations and executive appointments, though the Secretary of the Interior in Washington retains the right to cancel any law passed by the Fono, remove elected officials, and even cancel self-government itself without reference to the Samoans. The Secretary of the Interior appoints the Chief Justice of the High Court.

The Samoans have no desire to be brought under the jurisdiction of the U.S. Constitution, as this would mean an end to their system of chiefs and family-held lands and would open the territory to uncontrolled migration and business competition from the U.S. mainland. Neither are they interested in independence so long as Washington is holding the purse strings and a majority of their people reside in the U.S. itself.

Economy

Government, the largest employer, accounts for just over one-third of the workforce, followed by the tuna canneries with another third. The Government of American Samoa receives an annual US$80 million subsidy from Washington, 55% of its income. In fact, the territory gets twice as much money in U.S. aid as the entire budget of Western Samoa, although American Samoa has one-fifth the population. This, and diverging living standards, ensure that the two Samoas will never be reunited. Residents of the territory pay exactly the same level of income tax as stateside taxpayers (all such revenue is retained by the Government of American Samoa). Yet despite U.S. largess, the local government rings up multi-million-dollar budgetary deficits each year, due largely to overstaffing and the provision of free health and education services. Eighty percent of the local budget is spent on paying the salaries of the 4,500 government employees.

RICHARD EASTWOOD

These San Diego helicopter-equipped purse seiners based at Pago Pago each sweep millions in tuna from the South Pacific.

American Samoa's primary industry is tuna processing by the Samoa Packing Co., owned by the Prudential Insurance Company and user of the "Chicken of the Sea" label, and StarKist Samoa, a subsidiary of H.J. Heinz. The first cannery opened in 1954, and American Samoa today is the world's fourth-largest tuna processor. Canned fish, canned pet food (from the blood meat), and fish meal (from the skin, guts, and bones) now account for 93% of the territory's industrial output. Wastes from the canneries are barged out and dumped into the ocean.

Canneries thrive in this tiny U.S. territory because they allow Asian fishing companies to avoid U.S. import tariffs of up to 35% on processed fish. Goods have duty- and quota-free entry to the U.S. if 30% of their value is added in the territory. Federal law prohibits foreign commercial fishing boats from offloading tuna at U.S. ports; however, American Samoa is exempted. Thus the greater part of the South Pacific tuna catch is landed here, supplying the U.S. with about half its canned tuna, worth US$350 million a year.

Both canneries pay virtually nothing in taxes to the local government and employ 4,100 cheap nonunion Western Samoan workers who put in two shifts. American Samoans themselves aren't at all interested in cleaning fish for US$3.10 an hour and instead work in business or government. Though they make millions on their tuna operations, the canneries have threatened to relocate if the minimum wage is raised or if the workers became unionized (cannery workers

have several times voted against becoming members of the International Brotherhood of Teamsters). In March 1992 *Pacific Islands Monthly* reported that Heinz's chairman, Tony O'Reilly, made US$75,084,622 in 1990, nearly five times more than all 2,500 Heinz workers in Samoa combined! (American Samoa and the Northern Mariana Islands are the only U.S. jurisdictions where federal minimum wage legislation doesn't apply.)

The trend now is away from rust-eaten Korean and Taiwanese longline tuna boats, toward large California purse seiners worth a couple of million dollars apiece. StarKist has 35 purse seiners under contract, Samoa Packing about 10. A total of 82 Korean and 36 Taiwanese longline boats also work out of Pago Pago. Most of the fish are taken in Papua New Guinea and Federated States of Micronesia waters (the Samoa canneries don't can fish caught by setting nets around dolphins). In aggregate, the canneries contribute about US$25 million a year to the local economy in wages and spend another US$40 million on support services, fuel, and provisioning.

The Marine Railway near the canneries can dry-dock vessels up to 3,500 tons. In recent years harbor facilities have been upgraded through government investment as part of a scheme to make Pago Pago a transshipment center for surrounding countries.

The local government has recently established an industrial park at Tafuna near the airport where companies can lease land on which to build factories. Several American and Asian clothing manufacturers have expressed interest in setting up operations here to exploit the territory's low minimum wages and duty- and quota-free tariff relationship with the United States. With the local tuna canneries facing increasing competition from Mexican canneries under the North American Free Trade Agreement (NAFTA), this may be the way of the future for American Samoa's economy. One Chinese garment company, BCTC Inc., insisted on being allowed to bring in 320 Chinese "trainers" to work with 130 locals for three years, an indication that more is involved than meets the eye.

Tourism development has been hampered by the unstable air connection to Honolulu; a succession of carriers including Pan American Airways, Continental Airlines, Air Samoa, and South Pacific Island Airways have operated for a few years before pulling out or going broke. The present service on Hawaiian Airlines has also had problems. In 1992 American Samoa only got 4,710 "real" tourists, 2,540 of them from the U.S., 925 from New Zealand, 324 from Australia, 164 from Germany, and 103 from Britain. In addition, 12,933 persons arrived on business, 13,801 to visit relatives, 8,989 for employment, and 2,589 in transit. The government-owned Rainmaker Hotel has made a profit during only two years of its 25-year-history. It's hoped tourism will pick up if and when the National Park of American Samoa is properly developed.

The People

American Samoans are physically huge, comparable only to Nauruans. If you see a slim Samoan, chances are he or she is from Western Samoa. The people of the American and Western Samoan groups are homogeneous in blood, speech, and traditions. There has been considerable migration from west to east and much intermarriage: about 15,000 Western Samoans now live in American Samoa. Some 1,750 Tongans and 900 Caucasians are also present.

Between 1980 and 1990 the population grew 44.8%, from 32,297 to 46,773, an average of 3.8% a year. All of this growth was on Tutuila; the population of the Manu'a Group declined slightly. The population of the harbor area is growing 8.2% a year, and it's estimated that

within 18 years the total population will have doubled, the highest growth rate in Polynesia.

American Samoans are U.S. "nationals," not citizens, the main difference being that nationals can't vote in U.S. presidential elections nor be drafted. American Samoans have free entry to the U.S., and some 32,000 of them now live in California, 4,000 in Washington State, and another 15,000 in Hawaii, most in the lower income bracket. Nearly 70% of high school graduates leave American Samoa for the States within a year of graduation, many of them to voluntarily join the Armed Forces. About 1,175 students attend the American Samoa Community College at Mapusaga, a two-year institution established in 1970.

Although the young have largely forgotten their own culture in their haste to embrace that of the U.S., the fa'a Samoa is tenaciously defended by those who choose to remain in their home islands. For a complete description of the fa'a Samoa, see the Western Samoa "Introduction" section. Under treaties signed with the Samoan chiefs in 1900 and 1904, the U.S. government undertook to retain the matai system and protect Samoan land rights. To its credit, it has done just that. In addition, the innate strength and flexibility of "the Samoan way" has permitted its survival in the face of German, New Zealand, and American colonialism.

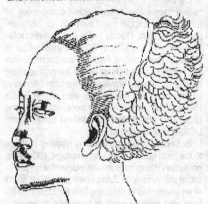

Samoan girl: The thick lips, moderately broad nose, and wavy hair are characteristic Samoan traits; the epicanthic fold at the corner of the eye is not.

On Tutuila the people live in 60 villages along the coast. After a hurricane in January 1966, the U.S. government provided funds to rebuild the thatched Samoan *fales* in plywood and tin, resulting in the hot, stuffy dwellings one sees today. The most farsighted act of the former naval administration was to forbid the sale of Samoan land to outsiders. Except for a small area owned by the government and the two percent freehold land alienated before 1900, 90% of all land in the territory is communally owned by Samoan extended families (*aiga*), who even bury relatives in the yards in front of their homes to reinforce their titles. The family *matai* assigns use of communal land to different members of the *aiga*. If American citizens were allowed to buy land, the Samoans would undoubtedly be exploited as they have little knowledge of property values. Non-Samoans can lease Samoan land for up to 55 years, however.

American Samoa's largest churches are the Congregational Christian Church (20,680 adherents), the Catholic Church (8,500 adherents), the Church of Jesus Christ of Latter-day Saints (4,950 adherents), the Methodist Church (3,900 adherents), the Assemblies of God (2,700 adherents), and the Seventh-Day Adventists (1,700 adherents).

Away from Pago Pago Harbor, if there's a village behind a beach, you're expected to ask permission before swimming. Never swim anywhere near a church on Sunday, and be aware that most Samoans don't wear bathing suits—they swim in shorts and T-shirts. Foreigners in swimsuits on a village beach could give offense, hence the necessity of asking permission first.

ON THE ROAD

Public Holidays and Festivals

All standard U.S. public holidays are observed in American Samoa: New Year's Day (1 January), Martin Luther King Day (third Monday in January), Presidents' Day (third Monday in February), American Samoa's Flag Day (17 April), Good Friday (March/April), Memorial Day (last Monday in May), Independence Day (4 July), Labor Day (first Monday in September), Veteran's Day (11 November), Thanksgiving (fourth Thursday in November), and Christmas Day (25 December). Although European explorers didn't find Samoa until 230 years after Christopher got to America, Columbus or "Discoverer's" Day (second Monday in October) is also a public holiday. In fact, it's one of the biggest holidays of the year because it happens to coincide with White Sunday, a major feast for the Samoans.

During Samoa Days in early April, schoolchildren perform traditional dances. American Samoa's Flag Day, 17 April, commemorates the first flying of the Stars and Stripes in 1900. This enthusiastic two-day celebration features *fautasi* (longboat) racing plus song and dance competitions in Fagatogo. Tourism Week in early July sees barbecues, canoe races, cultural demonstrations, fireworks, music, a parade, and the crowning of Miss American Samoa at Utulei Beach. The second Sunday in October is White Sunday, when children dress in snow-white clothes and walk to church in procession, singing as they go. The children take the seats of honor and lead the service. After church there are family feasts, and gifts are given to the kids.

Another important event is the rising of the *palolo* (coral worm) in late October or early November. When the moon and tide are just right and the *palolo* emerges to propagate, Samoans are waiting with nets and lanterns to scoop up this cherished delicacy, the caviar of the Pacific. During *sa* every afternoon around 1800 villagers pause in whatever they're doing for a brief prayer. If you hear a village bell around this time, stop walking, running, or riding to avoid raising the Samoans' ire.

Visas and Officialdom

No visa is required for a stay of 30 days. An onward ticket is required of U.S. citizens and foreign nationals alike. Everyone except Americans requires a passport for entry. Americans can enter by showing a certified birth certificate, though a passport will be necessary to visit Western Samoa. Due to previous abuse of subsidized medical facilities, "alien" women more than six months pregnant are refused entry to American Samoa. Entry requirements are set by the Government of American Samoa—the U.S. Immigration and Naturalization Service does not exercise jurisdiction here.

Visa extensions are difficult to obtain (US$25 a month up to 90 days total) and work permits almost impossible unless you have a special skill somebody needs, in which case your sponsor will have to post a bond. For more information write: Chief Immigration Officer, Box 7, Pago Pago, American Samoa 96799 (tel. 633-4203). Their office is in the Executive Office Building in Utulei.

If you're proceeding to Hawaii from Pago Pago and need a U.S. visa, be sure to pick it up at the U.S. embassy in Apia or elsewhere as there is no visa-issuing office here.

Those interested in employment in American Samoa should send a resume to: Director of Manpower Resources, American Samoa Government, Pago Pago, American Samoa 96799.

Before departing Hawaii for American Samoa, cruising yachts must obtain a U.S. Customs clearance. Pago Pago is the only port of entry for cruising yachts and few try to fight their way back to Ofu and Ta'u against the wind. At Pago Pago, US$25 clearance fees are charged, plus an additional US$25 departure fee. On both occasions you must take your boat to the customs dock, where the waves bang it against the rough concrete. Tutuila is infested with the Great African snail. Customs officials in neighboring countries know this and carefully inspect baggage and shipping originating in Pago Pago.

Money

U.S. dollars are used, and to avoid big problems and exorbitant commissions when changing money, non-U.S. residents should bring traveler's checks expressed in American currency. Western Samoan currency is not exchangeable in American Samoa.

North American tourism has introduced tipping to the territory. The local saying goes, "It's not only accepted, it's expected." There's no bargaining in markets or shops.

Post and Telecommunications

Because U.S. postal rates apply, American Samoa is a cheap place for airmailing parcels to the U.S. (sea mail takes months). The mail service is reported to be erratic, so mark all mail to or from Pago Pago "priority post." The U.S. postal code is 96799, and regular U.S. postage stamps are used.

Long-distance telephone calls to the U.S. are unexpectedly more expensive than from Apia. A three-minute call costs US$5.70 to New Zealand, US$6.50 to Australia, US$6.60 to the U.S., US$10 to Britain, and US$10.80 to Canada. Evenings and weekends you'll be eligible for a discount amounting to a few pennies on overtime charges to the U.S. but not elsewhere. Collect calls can be made to the U.S. only. More expensive but also available is AT&T's "USA-Direct" service at tel. 633-2872.

Local telephone calls from public telephones anywhere in American Samoa cost only 10 cents each and the phones do work—get into the habit of using them. Yes, it's only 10 cents to call the Manu'a Group from Tutuila. Local calls from private residences are free.

Local directory assistance is tel. 411. For the international operator, dial 0. American Samoa's telephone code is 684.

Media

The *Samoa Journal & Advertiser* (Box 3986, Pago Pago 96799; tel. 633-2399, fax 633-1439) comes out on Monday, Wednesday, and Friday, the *Samoa Daily News* (Box 909, Pago Pago 96799; tel. 633-5599, fax 633-4864) weekdays. Special deals on accommodations and airfares are sometimes advertised in the local newspapers and both papers provide interesting

insights. For example, one *Journal & Advertiser* editorial said this:

Hawaiian Airline is raping its South Pacific routes to make up for its losses. In recent test of customer satisfaction with major airlines comparing ground service, arrivals and departures, service, comfort and lost baggage HAL was rated the worse in all categories. Why do we have to settle for the worse and baddest (sic) airline in the business?

Rainforest Echoes (Box B, Pago Pago 96799; fax 633-7458) is the quarterly newsletter of **Le Vaomatua,** American Samoa's environmental group. One can become a member (and receive the newsletter) by sending in US$10.

Information Offices

The **American Samoa Office of Tourism** (Box 1147, Pago Pago, AS 96799, U.S.A.) mails out brochures upon request.

In the U.S. you could put your questions to American Samoa's congressman in Washington, the Hon. Eni F.H. Faleomavaega (tel. 202/225-8577, fax 202/225-8757). The territory also has an office in Honolulu, accessible at tel. (808) 545-7451, fax (808) 537-2837.

TRANSPORTATION

Getting There

Hawaiian Airlines (tel. 699-1875) connects Pago Pago to Honolulu twice a week, with connections in Honolulu to/from Los Angeles, San Francisco, and Seattle. Pago Pago-Honolulu costs US$554 roundtrip. Sometimes it's cheaper to buy separate tickets Los Angeles-Honolulu and Honolulu-Pago Pago instead of Los Angeles-Pago Pago direct, so compare. Don't forget to reconfirm your onward flight if you don't want to get bumped.

In past numerous problems have plagued Hawaiian's services, including delayed or canceled flights, lost baggage, etc. If their "stretched" narrow-body DC-8 is overbooked, residents and nonresidents are separated into two lines and local residents get priority. Beware of flights leaving three hours early! Things are said to have improved recently, though patience remains a virtue getting in or out on Hawaiian.

Samoa Air (Box 280, Pago Pago 96799; tel. 699-9106, fax 699-9751) has flights to Apia (US$64) four times a day and to Vava'u (US$165) twice a week. From Pago Pago to Apia, 30-day roundtrip excursion tickets are US$86 to Fagalii Airport or US$96 to Faleolo Airport (US$64 one-way to either). A 30-day excursion to Vava'u is US$300 roundtrip. Most Samoa Air flights to Western Samoa land at Fagalii Airstrip near Apia and only those connecting with Air New Zealand go to Faleolo International Airport. Always check carefully which airport you'll be using when booking.

Polynesian Airlines (tel. 699-9126) also has flights to Pago Pago from Apia seven times a day, two of them landing at Faleolo International Airport and five at Fagalii Airstrip. Polynesian and Samoa Air charge identical fares and due to currency differences, tickets for the Pago Pago-Apia flight are much cheaper when purchased in Apia than in American Samoa or elsewhere.

Polynesian Airlines has connections in Apia to and from Australia and New Zealand on their own aircraft, to and from Fiji on Air Pacific. Polynesian's 30-day Polypass (US$999) is valid for travel between the Samoas, Tonga, Cook Islands, Australia, and New Zealand.

If you're flying from Pago Pago to Nuku'alofa, you can stop on the Tongan islands of Vava'u and Ha'apai at little additional cost.

Local Flights
Samoa Air (tel. 699-9106) has two Twin Otter flights a day from Pago Pago to Ofu and Ta'u, leaving Pago Pago at 0600 and 1500 (US$39 one-way, US$78 return). The interisland flight *between* Ofu and Ta'u is US$20 and it's only guaranteed on Tuesday. Special fares are sometimes advertised in the local papers. The nine seats on these flights are often fully booked a week ahead, so inquire early. The baggage limit on flights to Manu'a is 20 kilograms.

By Ship
The Western Samoa Shipping Corporation's ferry *Queen Salamasina* leaves Pago Pago for Apia Thursday at 1600 (eight hours, US$25

one-way). On major public holidays the ship makes two weekly trips, departing Pago Pago at 1600 on Wednesday and Friday. Safety regulations limit the number of passengers aboard to 186, and when that number of tickets have been sold, the ship is "full." Thus it's wise to book before noon a day ahead (take your passport). If you have to buy your ticket at the wharf you'll be the last person allowed aboard and you won't find a proper place to sleep. The booking agent is **Polynesia Shipping** (Box 1478, Pago Pago 96799; tel. 633-1211) across from Sadie's Restaurant. Make sure your name is added to the passenger list or you won't be allowed onboard. As your departure date approaches keep in close touch with the agent as the schedule is subject to frequent change.

Boat fares are lower in Western Samoa, and it's cheaper to buy only a one-way ticket to Apia and purchase your return portion there, although the Western Samoan ticket-to-leave requirement makes it difficult to take advantage of this savings. Coming from Apia, get a roundtrip ticket if you intend to return. Go aboard early to get a wooden bunk. The action of the southeast trade winds makes this a smoother trip westbound toward Apia than vice versa (but it can be rough anytime). Immigration formalities at both ends are chaotic because everyone pushes to be the first person off.

We don't know of any scheduled passenger boats from Pago Pago to Tonga, the Cook Islands, or Fiji. The main season for hitching rides to Tonga or Fiji on yachts is mid-April to November.

The Port Administration, **Water Transportation Department** (tel. 633-5532), across the street from the Samoa News Building, runs a landing craft-type supply vessel, the *Manu'a Tele III,* to Manu'a about once a month. There's no set schedule for the eight-hour trip and they're not licensed to carry passengers, so it's up to the captain to decide if he'll take you. The ship from Pago Pago sails first to Ta'u and then to Ofu.

Airport
Pago Pago International Airport (PPG) is built over the lagoon at Tafuna, 11 km southwest of Fagatogo. Transport to town is 75 cents by public bus or US$10 by taxi (agree on the price before and be sure you have exact change—the

drivers *never* do). Public buses stop fairly frequently in front of the terminal (except on Sunday or after dark). The car rental booths in the terminal only open for flights from Hawaii.

There's no tourist information desk or bank at the airport. The restaurant (tel. 699-9981) around the corner behind the check-in counters serves filling American-style meals at reasonable prices.

The duty-free shop in the departure lounge is generally more expensive than the regular gift shop at the airport. Watch your tickets and baggage tags carefully when you check in here, as the agents will happily book you through to wherever or strand you. A US$3 departure tax is under discussion but at last report still had not been implemented.

TUTUILA

The main island of American Samoa, Tutuila, is 32 km long and anywhere from one to 10 km wide. Surprisingly, this is one of the most varied and beautiful islands in the South Pacific. Its long mountainous spine twists from east to west with wild coastlines and cliffs on the north side, gentler landscapes and plains on the south. There are lots of good beaches scattered around, but for a variety of reasons, finding a good place to swim takes some doing. When it's calm the snorkeling is fine off the empty golden beaches all along the north coast, and the reef-break surfing along the south coast is especially good from December to March.

Fagatogo, the largest town, looks out onto elbowlike Pago Pago Harbor, while government is centered at Utulei, just east of Fagatogo. Despite the oil slicks and continual flood of pollution from canneries, shipping, yachts, and residents, this harbor is dramatically scenic with many fine hikes in the surrounding hills. Among the seemingly incompatible elements thrown together here are slow-moving Samoan villagers, immigrant cannery workers, taciturn Asian fishermen, carefree yachties, and colorful American expatriates—only packaged tourists are missing. It's an unusual, unpretentious place to poke around for a few days.

SIGHTS

Utulei

At **Blunt's Point,** overlooking the mouth of Pago Pago Harbor, are two huge six-inch naval guns emplaced in 1941. To reach them from Utulei, start walking southeast on the main road past the oil tanks and keep watching on the right for a small pump house with two large metal pipes coming out of the wall. This pump is across the highway from a small beach, almost opposite two houses on the bay side of the road. The overgrown track up the hill begins behind the pump house. The lower gun is directly above a large green water tank, while the second is about 200 meters farther up the ridge. Concrete stairways lead to both guns but they're completely covered by vegetation, so be prepared. (Anywhere else these guns would be major tourist attractions but here they're totally abandoned.)

The new US$10-million **Executive Office Building** in Utulei is worth a visit to see how American tax dollars are being used here. Also in Utulei is the **Lee Auditorium** (1962) and American Samoa's **television studios,** which may be visited weekdays around 1030. In 1964 American Samoa became the first Pacific country to receive television, and although the original educational use has disappeared, KVZK-TV continues to broadcast commercially over two channels. Channel 2 is semi-educational, broadcasting PBS, CNN, and a couple of hours of local programming 0600-2400 daily (local programs are on in the evening). Channel 4 is strictly commercial television with ABC/CBS/NBC programs 1500-2400 weekdays, 1200-2400 weekends. Channel 5 was blown off the air by Hurricane Val in 1992 and its equipment cannibalized to keep the other two channels going. The TV tapes are broadcast with Hawaiian advertising. A few local ads appear occasionally on channel 2, but none are allowed on channel 4 as the station gets the Hawaiian tapes free on the understanding that the Hawaiian ads will not be cut and no local ads will be added. In 1995 satellite-generated cable television was introduced to the territory by three private companies, and

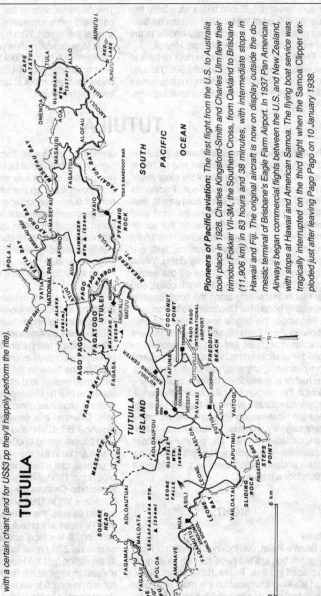

TUTUILA

TUTUILA ISLAND

Legends of Samoa: *Storytellers relate how once, at a time when food was scarce, a blind old woman took her granddaughter to a bluff at Vaitogi; and, holding hands, they leapt to the sea below. The young girl was transformed into a shark, while the old woman became a turtle. Villagers are still able to call the shark and the turtle to the shore with a certain chant (and for US$3 pp they'll happily perform the rite).*

Pioneers of Pacific aviation: *The first flight from the U.S. to Australia took place in 1928. Charles Kingsford-Smith and Charles Ulm flew their trimotor Fokker VII-3M, the Southern Cross, from Oakland to Brisbane (11,906 km) in 83 hours and 38 minutes, with intermediate stops in Hawaii and Fiji. The original aircraft is now on display outside the domestic terminal of Brisbane's Eagle Farm Airport. In 1937 Pan American Airways began commercial flights between the U.S. and New Zealand, with stops at Hawaii and American Samoa. The flying boat service was tragically interrupted on the third flight when the Samoa Clipper exploded just after leaving Pago Pago on 10 January 1938.*

DAVID STANLEY

although these cost about US$350 a year, dozens of channels are accessible 24 hours a day.

From the studios a road leads up to the **cable-car terminal,** where a monument recalls the 1980 air disaster in which a U.S. Navy plane hit the cables and crashed into the Rainmaker Hotel, killing the six servicemen aboard and two tourists at the hotel. The hotel manager refused to allow the memorial to be erected on the hotel grounds.

The cableway, one of the longest single-span aerial tramways in the world, was built in 1965 to transport TV technicians to the transmitters atop Mt. Alava (491 meters). The car sways for a kilometer and a half over Pago Pago Harbor, with mountains such as rugged Rainmaker (524 meters) in full view, making this the most spectacular aerial ride in the Pacific. In 1992 Hurricane Val put the cableway out of service and rumor has it that it will only be repaired when the national park finally opens and a park headquarters is established on Mt. Alava! Even now it's worth visiting the Utulei terminal for the excellent view of Rainmaker Mountain from the viewpoint (you'll have to search a bit to find the way up to the viewpoint—as usual it's completely overgrown and there's no sign).

Fagatogo

The **Governor's Mansion** (1903) stands on a hilltop just west of the Rainmaker Hotel but a large sign requests the public not to enter the grounds. The old Navy commissary (1917) now houses the **Jean P. Haydon Museum** (tel. 633-4347; open weekdays 0800-1500, admission free).

Facing the Malae-O-Le-Talu field, where local chiefs ceded the island to the U.S. in 1900, is the **Fono Building** (1973), in which the territory's legislature convenes for 45-day sessions twice a year. The **police station** across the field from the Fono was originally the barracks of the Fitafita Guard, the former Samoan militia.

Farther west just before the market is the old **courthouse** (1904), built in the U.S. Deep-South style. The **Fagatogo Public Market** is busiest early Saturday morning, when screaming red-faced evangelists backed up by ear-splitting gospel music harangue vendors selling tropical fruits and vegetables. Just inside the **Department of Marine and Wildlife Resources** office facing the bus station next to the market is a very good display of fish and birdlife of Samoa. Ask for a copy of their excellent booklet *American Samoa: Natural History and Conservation Topics.*

West of here is the former guesthouse where Somerset Maugham stayed in 1916, now **Sadie's Restaurant**. Today Maugham's tale of Sadie Thompson and the tormented missionary, set here, is discussed over upscale food.

Pago Pago

Continue west to Pila F. Patu Co. Inc. store, where a road runs up the hill into Happy Val-

Pago Pago Harbor as it looked in 1939 before roadbuilders broke out of the Bay Area

ley. On this side road you pass six WW II ammunition bunkers on the left before reaching a dirt road, also on the left, which leads to a large **concrete bunker** used during WW II as a naval communications headquarters. Many of these military structures are now inhabited, and you'll need to ask permission before approaching the bunker, which is in a backyard.

At the west end of the harbor is Pago Pago village, this whole area's namesake. **Korea House** in Pago Park is a center for Asian fishermen. Around on the north side of the harbor is the **Marine Railway,** which provides maintenance and repair facilities to the fishing fleet. The **tuna canneries** are nearby. To visit the Samoa Packing Plant (formerly owned by Van Camp) call the personnel manager at tel. 644-1347 and make an appointment. You could also try asking at the gate. Only persons wearing shoes and long pants are allowed inside the plant; flip-flops and shorts are banned for safety reasons. Star-Kist (H.J. Heinz) is less amenable to visitors.

High on the reef just east of the canneries are eight Taiwanese and Korean fishing boats thrown up by Hurricane Val in 1992.

The North Coast

The easiest way to escape the congested Pago Pago harbor area is to jump on a bus to **Vatia** on Tutuila's north coast in the center of the area designated as the **National Park of American Samoa.** Three buses shuttle (US$1.50 or US$2) back and forth via Aua and Afono all day, so getting there is easy. Vatia is a picturesque village with a nice beach, and the scenery around here is superb with jungle-covered peaks surrounding the village on all sides. Look across to unforgettable Pola Island (also known as the "Cockscomb") with its sheer 100-meter cliffs. If you're interested in some organized hiking or boating while at Vatia, call Roy West (tel. 644-1416) who offers boat trips at US$20 pp and who can arrange hiking guides at the same rate.

The East End

Two more six-inch WW II guns are on the hillside near **Breakers Point.** Walk up past Mr. Paleafei's house, the large two-story dwelling at the high point in the road. The hill directly opposite the guns bears a small lighthouse with a view, while by the water at the bottom of the hill on the bay side is a concrete ammunition bunker now used for dynamite storage.

Eastern Tutuila is easily accessible on the frequent Tula buses that wind along the southeast coast through the day. At Alao and **Tula** are wide sandy beaches, but beware of the undertow. Unfortunately empty milk cartons and other trash from the nearby elementary school litter the area. Mr. Haro M. Lesolo (tel. 622-7457) at Tula puts up visitors in his own house for a reasonable rate—great if you'd like to be near the beach. From Tula (the end of the bus route), the road continues around to the north side of Tutuila as far as Onenoa.

Aunu'u Island

There's a single village on Aunu'u Island off the southeast end of Tutuila, but no cars. Motorboats shuttle constantly between the small boat harbors at Auasi and Aunu'u, taking passengers for US$2 pp each way or US$10 one-way for a charter trip. Go over first thing in the morning and you shouldn't have any trouble getting back. Don't come on a Sunday though, as the locals don't appreciate *palagi* picnickers that day.

Aunu'u's eel-infested **Red Lake** in the sprawling crater is difficult to approach. Cliffs along the south coast and thick bushes make hiking around the island heavy going. Aunu'u's notorious stretch of red **quicksand** at Pala Lake is fairly close to the village, but you may have to wade through a swamp to get to it. The **taro swamps** just behind the village are easier to see, and a walk around to the new elementary school reveals an appealing slice of island life. At **Ma'ama'a Cove** on the east side of the island waves rush into "the teacup" with much slashing. It's picturesque, but don't swim here.

Ottoville

At Ottoville on the Tafuna plain is the new **Holy Family Catholic Cathedral** (1994) containing a wonderful picture of the Holy Family on a Samoan beach painted by Duffy Sheredi in 1991. Samoan carver Sven Ortquist did the woodcarvings in the cathedral and designed the stained glass windows.

Near the cathedral and adjacent to the Fatuoaiga Catholic Church Center is a small

historical park with restored stone *tia seu lupe* (pigeon-catching mound) that in many ways resembles the later *marae* of Eastern Polynesia. Similar (if usually smaller) *tia* dot the ridgelines and jungles of all of Tutuila. The park is well laid out and sits next to the only swatch of lowland rainforest still extant on Tutuila. It's accessible on the Tafuna bus and well worth a visit, especially around twilight if you're a birder.

Around Leone
The Leone bus will drop you between Vailoatai and Taputimu at **sliding rock** where the local kids take a running slide down the large, flat rocks covered by slimy algae. It's dangerous to imitate unless you know exactly how. From here you can hike east along the coast toward Fagatele Point, but only in dry weather at low tide as the rocks become extremely slippery and dangerous when it rains. There are several clear tidal pools here where you can swim at low tide and even a blowhole. This coast is lovely but Fagatele Bay, a drowned volcanic crater now designated a "national marine sanctuary," is difficult to reach due to high cliffs.

the monument to John Williams at Leone on Tutuila

From Sliding Rock it's a pleasant two km walk (or another bus) northwest to Leone village. Just before you reach the intersection with the main south coast road, ask someone to direct you to the former **Fagalele Boys School,** on the coast behind a row of large banyan trees. Built in the 19th century, this is the oldest European-style building on the island, unfortunately destroyed by Hurricane Val in 1992 (this place would make a fantastic restaurant—any entrepreneurs out there?).

Leone was the ancient capital of Tutuila and it was here that Samoa's first missionary, John Williams, landed on 18 October 1832. A monument to Williams is in front of **Zion Church** (1900) at Leone. The church is worth visiting for its finely carved wooden ceiling. Two km up the road beginning beside the nearby Catholic church is **Leone Falls** (closed Sunday), where there's freshwater swimming.

Both Fagalele and Zion were built by the London Missionary Society, and a couple of kilometers west of Leone is the former **Atauloma Girls School** (1900), a third relic of LMS activity. Today the school building is owned by the territory and used as government housing for *palagis*—Samoans refuse to live there out of fear that it's haunted. When the sea is calm you can snorkel on the reef in front of Atauloma Girls School, and since there isn't a church is this village, it's usually okay to swim there even on Sunday. There's also surfing off the beaches at Atauloma and nearby Fagamutu.

Cape Taputapu
There's beautiful scenery along the road west of Leone. Get off the bus just beyond Amanave where the road swings north to Poloa. At low tide you can hike along the south coast from Amanave to **Cape Taputapu** in about 30 minutes, passing several lovely isolated beaches and rocky offshore islets. At high tide look for the slippery, muddy trail that cuts behind several of the more difficult stretches. There's a lovely white-sand beach at uninhabited Loa Cove halfway to the cape. The cape itself is magnificent, and it's exciting to stand on the rocky westernmost headland and watch the ocean rise and fall before you as it crashes into the shore.

The Northwest Coast

Buses run fairly frequently between Pavaiai and Aoloaufou, high in the center of the island. It's a short walk up a paved road from Aoloaufou to the radio towers on **Mt. Olotele** (493 meters) for the view.

A muddy, slippery trail leads from beyond Aoloaufou down to Aasu village on **Massacre Bay,** about an hour each way. Only two families still live here and in front of one of the houses is a monument erected in 1883 and surmounted by a cross. This memorializes 11 French sailors from the ships *Astrolabe* and *Boussole* of the ill-fated La Pérouse expedition, who were killed here in an encounter with the Samoans on 11 December 1787. The French had come ashore to fill their casks with water, but as they were returning to their ships the two longboats became stranded on the reef due to a miscalculation of the tide, and the Samoans attacked. A Chinese member of the expedition and the 39 Samoans who also died are not mentioned on the monument. Ask someone at Aasu to indicate the way to the waterfalls (and remember that this whole area is private property).

Another trail from Aoloaufou goes down to **Aoloautuai;** the trailhead is behind a house on the left near the northwest end of the road. Aoloautuai is a deserted village site on a lovely bay where you can camp for a few days if you bring enough food.

SPORTS AND RECREATION

Visitors are welcome at the 18-hole **'Ili'ili Golf Course** (tel. 699-1832; open daily) maintained by the Department of Parks and Recreation at 'Ili'ili. You'll enjoy good views of the mountains and sea from the fairways, and inexpensive food and drink are available at the adjacent Country Club (tel. 688-2440). Green fees are US$6 weekdays, US$7 weekends and holidays for the 18 holes. The public tennis courts at Pago Pago and Tafuna are free.

Chuck Brugman's **Dive Samoa** (Box 3927, Pago Pago 96799; tel. 633-1701 or 633-1850) operates out of Safety Systems (tel. 633-1701), across from the beach park in Faga'alu. Chuck runs scuba trips at US$25 pp (minimum of two) for one tank, US$45 pp for two tanks, night dives US$30 (all gear is extra). Snorkelers can go along for reduced rates, and sightseeing boat rides are US$10 pp. Most of Chuck's clients are local divers, and there's almost always a trip on Saturday.

Deep-sea fishing is offered by **Mike Crook** (Box 3700, Pago Pago 96799; tel. 633-1701 or 622-7413), and you can also ask for Mike at Safety Systems. Mike will take up to six people out fishing in his *Tasi Two* at US$250 for five hours, US$400 for 12 hours.

The **windsurfing** in Pago Pago Harbor is good year-round, although there's more wind from June to October. The main drawback is the harbor's pollution. If you'd like to surf the wind and want some specific information contact Bill Hyman at the Island Business Center (tel. 633-2623) next to Pizza Time behind Tedi of Samoa in Fagatogo.

Roy West of **North Shore Tours** (General Delivery, Pago Pago 96799; tel. 644-1416) offers all kinds of hiking, mountain climbing, bird-watching, snorkeling, and boat trips at very reasonable prices. Most of Roy's ecotours cost US$20 pp for a full day, plus US$5 for lunch. If you want to hike along Tutuila's rugged north

the monument at Aasu to La Pérouse's massacred crew members

DAVID STANLEY

coast, climb Rainmaker Mountain, or get dropped off at an inaccessible bay for a few days of real Robinson Crusoe living, Roy is the person to call. He also has a good knowledge of Samoan plants. His base is at Vatia, so many of the trips leave from there.

Hiking

Mt. Matafao (653 meters), Tutuila's highest peak, can be climbed from the pass on the Fagasa road in half a day. Scramble up onto the ridge south of the road as best you can; the trail is much more obvious on top. It'll take about three hours up through a beautiful rainforest—stay on the ridge all the way. No special gear is required for this climb and you could even go alone, but avoid rainy weather when it gets slippery. In clear weather the view is one of the best in the South Pacific.

On the other side of the pass a jeep track leads northeast to the TV towers on **Mt. Alava** (491 meters), from whence there's a spectacular view of Pago Pago Harbor and Rainmaker Mountain. From Mt. Alava you can follow an overgrown trail through the National Park of American Samoa down to Vatia.

Snorkeling Locales

Snorkeling in the polluted waters off Utulei and Faga'alu is not recommended. The closest points outside the harbor are the open reefs opposite Aveina Bros. Market at Matu'u, or at Laulii. These can be treacherous in the usual fresh southeast tradewinds and rather heavy break. If the water is fairly quiet get into one of the *avas*—the channels going out—and enjoy undersea caves and canyons. Just beware of sneak bumper waves and strong undertow in the channels: you might have to come back in over the reef and the break varies considerably. Neither spot is outstanding, however, and you might see more trash than fish.

Better snorkeling locales are found at the east and west ends of Tutuila, but beware of strong currents and undertow. The north coast is best of all, as it's well protected from most pollution and the prevailing winds. Shark attacks are extremely rare around American Samoa—coral cuts and undertow or currents are much more of a hazard.

ACCOMMODATIONS

Budget Accommodations

Whether you love or hate Tutuila may well depend on the type of accommodations you get. Several good medium-priced places to stay have appeared recently, but you can still expect to pay more than you would for similar accommodations elsewhere in the South Pacific. Knowing this in advance, it won't come as quite as much of a shock, and many other things such as food, drinks, groceries, toiletries, clothes, transportation, admissions, and telephone calls are relatively cheap, so it averages out in a way.

There isn't any regular low-budget accommodation in the harbor area, and camping is not allowed in public parks. Some residents welcome paying guests, however, and Pago Pago village at the head of the harbor is a good place to start looking. For example, Mrs. Fetu Vaiuli (Box 792, Pago Pago 96799; tel. 633-1340) rents rooms to travelers by the week or month. It's the sixth house on the left past the huge derelict church up Fagasa Road from Pago Pago village.

Mr. Elmer "Sama" Nakiso (Box 152, Pago Pago 96799; tel. 633-4803) in Fagatogo village also rents rooms on a long-term basis (about US$150 a month). To find his house turn left at Herb & Sia's Motel and follow the road around to the end. The people in small corner grocery stores around the island may know of similar places, if they understand what you really want. These are private homes, so you ought to look upon it as a sort of cultural exchange and approach people with sensitivity. Your first question should not be the price.

The **Office of Tourism** (Box 1147, Pago Pago 96799; tel. 633-1091), next to the courthouse in Fagatogo, has a *Fale, Fala ma Ti* (house, mat, and tea) program of rather expensive accommodations with Samoan families starting at US$25-45 pp a day without food. Bargaining is sometimes possible. This is a nice way to meet people while finding a place to stay, but unfortunately it's very disorganized. Many of the families on the list have moved, changed their prices, or simply forgotten they were listed at all. Reconfirm everything by phone before

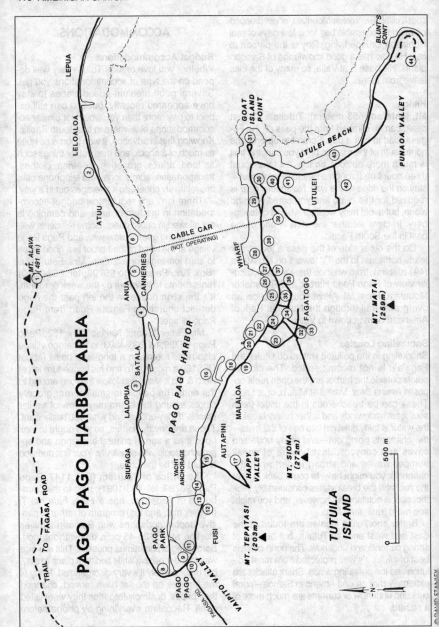

PAGO PAGO HARBOR AREA

TRAIL TO FAGASA ROAD

▲ MT. ALAVA (491 m)

CABLE CAR (NOT OPERATING)

MT. MATAI (259 m) ▲

LEPUA

LELOALOA

ATUU

CANNERIES

ANUA

SATALA

LALOPUA

SIUFAGA

PAGO PAGO

PAGO PARK

FUSI

VAIPITO VALLEY

AUTAPINI

HAPPY VALLEY

MALALOA

YACHT ANCHORAGE

WHARF

FAGATOGO

UTULEI

UTULEI BEACH

PUNAOA VALLEY

GOAT ISLAND POINT

BLUNT'S POINT

▲ MT. SIONA (272 m)

▲ MT. TEPATASI (203 m)

TUTUILA ISLAND

FAGASA RD.

500 m

© DAVID STANLEY

PAGO PAGO HARBOR AREA

1. Mt. Alava TV transmitters
2. Ramonna Lee's Restaurant
3. Power Plant
4. Marine Railway
5. StarKist Foods
6. Samoa Packing Plant
7. Korea House
8. Korean Food Huts
9. ATT Night Club
10. Spencer's
11. Pago Shopping Plaza
12. Motu O Fiafiaga Motel/Evalani's Cabaret Lounge
13. Senior Handicraft Fale
14. Pago Pago Bay Restaurant
15. Pila F. Patu Co.
16. Fisheries Dock
17. Wartime Concrete Bunker
18. Polynesia Shipping
19. Sadie's Restaurant
20. Icewich Fale
21. Market/Bus Station
22. Teo's Kitchen
23. Maria Laundromat
24. courthouse/Office of Tourism
25. Fono Building
26. Apia ferry landing
27. Jean P. Haydon Museum
28. Port Administration
29. Feleti Pacific Library
30. Governor's Mansion
31. Rainmaker Hotel
32. Mary's Laundromat
33. Herb and Sia's Motel
34. Office of Communications
35. Malae-O-Le-Talu
36. Police Station
37. Post Office/Bank of Hawaii
38. Wesley Bookshop/Samoa News Building
39. Cable Car Terminal
40. Television Studios
41. Lee Auditorium
42. Executive Office Building
43. Pago Pago Yacht Club
44. WW II Naval Guns

going anywhere. Be prepared for huge complimentary meals with lots of meat and breadfruit, friendly people, no privacy, free rides around town, outdoor showers called "watertaps," and remote locations. The Samoans are warm, hospitable people and if they like you you'll immediately become part of the family.

About the closest you'll come to backpackers' accommodations on Tutuila is offered by **Roy West** (General Delivery, Pago Pago 96799; tel. 644-1416) who lives in Vatia village on the north coast. He arranges places to stay in the village at US$10 pp and also has a secluded cabin at Amalau Bay, off the road to Vatia, which he rents at US$15/20 single/double. Several beach *fales* are also here at US$5 pp, but you'd need a mosquito net. (The Amalau Valley is a prime bird- and bat-watching area.) In addition, Roy has a plantation shack and accommodation in set tents at Tafeu Bay west of Vatia, accessible by trail in three hours or by boat in 10 minutes plus 20 minutes on foot. Roy is developing other low-budget accommodations around Tutuila, so call him up as soon as you arrive. If you get his answering machine and don't have a number to leave, just say you're on your way and catch a bus over to Vatia.

Tisa's Barefoot Bar (Box 3576, Pago Pago 96799; tel. 622-7447), at Alega Beach on the southeast coast between Lauli'i and Avaio villages, arranges bed and breakfast accommodations in the village at US$25/35 single/double, and there are two small *fales* right on the beach at US$10 pp for a pillow, mosquito net, and mat. Call ahead to check availability and prices.

Medium-Priced Accommodations

Tutuila's newest place to stay is Duke and Evalani's **Motu O Fiafiaga Motel** (Box 1554, Pago Pago 96799; tel. 633-7777, fax 633-4767). The 12 a/c rooms are US$60 single or double if you stay only one night, US$50 for two or more nights, or US$300 a week. This new two-story building overlooks a noisy highway, so ask for a room on the back side if traffic bothers you. The adjacent restaurant/bar under the same management serves excellent and inexpensive Mexican and American cuisine.

Herb and Sia's Motel (Box 430, Pago Pago 96799; tel. 633-5413) in the heart of Fagatogo has gone downhill in recent years, although the prices haven't followed. The rooms, six with shared bath (US$35/40/50 single/double/triple) and three with private bath (US$40/45 single/double), have a fridge in each but no cooking facilities. There's no hot water, the air-conditioning and fridges may be out of order, and to be frank, the whole hotel is a bit of a dump. Avoid rooms five and six, which are without outside windows, and lock your door securely when you go out to the toilet. Women traveling alone shouldn't stay here.

The 23 a/c rooms with bath and fridge at the 'Apiolefaga Inn (Box 336, Pago Pago 96799; tel. 699-9124), in Mesepa village back behind the Community College west of the airport, are US$40/50/65 single/double/triple. A bar and pool are on the premises.

About the best accommodation value on Tutuila is Barry's Bed & Breakfast (Box 5572, Pago Pago 96799; tel. 688-2488, 688-2400, or 699-5113, fax 633-9111). The five rooms in Barry's comfortable two-story house near the waterfalls at Leone go for US$35/40/50 single/double/triple including a good breakfast. There are full cooking facilities, hot water showers, a washing machine, TV, and large tropical garden at your disposal. You can even borrow a set of golf clubs to use at the local course. Local telephone calls are free. Barry Willis, a fifth generation European Samoan, will make you feel right at home. Give him a call from the airport and he'll come and pick you up at no charge if he has a room available (the house is often occupied by contract workers for extended periods).

Upmarket Hotel
Tutuila's only big hotel is the 167-room Rainmaker Hotel (Box 996, Pago Pago 96799; tel. 633-4241, fax 633-5959), erected in the mid-'60s by Pan American Airways but now government-owned. The oval neo-Samoan architecture echoes Rainmaker Mountain across the bay. Rates start at US$60 single or double standard, US$72 superior, US$85 deluxe (with TV). Children under 16 are free. Unfortunately it's rather run-down, so if the first room they give you is in bad condition, go back and ask for another. Request an upstairs room facing the beach. The Rainmaker sometimes offers "weekend getaway" packages that include an a/c room from anytime Friday until 1400 Sunday, plus the Friday dinner show at the hotel, all for US$85 per couple. Call and ask about this. The Rainmaker features the usual bars, restaurants, gift shops, swimming pool, surly desk staff, and garbage-littered grounds. There's even a golf driving range out into the lagoon featuring floating golf balls, which are collected by men in canoes (US$6 a basket). Swimming in the bay here is not recommended.

FOOD

Budget Places to Eat
Unlike accommodations, there's an excellent selection of inexpensive places to eat (although fried, high-sodium, and high-cholesterol foods are the norm). Most places provide the standard "bottomless" cup of coffee dear to the hearts of Americans.

Da Maks Island Style Restaurant (tel. 633-5838; open weekdays 0700-1630), by the bay behind the market, has lots of inexpensive breakfast and "ono" lunch specials, which you can consume on a terrace just above the water. You'll like Mel and Gretchen's mix of Samoan, Chinese, and Hawaiian foods. Next to Da Maks is the Sweete Shoppe (no sign) with good ice cream.

Teo's Kitchen (tel. 633-2250; open Saturday until 1600) beside the market has some of the cheapest meals in town. Get breakfast, hamburgers, etc., at the Icewich Fale (tel. 633-4414) just west of the market.

A small fast food counter called TFM Variety (open daily) opposite the Office of Communications in Fagatogo has Samoan-sized ice cream cones for about a dollar, and next door is a 24-hour diner with tasty, low-priced food.

Pinoy's Restaurant (tel. 633-2125), next to Luana's Handicrafts in the Samoa Daily News Building, serves tasty Filipino dishes Monday to Saturday from 0830 until the food runs out.

The Korean huts in Pago Park at the head of the bay dispense mammoth take-away lunches you can consume at adjacent picnic tables weekdays. Crab salads are 75 cents for a big scoop. Get there early for the best selection—by 1400 they're sold out.

Krystal's Burger (tel. 688-2335) on the main road out toward Leone has the best fast food on the island. Monday to Saturday they're open from 1100 until well after midnight (evenings only on Sunday).

Better Restaurants

The dining room at the **Rainmaker Hotel** (tel. 633-4241) offers a Samoan buffet lunch Friday 1130-1330 (US$10). Also try breakfast (0630-1100) or fish and chips in the surprisingly good hotel coffee shop (open daily until 1800).

Sadie's Restaurant (tel. 633-5981) just west of the market isn't cheap but the tuna dishes are good. Dress up for Sunday brunch here.

The upmarket menu at the **Pago Pago Bay Restaurant** (tel. 633-4197) in Pago Pago goes from hamburgers to Chinese food, with fresh seafood and U.S.-quality steak somewhere in between. Their fish and chips are worth asking for, and the weekday lunchtime working person's special is a bargain. The portions here are ample.

Ramonna Lee's Restaurant (tel. 644-2576; Monday to Saturday 1000-1400 and 1700-2300, Sunday 1600-2200), on the left east of the canneries, has medium-priced Chinese food.

Le Tausala (tel. 699-5128; Monday to Saturday 0900-2200) in Nu'uuli is perhaps the nicest restaurant outside the harbor area.

Vegetarians might like to know about **Paisano's Deli and Pizzeria** (tel. 633-2837; closed Sunday) at Matu'u between Nu'uuli and town. They bake some of the best pizza west of Santa Monica, plus huge submarine sandwiches jam-packed with corned beef, pastrami, and Italian sausage. Real mozzarella cheese is used. Owner Jimmy Stevens, an animated New Jersey Italian, is kept hopping feeding homesick crews off the big purse seiners based here.

ENTERTAINMENT

The **Wallace Theater** (tel. 699-5403) in Nu'uuli screens recent Hollywood films in two halls.

A.T.T. Night Club, next to the bowling alley across from Spencer's in Pago Pago, has live music Thursday to Saturday evenings. Fistfights between fishermen are routine here, so back off at the first sign of trouble. You can play bingo in the hall next to A.T.T. nightly except Sunday at 2000.

Evalani's Cabaret Lounge (tel. 633-4776; lunch 1130-1400, dinner 1800-2300) in Pago Pago has the best Mexican food in both Samoas, plus a spacious dance floor, karaoke videos, and a nice local crowd. Co-owner Duke Wellington plays Tutuila's only grand piano at happy hour (1800-2100). The purse seiner guys tend to stand at the bar and cause trouble among themselves under the watchful eye of the mountainous bouncer.

Have a happy happy hour at the **Pago Pago Restaurant** (tel. 633-4197) in Pago Pago weekdays from 1700 to 1900, with free *pupus* (snacks) and US$1.75 drinks—a yachtie hangout. Happy hours at **Sadie's Restaurant** (tel. 633-5981) are weekdays 1630-1800 (prices variable).

The Sadie Thompson Lounge off the main dining room at the Rainmaker Hotel has a consistently good happy hour band weekdays 1630-1830 (a favorite hangout of local politicians). Come early or you won't find a table. Shorts and bare feet are not permitted in the lounge after 1600; in fact, all of the places mentioned above except the bingo hall have strict dress codes in the evening. The drinking age in American Samoa is 21.

Fa'amao's Pago Bar (tel. 633-5633), across from the Office of Communications in Fagatogo, is the only nightspot where you don't have to dress up to get in—a good place to meet the locals. There are videos and cheap beer by day and dancing to a live band Thursday to Saturday evenings.

If you have wheels, the **Le'ala Resort** (tel. 688-1776) near the Sliding Rocks south of Leone is a safe place to dance to a great band on Friday and Saturday nights. Don't bother arriving before 2230 though, and call ahead to make sure they'll be open. Despite the name, this is only a local dance hall. Krystal's is just a five-minute drive away for a late night snack.

On Alega Beach between Lauli'i and Avaio villages is **Tisa's Barefoot Bar** (tel. 622-7447), which has gained notoriety recently due to a number of magazine articles about a certain fertility tattoo on the proprietress. At one point the U.S. Navy launched an investigation into alleged misconduct by the male-and-female crew of a visiting naval vessel during the regular all-night "Nude Friday" shenanigans here. Tisa was subpoenaed to testify in Hawaii, but nothing could be proved. Tisa's is open on Sunday and you can swim here—a good place to while away the day. Call to find out if they'll be serving a traditional *umu* meal that day, and ask about their seafood feast (US$25 pp). You might also inquire about the annual Nude Friday full moon party (actually, *lavalavas* are provided free). "Tisa's jungle hop," a three-hour guided romp through the bush behind the bar, is US$10 pp including a snack. Yes, it's a bit trendy, but several readers wrote in to say how much they enjoyed it.

Cultural Show for Visitors

A Polynesian variety show accompanies the Friday night Fia Fia buffet in the dining room at the Rainmaker Hotel (tel. 633-4241). Dinner is from 1830 and the show starts at 2000 (US$15 pp, reservations recommended). The food is excellent (prime rib, great salads), and you'll witness Maori war dances, Hawaiian hulas, and even a tropical version of "My Way!" The only other chance to see Samoan dancing is when a cruise ship arrives or leaves (which happens about four times a year), or on a local holiday.

SHOPPING

American Samoa is a poor place to shop for handicrafts. The **Samoan Women's Handicraft Fale** beside the Fono is worth a try, though many of the things here are imported from Tonga. Crafts are often made in the *fales* in front of the museum.

Much better is **Luana's Handicrafts** (tel. 633-1850) in the Samoa News Building at Fagatogo, which has a very good selection of crafts from Samoa, Tonga, and many other Pacific islands, but prices are high. They carry the excellent *Islands of Samoa* map.

In contrast, clothing is reasonable, and those long *puletasi* dresses make unique souvenirs. **Forsgren's** (tel. 633-5431) in Fagatogo has nice Samoan T-shirts and cut-rate clothes at the best prices in town. It's always crowded with Western Samoans who make the long pilgrimage just to shop here. **TK's Clothing** (tel. 633-2173) near Forsgren's is another place to shop for cheap tropical garb and *lavalavas*. **Tedi of Samoa** (tel. 633-4200) sells Samoan fashions

and Reebok shoes in their Hawaiian-style store across from the courthouse in Fagatogo. While other local stores sell Chinese products, Tedi has mostly American-made clothing but fewer bargains. **Spencer's** (tel. 633-4631) in Pago Pago also carries inexpensive garb.

The **Transpac Corporation** (tel. 699-9589) in the Nu'uuli Shopping Center and below Sadie's Restaurant has a good selection of imported goods. **The Record Store** (tel. 699-1283) sells cassette tapes of Samoan pop at three locations: Nu'uuli, Fagatogo, and Pago Shopping Plaza. **Tropik-Traders** (tel. 699-5077) near Transpac in Nu'uuli is the place to pick up magazines, compact discs, and gifts. Downtown closing time is inconveniently early at 1630, on Saturday at 1200.

Returning U.S. residents are allowed a duty-free exemption of US$800 (instead of US$400) on goods acquired in American Samoa. The next US$1000 worth of merchandise is liable to only five percent flat rate duty (instead of 10%). Four liters of alcoholic beverages may be brought back from American Samoa (instead of one liter). You can mail home gift parcels worth up to US$100 (instead of US$40). Keep invoices or bills of sale in case it's necessary to prove where you purchased the articles.

In general, American Samoa is a cheap place to shop because importers pay only three percent duty and there's no sales tax. Neighboring Western Samoa has a 10% sales tax and double-digit duties.

SERVICES AND INFORMATION

Money

Only the **Bank of Hawaii** (tel. 633-4226; weekdays 0900-1500), beside the post office in Fagatogo, will change foreign currency, but brace yourself for a rip-off US$7.50 commission (no commission on U.S.-dollar traveler's checks).

The **Amerika Samoa Bank** (tel. 633-1151) has branches next to the police station in Fagatogo and at Tafuna. The Tafuna branch is open Saturday morning 0900-1200. They cash U.S.-dollar traveler's checks without commission (as do most other businesses in the territory).

American Express is no longer represented in American Samoa.

Post and Telecommunications

The main post office (weekdays 0800-1600, Saturday 0800-1200) is in Fagatogo, with branches at Leone and Fagaitua. General delivery mail can be picked up at the main office weekdays 0930-1100 and 1300-1500, Saturday 1030-1130 (mail is held 30 days). If you're a yachtie, ask the clerk to also check under the name of your boat.

Place long-distance telephone calls at the **Office of Communications** (tel. 633-1126, fax 633-9111; open 24 hours) diagonally across from the Fono Building in Fagatogo. Go at odd hours as this office is jammed around mid-afternoon.

Laundromats and Toilets

Maria Laundromat (tel. 633-5980; open daily until midnight), up the street opposite Fagatogo Market, charges 75 cents to wash or dry. You'll save 25 cents on the washing by going to **Mary's Laundromat,** opposite Herb and Sia's Motel in Fagatogo, and there are many other laundromats around the island (ask locals where they are).

The nameless laundromat next to The Tool Shop opposite the fisheries dock in Malaloa has public showers (US$1) as well as washing machines.

Public toilets are next to the Jean P. Haydon Museum and near Da Maks Restaurant at the market.

Yachting Facilities

Harbormaster permitting, anchor your vessel as far away from the noise and smell of the canneries and power plant as you can. When all is calm, the stench can be almost unbearable. There's bad holding in the harbor because the soft oozy bottom is covered with plastic bags. Lock your dinghy when you go ashore.

The **Pago Pago Yacht Club** (tel. 633-2465; Monday to Thursday 1130-2000, Friday to Sunday 1130-2100) at Utulei is a friendly place worth frequenting in the late afternoon if you're looking to hitch a ride to Apia, Fiji, Wallis, Vava'u, or wherever. They can call any yachts in the vicinity over VHF channel 16 radio. Check their notice board, or borrow a book from their exchange. Friday at 1700 the whole yachting community

converges here for happy hour-priced drinks and free *pupus* (snacks). That's also the time when local members break out their longboats *(fautasi)* for a row around the harbor. The luncheon menu is also good and all visitors are most welcome (ignore the Members Only sign on the door).

Pago Pago is a good place for cruising yachts to provision—ask about case discounts. For example, **Tom Ho Ching Inc.** (tel. 633-2430; open Monday to Saturday 0700-2030, Sunday 0700-1900) in Faga'alu has good case lot prices on a variety of U.S. products. An even better place is **Cost-U-Less** (tel. 699-5975; weekdays 0900-2000, Saturday 0900-1900, Sunday 1100-1800), a warehouse-style bulk store in Tafuna on the road from 'Ili'ili to the airport. Manager Jim Lutgen swears he won't be undersold. It's also easy to order yacht supplies from the U.S. mainland, and they're imported duty-free.

Tom French of **Safety Systems** (tel. 633-1701) at Faga'alu can repair life rafts and fire prevention systems for yachts.

Information Offices

The **Office of Tourism** (weekdays 0730-1600; tel. 633-1091), next to the courthouse in Fagatogo, can supply the usual maps and brochures and answer questions. (This office has moved half a dozen times in as many years, so don't be surprised if they've moved again.)

You can get USGS topographical maps of American Samoa at the **Island Business Center** (tel. 633-4444), behind Tedi of Samoa in Fagatogo.

The **Wesley Bookshop** (Box 4105, Pago Pago 96799; tel. 633-2201) at Fagatogo carries books by Samoan novelist Albert Wendt.

The **Economic Development and Planning Office** (tel. 633-5155) in the Executive Office Building in Utulei sells the *American Samoa Statistical Digest* (US$7).

There's good reading at the **Feleti Pacific Library** (tel. 633-1182; weekdays 0730-1200 and 1300-1530) in Fagatogo. The Community College between Utulei and Leone has a library (tel. 699-1151), which is open Monday and Wednesday 0730-1800, Tuesday, Thursday, and Friday 0730-1600.

Hawaiian Airlines (tel. 699-1875), Polynesian Airlines (tel. 699-9126), and Samoa Air (tel. 699-9106) all have their offices at the airport. If possible, reconfirm your flight out as soon as you arrive. The travel agencies directly above the post office in Fagatogo sell air tickets for the same price as the airlines, and they are usually less crowded and more helpful.

Health

There are no private doctors on Tutuila. The 140-bed **LBJ Tropical Medical Center** (tel. 633-1222, fax 633-1869) in Faga'alu has doctors on call 24 hours a day in the Outpatients Department (US$2 fee). A dental checkup is also US$2 (appointment required). Inpatient rates at the hospital are US$60 a day. Prescription drugs are free, but no malaria pills are available.

The Drug Store (tel. 633-4630) has branches in Nu'uuli and on the road to the hospital.

GETTING AROUND

For an American territory, bus services on Tutuila are extremely good. Family-owned *aiga* buses offer unscheduled service from Fagatogo to all the outlying villages. You can flag them down anywhere along their route, and you bang on the roof when you want to get off. Not all the buses are marked with a destination, however; also, there's no service after 1600 on Saturday and very little on Sunday or after dark any day. No standing is allowed, so the rides are usually a lot of fun. Most buses play blaring music.

Bus fares are very reasonable. You pay as you leave and it's best to carry small change. A trip anywhere in the congested zone from the canneries to the hospital is 25 cents. Westbound to the airport intersection is 50 cents, 75 cents to Leone, US$1 to Amanave, US$1.25 to Fagamalo; eastbound it's 50 cents to Laulii, 75 cents to Avaio or Fagasa, US$1 to Aoloaufou or Tula. Service from Fagatogo to Leone is fairly frequent, and you can change buses there for points west. Change at Pavaiai for Aoloaufou. The bus across the island to Vatia leaves from in front of Da Mak Restaurant at Fagatogo market about once an hour (US$1.50 or US$2).

Taxis are expensive and it's important to agree on the price before getting into a meterless taxi anywhere on Tutuila. Expect to pay around US$1 a mile. You'll find taxi stands at the market and airport (tel. 699-1179), otherwise call **Island Taxi** (tel. 633-5645), **Pago Cab Service** (tel. 633-5545), or **Samoa Cab Service** (tel. 633-5870).

Royal Samoa Travel (tel. 633-2017), next to the Fono at Fagatogo, offers three-hour sightseeing tours of either the east or west sides of Tutuila at US$35 pp (two-person minimum).

Car Rentals

Bus service to the north coast villages of Fagamalo, Fagasa, Masefau, Aoa, and Onenoa is infrequent, so to reach them easily you'll need to rent a car. The three main rental car companies have counters at the airport. If no one is present, use the nearby public telephones to call around, checking current prices and requesting a car delivery to the airport.

Avis (tel. 699-4409 at the main office at Pavaiai, tel. 699-2746 at the airport, fax 699-4305) charges US$35 a day, plus US$8 insurance, for the cheapest car.

Royal Samoa Car Rental (tel. 633-4545 at the Rainmaker Hotel, tel. 688-7715 after hours) only staffs their airport counter for Hawaiian Airlines flights. They charge US$45 daily for a non-a/c car, plus US$5 for third-party liability insurance (collision insurance not available).

Pavitts U-Drive (tel. 699-1456 during business hours, tel. 699-1725 after hours) usually has a representative at the airport during the day and also for all Hawaiian Airlines flights. Pavitts charges US$45-50 a day.

All rates include unlimited mileage. Most of the agencies only rent to persons over the age of 25, although Avis will do business with you if you're 21 or older. Your home driver's license will be accepted. Lock your car and don't leave valuables in sight. One of the biggest problems with driving on Tutuila is the lack of places to pull over and get out. Most villages have open *fales* facing the beach, so you'll often feel like an intruder. Driving is on the right and seat belts are mandatory.

THE MANU'A GROUP

The three small islands of the Manu'a Group, 100 km east of Tutuila, offer spectacular scenery in a quiet village environment. Ta'u is the territory's most traditional island, but the beaches are far better and more numerous on Ofu and Olosega. All three islands feature stimulating hiking possibilities and an opportunity for the adventurer to escape the rat race on Tutuila. The biggest hassle is canine: a real or pretended stone will keep the dogs at bay.

Although a couple of small guesthouses are available, few tourists make it to Manu'a. Regular air service from Tutuila has now made these islands more accessible, but book early as local commuters fill the flights. Remember that telephone calls from Tutuila to the Manu'a Group cost only 10 cents each, so don't hesitate to call ahead to check accommodations.

OFU AND OLOSEGA

Ofu and Olosega appear to be the remaining northern portions of a massive volcano whose southern side disintegrated into the sea. Some of the best snorkeling is around the concrete bridge that links these soaring volcanic islands; just beware of currents. The strong current between Ofu and Nuutele islands makes snorkeling off Alaufau or Ofu villages risky, though the small-boat harbor just north of Alaufau is better protected than the one on Ta'u. The airstrip is by a long white beach on the south side of Ofu, about an hour's walk from Olosega village, and it's still possible to have all to yourself this quintessential Polynesian paradise of swaying palms, magnificent reef, and mountains rising out of the sea. Bring your own snorkeling gear as none is available locally.

To climb to the television tower atop Ofu's **Tumu Mountain** (494 meters), take the jeep track up the hill from near the floating docks at Alaufau village and continue up to the ridge top, then over the mountain to a spectacular lookout on Leolo Ridge (458 meters) above the airstrip. Notice how the vegetation changes as you rise.

For Olosega's **Piumafua Mountain,** follow the shoreline south almost to Maga Point, then cut back up along the ridge to the 639-meter summit. The cloud forest atop the steep hill *after* you think you've hit the peak is like the Old Forest in *The Lord of the Rings.* No goblins—only mosquitoes—but be very careful not to get turned around, as the trees cut off the view, though the forests on Ofu and Olosega are open and easy to cross after the trails give out. There is no trail along Olosega's forbidding east coast.

Accommodations and Food

Most visitors stay at **Vaoto Lodge** (Box 1809, Pago Pago 96799; tel. 655-1120), beside the airstrip on Ofu. The 10 fan-cooled rooms with private bath are US$35/40/50 single/double/triple. Cooking facilities are not available but hosts Tito, Marty, and Marge Malae will prepare good local meals for you (US$13 for all three). They make you feel just like one of the family; ask Tito to tell you a ghost story.

Don and Ilaisa's Motel (Box 932, Pago Pago 96799; tel. 655-1212) in Olosega village has five rooms at US$20/35 single/double. Not only is the price a little lower than at Vaoto Lodge but you'll get more of a feeling for outer island life. There's a small store in the village where you can get basic supplies. Often the whole building is rented out to contract workers for extended periods, so be sure to call ahead to check availability.

OFU AND OLOSEGA

Prior to arrival, you could also try calling Faufano Autele (tel. 655-1123), who can sometimes arrange budget accommodations on Ofu.

Rather than camp along Ofu's beautiful south coast beach, keep east toward the bridge, then just before you reach the bridge cut down to the deserted beach on the north side of the island. You'll be less likely to have visitors here than you would by the road, but bring all the food and water you'll need.

TA'U

Ta'u is a rectangular island 10 km long and five km wide. It's only 11 km southeast of Olosega, with a submarine volcano between the two. Eons ago the south side of Ta'u collapsed, leaving dramatic 500-meter-high cliffs that rise directly from the southern sea. Five smaller craters dot the steep northern slopes of Lata Mountain (995 meters), the highest peak in American Samoa. The entire southeast corner of Ta'u is to be included in the proposed National Park of American Samoa.

From Ta'u the Tui Manu'a ruled the entire group. In 1925, as a young woman of 24, Margaret Mead researched her book, *Coming of Age in Samoa*, at Luma village on Ta'u. The present inhabitants of Ta'u live in villages at the northeast and northwest corners of the island. The most sheltered anchorage for yachts is at Faleasao, while the small-boat harbor is at Luma. The reef pass is very narrow, and Luma harbor is used mostly by local fishing boats (not recommended for yachts). The airstrip is at Fitiuta in the northeast corner of the island.

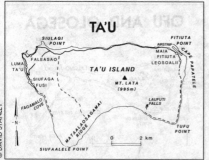

Sights

At Luma village, see the tomb of the Tui Manu'a and other chiefly burials near the **Sacred Water,** or "royal pool" (dry). Also of interest is the **cave of Ma'ava,** the legendary giant. There's a nice beach at **Fagamalo Cove** halfway down the west coast south of Fusi.

Waves crash into Ta'u's rocky, volcanic southern coast, and cliffs soar nearly 1,000 meters to Mt. Lata. It's possible to hike south along the coast from Fitiuta to 450-meter-high **Laufuti Falls** and return in a day, although fallen trees block the trail in places. Beyond Laufuti one must bushwhack. Craters punctuate the island's wild, thickly forested interior, known for its steep slopes and gullies. Terrain and bush can change suddenly from easy hiking to difficult, and most of the upland area is inaccessible.

Accommodations and Food

The most convenient place to stay is **Fitiuta Lodge** (Box 3953, Pago Pago 96799; tel. 677-3501 or 633-5841), in Fitiuta village a short walk from the airstrip. The eight rooms are US$25/30 single/double and cooking facilities are provided.

The **Ta'u Motel** (tel. 677-3467 or 677-3504, fax 677-3155), also known as "Niumata's Guest House," is near the small-boat harbor in Luma village, on the opposite side of the island from the airstrip. It has nine clean rooms at US$30/40 single/double, and you can cook your own food. Often the entire motel is booked out by local contractors for extended periods, so call ahead.

No restaurants are to be found on Ta'u, only four small stores and a bakery. If your baggage isn't overweight, bring some food with you on the plane from Tutuila.

CORAL ATOLLS

Rose Atoll

Discovered by French navigator Louis de Freycinet in 1819, Rose Atoll was visited by the U.S. Exploring Expedition under Commodore Charles Wilkes in 1839. In 1921 the U.S. claimed this uninhabited atoll, 125 km east of Ta'u. A reef of pink coral surrounds the square, three-by-three-km atoll with a pass into the lagoon. Of the atoll's two small islands, Rose is covered with coconut and other trees, while Sand is devoid of vegetation.

Large numbers of red-footed boobies and frigate birds nest near the top of Rose's large *buka* trees, while black noddies and white terns use the middle and lower branches. Green and hawksbill turtles lay eggs on the beach. To protect the turtles and seabirds, in 1974 Rose Atoll was included in the **Pacific Islands National Wildlife Refuges,** administered by the U.S. Fish and Wildlife Service (Box 50167, Honolulu, HI 96850, U.S.A.). Special permission is required to land.

Swains Island

Swains Island, 340 km northwest of Tutuila, is a circular coral atoll about two km across and 13 km around the fringing reef. There's a large lagoon in the center not connected to the sea. Swains is far closer to Tokelau than to the rest of Samoa. In fact, its customary owners were the Tokelauans of Fakaofo, who knew it as Olohega. In 1856 a New England whaling captain, Eli Jennings, arrived to set up a coconut plantation with the help of Polynesian labor; his descendants still run it as a private estate today. At present there are 16 resident humans on Swains, 10 men and six women.

Olohega was included in the Union Group (Tokelau), which Britain incorporated into the Gilbert and Ellice Islands Colony in 1916. In 1925, when Britain transferred Tokelau to N.Z. administration, the U.S. took advantage of the opportunity to annex Swains to American Samoa. Finally, in 1980 the U.S. government bullied the Tokelauans into signing a treaty recognizing American sovereignty over Swains as a condition for the withdrawal of U.S. "claims" to the entire Tokelau Group and recognition of Tokelau's 200-nautical-mile fisheries zone.

GORDON OHLIGER

WESTERN SAMOA

INTRODUCTION

The verdant, luxuriant isles of Western Samoa, two-thirds of the way between Hawaii and New Zealand, lie in the very heart of the South Pacific. Independent since 1962, the Western Samoans have retained their ancient customs as nowhere else in Polynesia, and the *fa'a Samoa,* or Samoan way, continues to flourish. Though both Western Samoa and nearby American Samoa spring from the same roots, their contrasting lifestyles permit a fascinating case study on the impact of differing patterns of development on a Pacific people.

This society has attracted poets rather than painters. Robert Louis Stevenson spent the last five years of his life here, and Rupert Brooke was enraptured by the islands and their people:

You lie on a mat in a cool Samoan hut, and look out on the white sand under the high palms, and a gentle sea, and the black line of the reef a mile out, and moonlight over everything. . . . And then among it all

are the loveliest people in the world, moving and dancing like gods and goddesses, very quietly and mysteriously, and utterly content. It is sheer beauty, so pure that it's difficult to breathe it in.

Travelers inbound from a dreary industrial world may be forgiven if they imagine they've arrived in paradise, but there's more to it. In a series of provocative novels, Samoan author Albert Wendt has portrayed the conflicting pressures of *palagi* (foreign) life on his people. The protagonist in *Sons for the Return Home* finds he can no longer accept the *fa'a*-sanctioned authority of his mother, while *Leaves of the Banyan Tree* explores the universal themes of a changing Samoan society. In *Pouliuli,* the complex social relationships of village life unravel in a drama of compelling force. Wendt's books bring us closer to the complexity of a third-world Samoa shaken by economic crises and searching desperately for a formula to reconcile timeworn traditions and contemporary consumer needs. Samoa is not a passive place: you'll be challenged to define your own role as an outsider looking in.

The Land

Western Samoa is made up of four inhabited and five uninhabited islands totaling 2,842 square km, a bit bigger than the American state of Rhode Island. Unlike most Pacific countries, which are scattered across vast areas, all of these islands are in one main cluster. Upolu, the most developed and populous, contains the capital, Apia; Savai'i is a much larger island. Between these sit well-populated Apolima and Manono, while the five islets off southeast Upolu shelter only seabirds. The fringing reefs around the two big islands protect soft, radiantly calm shores.

Samoa's volcanic islands increase in age from west to east. Savai'i, though dormant, spewed lava this century; the now-extinct cones of western Upolu erupted much more recently than those farther east. Well-weathered Tutuila and Manu'a in American Samoa are older yet, while 10-million-year-old Rose Island is a classic atoll.

Savai'i is a massive shield-type island formed by fast-flowing lava building up in layers over a long period. The low coast gradually slopes upward to a broad, 1,858-meter center of several parallel chains. Upolu's elongated dorsal spine of extinct shield volcanoes slopes more steeply on the south than the north. The eastern part of the island is rough and broken, while broad plains are found in the west.

Climate

Samoa is closer to the equator than Tonga and Rarotonga, thus it's noticeably hotter and more humid year-round. From May to October (winter) the days are cooled by the southeast trades; winds vary from west to north in the rainy season, November to April (summer). Practically speaking, the seasonal variations are not great, and long periods of sun are common even during the "rainy" months. Southern Upolu gets more rain than northern, but much of it falls at night.

December to March is hurricane time; ships at Apia should put to sea at the first warning, as the harbor is unsafe when a storm blows out of the north. In recent years, Samoa has suffered an increasing number of devastating hurricanes partially due to the greenhouse effect as the surrounding seas warm up.

Flora and Fauna

Rainforests thrive in the mountain areas, where heavy rainfall nurtures huge tree ferns and slow-growing, moss-laden hardwoods. The vegetation is sparse in the intermediate zones, where more recent lava flows fail to hold moisture or soil. The richer coastal strip is well planted in vegetable gardens and coconut plantations. The national flower is the *teuila* or red ginger, an elongated stalk with many red petals.

Although smaller than Savai'i, the rich volcanic soil of Upolu supports 72% of the population of Western Samoa; much of Savai'i is barren due to recent lava flows and the porousness of the soil, which allows rapid runoff of moisture. The rainforests of Samoa are threatened by exploitive logging operations for shortsighted economic gain and already 80% of the lowland tropical rainforests have been replaced by plantations or logged. Replanting is usually done in teak and mahogany, which native birds cannot use.

About 16 of 34 land bird species are unique to Samoa. One such species, the toothbilled

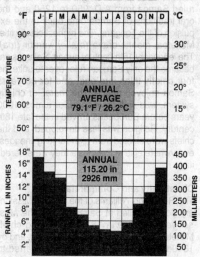

APIA'S CLIMATE

ANNUAL AVERAGE 79.1°F / 26.2°C

ANNUAL 115.20 in 2926 mm

pigeon or *manumea (Didunculus strigirostris),* is thought to be a living link with toothbilled birds of fossil times. Due to overhunting and habitat destruction, all native species of pigeons and doves are approaching extinction. In 1993 parliament banned all hunting of fruit bats (flying foxes) and Pacific pigeons for five years. There are no snakes on Upolu, although several harmless species are found on Savai'i.

HISTORY AND GOVERNMENT

Prehistory

Samoa was named for the sacred *(sa)* chickens *(moa)* of Lu, son of Tagaloa, the god of creation. Samoan tradition asserts that Savai'i was Hawaiki, the legendary Polynesian homeland where the Samoans originated. Archaeologists confirm that the Polynesians had settled in Samoa by 1000 B.C. and here evolved their distinctive culture. It was a beautiful, comfortable, productive place to live. Their vegetables thrived in the rich volcanic soil, and the lagoon provided ample fish. They had found their true home; not for another millennium did small groups push farther east from this "cradle of Polynesia" to colonize Tahiti and the Marquesas.

The ancient Samoans maintained regular contact with Fiji and Tonga; Tongan invaders ruled Samoa from A.D. 950 to 1250 and the oral traditions of Samoa date back to the expulsion of the Tongans. The highest chiefly title, Malietoa, means brave *(malie)* warrior *(toa).* The legendary 15th-century queen, Salamasina, became the only Samoan ruler ever to unite the four chiefly titles into one, and for 60 years Samoa enjoyed peace. The *matai,* or chiefly system, was well developed for almost 1000 years before Europeans arrived in the late 18th century. Religion was less developed, and the chiefs were elected from high-ranking lineages: everywhere else in Polynesia they were hereditary.

Christianity and Commercialization

The Rev. John Williams of the London Missionary Society called at Savai'i aboard the *Messenger of Peace* in 1830. The ruling chief, Malietoa Vai'inupo, welcomed Williams, and by 1840 most Samoans had been converted to Protestantism. The missionaries taught the need for clothing, and white traders were soon arriving to sell the required cotton cloth. The first copra trader in Samoa was John Williams Jr., son of the missionary, who exported six tons in 1842. In the 1840s Malua College was established by the church. In true Samoan fashion, Malietoa's rival Mata'afa Iosefo converted to Catholicism in 1845.

In 1856 the German trading firm Johann Godeffroy and Son opened a store at Apia, and within a few years over a hundred Europeans resided in the new town. The first central government was formed by a group of district chiefs at Mulinu'u in 1868. During the 1870s German businessmen purchased large tracts of family land from individual chiefs for the establishment of coconut plantations using Chinese and Melanesian labor. Germany, Britain, and the U.S. soon appointed consuls.

In 1873 an American, Col. A.B. Steinberger, assisted the Samoan chiefs in creating a constitution; two years later he had himself appointed premier. His role was not supported by the U.S., however, although he was an official State Department agent. After five months in the premiership, Steinberger was arrested and taken to Fiji by the captain of a British warship who suspected him of German sympathies. He never returned.

Instability and Intrigue

The new Samoan government fumbled on and signed treaties of friendship with the U.S. and Germany. An intermittent civil war between the chiefly orator groups Pule and Tumua over the four highest ceremonial titles dragged on through most of the late 19th century. Rival Europeans sided with the different factions, but no one was able to establish a single, stable government. In 1879 the European residents of Apia took advantage of the situation to enact a municipal convention, which put control of the town in their hands.

In 1887 the German company Deutsche Handels-und Plantagen-Gesellshaft (successor to Godeffroy), tiring of the vicissitudes of native government in an area where they controlled 80% of the business, staged an unofficial coup. The nominal king, Malietoa Laupepa, was forced to flee, and the Germans installed a puppet in his place. The German regime, supported by German naval units but not sanctioned by Berlin, soon alienated Samoans, British, and Americans.

In March 1889 an armed Samoan rebellion brought the warships of Germany, Britain, and the U.S. to Apia's port in a major international confrontation. This came to a ludicrous pass when the seven men-of-war refused to abandon Apia Harbor in the face of a hurricane, in fear of leaving the field to the opposing Great Powers. This colonial stupidity and arrogance caused the wreck of four ships; two others were beached and damaged; 92 German and 54 American lives were lost. The German ship *Adler* was thrown up onto the reef, and only the British *Calliope* escaped to the open sea. The Samoans saw it as an act of God.

After this disaster the military posturing abated, and in June 1889 a Tripartite Treaty was signed in Berlin under which the three powers agreed to the formation of a neutral government led by Malietoa Laupepa with the three consuls controlling Apia. Yet instability and open factional warfare alternated with ineffectual government until 1899 when new treaties were drawn up partitioning Samoa between Germany and the U.S. (see "American Samoa"). Britain withdrew completely in exchange for German concessions in Tonga and the Solomons.

The Colonial Period

On 1 March 1900 the German flag was raised over Western Samoa. Under Governors Wilhelm Solf (1900-1912) and Erich Schultz (1912-1914), the Germans created the first public school system, built and staffed a hospital, and constructed the only roads that existed right up until 1942. Though both Solf and Schultz tried to work according to the principle that the Samoans could be guided but not forced, they deported Samoan resisters to the Mariana Islands in 1909. The Germans carefully studied traditional Samoan culture in order to play rival factions off against each other.

On 29 August 1914, at the beginning of WW I, the last German governor surrendered without a fight to a New Zealand Expeditionary Force. The vast German plantations seized at the time are still held by the government-owned Western Samoa Trust Estates Corporation (WSTEC).

Most of the 2,000 Chinese the Germans had brought from southern China to work the plantations were repatriated.

The new N.Z. administrators were real bunglers compared to the Germans. In November 1918, they allowed the SS *Talune* to introduce influenza to the territory, and 8,000 Samoans—22% of the population—died; a stricter quarantine kept the epidemic out of American Samoa and Fiji. This awkward administration revived a strong opposition movement, the Mau, which had existed during colonial times. The Mau not only rejected colonial authority but turned away from Western development and culture. Boycotts of imported goods were organized. In 1929 New Zealand crushed the Mau by military force although the movement continued to enjoy the support of most of the villages, chiefs, and part-Samoan businessmen.

Only in 1947 was there a concrete step toward independence when a legislative assembly was created with some members elected from among the *matai* (chiefs). In 1960 a constitution was adopted; a year later both constitution and independence were approved in a plebiscite by universal ballot. And finally in 1962, with a Labour government in power in N.Z., Western Samoa became the first Polynesian nation to reestablish its independence in the 20th century. In 1976 Western Samoa joined the United Nations.

Government

Western Samoa has a parliamentary system with a prime minister elected by Parliament from its ranks. The prime minister chooses an eight-member Cabinet, also from among Parliament. Since independence, His Highness Malietoa Tanumafili II, Paramount Chief of Samoa, has been ceremonial head of state, a position he may hold for life. The next head of state will be chosen by Parliament for a five-year term from among the four *tama aiga* or paramount chiefs (Malietoa, Mata'afa, Tuimalealiifano, and Tupua Tamasese).

Until recently, 47 of the 49 members of parliament were elected every five years by the 18,000 registered chiefs or *matai* (most of them men) on a constituency basis, and only two by non-Samoan residents on the Individual Voters Roll. In October 1990 all citizens aged 21 and over were allowed to vote in a referendum that approved universal suffrage and an extension of the term of office from three to four years. The old system of allowing only *matai* to run for the 47 Samoan seats was retained, however. An untitled person *(tautaua)* can only be elected to parliament after he/she first becomes a *matai,* a situation that helps preserve traditional Samoan culture.

There are two main political parties, the Human Rights Protection Party and the Samoa National Development Party. As elsewhere in Anglophone Oceania, political parties revolve more around personalities than policies. Campaign funds are used to "buy" votes and official corruption is epidemic.

The 11 administrative districts (A'ana, Aiga-i-le-Tai, Atua, Fa'asaleleaga, Gaga'emauga, Gagaifomauga, Palauli, Satupa'itea, Tuamasaga, Va'a-o-Fonoti, and Vaisigano) are used only for the organization of government services, and district officers don't exist. Western Samoa has no army and very few police: those responsibilities are assumed by the *matai.*

ECONOMY

In recent years Western Samoa's economy has been battered by hurricanes, agricultural decline, and government mismanagement. Budget deficits and the foreign debt have blown out of all proportion, and by 1993 the country owed international agencies such as the Asian Development Bank and the World Bank WS$346 million, largely as a result of infrastructure and agricultural loans. In 1993-94 tens of millions went down the drain to support a reckless expansion program by Polynesian Airlines, and vast sums have been squandered on flashy new buildings in Apia. In early 1994 a 10% value-added tax was imposed to replenish government coffers; a few months later an auditor-general's report alleging high-level corruption was swept under the carpet. Two opposition politicians who organized a public protest over this situation were charged with "sedition" (the case was later thrown out of court).

Western Samoa's per-capita gross domestic product is A$936 (1990) whereas in nearby American Samoa it's A$6660 (1985). Thus many Western Samoans migrate to Pago Pago to seek employment in the tuna canneries where the starting rate is US$3 an hour (compared to a private-sector statutory minimum wage of WS$1.125 an hour in Western Samoa). Tens of thousands of Samoans now live in American Samoa, the U.S., New Zealand, and Australia, and remittances from them help keep the economy afloat.

Two-thirds of the workforce is engaged in subsistence agriculture, and fisheries and agriculture account for over a third of the gross domestic product, the highest such proportion in the Pacific except for that of Solomon Islands. Local fishermen go out in locally made aluminum *alia* catamaran fishing boats to catch tuna around FADS (fish aggregation devices). Western Samoans have to hustle to obtain cash money, perhaps one reason why they look thinner and healthier than American Samoans.

Although the *tala* is not a convertible currency, in 1989 Western Samoa launched an offshore banking center similar to that of Vanuatu and the Cook Islands. Foreign companies can pay a one-time registration fee that allows them to carry out tax-evasion operations for 20 years (local companies are barred from participating and face strict bureaucratic regulation). The biggest users of the tax-haven scheme are companies in Hong Kong, South Korea, Indonesia, and Eastern Europe.

Western Samoa receives around 40,000 overseas tourists a year, nearly half of them from American Samoa, 20% from New Zealand, and about 10% each from Australia, the U.S., and Europe. A large proportion of these arrivals are expatriate Samoans visiting relatives and friends. Tourist facilities are developing fast around the country and the collapse of Polynesian Airlines' U.S. routes in 1994 was a body blow to the country's fledgling tourist industry.

Industry

To stimulate light industry the government has established a Small Industries Center at Vaitele, on the airport highway five km west of Apia, where investing companies can obtain long-term leases at low rentals. Cheap labor and 15-year tax holidays are the main incentives to investing here. Most Western Samoan products have duty-free access to Australia and New

Zealand under SPARTECA, to Europe under the Lomé Convention, and to the U.S., Canada, and Japan under the Generalized System of Preferences (GSP) scheme.

The copra-crushing mill that opened at Vaitele in 1982 once accounted for a third of the country's export earnings, though falling prices for coconut oil and hurricane damage have reduced production to almost zero, and in 1993 the government privatized the mill. The nearby German-operated Western Samoa Breweries has been more successful with its excellent Vailima beer. Its rival, the Apia Bottling Company, produces the unpasteurized Manuia beer. The local Rothmans factory produces 50,000 cartons of cigarettes a month from raw materials imported from New Zealand.

In 1991 the Japanese corporation Yazaki transferred its automobile electrical wiring systems assembly plant from Melbourne to Vaitele, and Yazaki products now account for an estimated 82% of the country's exports. In 1993 a strike at Yazaki by workers protesting sweatshop conditions and WS$1.24-an-hour wages was quickly broken with government collusion. Since Yazaki pays no company taxes and only minimal wages to its 2,000 local employees, its real value to the Samoan economy is minimal.

Trade

Imports run 13 times higher than exports; food imports alone exceed all exports. Bony junk food not sold in its place of origin is dumped in Western Samoa: chicken backs and turkey tails from the U.S., mutton flaps and fatty canned corned beef from New Zealand. The only significant export items are automotive electrical systems, taro, coconut cream, and cocoa.

One of the largest of all insects, the rhinoceros beetle (Dynastinae) menaces the coconut plantations of the South Pacific.

During the 1950s Samoa exported 1.2 million cases of bananas a year to New Zealand but shipping problems, hurricanes, disease, and inefficiency cost them this market, which is now supplied by Ecuador. Cacao continues to decline, and taro shipments to the Polynesian community in N.Z. were halted in 1994 due to an outbreak of taro leaf blight. Copra production has also dwindled due to low prices and hurricane damage. Infestations by rhinoceros beetles and giant African snails have hurt Samoan agriculture, and some 7,000 hectares of the country's best land is held by the inefficient WSTEC.

New Zealand, Japan, the U.S., and Australia profit most from the trade imbalance—a classic case of economic neocolonialism. New Zealand exports five times as much to Western Samoa as it buys, the U.S. six times as much, Australia seven times as much, Japan 96,520 times as much! Foreign aid covers about 60% of the trade imbalance with the main donors being the Asian Development Bank, Japan, Australia, New Zealand, the United Nations Development Program, and the European Union, in about that order of importance.

THE PEOPLE

Samoans are the second-largest group of full-blooded Polynesians in the world, behind the Maoris. About 89% of the population is Samoan and another 10% is part-Samoan. Half of Western Samoa's people live in the northwest corner of Upolu, from Apia to the airport. Due to large-scale emigration to New Zealand and the U.S., the population growth rate is very low, averaging only 0.28% a year between 1974 and 1991. In all, 85,000 Samoans live in N.Z. and 50,000 in the U.S.

The Samoan approach to life is almost the opposite of the European: property, wealth, and success are all thought of in communal or family rather than individual terms. Eighty percent of the country's land is owned communally by family groups *(aiga)* and cannot be sold or mortgaged. The *matai* work to increase the prosperity and prestige of their *aiga*.

Samoans are very conservative and resist outside interference in village affairs. The Samoans have an almost feudal concern for protocol, rank, and etiquette. They lead a highly complex, stylized, and polished way of life. Today, however, they are being forced to reconcile the *fa'a Samoa* with the competitive demands of Western society, where private property and the individual come first. The greatest burden of adjustment is on the young; theirs is the highest suicide rate in the world.

Social Structure

Since ancient times, Samoan society has been based on the *aiga,* a large extended family group with a *matai* as its head, who is elected by consensus of the clan. The *matai* is responsible for the *aiga's* lands, assets, and distribution. He ensures that no relative is ever in need, settles disputes, sees to the clan's social obligations, and is the *aiga's* representative on the district or village council *(fono)*. A *pulenu'u* (village mayor) appointed by the government presides over the *fono.* The 1991 census reported that 85.7% of the total population were living under the direct authority of a *matai* with most of the rest residents of Apia.

The authority of traditional village law is enshrined in the Samoan constitution, and judges in the regular courts can take into account village fines or whether the offender has performed the traditional apology *(ifoga)* when passing sentence. A villager who chooses to ignore the rulings of his village *fono* faces ostracism, banishment, and worse. Stoning, arson, and even murder has resulted in exceptional cases.

Blood relationships count to a large extent in the elections of the *matai,* but even untitled persons can be elected on merit. In this formalized, ritualized society the only way a person can achieve place is to become a *matai.* This semidemocracy gives Samoan society its enduring strength.

A number of *aiga* comprise a village *(nu'u)* under an orator or talking chief *(tulafale)* and a titular or high chief *(ali'i).* The high chiefs are considered too grand to speak for themselves at ceremonies, thus the need for orators. The *tulafale* conduct eloquent debates, give ceremonial speeches, and are the real sources of authority in the community. Direct conflicts are avoided

through consensus decision-making. The villages are largely autonomous, and family welfare comes before individual rights—pure preindustrial socialism.

Villages

Western Samoans live in 362 villages near the seashore. Families share their work and food, and everyone has a place to live and a sense of belonging. Each immediate family has its own residence, called a *fale* (pronounced "fah-lay"), which may be round or oval. Without walls, it's the least private dwelling on earth. The only furniture may be a large trunk or dresser. A *fale* is built on a stone platform, with mats covering the pebble floor. Mats or blinds are let down to shelter and shield the *fale* from storms—a very cool, clean, fresh place to live.

Most food is grown in village gardens, and cooking is done in an earth oven *(umu).* Families are large, eight children being "about right." The men wear a vivid wraparound skirt known as a *lavalava.* The women of the village are often seen working together in the women's committee *fale,* making traditional handicrafts. The *fono* meets in the *fale taimalo.* Also a part of each village is the cricket pitch—looking like an isolated stretch of sidewalk. Notice too the *tia,* stone burial mounds with several stepped layers under which old chiefs are buried.

Kava and Tattoos

Unlike Fiji and Tonga, the Samoan kava ceremony is an exceptional occurrence held at important gatherings of *matai,* seldom witnessed by visitors. A *taupou* prepares the drink in a traditional wooden bowl; in the old days she was a fiercely guarded virgin daughter of a village high chief, a ceremonial princess. Chanting and dancing usually accompany this serving ceremony.

Tattooing is one of the few Polynesian cultural attributes adopted by Western civilization, and although missionaries a hundred years ago predicted its demise, it's still widespread among Samoan men. The tattoos, extending from waist to knees, are a visual badge of courage, as 16 or more highly painful sessions are required to apply a full *pe'a.* Once the tattooing begins it cannot end until completed, or the subject will be permanently marked with dishonor. Until recently a full body tattoo could only be applied to

SOUTHERN CROSS STARGAZING

Look for the Southern Cross (Crux), a constellation in the Milky Way near the south celestial pole. There's a much larger false cross to the right, but the real one is brighter. The "pointer stars," Alpha and Beta Centaurus, make it easy to positively identify the Southern Cross. Follow the longer axis of the Cross to the left about five times its length to locate the South Pole. When you are near the equator this line will intersect the horizon. As you move farther south the axis will indicate a location higher in the sky until it points directly overhead when you are

at the South Pole itself. Thus, Crux can be used both to find south and to determine latitude, which is 0° at the equator, 13° 50' at Apia, and 90° at the South Pole. At Apia, if you follow the axis line of the Southern Cross about five times its length to the left it will indicate a point of 13° 50' above the horizon, the latitude of Apia. Seen only from below about 20° north latitude, the Southern Cross is like a brilliant cluster of jewels in the southern sky. It appears on the national flags of Western Samoa, New Zealand, Australia, and Papua New Guinea.

a talking chief as a mark of his rank, but today anyone who can stand the pain is eligible. The designs originally represented a large fruit bat, although this is only recognizable today in the lines of the upper wings above the waist. This art dates back to ancient times, and contemporary Samoan tattoo designs are strikingly similar to incised decorations on *Lapita* pottery thousands of years old.

Religion

Ever since Rev. John Williams landed in 1830, the Samoans have taken Christianity very seriously and Samoan missionaries have gone on to convert residents of many other island groups (Tuvalu, the Solomons, and New Guinea). Many believe that Samoa was the biblical Garden of Eden. About 43% of the population belong to the Congregational Christian Church (successor of the London Missionary Society), 21% are Catholic, 17% Methodist, and 10% Mormon. The numbers of Mormons, Seventh-Day Adventists, and Assemblies of God are growing fast as the Congregational Christian Church declines. While the Samoans have embraced the rituals of Christianity, concepts such as individual sin are less accepted.

Each village has one or more churches, and the pastor's house is often the largest residence.

Minister of religion is usually the best-paying job in the village and many pastors enjoy an affluent lifestyle at the expense of their congregations. Some villages have regulations that *require* villagers to attend church as many as three times on Sunday, and choir practice weekly. Many of the schools are church-operated.

There's a daily vespers called *sa* around 1800 for family prayers. All movement is supposed to cease at this time; some villages are rather paranoid about it and levy fines on offenders. It only lasts about 10 minutes, so sit quietly under a tree or on the beach until you hear a gong, bell, or somebody beating a pan to signal "all's clear." Many villages also have a 2200 curfew.

CONDUCT AND CUSTOMS

Custom Fees

In many parts of Western Samoa it's an established village law that outsiders pay a set fee to swim at the local beach or waterhole, or to visit a cave, lava tube, waterfall, etc. Sometimes the amount is posted on a sign, but other times it's not. Although it may seem to Westerners that the Samoans have no *right* to charge for these things, the way the Samoans look at it, what *right* do visitors have to enjoy them free of charge? The best solution, if you don't wish to pay, is to just carry on quietly to some other beach or waterhole that is free or where no one's around. Don't argue with them: it's their country.

Be aware, however, that a few rip-offs have been associated with this—sometimes an unauthorized person will demand payment, and you can't really tell if it's for real. The charge should be WS$1 to WS$10 maximum. If someone asks more, try bargaining. Some tourists stupidly pay whatever is charged, so the locals figure there's no harm asking.

We recommend that you only pay customary fees of this kind if there's a sign clearly stating the amount or someone asks for the money *beforehand,* thus giving you the choice of going in or not. Resist paying anything if someone tries to collect as you're leaving (unless there's a sign), and *never* give the money to children. If there's a dispute or you're in doubt about the authenticity of a customary fee, politely say you want to pay the money directly to the *pulenu'u.* He will straighten things out quickly. Keep your cool in all of this—Samoans respect courtesy far more than anger or threats. All customary fees we know about are listed in this book. Please let us know if we missed any.

Culture Shock

This can work two ways in Samoa, both you being intimidated by the unfamiliar surroundings and the Samoans being put off by your seeming affluence and intrusiveness. Of course, this doesn't apply in Apia, but in remote villages you may be viewed with suspicion, especially if you arrive in a taxi or rental car, the daily hire of which costs more than a Samoan villager might earn in a month. You can easily smooth the situation over by smiling, waving, and saying *talofa* to those you meet. Be the first to say hello and everyone will feel a lot more comfortable.

Requests

Samoan culture is extremely manipulative, and there's a saying that you can buy anything with a *fa'amolemole* (please). Samoans are constantly asking each other for things; it's not just a game they play with foreigners. If you're staying in a village for long, somebody from another household may eventually come and ask you for

money or something you're carrying. It's important that you be firm with them. Explain that you're sharing what you have with your hosts, and you simply don't have money to give out. If you "loan" money, consider it a gift, for if you insist on being repaid you will only make an enemy without collecting anything. You have to form appropriate defenses in Samoa.

Theft and Violence

Nobody means any harm, and violent crime is almost unknown, but be careful: the concept of individual ownership is not entirely accepted by the Samoans. Don't leave valuables unattended. Someone might even steal your laundry off the line, so it's better to hang it up in your room. Theft from hotel rooms is also not unknown. The Bank of Western Samoa will keep a sealed envelope containing unneeded documents in their vault for about WS$5—a good precaution if you'll be staying long.

The best policy when visiting Western Samoa is to remain low-key. Don't put yourself in high-risk situations, and if you ever have to defend yourself, it's always better to try and run away. If confronted by a belligerent drunk (quite possible in the evening), humble yourself, apologize even if you did nothing wrong, and ease yourself out of the confrontation. If it ends in violence, you'll always lose, because the culture pressures relatives and friends to join in the attack even if their side is clearly wrong. Loyalty is priority number one, and proving that is a lifelong obligation.

Love and Marriage

After a few days in the country it'll become fairly obvious to male visitors that Samoan women like to marry Western men. Age is not an important factor here: teenagers smile invitingly at middle-aged bachelors. Samoans associate Europeans with the sort of affluence they see on television, and when a girl marries a *palagi* her economic situation, and that of her entire *aiga,* suddenly improves, or so they think.

If you're really smitten with a Samoan, you'll be expected to satisfy much more than just her needs. Be aware too that Samoan women are expert at stopping just short of lovemaking before they're married, and their brothers can be very hard on an insincere man who thinks he can play the game to his own advantage. Note too that marriage to a Samoan woman does not imply any legal right to stay in Samoa; in fact, the idea is that you take the woman *and* her family back and support them in your own home country. Somerset Maugham's story, "The Pool," in *The Trembling of a Leaf* deals with this subject.

Fa'a Samoa

It's considered impolite to eat while walking through a village, or to talk or eat while standing in a *fale*. Sit down cross-legged on a mat, *then* talk and eat. Don't stretch out your legs when sitting: it's bad form to point your feet at anyone or prop them up, and also a discourtesy to turn your back on a *matai*. Swaying from side to side indicates anger or contempt and gesturing with the hands is considered bad taste.

If you arrive at a house during the family prayer session, wait outside until they're finished. A sign that you are invited to enter is the laying out of mats for you to sit on. Walk around the mats, rather than over them. Shoes should be removed and left outside. Your host will give a short speech of welcome, to which you should reply by giving your impressions of the village and explaining your reason for coming, beginning with the words *susu mai* (listen). If you are offered food, try to eat a small amount even if you're not hungry.

Some villages object to the use of their beach on Sunday, and some object anytime. If someone's around, ask, or find a beach that's secluded. Public nudism is prohibited; cover up as you walk through a village. Women receive more respect when dressed in a *puletasi* (long dress) or *lavalava*, and not slacks or shorts. It's inappropriate to wear flowers or bright clothing to church.

This said, don't be intimidated by Samoan customs. Do your best to respect tradition, but rest assured the Samoans are indulgent with foreigners who make an honest blunder. Samoans are fiercely proud of the *fa'a Samoa* and will be honored to explain it to you. It's all part of the Samoan experience, not an inconvenience at all.

The *fa'a Samoa* is open to interpretation, and even "world authorities" such as Margaret Mead and Derek Freeman can create diametrically opposed theories as to just what Samoan customs were and are. Mead's version of happy, uninhibited sexuality presented in *Coming of Age in Samoa* has been challenged by Freeman's description of a violent, competitive society that prizes virginity and forbids premarital sex (see "Resources"). Albert Wendt's 1979 novel, *Pouliuli*, is a superb analysis of that "laboratory of contradictions" that is Samoa.

ON THE ROAD

Highlights

Your most long-lasting impression of Samoa may be of people living in harmony with nature, and there's no better way to experience it than by sleeping in a Samoan *fale* at Aleipata or Lepa on Upolu, or at Satuiatua on Savai'i. The bus rides from Apia to Aleipata and Lepa are also superb introductions to this exotic environment.

Samoa's most unforgettable sights draw their beauty from their natural surroundings, from the tomb of Robert Louis Stevenson on Mt. Vaea, to the Piula Cave Pool, the waterfall and pyramid at Savai'i's Letolo Plantation, and the nearby Taga blowholes. The *fia fia* dancing at Aggie Grey's Hotel in Apia is also memorable.

Sports and Recreation

Western Samoa has fewer organized recreational possibilities than some other Pacific countries, but there are unlimited opportunities to do your own thing. Hiking trails quickly become overgrown, which often makes local guides a good idea. Experienced hikers should be able to do the Lake Lanoto'o trip on their own.

The only two scuba diving companies are Samoa Marine in Apia and the scuba operator at Coconuts Beach Resort. Samoa Marine also offers deep-sea fishing. A good snorkeling locale, the Palolo Deep, is right in Apia, and Savai'i's Faga Beach is even better. There are fewer options elsewhere, due in part to narrow fringing reefs, deadly currents, and hurricane-impacted corals. Seek local advice.

Samoa is a true surfer's paradise and the best waves are off the north-facing coasts in summer, off the south-facing coasts in winter. Thus the best conditions are at Laulii, Solosolo, and Lano from December to March, and at Salani, Vaiula, and Salailua from May to August.

Golfers will enjoy the 18-hole course at Apia.

Public Holidays and Festivals

Public holidays include New Year's Days (1, 2 January), Good Friday, Easter Monday (March/April), ANZAC Day (26 April), Independence Days (1, 2, 3 June), White Monday (the Monday after the second Sunday in October), Arbor Day (the first Friday in November), and Christmas Days (25, 26 December).

On White Sunday, children dressed in white parade to church; after the service, they take the places of honor and eat first at family feasts. Many Western countries celebrate Mother's Day and Father's Day, but only Samoa has made Children's Day (White Monday, the day after White Sunday) a public holiday.

The big event of the year is the Independence Days celebrations during the first week of June with dancing, feasting, speeches by *tulafale* (talking chiefs), horse races, and other sporting events. A highlight is the *fautasi* race on the Saturday closest to Independence Days, with teams of dozens of men rowing great longboat canoes. Note that there are three public holidays in a row at this time, which means that banks, offices, and most stores will be closed for five consecutive days! Though Western Samoa actually attained independence on 1 January 1962, the celebrations are held in June to avoid total paralysis around Christmas. Many cultural activities also unfold at the Teuila Tourism Festival in early September.

Once a year the *palolo* reef worm *(Eunice viridis)* rises from the coral before dawn according to a lunar cycle (October on Upolu, November on Savai'i). The Samoans wait with lanterns and nets to catch this prized delicacy, the "caviar of the Pacific." This remarkable event takes place only in Samoa and Fiji.

Dance

The *sasa* is a synchronized group dance in which the rhythm is maintained by clapping or by beating on a rolled mat or drum. The *siva* is a graceful, flowing dance in which the individual is allowed to express him/herself as he/she sees fit. The *fa'ataupati* or slap dance employs body percussion. The knife and fire dances are done solo or in small groups, and they can be dangerous to the performers. Tradition holds that only men who are afraid will be burned during the fire dance.

Arts and Crafts

The Samoan love of elaborate ceremony is illustrated in the fine mat *(ie toga)*. Exquisitely and tightly plaited from finely split pandanus leaves, a good example might take a woman a year of her spare time to complete. Fine mats are prized family heirlooms used as dowries, etc. and they acquire value as they're passed from person to person at ceremonial exchanges *(lafo)*. Mats of this kind cannot be purchased.

Samoan tapa cloth *(siapo)* is decorated by rubbing the tapa over an inked board bearing the desired pattern in relief. In Samoa the designs are usually geometric but with a symbolism based on natural objects.

Traditional woodcarving includes kava bowls, drums, orator's staffs, and war clubs. In Tonga and Fiji, kava bowls have only four circular legs, but Samoan bowls are usually circular with a dozen or more round legs. A large kava bowl is an impressive object to carry home if you have six or seven kilograms to spare in your baggage allowance. Paradoxically, although carved from endangered trees such as the *ifilele*, the local production of kava bowls actually helps protect the rainforests as it greatly increases the value of the trees in the eyes of local villagers who become far less willing to sign away their timber rights for a pittance. A tree used to make handicrafts could be worth WS$2,000 while a logging company would only pay about WS$30 to cut it down.

It's also interesting to note that the tikis you see here are mock Maori or Hawaiian, not Samoan—don't buy the grotesque, grimacing little devils. Also beware of imitation tapa crafts in the Tongan style imported from Pago Pago, New Guinea-style masks, and turtle-shell jewelry, which is prohibited entry into many countries. If what you see in the craft shops of Samoa seems poor in comparison with other Pacific countries, remember that oratory and tattooing were the maximum expressions of Samoan culture, followed by the kava ceremony itself.

ACCOMMODATIONS

Accommodations

The higher-priced hotels usually quote their rates in U.S. dollars to make them seem lower, but in this book we've converted all prices into *tala* to make them easier to compare. Whenever a hotel mentions dollars when you ask the price of the room, be sure to clarify how they wish to be paid. If the amount is to be converted into *tala,* whether you're paying in *tala* cash or by credit card, expect to have your bill inflated about 15% due to the exchange rates used. You can usually avoid this by paying in U.S. dollars, cash or traveler's checks. In all cases, a 10% value added tax is charged and you should also ask if it's included. Failure to pay attention to these details could well result in a bill 25% higher than you'd expected!

Most of the hotels and guesthouses are still in Apia, but an increasing number of places to stay are found on eastern Savai'i and in southeastern Upolu. It's also quite possible to stay with the local people, though you'll have to arrange it for yourself. In the past few years a number of locally operated "ecotourism" resorts have opened in Aleipata and Lepa districts of Upolu and at Satuiatua on Savai'i. These offer mattresses, blankets, and mats in Samoan *fales* right on the beach, with local meals provided at reasonable cost. Virtually all are run by the villagers themselves, and they're an excellent way to combine hiking, snorkeling, swimming, surfing, and just plain relaxing with a sampling of Samoan life. They're covered in the accommodations sections of this chapter—highly recommended.

Staying in Villages

The Samoans are among the most hospitable people in the world, proud that a stranger can go to any house and request food or shelter and rarely be turned away. This admirable characteristic should not be abused, however. It's part of their culture that a gift will be reciprocated—if not now, then sometime in the future. Tourists who accept gifts (such as food and lodging) without reciprocating undermine the culture and cause the Samoans to be less hospitable to the next traveler who arrives.

For this reason it's strongly recommended that you look for a way of repaying their kindness. Thanks is not enough, and a casual offer of payment might be offensive. The Samoans are a very proud people, perhaps the proudest in the Pacific, and you must phrase this carefully to avoid misunderstandings. If your attitude is wrong, they will sense it.

Upon departure, sit down with your hosts for a formal thank you. Say something like, "Hospitality is not something that can be paid for, and I don't know how to show my appreciation fully, but I would like to leave a *mea alofa* (gift)." Then tender at least WS$10 pp per night, more if they've been especially helpful by taking you out fishing, guiding you through the mountains, etc. If you ask them to buy something for the children with the money, they'll smile and accept. At times the Samoans will refuse to accept anything from you, in which case you might take a roll of photos of the family and mail them prints when you get home. Thus at least you'd be able to reciprocate in a small way.

There's a Samoan proverb about guests who abuse hospitality, *ua afu le laufala* (the floor mats are sweating). Talk these matters over with your traveling companions before you set out, and don't go on a trip with one of the insensitive few.

Other Tips

It's best to make known the approximate length of your stay as soon as a family invites you. If one of your hosts' neighbors invites you to come stay with them, politely refuse. This would bring shame on the first family. It's a Samoan custom that travelers may spend the night at the pastor's house. If you do, make an appropriate contribution to the church. The pastor's views on religion, values, and development in general will fascinate you.

Samoans are still unfamiliar with camping and might be offended if they feel you're refusing their hospitality. A tactful explanation of your desire to be close to nature might be accepted, though Samoans are naturally suspicious of those who try to remain apart from the group. Always ask permission of a responsible adult, or camp well out of sight of all roads, trails, and villages. To do otherwise is to place yourself beyond the protection of village law.

FOOD

Try *palusami*—thick coconut cream, onions, canned corned beef *(pisupo),* and young taro leaves wrapped in a breadfruit leaf, then baked on hot stones and served on slices of baked

taro—a very tasty dish when well prepared. Other traditional Samoan specialties include *taofolo* (kneaded breadfruit and sweet coconut cream wrapped in taro leaves and baked), *fa'ausi* (grated-taro-and-coconut-cream pudding), *lua'u* (taro leaves cooked in coconut cream), *suafa'i* (ripe bananas with coconut cream), *faia'ife'e* (octopus in coconut cream), *faiaipusi* (sea eel in coconut cream), and *oka* (marinated raw fish).

If you spend a night in a village, notice how almost everything you eat is locally grown. Taro and breadfruit are the staples, but there's also pork, fish, chicken, *ta'amu,* and bananas. If you're a strict vegetarian, mention it at the outset. After a meal with a family linger a while; it's considered rude for a guest to get up and abruptly leave. Don't continue to occupy the table if others are awaiting their turn to eat, however. Samoans are big people. Most of us eat till we're full, but Samoans eat till they're tired.

SERVICES AND INFORMATION

Visas and Officialdom

No visa is required for a stay of up to 30 days although you *must* have a ticket to leave. They stamp your passport to the date of your flight out, but you can get the 30 days without a struggle.

Apia is the only port of entry for cruising yachts. Yachts may stop at Savai'i after checking out at Apia, provided they get prior permission.

Money

The Western Samoan *tala* is divided into 100 *sene.* There are coins of one, two, five, 10, 20, and 50 *sene* and one *tala,* and banknotes of two, five, 10, 20, 50, and 100 *tala.* The plastic WS$2 banknotes make nice souvenirs. Samoans often speak of dollars when they mean *tala,* and many tourism-related businesses add to the confusion by quoting prices in U.S. dollars. Always note the currency carefully as the difference is around US$1 = WS$2.46! For consistency, we've quoted most prices in Western Samoan currency (WS$).

Both banks charge 50 cents stamp duty per traveler's check, but only the Pacific Commercial Bank charges WS$3 commission (no commission at the Bank of Western Samoa). Traveler's checks attract an exchange rate about four percent higher than cash, but it's always good to have some U.S. currency in small bills in case you happen to run out of *tala,* as everyone will accept it willingly (though at a low rate). If you plan to go upmarket, also have an adequate supply of U.S. dollar traveler's checks in small denominations (see below).

Upmarket facilities that quote prices in dollars are cheaper if you pay them the exact amount in U.S. dollars, cash or traveler's checks. If you pay by credit card you risk having the charge inflated 15% because the dollar amount must be converted into *tala,* then the bank converts the *tala* into New Zealand dollars because all credit card charges are cleared through the Bank of New Zealand, then the NZ$ are converted into your own home currency, all at rates unfavorable to you. This situation definitely applies to bank cards such as Visa and MasterCard, however it may be possible to be charged the exact amount in U.S. dollars if you use a private card such as American Express (ask the merchant/hotel).

Tala are worthless outside Western Samoa, so change only what you think you'll need. If you overestimate, excess *tala* can be changed back into hard currency at airport bank without question. As you're doing so, pick up some Tongan or Fijian banknotes, if that's where you're headed.

Camera film is expensive here and the selection is poor, so bring a good supply. When buying drinks at a grocery store, be aware that there's a 30-cent deposit on large beer or soft drink bottles, 10 cents on small bottles. Tipping is discouraged, and avoid giving money to children on the streets of Apia as this only creates a nuisance. There's a 10% sales tax.

Post and Telecommunications

A reduced rate of postage applies to small packets under one kilogram. Express Mail Service (EMS) is available from Apia to Australia, Fiji, New Zealand, and the U.S.A. The charge to the U.S. is WS$40 for the first 500 grams, then another WS$8 for each additional 500 grams up to 20 kilos maximum. Delivery is guaranteed within less than one week.

To make an operator-assisted domestic call, dial 920. For the international operator, dial 900. If you have access to a direct-dial phone, the international access code is 0. For domestic directory assistance, dial 933; for international numbers, dial 910.

The country code for American Samoa is 684; for Western Samoa it's 685.

Business Hours and Time

Business hours are weekdays 0800-1200 and 1330-1630, Saturday 0800-1200, with government offices closed on Saturday. Banks open weekdays 0900-1500, the post office 0900-1630 weekdays. Expect most businesses to be closed on Sunday, although Samoa's Sunday closing laws are much more lenient than those of Tonga.

Both Samoas share the same hour, and since the international date line is just west of here, this is where the world's day really comes to an end. The Samoas are three hours behind California time, 21 hours behind eastern Australian time.

Weights and Measures

Unlike in American Samoa, where the electric voltage is 110 volts, in Western Samoa it's 240 volts AC, 50 cycles. In American Samoa Imperial measurements (yards, miles) are used, while in Western Samoa it's all metric (meters, kilometers).

Media

The English-language newspapers are the *Samoa Observer* (Box 1572, Apia; tel./fax 21-099), which appears on Wednesday, Friday, and Sunday; the *Samoa Bulletin* (Box 541, Apia; tel. 22-709), a Friday paper; and *Savali* (Private Bag, Apia; fax 26-396), issued on Wednesday and Friday. In early 1994 the *Observer*'s premises were burned to the ground in an arson attack presumably connected with its exposures of official corruption.

The free *Apia Hotline* (Box 508, Apia; tel. 24-926) often contains useful advertisements about special deals on food, transport, and accommodations.

In February 1993 the government enacted a law allowing the courts to require journalists to disclose their sources of information on pain of three months' imprisonment or a WS$5000 fine. Another law prohibits the publication of defamatory statements made about third parties during court cases. These challenges to freedom of the press were widely condemned.

Health

Although no vaccinations are required (except yellow fever or cholera in the unlikely case that you're arriving directly from an infected area), getting immune globulin or the hepatitis A vaccine, a typhoid fever shot, and a tetanus shot (in case a dog bites you) may be worthwhile. Body lice and intestinal parasites are widespread among Samoan villagers; any pharmacy will have a remedy for the former. Check the expiration date before buying any medicines. Take care with the tap water in Apia—beer is safer.

GETTING THERE

By Air

Polynesian Airlines (Box 599, Apia; tel. 685/21-261, fax 685/20-023), Western Samoa's national flag carrier, connects Apia to Auckland, Melbourne, Nuku'alofa, Pago Pago, Rarotonga, Sydney, and Wellington. Their Polypass allows 30 days unlimited travel over Polynesian's modest network (a roundtrip to/from Australia and New Zealand included) for a flat US$999. Details of this and their triangle fares are provided under "Getting Around" in the main Introduction to this book. Students under 26 are eligible for discounts of 25% on regular fares. Polynesian is the *only* Pacific airline that actually serves Pacific food (congratulations!), and their in-flight service is good, though the flights are often delayed. In 1991 Polynesian became the first South Pacific carrier to ban smoking on all flights (our compliments!).

Polynesian Airlines was founded by Australian aviator Reginald Barnewall in 1959. Daily return flights from Apia to Pago Pago began in 1960, and Polynesian had a monopoly on the route until 1975. In 1964 Polynesian extended service to Fiji, Tonga, and Wallis Island. The Western Samoan government bought a controlling interest in the fast-growing airline in 1971, and in 1977 flights began to Niue and Rarotonga, extending to Auckland and Tahiti in 1978. In 1981 Polynesian bought a new 737 directly from Boeing, but overly rapid expansion and cutthroat competition from other carriers soon led to a financial crisis. Thus in 1982 a five-year management contract was signed with Ansett Airlines of Australia, extended for a further 10 years in 1987. At this time Ansett was also managing Air Vanuatu, and in 1982 Polynesian and Air Vanuatu began joint flights from Sydney to Apia via Port Vila. Changes in Australian aviation laws led Ansett to abruptly

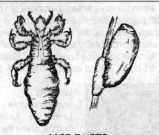

LICE FACTS

The louse *(Pediculus capitis)* is a small, wingless insect that can infest the hairy areas of all warm-blooded beasts. It's untrue that personal cleanliness prevents lice—anyone can get them, whether clean or dirty. The parasite attaches its egg securely to the side of hair shafts. By applying a solution available at any drugstore, you can zap the varmints in minutes.

terminate its contract in 1992 after it obtained authorization to fly internationally under its own colors. Soon after, Polynesian leased two 737s to service its South Pacific routes, and in May 1993 the airline launched direct air service from Apia to Honolulu and Los Angeles using a 767 leased from Air Canada. By mid-1994 losses totaled US$30 million and only government loan guarantees saved the company from bankruptcy. In late 1994 those responsible for this reckless growth were sacked, the 767 and one 737 withdrawn, and the money-losing U.S. routes dropped. Commercial assistance from Air New Zealand is now helping Polynesian get back on its feet.

Air Pacific (tel. 22-693) has flights to Apia from Suva and Nandi (often full) with connections in Fiji to/from Japan. **Air New Zealand** (tel. 20-825) arrives from Auckland, Honolulu, and Nuku'alofa with immediate connections in Honolulu to/from Los Angeles. See "Getting Around" in the main Introduction for information on circular tickets between Fiji, Apia, and Tonga.

Both Polynesian Airlines and **Samoa Air** (tel. 22-901) operate shuttles between Pago Pago and Apia several times a day. For the Pago Pago flights, check carefully which airport your service will be using as they alternate between Faleolo and Fagali'i and the ticket may only say "Apia." Both airlines charge identical fares from Apia to Pago Pago (WS$101 one-way, WS$153 roundtrip), and it's much cheaper to buy your ticket in Western Samoa than almost anywhere else due to currency differences. Samoa Air also offers through an excursion fare from Apia to Vava'u via Pago Pago which is the equivalent of the fare to Pago Pago plus US$165/300 oneway/roundtrip.

By Ship
The **Western Samoa Shipping Corporation** (Private Bag, Apia; tel. 20-935, fax 22-352) runs the car ferry *Queen Salamasina* from Apia to Pago Pago Wednesday at 2200 (nine hours, WS$30 one-way). Buy your ticket before 1200 Tuesday at their Vaea Street office and have your passport ready. If you wait to buy a ticket at the wharf you won't be allowed aboard until the last minute and all of the good places to sleep will have been taken (it's an overnight trip). During holiday periods the ship makes two trips,

leaving Apia at 2200 on Tuesday and Thursday, and at these times it's often fully booked. If you'll be returning to Apia, be sure to get a roundtrip ticket, as the fare is much higher in Pago Pago. But if you won't be returning change excess *tala* back into dollars at the bank the day before as there are no facilities on the wharf. By going by sea you save the WS$20 airport departure tax paid by air travelers.

For information on the supply ship to the Tokelau Islands, contact the **Office for Tokelau Affairs** (Box 865, Apia; tel. 20-822, fax 21-761) or the **New Zealand High Commission** (tel. 21-711, fax 24-844; weekdays 0800-1300/1400-1630) on Beach Road. There's about one a month, and a cabin would run NZ$528 roundtrip, but reservations are not accepted and tourists must travel on a "space available" basis only. Turn to the Tokelau chapter for more information.

AIRPORTS

Faleolo International Airport
Faleolo Airport (APW), Western Samoa's main international airport, is 35 km west of Apia. All flights to points outside the Samoas, as well as some services to Pago Pago, depart from here. The airport bus (WS$6) will take you right to your hotel, or you can wait on the highway for a public bus, which is only WS$1.30, but very scarce after 1600 and on Sunday. Airportbound, the airport bus departs Apia two hours before international flights. It picks up passengers in front on the Hotel Insel Fehmarn, then at Aggie Grey's Hotel, and finally at the Kitano Tusitala.

The airport taxi drivers often try to overcharge foreign tourists, so take the bus if you can. A taxi from the airport to Apia should cost WS$30 (30 *tala*) for the car but they will often insist on being paid US$30 in American currency, so be careful. It's a bit safer taking a taxi back to the airport as they'll know you're already familiar with Samoan currency and probably won't try this trick.

The Pacific Commercial Bank (WS$3 commission) and the Bank of Western Samoa (50 cents commission) in the arrivals area open for international flights (excluding those from Pago Pago) and change traveler's checks for similar rates. Another bank counter is in the departures hall for changing excess *tala* back.

The airport post office (weekdays 0900-1530) sells philatelic stamps, a good way to unload excess *tala*. The duty-free shop in the departure lounge sells only expensive luxury goods and imported alcohol (locally made wines and liqueurs not available), so don't wait to do your shopping here. In general, alcohol and beer are relatively cheap in Samoa.

The international departure tax is WS$20 (children ages five to nine pay WS$10). You don't have to pay the tax if you stay less than 24 hours (transit), and if you'll be departing Samoa twice within any 30-day period, keep your tax receipt as you can avoid paying the tax a second time if you have it.

Fagali'i Airport

Fagali'i Airport (FGI) is near the golf course on the east side of Apia, just five km from the center of town. All Polynesian Airlines flights to Savai'i leave from here. Some flights to Pago Pago use Fagali'i, others Faleolo, so check carefully to avoid disastrous mistakes. The local Fagali'i-tai bus runs between Apia Market and Fagali'i Airport throughout the day from Monday to Saturday. Taxi drivers charge US$5 from Fagali'i to Apia but WS$4 from Apia to Fagali'i. If you're unwilling to pay this arbitrary premium, try bargaining or just cross the street and wait for the bus. The Pacific Commercial Bank does have a counter at Fagali'i Airport but at last report it was unmarked and impossible to find without asking. The usual international departure tax applies.

UPOLU

APIA AND ENVIRONS

Central Apia has been transformed in recent years, with huge government buildings overshadowing the older churches and trading companies that still line the waterfront in the traditional South Seas manner. Yet away from the center this city of 34,000 is only a cluster of villages. In Apia Harbor, where the Vaisigano River has cut an opening in Upolu's protective reef, are a motley assortment of interisland ferries, container ships, fishing boats, and cruising yachts. As at Papeete, you'll see teams of men paddling outrigger racing canoes around the harbor at sunset, about the only two towns in the South Pacific where this remains true.

Apia makes a good base from which to explore northern Upolu, and there's lots of accommodation in all price brackets. The food and entertainment possibilities are also very good, so take a break in your transpacific odyssey and see the city one step at a time. Get into the culture and prepare yourself for that big trip around Savai'i. Samoa is the most Polynesian place in the Pacific, and Apia is the exciting bright light around which Samoa revolves.

Like Suva, Nuku'alofa, Avarua (Rarotonga), and most other South Pacific "Bible Belt" towns, Apia is pretty dead on Saturday afternoon and Sunday. Luckily a number of beach resorts have opened around Upolu and Savai'i in recent years, giving visitors the option of escaping legislated piety by evacuating Apia on Saturday morning. Upolu has a much more varied landscape than Savai'i, with winding roads around the coast and several across the center of the island. Be on one of those roads before noon.

Central Apia

By the harbor side where Falealili Street meets Beach Road is the **John Williams Memorial,** dedicated to the missionary who implanted Protestantism in Samoa in 1830. Nine years later Williams was killed and eaten by cannibals on Erromango Island in present Vanuatu. Later his remains were returned to Samoa and buried beneath the porch of the old **Congregational Christian Church** (1898) across the street.

A block west on Beach Road is the historic wooden **Courthouse** dating from German times, which served as government headquarters until 1994. On Black Saturday, 29 December 1929, Tupua Tamasese Lealofi III, leader of the Mau Movement (see "History and Government," above), was shot in the back by the N.Z. Constabulary while trying to calm his people during a demonstration against the colonial regime in front of this building. Eight other Samoans were also killed and five years of severe repression began, only ending with a change of government in New Zealand.

West again is imposing **Mulivai Catholic Cathedral** (1905), formerly a landmark for ships entering the harbor, and **Matafele Methodist Church,** a fine building where marvelous singing

Apia's Catholic cathedral on Beach Road

DAVID STANLEY

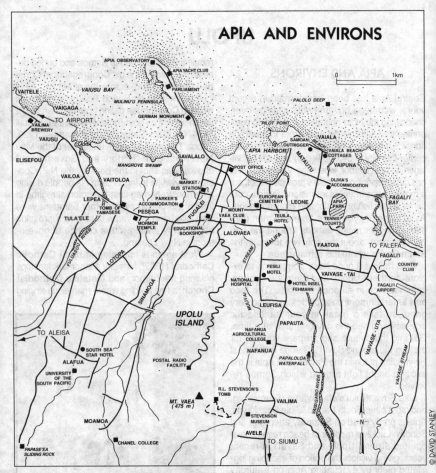

APIA AND ENVIRONS

0   1km

© DAVID STANLEY

may be heard during services. Across the street is the gigantic eight-story **Government Building,** erected in 1994 with a WS$35-million interest-free loan from the People's Republic of China. It and the neighboring seven-story **Central Bank of Samoa** wouldn't be out of place in Abu Dhabi, Dubai, or Kuwait and stand as stunning examples of third-world megalomania. Earthquakes are common at Apia and both of these massive buildings stand on unstable reclaimed land, which tends to magnify the impact of quakes, so you could be looking at a

disaster waiting to happen. If you're brave, enter and take the elevator up to the Government Building's fifth floor, then mount the stairway onto the roof, for some great photos of central Apia. The police band plays the national anthem at the raising of the flag on weekday mornings at 0750.

Nearby is the new **Chief Post Office** with the modern headquarters of the **Bank of Western Samoa** opposite. The old post office on the site of the bank burned down mysteriously in 1986, just as an official inquiry into hundreds of thousands of dollars in missing funds was about to begin. A block west in the center of the traffic circle where Vaea Street meets Beach Road is a **Clock Tower** built as a WW I memorial. On opposite corners of Vaea Street and Beach Road are the former Burns Philp store, now **Chan Mow Supermarket,** and the new **National Provident Fund** building housing the agency that administers the country's pension fund.

Mulinu'u Peninsula

Just northwest of town is the **Kitano Tusitala Hotel,** which is well worth entering to appreciate the great hand-tied roofs of the main *fale*-like neo-Samoan buildings erected in 1974.

Continue northwest on Mulinu'u Street, past two monuments on the left commemorating the disastrous 1889 naval debacle (see "History," earlier in this chapter) when the German cruiser *Adler* and several other ships sank during a hurricane. There's also a monument on the right that recalls the raising of the German flag on 1 March 1900 *("die deutsche Flagge gehisst").*

The large beehive-style building farther along on the left is the neo-Samoan **Parliament of Samoa** (1972). In 1990 the building was closed after cancer-causing asbestos fibers began drifting down from the ceiling onto the assembled legislators. Beyond the old Fono House across the field is the **Independence Memorial** (1962), which declares, "The Holy Ghost, Council of all Mankind, led Samoa to Destiny."

At the end of the Mulinu'u Peninsula is the **Apia Observatory,** founded by the Germans in 1902. After the unexpected hurricane of 1889, the Germans weren't taking any more chances. Note the many impressive **royal tombs** of former paramount chiefs both here and down the road to the left. Mulinu'u is the heartland of modern Samoan history.

Vailima

In 1889 Robert Louis Stevenson, Scottish author of the adventure classic *Treasure Island,* purchased approximately 162 hectares of bushland at the foot of Mt. Vaea, three and a half km inland from Apia and high above the sea, for US$4000. Stevenson named the place Vailima, meaning "five waters," for the small streams that ran across the property, and here he built his home and spent the last five years of his life.

During a power struggle between rival Samoan factions, some chiefs were imprisoned at Mulinu'u. Stevenson visited them in confinement, and to show their gratitude, these chiefs built him a road up to Vailima when they were released. The Samoans called Stevenson Tusitala, or "Teller of Tales." On 3 December 1894, at the age of 44, Stevenson suffered a fatal brain hemorrhage while helping his wife Fanny fix dinner. He's buried just below the summit of Mt. Vaea, overlooking Vailima, as he'd requested.

The stately mansion with its beautiful tropical gardens was first sold to a retired German businessman, then bought by the German government as the official residence of their Governor. The Germans built the westernmost wing of the present building. The N.Z. regime took it over when they assumed power. Until recently the structure was Government House, official residence of Samoa's head of state. Inscribed "Samoa 1889," the old-fashioned mahogany steering wheel of the British ship *Calliope,* the only one to survive the naval debacle of that year, is in the building. Britain donated the wheel to Samoa when the ship was broken up after WW II.

In early 1992, after Hurricane Val did serious damage to Vailima, Mormon businessmen from Utah and Arizona obtained a 60-year lease on the property with the intention of creating a museum. Fortunately sanity prevailed and early plans to build a cable car to Stevenson's tomb on Mt. Vaea and to install life-sized mechanical figures of the writer, his wife, and family pets in the house were scrapped, and in December 1994 the **Robert Louis Stevenson Museum** opened on the centenary of the writer's death. The building is open Tuesday to Friday 0900-1600, Saturday 0900-1200, with the last tour commencing 30 minutes before closing (admission WS$15 for adults or WS$5 for children under 12). The Avele or Vaoala bus will bring you directly here from the market.

Mount Vaea

An almost obligatory pilgrimage for all visitors to Samoa is the 45-minute climb along a winding trail to the tomb of Robert Louis Stevenson, just below the 475-meter summit of Mt. Vaea (admission free). After the small bridge turn left. Five hundred meters up, the trail divides with a

Fanny Osborne and Robert Louis Stevenson with friends at Vailima

AUCKLAND MUSEUM AND INSTITUTE

shorter, steeper way to the right and a much longer less-used trail to the left. A good plan is to go up by the short trail and come back down the longer way. After rains, the trail can get muddy. The area at the bottom of the hill adjoining Vailima has been developed with botanical gardens, a swimming hole, and a small waterfall (dry except during the wet months).

The path to the top was cut by 200 sorrowful Samoans as they carried the famous writer's body up to its final resting place in 1894. From the tomb there's a sweeping panorama of the verdant valley to the east with the misty mountains of Upolu beyond, and in the distance the white line of surf breaking endlessly on the reef. The red roof of Vailima directly below is clearly visible. It's utterly still—a peaceful, poignant, lonely place. Stevenson's requiem reads:

Under the wide and starry sky,
Dig the grave and let me lie.
Glad did I live and gladly die,
And I laid me down with a will.

This be the verse you grave for me:
Here he lies where he longed to be;
Home is the sailor, home from the sea,
And the hunter home from the hill.

Stevenson's wife Fanny died in California in 1914. Her ashes were brought back to Samoa and buried at the foot of her husband's grave.

The bronze plaque bears her Samoan name, Aolele, and the words of Stevenson:

Teacher, tender comrade, wife,
A fellow-farer true through life
Heart-whole and soul free,
The August Father gave to me.

Side-Trip Southwest

Catch a Tafaigata, Seesee, or Siusega bus at the market and ask the driver to drop you at the closest point to **Papae'ea Sliding Rocks.** You can also come on the Alafua bus to the university (see below), but this will add about 15 minutes to your walking time. Even from the closest bus stop you'll still have to hike uphill two km and pay WS$2 admission (don't give the money to children—only to the adult at the entrance). You slide down three rocks into freshwater pools—don't forget your bathing suit. It's open daily (Sunday included!).

At Alafua, below and to the east of this area, is the 30-hectare Western Samoan campus of the **University of the South Pacific** (the main campus is in Fiji). In 1977 the university's School of Agriculture was established here, with assistance from New Zealand. To the left of the main gate is an agricultural training center funded by the European Union. The university's two semesters run from February to the end of June and late July to mid-November. Annual tuition for students from outside the region is WS$11,400 (see the "Suva" section in the Fiji Islands chapter for more information).

On the way back to Apia notice the **Mormon Temple** (1983) on the airport highway. The golden angel Moroni trumpets The Word from above but tourists aren't allowed inside. The Church of Latter-day Saints established its Samoan headquarters here in 1902. Just a few minutes' walk west along the highway from the temple is the impressive four-tier **tomb of Tupua Tamasese Lealofi III,** the Mau Movement leader mentioned above.

Beer lovers might like to visit the **Vailima Brewery** at Vaitele on the road to the airport. You'll only be allowed in on Thursday, and it's a good idea to call the Personnel Manager (tel. 20-200) beforehand to make sure he'll be available for a tour (no tasting). Plenty of buses run out this way (including those marked Puipa'a, Toamua, Vaigaga, or Vaitele-uta).

Central Upolu

For a bit of heavy hiking, catch a Siumu, Falealili, or Salani bus up the Cross Island Highway to a turnoff on the right for **Lake Lanoto'o,** otherwise known as "Goldfish Lake," high in the center of Upolu at 590 meters above sea level. Walk straight west on the dirt access road for just under an hour until you see the power lines end abruptly at a transformer on a pole, plus several radio towers down a road to the left. Continue straight ahead another 500 meters to a point where the access road turns left (south). Walk 400 meters south on this road until the radio towers are visible again on the left. On the right directly opposite here an overgrown trail runs due west to the lake, another one-hour walk.

When you arrive at a destroyed microwave reflector on top of a hill, the lake is just below you to the left.

The unmarked way takes a bit of intuition to find and some of the locals living on the main road to the trail ask exorbitant fees such as WS$40 to act as guides. Just take your time and follow the instructions provided above and you'll be okay. The route to the lake is very muddy following heavy rains, so only go after a couple of days of sunny weather. Expect fallen trees across the route and some confusion about the way toward the end. This is a *very* strenuous hike, so be prepared.

The opaque green waters of this seldom-visited crater lake are surrounded by a mossy green bush dripping from the mist. Swimming in the lake is an eerie experience. To add to the otherworldliness of the place, Lake Lanoto'o is full of goldfish, but you'll have to wait patiently if you want to see any from shore (bread crumbs might help). This hike is ideal for seeing Upolu's high-altitude vegetation without going too far from town, but sturdy shoes and long pants are essential.

On the right near the road, three km south of the Lanoto'o turnoff (and 13.5 km from Apia), are **Papapapaitai Falls,** also known as Tiavi Falls. The viewpoint beside the road is free but it's only worth going if you have your own transportation. Some 21 km south of Apia the Cross Island Highway meets the South Coast Road.

On your way back to Apia stop to visit the **Baha'i House of Worship** (1984), Mother Temple to all Baha'is in the region, and one of the most impressive modern buildings in the South

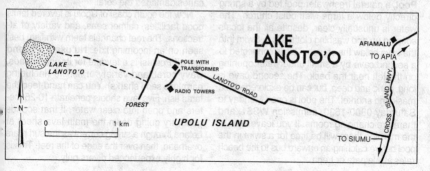

LAKE LANOTO'O

AFIAMALU
TO APIA

LAKE LANOTO'O

POLE WITH TRANSFORMER

LANOTO'O ROAD

RADIO TOWERS

FOREST

-N-

0   1 km

UPOLU ISLAND

CROSS ISLAND HWY.

TO SIUMU

Pacific. The temple is at Tiapapata, eight km from Apia and 30 minutes down the highway from the Lanoto'o turnoff. The monumental dome soars 30 meters above the surrounding area and has nine sides, symbolizing the unity of the nine major religions of the world. Inside, the latticework of ribs forms a nine-pointed star at the apex of the dome. The seating is arranged facing the Holy Land (Israel) because this is the final resting place of Baha 'Ullah (1817-92), Prophet-Founder of the Baha'i Faith. This majestic building, funded by Baha'is around the world, is open to all for prayer and meditation daily 0900-1700. Also visit the information center (tel. 24-192), to the left as you approach the temple. Another 30-minute walk down the highway toward Apia is the Island Styles Factory Showroom (see "Shopping" below). The Vaoala bus comes up this far.

Side-Trip East

Buses marked Falevao or Falefa depart Apia Market every hour or so for Falefa, 29 km east (you can also pick up these buses on Matautu Street near Betty Moors or Olivia's Accommodation). You'll get many fine views of Upolu's north coast as you pass along Upolu's finest summer surfing beaches, Laulii and Solosolo (beware of undertow). No barrier reef breaks the waves that crash onto these black sandy shores. Change rooms and showers (WS$1 pp) are provided at Saoluafata Beach, but no visitors are allowed on Sunday. Most of the coral here was destroyed during Hurricane Val in late 1991, so the snorkeling is rather poor.

A km east of Saoluafata Beach is Piula Theological College with the superb Piula Cave Pool, a natural freshwater pool fed by a spring directly below a large Methodist church. The water is unusually clear, despite all the locals soaping up and washing clothes in it. Swim into the cave below the church. This is connected to a second cave by a small underwater opening on the left near the back. The second cave is long, dark, and deep, but can be explored with a mask and snorkel. The pool is open Monday to Saturday 0800-1630, admission WS$1, and there are changing rooms. If you leave Apia in the morning there will be time for a swim in the pool before catching an onward bus to the beach *fales* at Aleipata or Lepa.

Falefa Falls, two km east of Piula through beautiful Falefa village, is impressive during the rainy season and it's freely visible beside the road. The Falefa bus turns around here.

Palolo Deep

One of Apia's nicest attractions is the **Palolo Deep Marine Reserve** (daily 0800-1800, admission WS$1), a natural reef aquarium operated by the Division of Environment and Conservation. The signposted entrance to the reserve is near the main wharf at Matautu, in fact, the Deep's main draw is its convenience to Apia. You can easily wade out to the Deep at low tide, and although the reef has been heavily damaged by hurricanes, much of the coral has regenerated and there are plenty of colorful fish (bring along bread to feed to them). Even if you don't intend to swim, the reserve garden is a very nice place to sit and read with lots of benches and relaxing lagoon views. This place is so peaceful it's hard to believe you're just a five-minute walk from the center of a capital city. The helpful staff do their best to serve visitors, but they also let you relax in privacy. Facilities include toilets, showers, and changing rooms. You can rent snorkeling gear (WS$10), scooters (WS$30), and bicycles (WS$12) and buy cold soft drinks (no beer). The Deep is a perfect escape on Sunday—make an afternoon of it.

Scuba Locales

Five Mile Reef, an ocean reef eight km straight out to sea from Apia Harbor, was one of Samoa's best dive sites until the locals started using dynamite to bring up the fish and hurricanes damaged the coral.

Now the south coast of Upolu is favored for its good facilities, calmer seas, and variety of attractions. The reef channels teem with fish, best seen on an incoming tide. **Nu'usafe'e Island** just off Poutasi is a favorite for its coral heads, wavy coral, and variety of fishlife (including harmless sand sharks). You can hand-feed the tame fish. Five lava shoots penetrate 10-25 meters and open into clear water. If that sounds good, try going down the main lava shoot at Lefaga through a strong current as the surf roars overhead, then over the edge of the reef. This is for highly experienced divers only.

Other good spots are the drop-offs at Nu'utele and Nu'ulua Islands in Aleipata, the western reef areas off Manono, and the edge of the barrier reef, three km offshore from Lalomalava, Savai'i.

Sports and Recreation

The 18-hole golf course of the **Royal Samoa Country Club** (tel. 20-120) is just beyond Fagali'i Airport east of Apia (Fagali'i-tai bus). The clubhouse bar has a pleasant balcony overlooking the course and the sea—highly recommended for an afternoon drink. The course is open daily, Sunday included, and all visitors are warmly welcomed (green fees WS$20). The big tournament of the year is the Samoa Open in August.

Samoa Marine (Box 4700, Apia; tel. 22-721, fax 20-087), next to the Seaside Inn near the main wharf, offers scuba diving at WS$125 for a one-tank dive, WS$150 for two tanks, gear included. All dives are boat dives. Certified, equipped divers can also rent tanks and organize their own trips. They may ask you to leave your passport as security.

Samoa Marine's game fishing boat, the *Ole Pe'a,* is available for charter at WS$875 a half day (0500 to 1400) or WS$1250 a full day (0500-2100). Night fishing from 1630 to 0100 costs WS$750. Five anglers can go for that price, and fishing gear and snacks are provided—you bring the beer. Their guarantee is "no fish, no pay!"

Saturday at 1600 see exciting rugby (March to June) or soccer (July and August) from the grandstand at **Apia Park.** The gymnasium at Apia Park was a gift of the People's Republic of China for the 1983 South Pacific Games. You can observe basketball (Tuesday and Thursday at 1700), badminton (Wednesday and Friday at 1900), and volleyball (Saturday from May to July) in the gym (tel. 20-278). The **tennis courts** behind Apia Park are open to the public daily 0800-1600.

Cricket *(kirikiti)* is played mostly in rural villages at 1400 on Saturday throughout the year.

AROUND UPOLU

Eastern Upolu

There's no bus service right around Upolu, and if you want to do a circle trip without renting a car you'll need several days and a willingness to walk for long stretches. Some eight km south of Falefa Falls, the road works its way up to **Mafa Pass** (276 meters), beyond which is a junction, with Aleipata to the left and Lepa to the right. If you take the left-hand road toward Amaile (Aleipata bus) you'll pass alongside the **Afulilo Reservoir** where in 1993 Afulilo Falls above Fagaloa Bay was harnessed in a US$33-million, four-megawatt hydroelectric development.

Aleipata and **Lepa** districts feature many excellent and unspoiled white-sand beaches with good swimming but only average snorkeling. The ecotourism resorts of this area are covered under "Accommodations" below, and a stay at one of them would allow the time to explore this attractive area. Visit the beautiful offshore islands at high tide with fishermen from Lalomanu. **Nu'utele Island,** a leper colony from 1916 to 1918, is now uninhabited, and two beautiful beaches flank the steep forested slopes. Hiring a boat out to Nu'utele would run about WS$50 roundtrip.

The Aleipata buses finish their runs at Lalomanu, from whence it's a level, seven-km walk along the south coast to Saleapaga (no bus service and little traffic). The Lepa buses run from Apia to Saleapaga via Mafa Pass and Lotofaga. Five km south of the pass, deep in the interior, are **Fuipisia Falls** (WS$2 admission), signposted on the west side of the road. Just a 300-meter walk inland from the road, the falls plunge 56 meters down into a fern-filled valley of which you can get a good view from on top.

Three km south of Fuipisia, the same river plummets over 53-meter-high **Sopo'aga Falls** (admission WS$3 per car, WS$6 per bus). The signposted viewpoint is just a few hundred meters south of the junction with the westbound road to O Le Pupu-Pu'e National Park. A trail heads down to the falls from the viewpoint.

If you don't have your own transportation, you'll probably have to walk the four km from Sopo'aga Falls to the Salani turnoff. Buses run along the south coast from Salani to the National Park and Apia, but they're infrequent, and there's next to no traffic, so you're not likely to hitch a ride. The south coast of Upolu is more traditional than the north, and the people take pride in keeping their villages clean and attractively decorated with flowers.

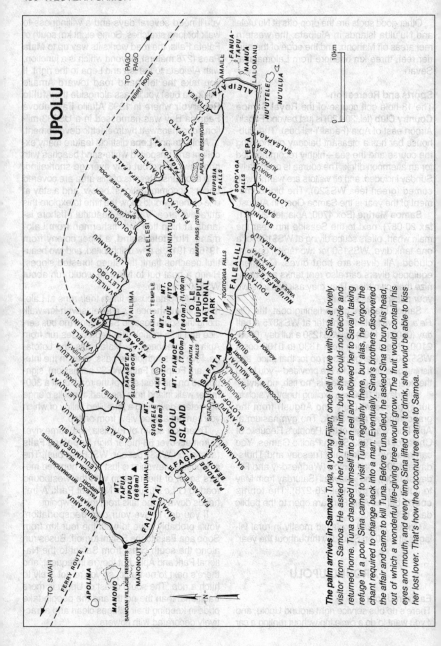

UPOLU

TO PAGO
PAGO

FERRY ROUTE

ALEIPATA
TIAVEA
AMAILE
FANUA-
TAPU
NAMU'A
LALOMANU
NU'UTELE
NU'ULUA

(UAFATO)
AFULILO RESERVOIR

UTUALOA BAY

TAGA'LOA
FALLS

FUIPISIA
FALLS

SOPO'AGA
FALLS

LEPA
LEPA

AUFAGA

SALEAPAGA

SALATELE
(SALATELE
FALLS)

PULA CAVE POOL
FALEFA CAVE POOL
SAULUATAGA BEACH
SOLOSOLO

FALEVAO

MAFA PASS (276 m)

SALEILUA
SALELESI

SAUNIATU

VAVAU
SAPOE
LOTOFAGA
SALANI
MALAEMALU
TAFATAFA
FALEALILI

TOGITOGIGA FALLS

POUTASI
NU'USAFE'E HOTEL
VAIULA BEACH HOTEL
SATITOA

O LE
PUPU-PU'E
NATIONAL
PARK

LUATUANU'U
LUFILUFI
LAULI'I
VAILELE
LETOGO

MULINU'U
APIA
VAIUSU
MT. VAEA
(350m)
VAILIMA
BAHA'I TEMPLE
VAITELE
FALEULA
MT. LE PUE
(840 m)
MT. FITO
(1,100 m)
FALEASI'U
LE AUVA'A
SAANAPU
PAPASE'EA
SLIDING ROCK
LAKE
LANOTO'O
MT. FIAMOE
(700 m)
PAPAPAPAITAI
FALLS
SIUMU

AGANOA BEACH

TAFITOALA
MULIVAI
COCONUT BEACH RESORT

NU'USUATIA
SA'ANAPU
TAPUATA
SATAOA

SAFATA

MT.
SIGAELE
(868m)

MT.
TAFUA
UPOLU
(669m)

MALUA
FALEULA
ALEISA

LEPALE
LEPALE

LEFAGA

FALELATAI

MULIFANUA
WHARF
MT.
TAFUA
UPOLU
(669m)
FALEOLO
INTERNATIONAL
TANUMALALA

SATAPUALA BEACH RESORTS

PARADISE
BEACH
FALEASE'ELA
SALAMUMU

10 km

TO PAGO
PAGO

FERRY ROUTE

TO SAVAI'I

APOLIMA
MANONO
MANONOUTA
SAMOAN VILLAGE RESORTS

N

The palm arrives in Samoa: Tuna, a young Fijian, once fell in love with Sina, a lovely visitor from Samoa. He asked her to marry him, but she could not decide and returned home. Tuna changed himself into an eel and followed her to Savai'i, taking refuge in a pool. Sina came to visit Tuna regularly there, but alas, he forgot the chant required to change back into a man. Eventually, Sina's brothers discovered the affair and came to kill Tuna. Before Tuna died, he asked Sina to bury his head, out of which a wonderful life-giving tree would grow. The fruit would contain his eyes and mouth, and every time Sina lifted one to drink, she would be able to kiss her lost lover. That's how the coconut tree came to Samoa.

O Le Pupu-Pu'e National Park

This large 2,850-hectare national park (tel. 24-294), created in 1978, stretches along the insular divide from the summits of Mt. Le Pu'e, the double-cratered peak east of Afiamalu, and Mt. Fito (1,100 meters), highest point on Upolu, right down to the lava fields of O Le Pupu and the south coast. The park provides a habitat for the endangered Tongan fruit bat, or flying fox (*Pteropus tonganus*). At dusk these giant bats with one-and-a-half-meter wingspans are seen soaring above the treetops.

At Togitogiga, 28 km south of Apia via the Cross Island Highway, five km east of the Siumu junction and just a short walk from the main road, are beautiful **Togitogiga Falls**, good for swimming, wading, and diving (middle pool). There are toilets, changing rooms, and shelters at the falls. After heavy rains Togitogiga Falls becomes a raging torrent.

An overgrown trail from the falls leads up to **Peapea Cave**, two hours roundtrip. It's hard to find the way on your own. Good views of the lava fields and the coast are obtained on the **O Le Pupu Trail,** which begins two km west of the falls. The easiest way to get to this national park is to ask for a Falealili or Salani bus behind the RSA Club in Apia.

MANONO ISLAND

Three-km-square Manono Island, four km off the west end of Upolu, is sheltered within the larger island's protective reef. Four villages are on Manono (Faleu, Lepuia'i, Apai, and Salua) but cars, dogs, and hotels aren't present, which makes it a delightful place. Electricity was installed on Manono in 1995, but as yet there are only a few small village stores, which are closed most of the time. Unfortunately there's no regular place to stay on Manono, so before going ask the Western Samoa Visitors Bureau in Apia for the name of a local resident who might be willing to put you up—the locals tend to be a little sensitive about visitors who just show up presuming automatic hospitality.

CENTRAL APIA

PILOT POINT

MAIN WHARF

APIA HARBOR

RECLAIMED AREA

YACHT ANCHORAGE

MULINUU RD

FUGALEI ST

CONVENT ST

SAVALALO RD

SALEUFI ST

VAEA ST

BEACH RD

BEACH RD

MATAUTU ST

VAISIGANO RIVER

VIVI ST

FALEALILI ST

TO SIUMU

UPOLU ISLAND

0   200 m

—N—

TO FALEOLO INTERNATIONAL AIRPORT

© DAVID STANLEY

1. Le Godinet Hotel and Restaurant
2. Beachcomber Nightclub
3. Kitano Tusitala Hotel
4. Fish Market
5. Eastern Bus Station
6. Morris Hedstrom Department Store
7. RSA Club
8. Clock Tower
9. Central Bank of Samoa
10. New Government Building
11. Clothing Market
12. Polynesian Airlines
13. St. Mary's Convent
14. Shipping Corporation
15. The Town Clock Tower Coffee Shop
16. Chan Mow Supermarket
17. Bank of Western Samoa
18. Lotemau Center
19. Gourmet Seafood and Grill
20. Chief Post Office
21. Jane's Tours/Mandarin Palace Restaurant
22. Betty's Restaurant
23. Cam's Food Bar
24. Feiloaimauso Bingo Hall
25. Wesley Book Store
26. Catholic Cathedral
27. Visitors Bureau
28. Tauesi Cinema/Kava and Kavings Handicrafts
29. Otto's Reef/Wong Kee Restaurant
30. Office for Tokelau Affairs
31. Treasure Garden Restaurant
32. Ah Kam's Motel
33. Western Bus Station
34. Market
35. Bank of Western Samoa Saleufi Agency
36. Police Station
37. Immigration Office
38. Courthouse
39. Lands and Survey Department/New Zealand High Commission
40. John Williams Building
41. Australia High Commission
42. Aggie Grey's Hotel
43. Peace Corps Office/Avis Rent-a-Car
44. Klub Lodge
45. Betty Moors Accommodation
46. Sapolu Laundrette
47. Margrey-Ta's Beer Garden
48. Samoa Marine
49. Seaside Inn
50. Harbour Light Hotel
51. Palolo Deep Marine Reserve

The trail around the island can be covered on foot in a little over an hour. Near the landing at Faleu is a monument commemorating the arrival of the first European Methodist missionary to Samoa, Rev. Peter Turner, who landed here on 18 June 1835. A five-minute walk west of the missionary monument is the **Grave of 99 Stones** (Pa Le Soo) at Lepuia'i, with one stone for each of the dead man's wives. On a hill in the center of the island is an ancient **star mound** (Mauga Fetu), but a guide will be necessary to find it. Manono has a few nice beaches, and the tour groups use one on the less-populated northern side of the island facing Apolima.

Getting There

Village boats to Manono depart from a landing just south of the Samoa Village Resorts at the west tip of Upolu. The Manono and Falelatai buses from Apia will bring you to the landing, and the boat leaves soon after the bus arrives, provided there are enough passengers (WS$1.50 pp). The operators try to charge tourists WS$20 for a special charter, but arrive early and show no impatience. Once they realize you're not about to pay the higher price, they'll tell everyone to get aboard and leave (have small bills ready so there's no argument over change).

There are two landings on Manono, at Faleu on the south side of the island and at Salua on the northeast side. Get off at the first stop they visit, and when you want to return to Upolu, go back to the landing (before 1600) and wait patiently. When the boat finally arrives just get on with the others and pay the same exact fare when you reach the other side.

Some travel agencies in Apia offer full-day tours to Manono at WS$78 pp, lunch included. Rather than taking the tour, get a small group together and charter a boat to Manono from the landing at WS$20 each way for the whole boat. Agree upon a time and place for the return trip, and pack a picnic lunch as little is available on the island. You could also visit nearby Apolima Island, in the strait between Upolu and Savai'i, this way by paying WS$50 return to charter a boat.

ACCOMMODATIONS AROUND APIA

Budget Accommodations

The 12-room **Seaside Inn** (Cyril Curry, Box 3019, Apia; tel. 22-578, fax 22-918), near the wharf at Matautu, offers rooms with shared bath at WS$35/47/60 single/double/triple, rooms with private bath at WS$40/50/65, or two-bedroom flats with private cooking facilities at WS$50/61/75, all including tax and breakfast (served from 0700-0830 only). If you're not out of your room by noon you'll be charged for an extra night. Communal cooking facilities are available (shortage of utensils). Breakfast is only toast and tea or coffee, and sometimes the Inn has water problems. Don't leave valuables lying around as there have been reports of petty theft from the rooms. A small bar is attached and there's a nice veranda overlooking the harbor (a great place to pass a rainy afternoon). Many travelers stay here, so it's a good place to meet people, although the staff is often moody and the toilets could use a cleaning. The Seaside rents cars at WS$110 a day all inclusive.

Around the corner, just before the Shell station on Matautu Street, is **Betty Moors Accommodation** (Box 18, Apia; tel. 21-085), where the 13 cell-like cubicles with shared bath are WS$20 pp (you'll almost certainly get one to yourself). Ask for a better room behind the main building. No cooking facilities are provided out of safety considerations. On weekends, loud music spills over from a nightclub near the Seaside Inn. Get there on the Letogo bus from the market. If you come back on foot at night, beware of a sudden attack by dogs from the nearby laundromat. Have a few stones ready. Betty's an interesting person to chat with, and her husband was the son of trader J.J. Moors, with whom Robert Louis Stevenson stayed when he first arrived in Samoa. She'll hold excess luggage while you're off touring Savai'i or south Upolu.

Farther along in the same direction, behind the BP gasoline station beyond the bank, is **Olivia's Accommodation** (Box 4089, Apia; tel./fax 23-465). There are eight three-bed rooms with shared bath in the main building at WS$16.50 per bed in a shared room. A large communal kitchen and lounge are provided, and music plays from loudspeakers throughout the day. Peace and quiet at night depend on who your neighbors are. Olivia's roosters and pigs will wish you a good morning. It's the cheapest place in town, and young backpackers like the convivial atmosphere. For more privacy ask for one of the two self-catering units in a three-unit block at back that cost WS$44/55 double/triple. These are a little grungy but at that price you can't complain. Olivia's is near Apia Park, which should be avoided for evening walks as there have been reports of incidents.

Valentine Parker's Accommodation (Box 395, Apia; tel. 22-158) at Fugalei, near the new market, has nine double rooms on the airy second floor of a large building at WS$20/30 single/double. Showers, toilets, and TV room are downstairs, but no "visitors" are allowed in the rooms. In theory you can cook simple meals in the family kitchen downstairs, but in practice they don't like it, and you'll be charged WS$5 for gas and electricity if your meals are too "complicated." A sign advises that cooking is not allowed after 1800, but it's no problem asking for hot water to make instant noodles or tea. Squealing pigs below and a disco beat from the adjacent Talofa Bar add their exotic flavor to this place.

The **Travelers Inn** (Box 5214, Apia; tel. 26-055, fax 20-110), directly opposite the Mormon Temple at Pesega, has 15 fan-cooled rooms with shared bath at WS$33/47/61 single/double/triple, eight a/c rooms with private bath at WS$50/69 single/double, breakfast included.

The **South Sea Star Hotel** (Box 800, Apia; tel. 25-341, tel./fax 21-667), at Alafua near the entrance to the University of the South Pacific, has 34 fan-cooled rooms with shared bath at WS$33/55 single/double. The minimum stay is two nights and there are weekly and monthly discounts. This new two-story building in a garden setting is a good choice if you'd like to be a bit outside the city while having the regular Alafua bus available to take you into town (taxi WS$4). A store is nearby and unlimited free hot water is available to make instant noodles, tea, or coffee.

You can pitch a tent or hang a mosquito net under a thatched *fale* roof at the **Palolo Deep Marine Reserve** at WS$15 pp. Toilets, showers, and picnic tables are provided, and there's a nice sea breeze.

Medium-Priced Hotels

Almost opposite the entrance to the main wharf at Matautu is the two-story **Harbour Light Hotel** (Box 5214, Apia; tel. 21-103). Its 18 motel-style a/c rooms with private bath and fridge are WS$63/75/88 single/double/triple, a spaghetti-and-eggs breakfast included. If the air conditioning is important to you, check that it works before taking the room. There's 24-hour service here, so give it a try if you arrive late on the ferry from Pago Pago.

Nearby is the **Samoan Outrigger Hotel** (Box 4074, Apia; tel./fax 20-042) in a stately old residence facing Vaiala Beach, a six-minute walk from the main wharf in the opposite direction as central Apia. Rooms are WS$44/55 single/double with shared bath, WS$88 double with private bath, or WS$28 pp in the dorm,

breakfast and tax included. Facilities include a communal kitchen, lounge, bar, and a washing machine. You'll enjoy sitting on the steps in the evening chatting with the other guests. This Danish-operated guesthouse only opened in December 1994 and it seems destined to become *the* favorite place to stay in Apia.

Klub Lodge (Box 2201, Apia; tel. 25-611, fax 25-610), also known as Manu Sina Lodge, on Matautu Street near Betty Moors, has 14 a/c rooms with bath at WS$75/100 single/double, breakfast included. It's overpriced for what you get.

Ah Kam's Motel (Box 1299, Apia; tel. 20-782, fax 20-782), on Savalalo Road in downtown Apia, has 10 fan-cooled rooms with fridge at WS$75/100/125 single/double/triple, plus 10% tax. An a/c room will be about WS$25 more. This two-story motel has a nice little bar in the courtyard (island night on Tuesday)—drop in for a drink even if you're not staying there.

Out on the Mulinu'u Peninsula, northwest of the Kitano Tusitala, is **Le Godinet Beachfront Hotel** (Box 9490, Apia; tel. 23-690, fax 25-436), the "biggest little hotel in Western Samoa." The nine clean a/c rooms with bath are WS$110/138/165 single/double/triple, including breakfast and tax. Owner Derek Godinet serves Apa's best lobster and maybe the world's best seafood spaghetti in the hotel restaurant (open 1200-1400 for lunch weekdays, for dinner daily). A band plays Saturday night 2030-2200. Despite the name, you can't swim here.

Across the street from the National Hospital is **Fesili Motel** (Box 1062, Apia; tel. 26-476, fax 22-517), a bizarre five-story building with a laundromat in the basement, a supermarket on the second floor, motel rooms on the third and fourth floors, and "Faupepe's Sky Village" restaurant/bar and swimming pool on the roof. The 10 a/c rooms with private bath, fridge, and TV are WS$100/125 single/double.

Apia's nicest little hideaway is the **Plantation Homestead Bed & Breakfast** (Box 5500, Apia; tel. 25-244, fax 27-037), nine km southwest of town. The three rooms with shared bath upstairs in an old plantation house (not unlike those depicted in the film *Gone With The Wind*) are WS$55 single or double, WS$72 triple. The gracious restaurant downstairs is open for dinner on Thursday, Friday, and Saturday nights, and on Sunday Devonshire cream teas (WS$6.60) and a buffet lunch (WS$33) are served in the large tropical garden. The Aleisa and Tanumapua buses pass this way, but you'll probably need to rent a car to stay here as bus service is sporadic. A taxi from town costs WS$9. The Homestead would certainly make a wonderful central base from which to explore western Upolu by car, but they're often fully booked, so try to reserve.

Upmarket Hotels

The **Vaiala Beach Cottages** (Box 2025, Apia; tel. 22-202), facing the lagoon at Vaiala, offers seven pleasant, fan-cooled bungalows with cooking facilities and fridge at WS$166/188/213 single/double/triple, plus 10% tax. Parents with children 12 and under are charged WS$24 extra. Discounts are possible for long stays if you book direct, and bookings made through a travel agent or airline are 10% higher. The aggressive guard dogs of this neighborhood make it unwise to walk back here from town late at night, so take a taxi. Manageress Helen Mihelovich is very helpful.

Aggie Grey's Hotel (Box 67, Apia; tel. 22-880, fax 25-484), on the east side of the harbor, began in March 1942 as a hamburger stand catering to U.S. servicemen stationed in the area. The main waterfront building has recently been reconstructed in mock-colonial style by Alan Grey and Japanese investors, and the 154 rooms begin at WS$188/213/238 single/double/triple in the old section around the pool. Bungalows are about WS$50 more, rooms in the main lobby wing 50% more, suites 100% more. Children aged four to 11 are charged half rate, those 12 and over full rate. Add 10% tax to these prices. Meals used to be included in the tariff, but they're now WS$88 pp extra. Weekly events include the barbecue on Friday and Sunday nights, and the Samoan feast on Wednesday. Aggie's is the darling of the packaged travel set and it's always crowded with tourists. There's even an island in the swimming pool!

The Japanese-owned **Hotel Kitano Tusitala** (Box 101, Apia; tel. 21-122, fax 23-652), at the beginning of the Mulinu'u Peninsula, is a complex of two-story blocks containing 96 a/c rooms with private bath beginning at WS$175/200/225 single/double/triple, plus 10% tax, with children under 12 free. The open *fale* architecture of the main buildings is pleasant, and perhaps because it's a little disorganized, the atmosphere is surprisingly relaxed. The snack bar serves good food at reasonable prices, but waiters may try to shortchange you or ask for a loan or a free trip to America. Mosquitoes permitting, the poolside bar is a pleasant place to visit in the afternoon or early evening. It's not at all as stuffy as Aggie's, just don't expect everything to work perfectly. For example, don't count on receiving your telephone messages or having your faxes go out.

The two-story **Teuila Hotel** (Box 182, Apia; tel. 23-959, fax 26-887), on Vaitele Street opposite the Teachers College, has 16 overpriced a/c rooms with fridge and private bath at WS$138/213 single/double, breakfast included. There's live music in their lounge Tuesday to Sunday evenings.

The three-story **Hotel Insel Fehmarn** (Box 3272, Apia; tel. 23-301, fax 22-204), up Falealili Street in Moto'otua, has 54 rooms at WS$163/188/213 single/double/triple, plus 10% tax. Each a/c unit has a fridge, full cooking facilities, video/TV, balcony, and private bath. The Insel Fehmarn caters mostly to business travelers; typing, photocopying, and fax services are available. A swimming pool, tennis court, guest laundromat, restaurant, and bar are on the premises.

ACCOMMODATIONS AROUND UPOLU

Beach *Fales* at Aleipata and Lepa

During the past few years a dozen or so basic ecotourism resorts have sprung up at Lalomanu (Aleipata), on the golden sands facing Nu'utele Island, and on a less-frequented beach at Saleapaga (Lepa). These clusters of small two-person beach *fales* are still developing and amenities like electricity, toilets, and running water are provided at some but not at others. As well as being great places to stay, it's a wonderful introduction to Samoan culture.

For about WS$15 pp you'll get *fale* accommodation with a mat, pillow, and mosquito net but no bed. Food can cost anywhere from WS$5 pp to WS$26 pp for all meals. Of course, these are open thatched *fales* with no walls or doors, so keep valuables well stowed at night, and if you go off during the day, it might be a good idea to pack your bags and leave them with the owner. Hurricanes tend to wipe these places out, but they are quickly rebuilt. There's always lots of space for visitors who just show up. Picnickers pay WS$2 pp or WS$10 per car to use the facilities for the day. Most day-trippers arrive on weekends, so during the week you could have the entire beach to yourself. It's lovely—the perfect escape from Apia.

As you come down from Lalomanu village (Aleipata bus) and go west along the coast you'll pass Twin Huts, Lusi and Gata's, Litia Sini's, Taufua's, Sieni & Robert's, and Romeo's. **Lusi and Gata's Beach Fales** have a secluded beach all to themselves, whereas the last four share the same long beach. A few hundred meters west along the road from Romeo's is Malo Beach Fales. **Litia Sini's Beach Fales** is the most developed with the best facilities, and **Taufua's Beach Fales** has a bar. There have been several reports of theft at **Sieni & Robert's Beach Fales.**

Facing the white sands of Saleapaga (Lepa bus), seven km west of Lalomanu, you'll find another row of small *fale* resorts, including Gogosiva, Vaotea, Le Ta'alo, Banana Beach, Faofao, Fagiilima, Malaefono, Manusina, and Saleapaga Ocean View. For example, **Gogosiva Beach Fales** offers five thatched *fales* right on the beach at WS$15 pp, meals WS$5 each. Electricity and running water are available, and the family that runs the place is very helpful. Several readers wrote in strongly endorsing Tapu Legalo's **Faofao Beach Fales,** where you'll pay WS$40 pp including all meals. ("When we had a cloudburst one night, they ran out immediately and insisted that we stay inside while they arranged the blinds for us, getting soaked in the process.") No alcohol is allowed at Saleapaga village. There are hiking possibilities in the hills overlooking the village.

At Aufaga, a few km west of Saleapaga, are three adjacent *fale*-style resorts, but these are different in that they're at the bottom of a high cliff. Although all three charge WS$15 pp to sleep, food prices tend to be considerably higher than at Saleapaga. The largest such resort is **Fagatele Beach Fales** with 16 *fales* facing a wide sandy beach. Picnickers pay WS$2 for day use of this beach and there's a large parking lot at the top of the cliff. Avoid this place on Sunday. Meals at Fagatele are WS$10 each. Near-

by is **Faga Beach** (formerly called Vailaasia Beach), which has 14 *fales,* including one on a tiny island accessible by canoe and another on an isolated hill. The beach here is only so-so and the meals are overpriced. **Sinalele Beach** is separated from Faga by a rocky headland and features 12 *fales.* Check in at the grocery store across the street. All three of these have electricity and running water.

The **Vava'u Beach Fales** (Box 3026, Apia; tel. 26-266), a 10-minute walk west of Aufaga, is by far the most upmarket operation in this area—perfect if you want to experience the unspoiled beauty of southern Upolu without sacrificing creature comforts. The six attractive thatched bungalows on a private beach each have a private bath and shower, kitchenette, fridge, fan, table and chairs, windows, walls, and door. The price is WS$163 whether you're alone or a family of four. There's no restaurant so you ought to bring fresh vegetables from Apia, although basic supplies can be purchased at the small grocery stores in Lotofaga and Aufaga (the best store is at the east end of Aufaga). If you can afford to stay here you might consider renting a car in Apia and driving down as bus service is minimal. Vava'u would make a much nicer base than Apia for exploring Upolu by rental car, just fill the tank before leaving town. Don't expect the resort managers to provide "free" transportation to Apia or anywhere else, even if they offer.

Beach *Fales* at Falealili

The **Salani River Fales** at the end of the paved road in Salani village (Salani or Falealili buses) has seven thatched *fales* beside the Salani River and near the beach at WS$8 pp, meals WS$5 each. Ask for Rev. Vaolotu Taulapapa. This resort is mostly of interest to surfers who frequent the long lefthander in the channel. Other activities include canoeing in the mangroves or up the jade green river to a waterfall, crab fishing, using the nearby village bathing pool, and exploring the south coast.

Backpackers and anyone interested in finding a quiet little hideaway are welcome at **Vaiula Beach** (Box 189, Apia; no phone), one and a half km off the main highway at Tafatafa, nine km east of the junction of the Cross Island and South Coast Highways. There are four rooms in a run-down European-style house at WS$15 pp. You can use a communal kitchen, but the shared toilets and showers are outside. Camping is WS$5 pp (in your own tent) and picnic tables, toilets, and shelters are provided. The place fills up with picnickers on Saturday and Sunday (WS$5 per car) but during the week it's usually empty. The snorkeling off their beach is only mediocre, but there's the possibility of surfing the hollow, fast righthander out on the reef (boat required). Owner David Petersen is the grandson of a Danish sea captain and a bit of a character. Vaiula Beach makes an excellent base from which to explore O Le Pupu-Pu'e National Park and it's an okay stop on your way around the island.

Beach *Fales* near Faleolo Airport

Satapuala Beach Resorts (Box 1539, Apia; tel. 42-212, fax 42-386), on Fusive'a Beach near Satapuala village, is a 15-minute walk or a WS$6 taxi ride east from the airport. There are three fan-cooled bungalows with private bath and fridge at WS$59/79/99 single/double/triple, and for low-budgeteers there's an open Samoan *fale* costing WS$15 pp a night. Camping is WS$5 pp (own tent). Add 10% tax to all rates. High Chief To'alepaialii or his wife Teri can also arrange for you to stay in the local village, if you'd like. The adjacent restaurant specializes in local dishes, and there's also a seaside bar with live music on Friday and Saturday nights. On Sunday an *umu* is prepared (WS$20 pp). Since it's right on the main road to Apia, getting around is fairly easy, and it's also a good choice if you're only in transit through Samoa for one night and don't want to go into Apia from the airport. A drawback is that the reef is far away and you have to go quite a distance from shore before the water gets deep.

It's also possible to camp at **Paradise Beach** in Lefaga at WS$10 pp. Obtaining drinking water is sometimes a problem. In early 1995 it was announced that a 300-room hotel and competition golf course was to be erected at Lefaga by the Intercontinental chain.

Upmarket Beach Resorts

The **Samoan Village Resorts** (Bob Roberts, Box 3495, Apia; tel. 20-749), on Cape Fatuosofia opposite Manono Island, has confronted devastating hurricanes, undercapitalization, and a shortage of tourists in its protracted quest to erect Samoa's biggest beach resort. At last report the resort had 10 thatched a/c bungalows, each complete with private bathroom, cooking facilities, veranda, living room, and jacuzzi. Eventually there will be 32 bungalows, but while construction continues, the existing units are rented at WS$188 single, double, or triple, plus 10% tax. There's a swimming pool and restaurant/bar. Airport transfers are WS$24 each way but bicycles, canoes, and snorkeling gear are loaned free.

The most upscale place to stay in Western Samoa is the American-operated **Coconuts Beach Resort** (Jennifer and Barry Rose, Box 3684, Apia; tel. 24-849, fax 20-071), which opened in 1992 on a white-sand beach at Maninoa on the south side of Upolu, a km west of Siumu (Siumu, Safata, and Sataoa buses). There are five different categories of accommodations, varying in price from WS$260/300 single/double in an eight-room cluster to WS$555/650 for a two-bedroom beachfront bungalow (three-night minimum stay). The spacious treehouse rooms are cleverly designed with good ventilation and large covered balconies. Airport transfers are free for house guests. Their tariff is listed in U.S. dollars and that's how they prefer to be paid (cash or traveler's checks). Visa and MasterCard are accepted but you'll lose about 15% due to the way the banks clear the charges; use of an American Express card involves no loss. Gayle and Roger at the water sports hut offer scuba diving at WS$132 (snorkeling WS$48), two hours of deep-sea fishing at WS$270 for two people, kayak or paddle boat rentals at WS$22 an hour, and a sunset cruise at WS$60 pp. Roger is friendly but he'll often cancel a scheduled trip if fewer than six people sign up or if the boat is required for a more lucrative fishing expedition. On Saturday night, Coconuts has a *fia fia* on the beach under the stars. Day visitors who patronize their beachside bar and excellent seafood restaurant are welcome to use the beach, otherwise they'll be asked to leave. Day-trippers certainly aren't allowed to bring their own food or drink into the resort. For picnics, the adjacent village beach is available at WS$10 for adults, WS$5 for children. Several readers have commented on "a certain edgy, underlying tension" at Coconuts.

FOOD

Budget Places to Eat

The food stalls at the **Apia Market** are the cheapest places to eat (WS$3-5), and it's hard to beat a breakfast of hot chocolate with buttered bread, or a large bowl of cocoa and rice.

As you walk east along Beach Road it's worth noting **Le Rendez-Vous/Fale Aiga Coffee Bar** next to Samoa Air—it serves fresh coconuts at lunchtime. **Value City** (tel. 26-528) next to the Gold Star Building has a small lunch counter where you can get a good cup of coffee. **Skippy's** (tel. 25-050; closed Sunday) in the arcade beside the Pacific Commercial Bank has fish and chips, hamburgers, and local meals.

The **Town Clock Coffee Shop** (tel. 20-941; Monday to Thursday 0700-2000, Friday 0700-2200, Saturday 0700-1400/1800-2200, Sunday 1600-2100) on Vaea Street near Beach Road, is good for burgers, homemade meat pies, pancakes, coffee (free refill), and soft ice cream. The special Sunday roast dinner is WS$10. They bake their own bread and are very friendly (ask to see the visitors book).

Nearby at the corner of Vaea and Convent streets is **Betty's Restaurant** (open Monday to Friday 0630-1600, Saturday 0630-1300), which serves huge Samoan lunches, but you'll need a strong stomach to eat here.

A step up is the **Gourmet Seafood and Grill** (tel. 24-625; closed Sunday), on Convent Street a block back from the Chief Post Office, with lunch specials by the scoop and upmarket steaks. Their burgers are said to be the best in town. Right next door is **Isa's Ice Cream Shoppe** (tel. 23-728) with more fast food.

It's worth taking the trouble to seek out **Cam's Food Bar** (tel. 22-629; Monday to Thursday 0700-2100, Friday and Saturday 0700-2200), a block and a half behind the Chief Post Office (see the Central Apia map). Cam's is great for lunch and passable at breakfast.

Pele Rose Mini Market (tel. 24-062), opposite the Western Samoa Visitors Bureau, has coffee, sandwiches, and other takeaway foods, and they're open 24 hours a day seven days a week. **G.M. Bakery** (tel. 21-208; Monday to Saturday 0530-2200, Sunday 0530-0800 and 1600-2200), farther east on Beach Road next to the John Williams Building, sells cakes, ice cream cones, pies, and pastries.

The nameless snack bar next to Margrey-Ta's Beer Garden is open on Sunday, and when the beer garden's open you can consume the food in there. The *oka* (raw fish) is excellent.

Better Restaurants

The German-operated **Apia Inn** (tel. 21-010; weekdays 1200-1400, Monday to Saturday 1900-2300), on the second floor of the John Williams Building on Beach Road, is the place to splurge on fresh fish, lobster, mussels, and shrimp (small portions). Main courses average around WS$30—the menu is posted in the window. Avoid Daphne's Coffee Shoppe downstairs, where you can expect to be overcharged for a lousy cup of coffee.

Wong Kee's Restaurant (tel. 26-775), in a ramshackle building behind Otto's Reef, has some of the best Chinese food in town. The *aiga* lunch served weekdays is reasonable but the dinner menu is considerably more expensive. It's a good idea to order extra rice and share one main dish between two people.

The **Mandarin Palace Restaurant** (tel. 21-996) off Vaea Street has a WS$5 lunch special weekdays. Substantial Chinese meals are served at the upmarket **Treasure Garden Restaurant** (tel. 22-586) on Fugalei Street.

WESTERN SAMOA BREWERIES LTD. APIA, WESTERN SAMOA

NET CONTENTS
25.4 FL. OZ.
750 ml

ALCOHOLIC CONTENT
4.9 % VOL.

LAGER BEER

Vailima

BREWED AND BOTTLED UNDER GERMAN MANAGEMENT

The **Canton Restaurant** (tel. 22-818), on Matautu Street near Betty Moors, gets varied reports, but it's one of the few places that opens for dinner on Sunday (1730-2100). Try the saltwater crabs.

Another option for Sunday night dinner is the barbecue at **Aggie Grey's Hotel,** which offers a good selection of Samoan dishes at WS\$32 including wine. There's no traditional dancing but a corny hotel band is on the stage.

ENTERTAINMENT

Fale Tifaga Tauese Nos. 1 & 2 mini cinemas on Beach Road near Otto's Reef shows the usual adventure and romance films popular throughout the third world.

Friday nights a rock band shakes **Beachcomber Nightclub** (tel. 20-248; WS\$3 cover charge), just up the Mulinu'u Peninsula from the Kitano Tusitala, and Pale's Polynesian Show comes on at 2100 (check, as some weeks this show is on Thursday or Saturday). Drinks are reasonable—just take care with the doorman, who is known for his unpredictable nature.

The **Mount Vaea Nightclub** (tel. 21-627; Monday to Saturday 1900-midnight) on Vaitele Street has been the place to pick up or get picked up in Apia since 1968. It's loud, rough, and fast, and there are lots of girls/boys. Things don't get going until late, and drunks often get into squabbles, so stay out of the middle and be really polite to everyone. The trouble is usually between local Samoans, rarely tourists.

Other nightclubs around town include the **Talofa Bar** next to Parker's Accommodation, the **Korean Night Club** also near Parker's, and **Tijuana Night Club** on Vaea Street.

Most of the problematical situations at these places revolve around the Samoan "nightclub custom" of asking any female to dance who is not currently dancing, whether she came with a date or not. It can be taken as an insult to say no in this situation, so a female who only wants to dance with her date must dance every dance with him or be bombarded with requests she cannot lightly refuse. Otherwise she can say that her foot hurts and forgo dancing with anyone, including her date.

A dance band plays at the **Kitano Tusitala Hotel** most nights, with a cover charge on weekends. On Sunday everything's shut except the hotel bars, and you're supposed to be a hotel guest in order to patronize them.

Apia's favorite drinking place is the **RSA Club** (tel. 20-171; Monday to Saturday 1000-midnight) on Beach Road in the center of Apia. Happy hour is 1700-1900 with free *pupu*s (snacks) at 1800. Visitors are welcome here.

Otto's Reef (tel. 22-691) on Beach Road is a safe, casual place to drink. Check out their Samoan *oka* (spicy raw fish) Thursday to Saturday. **Don't Drink the Water** (tel. 20-093) is a No Smoking bar!

Margrey-Ta's Beer Garden (tel. 25-395; Monday to Saturday 1000-midnight), a collection of small *fales* near the Seaside Inn on Beach Road, is always rowdy and fun.

At the **Apia Yacht Club** (tel. 21-313) out on the Mulinu'u Peninsula, you can get a great cheeseburger and a drink on Friday night, a barbecue on Sunday 1100-1600. All visitors are welcome *with* a member; polite, nicely dressed visitors *without* a member are usually invited in too.

Weekday mornings at 0750 the police band marches up Beach Road to the new Government Building for the flag-raising ceremony at 0800, and all traffic is stopped. Late Friday night or very early Saturday morning you can sometimes see a great show for free by the market as evangelists preach and a choir sings joyful religious songs, all the hands moving gracefully just as if this were a *fia fia*. Church choirs are good Sunday morning too (dress neatly and avoid bright clothing or shorts).

Cultural Shows for Visitors

An essential part of any visit to Samoa is attendance at a *fia fia* where the Polynesian dancing on stage comes with a buffet dinner of local foods (look over the whole spread before getting in line). Sometimes the show is before dinner, sometimes after. If you're not hungry, a drink at the bar should admit you. Patrons wearing T-shirts or shorts are not allowed.

There's usually a *fia fia* at Ah Kam's Motel on Tuesday (WS\$30), at Aggie Grey's Hotel on Wednesday (WS\$40), at the Kitano Tusitala on Thursday (WS\$45), and at Margrey-Ta's Beer Garden or Beachcomber Nightclub on Friday.

The show at the Kitano Tusitala includes dances from several Pacific countries, while the "We Are Samoa" program put on by the hotel staff at Aggie Grey's is strictly Samoan and usually includes an appearance by a female member of the Grey clan, carrying on a tradition established by Aggie herself. The show at Aggie's is before dinner and it's no problem dropping in and ordering a few drinks. The buffet is served later by the pool.

SHOPPING

Kava & Kaving Handicrafts (Box 853, Apia; tel. 24-145) on Beach Road has war clubs (WS$70), kava bowls (WS$115-300), baskets, shell necklaces, and coconut shell jewelry. They carry mostly authentic traditional handicrafts at good prices. Also compare **Aggie's Gift Shop** next to Aggie Grey's Hotel and **Chan Mow Supermarket** opposite the Government Building, both of which have handicrafts.

Apia's colorful new **market** three blocks inland on Fugalei or Saleufi Streets throbs with activity 24 hours a day—families spend the night here rather than abandon their places. You'll see a marvelous array of local produce, all with prices clearly marked, plus handicrafts, local foods, an eating area, and a great assortment of classic Polynesian types.

Go native in Samoa by changing into some colorful, eye-catching clothing. Female travelers especially will enhance their appearance and acceptance by wearing a long *mu'umu'u* gown, a two-piece *puletasi,* or a simple wraparound *lavalava.* The **Island Styles Factory Showroom** (tel. 21-436) on the Cross Island Highway, six and a half km from Apia (Vaoala bus), displays lovely hand-printed fabrics ready-made into the above items and more. The locally made Talofa ginger or passion fruit wines, and coconut cream, ginger, or coffee liqueurs can also be tasted here. Island Styles has a small sales outlet in the arcade behind Wesley Bookshop in central Apia. Most shops are closed Saturday afternoon and Sunday.

The Western Samoa **Philatelic Bureau** (tel. 20-720) is in the Chief Post Office and at the airport—beautiful stamps at face value.

SERVICES AND INFORMATION

Money

The **Bank of Western Samoa** (a joint venture between the government and the ANZ Bank) gives cash advances on Visa credit cards, while the **Pacific Commercial Bank** (a joint venture of the Bank of Hawaii and the Westpac Bank) takes MasterCard. Obtaining money this way is expensive as you'll lose about 15% on the exchange and interest is charged from the moment you collect the money.

The main branch of the Bank of Western Samoa opposite the Chief Post Office changes traveler's checks weekdays 0900-1500, Saturday 0830-1130. Several small agencies of the Bank of Western Samoa around Apia will also change traveler's checks at the same rate. The Bank of Western Samoa charges 50 cents commission on traveler's checks, whereas the Pacific Commercial Bank deducts WS$3.

The rate of exchange for traveler's checks is considerably better than that for cash. Changing foreign currency outside Apia can be a nuisance, so do it here. On Saturday afternoon and Sunday, Aggie Grey's Hotel and the Kitano Tusitala will change traveler's checks for a rate about 10% lower than the bank.

There's no real American Express representative in Apia, although **Retzlaff Travel** (tel. 21-724, fax 23-038) will help you report lost traveler's checks and credit cards. Due to financial restrictions imposed by the Central Bank of Western Samoa, Retzlaff Travel is unable to provide any of the regular Amex services.

Post and Telecommunications

The Chief Post Office in central Apia is open weekdays 0900-1630. Poste restante main is held one month at a counter in the room with the post office boxes. Branch post offices exist at Matautu, Pesega, and Faleolo Airport.

Make long-distance telephone calls from the **International Telephone Bureau** (daily 0800-2200), inside the Chief Post Office. Station-to-station calls are WS$4.50 to American Samoa, WS$9 to Australia or New Zealand, and WS$13.50 to North America or Europe, all for three minutes. These prices are about the lowest in the South Pacific. Public telephones for local calls are available at the Chief Post Office but they're always occupied.

Immigration Office

For a visa extension, go to the Immigration office (tel. 20-291) on Beach Road (top floor) with WS$50, two photos, your onward ticket, sufficient funds, proof that you're staying at a hotel, and a good reason. You may also be asked to obtain a local sponsor who'll accept responsibility for you. If these requirements seem strict, consider that about 1,000 Samoans are deported from New Zealand each year.

Embassies

The U.S. Consulate (tel. 21-631 or 22-696; weekdays 0930-1230) is on the fifth floor of the John Williams Building on Beach Road. As usual, it's there mostly for official purposes and has little interest in protecting or defending individual Americans, unless there's some political mileage to be made out of it.

The **Australian High Commission** (tel. 23-411; Monday to Thursday 0830-1600, Friday 0830-1200) on Beach Road near Aggie Grey's Hotel issues free tourist visas mandatory for everyone other than New Zealanders.

Other countries with representation in Apia include China (tel. 22-474), Germany (tel. 22-695), New Zealand (tel. 21-711), and the European Union (tel. 20-070).

Laundromats and Public Toilets

Sapolu Laundrette (tel. 21-934; Monday to Saturday 0600-2200, Sunday 0600-2000), on Matautu Street between Betty Moors and the harbor, charges WS$2.50 to wash, WS$3.50 to dry. Bring your own laundry soap. At night, beware of vicious dogs here that often attack pedestrians headed for the guesthouses down the road.

If you're staying at Parker's Accommodation or Ah Kam's Motel try **Homestyle Laundromat** (tel. 21-551; open daily 0700-1900) behind A.S. Hunt Service Center on Fugalei Street. There's also a mini-cinema here that shows mostly worthless trash. **Laundrette Sil** is across the street.

Public toilets are behind the clock tower in the center of town.

Information

The overstaffed **Western Samoa Visitors Bureau** (tel. 20-878; weekdays 0800-1630, Saturday 0800-1200), in a *fale* on Beach Road between the Government Building and the Catholic cathedral, has brochures and can answer questions.

The **Department of Statistics** (Box 1151, Apia; tel. 21-371, fax 21-373) sells the *Annual Statistical Abstract* and *Quarterly Statistical Bulletin*.

Get large maps of Apia and Samoa at the **Lands and Survey Department** (tel. 22-481) for WS$7 each. The *Western Samoa* map published by Hema Maps (WS$10) is excellent and it's available both here and at Aggie's Gift Shop.

The **Wesley Bookshop** (tel. 24-231) on Beach Road carries Michael Shield's noted book *The Mau,* but proprietors have long refused to stock the works of Samoa's leading novelist, Albert Wendt, which are too critical for their taste. For Wendt's novels and other excellent books on the Pacific, you must go to the **Educational Bookstore** (tel. 20-817) at the south end of Vaea Street.

The place to buy overseas newspapers and magazines is **Le Moana Cafe** (tel. 25-170) in the Lotemau Center on Convent Street.

The **Public Library** (tel. 21-208; Monday to Thursday 0900-1630, Friday 0800-1600, Saturday 0830-1200) is on the ground floor of the monumental new Government Building on the waterfront.

Western Samoa's environmental group, the **Siosiomaga Society** (Box 5774, Matautu-uta, Upolu; tel./fax 21-993), in the office building above the Educational Bookstore at the south end of Vaea Street, has a large library of environmentally oriented videos, which you can view at their office weekdays 0800-1630.

The **South Pacific Regional Environmental Program** (Box 240, Apia; tel. 21-929, fax 20-231), opposite the Yazaki Samoa plant near the Vailima Brewery at Vaitele, sells many specialized publications on the South Pacific environment. (There are plans to eventually move this office to a new site near the Robert Louis Stevenson Museum—ask before making the long trip out to Vaitele.)

Air New Zealand (tel. 20-825) and **Samoa Air** (tel. 22-901) are next to Morris Hedstrom Department Store. **Polynesian Airlines** (tel.

21-261) is opposite the clock tower with **Air Pacific** (tel. 22-693) in the same building.

Health

You can see a doctor at the **National Hospital** (tel. 21-212) almost anytime for WS$20 (bring along a book to read while you're waiting). You can call an ambulance at the number provided. The Public Health Clinic in the dilapidated section of the same complex offers vaccinations weekdays 0800-1200 and 1300-1630. Chemists in Apia are closed weekends and holidays, and the pharmacy at the National Hospital is useless. The Moto'otua bus passes the hospital.

A good alternative to trekking out to the hospital is visiting **Dr. I.M. Alama** (tel. 24-120, after hours tel. 21-908), whose office is directly behind Beachcomber Night Club (same building) near the Kitano Tusitala Hotel.

TRANSPORTATION

By Bus

Local buses for Apia and vicinity, and those to points along Upolu's north or west coasts, leave from the main bus station adjacent to Apia Market. Come here to catch a bus to the Robert Louis Stevenson Museum (marked Avele or Vaoala), the Papase'ea Sliding Rocks (Seesee, Siusega, or Tafaigata), the University of the South Pacific (Alafua), the main wharf (Mataututai), Fagali'i Airport or the Royal Samoa Country Club (Fagali'i-tai), the National Hospital (Moto'otua), Piula Cave Pool (Falefa or Falevao), Faleolo Airport or the Savai'i ferry wharf (Falelatai, Mulifanua, Manono, Pasi Ole Vaa, or Satui), or Manono Island (Falelatai or Manono).

Long-distance buses to southern and eastern Upolu generally leave from the parking lot behind the RSA Club near the clock tower in central Apia. Here you'll find the Uafato, Tiavea, Aleipata, Lepa, Salani, Falealili, Siumu, Safata, Sataoa, and Lefaga buses. You can find a bus to virtually any of them so long as you're there by 1000 Monday to Saturday.

The police do not allow buses to sit waiting for passengers for long periods at the overcrowded market bus station, so the buses usually make a loop around the block and return to the station every 10 minutes or so until they're full. The

long-distance buses from south or east Upolu first call at the market bus station to drop off passengers, then park behind the RSA Club until they're ready to leave. Long-distance buses have been known to drive around town for an hour looking for passengers. There are no set schedules.

On Friday afternoon all buses departing Apia tend to be crowded with workers headed home. Saturday morning is a good time for buses, but on Saturday afternoon, Sunday, and evenings, service is very limited. It's not possible to make a day-trip to Aleipata or Lepa from Apia by bus—you must spend the night there.

In outlying villages only bus drivers are reliable sources of information about bus departure times. Others can give misleading information, so ask three or four people. On weekdays buses to Apia often leave villages in south and east Upolu at 0500, and then again at 1130. They often set out from behind the RSA Club in Apia to return to their villages at 1200 and 1600.

The Salani or Falealili buses follow the Cross Island Highway to Siumu, then run along the south coast via Poutasi to Salani. Four buses serve this route, but they all seem to run about the same time, making three or four trips a day. The last bus back to Apia from Salani is at 1400 (important to know if you're making a day-trip to O Le Pupu-Pu'e National Park).

Most of these colorful homemade wooden buses are village-owned. Trying to use them to go right around Upolu is very difficult, as they serve outlying villages by different routes that don't link up. The Lalomanu or Aleipata bus goes via Falevao and Amaile, while the Lepa bus goes via Lotofaga to Saleapaga. There's no bus from Lalomanu to Saleapaga (a seven-km walk).

There's a good paved road from Mafa Pass to Amaile, but only a rough gravel road from Mafa Pass to Lepa. The road along the south coast is paved from Siumu to Salani, but there a river blocks eastbound vehicular traffic and cars must make a loop up and around via Sopo'anga Falls (no bus service). There's very little traffic along the south coast of Upolu if you intended to hitch.

Bus service is also very limited west of Siumu on the south coast with no service between Sataoa and Lefaga. The Lefaga bus follows the north coast west to Leulumoega, then drives south through Tanumalamala to Matautu (Paradise Beach). There's no service between Lefaga and Falelatai. The only convenient way to go right around Upolu is to rent a car.

The buses are without cushions, but they do have destination signs and set fares. Buses around Apia cost 50 *sene;* WS$1.50 to the Savai'i ferry wharf or Falefa; WS$2 to Lefaga or Mafa Pass; WS$2.50 to Siumu; WS$3 to Lalomanu or Saleapaga. The bus fare from Apia to Aleipata is usually WS$3, although some drivers collect WS$5. The stereo music is a bus plus.

Taxis

Taxis have license plates bearing the prefix "T." Taxis parked outside the two airports and at the upmarket hotels tend to be a rip-off, while those waiting at taxi stands used mostly by local people are often okay. Average taxi prices from the taxi stand adjacent to the market bus station are WS$3 to the main wharf, WS$4 to Fagali'i Airport, or WS$5 to the Robert Louis Stevenson Museum.

Since the taxis don't have meters, always agree on the price before you get in and make sure you're both talking Western Samoa *tala,* otherwise the driver could insist on the same amount in U.S. dollars (a favorite trick). If you intend to get out and have the driver wait awhile, ask the price of that too. Failure to do so will lead to unpleasant demands for extra money at the end of the trip and ugly threats if you resist. There should be no additional charge for luggage, and tipping is unnecessary.

Beware of the taxis parked in front of Aggie Grey's Hotel, as these drivers are some of the most seasoned hustlers you'll ever meet. If you're staying at Aggie's and want a taxi, turn right as you come out the door, cross the bridge, and about a hundred meters in front you'll see a regular taxi stand.

Car Rentals

The international driver's license isn't recognized in Western Samoa. Officially you're supposed to get a local driver's license (WS$20 and one photo) at the licensing office opposite the main police station in Apia. Some car rental agencies require a Samoan driver's license, while others don't. According to the Western Samoa Visitors Bureau, it's actually up to the agency!

Many side roads are too rough for a car and most agencies will tell you the insurance isn't valid if you drive on them. Make reservations well ahead if you want a Jeep. A few of the car rental agencies are evasive about what is and isn't covered by the optional collision insurance, and some rental cars don't carry any collision insurance at all. Check the car *very carefully* before you drive off, and don't under any circumstances leave your passport as security on a car rental, although some agencies have the cheek to suggest it. Be suspicious, as we get more than the usual number of complaints about car rentals at Apia.

Speed limits are 40 kph around Apia or 56 kph on the open road. Drive very slowly and avoid hitting any people or animals—it can be as bad as in Mexico. If you do hit something valuable like a large pig, drive straight to the nearest police station and turn yourself in. If you stop you could get stoned. Heaven help you if you hit a Samoan! If you park a rental car in a village, you risk having it vandalized.

Except for one gas station near the airport and another at Siumu, fuel isn't usually available outside Apia, so plan ahead. Ask the car rental company which gas station they recommend, as some stations have tanks that let rainwater leak in. If you want to take the car to Savai'i make sure it's allowed before signing the rental contract (most agencies won't allow you to do this). You can reserve a car space on the ferry at the office of the Western Samoa Shipping Corporation on Vaea Street in Apia. As in American Samoa, driving is on the right. Add 10% tax to all rates quoted below.

Budget Rent-a-Car (tel. 20-561, fax 22-284), between Polynesian Airlines and the Pacific Commercial Bank in the center of town, is expensive at WS$125 daily, unlimited mileage included. You'll not be allowed to take the car to Savai'i and they'll really sock it to you if any damage is done to the car (don't accept a substandard car from them).

Avis Rent-a-Car (tel. 20-486, fax 26-069), next to the Peace Corps office on Matautu Street, also charges WS$125 for their cheapest car with unlimited mileage. Their WS$25 collision insurance is of dubious value and Avis cars cannot be taken to Savai'i.

G & J Transport (Box 1707, Apia; tel. 21-078, fax 21-078), next to Kava & Kavings on Beach Road, has cars at WS$130. Unlimited mileage and WS\$600 deductible collision insurance are included and it's okay to take the car to Savai'i.

P & K Filo Car Rentals (Box 4310, Matautu; tel. 23-031 or 22-046, fax 25-574), opposite the Canton Restaurant on Matautu Street, has cars at WS\$110 a day for one or two days, WS\$88 a day for three days or more, including tax, mileage, and insurance (WS\$600 deductible). You must leave WS\$200 deposit and you may take the car to Savai'i.

Funway Rentals (Box 6075, Apia; tel. 22-045) rents Suzuki Sidekick jeeps at WS\$135/810 daily/weekly with unlimited mileage and it's okay to take the vehicle to Savai'i. At last report, their jeeps were in good shape. Call them up for free delivery.

Billie's Car Rentals (Box 1863, Apia; tel. 21-724 or 25-363, fax 23-038) on Vaea Street has cars at WS\$100 a day for one or two days, WS\$90 for three or four days, WS\$80 for five days or more. Billie's cars may be taken to Savai'i by ferry. This company is owned by Retzlaff Travel, thus it can be considered one of the more reliable independent car rental operators.

Another local company with a good reputation is **Pavitt's-U-Drive** (tel. 21-766, fax 24-667), near the National Hospital, with cars beginning at WS\$115 daily. Also try **Apia Rentals** (Box 173, Apia; tel. 24-244, fax 26-193) on Palisi Moamoa Road, **Hibiscus Rentals** (tel. 27-039, fax 20-162) near Hotel Insel Fehmarn, and **Le Car Rentals** (Box 3669, Apia; tel./fax 22-754) on Fugalei Street.

Emka Rental Cars (tel. 23-266, fax 25-265), on Vaitele Street near the Mount Vaea Club (in the small store opposite the Adventist Youth Welfare Center), has cars at WS\$100 a day (WS\$100 deposit) and it's okay to take them to Savai'i. Emka offers no collision insurance.

Scooter and Bicycle Rentals

The agencies renting motorbikes and bicycles changes all the time, so ask at the visitors bureau for current locations. With scooters the in-

surance is usually included, but the gas is extra. A cash deposit will be required. The caretaker at the Palolo Deep Marine Reserve rents bicycles.

Tulei Rentals (tel. 24-145), at Kava & Kavings Handicrafts on Beach Road, rents Yamaha 175 motorbikes at WS\$50 a day plus WS\$5 for a helmet (motorcycle license required).

Tours

Several companies offer organized day tours of Upolu from Apia. Prices vary according to the number of participants, whether you travel by private car or minibus, if lunch is included, etc. Don't expect much "narration" from the guide—it's mainly a way of getting around. The tours don't operate unless at least eight people sign up, so ask about that, and if it looks questionable, ask elsewhere. Even if organized sightseeing isn't your usual thing, it's worth considering here.

Samoa Scenic Tours (Box 669, Apia; tel. 22-880, fax 23-626) at Aggie Grey's Hotel charges WS\$33 pp for an afternoon tour around town. Full-day trips including lunch cost WS\$66 pp to Lefaga's Paradise Beach (Tuesday and Friday) or Aleipata (Wednesday and Saturday). Their full-day Manono Island excursion on Monday and Thursday is WS\$78 pp, lunch included. **Jane's Tours** (Box 70, Apia; tel. 20-954, fax 22-680) on Vaea Street offers full-day trips to Coconuts Beach Resort on Tuesday and Friday, Aleipata on Wednesday, and Paradise Beach on Thursday, all WS\$55 pp including lunch. The Manono trip on Tuesday is WS\$65 (half price for children under 12).

Eco-Tour Samoa Ltd. (Box 4609, Matautu-tai, Apia; tel./fax 25-993) offers adventuresome hiking tours to remote natural locations on Upolu and two different overnight trips around Savai'i. Contact them through the Western Samoa Visitors Bureau. **Oceania Tours** (Box 9339, Apia; tel. 24-443, fax 22-255), next to the Kitano Tusitala Hotel, also has a variety of overnight tours to Savai'i. These trips are reasonable value for those with limited time, but compare prices and book ahead.

SAVAI'I

Savai'i is just 20 km northwest of Upolu across the Apolima Strait. Although half again larger and higher than its neighbor, Savai'i has under two-fifths as many people. This totally unspoiled big island offers ancient Polynesian ruins, waterfalls, clear freshwater pools, white beaches, vast black lava fields, massive volcanoes, and traditional Samoan life. Robert Flaherty's classic, *Moana of the South Seas* (1926), was filmed on Savai'i. Most of the villages are by the seashore, strung along the circumsular highway, and they're a pleasure to stroll through. Yet for an island, a visit to Savai'i is not sea-oriented as many of the attractions are away from the coast.

Savai'i is the largest island in Polynesia (outside of Hawaii and New Zealand). Most of the north side of this high volcanic island was transformed in the great eruptions of Mt. Matavanu between 1905 and 1911, which buried much fertile land and sent refugees streaming across to Upolu. Even today vast tracts of virgin rain-

forest survive despite logging and agricultural clearings. Coral reefs are present along the east coast from Saleloaga to Pu'apu'a, on the north coast from Saleaula to Sasina, then from Asau to Vaisala, and on the south coast at Palauli. Expect to pay a custom fee of anywhere from WS$1 pp to WS$10 per car to a responsible adult (not a child or teenager) to use a village beach.

Orientation

Other than Salelologa, there's nothing that could be called a town on Savai'i; it's just one village after another around the coast, with large gaps on all sides. In recent years Salelologa has developed into a busy little town with a market, stores, laundromat, bookshop, several small restaurants and takeaways, and a couple of places to stay. From the wharf where the Upolu ferry lands it's less than a km straight up to the market and main bus station. The **Bank of Western Samoa** (tel. 51-213) is next to the market and the **Pacific Commercial Bank** (tel. 51-

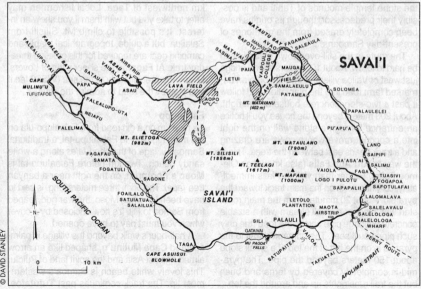

SAVAI'I

208) is farther up the same way, near the T-junction with the circuminsular road.

Police stations are found at Asau and Fagamalo, but the main police station (also handling immigration matters) is in the small government complex at Tuasivi, about 10 km north of Salelologa. There are post offices at Salelologa, Tuasivi, Fagamalo, Asau, and Salailua, and district hospitals at Sataua and Tuasivi.

SIGHTS

Letolo Plantation

Catch a bus from the Salelologa ferry wharf to Letolo Plantation, eight km west in Palauli District. The largest remaining prehistoric monument in Polynesia is here, as well as an idyllic waterfall and pool. The huge **Pulemelei stone pyramid** *(tia)*, on a slope about two km from the main circuminsular highway, was concealed by thick undergrowth until the 1960s. This immense stone platform on a hillside in the middle of the coconut plantation is 73 meters long, 60 meters wide, and 15 meters high, and stones used in religious ceremonies are scattered around it. The structure is similar to some of the stone temple mounds of Tahiti and is possibly their predecessor, though its origins have been completely erased from the memories of present-day Samoans.

The route to the still-overgrown pyramid can be hard to follow. About 100 meters after a bridge just west of Vailoa village, turn right onto an unmarked farm road into the plantation and follow it past a two-story concrete house on the right. About 200 meters beyond the house you'll notice an entrance through a stone wall on the right into a coconut grove where cows are grazing and a track heads east between the trees. This is the way to **Afu Aua Falls** (also known as Olemoe Falls). Rather than visit the falls immediately, continue north on the main track toward the pyramid. About 20 minutes from the main road, start watching for a small stream with a sizable concrete drainage pipe across the road (the only such pipe you'll see). The unmarked trail to the pyramid is on the left at the top of a small slope about 150 meters beyond the pipe. The pyramid is completely covered by ferns and bush but the trail runs rights up and around the top.

After exploring the pyramid return to the falls for a well-deserved swim. The edge of the ravine is 400 meters straight east through the coconut plantation, and the steep path down to the pool is fairly obvious. The crystal-clear waters of the river running down the east side of the plantation plunge over a cliff into a large, deep pool into which you can dive from the sides. Brown prawns live in the pool: drop in bread crumbs and wait for them to appear.

During your visit here, keep in mind that you're on private property, courtesy of the Nelson family. Politely ask permission to proceed of any people you meet along the way. Admission should be free.

The Southwest Coast

There's a series of rather spectacular **blowholes** *(pupu)* along the coast near Cape Asuisui, just a short walk from **Taga** village some 40 km west of the wharf. These blowholes (WS$1 admission) are at their best at high tide. Throw in a coconut and watch the roaring jet propel it skyward. (If you allow a boy to perform this trick for you he'll want a substantial tip.)

There's good surfing in winter (May to August) at high tide just off the point at **Salailua,** 13 km northwest of Taga. Local fishermen may offer to take you out with them if you show an interest. It's possible to climb Mt. Silisili from Salailua, but a guide, topographical maps, and camping gear are required for this grueling three-day trek. At **Fagafau** the sheer cliffs of Lovers' Leap drop precipitously to the sea (WS$2 fee if you stop by the road to admire the cliffs).

Falealupo

It's nine km on a dirt road from Falealupo-uta on the main highway to Falealupo-tai, a traditional Samoan village of thatched *fales* along a white sandy beach. Two km before Falealupo-tai is **Moso's Footprint,** on the right near a banyan tree *(aoa)*. The print, three meters long, is said to have been left when Moso, the war god, leaped from Samoa to Fiji. It's now enclosed by a cover which you must pay to have opened.

A half-hour's walk beyond the village is palm-covered **Cape Mulinu'u,** shaped like an arrow aimed against Asia and the spirit land of Pulotu. This lovely white beach is Samoa's westernmost tip. The track continues past **Tufutafoe,** one km from the cape, to Neiafu on the main highway, a couple of hours walk.

Several rather stiff admission fees are charged to visit this idyllic area. You'll pay WS$5 to enter Falealupo-tai village, plus an extra WS$5 to see Moso's Footprint (not worth it). If you enter the domain of nearby Tufutafoe village, an additional WS$10 must be paid. No services are provided for this money. If you're driving you can usually bargain for a group rate and get everyone in your vehicle in for these amounts, but individuals roughing it on public transport may have to pay the same per person. Unless you have your own transport, getting to Falealupo is difficult—there's only one bus a day, which leaves the village for the wharf at 0300 every morning, although it's usually possible to hitch a ride in a pickup.

The North Coast

The paved road ends at **Asau,** the main center on the north side of Savai'i. Attractive Asau has a disused airstrip on the breakwater enclosing Asau Bay, a wharf, and a large sawmill belonging to Samoa Forest Products. There's good holding for yachts in the well-protected small boat harbor, but the channel is subject to silting, so seek local advice before attempting to enter. A safe, though exposed, yacht anchorage is found at Matautu Bay farther east from May to October.

From Asau, continue east as best you can (see "Getting Around," below). Stop at **Matavai,** where there's swimming in a large freshwater spring *(mata ole alelo).* Find more freshwater pools *(vaisafe'e)* at **Safotu** village, three km east of Matavai. Safotu also has a large Catholic church opposite a picturesque beach lined with small dugout fishing canoes.

Three km inland from Safotu is **Paia** village, where the *pulenu'u* collects WS$1 pp from visitors. An old Samoan fort is on a mound just above the village, but more interesting is the lava tube *(nu'uletau),* the "short people's cave," another three km inland from Paia. You'll need guides and kerosene lamp to visit it (WS$20 fee). Meter-high midgets are said to live inside.

A stiff two-and-a-half-hour walk inland from Paia brings you to **Mt. Matavanu** (402 meters), which the locals call *mata ole afi* (eye of the fire). This was the source of the 1905-11 volcanic outbreak that covered much of northeast

Savai'i with black lava. You don't really need a guide to find the crater—just look for a trail to the left where the road dips, about two and a half hours out of Paia. Beware of deep crevices and crumbling edges as you near the crater; they have claimed at least one life. There's no charge to come up here.

The Lava Field

The road south of Saleaula runs right across a wide, barren lava flow. A large stone church, nearly engulfed by the lava at the beginning of the century, is on the northeast side of the road under a large tree about 100 meters off the road near the flow's north edge. The so-called **Virgin's Grave** is about 150 meters east of the church near a mango tree. Look for a rectangular depression about two meters deep in the lava; the grave is clearly visible at the bottom. Someone will collect WS$5 admission per group (it's not worth the trouble stopping unless you're driving).

As the fast-flowing *pahoehoe* lava approached the coast here in the early years of this century, it built up behind the reef and spread out in both directions. The highway now runs across it for eight km. Walk on the lava to get a feel for this awesome geological event.

The East Coast

Picturesque villages and intermittent white beaches run all the way south from Pu'apu'a to the wharf. **Lano** is a favorite surfing beach in summer (December to March), and there's good snorkeling at **Faga.** At **Sapapalii** is a large monument to John Williams in front of the large Congregational Christian Church. This marks the site where the missionary arrived in 1830 and converted the local chiefs to Christianity in a couple of days. Several hotels are found around here (see "Accommodations and Food," below).

ACCOMMODATIONS AND FOOD

Accommodations at Salelologa

A few minutes walk from the ferry wharf is the **Savai'i Ocean View Motel** (Tui and Maselina Retzlaff, Box 195, Apia; tel. 51-258), with four self-contained bungalows at WS$88/113/138 single/double/triple, plus 10% tax. The Ocean View caters mostly to Samoan government officials with fat expense accounts—everyone else will do better elsewhere.

Next door to the Ocean View is Manumalo Baptist Church where Rev. Seumanu Alofa operates **Rita's Accommodation** (Box 5066, Salelologa, Savai'i; tel. 51-257) with four small two-room *fales* facing the coast at WS$30 pp including all meals. Reverend Seumanu also organizes island tours in his pickup at negotiable rates. This place makes a good base for visiting the island thanks to the radiating bus services, but it's still developing, so let us know how you liked it. Sometimes the family occupies part of the guest accommodations, which creates a lot of noise and eliminates privacy.

A little farther up the road from Rita's, before the market, is **Taffy's Paradise Inn** (Box 3044, Apia; no phone) with shared-bath rooms at WS$60/80/113 single/double/triple, or WS$70/138/188 with private bath, plus tax. There's a bar, and meals are served. The seven rooms in this Western-style building are pleasant enough, but it's poorly managed and you may arrive to find it padlocked. Ask at the restaurant/store upstairs in the ferry terminal.

Accommodations in Eastern Savai'i

The **Safua Hotel** (Private Mail Bag, Salelologa; tel. 51-271, fax 51-272), in a garden setting at Lalomalava, six km north of the wharf, was the first hotel on Savai'i. The nine fan-cooled Samoan *fales* with private facilities are WS$100/113/138 single/double/triple, plus tax, and camping is WS$15 pp. Three mammoth meals (WS$56 pp extra) are served at a long table where the gracious owner/hostess Moelagi Jackson and her family eat with guests. Sunday dinner is a special treat. (Campers may use the kitchen to prepare their own breakfast and lunch.) Moelagi, one of the very few female *failauga* in Samoa, is an expert on tapa making, and she usually keeps a few high-quality pieces on hand to sell. Island tours by minibus are arranged, or just ask to be shown around the family plantation. The Safua is not on the beach but an informal bar faces a shady garden, and there's a large library. This characterful hotel is a perennial favorite of international travelers and you'll enjoy sitting in the lounge chatting with the other guests.

The **Savaiian Hotel** (Roger and Ama Gidlow, Box 5082, Salelologa; tel. 51-206, fax 51-

291), behind the Mobil service station just south of the Safua at Lalomalava, has less Samoan atmosphere. The six a/c duplex units with cooking facilities, fridge, and private bath (hot water) are WS$95/115/135 single/double/triple. It's on a rocky shore and is clean but rather sterile.

If you want to be right at the beach, pick the **Siufaga Beach Resort** (Box 8002, Tuasivi; tel. 53-518, fax 53-535), just a km north of the new hospital at Tuasivi and about six km north of Lalomalava. Created by an Italian doctor and his Samoan family, the resort has a large green lawn that faces lovely Faga Beach, one of the best swimming/snorkeling locales in Samoa. It's in something of a rain shadow so it's drier than Salelologa. The six attractive *fales* with private bath, kitchenette, and local Samoan decor go for WS$88/100/113 single/double/triple, and campers are also welcome at WS$12 pp. There's a good grocery store opposite the post office, a 10-minute walk south of the resort, but no cooking facilities for campers. Dr. Peter Caffarelli is an interesting character who enjoys chatting with guests on his veranda. The Puapua bus (WS$1) will bring you here from Salelologa wharf, otherwise a taxi from the wharf will run WS$15. Highly recommended.

In 1994 a new tourist resort appeared at Manase village on Savai'i's north side. **Stevenson's at Manase** (Box 210, Apia; tel./fax 58-219) has 18 rather stuffy a/c rooms in a long prefabricated block at WS$70/75/85 single/double/triple. The one family-size suite is WS$165. Stevenson's also caters to backpackers and adventure groups with six *fales* and eight set tents at WS$30 including one mattress, plus WS$10 for each additional mattress. There are no cooking facilities, and meals in the hotel restaurant are expensive. The well-fenced beach is only fair, and pedalboats are WS$10 an hour (outrigger canoes are free). Rental cars are WS$100 a day. Stevenson's might be okay if you enjoy a resort atmosphere, though there aren't usually a lot of people staying there. It does make a good base for visiting Mt. Matavanu and is a convenient place to stop on your way around the island.

A more-do-it-yourself place is **Lagoto Beach Fales** (Box 34, Fagamalo; no phone), a couple of km east near Fagamalo Post Office. The four individual *fales* facing a better beach are WS$100/125/150 single/double/triple. Each fan-cooled unit has a tiny kitchenette, fridge, and private bath (hot water), and there's a large store on the premises where you can buy groceries and drinks. In Samoan, "lagoto" means sunset and you can often enjoy good ones sitting outside your unit. Retzlaff Travel in Apia owns this place.

Accommodations in Western Savai'i

Backpackers and anyone looking for a hassle-free beachfront place to stay won't go wrong at the **Satuiatua Beach Resort** (Box 5623, Salailua; no phone) at Satuiatua, 55 km west of Salelologa wharf. For WS$33 pp you get a mattress in an open Samoan *fale* with electric lighting right on the beach itself, plus breakfast, lunch, and dinner. The meals are huge with the emphasis on Samoan cuisine, and if you decide to go off on an excursion for the day, they'll give you a box lunch. Their small store across the road sells cold beer at normal prices. Security is good as you can lock your luggage below your *fale*. The beach is protected by a long lava ledge, which makes it safe for children, and one of Samoa's best surfing spots is nearby. You can snorkel here but it isn't quite as good as at the Siufaga Beach Resort on the east side of the island. Tutogi and Mamate, the two sisters who run this place, lived in New Zealand for many years, so they understand the *palagi* need for privacy, peace, and quiet. They also warmly welcome guests to participate in the activities of their extended family across the street, so you get the best of both worlds here. A pickup truck is available for tours to Falealupo at WS$80 for the truck. Guests are expected to attend an evening vespers around sunset daily, and it's prudent to comply rather than risk a WS$2 fine from the red-clad village "morality police" who patrol the main highway at these times. Guests must also present themselves at church on Sunday morning. There's a 2200 curfew in the village. Actually, these quaint formalities have a charm of their own. The Fagafau bus that meets all ferries from Upolu will bring you directly here for WS$2. Highly recommended.

A hundred meters east of the Satuiatua Beach Resort are the **Flying Fish Fales** (Box 5651, Salailua; no phone), which are similar though they're on the inland side of the road. The rates at Flying Fish are slightly lower but it's well worth spending a few extra *tala* to be right on the beach at the resort. Many surfers stay with the Methodist pastor at Salailua.

To date the only official place to stay on northwestern Savai'i is the **Vaisala Hotel** (Box 570, Apia; tel. 58-016, fax 58-017), four km west of Asau on the north coast. The 33 rooms in a European-style building overlooking the beach go for WS$132/146/160 single/double/triple, plus 10% tax. Although the rooms are good, with private bath, coffee-making facilities, and fridge (but no cooking), meals in the restaurant are exorbitant, and the rental scooters and nautical gear unreliable. Transfers from Maota airstrip or Salelologa wharf are WS$48 pp return. The Vaisala is a convenient base for exploring the northwest coast.

Food

A restaurant upstairs in the ferry terminal at Salelologa serves basic meals. It's closed on Sunday but the small shop here remains open. The store opposite the Ocean View Motel at Salelologa serves a good plate lunch for about WS$4.

GETTING THERE

By Air

Polynesian Airlines (Box 599, Apia; tel. 21-261) has domestic flights to Maota Airstrip, just west of Salelologa, three times a day (10 minutes, WS$34 one-way, WS$60 roundtrip) from Fagali'i Airstrip (FGI) just east of Apia. When booking, ask how much checked baggage you'll be allowed on this eight-passenger Islander aircraft. You'll also be stuck with a steep taxi fare from Maota airstrip to your hotel, so these flights are really only for those who turn deep green at the thought of an hour-and-a-half boat ride.

By Boat

The **Western Samoa Shipping Corporation** (tel. 51-477) operates the car ferry *Lady Samoa* between the wharfs at Mulifanua (Upolu) and Salelologa (Savai'i), departing each end two or three times daily. At last report, the ferry left Mulifanua weekdays at 0800, 1200, and 1600, Saturday at 0800 and 1400, and Sunday at 1200 and 1600. Departure times from Salelologa were weekdays at 0600, 1000, and 1400, Saturday at 0600 and 1200, Sunday at 1000 and 1400. Passenger fares are WS$6 pp each way (students WS$3); bicycles and motorcycles are WS$15, cars WS$40. Reservations are recommended for vehicles (and sometimes even foot passengers have to fight to get a ticket). The trip takes an hour and a half. On the way across, you get a good view of Apolima Island's single village cradled in the island's classic volcanic crater, and dolphins are often spotted.

Recently this service was disrupted due to construction work on the wharf at Mulifanua and the ferries were departing directly from Apia, but this is only temporary, so ask.

GETTING AROUND

Travel up the southwest side of Savai'i is easy thanks to the broad paved highway from Salelologa to Asau via Salailua built with Australian aid in the early 1980s. The east coast road is also paved as far as Sasina and bus service between the wharf and Sasina is good. But from Asau to Sasina there's only a steep gravel road, extremely rough in places, with no bus service, and getting over this stretch is the biggest challenge of any round-the-island excursion.

One useful thing to know about is the flatback truck jammed with plantation laborers, which leaves the sawmill at Asau for Sasina and beyond weekdays at 1600. The driver is usually willing to give travelers a lift, in which case a pack of cigarettes would be welcome. Weekday mornings this truck departs Safotu for Asau at 0500. With a little luck you can go right around Savai'i, visiting most of the places described above, in three or four days.

All public transportation on Savai'i is a bit irregular, so don't plan tight itineraries and never expect to be able to get back to Upolu to catch an international flight the same day. If a storm came up and the ferries were canceled, you'd be as stranded as everyone else.

By Bus

Bus service on Savai'i focuses on the wharf at Salelologa, with departures to almost any point on the island. Over a dozen buses will be waiting when the ferry arrives at Salelologa from Upolu. They fill up fast, so jump on the bus of your choice quickly (marked "Pu'apu'a" or "Tuasivi" for the east coast, "Sasina," "Manase," or "Avao" for the north coast, "Palauli," "Gataivai," or "Sili" for the south coast, or "Fagafau" or "Asau" for the west coast).

The buses leave as soon as they're full, and you'll see as many as five buses all going the same way, one right after another, then none until another ferry comes in. Going back toward the ferry is more inconvenient, with very early morning departures from villages in the northwest corner of Savai'i the norm. The last bus leaving Asau for the wharf via the west coast starts out at 0700 and some buses leave Asau at 0300 and 0500!

Hitchhiking

There's no such thing as hitchhiking on Savai'i: truck drivers expect their passengers to pay. They only ask for the equivalent of bus fare and make getting around a lot easier, so don't spoil things by not offering. There are already a few drivers who won't stop for *palagis* because of previous unpleasant encounters, which is rather a pity. Many drivers will refuse any payment from foreigners. Traffic diminishes greatly after 1400.

Others

Taxis are expensive on Savai'i, so be sure to settle the price before setting out. Rental vehicles are scarce, yet some of the car rental agencies in Apia won't allow you to bring one of their vehicles over on the ferry (be sure to ask). In Salelologa, **Savai'i Car Rentals** (tel. 51-206, fax 51-291), opposite the Pacific Commercial Bank, rents cars at WS$110 a day all inclusive.

The easiest way to get around is on an organized sightseeing tour conducted by retired geologist Warren Jopling from the **Safua Hotel.** They'll do trips north across the lava fields to Mt. Matavanu and the "short people's cave," or along the south coast to the Pulemelei stone pyramid and Taga blowholes, but only if four or five people sign up. The cost is around WS$33 pp for a half day, WS$66 a full day (including lunch). Warren conducts his tours with sensitivity and they're worth every *sene.*

Eco-Tour Samoa Ltd. (tel./fax 25-993) operates out of Stevenson's at Manase with tours to the Satoalepai wetlands on Thursday (WS$40) and Mount Matavanu on Saturday (WS$100).

CAPSULE SAMOAN VOCABULARY

Although you can get by with English in both American and Western Samoa, knowing a few words of the Samoan language will make things more enjoyable. Written Samoan has only 14 letters. Always pronounce g as "ng," and t may be pronounced "k." Every letter is pronounced, with the vowels sounding as they do in Spanish. An apostrophe indicates a glottal stop between syllables.

afakasi—half-caste
afio mai—a Samoan greeting
afu—waterfall
'ai—eat
aiga—extended family
aitu—ghost, spirit
alia—catamaran fishing boat
ali'i—high chief
alofa—love
alu—go
alu i fea?—where are you going?
'ata—laugh

fa'afafine—transvestite
fa'afetai—thank you
fa'afetai tele—thank you very much
fa'amafu—home-brewed beer
fa'amolemole—please
fa'apefea mai oe?—how are you?
fa'a Samoa—the Samoan way
fa'a se'e—surfing
fafine—woman
fa'i—banana
faia—sacred
faife'au—an ordained church minister
failauga—orator
fai se miti lelei—have a nice dream
fale—house
faleoloa—store
fautasi—a Samoan longboat
fia fia—happy; a Samoan feast
fono—council

i—to, toward
i'a—fish
ietoga—fine mat
inu—drink
ioe—yes

lafo—a ceremonial exchange of gifts
lali—a large wooden drum
lavalava—traditional men's skirt
le—the
leai—no
leaga—bad
lelei—good
lelei tele—very good
le tau—the cost, price
lotu—religion

maamusa—girlfriend
malae—meeting ground
malaga—journey
malo—hi
malo lava—response to *malo*
manaia tele Samoa—Samoa is very beautiful
manogi—smell
manuia!—cheers!
manuia le po—good night
matafaga—beach
matai—head of an *aiga*
mau—opposition
mea alofa—gift
moe—sleep
motu—small island
musu—to be sullen

niu—coconut
nofo—sit
nu'u—village

oi fea—where is
ou te alofa ia te oe—I love you
ou te toe sau—I shall return

paepae—the stone foundation of a *fale*
palagi—a non-Samoan; also *papalagi*
paopao—canoe
pe fia?—how much?
pisupo—canned corned beef

poo fea a alu iai?—where are you going?
pule—authority, power
pulenu'u—village mayor
puletasi—traditional women's dress
pupu—blowhole

sa—taboo, sacred
sau—come
savali—walk
sene—a cent
siapo—tapa cloth
sili—best
siva—dance
soifua—good luck
sua—an important ceremonial presentation

taamu—giant taro
taavale—car
tai—sea
tala—dollar
talofa—hello
talofa lava—hello to you
tama—a boy
tamaloa—a man
tamo'e—run
tanoa—kava bowl
taulealea—untitled man
taupou—ceremonial virgin
tautau—untitled people, commoners
tele—much
tofa—goodbye
tofa soifua—fare thee well
tulafale—talking chief, orator

uku—head lice
ula—lei (flower necklace)
uma—finished
umu—earth oven

va'a—boat

TOKELAU

INTRODUCTION

Tokelau, a dependent territory of New Zealand, consists of three large atolls 480 km north of Western Samoa (Tokelau means "north"). In British colonial times it was known as the Union Group. The central atoll, Nukunonu, is 92 km from Atafu and 64 km from Fakaofo. Swains Island (Olohenga), 200 km south of Fakaofo, traditionally belongs to Tokelau but it is now part of American Samoa.

Each atoll consists of a ribbon of coral *motus* (islets), 90 meters to six km long and up to 200 meters wide, enclosing a broad lagoon. At no point does the land rise more than five meters above the sea, which makes the territory uniquely vulnerable to rising sea levels caused by the greenhouse effect. Together Atafu (three and a half square km), Fakaofo (four square km), and Nukunonu (4.7 square km) total only 12.2 square km of dry land, but they also include 165 square km of enclosed lagoons and 290,000 square km of territorial sea.

Life is relaxed in Tokelau. There are no large stores, hotels, restaurants, or bars, just plenty of sand and sun, coconuts, and a happy, friendly people. This is outer-island Polynesia at its best.

Climate

There is little variation from the 28° C annual average temperature. Rainfall is irregular but heavy (2,900 mm annually at Atafu); downpours of up to 80 mm in a single day are possible anytime. Tokelau is at the north edge of the main hurricane belt, but tropical storms sometimes sweep through between November and February. Since 1846 Tokelau has only experienced three recorded hurricanes; then in 1989 waves from Hurricane Ofa broke across the atolls, washing topsoil away and contaminating the freshwater lens. Residual salt prevented new plant growth for months. The recent increase in such storms is suspected of being related to global warming.

History

Legend tells how the Maui brothers pulled three islands out of the ocean while fishing far from shore. Later the Polynesians arrived with taro, which supplemented the abundance of fish and coconuts. The warriors of Fakaofo brought the other atolls under the rule of the Tui Tokelau.

The first European on the scene was Captain Byron of HMS *Dolphin,* who saw Atafu in 1765. Ethnologist Horatio Hale of the U.S. Exploring Expedition of 1841 spent several days at Fakaofo and wrote an account of the inhabitants. Catholic and Protestant missionaries arrived between 1845 and 1863. In 1863 Peruvian slavers kidnapped several hundred Tokelauans, including nearly all the able-bodied men, for forced labor in South America. Those who resisted were killed. A terrible dysentery epidemic from Samoa hit Tokelau the same year, reducing the total population to only 200.

The British officially extended belated protection in 1877, but not until 1889, when it was decided that Tokelau might be of use in laying a transpacific cable, did Commander Oldham of the *Egeria* arrive to declare a formal protectorate. The British annexed their protectorate in 1916 and joined it to the Gilbert and Ellice Islands Colony. This distant arrangement ended in 1925, when New Zealand, which ruled Western Samoa at that time, became the adminis-

tering power. With the Tokelau Act of 1948, N.Z. assumed full sovereignty, and the islanders became N.Z. citizens. A N.Z. proposal for Tokelau to unite with either Western Samoa or Cook Islands was rejected by the Tokelauans in 1964. In a 1980 treaty signed with N.Z., the U.S. government formally renounced claims to the group dating back to 1856. Tokelau's fourth atoll, Olohenga (Swains Island), was retained by the U.S.

The Riddle of the *Joyita*

One of the strangest episodes in recent Pacific history is indirectly related to Tokelau. On 10 November 1955, the crew of the trading ship *Tuvalu* sighted the drifting, half-sunken shape of the 70-ton MV *Joyita,* which had left Apia on 3 October bound for Fakaofo, carrying seven Europeans and 18 Polynesians. The *Joyita* had been chartered by Tokelau's district officer to take badly needed supplies to the atolls and pick up their copra, which was rotting on the beach. When the vessel was reported overdue, a fruitless aerial search began, which only ended with the chance discovery by the *Tuvalu* some 150 km north of Fiji. There was no sign of the 25 persons aboard, and the ship had been looted of sacks of flour, rice, and sugar. Also missing

weaving preparation

reef fishing

canoe making

a kitchen

were forty drums of kerosene, seven cases of aluminum strips, and the three life rafts.

The ghost ship was towed to Fiji and beached. Investigators found that the rudder had been jammed, the radio equipment wrecked, and the engines flooded due to a broken pipe in the saltwater cooling system. The navigation lights and galley stove were switched on. The *Joyita* hadn't sunk because the holds were lined with eight centimeters of cork. Though several books and countless newspaper and magazine articles have been written about the *Joyita* mystery, it has never been learned what really happened, nor have any of the missing persons ever been seen again.

Government

New Zealand policy has been to disturb traditional institutions as little as possible. The administrator of Tokelau is appointed by the N.Z. Ministry of Foreign Affairs and Trade and resides in Wellington. He works through the Office for Tokelau Affairs (the Tokalani), a liaison office presently in Apia, Western Samoa, but scheduled to be transferred to Tokelau. The administrator is represented on each island by a *faipule* (headman), who is elected locally every three years.

All three atolls have a *pulenuku* (mayor), also elected for a three-year term, who directs *nuku* (village) activities. Each island has a *taupulega* (island council) comprised of village elders or heads of families. Each *taupulega* chooses nine delegates to the 27-member General Fono, which meets twice a year (April and October) on alternate islands and has almost complete control over local matters. In December 1992 Tokelau received an added degree of self-government when a Council of Faipule was created to act on behalf of the General Fono between sessions. The new position of *Ulu o Tokelau* (titular leader) is rotated annually among the Council's three members, all of whom act as government ministers. In January 1994 the powers of the Administrator were delegated to the General Fono and the Council of Faipule, giving Tokelau de facto internal self-government. In the near future the Parliament of New Zealand is to amend the Tokelau Act of 1948 to make this system official.

There are plans to move the Office for Tokelau Affairs from Apia to one of the atolls, but which atoll? Although Fakaofo seems the likely choice, there is great rivalry between the three and little "national" feeling as yet. New Zealand would give Tokelau independence for the asking, but without a source of income the prospect seems unlikely; free association with N.Z. on the Niue model seems more probable.

Economy

In 1994 Tokelau received NZ$5 million in N.Z. budgetary support and project assistance, NZ$3170 per capita. This subsidy is six times greater than all locally raised revenue, and imports exceed exports of copra and handicrafts by 11 times. In addition, the U.N. Development Program contributed just over US$1 million in 1992-96, mostly for telecommunications development.

Tokelau earns several hundred thousand dollars a year from the sale of postage stamps and coins, but a more important source of revenue is licensing fees from American purse seiners, which pull tuna from Tokelau's 200-nautical-mile Exclusive Economic Zone (EEZ). Inshore waters within 40 km of the reef are reserved for local fishing. New Zealand has declared that all income from the EEZ will go to Tokelau (US$705,496 was paid by American vessels in 1994).

The 216 government jobs funded by New Zealand are the only regular source of monetary income in Tokelau today. Almost all these jobs are held by Tokelauans—there are few resident expatriates—and to avoid the formation of a privileged class, nearly half are temporary or casual positions which are rotated among the community. Taxes collected from wage earners are used to subsidize copra and handicraft production, further distributing the wealth. Island families provide for their old and disabled.

Yet, limited resources have prompted many islanders to emigrate to New Zealand. Tokelauans are not eligible for N.Z. welfare payments unless they live in New Zealand and pay taxes there. They may now receive 50% of their pensions in Tokelau, however, and this has stimulated some return migration.

The Changing Village

To be in the lee of the southeast trades, the villages are on the west side of each atoll. The sandy soil and meager vegetation (only 61 species) force the Tokelauans to depend on the sea for protein. Coconut palms grow abundantly on the *motus*: what isn't consumed is dried and exported as copra. The islands are gradually being replanted with a high-yield coconut species from Rotuma. *Pulaka* (swamp taro) is cultivated in man-made pits up to two meters deep. Breadfruit is harvested from November to March, and some bananas and papaya are also grown. Pandanus is used for making mats and other handicrafts, or thatching roofs; pandanus fruit is also edible. Pigs, chickens, and ducks are kept. Land and coconut crabs are a delicacy. Most land is held by family groups *(kainga)* and cannot be sold to outsiders.

Now, as Tokelau enters a cash economy, imported canned and frozen foods are gaining importance. Aluminum motorboats are replacing dugout sailing canoes, and when gasoline is scarce the islanders cannot travel to the *motus* to collect their subsistence foodstuffs. Also, the people now want appliances such as washing machines, electric irons, freezers, and VCRs. European-style concrete housing is becoming common, and catchments from the tin roofs are used to alleviate water shortages. Trousers are gaining preference over the traditional *kie* (loincloth).

The changing values have also meant a decline in the traditional sharing system *(inati)*. Outboard motors and electricity cost money: the rising standard of living has paralleled an increasing dependency on aid and remittances from relatives in New Zealand. A 1990 survey showed that 80% of the adult population smoked. Surveyors blamed the rapid increase in noncommunicable diseases such as hypertension, diabetes, heart disease, and gout on imported foods and the changing lifestyle. An average of one kilogram of sugar per person is consumed weekly.

The People

The Tokelauans are closely related to the people of Tuvalu. In 1991 there were 543 people on Atafu, 597 on Fakaofo, and 437 on Nukunonu, totaling 1,577. Another 4,000 Tokelauans live "beyond the reef" in New Zealand, the result of a migration that began in 1963, following overpopulation in Tokelau itself. A good many of the present islanders have been to New Zealand. Dengue fever, influenza, and hepatitis are endemic in the population.

Due to the work of early missionaries, Atafu is Congregationalist (LMS), Nukunonu Catholic, and Fakaofo a combination of the two. Since the Samoan Bible is used, all adults understand Samoan. Young people learn English at school, but everyone speaks Tokelauan at home. In Tokelau, authority is based on age, rather than lineage. Arguably, nowhere else in the world are senior citizens as respected. Traditionally the women controlled family resources, but in recent years monetarism has led to this role being appropriated by men.

Conduct and Customs

In Tokelau, as elsewhere, proper conduct is mostly common sense. Take care not to expect better service or facilities than anyone else and avoid causing a disturbance. Keep in mind that you're a guest in someone's home. Bad reports or complaints could well deprive others of the opportunity to visit. Step aside for the elders and *never* tell them what to do. When passing in front of another person, bow slightly and say *tulou.*

If people invite you into a house for a cup of coffee or a meal, politely refuse, saying that you have just finished eating. Such invitations are usually only a form of greeting, and they may not even have what is offered. If they insist a second or third time, or it's someone you know quite well, then they probably mean it. Sit on the mat with your legs crossed or folded, not stretched out.

Village men work together a day or two a week on communal projects. Join in with the group (known as the *aumaga)* or you'll feel left out, not fitting into the community. You should also accompany your hosts to church on Sunday. Overt flirtations with members of the opposite sex are frowned upon. If you feel an attraction, simply mention it to one of his/her friends, and the word will be passed on. The women are crazy about bingo and stay up half the night playing it. You'll have to learn how to count *(helu, tahi, lua, tolu, fa, lima, ono, fitu, valu, iva)* if you want to join them (two *sene* a game, nice prizes). The men may offer to take you line fishing, rod fishing, spearfishing, net fishing, trolling (for bonito), etc.

ON THE ROAD

Arts and Crafts

Some of the best traditional handicrafts in the Pacific are made in the Tokelau Islands, especially high-quality coconut-fiber hats and handbags, fans, and exquisite model canoes. Some of the handbags have a solid coconut-shell liner—handy for women wishing to tranquilize over-enthusiastic males! The coconut-shell water bottles are authentic and unique. The most distinctive article on display is the *tuluma,* a watertight wooden box used to carry valuables on canoe journeys; its buoyancy also makes it an ideal lifesaver. All the above are genuine collectors' items.

Accommodations

Since there aren't any hotels or rest houses, you have to stay with a family. To stay on an island between ship arrivals you must first obtain an entry permit from the **Office for Tokelau Affairs** (Box 865, Apia, Western Samoa; tel. 20-822, fax 21-761). They will cable the island council for permission, and you'll have to pay for food and accommodations, about 20 Western Samoan *tala* pp a day (negotiable). You could also write in advance to the *faipule* or *pulenuku* of the island of your choice to let them know your intentions—having a contact or local friend makes everything easier.

When you go, take along a bottle of spirits for whoever made the arrangements, as well as gifts for the family. Suggested items are rubber thongs, housewares, tools, fishing gear (galvanized fishhooks, fishing line, swivels, sinkers, lures, mask and snorkel, and speargun rubbers), and perhaps a rugby ball or volleyball. The women will appreciate perfumes, deodorants, cosmetics, and printed cloth. Kitchen knives and enamel mugs are always welcome.

You'll probably have to sleep on the floor and use communal toilets over the lagoon—there'll be little privacy. Most families own land on one of the *motus,* so you could spend a few days camping on your own if you have a tent and a large enough water container.

Food

There's only one cooperative store on each atoll, selling rice, flour, sugar, canned fish and meat, spaghetti, gasoline, etc. Take as much food as you can—bags of taro, a sack of bananas, fruit such as pineapples and mangoes, garlic, instant coffee, and tea. Ask at the Office for Tokelau Affairs about agricultural import restrictions. Cigarettes are in short supply, and camera film is not available.

Only the co-op on Nukunonu (and possibly Fakaofo) sells liquor. Instead, the locals drink sour toddy. This is obtained by cutting the flower stem of a coconut tree and collecting the sap in a half-coconut container. The whitish fluid *(kaleve)* has many uses. It can be drunk fresh, or boiled and stored in a fridge. If kept in a container at room temperature for two days, it ferments into sour toddy beer. Boil fresh *kaleve* to a brown molasses for use in cooking or as a sauce. A tablespoon of boiled *kaleve* in a cup of hot water makes an island tea. You can even make bread out of it by adding saltwater, flour, and fat, as all Tokelauan women know.

Services and Information

The New Zealand dollar is the currency used on the islands. Since 1978, a limited number of Tokelauan one-dollar coins have been issued each year. You can change money at the Administration Center on each island.

Collectors can order Tokelau postage stamps from the Tokelau Philatelic Bureau, Box 68, Wellington, New Zealand.

There's a hospital on all three atolls, and treatment is free. Take a remedy for diarrhea.

Getting There

The only way to go is on a ship chartered by the **Office for Tokelau Affairs,** leaving Apia, Western Samoa, for the three atolls every month or so, taking about two days to reach the first island or seven to nine days roundtrip. Cabin class is NZ$528 roundtrip, deck class NZ$286 roundtrip, including meals. Deck passengers can take cabin-class meals for a little extra, though those prone to seasickness won't be eating much. The ship often runs out of food on the way back to Apia, so carry a reserve supply.

This is not a trip for the squeamish or faint-hearted. Every available space on deck will be packed with the Tokelauans and their belongings. The cabins are usually without ventilation, and washing facilities are minimal. There's merry feasting when the ship arrives, and usually time for snorkeling and picnicking on the *motus*. The passengers are an interesting mix.

Tokelauans and officials get priority on these trips, and tourists are only taken if there happens to be space left over. Advance reservations from tourists are not accepted, and cabins will be confirmed only a week prior to sailing. Check with the Office for Tokelau Affairs or the New Zealand High Commission when you reach Apia—you may be lucky. You pass Western Samoan Immigration on the wharf in Apia, an easy way of renewing your Samoan tourist visa. Some of the Tokelau ships are based at Suva, Fiji, or Nuku'alofa, Tonga, in which case you could continue on to there if you wished. In 1993 a regular supply ship, the MV *Wairua,* sank off Fiji. The seaplane service to Tokelau was suspended in 1983, but there's talk of building an airstrip on Fenuafala (Fakaofo).

Internal Transport

Passes for small boats have been blasted through the reefs, but ships must stand offshore; passengers and cargo are transferred to the landings in aluminum whaleboats, which roar through the narrow passes on the crest of a wave. In offshore winds there is poor anchorage at Fakaofo and Nukunonu, and none at all off Atafu. For safety's sake, inter-atoll voyages by canoe are prohibited, and the 19-meter, 50-passenger catamaran *Tu Tolu,* especially built for this purpose, entered service in 1992. There are no cars or trucks in Tokelau, but most canoes are now fitted with outboards.

THE TOKELAU ISLANDS

Atafu

The smallest of the atolls, Atafu's lagoon totals only 17 square km (compared to 50 square km on Fakaofo and 98 square km at Nukunonu). This is the most traditional of the islands, the only one where dugout canoes are still made. The village is at the northwest corner of the atoll. There's a ceramic history of Tokelau on the side wall of Matauala Public School. A small plant to process fresh tuna into marinated, sun-dried tuna flakes was opened in 1990 with U.S. fisheries aid money. Atafu is officially "dry," but a homebrew of yeast and sugar compensates. Be prepared for a NZ$35 fine if you get caught partaking.

Nukunonu

This largest atoll in both land and lagoon area sits in the center of the group. Since Nukunonu is Catholic (see the large whitewashed stone church), life is less restricted than on the Congregationalist islands. The village is divided into two parts by a reef pass spanned by a bridge. No dugout canoes are left on Nukunonu; everyone has switched to aluminum outboards. The rhinoceros beetle, a pest that attacks coconut trees, has established itself here. Luhi'ano

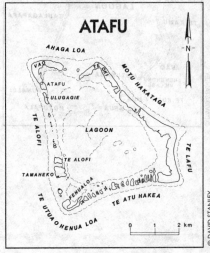

© DAVID STANLEY

Perez, headmaster of the local school, can answer questions about the atoll.

Fakaofo

Some 400 people live on tiny four-and-a-half-hectare Fale Island, which is well shaded by breadfruit trees. Fale resident Vaopuka Mativa (Bob) is knowledgeable about Polynesian history and language links to other islands. In 1960, a second village was established on the larger island of Fenuafala, about three km northwest, to relieve the overcrowding. At low tide you can walk across the reef between the two. The school and hospital are now on Fenuafala. A two-story administration building housing the health clinic, police station, post office, and village store was completed in 1989.

FAKAOFO

© DAVID STANLEY

NUKUNONU

© DAVID STANLEY

An ancient coral slab erected to the Tui Tokelau stands in the meetinghouse at Fale. This stone may once have exercised supernatural power, but the head you see on it today is a recent addition. On the lagoonside beach opposite the *hakava* (family meeting place) is a huge rock, which takes a dozen men to lift it, once used to crush wrongdoers.

The freighter *Ai Sokula* can be seen wrecked on the reef at Ahaga Loa. Guano, a fertilizer formed from bird droppings, is collected on Palea, a tiny *motu* on the east side of the atoll, for use in nearby taro pits. Pigs swim and forage for shellfish in pools on the reef near the settlements on Fakaofo (the only swimming pigs in the Pacific).

GORDON OHLIGER

WALLIS AND FUTUNA
INTRODUCTION

This little-known corner of Polynesia lies 600 km northeast of Fiji and 300 km west of Samoa. Smallest of France's three South Pacific territories, Wallis and Futuna is isolated from its neighbors geographically, culturally, and politically. All the marks of French colonialism are here, from overpaid European officials controlling functionless staff to little French *gendarmes* in round peaked caps and shorts.

Although weekly flights and a regular shipping service make the islands accessible from Nouméa, Fiji, and Tahiti, the lack of moderately priced facilities and resorts limits visitors to French officials, the eccentric, the adventuresome, and yachts' crews. Wallis and Futuna is still well off the beaten track.

The Land
The islands of Wallis and Futuna, 200 km apart, are quite dissimilar. Wallis (159 square km including adjacent islands) is fairly flat, with verdant volcanic hillsides rising gently to Mt. Lulu Fakahega (145 meters). There are freshwater crater

lakes (Lalolalo, Kikila, and Lanutavake). The main island, Uvéa, is surrounded by a barrier reef bearing 22 smaller islands, many with fine beaches. Ships bound for Mata Utu wharf enter the lagoon through Honikulu Pass, the southernmost. Few fish remain in the broad lagoon—the locals have been fishing with dynamite.

Futuna and Alofi, together totaling 115 square km, are mountainous, with Mt. Puke on Futuna reaching 524 meters. Though there are many freshwater springs on Futuna, Alofi two km to the southeast is now uninhabited, due to a lack of water. A reef fringes the north coast of Alofi; the south coast features high cliffs. Futuna is completely surrounded by a narrow fringing reef.

Climate
The hurricane season on the islands is November to March, and many storms form in the area between Wallis and Samoa. During the drier season, May to October, the islands are cooled by the refreshing southeast trades.

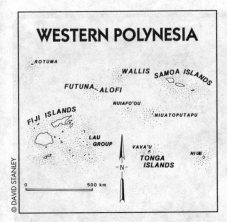

WESTERN POLYNESIA

ROTUMA

WALLIS SAMOA ISLANDS

FUTUNA - ALOFI

NUIAFO'OU

FIJI ISLANDS   NIUATOPUTAPU

LAU GROUP

VAVA'U

TONGA ISLANDS   NIUE

-N-

0   500 km

© DAVID STANLEY

Fauna

Wallis and Futuna is one of the few countries of the world where pigs outnumber people. The 25,000 swine have free run of the land; they're often seen foraging for shellfish on the beaches. In the early evening they are called back for feeding and penning: one can hear bells ringing, people shouting, the beating of drums, gongs, etc., as the owners utilize different methods of calling home *les cochones*. A fantastic array of sounds!

Beware of "electric" ants *(loimimi utiuti)* when hiking or camping on either Wallis or Futuna as these one-mm-long brown ants deliver a painful bite. Wallis is also overrun by African snails, although they won't harm you.

History

Although these islands were discovered by the Polynesians some 3,000 years ago, not until 28 April 1615 did the Dutch navigators Schouten and Le Maire arrive at Futuna and Alofi. They named Futuna Hoorn after their home port of Hoorn on the IJsselmeer, 42 km north of Amsterdam. The name of Cape Horn, in South America, is derived from the same old port. Captain Samuel Wallis of HMS *Dolphin* was the first European to contact Wallis (on 16 August 1767). American whalers began to visit from 1820 onward.

Marist missionaries arrived on both Futuna and Wallis in 1837, and today 98% of the inhabitants are Catholic. Wallis was declared a French protectorate in 1886, Futuna in 1887.

In 1924 the protectorate officially became a colony. This was the only French colony in the Pacific to remain loyal to the collaborating government in Vichy France right up until Pearl Harbor. From 1942 to 1944, Wallis was an important American military base, with 6,000 troops on the island. Hihifo airport dates from the war, as does an abandoned airstrip just south of Lake Kikila. In a 1959 referendum, the populace voted to upgrade Wallis and Futuna's status to that of an overseas territory, and this status was granted by the French Parliament in 1961.

Government

The French High Commissioner in Nouméa selects a senior administrator to control the local bureaucracy from Mata Utu on Wallis. An elected Territorial Assembly (20 members) has limited legislative powers over local matters. The policy-making Territorial Council is comprised of the king of Wallis, two kings of Futuna (from Sigave and Alo), and three members appointed by the French administrator, who presides. The territory elects a deputy and a senator to the French Parliament in Paris. The traditional Polynesian monarchy and the Catholic Church continue to be powerful forces in the islands.

Economy

The only exports are a few bags of trochus shells. Of the 900 people employed on the island, 750 work for the French government. What they produce is perhaps the most invisible export of all—the illusion of colonial glory. Yet the strategic position of Wallis and Futuna in the heart of the South Pacific indicates a future role of increasing importance as France develops its global empire.

The A$40 million annual budget mostly comes out of the pockets of French taxpayers, although some revenue is collected in customs duties. French civil servants on Wallis make three times as much as they'd earn back in France, plus a respectable lump sum upon completion of their three-year contract. All prices on Wallis are set accordingly. The locals get free medical and dental care, and free education (in French) up to university level: with such French largess, independence is unthinkable. Money also arrives in the form of remittances from Wallisian emigrants in New Caledonia.

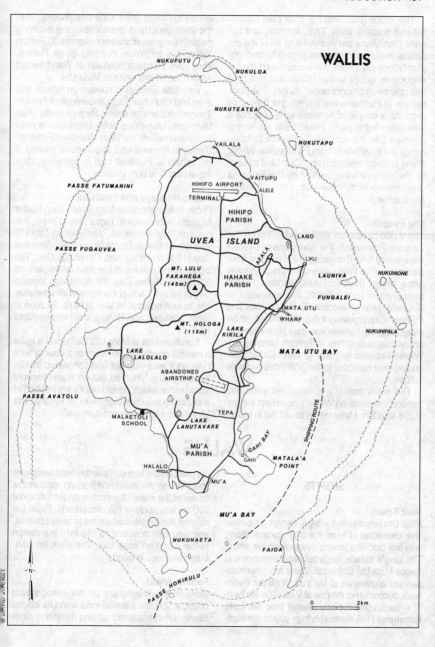

WALLIS

NUKUFUTU
NUKULOA
NUKUTEATEA
NUKUTAPU

PASSE FATUMANINI

VAILALA
VAITUPU
ALELE

HIHIFO AIRPORT
TERMINAL

HIHIFO
PARISH

PASSE FUGAUVEA

UVEA ISLAND

LANO
LIKU

AFALA

HAHAKE
PARISH

LAUNIVA
FUNGALEI

MT. LULU
FAKAHEGA
(145m)

NUKUHIONE

MATA UTU

NUKUHIFALA

WHARF

LAKE
KIKILA

MATA UTU BAY

LAKE
LALOLALO

PASSE AVATOLU

ABANDONED
AIRSTRIP

SHIPPING ROUTE

TEPA
MALAETOLI
SCHOOL

GAHI BAY

LAKE
LANUTAVAKE

GAHI

MATALA'A
POINT

HALALO

MU'A
PARISH

MU'A

MU'A BAY

NUKUHAETA

FAIOA

N

PASSE HONIKULU

0   2km

PASSE FATUMANINI

© DAVID STANLEY

The locals grow most of their own food in the rich volcanic soils. Taro, manioc, and banana plantations are everywhere. All of the coconuts are used to feed the pigs. The coconut plantations on Wallis were destroyed by the rhinoceros beetle in the 1930s, but this pest has now been brought under control. The plantations of Futuna were saved, but they only produce a couple of hundred tons of copra a year (also fed to pigs). Handicrafts are so expensive that it's actually profitable to bring things like kava bowls from Fiji to sell on Wallis. Plans to install television and Club Med tourism to the territory were vetoed by the kings as dangerous outside influences, although videos have arrived.

The People

The 9,000 people on Wallis and 5,000 on Futuna are Polynesian: the Wallisians or Uvéans descended from Tongans, the Futunans from Samoans. The Wallis Islanders are physically huge, bigger than Tongans. Another 14,000 people from both islands live and work in Nouméa, New Caledonia. These Uvéans and Futunans, recognizing the great difficulty of reintegrating themselves into their home islands, are strong supporters of French colonialism. Whole families migrate to New Caledonia, adding their numbers to the anti-independence faction.

The many partially constructed and uninhabited dwellings on Wallis also reflect the unstable situation. Many residents still live in round-ended thatched *fales*. One compromise with the 20th century is the electric line entering through the peak of the roof. Some 400 French expats live on Wallis, but only 20 on Futuna. They have a small subdivision on Wallis named Afala on a hill just north of Mata Utu.

Very little English is spoken on Wallis, and even less on Futuna, so a knowledge of French, Tongan, or Samoan makes life a lot easier. Wallisian and Futunan are distinct: welcome is *malo te kataki/malo le ma'uli* in Wallisian/Futunan. Similarly, farewell said to someone leaving is *alu la/ano la*. Farewell said to someone staying is *nofo la* in both dialects.

Public Holidays and Festivals

Public holidays include New Year's Day, Easter Monday (March/April), Labor Day (1 May), Ascension Day, Pentecost, Assumption Day (15 August), All Saints' Day (1 November), Armistice Day (11 November), and Christmas Day. The biggest celebrations of the year center around St. Pierre Chanel Day (28 April) and Bastille Day (14 July). Each of the three Wallis parishes has its own holiday: 14 May at Mu'a, 29 June at Hihifo (Vaitupu), and 15 August at Hahake (Mata Utu).

Sunday mass at Mata Utu Cathedral is quite a colorful spectacle, but sit near a door or window, as it gets very hot and congested inside. Kava drinking has died out on Wallis (people would rather watch videos) but it's still imbibed at a *tau'asu* (kava meetinghouse) on Futuna. The Uvéans are expert sword dancers.

WALLIS

SIGHTS

Near Town

Mata Utu resembles a village, except for a massive **cathedral** of hand-cut blue volcanic stone with two blocklike towers overlooking the wharf. The **king's palace**, large but not ostentatious, is beside Mata Utu Cathedral. There are other massive stone churches at Mu'a and Vaitupu; the interior decoration of the one at Vaitupu is the best.

A track up to the tiny chapel atop **Mt. Lulu Fakahega** (145 meters) brings you to the highest point on the island. Take the road west from Mata Utu to the main north-south road in the center of the island: the track is on the left about 500 meters north of the crossroads. From the summit the jungle-clad crater is fairly obvious, and you can descend to the taro plantation below along an easy trail. The view from Mt. Lulu Fakahega is good.

Farther Afield

Most of the villages are on the island's east coast, which has a paved road along its length. Buses run sporadically up and down this high-

The massive stone hulk of Mata Utu Cathedral is a very visible bulwark of Gaulish Catholicism.

DAVID STANLEY

way from Halalo to Vailala. Fares are about CFP 150 from Mata Utu to either end. Hitching is easy.

Lake Lalolalo on the far west side of Wallis is spectacular: it's circular, with vertical walls 30 meters high, which make the water inaccessible. Flying foxes swoop over Lake Lalolalo from their perches on overhanging trees in the late afternoon, and there are blind snakes in the lake. Another of the crater lakes, **Lake Lanutavake**, is less impressive, but you can swim (approach it from the west side). The Americans dumped their war equipment into the lakes just before they left.

There are no good beaches on the main island of Uvéa, but **Faioa Island** on the reef southeast of Mu'a has the white sands bordering a turquoise lagoon of which South Seas dreams are made. When the easterlies are blowing hard, this is a protected place to anchor; nearby Gahi Bay is another good protected anchorage for yachts.

PRACTICALITIES

Accommodations

The two-story **Hôtel Lomipeau** (Paola et Christian Ruotolo, B.P. 84, Mata Utu, 98600 Uvéa, Wallis; tel. 72-20-21, fax 72-26-95), beside the hospital 800 meters from Mata Utu, has 15 a/c rooms with private bath and balcony at CFP 7500/8500 single/double, slightly reduced if you stay a week. Meals cost CFP 800 for breakfast, CFP 2000 for lunch, CFP 2500 for dinner. The Lomipeau arranges lagoon excursions by boat at CFP 1500 pp, water-skiing at CFP 2000, and car rentals at CFP 5000 a day. Airport transfers are free for guests.

The 10-room **Hôtel Moana Hou** (M. Kulikovi, B.P. 136, Mata Utu, 98600 Uvéa, Wallis; tel. 72-21-35), at Liku between Mata Utu and the airport, is a bit cheaper at CFP 4000 per night per room, plus CFP 500 for breakfast and CFP 1500 for dinner.

Hôtel-Restaurant Teone (tel. 72-29-19), also at Liku, has five a/c bungalows with TV at CFP 7500 daily including breakfast, or CFP 4500 daily on a weekly basis without breakfast. The meals served in their thatched restaurant on the waterfront are good. There's also the five-room **Hôtel Albatros** (tel. 72-27-37) beside the airport.

About the only alternative is to camp in the interior; the Uvéans are hospitable, and a request for permission to camp sometimes leads to an invitation to stay in their homes. Otherwise you might be able to stay at a Catholic mission. Père Perret at Lano occasionally allows travelers to stay at the bishop's house for CFP 500 a night. It's a Samaritan's work, not a hotel.

Food and Shopping

Together, the two general stores at Mata Utu offer a reasonable selection of goods. Fresh meat is flown in from Nouméa weekly. **Restaurant Les Alizés** serves lunch and dinner. Drop in to the **Bar Hatutori Molihina** to meet Simi, a friendly Fijian, and Mele, his Wallisian wife. This is about the only place in town where English is spoken.

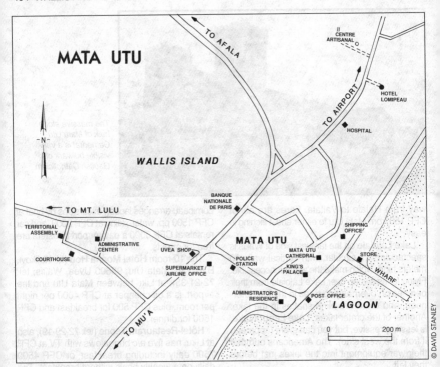

MATA UTU

WALLIS ISLAND

TO AFALA

CENTRE ARTISANAL

HOTEL LOMIPEAU

TO AIRPORT

HOSPITAL

BANQUE NATIONALE DE PARIS

TO MT. LULU

TERRITORIAL ASSEMBLY

ADMINISTRATIVE CENTER

COURTHOUSE

UVEA SHOP

SUPERMARKET/ AIRLINE OFFICE

MATA UTU

POLICE STATION

MATA UTU CATHEDRAL

KING'S PALACE

SHIPPING OFFICE

STORE

WHARF

ADMINISTRATOR'S RESIDENCE

POST OFFICE

LAGOON

TO MU'A

0   200 m

© DAVID STANLEY

There's a **Centre Artisanal** near the hospital selling handicrafts such as tapa cloth, handbags, and colored mats. **Boutique Tropical** across from the bank has nice clothing and perfume. Owner Michel Goepfert speaks acceptable English and is a good contact. The **Philatelic Bureau** adjoining Mata Utu Post Office sells first-day covers. Wallis and Futuna issues its own colorful postage stamps. Ask at the **Uvéa Shop** in Mata Utu for cassettes of the music of the well-known Wallisian singer/composer Palisio Tuauli.

Visas

Entry requirements are the same as those of New Caledonia and Tahiti-Polynesia. If you arrive by ship, go straight to the police station in Mata Utu (weekdays 0700-1130 and 1500-1700) for a passport stamp. If you're going on to Futuna, return here for a *sortie* stamp, otherwise you could have trouble when you apply for an *entrée* stamp on Futuna.

Services

The **Banque Nationale de Paris** (tel. 72-21-24) in Mata Utu opens Monday, Tuesday, Thursday, and Friday 0900-1200 and 1300-1500. This is a nuisance, as the weekly flight from Fiji arrives on Wednesday. If you'll be visiting Tahiti or New Caledonia before going to Wallis and Futuna, buy your Pacific francs (CFP) there, as exactly the same currency is used in all three French territories. Otherwise try the Administrative Center, which will change French francs in cash into CFP. Though expensive, Wallis and Futuna has the lowest inflation rate in the South Pacific.

Place long-distance calls at the post office near Mata Utu wharf. Wallis and Futuna's telephone code is 681. Mata Utu **hospital** offers free consultations weekdays 0800-1000 and 1500-1600. The airline office is next to the supermarket.

There's no tourist information but the Affaires Culturelles office in the Administrative Center (weekdays 0730-1330) handles general inquiries. The territory's representative office in New Caledonia is the **Bureau des Wallis et Futuna** (B.P. C5, Nouméa Cedex; tel. 687/28-19-35, fax 687/28-42-83).

GETTING THERE

By Air

The New Caledonian carrier **Air Calédonie International** (tel. 72-28-80, fax 72-27-11) flies to Hihifo Airport (WLS) on Wallis twice a week from Nouméa, weekly from Nandi (F$463 one-way, F$570 return) and Papeete. (Though the territory is actually east of the 180th meridian, the international date line swings east around the territory so it can share New Caledonia's day. Thus it's the same day here as in Nouméa, but one day later than in Papeete.)

In dollar areas such as Fiji you pay 25% more for the same air ticket to Wallis than you would in a French territory, where prices are fixed. Fares between the French territories are also relatively lower: for instance, Wallis-Nandi is CFP 44,800, while the much longer Wallis-Papeete flight is only CFP 50,200. Since a "ticket to leave" is required to enter the French territories, it's hard to take advantage of this situation. Spe-

cial one-year roundtrip excursion fares between Nouméa and Wallis are CFP 46,900.

Air Calédonie International also flies four times a week between Wallis and Futuna (CFP 8900 one-way). Only 10 kilos of baggage is allowed on the 20-passenger Twin Otter turboprop that does the Wallis-Futuna run, and it's often full.

By Ship

Other than arriving by private yacht, the only inexpensive way to visit Wallis and Futuna is to book round-trip passage on the MV *Moana III* and MV *Moana IV* of the **Compagnie Wallisienne de Navigation.** These passenger-carrying freighters depart Nouméa monthly for Wallis via Futuna, with occasional stops at Suva, Fiji. Fares are reasonable: Nouméa-Wallis is CFP 14,610 deck, Suva-Wallis CFP 8348 deck. Passage between Futuna and Wallis is CFP 1170 deck (14-16 hours). Meals are included and, as they're prepared on a French ship, they're good. One cabin is available at about double the above rates, or sleep on a steel bunk on the upper deck. Through passengers pay CFP 1770 a day to live onboard while in port. The *Moana* is empty between Nouméa and Wallis, but fills up on the return trip. The ship's agent in Nouméa is Amacal Agence Maritime Caledonienne (5 rue d'Austerlitz; tel. 687/28-72-22); in Suva it's Carpenters Shipping.

FUTUNA

Futuna (not to be confused with an island of the same name in Vanuatu) is a volcanic island five km wide by 20 km long (64 square km). The narrow coastal strip from Alo to Sigave and beyond is 200 meters wide at most. Gardens are planted on the mountainside, which rises abruptly from the sea. The terraced taro fields are quite ingenious. High cliffs on the northeast side of Futuna delayed completion of the road around the island until 1992, and the steep, narrow road from Alo to the airstrip and beyond is quite a feat of engineering.

Most of the people live at **Sigave,** which has the only anchorage for ships. A few shops are opposite the wharf; the police station is just outside Sigave on the road to Alo. For a place to stay at Sigave, ask for Julien Brual. At **Poi,** on the eastern coast, a peculiar church with a stepped tower has been erected to honor Pierre

Chanel, Polynesia's first and only Catholic saint (canonized 1954). Relics of the saint, including some of his bodily remains, clothes, and the war club that killed him, are kept in a room near the chapel. King Niuliki, who feared the missionary was usurping his position, had Chanel martyred in 1841, four years after he had arrived on the island.

Alofi (51 square km) is under the control of the chief of Alo. People from Futuna travel to their gardens on Alofi in small boats kept on the beach near the airstrip. They spend the week tending their gardens and come back to Futuna Sunday for church.

Large ships can pass between Futuna and Alofi, so long as they keep to the middle of the passage. With no organized accommodations on Futuna, plan on staying with the locals or camping.

FUTUNA AND ALOFI

NORTH POINT · SOMALOMA ROCKS

PYRAMID POINT

▲ MT. MATSI

▲ MT. PUKE (524 m)

FUTUNA

SIGAVE · POI

TAOA · ALO · AIRSTRIP · VELE POINT

SALONGA

ALOFITAI · ALOFI · VOLTA POINT

▲ MT. KOLOFAU (417 m)

0 — 5 km

© DAVID STANLEY

St. Pierre Chanel, Polynesia's only Catholic saint

WALLIS ET FUTUNA — RF POSTES 1991 — TRADITION — 7F · 54F · 62F · 72F · 90F

GORDON OHLIGER

TUVALU

INTRODUCTION

One of the world's smallest and most isolated independent nations, Tuvalu was known as the Ellice Islands until quite recently. The name Tuvalu means "cluster of eight," although there are actually nine islands in all. Niulakita, the smallest, was resettled by people from Niutao in 1949. Due to high airfares, this remote group of low coral atolls gets only a few hundred tourists a year, most of whom never get beyond the crowded little government center on Funafuti. In contrast, time seems to be standing still on the almost inaccessible outer islands, which rank among the most unspoiled and idyllic in the Pacific. Internationally, Tuvalu is best known for its colorful postage stamps. For the traveler, Tuvalu can be a rather expensive stepping stone between Fiji and Micronesia.

The Land

Legend tells how an eel *(te Pusi)* and a flatfish *(te Ali)* were carrying home a heavy rock and began to quarrel. The eel killed the flatfish and fed on his body, just as the tall coconut trees still feed on the round, flat islands. Then *te Pusi* broke the rock into eight pieces and disappeared into the sea.

The nine islands that make up Tuvalu today total about 25 square km in land area, curving northwest-southeast in a chain 579 km long on the western edge of Polynesia. Funafuti, the Administrative Center, is over 1,000 km north of Suva, Fiji. Funafuti, Nanumea, Nui, Nukufetau, and Nukulaelae are true atolls, with multiple islets under four meters high and central lagoons, while Nanumaga, Niulakita, and Niutao are single table-reef islands, with small land-locked interior lakes. Vaitupu is also closer to the table-reef type, though its interior lake or lagoon is connected to the sea. In all, the nine islands are composed of 129 islets, of which Funafuti accounts for 34 and Nukufetau 37. Ships can enter the lagoons at Nukufetau and Funafuti; elsewhere they must stand offshore.

It's feared that within a century rising ocean levels will inundate these low-lying atolls and Tuvalu will cease to exist. Coastal erosion is already eating into shorelines, and seawater has

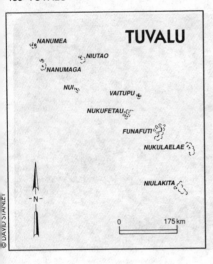

TUVALU AT A GLANCE		
	POPULATION (1991)	AREA (HECTARES)
Nanumea	818	361
Nanumaga	644	310
Niutao	749	226
Nui	608	337
Vaitupu	1,205	509
Nukufetau	756	307
Funafuti	3,836	254
Nukulaelae	370	166
Niulakita	75	41
Tuvalu	**9,061**	**2,511**

seeped into the groundwater, killing coconut trees and flooding the taro pits. Sea walls may slow the erosion, but as ocean levels continue to rise, the entire population of Tuvalu may eventually have to evacuate, third-world victims of first-world affluence.

Climate
The climate is generally warm and pleasant. The mean annual temperature is 29° C and the average annual rainfall 3,000 mm. Rain falls on over half the days of the year, usually heavy downpours followed by sunny skies. The trade winds blow from the east much of the year. Strong west winds and somewhat more rain come between October and March, the hurricane season. Tuvalu is near the zone of hurricane formation, and these storms can appear with little warning and cause considerable damage. Otherwise, few seasonal variations disturb the humid, tropical weather. The waters lapping these shores are among the warmest in the world, and those of the interior lagoons are several degrees warmer again.

History
The Polynesians colonized Tuvalu some 2,000 years ago; Samoans occupied the southern

atolls, while Tongans were more active in the north. Groups of warriors also arrived from Kiribati, and their language is still spoken on Nui. Polynesian migrants reached the outliers of the Solomons and the Carolines from bases in Tuvalu.

Although the Spaniard Mendaña reportedly saw some of the islands in the 16th century, regular European contact did not occur until the 19th century. Slavers kidnapped 450 people from Funafuti, Nanumea, and Nukulaelae in 1863 to dig guano on the islands off Peru—none returned. In 1861 a Cook Islands castaway named Elekana was washed up on Nukulaelae. He taught Christianity to the islanders, and after reporting back to Protestant missionaries in Samoa, returned in 1865 with Rev. A.W. Murray and an organized LMS missionary party. Soon, most Tuvaluans were converted, and they remained under the spiritual guidance of Samoan pastors right up to 1969. The LMS-descended Ekalesia Kelisiano Tuvalu retains the loyalty of 92% of the population today.

To keep out American traders, Britain declared a protectorate over Tuvalu in 1892, upgrading it to colonial status in 1916. The ensuing period was fairly uneventful, except for the American military bases established at Funafuti, Nukufetau, and Nanumea during WW II. Funafuti was home to B-24 Liberator bombers of the U.S. Seventh Air Force, which launched raids against Japanese bases in the Gilberts and Marshalls. Warplanes en route from Wallis Island to the Gilberts were refueled here. Japanese planes did manage to drop a few bombs back, but Tuvalu was spared the trauma of a Japanese invasion.

The U.S. built its airfield across the most fertile land on Funafuti, reducing the area planted in coconuts and *pulaka* (swamp taro) by a third. The enduring impact of this loss is reflected in the fact that *pulaka* is no longer a staple food of the Tuvaluans on Funafuti. The Americans left behind a few wrecked cranes and huge "borrow" pits where they extracted (borrowed) coral. Today garbage is dumped into the stagnant lakes in the American pits, forming perfect breeding grounds for mosquitoes and rats. A plan to fill the pits and reclaim the land has been under discussion for decades.

Until 1975, Tuvalu was part of the Gilbert and Ellice Islands Colony. In the early 1970s the Polynesian Ellice Islanders expressed their desire to separate from the Micronesian Gilbertese and proceed toward true independence. In a 1974 referendum, the Tuvaluans voted overwhelmingly to become a separate unit. Britain acceded to the wish in 1975, and on 1 October 1978, after only five months of full internal self-government, Tuvalu became a fully independent nation. Political independence has greatly benefitted Tuvalu, as it would receive much less attention and economic aid as an outer island group of Kiribati.

Government

Tuvalu has an elected 12-member parliament headed by a prime minister chosen from its ranks. The four cabinet ministers and the speaker of the house must also be elected members of parliament. There are no political parties. A Tuvaluan governor-general represents the British Crown. Decisions of the High Court of Tuvalu may be appealed to the Fiji Court of Appeal and finally the Privy Council in London.

Since 1966 elected island councils have provided local government on each outer island; in 1977 a town council replaced the island council on Funafuti. Previously the heads of families had met in a *maneapa* (community hall) to discuss island affairs.

Economy

Tuvalu's gross domestic product (A$11.5 million in 1990) is the smallest of any independent state. Only small quantities of locally made clothing are exported, whereas most food, fuel, and manufactured goods are imported. In 1991 imports exceeded exports by 20 to one (compared to three to one at independence). This negative balance of trade makes Tuvalu highly dependent on foreign aid, provided mostly by Australia, New Zealand, Japan, and Britain, in that order. Government services account for nearly half of total economic output, a situation only possible due to outside aid.

The Tuvalu Trust Fund, created in August 1987 with grants of A$27.1 million (now worth A$37 million) from the governments of Australia, N.Z., and the U.K., provides Tuvalu with a regular income of around A$2 million a year. Remittances from Tuvaluans overseas, such as those working as crew on foreign ships or at the phosphate works on Nauru, bring in another A$2 million a year. The sale of postage stamps to collectors provides a further five percent of government revenue.

This Tuvaluan, strips of pandanus around head and waist, came aboard a ship of the U.S. Exploring Expedition, which visited Nukufetau in 1841.

A.T. AGATE

typical house, Tuvalu

HEINZ GEISER

American, Korean, and Taiwanese tuna-fishing boats pay about half a million dollars in licensing fees to exploit Tuvalu's 900,000-square-km Exclusive Economic Zone. Japan has also donated six 10-meter fishing boats to Tuvalu, and these supply the local fish market. Tourism has long been hampered by high air fares, and in early 1995 the government sharply increased its room and airport taxes, effectively eliminating all but the most determined travelers. Of the 976 overseas visitors to Tuvalu in 1991, only 137 declared their purpose as tourism.

The People

All nine atolls are inhabited, with one or two villages on each. The villages are often divided into two "sides" to foster competition. Over 70% of the people on the outer islands still live in traditional-style housing. The life of the people is hard—only coconuts and pandanus grow naturally, though bananas, papayas, and breadfruit are cultivated. A variety of taro *(pulaka)* has to be grown in pits excavated from coral rock. Reef fish and tuna are the main protein components in the diet. Chicken, both local and imported, is eaten quite regularly on Funafuti; pork is eaten on special occasions.

Tuvalu's population density (361 persons per square km) is the highest in the South Pacific and one of the highest in the world. Between 1985 and 1991 the number of persons per

square km on Funafuti increased from 1,124 to 1,510. Over 40% of the country's population now lives on this one atoll, and room to breathe is rapidly disappearing as additional people arrive continuously in search of government jobs. About 75% of the food consumed on Funafuti is now imported, and diet-related diseases such as diabetes, hypertension, and vitamin deficiency are on the increase. The infant mortality rate of 41 per thousand is the highest in Polynesia.

While some 9,061 people (1991) live in Tuvalu, another 2,000 Tuvaluans reside abroad. After the separation from the Gilbert Islands in 1975, many Tuvaluans who had previously held government jobs on Tarawa or worked at the phosphate mine on Banaba returned home. A second influx is expected when phosphate mining ends on Nauru where 750 Tuvaluans are presently employed.

Mostly Polynesian, related to the Samoans and Tongans, the Tuvaluans' ancestry is evident in their language, architecture, customs, and *tuu mo aganu Tuvalu* (Tuvaluan way of life). Nui Island is an exception, with some Micronesian influence. Before independence, many Tuvaluans working on Tarawa took an I-Kiribati husband or wife, and there's now a large Gilbertese community on Funafuti. The Tuvaluan language is almost identical to that spoken in neighboring Tokelau, Wallis and Futuna, and Tikopia in the Solomons.

Conduct and Customs

If you're planning on stopping at an outer island, take along things like sticks of tobacco, cigarettes, matches, chewing gum, volleyballs, fishhooks, T-shirts, cloth, and cosmetics to give as gifts. Don't hand them out at random as if you're Santa Claus—give them to people you know as a form of reciprocation. It's the custom.

Scanty dress is considered offensive everywhere, so carry a *sulu* to wrap around you. Women should cover their legs when seated and their thighs at all times. Never stand upright before seated people, and try to enter a house or *maneapa* shoeless, and from the lagoon side rather than the ocean side.

ON THE ROAD

Entertainment

Tuvaluans love dancing, be it their traditional *fatele,* more energetic than Gilbertese dancing, or the predictable twist. Traditional dancing is performed on special occasions, such as when opening a building, greeting special visitors, or celebrating holidays. Get in on the singing, dancing, and general frivolity taking place at the *maneapas* almost every night. On Funafuti migrants from each outer island have their own *maneapa,* so ask around to find out if anything is on. Or just listen for the rhythmic sounds and head that way. Sometimes the local I-Kiribati do Gilbertese dances. On festive occasions many people wear flower garlands called *fou* (rhymes with Joe) in their hair. Each island has its own style.

Ask where you can watch *te ano* (the ball), the national game. Two teams line up facing one another and competition begins with one member throwing the heavy ball toward the other team, who must hit it back with their hands. Points are scored if the opposing team lets the ball fall and the first team to reach 10 wins. Obviously, weak players are targeted and the matches can be fierce (but usually friendly).

Public Holidays and Festivals

Public holidays include New Year's Day, Commonwealth Day (second Monday in March), Good Friday, Easter Monday (March/April), Gospel Day (2nd Monday in May), the Queen's Birthday (June), National Children's Day (early August), Tuvalu National Days (1 and 2 October), Prince Charles' Birthday (November), Christmas (25 December), and Boxing Day (28 December). The period 25-28 December is the Christmas-Boxing Day Break.

Local Funafuti holidays include Bomb Day, which commemorates 23 April 1943, when a Japanese bomb fell through Funafuti's church roof and destroyed the interior. An American corporal had shooed 680 villagers out of the building only 10 minutes before, thus averting a major tragedy. Children's Day features kids' sports and crafts; dancing and a parade on Funafuti airstrip mark Independence Day (1 October). On 21 October, Hurricane Day, Tuvaluans recall 1972's terrible Hurricane Bebe.

Accommodations

One upmarket hotel and nearly a dozen small private guesthouses exist on Funafuti, but camping is not allowed. A 10% government room tax is added to all accommodations charges. The Vaiaku Lagi Hotel will accept traveler's checks but most of the other places prefer to be paid in cash. Don't count on anyone taking a credit card. If you'd like to be picked up at the airport you can fax virtually all of the guesthouses on Funafuti over the "public fax" 688/20800.

All of the outer islands except Niulakita and Nukufetau have guesthouses run by the island councils, where you can stay for A$5-15 pp, or A$20-32 including meals. The guesthouse attendants will do laundry for an additional charge. It's *essential* to announce your arrival by sending a telegram to the particular island council (you'd get there before a letter). This can be done either at the Telecom Center opposite the post office in Vaiaku or at the Department of Rural Development (tel. 20177) in the Ministry of Natural Resources building just south of the main government building next to the lagoon. Otherwise, it's possible to arrange accommodations with local outer-island families but be prepared to renounce all privacy. Don't count on being able to buy *any* imported goods on the outer islands: take with you what you'll need.

Food

Pulaka (swamp taro) is eaten boiled or roasted or is made into pudding. Breadfruit, a staple, is boiled with coconut cream, baked, or fried in oil as chips. Plantain (cooking bananas) may also be boiled or chipped. Sweet potatoes, though becoming popular, are still only served on special occasions. Fish is eaten every day, both whitefish and tuna; pork, chicken, and eggs add a little variety. Reddish-colored fish caught in the lagoons may be poisonous. If you're interested in fishing, make it known and someone will take you out in their canoe. Imported foods such as rice, corned beef, sugar, and a variety of canned foods are used in vast amounts.

When eating on the outer islands, ask for some of the local dishes such as *laulu* or *lolo* (a leaf in coconut cream, not unlike spinach and delicious), *palusami (laulu*, onions, and fish, usually wrapped in banana leaves), *uu* (coconut crab, only readily available on Nukulaelae and Nukufetau), and *ula* (crayfish). Quench your thirst with *pi* (drinking coconut), *kaleve* (sweet coconut toddy, generally extracted morning and night), or supersweet coffee and tea. *Kao* is sour toddy produced by fermenting *kaleve* two or three days. Take care, as *kao* can quickly render you senseless and produces a vicious hangover. Drinking alcohol in public is prohibited.

Visas and Officialdom

Funafuti is the only port of entry. There are no visa requirements for any nationality, but make sure you have a passport valid for another six months and an onward ticket. Those arriving/departing by boat also require an air ticket to leave. Upon arrival by boat, immigration will inform you that it's prohibited to stay with the locals or to leave Funafuti. Diplomacy can usually overcome both obstacles.

The maximum stay is four months, but visitors are usually given only the time until their onward flight or 28 days. Sometimes you only get a week on arrival, with an extension to one month available for A$10 at the Immigration office (tel. 20240, fax 20241) in the government stores building near the library. Two additional months cost A$10 each (return ticket essential). Further extensions require government approval.

Most government offices are open Monday to Thursday 0800-1615, Friday 0800-1245.

Money

Australian currency is used, with Tuvaluan coins (about US$1 = A$1.35). The Tuvaluan one-dollar coin is of the same size and edging as the Australian 50-cent piece. It pays to be alert when handling these coins, or face a 50% devaluation.

The National Bank of Tuvalu (tel. 20803, fax 20802; open Monday to Thursday 0930-1300, Friday 0830-1200) at Funafuti charges A$1 commission to change traveler's checks. They'll give cash advances on Visa and MasterCard.

Tuvaluans do not expect to be tipped.

Health

Princess Margaret Hospital (tel. 20481) on Funafuti has a pharmacist and dentist, but on the outer islands there are only "dressers." Hepatitis, cholera, dengue fever, and tuberculosis are occasional problems. Cuts can turn septic quickly, so one should pack and use antiseptic cream such as hydrogen peroxide. Water should be considered suspect and boiled.

Recommended (but not compulsory) vaccinations for those who will be spending much time here include typhoid fever and immune globulin or the hepatitis A vaccine. The cholera vaccination is only 50% effective but you may be required to prove you've had it if you're arriving from an infected area. At last report Fiji-bound passengers were being refused permission to board Air Marshall Islands flights at Funafuti unless they had a cholera vaccination certificate not over six months old. If need be, vaccinations and certificates can be obtained at the hospital.

What to Take

Bring plenty of film, as that which is sold locally is often expired. Only color print film is available (no black and white or color slides). Snorkelers should arrive with their own gear. Bring coffee too—it's priced out of reach here. Tampons can also be a problem. On the outer islands even staples such as rice, flour, and sugar can be sold out.

TRANSPORTATION

Getting There

Air Marshall Islands (Box 1319, Majuro, MH 96960, U.S.A.; tel. 692/625-3731, fax 692/625-3730) flies Majuro-Tarawa-Funafuti-Fiji and return twice a week using a 50-seat jetprop Saab 2000 aircraft. Once a week AMI does an extra Fiji-Funafuti-Fiji run. Different AMI flights may use Suva or Nadi airport in Fiji, so check. One-way fares to Funafuti are F$428 from Fiji, A$357 from Tarawa, US$429 from Majuro. Seven-day roundtrip excursion fares to Funafuti cost F$645 from Nadi or Suva or A$576 from Tarawa. Ask about advance-booking discounts.

Air Marshall Island doesn't allow free stopovers on their through tickets, so if you want to stop at both Tarawa and Funafuti between Majuro and Fiji you must pay US$715 instead of the usual US$535 direct fare Fiji-Majuro! How expensive they are is illustrated by Air Nauru's fare of US$312 Tarawa-Nauru-Fiji, compared with about US$536 Tarawa-Funafuti-Fiji on Air Marshall Islands! Unfortunately, Air Marshall Islands has a monopoly on flights to Tuvalu (which is how they can get away with this sort of pricing).

You don't receive a seat number on AMI flights, so be near the door when the flight is called if you want to sit in a certain place. These flights are often heavily booked by people on some sort of official business. All passengers continuing from Funafuti to Tarawa or Majuro should check Kiribati and Marshall Islands visa requirements well before leaving Fiji (don't wait to ask the extremely rude woman who works the AMI check-in counter at Nadi). For toll-free information on Air Marshall Islands in the U.S., call 800/543-3898. In Australia check with Qantas, which has AMI schedules and fares in their computers.

The government-owned *Nivaga II* travels Suva-Funafuti (1,020 km) about four times a year. One-way fares are F$70 deck, F$124 2nd class, F$139 first class without meals, or F$200 2nd class, F$215 first class including meals. For information in Fiji, inquire at the Tuvalu Embassy (16 Gorrie St., Suva; tel. 679/301-355, fax 679/301-023). In Funafuti, ask about ships at the Travel Office (tel. 20737) beside the post office in Vaiaku. The *Nivaga II* also makes occasional trips to Nauru (1,400 km), Tarawa, Tokelau, and Apia (1,000 km), carrying both passengers and cargo.

Tuvalu collects a A$20 departure tax, which yachties must also pay.

Getting Around

There are no internal flights. In 1988 the British government donated the 58-meter interisland ship *Nivaga II* to mark Tuvalu's 10 years of independence. This ship makes the rounds of the outer islands roughly every fortnight stopping at each atoll for about an hour, depending on the tides. The southern trip to Nukulaelae and Niulakita takes three days; the northern trip visits about three of the six islands up that way in four

the interisland ship,
Nivaga II

JACK D. HADEN

days. If you decide to stop off at one of the islands, you could be there two weeks or more before the ship returns. Distances from Funafuti are 112 km to Nukulaelae, 221 km to Niulakita, 102 km to Nukufetau, 118 km to Vaitupu, 242 km to Nui, 301 km to Niutao, 352 km to Nanumaga, and 400 km to Nanumea.

There are three twin first class cabins with private bath and eight second class cabins with shared facilities. The 120 deck passengers must bring their own mats, eating utensils, and food (unless meals have been ordered beforehand). No booze is sold aboard, though it's okay to bring your own (no refrigerators available). Don't offer alcohol to the crew, however, as disciplinary action would be taken against them if they imbibed. If you must drink, do it in your cabin.

Roundtrip fares from Funafuti to the central islands of Vaitupu, Nui, and Nukufetau are A$94/154/184 deck/second/first class. Otherwise it's A$115/194/234 to the northern islands of Nanumaga, Nanumea, and Niutao. Meals are charged extra. Tuvaluans pay cheaper fares, so make sure you're being quoted the right amount. In busy periods women have a slightly better chance of getting cabin space on the *Nivaga II* than men, but even if you've booked and paid for a cabin you're not safe until the ship has actually sailed, since a VIP such as the prime minister or a member of parliament can requisition your cabin on short notice, and all the kicking and screaming in the world won't help a bit. The schedule is erratic and unreliable, so you really have to be lucky to be able to go!

FUNAFUTI

Captain Arent De Peyster "discovered" Funafuti in 1819 and named it Ellice, for Edward Ellice, the British member of parliament who owned the cargo he was carrying in his ship, the *Rebecca*. In 1841 Charles Wilkes, commander of the United States Exploring Expedition, applied the name to the entire Tuvalu group.

The government offices are at Vaiaku, 50 meters west of the airstrip, the Funafuti Fusi cooperative supermarket is a kilometer northeast, and the deepwater wharf (built with Australian aid in 1981) is a little over a kilometer beyond that. A Japanese fishing boat wrecked during a hurricane in 1972 is in the lagoon just north of the wharf. Most of the homes on Funafuti are prefabs put up after this same storm, which also left a beach of coral boulders along the island's east side.

The area between Vaiaku and the wharf is developing into a busy little township with street lighting installed by New Zealand in 1990, the roads paved by the U.S. in 1991, the airstrip sealed by the European Union in 1992, and a new airport terminal erected by Australia in 1993. Heavy motorcycle traffic circulates on the one main street, and the litter is piling up along the lagoon as consumerism stifles the South Seas dream. The unsupervised men in blue loincloths seen sweeping the streets and gardening around Vaiaku are doing community service as inmates from the prison across the airstrip.

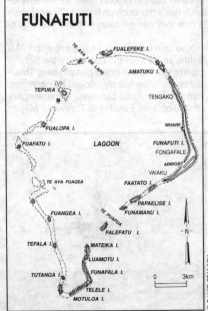

Sights

Sights around Vaiaku include the open-sided government *maneapa* next to the airport building and the former lighthouse next to the governor-general's residence. In the northeastern part of the Fongafale village directly across from the Nanumaga *maneapa,* not far from the hospital, is a borehole known as **David's Drill**. In 1896-98 scientists sent by the Royal Society of London conducted experimental drilling at Funafuti to test Darwin's theory of atoll formation. The deepest bore (340 meters) failed to reach Funafuti's volcanic base.

At the north end of Funafuti Island, 10 km from Vaiaku, is a white sandy beach on the lagoon side and a wartime bunker. Farther north is the **Tuvalu Maritime Training School** (tel. 20849) on Amatuku, which prepares young Tuvaluans for employment on oceangoing ships. Since the school opened in 1979, several hundred young Tuvaluans have completed 12-month courses here. At low tide you can walk across the reef to Amatuku.

Some of the best snorkeling on Funafuti can be found in the huge oceanside pits blasted by the Americans during the war. At low tide the pits are like immense swimming pools trapping thousands of fish until high tide returns. Otherwise one should use extreme caution when swimming on the ocean side of the atoll due to the big surf, currents, coral heads, etc. Lagoon beaches in the populated areas are often used as toilets by the locals, which makes swimming or simply walking along the shore hazardous.

Of the outlying *motus* on the atoll's coral ring, Funafala, Amatuku, and Fualefeke are inhabited. You can stay in a small guesthouse on the beach at Funafala; local families also take guests. This little tropical paradise only an hour away by boat is a perfect escape from town. Rolf Koepke and the other guesthouse managers will be able to help with the arrangements. A maritime park is being established on the western side of the lagoon.

Te Ava Fuagea is the deepest (13 meters) of the three passes into the 14-by-18 km Funafuti lagoon; the others are only about eight meters deep. Yachties beware: Funafuti is probably the most poorly beaconed port of entry in the Pacific. At last report all the navigation buoys had disappeared from Te Ava Fuagea, making

it an eyeball entrance. Navigation within the lagoon is also dangerous as it's studded with unmarked shoals, so yachts should proceed carefully along the marked channel to the anchorage off the main wharf to clear customs. From October to March, westerly winds make this anchorage risky.

Accommodations

In 1992 the government spent A$2.5 million rebuilding the two-story **Vaiaku Lagi Hotel** (Mamani O'Brien, Box 10, Funafuti; tel. 20733, fax 20503), facing the lagoon near the Funafuti airstrip. The 16 a/c rooms with private bath in the new wing are A$70/80/90 single/double/triple (children under 12 free). Two non-a/c rooms in the old wing are A$35/40/50. Credit cards are not accepted, and meals in the hotel restaurant are expensive. Traditional dancing is performed on Thursday nights if sufficient guests are present (ask) and there's no cover charge. The Friday night "twist" (disco) at the hotel continues until midnight. Rowdy locals (often seamen on leave) demolish can after can of Foster's in the hotel's old wing bar (the bar in the new wing is more expensive). The hotel staff are nice, friendly people who don't really put themselves out for their guests in any way. You must make all your transportation or tour arrangements yourself.

Su's Place (Susana Taafaki, tel. 20612), 250 meters northeast of Vaiaku post office, has five fan-cooled rooms at A$25/35/48 single/double/triple, plus one self-catering a/c apartment at A$58 double plus a surcharge for gas and electricity (this can be substantial—ask about it). Breakfast costs A$3.50 pp. They rent bicycles at A$4 per day, a small truck at A$2 per kilometer, and a boat at A$120 a day. A VCR is available, and you can rent videos at the Sagale Tutasi Bakery next door. A restaurant/bar is on the premises.

Filamona Lodge (Box 44, Funafuti; tel. 20864) is in the center of the village 100 meters due east of the Funafuti Fusi. It's a bit hidden, so ask for the proprietors, Lotoala Metia or Penieli Tealofi. The four fan-cooled rooms are A$30/40 single/double. Though only the downstairs room has private bath, the two upstairs rooms with a shared bath get more breeze. They have laundry facilities, and you can watch videos on their VCR if you rent your

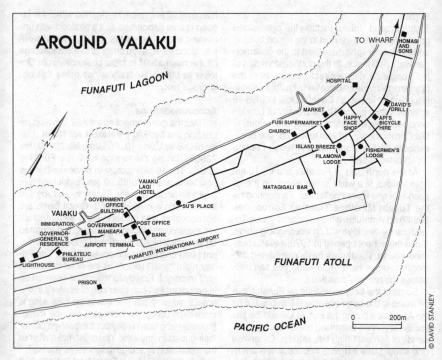

AROUND VAIAKU

TO WHARF — HOMASI AND SONS

FUNAFUTI LAGOON

HOSPITAL

DAVID'S DRILL

MARKET

FUSI SUPERMARKET

HAPPY FACE SHOP

API'S BICYCLE HIRE

CHURCH

ISLAND BREEZE

FISHERMEN'S LODGE

FILAMONA LODGE

VAIAKU LAGI HOTEL

MATAGIGALI BAR

GOVERNMENT OFFICE BUILDING

SU'S PLACE

VAIAKU

IMMIGRATION

POST OFFICE

GOVERNMENT MANEAPA

BANK

GOVERNOR-GENERAL'S RESIDENCE

AIRPORT TERMINAL

FUNAFUTI INTERNATIONAL AIRPORT

PHILATELIC BUREAU

LIGHTHOUSE

FUNAFUTI ATOLL

PRISON

PACIFIC OCEAN

0   200m

© DAVID STANLEY

own cassettes at the Funafuti Fusi (second floor). The Kai Restaurant downstairs serves local foods.

Near Filamona is the **Island Breeze Motel** (Mr. Fanoga, tel. 20606, fax 20708), which is a bit of a misnomer as a hurricane would have to be raging for any breeze to reach there. Perhaps they're referring to the fans in the rooms! The four rooms are A$30/35 single/double (no hot water). Meals can be arranged.

Fishermen's Lodge (tel. 20735, fax 20800), deeper east in the village not far from Filamona Lodge, has three fan-cooled rooms with shared bath, cooking facilities, and videos at A$30/40 single/double. The manager, Elesene Lafita, lives next door, and meals can be ordered. The whole house is often rented out to contract workers who pay by the month.

Also in this area but closer to the lagoon is **Mele Mele Guesthouse** (Willy Telavi, tel. 20146) with four fan-cooled rooms with shared cooking and bathing facilities at A$30-40.

A 10-minute walk north of the main wharf is **Laisini's Guest House** (Box 82, Funafuti; fax 20723) where Laisini and Alexandra accommodate visitors at A$15/20 single/double including breakfast. Dinner is A$5 extra. At last report there was no electricity and only a bucket shower, but things should get better. For rent are bicycles (A$2 a day), mask/snorkel sets (A$3 a day), a sailboard (A$10 an hour), and bathing suit/towel (A$1). They can arrange a large motorized canoe at A$60 a day for up to six people or A$10 pp for up to 15 people.

German expat Rolf Koepke and his Tuvaluan wife Emily operate **Hide-Away Guest House** (Box 59, Funafuti; tel. 20829, fax 20835), a two-story European-style house in spacious surroundings about five km north of Vaiaku. Take a bus to the deepwater wharf, then walk along the lagoon 30 minutes (some buses continue this far). Rolf offers a self-catering apartment with private bath at A$30/35/40 single/double/triple, plus two rooms with private bath in the annex at A$25/30/35. Cooking facilities are available and a small restaurant is on the premises. Rolf's dog, Spottie, will accompany you on walks; bicycles (A$4) or a motorbike (A$10) can also be arranged. Hide-Away is just 30 meters from both lagoon and ocean beaches with a thatched hut provided for relaxing. This is certainly your best bet if you want a restful holiday.

Food
The **Kai Restaurant** serves tasty local meals in their open-air pavilion beneath Filamona Lodge. Typical dishes include fish in coconut cream, heart of banana (from the purple leaf surrounding the flower), and breadfruit. Ask about the special menu on Wednesday and the *umu* feast on Friday. There could be a guitarist singing Tuvaluan songs or local children performing a *fatele* (local dance) these nights.

Su's Restaurant (tel. 20612) at Su's Place serves lunch and dinner. Reservations are required at both Kai and Su's (they mightn't bother opening otherwise).

The **Futimai Restaurant** (tel. 20618), next to the Funafuti Fusi Supermarket and opposite the market, serves local favorites like chicken and rice, or raw fish with cooked bananas and breadfruit. It's clean and the portions are large, about A$2.50 a plate (lunch only). Cold water is provided (but no beer). The snack bar at the airport is similar, and they also have a cordial made from *kaleve* and water.

Entertainment
The **V.K. Public Bar** (tel. 20741), 500 meters south of the wharf, is an open-walled establishment serving mostly beer. There's a small pool table, and Vaitupu men on Funafuti often hang out here, occasionally mixing it up with one another.

Near the old seaplane hangar on the northwest side of the airstrip is the **Matagigali Bar** (the name means "Lovely Wind"). This one has two pool tables and more space to move around. The Friday and Saturday night "twists" often resemble saloon scenes out of Wild West movies. It's okay for males, but unescorted women may have problems with overenthusiastic local men.

Catch the singing in the church not far from the Funafuti Fusi on Sunday. Cricket (*kilikiti*) and soccer are played on Funafuti airstrip in the evenings and on weekends, as is *te ano*—a sort of 50-per-side elongated volleyball. If you wish to use the tennis courts near the airport terminal, bring your own rackets and ball (the lights will be turned on at night for a small fee). This tennis court doubles as a basketball and volleyball court. Other tennis courts are near the Matagigali Bar.

Shopping
Some of the best handicrafts in the Pacific are available here. The **Women's Handicraft Center** (tel. 20852, fax 20643) behind the airport terminal (open office hours and at flight times) has baskets, bags, mats, hats, fans, necklaces,

Hide-Away Guest House, Funafuti

JACK D. HADEN

and model canoes from Funafuti and the outer islands. A fisherman's watertight wooden box *(tuluma)* is a unique souvenir. A booklet on Tuvaluan handicrafts is available at A$5.

The **Funafuti Fusi** (tel. 20867), halfway between Vaiaku and the deepwater wharf, is the biggest self-service supermarket on Funafuti. The small municipal market across the street is open daily except Sunday. Bread is available after 1600, fresh fish in the early morning and 1630-1700. A limited selection of food and merchandise is also available from stores owned by the various outer-island communities on Funafuti, most of them along the lagoonside road between the Funafuti Fusi and the wharf.

Happy Face Garments (tel. 20622), between the Funafuti Fusi and the hospital, sells colorful T-shirts, shirts, shorts, towels, and *sulus* at reasonable prices. Ask the manager, Melina, to custom print you a Tuvalu T-shirt of your own design. Nearby is **Togolands** (tel. 20708), a unique merchandising combination where you can rent a motorbike or purchase eggs.

If you're a yachtie, buy your diesel oil at BP just north of the main wharf, as depot prices are 35% less than those charged at the Funafuti Fusi supermarket. Sammy's Service Station next to the Fusi also sells gasoline and diesel.

Post and Telecommunications

When writing, address your letter: Funafuti, Tuvalu, Central Pacific (via Fiji Islands). Important messages should be sent to you via the "public fax" at 688/20800. The post office sells very attractive Tuvalu aerogrammes for 50 cents each. The **Philatelic Bureau** (tel. 20224, fax 20712) is a few doors southwest of the library.

Normal telephone, fax, and telex facilities are provided by satellite on a 24-hour basis at the Telecom Center opposite the post office. Local calls are 10 cents each. Long-distance calls are 50 cents a minute to other atolls of Tuvalu, A$2 a minute to Australia, or A$4 a minute to North America or Europe (three-minute minimum). Faxes can be sent for A$4 for the first page and 50 cents for each additional page, plus the regular telephone charge.

If you have access to a direct-dial telephone, you'll need to know the international access code is 00. For the local operator dial 010, for the international operator 012. Tuvalu's telephone code is 688.

Information

The **Tourism Office** (Box 33, Funafuti; tel. 20184, fax 20829) in the Customs office in Vaiaku sells postcards. Other postcards are available at Broadcasting House, the Funafuti Fusi, and the post office.

Excellent maps of each of the atolls are available from the **Lands & Survey Department** (tel. 20836), just north of the Library and Archives building fronting the lagoon.

The **USP Extension Center** (tel. 20811, fax 20704) near the hospital sells books on Tuvalu and the region. The excellent Tuvalu-English dictionary (A$8) produced by the Jehovah's Witnesses is available at the National Bank, the USP Center, and the Fusi.

Nui Store (tel. 20623) sells the regional news magazines.

A good **National Library** (tel. 20711) is near the government offices in Vaiaku (the USP also has a library).

Reconfirm your flight reservations not less than 72 hours in advance at the computerized Travel Office (tel. 20737) beside the post office in Vaiaku. There can be long waiting lists, and you'll get bumped if you forget to reconfirm.

Getting Around

Privately owned 26-seat buses run hourly between the Government Center at Vaiaku and the deepwater wharf on Funafuti from 0700-2100 daily (20 cents per zone to 60 cents maximum). The buses marked "Vao" continue to the north end of the island, usually in the morning and late afternoon. There are no bus stops—you just wave the buses down.

Api's Bicycle Hire (tel. 20626) is on the main road near the hospital. **Togolands** nearby rents small motorbikes at A$10 a day. Motorbikes are also available from a guy named Sakaio who lives near Fishermen's Lodge. Several places rent pick-up trucks. At night bicycles must carry a light, though a flashlight in hand will do—this regulation *is* enforced. Driving is on the left.

The **Fisheries Department** (tel. 20742) near the main wharf has the only compressor on the island for filling scuba tanks. Government fishing boats are available for outer-island charters at A$1000 per day including meals (deck accommodation only). Contact the Ministry of Natural Resources (tel. 20827) or phone the Fisheries Department direct.

One privately owned catamaran capable of carrying 25 adults is also available at A$120 a day for the boat. On Monday and Thursday there is a regular trip to Funafala Island (locals A$6 pp each way, tourists A$20 pp each way). Many other private boats are available for rent.

OTHER ISLANDS OF TUVALU

Nanumaga

Nanumaga is a single island with only a narrow fringing reef. The main village is divided into the Tokelau (north) and Tonga (south) quarters, representing the island's two social groups. The Nanumaga people are conservative, but those few visitors who happen to call are warmly welcomed. If you happen to visit, pay a courtesy call on the island chief, who belongs to the Mouhala clan. Fishing is prohibited on Tuesday and Wednesday.

Stay at the guesthouse for A$6 pp, plus A$13.50 for all meals.

Nanumea

Nanumea is the northwesternmost of the Tuvalu group, and its lagoon is considered by many to be the most beautiful. On Lakena Island is a freshwater lake surrounded by palm and pandanus. A U.S. landing craft still sits wrecked on the reef as a reminder of the wartime U.S. base here. Other aircraft wreckage (mainly B-24s) is strewn around the island. American Passage just west of the village was cut through the reef for 500 meters by the U.S. Army to allow small boats to enter the lagoon. If you have a head for heights, climb the pointed spire of the church—the view is worth it—but get permission from the pastor first. This German-style tower is one of the highest in the South Pacific.

The Nanumea island council guesthouse is A$15 pp without meals. Guests may cook for themselves, otherwise the attendant will prepare meals for an additional charge.

Niulakita

The southernmost, smallest, and least inhabited of the Tuvalu group, Niulakita is only a tiny coral dot just over a kilometer long. Niulakita sits up slightly higher than the other atolls, and the vegetation is lush. During the 19th century, the island was exploited by miners digging guano left by countless generations of seabirds. In 1926 the trading company Burns Philp set up a copra plantation here, which was sold to the British government in 1944. In 1946 the government ceded Niulakita to the people of Niutao, who have kept rotating groups here since 1949 (there never was any permanent population). They now live here making copra in shifts of a couple of years each. There's no guesthouse here but you can stay with local families.

Niutao

Legend has it that Pai and Vau, the two women who created Nanumea, also made Niutao, a tiny rectangular island about two km long. The people were converted by Protestant missionaries who arrived in 1870, and in 1991 a sturdy new church was completed, yet many traditional beliefs survive. Niutao is known for its decorative and durable pandanus floor mats.

Room and board at the island council guesthouse costs A$20 pp.

Nui

A string of coconut-covered islands surrounds the closed Nui lagoon on the northern, eastern, and southern sides. This six-km-long oval body of water is flanked by lovely white beaches. Terikiai islet is especially beautiful. Nui was the first of the Tuvalu islands to be spotted by Europeans (Mendaña in 1568). Though the Nui people are known to be of Micronesian origin and still speak Gilbertese, today their culture is thoroughly Tuvaluan. The main, or "old," village (Tekawa Nikawai in Gilbertese) has recently been joined by Fakaifou, which means "new village" in Tuvaluan. The village houses sit in orderly rows.

The island council guesthouse is A$26 pp including meals or A$6.50 only to sleep. There's also a guesthouse without toilet facilities on Terikiai islet, which is usually only for locals (A$1.50 pp), but special permission may be granted to stay there.

Nukufetau

Nukufetau is the closest outer atoll to Funafuti (102 km). Unlike Funafuti's, the lagoon at

Nukufetau is relatively safe for navigation and offers some protection from the westerlies. During WW II, the Americans constructed a wharf and an X-shaped airfield on Motolalo Island, eight km east of the present village across the lagoon. Quite a bit of debris remains.

There's no island council guesthouse on this island, but you can stay with the pastor for a similar price.

Nukulaelae

Nukulaelae is the easternmost of Tuvalu's nine islands, only a half degree west of the 180th meridian and the international date line, its 10-km-long lagoon partly surrounded by long, sandy islands. Today climatic change threatens this isolated atoll and flooding has become a problem. Though the European Union has funded a seawall to slow the increasing erosion, salt water has already seeped into the large taro pits in the center of the main island. Pig pens stand on the mounds created when the pits were dug. The Nukulaelae people are renowned dancers.

It was here in 1861 that a Cook Islander named Elekana made an unscheduled landfall after drifting west in his canoe from the Cook Islands. Elekana introduced Tuvalu to Christianity, as a monument on Nukulaelae now records, and it was here too that the first organized missionary party from Samoa landed in 1865.

In 1863 visitors of a different kind called, as three Peruvian ships appeared off the atoll. An old man came ashore to tell the islanders they were mission ships and everyone was invited aboard for religious services. The trusting Polynesians accepted, and after all the men were aboard and locked in the hold, the same rascal returned to the beach to say that the men had asked that the women and children join them. The ships then sailed off with 250 of Nukulaelae's 300 inhabitants to be used as slave labor in the mines of Peru. Only two men, who managed to jump overboard and swim 10 km back, ever returned.

The island council guesthouse is A$5 pp to stay, plus another A$25 pp for three meals and

---

CAPSULE TUVALUAN VOCABULARY

ao—yes

ea koe—how are you?
e fia?—how much? how many?

fafine—women
fakafetai—thank you
fakafetai lasi—thank you very much
fakamolemole—please, sorry
fakatali—wait
fale—house
falefoliki—toilet
fesoasoani—help
fiafia—happy
foliki—small

gali—nice, good

igoa—name
ika—fish
ikai—no
inu—drink
kai—to eat

koe e fano ki fea?—where are you going?
koi tou igoa?—what is your name?
kou kou—to wash, bathe

lasi—big, large
lei—fine, well

makalili—cold
makona—full
malosi fakafetai—I am well, thank you
masaki—sick
masei—bad
mataku—afraid
meakai—food
meakaigali—good food
mea pusi—cigarettes
moa—chicken
moe—sleep

niu—coconut
palagi—non-Tuvaluan

pi—drinking coconut
poo—night

seai—none, none left
seiloa ne au—I don't know
sene—cent

taala—dollar
tagata—man
tai—salt water
taimi—time
talofa—hello
tamaliki—child
tapu—forbidden
ti—tea
tofaa—goodbye
toku igoa ko . . .—my name is . . .

vai—fresh water
vaka—boat, canoe
vakalele—airplane
vela—hot

morning and afternoon tea. Unless you're really big on food, ask if they can cut some of those meals from your bill. This island is dry, so don't carry any alcohol with you if you go ashore here.

Vaitupu

Vaitupu is the largest of the nine Tuvalu atolls in land area and, after Funafuti, the most Europeanized. The house of Herr Nitz, representative on Vaitupu of the German trading company J.C. Godeffroy for a quarter century in the late 19th century, still stands. In 1905 the London Missionary Society opened a primary school at Motufoua on Vaitupu to prepare young men for entry into the seminary in Samoa. Over the years this has developed into the large church/government secondary school, until recently the only one in Tuvalu (in 1992 the Tuvalu Christian Church opened the Fetu Valu Secondary School on Funafuti). There are a few expatriates, primarily teachers at the secondary school. In 1946 the *matai* (chiefs) of Vaitupu purchased Kioa Island in Fiji, where some 300 Vaitupu people now live.

The island council guesthouse is A$6.50 pp to stay, but meals bring the total up to A$32 pp. Ask if you'll be allowed to prepare your own food and only pay to sleep. A local school teacher named Faleefa occasionally accepts paying guests in her own home.

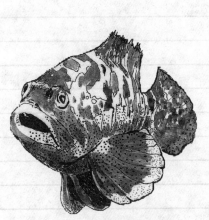

marbled grouper
(Epinephelus microdon)

MELANESIA

FIJI ISLANDS, NEW CALEDONIA, VANUATU, SOLOMON ISLANDS

Named for its "black" inhabitants, Melanesia encompasses the hulking island chains of the Western Pacific from Fiji to New Guinea. A tremendous variety of cultures, peoples, languages, and attractions make up this relatively large region of mountainous islands. Prior to European colonization in the late 19th century, the 900 linguistic groups of Melanesia had little contact with one another, and unlike Polynesia, this was a largely classless society. Today parts of New Caledonia are as cosmopolitan as southern France, but on the outer islands of Vanuatu and Solomon Islands people cling to their traditional ways. Custom and land ownership are everywhere decisive issues.

Compared to Polynesia, the population and islands are large. Densely populated Fiji is equal in inhabitants to New Caledonia, Vanuatu, and Solomon Islands combined, yet in land area both New Caledonia and Solomon Islands are bigger than Fiji. In Vanuatu and Solomon Islands, few foreigners are seen outside the capitals. British and French colonialism introduced new ethnic groups to Fiji and New Caledonia, leading to their present political instability. During WW II northern Melanesia became a pivotal battlefield. Today all of the countries of Melanesia except New Caledonia are independent. We don't include Papua New Guinea herein, because its extensive area and variety of cultures merit a separate guidebook. For North Americans and Europeans, Fiji is the gateway to this exciting area.

GORDON OHLIGER

FIJI ISLANDS
INTRODUCTION

Once notorious as the "Cannibal Isles," Fiji is now the colorful crossroads of the Pacific. Of the 322 islands that make up the Fiji Group, over 100 are inhabited by a rich mixture of vibrant, exuberant Melanesians, East Indians, Polynesians, Micronesians, Chinese, and Europeans, each with a cuisine and culture of their own. Here Melanesia mixes with Polynesia, ancient India with the Pacific, and tradition with the modern world in a unique blend.

Fiji preserves an amazing variety of traditional customs and crafts such as kava or *yanggona* drinking, the presentation of the whale's tooth, firewalking, fish driving, turtle calling, tapa beating, and pottery making. Alongside this fascinating human history is a dramatic diversity of landforms and seascapes, all concentrated in a relatively small area. Fiji's sun-drenched beaches, blue lagoons, panoramic open hillsides, lush rainforests, and dazzling reefs are truly magnificent. Such things are duplicated on continents such as Africa, but over there you'd have to travel weeks or months to see what you can see in Fiji in days.

Fiji offers posh resorts, good food and accommodations, nightlife, historic sights, outer-island living, hiking, camping, surfing, snorkeling, scuba diving, and river-running, plus easy travel by small plane, interisland ferry, copra boat, outboard canoe, open-sided bus, and air-conditioned coach. Even in a month you'd barely scratch the surface of all there is to see and do.

Best of all, Fiji is a hassle-free country with uncrowded, inexpensive facilities available almost everywhere. There's something for everyone in Fiji and prices are affordable, with a wide range of accommodation and travel options. In a word, Fiji is a traveler's country *par excellence,* and whatever your budget, Fiji gives you good value for your money and plenty of ways to spend it. *Mbula,* welcome to Fiji, everyone's favorite South Pacific country.

Important Note

There are two different systems for spelling Fijian words, one phonetic, the other historic. To relieve readers of the need to learn the complicated orthographic rules invented by early British

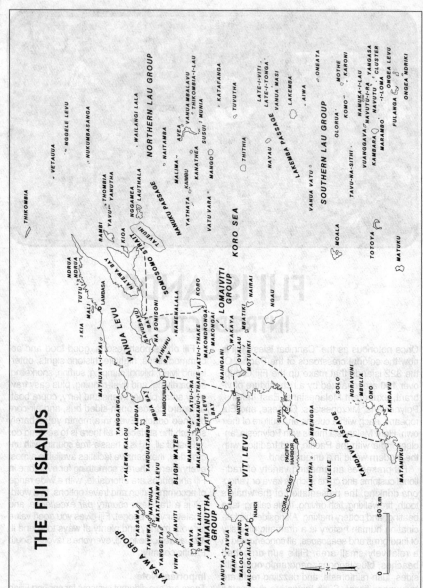

THE FIJI ISLANDS

© DAVID STANLEY

FIJI AT A GLANCE

ISLAND	AREA (square km)	HIGHEST POINT (m)	POPULATION (mid-1988 est.)	PERCENT FIJIAN*
Viti Levu	10,429	1,323	508,777	40.5
Vanua Levu	5,556	1,032	117,790	43.3
Taveuni	470	1,241	8,799	72.7
Kandavu	411	838	9,936	98.1
Ngau	140	747	3,054	99.4
Koro	104	522	3,654	98.5
Ovalau	101	626	6,660	88.3
Rambi	69	463	2,771	5.0
Lakemba	54	215	2,444	97.4
Rotuma	47	256	3,204	1.9
Mbengga	36	439	1,488	98.6
Fiji Islands	**18,272**	**1,323**	**758,275**	**49.7**

* Viti Levu, Vanua Levu, and Taveuni have sizeable Fiji Indian populations, while Rambi is Micronesian and Rotuma is Polynesian.

missionaries, all words and place names in this book are rendered phonetically. However, we use historic spelling for the personal names of individuals. In Fiji itself, historic spelling is consistently used on signboards and in printed texts, thus an *mb* in this book is written *b* locally, *nd* is *d*, *ng* is *g*, *ngg* is *q*, and *th* is *c*. Turn to "Language," which follows, for more information.

The Land

Fiji sits astride the main air route between North America and Australia, 5,100 km southwest of Hawaii and 3,150 km northeast of Sydney. Nandi is the hub of Pacific air routes, while Suva is a regional shipping center. The 180th meridian cuts through Fiji, but the international date line swings east so the entire group can share the same day. Together the Fiji Islands are scattered over 1,290,000 square km of the South Pacific Ocean.

The name Fiji is a Tongan corruption of the indigenous name "Viti." The Fiji Islands are arrayed in a horseshoe configuration with Viti Levu ("Great Fiji") and adjacent islands on the west, Vanua Levu ("Great Land") and Taveuni to the north, and the Lau Group on the east.

This upside-down U-shaped archipelago encloses the Koro Sea, which is relatively shallow and sprinkled with the Lomaiviti, or central Fiji, group of islands.

If every single island were counted, the isles of the Fiji archipelago would number in the thousands. A mere 322 are judged large enough for human habitation, however, and of these only 106 are inhabited. That leaves 216 uninhabited islands, most of them prohibitively isolated or lacking fresh water.

Most of the Fiji Islands are volcanic, remnants of a sunken continent that stretched through Australia. This origin accounts for the mineral deposits on the main islands. None of Fiji's volcanoes are presently active, though there are a few small hot springs. The two largest islands, Viti Levu and Vanua Levu, together account for 87% of Fiji's 18,272 square km of land. Viti Levu has 50% of the land area and three-quarters of the people, while Vanua Levu, with 30% of the land, has 18% of the population. Viti Levu alone is bigger than all five archipelagos of Tahiti-Polynesia put together; in fact, Fiji has more land and people than all of Polynesia combined.

The 1,000-meter-high Nandrau Plateau in central Viti Levu is cradled between Tomanivi (1,323 meters) on the north and Monavatu (1,131 meters) on the south. On different sides of this elevated divide are the Tholo-East Plateau drained by the Rewa River, the Navosa Plateau drained by the Mba, the Tholo-West Plateau drained by the Singatoka, and the Navua Plateau drained by the Navua. Some 29 well-defined peaks rise above Viti Levu's interior; most of the people live in the river valleys or along the coast.

The Nandi River slices across the Nausori Highlands, with the Mount Evans Range (1,195 meters) towering above Lautoka. Other highland areas of Viti Levu are cut by great rivers like the Singatoka, the Navua, the Rewa, and the Mba, navigable far inland by outboard canoe or kayak. Whitewater rafters shoot down the Navua and the Mba, while the lower Singatoka flows gently through Fiji's market garden "salad bowl." Fiji's largest river, the Rewa, pours into the Pacific through a wide delta just below Nausori. After a hurricane the Rewa becomes a dark torrent worth a special visit to Nausori just to see. Sharks have been known to enter both the Rewa and the Singatoka and swim far upstream.

Vanua Levu has a peculiar shape, with two long peninsulas pointing northeastward. A mountain range between Lambasa and Savusavu reaches 1,032 meters at Nasorolevu. Navotuvotu (842 meters), east of Mbua Bay, is Fiji's best example of a broad shield volcano, with lava flows built up in layers. The mountains are closer to the southeast coast, and a broad lowland belt runs along the northwest. Of the rivers only the Ndreketi, flowing west across northern Vanua Levu, is large; navigation on the Lambasa is restricted to small boats. The interior of Vanua Levu is lower and drier than Viti Levu, yet scenically superb: the road from Lambasa to Savusavu is a visual feast.

Vanua Levu's bullet-shaped neighbor Taveuni soars to 1,241 meters, its rugged east coast battered by the southeast trades. Taveuni and Kandavu are known as the finest islands in Fiji for their scenic beauty and agricultural potential. Geologically, the uplifted limestone islands of the Lau Group have more in common with Tonga than with the rest of Fiji. Northwest of Viti Levu is the rugged limestone Yasawa Group.

Fringing reefs are common along most of the coastlines, and Fiji is outstanding for its many barrier reefs. The Great Sea Reef off the north coast of Vanua Levu is the fourth longest in the world, and the Astrolabe Reef north of Kandavu is one of the most colorful. Countless other unexplored barrier reefs are found off northern Viti Levu and elsewhere. The many cracks, crevices, walls, and caves along Fiji's reefs are guaranteed to delight the scuba diver.

Climate

Along the coast the weather is warm and pleasant, without great variations in temperature. The southeast trades prevail from June to October, the best months to visit. In February and March the wind often comes directly out of the east. These winds dump 3,000 mm of annual rainfall on the humid southeast coasts of the big islands, increasing to 5,000 mm inland. The drier northwest coasts, in the lee, get only 1,500 to 2,000 mm. Yet even during the rainy months (December to April), bright sun often follows the rains.

The official dry season (June to October) is not always dry at Suva, although much of the rain falls at night. In addition, Fiji's winter (May to November) is cooler and less humid, the best

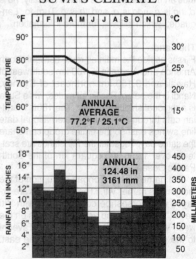

SUVA'S CLIMATE

NANDI'S CLIMATE

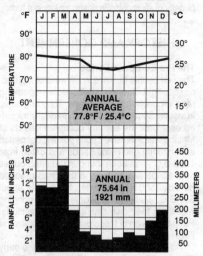

months for mountain trekking. During the drier season the reef waters are clearest for the scuba diver. Summer (December to April) is hurricane season, with Fiji, Samoa, and Tonga receiving up to five tropical storms annually. But even in summer the refreshing trade winds relieve the high humidity.

In Fiji you can obtain prerecorded weather information by dialing 301-642.

Flora

There are over 3,000 species of plants in Fiji, a third of them endemic. One of the only poisonous plants is the *salato*, a tree with large, hairy leaves that inflict painful wounds when touched. Patterns of rainfall are in large part responsible for the variety of vegetation here. The wetter sides of the high islands are heavily forested, with occasional thickets of bamboo and scrub. Natural forests cover 40% of Fiji's total land area and about a quarter of this is classified as production forest suitable for logging. The towering *ndakua* tree, once carved into massive Fijian war canoes, has already disappeared from Viti Levu, and the last stands are now being logged on Vanua Levu.

Coconut groves fill the coastal plains. On the drier sides open savanna or *talasinga* of coarse grasses predominates where the original vegetation has been destroyed by slash-and-burn agriculture. Sugarcane is now cultivated in the lowlands here, and Caribbean pine has been planted in many dry hilly areas, giving them a Scandinavian appearance. The low islands of the Lau Group are restricted to a few hardy, drought-resistant species such as coconuts and pandanus.

Fauna

Of the 70 species of land birds, 22 are endemic, including broadbills, cuckoos, doves, fantails, finches, flycatchers, fruitdoves, hawks, herons, honey eaters, kingfishers, lorikeets, parrots, pigeons, rails, silktails, and warblers. The Fijian names of some of these birds, such as the *kaka* (parrot) and *kikau* (giant honey eater), imitate their calls. Of the seabirds, boobies, frigate birds, petrels, and tropic birds are present. More in evidence is the introduced Indian mynah, with its yellow legs and beak, the bulbul, and the Malay turtledove.

The only native mammals are the monkey-faced fruit bat or flying fox, the insect-eating bat, and the Polynesian gray rat. Two species of snakes inhabit Fiji: the very rare, poisonous *bolo loa,* and the harmless Pacific boa, which can grow up to two meters long. Venomous sea snakes are common on some coasts, but they're docile and easily handled. Fijians call the common banded black-and-white sea snake the *ndandakulathi.* The land- and tree-dwelling native frogs are noteworthy for the long suction discs on their fingers and toes. Because they live deep in the rainforests and feed at night, they're seldom seen. Some Fijian clans have totemic relationships with eels, prawns, turtles, and sharks, and are able to summon these creatures with special chants.

One of the more unusual creatures found in Fiji and Tonga is the banded iguana, a lizard that lives in trees and can grow up to 70 centimeters long (two-thirds of which is tail). The iguanas are emerald green, and the male is easily distinguished from the female by his bluish-gray cross stripes. Banded iguanas change color to control their internal temperature, becoming darker when in the direct sun. Their nearest relatives are found in South America and Madagascar, and no lizards live farther

banded iguana

east in the Pacific than these. In 1979 a new species, the crested iguana, was discovered on Yanduatambu, a small island off the west coast of Vanua Levu.

The Indian mongoose was introduced by planters in the 1880s to combat rats, which were damaging the plantations. Unfortunately, no one realized at the time that the mongoose hunts by day, whereas the rats are nocturnal; thus, the two seldom meet. Today, the mongoose is the scourge of chickens, native ground birds, and other animals, though Kandavu, Ngau, Ovalau, and Taveuni are mongoose-free (and thus the best islands for birdwatching). In 1936 the giant toad was introduced from Hawaii to control beetles, slugs, and millipedes. When this food source is exhausted, they tend to eat each other. At night gardens and lawns may be full of them.

Four of the world's seven species of sea turtles nest in Fiji: the green, hawksbill, loggerhead, and leatherback. Nesting occurs between November and February, at night when there is a full moon and a high tide. The female struggles up the beach and lays as many as 100 eggs in a hole, which she digs and then covers with her hind flippers. The turtles and their

eggs are now protected by law in Fiji (maximum penalty of six months in prison for killing a turtle).

HISTORY AND GOVERNMENT

The Pre-European Period
The first people to arrive in Fiji were of a broadnosed, light-skinned Austronesian-speaking race, probably the Polynesians. They originated in insular Southeast Asia and gradually migrated east past the already occupied islands of Melanesia. Distinctive *Lapita* pottery, decorated in horizontal geometric bands and dated from 1290 B.C., has been found in the sand dunes near Singatoka, indicating they had reached here by 1500 B.C. or earlier. Much later, about 500 B.C., Melanesian people arrived, bringing with them their own distinct pottery traditions. From the fusion of these primordial peoples the Fijian race was born.

The hierarchical social structure of the early Fijians originated with the Polynesians. Status and descent passed through the male line, and power was embodied in the *turanga* (chief). The hereditary chiefs possessed the mana of an ancestral spirit or *vu*. This feudal aristocracy combined in confederations, or *vanua*, which extended their influence through war. Treachery and cannibalism were an intrinsic part of these struggles; women were taken as prizes or traded to form alliances. For defense, villages were fortified with ditches, or built along ridges or terraced hillsides.

The native aristocracy practiced customs that today seem barbarous and particularly cruel. The skull cap of a defeated enemy might be polished and used as a *yanggona* (kava) cup to humiliate the foe. Some chiefs even took delight in cooking and consuming bodily parts as their agonized victims looked on. Men were buried alive to hold up the posts of new houses, war canoes were launched over the living bodies of young girls, and the widows of chiefs were strangled to keep their husbands company in the spirit world. The farewells of some of these women are remembered today in dances and songs known as *meke*.

These feudal islanders were, on the other hand, guardians of one of the highest material cultures of the Pacific. They built great ocean-

(top) Mele Peha preparing pandanus fruit for cooking, Nukunonu, Tokelau (Robert Kennington);
((bottom left) Luhi'ano Perez cleaning giant clams, Nukunonu, Tokelau (Robert Kennington);
(bottom right) removing coconut meat, Tonga (Phil Esmonde)

(top left) tattooed man, Tikopia, Solomon Islands (Robert Kennington); (top right) Ariki Tafua, a chief of Tikopia, Solomon Islands, grating taro (Robert Kennington); (bottom left) Polynesian woman, Mauke, Cook Islands (David Stanley); (bottom right) girl at Aitu, Cook Islands (David Stanley)

going double canoes *(ndrua)* up to 30 meters long, constructed and adorned large solid thatched houses *(mbures),* performed marvelous song-dances called *meke,* made tapa, pottery, and sennit (coconut cordage), and skillfully plaited mats. For centuries the Tongans came to Fiji to obtain great logs from which to make canoes, and sandalwood for carving.

European Exploration
In 1643 Abel Tasman became the European discoverer of Fiji when he sighted Taveuni, although he didn't land. In 1774, Captain Cook anchored off Vatoa (which he named Turtle Island) in southern Lau. Like Tasman he failed to proceed farther or land, and it was left to Capt. William Bligh to give Europeans an accurate picture of Fiji for the first time. After the *Bounty* mutiny in May 1789, Bligh and his companions were chased by canoe-loads of Fijian warriors just north of the Yasawa Islands as they rowed through on their escape route to Timor. Some serious paddling, a timely squall, and a lucky gap in the Great Sea Reef saved the Englishmen from ending up as the main course at a cannibal feast. The section of sea where this happened is today known as Bligh Water. Bligh cut directly across the center of Fiji between the two main islands, and his careful observations made him the first real European explorer of Fiji, albeit an unwilling one. Bligh returned to Fiji in 1792, but once again he stayed aboard his ship.

Beachcombers and Chiefs
All of these early explorers stressed the perilous nature of Fiji's reefs. This, combined with tales told by the Tongans of cannibalism and warlike Fijian natives, caused most travelers to shun the area. Then in 1804 a survivor from the shipwrecked American schooner *Argo* brought word that sandalwood grew abundantly along the Mbua coast of Vanua Levu. This precipitated a rush of traders and beachcombers to the islands. A cargo of sandalwood bought from the islanders for $50 worth of trinkets could be sold to the Chinese at Canton for $20,000. By 1814 the forests had been stripped to provide joss sticks and incense, and the trade collapsed.

During this period Fiji was divided among warring chieftains. The first Europeans to actually mix with the Fijians were escaped convicts from Australia, who instructed the natives in the use of European muskets and were thus well received. White beachcombers such as the Swedish adventurer Charles Savage and the German Martin Bushart acted as middlemen between traders and Fijians and took sides in local conflicts. In one skirmish Savage was separated from his fellows, captured, and eaten. With help from the likes of Savage, Naulivou, the cannibal chief of tiny Mbau Island just off eastern Viti Levu, and his brother Tanoa extended their influence over much of western Fiji.

From 1827 to 1850 European traders collected bêche-de-mer, a sea slug which, when

M.G.L. DOMENY DE RIENZI

Rotuma islanders signaling to European vessel

smoked and dried, also brought a good price in China. While the sandalwood traders only stayed long enough to take on a load, the bêche-de-mer collectors set up shore facilities where the slugs were processed. Many traders such as David Whippy followed the example of the beachcombers and took local wives, establishing the part-Fijian community of today. By monopolizing the bêche-de-mer trade and constantly warring, Chief Tanoa's son and successor, Ratu Seru Cakobau (pronounced Thakombau), became extremely powerful in the 1840s, proclaiming himself Tui Viti, or king of Fiji.

The beginnings of organized trade brought a second wave of official explorers to Fiji. In 1838 Dumont d'Urville landed on Mbau Island and met Tanoa. The Frenchmen caused consternation and confusion by refusing to drink yanggona (kava), preferring their own wine. The American Exploring Expedition of 1840, led by Commodore Charles Wilkes, produced the first recognizable map of Fiji. When two Americans, including a nephew of Wilkes, were speared in a misunderstanding on a beach at Malolo Island, Wilkes ordered the offending fortified village stormed and 87 Fijians were killed. The survivors were made to water and provision Wilkes's ships as tribute. Captain H.M. Denham of the HMS Herald prepared accurate navigational charts of the island group in 1855-56, making regular commerce possible.

European and Tongan Penetration

As early as the 1830s an assortment of European and American beachcombers had formed a small settlement at Levuka on the east coast of Ovalau Island just northeast of Mbau, which whalers and traders used as a supply base. In 1846 John Brown Williams was appointed American commercial agent. On 4 July 1849 Williams's home on Nukulau Island near present-day Suva burned down. Though the conflagration was caused by the explosion of a cannon during Williams's own fervent celebration of his national holiday, he objected to the way Fijian onlookers carried off items they rescued from the flames. A shameless swindler, Williams had purchased Nukulau for only $30, yet he blamed the Tui Viti for his losses and sent Cakobau a $5001.38 bill. American claims for damages eventually rose to $44,000, and in 1851 and

1855 American gunboats called and ordered Cakobau to pay up. This threat hung over Cakobau's head for many years, the 19th-century equivalent of 20th-century third world debt.

The early 1830s also saw the arrival from Tonga of the first missionaries. Though Tahitian pastors were sent by the London Missionary Society to Oneata in southern Lau as early as 1830, it was the Methodists based at Lakemba after 1835 who made the most lasting impression by rendering the Fijian language into writing. At first Christianity made little headway among these fierce, idolatrous people, and only after converting the powerful chiefs were the missionaries successful. Methodist missionaries Cargill and Cross were appalled by what they saw during a visit to Mbau in 1838. A white missionary, Rev. Thomas Baker, was clubbed and eaten in central Viti Levu by the kai tholo (hill people) as late as 1867.

In 1847 Enele Ma'afu, a member of the Tongan royal family, arrived in Lau and began building a personal empire under the pretense of defending Christianity. In 1853 King George of Tonga made Ma'afu governor of all Tongans resident in Lau. Meanwhile, there was continuing resistance from the warlords of the Rewa River area to Cakobau's dominance. In addi-

Cakobau of Fiji: A drawing from a photo taken in 1877, now in the possession of the Museum of Archaeology and Ethnology, Cambridge, England

tion the Europeans at Levuka suspected Cakobau of twice ordering their town set afire and were directing trade away from Mbau. With his power in decline, in 1854 Cakobau accepted Christianity in exchange for an alliance with King George, and in 1855, with the help of 2,000 Tongans led by King George himself, Cakobau was able to put down the Rewa revolt. In the process, however, Ma'afu became the dominant force in Lau, Taveuni, and Vanua Levu.

During the early 1860s, as Americans fought their Civil War, the world price of cotton soared, and large numbers of Europeans arrived in Fiji hoping to establish cotton plantations. In 1867 the USS *Tuscaroga* called at Levuka and threatened to bombard the town unless the still-outstanding American debt was paid. The next year an enterprising Australian firm, the Polynesia Company, paid off the Americans in exchange for a grant from Cakobau of 80,000 hectares of choice land, including the site of modern Suva. The British government later refused to recognize this grant, though they refunded the money paid to the Americans and accepted the claims of settlers who had purchased land from the company. Settlers soon numbered about 2,000 and Levuka boomed.

It was a lawless era and a need was felt for a central government. An attempt at national rule by a council of chiefs failed in 1867, then three regional governments were set up in Mbau (western), Lau (eastern), and Mbua (northern), but these were only partly successful. With cotton prices collapsing as the American South resumed production, a national administration under Cakobau and planter John Thurston was established at Levuka in 1871.

However, Cakobau was never strong enough to impose his authority over the whole country, so with growing disorder in western Fiji, infighting between Europeans and Fijian chiefs, and a lack of cooperation from Ma'afu's rival confederation of chiefs in eastern Fiji, Cakobau decided he should cede his kingdom to Great Britain. The British had refused an invitation to annex Fiji in 1862, but this time they accepted rather than risk seeing the group fall into the hands of another power, and on 10 October 1874 Fiji became a British colony. In 1877 the Western Pacific High Commission was set up to protect British interests in the surrounding unclaimed island groups as well. At first Levuka was the colony's capital, but in 1882 the government moved to a more spacious site at Suva.

The Making of a Nation

The first British governor, Sir Arthur Gordon, and his colonial secretary and successor, Sir John Thurston, created modern Fiji almost single-handedly. They realized that the easiest way to rule was indirectly, through the existing Fijian chiefs. To protect the communal lands on which the chieftain system was based, they ordered that native land could not be sold, only leased. Not wishing to disturb native society, Gordon and Thurston ruled that Fijians could not be required to work on European plantations. Meanwhile the blackbirding of Melanesian laborers from the Solomons and New Hebrides had been restricted by the Polynesia Islanders Protection Act of 1872.

By this time sugar had taken the place of cotton and there was a tremendous labor shortage on the plantations. Gordon, who had previously served in Trinidad and Mauritius, saw indentured Indian workers as a solution. The first arrived in 1879, and by 1916, when Indian immigration ended, there were 63,000 present. To come to Fiji the Indians had to sign a labor contract *(girmit)* in which they agreed to cut sugarcane for their masters for five years. During the next five years they were allowed to lease small plots of their own from the Fijians and plant cane or raise livestock. Over half the Indians decided to remain in Fiji as free settlers after their 10-year contracts expired, and today their descendants form about half the population, many of them still working small leased plots.

Though this combination of European capital, Fijian land, and Indian labor did help preserve traditional Fijian culture, it also kept the Fijians backward—envious onlookers passed over by European and (later) Indian prosperity. The separate administration and special rights for indigenous Fijians installed by the British over a century ago continue in force today. In early 1875 Cakobau and two of his sons returned from a visit to Australia infected with measles. Though they themselves survived, the resulting epidemic wiped out a third of the Fijian population. As a response to this and other public health problems the Fiji School of Medicine was founded in 1885. At the beginning of European colonization there were about 200,000 Fijians, approximately 114,748 in 1881, and just 84,000 by 1921.

The Colonial Period

In 1912 a Gujerati lawyer, D.M. Manilal, arrived in Fiji from Mauritius to fight for Indian rights, just as his contemporary Mahatma Gandhi was doing in South Africa. Indentured Indians continued to arrive in Fiji until 1916, but the protests led to the termination of the indenture system throughout the empire in 1920 (Manilal was deported from Fiji after a strike that year).

Although Fiji was a political colony of Britain, it was always an economic colony of Australia: the big Australian trading companies Burns Philp and W.R. Carpenters dominated business. (The ubiquitous Morris Hedstrom is a subsidiary of Carpenters, though both are now owned by Malaysians.) Most of the Indians were brought to Fiji to work for the Australian-owned Colonial Sugar Refining Company, which controlled the sugar industry from 1881 right up until 1973, when it was purchased by the Fiji government for $14 million.

No representative government existed in Fiji until 1904, when a Legislative Council was formed with six elected Europeans and two Fijians nominated by the Great Council of Chiefs *(Mbose Levu Vakaturanga)*, itself an instrument of colonial rule. In 1916 the governor appointed an Indian member to the council. A 1929 reform granted five seats to each of the three communities: three elected and two appointed Europeans and Indians, and five nominated Fijians. The council was only an advisory body and the governor remained in complete control. The Europeans generally sided with the Fijians against any demands for equality from the Indians—typical colonial divide and rule.

During WW I an indigenous resistance movement to this colonial exploitation emerged in the form of the Viti Kabani, or Fiji Company, led by Apolosi Ranawai, a commoner from western Viti Levu. The company began as a reaction to profiteering by Fijian chiefs and white traders who bought and sold village products, but it soon moved beyond economic matters to question the whole eastern-dominated chiefly system, which allowed the British to rule so easily.

The chiefs reacted by having the movement branded seditious and Apolosi exiled.

Fijians were outstanding combat troops on the Allied side in the Solomon Islands campaign during WW II, and again in 1952-56 suppressing Malaya's national liberation struggle. So skilled were the Fijians at jungle warfare against the Japanese that it was never appropriate to list a Fijian as "missing in action"—the phrase used was "not yet arrived." Until 1952, Suva, the present Fijian capital, was headquarters for the entire British Imperial Administration in the South Pacific.

In 1963 the Legislative Council was expanded but still divided along racial lines; women and indigenous Fijians got the vote for the first time. Wishing to be rid of the British, whom they blamed for their second-class position, the Indians pushed for independence, but the Fijians had come to view the British as protectors and were somewhat reluctant. After much discussion, a constitution was finally adopted in 1970. Some legislature members were to be elected from a common roll (voting by all races), as the Indians desired, while other seats remained ethnic (voting in racial constituencies) to protect the Fijians. On 10 October 1970 Fiji became a fully independent nation and the first Fijian governor-general was appointed in 1973—none other than Ratu Sir George Cakobau, great-grandson of the chief who had ceded Fiji to Queen Victoria 99 years previously.

Political Development

During the 1940s Ratu Sir Lala Sukuna, paramount chief of Lau, played a key role in the creation of a separate administration for indigenous Fijians, with native land (83% of Fiji) under its jurisdiction. In 1954 he formed the Fijian Association to support the British governor against Indian demands for equal representation. In 1960 the National Federation Party (NFP) was formed to represent Indian cane farmers.

In 1966 the Alliance Party, a coalition of the Fijian Association, the General Electors' Association (representing Europeans, part-Fijians, and Chinese), and the Fiji Indian Alliance (a minority Indian group) won the legislative assembly elections. In 1970 Alliance Party leader Ratu Sir Kamisese Mara led Fiji into independence and in 1972 his party won Fiji's first post-independence elections. Ratu Mara served as prime minister almost continuously until the 1987 elections.

In 1975 Mr. Sakeasi Butadroka, a member of parliament previously expelled from the Alliance Party, presented a motion calling for all Indians to be repatriated to India at British expense. This was rejected but during the April 1977 elections Butadroka's Fijian Nationalist Party took enough votes away from the Alliance to allow the predominantly Indian NFP to obtain a majority in parliament. After a few days' hesitation, the governor-general reappointed Ratu Mara as prime minister, but his minority Alliance government was soon defeated. Meanwhile, Butadroka had been arrested for making racially inflammatory statements in violation of the Public Order Act, and in new elections in September 1977 the Alliance recovered its majority, due in part to a split of the NFP into Hindu and Muslim factions.

The formation of the Fiji Labor Party (FLP), headed by Dr. Timoci Bavadra, in July 1985 dramatically altered the political landscape. Fiji's previously nonpolitical trade unions had finally come behind a party that campaigned on bread-and-butter issues rather than race. Late in 1986 Labor and the NFP formed a coalition with the aim of defeating the Alliance in the next election. Dr. Bavadra, a former director of Primary and Preventive Health Services and president of the Fiji Public Service Association, was chosen as Coalition leader. In the 12 April 1987 elections the Coalition won 28 of 52 House of Representatives seats; 19 of the 28 elected Coalition members were Indians. What swung the election away from Alliance was not a change in Indian voting patterns but support for Labor from urban Fijians and part-Fijians, which cost Alliance four previously "safe" seats around Suva.

The Coalition had a broad base of public support, and all cabinet positions of vital Fijian interest (Lands, Fijian Affairs, Labor and Immigration, Education, Agriculture and Rural Development) went to indigenous Fijian legislators, though none of them was a traditional chief. Coalition's progressive policies marked quite a switch from the conservatism of the Alliance—a new generation of political leadership dedicated to tackling the day-to-day problems of people of all races rather than perpetuating the privileges of the old chiefly oligarchy. Medical care was expanded, an Institute for Fijian Language and Culture was created, and Fijians were given greater access to Fiji Development Bank loans, which had previously been going mostly to foreign corporations.

The new government also announced that nuclear warships would be banned from a nonaligned Fiji. Foreign Minister Krishna Datt said he would join Vanuatu and New Zealand in pressing for a nuclear-free Pacific at the 24 May 1987 meeting of the South Pacific Forum. Alleged corruption in the previous administration was also to be investigated. Ratu Mara himself had allegedly accumulated a personal fortune of $4-6 million on his annual salary of $100,000. Given time the Coalition might have required the high chiefs to share the rental monies they received for leasing lands to Indians more fairly with ordinary Fijians. Most significant of all, the Coalition would have transformed Fiji from a plural society where only indigenous Melanesian Fijians were called Fijians into a truly multiracial society where all citizens would be Fijians.

The First Coup

After the election the extremist Fiji-for-Fijians Taukei (landowners) movement launched a destabilization campaign by throwing barricades across highways, organizing protest rallies and marches, and carrying out firebombings. On 24 April 1987 Senator Inoke Tabua and former Alliance cabinet minister Apisai Tora organized a march of 5,000 Fijians through Suva to protest "Indian domination" of the new government. Mr. Tora told a preparatory meeting for the demonstration that Fijians must "act now" to avoid end-

IF YOU ARE NEUTRAL IN SITUATIONS OF INJUSTICE, YOU HAVE CHOSEN THE SIDE OF THE OPPRESSOR.

IF AN ELEPHANT HAS HIS FOOT ON THE TAIL OF A MOUSE AND YOU SAY THAT YOU ARE NEUTRAL, THE MOUSE WILL NOT APPRECIATE YOUR NEUTRALITY.
Bishop Desmond Tutu

ing up as "deprived as Australia's aborigines." (In fact, under the 1970 constitution the Coalition government would have had no way of changing Fiji's land laws without indigenous Fijian consent.) During the following weeks five gasoline bombs were thrown against government offices, though no one was injured. On 13 May 1987 Alliance Senator Jona Qio was arrested for arson.

At 1000 on Thursday 14 May 1987 Lt. Col. Sitiveni Rabuka (pronounced Rambuka), an ambitious officer whose career was stalled at number three in the Fiji army, and 10 heavily armed soldiers dressed in fatigues, their faces covered by gas masks, entered the House of Representatives in Suva. Rabuka ordered Dr. Bavadra and the Coalition members to follow a soldier out of the building, and when Dr. Bavadra hesitated the soldiers raised their guns. The legislators were loaded into army trucks and taken to Royal Fiji Military Forces headquarters. There was no bloodshed, though Rabuka later confirmed that his troops would have opened fire had there been any resistance. At a press conference five hours after the coup, Rabuka claimed he had acted to prevent violence and had no political ambitions of his own.

Most Pacific governments promptly denounced the region's first military coup. Governor-General Ratu Sir Penaia Ganilau attempted to reverse the situation by declaring a state of emergency and ordering the mutineers to return to their barracks. They refused to obey. The next day the *Fiji Sun* ran a black-bordered editorial that declared, "Democracy died in Fiji yesterday. What right has a third-ranking officer to attack the sacred institutions of Parliament? What right has he to presume he knows best how this country shall be governed? The answer is none." Soon after, Rabuka's troops descended on both daily papers and ordered publication suspended. Journalists were evicted from the buildings.

Later that day Rabuka named a 15-member Council of Ministers, chaired by himself, to govern Fiji, with former Alliance prime minister Ratu Mara as foreign minister. Significantly, Rabuka was the only military officer on the council; most of the others were members of Ratu Mara's defeated administration. Rabuka claimed he had acted to "safeguard the Fijian land issue and the Fijian way of life."

On 19 May Dr. Bavadra and the other kidnapped members of his government were released after the governor-general announced a deal negotiated with Rabuka to avoid the possibility of foreign intervention. Rabuka's Council of Ministers was replaced by a 19-member caretaker Advisory Council appointed by the Great Council of Chiefs, which would govern until new elections could take place. The council would be headed by Ratu Ganilau, with Rabuka in charge of Home Affairs and the security forces. Only two seats were offered to Dr. Bavadra's government and they were refused.

The Sunday before the coup Ratu Mara was seen playing golf with Rabuka at Pacific Harbor. At the time of the coup he was at the Fijian Hotel chairing a meeting of the Pacific Democratic Union, a U.S.-sponsored grouping of ultraright politicians from Australia, New Zealand, and elsewhere. Though Ratu Mara expressed "shock" at the coup, he accepted a position on Rabuka's Council of Ministers the next day, prompting New Zealand Prime Minister David Lange to accuse him of treachery under Fiji's constitution by acquiescing to military rule. Lange said Ratu Mara had pledged allegiance to the Queen but had brought about a rebellion in one of her countries. Ratu Ganilau was also strongly criticized for legitimizing a traitor by accepting Rabuka on his Advisory Council.

Behind the Coup

In 1982 American interest in the South Pacific picked up after the U.S. ambassador to Fiji, William Bodde, Jr., told a luncheon audience at the Kahala Hilton in Hawaii that the creation of a South Pacific nuclear-free zone would be "the most potentially disruptive development to U.S. relations with the region . . . I am convinced that the United States must do everything possible to counter this movement. It will not be an easy task, but it is one that we cannot afford to neglect." In 1983 Bodde's diplomacy resulted in the lifting of a ban on visits to Fiji by U.S. nuclear warships, and Fiji was soon rewarded by becoming the first South Pacific country to receive direct American aid. Substantial grants to the Fiji army for "weapons standardization" soon followed, and from 1984 to 1986 U.S. aid to Fiji tripled.

Immediately after the coup, rumors circulated throughout the South Pacific that the U.S.

government was involved. On 16 June 1987 at a press conference at the National Press Club in Washington, D.C., Dr. Bavadra publicly accused the director of the South Pacific regional office of the U.S. Agency for International Development of channeling US$200,000 to right-winger Apisai Tora of the Taukei movement for destabilization purposes, something they both denied.

From 29 April to 1 May 1987 Gen. Vernon A. Walters, U.S. ambassador to the United Nations and a former CIA deputy director, visited Fiji. At a long meeting with Foreign Minister Datt, Walters tried to persuade the new government to give up its antinuclear stance. Walters told the Fiji press that the U.S. "has a duty to protect its South Pacific interests." Walters is believed to have been involved in previous coups in Iran (1953) and Brazil (1964), and during his stay in Fiji he also met with Rabuka and U.S. AID officials. During his 10-country Pacific trip Walters spread fanciful rumors of Libya subversion, diverting attention from what was about to happen in Fiji.

On 22 October 1987 the U.S. Information Service in New Zealand revealed that the amphibious assault ship USS *Belleau Wood* was just west of Fiji immediately after the coup, supported by three C-130 Hercules transport planes, which staged through Nandi Airport 20-22 June. The same release mentioned four other C-130s at Nandi that month to support the gigantic hospital ship USNS *Mercy*, which was at Suva 23-27 June—an unprecedented level of U.S. military activity. By chance or design the U.S. would have been ready to intervene militarily within hours had anything gone wrong. Yet American involvement in the coup has never been conclusively proven and the full story may never be told. The events caught the Australian and New Zealand intelligence services totally by surprise, indicating that few knew of Rabuka's plans in advance.

Until the coup the most important mission of the Royal Fiji Defense Force was service in South Lebanon and the Sinai with peacekeeping operations. Half of the 2,600-member Fiji army was on rotating duty there, the Sinai force financed by the U.S., the troops in Lebanon by the United Nations. During WW II Fiji Indians refused to join the army unless they received the same pay as European recruits; indigenous Fijians had no such reservations and the force has been 95% Fijian ever since. Service in the strife-torn Middle East gave the Fiji military a unique preparation for its destabilizing role in Fiji itself.

The mass media presented the coup in simplistic terms as a racial conflict between Indians and Fijians, though commentators with a deeper knowledge of the nature of power in Fiji saw it quite differently. Anthony D. van Fossen of Griffith University, Queensland, Australia, summed it up this way in the *Bulletin of Concerned Asian Scholars* (Vol. 19, No. 4, 1987):

> *Although the first coup has been most often seen in terms of ethnic tensions between indigenous Fijians and Fijian Indians, it may be more accurately seen as the result of tensions between aristocratic indigenous Fijians and their commoner allies defending feudalism, on the one hand, and the cause of social democracy, small-scale capitalism, and multi-ethnic nationalism represented by middle-class indigenous Fijian commoners and Hindus on the other.*

In their October 1987 issue, *Pacific Islands Monthly* published this comment by noted author Brij V. Lal of the Australia National University:

> *More than anything else, the coup was about power. The emergence in an incipient form of a class-minded multi-racial politics, symbolized by the Labor Party and made possible by the support of many urban Fijians, posed a grave threat to the politics of race and racial compartmentalization preached by the Alliance and thus had to be nipped in the bud. The ascent of Dr. Bavadra, a chief from the long-neglected western Viti Levu, to the highest office in the land posed an unprecedented challenge to the traditional dominance of eastern chiefs, especially from Lau and Thakaundrove.*

The Second Coup

In July and August 1987 a committee set up by Governor-General Ganilau studied proposals for constitutional reform, and on 4 September talks began at Government House in Suva between Alliance and Coalition leaders under the chairmanship of Ratu Ganilau. With no hope of a consensus on a revised constitution the talks were aimed at preparing for new elections.

Then, on Friday, 26 September 1987, Rabuka struck again, just hours before the governor-general was to announce a Government of National Unity to rule Fiji until new elections could be held. The plan, arduously developed over four months and finally approved by veteran political leaders on all sides, would probably have resulted in Rabuka being sacked. Rabuka quickly threw out the 1970 constitution and pronounced himself "head of state." Some 300 prominent community leaders were arrested and Ratu Ganilau was confined to Government House. Newspapers were shut down, trade unions repressed, the judiciary suspended, the public service purged, the activities of political opponents restricted, a curfew imposed, and the first cases of torture reported.

At midnight on 7 October 1987 Rabuka declared Fiji a republic. Rabuka's new Council of Ministers included Taukei extremists Apisai Tora and Filipe Bole, Fijian Nationalist Party leader Sakeasi Butadroka, and other marginal figures. Rabuka appeared to have backing in the Great Council of Chiefs, which wanted a return to the style of customary rule threatened by the Indian presence and Western democracy. Regime ideologists trumpeted traditional culture and religious fundamentalism to justify their actions. Rabuka said he wanted Christianity adopted as Fiji's official religion and henceforth all trading (except at tourist hotels), sports, and public transport would be banned on Sunday. Rabuka even called for the conversion of Hindu and Muslim Indians to Christianity.

On 16 October Ratu Ganilau resigned as governor-general and two days later Fiji was expelled from the British Commonwealth (perhaps for good, as Commonwealth rules require a unanimous vote from other members for readmission). On 6 November Rabuka allowed the *Fiji Times* to resume publication after it pledged self-censorship, but the more independent *Fiji Sun* has never appeared again. Nobody accused the U.S. of having anything to do with Rabuka's second coup, and even Ratu Mara seemed annoyed that Rabuka had destroyed an opportunity to salvage the reputations of himself and Ratu Ganilau. Clearly Rabuka had become his own man.

The Republic of Fiji

Realizing that Taukei/military rule was a recipe for disaster, on 5 December 1987 Rabuka appointed Ratu Ganilau president and Ratu Mara prime minister of his new republic. The 21-member cabinet included 10 members of Rabuka's military regime, four of them army officers. Rabuka himself (now a self-styled brigadier) was once again Minister of Home Affairs. This interim government set itself a deadline of two years to frame a new constitution and return Fiji to freely elected representative government. By mid-1988 the army had been expanded into a highly disciplined 6,000-member force loyal to Brigadier Rabuka, who left no doubt he would intervene a third time if his agenda was not followed. The Great Council of Chiefs was to decide on Fiji's republican constitution.

The coups transformed the Fijian economy. In 1987 Fiji experienced 11% negative growth in the gross domestic product. To prevent a massive flight of capital the Fiji dollar was devalued 17.75% on 30 June 1987 and 15.25% on 7 October, and inflation, which had been under two percent before the coups, was up to 11.9% by the end of 1988. At the same time the public service (half the workforce) had to accept a 25% wage cut as government spending was slashed. Food prices skyrocketed, causing serious problems for many families. At the end of 1987 the per capita average income was 11% *below* what it had been in 1980. Thousands of Indian professionals—accountants, administrators, dentists, doctors, lawyers, nurses, teachers—left for Australia, Canada, New Zealand, and the United States. In 1987 there were 18,359 emigrants, in 1988 another 10,360, crippling losses for a country with a total population of under 750,000. From January 1990 to June 1993 a further 16,118 Indians left.

On the other hand, the devaluations and wage-cutting measures, combined with the creation of a tax-free exporting sector and the encouragement of foreign investment, brought about a full economic recovery by 1990. At the expense of democracy, social justice, and racial harmony, Fiji embarked on the IMF/World Bank-style structural readjustment program which continues today. The imposition of a 10% value added tax (VAT) in 1992 has shifted the burden of taxation from rich to poor, standard IMF dogma. In effect, Rabuka and the old oligarchs have pushed Fiji squarely back into the third world, and even the Fiji Visitors Bureau has had to scrap their former marketing slogan, "The Way the World Should Be."

Interim Government

In May 1989 the interim government eased Sunday restrictions on work, trading, and sports. This drew loud protests from Rev. Manasa Lasaro, fundamentalist general secretary of the Methodist Church of Fiji, who organized Sunday roadblocks in Lambasa, leading to the arrest and conviction of himself and 56 others for unlawful obstruction. On August 9 Rabuka flew to Lambasa by helicopter and arranged the release of Reverend Lasaro and the others on his own authority. On Sunday 15 October 1989 members of a Methodist youth group carried out firebombings against Hindu and Sikh temples and a Muslim mosque at Lautoka.

In November 1989 Dr. Bavadra died of spinal cancer at age 55 and 60,000 people attended his funeral at Viseisei, the largest in Fijian history. Foreign journalists were prevented from covering the funeral. The nominal head of the unelected interim government, Ratu Mara, considered Rabuka an unpredictable upstart and insisted that he choose between politics or military service. Thus in late 1989, the general and two army colonels were dropped from the cabinet, though Rabuka kept his post as army commander.

In May 1990 Fiji expelled the entire staff of the Indian Embassy in Suva in preparation for the launching of a new constitution approved by the Great Council of Chiefs in June and promulgated by President Ganilau on 25 July 1990. This constitution (still in force today) gives the chiefs the right to appoint the president and 24 of the 34 members of the Senate. In addition, one senator is appointed by the Rotuman Council and nine senators are appointed by the president

to represent the other communities. The president has executive authority and appoints the prime minister from among the ethnic Fijian members of the House of Representatives. Cabinet ministers may be from either house.

Under the constitution the 70-member House of Representatives is elected directly, with voting racially segregated. Ethnic Fijians are granted 37 seats, 32 from 14 provincial constituencies and only five from five urban constituencies, despite the fact that 33% of indigenous Fijians live in towns and cities. The provincial Fijian constituencies are gerrymandered to ensure eastern dominance. For example, Mba with an ethnic Fijian population of 55,000 gets three Fijian seats, the same number as Lau with only 14,000 inhabitants. Fiji Indians (nearly half the population) get 27 seats based on 27 constituencies, while there is a Rotuman seat and five for other races (Chinese, part-Fijians, Europeans, etc.).

The constitution not only guarantees ethnic Fijians a majority in both houses, but explicitly reserves for them the posts of president, prime minister, and army chief. Christianity is the official religion and Rabuka's troops are granted amnesty for any crimes committed during the 1987 coups. Fijian customary laws have become the law of the land, and all decisions of the Native Lands Commission are final, with no further recourse to the courts. Continued military interference in civilian government is covered by the vague identification of the army as the final arbiter in determining "the security, defense, and well-being of Fiji and its peoples."

The Coalition promptly rejected this supremacist constitution as undemocratic and racist, and threatened to boycott elections held under it unless a referendum took place. They claimed the rigged voting system used race as a device to divide Fijians and perpetuate the power of the eastern elite. Urban and western Fijians, the very groups that challenged the status quo by voting Labor in 1987, are discriminated against, and Indians are relegated to the fringes of political life. Complicated registration requirements also deprive many rural Fijian commoners of the vote.

Not satisfied with control of the Senate, in early 1991 the Great Council of Chiefs decided to project their power into the lower house through the formation of the Songgosonggo ni Vakavulewa ni Taukei (SVT), meaning "Group of Decision Makers for the Indigenous People" but commonly called the Fijian Political Party. To avoid thé embarrassment of a defeat for the chiefs and to allow more time for voter registration, the interim government postponed the elections several times. Meanwhile Fiji's multi-ethnic unions continued to rebuild their strength by organizing garment workers and leading strikes in the mining and sugar industries.

In June 1991 Major-General Rabuka rejected an offer from Ratu Mara to join the cabinet as Minister of Home Affairs and co-deputy prime minister, since it would have meant giving up his military power base. Instead Rabuka attempted to widen his political appeal by making public statements in support of striking gold miners and cane farmers, and even threatening a third coup. By now Rabuka's ambition to become prime minister was obvious, and his new role as a populist rabble-rouser seemed designed to outflank both the Labor Party and the chiefs (Rabuka himself is a commoner). President Ganilau (Rabuka's paramount chief) quickly applied pressure, and in July the volatile general reversed himself and accepted the cabinet posts he had so recently refused. As a condition for reentering the government, Rabuka was forced to resign as army commander and the president's son, Major-Gen. Epeli Ganilau, was appointed his successor. With Rabuka out of the army everyone breathed a little easier, and the chiefs decided to co-opt a potential troublemaker by electing Rabuka president of the SVT.

Recent Elections

In July 1991 the NFP decided at its annual meeting that it would field candidates for the 27 Indian seats after all, to avoid their being won by "irresponsible persons." After a bitter internal debate the Fiji Labor Party (FLP), now led by Mahendra Chaudhry, also decided not to boycott the elections.

The long-awaited parliamentary elections took place in late May 1992, and the SVT captured 30 of the 37 indigenous Fijian seats, with another five going to Sakeasi Butadroka's Fijian Nationalist United Front (FNUF) and two to independents. The 27 Indian seats were split between the NFP with 14 and the FLP with 13.

The five other races' seats went to the General Voters Party (GVP).

Just prior to the election, Ratu Mara (who had retired from party politics) was named vice-president of Fiji by the Great Council of Chiefs. An intense power struggle developed in the SVT between Ratu Mara's chosen successor, former finance minister Josevata Kamikamica, and ex-general Rabuka. Since the party lacked a clear majority in the 70-seat house, coalition partners had to be sought, and after much repositioning the pro-big business camp lined up behind Kamikamica, with NFP and GVP support. Rabuka had the backing of the FNUF, but most SVT members opposed a coalition with Butadroka's racial extremists, and in a remarkable turn of events populist Rabuka gained the support of the FLP by offering concessions to the trade unions and a promise to review the constitution and land leases. Thus Sitiveni Rabuka became prime minister thanks to the very party he had ousted from power at gunpoint exactly five years before!

The SVP formed a coalition with the GVP, and to consolidate his position, Rabuka called for a "government of national unity," but this concept failed to win approval by the powerful Great Council of Chiefs (which now holds a virtual power of veto on all matters of national interest). In November 1993 the Rabuka government was defeated in a parliamentary vote of no confidence over the budget, leading to fresh elections in February 1994. In these, Rabuka's SVT increased its representation to 31 seats, and both Kamikamica and Butadroka lost their parliamentary seats. Many Indians had felt betrayed by FLP backing of Rabuka's prime ministership in 1992, and FLP representation dropped to seven seats, compared to 20 for the NFP..

Ratu Ganilau died of leukemia in December 1993, and Ratu Mara was sworn in as president in January. Meanwhile, Rabuka has tried to cultivate a pragmatic image to facilitate his international acceptance in the South Pacific. Yet the legacy of the coups continues to hang over Fiji. In early 1995 the government attempted to repeal the controversial Sunday Observance Decree imposed in 1988, but passage of the bill was blocked in the Senate after 12,000 Methodists marched through Suva in protest. Indian resentment over their second-class position continues, and a lot is hanging on the constitutional review presently underway to restore business and social confidence.

Government

Aside from the national government described above, there's a well-developed system of local government. On the Fijian side, the basic unit is the village (koro) represented by a village herald (turanga-ni-koro) chosen by consensus. The villages are grouped into districts (tikina), the districts into 14 provinces (yasana), the provinces into four administrative divisions: central, eastern, northern, and western. The 14 provinces with the locations of their offices in parenthesis are Kandavu (Vunisea), Lau (Lakemba), Lomaiviti (Levuka), Mathuata (Lambasa), Mba (Lautoka), Mbua (Nambouwalu), Naitasiri (Vunindawa), Namosi (Navua), Nandronga (Singatoka), Ra (Nanukuloa), Rewa (Nausori), Serua (Navua), Tailevu (Nausori), and Thakaundrove (Savusavu). The executive head of a provincial council is known as a roko tui, and each division except Eastern is headed by a commissioner assisted by a number of district officers. The Micronesians of Rambi govern themselves through a council of their own. City and town councils also function.

ECONOMY

Economic Development

Fiji has a diversified economy based on tourism, sugar production, garment manufacturing, gold mining, timber, commercial fishing, and coconut products. From WW II until 1987 a series of five-year plans guided public investment, resulting in the excellent modern infrastructure and ad-

vanced social services Fiji enjoys today. Devaluation of Fiji's currency immediately after the 1987 coups increased the country's competitiveness by giving exporters more Fiji dollars for their products. This lowered the real incomes of ordinary Fijians, but also led to a mini-economic boom which is now beginning to level out.

While eastern Viti Levu and the Lau Group dominate the country politically, western Viti Levu is Fiji's economic powerhouse, with sugar, tourism, timber, and gold mining all concentrated there. Almost all of Fiji's sugar is produced by small independent Indian farmers on contract to the government-owned Fiji Sugar Corporation, which took over from the Australian-owned Colonial Sugar Refining Company in 1973. Some 23,000 farmers cultivate cane on holdings averaging 4.5 hectares leased from indigenous Fijians. The corporation owns 644 km of 0.610-meter narrow-gauge railway, which it uses to carry the cane to the mills at Lautoka, Mba, Rakiraki, and Lambasa. Nearly half a million metric tonnes of sugar are exported annually to Britain, Malaysia, Japan, and other countries, providing employment for 40,000 people. A distillery at Lautoka produces rum and other liquors from the by-products of sugar. Over the next few years the viability of Fiji's sugar industry may be badly shaken as European Union import quotas are phased out (under the Lomé Convention, 163,000 metric tonnes of Fijian sugar are sold to the E.U. each year at fixed prices far above world market levels). If lease payments were concurrently increased, thousands of Fiji's cane growers would face bankruptcy.

Timber is increasingly important as tens of thousands of hectares planted in western Viti Levu and Vanua Levu by the Fiji Pine Commission and private landowners in the late 1970s reach maturity. Each year Fiji exports about F$26 million in sawed lumber and wood chips (the export of raw logs was banned in 1987). Yet Fiji's native forests are poorly protected from the greed of foreign logging companies and shortsighted local landowners, and each year large tracts of pristine rainforest are lost. Now that all of the lowland forests have been cleared, attention is turning to the highlands. The pine project has had the corollary benefit of reducing pressure on the natural forests to supply Fiji's timber needs.

Commercial fishing is booming, with a major tuna cannery at Levuka supplied in part by Fiji's own fleet of 17 longline vessels. The 15,000 metric tonnes of canned tuna produced each year comprise Fiji's fourth-largest export, shipped mostly to Britain and Canada (see "Ovalau Island" in the "Lomaiviti Group" section for more information). In addition, chilled yellowfin tuna is air freighted to Hawaii and Japan to serve the *sashimi* (raw fish) market.

Mining activity centers on gold at Vatukoula on northern Viti Levu, but extensive low-grade copper deposits exist at Namosi, 30 km northwest of Suva. In mid-1995 the Canadian company, Placer Pacific, announced it was putting development of the site on hold after a dispute with the Fiji government over taxation. If the US$1-billion Namosi mine ever goes ahead it will be one of the largest in the world, totally altering Fiji's economy and the country with it. Fiji now grows almost half its own rice needs and is trying to become self-sufficient. Much of the rice is grown around Nausori and Navua. Most of Fiji's copra is produced in Lau, Lomaiviti, Taveuni, and Vanua Levu, half by European or part-Fijian planters and the rest by indigenous Fijian villagers.

Yet, in spite of all this potential, unemployment is a major social problem as four times more young people leave school than there are jobs to take them. To stimulate industry, firms that export 95% of their production are granted 13-year tax holidays, the duty-free import of materials, and freedom to repatriate capital and profits. The garment industry is growing fast and already employs 11,000, with female workers earning an average of F$30 a week. At peak periods the factories operate three shifts, seven days a week. Women working in the industry have complained of being subjected to body searches and sexual harassment, with those who protest or organize collective action being fired and blacklisted. The clothing produced by the 200 foreign-owned and 12 locally owned companies in the sector is exported mostly to Australia and New Zealand, where partial duty- and quota-free entry is allowed under the South Pacific Regional Trade and Economic Cooperation Agreement (SPARTECA) for products with at least 50% local content, and many manufacturers in those countries have moved their fac-

tories to Fiji to take advantage of the low labor costs. SPARTECA rules prevent local manufacturers from importing quality fabrics from outside the region, limiting them to the bottom end of the market.

Food processors and furniture and toy makers are also prominent in the tax-free exporting sector. Until recently it was believed that manufacturing would eventually overtake both sugar and tourism as the main source of income for the country, but current worldwide trade liberalization trends are cutting into Fiji's competitiveness. SPARTECA's local-content rule discourages local companies from cutting costs by introducing labor-saving technology, condemning them to obsolescence in the long term.

Aside from this cash economy, subsistence agriculture makes an important contribution to the life of indigenous Fijians in rural areas. About 40% of the workforce has paid employment; the remainder is involved in subsistence agriculture, with manioc, taro, yams, sweet potato, and corn the principal subsistence crops. Kava gardens produce cash income.

Trade and Aid

Fiji is an important regional trading center. Although Fiji imports 50% more than it exports, some of the imbalance is resold to tourists who pay in foreign exchange. In the Pacific islands, Fiji's trade deficit is exceeded only by that of the French colonies and it has grown much larger in recent years due to sharply increased imports of machinery and textiles by tax-free zone industry. Raw sugar accounts for nearly half of the nation's visible export earnings, followed by garments, unrefined gold, canned fish, wood chips, molasses, sawed timber, and ginger, in that order. Huge trade imbalances exist with Australia, Japan, and New Zealand.

Mineral fuels used to eat up much of Fiji's import budget, but this declined as the Monasavu Hydroelectric Project and other self-sufficiency measures came on-line a decade ago. Petroleum products, manufactured goods, food, textiles, and motor vehicles account for most of the import bill.

Fiji is the least dependent Pacific nation (excluding Nauru). In 1989 overseas aid totaled only A$75 per capita (as compared to A$1875 per capita in Tahiti-Polynesia); it accounts for just 11% of government expenditures. Development aid is well diversified among over a dozen donors; the largest amounts come from Australia, Japan, New Zealand, France, the Asian Development Bank, the European Union, Germany, and the United Kingdom, in that order, with Australia alone contributing nearly half. North American aid to Fiji is negligible. Increasingly Fiji is looking to Asian countries such as Japan, China, Taiwan, South Korea, and Singapore for development assistance. Fiji is fortunate in its low level of foreign indebtedness, a result of cautious fiscal management during the 1980s, and government financing has largely come from domestic sources. In June 1995, however, Fiji's financial standing was severely shaken when it was announced that the National Bank of Fiji was holding F$100 million in bad debts, most of it resulting from politically motivated loans to indigenous Fijians and Rotumans. The subsequent run on deposits cost the bank another F$20 million, and the government was forced to step in to save the bank.

Tourism

Tourism is the leading money-maker, earning over F$400 million a year—more than sugar and gold combined. In 1994 some 318,000 tourists visited Fiji—more than twice as many as visited Tahiti and 15 times as many as visited Tonga. Things appear in better perspective, however, when Fiji is compared to Hawaii, which is about the same size in surface area. Overpacked Hawaii gets seven million tourists, 25 times as many as Fiji. Gross receipts figures from tourism are often misleading, as 56 cents on every dollar is repatriated overseas by foreign

investors or used to pay for tourism-related imports. In real terms, sugar is far more profitable for Fiji. In 1994 paid employment in the hotel industry totaled 5,996 (3,556 male and 2,440 female employees) and an estimated 40,000 jobs in all sectors are related to tourism.

The main tourist resorts are centered along the Coral Coast of Viti Levu and in the Mamanutha Islands off Nandi/Lautoka. For years the Fiji government swore there would be no hotel development in the Yasawa and Lau groups, but several resorts now exist there. Japanese companies have investments in Fiji worth a half billion dollars, including the Sheraton and Regent hotels at Nandi. About 32% of Fiji's tourists come from Australia, 14% from New Zealand, 13% each from the U.S. and Japan, 11% from continental Europe, six percent from Britain, and five percent from Canada. The vast majority of visitors arrive in Fiji to/from Auckland, Sydney, Honolulu, and Los Angeles.

Most of the large resort hotels in Fiji are foreign-owned, and 80% of their purchases for food, beverages, linen, glassware, etc., are imported at concessional rates. The Fiji government has diverted large sums from its capital-improvements budget to provide infrastructure such as roads, airports, and other services to the resorts, yet the hotels can write off 55% of their capital expenditures against taxes over six-year periods. Management of the foreign-owned hotels is usually European, with Fiji Indians filling technical positions such as maintenance, cooking, accounting, etc., and indigenous Fijians working the high-profile positions such as receptionists, waiters, guides, and housekeepers.

THE PEOPLE

The Fijians

Fiji is a transitional zone between Polynesia and Melanesia. The Fijians bear a physical resemblance to the Melanesians, but like the Polynesians, the Fijians have hereditary chiefs, patrilineal descent, a love of elaborate ceremonies, and a fairly homogeneous language and culture. Fijians have interbred with Polynesians to the extent that their skin color is lighter than that of other Melanesians. In the interior and west of Viti Levu where the contact was less, the people tend to be somewhat darker than the easterners. Yet Fijians still have Melanesian frizzy hair, while most—but not all—Polynesians have straight hair.

The Fijians live in villages along the rivers or coast, with anywhere from 50 to 400 people led by a hereditary chief. To see a Fijian family living in an isolated house in a rural area is rare. *Matanggali* (clans) are grouped into *yavusa* of varying rank and function. Several *yavusa* form a *vanua*, a number of which make up a *matanitu*. Chiefs of the most important *vanua* are known as high chiefs. In western Viti Levu the groups are smaller, and outstanding commoners can often rise to positions of power and prestige reserved for high chiefs in the east. Away from the three largest islands the population is almost totally Fijian. The traditional thatched *mbure* is fast disappearing from Fiji as villagers rebuild in tin and panel (often following destructive cyclones). Grass is not as accessible as cement, takes more time to repair, and is less permanent.

Fijians work communal land individually, not as a group. Each Fijian is assigned a piece of native land. They grow most of their own food in village gardens, and only a few staples such as tea, sugar, flour, etc., are imported from Suva and sold in local co-op stores. A visit to one of these stores will demonstrate just how little they import and how self-sufficient they are. Fishing, village maintenance work, and ceremonial presentations are done together. While village life provides a form of collective security, individuals are discouraged from rising above the group. Fijians who attempt to set up a business are often stifled by the demands of relatives and friends. The Fijian custom of claiming favors from members of one's own group is known as *kerekere*. This pattern makes it difficult for Fijians to compete with Indians, for whom life has always been a struggle.

The Indians

Most of the Indians now in Fiji are descended from indentured laborers recruited in Bengal and Bihar a century ago. In the first year of the system (1879) some 450 Indians arrived in Fiji to work in the cane fields. By 1883 the total had risen to 2,300 and in 1916, when the last indentured laborers arrived, 63,000 Indians were present in the colony. In 1920 the indenture system was finally terminated, the cane fields were divided into four-hectare plots, and the Indian workers became tenant farmers on land owned by Fijians. Indians continued to arrive until 1931, though many of these later arrivals were Gujerati or Sikh businesspeople.

Fijian boys, Singatoka Valley

DAVID STANLEY

In 1940 the Indian population stood at 98,000, still below the Fijian total of 105,000, but by the 1946 census Indians had outstripped Fijians 120,000 to 117,000—making Fijians a minority in their own home. In the wake of the coups the relative proportions changed when some 30,000 Indians emigrated to North America and Australia, and by early 1989 indigenous Fijians once again outnumbered Fiji Indians. At the end of 1992, Fiji's estimated total population was 758,275, of which approximately 49.7% were Fijian while 45.3% were Indian (compared to 46% Fijian and 48.7% Indian at the 1986 census). Compared to indigenous Fijian women, twice as many Fiji Indian women take contraceptives, thus their fertility rate is considerably lower.

Unlike the village-oriented Fijians, a majority of Indians are concentrated in the cane-growing areas and live in isolated farmhouses, small settlements, or towns. Many Indians also live in Suva, as do an increasing number of Fijians. Within the Fiji Indian community there are divisions of Hindu (80%) versus Muslim (20%), north Indian versus south Indian, and Gujerati versus the rest. The Sikhs and Gujeratis have always been somewhat of an elite as they immigrated freely to Fiji outside the indenture system.

The different groups have kept alive their ancient religious beliefs and rituals. Hindus tend to marry within their caste, although the restrictions on behavior, which characterize the caste system in India, have disappeared. Indian marriages are often arranged by the parents, while Fijians generally choose their own partners. Rural Indians still associate most closely with other members of their extended patrilineal family group, and Hindu and Muslim religious beliefs still restrict Indian women to a position subservient to men.

It's often said that Indians concentrate on accumulation while Fijians emphasize distribution. Yet Fiji's laws themselves encourage Indians to invest their savings in business by preventing them or anyone else from purchasing native communal land. High-profile Indian dominance of the retail sector has distorted the picture and the reality is that the per capita incomes of ordinary indigenous Fijians and Fiji Indians are not that different. Big business remains the domain of government and foreign investors. Fijians are not "poor" because they are exploited by Indians; the two groups simply amass their wealth in different ways. And if some Indians seem money-minded, it's largely because they have been forced into that role. In large measure, Fiji's excellent service and retail industries exist thanks to the thrift and efficiency of the Indians. When you consider their position in a land where most have lived four generations and where they form almost half the population, where the constitution precludes them from ever governing, and where all natural resources are in the hands of others, their industriousness and patience are admirable.

Land Rights

When Fiji became a British colony in 1874, the land was divided between white settlers who had bought plantations and the *taukei ni ngele*, the Fijian "owners of the soil." The government assumed title to the balance. Today the alienated (privately owned) plantation lands are known as "freehold" land—about 10% of the total. Another seven percent is Crown land and the remaining 83% is inalienable Fijian communal land, which can be leased (about 30% is) but may never be sold. Compare this 83% (much of it not arable) with only three percent Maori land in New Zealand and almost zero native Hawaiian land. Land ownership has provided the Fijians with a security that allows them to preserve their traditional culture, unlike most indigenous peoples in other countries.

Communal land is administered on behalf of some 6,600 clan groups *(matanggali)* by the Native Land Trust Board (Box 116, Suva; fax 679/303-164), a government agency established in 1940. The NLTB retains 25% of the lease money to cover administration, and a further 10% is paid directly to regional hereditary chiefs. In 1966 the Agricultural Landlords and Tenants Act increased the period for which native land can be leased from 10 to 30 years. The 30-year leases will begin coming up for renewal in 1997, and Fiji's 23,000 Indian sugarcane farmers are apprehensive about the new terms they'll receive. If rents are greatly increased or the leases terminated, Fiji's sugar industry could be badly damaged and an explosive social situation created.

At the First Constitutional Conference in 1965, Indian rights were promulgated, and the 1970 independence constitution asserted that everyone born in Fiji would be a citizen with equal rights. But land laws, right up to the present, have very much favored "Fiji for the Fijians." Fiji Indians have always accepted Fijian ownership of the land, provided they are granted satisfactory leases. Now that the leases seem endangered, many Indians fear they will be driven from the only land they've ever known. The stifling of land development may keep Fiji quaint for tourists, but it also condemns a large portion of the population of both races to backwardness and poverty.

Other Groups

The 5,000 Fiji-born Europeans or *Kai Viti* are descendants of Australians and New Zealanders who came to create cotton, sugar, or copra plantations in the 19th century. Many married Fijian women, and the 13,000 part-Fijians or *Kai Loma* of today are the result. There is almost no intermarriage between Fijians and Fiji Indians. Many other Europeans are present in Fiji on temporary contracts or as tourists.

Most of the 5,000 Chinese in Fiji are descended from free settlers who came to set up small businesses a century ago, although since 1987 there has been an influx of about a thousand Chinese from mainland China who were originally admitted to operate market gardens but who have since moved into the towns. Fiji Chinese tend to intermarry freely with the other racial groups.

The people of Rotuma, a majority of whom now live in Suva, are Polynesians. On neighboring islands off Vanua Levu are the Micronesians of Rambi (from Kiribati) and the Polynesians of Kioa (from Tuvalu). The descendants of Solomon Islanders blackbirded during the 19th century still live in communities near Suva, Levuka, and Lambasa. The Tongans in Lau and other Pacific islanders who have immigrated to Fiji make this an ethnic crossroads of the Pacific.

Social Conditions

Some 98% of the country's population was born in Fiji. The partial breakdown in race relations after the Rabuka coups was a tragedy for Fiji,

though racial antagonism has been exaggerated. Despite the rhetoric, the different ethnic groups have always gotten along well together, with remarkably little animosity. You may hear individuals make disparaging remarks about the other group, but it's highly unlikely you'll witness any local confrontations. Though there are few problems in everyday life, the attitude has changed since 1987. Most Fiji Indians seem to have resigned themselves to their second-class position in Fiji, and some of the brightest and best have left.

As important as race are the variations between rich and poor, or urban (39%) and rural (61%). The imposition in 1992 of a 10% value-added tax combined with reductions in income tax and import duties shifted the burden of taxation from the haves to the have nots, and about nine percent of the population lives in absolute poverty. Avenues for future economic growth are limited, and there's chronic unemployment. The population is growing at an annual rate of three percent (compared to 0.9% in the U.S.) and the subsistence economy has difficulty absorbing these numbers. The lack of work is reflected in an increasing crime rate.

Literacy is high at 87%. Although not compulsory, primary education is free and accessible to most children. Most schools are still racially segregated. Over 100 church-operated schools receive government subsidies. The Fiji Institute of Technology was founded at Suva in 1963, followed by the University of the South Pacific in 1968. The university serves the 12 Pacific countries that contribute to its costs. Medical services in Fiji are heavily subsidized. The main hospitals are at Lambasa, Lautoka, and Suva, though smaller hospitals, health centers, and nursing stations are scattered around the country. The most common infectious diseases are influenza, gonorrhea, and syphilis.

Religion

The main religious groups in Fiji are Hindus (290,000), Methodists (265,000), Catholics (70,000), Muslims (62,000), Assemblies of God (33,000), and Seventh-Day Adventists (20,000). About 78% of indigenous Fijians are Methodist, 8.5% Catholic. Only two percent of Indians have converted to Christianity despite Methodist missionary efforts dating back to 1884.

After the 1987 military coups extremist elements seized control of the Methodist Church and there have been allegations of thousands of dollars in German aid to the church being diverted for political purposes. Membership in the Assemblies of God and some other new Christian sects is growing quickly at the expense of the Methodists. Due to a change in government policies, the number of Mormon missionaries granted Fijian visas has increased tenfold since 1987, and 90% of the money used to support Mormon activities in Fiji comes from the church headquarters in Utah.

LANGUAGE

Fijian, a member of the Austronesian family of languages spoken from Easter Island to Madagascar, has more speakers than any other indigenous Pacific language. Fijian vowels are pronounced as in Latin or Spanish, while the consonants are similar to those of English. Syllables end in a vowel, and the next-to-last syllable is usually the one emphasized. Where two vowels appear together they are sounded separately. In 1835 two Methodist missionaries, David Cargill and William Cross, devised the form of written Fijian used in Fiji today. Since all consonants in Fijian are separated by vowels, they spelled mb as b, nd as d, ng as g, ngg as q, and th as c. (For convenience, this book employs phonetic spelling for placenames and words, but Fijian spelling for the names of individuals.)

Though Cargill and Cross worked at Lakemba in the Lau Group, the political importance of tiny Mbau Island just off Viti Levu caused the Mbauan dialect of Fijian to be selected as the "official" version of the language, and in 1850 a dictionary and grammar were published. When the Bible was translated into Mbauan that dialect's dominance was assured, and it is today's spoken and written Fijian. From 1920 to 1970 the use of Fijian was discouraged in favor of English, but since independence there has been a revival. In 1973 a project was set up to create a definitive monolingual Fijian dictionary, and in 1987 the short-lived Coalition government restructured this work to create the Fijian Institute of Culture under the Ministry of Fijian Affairs.

Hindustani or Hindi is the household tongue of most Fiji Indians. Fiji Hindi has diverged from that spoken in India with the adoption of many words from English and other Indian languages such as Urdu. Though a quarter of Fiji Indians are descended from immigrants from southern India where Tamil and Telegu are spoken, few use these languages today, even at home. Fiji Muslims speak Hindi out of practical considerations, though they might consider Urdu their mother tongue. In their spoken forms, Hindi and Urdu are very similar. English is the second official language in Fiji and is understood by almost everyone. All schools teach exclusively in English after the fourth grade. Fiji Indians and indigenous Fijians usually communicate with one another in English.

CUSTOMS

Fijians and Fiji Indians are very tradition-oriented people who have retained a surprising number of their own ancestral customs despite the flood of conflicting influences that have swept the Pacific over the past century. Rather than a melting pot where one group assimilated another, Fiji is a patchwork of varied traditions.

The obligations and responsibilities of Fijian village life include not only the erection and upkeep of certain buildings, but personal participation in the many ceremonies that give their lives meaning. Hindu Indians, on the other hand, practice firewalking and observe festivals such as Holi and Diwali, just as their forebears in India did for thousands of years.

Fijian Firewalking

In Fiji, both Fijians and Indians practice firewalking, with the difference being that the Fijians walk on heated stones instead of hot embers. Legends tell how the ability to walk on fire was first given to a warrior named Tui-na-vinggalita from Mbengga Island, just off the south coast of Viti Levu, who had spared the life of a spirit god he caught while fishing for eels. The freed spirit gave to Tui-na-vinggalita the gift of immunity to fire. Today his descendants act as mbete (high priests) of the rite of vilavilairevo (jumping into the oven). Only members of his tribe, the Sawau, perform the ceremony. The

a tanoa *carved from a single block of* vesi *wood*

Tui Sawau lives at Ndakuimbengga village on Mbengga, but firewalking is now only performed at the resort hotels on Viti Levu.

Fijian firewalkers (men only) are not permitted to have contact with women or to eat any coconut for two weeks prior to a performance. In a circular pit about four meters across, hundreds of large stones are first heated by a wood fire until they're white-hot. If you throw a handkerchief on the stones, it will burst into flames. Much ceremony and chanting accompanies certain phases of the ritual, such as the moment when the wood is removed to leave just the red-hot embers. The men psych themselves up in a nearby hut, then emerge, enter the pit, and walk briskly once around it. Bundles of leaves and grass are then thrown on the stones and the men stand inside the steaming pit again to chant a final song. They seem to have complete immunity to pain and there's no trace of injury. The men appear to fortify themselves with the heat, to gain some psychic power from the ritual.

Indian Firewalking

By an extraordinary coincidence, Fiji Indians brought with them the ancient practice of religious firewalking. In southern India, firewalking occurs in the pre-monsoon season as a call to the goddess Kali (Durga) for rain. Fiji Indian firewalking is an act of purification, or fulfillment of a vow to thank the god for help in a difficult situation.

In Fiji there is firewalking in most Hindu temples once a year, at full moon sometime between May and September according to the Hindu calendar. The actual event takes place on a Sunday at 1600 on the Suva side of Viti Levu, and at 0400 on the Nandi/Lautoka side. In August there is firewalking at the Sangam Temple on Howell Road, Suva. During the 10 festival days preceding the walk, participants remain in isolation, eat only unspiced vegetarian food, and spiritually prepare themselves. There are prayers at the temple in the early morning and a group singing of religious stories at about 1900 from Monday through Thursday. The yellow-clad devotees, their faces painted bright yellow and red, often pierce their cheeks or other bodily parts with spikes as part of the purification rites. Their faith is so strong they feel no pain.

The event is extremely colorful; drumming and chanting accompany the visual spectacle. Visitors are welcome to observe the firewalking, but since the exact date varies from temple to temple according to the phases of the moon (among other factors), you just have to keep asking to find out where and when it will take place. To enter the temple you must remove your shoes and any leather clothing.

The *Yanggona* Ceremony

Yanggona (kava), a tranquilizing, nonalcoholic drink that numbs the tongue and lips, comes from the *waka* (dried root) of the pepper plant *(Macropiper methysticum)*. This ceremonial preparation is the most honored feature of the formal life of Fijians, Tongans, and Samoans. It is performed with the utmost gravity according to a sacramental ritual to mark births, marriages, deaths, official visits, the installation of a new chief, etc.

New mats are first spread on the floor, on which is placed a handcarved *tanoa* (wooden bowl) nearly a meter wide. A long fiber cord decorated with cowry shells leads from the bowl to the guests of honor. To step over this cord during the ceremony is forbidden. As many as 70 men take their places before the bowl. The officiants are adorned with tapa, fiber, and croton leaves, their torsos smeared with glistening coconut oil, their faces usually blackened.

The guests present a bundle of *waka* to the hosts, along with a short speech explaining their visit, a custom known as *sevusevu*. The *sevusevu* is received by the hosts and acknowledged with a short speech of acceptance. The *waka* are then scraped clean and pounded in a *tambili* (mortar). Formerly they were chewed. Nowadays the pulp is put in a cloth sack and mixed with water in the *tanoa*. In the chiefly ceremony the *yanggona* is kneaded and strained through *vau* (hibiscus) fibers.

The mixer displays the strength of the grog (kava) to the *mata ni vanua* (master of ceremonies) by pouring out a cupful into the *tanoa*. If the *mata ni vanua* considers the mix too strong, he calls for *wai* (water), then says *"lose"* ("mix"), and the mixer proceeds. Again he shows the consistency to the *mata ni vanua* by pouring out a cupful. If it appears right the *mata ni vanua* says *"lomba"* ("squeeze"). The mixer squeezes the remaining juice out of the pulp, puts it aside, and announces, *"Sa lose oti saka na yanggona, vaka turanga"* ("The kava is ready, my chief"). He runs both hands around the rim of the *tanoa* and claps three times.

The *mata ni vanua* then says *"talo"* ("serve"). The cupbearer squats in front of the *tanoa* with a *mbilo* (half coconut shell), which the mixer fills. The cupbearer then presents the first cup to the guest of honor, who claps once and drains it, and everyone claps three times. The second cup goes to the guests' *mata ni vanua*, who claps once and drinks. The man sitting next to the mixer says *"aa,"* and everyone answers *"matha"* ("empty"). The third cup is for the first local chief, who claps once before drinking, and everyone claps three times after. Then the *mata ni vanua* of the first local chief claps once and drinks, and everyone says *"matha."* The same occurs for the second local chief and his *mata ni vanua*.

After these six men have finished their cups, the mixer announces, *"Sa matha saka tu na yanggona, vaka turanga"* ("The bowl is empty, my chief"), and the *mata ni vanua* says *"thombo"* ("clap"). The mixer then runs both hands around the rim of the *tanoa* and claps three times. This terminates the full ceremony, but then a second bowl is prepared and everyone drinks. During the drinking of the first bowl complete silence must be maintained.

Social Kava Drinking

While the above describes one of several forms of the full *yanggona* ceremony, which is performed only for high chiefs, abbreviated versions are put on for tourists at the hotels. However, the village people have simplified grog sessions almost daily. Kava drinking is an important form of Fijian entertainment and a way of structuring friendships and community relations. Even in government offices a bowl of grog is

kept for the staff to take as a refreshment at *yanggona* breaks. Some say the Fijians have *yanggona* rather than blood in their veins. Excessive kava drinking over a long period can make the skin scaly and rough, a condition known as *kanikani*.

Visitors to villages are invariably invited to participate in informal kava ceremonies, in which case it's customary to present a bunch of kava roots to the group. Do this at the beginning, before anybody starts drinking, and make a short speech explaining the purpose of your visit (be it a desire to meet the people and learn about their way of life, an interest in seeing or doing something in particular on their island, or just a holiday from work). Don't hand the roots to anyone, just place them on the mat in the center of the circle. The bigger the bundle of roots, the bigger the smiles. (The roots are easily purchased at any town market for about F$7 a half kilo.) Kava doesn't grow well in dry, cane-growing areas or in the Yasawas, so carry a good supply with you when traveling there, as it can be hard to buy more.

Clap once when the cupbearer offers you the *mbilo*, then take it in both hands and say *"mbula"* just before the cup meets your lips. Clap three times after you drink. Remember, you're a participant, not an onlooking tourist, so don't take photos if the ceremony is rather formal. Even though you may not like the appearance or taste of the drink, do try to finish at least the first cup. Tip the cup to show you're done.

It's considered extremely bad manners to turn your back on a chief during a kava ceremony, to walk in front of the circle of people when entering or leaving, or to step over the long cord attached to the *tanoa*. At the other end of the cord is a white cowry, which symbolizes a link to ancestral spirits.

Presentation of the *Tambua*

The *tambua* is a tooth of the sperm whale. It was once presented when chiefs exchanged delegates at confederacy meetings and before conferences on peace or war. In recent times, the *tambua* is presented during chiefly *yanggona* ceremonies as a symbolic welcome for a respected visitor or guest or as a prelude to public business or modern-day official functions. On the village level, *tambuas* are still commonly presented to arrange marriages, to show sympathy at funerals, to request favors, to settle disputes, or simply to show respect.

Old *tambuas* are highly polished from continuous handling. The larger the tooth, the greater its ceremonial value. *Tambuas* are prized cultural property and may not be exported from Fiji. Endangered species laws prohibit their entry into the United States, Australia, and many other countries.

Stingray Spearing and Fish Drives

Stingrays are lethal-looking creatures with caudal spines up to 18 cm long. To catch them, eight or nine punts are drawn up in a line about a kilometer long beside the reef. As soon as a stingray is sighted, a punt is paddled forward with great speed until close enough to hurl a spear.

Another time-honored sport and source of food is the fish drive. An entire village participates. Around the flat surface of a reef at rising tide, sometimes as many as 70 men and women group themselves in a circle a kilometer or more in circumference. All grip a ring of connected liana vines with leaves attached. While shouting, singing, and beating long poles on the seabed, the group slowly contracts the ring as the tide comes in. The shadow of the ring alone is enough to keep the fish within the circle. The fish are finally directed landward into a net or stone fish trap.

The Rising of the *Mbalolo*

Among all the Pacific island groups, this event takes place only in Samoa and Fiji. The *mbalolo (Eunice viridis)* is a segmented worm of the Coelomate order, considered a culinary delicacy throughout these islands. It's about 45 cm long and lives deep in the fissures of coral reefs, rising to the surface only twice a year to propagate and then die. This natural almanac keeps both lunar and solar times, and has a fixed day of appearance—even if a hurricane is raging—one night in the third quarter of the moon in October, and the corresponding night in November. It has never failed to appear on time for over 100 years now, and you can even check your calendar by it.

Because this thin, jointed worm appears with such mathematical certainty, Fijians are waiting in their boats to scoop the millions of writhing, reddish brown (male) and moss green (female) spawn from the water when they rise to the surface just before dawn. Within an hour after the rising the sacs burst, and the fertile milt spawns the next generation of *mbalolo*. This is one of the most bizarre curiosities in the natural history of the South Pacific, and the southeast coast of Ovalau is a good place to observe it.

CONDUCT

It's a Fijian custom to smile when you meet a stranger and say something like "Good morning," or at least "Hello." Of course, you needn't do this in the large towns, but you should almost everywhere else. If you meet someone you know, stop for a moment to exchange a few words. Men should always wear a shirt in town, and women should forgo halter tops, see-through dresses, and short shorts. Scanty dress in public shows a lack of respect; notice how the locals are dressed. Shorts are not proper dress for women in villages, so carry a *sulu* to cover up. Topless sunbathing by women is not allowed in Fiji.

Fijian villages are private property and it's important to get permission before entering one. Of course it's okay to continue along a road that passes through a village, but do ask before leaving the road. It's good manners to take off your hat while walking through a village, where only the chief is permitted to wear a hat. Some villagers also object to sunglasses. Objects such as backpacks, handbags, and cameras are best carried in your hands rather than slung over your shoulders. Don't point at people in villages.

If you wish to surf off a village, picnic on their beach, or fish in their lagoon, you should also ask permission. You'll almost always be made most welcome and granted any favors you request if you present a *sevusevu* of kava roots to the village headman or chief (see "Staying in Villages" in the "Accommodations" section that follows for the correct way to present a *sevusevu).* If you approach the Fijians with respect you're sure to be so treated in return.

Take off your shoes before entering a *mbure* and stoop as you walk around inside. Clap three times when you join people already seated on mats on the floor. Men should sit cross-legged, women with their legs to the side. Sitting with your legs stretched out in front is insulting. Fijian villagers consider it offensive to walk in front of a person seated on the floor (pass behind) or to fail to say *"Tulou"* ("Excuse me") as you go by. Don't stand up during a *sevusevu* to village elders. When you give a gift hold it out with both hands, not one hand. Never place your hand on another's head and don't sit in doorways.

There's no running or shouting when you arrive in a village, and they leave you alone if you wish. Fijian children are very well behaved, and all Fijians love children, so don't hesitate to bring

your own. You'll never have to worry about finding a babysitter. Do you notice how Fijians rarely shout? Keep your voice down.

In a main tourist center such as Nandi or Suva, take care if a local invites you to visit his home as you may be seen mainly as a source of beer and other goods. Surprisingly friendly people at bars may expect you to buy them drinks. Alcohol is forbidden in many Fijian villages. Women should have few problems traveling around Fiji on their own, so long as they're prepared to cope with frequent offers of marriage. Littering is punished by a minimum F$40 fine and breaking bottles in public can earn six months in jail (unfortunately seldom enforced).

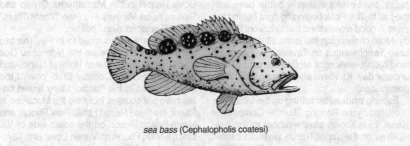

sea bass (Cephalopholis coatesi)

ON THE ROAD

HIGHLIGHTS

Fiji's many attractions are hard to shortlist but two outstanding natural features on the south side of Viti Levu are the Singatoka sand dunes and the Navua River with its cliff-hugging rapids. The three waterfalls at Mbouma Falls on the northeastern island of Taveuni are also magnificent. Fiji's finest bus rides take you through open rolling countryside from Lautoka to Rakiraki, or across the mountains of Vanua Levu from Savusavu to Lambasa. Without doubt, the most appealing town is the old capital Levuka. There are many candidates for best beach, reef, and outer island: all are tops. Two weeks is the absolute minimum amount of time required to get a feel for Fiji, and one month is much better.

SPORTS AND RECREATION

All of the high islands offer good, safe **hiking** possibilities and many remote villages are linked by well-used trails. The most important hike described in this chapter is the two-day Singatoka River Trek down the Singatoka River from Nandarivatu. Tholo-i-Suva Forest Park behind Suva is one of Fiji's most accessible hiking areas, but Levuka makes a better base with the trail to The Peak beginning right behind the town. A good cross-island trail to Lovoni is nearby. More challenging still is the all-day climb to Lake Tangimauthia on Taveuni. For some island hiking, walk right around Nananu-i-Ra in under a day. Kandavu also offers many hiking possibilities.

Exciting **whitewater rafting** on the Mba River is offered by the Roaring Thunder Company at Nandi. Less known are the rubber rafting possibilities on the upper Navua River. In central Viti Levu, villagers will pole you through the Waingga Gorge on a bamboo raft from Naitauvoli to Naivuthini villages.

Fiji has four important **surfing** camps. The more upmarket is Tavarua Island in the Mamanutha Group, which receives mostly American surfers on package deals. You can also use speedboats from Seashell Cove Resort to surf the same breaks at less expense. Fiji's best budget surfing is available at the Club Masa Sports Resort near Singatoka. A new surfing camp called Frigate Surfriders has opened on Yanutha Island off southern Viti Levu.

Windsurfing is possible at a much wider range of locales, and many upmarket hotels include equipment in their rates. Windsurfing is possible at most of the Mamanutha resorts, including Plantation Island, Musket Cove, Naitasi Resort, Castaway, Tokoriki, and Treasure Island. Other offshore resorts around Fiji offering windsurfing are Vatulele, Tomberua Island, Mbekana Island, Turtle Island, Naingani Island, and Nggamea Beach. For those on a budget, check out the windsurfing at Nandi's Club Fiji or Singatoka's Club Masa.

In the past, organized **ocean kayaking** expeditions have been offered among the Yasawa Islands, down the northeast coast of Taveuni, and in Vanua Levu's Natewa Bay. Those who only want to dabble can hire kayaks at Lautoka's Mbekana Island, Taveuni's Garden Island Resort, and Kandavu's Albert's Place.

Get in some **sailing** by taking one of the day cruises offered from Nandi by yacht. Fiji's two main bases for chartered yachts are Musket Cove Resort in the Mamanutha Group and Savusavu on Vanua Levu (see "Yacht Tours" under "Transportation," below).

Golfers are well catered to in Fiji. The two most famous courses are the Ndenarau Golf Club, next to the Sheraton Hotel at Nandi, and the Pacific Harbor Country Club, one of the finest courses in the Pacific. Many tourist hotels have golf courses, including the Mocambo at Nandi; the Fijian Resort Hotel, Reef Resort, and Naviti Beach Resort on the south side of Viti Levu; Kontiki Resort on Vanua Levu; and Taveuni Estates on Taveuni. More locally oriented are the city golf courses at Nandi Airport and in Suva, and the company-run courses near Rakiraki, Lautoka, and Lambasa sugar mills and at the Vatukuola gold mine, all built to serve former expatriate staffs. All are open to the public and only the Sheraton and Pacific Harbor courses could be considered expensive.

The soccer season in Fiji is February to November, while rugby is played from April to September. Rugby is played only by Fijians, while soccer teams are both Fijian and Indian. Cricket is played from November to March, mostly in rural areas. Lawn bowling is also popular. Sports of any kind are forbidden on Sunday.

Scuba Diving

Diving is possible year-round in Fiji, with the marinelife most profuse from July to November. Fiji has been called "the soft coral capital of the world" and many fantastic dives are just 10 or 15 minutes away from the resorts by boat (whereas at Australia's Great Barrier Reef the speedboats often have to travel over 60 km to get to the dive sites). The worst underwater visibility conditions in Fiji are the equivalent of the very best off Florida. In the Gulf of Mexico you've about reached the limit if you can see for 15 meters; in Fiji visibility begins at 15 meters and increases to 45 meters in some places. Water temperatures vary from 24° C in June, July, and August to 30° C in December, January, and February.

Facilities for scuba diving exist at most of the resorts in the Mamanutha Group, along Viti Levu's Coral Coast, on Mbengga, Kandavu, Nananu-i-Ra, Leleuvia, at Nandi, Lautoka, Suva, and Savusavu, and on Taveuni and adjacent islands. Low-budget divers should turn to the Leleuvia, Kandavu, and Taveuni sections in this book and read. If you've never dived before, Fiji is an excellent place to learn, and the Nandi, Leleuvia, Kandavu, and Taveuni scuba operators offer certification courses from budget accommodations. Even if you aren't willing to put the necessary money and effort into scuba diving, you'd be foolish not to check out the many free snorkeling possibilities. Some dive shops take snorkelers out in their boats for a nominal rate.

Four live-aboard dive boats ply Fiji waters: the *Matangi Princess II,* a 26-meter cruise vessel operating around Taveuni, the 34-meter, eight-cabin *Nai'a* based at Suva, the five-stateroom *Mollie Dean II* also based at Suva, and the 18-meter cabin cruiser *Beqa Princess* based at Pacific Harbor. A seven-night stay on one of these vessels will run F$2775 pp (airfare extra), but the boat anchors right above the dive sites so no time is wasted commuting back and forth, all meals are included, and the diving is unlimited. Bookings can be made through any of the scuba wholesalers listed in the main introduction.

ENTERTAINMENT

There are cinemas in towns such as Lambasa, Lautoka, Mba, Nandi, Nausori, Suva, and Tavua showing adventure and romance films for low admissions. These same four towns have local nightclubs where you can enjoy as much drinking and dancing as you like without spending an arm and a leg. When there's live music, a cover charge is collected.

A South Pacific institution widespread in Fiji is the old colonial clubs that offer inexpensive beer in safe, friendly surroundings. Such clubs are found in Nandi, Singatoka, Lautoka, Levuka, Lambasa, Savusavu, and Taveuni, and although they're all private clubs with Members Only signs on the door, foreign visitors are allowed entry (except at Suva). Occasionally the bartender will ask you to sign the guest book or tell you to request authorization from the club secretary.

Fiji's one unique spectacle is the **Fijian firewalking** performed several times a week at the large hotels along the southwest side of Viti Levu: Mocambo (Saturday), Sheraton (Thursday), Fijian Resort Hotel (Monday and Friday), Reef Resort (Friday), and Pacific Harbor (Tuesday and Saturday). A fixed admission price is charged but it's well worth going at least once, if you have the chance. For more information on firewalking, see "Customs" in the Fiji Islands introduction. The same hotels that present firewalking usually stage a Fijian *meke* (described below) on an alternate night.

Fijian Dancing *(Meke)*

The term *meke* describes the combination of dance, song, and theater performed at feasts and on special occasions. Brandishing spears, their faces painted with charcoal, the men wear frangipani leis and skirts of shredded leaves. The war club dance reenacts heroic events of the past. Both men and women perform the *vaka-malolo,* a sitting dance, while the *seasea* is danced by women flourishing fans. The *tralala,* in which visitors may be asked to join, is a simple two-step shuffle danced side-by-side (early missionaries forbade the Fijians from dancing face-to-face). As elsewhere in the Pacific the dances tell a story, though the music now is strongly influenced by Christian hymns and contemporary pop. Less sensual than Polynesian dancing, the rousing Fijian dancing evokes the country's violent past. Fijian *meke* are often part of a *mangiti* or feast performed at hotels. The Dance Theater of Fiji at Pacific Harbor is well regarded.

PUBLIC HOLIDAYS AND FESTIVALS

Public holidays in Fiji include New Year's Day (1 January), National Youth Day (a Friday in early March), Good Friday and Easter Monday (March/April), Ratu Sukuna Day (a Monday around 29 May), Queen Elizabeth's Birthday (a Friday around 14 June), Constitution Day (a Saturday around 27 July), Prophet Mohammed's Birthday (anytime from August to December), Fiji Day (a Monday around 10 October), Diwali (October or November), and Christmas Days (25 and 26 December). Constitution Day commemorates promulgation of the racially weighted 1990 constitution.

Check with the Fiji Visitors Bureau to see if any festivals are scheduled during your visit. The best known are the Mbula Festival in Nandi (July), the Hibiscus Festival in Suva (August), and the Sugar Festival in Lautoka (September). Before Diwali, the Hindu festival of lights, Hindus clean their homes, then light lamps or candles to mark the arrival of spring. Fruit and sweets are offered to Lakshmi, goddess of wealth. Holi is an Indian spring festival in February or March.

ARTS AND CRAFTS

The traditional art of Fiji is closely related to that of Tonga. Fijian canoes, too, were patterned after the more advanced Polynesian type, although the Fijians were timid sailors. War clubs, food bowls, *tanoas* (kava bowls), eating utensils, clay pots, and tapa cloth *(masi)* are considered Fiji's finest artifacts.

There are two kinds of woodcarvings: the ones made from *vesi (Intsia bijuga)*—ironwood in English—or *nawanawa (Cordia subcordata)* wood are superior to those of the lighter, highly breakable *vau (Hibiscus tiliaceus).* In times past it often took years to make a Fijian war club, as the carving was done in the living tree and left to grow into the desired shape. The best *tanoas* are carved in the Lau Group.

Though many crafts are alive and well, some Fijians have taken to carving "tikis" or mock New Guinea masks smeared with black shoe polish to look like ebony for sale to tourists. Also avoid crafts made from endangered species such as sea turtles (tortoise shell) and marine mammals (whales' teeth, etc.). Prohibited entry into most countries, they will be confiscated by customs if found.

Pottery Making

Fijian pottery making is unique in that it is a Melanesian artform. The Polynesians forgot how to make pottery thousands of years ago. Today the main center for pottery making in Fiji is the Singatoka Valley on Viti Levu. Here, the

a Fijian woman wrapped in a tapa blanket

HUNGARIAN ETHNOGRAPHICAL MUSEUM, BUDAPEST

women shape clay using a wooden paddle outside against a rounded stone held inside the future pot. The potter's wheel was unknown in the Pacific.

A saucerlike section forms the bottom; the sides are built up using slabs of clay, or coils and strips. These are welded and battered to shape. When the form is ready the pot is dried inside the house for a few days, then heated over an open fire for about an hour. Resin from the gum of the *dakua* (kauri) tree is rubbed on the outside while the pot is still hot. This adds a varnish that brings out the color of the clay and improves the pot's water-holding ability.

This pottery is extremely fragile, which accounts for the quantity of potsherds found on ancient village sites. Smaller, less breakable pottery products such as ashtrays are now made for sale to visitors.

Tapa Cloth

This is Fiji's most characteristic traditional product. Tapa is light, portable, and inexpensive, and a piece makes an excellent souvenir to brighten up a room back home. It's made by women on Vatulele Island off Viti Levu and on certain islands of the Lau Group.

To make tapa, the inner, water-soaked bark of the paper mulberry *(Broussonetia papyrifera)* is stripped from the tree and steeped in water. Then it's scraped with shells and pounded into a thin sheet with wooden mallets. Four of these sheets are applied one over another and pounded together, then left to dry in the sun.

While Tongan tapa is decorated by holding a relief pattern under the tapa and overpainting the lines, Fijian tapa *(masi kesa)* is distinctive for its rhythmic geometric designs applied with stencils made from green pandanus and banana leaves. The stain is rubbed on in the same manner in which temple rubbings are made from a stone inscription.

The only colors used are red, from red clay, and a black pigment obtained by burning candlenuts. Both powders are mixed with boiled gums made from scraped roots. Sunlight deepens and sets the colors. Each island group had its characteristic colors and patterns, ranging from plantlike paintings to geometric designs. Sheets of tapa feel like felt when finished.

SHOPPING

Shops in Fiji close at 1300 on Saturday, except in Nausori town where they stay open all day Saturday but only half a day on Wednesday. The 1987 military coups placed Fiji firmly in the South Pacific Bible Belt, which also encompasses Tonga, Western Samoa, and the Cook Islands, so most commercial business is suspended on Sunday (hotels excepted). Fiji Indians dominate the retail trade. If you're buying from an Indian merchant, always bargain hard and consider all sales final. Indigenous Fijians usually begin by asking a much lower price, in which case bargaining isn't so important.

Fiji's duty-free shops such as Prouds or Tappoo are not really duty-free, as all goods are subject to various fiscal duties plus the 10% value-added tax. Bargaining is the order of the day, but only in Suva is the selection really good. To be frank, Americans can usually buy the sort of Japanese electrical merchandise sold "duty-free" in Fiji cheaper in the States, where they'll get more recent models. If you do buy something, get an itemized receipt and international guarantee, and watch that they don't switch packages and unload a demo on you. Once purchased, items cannot be returned, so don't let yourself be talked into something. Camera film is cheap, however, and the selection good—stock up.

If you'd like to do some shopping in Fiji, locally made handicrafts such as tapa cloth, mats, kava bowls, war clubs, woodcarvings, etc., are a much better investment (see "Arts and Crafts," above). The four-pronged cannibal forks available everywhere make unique souvenirs. The Government Handicraft Center in Suva is a place to learn what's available, and if you're spending serious money for top-quality work, visit the Fiji Museum beforehand.

Try to purchase your souvenirs directly from the Fijian producers at street markets, etc. Just beware of aggressive Fijian "sword sellers" on the streets of Suva who sell fake handicrafts at high prices, high-pressure duty-free touts who may try to pull you into their shops, and self-appointed guides who offer to help you find the "best price." If you get the feeling you're being hustled, walk away.

ACCOMMODATIONS

A 10% government tax is added to all accommodations prices. Some hotels include the tax in their quoted rates, while others don't. You can often tell whether tax is included by looking at the amount: if it's F$33 tax is probably included, whereas if it's F$30 it may not be. We've tried to include the tax in all prices quoted herein. When things are slow, specials are offered and some prices are negotiable. Occasionally you'll pay less than the prices quoted in this book.

Fiji offers a wide variety of places to stay, from low-budget to world-class, and in this book we list them all. Standard big-city international hotels are found in Nandi and Suva, while most of the huge upmarket beach resorts are on small islands in the Mamanutha Group off Nandi and along the Coral Coast on Viti Levu's south side.

In recent years smaller luxury resorts have multiplied on the outer islands, from the guest-accepting plantations near Savusavu and on Taveuni to isolated beach resorts on remote islands such as Turtle, Yasawa, Vatulele, Mbengga, Tomberua, Kandavu, Naingani, Wakaya, Nukumbati, Namenalala, Nggamea, Matangi, Lauthala, Kaimbu, and Vanua Mbalavu. Prices at these begin at several hundred dollars a day. A few such as Mbengga, Matana, and Matangi are marketed almost exclusively to scuba divers. If heading for any of these, pick up a bottle of duty-free liquor on the way as bar prices are high.

The **Mamanutha resorts** are secluded, with fan-cooled *mbure* accommodations, while at the **Coral Coast hotels** you often get an a/c room in a main building. The Coral Coast has more to offer in the way of land tours, shopping, and entertainment/eating options, while the offshore resorts are preferable if you want a rest or are into water sports. The Coral Coast beaches are only good at high tide. Most guests at the deluxe hotels in both areas are on package tours. For economy and flexibility, avoid prepaying hotel accommodations from home.

Many hotels, both in cities and at the beach, offer **dormitory beds** as well as individual rooms. Most of the dorms are mixed. Women can sometimes request a women-only dorm when things are slow, but it's not usually guaranteed.

Low-budget accommodations are spread out, with concentrations in Nandi, Korolevu, Suva, Lautoka, Levuka, and Savusavu, and on Taveuni. Low-cost outer island beach resorts exist on Kandavu, Ono, Leleuvia, Naingani, Nananu-i-Ra, and Tavewa. Some Suva hotels lock their front doors at 1100, so ask first if you're planning a night on the town. A few of the cheapies double as whorehouses, making them cheap in both senses of the word. Some islands with air service from Suva, including Koro, Moala, Ngau, Rotuma, and Thithia, have no facilities whatsoever for visitors, so it really helps to know someone before heading that way.

Camping facilities (bring your own tent) are found at Momi Bay south of Nandi, on Nukulau Island off Suva, and on Kandavu, Ono, Ovalau, and Taveuni islands. Elsewhere, get permission before pitching your tent as all land is owned by someone and land rights are sensitive issues in Fiji. Some freelance campers on beaches such as Natandola near Nandi have been robbed, so take care. Don't ask a Fijian friend for permission to camp beside his house in the village itself. Although he may feel obligated to grant the request of a guest, you'll be proclaiming to everyone that his home isn't completely to your liking. Of course, in places (like Tavewa Island) that receive visitors regularly this isn't a problem; elsewhere if all you really want is to camp, make this clear from the start and get permission to do so on a beach or by a river, but *not* in the village. A *sevusevu* should always be presented in this case.

Staying In Villages

A great way to meet the people and learn a little about their culture is to stay in a village for a few nights. A number of hiking tours now offer overnighting in remote villages, and it's also possible to arrange it for yourself. If you befriend someone from a remote island, ask them to write you a letter of introduction to their relatives back in the village. Mail a copy of it ahead with a polite letter introducing yourself, then start slowly heading that way.

In places off the beaten tourist track, you could just show up in a village and ask permission of the *turanga-ni-koro* (village herald) to spend the night. Rarely will you be refused. Similarly, both Fiji Indians and native Fijians will spontaneously invite you in. The Fijians' innate dignity and kindness should not be taken for granted, however.

All across the Pacific it's customary to reciprocate when someone gives you a gift—if not now, then sometime in the future. Visitors who accept gifts (such as meals and accommodations) from islanders and do not reciprocate are undermining traditional culture and causing resentment, often without realizing it. It's sometimes hard to know how to repay hospitality, but Fijian culture has a solution: the *sevusevu*. This can be money, but it's usually a 500-gram bundle of kava roots *(waka)*, which can be easily purchased at any Fijian market for about F$7. *Sevusevus* are more often performed between families or couples about to be married, or at births or christenings, but the custom is certainly a perfect way for visitors to show their appreciation.

We recommend that travelers donate between F$10 and F$15 pp per night to village hosts (carry sufficient cash in small denominations). The *waka* is additional, and anyone traveling in remote areas of Fiji should pack some (take whole roots, not powdered kava). If you give the money up front together with the *waka* as a *sevusevu*, they'll know you're not a freeloader and you'll get better treatment, though in all cases it's absolutely essential to contribute something.

The *sevusevu* should be placed before (not handed to) the *turanga-ni-koro* or village chief so he can accept or refuse. If he accepts (by touching the package), your welcome is confirmed and you may spend the night in the village. It's also nice to give some money to the lady of the house upon departure, with your thanks. Just say it's your goodbye *sevusevu* and watch the smile. A Fijian may refuse the money, but he/she will not be offended by the offer if it is done properly.

In addition you could also take some gifts along, such as lengths of material, T-shirts, badges, pins, knitting needles, hats, acoustic guitar strings, school books, colored pens, toys, playing cards, fishhooks, line, or lures, or a big jar of instant coffee. Keep in mind, however, that Seventh-Day Adventists are forbidden to have coffee, cigarettes, or kava, so you might ask if there are any SDAs around in order to avoid embarrassment. Uncontroversial food items to donate include sugar, flour, rice, corned beef, matches, chewing gum, peanuts, and biscuits. One thing *not* to take is alcohol, which is always sure to offend somebody.

When choosing your traveling companions for a trip that involves staying in Fijian villages, make sure you agree on this before you set out. Otherwise you could end up subsidizing somebody else's trip, or worse, have to stand by and watch the Fijian villagers subsidize it. Never arrive in a village on a Sunday, and don't overstay your welcome.

Village Life

When you enter a Fijian village, people will usually want to be helpful and will direct or accompany you to the person or place you seek. If you show genuine interest in something and ask to see how it is done, you will usually be treated with respect and asked if there is anything else you would like to know. Initially, Fijians may hesitate to welcome you into their homes because they fear you will not wish to sit on a mat and eat native foods with your fingers. Once you show them that this isn't true, you'll receive the full hospitality treatment.

Consider participating in the daily activities of the family, such as weaving, cooking, gardening, and fishing. Your hosts will probably try to dissuade you from "working," but if you persist you'll become accepted. Staying in a village is definitely not for everyone. Most houses contain no electricity, running water, toilet, furniture, etc., and only native food will be offered. Water and your left hand serve as toilet paper.

You should also expect to sacrifice most of your privacy, to stay up late drinking grog, and to sit in the house and socialize when you could be out exploring. On Sunday you'll have to stay put the whole day. The constant attention and lack of sanitary conditions may become tiresome, but it would be considered rude to attempt to be alone or refuse the food or grog. Staying in the villages of Fiji offers one of the most rewarding travel experiences in the South Pacific, and if everyone plays fair it will always be so.

FOOD AND DRINK

Unlike some other South Pacific nations, Fiji has many good, inexpensive eateries. Chinese restaurants are everywhere. On the western side of Viti Levu, Indian restaurants sometimes use the name "lodge." Indian dishes are spicy, often curries with rice and *dhal* (lentil) soup. Mutton or goat curry are common Indian dishes, but orthodox Hindus don't eat beef and Muslims forgo pork. If you have the chance, try South Indian vegetarian dishes like *idly* (rice cake with soup) and *masala dosa* (filled rice pancake with sauce). Instead of bread Indians eat roti, a flat, tortilla-like pancake. If you have a delicate stomach you might avoid "exotic" meats like mutton and goat often served in Indian restaurants.

Real Fijian dishes such as baked fish *(ika)* in coconut cream *(lolo)* with cassava *(tavioka),* taro *(ndalo),* breadfruit *(uto),* and sweet potato *(kumala)* take a long time to prepare and must be served fresh, which makes it difficult to offer them in a restaurant. Try *nduruka,* a native vegetable tasting something like a cross between artichoke and asparagus. Taro leaves are used to make *palusami* (with coconut cream) and *rourou* (the local spinach). *Kokonda* is an appetizing dish made of diced raw fish marinated in coconut cream and lime juice. *Miti* is a sauce made of coconut cream, oranges, and chilies. "Bird meat" means chicken.

A good opportunity to taste the local food and see traditional dancing is at a *lovo* or underground oven feast staged weekly at one of the large hotels around Nandi or on the Coral Coast for about F$40. These are usually accompanied by a Fijian *meke* or song and dance performance in which legends, love stories, and historical events are told in song and gesture. Alternatively, firewalking may be presented.

Many restaurants are closed on Sunday, and a 10% tax is added to the bill. Fijians have their own pace and trying to make them do things more quickly is often counterproductive. Their charm and the friendly personal attention you receive more than make up for the occasionally slow service at restaurants.

The Hot Bread Kitchen chain of bakeries around Fiji serves delicious fresh fruit loaves, cheese and onion loaves, muffins, and other assorted breads. The Morris Hedstrom supermarket chain is about the cheapest, and many have milk bars with ice cream and sweets.

The famous Fiji Bitter beer is brewed by Australian-owned Carlton Brewery Ltd., with breweries in Suva and Lautoka. South Pacific Distilleries Ltd. in Lautoka produces brandy, gin, rum, vodka, and whisky under a variety of brand names. What could be better than a vodka and tonic in the midday heat or a rum and coke at sunset? Supermarkets in Fiji usually only sell beer and other alcohol weekdays 0800-1800, Saturday 0800-1300. Drinking alcoholic beverages on the street is prohibited.

preparing a lovo *(earthen pit oven)* at Korovou on the Wainimata River, Viti Levu, to celebrate the opening of the primary school

SERVICES AND INFORMATION

Visas and Officialdom

Everyone needs a passport valid at least three months beyond the date of entry. No visa is required of visitors from Western Europe, North America, or most Commonwealth countries for

stays of 30 days or less, although everyone needs a ticket to leave. Tourists are forbidden to become involved in any sort of political activity, to engage in political studies, or to conduct research. The required vaccination against yellow fever or cholera only applies if you're arriving directly from an infected area, such as the Amazon jungles or the banks of the Ganges River.

Fiji has diplomatic missions in Auckland, Brussels, Canberra, Jakarta, Kuala Lumpur, London, New York, Ottawa, Port Moresby, Seoul, Sydney, Tokyo, Washington, Wellington, and Vancouver.

Extensions of stay are given out two months at a time up to a maximum of four months free of charge by the immigration offices in Suva and Lautoka, and at Nandi Airport. If you extend your stay somewhere else the police have to send your passport to Suva, and this process will take a week at least. You must apply before your current permit expires. After the first four months, you can get another two months to bring your total stay up to six months by paying a F$55 fee. Bring your passport, onward or return ticket, and proof of sufficient funds. After six months you must leave and aren't supposed to return until another six months have passed.

Fiji has three ports of entry for yachts: Suva, Lautoka, and Levuka. Calling at an outer island before clearing customs is prohibited. Levuka is by far the easiest place to check in or out, as all of the officials have offices right on the main wharf.

To visit the outer islands, yachts require a letter of authorization from the Secretary of Fijian Affairs in Suva or the commissioner (at Lambasa, Lautoka, or Nausori) of the division they wish to visit.

Money

The currency is the Fiji dollar, which is lower than the U.S. dollar in value (about US$1 = F$1.39) but almost one to one with Australian and Canadian dollars. It's based on a basket of currencies, which means it doesn't fluctuate much. The first Fijian coins were minted in London in 1934, but Fiji continued to deal in British pounds, shillings, and pence until 1969 when dollars and cents were introduced (at the rate of two Fiji dollars to one pound). There are bills of F$1, F$2, F$5, F$10, F$20, and F$50, and despite Fiji's expulsion from the Commonwealth in 1987, the portrait of Queen Elizabeth still appears on them (and the Union Jack still forms part of the country's flag).

Banking hours are Monday to Thursday 0930-1500, Friday 0930-1600. Commercial banks operating in Fiji include the ANZ Bank, Indian-owned Bank of Baroda, Pakistani-owned Habib Bank, National Bank of Fiji, Bank of Hawaii, and Westpac Banking Corporation. Don't expect to change foreign currency outside the main towns. There are banks in all the towns, but it's usually not possible to change traveler's checks on remote outer islands; credit cards are strictly for the cities and resorts (the best cards to bring are American Express, Diners Club, MasterCard, and Visa), though most banks give cash advances. Take care changing at hotels, which often give a much lower rate than the banks.

The import of foreign currency is unrestricted, but only F$100 in Fijian banknotes may be exported. Avoid taking any Fijian banknotes out of the country at all, as Fijian dollars are difficult to change and heavily discounted outside Fiji. Change whatever you have left over into the currency of the next country on your itinerary or spend it on duty-free camera film.

The bulk of your travel funds should be in traveler's checks. American Express is probably the best kind to have, as they're represented by Tapa International in Suva (4th Floor, ANZ House, 25 Victoria Parade; tel. 302-333, fax 302-048) and Nandi (Nandi Airport Concourse; tel. 722-325). If your American Express checks are lost or stolen, contact either of these. Thomas Cook has an office of their own at 21 Thomson St., Suva (tel. 301-603, fax 300-304).

If you need money sent, have your banker make a telegraphic transfer to any Westpac Bank branch in Fiji. Many banks will hold a sealed envelope for you in their vault for a nominal fee—a good way to avoid carrying unneeded valuables with you all around Fiji.

On 1 July 1992 Fiji introduced a 10% value-added tax (VAT), which is usually (but not always) included in quoted prices. Among the few items exempt from the tax are unprocessed local foods and bus fares. Despite VAT, Fiji is perhaps the least expensive country in the South Pacific and inflation is low. Tipping isn't customary in Fiji, although some luxury resorts have a staff Christmas fund, to which contributions are welcome.

Post and Telecommunications

Post offices are generally open weekdays 0800-1600 and they hold general delivery mail two months. Fiji's postal workers are amazingly polite and efficient, and postage is inexpensive, so mail all of your postcards from here! Consider using air mail for parcels, however, as surface mail takes up to six months. If time isn't important, however, most surface parcels do eventually arrive and small packets weighing less that one kilogram benefit from an especially low tariff. The weight limit for overseas parcels is 10 kilograms. Express mail service (EMS) is more expensive but much faster and up to 20 kilograms may be sent (only available to Australia, Canada, France, Great Britain, New Zealand, U.S.A., Western Samoa, and Singapore). The only post offices accepting EMS mail are Lambasa, Lautoka, Mba, Nandi, Nandi Airport, and Suva. When writing to Fiji, use the words "Fiji Islands" in the address (otherwise the letter might go to Fuji, Japan) and underline Fiji (so it doesn't end up in Iceland).

Most post offices have public telephones. Lift the receiver, wait for a dial tone, then deposit a coin and dial. Some coin telephones only accept new coins minted in 1990 or later. Card phones are much more convenient than coin phones, and a telephone card is a very wise investment. The cards come in denominations of F$2, F$5, F$10, and F$20, and all post offices and many shops have them. In emergencies, dial 000. Domestic directory assistance is 011, international directory assistance 022, the domestic operator 010, the international operator 012. Domestic calls from public telephones are half price 1800-0600, and all day on Saturday, Sunday, and public holidays.

Fiji's international access code from public telephones is 05, so insert your card, dial 05, the country code, the area code, and the number. To call overseas collect (billed at the higher person-to-person rate), dial 031, the country code, the area code, and the number. If calling Fiji from abroad, dial your own international access code, Fiji's telephone code 679, and the local six-digit number listed in this book (there are no area codes in Fiji). If the line is inaudible, hang up immediately and try again.

A good way to place a long-distance call is to go to the FINTEL (Fiji International Telecommunications Ltd.) office on Victoria Parade, Suva, or to any post office. The basic charge for three minutes is F$5.28 to Australia or New Zealand, F$8.91 to North America, Europe, or Japan. All operator-assisted international calls have a three-minute minimum charge and additional time is charged per minute, whereas international calls made using telephone cards have no minimum and the charges are broken down into flat six-second units (telephone cards with less than F$3 credit on them cannot be used for international calls). International calls placed from hotel rooms are always much more expensive (ask the receptionist for the location of the nearest card phone).

In 1994 AT&T's "USADirect" service was introduced to Fiji, at tel. 004-890-100-1. This is about 40% more expensive than using a local telephone card for international calls as described above, and there are surcharges if you use a calling card or call collect. The advantage is that you're immediately connected to an AT&T operator or automated voice prompt, so it might be useful if you already have an AT&T calling card and don't mind paying extra for the convenience.

Faxes can be sent from the following main post offices: Lambasa, Lautoka, Mba, Nandi, Singatoka, and Suva. Outgoing faxes cost F$6.50 a page to regional countries, F$7.70 to other countries, both plus a F$3.30 handing fee. You can also receive faxes at these post offices for F$1.10 a page.

Media

The *Fiji Times* (G.P.O. Box 1167, Suva; tel. 304-111, fax 302-011), "the first newspaper published in the world today," was founded at Levuka in 1869 but is now owned by publishing mogul Rupert Murdoch's estate. The *Daily Post* (Box 7010, Valelevu, Nasinu; tel. 313-342, fax 340-455) is a Government-owned morning newspaper with a local focus. The *Times* has a daily print run of 37,000, the *Post* about 10,000. Since 1987 the press in Fiji has had to walk a narrow line, and in late 1994 Fiji's Minister of Information called for 51% local ownership of the *Times* after mild criticism of his government appeared in the paper.

Two regional newsmagazines are published in Suva: *Pacific Islands Monthly* (tel. 304-111, fax 303-809), also part of the Murdoch empire, and *Islands Business Pacific* (tel. 303-108, fax 301-423), owned by several local European businessmen. As well, there's a monthly Fijian business magazine called *The Review* (G.P.O. Box 12095, Suva; tel. 305-916, fax 305-256), owned by Fiji journalist Yashwant Gaunder. The *Review* has been threatened with suspension by the government due to its independent coverage.

The government-owned Fiji Broadcasting Commission (Box 334, Suva; tel. 314-333, fax 301-643) operates three public AM radio stations heard throughout the islands, Radio Fiji 1 in English and Fijian (BBC world news at 0800), Radio Fiji 2 in English and Hindi (local news in English at 0700 and 1900), and Radio Fiji 3 in English. They also run music-oriented FM 104. Privately owned Communications Fiji Ltd. (Private Mail Bag, Suva; tel. 314-766) operates two commercial FM stations, which broadcast around the clock, FM 96 in English and Fijian, and Radio Navtarang in Hindi. The latter two are not heard everywhere in the country.

Television broadcasting only began in Fiji in 1991, and at last report Fiji One was on the air weekdays 1700-2300, Saturday 1200-2400, and Sunday 1200-2300. The Fiji Government owns 65% of the company and another 15% is owned by TV New Zealand, which manages the station. A clause in Fiji TV's license forbids them from broadcasting "anything offensive to the Great Council of Chiefs." Local content is negligible and the steady stream of American sitcoms spreads alien cultural values in Fiji. News broadcasts on all of the government-owned radio stations are prepared by employees of the Ministry of Information, and government control of large segments of the media in Fiji is a matter of growing concern.

Information

The government-funded **Fiji Visitors Bureau** (G.P.O. Box 92, Suva; fax 300-970) sends out free upon request general brochures and a list of hotels with current prices. In Fiji they have walk-in offices in Suva and at Nandi Airport. For a list of their overseas offices see the Appendix at the end of this book.

The **Fiji Hotel Association** (Private Mail Bag, G.P.O. Suva; fax 300-331) will mail you a brochure listing all upmarket hotels with specific prices, though low-budget accommodations are not included.

The free *Fiji Magic* magazine (Box 12511, Suva; tel. 313-944, fax 302-852) is very useful to get an idea of what's on during your visit. Also browse the local bookstores, **Desai Bookshops, Zenon Book Shops,** and the **Singatoka Book Depot,** with branches all over Fiji.

Travel Agencies

If you want the security of advance reservations but aren't interested in joining a regular packaged tour, there are several companies specializing in prebooking Blue Lagoon cruises, first-class hotel rooms, airport transfers, sightseeing tours, rental cars, etc. Their prices are competitive with what you'd pay on the spot, and they're sometimes cheaper.

The Nandi Airport office of **Rosie The Travel Service** (Box 9268, Nandi Airport; tel. 722-935, fax 722-607) can arrange hotels, transfers, cruises, bus tours, etc., for you upon arrival in Fiji. Be aware however, that if your flight arrives at Nandi in the middle of the night, their airport office only opens at 0800. Rosie's bus tours from Nandi and all the Coral Coast hotels are cheaper than those of other companies because lunch and admissions aren't included (lunch is included on all the cruises). In Australia bookings can be made through Rosie The Travel Service (Level

5, Ste. 505, 9 Bronte Rd., Bondi Junction, Sydney, NSW 2022, Australia; tel. 61-2/9389-3666, fax 61-2/9369-1129), in North America through Goway Travel (Suite 300, 3284 Yonge St., Toronto, ON M4N 3M7, Canada; tel. 800/387-8850). For information of hiking tours offered by **Adventure Fiji,** a division of Rosie The Travel Service, see "Organized Tours" under "Getting There" in this book's main introduction. This locally owned business has provided efficient, personalized service since 1974.

Another large wholesaler handling Fiji bookings is **A.T.S. Pacific** with offices in the U.S. (Ste. 325, 2381 Rosecrans Ave., El Segundo, CA 90245, U.S.A.; tel. 310/643-0044), Australia (3rd Floor, 40 Miller St., North Sydney, NSW 2060, Australia; tel. 61-2/9957-3811, fax 61-2/9957-1385), and New Zealand (48 Emily Place, 10th Floor Jetset Center, Auckland 1, New Zealand; tel. 64-9/379-7105, fax 64-9/309-3239). The A.T.S. Pacific representative in Fiji is United Touring Company with an office (Box 9172, Nandi Airport; tel. 722-811, fax 790-389) in the arrival concourse at Nandi Airport, open around-the-clock. A.T.S. Pacific can put together any itinerary you may wish, but you must work through your regular travel agent as they don't deal directly with the public.

One of the top North American wholesalers specializing in Fiji is **Fiji Travel** (3790 Dunn Dr., Suite A, Los Angeles, CA 90034, U.S.A.; tel. 800/500-FIJI, fax 310/202-8233).

Health

Fiji's climate is a healthy one, and the main causes of death are noncommunicable diseases such as heart disease, diabetes, and cancer. There's no malaria here, but a mosquito-transmitted disease known as dengue fever is endemic, so try to avoid getting bitten. AIDS is now present in Fiji (seven confirmed cases of AIDS and 21 HIV infections by November, 1994), and sexually transmitted diseases such as syphilis, gonorrhea, and herpes have reached almost epidemic proportions in urban areas. Turn to the section on AIDS in this book's main introduction for more information.

The tap water in Fiji is usually drinkable except immediately after a cyclone or during droughts, when care should be taken. Health care is good, with an abundance of hospitals, health centers,

and nursing stations scattered around the country. The largest hospitals are in Lambasa, Lautoka, Levuka, Mba, Savusavu, Singatoka, Suva, and Taveuni. Attention at these is inexpensive, but in the towns it's less time-consuming and much simpler to visit a private doctor. Their fees are also reasonable.

To call an ambulance dial 000. In case of scuba diving accidents, an operating dive recompression chamber (tel. 305-154) is available in Suva. The 24-hour recompression medical evacuation number is 362-172.

TRANSPORTATION

Getting There

Fiji's geographic position makes it the hub of transport for the entire South Pacific, and Nandi Airport is the region's most important international airport, with long-haul services to points all around the Pacific Rim. Eight international airlines fly into Nandi: Air Calédonie International, Air Marshall Islands, Air Nauru, Air New Zealand, Air Pacific, Air Vanuatu, Qantas Airways, and Solomon Airlines. Air Marshall Islands, Air Nauru, and Air Pacific also use Suva's Nausori Airport, a regional distribution center with flights to many of the nearby Polynesian countries to the east.

Fiji's national airline, **Air Pacific,** was founded as Fiji Airways in 1951 by Harold Gatty, a famous Australian aviator who had set a record in 1931 by flying around the world in eight days with American Willy Post. In 1972 the airline was reorganized as a regional carrier and the name changed to Air Pacific. Thanks to careful management, the Nandi-based company has made a profit every year since 1985. The carrier arrives at Nandi from Apia, Auckland, Brisbane, Christchurch, Honiara, Los Angeles, Melbourne, Osaka, Port Vila, Sydney, Tokyo, and Tongatapu, and at Suva from Apia, Auckland, and Tongatapu. Air Pacific's U.S. office is at 6151 West Century Blvd., Suite 524, Los Angeles, CA 90045, U.S.A. (tel. 310/417-2236). Flying with Air Pacific means you enjoy the friendly flavor of Fiji from the moment you leave the ground.

Air Pacific flies nonstop from Los Angeles to Fiji, and Air New Zealand arrives direct from Honolulu, Los Angeles, Papeete, and Raroton-

(top) northern Viti Levu, Fiji (Don Pitcher);
(bottom) Oneroa, Mangaia, Cook Islands (David Stanley)

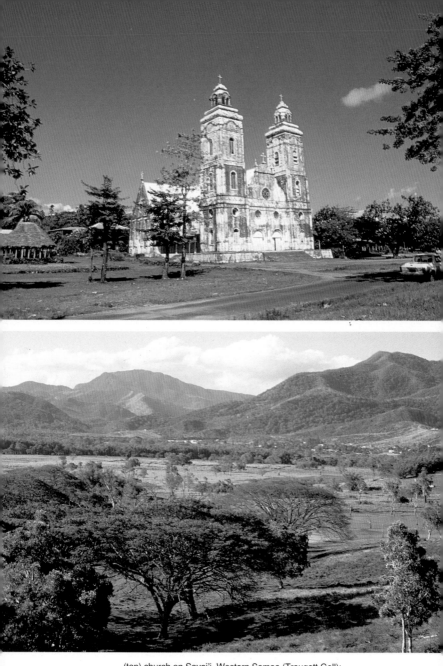

(top) church on Savai'i, Western Samoa (Traugott Goll);
(bottom) Grande Terre, New Caledonia (Robert Leger)

ga. Unfortunately Canadian Airlines International passengers originating in Toronto and Vancouver must change planes in Honolulu. Europeans must transfer at Los Angeles. It's a five-and-a-half-hour flight from California to Hawaii, then another six and a half hours from Hawaii to Fiji. The nonstop flights from Los Angeles take only 11 hours and you also save all the time Air New Zealand spends on the ground in Hawaii.

From Australia, you can fly to Nandi on Air Pacific and Qantas, both of which arrive from Brisbane, Melbourne, and Sydney. From New Zealand, both Air New Zealand and Air Pacific fly to Nandi, but Air Pacific also flies from Christchurch to Nandi and Auckland to Suva. From Japan, both Air New Zealand and Air Pacific arrive from Tokyo, and Air New Zealand also arrives from Nagoya and Air Pacific from Osaka.

Other regional carriers landing at Nandi include Air Calédonie International (from Nouméa and Wallis), Air Marshall Islands (from Funafuti, Majuro, and Tarawa), Air Nauru (from Nauru and Tarawa), Air Vanuatu (from Port Vila), and Solomon Airlines (from Honiara and Port Vila).

Airlines offering direct flights to Suva include Air Marshall Islands (from Funafuti, Majuro, and Tarawa), Air Nauru (from Nauru and Tarawa), and Air Pacific (from Apia, Auckland, and Tongatapu).

For special airfares from Fiji to other South Pacific countries, see "Getting Around" in the main introduction. A F$15 turnover tax is charged on all international air tickets purchased in Fiji.

Getting Around by Air

While most international flights are focused on Nandi, Fiji's domestic air service radiates from Suva. **Air Fiji** (Box 1259, Suva; tel. 314-666, fax 300-771) flies their fast Brazilian-made Bandeirantes and sturdy Canadian-made Twin Otters from Nausori Airport four times a week to Kandavu (F$52) and twice a week Lakemba (F$98). More common destinations such as Lambasa (F$73), Levuka (F$33), Nandi (F$63), Savusavu (F$68), and Taveuni (F$87) are served several times daily (all fares one-way).

Air Fiji's **Air Fiji Holiday Pass** allows you to fly from Suva to Kandavu, Levuka, Nandi,

Savusavu, Taveuni and back anytime within 30 days for F$253 (or US$150 if sold abroad). You can also use it to go Savusavu-Taveuni. If you were to fly Nandi-Suva-Kandavu-Suva-Taveuni-Savusavu-Suva-Levuka-Suva-Nandi on regular tickets you'd pay a total of F$496, so the pass does offer savings if you love flying and want to see a lot in one month. Some services are infrequent and heavily booked, so you should reserve all sectors when the ticket is issued and be prepared to show your passport every time you use the pass. This pass is sold at Air Fiji offices in Nandi and Suva, or by travel agents worldwide. If you're sure you want this pass, order it from your travel agent well ahead, as some sectors could be full by the time you reach Fiji.

Sunflower Airlines (Box 9452, Nandi Airport; tel. 723-016, fax 790-085) bases much of its domestic network in Nandi, with daily flights to Lambasa (F$96), Savusavu (F$96), Suva (F$60), and Taveuni (F$116). Kandavu (F$66) and Vatulele (F$62) are served from Nandi four times a week. Sunflower's seven-day round-trip excursion fare between Nandi and Lambasa is F$140. From Suva, Sunflower has flights to Lambasa (twice daily, F$72), Moala (three weekly, F$77), Nandi (twice daily, F$60), Ngau (three weekly, F$42), Koro (three weekly, F$60), and Rotuma (twice weekly, F$250). From Taveuni, they go to Savusavu (daily, F$45) and Lambasa (three weekly, F$45). Flying in their 10-seat Britten Norman Islanders and Twin Otters is sort of fun.

Fiji's third domestic carrier, **Vanua Air** (Box 2523, Government Buildings, Suva; tel. 381-226, fax 386-460), flies from Suva to Lambasa twice daily (F$66), to Lakemba twice weekly (F$98), to Moala twice weekly (F$73), to Rotuma twice weekly (F$250), to Savusavu twice daily (F$67), to Taveuni twice daily (F$87), to Thithia twice weekly (F$95), and to Vanua Mbalavu twice weekly (F$98). Unlike Sunflower Airlines, however, Vanua Air also flies between the different islands themselves: Thithia to/from Vanua Mbalavu twice weekly (F$22), Lakemba to/from Moala twice weekly (F$39), and Savusavu to/from Taveuni twice daily (F$42). When traffic warrants, they schedule flights from Suva to Koro (F$52), Ngau (F$44), and Rambi (F$94). It should be noted that Vanua Air is mainly an air charter operator and their schedules are far more "flexible" than those of the other two carriers mentioned above.

The busy little resort island of Malololailai gets eight flights a day by Sunflower Airlines (F$28) and five by **Island Air** (Office Suite 30, The Concourse, Nandi Airport, Nandi; tel. 722-077). Sunflower's day excursion from Nandi to Malololailai is F$58 roundtrip, lunch included. **Turtle Airways Ltd.** (Private Mail Bag, Nandi Airport, Nandi; tel. 722-988) flies their five Cessna floatplanes three times a day from Nandi to Castaway and Mana Islands (F$90 one-way, F$180 roundtrip).

All flights are during daylight hours. Always reconfirm your return flight immediately upon arrival at an outer island, as the reservation lists are sometimes not sent out from Suva. Failure to do this could mean you will be "bumped" without compensation. Student discounts are for local students only and there are no standby fares. Children aged 12 and under pay 50%, infants two and under carried in arms 10%. All of the local airlines allow 15 kilograms of baggage only (overweight costs one percent of the full one-way fare per kilogram with a F$5 minimum).

Getting Around by Boat

Since most shipping operates out of Suva, passenger services by sea both within Fiji and to neighboring countries are listed in the "Suva" section under "Transportation."

The largest company is **Patterson Brothers Shipping,** set up by Levuka copra planter Reg Patterson and his brother just after WW I. Patterson's four Japanese-built ferries are the barge *Yaumbula,* which shuttles between Natuvu and Taveuni; the 40-meter car ferries *Jubilee* and *Princess Ashika,* usually used on the Mburesala-Natovi-Nambouwalu-Ellington Wharf run; and the large car ferry *Ovalau,* which sails Suva-Ngau-Koro-Savusavu-Taveuni weekly. Delays due to the mechanical failures of Patterson's aging fleet are routine.

Consort Shipping Line runs the large car ferry *Spirit of Free Enterprise* from Suva to Koro, Savusavu, and Taveuni once or twice a week.

In August 1995 **Beachcomber Cruises** (Box 364, Lautoka; tel. 661-500, fax 664-496) launched a direct service from Lautoka to Savusavu and Natovi on the 60-passenger, 18-meter high-speed catamaran *Ndrondrolangi* ("Rainbow"). Turn to the "Lautoka," "Savusavu," and "Suva" sections for details.

Getting Around by Bus

Scheduled bus service is available all over Fiji, and fares are low. If you're from the States you'll be amazed how accessible, inexpensive, and convenient the bus service is. Local people are always happy to supply information about buses and to help you catch one. Right after the Rabuka coups, buses were prohibited on Sunday, but this is no longer the case and most long-distance services now operate daily. Bus stations are usually adjacent to local markets. Unfortunately the times of local buses are not posted at the bus stations, so you always have to ask (the times of express buses *are* posted and it's often possible to pick up express bus timetables at tourist offices). Buses with a signboard in the window reading Via Highway are local "stage" buses that will stop anywhere along their route. Fares average about F$1.50 for each hour of travel.

On Viti Levu, the most important routes are between Suva and Lautoka, the biggest cities. If you follow the southern route via Singatoka you'll be on Queens Road, the faster and smoother of the two. Kings Road via Tavua is longer and can be rough and dusty, but you get to see a little of the interior. Fares from Suva are F$2 to Pacific Harbor, F$4.70 to Singatoka, F$6.80 to Nandi, F$7.10 to Nandi Airport, F$7.80 to Lautoka, and F$9 to Mba. Express buses are 20 cents extra and to reserve a seat on a bus costs another 50 cents (usually unnecessary).

Pacific Transport Ltd. (G.P.O. Box 1266, Suva; tel. 304-366, fax 303-668) has nine buses a day along Queens Road, with expresses leaving Suva for Lautoka at 0645, 0930, 1210, 1500, and 1730 (five hours). Eastbound, the expresses leave Lautoka for Suva at 0630, 0700, 1210, and 1730. An additional Suva-bound express leaves Nandi at 0900. These buses stop at Navua, Pacific Harbor, Singatoka (coffee break), Nandi, and Nandi Airport only. The 1500 bus continues on to Mba. If you want off at a Coral Coast resort or some other smaller place, you must take one of the five local "stage" buses, which take six and a half hours to reach Lautoka via Queens Road.

Sunbeam Transport Ltd. (tel. 382-122) services the northern Kings Road from Suva to Lautoka five times a day, with expresses leaving Suva at 0645, 1330, and 1715 (six hours). From Lautoka, they depart at 0630, 1215, and 1630. A Sunbeam express bus along Kings Road is a comfortable way to see Viti Levu's picturesque back side. These expresses only stop at Nausori, Korovou, Vaikela (Rakiraki), Tavua, and Mba. If you want off anywhere else you must take one of the two local buses, which take nine fun-filled hours to reach Lautoka via Kings Road. Another local Sunbeam bus leaves Suva for Vatukoula via Tavua daily at 0730 (seven hours). **Reliance Transport** (tel. 382-296) also services Kings Road.

K.P. Latchans Ltd. (tel. 477-268) also runs express buses around Viti Levu. Their buses often run about 30 minutes ahead of the scheduled Sunbeam or Pacific Transport services and scoop all their passengers. Latchans buses are newer and more comfortable than Sunbeam's.

There are many other local buses, especially closer to Suva or Lautoka. The a/c tourist expresses such as UTC's "Fiji Express" cost twice as much and are not as much fun as the ordinary expresses, whose big open windows with roll-down canvas covers give you a panoramic view of Viti Levu. Bus service on Vanua Levu and Taveuni is also good. Local buses often show up late, but the long-distance buses are usually right on time. Passenger trucks serving as "carriers" charge set rates to and from interior villages.

Shared "running" taxis also shuttle back and forth between Suva, Nandi, and Lautoka, leaving when full and charging only a little more than the bus. Look for them in the markets around the bus stations. It's possible to hire a complete taxi from Nandi Airport to Suva for about F$50 for the car, with brief stops along the way for photos, resort visits, etc.

Often the drivers of private or company cars and vans try to earn a little money on the side by stopping to offer lifts to persons waiting for buses beside the highway. They ask the same as you'd pay on the bus but are much faster and will probably drop you off exactly where you want to go. If you're hitching, be aware that truck drivers who give you a lift may also expect the equivalent of bus fare; locals pay this without question.

Taxis

Fijian taxis are plentiful and among the cheapest in the South Pacific, usable even by low-budget travelers. This could soon change, however, due to a government decision to force taxi drivers to take cars over 10 years old out of service. There's also a move to force Fiji Indians out of the taxi business by issuing new permits only to ethnic Fijians.

Many taxis have meters but it's usually easier to ask the driver for a flat rate before you get in. If the first price you're quoted is too high you can often bargain (although bargaining is much more accepted by Fiji Indian than by ethnic Fijian drivers). A short ride across city can cost F$1-2, a longer trip into a nearby suburb about F$3. Taxis returning to their stand after a trip will pick up passengers at bus stops and charge the regular bus fare (ask if it's the "returning fare"). Taxis are sometimes hard to find in Suva after dark or on Sunday, though this is less of a problem in Nandi/Lautoka.

Don't tip your driver; tips are neither expected nor necessary. And don't invite your driver for a drink or become overly familiar with him as he may abuse your trust. If you're a woman taking a cab alone in the Nandi area, don't let your driver think there is any "hope" for him, or you could have problems (videos often portray Western women as promiscuous, which leads to mistaken expectations).

Car Rentals

Rental cars are expensive in Fiji, due in part to high import duties on cars, and a 10% government tax is added, so with public transportation as good as it is here, you should think twice before renting a car. By law, third-party public liability insurance is compulsory for rental vehicles and is included in the basic rate, but collision damage waiver (CDW) insurance is about F$16 per day extra. Even with CDW, you're often still responsible for a "non-waivable excess," which can be as high as the first F$1500 in damage to the car! Many cars on the road have no insurance, so you could end up paying even if you're not responsible for the accident.

Your home driver's license is recognized for your first six months in Fiji, and driving is on the left (as in Britain and Japan). Seat belts must be worn in the front seat and the police are empowered to give roadside breath-analyzer tests. The police around Viti Levu occasionally employ hand-held radar. Speed limits are 50 kph in towns, 80 kph on the highway. Pedestrians have the right of way at crosswalks.

Unpaved roads can be very slippery, especially on inclines, and gravel roads throw up stones. Beware of poorly marked speed humps on roads through villages and narrow bridges, and take care with local motorists, who sometimes stop in the middle of the road, pass on blind curves, and drive at high speeds. Driving can be an especially risky business at night. Many of the roads are atrocious (check the spare tire), although Queens Road, which passes the Coral Coast resorts, is now completely paved from Lautoka to Suva, and there isn't a lot of traffic.

If you plan to use a rental car to explore rough country roads in Viti Levu's mountainous interior, think twice before announcing your plans to the agency, as they may suddenly decline your business. The rental contracts all contain clauses stating that the insurance coverage is not valid under such conditions. Some companies offer four-wheel-drive Suzukis just made for mountain roads. Tank up on Saturday, as many gas stations are closed on Sunday. If you run out of gas in a rural area, small village stores sometimes sell fuel from drums.

All of the international car rental chains are represented in Fiji, including Avis, Budget, Hertz, National, and Thrifty. Local companies like Beta Rent-A-Car, Central Rent-A-Car, Dove Rent-A-Car, Khan's Rental Cars, Letz Rent-A-Car, Nandroga Car Hire, Roxy Rentals, Satellite Rentals, Sharmas Rental Cars, Sheik's Rent-A-Car, Skyline Car Rental, and UTC Rent-A-Car are often cheaper, but check around as prices and service vary. The international companies rent only new cars, while the less expensive local companies may offer secondhand vehicles. If in doubt, check the vehicle carefully before driving off. Budget, Central, and National won't rent to persons under age 25, while Avis, Hertz, and Thrifty will, so long as you're over 21.

A dozen companies have offices in the concourse at Nandi Airport and three are also at Nausori Airport. Agencies with town offices in Suva include Avis on Scott Street (tel. 313-833); Budget, 123 Forster Rd., Walu Bay (tel. 315-899); Central, 293 Victoria Parade (tel. 311-

908); Dove, Harifam Center, Greig Street (tel. 311-755); and Hertz, 56 Grantham Rd., Raiwannga (tel. 370-518). In Lautoka you'll find Budget on Marine Drive (tel. 666-166) and Central at 73 Vitongo Parade (tel. 664-511). Avis and Thrifty also have desks in many resort hotels on Viti Levu. On Vanua Levu, Avis, Budget, and Thrifty are at Savusavu, and Budget is also at Lambasa.

Both unlimited-kilometer and per-kilometer rates are available. **Thrifty Car Rental** (tel. 722-755) offers good unlimited-kilometer prices from F$85 daily, F$510 weekly), which include CDW (F$600 nonwaivable) and tax, but there's a 150-km limit on one-day rentals. Prices at Avis start at F$88 a day (plus F$16.50 CDW), at Hertz F$85 (plus F$17 CDW plus 10% tax). **Sharmas Rental Cars** (tel. 701-055) at Nandi Airport and near the ANZ Bank in Nandi town advertises unlimited-kilometer rates of F$222 a week or F$700 a month (10% tax and F$10 a day insurance extra). On a per-kilometer basis, rates at Sharmas begin at F$14 a day, plus 14 cents per kilometer, plus F$10 CDW, plus tax. **Khan's Rental Cars** (tel. 701-009) in Nandi is also good at F$15 daily plus 17 cents per km and F$10 CDW (F$1500 nonwaivable).

On a per-kilometer basis, you'll only want to use the car in the local area, as a drive around Viti Levu is 486 km. If you want the cheapest economy subcompact, reserve ahead. Beware of companies like Central, which list extremely low prices in their brochure, only mentioning in very small type at the bottom that these are the "off-season" rates (period not specified). Others, such as Budget and National, also advertise low prices with the qualification in tiny type below that these apply only to rentals of three days or more. Most companies charge a F$30 delivery fee if you don't return the vehicle to the office where you rented it.

Yacht Tours

Moorings Rainbow Yacht Charters offers bareboat yacht charters among the Mamanutha and Yasawa islands from their base at Musket Cove Resort on Malololailai Island in the Mamanutha Group. Prices begin at F$510 a day for a Rainbow 350 yacht and increase to F$1015 for a Beneteau 51. Due to the risks involved in navigating Fiji's poorly marked reefs, all charter boats are required by law to carry a Fijian guide (included in the basic charter price). Extras include F$156 daily for an optional skipper, F$94 daily for an optional cook, F$47 pp a day for provisioning, F$28 daily security insurance, and F$78-125 for a starter kit. Alcohol is not included. As will be seen, chartering isn't for the budget-minded traveler, though small groups planning on staying at a luxury resort may find prices comparable and the experience more rewarding. For more information contact The Moorings (4th Floor, 19345 U.S. 19 North, Clearwater, FL 34624, U.S.A.; tel. 800/535-7289); Moorings Rainbow Yacht Charters (Box 8327, Symonds St., Auckland, New Zealand; tel. 64-9/377-4840, fax 64-9/377-4820); or Adventure Holidays (Postfach 920113, 90266 Nürnberg, Germany; fax 49-911/979-9588).

Perhaps the finest charter yacht available at Fiji is the 14-meter ketch *Seax of Legra,* based at Taveuni (Box 89, Waiyevo, Taveuni; tel./fax 679/880-141). The charge is F$930 daily for two persons, F$985 for three, F$1035 for four, all-inclusive. Warwick and Dianne Bain who live next to Lisi's Campground on Taveuni will be your distinguished hosts on an unforgettable cruise. Larger groups could consider the 27-meter ketch *Tau* at the Raffles Tradewinds Hotel, Suva, which charges F$13,600 a week for up to six persons, meals included. For full information on these and other boats available in Fiji waters, write the **Fiji Yacht Charter Association** (Box 3084, Lami, Fiji Islands; tel. 361-256, fax 880-141).

Mini-Cruise Ships
Blue Lagoon Cruises Ltd. (Box 130, Lautoka; tel. 661-622, fax 664-098) has been offering upmarket minicruises from Lautoka to the Yasawa Islands since its founding in 1950 by Captain Trevor Withers. The three-night "original" trips (from F$605) leave daily, while the six-night "club" cruise (from F$1350) is weekly. Prices are per person, double or triple occupancy, and include meals (excluding alcohol), entertainment, and shore excursions. On the three-night cruises they use older three-deck, 40-passenger vessels, while larger four-deck, 60-passenger mini-cruise ships are used on the six-night (and some of the three-night) voyages. In July 1996 a new 72-passenger, US$8-million luxury cruiser is

to begin operating trips to more remote island groups. The meals are often beach barbecue affairs, with Fijian dancing. You'll have plenty of opportunities to snorkel in the calm, crystal-clear waters (bring your own gear). Though expensive, these trips have a good reputation. There are daily departures but reservations are essential, as they're usually booked solid months ahead—they're that popular.

Captain Cook Cruises (Box 23, Nandi; tel. 701-823, fax 702-045), on Narewa Road near the bridge into Nandi town, also offers luxury three-day cruises to the southern Yasawa Islands aboard the 38-meter MV *Duchess of the Isles,* departing Nandi Tuesday and Friday. The 31 double-occupancy staterooms cost F$695 pp on the upper deck (with TV), or F$590 pp on the lower deck (without TV).

In addition, Captain Cook operates three-day cruises to the southern Yasawas on the square-rigged brigantine *Ra Marama*. These depart Nandi every Monday morning and cost F$378 pp. You sleep in large tents at night, the food is good with lots of fresh vegetables and salads, and the staff friendly and well organized. The snorkeling is extraordinary, and scuba diving off Waya Island is possible at F$130 extra for three tanks. Your biggest disappointment will probably be that they have the diesel engine on all the time, and they don't bother trying to use the sails (logical—they haven't got a clue how to sail). Still, the *Na Marama* is a fine vessel built of teak planks at Singapore in 1957 for a former governor-general of Fiji. These trips can be booked through most travel agents; readers who've gone report having a great time.

AIRPORTS

Nandi International Airport
Nandi Airport (NAN) is between Lautoka and Nandi, 22 km south of the former and eight km north of the latter. There are frequent buses to these towns until around 2200. To catch a bus to Nandi (45 cents), cross the highway; buses to Lautoka (90 cents) stop on the airport side of the road. A few express buses drop passengers right outside the international departures hall. A taxi from the airport should be F$6 to downtown Nandi, F$20 to Lautoka.

Most hotels around Nandi have their rates listed on a board inside the customs area, so peruse the list while you're waiting for your baggage. The Fiji Visitors Bureau office (fax 720-141) is to the left as you come out of customs. They open for all international arrivals and can advise you on accommodations. Pick up brochures, hotel lists, and the free tourist magazines.

There's a 24-hour ANZ Bank (F$2 commission) in the commercial arcade near the visitors bureau and another bank in the departure lounge. Many travel agencies, car rental companies, and airline offices are also located in the arrivals arcade. The rent-a-car companies you'll find here are Avis, Budget, Central, Hertz, Khan's, Letz, National, Roxy, Sharmas, and Thrifty.

The post office is across the road from the terminal (ask). The luggage storage service near the snack bar in the departure terminal charges F$1 per bag per day. Most hotels around Nandi will also store luggage. The airport never closes. NAN's 24-hour flight arrival and departure information number is 722-076.

Duty-free shops are found in both the departure lounge and the arrivals area near the baggage pickup. Prices in the duty-free shop for arriving passengers are higher than those in the much larger shop in the departure lounge. You can use leftover Fijian currency to stock up on cheap film and cigarettes just before you leave (film prices here are the lowest in the South Pacific).

A departure tax of F$20 is payable on all international flights, but transit passengers connecting within 12 hours and children under the age of 16 are exempt (no airport tax on domestic flights). Have a look at the museum exhibits near the departures gates upstairs as you're waiting for your flight. There's zero tolerance for drugs in Fiji and a three-dog sniffer unit checks all baggage passing through NAN.

Nausori Airport

Nausori Airport (SUV) is on the plain of the Rewa River delta, 23 km northeast of downtown Suva. After Hurricane Kina in January 1993 the whole terminal was flooded by Rewa water for several days. There's no special airport bus and a taxi direct to/from Suva will run about F$17. You can save money by taking a taxi from the airport only as far as Nausori (four km, F$4), then a local bus to Suva from there (19 km, 80 cents, with services daily every 10 minutes until 2100). Airport-bound, catch a local bus from Suva to Nausori, then a taxi to the airport (only F$2 in this direction). It's also possible to catch a local bus to Nausori from the highway opposite the airport about every 15 minutes (35 cents).

Avis, Budget, and Hertz all have car rental offices in the terminal, and a lunch counter provides light snacks. You're not allowed to sleep overnight at this airport. The departure tax is F$20 on all international flights, but no tax is levied on domestic flights. The inevitable duty-free shop is on the premises.

NANDI AND VICINITY

NANDI

Nandi (population 16,000), on the dry side of Fiji's largest island, offers a multitude of places to stay for incoming visitors landing at Nandi International Airport. A small airstrip existed at Nandi even before WW II, and after Pearl Harbor the Royal New Zealand Air Force began converting it into a fighter strip. Before long the U.S. military was there, building a major air base with paved runways for bombers and transport aircraft serving Australia and New Zealand. In the early 1960s, Nandi Airport was expanded to accommodate jet aircraft, and today the largest jumbo jets can land here. This activity has made Nandi what it is today.

All around Nandi are cane fields worked by the predominantly Indian population. There aren't many sandy, palm-fringed beaches on the western side of Viti Levu—for that you have to go to the nearby Mamanutha Group where a string of sun-drenched "Robinson Crusoe" resorts soak up vacationers in search of a place to relax. The long gray mainland beaches near Nandi face shallow murky waters devoid of snorkeling possibilities but fine for windsurfing and water-skiing. Fiji's tropical rainforests are on the other side of Viti Levu.

Nandi town has a kilometer of concrete duty-free tourist shops with high-pressure sales staffs peddling mass-produced souvenirs. Yet there's also a surprisingly colorful market (best on Saturday morning). It's a rather touristy town, so if you're not that exhausted after your transpacific flight you'd do better to head for Lautoka (see the separate Lautoka section later in this chapter). All of the hotels around Nandi tend to experience quite a bit of aircraft/traffic/disco noise, while those at Lautoka are out of range.

Sights

Nandi's only substantial sight is the **Sri Siva Subramaniya Swami Temple** at the south entrance to town, erected by local Hindus in 1994 after the lease on their former temple property expired. This colorful South Indian-style temple, built by craftspeople flown in from India itself, is the largest and finest of its kind in the South Pacific.

Sports and Recreation

Aqua-Trek (Box 10215, Nandi Airport; tel. 702-413, fax 702-412), located at 465 Queens Rd., opposite the Mobil station in Nandi town, arranges scuba diving at Mana Island and elsewhere. **Tropical Divers** (Box 9063, Nandi; tel. 750-777) in the beach hut at the Sheraton offers overpriced scuba diving at F$95 one tank, F$135 two tanks, or F$585 for a PADI certification course.

Much less expensive diving is offered by **Inner Space Adventures** (Box 9535, Nandi Airport; tel./fax 723-883), between the Horizon and Travellers beach resorts at Wailoaloa Beach. They go out daily at 0900, charging F$44/77/99 for one/two/three tanks, equipment and pickup anywhere around Nandi included. Snorkelers are welcome to tag along at F$25 pp, gear included. The four-day open-water PADI certification course costs F$299.

The **Roaring Thunder Company** (Box 545, Nandi; tel. 780-029, fax 790-094) offers white-water rubber rafting on the Mba River (F$70). The trips are designed for those aged 15-45, although physically fit older persons can join by signing a liability disclaimer. Bookings can be made at Cardo's Restaurant in Nandi town, which is owned by the same company. The degree of excitement will depend on how much rain they've been getting in the mountains, and during droughts the ride will be rather placid. Even then, it's a very scenic trip.

Thirty-minute jet boat rides around the mouth of the Nandi River are offered by **Shotover Jet** (Box 1932, Nandi; tel. 750-400, fax 750-666) about every half hour from the Ndenarau Island Marina (adults F$55, children under 16 years F$24). It's fairly certain the birds and fish of this mangrove area are less thrilled by these energy-guzzling, high-impact craft than the tourists seated therein. The raft trips mentioned above are better value and more environmentally friendly.

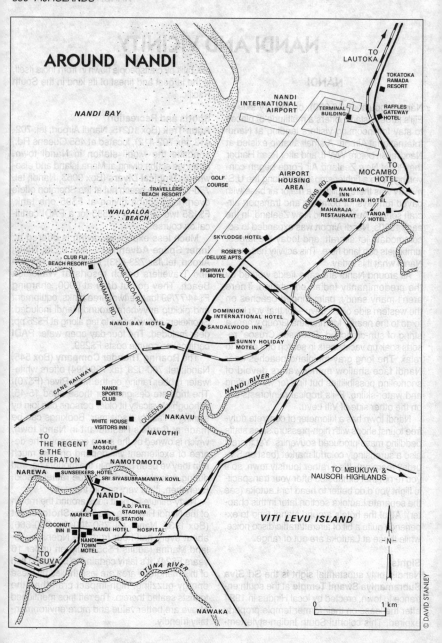

AROUND NANDI

TO LAUTOKA

NANDI BAY

NANDI INTERNATIONAL AIRPORT

TERMINAL BUILDING

TOKATOKA RAMADA RESORT

RAFFLES GATEWAY HOTEL

GOLF COURSE

TRAVELLERS BEACH RESORT

WAILOALOA BEACH

CLUB FIJI BEACH RESORT

ENANAMU RD.

WAILOALOA RD.

AIRPORT HOUSING AREA

QUEENS RD.

TO MOCAMBO HOTEL

NAMAKA INN MELANESIAN HOTEL

MAHARAJA RESTAURANT

SKYLODGE HOTEL

ROSIE'S DELUXE APTS.

HIGHWAY MOTEL

NAMAKA

TANOA HOTEL

NANDI BAY MOTEL

DOMINION INTERNATIONAL HOTEL

SANDALWOOD INN

SUNNY HOLIDAY MOTEL

NANDI RIVER

CANE RAILWAY

NANDI SPORTS CLUB

QUEEN'S RD.

NAKAVU

WHITE HOUSE VISITORS INN

NAVOTHI

JAM-E MOSQUE

NAMOTOMOTO

TO THE REGENT & THE SHERATON

NAREWA

SUNSEEKERS HOTEL

SRI SIVASUBRAMANIYA KOVIL

NANDI

A.D. PATEL STADIUM

MARKET

BUS STATION

COCONUT INN II

NANDI HOTEL

HOSPITAL

NANDI TOWN MOTEL

TO SUVA

OTUNA RIVER

TO MBUKUYA & NAUSORI HIGHLANDS

VITI LEVU ISLAND

NAWAKA

0   1 km

-N-

© DAVID STANLEY

The 18-hole, par-71 **Nandi Airport Golf Club** (Box 9015, Nandi; tel. 722-148), between the airport runways and the sea at Wailoaloa Beach, is said to be the toughest course in Fiji. Green fees are F$13.50 plus F$12 for a half set of clubs. There's a bar and pool table in the clubhouse.

Other golf courses are available at the Mocambo and Sheraton hotels. The 18-hole, par-72 course at the Japanese-owned **Ndenarau Golf & Racquet Club** (Box 9081, Nandi Airport; tel. 750-477, fax 750-484) opposite the Sheraton was designed by Eiichi Motohashi. The course features bunkers shaped like a marlin, crab, starfish, and octopus, and water shots across all four par-three holes (the average golfer loses four balls per round). Green fees are F$77 and cart hire is mandatory. Ask about their special "nine, wine & dine" deal on Friday and Saturday afternoons: tee time for the nine holes is at 1500, followed by the barbecue and wine at 1830 (F$35). Ten tennis courts are available. Higher prices may apply for those not staying at the Sheraton or Regent, so call ahead for information.

During the February-to-November sports season, see rugby or soccer on Saturday afternoon at the A.D. Patel Stadium, near the bus station.

Budget Accommodations in Town

Most of the hotels offer free transport from the airport, which is lucky because there aren't any budget places within walking distance of the airport itself. As you leave customs you'll be besieged by a group of men representing the hotels. If you know which one you want, call out the name; if a driver from that hotel is there, you'll get a free ride. If not, the Fiji Visitors Bureau (tel. 722-433, fax 720-141) to the left will help you telephone them for a small fee. Don't be put off by the hotel drivers at the airport, but do question them about the rates and facilities before you let them drive you to their place.

There are three choices in the downtown area, two with confusingly similar names but under separate managements. The seedy **Nandi Town Motel** (Box 1326, Nandi; tel. 700-600, fax 701-541), occupying the top floor of an office building opposite the BP service station in the center of Nandi, is a bit of a dive and the only attraction here is price: F$20/22 single/double with fan, F$23/28 with a/c, both with private bath. The five-bed dormitory is just F$6 pp and basic rooms with shared bath are F$11/15. Breakfast is supposed to be included in all rates but don't be surprised if they try to charge extra. Definitely ask to see the room before accepting, expect dirty sheets, and, if you're a woman, don't tolerate any nonsense from the male motel staff. The adjacent Rupeni's Nightclub sends out a steady disco beat well into the morning. The travel agency below the motel arranges transport to Nananu-i-Ra Island for F$26 pp.

Around the corner on Koroivolu Street is the two-story, 36-room **Nandi Hotel** (Box 91, Nandi; tel. 700-000, fax 700-280). Rooms with private bath here begin at F$22/28 single/double with fan, F$33/39 with a/c, or F$11 pp in an eight-bed dorm. The neat courtyard with a swimming pool out back makes this a pleasant, convenient place to stay. Nice people too. Some rooms are also subjected to nightclub noise though, so ask for a room in the block farthest away from Rupeni's.

The two-story **Coconut Inn II** (Box 2756, Nandi; tel. 701-011, fax 701-169) is down the side street opposite the Nandi Handicraft Market, a block from the Nandi Hotel and the Nandi Town Motel. The 22 a/c rooms with private bath upstairs begin at F$30/35 single/double, and downstairs is a F$10 dorm. Until recently this was the dodgy Fong Hing Hotel, but things have changed and prostitutes are no longer admitted. The restaurant downstairs still serves good Chinese food, however.

On Narewa Road at the north edge of Nandi town is **Sunseekers Hotel** (Box 100, Nandi; tel. 700-400, fax 702-047). The 20 rooms here are F$25 single or double with fan, F$35 single or double with a/c, F$6 dorm (extra charge if you want a sheet, F$1 surcharge for one night, airport transfers F$3). There's a tiny pool (dry) out back. Despite the prominent Youth Hostel signs outside, there's no YHA discount. Unfortunately this poorly managed hotel has fallen on hard times and can no longer be recommended.

Much better is the two-story **White House Visitors Inn** (Box 2150, Nandi; tel./fax 700-022), at 40 Kennedy Ave., up Ray Prasad Road just off Queens Road, a 10-minute walk north of central Nandi. The 12 fan-equipped rooms are F$20 double with shared bath, F$25/30 single/

double with private bath, or F$8 pp in the dorm. Rooms with a/c cost F$5 extra. The beds are comfortable, and a weight-watchers' toast-and-coffee breakfast is included in the price. You can cook your own meals in the communal kitchen, and there's a grocery store across the street. This new hotel is a fairly peaceful place to stay with a small swimming pool, video lounge, and free airport pickup. Baggage storage is F$1 per day. Though you'll hear a bit of traffic and animal noise, you won't be bothered by disco music. It's very popular and might be full.

Half a block up Kennedy Avenue from the White House is the three-story **Kennedy Hotel** (Box 9045, Nandi Airport; tel. 702-360, fax 702-218), the highest-priced hotel in this category. At F$44/50 single/double with bath, tax included, the 16 a/c rooms are a reasonable value. Deluxe two-bedroom apartments with cooking facilities are F$99. They've converted a few less appealing rooms near the reception area into three-bed dorms at F$10 pp. All rooms at the Kennedy have a/c, TV, fridge, and coffee-making facilities. Another big plus are the spacious gardenlike grounds with a large swimming pool, and there's a restaurant/bar on the premises.

Budget Airport Hotels

The listings below are arranged from the airport into town. The low-budget hotel closest to the terminal is the **Kon Tiki Private Hotel** (tel. 722-836), set in cane fields a 15-minute walk in from the main highway, past the Mocambo Hotel. The 16 rooms go for F$17/22 single/double with private bath and fan, F$7 pp dormitory. Some hard drinking goes on at the bar, so don't accept a room near it. Kon Tiki is all by itself down a side road, so you're dependent on the hotel restaurant for food. Considering the many other budget accommodations around Nandi, Kon Tiki doesn't have much going for it. They do arrange daily transfers to Nananu-i-Ra Island at F$22 each way.

The **Melanesian Hotel** (Box 9242, Nandi Airport; tel. 722-438, fax 720-425) has 16 rooms beginning at F$26/31 single/double, F$9 extra for a/c. A mixed five-bed dorm (F$8 pp) is also available. The rooms are okay and the Melanesian looks fine, but it's got a reputation for occasional shenanigans suggested by the name of the hotel restaurant, the "Jolly Jumpbuck!"

More basic is the **Highway Motel** (Box 9236, Nandi; tel. 723-761), a single-story block with rooms at F$20/25 single/double, all with private facilities. Rooms with a/c are F$5 more. The Highway offers shared cooking facilities for F$3 extra and luggage storage. You can bargain for a discount when things are slow, but it's rather basic and unpleasant.

A newer place to stay is the **Valentino Hotel** (Box 9609, Nandi Airport; tel. 720-640), behind Ed's Cocktail Bar, with nine fan-cooled rooms with bath at F$20/25 single/double. Their restaurant specializes in seafood and Italian food.

The two-story **Sandalwood Inn** (John and Ana Birch, Box 9454, Nandi Airport; tel. 722-044, fax 790-103), on Ragg Street beside the Dominion International Hotel, is F$22/28/34 single/double/triple for one of the five rooms with shared bath in the old wing, or F$29/35 single/double for one of the 20 rooms with fridge and private bath in the new wing (a/c rooms F$42/48). The cheaper rooms may all be full and the a/c rooms aren't worth the price. The atmosphere is pleasant and the layout attractive with pool, bar, and a restaurant serving authentic Fijian dishes! The food and drinks are a little overpriced.

Close by and less expensive is the 14-room **Sunny Holiday Motel** (Box 1326, Nandi Airport; tel. 722-158, fax 701-541), located at 67 Northern Press Rd. behind Hamacho Japanese Restaurant. It's F$11/16 single/double with shared bath, F$20/22 with private bath, or F$5 dorm (five beds). Self-contained apartments with cooking facilities are F$28/33. Show your Youth Hostel card for a 10% discount. Inveterate campers may like to know that this is about the only place around Nandi where you're allowed to unroll your tent (F$3 pp). There's a pool table, TV room, bar, and luggage storage. It's all a little run-down, but friendly, uncrowded, and fine for those on the lowest of budgets. They book the daily shuttle to Nananu-i-Ra Island (F$26 one-way).

A few hundred meters down Wailoaloa Beach Road off the main highway, in the opposite direction from the Sunny Holiday, is the **Nandi Bay Motel** (Private Mail Bag, Nandi; tel. 723-599, fax 720-092), a two-story concrete edifice enclosing a small swimming pool. The 25 rooms are F$21/28 single/double with fan, F$7 extra for private bath, F$15 extra for private bath and a/c. An apartment with cooking facilities is F$49. There's also a F$8 dorm with a 10% discount on dormitory beds to YHA cardholders. Washing machines are available, plus a congenial bar, inexpensive restaurant, and luggage room. This uninteresting place is always full of bored tourists reading Lonely Planet as they hang around waiting for their flights out of Fiji. The airport flight path passes right above Nandi Bay and the roar of jets on the adjacent runway can be jarring. Don't agree to take any scuba lessons in the motel swimming pool unless you're prepared for a steady stream of wisecracks from the jerks lounging by the pool. We've heard that the scuba instruction arranged by this hotel isn't up to scratch.

Budget Beach Hotels

There are four inexpensive places to stay on Wailoaloa Beach, also known as Newtown Beach, on the opposite side of the airport runway from the main highway. The first three places are adjacent to the seaplane base and golf club, a three-km hike from the Nandi Bay Motel, so ask for their free shuttle buses at the airport or take a taxi (F$6). The Wailoaloa Newtown bus from Nandi market also passes nearby three times a day. These places are probably your best bet on the weekend, and sporting types can play a round of golf on the public course or go jogging along the beach (the swimming in the knee-deep water isn't great). The main base of Inner Space Adventures is here, with scuba diving and horseback riding on offer.

The cheapest of the lot is the **Horizon Beach Resort** (Box 1401, Nandi; tel. 722-832, fax 720-662), a large wooden two-story house just across a field from the beach. The 14 rooms with shared bath are F$18/26 single/double with fan, F$29/34 with a/c. Horizon's 10-bed dormitory is F$5 pp. No cooking facilities are provided but there's a restaurant/bar.

A hundred meters inland from the Horizon is the two-story **Newtown Beach Motel** (Box 787, Nandi; tel. 723-332, fax 720-087). The seven clean rooms with fan are F$19/25/30 single/double/triple. There's no cooking, but a huge dinner is offered for F$7.

A hundred meters along the beach from the Horizon is **Travellers Beach Resort** (Box 700,

Nandi; tel. 723-322, fax 720-026). The 20 rooms with private bath are F$25/30 single/double with fan, F$5 extra for a/c; dorm is F$10 pp. The restaurant/bar and pool make this a self-contained resort. It's good value and often full, so call ahead.

Also on Wailoaloa Beach, about one km southwest of the three places mentioned above, is **Club Fiji Beach Resort** (Box 9619, Nandi Airport; tel. 702-189, fax 720-350). The 22 attractive thatched bungalows with veranda, private bath, solar hot water, and fridge cost F$55 double (garden) or F$65 (beachfront). One bungalow has been converted into a four-bunk, eight-person dormitory at F$11 pp. Club Fiji's staff does its best to keep the accommodations and grounds spotless. The units have only tea- and coffee-making facilities (no cooking), but the restaurant serves authentic Fijian food and a variety of dishes, which are good when the cook resists the urge to put sugar in everything. The continental breakfast is F$5. Special evening events include the *lovo* on Wednesday, the *meke* and Italian buffet on Saturday, and the beach barbecue on Sunday night. Horseback riding (F$10), sailing, water-skiing (F$15), and windsurfing (free) are also available. At low tide the beach resembles a tidal flat, but there's a small clean swimming pool, and the location is lovely—the equivalent of the Sheraton at a fifth the price and without the stuffy upmarket atmosphere. Club Fiji is highly recommended as your best choice in this price range. Call ahead as they're often full and book well ahead if you're sure it's where you want to stay.

Medium-Priced Airport Hotels

Back at the airport, let's work our way into Nandi again looking at the medium-priced properties. The two-story, colonial-style **Raffles Gateway Hotel** (Box 9891, Nandi Airport; tel. 722-444, fax 720-620) is just across the highway from the terminal, within easy walking distance. Its 93 a/c rooms begin at F$90/100/110 single/double/triple. Happy hour in the Flight Deck Bar is 1800-1900 (half-price drinks)—worth checking out if you're stuck at the airport waiting for a flight.

The **Tokatoka Resort Hotel** (Box 9305, Nandi Airport; tel. 790-222, fax 790-400), right next to the Raffles Gateway, caters to families by offering 70 villas with cooking facilities and video for F$127 double and up. A small supermarket and a large swimming pool with water slide are on the premises.

Four km from the airport is the **Skylodge Hotel** (Box 9222, Nandi Airport; tel. 722-200, fax 720-212), which was constructed in the early 1960s as Nandi Airport was being expanded to take jet aircraft. Airline crews on layovers originally stayed here, and business travelers still make up 50% of the clientele. The 53 a/c units begin at F$100 single or double; children under 16 are free, provided the bed configurations aren't changed. It's better to pay F$25 more and get a room with cooking facilities in one of the four-unit clusters well-spaced among the greenery, rather than a smaller room in the main building or near the busy highway. The six family units cost F$500 a week. If you're catching a flight in the middle of the night there's a half-price "day use" rate valid until 2300. Pitch-and-putt golf, half-size tennis facilities, and a swimming pool are on the premises. Airport transfers are free.

Rosie's Serviced Apartments (Box 9268, Nandi Airport; tel. 722-755, fax 722-607) near Ed's Cocktail Bar offers studio apartments accommodating four at F$55, one-bedrooms for up to five at F$88, and two-bedrooms for up to seven at F$99. All eight units have cooking facilities and private balcony. Rosie The Travel Service at the airport arranges special car/apartment packages here (minimum stay four nights). Rosie's is fine for families and small groups looking for comfortable accommodations near the airport for a night or two, but don't spend your whole holiday in this busy commercial area.

The **Dominion International Hotel** (Box 9178, Nandi Airport; tel. 722-255, fax 720-187), an appealing three-story building facing a pool, is halfway between the airport and town. The Dominion was built in 1973, but they've done their best to keep the place up. The 85 a/c rooms with bright bedspreads and curtains are good value at F$89/94/99 single/double/triple. Their 50% "day rate" allows you to keep your room until 1800 only. There's a Rosie The Travel Service desk in this hotel and a barber shop/beauty salon.

The two-story **New Westgate Hotel** (Box 10097, Nandi Airport; tel. 720-044, fax 720-071), next to the Dominion International, is affiliated with the Best Western chain. The 62 rooms begin at F$65 single or double with fan, or F$85/95 single/double with a/c. A swimming pool, restaurant, business center, and "adult" disco are on the premises.

The **Metro Inn** (Box 9043, Nandi Airport; tel. 790-088, fax 720-522), between the New Westgate Hotel and Hamacho Japanese Restaurant, consists of two-story blocks surrounding a swimming pool with a nice grassy area on which to sunbathe. The 60 a/c rooms with fridge are F$50/55 single/double. Cooking facilities are not provided, but there's a restaurant/bar on the premises. It's a good medium-priced choice if you only need somewhere for one night.

Upmarket Airport Hotels

Three upmarket places off Votualevu Road, a 15-minute walk inland from the airport (take a taxi), cater mostly to people on brief prepaid stopovers in Fiji. The first is **Tanoa Apartments** (Box 9203, Nandi Airport; tel. 721-144, fax 721-193), on a hilltop overlooking the surrounding countryside, two km from the airport. The 23 self-catering apartments begin at F$140 (weekly and monthly rates available).

A few hundred meters more inland from Tanoa Apartments is the Malaysian-owned **Fiji Mocambo Hotel** (Box 9195, Nandi Airport; tel. 722-000, fax 720-324), a sprawling two-story hotel that is probably the best in its category. The 128 a/c rooms with patio or balcony begin at F$155 single or double. Secretarial services can be arranged for businesspeople, and there's a par-27, nine-hole executive golf course on the adjacent slope (green fees F$10, clubs F$8). Their much-touted restaurant is said to be overrated, so ask another guest about it before sitting down to a pricey meal. Alternatively, stick to the salads. Lots of in-house entertainment is laid on, including *mekes* four nights a week. A live band plays in the Vale ni Marau Lounge Thursday, Friday, and Saturday 2100-0100.

Across the street from the Mocambo is the two-story **Tanoa International Hotel** (Box 9203, Nandi Airport; tel. 720-277, fax 720-191), formerly the Nandi Travelodge Hotel and now owned by local businessman Yanktesh Permal Reddy. The 114 a/c rooms are F$160 single or double, F$190 suite, and children under 16 may stay free. They also have a half-price day-use rate, which gives you a room from noon until midnight if you're leaving in the middle of the night (airport transfers free), and the coffee shop here is open 24 hours a day. A swimming pool, fitness center, and floodlit tennis courts are on the premises.

Grande Luxe Beach Hotels

Nandi's two big transnational hotels, The Regent and the Sheraton, are on Ndenarau Beach opposite Yakuilau Island, seven km west of the bridge on the north side of Nandi town and a 15-minute drive from the airport. These are Nandi's only upmarket hotels right on the beach, though the gray sands here can't compare with those of the Mamanutha Islands. The murky waters lapping Sheraton and Regent shores are okay for swimming, and two pontoons are anchored in deeper water, but there'd be no point in snorkeling here. Windsurfing, water-skiing, and sailboating are more practicable activities.

Sidestepping the Waikiki syndrome, neither hotel is taller than the surrounding palms, though the manicured affluence has a dull Hawaiian neighbor-island feel. The Regent opened in 1975 and its vegetation is lush and dense compared to that surrounding the newer Sheraton. In mid-1988 a Japanese company bought control of both The Regent and the Sheraton, and in 1993 a F$15-million championship golf course opened on the site of a former mangrove swamp adjacent to the Sheraton. Two-thirds of the hotel staffs and all of the taxi drivers based here belong to the landowning clan.

Almost all the tourists staying at these places are on a package tour and they pay only a fraction of the rack rates quoted below. Both hotels are rather isolated, and restaurant-hopping possibilities are restricted to the pricey hotel restaurants, so you should take the meal package if you intend to spend most of your time here. Also bring insect repellent unless you yourself want to be on the menu!

The Regent of Fiji (Box 9081, Nandi Airport; tel. 750-000, fax 750-259) is arguably Fiji's finest (and most pretentious) hotel. The 285 spacious a/c rooms in this sprawling series of two-story clusters between the golf course and the beach begin at F$253 single or double. Facilities include an impressive lobby with shops to one side, a thatched pool bar you can swim right up to, and 10 floodlit tennis courts. Yachties anchored offshore are not welcome at this hotel.

The Regent's neighbor, the **Sheraton-Fiji Resort** (Box 9761, Nandi Airport; tel. 750-777, fax 750-818), has 300 a/c rooms that begin at F$295 single or double including a buffet breakfast. This $60-million two-story hotel complex opened in 1987, complete with a 16-shop arcade and an 800-seat ballroom.

There's no bus service to either the Sheraton or The Regent. A taxi to/from Nandi town should be around F$6, though cabs parked in front of the hotels may expect much more. Avis Rent A Car has a desk in each of the hotels. If your travel agent didn't book you into one of these enclaves, don't bother taking the trouble to visit.

Food

Several excellent places to eat are opposite the Mobil service station on Queens Road at the north end of Nandi town. For Cantonese and European food try the upstairs dining room at **Poon's Restaurant** (tel. 700-896; closed Sunday), which is recommended for its filling meals at reasonable prices, pleasant atmosphere, and friendly service. **Mama's Pizza Inn** (tel. 700-221), just up the road from Poon's, serves pizzas big enough for two or three people for F$8-20. **Cardo's Chargrill Restaurant** (tel. 702-704), a few doors away from Mama's, specializes in steaks costing anywhere from F$13-20 depending on size and type. It's popular among the local expat community who drop in around 1800 for happy hour drinks.

The new **Gelato Restaurant,** next to the ANZ Bank on the main street, offers a filling six-course Indian lunch 1000-1400 for F$3.50. Only pure vegetarian food is served here, and you'll like the clean, attractive decor. It's a bit cheaper than the famous Hari Krishna Vegetarian Restaurant in Suva, and the ice cream is excellent.

The **Curry Restaurant** (closed Sunday) on Clay Street has a wide range of inexpensive Indian dishes (though they close at 1800). **Bombay Lodge** on Queens Road near the Nandi

Town Motel looks basic but they serve good curries at the right price.

The **Kababish Restaurant** (tel. 723-430), next to the Shell service station opposite the Dominion International Hotel, features upmarket Indian and Pakistani cuisine. They claim to offer authentic India Indian dishes different from Fiji Indian food, and you pay tourist-level prices to try it.

The **Maharaja Restaurant** (tel. 722-962; closed Sunday), out near the Skylodge Hotel is popular with flight crews who come for the good Indian curries. It's expensive but good. The **Namaka Inn** (tel. 722-276), near the Melanesian Hotel a bit closer to the airport, serves large portions of quality food.

Entertainment

There are three movie houses in Nandi: Westend Twin Cinema on Ashram Road, Karishma Cinema next to the Coconut Inn on Vunavau Street, and Novelty Cinema (formerly Lotus Cinema), upstairs from a mall next to the Nandi Town Council, not far from the post office. All show an eclectic mix of Hollywood and Indian films.

Rupeni's Night Club, formerly the Bamboo Palace, next to the Nandi Hotel, has a live band 2100-0100 on Thursday, Friday, and Saturday nights. Locals call it "the zoo."

The **Nandi Farmers Club** (tel. 700-415), just up Ashram Road from the Mobil station, is a good local drinking place.

Entertainment possibilities out on the hotel strip toward the airport include **Ed's Cocktail Bar** (tel. 720-373), a little north of the Dominion International Hotel, and **Jessica's Disco** in the New Westgate Hotel (tel. 720-044; Thursday, Friday, and Saturday 2100-0100).

Cultural Shows for Visitors: The **Sheraton** (tel. 750-777) has a free *meke* Tuesday and Saturday at 2100. Thursday at 1900 Fijian firewalking comes with the *meke* and a F$11 fee is charged. The *meke* and *mangiti* (feast) at **The Regent** (tel. 750-000) happen Monday and Friday at 1830 (F$44).

At the **Fiji Mocambo Hotel** (tel. 722-828) there's Fijian firewalking Saturday at 1830 (F$13.50), followed by a *lovo* feast and *meke* (F$27.50). The **Dominion International Hotel** (tel. 722-255) stages a *meke* on Thursday night

and Polynesian dancing on Saturday night when the house is full (call to ask).

Shopping

The **Nandi Handicraft Market** opposite the Nandi Hotel just off Queens Road is worth a look. Before going there, have a look around **Jack's Handicrafts** (tel. 700-744) on the main street to get an idea of what is available and how much things cost. Beware the friendly handshake in Nandi, for you may find yourself buying something you neither care for nor desire.

If you have an interest in world literature, you can buy classical works of Indian literature and books on yoga at very reasonable prices at the **Ramakrishna Mission** (Box 716, Nandi; tel. 702-786), across the street from the Farmers Club. It's open weekdays 0900-1300 and 1500-1700, Saturday 0900-1300.

Services

The **Westpac Bank** opposite the Nandi Handicraft Market and the **ANZ Bank** near Morris Hedstrom change traveler's checks without commission. Both are open Monday to Thursday 0930-1500, Friday 0930-1600.

Tapa International (tel. 722-325) in the concourse at Nandi Airport is the American Express representative. If you buy traveler's checks from them using a personal check and your American Express card, you'll have to actually pick up the checks at the ANZ Bank in Nandi town, so go early.

There are two large post offices, one next to the market in central Nandi, and another between the cargo warehouses directly across the park in front of the arrivals hall at Nandi Airport. Check both if you're expecting general delivery mail; open weekdays 0800-1600.

The public health clinic is up the street from the Nandi Hotel, but you'll save time by visiting Dr. Ram Raju, 36 Clay St. (tel. 701-375).

There are public toilets on the corner of Nandi Market closest to the post office.

Transportation

Turtle Airways (Box 717, Nandi; tel. 722-988), next to the golf course at Wailoaloa Beach, runs a seaplane shuttle to the offshore resorts at F$90 one-way, F$180 roundtrip (baggage limited to one 15-kg suitcase plus one carry-on). Combined catamaran/seaplane trips to the resorts are F$116 roundtrip. Scenic flights with Turtle are F$49 pp for 10 minutes, F$100 for 30 minutes (minimum of three persons). See "Getting Around by Air" in the Fiji Islands chapter introduction for information on regular flights to Malololailai Island and other parts of Fiji.

If you're headed for the offshore resorts on Malololailai, Malolo, Castaway, or Mana islands, the 300-passenger catamaran *Island Express* of **South Sea Cruises** (Box 718, Nandi; tel. 722-988, fax 720-346) departs Nandi's Ndenarau Marina twice daily at 0900 and 1330 (F$40 one-way, F$72 roundtrip). Interisland hops are F$20 each. A four-hour, four-island, nonstop roundtrip cruise on this 25-meter boat provides a fair glimpse of the lovely Mamanutha Group for F$35, or pay F$69 for a day-trip to Mana Island including lunch and nonmotorized activities. Be prepared to wade on and off the boat. Bookings with free twice-daily hotel transfers can be made through Rosie The Travel Service.

Pacific Transport (tel. 701-386) has express buses to Suva via Queens Road daily at 0720, 0750, 0900, 1300, and 1820 (four hours, F$6.80). The 0900 bus is the most convenient, as it begins its run at Nandi (the others all arrive from Lautoka). Four other "stage" buses also operate daily to Suva (five hours). Nandi's bus station adjoining the market is an active place.

You can bargain for fares with the collective taxis cruising the highway from the airport into Nandi. They'll usually take what you'd pay on a bus, but ask first. Collective taxis take five passengers nonstop from Nandi to Suva in three hours for F$10 pp.

For information on car rentals, turn to "Transportation" in this chapter's introduction.

Tours

Many day cruises and bus tours that operate in the Nandi area are listed in the free tourist magazine *Fiji Magic*. Reservations can be made through hotel reception desks or at Rosie The Travel Service, with several offices around Nandi. Bus transfers to/from your hotel are included in the price, though some trips are arbitrarily canceled when not enough people sign up. The actual vessels used to operate the cruises vary, and the trips described below are only an indication of the sort of thing to expect.

South Sea Cruises (tel. 722-988, fax 720-346) operates day-trips to Plantation Resort on the two-masted schooner *Seaspray* (F$59 including lunch). The sunset cruise on the *Seaspray* is F$32 pp. The same company has day cruises to Castaway Island Resort on the 22-meter ketch *Ariadne*.

Captain Cook Cruises (tel. 701-823) runs day cruises to Plantation Island Resort on Thursday, Friday, and Sunday aboard the 34-meter brigantine *Ra Marama* for F$54 including a picnic lunch. Sunset cruises on the same vessel are every Wednesday afternoon.

Every Tuesday and Friday the 30-meter schooner *Whale's Tale,* built at Suva's Whippy Shipyard in 1985, does a one-day cruise to Malamala Island, or "Daydream Island" as they call it. The cost is F$69 pp, including a beach buffet lunch, snorkeling, sailing, and hotel transfers. Book through **Daydream Cruises** (Box 9777, Nandi Airport; tel. 723-375, fax 790-441) or Rosie The Travel Service. The **Oceanic Schooner Co.** (Box 9626, Nandi Airport; tel. 723-590, fax 720-134) runs more upscale cruises on the *Whale's Tale,* which also include champagne breakfast, gourmet lunch served aboard, open bar, sunset cocktails, and limited participation for F$150 pp.

Mediterranean Villas (tel. 664-011, fax 661-773) offers day-trips (F$50 pp) to "Mediterranean Island," a typical Mamanutha speck of sand also known as Tivoa Island, 10 km west of Lautoka. The clean, clear water (except when it rains), abundant fish, and beautiful coral make this an excellent place to snorkel or scuba dive. Ask about camping possibilities here. Avoid the day cruise to "Aqualand" as the snorkeling is only fair, and there are very few support staff on the island.

Young travelers will enjoy a day cruise to **Beachcomber Island** (tel. 661-500), Fiji's unofficial Club Med for the under 35 set. Operating daily, the F$58 pp fare includes bus transfers from Nandi hotels, the return boat ride via Lautoka, and a buffet lunch. Large families especially should consider Beachcomber because after two full adult fares are paid, the first child under 16 is half price and additional children are quarter price. Infants under two are free.

Rosie The Travel Service (tel. 722-935), at Nandi Airport and opposite the Nandi Handicraft Market in town, offers the cheapest "road tours" because lunch and some admissions aren't included. Their day-trips to Suva (F$59) involve too much time on the bus, so instead go for the Singatoka Valley/Tavuni Hill Fort (F$52) or Emperor Gold Mine (F$39) full-day tours. If you're looking for a good morning tour around Nandi, sign up for the four-hour Vunda Lookout/Viseisei Village/Garden of the Sleeping Giant tour, which costs F$29 pp, plus F$10 admission to the garden; other than Viseisei, these places are not accessible on public transport. These trips only operate Monday to Saturday, but on Sunday Rosie offers a half-day drive to the Vunda Lookout and Lautoka for F$36 pp. Also ask about the full-day hiking tours to the Nausori Highlands (daily except Sunday, F$55), the easiest way to see this beautiful area.

The **Tourist Information Center** (Box 251, Nandi; tel. 700-243, fax 702-746), with offices in central Nandi (daily 0800-1700, Sunday until 1500) and opposite the Dominion International Hotel, is actually a commercial travel agency run by Victory Tours. Also known as "Fiji Island Adventurers," they offer a variety of 4WD and trekking excursions into the Nausori Highlands, and book low-budget beach resorts on Mana, Malolo, Waya, Leleuvia, and Kandavu islands. Their prices are often lower than those charged by the more upmarket tour companies mentioned above, but we suggest you approach this agency with caution as you only get what you pay for. **PVV Tours** (tel. 701-310) at the Nandi Town Motel is similar (their specialty is Nananu-i-Ra bookings and transfers).

Peni's Waterfall Tours (Box 474, Nandi; tel. 701-355), in the Westpoint Arcade off Queens Road in central Nandi, promises three nights of "real Fijian life" at Mbukuya, a mountain village in the Nausori Highlands, for F$160 pp. We've received varying reports about these trips, which seem to be a mixture of good and bad. Reader Andy Bray of Hampshire, England, sent us this:

Peni's tour is very much what you make of it. We got three good meals a day, transportation, a wild pig hunt, eel fishing, a waterfall trip, visits to neighboring villages, and various river and jungle treks. If you're content to settle into the typically slow Fi-

jian pace and be satisfied with maybe one good activity a day, you'll enjoy it. If you're used to hot running water, electricity, and constant activity, it's not for you. I found it helped to gently badger the hosts so they wouldn't forget we had activities in mind.

Similar hiking trips offered by Adventure Fiji, a division of Rosie The Travel Service, are more expensive but the quality is superior (see "Hiking Tours" under "Organized Tours" in the "Getting There" section of the main introduction).

THE MAMANUTHA GROUP

The Mamanutha Group is a paradise of eye-popping reefs and sand-fringed isles shared by traditional Fijian villages and jet-set resorts. The white coral beaches and super snorkeling grounds attract visitors aplenty; boats and planes arrive constantly, bringing folks in from nearby Nandi or Lautoka. These islands are in the lee of big Viti Levu, which means you'll get about as much sun here as anywhere in Fiji. Some of the South Pacific's best skin diving, surfing, game fishing, and yachting await you, and many nautical activities are included in the basic rates. Dive spots include the Pinnacles, Sunflower Reef, Wilkes Passage, and Land of the Giants. As yet only a few have noticed the potential for ocean kayaking in this area. Unpack your folding kayak on the beach a short taxi ride from the airport, and you'll be in for some real adventure. The Mamanuthas are fine for a little time in the sun, though it's mostly a tourist scene irrelevant to the rest of Fiji.

Malololailai Island
Malololailai, or "Little Malolo," 22 km west of Nandi, is the first of the Mamanutha Group. It's a fair-sized island eight km around (a nice walk). In 1860 an American sailor named Louis Armstrong bought Malololailai from the Fijians for one musket; in 1966 Dick Smith purchased it for many muskets. You can still be alone at the beaches on the far side of the island, but with two growing resorts, projects for a golf course and marina, and lots more time-share condominiums in the pipeline it's in danger of becom-

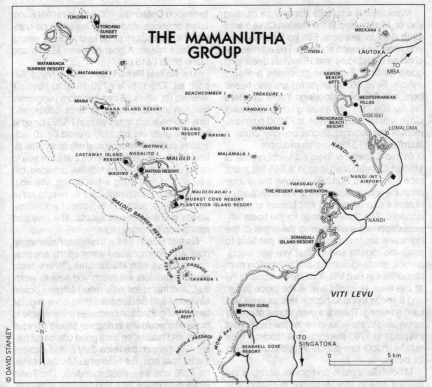

THE MAMANUTHA GROUP

© DAVID STANLEY

ing overdeveloped. An airstrip across the island's waist separates its two resorts; inland are rounded, grassy hills.

Plantation Island Resort (Box 9176, Nandi Airport; tel. 722-333, fax 720-163), on the southwest side of Malololailai, is one of the largest of the resorts off Nandi. The 110 rooms (beginning at F$160 single or double) are divided between 40 a/c hotel rooms in a two-story building and 70 individual *mbures*. Add F$49 pp for breakfast and dinner, as no cooking facilities are provided. Snorkeling gear, rowboats, and windsurfing are free, but boat trips cost extra. Coral viewing on Plantation's 30-passenger "yellow submarine" is F$33.

Also on Malololailai Island is **Musket Cove Resort** (Private Mail Bag NAPO352, Nandi Airport; tel. 662-215, fax 662-633), which opened as Dick's Place way back in 1977. The 24 fully

equipped *mbures* and six two-bedroom villas are F$250 single or double, or F$345 for six adults. Unlike Plantation, at Musket Cove the units have small kitchenettes where you can cook, and a well-stocked grocery store selling fresh fruit and vegetables is on the premises. There's also a bar and restaurant by the pool, with a F$71 meal package available. Entertainment is provided at the Thursday night pig roast.

Activities at Musket Cove such as snorkeling, windsurfing, water-skiing, line fishing, and boat trips are free for guests. Scuba diving with Musket Cove Divers costs F$55/88 one/two tanks, or F$390 for the four-day PADI certification course, which begins every Monday. Certified divers can also rent tanks and other gear and organize their own beach diving for much less.

Malololailai is a favorite stopover for cruising yachts. Membership in the **Musket Cove Yacht Club** (F$1 for skippers, F$5 pp for crew) gets you water and clean showers. The marked anchorage is protected and 15 meters deep, with good holding. Fuel and groceries are sold ashore. Several charter yachts are also based here, and **Rainbow Moorings Yacht Charters** (tel./fax 666-710) runs a sailing school at Musket Cove with two-day courses at F$200 pp (maximum of four persons). Shorter one-day "cruise 'n learn" sailing (F$135) is also available.

In mid-September there's a yacht regatta at Musket Cove, culminating in a 965-km yacht race from Fiji to Port Vila. Among the unique rules: the first yacht to arrive at Vila is disqualified unless it can be proven that blatant cheating occurred. The "race" is timed for the boats' annual departure east, prior to the onset of the hurricane season. It costs F$100 per boat to enter the regatta and for that you get feasts, parties, prizes, groceries, and exemption from harbor fees at Port Vila. If you're on a boat in Fiji at this time, Musket Cove is *the* place to be, and if you're trying to hitch a ride as crew you can't go wrong. There are even stories of people being *paid* to serve as crew for the race! Most evenings at 1700 there's also a "cocktail hour race" with four rum-punch-primed boats racing for prizes.

Malololailai's grass-and-gravel airstrip is the busiest one in the Mamanutha Group and serves as a distribution point for the other resorts. You can fly to Malololailai from Nandi Airport (F$28 one-way, F$44 same day return) eight times a day on Sunflower Airlines and five times a day on Island Air. Otherwise take the twice-daily 25-meter catamaran *Island Express* from Nandi's Ndenarau Marina for F$31 one-way, F$62 roundtrip; call 722-988 for free pickup.

Malolo Island

At low tide you can wade from Malololailai to nearby Malolo Island, largest of the Mamanutha Group, which has two Fijian villages. One of them is known to tourists as "shell village" for what the locals offer for sale. Camping is possible in the villages at F$8 pp; dormitory accommodations are available for F$12 pp, plus another F$10 pp for all meals. The **Tourist Information Center** (tel. 700-243) in central Nandi takes bookings, and a stay here can be combined with a sojourn at the backpackers' places on Mana Island. A boat between Malolo and Mana costs F$15 pp.

The **Naitasi Resort** (Box 10044, Nandi Airport; tel. 720-178, fax 720-197), at Malolo's western tip, offers 28 one-bedroom bungalows with fan at F$275 for up to three adults, and nine two-bedroom family villas at F$385 for up to six. The units are privately owned by 10 individuals, and each is decorated differently. The Island Store sells basic groceries that allow you to make use of the cooking facilities provided, but you should also bring a few things with you. The Terrace Restaurant does its best to serve local produce, such as five types of edible seaweeds and six different salads. The *lovo* and *meke* is on Saturday night.

Naitasi Resort has a freshwater swimming pool, and nonmotorized water sports are free; scuba diving with Mamanutha Divers costs extra. Instructors will teach you how to windsurf, and this is the only resort offering ocean kayaking and horseback riding on a regular basis. Self-guided trail brochures are available to those who would like to discover Malolo's unique plant- and birdlife, so it's a good choice for hikers. Get there on the twice-daily *Island Express* tourist boat from the Ndenarau Marina, Nandi, for F$36 one-way, F$62 roundtrip. The Turtle Airways seaplane from Nandi is F$90 one-way, and there are also speedboats from Malololailai. No day-trippers are allowed at the resort. Due to pressure from resort owners, campers wishing to stay at one of the villages on Malolo may have difficulty using the *Island Express,* in which case it might be better to arrive via Malololailai (call the numbers provided above to check).

Tavarua Island

Tavarua Island Resort (Box 1419, Nandi; tel. 723-513, fax 720-395), just south of Malololailai, operates as a surfing base camp. Guests are accommodated in 12 beach *mbures* at F$210/360 single/double a day, including meals, boat transfers from the landing, and most activities (three-night minimum stay). A small reduction is available from December to February, and children under 16 pay F$78 each, so long as they sleep in the same *mbure* as their parents and don't surf. Couples get preference. There are both lefts and rights in Malolo Passage at Tavarua, although the emphasis is usually on the lefts. When the swell is high enough you'll have some of the best surfing anywhere. On the off days you can get in some deep-sea fishing, windsurfing, snorkeling, or scuba diving (extra charge).

Bookings must be made through **Tavarua Tours** (Box 60159, Santa Barbara, CA 93160, U.S.A.; tel. 805/686-4551, fax 805/683-6696). They're usually sold out, especially in June, July, and August. You can always try calling upon arrival, and they'll probably take you if vacancies have materialized. If not, or if you simply can't afford those prices, stay at Seashell Cove Resort south of Nandi and charter one of their boats out to Wilkes Passage or nearby Namotu Island. Registered guests are transferred out to Tavarua from Seashell Cove.

Castaway Island
Castaway Island Resort (Private Mail Bag, Nandi Airport; tel. 661-233, fax 665-753), on 174-hectare Nggalito Island just west of Malolo and 15 km from Nandi, was erected in 1966 as Fiji's first outer-island resort. The 66 thatched *mbures* sleep four—F$310 and up including breakfast. No cooking facilities are provided. Among the free water sports are sailing, windsurfing, canoeing, tennis, and snorkeling, but scuba diving and game fishing are extra. There's the daily catamaran from Nandi's Ndenarau Marina (F$36 one-way, F$60 roundtrip), and Turtle Airways has three seaplane flights a day from Nandi for F$90. Many Australian holidaymakers return to Castaway year after year; families with small children are welcome.

Mana Island
Mana Island, 32 km west of Lautoka, is best known for the **Mana Island Resort** (Box 610, Lautoka; tel. 661-455, fax 661-562). This is by far the biggest of the resorts off Nandi, with 32 hotel rooms and 128 tin-roofed bungalows clustered between the island's grassy rounded hilltops, white sandy beaches, and crystal-clear waters. Standard bungalows begin at F$260 single or double, F$300 triple, while deluxe beachfront bungalows and hotel rooms are around F$100

more, breakfast included. Cooking facilities are not provided, so you'll have to patronize either the Mamanutha Restaurant, the Bulamakau Steak House, or the North Beach Barbecue Buffet (breakfast and dinner plan F$62 pp). Mana Island Resort should be your choice if you like the excitement of large crowds and a wide range of organized activities. Live entertainment is presented nightly except Sunday, and three nights a week there's a Fijian or Polynesian floor show.

The room rates include all nonmotorized water sports, although the 45-minute semisubmersible rides (F$29 pp), water-skiing, para-flying, water scooters, game fishing, and scuba diving are all extra. The **Aqua-Trek** base here is one of only two five-star PADI scuba diving centers in Fiji (the other is Suva's Scubahire), and it offers a great variety of dive courses, beginning with a four-day open-water certification course (F$572). Boat dives cost F$66 for one tank or F$363 for a six-dive package. The Mana Main Reef is famous for its drop-offs with visibility never less than 25 meters, and you'll see turtles, fish of all descriptions, and the occasional crayfish. Divemaster Apisi Bati specializes in underwater shark feeding at a dive site called "Supermarket," a 30-minute boat ride away.

The *Island Express* catamaran from Ndenarau Marina, Nandi, calls at Mana Island Resort twice a day (F$70 roundtrip). In 1995 an airstrip opened on Mana, and Sunflower Airlines now has six flights a day from Nandi.

There are lots of lovely beaches all around Mana, most of them empty because the tourists seldom stray far from their resort. This works to your advantage because on the other side of the island is a place known as **Mana Island Backpackers** where you can sleep in an eight-bed dormitory for F$17 pp, plus another F$11 pp for three buffet-style meals; cooking for yourself is also possible. Activities include deep-sea fishing trips (F$33 an hour), four-island boat excursions (F$25), and a *lovo* picnic on a small island (F$25—free for guests staying a week). Those staying two weeks get an extra night free and several complimentary trips. There's a great view from the highest point on Mana, a 15-minute hike away. Bookings can be made by calling 667-520 on Mana, at which time transfers from Nandi on the *Tui Mana* (one hour, F$50 roundtrip) will be arranged.

In the Fijian village a couple of hundred meters from Backpackers is **Ratu Kini Boko's Hostel** (Box 5818, Lautoka; tel. 667-520), also known as "Mama's Place." Here you can rent a pleasant thatched *mbure* at F$77 double, or stay in a dormitory at F$28 pp, both including three filling meals. It's cleaner and nicer than Backpackers for about the same price, and Ratu Kini and his wife Veronica prepare very good meals, which you take with the family. Sometimes it gets a little crowded.

Ratu Kini is an interesting character. He's the chief of 20 islands in the Mamanutha Group, but he made the mistake of leasing part of Mana Island to an Australian company that sublet their property to the Japanese investors who now run Mana Island Resort, and of course the resort people would like nothing better than to oust the backpackers and Fijian villagers from the island. Ratu Kini claims his main purpose in running the hostel is "to show the world the way Fijians live and to teach visitors about Fijian customs and culture."

For information on the current situation, call the hostel or their Lautoka office (tel. 663-724), or ask at **Margaret Travel Service** (Box 9831, Nandi Airport; tel. 721-988, fax 721-992). In light of the above, it's obvious that people staying at Backpackers or Ratu Kini's aren't welcome at Mana Island Resort, and these problems even extend to the use of the *Island Express* to get to Mana. (The resort management warns their upscale clientele not to visit the Fijian village after dark because "hippies" are staying there!) It's all a bit of an adventure, and the chance to enjoy Mana's stunning beauty at a fraction of the price tourists at the Japanese resort are paying makes it worth the intrigue.

Matamanoa Island
Matamanoa Sunrise Resort (Box 9729, Nandi Airport; tel. 660-511, fax 720-679), to the northwest of Mana Island, has four a/c rooms for F$170 single or double, or F$297 for one of the 20 fan-cooled *mbures* sleeping four. Meals are F$99 extra for all three (no cooking facilities). Matamanoa's rugged volcanic core gives it a certain character, and as if the tiny island's fine white beach and blue lagoon weren't enough, there's also a swimming pool and lighted tennis court. It's more expensive to reach because the

launch transfers from Mana to Matamanoa (F$30 pp each way) are in addition to the catamaran from Nandi.

Tokoriki Island
Tokoriki Sunset Resort (Box 9729, Nandi Airport; tel. 661-999, fax 665-295), 27 km due west of Lautoka, is the farthest offshore resort from Nandi. There are 20 fan-cooled *mbures* at F$250 for four adults and two children (no cooking facilities). The resort faces west on a kilometer-long beach and water sports such as reef fishing, windsurfing, and Hobie Cats are free (water-skiing, scuba diving, and sportfishing available at additional charge). At the center of the island is a 94-meter-high hill offering good views of the Yasawa and Mamanutha groups. Tokoriki is under the same management as Matamanoa, and as on Matamanoa, you must take the catamaran to Mana, then a launch to Tokoriki (F$33 pp each way). The regular launch to Matamanoa and Tokoriki leaves Mana daily at 1100.

Vomo Island
Standing alone midway between Lautoka and Waya Island (see the "Yasawa Islands" map), 91-hectare Vomo has since 1993 been the site of the **Sheraton Vomo Island Resort** (Box 9761, Nandi Airport; tel. 667-955, fax 667-997). The 30 a/c villas run F$700 single or double, F$987 triple, breakfast included. Other meals are additional (no cooking facilities). Add F$585 per couple for return helicopter transfers from Nandi Airport and you've got the most expensive resort in the Mamanutha Group.

Navini Island
Navini Island Resort (Box 9445, Nandi Airport; tel. 662-188, fax 665-566) is the smallest of Mamanutha resorts, a tiny coral isle with only seven thatched *mbures*. Rates vary from F$255 double for a fan-cooled beachfront unit to F$375 for the honeymoon *mbure* with spa and enclosed courtyard. Discounts are available for stays over a week. The meal package is F$57 pp a day (no cooking facilities). Everyone gets to know one another by eating at a long table (private dining is also possible). Complimentary morning boat trips are offered, as are snorkeling gear, windsurfers, and kayaks. Car/boat transfers from Nandi via Vunda Point (one hour, F$96

return for adults, F$48 for children under 13) are arranged anytime upon request.

Beachcomber Island

Beachcomber Island (Box 364, Lautoka; tel. 661-500, fax 664-496), 18 km west of Lautoka, is Club Med at a fraction of the price. The resort caters mostly to young Australians, and it's a good place to meet travelers of the opposite sex. You'll like the informal atmosphere and late-night parties; there's a sand-floor bar, dancing, and floor shows four nights a week. The island is so small you can stroll around it in 10 minutes, but there's a white sandy beach and buildings nestled among coconut trees and tropical vegetation. A beautiful coral reef extends far out on all sides and scuba diving is available with Subsurface Fiji (F$65 for one tank). A full range of sporting activities is available at an additional charge (parasailing F$45, windsurfing F$20, water-skiing F$26, jet skis F$32 for 15 minutes).

Accommodations include all meals served buffet style. Most people opt for the big, open mixed dormitory where the 40 double-decker bunks cost F$69 each a night, but you can also get one of 18 thatched *mbures* with ceiling fan and private facilities for F$182/242/302 single/double/triple. A good compromise for the budget-conscious traveler is one of the 14 lodge rooms with shared bath at F$146/189 single/double (fridge and fan provided). Former water problems have been solved by laying pipes from the mainland and installing solar water heating.

Of course, there's also the F$58 roundtrip boat ride from Lautoka to consider, but that includes lunch on arrival day. You can make a day-trip to Beachcomber for the same price if you only want a few hours in the sun. There's a free shuttle bus from all Lautoka/Nandi hotels to the wharf; the connecting boat leaves daily at 1000. Beachcomber has been doing it right since the 1960s, and the biggest drawback is its very popularity, which makes it crowded and busy. Reserve well ahead at their Lautoka or Nandi Airport offices, or at any travel agency.

Treasure Island Resort

Beachcomber's neighbor, **Treasure Island** (Box 2210, Lautoka; tel. 661-599, fax 663-577), caters to couples and families less interested in an intense singles' social scene. Instead of helping yourself at a buffet and eating at a long communal picnic table, you'll eat regular meals in Treasure's restaurant (meal plan F$60 pp daily). Cooking facilities are not provided. The 68 units, each with three single beds (F$240 single or double), are contained in 34 functional duplex bungalows packed into the greenery behind the island's white sands. Some nautical activities such as windsurfing, sailing, canoes, and spy board, which cost extra on Beachcomber, are free on Treasure Island. Guests arrive on the Beachcomber Island shuttle boat from Lautoka (which leaves daily at 1000 and 1400, F$58 roundtrip), but unlike Beachcomber, Treasure doesn't get any day-trippers. There's no wharf here, so be prepared to wade ashore. Formerly owned by the same company, Beachcomber and Treasure have been under separate managements since 1991.

SOUTHERN VITI LEVU

SOUTH OF NANDI

Sonaisali Island Resort

Opened in June 1991, this upmarket resort (Box 2544, Nandi; tel. 720-411, fax 720-392), down Nathombi Road from Queens Road, is on a long, low island in Momi Bay, just 300 meters off the coast of Viti Levu. The 32 a/c rooms in the main two-story building are F$190 single or double, and there are six thatched two-bedroom *mbures* at F$260 (no cooking facilities). The meal plan is F$48 pp and guests are expected to dress up for dinner in the restaurant. The resort features a full-service marina, a swimming pool with swim-up bar, tennis courts, a children's program, and water sports, but the snorkeling off their beach is poor. A shuttle boat provides free access to the island 24 hours a day.

Momi Bay

On a hilltop overlooking Momi Bay 28 km from Nandi are two **British six-inch guns,** one named Queen Victoria (1900), the other Ed-

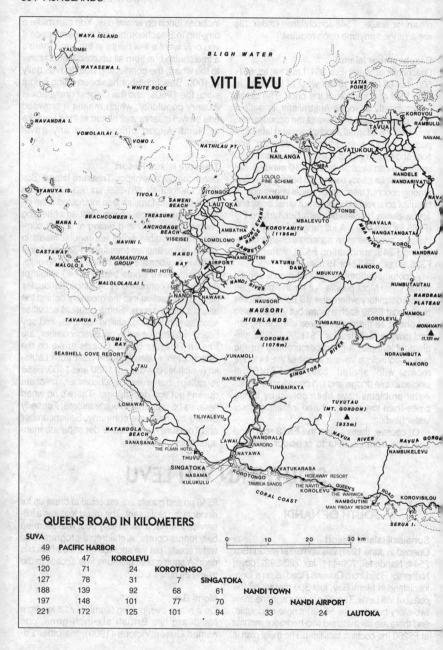

QUEENS ROAD IN KILOMETERS

SUVA						
49	**PACIFIC HARBOR**					
96	47	**KOROLEVU**				
120	71	24	**KOROTONGO**			
127	78	31	7	**SINGATOKA**		
188	139	92	68	61	**NANDI TOWN**	
197	148	101	77	70	9	**NANDI AIRPORT**
221	172	125	101	94	33	24	**LAUTOKA**

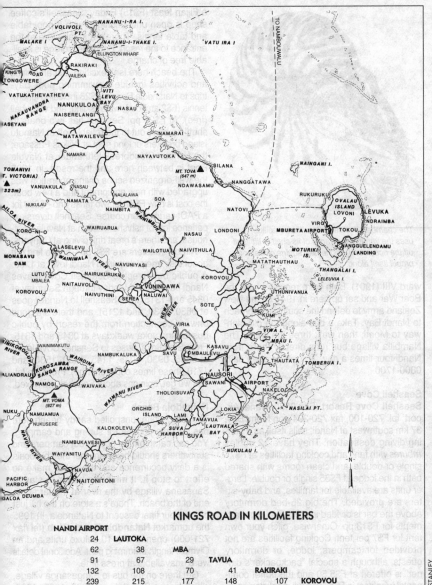

KINGS ROAD IN KILOMETERS

NANDI AIRPORT								
24	LAUTOKA							
62	38	MBA						
91	67	29	TAVUA					
132	108	70	41	RAKIRAKI				
239	215	177	148	107	KOROVOU			
270	246	208	179	138	31	NAUSORI		
289	265	227	198	157	50	19	SUVA	

© DAVID STANLEY

The chambered nautilus (Nautilis pompilius) uses the variable buoyancy of its shell to lift itself off the ocean bed, and jet-like squirts of water to propel itself along.

ward VIII (1901). Both were recycled from the Boer War and set up here in 1941 by the New Zealand army to defend the southern approach to Nandi Bay. Take a bus along the old highway to Momi, then walk three km west. The Nambilla village bus runs directly there from Nandi four times a day. The site is open daily 0800-1700.

Seashell Cove

Seashell Cove Resort (Box 9530, Nandi Airport; tel. 720-100, fax 720-294), on Momi Bay, 37 km southwest of Nandi, sells itself as a surfing/diving destination. They have 12 duplex *mbures* with fans and cooking facilities at F$77 single or double, and clean rooms with shared bath in the lodge at F$35 single or double. Larger units are available for families, and baby-sitters are provided. The big 25-bed dormitory above the bar is divided into five-bed compartments for F$13 pp. Otherwise, pitch your own tent for F$7 per tent. Cooking facilities are not provided for campers, lodge, or dormitory guests, although a special "backpacker's dinner" is offered at F$5.50 and the buffet continental breakfast is F$4.50; a full meal plan costs F$17.50. A *meke* (F$16) occurs Wednesday,

a Fijian feast (F$15) Friday. Seashell's coffee shop is open until midnight, with a pool table and table tennis. There's a small store at the entrance to the resort. Baggage storage is available free of charge.

The beach here isn't exciting, but amenities and activities include a swimming pool, day-trips to Natandola Beach (F$28 including lunch), tennis (F$2 an hour), water-skiing, and volleyball (free). At F$20 pp, Seashell has two boats to shuttle surfers out to the reliable left at Namotu Island breakers or long right at Wilkes Passage; the famous Cloudbreak lefthander at Navula Reef is between here and the resort. In 1995 the well-organized scuba diving operation was upgraded with new equipment and a new boat; the cost is now F$77 for two tanks and F$330 for a PADI certification course. Seashell divers experience lots of fish/shark action at Navula Lighthouse, and there's great drift diving at Canyons.

Airport transfers are F$8 pp—call to find out about their free pickup from Nandi town at 1100. A public bus direct to Seashell Cove leaves Nandi bus station Monday through Saturday at 0845 and 1315 (from Seashell to Nandi it goes at 0630, 0830, and 1215), and there's a good onward connection from the resort by public bus to Singatoka weekdays at 0845 and 1315. From Singatoka, buses to Seashell Cove leave at 0645, 0930, 1045, 1145, 1230, 1530, and 1710 (these times could change). From the letters we get, opinions about Seashell are mixed.

Natandola Beach

The long, white, unspoiled sandy beach here has become popular for surfing and camping. You can camp on the beach, but campers and sunbathers should be aware that theft by locals is a daily occurrence and the police make no effort to stop it. It might be better to stay at Sanasana village by the river at the far south end of the beach. There's a store on the hill just before your final descent to Natandola. In 1995 the upmarket **Natandola Beach Club** (tel./fax 721-000) opened with 10 deluxe units and an Olympic-length swimming pool. Additional details were unavailable at press time.

Get there on the bus to Sangasanga village, which leaves Singatoka at 0900, 1300, 1500, and 1745. You have to walk the last three km to the beach. Otherwise get off at the Maro School stop on the main highway and hitch 10 km to the beach. The sugar train passes close to Natandola, bringing day-trippers from the Coral Coast.

THE CORAL COAST

Yanutha Island

Shangri-La's Fijian Resort Hotel (Private Mail Bag NAPO353, Nandi Airport; tel. 520-155, fax 500-402) occupies all 40 hectares of Yanutha Island, not to be confused with another island of the same name west of Mbengga. This Yanutha Island is connected to the main island by a causeway 10 km west of Singatoka and 61 km southeast of Nandi Airport. Opened in 1967, the 436-room complex of three-story Hawaiian-style buildings was Fiji's first large resort and is still Fiji's biggest hotel, catering to a predominantly Japanese clientele. In 1995 the entire complex was renovated by its Malaysian owners. The a/c rooms begin at F$275 single or double, F$320 triple, or F$703 for a deluxe beach *mbure*. There's no charge for two children 15 or under sharing their parents' room. The Fijian offers a nine-hole golf course (par 31), five tennis courts, four restaurants and five bars, two swimming pools, and a white sandy beach. Weekly events include a *meke* on Tuesday and Friday (and sometimes Thursday), and firewalking on Monday and Friday nights. Scuba diving is arranged by Sea Sports Limited. Avis Rent A Car has a desk in The Fijian.

A local attraction is the Fijian Princess, a restored narrow-gauge railway originally built to haul sugarcane but that now runs 16-km day-trips to Natandola Beach daily at 1000. The train station is on the highway opposite the access road to The Fijian Hotel, and the ride costs F$55 pp including a barbecue lunch if you book here. Otherwise pay F$59 pp including bus transfers from any Coral Coast hotel or F$69 from Nandi-area hotels. For information call the **Coral Coast Railway Co.** (Box 571, Singatoka; tel. 520-599). Across the road from the train station is the **Ka Levu Center,** a mock-Fijian village dispensing instant Fijian culture to tourists for F$10 pp admission.

Kulukulu

Fiji's best **surfing beach** is at Kulukulu, five km south of Singatoka, where the Singatoka River breaks through Viti Levu's fringing reef. The surf is primarily a rivermouth point break with numerous beachbreaks down the beach. It's one of the only places for beachbreak surfing on Viti Levu, and unlike most other surfing locales around Fiji, no boat is required here. The **windsurfing** in this area is fantastic, as you can either sail "flat water" across the rivermouth or do "wave jumping" in the sea (all-sand bottom and big rollers with high wind). The surfing is good all the time, but if you want to combine it with windsurfing, it's best to surf in the morning and windsurf in afternoon when the wind comes up. Be prepared, however, as these waters are treacherous for novices. You can also bodysurf here. There's a nice place nearby where you can swim in the river and avoid the currents in the sea.

Incredible 20-meter-high **sand dunes** separate the cane fields from the two-km-long beach, and giant sea turtles come ashore here now and then to lay their eggs. Winds sometimes uncover human bones from old burials, and potsherds lie scattered along the seashore—these fragments have been carbon dated at up to 3,000 years old. It's a fascinating, evocative place, now protected as a national park. Please show some sensitivity in the way you approach this unique environment.

Because it and its eggs are taken for human food, the green sea turtle (Chelonia mydas) *is in danger of extinction. Fortunately the shell is too thin to be made into jewelry.*

American surfer Marcus Oliver has opened a base camp behind the dunes called **Club Masa Sports Resort** (Box 710, Singatoka; no telephone), also known as "Sand Dunes Lodge." So far there's a 10-bed dormitory (F$11 pp), double rooms (F$15 pp), and fenced camping area (F$6). There's no electricity, but the layout is attractive. No cooking facilities are provided, but the three-meal plan is worth taking at F$5.50 (otherwise you go hungry). Have a beer on their pleasant open porch. Boogie boards are for hire at F$5 a day. It's a nice place to hang out—friendly people.

There are buses from Singatoka to Kulukulu village seven times a day on Wednesday and Saturday, five times on other weekdays, but none on Sunday and holidays. Taxi fare to Club Masa should be around F$4, and later you may only have to pay 50 cents for a seat in an empty taxi returning to Singatoka.

Singatoka

Singatoka is the main center for the Coral Coast tourist district and the headquarters of Nandronga/Navosa Province. The town's setting is made picturesque by the long single-lane highway bridge crossing the Singatoka River here, and it's pleasant to stroll around. You'll find the ubiquitous duty-free shops and a colorful local market (best on Wednesday and Saturday) with a large handicraft section. Jack's Handicrafts (tel. 500-810) on the main street is also worth a look.

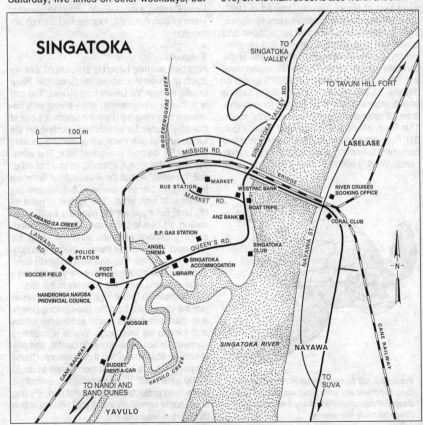

Strangely, the traditional handmade **Fijian pottery** for which Singatoka is famous is not available here. Find it by asking in Nayawa (where the clay originates), Yavulo, and Nasama villages near Singatoka. Better yet, take the two-hour **Bounty Cruise** (tel. 500-669) up the river from Singatoka to Nakambuta and Lawai villages, where the pottery is displayed for sale. Cruises leave daily except Sunday at 1000, 1200, and 1430 (F$16).

Upriver from Singatoka is a wide valley known as Fiji's "salad bowl" for its rich market gardens by Fiji's second-largest river. Vegetables are grown in farms on the west side of the valley, while the lands on the east bank are planted with sugarcane. Small trucks use the good dirt road up the west side of the river to take the produce to market, while a network of narrow-gauge railways collects the cane from the east side. You can drive right up the valley in a normal car. The locals believe that Dakuwangga, shark god of the Fijians, dwells in the river.

Also near Singatoka, five km up the left (east) bank of the river from the one-way bridge, is the **Tavuni Hill Fort** on a bluff at Naroro village. The fort was established by the 19th-century Tongan chief Maile Latemai and destroyed by native troops under British control in 1876. An interpretive center and walkways have been established, and F$6 admission is collected. There's a good view of the river and surrounding countryside from here. Those without transport could take a taxi from Singatoka to the reception area (about F$5), then walk back to town in an hour or so.

Practicalities at Singatoka

The **Singatoka Club** (Box 38, Singatoka; tel. 500-026) has four pleasant fan-cooled rooms with private bath at F$22/33 single/double. It's a good untouristy place to stay, and the bar here is perfect for a beer or a game of pool (three tables). The bar is open Monday to Saturday 1000-2200. In contrast to drinks, meals at the Club are expensive.

The basic **Singatoka Accommodations** (Box 35, Singatoka; tel. 500-833), opposite the BP service station on Queens Road, has nine rooms at F$20/25 single/double, and a six-bed dorm at F$10 pp. Bargaining should quickly lower these prices, and camping on the back lawn is possible. Check the lock on your door. Singatoka Accommodations should be considered only a place to crash.

The **Oriental Pacific Restaurant** (tel. 520-275) in front of the bus station dispenses fast food to bus passengers during their 15-minute stop here. If you have more time, you're better off seeking out **Eddie Hin Ching's Restaurant** (tel. 500-376), upstairs in a row of shops behind the market. There's also the darker and more expensive **Rattan Restaurant** (tel. 500-818) and unmarked **Reddy's Restaurant,** both by the market.

Of the four **banks** in Singatoka, the Westpac is the most convenient since they have a separate overseas section upstairs and you don't have to join the long queue of local customers.

Pacific Transport (tel. 500-088) express buses leave Singatoka for Suva at 0845, 0910, 1025, 1425, and 1945 (3.5 hours, F$4.70), for Nandi Airport at 0935, 1220, 1500, 1800, and 2020 (1.5 hours, F$2.75).

Scuba Diving

Sea Sports Ltd. (Box 688, Singatoka; tel. 500-225, fax 520-239) offers scuba diving from their dive shops at The Fijian, Hideaway, and Warwick hotels. Their free red-and-blue minibus picks up clients at all the other Coral Coast resorts just after 0700 (just after 0900 on Sunday). The charge is F$52 for one tank, F$90 for two tanks (both on the same morning), plus tax. Sea Sports runs NAUI open-water certification courses (F$422), and night dives are possible. Most dive sites are within 15 minutes of the resort jetties, so you don't waste much time commuting.

Korotongo

The south side of Viti Levu along the Queens Road east of Singatoka is known as the Coral Coast. East of Korotongo the sugar fields of western Viti Levu are replaced by coconut plantations merging into rainforests on the green slopes behind.

This shoreline is heavily promoted as one of the top resort areas in Fiji, probably because of its convenient location along the busy highway between Nandi and Suva, but to be frank, the beaches here are second rate, with good swimming and snorkeling conditions only at high tide. To compensate, most of the hotels have swimming pools and in some places you can go reef walking at low tide. All the hotels at Korolevu farther east are quite upmarket, but there are nearly a dozen inexpensive self-catering places to stay at Korotongo, eight km east of Singatoka.

Korotongo Accommodations

The first place you come to as you enter Korotongo from Singatoka is **Shiu's Coral Coast Lodge** (Box 389, Singatoka; tel. 500-237), with five rooms with bath at F$30 double (or F$20 double after bargaining). A shared "dormitory" room is F$10 pp. You can cook here, but the whole place has an abandoned feel to it. A backyard overlooks the bay.

Korotongo Lodge (Box 37, Singatoka; tel. 500-755, fax 520-182), next to Tom's Restaurant at the west end of Korotongo, a few minutes away from Shiu's, has four rooms at F$22/25 single/double or F$11 pp in the dorm. You can use the communal kitchen, but it's all rather basic and the lodge is not on the beach. This place has been around for quite a while, and it shows.

The **Crow's Nest Motor Lodge** (Box 270, Singatoka; tel. 500-513, fax 520-354), 500 meters east of Korotongo Lodge, offers 18 split-level duplex bungalows with cooking facilities at F$82/110 single/double. Reduced rates of F$55 single or double are possible if you just stroll in without reservations at a time when things are slow. The **Crow's Nest Dormitory** at the bottom of the hill is F$11 pp for the 10 beds. The nautical touches in the excellent moderately priced restaurant behind the swimming pool spill over into the rooms, and good views over the lagoon are obtained from the Crow's Nest's elevated perch.

The **Vakaviti Motel** (Box 5, Singatoka; tel. 500-526, fax 520-319), next to the Crow's Nest, has six self-catering units at F$50/55 single/double and a six-bed dorm at F$13 pp. A five-bed family cabin is F$66 double, plus F$6 per additional person. They have a swimming pool, and the manager's half dozen dogs greet newcomers enthusiastically. It's often full.

The **Casablanca Hotel** (Box 86, Singatoka; tel. 520-600) next door is a two-story building on a hillside on the inland side of Queens Road. Its eight a/c rooms with cooking facilities and arched balconies begin at F$80 single or double. This place has gone through several changes of ownership in recent years as it tries to find its market niche.

A new upmarket place to stay is **Bedarra House** (Box 1213, Singatoka; tel. 500-476, fax 520-116), with only four rooms at F$125 double including breakfast and dinner. This spacious two-story hotel prides itself on the personalized service and it's a mystery how they can afford to keep such a large staff for only a dozen guests maximum. There isn't even a reception; you check in at the bar. A swimming pool, video room, and upstairs lounge round out the facilities of this unusual hotel.

Just a few hundred meters east near the Reef Resort is **Waratah Lodge** (Box 86, Singatoka; tel. 500-278, fax 520-219), with five very nice self-catering units—good value at F$33/44 single/double. The swimming pool and charming management add to the allure. Recommended.

The **Reef Resort** (Box 173, Singatoka; tel. 500-044, fax 520-074), about a kilometer east of the Crow's Nest, is a three-story building facing right onto a white sandy beach. The 72 a/c rooms are F$140 for up to three persons, family suites F$160; most nonmotorized recreational activities are free. The hotel tennis courts, nine-hole par-31 golf course, and horses are available to both guests and nonguests at reasonable rates. Even if you're not staying there, check out the firewalking (F$12) on Friday and the Fijian dancing (F$3) on Wednesday and Saturday nights. Meals in the hotel restaurant are prepared to please the mostly Australian clientele, and the all-you-can-eat buffet (F$16) is excellent value. Thrifty Car Rental and Sea Sports Ltd. have desks here. For a large hotel it's fairly pleasant.

Sandy Point Beach Cottages (Box 23, Singatoka; tel. 500-125, fax 520-147) shares the same beach with the adjacent Reef Resort. Three fan-cooled double units with full cooking facilities are offered at F$55 single, F$72 double or triple, and a five-bed cottage is F$127. Set in spacious grounds right by the sea, Sandy Point has its own freshwater swimming pool. It's a good choice for families or small groups, but it's often full so you must reserve well ahead.

A bit east again is **Tumbakula Beach Resort** (Box 2, Singataka; tel. 500-097, fax 340-236). The 27 pleasant A-frame bungalows with fan, cooking facilities, and private bath, each capable of sleeping three or more, are F$48 in the garden or F$58 facing the beach. Their "Beach Club" consists of eight rooms, each with three or four beds at F$11 a bed. A communal kitchen is available, plus a swimming pool, game room, nightly videos, minimarket, and Tuesday *lovo* (F$15). The snorkeling here is good, there's surfing and scuba diving nearby, and bus excursions are available. What more do you want? Basically, Tumbakula is a quiet, do-your-own-thing kind of place for people who don't need lots of organized activities. Seated on your terrace watching the sky turn orange and purple behind the black silhouettes of the palms along the beach, a bucket of cold Fiji Bitter stubbies close at hand, you'd swear this was paradise! It's one of the most popular backpacker's resorts in Fiji and well worth a couple of nights.

All of the hotels mentioned above to the west of the Reef Resort are on the inland side of the highway; in contrast, the Reef, Sandy Beach, and Tumbakula are right on the beach.

Korotongo Food

Opposite the Reef Resort is a small grocery store and two paltry restaurants, one with pizza and the other Chinese. These cater mostly to hungry tourists staying at the Reef who don't have access to cooking facilities. Unless all you want is to fill your stomach, it's better to walk 800 meters west to the more atmospheric **Crow's Nest Restaurant** (tel. 500-670).

Tom's Restaurant (Tom Jacksam, tel. 520-238) at the west entrance to Korotongo specializes in Chinese dishes, but there are four vegetarian items on the menu and six grilled choices such as steaks. They're open Monday to Saturday 1200-1500/1800-2200, Sunday 1800-2200, and to date all reviews have been good.

Vatukarasa

This small village between Korotongo and Korolevu is notable for its quaint appearance and the **Baravi Handicraft Boutique** (tel. 520-364), which carries a wide selection of Fijian handicrafts at fixed prices. They buy directly from the craftspeople themselves and add only a 20%

markup, plus tax. It's a good place to get an idea of how much things should cost and is worth an outing by local bus if you're staying at one of the Coral Coast resorts.

Korolevu Accommodations

At Korolevu, east of Korotongo, the accommodations cater to a more upscale crowd, and cooking facilities are not provided for guests. These places are mostly intended for people on package holidays who intend to spend most of their time unwinding on the beach. Distances between the resorts are great, so for sightseeing you'll be dependent on your hotel's tour desk.

The **Tambua Sands Beach Resort** (Box 77, Singatoka; tel. 500-399, fax 520-265), in an attractive location facing the sea about 10 km east of the Reef Resort, has 31 beach bungalows at F$81/104 single/double (plus F$35 pp for breakfast and dinner). Ask for a unit near the beach—they all cost the same. There's a very nice swimming pool, live music most evenings, and a *meke* on Tuesday and Friday nights. Thrifty Car Rental has a desk in this hotel. It's recommended as a good medium-priced choice for a couple of nights of relaxation.

The 56-room **Hideaway Resort** (Box 233, Singatoka; tel. 500-177, fax 520-025) at Korolevu, three km east of Tambua Sands and 20 km east of Singatoka, tries to cater to both ends of the market. Set on a palm-fringed beach before a verdant valley, the smaller fan-cooled *mbures* are F$110 single or double; larger units suitable for up to six people go for F$154. Where Hideaway differs from its neighbors is in the F$30-a-night dormitories—men and women are mixed here with 15 beds downstairs and nine upstairs. Cooking your own food is not possible and no grocery stores are to be found nearby, but three meals are included in the dorm rates (though not in the *mbure* rates). Hideaway provides free entertainment nightly, including a real *meke* on Tuesday and Friday, and an all-you-can-eat Fijian feast Sunday night (F$18). Valuables can be left in safety deposit boxes at the reception area for a refundable F$2 deposit. An afternoon excursion to a rainforest waterfall departs at 1330 on Tuesday and Saturday (F$15). Surfing is possible in the pass here (not for beginners), and you can scuba dive with Sea Sports Limited. Thrifty Car Rental is represented.

The **Naviti Beach Resort** (Box 29, Korolevu; tel. 530-444, fax 530-343), just west of Korolevu and 100 km from Nandi Airport, has 140 spacious a/c rooms in a series of two-story blocks beginning at F$182 single or double. There's a *lovo* (F$25) on Friday night, and nonguests may use the nine-hole golf course for F$10. Scuba diving is arranged by Sea Sports Limited. This resort has difficulty competing with other medium-priced properties such as the Tambua Sands, Hideaway, and Reef Resort, and a good percentage of the rooms lie empty most of the time.

The **Warwick Fiji** (Box 100, Korolevu; tel. 530-555, fax 530-010), on the Queens Road just east of Korolevu, 107 km from Nandi Airport, is the second-largest hotel on the Coral Coast (after The Fijian). Erected in 1979 and part of the Hyatt Regency chain until 1991, it's now under the same ownership as the Naviti Beach; there's a shuttle bus between the two. The 246 a/c rooms in three-story wings running east and west from the lobby begin at F$191 single or double, F$215 triple, and rise to F$347 for a club suite. In 1995 the rooms were completely refurbished. There's live music in the Hibiscus Lounge nightly until 0100 and disco dancing on Sunday. This plush resort also offers a complete sports and fitness center, an excellent beach, and scuba diving with Sea Sports Limited. There's even a small offshore island connected to the main beach by a causeway. Avis Rent A Car has a desk in the Warwick.

The **Man Friday Resort** (Box 20, Korolevu; tel. 500-185, fax 520-666), right by the beach, six km off Queens Road at Namboutini, is the most secluded place to stay on the Coral Coast. The 30 thatched *mbures* are F$66 double, with cooking facilities F$10 extra. The footprint-shaped freshwater swimming pool alludes to Daniel Defoe's novel *Robinson Crusoe,* which gave Man Friday its name.

Coral Village Resort (Box 104, Korolevu; tel./fax 500-807), also known as Gaia Beach Resort, is on the side of Namanggumanggua village opposite Man Friday. This 12-bungalow property on a lovely beach functions as a health resort dedicated to "permaculture," a system dedicated to earth-friendly agriculture and energy use. Special programs to help you lose weight or stop smoking are available.

Getting Around

An easy way to get between the Coral Coast resorts and Nandi/Suva is on the a/c **Fiji Express** shuttle bus run by United Touring Company (tel. 722-811). The bus leaves the Travelodge and Courtesy Inn hotels in Suva (F$25) at 0800 and calls at the Pacific Harbor Hotel (F$22), Warwick Hotel (F$17), Naviti Resort, Hideaway, Tambua Sands, Reef Resort (F$16), Fijian Hotel (F$14), Sheraton Resort (F$5), and The Regent, arriving at Nandi Airport at 1230 (quoted fares are to the airport). It leaves Nandi Airport at 1330 and returns along the same route, reaching Suva at 1800. Bookings can be made at the UTC office in the airport arrival concourse or at hotel tour desks.

Also ask about the a/c **Queen's Deluxe Coach,** which runs in the opposite direction, leaving The Fijian Hotel for Suva at 0910, the Warwick and Naviti Beach at 1030, and Pacific Harbor at 1115. The return trip departs the Suva Travelodge around 1600.

Many less expensive non-a/c buses pass on the highway, but make sure you're waiting somewhere they'll stop. Pacific Transport's "stage" or "highway" buses between Lautoka/Nandi and Suva will stop at any of the Coral Coast resorts, but the express buses call only at Singatoka, Pacific Harbor, and Navua. If you're on an express, get a ticket to Singatoka and look for a local bus (or taxi) from there.

NAVUA AND VICINITY

Southeastern Viti Levu from Deumba to Suva is wetter and greener than the Coral Coast, and the emphasis changes from beach life to cultural and natural attractions. Pacific Harbor satisfies both sporting types and culture vultures, while Fiji's best river trips begin at Navua. Here, too, scattered Fiji Indian dwellings join the Fijian villages that predominate farther west. All of the places listed below are easily accessible on the fairly frequent Ngaloa bus from Suva market.

Deumba

The **Coral Coast Christian Camp** (Box 36, Pacific Harbor; tel. 450-178), 13 km west of Navua near Pacific Harbor, offers four five-bed Kozy

Korner dormitories with a good communal kitchen and cold showers at F$13/22/31 single/double/triple. The six adjoining motel units go for F$22/40/58, complete with private bath, kitchen, fridge, and fan. Camping costs F$7 pp. No dancing and no alcoholic beverages are permitted on the premises; on Sunday at 1930 you're invited to the Fellowship Meeting in the manager's flat. The Camp is just across the highway from long golden Loloma Beach, the closest public beach to Suva, but if you swim here, watch your valuables. Technically you can camp free on this beach, but rampant theft has made this impractical. The Christian Camp is useful as a base from which to visit Pacific Harbor, and it's a good budget place to spend the night while arranging to get out to the surfers' camp on Yanutha Island, but avoid arriving on a weekend as it's often fully booked by church groups from Friday afternoon until Monday morning.

Right next door to the Christian Camp is the **Deumba Inn** (Box 132, Pacific Harbor; tel. 450-544, fax 361-337), which opened in 1994. They have 10 rooms with shared bath at F$17/27 single/double and five self-catering units at F$50 double. The Inn's main drawback is that you can't cook your own food in the cheaper rooms and meals at the restaurant are expensive. However, inexpensive snacks are available at the takeaway counter at lunchtime and the Inn is a useful backup if you happen to arrive on a day when the Camp is full.

The grocery stores nearest the above are by the bridge, one km toward Pacific Harbor. For fruit and vegetables you must go to Navua.

Pacific Harbor

Pacific Harbor is a sprawling, misplaced Hawaiian condo development and instant culture village, 152 km east of Nandi Airport and 44 km west of Suva. In July 1988 the Japanese corporation South Pacific Development purchased Pacific Harbor, and many of the 180 individual villas are owned by Australian or Hong Kong investors.

Pacific Harbor's imposing **Cultural Center** (Box 74, Pacific Harbor; tel. 450-177, fax 450-083) offers the chance to experience some freeze-dried Fijian culture. This re-created Fijian village on a small "sacred island" is complete with a 20-meter-tall temple and natives attired in jungle garb. Visitors tour the island hourly, seated in a double-hulled *ndrua* with a tour guide "warrior" carrying a spear, and at various stops village occupations such as canoe making, weaving, tapa, and pottery are demonstrated for the canoe-bound guests. At 1500 there are one-hour performances by the Dance Theater of Fiji (Monday, Wednesday, Thursday, and Friday) and Fijian firewalking (Tuesday and Saturday), and if you want to see one of the shows it's best to arrive with the tour buses in the early afternoon. Admission is F$17 pp for the village tour (Monday to Saturday 0930-1330), then another F$17 to see the dancing or firewalking, or F$28 for village tour and show combined. Rosie The Travel Service runs full-day bus tours to the Cultural Center from Nandi at F$84 pp including the tour and show but not lunch. The Dance Theater has an international reputation, with several successful North American tours to their credit.

Entry to the Waikiki-style **Marketplace of Fiji** at the Cultural Center, made up of mock-colonial boutiques and assorted historical displays, is free of charge. If you arrive here after 1630, all of the tourist buses will have left, and you'll be able to see quite a bit of the Cultural Center for nothing. The main Pacific Harbor post office is next to the Cultural Center.

Pacific Harbor's other main claim to fame is its 18-hole, par-72 championship **Country Club Golf Course** (Box 144, Pacific Harbor; tel. 450-048, fax 450-262), designed by Robert Trent Jones Jr. and said to be the South Pacific's finest. It's Fiji's only fully sprinklered and irrigated golf course. Course records are 69 by Bobby Clampett of the U.S. (amateur) and 64 by Greg Norman of Australia (professional). Green fees are F$22 for hotel guests, F$44 for others; the hire of clubs is F$16.50, an electric golf cart F$33. Take along an extra pair of socks in case you get a hole in one. You'll find a restaurant and bar in the clubhouse, about two km inland off Queens Road. Rosie The Travel Service runs full-day golfing tours from Nandi with time for nine holes at F$44 (lunch and green fees not included).

Although golfing is the resort's main sporting draw, **Beqa Divers** (tel. 450-323), a branch of Suva's Scubahire, is based at the Pacific Harbor International Hotel's marina and organizes diving on the nearby Mbengga Lagoon daily at 0900. Excursions cost F$127 with two tanks and a mediocre lunch.

Serious divers also have at their disposal the 18-meter live-aboard *Beqa Princess* operated by **Tropical Expeditions** (Box 271, Deumba; tel. 450-188, fax 450-426) from their Pacific Harbor base. The *Princess* specializes in three-night scuba cruises to the islands south of Viti Levu and day-trips to the Mbengga Lagoon.

There are three expensive hotels at Pacific Harbor. The 84 a/c rooms at the three-story **Pacific Harbor International Hotel** (Box 144, Pacific Harbor; tel. 450-022, fax 450-262) are F$143/165/198 single/double/triple, breakfast included. This hotel is at the mouth of the Nggaraninggoi River, between Queens Road and a long sandy beach. There's a *lovo* (F$28) with island entertainment here every Saturday night.

The advantage of the **Fiji Palms Beach Club Resort** (Box 6, Pacific Harbor; tel. 450-050, fax 450-025), right next to the Pacific Harbor International Hotel, is that the 14 two-bedroom apartments (F$150 single or double) have cooking facilities, which allows you to skip the many expensive restaurants in these parts. Many of the units have been sold as part of a time-share scheme.

Equally upmarket is the **Atholl Hotel** (Box 14, Pacific Harbor; tel. 450-100, fax 450-153), alongside the golf course, inland a couple of kilometers behind the Cultural Center, with 22 plush rooms at F$150 double.

Kumarans Restaurant (tel. 450-294), across the highway from the Pacific Harbor International Hotel, has some cheap curries at lunchtime, but the dinner menu is pricey. There are three small grocery stores beside Kumarans, and the self-service Trading Post Supermarket at the Marketplace of Fiji has a good selection.

Only charter flights from Nandi Airport land at Pacific Harbor's airstrip, but all of the Queens Road express buses stop here. If coming to Pacific Harbor from Suva by express bus, you'll be dropped at the Pacific Harbor International Hotel, a kilometer from the Cultural Center. The slower Ngaloa buses will stop right in front of the Cultural Center itself.

Navua

This bustling river town 39 km west of Suva is the market center of the rice-growing delta area near the mouth of the Navua River and the headquarters of Serua and Namosi provinces. If low-grade copper deposits totaling 1,000 million metric tonnes just inland at Namosi are ever developed, Navua will become a major mining port, passed by a huge drain pipe for copper tailings, ore conveyors, and four-lane highways. The present quiet road between Navua and Suva will bustle with new housing estates and heavy traffic, and the change from today will be total!

All of the express buses between Suva and Nandi stop at Navua. Village boats leave from the wharf beside Navua market for Mbengga Island south of Viti Levu daily except Sunday, but more depart on Saturday. Flat-bottomed punts to **Namuamua** village, 25 km up the Navua River, depart on Thursday, Friday, and Saturday afternoons, but almost anytime you can charter an outboard from Navua wharf to Namuamua at F$50 for the boat roundtrip. The hour-long ride takes you between high canyon walls and over boiling rapids with waterfalls on each side. Above Namuamua is the fabulous **Navua Gorge**, accessible only to intrepid river-runners in rubber rafts who go in by helicopter. It's also possible to reach the river by road at Nambukelevu.

A great way to experience the picturesque lower Navua is with **Wilderness Adventures** (Box 1389, Suva; tel. 386-498, fax 300-584), which runs full-day canoe trips (F$59 pp) down the river. Their minibus collects participants at Suva hotels around 0900, then there's a two-hour scenic drive to the embarkation point on the upper river, where the canoes and a rubber raft will be waiting. A stop is made halfway down the river for swimming and a picnic lunch (included). The canoe trips are intended for those aged 15-45, although physically fit older folks may join by signing a liability disclaimer. Everyone is welcome on Wilderness Adventures' motorized boat trips (adults F$54, children F$33) 20 km up the river from Navua to Nukusere village, where lunch is taken and visitors get an introduction to Fijian culture. These are probably the best day tours available in Fiji for the adventurous traveler, and any travel agent in Suva can make the bookings. In Nandi, book through Rosie The Travel Service. (If saving money is a priority and you can get a small group together, it's much cheaper to go to Navua by public bus and hire a market boat there.)

The building of the former Farmers Club, by the river in the center of Navua, 200 meters from the bus stand, was the four-room Heartbreak Hotel until recently when it closed due to financial difficulties. Check to see if they've reopened, and whether the large public bar downstairs is back in service.

Toward Suva

The **Ocean Pacific Club** (Box 3229, Lami; tel. 304-864, fax 361-577), near Nambukavesi village on a hillside between Navua and Suva, is an upmarket sportfishing camp with eight bungalows at F$85 single or double if you book direct. Their nine-meter cruiser goes out for wahoo, mahimahi, giant trevally, yellowfin tuna, marlin, and sailfish each morning at 0830 (F$110 pp). Scuba diving is also offered here.

OFFSHORE ISLANDS

Vatulele Island

This small island, just south of Viti Levu, is famous for its tapa cloth. Vatulele reaches a height of only 34 meters on its north end; there are steep bluffs on the west coast and gentle slopes facing a wide lagoon on the east. Both passes into the lagoon are from its north end. Five different levels of erosion are visible on the cliffs from which the uplifted limestone was undercut. There are also rock paintings, but no one knows when they were executed.

Other unique features of Vatulele are the sacred **red prawns**, which are found in a tidal pool at Korolamalama Cave near the island's rocky north coast. These scarlet prawns with remarkably long antennae are called *ura mbuta,* or cooked prawns, for their color. The red color probably comes from iron oxide in the limestone of their abode. It's strictly *tambu* to eat them or remove them from the pools. If you do, it will bring ill luck or even shipwreck. The story goes that a princess of yesteryear rejected a gift of cooked prawns from a suitor and threw them in the pools, where the boiled-red creatures were restored to life. Villagers can call the prawns by repeating a chant.

Village boats leave for the villages on the east side of Vatulele from Paradise Point near Korolevu Post Office on Tuesday, Thursday, and Saturday if the weather is good. Sunflower Airlines flies to Vatulele from Nandi four times a week (F$62 one-way). The island's small private airstrip is near the villages, six km from the resort described below, to which tourists are transferred by bus.

In 1990 Vatulele got its own luxury resort, the **Vatulele Island Resort** (Box 9936, Nandi Airport; tel. 520-300, fax 520-062) on Vatulele's west side. The 12 futuristic villas in a hybrid Fijian/New Mexico style sit about 50 meters apart on a magnificent white sand beach facing a protected lagoon. The emphasis is on luxurious exclusivity: villas cost F$1000 double per day, including all meals. The minimum stay is five nights, and children are only accepted at certain times of the year. To preserve the natural environment, motorized water sports are not offered, but there's lots to do, including sailing, snorkeling, windsurfing, paddling, tennis, and hiking, with guides and gear provided at no additional cost. The only thing you'll be charged extra for is scuba diving. This world-class resort is a creation of Australian TV producer Henry Crawford and local promoter Martin Livingston, a former manager of Turtle Island Resort in the Yasawas.

Yanutha Island

In 1994 a new surfers' camp opened on a splendid beach on Yanutha Island, to the west of Mbengga (not to be confused with the Yanutha Island on which The Fijian Resort Hotel is found). **Frigate Surfriders** (Ratu Penaia Drekeni, Box 39, Pacific Harbor; tel. 450-472) offers cots in a 10-bed dorm at F$55 pp for surfers, F$25 pp for nonsurfers, plus tax. Included are accommodations and all meals, windsurfing, surfing, and sportfishing. The lefthander in Frigate Passage has been called the most underrated wave in Fiji: "fast, hollow, consistent, and deserted." For information ask for Inoke at the video rental shop in the Marketplace of Fiji at Pacific Harbor's Cultural Center. Boat transfers are F$20 pp return. Village boats to the one Fijian village on Yanutha depart on Tuesday and Saturday afternoons from the bridge near the Pacific Harbor International Hotel.

Mbengga Island

Mbengga is the home of the famous Fijian fire-walkers; Rukua, Natheva, and Ndakuimbengga are firewalking villages. Nowadays, however, they perform only at the hotels on Viti Levu. At low tide you can walk the 27 km around the island: the road only goes from Waisomo to Ndakuni. There are caves with ancient burials near Suliyanga, which can be reached on foot from Mbengga at low tide, but to visit you'll need permission from the village chief. Have your *sevusevu* ready. Malumu Bay, between the two branches of the island, is thought to be a drowned crater. Climb Korolevu (439 meters), the highest peak, from Waisomo or Lalati.

Frigate Passage on the west side of the barrier reef is one of the best dive sites near Suva. There's a vigorous tidal flow in and out of the passage, which attracts large schools of fish, and there are large coral heads. **Sulfur Passage** on the east side of Mbengga is equally good. Kandavu Island is visible to the south of Mbengga.

The **Marlin Bay Resort** (Box 112, Deumba; tel. 304-042, fax 304-028) opened in 1991 on a golden beach between Raviravi and Rukua villages on the west side of Mbengga. The 12 luxurious *mbures* (no cooking facilities) go for F$178/220/260 single/double/triple. The meal plan is F$78 pp a day, and boat transfers from Pacific Harbor cost F$70 return. The area is a favorite of scuba divers (F$100 a dive) and horseback riding is also available. Boat pickups for the Marlin Bay Resort take place at The Pub Restaurant, Pacific Harbor.

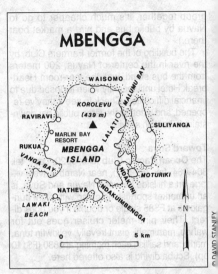

The best beach is Lawaki to the west of Natheva. Present the village chief of Natheva with a nice bundle of *waka* if you want to camp. It's quite possible to stay in any of the Fijian villages on Mbengga by following the procedure outlined in "Staying in Villages" in the Fiji Islands chapter introduction. Ask around the wharf at Navua around noon any day except Sunday and you'll soon find someone happy to take you. Alcohol is not allowed in the villages on Mbengga, so if you're asked to buy a case of beer, politely decline and offer to buy other groceries instead.

SUVA AND VICINITY

The pulsing heart of the South Pacific, Suva is the largest and most cosmopolitan city in Oceania. The port is always jammed with ships bringing goods and passengers from far and wide, and busloads of commuters and enthusiastic visitors constantly stream into the busy market bus station. In the business center are Indian women in saris, large sturdy chocolate-skinned Fijians, Australians and New Zealanders in shorts and knee socks, and wavy-haired Polynesians from Rotuma and Tonga.

Suva squats on a hilly peninsula between Lauthala Bay and Suva Harbor in the southeast corner of Viti Levu. The verdant mountains north and west catch the southeast trades, producing damp conditions year-round. Visitors sporting a sunburn from Fiji's western sunbelt resorts may appreciate Suva's warm tropical rains (most of which fall at night). In 1870 the Polynesia Company sent Australian settlers to camp along mosquito-infested Numbukalou Creek on land obtained from High Chief Cakobau. When efforts to grow sugarcane here failed, the company convinced the British to move their headquarters here, and since 1882 Suva has been the capital of Fiji.

Today this exciting multiracial city of 175,000—a fifth of Fiji's population—is also about the only place in Fiji where you'll see a building taller than a palm tree. High-rise office buildings and hotels overlook the compact downtown area. The British left behind imposing colonial buildings, wide avenues, and manicured parks as evidence of their rule. The Fiji School of Medicine, the University of the South Pacific, the Fiji Institute of Technology, the Pacific Theological College, and the headquarters of many regional organizations have been established here. In addition, the city offers some of the best nightlife between Kings Cross (Sydney) and North Beach (San Francisco), plus shopping, sightseeing, and many good-value places to stay and eat.

Keep in mind that on Sunday all shops will be closed, restaurants keep reduced hours, and far fewer taxis or buses will be operating. In short, the city will be dead. An excellent plan is to catch the Saturday bus/boat service to Levuka and spend the rest of the weekend there (book your ticket a day or two in advance). However, if you do find yourself in Suva, the fantastic choral singing makes dressing up and attending church worthwhile. Most churches have services in English, but none compare with the 1000 Fijian service at Centenary Methodist Church on Stewart Street.

The lovely *Isa Lei,* a Fijian song of farewell, tells of a youth whose love sails off and leaves him alone in Suva, smitten with longing.

SIGHTS

Central Suva

Suva's wonderful, colorful **municipal market,** the largest retail produce market in the Pacific, is a good place to dabble. If you're a yachtie or backpacker, you'll be happy to know that the market overflows with fresh produce of every kind. It's worth some time looking around, and consider having kava at the *yanggona* dens at the back of the market for about F$2 a bowl (share the excess with those present). Fijian women sell fresh pineapple and guava juice from glass "fish tank" containers.

From the market, walk south on Scott Street, past the colorful old Metropole Hotel, to the **Fiji Visitors Bureau** in a former customs house (1912) opposite Suva's General Post Office. At the corner of Thomson and Pier streets opposite the visitors bureau is the onetime **Garrick Hotel** (1914) with a Sichuan Chinese restaurant behind the wrought-iron balconies upstairs. Go east on Thomson to Morris Hedstrom Supermarket and a picturesque colonial-style arcade (1919) along **Numbukalou Creek,** a campsite of Suva's first European settlers. You'll get good photos from the little park just across the bridge.

Cumming Street, Suva's main duty-free shopping area, runs east from the park on the site of Suva's original vegetable market before it moved to its present location just prior to WW II. During the war the street became a market of a different sort as Allied troops flocked here in

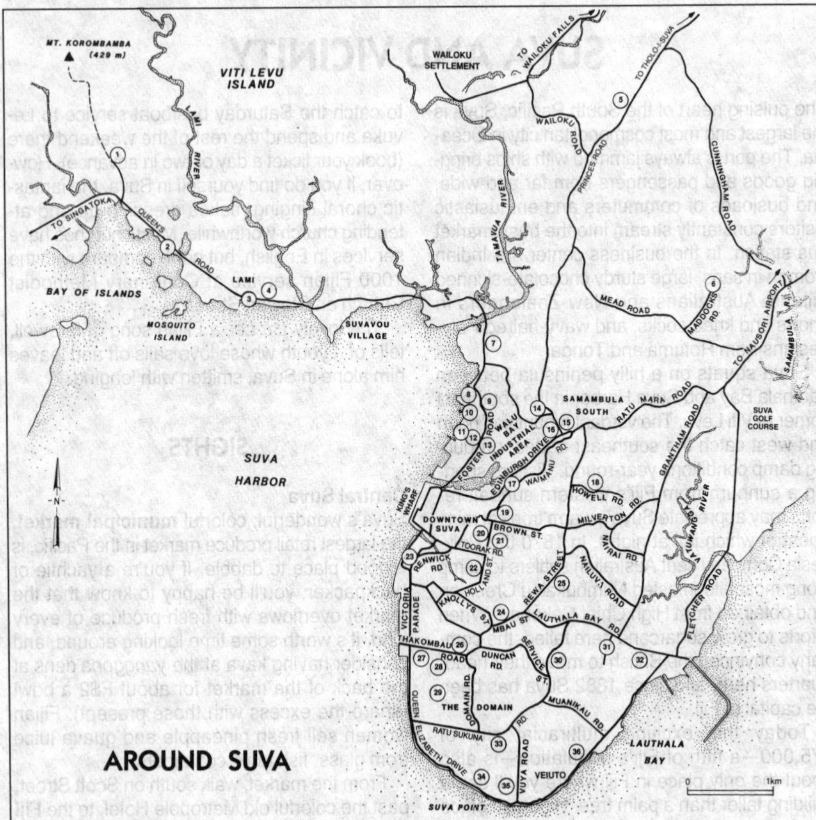

AROUND SUVA

1. cement factory
2. Raffles Tradewinds Hotel
3. Scubahire
4. Castle Restaurant
5. Fiji School of Medicine
6. Queen Elizabeth Barracks
7. Suva Cemetery
8. Royal Suva Yacht Club
9. Suva Prison
10. Carpenters Shipping
11. Muaiwalu Jetty
12. Dive Center Ltd.
13. Carlton Brewery
14. Australian Embassy
15. Fiji Institute of Technology
16. Tanoa House Private Hotel
17. Outrigger Hotel
18. Sangam Temple
19. C.W.M. Hospital
20. Pacific Concerns Resource Center
21. Amy Apartment Hotel
22. Jame Mosque
23. General Post Office
24. Suva Apartments
25. Flagstaff Boarding House
26. South Seas Private Hotel
27. Thurston Botanical Gardens
28. Fiji Museum
29. Government House
30. Forum Secretariat
31. University of the South Pacific
32. National Stadium
33. Parliament
34. Divisional Surveyor
35. Pacific Theological College
36. Pacific Regional Seminary

search of evening entertainment. When import duties were slashed in the early 1960s to cater to an emerging tourist market, Cumming assumed its present form. To continue your walk, turn right on Renwick Road and head back into the center of town.

At the junction of Thomson Street, Renwick Road, and Victoria Parade is a small park known as **The Triangle** with five concrete benches and a white obelisk bearing four inscriptions: "Cross and Cargill first missionaries arrived 14th October 1835; Fiji British Crown Colony 10th October 1874; Public Land Sales on this spot 1880; Suva proclaimed capital 1882." Inland a block on Pratt Street is the **Catholic cathedral** (1902), one of Suva's finest buildings. Between The Triangle and the cathedral is the towering **Reserve Bank of Fiji** (1984), which is worth entering to see the currency exhibition.

Return to Suva's main avenue, Victoria Parade, and walk south past **Sukuna Park,** site of public protests in 1990 against Fiji's gerrymandered constitution; the colonial-style **Fintel Building** (1926), nerve center of Fiji's international telecommunications links; the picturesque **Queen Victoria Memorial Hall** (1904), later Suva Town Hall and now the Ming Palace restaurant; and the **City Library** (1909), which opened in 1909 thanks to a grant from American philanthropist Andrew Carnegie. All these sights are on your right.

South Suva

Continue south on Victoria Parade past the somber headquarters of the **Native Land Trust Board,** which administers much of Fiji's land on behalf of indigenous landowners. Just beyond and across the street from the Travelodge Hotel is Suva's largest edifice, the imposing **Government Buildings** (1939), once the headquarters of the British colonial establishment in the South Pacific. Here on 14 May 1987 Col. Sitiveni Rabuka carried out his assault on parliament and for the next five years Fiji had no representative government. The statue of Chief Cakobau faces the door where the legislators were led out. The building's clock tower is a symbol of Suva.

The main facade of the Government Buildings faces **Albert Park,** where aviator Charles Kingsford Smith landed his trimotor Fokker VII-3M on 6 June 1928 after arriving from Hawaii on the first-ever flight from California to Australia. (The first commercial flight to Fiji was a Pan Am flying boat, which landed in Suva Harbor in October 1941.) Facing the west side of the park is the elegant, Edwardian-style **Grand Pacific Hotel,** built by the Union Steamship Company in 1914 to accommodate their transpacific passengers. The 75 rooms were designed to appear as shipboard staterooms, with upstairs passageways surveying the harbor, like the promenade deck of a ship. For decades the Grand Pacific was the social center of the city, but it has been closed since 1992. The building's owners, the phosphate-rich Republic of Nauru, have announced that the building is soon to be fully renovated and expanded into a five-star luxury hotel managed by the French Accor chain, though that remains to be seen.

South of Albert Park are the pleasing **Thurston Botanical Gardens,** opened in 1913, where tropical flowers such as cannas and plumbagos blossom. The original Fijian village of Suva once stood on this site. On the grounds of the gardens is a clock tower dating from 1918 and the **Fiji Museum** (tel. 315-944, fax 305-143), founded in 1904 and the oldest in the South Pacific. Small but full, this museum is renowned for its maritime displays: canoes, outriggers, the rudder from HMS *Bounty,* and *ndrua* steering oars that were manned by four Fijians. The collection of Fijian war clubs is outstanding and the history section is being expanded as artifacts in overseas collections are returned to Fiji. The museum is open daily except Sunday, 0830-1630, admission F$3.30. (While you're there, pick up a copy of *Life in Feejee—Five Years Among the Cannibals* at the museum shop—one of the most fascinating books about the South Seas you'll ever read.)

South of the gardens is **Government House,** formerly the palace of the British governors of Fiji and now the residence of the president. The original building, erected after 1882, burned after being hit by lightning in 1921, and the present edifice, which dates from 1928, is a replica of the former British governor's residence in Colombo, Sri Lanka. The grounds cannot be visited. The sentry on ceremonial guard duty wears a belted red tunic and an immaculate white *sulu* (kilt). Military officers on duty here do not care to

fishing for matu and kaikai on the Nasese Seawall, just south of Suva's Botanical Garden

THE FIJI TIMES

be photographed, though the sentry won't mind having his picture taken. The changing of the guard takes place daily at noon with an especially elaborate ceremony the first Friday of every month to the accompaniment of the military band.

From the seawall south of Government House you get a good view across Suva Harbor to Mbengga Island (to the left) and the dark, green mountains of eastern Viti Levu punctuated by Joske's Thumb, a high volcanic plug (to the right). Follow the seawall south past a few old colonial buildings, and turn left onto Ratu Sukuna Road, the first street after the Police Academy. About 500 meters up this road is the new **Parliament of Fiji** (1992), an impressive, traditional-style building with an orange pyramid-shaped roof. From here it's a good idea to catch a taxi to the University of the South Pacific (a description of which follows). The Nasese bus does a scenic loop through the beautiful garden suburbs of South Suva: just flag it down if you need a ride back to the market.

University of the South Pacific

A frequent bus from in front of Zenon Bookstore, next to the National Bank of Fiji on Victoria Parade opposite Sukuna Park, will bring you direct to the University of the South Pacific (USP). Founded in 1968, this beautiful 72.8-hectare campus on a hilltop overlooking Lauthala Bay is jointly owned by 12 Pacific countries. Although over 70% of the almost 2,000 full-time and more than 600 part-time students are from

Fiji, the rest are on scholarships from every corner of the Pacific.

The site of the Lauthala Campus was a Royal New Zealand Air Force seaplane base before the land was turned over to USP. As you enter from Lauthala Bay Road you'll pass the Botanical Garden (1988) and an information office on the right, then the British-built Administration Building on the left. Next comes the $3.5-million university library (1988), erected with Australian aid. The design of the Student Union Building (1975), just across a wooden bridge from the library, was influenced by traditional Pacific building motifs of interlocking circles. Look for the pleasant canteen in the Student Union (open Monday to Saturday 0800-2030 during the school year). It's interesting to observe the mixed batch of students and the ways they cope with the inconvenience of tiny chairs. There's a choice of Indian or island food.

Several buildings south of this is the **Institute of Pacific Studies** (Box 1168, Suva; tel. 314-306), housed in the former RNZAF officers' mess. Every available space on the walls of the IPS building has been covered with murals by Pacific painters. This Institute is a leading publisher of insightful books written by Pacific islanders; these books may be purchased at their bookroom without the markup charged by commercial bookstores in town. Don't confuse this bookroom with the regular USP bookstore nearby.

Students from outside the Pacific islands pay about F$9500 a year tuition to study at USP. Room and board are available at around F$3360 and books will run another F$400. There are academic minimum-entry requirements and applications must be in by 31 December for the following term. The two semesters are late February to the end of June, and late July until the end of November. Many courses in the social sciences have a high level of content pertaining to Pacific culture, and postgraduate studies in a growing number of areas are available. To obtain a calendar, application for admission, and other materials send US$20 to: The Registrar, University of the South Pacific, Box 1168, Suva, Fiji Islands (tel. 313-900, fax 302-556).

The USP is always in need of qualified staff, so if you're from a university milieu and looking for a chance to live in the South Seas, this could be it. The maximum contract is six years (you need seven years of residency to apply for Fijian citizenship). If your credentials are impeccable you should write to the registrar from home. On the spot it's better to talk to a department head about his/her needs before going to see the registrar. All USP staff, both local and expatriate, must leave the university if they run for political office or become officers of political parties.

Northwest of Suva

The part of Suva north of Walu Bay accommodates much of Suva's shipping and industry. Carlton Brewery on Foster Road cannot be visited. About 600 meters beyond the brewery is the vintage **Suva Prison** (1913), a fascinating colonial structure with high walls and barbwire. Opposite is the **Royal Suva Yacht Club,** where you can sign in and buy a drink, meet some yachties, and maybe find a boat to crew on. Their T-shirts (F$12-18) are hot items. In the picturesque **Suva Cemetery,** just to the north, the Fijian graves are wrapped in colorful *sulus* and tapa cloth, and make good subjects for photographers.

Catch one of the frequent Shore, Lami, or Ngaloa buses west on Queens Road, past **Suvavou** village, home of the Suva area's original Fijian inhabitants (and most contemporary "sword sellers"), and past Lami town to the **Raffles Tradewinds Hotel,** seven km from the market. Many cruising yachts tie up here, and the view of the Bay of Islands from the hotel is good.

Orchid Island

Seven km northwest of Suva is the **Orchid Island Cultural Center** (Box 1018, Suva; tel. 361-128, fax 361-064). In the past it offered a good synopsis of Fijian customs through demonstrations, dancing, and historical exhibits, affording a glimpse into traditions such as the kava ceremony, tapa and pottery making, etc. At the miniature zoo you could see and photograph Fiji's rare banded and crested iguanas up close. Replicas of a Fijian war canoe and thatched temple *(mbure kalou)* were on the grounds. We've used the past tense here because Orchid Island has gone downhill and now looks abandoned, although some readers report being admitted and shown around the empty, decaying buildings by residual staff who were only too happy to pocket their F$10 pp admission fee. You might check Orchid Island's current status at the Fiji Visitors Bureau (and don't bother going on a Sunday). The Shore and Ngaloa buses pass this way.

Tholo-i-Suva Forest Park

This lovely park, at an altitude of 150-200 meters, offers 3.6 km of trails through the beautiful mahogany forest flanking the upper drainage area of Waisila Creek. Enter from the Forestry Station along the Falls Trail. A half-km nature trail begins near the Upper Pools, and aside from waterfalls and natural swimming pools there are thatched pavilions with tables at which to picnic. With the lovely green forests behind Suva in full view, this is one of the most breathtaking places in all of Fiji and you may spot a few native butterflies, birds, reptiles, and frogs. The park is so unspoiled it's hard to imagine you're only 11 km from Suva.

When the park first opened in 1973, camping was allowed near the upper and lower pools. Then in the mid-1980s the rangers were forced to prohibit camping due to thefts from both campers and swimmers. Recently security patrols have been stepped up and camping is once again allowed, but someone must still keep watch at the campsite at all times, especially on weekends. You must also keep an eye on your gear if you go swimming. There's been talk of imposing a F$5 pp entry fee to cover park maintenance and management, but even with such a fee Tholo-i-Suva would still be worth

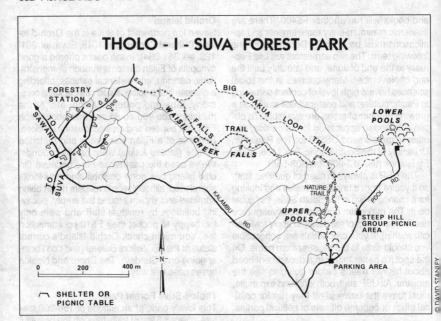

THOLO - I - SUVA FOREST PARK

FORESTRY STATION

BIG NDAKUA LOOP TRAIL

WAISILA FALLS TRAIL

WAISILA CREEK FALLS

LOWER POOLS

TO SAWANI

TO SUVA

KALAMBU RD.

NATURE TRAIL

UPPER POOLS

POOL RD.

STEEP HILL GROUP PICNIC AREA

PARKING AREA

-N-

0   200   400 m

⌒ SHELTER OR PICNIC TABLE

© DAVID STANLEY

visiting. Get there on the Sawani or Serea bus (55 cents), which leave from Lane No. 3 at Suva Bus Station every hour, but come on a dry day as it's even rainier than Suva and the creeks are prone to flooding.

On your way back to Suva from Tholo-i-Suva ask the bus driver to drop you at Wailoku Road, just past the Fiji School of Medicine in Tamavua Heights. Every half hour the Wailoku bus runs down the hill: stay on till the bus stops and turns around, then continue down the road a few hundred meters to a bridge. Take the trail on the left just across the bridge and hike about five minutes upstream to **Wailoku Falls**, where you can swim in a deep pool of cold, clear water amid the idyllic verdant vegetation. This nice picnic spot is government land and no admission is charged. The nearby Wailoku Settlement is inhabited by descendants of blackbirded Solomon Islanders. If you only want to visit the falls, look for the Wailoku bus in Lane No. 2 at the market bus station.

Sports and Recreation
At the 18-hole, par-72 **Suva Golf Club** (tel. 382-872), 15 Rifle Range Rd., Vatuwangga, the course record is 65. Green fees are F$6 for nine holes, F$12 for 18 holes, plus F$12 for club and trolley hire. Visitors are welcome, though Tuesday and Saturday afternoons are reserved for club competitions (General Rabuka and Ratu Mara are regulars).

Scubahire (G.P.O. Box 777, Suva; tel. 361-088, fax 361-047), 75 Marine Dr., opposite the Lami Shopping Center, is the country's oldest dive shop (established 1970) and one of only two PADI five-star dive centers in Fiji. Also known as "Beqa Divers," they arrange full-day diving trips to the Mbengga Lagoon from their Pacific Harbor base for F$127, including two tanks, weight belt, backpack, and lunch. Other equipment can be rented. Scubahire will also take snorkelers out on their full-day dive trips for F$66 pp, snorkeling gear and lunch included. The 65 km of barrier reef around the Mbengga Lagoon features multicolored soft corals and fabulous sea fans at Side Streets, and an exciting wall and big fish at Cutter Passage. Scubahire's four-day PADI certification course (F$450) involves six boat dives, an excellent way to learn while getting in some great diving.

An introductory dive is F$138. Fiji's only pur-pose-built diver training pool is on their Lami premises. You'll need to show a medical cer-tificate proving you're fit for diving.

Dive Center Ltd. (Box 3066, Lami; tel. 300-599, fax 302-639), 4 Matua St., Walu Bay (op-posite Carlton Brewery), rents and sells scuba gear at daily and weekly rates, and fills tanks.

Surfers should call Matthew Light (tel. 361-560), who runs a shuttle out to Sandspit Light-house where there's good surfing at high tide. He'll pick you up at the Raffles Tradewinds Hotel in Lami for F$15 pp roundtrip.

The Suva **Olympic Swimming Pool,** 224 Victoria Parade, charges F$1.10 admission. It's open Monday to Friday 1000-1800, Saturday 0800-1800 (April to September), or Monday to Friday 0900-1900, Saturday 0600-1900 (Octo-ber to March). Lockers are available.

The Fijians are a very muscular, keenly ath-letic people who send champion teams far and wide in the Pacific. You can see rugby (April to September) and soccer (March to October) on Saturday afternoons at 1500 at the **National Stadium** near the University of the South Pacific. Rugby and soccer are also played at Albert Park Saturday, and you could also see a cricket game here (mid-October to Easter).

ACCOMMODATIONS

There's a wide variety of places to stay and the low-budget accommodations can be divided into two groups. The places on the south side of the downtown area near Albert Park are mostly de-cent and provide communal cooking facilities to bona fide travelers. However, many of those northeast of downtown are dicey and cater most-ly to "short-time" guests; few of these bother providing cooking facilities. Many of the medi-um-priced hotels and self-catering apartments are along Gordon Street and its continuation MacGregor Road. In this book we include every known hotel, regardless of its category or lack thereof. If you want to spend some time in Suva to take advantage of the city's good facilities and varied activities, look for something with cooking facilities and weekly rates. Many apart-ments are available on a short-term basis.

Budget Accommodations
Around Albert Park

Women are accommodated at the big, mod-ern **YWCA** (Box 534, Suva; tel. 304-829, fax 303-004) on Sukuna Park—a good place to meet Fijian women. There are only two singles and one double available for foreign visitors (F$10 pp).

Suva's original backpacker's oasis is the **Co-conut Inn** (Box 12539, Suva; tel. 312-904, fax 701-169), 8 Kimberly St., which charges F$8.50 per bunk in the stuffy four-bed dormitories. The four double rooms are F$22, and there's a small flat upstairs for up to six persons at F$38 double. The Inn offers cooking facilities and luggage storage, though it's sometimes a little dirty and disorganized (take care with your gear here). It's far less crowded now than it was back in the days when it was the only cheap place to stay.

The 42-room **South Seas Private Hotel** (Box 2086, Government Buildings, Suva; tel. 312-296, fax 340-236), 6 Williamson Rd., one block east of Albert Park, has clean singles/doubles with fan and shared bath at F$11/18, or F$8 pp in the five-bed dorms. A room with private bath is F$26 double—good value. This quiet hotel has a pleasant veranda and a large communal kitchen that may be used 0700-2000 only. For a refundable F$10 deposit, you may borrow a plate, mug, knife, fork, and spoon, but there's a longstanding shortage of pots and pans (blan-kets in the rooms and toilet paper in the toilets are two other things in short supply here). They have a solar hot water system, so you'll proba-bly have hot water in evening but not in the morning. It's possible to leave excess luggage at the South Seas while you're off visiting other islands, but lock your bag securely with a pad-lock that can't be picked. Traveler's checks are changed at bank rates. Since this hotel received rave reviews in the Australian guidebooks (which they also sell) it has always been crowded with travelers (not all of them friendly), and you may arrive to find it full. Catch a taxi here from the market the first time (F$2). The staff can arrange minibus transfers to Nandi at F$10.

Travel Inn (Box 2086, Government Build-ings, Suva; tel. 304-254, fax 340-236), formerly known as Loloma Lodge and Pacific Grand Holi-day Apartments, an older two-story building at 19

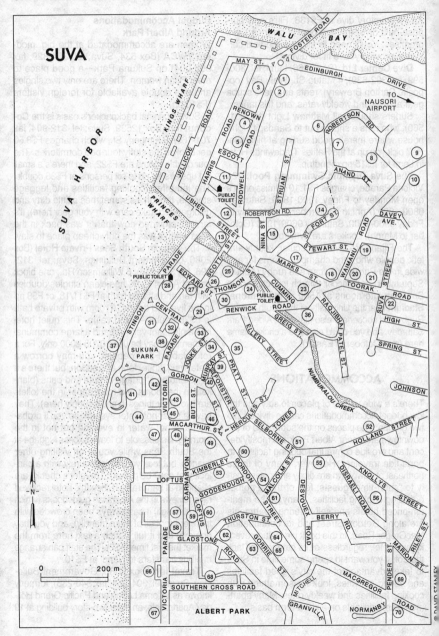

SUVA

WALU BAY

FOSTER ROAD

EDINBURGH DRIVE

TO NAUSORI AIRPORT

KINGS WHARF

SUVA HARBOR

PRINCES WHARF

MAY ST.

RENOWN ROAD

ESCOTT ROAD

RODWELL ROAD

JELLICOE ROAD

HARRIS ROAD

USHER STREET

ROBERTSON RD.

ROBERTSON RD.

STRUAN ST.

ANAND ST.

NINA ST.

ST FORT ST.

WAIMANU ROAD

DAVEY AVE.

STEWART ST.

MARKS ST.

TOORAK ROAD

SUVA ST.

HIGH ST.

SPRING ST.

SCOTT ST.

THOMSON ST.

CUMMING ST.

RENWICK ROAD

RAQUIBAI PATEL ST.

GREIG ST.

ELLERY STREET

EDWARD STREET

CENTRAL ST.

STINSON PARADE

SUKUNA PARK

VICTORIA PARADE

GORDON ST.

JOSKE ST.

MURRAY ST.

PRATT ST.

FORSTER ST.

HERCULES ST.

SELBORNE ST.

TOWER ST.

NUMBUKALOU CREEK

HOLLAND STREET

JOHNSON

MACARTHUR ST.

BUTT ST.

KIMBERLEY ST.

CARNARVON ST.

LOFTUS ST.

GOODENOUGH ST.

GORDON STREET

MALCOLM ST.

DESVOEUX ROAD

BERRY RD.

KNOLLYS STREET

DISRAELI ROAD

MARION ST.

RILEY ST.

GLADSTONE ROAD

THURSTON ST.

GORRIE ST.

MACGREGOR ROAD

PENDER ST.

VICTORIA PARADE

SOUTHERN CROSS ROAD

MITCHELL

GRANVILLE

NORMANBY ROAD

ALBERT PARK

-N-

0   200 m

PUBLIC TOILET

DAVID STANLEY

SUVA

1. Bali Hai Nightspot	25. Harbor Center/Dominion Arcade	48. Air Nauru/Government Handicraft Center
2. Phoenix Cinema	26. Fiji Visitors Bureau	49. Anglican Cathedral
3. Pacific Forum Line	27. General Post Office	50. Southern Cross Hotel
4. Health Office	28. Curio and Handicraft Market	51. The Playhouse
5. buses to Lautoka	29. The Triangle	52. Laxmi Narayan Temple
6. Motel Capital	30. Sunflower Airlines	53. Coconut Inn
7. Tropic Towers Apartment Motel	31. Y.W.C.A.	54. Elixir Motel Apartments
8. Motel Crossroad	32. Air Pacific	55. Coconut Frond Bookstore
9. New Haven Motel	33. Hare Krishna Vegetarian Restaurant	56. Victoria Tennis Courts
10. Suva Oceanview Hotel	34. Central Police Station	57. Golden Dragon
11. bus station	35. Catholic Cathedral	58. Native Land Trust Board
12. market	36. Travelworld Services	59. Old Mill Cottage Cafe
13. Metropole Hotel	37. Tiko's Floating Restaurant	60. U.S. Embassy/Tourism Council
14. Capricorn Apartment Hotel	38. Regal Cinema	61. Berjaya Hotel
15. Patterson Brothers Shipping	39. Town House Apartment Hotel	62. Pacific Conference of Churches
16. Centenary Methodist Church	40. Sunset Apartment Motel	63. Tuvalu Embassy
17. Century Cinema	41. Suva Civic Auditorium	64. Gordon St. Medical Center
18. Kings Suva Hotel	42. Fiji International Telecommunications office	65. Travel Inn
19. Karishma Cinema	43. Air Fiji	66. Suva Travelodge
20. New Lilac Cinema	44. Suva Olympic Pool	67. Grand Pacific Hotel
21. Bouganvillia Motel	45. Lucky Eddie's	68. Government Buildings
22. Immigration office	46. Emosi Ferry Service	69. Pender Court
23. Chequer's Nightspot	47. Suva City Library	70. Suva Peninsula Hotel
24. Morris Hedstrom Supermarket		

Gorrie St., is owned by the same company as the South Seas Private Hotel. There are 16 fan-cooled rooms with shared bath at F$17/22 single/double, all with access to communal cooking facilities, and four self-contained apartments for F$40 triple daily (weekly rates available). Again, the solar heating means no hot water unless the sun shines but there are plenty of blankets and good locks on the doors. Visitors from other Pacific islands often stay here, as this is one of Suva's best buys. For a longer stay check **Nukurua Apartments** (tel. 312-343) nearby at 25 Gorrie Street.

Budget Accommodations Northeast of Downtown

The **Metropole Hotel** (Box 404, Suva; tel. 304-112), on Scott Street opposite the market, is an old-fashioned British pub gone native. There are four rooms with shared bath at F$17/25 single/double. The bars next to and below the hotel

section are extremely noisy, but they usually close at 2100 (ask).

The **Kings Suva Hotel** (Box 5141, Raiwangga; tel. 304-411, fax 304-384) on Waimanu Road is rougher, and the four noisy bars make it more appealing to hookers than travelers. The 24 rooms are F$17/20 single/double without bath, F$25/30 with bath, but have a look beforehand as quality varies. In short, this place is a dive.

The 42-room **Oceanview Private Hotel** (Box 16037, Suva; tel. 312-129), 270 Waimanu Rd., charges F$14/20 single/double, F$30 for a four-person family room, or F$8 in the dorm. It has a pleasant hillside location, but avoid the noisy rooms over the reception area and bar. The new management has tried to clean the place up, but because of its former reputation, the Oceanview isn't listed in any travel guidebook to Fiji, so here's your chance to escape the backpack brigade without going upmarket.

Just up the hill at 587 Waimanu Rd. is the 14-room **New Haven Motel** (G.P.O. Box 992, Suva; tel. 315-220), which is cheap (F$17 single or double downstairs, F$20 upstairs) but rather dirty, and it hosts a lot of couples for *very* short stays. The **Motel Crossroad** (tel. 300-089), 124 Robertson Rd. (F$15 single or double), and the 22-room **Motel Capital** (tel. 313-246), 91 Robertson Rd. (F$18 single or double with bath), are similar. Only consider these three if your main interest is Suva's seedier side.

The 23 units at **Amy Apartments Motel** (Box 3985, Samambula; tel. 315-113), at 98 Amy St. several blocks east of Waimanu Road, are F$20/25 single/double on the first floor, F$30/33 on the second and third floors. A larger "family unit" is F$66. Many of the people staying here seem to have more on their minds than sleep, and it can be rather noisy with shouts and laughter echoing through the halls.

Another place to avoid is the **Flagstaff Boarding House** (Box 1328, Suva; tel. 313-873), 62 Rewa St., which is also well frequented by "short time" guests.

The **Tanoa House Private Hotel** (Box 704, Suva; tel. 381-575), 5 Princes Rd. in Samambula South, is a totally respectable guesthouse run by an ex-colonial from the Gilberts. The place has a garden with a view, and you meet genuine island characters. The 10 rooms with shared bath are F$15/25/30 single/double/triple; breakfast is F$5 extra, and other meals are available. It's situated across from the Fiji Institute of Technology near the end of Waimanu Road, too far to walk from downtown, but you can get there easily on the Samambula bus.

Apartment Hotels

Two apartment hotels behind the Central Police Station are worth a try. The congenial **Town House Apartment Hotel** (G.P.O. Box 485, Suva; tel. 300-055, fax 303-446), 3 Forster St., is a five-story building with panoramic views from the bar on the roof. The 28 a/c units with cooking facilities are good value at F$44/55 single/double and up.

Nearby and under the same management is the **Sunset Apartment Motel** (G.P.O. Box 485, Suva; tel. 301-799, fax 303-446), corner of Gordon and Murray streets. The 15 self-catering apartments in this normal four-story suburban apartment block begin at F$40/49 single/double. Some of the singles lack cooking facilities, are noisy, and have uncomfortably soft beds.

Four-story **Elixir Motel Apartments** (Box 2347, Government Buildings, Suva; tel. 303-288, fax 303-383), on the corner of Gordon and Malcolm streets, has 14 two-bedroom apartments with cooking facilities and private bath at F$55 without a/c, F$66 with a/c for up to three people. Weekly and monthly rates are also available, so check it out for a long stay (on a daily basis you can do better elsewhere).

Also consider the apartments with fan at **Pender Court** (31 Pender St., Suva; tel. 313-973, fax 300-381). The 13 studios with kitchenettes begin around F$35 single or double (10% reduction by the week), and there are also six one-bedroom apartments with kitchens for F$45. It's sometimes a little noisy, so don't make it your first choice.

Eleven better self-catering units owned by the National Olympic Committee are available at **Suva Apartments** (Box 12488, Suva; tel. 304-280, fax 303-446), 17 Mbau St., a block or two east of Pender Court. They're F$28/33/43 single/double/triple daily, with 10% off on weekly rentals. Be prepared for some traffic noise.

Up in the Waimanu Road area, the **Capricorn Apartment Hotel** (G.P.O. Box 1261, Suva; tel. 303-732, fax 303-069), 7 St. Fort St., has 25 spacious a/c units with cooking facilities beginning at F$75 single or double, F$85 triple. It's very clean, comfortable, and good value. The three- and four-story apartment blocks edge the swimming pool, and there are good views of the harbor from the individual balconies.

Tropic Towers Apartment Motel (G.P.O. Box 1347, Suva; tel. 304-470, fax 304-169), 86 Robertson Rd., has 34 a/c apartments with cooking facilities in a four-story building at F$50/61/72 single/double/triple. Ask about the 13 "budget" units without air-conditioning in the annex, which are about F$15 cheaper. Washing machines (F$5) and a swimming pool are available for guests; screened windows or mosquito nets are not. This and the Capricorn are good choices for families.

Medium-Priced Hotels

The **Bougainvillea Motel** (Box 15030, Suva; tel. 303-690, fax 303-289), 55 Toorak Rd., tries to cater to businesspeople. The 13 spacious self-contained rooms with balcony, phone, TV, and coffee-making facilities are F$39 double with fan, F$50 with a/c.

Up the hill beyond the hospital is the two-story **Outrigger Hotel** (Box 750, Suva; tel. 314-944, fax 302-944), 349 Waimanu Road. The 20 a/c rooms with bath are F$43/50 single/double; a four-person suite is F$66. Most of the rooms have an excellent view of Suva Harbor, and there's a swimming pool. **Papa La Pizza** on the premises is said to serve the best pizza in Suva. Get there on the frequent Hospital bus from the bus station.

The **Suva Peninsula Hotel** (Box 888, Suva; tel. 313-711, fax 300-804), at the corner of Macgregor Road and Pender Street, is a stylish four-floor building with swimming pool. The 32 a/c rooms begin at F$55/65 single/double, while the eight suites with kitchenettes run F$77.

Upmarket Hotels

Suva's largest and most expensive hotel is the **Suva Travelodge** (Box 1357, Suva; tel. 301-600, fax 300-251), on the waterfront opposite the Government Buildings. It's a big American-style place with 132 a/c rooms beginning at F$176 single or double. The swimming pool behind the two-story buildings compensates for the lack of a beach. Special events here include "island night" (F$25) on Wednesday with a *meke* at 2000, and the Sunday poolside barbecue lunch (F$11). This is the only Suva hotel where reservations are often necessary.

The **Southern Cross Hotel** (G.P.O. Box 1076, Suva; tel. 314-233, fax 302-901) is a high-rise concrete building at 63 Gordon Street. At F$83/96/116 single/double/triple, the price of the 34 a/c rooms has increased sharply in recent years. Beware of rooms on the lower floors, which are blasted by band music six nights a week. The hotel restaurant on the 6th floor serves delicious Fijian and Korean dishes.

The eight-story **Berjaya Inn** (G.P.O. Box 112, Suva; tel. 312-300, fax 301-300), formerly the Suva Courtesy Inn, at the corner of Malcolm and Gordon streets, is the tallest hotel in Fiji. The 56 a/c rooms all face the harbor, but at F$134 single or double they're overpriced. Ask for the F$99 "local rate." This Malaysian-owned hotel hosts Suva's only Malaysian restaurant.

The 110-room **Raffles Tradewinds Hotel** (Box 3377, Lami; tel. 362-450, fax 361-464), at Lami on the Bay of Islands just west of Suva, reopened in August 1992 after a US$4-million renovation, complete with a convention center and floating seafood restaurant. Rates are F$130/150/170 single/double/triple with private bath and a/c. Many cruising yachts anchor here. Though bus service into Suva is good, the location is inconvenient for those without a car.

Camping

There's camping on Nukulau, a tiny reef island southeast of Suva. For many years Nukulau was the government quarantine station where most indentured laborers spent their first two weeks in Fiji. Now it's a public park. Get free three-day camping permits from the Divisional Surveyor, Central/Eastern Office, Lands and Surveys Department, Suva Point (Nasese bus), during office hours. The island has toilets and drinking water, and the swimming is good. Problem is, the only access is the F$52 tourist boat (includes lunch) departing Suva at 0930 when there are at least eight passengers. Contact **Coral See Cruises** (Box 852, Suva; tel. 321-570) for information. You're allowed to return to Suva a couple of days later at no extra charge, provided there's a trip.

FOOD

Budget Eateries

Choy's Cafeteria (tel. 315-127) at 151 Victoria Parade opposite Fintel has good breakfast specials, and **Judes** (tel. 315-461), in the arcade opposite Sukuna Park, has good sandwiches at lunchtime. A good inexpensive snack bar with concrete outdoor picnic tables is at the back side of the Handicraft Market facing harbor.

If you just want a snack, check out **Donald's Kitchen** (tel. 315-587), 103 Cumming Street. One block over on Marks Street are cheaper Chinese restaurants, such as **Kim's Cafe** (tel. 313-252), 128 Marks St., where you can get a toasted egg sandwich and coffee for just over a dollar. There are scores more cheap milk bars around Suva, and you'll find them for yourself as you stroll around town.

pick of the produce at Suva's colorful market

DAVID STANLEY

Fijian Restaurants

The **YWCA cafeteria** (tel. 311-617; Monday to Saturday 0800-1700) on Sukuna Park is the place to try native Fijian food, such as *wathi poki* (palusami) or *kuita* (octopus) in *lolo* (coconut cream). You have to come early to get the best dishes.

Another excellent place to sample Fijian food is the **Old Mill Cottage Cafe** (tel. 312-134; closed Sunday and evenings), 49 Carnarvon St.—the street behind the Golden Dragon nightclub. Government employees from nearby offices descend on this place at lunchtime for the inexpensive curried freshwater mussels, curried chicken livers, fresh seaweed in coconut milk, taro leaves creamed in coconut milk, and fish cooked in coconut milk. It's great, but don't come here for coffee as it's cold and overpriced.

Indian Restaurants

The **Hare Vegetarian Krishna Restaurant** (tel. 314-154; closed Sunday), at the corner of Pratt and Joske streets, serves ice cream (12 flavors), sweets, and snacks downstairs, main meals upstairs. If you want the all-you-can-eat vegetarian *thali* (F$6.50), just sit down and they'll bring it to you. But if you're not that starved, go up to the self-service counter and pick up a couple of vegetable dishes which you can have with one or two rotis. This will cost about half as much as the full meal, though ordering individual dishes can be unexpectedly expensive, so unless you want the full meal it's better to look elsewhere. No smoking or alcohol are allowed.

Another excellent Indian place is the **Curry House** (tel. 313-000), in the old town hall on Victoria Parade next to the Ming Palace, with vegetarian curries for F$3 and meat curries from F$5.

Chinese Restaurants

Suva has many excellent, inexpensive Chinese restaurants. The **Diamond Restaurant,** upstairs at 30 Cumming St., in the heart of the duty-free shopping area, serves generous portions, and the staff and surroundings are pleasant. **Geralyne's Restaurant** (tel. 311-037; closed Sunday), 160 Renwick Rd., is similar.

The **Sichuan Pavilion Restaurant** (tel. 315-194), upstairs in the old Garrick Hotel building at 6 Thomson St., is perhaps Suva's finest Asian restaurant. Employees of the Chinese Consulate frequent it for the spicy-hot Chinese dishes (though not as hot as Sichuan food elsewhere). Weekdays they have a lunchtime buffet that allows you to sample six dishes. Weather permitting, sit outside on the balcony and watch all Suva go by.

Also try the good-value **Lantern Palace Restaurant** (tel. 314-633) at 10 Pratt St. near Hare Krishna. The **Phoenix Restaurant** (tel. 311-889), 165 Victoria Parade, has inexpensive Chinese food and cheap beer. Their takeaways are good. The upmarket **New Peking Restaurant** (tel. 312-714), 195 Victoria Parade, has a weekday lunchtime smorgasbord worth checking out.

Suva's most imposing Chinese restaurant is the **Ming Palace** (tel. 315-111; closed Sunday) in the Old Town Hall next to the public library on Victoria Parade.

The best place to eat Chinese style near the Raffles Tradewinds Hotel yacht anchorage is the **Castle Restaurant** (tel. 361-223) in the Lami Shopping Center.

Expensive Restaurants

Leonardo's Restaurant (tel. 312-884; closed Sunday), 215 Victoria Parade, is Suva's upmarket Italian specialist. If it fails to please, you can always fall back on **Pizza Hut** (tel. 311-825; Monday to Saturday 1100-2230, Sunday 1900-2200), nearby at 207 Victoria Parade. In the past we've been critical about this place, but several readers disagreed and said they thought it was fine (no connection with the Pizza Hut chain).

For German or French cuisine it's the **Swiss Tavern** (tel. 303-233; closed Sunday), 16 Kimberly St. at Gordon (say hello to Hans).

Tiko's Floating Restaurant (tel. 313-626) is housed in the MV *Lycianda,* an ex-Blue Lagoon cruise ship launched at Suva in 1970 and now anchored off Stinson Parade behind Sukuna Park. Their steaks and seafood (dinner only) are good for a splurge.

ENTERTAINMENT AND EVENTS

Movie houses are plentiful downtown, charging F$2 for a hard seat, F$3 for a soft seat. The selection of films is fairly good, and they change every three days, which makes Suva a paradise for movie lovers. Regal Cinema near Sukuna Park is very comfortable, but rats run freely beneath the seats as soon as they lights go out at Century Cinema on Marks Street.

The **Fiji Indian Cultural Center,** 271 Toorak Rd., offers classes in Indian music, dancing, art, etc. It's well worth dropping in to find out if any public performances are scheduled during your visit.

The best time to be in Suva is around the end of August or early September, when the **Hibiscus Festival** fills Albert Park with stalls, games, and carnival revelers.

Nightclubs

There are many nightclubs, all of which have cover charges of around F$4 and require neat dress, but nothing much happens until after 2200, and women shouldn't enter alone.

Gays will feel comfortable at **Lucky Eddie's** (tel. 312-884; daily except Sunday after 2000), 217 Victoria Parade, but it's not really a gay bar, as the Fijian women present try to prove.

The Lucky Eddie's cover charge is also valid for the more sedate **Urban Jungle Night Club** (Thursday to Saturday after 2100) in the same building.

Signals Night Club, also on Victoria Parade, is a new place. **Traps** (tel. 312-922), at 305 Victoria Parade next to the Shell service station, has loud live jazz and pitchers of beer from 2130 on Monday, Wednesday, and Saturday (free admission but reasonable dress required). Sometimes it's a groupie Suva social scene. One reader recommended a new spot on Carnarvan Street, the **Birdland Jazz Club,** which has live music on weekends and recorded jazz other nights.

A shade rougher but also very popular is the **Golden Dragon** (tel. 311-018; open Monday to Saturday 1930-0100), 379 Victoria Parade.

The most interracial of the clubs is **Chequers Nightspot** (tel. 313-563), 127 Waimanu Rd., which has live music Tuesday to Saturday after 2100. Hang onto your wallet here.

For real earthy atmosphere try the **Bali Hai** (tel. 315-868) on Rodwell Road, the roughest club in Suva. Friday and Saturday nights the place is packed with Fijians (no Indians) and tourists are rare, so beware. If you're looking for action, you'll be able to pick a partner within minutes, but take care with aggressive males. The dance hall on the top floor is the swingingest, with body-to-body jive—the Bali Hai will rock you.

Bars

O'Reilly's Pub (tel. 312-968), 5 MacArthur St., just around the corner from Lucky Eddie's, has a happy hour with local beer at F$1 a mug weekdays 1700-1945, Saturday 1800-1945. It's a nice relaxed way to kick off a night on the town.

Unescorted female travelers and those in search of more subdued drinking should try the bar at Tiko's Floating Restaurant or the lounge at the Southern Cross Hotel. The piano bar at the Travelodge is even more upmarket.

SHOPPING

The **Government Handicraft Center** behind Ratu Sukuna House, MacArthur and Carnarvon streets, is a low-pressure place to familiarize yourself with what is authentic, though prices have jumped sharply here in recent years, making it better to do your buying elsewhere. The large **Curio and Handicraft Market** (Monday to Saturday 0800-1700) on the waterfront behind the post office is a good place to haggle over crafts, so long as you know what is really Fijian (avoid masks and "tikis").

For clothing see the fashionable hand-printed shirts and dresses at **Tiki Togs** (tel. 304-381), 38 Thomson St. across from the post office, or at their second location at 199 Victoria Parade next to the Pizza Hut. You could come out looking like a real South Seas character at a very reasonable price. Also check **Sogo Fiji** (tel. 313-941), 189 Victoria Parade.

Cumming Street (site of the main Suva produce market until the 1940s) is Suva's duty-free shopping area. The wide selection of goods in the large number of shops makes this about the best place in Fiji to shop for electrical and other imported goods. Expect to receive a 10-40% discount by bargaining, but *shop around* before you buy. Be wary when purchasing gold jewelry, as it might be fake. And watch out for hustlers who will try to take you around to the shops and get you a "good price." Dealers with a sticker from the Fiji National Duty Free Merchants Association in the window tend to be more reliable. Never buy anything on the day when a cruise ship is in port—prices shoot up.

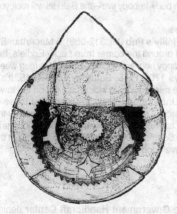

This Fijian breastplate of sperm whale ivory bears a pearl-shell plaque with perforated star and birds.

Some of the most offbeat buys in Suva are in the pawn shops, most of which are off Marks or Cummings streets. Ask for the behind-the-counter selection.

J.R. White & Co. (tel. 302-325), in the mall behind Air New Zealand, has all kinds of sporting equipment (but not camping gear or backpacks). They can repair worn-out zippers.

The **Philatelic Bureau** (G.P.O. Box 100, Suva; tel. 312-928) at the General Post Office sells the stamps of Tuvalu, Western Samoa, Pitcairn, Solomon Islands, and Vanuatu, as well as those of Fiji.

Beware of the seemingly friendly men (usually with a small package or canvas bag in their hands) who will greet you on the street with a hearty *"Mbula!"* These are "sword sellers" who will ask your name, quickly carve it on a sword, and then demand F$15 for a set that you could buy at a Nandi curio shop for F$5. Try to avoid people like this, as they can become suddenly aggressive. Their swords and masks themselves have nothing to do with Fiji.

SERVICES

Money
The **Westpac Bank** (tel. 300-666), 1 Thomson St., usually gives the best rate on exchanges. **Thomas Cook Travel** (tel. 301-603), 21 Thomson St. next to the post office, will change foreign currency weekdays 0830-1700, Saturday 0830-1200, at a comparable rate. On Sunday you may be able to change money at the Travelodge for a rate about three percent lower than the bank's.

Telecommunications
Fintel, the **Fiji International Telecommunications** office (tel. 312-933), 158 Victoria Parade, is open Monday to Saturday 0800-2200 for trunk calls and telegrams. The basic charge for three minutes is F$5.28 to Australia or New Zealand, F$8.91 to North America and Europe (no minimum when using card phones). The card phones at Fintel require a different type of magnetic card than the public telephones on the street, such as those outside the post office.

Immigration and Consulates

The **Immigration Office** for extensions of stay, etc., is at the corner of Toorak Road and Suva Street (tel. 312-622; open Monday to Friday 0830-1200/1400-1530). Bring along your ticket to leave Fiji and traveler's checks/credit cards.

Cruising yachts wishing to visit the outer islands must first obtain a permit at the **Ministry of Fijian Affairs** (Box 2100, Government Buildings, Suva; tel. 304-200), 61 Carnarvon Street. They'll want to see the customs papers for the boat and all passports. (Yachties anchoring off a Fijian village should present a *sevusevu* of kava to the chief.)

The following countries have **diplomatic missions** in Suva: Britain (tel. 311-033), Canada (tel. 300-589), China (tel. 300-215), the Federated States of Micronesia (tel. 304-566), France (tel. 312-233), Israel (tel. 303-420), Japan (tel. 304-633), Korea (tel. 300-977), Malaysia (tel. 312-166), Marshall Islands (tel. 387-899), Nauru (tel. 313-566), Netherlands (tel. 301-499), New Zealand (tel. 311-422), Papua New Guinea (tel. 304-244), Taiwan (tel. 315-922), Tuvalu (tel. 301-355), and the U.S.A. (tel. 314-466).

Everyone other than New Zealanders requires a visa to visit Australia, and these are readily available free of charge at the Australian Embassy, 10 Reservoir Rd., off Princes Road, Samambula (Box 214, Suva; tel. 382-219; weekdays 0830-1200). It's probably easier to take a taxi there and return to town on the Samambula bus.

Public Toilets

Free public toilets are just outside the Handicraft Market on the side of the building facing the harbor; beside Numbukalou Creek off Renwick Road; and between the market and the bus station.

Yachting Facilities

The Royal Suva Yacht Club (G.P.O. Box 335, Suva; tel. 312-921, fax 304-433) on Foster Road between Suva and Lami offers visiting yachts such amenities as mooring privileges, warm showers, laundry facilities, cheap drinks, Sunday barbecues, and the full use of facilities by the whole crew for F$25 a week. There have been reports of thefts from boats anchored here, so watch out. Many yachts anchor off the Raffles Tradewinds Hotel in Lami.

INFORMATION

The **Fiji Visitors Bureau** (tel. 302-433) is on Thomson Street across from the General Post Office, open Monday to Friday 0800-1630, Saturday 0800-1200.

The **Tourism Council of the South Pacific** (tel. 304-177, fax 301-995), 35 Loftus St. next to the U.S. Embassy, provides general brochures on the entire South Pacific.

The Publications Division of the **Ministry of Information** (tel. 211-305), Ground Floor, Government Buildings, hands out a few official brochures on the country. Nearby in the same building is the **Maps and Plans Room** (tel. 211-395) of the Lands and Survey Department, which sells excellent maps of Fiji (Monday to Thursday 0900-1300/1400-1530, Friday 0900-1300/1400-1500).

Carpenters Shipping (tel. 312-244), 4th Floor, Neptune House, Tofua Street, Walu Bay, sells navigational charts (F$43 each). Nearby is the **Fiji Hydrographic Office,** Top Floor, Freeston Road, Walu Bay (tel. 315-457; weekdays 0830-1300 and 1400-1600), with local navigational charts.

Bookstores

Suva's best bookstore by far is the **USP Book Center** (Monday to Thursday 0830-1615, Friday 0830-1545) at the Lauthala Bay university campus. While you're in the area visit the Book Display Room in the Institute of Pacific Studies building, not far from the Book Center. They sell interesting books by local authors published by the IPS itself.

The **Desai Bookshop** (tel. 314-088), on Thomson Street opposite the post office, and the **Zenon Bookshop** (tel. 312-477), on Victoria Parade opposite Sukuna Park, also have books on Fiji. The **Fiji Museum** shop sells a number of excellent books at reasonable prices.

You can purchase the hard-to-find *Pacific Islands Yearbook* at the **Fiji Times Limited Circulation Office** (tel. 304-111), 177 Victoria Parade. Several other good books on the Pacific are sold here.

Lotu Pasifika Productions (Box 208, Suva; tel. 301-314, fax 301-183), in the Pacific Conference of Churches building, 4 Thurston St., publishes a number of excellent books on regional social issues and carries Nuclear-Free Pacific posters. If you are at all interested in contemporary religion, pick up a copy of Manfred Ernst's *Winds of Change* here.

The **Government Bookshop**, shop No. 38 in the arcade at 68 Rodwell Rd. opposite the bus station (tel. 311-711; Monday to Thursday 0830-1630, Friday 0800-1600, Saturday 0800-1500), sells Fijian school textbooks, a Fijian dictionary, and official reports at very reasonable prices.

The **Pacific Concerns Resource Center** (tel. 304-649, fax 304-755), 83 Amy St. off Toorak Road (enter from the rear of the building), sells a number of issue-related books and booklets on social and political problems in the South Pacific.

The **Coconut Frond** (tel. 311-963), 8 Disraeli Rd., looks like a fast-food place, but in a room in back they run the largest secondhand book exchange in Suva, though most of the books here are adventure or romance. Better titles are obtained at the **Missions to Seamen** on the main wharf (inside—go through the security gate), which trades paperback books one for one (tel. 300-911; open weekdays 0900-1300 and 1330-1600).

Libraries

The **Suva City Library** on Victoria Parade is worth a look (tel. 313-433; Monday, Tuesday, Thursday, Friday 0930-1800, Wednesday 1200-1800, Saturday 0900-1300). Visitors can take out books upon payment of a F$11 fee, plus a F$10 refundable deposit (there's no charge to sit and read inside the library itself).

The **Alliance Française** (tel. 313-802), 77 Thakombau Rd., has an excellent selection of French books, magazines, and newspapers. You're welcome to peruse materials in the reading room weekdays 0830-1200 and 1300-1700. Ask about their video and film evenings.

Travel Agents

Hunts Travel (Box 686, Suva; tel. 315-288), in the Dominion Building arcade behind the Fiji Visitors Bureau, is the place to pick up air tickets. They often know more about Air Pacific flights than the Air Pacific employees themselves!

Also compare **Travelworld Services** (tel. 315-870), 18 Waimanu Rd., which gives five percent discounts on plane tickets to other Pacific countries.

For domestic tickets on **Vanua Air** go to **Macquarie Tours & Travel** (Box 1170, Suva; tel. 315-855, fax 303-856), 12 Pier St. (opposite Sunflower Airlines).

Airline Offices

Reconfirm your onward flight at your airlines' Suva office: **Air Calédonie International** (tel. 302-133), 64 Renwick Rd. (in the arcade); **Air Fiji** (tel. 314-666), 185 Victoria Parade (also represents Air Vanuatu and Solomon Airlines); **Air Marshall Islands** (tel. 303-888), 30 Thomson St.; **Air Nauru** (tel. 312-377), Ratu Sukuna House, 249 Victoria Parade; **Air New Zealand** (tel. 313-100), Queensland Insurance Centre, Victoria Parade; **Air Pacific** (tel. 384-955), CML Building, Victoria Parade; **Qantas Airways** (tel. 313-888), CMLA Building, Victoria Parade; and **Sunflower Airlines** (tel. 315-755), corner of Renwick Road and Pier Street (also represents Royal Tongan Airlines). While you're there, check your seat assignment.

HEALTH

You'll receive good attention at the **Gordon St. Medical Center** (tel. 313-355, fax 302-423), Gordon and Thurston Streets (consultations F$17). There's a female doctor there. Fiji's only recompression chamber (tel. 305-154) is adjacent to this clinic (donated by the Cousteau Society in 1992).

The **J.P. Bayly Clinic** (tel. 315-888), 190 Rodwell Rd. opposite the Phoenix Cinema, is a church-operated low-income clinic.

The poorly marked **Health Office** (tel. 314-988; open weekdays 0800-1630), beside the bus stand on Rodwell Road, gives tetanus, polio, cholera, typhoid, and yellow fever vaccinations. They're F$6 each, except yellow fever, which is F$16.

Two recommended dentists are Dr. Abdul S. Haroon (tel. 313-870), Suite 12, Epworth House off Nina Street (just down the hall from Patterson Shipping); and Dr. (Mrs.) S. Khan (tel. 302-289), Jannif Building, Victoria Parade.

TRANSPORTATION

Although nearly all international flights to Fiji arrive at Nandi, Suva is still the most important transportation center in the country. Interisland shipping crowds the waterfront, and if you can't find a ship going precisely your way at the time you want to travel, Air Fiji and Sunflower Airlines fly to all the major Fiji islands, while Air Pacific serves New Zealand, Tonga, and Samoa—all from Nausori Airport. Make the rounds of the shipping offices listed below, then head over to Walu Bay to check the information. Compare the price of a cabin and deck passage, and ask if meals are included. Start checking early, as many domestic services within Fiji are only once a week and trips to other countries are far less frequent.

A solid block of buses await your patronage at the market bus station near the harbor, with continuous local service, and frequent long-distance departures to Nandi and Lautoka. Many of the points of interest around Suva are accessible on foot, but if you wander too far, jump on any bus headed in the right direction and you'll end up back in the market. Taxis are also easy to find and relatively cheap (F$2 in the city center, F$3 to the suburbs).

Suva's bus station can be a little confusing as there are many different companies, and timetables are not posted. Most drivers know where a certain bus will park, so just ask. For information on bus services on Viti Levu and domestic flights from Nausori Airport, see "Getting Around" in the Fiji Islands' introduction. Shipping services from Suva are covered below.

Ships to other Countries

The Wednesday issue of the *Fiji Times* carries a special section on international shipping, though most are container ships that don't accept passengers. Most shipping is headed for Tonga and Samoa—there's not much going westward, and actually getting on any of the ships mentioned below requires considerable persistence. It's often easier to sign on as crew on a yacht. Try both yacht anchorages in Suva: put up a notice, ask around, etc.

Carpenters Shipping (tel. 312-244, fax 301-572), 4th Floor, Neptune House, Tofua Street,

Walu Bay, is an agent for the *Moana III* and *Moana IV*, which sail occasionally from Suva to Wallis and Futuna, then on to Nouméa. They can't sell the ticket but will tell you when the ship is expected in, and you can book with the captain. This is a beautiful trip, not at all crowded between Fiji and Wallis. Book a cabin, however, if you're going right through to Nouméa.

Carpenters is also an agent for the monthly **Banks Line** service to Lautoka, Nouméa, Port Vila, Honiara, Port Moresby, and on to Great Britain. They cannot sell you a passenger ticket and will only tell you when the ship is due in and where it's headed. It's up to you to make arrangements personally with the captain, and the fare won't be cheap.

The **Tuvalu Embassy** (Box 14449, Suva; tel. 301-355, fax 301-023), 16 Gorrie St., runs the *Nivaga II* to Funafuti about four times a year, but the dates are variable. Tickets are sold by the **Pacific Forum Line** (tel. 315-444, fax 302-754), 187 Rodwell Rd., at F$124 without meals or F$200 with meals second class, F$139 without meals or F$215 with meals first class, F$70 deck. They only know about a week beforehand approximately when the ship may sail. After reaching Funafuti, the ship cruises the Tuvalu Group.

The Pacific Forum Line also knows about ships from Suva to Apia, Pago Pago, and Nuku'alofa, such as the Samoan government-owned *Forum Samoa* (every three weeks) and the Tongan government-owned *Fua Kavenga* (monthly service). They don't sell passenger tickets, so just ask when these ships will be in port, then go and talk to the captain, who is the only one who can decide if you'll be able to go.

Shipping Services Limited (G.P.O. Box 12671, Suva; tel. 313-354, fax 301-615), corner of Robertson and Rodwell roads (behind Suva Supermarket), also knows the departure dates of container ships to Tonga and Samoa. Again, they don't sell passenger tickets and you must see the captain in person to arrange passage.

When they need hands, **Sofrana Unilines** ships sometimes accept work-a-passage crew for New Zealand, Australia, or other ports. You must arrange this with the captain. Their Suva office (tel. 304-528, fax 300-951) is in the same building as Carpenters Shipping.

Ships to other Fijian Islands

Quite a few ships leave Suva on Saturday, but none depart on Sunday. **Patterson Brothers** (G.P.O. Box 1041, Suva; tel. 315-644, fax 301-652), Suite 1, 1st Floor, Epworth Arcade off Nina Street, takes obligatory reservations for the Suva-Natovi-Nambouwalu-Lambasa ferry/bus combination, which departs Suva's Western Bus Stand Tuesday to Saturday at 0400. Fares from Suva are F$30 to Nambouwalu or F$38 right through to Lambasa, an excellent 10-hour trip.

Patterson's *Princess Ashika* or *Ovalau II* links Suva to Ngau (five hours, F$29), Koro (10 hours, F$31), Savusavu (14.5 hours, F$31), and Taveuni (22 hours, F$36) weekly, departing Muaiwalu Jetty, Walu Bay, at midnight Monday. Thursday at 2200 one of these ships departs Suva for Kandavu (six hours, F$34). Forthcoming departures are listed on a blackboard in their Suva office and the schedule varies slightly each week. Patterson Brothers also has offices in Lambasa, Lautoka, Levuka, Savusavu, and Taveuni.

Consort Shipping Line (G.P.O. Box 152, Suva; tel. 302-877, fax 303-389), in the Dominion House arcade on Thomson Street, operates the MV *Spirit of Free Enterprise* (popularly known as the "Sofe"), a 450-passenger car ferry that formerly shuttled between the north and south islands of New Zealand. The *Sofe* leaves Suva on Wednesday at 0500 and Saturday at 1800 for Savusavu (13 hours, F$30 one-way) and Taveuni (23 hours, F$35). The ship also calls at Koro. The northbound Saturday voyage spends all day Sunday tied up at Savusavu and Taveuni passengers can get off and walk around. The two-berth cabins of the *Sofe* are quite comfortable and excellent value at F$55 pp to Savusavu or F$66 pp to Taveuni. For a refundable F$20 deposit the purser will give you the key to your cabin, allowing you to wander around the ship without worrying about your luggage. Another advantage of taking a cabin is that you're able to order meals in the pleasant first-class restaurant. Only cabin passengers may do this and the meals are excellent value at F$3.

Beachcomber Cruises offers a bus/ferry connection from Suva to Savusavu via Natovi every morning except Sunday (F$60). Their high-speed catamaran *Ndrondrolangi* takes only two hours for the crossing from Natovi to Vanua Levu. The Fiji Visitors Bureau will have the address of their booking office.

Ask on the smaller vessels tied up at Muaiwalu Jetty, Walu Bay, for passage to Nairai, Ngau, Kandavu, etc. Don't believe the first person who tells you there's no boat going where you want—*ask around.* **Walu Shipping** (tel. 312-668) at the Ports Authority Building, Rona St., Walu Bay, has regular services to the Lau Group on the MV *Katika,* costing F$65 deck (no cabins) to any island in Lau. Food is included in the price and on the outward journey it will probably be okay, but on the return don't expect much more than rice and tea.

The **Marine Department** (tel. 315-266) at Walu Bay handles government barges to all of the Fiji Islands, but tourists are not usually accepted on those boats. If you're planning a long voyage by interisland ship, a big bundle of kava roots to captain and crew as a token of appreciation for their hospitality works wonders.

Keep in mind that all of the ferry departure times mentioned above and elsewhere in this book are only indications of what was true in past. It's essential to check with the company office for current departure times during the week you wish to travel.

To Ovalau Island

Air Fiji flies from Suva to Levuka (F$33) two or three times a day, but the most popular trips are the bus/launch/bus combinations via Natovi or Mbau Landing. Two different companies operate these trips, which take four or five hours right through. Reservations are recommended on Saturday and public holidays.

The **Patterson Brothers** service (book at their office mentioned above) leaves from the Western Bus Stand in Suva Monday to Saturday at 1400 (F$19). This express bus goes from Suva to Natovi, where it drives onto a ferry to Mburesala on Ovalau, then continues on to Levuka, where it arrives around 1730. For the return journey you leave the Patterson Brothers office in Levuka Monday to Saturday at 0500, arriving in Suva at 0830. Tickets must be purchased in advance at the office—no exceptions.

A second choice is the ***Emosi Express,*** departing Suva Monday, Wednesday, Friday, and Saturday at 1200 for Mbau Landing, where you board a speedboat powered by two 40-horsepower Yamaha engines to Leleuvia Island and Levuka (four hours, F$18 one-way). A free stopover on Leleuvia is possible. To book this, go to Rosie Tours, 46 Gordon St. (tel. 313-366). For variety and the most convenient timings, we recommend traveling with Patterson northbound and Emosi southbound. It's a beautiful circle trip not to be missed (sit up on the boat's roof if it's nice weather).

Tours

For information on the exciting day-trips from Suva offered by **Wilderness Adventures** (Box 1389, Suva; tel. 386-498, fax 300-584), turn to the "Around Navua" and "Around Nausori" sections in this chapter. Wilderness also runs excellent two-hour city sightseeing tours three times a day (adults F\$25, children under 12 years F\$15). These trips can be booked through any travel agency in Suva. Another company called **Livai Tours** (tel. 394-251) offers almost identical trips.

NAUSORI

In 1881 the Rewa River town of Nausori, 19 km northeast of Suva, was chosen as the site of Fiji's first large sugar mill, which operated until 1959. In those early days it was incorrectly believed that sugarcane grew better on the wetter eastern side of the island. Today cane is grown only on the drier, sunnier western sides of Viti Levu and Vanua Levu. The old sugar mill is now a rice mill and storage depot, as the Rewa Valley has become a major rice-producing area.

Nausori is Fiji's fifth-largest city (population 15,000) and the headquarters of Central Division, plus Rewa and Tailevu provinces. The nine-span bridge across the river here was built in 1937. The town is best known for its large international airport three km southeast, built as a fighter strip to defend Fiji's capital during WW II. There are several banks in Nausori.

Accommodations and Food

The **Kings Nausori Hotel** (Box 67, Nausori; tel. 478-833), 99 Kings Rd., beside the rice mill, has three grubby rooms with private bath and hot water at F\$25 single or double. The dingy rooms are attached to the noisy bar and are rented mostly for "short times"—only of interest to people on the make. Due to licensing restrictions, women are not admitted to the hotel bar.

A far nicer drinking place is the **Whistling Duck Pub,** a block from the bus station in the center of town (ask directions). Upstairs in the adjacent building is a good, inexpensive restaurant where you can get cold beer with your curries (Monday to Wednesday 1200-1430, Thursday to Saturday 1200-1430/1800-2100).

From Nausori

Local buses to the airport (35 cents) and Suva (80 cents) are fairly frequent, but the last bus to Suva is at 2100. You can also catch Sunbeam Transport express buses to Lautoka from Nausori at 0715, 1400, and 1745 (5.5 hours).

AROUND NAUSORI

Rewa Delta

Take a bus from Nausori to Nakelo Landing to explore the heavily populated Rewa River Delta. Many outboards leave from Nakelo to take villagers to their riverside homes, and passenger fares are under a dollar for short trips. Larger boats leave sporadically from Nakelo for Levuka, Ngau, and Koro, but finding one would be pure chance. Some also depart from nearby Wainimbokasi Landing.

Wilderness Adventures (Box 1389, Suva; tel. 386-498) runs half-day boat tours of the Rewa Delta, with stops at Nailili Catholic Mission to visit St. Joseph's Church (1901), and at Nambua village, where Fijian pottery is still made. The tour leaves twice daily at 0930 and 1300, and the F\$35 pp price includes minibus transfers from Suva hotels (it only operates if at least four people sign up). A full-day delta trip with lunch at Nasilai village is F\$49 (F\$25 for children). This is a refreshing change of pace.

Mbau Island

Mbau, a tiny, eight-hectare island just east of Viti Levu, has a special place in Fiji's history as this was the seat of High Chief Cakobau, who used European cannons and muskets to subdue most of western Fiji in the 1850s. At its pinnacle Mbau had a population of 3,000, hundreds of war canoes to guard its waters, and over 20 temples on the island's central plain. After the Battle of Verata on Viti Levu in 1839, Cakobau and his father, Tanoa, presented 260 bodies of men, women, and children to their closest friends and allied chiefs for gastronomical purposes. Fifteen years after this slaughter, Cakobau converted to Christianity and prohibited cannibalism on Mbau. In 1867 he became a sovereign, crowned by European traders and planters desiring a stable government in Fiji to protect their interests.

For a lively account of Mbau in the mid-19th century read *Life in Feejee—Five Years Among the Cannibals* by Mary Wallis (available at the Fiji Museum in Suva).

Sights of Mbau

The great stone slabs that form docks and seawalls around much of the island once accommodated Mbau's fleet of war canoes. The graves of the Cakobau family and many of the old chiefs lie on the hilltop behind the school. The large, sturdy stone church located near the provincial offices was the first Christian church in Fiji. Inside its nearly one-meter-thick walls, just in front of the altar, is the old sacrificial stone once used for human sacrifices, today the baptismal font. Now painted white, this font was once known as King Cakobau's "skull crusher." It's said a thousand brains were splattered against it. Across from the church are huge ancient trees and the thatched Council House on the site of the onetime temple of the war god Cagawalu. The family of the late Sir George Cakobau, governor-general of Fiji 1973-82, has a large traditional-style home on the island. You can see everything on the island in an hour or so.

Getting There

Take the Mbau bus (five daily, 50 cents) from Nausori to Mbau Landing where there are outboards to cross over to the island. Be aware that Mbau is not considered a tourist attraction, and from time to time visitors are prevented from going to the island. It's important to get someone to invite you across, which they'll do willingly if you show a genuine interest in Fijian history. Like most Fijians, the inhabitants of Mbau are very friendly people. Bring a big bundle of *waka* for the *turanga-ni-koro,* and ask permission very politely to be shown around. There could be some confusion about who's to receive the *sevusevu,* however, as everyone on Mbau's a chief! The more respectable your dress and demeanor, the better your chances of success. If you're told to contact the Ministry of Fijian Affairs in Suva, just depart gracefully as that's only their way of saying no. After all, it's up to them. Alternatively, you get a good close look at Mbau from the *Emosi Express* ferry service to/from Levuka via Leleuvia.

Viwa Island

Before Cakobau adopted Christianity in 1854, Methodist missionaries working for this effect resided on Viwa Island, just across the water from Mbau. Here the first Fijian New Testament was printed in 1847; Rev. John Hunt, who did the translation, lies buried in the graveyard beside the church that bears his name.

Viwa is a good alternative if you aren't invited to visit Mbau itself. To reach the island, hire an outboard at Mbau Landing. If you're lucky, you'll be able to join some locals who are going. A single Fijian village stands on the island.

Tomberua Island

Tomberua Island Resort (Michael Dennis, Box 567, Suva; tel. 479-177, fax 302-215), on a tiny reef island off the east tip of Viti Levu, caters to upmarket honeymooners, families, and professionals. Built in 1968, this was one of Fiji's first outer-island resorts. The 14 thatched *mbures* are designed in the purest Fijian style, yet it's all very luxurious and the small size means peace and quiet. The tariff is F$319/352/404 single/double/triple, plus F$81 pp for three gourmet meals, F$68 pp for two meals; baby-sitters are F$13 a day. Two children under 16 sharing with adults are accommodated free and they're fed for half price or less. Tomberua is out of eastern Viti Levu's wet belt, so it doesn't get a lot of rain like nearby Suva, and weather permitting, all meals are served outdoors. Friday nights there's a *lovo* and *meke.*

Don't expect tennis courts or a golf course at Tomberua, though believe it or not, there's tropical golfing on the reef at low tide! (Nine holes from 90-180 meters, course par 27, clubs and balls provided free.) Deep-sea fishing is F$44 an hour and scuba diving F$60 a dive. All other activities are free, including snorkeling, sailing, windsurfing, and boat trips to a bird sanctuary or mangrove forest. The launch transfer from Nakelo landing to Tomberua is F$24 pp each way; a Turtle Airways seaplane from Nandi will be F$330 pp one-way (minimum of three persons).

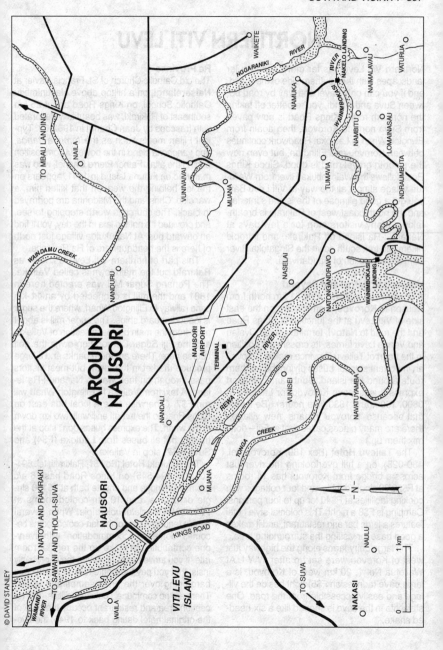

AROUND NAUSORI

© DAVID STANLEY

NORTHERN VITI LEVU

Northern Viti Levu has far more spectacular landscapes than the southern side of the island, and if you can only travel one way by road between Suva and Nandi, you're better off taking the northern route. Kings Road is now paved from Suva north to Korovou, then again from Ellington Wharf to Lautoka. Roadwork continues between Korovou and Ellington, but even now the smooth gravel road is good. Since Kings Road follows the Wainimbuka River from Wailotua village almost all the way to Viti Levu Bay, you get a good glimpse of the island's interior, and the north coast west of Rakiraki is breathtaking. Many visitors stop for a few days at Nananu-i-Ra Island off Rakiraki, and intrepid hikers can trek south down the Singatoka River from the hill station of Nandarivatu.

Korovou to Natovi and Beyond

A good paved highway runs 31 km north from Nausori to **Korovou,** a small town on the east side of Viti Levu at the junction of Kings Road and the road to **Natovi,** terminus of the Ovalau and Vanua Levu ferries. Its crossroads position in the heart of Tailevu Province makes Korovou an important stop for buses plying the northern route around the island. Sunbeam Transport express buses leave Korovou for Lautoka at 0800, 1500, and 1830 (five hours). (Be aware that because "korovou" means "new village," there are many places called that in Fiji—don't mix them up.)

The **Tailevu Hotel** (Box 189, Korovou; tel. 430-028), on a hill overlooking the river just across a bridge from Korovou, has 14 rooms at F$22/30 single/double, and four cottages with cooking facilities at F$40 for up to four persons. Camping is F$8 a night. This colonial-style hotel features a large bar and restaurant, and it makes a good base for visiting the surrounding area.

The large dairy farms along the highway just west of Korovou were set up after WW I. At Wailotua No. 1, 20 km west of Korovou, is a large **cave** (admission F$5) right beside the village and easily accessible from the road. One stalactite in the cave is shaped like a six-headed snake.

Ra Province

The old Catholic Church of St. Francis Xavier at **Naiserelangi,** on a hilltop above Navunimbitu Catholic School, on Kings Road about 25 km southeast of Rakiraki, was beautifully decorated with frescoes by Jean Charlot in 1962-63. Typical Fijian motifs such as the *tambua, tanoa,* and *yanggona* blend in the powerful composition behind the altar. Father Pierre Chanel, who was martyred on Futuna Island in 1841, appears on the left holding the weapon that killed him, a war club. Christ and the Madonna are portrayed in black. The church is worth stopping to see, and provided it's not too late in the day, you'll find an onward bus. At Nanukuloa village just north of here is the headquarters of Ra Province.

This part of northern Viti Levu is known as **Rakiraki** but the main town is called **Vaileka.** The Penang Sugar Mill was erected here in 1881 and the mill is connected by an 11-km cane railway to Ellington Wharf, where the sugar is loaded aboard ships. The sugar mill is about a km from the main business section of Vaileka, and the Fiji Sugar Corporation owns the golf course here. There are three banks and a large produce market in the town, but most visitors pass through on their way to Nananu-i-Ra Island. A taxi from Vaileka to Ellington Wharf will run F$7. Otherwise take a local bus east on Kings Road to the turnoff and walk two km down to the wharf. The express buses don't stop at the turnoff, but all buses from Lautoka (F$4) and Suva (F$7) stop in Vaileka.

The **Rakiraki Hotel** (Box 31, Rakiraki; tel. 694-101, fax 694-545) on Kings Road has 36 a/c rooms with fridge and private bath at F$100 single or double, and 10 fan-cooled rooms at F$33/38/44 single/double/triple. When several people request it, one of the fan-cooled rooms becomes "dormitory accommodation" with everyone contributing to make up the regular room rate. If you arrive alone, however, they'll probably insist that you pay the single rate, in which case bargaining over the price sometimes works. There are no communal cooking facilities. The reception area and restaurant occupy the core of the original hotel dating back to 1945; the two-story accommodations blocks were added much later. Extensive gardens surround the hotel. The Rakiraki's outdoor bowling green draws middle-aged lawn bowling enthusiasts from Australia and New Zealand, the sort that like old-fashioned "colonial" touches like the typed daily menu featuring British-Indian curry dishes, and gin and tonic in the afternoon. This hotel is a couple of kilometers north of Vaileka and only the local or "stage" buses will drop you off on Kings Road right in front of the hotel (the express buses will drop you in Vaileka).

Wananavu Beach Resort (General Delivery, Rakiraki; tel. 694-433, fax 694-499), on Volivoli Road facing Nananu-i-Ra Island, four km off Kings Road, opened in 1994. There are 14 self-contained rooms at F$85 for up to three people, and two eight-bedded dormitories at F$16 pp, breakfast included. No cooking facilities are provided, but each regular room does have a fridge. Ra Divers offers scuba diving from the resort, and a variety of other water sports are available.

Right beside Kings Road, just a hundred meters west of the turnoff to Vaileka, is the grave of **Ratu Udre Udre,** the cannibal king of this region who is alleged to have consumed 99 corpses. **Navatu Rock,** a few kilometers west of Vaileka, was the jumping-off point for the disembodied spirits of the ancient Fijians. A fortified village once stood on its summit. Navatu's triangular shape is duplicated by a small island just offshore.

The **Nakauvandra Range,** towering south of Rakiraki, is the traditional home of the Fijian serpent-god Degei, who is said to dwell in a cave on the summit of Mt. Uluda (866 meters). This "cave" is little more than a cleft in the rock. To climb the Nakauvandra Range, which the local Fijians look upon as their primeval homeland, permission must be obtained from the chief of Vatukathevatheva village who will provide guides. A *sevusevu* should be presented.

NANANU-I-RA ISLAND

This small 355-hectare island, three km off the northernmost tip of Viti Levu, is a good place to spend some time amid perfect tranquility and beauty without the commercialization of the resorts off Nandi. Here too the climate is dry and

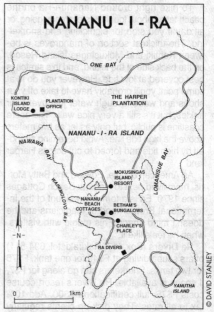

sunny, and there are great beaches, reefs, snorkeling, walks, sunsets, and moonrises over the water—only roads are missing. Seven or eight separate white sandy beaches lie scattered around the island. The island is large enough that you won't ever feel confined. In the early 19th century Nananu-i-Ra's original Fijian inhabitants were wiped out by disease and tribal warfare, and an heir sold the island to the Europeans whose descendants now operate small resorts and a 219-hectare plantation on the island.

The northern two-thirds of Nananu-i-Ra Island, including all of the land around Kontiki Island Lodge, is owned by Mrs. Louise Harper of southern California, who bought it for a mere US$200,000 in 1966 (she also owns a sizable chunk of Proctor & Gamble back in the States). Today some 22 head of Harper cattle graze beneath coconuts on the Harper Plantation, and the plantation management actively discourages trespassing by tourists. The plantation manager lives in a house adjoining Kontiki, and it's common courtesy to ask his permission before climbing the hill behind the lodge.

To hike right around Nananu-i-Ra on the beach takes about four hours of steady going, or all day if you stop for picnicking and snorkeling. The thickest section of mangroves is between Kontiki and Mokusingas Island Resort, on the back side of the island, and this stretch is best covered at low tide. However you do it, at some point you'll probably have to take off your shoes and wade through water just over your ankles, but it's still a very nice walk. The entire coastline is public, but only as far as two meters above the high tide line. Avoid becoming stranded by high tide and forced to cut across Harper land.

An American couple, Edward and Betty Morris, have lived next to Nananu Beach Cottages since 1970. Ed is a former president of the International Brotherhood of Magicians and he doesn't mind sharing his magic with visitors, when he feels like it.

Ra Divers (Box 417, Rakiraki; tel. 694-511) offers scuba diving at F$40 for one tank, F$75 for two tanks. Snorkelers can go along for F$7, if space is available. Ra Diver's resort course costs F$75, full certification F$300. Add 10% tax to all rates. They pick up clients regularly from Betham's, Charley's, and Kontiki.

Accommodations

The number of beds on Nananu-i-Ra is limited, and with the island's growing popularity, it's strongly recommended that you call ahead to one of the resorts and arrange to be picked up at Ellington Wharf. Of course, none of the innkeepers bother coming over in search of guests when they're fully booked. There's no public telephone at Ellington Wharf.

If you want an individual room or *mbure* make 100% sure one is available, otherwise you could end up spending quite a few nights in the dormitory waiting for one to become free. All the budget places have cooking facilities, but it's necessary to take most of your own supplies, as shopping possibilities on the island are very limited. There's a large market and several supermarkets in Vaileka where you can buy all the supplies you need. If you run out, groceries can be ordered from Vaileka for a small service charge and Betham's Bungalows runs a small grocery store with a few things (including beer). Also bring enough cash, as only the Mokusingas

Island Resort accepts credit cards. Add 10% tax to all prices quoted below.

Of all the budget places on Nananu-i-Ra, **Kontiki Island Lodge** (Box 87, Rakiraki; tel. 694-290) has more of the feeling of a genuine resort, with ample opportunity for group activities. Because they cater mostly to backpackers, the dormitory guests are treated the same as everyone else, and the atmosphere is friendly and congenial. It's also ideal if you want to do your own thing, as the long deserted beach facing One Bay is just a 20-minute walk away. Kontiki is at the unspoiled north end of the island, with no other resorts or houses (except the Harper caretaker) nearby. It's quite popular and on Saturday night they're full (reservations essential).

Kontiki offers three modern self-catering bungalows, each with two double rooms and three dorm beds. If you want privacy ask for one of the four rooms in the two thatched duplex *mbures.* Either way, dormitory beds are F$12 pp and double rooms F$26. Camping is not allowed. It's basic but well maintained. All guests have access to fridges and cooking facilities, and a few very basic supplies are sold, as well as cold beer. The staff will serve you a generous breakfast (F$2.50) and dinner (F$5) upon request. In the evening everyone gets together and swaps stories around the kava bowl. The generator runs until 2200. Enjoy the beach, snorkel, and rest—four nights is the average stay, though some people stay four weeks. If you get the right room, this could be one of the nicest low-budget places you'll encounter on your South Pacific trip.

At the other end of Nananu-i-Ra, a one-hour walk along the beach at low tide, are three other inexpensive places to stay, all offering cooking facilities, but no camping. They experience more speedboat noise than Kontiki but are less crowded and perhaps preferable for a restful holiday. They almost always have a few free beds in the dorms.

Nananu Beach Cottages (Box 140, Rakiraki; tel. 694-633), also known as "MacDonald's" and "Dive Lodge," offers three individual houses at F$50 single or double, plus F$6 pp for additional persons, and two five-bed dormitory rooms at F$13 pp. The dorms feature bunk beds and the cooking facilities are in the same room. It's peaceful and attractive with a private wharf and pontoon off their beach. The scuba diving operation based here is not always functioning, so check when booking if it makes a difference.

Right next to MacDonald's is **Betham's Bungalows** (Box 5, Rakiraki; tel. 694-132) with four cement-block duplex houses at F$44 single or double, F$53 triple, plus two dormitories, one with 10 beds and another with eight beds, at F$13 pp.

Sharing the same high sandy beach with MacDonald's and Betham's is **Charley's Place** (Charley and Louise Anthony, Box 407, Rakiraki; tel. 694-676) run by a delightful, friendly family. The dormitory building has six beds (F$12 each) in the same room as the cooking facilities, plus one double room (F$30). The adjacent bungalow can sleep up to six people at F$50 for two, plus F$5 for each additional person. Both buildings are on a hill and you can watch the sunrise on one side and the sunset on the other. Charley's also rents two other houses further down the beach, one at F$40 double, another at F$50 double.

In August 1991 **Mokusingas Island Resort** (Box 268, Rakiraki; tel. 694-449, fax 694-404) opened on Nananu-i-Ra. The 20 comfortable bungalows with fridge are F$175 for up to three persons, but cooking facilities are not provided and meals at the restaurant/bar are extra (F$74 pp meal plan). The resort's dive shop offers scuba diving at F$55 from a boat or F$26 from shore. A five-day PADI certification course costs F$400. To create a diving attraction, the 43-meter *Papuan Explorer* was scuttled in 25 meters of water, 60 meters off the 189-meter Mokusingas jetty, which curves out into the sheltered lagoon. The snorkeling off the wharf is good, especially at low tide, with lots of coral and fish. Don't be disappointed by the skimpy little beach facing a mudflat you first see when you arrive at the jetty: the mile-long picture-postcard beach in their brochure is a few minutes away over the hill on the other side of the island. All the resort facilities, including the restaurant, bar, and dive shop, are strictly for house guests only.

Getting There
Boat transfers from Ellington Wharf to Nananu-i-Ra are F$14-18 pp return (20 minutes), though the resorts may levy a surcharge if you're alone.

Check prices when you call to make your accommodation booking. A taxi to Ellington Wharf from the express bus stop next to the market in Vaileka is F$7 for the car. Several budget hotels in Nandi (including Sunny Holiday Motel, the Nandi Town Motel, and Kontiki Nandi) arrange minibus rides from Nandi direct to Ellington Wharf at F$26 pp, though it's cheaper to take an express bus from Lautoka to Vaileka, then a taxi to the landing.

As you return to Ellington Wharf from Nananu-i-Ra, taxis will be waiting to whisk you to Vaileka where you'll connect with the express buses (share the F$7 taxi fare with other travelers to cut costs). You could also hike two km out to the main highway and try to flag down a bus, but only local buses will stop at this junction.

Patterson Brothers operates a car ferry service between Ellington Wharf and Nambouwalu on Tuesday, Thursday, and Saturday, a great shortcut to/from Vanua Levu (F$26.40 one-way). The ferry leaves Ellington Wharf at the difficult hour of 0600, so it's more useful as a way of coming here from Vanua Levu since it departs Nambouwalu at 1130. There's a connecting bus to/from Lambasa. Sometimes you can arrange to spend the night on the boat at Ellington (ask at the Patterson Brothers office in Lautoka).

NORTHWESTERN VITI LEVU

Tavua
West of Rakiraki, Kings Road gets much better, and you pass the Yanggara Cattle Ranch where Fijian cowboys keep 5,500 head of cattle and 200 horses on a 7,000-hectare spread enclosed by an 80-km fence. At Tavua, an important junction on the north coast, buses on the north coast highways meet the daily service to Nandarivatu. Catching a bus from Tavua to Vaileka, Vatukoula, or Lautoka is no problem, but the bus to Nandarivatu only leaves at 1500. There are two banks in Tavua.

The two-story **Tavua Hotel** (Box 81, Tavua; tel. 680-522, fax 680-390), an old wooden building on a hill, a five-minute walk from the bus stop, has 11 rooms with bath at F$33/44 single/double. The **Golden Eagle Restaurant** (tel. 680-635) on Kings Road in Tavua serves standard Indian curries.

Vatukoula

In 1932 gold was discovered at Vatukoula, eight km south of Tavua, by an old Australian prospector named Bill Borthwick. Two years later Borthwick and his partner, Peter Costello, sold their stake to an Australian company, and in 1935 the **Emperor Gold Mine** opened. In 1977 there was a major strike at the mine and the government had to step in to prevent it from closing. In 1983 the Western Mining Corporation of Australia bought a 20% interest in the mine and took over management. Western modernized the facilities and greatly increased production, but after another bitter strike in 1991 they sold out and the mine is now operated by the Emperor Gold Mining Company once again. At last report, the 700 miners who walked out in 1991 were still on strike and the Emperor was refusing to recognize their union.

The ore comes up from the underground area through the Smith Shaft near "Top Gate." It's washed, crushed, and roasted, then fed into a flotation process and the foundry where gold and silver are separated from the ore. Counting both underground operations and an open pit, the mine presently extracts 135,000 ounces of gold annually from 600,000 metric tonnes of ore. A tonne of silver is also produced each year and waste rock is crushed into gravel and sold. Proven recoverable ore reserves at Vatukoula are sufficient for another decade of mining, and in 1985 additional deposits were discovered at nearby Nasomo, where extraction began in 1988.

Vatukoula is a typical company town, with education and social services under the jurisdiction of the Emperor. Company housing consists in part of WW II-style Quonset huts. The 2,000 miners employed here, most of them indigenous Fijians, live in racially segregated ghettos and are paid low wages. In contrast, tradespeople and supervisors, most of them Rotumans and part-Fijians, enjoy much better living conditions, and senior staff and management live in colonial-style comfort. Sensitive to profitability, the Emperor has tenaciously resisted the unionization of its workforce.

To arrange a guided tour of the mine you must contact the Public Relations Officer, Emperor Gold Mining Co. Ltd. (tel. 680-477, fax 680-772), at least one week in advance. It's not possible to just show up and be admitted. There's bus service from Tavua to Vatukoula every half hour, and even if you don't get off, it's well worth making the roundtrip to "Bottom Gate" to see the varying classes of company housing, to catch a glimpse of the golf course and open pit, and to enjoy the lovely scenery. Rosie Tours in Nandi runs gold mine tours (F$39 without lunch), but these do not enter the mine itself and you can see almost as much from the regular bus at a fraction the cost.

Mba

The large Indian town of Mba (population 11,000) on the Mba River is seldom visited by tourists. As the attractive mosque in the center of town indicates, nearly half of Fiji's Muslims live in Mba Province. Small fishing boats depart from behind the Shell service station opposite the mosque, and it's fairly easy to arrange to go along on all-night trips. A wide belt of mangroves covers much of the river's delta. Mba is better known for the large Rarawai Sugar Mill, opened by the Colonial Sugar Refining Co. in 1886.

The **Mba Hotel** (Box 29, Mba; tel. 674-000, fax 670-139), 110 Bank St., is the only organized accommodations. The 14 a/c rooms with bath are F$40/52 single/double—very pleasant with a swimming pool, bar, and restaurant. Many inexpensive restaurants serving Indian and Chinese meals are found along Kings Road.

If you're spending the night here check out Venus Cinema beside the Mba Hotel, and the Metro and Civic cinemas on opposite sides of Tambua Park near the post office. The Central Club is also in Tambua Park. Four banks have branches in Mba.

Three buses a day (except Sunday) run from Mba to Mbukuya in Viti Levu's high interior. If you'd like to stay in a village, you'll be welcome at **Navala** on the road to Mbukuya. Take along a *sevusevu* for the *turanga-ni-koro* and be prepared to pay your way (just don't arrive on a Sunday). Navala's thatched *mbures* stand picturesquely against the surrounding hills. When water levels are right, whitewater rafters shoot the rapids through the Mba River Gorge near here.

Important express buses leaving Mba daily are the Pacific Transport bus to Suva via Singatoka at 0615 (six hours, F$9), and the Sunbeam Transport buses to Suva via Tavua at 0715, 1300, and 1715 (five hours).

INTO THE INTERIOR

Nandarivatu

An important forestry station is at Nandarivatu, a small settlement above Tavua. Its 900-meter altitude means a cool climate and a fantastic panorama of the north coast from the ridge. Beside the road right in front of the Forestry Training Center is **The Stone Bowl,** official source of the Singatoka River, and a five-minute walk from the Center is the **Governor General's Swimming Pool** where a small creek has been dammed. Go up the creek a short distance to the main pool, though it's dry much of the year and the area has not been maintained. The trail to the fire tower atop **Mt. Lomalangi** (Mt. Heaven) begins nearby, a one-hour hike each way. The tower itself has collapsed and is no longer climbable, but the forest is lovely and you may see and hear many native birds. Pine forests cover the land.

In its heyday Nandarivatu was a summer retreat for expatriates from the nearby Vatukoula gold mine, and during the 1980s their large bungalow served as a Forestry Rest House. This ended after a small kitchen fire in 1989, and although the building is still there, it's in a dilapidated state and remains officially closed. Hopefully some local entrepreneur will recognize the possibilities for mountain tourism in this area, lease the building from the government, and carry out much-needed repairs. Meanwhile visitors with tents are allowed to camp at the Forestry Training Center. Ask permission at the Ministry of Forests office as soon as you arrive. Some canned foods are available at the canteen opposite the former Rest House, but bring food from Suva or Lautoka. Cabin crackers are handy.

There's only one bus a day (excluding Sunday) between Tavua and Nandarivatu, leaving Tavua at 1500, Nandarivatu at 0700—a spectacular one-and-a-half-hour bus ride. Arrive at the stop in Tavua at least 30 minutes ahead, as this bus does fill up. This bus originates/terminates in Nandrau. It's also quite easy to hitch.

Mount Victoria

The two great rivers of Fiji, the Rewa and the Singatoka, originate on the slopes of Mt. Victoria (Tomanivi), highest mountain in the country (1,323 meters). The climb begins near the bridge at Navai, 10 km southeast of Nandarivatu. Turn right up the hillside a few hundred meters down the jeep track, then climb up through native bush on the main path all the way to the top. Beware of misleading signboards. There are three small streams to cross; no water after the third. On your way down, stop for a swim in the largest stream. There's a flat area on top where you could camp—if you're willing to take your chances with Mbuli, the devil king of the mountain. Local guides are available, but allow about six hours for the roundtrip. Bright red epiphytic orchids *(Dendrobium mohlianum)* are sometimes in full bloom. Mount Victoria is on the divide between the wet and dry sides of Viti Levu, and from the summit you should be able to distinguish the contrasting vegetation in these zones.

Monasavu Hydroelectric Project

The largest development project ever undertaken in Fiji, this massive F$234 million scheme at Monasavu, on the Nandrau Plateau near the center of Viti Levu, took 1,500 men and six years to complete. An earthen dam, 82 meters high, was built across the Nanuka River to supply water to the four 20-megawatt generating turbines at the Wailoa Power Station on the Wailoa River, 625 meters below. The dam forms a lake 17 km long, and the water drops through a 5.4-km tunnel at a 45-degree angle, one of the steepest engineered dips in the world. Overhead transmission lines carry power from Wailoa to Suva and Lautoka. Monasavu is capable of filling Viti Levu's needs well into the 1990s, representing huge savings on imported diesel oil.

The Cross-Island Highway that passes the site was built to serve the dam project. Bus service ended when the project was completed and the construction camps closed in 1985. Traffic of all kinds was halted in 1993 when a hurricane took out the bridge at Lutu, although 4WD vehicles can still ford the river when water levels are low. At the present time there are only buses from Tavua to Nandrau and from

Suva to Naivuthini, although occasional carriers go farther.

The Singatoka River Trek

One of the most rewarding trips you can make on Viti Levu is the three-day hike south across the center of the island from Nandarivatu to Korolevu on the Singatoka River. There are many superb campsites along the trail, and luckily this trek is not included in the Australian guidebooks, so the area isn't overrun by tourists. Even so, villages like Numbutautau, Namoli, and Korolevu have hosted overnight visitors far too often for it to be pure Fijian hospitality anymore: a monetary *sevusevu* spiced with a generous bundle of *waka* are in order. (Kava for presentations on subsequent days can be purchased at villages along the way.) Set out from Nandarivatu early in the week, so you won't suffer the embarrassment of arriving in a village on Sunday. Excellent topographical maps of the entire route can be purchased at the Maps and Plans Room of the Lands and Survey Department in Suva.

Follow the dirt road south from Nandarivatu to **Nangatangata** where you should fill your canteen as the trail ahead is rigorous and there's no water to be found. From Nangatangata walk south about one hour. When you reach the electric high-power line, where the road turns right and begins to descend toward Koro, look for the well-worn footpath ahead. The trail winds along the ridge, and you can see as far as Mba. The primeval forests that once covered this part of Fiji were destroyed long ago by the slash-and-burn agricultural techniques of the Fijians.

When you reach the pine trees the path divides, with Nanoko to the right and Numbutautau down to the left. During the rainy season it's best to turn right and head to Nanoko, where you may be able to find a carrier to Mbukuya or all the way to Nandi. There's bus service between Mbukuya and Mba three times a day. If you do decide to make for Nanoko, beware of a very roundabout loop road on the left. Another option is to skip all of the above by staying in the bus from Tavua right to the end of the line at Nandrau, from whence your hike would then begin.

Reverend Thomas Baker, the last missionary to be clubbed and devoured in Fiji (in 1867), met his fate at **Numbutautau.** Jack London

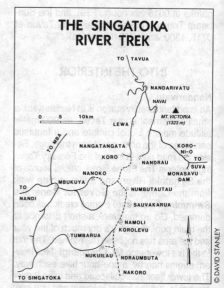

THE SINGATOKA RIVER TREK

© DAVID STANLEY

wrote a story, "The Whale Tooth," about the death of the missionary, and the axe that brought about Reverend Baker's demise is still kept in the village. You should be able to stay in the community center in Numbutautau. The Numbutautau-Korolevu section of the trek involves 22 crossings of the Singatoka River, which is easy enough in the dry season (cut a bamboo staff for balance), but almost impossible in the wet (December to April). Hiking boots will be useless in the river, so wear a pair of old running shoes.

It's a fantastic trip down the river to **Korolevu** if you can make it. The Korolevu villagers can call large eels up from a nearby pool with a certain chant, and a few hours' walk away are the **pottery villages,** Ndraumbuta and Nakoro, where traditional, long Fijian pots are still made. From Korolevu you can take a carrier to Tumbarua, where there are two buses a day to Singatoka (F$2). A carrier leaves Korolevu direct to Singatoka every morning except Sunday, departing Singatoka for the return around 1400 (if you want to do this trip in reverse). Reader Bruce French of Edgewood, Kentucky, wrote that "this trek was a big highlight of my South Pacific experience."

LAUTOKA AND VICINITY

Fiji's second-largest city, Lautoka (population 50,000) is the focus of the country's sugar and timber industries, a major port, and the Western Division and Mba Province headquarters. It's an amiable place with a row of towering royal palms along the main street. Though Lautoka grew up around the Fijian village of Namoli, it's a predominantly Indian town today, with temples and mosques standing prominently in the center of town. Shuttle boats to Beachcomber and Treasure islands depart from Lautoka, and this is the gateway to the Yasawa Islands with everything from Blue Lagoon cruises to village boats. Yet because Lautoka doesn't depend only on tourism, you get a truer picture of ordinary life, and the town has a rambunctious nightlife. There's some duty-free shopping, but mainly this is just a nice place to wander around. Unless you're hooked on tourist-oriented activities, Lautoka is a good alternative to Nandi for a stay.

SIGHTS OF LAUTOKA AND VICINITY

South of the Center

Begin next to the bus station at Lautoka's big, colorful **market,** which is busiest on Saturday (open weekdays 0700-1730, Saturday 0530-1600). From here, walk south on Yasawa Street to the photogenic **Jame Mosque.** Five times a day local male Muslims direct prayers toward a small niche known as a *mihrab,* where the prayers fuse and fly to the *Kabba* in Mecca, thence to Allah. During the crushing season (June to November) narrow-gauge trains rattle past the mosque along a line parallel to Vitongo Parade, bringing cane to Lautoka's large sugar mill.

Follow the line east a bit to the **Sikh Temple,** rebuilt after a smaller temple was burned by Methodist youths in October 1989. To enter you must wash your hands and cover your head (kerchiefs are provided at the door), and cigarettes and liquor are forbidden inside the compound. The teachings of the 10 Sikh gurus are contained in the Granth, a holy book prominently displayed in the temple. Sikhism began in the Punjab region of northwest India in the 16th century as a reformed branch of Hinduism much influenced by Islam: for example, Sikhs reject the caste system and idolatry. The Sikhs are easily recognized by their beards and turbans.

Follow your map west along Ndrasa Avenue to the **Sri Krishna Kaliya Temple** on Tavewa Avenue, the most prominent Krishna temple in the South Pacific (open daily until 2030). The images inside are Radha and Krishna on the right, while the central figure is Krishna dancing on the snake Kaliya to show his mastery over the reptile. The story goes that Krishna chastised Kaliya and exiled him to the island of Ramanik Deep, which Fiji Indians believe to be Fiji. (Curiously, the indigenous Fijian people have also long believed in a serpent-god, named Degei, who lived in a cave in the Nakauvandra Range.) The two figures on the left are incarnations of Krishna and Balarama. At the front of the temple is a representation of His Divine Grace A.C. Bhaktivedanta Swami Prabhupada, founder of the International Society for Krishna Consciousness (ISKCON). On Sunday, 15 October 1989, members of a Methodist youth group carried out a firebomb attack on this and three other Indian places of worship in Lautoka. The damage has since been repaired but a security guard is now posted at the gate.

Nearby off Thomson Crescent is the entrance to Lautoka's **botanical garden** (closed Sunday). It will be a few more years before the plants in the garden reach maturity, but the landscaping here is attractive.

Sugar and Spirits

Continue up Ndrasa Avenue a block from the garden and turn right on Mill View Road. The large Private Property sign at the beginning of the road is intended mostly to keep out heavy vehicles, and tourists are allowed to walk through this picturesque neighborhood, past the colonial-era residences of sugar industry executives and century-old banyan trees. Just beyond the Fiji Sugar Corporation offices is the **Lautoka Sugar Mill,** one of the largest in the Southern Hemisphere. The mill was founded in

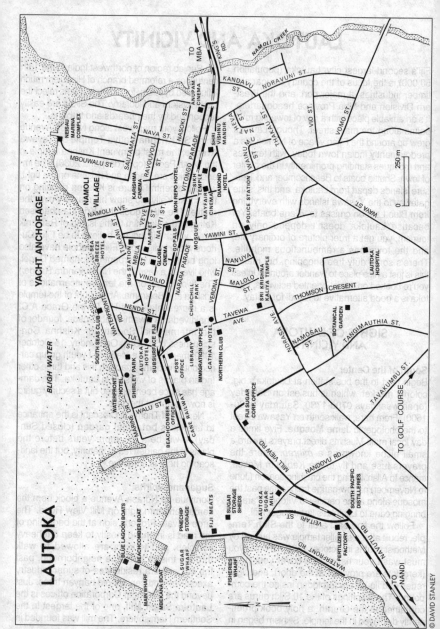

LAUTOKA

BLIGH WATER

YACHT ANCHORAGE

NAMOLI VILLAGE

TO MBA

TO GOLF COURSE

TO NANDI

© DAVID STANLEY

0   250 m

NEISAU MARINA COMPLEX

MBOUWALU ST.

SAUTAMATA ST.

NAVA ST.

KARISHNA CINEMA

RAVOUVOU ST.

NASOKI ST.

ANUPAM CINEMA

KING'S RD.

NAMOLI CREEK

KANDAVU ST.

NDRAVUNI ST.

VIO ST.

VOMO ST.

HEVAI ST.

THAKAU ST.

NAI ST.

WAINUMU ST.

WAYA ST.

NAMOLI AVE.

NAMOLI ST.

VEVE ST.

TUKANI ST.

SEA BREEZE HOTEL

BUS STATION

MBILA ST.

MARKET ST.

NAVITI ST.

GLOBE CINEMA

VINDILIO ST.

NENDE ST.

VITONGO PARADE

MON REPO HOTEL

GOPALS

SHRI VISHNU MANDIR

SIKH TEMPLE

MAYFAIR CINEMA

DIAMOND HOTEL

MOSQUE

YAWINI ST.

POLICE STATION

NANUYA ST.

MALOLO ST.

VERONA ST.

SRI KRISHNA KALIYA TEMPLE

LAUTOKA HOSPITAL

THOMSON CRESENT

NARARA PARADE

CHURCHILL PARK

SOUTH SEAS CLUB

WATERFRONT RD.

SHIRLEY PARK

LAUTOKA HOTEL

SUBSURFACE FIJI

TUI ST.

WATERFRONT HOTEL

MARINE DR.

WALU ST.

POST OFFICE

LIBRARY

IMMIGRATION OFFICE

CATHAY HOTEL

NORTHERN CLUB

TAVEWA AVE.

CANE RAILWAY

BEACHCOMBER OFFICE

NORASA AVE.

NAMOSAU ST.

BOTANICAL GARDEN

TANGIMAUTHIA ST.

FIJI SUGAR CORP. OFFICE

TAVAKUMBU ST.

MILL VIEW RD.

NANDOVU RD.

SUGAR STORAGE SHEDS

LAUTOKA SUGAR MILL

VEITARI ST.

SOUTH PACIFIC DISTILLERIES

NAVUTU RD.

WATERFRONT RD.

FERTILIZER FACTORY

FIJI MEATS

PINECHIP STORAGE

SUGAR WHARF

MAIN WHARF

MBEKANA BOAT

BLUE LAGOON BOATS

BEACHCOMBER BOAT

FISHERIES WHARF

N

1903, and until the 1987 military coups it was possible to visit. Although the security situation in Fiji is now about back to normal, the mill tours remain suspended, though you can see quite a lot of the operation (busiest from June to November) as you walk down Mill View Road toward the main gate.

Continue straight ahead on Navutu Road (the dirt road beside the railway line) to **South Pacific Distilleries** (Box 1128, Lautoka; tel. 662-088, fax 664-361), where free plant tours can be arranged on the spot weekdays during business hours. This government-owned plant bottles rum, whisky, vodka, and gin under a variety of labels and, of course, molasses from the sugar mill is the distillery's main raw material. The **fertilizer factory** across the highway uses mill mud from the sugar-making process.

The Waterfront
Backtrack to the sugar mill and turn left toward **Fisheries Wharf,** from which you'll have a fine view of the huge sugar storage sheds next to the mill and many colorful fishing boats. If you were thinking of taking a village boat to the Yasawa Islands, this is where you'll board.

To the north, just beyond the conveyor belts used to load raw sugar onto the ships, is a veritable mountain of **pine chips** ready for export to Japan where they are used to make paper. Forestry is becoming more important as Fiji attempts to diversify its economy away from sugar. The **Main Wharf** behind the chips is the departure point for the famous Blue Lagoon Cruises to the Yasawa Islands, plus the 39-meter Beachcomber Island shuttle boat *Tui Tai.* If you have time, take the **Mbekana Island** shuttle boat from just inside the main gate over to the small resort (see "Mbekana Island" under "Accommodations," below) on the only beach right at Lautoka—it only costs F$1 each way. As you return to central Lautoka, turn left onto **Marine Drive** for its view of the harbor, especially enchanting at sunset.

North of Lautoka
One of the largest reforestation projects yet undertaken in the South Pacific is the **Lololo Pine Scheme,** eight km off Kings Road between Lautoka and Mba. The logs are sawn into timber if straight or ground into chip if twisted and then

exported from Lautoka. There's a shady picnic area along a dammed creek at the forestry station where you could swim, but even if you don't stop, it's worthwhile taking the one-and-a-half-hour roundtrip bus ride from Lautoka to see this beautiful area and to learn how it's being used. The buses follow a circular route, returning by a different road.

South of Lautoka
A popular legend invented in 1893 holds that **Viseisei village,** between Lautoka and Nandi, is the oldest settlement in Fiji. It's told how the first Fijians, led by Chiefs Lutunasobasoba and Degei, came from the west, landing their great canoe, the *Kaunitoni,* at Vunda Point, where the oil tanks are now. A Centennial Memorial (1835-1935) in front of the church commemorates the arrival of the first Methodist missionaries in Fiji, and opposite the memorial is a traditional Fijian *mbure*—the residence of the present Tui Vunda.

Near the back of the church is another monument topped by a giant war club, the burial place of the village's chiefly family. The late Dr. Timoci Bavadra, the former prime minister of Fiji who was deposed by the Rabuka coup in 1987, hailed from Viseisei and is interred here in an unmarked grave. Dr. Bavadra's traditional-style home faces the main road near the church. His son presently lives there, and with his permission you'll be allowed to enter to see the photos hanging from the walls.

All this is only a few minutes' walk from the bus stop (frequent service), but you're expected to have someone accompany you through the village. Ask permission of anyone you meet at the bus stop and they will send a child with you. As you part, you could give the child a pack of chewing gum (give something else if your escort is an adult). Nearby is a **Memorial Cultural Center,** where souvenirs are sold to cruise ship passengers. There's a fine view of Nandi Bay from the Center.

A couple of kilometers from the village on the airport side of Viseisei, just above Lomolomo Public School, are two **British six-inch guns** set up here during WW II to defend the north side of Nandi Bay. It's a fairly easy climb from the main highway, and you get an excellent view from the top.

Sports and Recreation

Subsurface Fiji (Box 5202, Lautoka; tel. 664-422, fax 664-496) at the corner of Nende and Naviti streets near the Lautoka Hotel, arranges scuba diving at F$65 for one tank, F$115 for two tanks. Trips to Waya Island in the Yasawas are offered for scuba divers and snorkelers on Thursday, Friday, and Saturday. Divers should call for free pickup at Nandi/Lautoka hotels. Tank air fills at offshore islands can also be arranged.

You can rent tanks and have them filled at **Dive Center Ltd.** (Box 5015, Lautoka; tel. 663-797, fax 662-211), 11 Walu Street.

Saturday you can catch an exciting rugby or soccer game at the stadium in Churchill Park. Admission is reasonable—check locally for the times of league games.

ACCOMMODATIONS

Accommodations in Town

A good choice is the clean, quiet, three-story **Sea Breeze Hotel** (Box 152, Lautoka; tel. 660-717), at 5 Mbekana Lane on the waterfront near the bus station. They have 26 rooms with private bath from F$25/30 single/double (rooms with a/c cost F$4 more). A larger family room accommodating four adults is F$50. At first they'll try to give you an a/c room; then if you convince them to let you have a fan-cooled room, they may want to stick you in a noisy room near the reception, even when the top floor is completely empty. Ask to see the room before signing the register. For reasons unknown, they'll occasionally claim they're fully booked even when the place is almost empty. There's a very pleasant lounge and swimming pool overlooking the lagoon.

To be closer to the action, stay at the 38-room **Lautoka Hotel** (Box 51, Lautoka; tel. 660-388, fax 660-201), 2 Naviti St., which has a good restaurant and nightclub on the premises. There's also a swimming pool. Room prices vary from F$17/22 single/double for a fan-cooled room with shared bath to F$44 single or double for a/c and private bath, F$66 for a/c, private bath, fridge, and waterbed, or F$9 pp in the dorm.

Also recommended are the 40 rooms at the friendly **Cathay Hotel** (Box 239, Lautoka; tel. 660-566, fax 340-236) on Tavewa Avenue, which features a small swimming pool, TV room, and bar. The charge is F$25/33 single/double with fan and private bath, F$33/41 with a/c. There are several dormitories of varying size, cleanliness, and facilities at F$10 pp. They offer free luggage storage for guests.

The 18-room **Diamond Hotel** (Box 736, Lautoka; tel. 661-920) on Nathula Street charges F$8 pp in the dorm (three beds), or F$19/25 single/double for a room with fan. Though plain and basic, it's okay for one night if everything else is full.

Another step down is the **Mon Repo Hotel** (Box 857, Lautoka; tel. 661-595), 75 Vitongo Parade, at F$14/22 single/double with shared bath. This building is a former police station and the cells (guest rooms) are still frequented by prostitutes.

Lautoka's most expensive hotel is the **Waterfront Hotel** (Box 4653, Lautoka; tel. 664-777, fax 665-870), a two-story building erected in 1987 on Marine Drive. The 41 waterbed-equipped a/c rooms are F$100 single or double, F$120 triple (children under 16 are free if no extra bed is required). There's a swimming pool, and members of tour groups departing Lautoka booked on Blue Lagoon cruises often stay here.

South of Lautoka

Saweni Beach Apartments (Box 239, Lautoka; tel. 661-777, fax 340-236), a kilometer off the main highway south of Lautoka, offers a row of 12 self-catering apartments with fan at F$38/44 single/double, plus a F$11 pp dorm. You can pitch your own tent here at F$5 pp (provided the communal toilets are working). Fishermen on the beach sell fresh fish every morning, and cruising yachts often anchor off Saweni Beach. Saweni is quieter than the Anchorage mentioned below, and the so-so beach only comes alive on weekends when local picnickers arrive. A bus runs right to the hotel from Lautoka three times a day. Otherwise any of the local Nandi buses will drop you off a 10-minute walk away.

The **Anchorage Beach Resort** (Box 9472, Nandi Airport; tel. 662-099, fax 665-571), between Viseisei and Vunda Point, a few kilometers south of the Saweni Beach, has 10 rooms at F$70/75 single/double, and a F$17 pp dorm with cooking facilities. A swimming pool, washing machine, and panoramic views are among the other attractions. Stay at the Anchorage if you like meeting people, at the Saweni if you want to regenerate. It's about a 15-minute walk from the highway to Anchorage Resort.

Mediterranean Villas (Box 5240, Lautoka; tel. 664-011, fax 661-773), on Vunda Hill overlooking Viseisei village, has six attractive villas beginning at F$77/88 single/double. Cooking facilities are not provided, but a licensed Italian seafood restaurant is on the premises. The beach is far from here.

For information on Beachcomber Island and Treasure Island resorts, both accessible from Lautoka, turn to "The Mamanutha Group," previously covered under "Southwest Viti Levu."

Mbekana Island

The most easily accessible island resort in Fiji is **Mbekana Island Resort** (Tracy and Robert Walker, Box 4091, Lautoka; tel. 665-222, fax 665-409), formerly known as "Paradise Island," just offshore from Lautoka. They offer 12 thatched fan-cooled *mbures* with private bath and fridge (but no cooking facilities) at F$115 for up to four persons. A six-bed dormitory lodge is F$38 pp including breakfast and dinner. Water taxi transfers from Lautoka's main wharf are F$1 pp each way. Mbekana's biggest draw is its easy access to Lautoka, allowing you to combine beach life with organized shopping and sightseeing, and a night here can be memorable if you don't mind spending more than you would at the city hotels. It's peaceful and the view of the Lautoka skyline backed by the Mount Evans Range is unsurpassed. Mbekana itself is an uninteresting flat island with nothing to see beyond the boundaries of the resort (although it's fascinating to kayak through the nearby mangroves). Water sports such as windsurfing, kayaking, and sailing are freely available to guests, and the clean swimming pool makes up for the lack of snorkeling possibilities around here. Even if you aren't staying, their F$10 Sunday barbecue at 1230 is a good way to put in a Sunday afternoon.

FOOD

Several inexpensive local restaurants are opposite the bus station. The **Pacific Restaurant** (Monday to Saturday 0700-1900, Sunday 1000-1600), on Yasawa Street near the Singatoka Bookshop, has some of the hottest (spiciest) food you'll find anywhere in the Pacific—excellent if that's to your taste. This is also a good place to get a coffee or breakfast.

For the best vegetarian food and ice cream in town, it's **Gopal's** (tel. 662-990; closed Sunday). It's on the corner of Naviti and Yasawa streets near the market, with a second location at 117 Vitongo Parade (tel. 660-938) opposite Churchill Park. This is the Lautoka equivalent of Suva's Hare Krishna Restaurant.

Rennee's Restaurant (tel. 662-473; also open Sunday night), 62 Naviti St., has the standard curry- and chop suey-type stuff, but tasty big portions and reasonable prices (add 10% tax to what it says on the menu). Cold beer is available with the meal. The **Hot Snax Shop,** 56 Naviti St., is also good for Indian dishes.

Enjoy ample servings of Cantonese food at the a/c **Sea Coast Restaurant** (tel. 660-675; closed Sunday) on Naviti St. near the Lautoka Hotel. (Conversely, avoid the nearby Great Wall of China Restaurant, notable for its poor service, miserly portions, and erratic pricing.)

Eat Italian at the **Pizza Inn** (tel. 660-388) in the Lautoka Hotel, 2 Naviti Street.

On Sunday the best thing to do is attend a barbecue, and the **Mbekana Island Resort** (tel. 665-222) puts one on at 1230 (F$10, plus F$2 pp for boat transfers from the main wharf). The **Neisau Marina** (tel. 664-858) has another barbecue at 1800 (also F$10).

ENTERTAINMENT

There are four movie houses with several showings daily except Sunday.

The disco scene in Lautoka centers on the **Hunter's Inn** at the Lautoka Hotel (tel. 660-388; open Friday and Saturday 2100-0100 only; F$4 cover). There's also **Coco's** (tel. 667-900) at 91 Naviti St., above the Great Wall of China

Restaurant, but you won't be admitted if you're wearing a T-shirt, jeans, shorts, running shoes, or flip-flops.

The roughest place in town is **Kings Nite Club,** above Gopal's in the center of town (tel. 665-822). It's open Monday to Saturday 1800-0100, but nothing much happens at Kings before 2200. The cover charge on Thursday, Friday, and Saturday is F$3, and flip-flop shoes aren't allowed.

Lautoka's old colonial club is the **Northern Club** (tel. 662-469) on Tavewa Avenue opposite the Cathay Hotel. The sign outside says Members Only, but the club secretary is usually happy to sign in foreign visitors. Lunch and dinner are available here from Monday to Saturday; there's tennis and a swimming pool. Happy hour is Tuesday 1800-1900.

The **Lautoka Club** (tel. 660-637), at 17 Tukani St. next to the Sea Breeze Hotel, is another good drinking place with a sea view.

Day cruises to Beachcomber Island (F$58 pp including lunch, reductions for children) depart Lautoka daily at 1000—a great way to spend a day. Any travel agency can book them.

Sunday *Puja*

The big event of the week is the Sunday evening *puja* (prayer) at the **Sri Krishna Kaliya Temple** on Tavewa Avenue from 1630-2030, followed by a vegetarian feast. Visitors may join in the singing and dancing, if they wish. Take off your shoes and sit on the white marble floor, men on one side, women on the other. The female devotees are especially stunning in their beautiful *saris.* Bells ring, drums are beaten, conch shells blown, and stories from the Vedas, Srimad Bhagavatam, and Ramayana are acted out as everyone chants, *"Hare Krsna, Hare Krsna, Krsna Krsna, Hare Hare, Hare Rama, Hare Rama, Rama, Rama, Hare, Hare."* It's a real celebration of joy and a most moving experience. At one point children will circulate with small trays covered with burning candles, on which it is customary to place a modest donation; you may also drop a dollar or two in the yellow box in the center of the temple. You'll be readily invited to join the vegetarian feast later, and no more money will be asked of you.

OTHER PRACTICALITIES

Services and Information

The ANZ Bank, National Bank, and Westpac Bank are all on Naviti Street near the market. The receptionist at the Cathay Hotel will change traveler's checks anytime at the regular bank rate without commission.

The **Immigration Department** (tel. 662-283) is in the Housing Authority building near the Cathay Hotel.

Public toilets are on the back side of the bus station facing the market.

The **Book Exchange,** 19 Yasawa St., trades and sells used books. The **Western Regional Library** (tel. 660-091) on Tavewa Avenue is open weekdays 1000-1700, Saturday 0900-1200.

Yachting Facilities

The **Neisau Marina Complex** (Box 3831, Lautoka; tel. 664-858, fax 663-807), at the end of Mbouwalu Street, provides complete haul-out facilities for yachts in need of repair. There's also an authentic token-operated **laundromat** here (F$3 to wash, F$3 to dry), and Spencer's Bar, which puts on a barbecue Sunday at 1800 (F$10). The bar's terrace is a great place to enjoy a beer while your clothes are washing.

Health

There's an outpatient service and dental clinic at the **Lautoka Hospital** (tel. 660-399; Monday to Friday 0800-1600, Saturday 0800-1100), off Thomson Crescent south of the center. A consultation with a private doctor is more convenient.

Vaccinations for international travelers are available at the **Health Office** (tel. 663-542) on Naviti Street opposite the Lautoka Hotel on Tuesday and Friday 0800-1200.

Transportation

Sunflower Airlines (tel. 664-753) is at 27 Vindilo Street.

Anyone headed toward Vanua Levu should check with **Beachcomber Cruises** (tel. 661-500), which runs the high-speed catamaran *Ndrondrolangi* from Lautoka to Savusavu daily except Sunday at 0600 (three hours, F$55).

Patterson Brothers (tel. 661-173), on Tukani Street opposite the bus station, runs a bus/ferry/bus service between Lautoka, Ellington Wharf, Nambouwalu, and Lambasa (F$34), departing Lautoka on Tuesday, Thursday, and Saturday around 0400.

Buses, carriers, taxis—everything leaves from the bus stand beside the market. **Pacific Transport** (tel. 660-499) has express buses to Suva daily at 0630, 0700, 1210, and 1730 (five hours, F$7.80) via Singatoka (Queens Road). Four other "stage" buses also operate daily along this route (six hours). **Sunbeam Transport** (tel. 662-822) has expresses to Suva at 0630, 1215, and 1630 (six hours) via Tavua (Kings Road), plus two local buses on the same route (nine hours). The northern route is more scenic than the southern. Local buses to Nandi (F$1.15) and Mba (F$1.25) depart every half hour or so.

THE YASAWA ISLANDS

The Yasawas are a chain of 16 main volcanic islands and dozens of smaller ones, stretching 80 km in a north-northeast direction, roughly 35 km off the west coast of Viti Levu. In the lee of Viti Levu, the Yasawas are dry and sunny, with beautiful, isolated beaches, cliffs, bays, and reefs. The waters are crystal clear and almost totally shark-free. The group was romanticized in two movies titled *The Blue Lagoon:* a 1949 original starring Jean Simmons and the 1980 remake with Brooke Shields. It was from the north end of the Yasawas that two canoe-loads of cannibals sallied forth in 1789 and gave chase to Capt. William Bligh and his 18 companions less than a week after the famous mutiny.

Two centuries later, increasing numbers of mini-cruise ships ply the chain. Though an abundance of luxury resorts dot the Mamanutha Islands off Nandi and a couple have appeared in the Yasawas, there aren't many regular, inexpensive places to stay. The backpackers' usual routine is to take a village boat to Tavewa or Waya (see below). If you'll be going off on your own trekking or kayaking, you should take along a good supply of *yanggona* (which doesn't grow in the Yasawas) for use as a *sevusevu* to village chiefs. All access to the Yasawas is via Lautoka. In the local dialect, *thola* is "hello" and *vina du riki* is "thank you."

Waya Island

Just 60 km northwest of Lautoka is Waya, the closest of the larger Yasawas to Viti Levu and also the highest island (579 meters). A sheer mass of rock rises above Yalombi village. Yalombi has a beautiful beach, and the offshore reef features cabbage coral, whip coral, and giant fan corals in warm, clear waters teeming with fish. At low tide you can wade from Waya across to neighboring Wayasewa Island: there's good snorkeling there and a remarkable 354-meter-high volcanic thumb that overlooks the south coast. Also from Yalombi, it's a 30-minute hike across the ridge to Natawa village on the east side of Waya. There's a deserted beach another 20 minutes north of Natawa. In a long day you can hike right around Waya, passing two villages and many friendly people along the way.

Andi Sayaba's Place (Box 1163, Lautoka) at Yalombi on the south side of Waya consists of a former schoolhouse partitioned into 10 "rooms" at F$8 pp in a five- to 10-bed dorm, or F$20 double. Campers pay F$6 pp, and three decent meals are an additional F$10 pp, but bring your own drinks. The rooms are usually used by scuba divers sent over by **Subsurface Fiji Ltd.** (Box 502, Lautoka; tel. 664-422) near the Lautoka Hotel, and you can get full information about Andi's Place from Harry in Subsurface Fiji's Lautoka office on the corner of Nende and Naviti streets. Subsurface provides speedboat transportation to Waya from Lautoka's Fisheries Wharf at 1000 on Thursday, Friday, and Saturday (two hours, F$66 pp return). This local resort makes a good base for observing traditional Fijian life and enjoying nature, while retaining some privacy.

On a lovely white-sand beach in Likuliku Bay on northwestern Waya is **Octopus Club Fiji** (Box 1861, Lautoka; tel. 666-337, fax 666-210), run by Ingrid and Wolfgang Denk. They have three thatched *mbures* with private bath at F$49 pp double occupancy, or F$29 pp in a four-bed

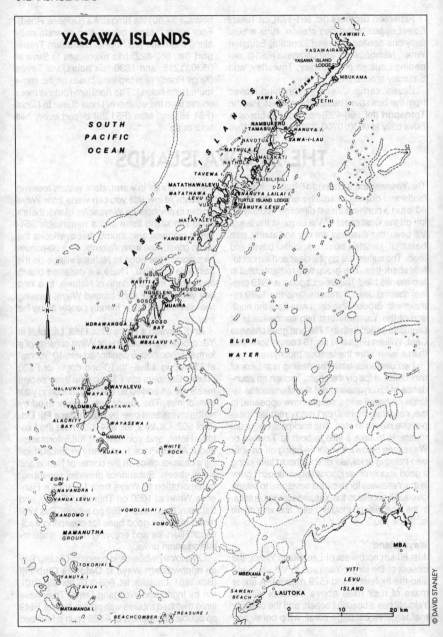

YASAWA ISLANDS

SOUTH
PACIFIC
OCEAN

YASAWA ISLANDS

YAWINI I.

YASAWAIRARA

YASAWA ISLAND
LODGE

YASAWA I.

MBUKAMA

VAWA I.

TETHI

NAMBUKERU

TAMASUA
NANUYA I.

SAWA-I-LAU

NAVOTUA

MALAKATI

NATHULA I.

NATHULA

NAISILISILI

TAVEWA I.

MATATHAWALEVU

MATATHAWA
LEVU

NANUYA LAILAI I.

VUXKE

TURTLE ISLAND LODGE

NANUYA LEVU

MATAYALEVU

YANGGETA

BLIGH
WATER

NGUNU

NAVITI I.

NGGELENI

KESE

SOSO

MUAIRA

SOMOSOMO

NDRAWANGGA I.

SOSO
BAY

NANUYA
MBALAVU I.

NARARA I.

NALAUWAKI

WAYALEVU

WAYA I.

NATAWA

YALOMBI

ALACHITY
BAY

NAMARA

KUATA I.

WHITE
ROCK

EORI I.

NAVANDRA I.

VANUA LEVU I.

KANDOMO I.

VOMOLAILAI I.

VOMO I.

MAMANUTHA
GROUP

MBA

TOKORIKI I.

YANUYA I.

TAVUA I.

MBEKANA I.

VITI
LEVU
ISLAND

MATAMANOA I.

SAWENI
BEACH

LAUTOKA

TREASURE I.

BEACHCOMBER I.

0   10   20 km

© DAVID STANLEY

dorm, breakfast and dinner included. They organize a *meke* every Tuesday evening (F$15 for guests, F$25 for nonguests). Fishing trips and island visits are F$17 pp including lunch. Hike to Waya's highest point for a splendid view. Yachts are welcome to anchor offshore and use the facilities. Transfers depart Lautoka's Neisau Marina Monday at 1400 and Thursday at 1000, departing Waya for the return Monday and Wednesday at 0800 (F$66 roundtrip). Information should be available at the Cathay Hotel reception in Lautoka.

Dive Trek Nature Lodge (Semi Koroilavesau, Box 23, Nandi; tel. 720-977, fax 720-978), adjacent to old Namara village on the south side of neighboring Wayasewa Island, opened in June 1994. The former village school building on a hill overlooking the beach has been partitioned into 14 tiny double rooms costing F$30 pp, including ample Fijian meals. Toilets, showers, and the eating area are in separate buildings nearby, and lighting is by hurricane lamp. There are also 10 traditional guest *mbures* with private bath and a small porch at F$100 double, meals included. Add 10% tax to all rates. Beer and soft drinks are sold, kava is served three evenings a week, and on Sunday afternoon a *lovo* is prepared. Informal musical entertainment occurs nightly. Three different guided hikes into the nearby hills are arranged; the extra charge for this service is worth it. Good snorkeling is available right off their beach—giant clams—and daily boat trips to nearby Kuata Island are organized. Scuba diving is also offered (F$65/100/130 one/two/three tanks, equipment included), as is a PADI scuba certification course (F$330). Boat transfers from Nandi depart Tuesday, Thursday, and Saturday at 1330 (F$35 pp each way including bus transfers to Nandi/Lautoka hotels). At Nandi Airport inquire about the lodge at Fiji Holiday Connections in Suite 8 in the international arrivals area. This sensitively planned ecotourism resort operated in partnership with the local villagers is highly recommended.

Naviti Island

Naviti, at 33 square km, is the largest of the Yasawas. Its king, one of the group's highest chiefs, resides at Soso, and the church there houses fine woodcarvings. Every Wednesday at noon the people of Soso gather to sell shells to a button factory. On the hillside above Soso are two caves containing the bones of ancestors. Yawesa, the secondary boarding school on Naviti, is a village in itself. There's no wharf on Naviti, so you must wade ashore from the boat.

Tavewa Island

Tavewa is much smaller than Waya and twice as far from Lautoka, yet it's also strikingly beautiful with excellent bathing in the warm waters off a picture-postcard beach on the southeast side, and a good fringing reef with super snorkeling. Tall grass covers the hilly interior (splendid sunsets from the hill). It's a small island about two km long, with a population of around 50 souls. There's no chief here, as this is freehold land. The people are friendly and welcoming; in fact, accommodating visitors is their main source of income. Most of their guests are backpackers who usually stay six nights, and most are sorry to leave. It's idyllic if you don't mind a non-Fijian atmosphere and a lack of privacy. Bring along mosquito coils, toilet paper, a flashlight (torch), and a *sulu* to cover up.

There's a reasonable choice of places to stay. **David and Kara Doughty's Place** (tel. 663-939), in a coconut grove near the small church, has several quite acceptable *mbures* for travelers at F$40 double, or F$18 pp in the dorm, three huge meals included. Camping is F$8 pp with your own tent, or F$13 pp to sleep in one of their tents, meals included (occasional extra charge for special barbecues). There's no electricity in the *mbures*, but David runs a generator in the house and his small store sells cold beer, drinks, and cigarettes. Since they started cutting the grass the mosquito problem has declined, but the communal toilets could use a cleaning. David and Kara will invite you to join in family activities, and the results of David's fishing trips often appear at dinner. He'll take you to a scenic cave or drop you off on an isolated beach, and in the evening men can sit around playing backgammon and drinking kava with David, or women might help Kara weave a mat. Often someone sings a couple of songs. In short, it's a good escape from civilization, and you'll be made most welcome. Their boat leaves Lautoka Tuesday and Saturday at 0700, returning Monday and Friday (F$30 pp each way). Bookings can be made at the reception of the Lautoka Hotel (though we've heard the system is erratic, with people who didn't book ahead occasionally given priority).

The other main accommodation on Tavewa is **Coral View Resort** (Box 3764, Lautoka), also known as "Uncle Robert de Bruce's Place." Prices here are similar at F$49 double, F$22 in the dorm, or F$16 pp to camp, including all meals and one organized activity a day. It's a bit more primitive than David's and the food isn't quite as good, but it's still quite okay and mosquito nets are supplied. Their Thursday morning village excursion with lunch and "folkloric entertainment" (F$12 pp) is better than David's, and there are also boat trips to the Sawa-i-Lau cave (F$20 pp). A German reader who stayed at Robert's liked Meca's meals of fresh fish seasoned with garlic and ginger, and enjoyed Robert's evening tales of 10-headed snakes and buried treasure. Their boat leaves Lautoka Tuesday and Saturday at 0800, and Wednesday at 1400, departing Tavewa for the return on Monday, Wednesday, and Friday mornings (F$66 pp roundtrip). Bookings are handled at the reception of the Cathay Hotel in Lautoka.

Village boats such as the *Calm Sea, Babale,* and *Nukunindreke* leave from Lautoka's Fisheries Wharf near Fiji Meats very early Tuesday and Saturday mornings, returning to Lautoka on Monday and Friday (F$30 oneway). This schedule means you can spend either two, three, six, or more nights in the Yasawas. Any boat headed for Nathula village on Nathula Island will drop you off on Tavewa and there are always Yasawans around Lautoka market on Friday. The boat ride from Lautoka can take anywhere from three to six hours (or more) depending on weather conditions, and it's a scenic trip across Bligh Water through the Yasawa Group to Tavewa. Just don't expect luxuries such as toilets on these boats, so limit how much you drink before boarding. Also limit what you eat, or take seasickness pills if you're a poor sailor. The boats can become very crowded, and if it's a nice day you ought to sit on the roof (bring sunscreen). Be prepared to wade ashore with your pack over your head at Tavewa.

Nanuya Levu Island

In 1972 an eccentric American millionaire named Richard Evanson bought 200-hectare Nanuya Levu Island in the middle of the Yasawa Group for US$300,000. He still lives there, and his **Turtle Island Lodge** (Box 9317, Nandi Airport; tel. 722-921, fax 720-007) has gained a reputation as one of the South Pacific's ultimate hideaways. Only 14 fan-cooled, two-room *mbures* grace Turtle, and Evanson swears there'll never be more.

Turtle is Tavewa at 25 times the price. The 28 guests (English-speaking mixed couples only, please) pay around F$1000 per couple per night, but that includes all meals, drinks, and activities. You'll find the fridge in your cottage well stocked with beer, wine, soft drinks, and champagne, refilled daily, with no extra bill to pay when you leave. Sports such as sailing, snorkeling, scuba diving, canoeing, windsurfing, glass-bottom boating, deep-sea fishing, catamaraning, horseback riding, guided hiking, and moonlight cruising are all included in the tariff. Lodge staff will even do your laundry at no charge.

If you want to spend the day on any of the dozen secluded beaches, just ask and you'll be dropped off. Later someone will be back with lunch and a cooler of wine or champagne (or anything else you'd care to order over the few walkie-talkie). Otherwise use the beach a few steps from your door. Meals are served at remote and romantic dine-out locations, or taken at the community table; every evening Richard hosts a small dinner party. He's turned down many offers to develop the island with hundreds more units or to sell out for a multimillion-dollar price. That's not Richard's style, and he's quite specific about who he *doesn't* want to come: "Trendies, jetsetters, obnoxious imbibers, and plastic people won't get much out of my place. Also, opinionated, loud, critical grouches and anti-socials should give us a miss."

Of course, all this luxury and romance has a price. Aside from the per diem, it's another F$750 per couple for roundtrip seaplane transportation to the island from Nandi. There's also a seven-night minimum stay, but as nearly half the guests are repeaters that doesn't seem to be an impediment. (Turtle Island is off-limits to anyone other than hotel guests.) Turtle's success may be measured by its many imitators, including the Vatulele Island Resort, the Wakaya Club, Lauthala Island, Kaimbu Island, and the Yasawa Island Lodge.

Turtle Island has also set the standard for environmentally conscious resort development. Aside from planting thousands of trees and providing a safe haven for birds, Evanson has preserved the island's mangroves, cleverly erecting a boardwalk to turn what others may have considered an eyesore into a major attraction. The beach on neighboring **Nanuya Lailai Island** is used by passengers on Blue Lagoon cruises.

Sawa-i-Lau Island

On Sawa-i-Lau is a large limestone cave illuminated by a crevice at the top. There's a clear, deep pool in the cave where you can swim, and an underwater opening leads back into a smaller, darker cave (bring a light). A Fijian legend tells how a young chief once hid his love in this cave when her family wished to marry her off to another. Each day he brought her food until both could escape to safety on another island. All the cruise ships stop at this cave. If you get there on your own, present a *sevusevu* to the chief of Nambukeru village, just west of the cave, to visit.

Yasawa Island

The Tui Yasawa, highest chief of the group, resides at Yasawairara village at the north end of Yasawa, northernmost island of the Yasawa group.

For many years the Fiji government had a policy that the Yasawas were "closed" to land-based tourism development, and it was only after the 1987 coups that construction of **Yasawa Island Lodge** (Box 10128, Nandi Airport; tel. 663-364, fax 665-044) was approved. This $8.5-million Australian-owned resort opened in 1991 on a creamy white beach on Yasawa's upper west side. Most of the resort's employees come from Mbukama village, which owns the land.

The 16 thatched a/c *mbures* with private baths consist of four duplexes at F$798 double, 10 deluxes at F$886, a two-bedroom unit at F$1025, and a honeymoon unit also at F$1025. All meals are included, but unlike at most other resorts in this category, alcoholic drinks are *not*. Scuba diving and game fishing also cost extra. Guests arrive on a chartered flight (F$165 pp each way), which lands on the resort's private airstrip. Here they're met by a thatched six-wheel-drive truck called the "*mbula* bus" that seats them on padded wooden benches in back and carries them to the resort. Children under 14 are only admitted during school holiday periods four times a year.

KANDAVU

This big, 50-by-13-km island 100 km south of Suva is the fourth largest in Fiji. A mountainous, varied island with waterfalls plummeting from the rounded hilltops, Kandavu is outstanding for its vistas, beaches, and reefs. The three hilly sections of Kandavu are joined by two low isthmuses, with the sea biting so deeply into the island that on a map its shape resembles that of a wasp. Just northeast of the main island is smaller Ono Island and the fabulous Astrolabe Reef, stretching halfway to Suva. The famous red-and-green Kandavu parrots may be seen and heard.

In the 1870s steamers bound for New Zealand and Australia would call at the onetime whaling station at Ngaloa Harbor to pick up passengers and goods, and Kandavu was considered as a possible site for a new capital of Fiji. Instead Suva was chosen and Kandavu was left to lead its sleepy village life; only today is the outside world making a comeback with the arrival of roads, planes, and a handful of visitors. Some 8,000 indigenous Fijians live in 60 remote villages scattered around the island.

KANDAVU

NORTH ASTROLABE REEF

SOLO LIGHTHOUSE

D'URVILLE CHANNEL

NDRAVUNI I.

YAUKUVELEVU I.

MBULIYA I.

NANGGARA

ONO I.

VAMBEA

KANDAVU PASSAGE

KAVALA BAY

RAKIRAKI

NGASELE

NDAKU BAY

MALAWAI RESORT

NDAKU

LOMANIKORO

KAVALA

TILIVA

ALBERT'S PLACE

ONO CHANNEL

GREAT ASTROLABE REEF

KANDAVU ISLAND

SOSO

SOSO BAY

NAMARA

KANDAVU

NATHOMOTO

NDRUIE (MATANA RESORT)

YUNISEA

YANDAKU FALLS

NAMALATA BAY

NAMUANA

AIRPORT

REECE'S PLACE

NGALOA I.

WAIKANA BAY

FALLS

TAVUKI

WAILEVU

NGALOA HARBOR

NALOTU

YAKITA

NANGGALOTO

YAWE DISTRICT

LOMATI

NAMBUKELEVU (MT. WASHINGTON)

NAMBUKELEVUIRA

NDAVINGGELE

MUANI

MBURELEVU

MATANUKU I.

-N-

0   5   10 km

© DAVID STANLEY

SIGHTS

The airstrip and wharf are each a 10-minute walk, in different directions, from the post office and hospital in the tiny government station of **Vunisea,** the largest of Kandavu's 60 Fijian villages and headquarters of Kandavu Province. Vunisea is strategically located on a narrow, hilly isthmus where Ngaloa Harbor and Namalata Bay almost cut Kandavu in two.

The longest sandy beach on the island is at **Ndrue,** an hour's walk north from Vunisea. Another good beach is at **Muani** village, eight km south of Vunisea by road. Just two km south of the airstrip by road and a 10-minute hike inland is **Waikana Falls.** Cool spring water flows over a 10-meter-high rocky cliff between two deep pools, the perfect place for a refreshing swim on a hot day. A second falls six km east of Vunisea is even better.

The women of **Namuana** village just west of the airstrip can summon **giant turtles** up from the sea by singing traditional chants to the *vu* (ancestral spirits) Rauninidalithe and Tinandi Thambonga. On a bluff 60 meters above the sea, the garlanded women begin their song, and in 15 minutes a large turtle will appear. This turtle, and sometimes its mates, will swim up and down slowly offshore just below the overhanging rocks. For various reasons, the calling of turtles is performed very rarely these days.

A Hiking Tour

Hike over the mountains from Namuana to **Tavuki** village, seat of the Tui Tavuki, paramount chief of Kandavu. A couple of hours beyond is the **Yawe** District, where large pine tracts have been established. In the villages of Nalotu, Yakita, and Nanggalotu at Yawe, traditional Fijian **pottery** is still made. Without potter's wheel or kiln, the women shape the pots with a paddle and fire them in an open fire. Sap from the mangroves provides a glaze.

Carry on from Yawe to **Lomati** village, from where you begin the ascent of **Nambukelevu** (838 meters). There's no trail—you'll need a guide to help you hack a way. The abrupt extinct cone of Nambukelevu (Mt. Washington) dominates the west end of Kandavu and renders hiking around the cape too arduous. Petrels nest in holes on the north side of the mountain.

There's **surfing** off Nambukelevuira village at the island's west point, but you'll need a boat. It's strongly suggested that you present a *sevusevu* to the village chief before engaging in this activity. Unfortunately, the villagers have become rather hostile to stray tourists who turn up unannounced and pay no heed to local customs.

Cut south from Lomati to **Ndavinggele** village, where another trail leads east along the coast to **Mburelevu,** end of the road from the airstrip. This whole loop can be done in three days without difficulty, but take food and be prepared to sleep rough.

The Great Astrolabe Reef

The Great Astrolabe Reef stretches unbroken for 30 km along the east side of the small islands north of Kandavu. One km wide, the reef is unbelievably rich in coral and marinelife, and because it's so far from shore, it still hasn't been fished out. The reef surrounds a lagoon containing 10 islands, the largest of which is Ono. The reef was named by French explorer Dumont d'Urville, who almost lost his ship, the *Astrolabe,* here in 1827.

There are frequent openings on the west side of the reef and the lagoon is never over 10 fathoms deep, which makes it a favorite of scuba divers and yachties. The Astrolabe also features a vertical drop-off of 10 meters on the inside and 1,800 meters on the outside, with visibility of about 75 meters. The underwater caves and walls here must be seen to be believed.

PRACTICALITIES

Accommodations near Vunisea

Reece's Place (Bill and Sarah Reece, Box 6, Vunisea, Kandavu; tel. 315-703), on tiny Ngaloa Island just off the northwest corner of Kandavu, was the first to accommodate visitors to Kandavu, and it's still the only inexpensive place to stay at Vunisea station. Conditions are said to have improved since a new management took over in 1994. It's a 15-minute walk from the airstrip to the dock, then a short launch ride to Ngaloa itself (F$6 pp return). There are eight beds (F$12 pp) in four Fijian *mbures,* and a F$9 dormitory; or pitch your tent for F$4 pp. Three good meals cost F$24 pp, and unless you have a camp stove, cooking your own food is not possible. They use an electric generator in the evening. The view of Ngaloa Harbor from Reece's Place is excellent, and there's a long, dark beach a 10-minute walk away, but the snorkeling in the murky water is only fair. For F$8 pp (minimum of four), you can ride to the Ngaloa Barrier Reef, where the snorkeling is vastly superior. Scuba diving (F$50/75 one/two tanks) and even PADI certification courses (F$295) are offered. If you're there on Sunday, consider attending the service in the village church to hear the wonderful singing.

A more upscale operation is **Matana Resort** (Box 8, Vunisea, Kandavu; tel. 311-780, fax 303-860) at Ndrue, six km north of Vunisea. The four "budget rooms" with shared bath in the beachfront *mbure* are F$55/78/110 single/double/triple, or F$40 pp in a shared three-bed dormitory. An attractive thatched *mbure* with private bath will run F$110 double on the hillside, or F$140/172/203 double/triple/quad for the two larger units on the beach (the only accommodations in which children are accepted). Add F$63 pp a day for the meal plan as no cooking facilities are available. Sunsets over Mt. Washington from the bar's open terrace can be spectacular. Matana caters mostly to scuba divers who've booked from abroad to dive with **Dive Kandavu,** and diving is available Monday to Saturday at 0930 and 1430 (F$55 per boat dive). Their open-water certification course is F$400. Windsurfers and paddle-boards are free. The snorkeling off Matana's white-sand beach is good, and the fantastic Namalata Reef is straight out from the resort. Airport transfers by boat are F$16 pp.

Malawai Resort (Box 1277, Suva; tel. 361-159, fax 361-536) offers colonial-style cottages on a 140-hectare plantation owned by the McLauchlan family, on the north side of Kandavu 15 km east of Vunisea and accessible only by boat. The package price is F$297/390 single/double including meals and airport transfers (three-night minimum stay). Aside from quiet country life, the main attractions here are scuba diving (F$110 for two tanks) and deep-sea fishing (F$500 for four hours). If you don't mind paying top dollar for the ultimate in comfort, convenience, and elegance, Malawai is for you.

Accommodations on North Kandavu

Albert's Place (Albert O'Connor, c/o P.O. Naletha, Kandavu; tel. 302-896), at Langalevu at the east end of Kandavu, is similar to Reece's Place but more remote, more laid-back, and less crowded. Each of the 10 *mbures* has a double and a single bed, coconut mats on the floor, and a kerosene lamp for light. Accommodations are F$15 pp (share twin); camping is F$6 pp. The units share rustic flush toilets and cold showers with plenty of running water (except during droughts), and everything is kept fairly clean. Mosquito nets and coils are supplied.

Meals cost another F$29 pp for all three, but Ruth O'Connor and her daughter Ramona serve huge portions, so breakfast and dinner (F$19) should suffice. Their meals are exceptional, consisting of fresh fish, lobster, chicken curry, or seafood soup, and they bake their own bread daily. Campers who wish to do their own cooking should bring their own food and cooking equipment, as little is available in Michel and Jesse's small store on the premises. There are several lovely waterfalls nearby where you can swim, and in the evening everybody sits around the kava bowl and swaps stories. As there are never more than 20 guests here at a time, it gets very chummy. The snorkeling right off Albert's beach is excellent, and scuba with **Naiqoro Divers** (run by Albert's sons Bruce and Julian) is F$50/88 for a one/two tank boat dive, shore dives F$25. The equipment is new, the prices as good as you'll find anywhere, and these guys know their waters.

The easiest way to get there is on Whippy's twice-weekly boat from Suva (F$38 one-way), which will bring you directly to Albert's Place. The larger and more comfortable Patterson Brothers ferry *Princess Ashika* should leave Suva for Kavala Bay (a good hour west of Albert's on foot) Thursday at midnight every other week (weekly to Vunisea). Albert will pick you up at Vunisea Airport for F$55 each way for two persons, F$25 pp for three or more for the two-hour boat ride (these prices are fixed, so don't bother bargaining). Be sure to let him know you're coming. It's best to allow plenty of time coming and going, so plan a stay at Albert's Place early on in your visit to Fiji so you don't have to be in a big rush to leave. People rave about this property, and we have no hesitation in recommending it as one of the South Pacific's top resorts—just don't expect luxuries like electricity at those prices!

The **Nukumbalavu Resort** (Box 228, Suva; tel. 520-089, fax 303-160) faces a two-km stretch of white sandy beach on the north side of Kandavu, between Albert's and Kavala Bay. Originally a backpackers' camp, the resort has recently been upgraded, and the estate subdivided into 31 lots and sold to American and Australian investors. Two-week dive vacationers are now the target market. With electricity, hot water, and private baths installed, rates for the beachfront *mbures* have quadrupled to F$55/86/110 single/double/triple, F$32 dorm beds, or F$8 pp for camping. The three-meal package is another F$43. Scuba diving costs F$63/118 one/two tanks for boat dives, F$39 for beach dives, or F$78 for night dives, and a wide range of PADI certification courses are offered at prices that are high for Fiji. The gorgeous Great Astrolabe Reef is only a five-minute boat ride away, and Nukumbalavu claims to have purchased the exclusive right to dive on 50 different sites there! It's still cheaper than Dive Kandavu, though they don't have the same kind of boats available. Every Wednesday there are three-night trekking expeditions at F$255 pp including village accommodations and guides. The Nukumbalavu launch can pick you up at Vunisea airport (F$35 pp each way), or come on Whippy's boat (see "Getting There," below), which will drop you directly at the resort. (Incidentally, there's intense rivalry between Nukumbalavu and Albert's Place, so take whatever you hear from one side or the other with a grain of salt.)

Accommodations on Ono

Jona's Paradise Resort (Box 15447, Suva; tel. 315-889, fax 315-992), formerly known as "Kenia Paradise," at Vambea on the south side of Ono Island, offers accommodation in traditional *mbures* at F$40 pp or camping at F$25 pp. All prices include three hearty meals a day. It's a small, family-style resort with a fine white-sand beach, good snorkeling, and scuba diving. Boat trips are F$65/100 per half/full day and you can also go hiking in the hills. Husband Jona is the best fisherman around (expect fresh fish and lobster every day), wife Ledua is a super cook, young son Veita is an expert guide, and grandfather Villame is a master builder. One reader called this place "the image of paradise." Whippy's boat drops passengers here twice a week, or you can arrange to be collected at Vunisea airport (F$25 pp).

Other Practicalities

There are no restaurants at Vunisea, but a coffee shop at the airstrip opens mornings, and two general stores sell canned goods. A woman at the market serves tea and scones when the market is open, Tuesday through Saturday. Buy *waka* at the co-op store for formal presentations to village hosts.

Occasional carriers ply the roads of Kandavu, but no buses. No banks are to be found on Kandavu either, so change enough money before coming.

Getting There

The easy way to come is on **Air Fiji** from Suva (F$52) four times a week (air pass accepted). **Sunflower Airlines** (tel. 42-010, ext. 42) flies Nandi-Kandavu four times a week (F$66 one-way). The agent at Kandavu watches closely for overweight baggage and sometimes sells more seats than there are in the plane, in which case the locals get priority. Be sure to reconfirm your return flight immediately upon arrival. Only Reece's Place meets all flights—pickups by the resorts on north Kandavu and Ono must be prearranged.

Boats arrive at Vunisea from Suva about twice a week, calling at villages along the north coast. The **Patterson Brothers** ferry *Princess Ashika* departs Suva's Muaiwalu Wharf at Walu Bay every Thursday night at midnight (F$34), returning to Suva on Friday morning. This ship gets crowded so arrive early. The MV *Gurawa* of **Whippy's Shipping Co.** (G.P.O. Box 9, Suva; tel./fax 340-015) leaves Suva for Ono and northern Kandavu Tuesday and Friday at 0600 (F$38 pp), returning to Suva on Wednesday and Saturday. Ask if lunch is included in the fare. Also ask about the new *Kandavu Ferry* that leaves Suva for Kavala Bay on Monday and Wednesday, a comfortable three-and-a-half-hour trip.

THE LOMAIVITI GROUP

The Lomaiviti ("Central Fiji") Group lies in the Koro Sea near the heart of the archipelago, east of Viti Levu and south of Vanua Levu. Of its nine main volcanic islands, Ngau, Koro, and Ovalau are among the largest in Fiji. Lomaiviti's climate is moderate, neither as wet and humid as Suva, nor as dry and hot as Nandi. The population is mostly Fijian, engaged in subsistence agriculture and copra making.

The old capital island, Ovalau, is by far the best known and most visited island of the group, and several small islands south of Ovalau on the way to Suva bear popular backpackers' resorts. Naingani also has a tourist resort of its own, but Koro and Ngau are seldom visited, due to a lack of facilities for visitors. Ferries ply the Koro Sea to Ovalau, while onward ferries run to Vanua Levu a couple of times a week.

OVALAU ISLAND

Ovalau, a large volcanic island just east of Viti Levu, is the main island of the Lomaiviti Group. Almost encircled by high peaks, the Lovoni Valley in the center of Ovalau is actually the island's volcanic crater and about the only flat land. The crater's rim is pierced by the Mbureta River, which escapes through a gap to the southeast. The highest peak is 626-meter Nandelaiovalau (meaning, "the top of Ovalau"), behind Levuka. Luckily Ovalau lacks the magnifi-

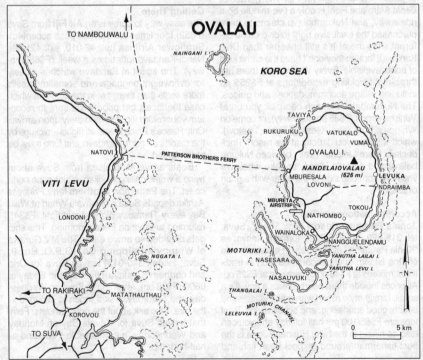

OVALAU

TO NAMBOUWALU

NAINGANI I.

KORO SEA

TO NAMBOUWALU

TAVIYA

RUKURUKU   VATUKALO
                         VUMA

OVALAU I.

NATOVI   PATTERSON BROTHERS FERRY

NANDELAIOVALAU
(626 m)

MBURESALA   LEVUKA
LOVONI   NDRAIMBA

VITI LEVU

MBURETA
AIRSTRIP   TOKOU

LONDONI   NATHOMBO

WAINALOKA

NANGGUELENDAMU

MOTURIKI I.

NGGATA I.   NASESARA   YANUTHA LAILAI I.
                                  YANUTHA LEVU I.
                  NASAUVUKI

TO RAKIRAKI   MATATHAUTHAU   THANGALAI I.

KOROVOU   MOTURIKI CHANNEL
                  LELEUVIA I.
TO SUVA

0   5 km

-N-

© DAVID STANLEY

cent beaches found elsewhere in Fiji, which has kept the packaged-tour crowd away, and it's still one of the most peaceful, pleasant, and picturesque places to visit in Fiji.

Levuka

The town of Levuka on Ovalau's east side was Fiji's capital until the shift to Suva in 1882. Founded as a whaling settlement in 1830, Levuka became the main center for European traders in Fiji, and a British consul was appointed in 1857. The cotton boom of the 1860s brought new settlers and Levuka quickly grew into a boisterous town with over 50 hotels and taverns along Beach Street. Escaped convicts and debtors fleeing creditors in Australia swelled the throng, until it was said that a ship could find the reef passage into Levuka by following the empty gin bottles floating out on the tide. The honest traders felt the need for a stable government, so in 1871 Levuka became capital of Cakobau's Kingdom of Fiji. The disorders continued, with extremist elements forming a "Ku Klux Klan," defiant of any form of Fijian authority.

On 10 October 1874, a semblance of decorum came as Fiji was annexed by Great Britain and a municipal council was formed in 1877. Ovalau's central location seemed ideal for trade, and sailing boats could easily reach the port from Lau or Vanua Levu. Yet the lush green hills that rise behind the town were its downfall, as colonial planners saw that there was no room for the expansion of their capital, and in August 1882 Gov. Sir Arthur Gordon moved his staff to Suva. After a hurricane in 1886, Levuka's devastated buildings were not replaced.

Levuka remained the collection center for the copra trade right up until 1957, but the town seemed doomed when that industry, too, moved to a new mill in Suva. With the establishment of a fishing industry in 1964 things picked up, and today Levuka is a minor educational center, the headquarters of Lomaiviti Province, and a low-impact tourist center. The false-fronted buildings and covered sidewalks along Beach Street give this somnolent town of 3,000 inhabitants a 19th-century, Wild West flavor. It's a perfect base for excursions into the mountains, along the winding coast, or out to the barrier reef a kilometer offshore.

It's customary to say "Good morning," "Mbula," or simply "Hello" to people you meet while strolling around Levuka, especially on the backstreets, and the locals have been rather put off by tourists who failed to do so. This is one of the little adverse effects of tourism, and a very unnecessary one at that.

Sights

Near Queen's Wharf is the old Morris Hedstrom Ltd. store, erected by Percy Morris and Maynard Hedstrom in 1878, great-granddaddy of today's Pacific-wide Morris Hedstrom chain. In 1980 the building was restored and converted into the **Levuka Community Center** with a museum and library (closed Sunday), where cannibal forks vie with war clubs and clay pots for your attention. Ask at the Community Center next to the museum about guided walking tours of historic Levuka and hikes to Lovoni. The YWCA here sells handicrafts with most of the money going to the craftspeople themselves.

Stroll along Levuka's sleepy waterfront. The **Church of the Sacred Heart,** with its square stone clock tower, was erected by French Marist priests who arrived in 1858. The green neon cross on the tower lines up with another green light farther up the hill to guide mariners into port. When you reach the former movie house, turn left onto Hennings Street and head inland on the left side of Totonga Creek to the **Levuka Public School** (1879), the birthplace of Fiji's present public educational system. Before WW I the only Fijians allowed to attend this school were the sons of chiefs. Other Levuka firsts include Fiji's first newspaper (1869), first Masonic Lodge (1875), and first bank (1876).

Continue straight up Garner Jones Road for about 10 minutes, past the lovely colonial-era houses, and you'll eventually reach the source of the town's water supply, from which there's a good view. The path to **The Peak** branches off to the left between the steel water tank and the gate at the end of the main trail. It takes about an hour to scale The Peak, preferably with the guidance of some of the local kids.

As you come back down the hill, turn left across a small bridge to the **Ovalau Club** (see "Entertainment," below), adjoining the old **Town Hall** (1898) and **Masonic Lodge.** A few blocks north of the Club, past the Royal Hotel, are the

199 steps up **Mission Hill** to an old Methodist school with a fine view.

North of Levuka

On a low hill farther north along the waterfront is the **European War Memorial,** which recalls British residents of Levuka who died in WW I. Before Fiji was ceded to Britain, the Cakobau government headquarters was situated on this hill. **Holy Redeemer Anglican Church** (1904) beyond has period stained-glass windows.

Follow the coastal road north from Levuka to a second yellow bridge, where you'll see the **old Methodist church** (1869) on the left. In the small cemetery behind the church is the grave of the first U.S. consul to Fiji, John Brown Williams. For the story of Williams's activities, see "History and Government" in the chapter introduction. Across the bridge and beneath a large *ndilo* tree is the tomb of an old king of Levuka. The large house in front of the tree is the residence of the present Tui Levuka.

Directly above is **Gun Rock,** which was used as a target in 1849 to show Cakobau the efficacy of a ship's cannon so he might be more considerate to resident Europeans. The early Fijians had a fort atop the Rock to defend themselves against the Lovoni hill tribes. Ask permission of the Tui Levuka (the "Roko") or a member of his household to climb Gun Rock for a splendid view of Levuka. If a small boy leads you up and down, it wouldn't be out of place to give him something for his trouble. From the summit, let your eyes follow the horizon from right to left to view the islands of Ngau, Mbatiki, Nairai, Wakaya, Koro, Makongai, and Vanua Levu, respectively.

Continue north on the road, round a bend, pass the ruin of a large concrete building, and you'll reach a cluster of government housing on the site of a cricket field where the Duke of York (later King George V) played in 1878.

There's a beautiful deep pool and waterfall behind **Waitovu** village, about two km north of Levuka. You may swim here, but please don't skinny-dip; this is offensive to the local people and has led to serious incidents in the past. Since they're good enough to let you use this idyllic spot (which they own), it's common courtesy to respect their wishes.

South of Levuka

The **Pacific Fishing Company** tuna cannery (Box 41, Levuka; tel. 440-005, fax 440-400) is south of Queen's Wharf. A Japanese cold-storage facility opened here in 1964, the cannery in 1975. After sustaining losses for four years, the Japanese company involved in the joint venture pulled out in 1986, turning the facility over to the government, which now owns the cannery. In 1989 a F$2 million state-of-the-art can-making factory opened alongside the cannery, and major improvements to the wharf, freezer, storage, and other facilities were completed in 1992. The plant is supplied with albacore tuna caught in Kiribati and Solomons waters by Taiwanese longline fishing boats, and with skipjack and yellowfin by pole-and-line ships of the government-owned Ika Corporation. For both environmental and quality-control reasons, fish caught with nets are not accepted here. Most of the F$50 million worth of canned tuna produced each year is marketed in Britain by Sainsbury and John West, and in Canada by B.C. Packers. A thousand residents of Ovalau have jobs directly related to tuna canning, and a rumored privatization and shift of the whole operation to Suva would have devastating consequences for Levuka.

A little farther along is the **Cession Monument,** where the Deed of Cession, which made Fiji a British colony, was signed by Chief Cakobau in 1874. A traditional *mbure* used for Provincial Council meetings is on the other side of the road.

One of Fiji's best hikes begins at Ndraimba village, a kilometer south of the Cession Monument. A road to the right, just before four single-story rows of apartments, marks the start of the four-and-a-half-hour hike through enchanting forests and across clear streams to **Lovoni** village. Go straight back on the road, pass a metal scrapyard, cut up the hill, and follow the beaten path ahead. The trail is no longer used by the locals and requires attentiveness to follow, so consider hiring a guide at the Community Center next to the museum if you're not an experienced hiker. Be sure to reach Lovoni before 1500 to be able to catch the last bus back to Levuka. It's also possible to hike to Lovoni from Rukuruku. In 1855 the fierce Lovoni tribe, the Ovalau, burned Levuka, and they continued to threaten the town right up until 1871 when they were finally captured during a truce and sold to European planters as laborers. In 1875 the British government allowed the survivors to return to their valley, where their descendants live today.

If you forgo this hike and continue on the main road, you'll come to an old **cemetery** a little south of Ndraimba. A few kilometers farther is the **Devil's Thumb,** a dramatic volcanic plug towering above **Tokou** village, one of the scenic highlights of Fiji. Catholic missionaries set up a printing press at Tokou in 1889 to produce gospel lessons in Fijian. In the center of the village is a sculpture of a lion made by one of the early priests. It's five km back to Levuka.

Wainaloka village on the southwest side of Ovalau is inhabited by descendants of Solomon Islanders from the Lau Lagoon region who were blackbirded in Fiji over a century ago.

PRACTICALITIES

Accommodations

There's a good choice of inexpensive places to stay around Levuka. The **Old Capital Inn I** (Box 50, Levuka; tel. 440-057) on Convent Road is one of the cheapest, with six double rooms above the restaurant at F$9/16 single/double, and dorm beds at F$8 pp, a cooked breakfast included (if you want to skip the breakfast you'll save a dollar). There's no hot water.

The low-budget travelers' best bet is the Inn's annex, the **Old Capital Inn II** (tel. 440-013) on Beach Street. The 15 fan-cooled rooms cost the same as rooms at Inn I (where guests at both places take their breakfast). A separate cottage with cooking facilities is F$13/24/29 single/double/triple—good value. It's quieter than Inn I, but the quality of the beds in the dorm section here is poor. A cool breeze blowing in from the east keeps the mosquitoes away.

Mavinda Guesthouse (Box 4, Levuka; tel. 440-477) on Beach Street, which has been functioning since 1869, is Fiji's oldest guesthouse. This old-fashioned English bed and breakfast owned by Patterson Brothers Shipping occupies a spacious colonial house on the waterfront near the Levuka Club. The 12 rooms are F$12/24 single/double, or F$8 in the dormitory, cooked breakfast included. You can order

LEVUKA

TO OVALAU HOLIDAY RESORT
GUN ROCK
LEVUKA CREEK
OLD METHODIST CHURCH
BEACH ST.
ANGLICAN CHURCH
MISSION HILL
HOSPITAL
WAR MEMORIAL
LEVUKA CLUB
MAVINDA GUEST HOUSE
HILL RD.
MISSION
CHURCH ST.
CHAPEL ST.
KING ST.
LANGHAM
MARKET
SPORTS FIELD
ROYAL HOTEL
ROBBIES LN.
TOWN HALL
OVALAU CLUB
TOTONGO CREEK
HENNINGS ST.
GARNER JONES LN.
TOTONGA LN.
CONVENT LN.
OLD CAPITAL INN II
OLD CAPITAL INN I
LEVUKA PUBLIC SCHOOL
BENTLEY'S LN.
WHALE'S TALE RESTAURANT
LEVUKA COMMUNITY CENTER
VULCAN LN.
BEACH ST.
POST OFFICE
QUEEN'S WHARF
-N-
OVALAU ISLAND
AIR FIJI
TUNA CANNERY
0   200m
TO AIRPORT

KORO
SEA

© DAVID STANLEY

an excellent dinner here for F$5. It's worth asking to see the room beforehand as all are different, and they're sometimes reluctant to give out their best rooms for some reason. Ask for a mosquito net. If you do get a good room, it's excellent, otherwise you'll probably do better elsewhere. Backpackers are accepted here, but if you quibble over the rates they'll suggest you try the Old Capital Inn.

For the full Somerset Maugham flavor, stay at the 15-room **Royal Hotel** (Box 47, Levuka; tel. 440-024). Built in 1852 and renovated in the 1890s, this is Fiji's oldest regular hotel, now run by the Ashley family. In the lounge, ceiling fans revolve above the rattan sofas and potted plants, and the fan-cooled rooms upstairs with private bath are pleasant, with much-needed mosquito nets provided. At F$16/23/27 single/double/triple, the colonial atmosphere and impeccable service make it about the best value in Fiji. There's also a F$7 dorm, and they have one two-bedroom cottage with cooking facilities at F$55. Checkout time is 1000, but you can arrange to stay until 1500 by paying another 50% of the daily rate. Hotel staff will do your laundry for about F$5. Everybody loves this place, but don't order dinner (F$8) here as the food isn't highly rated. The bar, beer garden, snooker tables, and videos are strictly for guests only.

Beach Resorts

A good choice for families is the **Ovalau Holiday Resort** (Stephen and Rosemary Diston, Box 113, Levuka; tel. 440-329) on a rocky beach at Vuma, four km north of Levuka (taxi F$5). *Mbures* are F$22/35/45 single/double/triple, or F$8 pp in the dorm. Camping is F$5 pp, with the use of the dorm facilities. Cooking facilities and hot showers are provided, and there's the Mbula Beach Bar in a converted whaler's cottage. The restaurant does some fine home cooking, and the snorkeling here is good. The swimming pool is the only one on Ovalau. The resort has a six-passenger boat for rent for full-day excursions to Makongai (F$100) or fishing trips (F$25 for three hours).

On the northwest side of Ovalau is quiet, lovely **Rukuruku Resort** (Box 112, Levuka), 20 km from Levuka. There's a large campground (F$6 pp), complete with toilets, showers, barbecue, and kitchen. Dormitory-style accommodations (F$8 pp including breakfast) are also available, or stay in a four-person *mbure* for F$15 pp a day. The restaurant/bar is somewhat overpriced, but basic groceries may be purchased in the adjacent Fijian village, though there are no cooking facilities. The black-sand beach is only so-so, but the snorkeling out on the reef is good, and there's a natural freshwater swimming pool in the river adjacent to the resort. A vanilla plantation and beautiful verdant mountains cradle Rukuruku on the island side. Rukuruku bookings can be made at the Whale's Tale Restaurant in Levuka, but be aware, poor management has allowed it to become run-down and the service is lackadaisical.

Food

Few of the guesthouses in Levuka provide cooking facilities, but the recent influx of backpackers has caused a half dozen small restaurants to blossom where there was formerly nowhere to eat out. All of these places are patronized mostly by foreigners, and prices are higher than what you may have paid in Suva or Lautoka, but with luck you'll enjoy some superior meals.

An inexpensive place for lunch is the little **takeaway stand** in Patterson Gardens, between the Levuka Community Center and the power plant. It serves fish and curry plates and tasty homemade desserts, which you can consume seated at one of the picnic tables overlooking the sea. It's closed on Sunday.

Cafe Levuka (tel. 440-095), on Beach Street adjacent to the Community Center, serves a three-course dinner (F$7) daily until 2000. When this place opened in 1990, it quickly became the town's premier eatery. Since then it has been rather eclipsed by newer places, although it's still a good place to find out what's happening around town over coffee and cakes. Their fruit pancakes are great for breakfast. This place recently changed ownership and things could be different.

Kim's Restaurant (Monday to Saturday 0800-1400/1800-2000), on Beach Street diagonally opposite the Community Center, is slightly cheaper than some of the other tourist-oriented restaurants, but the food is excellent with each dish individually prepared. Peruse their extensive menu posted over the counter—recommended.

The Chinese restaurant at **Old Capital Inn I** (tel. 440-057; daily 0700-2100) on Convent Road is famous for its all-you-can-eat dinner Sunday at 1800 (F$7), a long-running local institution. There's a good selection of items in their buffet, and cold beer is available.

The **Whale's Tale Restaurant** (tel. 440-235; daily 1130-2100) on Beach Street is the current favorite for its real home cooking at medium prices (delicious mahimahi and salad for F$7). They're fully licensed so you can get a beer with your meal, but it's also a nice place to stop for a coffee. They sell bags of kava and genuine Fijian handicrafts (no bizarre devil masks).

The **Shipwreck Restaurant,** another component of the Old Capital Inn empire, on Beach

Street next to the Church of the Sacred Heart, posts its menu in the window. Their prices are just a bit above Kim's, and the food is also good.

Deepak's Restaurant (tel. 440-314), on Beach Street just north of the Church of the Sacred Heart, is cheap but basic and not very inviting.

Entertainment

Despite the Members Only sign, you're welcome to enter the **Ovalau Club** (tel. 440-102), said to be the oldest membership club in the South Pacific. You'll meet genuine South Seas characters here, and the place is brimming with atmosphere. Ask the bartender to show you the framed letter from Count Felix von Luckner, the WW I German sea wolf. Von Luckner left the letter and some money at the unoccupied residence of a trader on Katafanga Island in the Lau Group, from which he took some provisions. In the letter, Count von Luckner identifies himself as Max Pemberton, an English writer on a sporting cruise through the Pacific.

A good place for sunsets is the **Levuka Club** (tel. 440-272) on Beach Street, which has a nice backyard with picnic tables beside the water. It's less visited by tourists and a better choice than the Ovalau Club if you only want a quick beer.

Services

The **Westpac Bank** (tel. 440-346) and the **National Bank** on Beach Street change traveler's checks; the Westpac gives a slightly better rate. Cafe Levuka will change traveler's checks anytime at the bank rate less a three percent commission.

Cafe Levuka will wash, dry, and fold your laundry within three hours for F$7.

Public toilets are available behind the Levuka Community Center (ask directions).

Information

Lisa at the Whale's Tale Restaurant (tel. 440-235) will be happy to give you her frank opinion of the offshore resorts—invaluable when planning a trip. Cafe Levuka (tel. 440-095) maintains a "Visitors' Information Book" containing current information about almost every aspect of travel around Ovalau. The restaurant staffs are probably the most likely people to give you a straight answer to any question you may have about Levuka. Cafe Levuka also runs a one-for-one book exchange.

Transportation

Air Fiji (tel. 440-139), across the street from the museum, has two or three flights a day from Mbureta Airport to Suva (F$33). The Ovalau Tours minibus from Levuka to the airstrip is F$3 pp (a taxi will run F$17).

Inquire at **Patterson Brothers** (tel. 440-125) beside the market on Beach Street about the direct ferry from Ovalau to Nambouwalu, Vanua Levu, via Natovi. The connecting bus departs Levuka at about 0500 Monday to Saturday. At

The Ovalau Club at Levuka was once the reserve of British colonials. Although the sign by the door says Private—Members Only, the bartenders will sign you in.

RICHARD EASTWOOD

Nambouwalu, there's an onward bus to Lambasa, but bookings must be made in advance (F$35 straight through).

The bus/ferry/bus service between Suva and Levuka was discussed previously under "Transportation" in the Suva section. Two competing services are available, each taking around five hours right through and costing around F$19. The Patterson Brothers combination involves an express bus from Levuka to Mburesala daily except Sunday at 0500, a 45-minute ferry ride from Mburesala to Natovi, then the same bus on to Suva (change at Korovou for Lautoka). The other choice is the *Emosi Express* leaving Queen's Wharf, Levuka, at 0900 on Monday, Wednesday, Friday, and Saturday to Mbau Landing, then a minibus to Suva (arriving at 1400). Southbound you can get off in Nausori and connect with the Sunbeam Transport bus to Lautoka at 1400. Inquire at the Old Capital Inn. From Levuka, Emosi's boat is more conveniently timed and there's a brief stop at Leleuvia Island, where free stopovers are possible. Advance bookings are required on the Patterson Brothers ferry/bus service but not on Emosi's boat. Use a different service each way for a scenic circle trip from Suva.

Both taxis and carriers park across the street from the Church of the Sacred Heart in Levuka. Due to steep hills on the northwest side of Ovalau, there isn't a bus right around the island. Carriers leave from Levuka at 0715 or 1200 for Rukuruku village (F$1.30) along a beautiful, hilly road. There are also occasional buses and carriers to Lovoni (F$1). There's no service on Sunday or late in the afternoon.

The YWCA next to Cafe Levuka rents mountain bikes at F$12 a day, but most are in bad shape.

Tours

Ratu Niumaia Turaganicolo at the Levuka Community Center (Box 124, Levuka; tel. 440-356) on Beach Street offers 15 different guided tours around Levuka and Ovalau. His guided hike from Levuka or Rukuruku to Lovoni is F$16 pp including lunch. The bus tour to Lovoni is also F$16, or pay F$21 for a trip right around Ovalau, both including lunch. The reef tours (F$10 pp including lunch) are great for swimming and snorkeling, and you'll be shown sharks if you ask. Four people are required for any of these tours. If you'd like to climb the peak that towers behind Levuka, a guide can be arranged. Ratu Niumaia welcomes visitors who want to drop into his office Monday to Saturday around 1700 for a chat about the history of Ovalau. There's no charge for this, it's just of a way of drumming up business for his trips. Soft drinks are sold at normal Fijian prices. A guided walk around Levuka with Ratu Niumaia is F$5 pp.

ISLANDS OFF OVALAU

Yanutha Lailai Island

It was on tiny Yanutha Lailai Island, just off the south end of Ovalau, that the first 463 indentured Indian laborers to arrive in Fiji landed from the ship *Leonidas* on 14 May 1879. To avoid the introduction of cholera or smallpox into Fiji, the immigrants spent two months in quarantine on Yanutha Lailai. Later Nukulau Island off Suva became Fiji's main quarantine station.

It's possible to stay on Yanutha Lailai at **Lost Island Resort.** Dorm beds cost F$7 pp, *mbures* F$9 pp, camping F$6 pp, and three meals a day are another F$8 (F$5 for the *lovo* special). Reef tours from Lost Island are F$5 pp, and transfers from Levuka F$11 pp each way. It's also possible to visit on a day-trip from Levuka at F$25 pp, lunch included. For information contact Levi at the Levuka Community Center.

Moturiki Island

Small outboards to Moturiki Island depart Nangguelendamu Landing most afternoons. The best beaches are on the east side of Moturiki. Camping is officially discouraged, but possible.

Thangalai Island

Thangalai is owned by the Methodist Church of Fiji, which operates a small backpackers' resort on this palm-fringed island. The 12 *mbures* are F$12 pp (triple occupancy), otherwise pay F$7 pp in the dormitory without meals, or camp for F$7 pp. Three meals are another F$10 pp. It's primitive but adequate, and the island and people are great. Dress up for Sunday service in the village church. Information should be available at Cafe Levuka (boat from Levuka daily at 1000, F$10 pp).

Leleuvia Island

Emosi Yee Show of Levuka's Old Capitol Inn runs a small backpackers' resort (tel. 301-584) on Leleuvia, a lovely isolated reef island with nothing but coconut trees, sandy beaches, and a ramshackle assortment of tourist huts scattered across the island. Accommodations run F$19 pp in the dorm, F$22 pp in a thatched hut, F$28 pp in a wooden bungalow, or F$17 pp if you camp. Included are three basic meals (rationed, not buffet) served punctually at 0800, 1200, and 1800. You get lots of fried food and repeats of the same dishes, but vegetarian food is possible. Water is in short supply on Leleuvia, and bathing is with a bucket of brackish water. The small shop sells candy, cake, and drinks. The owners send as many people as they can to Leleuvia, and it can get *very* crowded (pick Thangalai instead if you'd rather do your own thing).

Leleuvia is popular among backpackers who like to drink beer and party a lot (live music in the evening), so don't come expecting a rest. Actually, it sort of depends on who is on the island at the time. Sometimes it's great fun with lots of neat people, but other times the scene is dominated by "groupies," and newcomers are excluded. One reader called it "a Boy Scout holiday camp." Peace returns around 2230 when the generator switches off.

Plenty of activities are laid on, especially reef trips by boat (F$5 pp) and scuba diving (F$44/66 one/two tanks on the same day), and on Sunday they'll even take you to church! For a nominal amount they'll drop you off on one-tree "Honeymoon Island." Leleuvia is the only Lomaiviti resort offering scuba diving, and resident instructors Nobi and Andrea have taught diving to quite a few guests. This isn't surprising because at F$298, it's about the cheapest PADI open-water certification course available in Fiji (this price only applies if several people are taking lessons at the same time). If you just want a taste of diving their resort course is F$44 from shore, or F$77 from boat and shore. The snorkeling is also excellent though the sea is sometimes cold.

Getting there is easy on the *Emosi Express* from Levuka at 0800 daily except Sunday. From Suva, you can catch the bus at 46 Gordon St. Monday, Wednesday, Friday, and Saturday at 1200 and arrive via Mbau Landing (F$18 roundtrip). Leleuvia is a free stopover on all of Emosi's regular trips between Levuka and Suva. Day-trips to Leleuvia from Levuka with lunch are also possible. All bookings should be made through the Old Capital Inn in Levuka, or at Rosie Tours (tel. 313-366), 46 Gordon St., Suva.

Naingani

Naingani, 11 km off Viti Levu, is a lush tropical island near Ovalau at the west end of the Lomaiviti Group, with pristine beaches and only one Fijian village in the southwest corner. It's just the right size for exploring on foot, and there's a medium-priced place to stay.

Naingani Island Resort (Box 12539, Suva; tel. 300-925, fax 300-539), also known as Mystery Island Resort, offers 12 comfortable fancooled bungalows sleeping up to six persons at F$180. Children under 12 get a 50% discount, so this is a good place for families, and lower off-season rates sometimes apply from mid-September to March (excepting Christmas)—ask. Unfortunately the cooking facilities have been removed from the units and you're now required to take the F$35 pp meal plan. Some nonmotorized water sports are free. The minibus/launch connection from Suva daily at 1000 is F$55 roundtrip, and bookings can be made at their Suva office at 22 Cumming St., 2nd Floor. From Levuka, call them up and arrange to be collected by the speedboat at Taviya village on the northwest side of Ovalau (accessible on the Rukuruku truck) at F$12 pp each way.

OTHER ISLANDS OF THE LOMAIVITI GROUP

Makongai

Makongai shares a figure-eight-shaped barrier reef with neighboring Wakaya. The anchorage is in Dalithe Bay on the northwest side of the island. From 1911 to 1969 this was a leper colony staffed by Catholic nuns; the colony also received patients from various other Pacific island groups. Many of the old hospital buildings still stand. Today Makongai is owned by the Department of Agriculture, which runs an experimental sheep farm here, with some 2,000 animals. A new breed obtained by crossing British and Caribbean sheep bears little wool and is intended as a source of mutton.

Wakaya

A high cliff on the west coast of Wakaya is known as Chieftain's Leap, for a young chief who threw himself over the edge to avoid capture by his foes. Chief Cakobau sold Wakaya to Europeans in 1840, and it has since had many owners. In 1862 David Whippy set up Fiji's first sugar mill on Wakaya. Red deer imported from New Caledonia run wild across the island.

In 1976 Canadian industrialist David Harrison Gilmour bought the island for US$3 million, and in 1990 he opened **The Wakaya Club** (Box 15424, Suva; tel. 440-128, fax 440-406), with eight spacious cottages at F$1050/1375 single/double, all-inclusive (three-night minimum stay). Children under 16 are not accommodated. There's a nine-hole golf course open to guests, scuba diving, and an airstrip for charter flights (F$1200 roundtrip per couple from Nandi). As you might expect at these prices (Fiji's highest!), it's all very tasteful and luxurious. The rest of Wakaya has been subdivided into 150 parcels, which are being sold to foreigners as homesites at US$385,000 and up (contact René Boehm in Hamburg, Germany at fax 040-340-568).

The German raider Count Felix von Luckner was captured on Wakaya during WW I. His ship, the *Seeadler,* had foundered on a reef at Maupihaa in the Society Islands on 2 August 1917. The 105 survivors (prisoners included) camped on Maupihaa while on 23 August von Luckner and five men set out in an open boat to capture a schooner and continue the war. On 21 September 1917 they found a suitable ship at Wakaya. Their plan was to go aboard pretending to be passengers and capture it, but a British officer and four Indian soldiers happened upon the scene. Not wishing to go against the rules of chivalry and fight in civilian clothes, the count gave himself up and was interned at Auckland as a prisoner of war. He later wrote a book, *The Sea Devil,* about his experiences.

Mbatiki

Mbatiki has a large interior lagoon of brackish water surrounded by mudflats. Four Fijian vil-

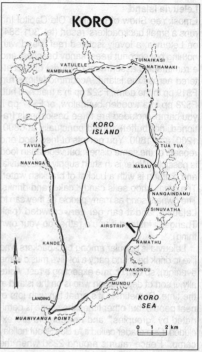

KORO

© DAVID STANLEY

lages are on Mbatiki, but due to hazardous reefs there's no safe anchorage for ships. Fine baskets are made here.

Nairai

Seven Fijian villages are found on this 336-meter-high island between Koro and Ngau. The inhabitants are known for their woven handicrafts. Hazardous reefs stretch out in three directions, and in 1808 the brigantine *Eliza* was wrecked here. Among the survivors was Charles Savage, who served as a mercenary for the chiefs of Mbau for five years until falling into the clutches of Vanua Levu cannibals.

Koro

Koro is an eight-by-16-km island shaped like a shark's tooth. A ridge traverses the island from northeast to southwest, reaching 561 meters near the center. High jungle-clad hillsides drop sharply to the coast. The best beach is along the south coast between Mundu and the lighthouse at Muanivanua Point. Among Koro's 14 large Fijian villages is **Nasau,** the government center with post office, hospital, and schools.

The road to **Vatulele** village on the north coast climbs from Nasau to the high plateau at the center of the island. The coconut trees and mangoes of the coast are replaced by great tree ferns and thick rainforest. Mr. Amena Tave, chief of Vatulele, can arrange accommodations in the village or give you a place to camp.

At **Nathamaki** village, in the northeast corner of Koro, turtle calling is still practiced. The caller stands on Tuinaikasi, a high cliff about a kilometer west of the village, and repeats the prescribed words to bring the animals to the surface. The ritual does work, although the turtles are becoming scarce and only one or two may appear. If anyone present points a finger or camera at a turtle, they quickly submerge. Actually, it's not possible to photograph the turtles, as magic is involved—the photos wouldn't show any turtles. Anyway, you're so high above the water you'd need the most powerful telephoto lens just to pick them out. (One reader wrote in to report that no turtles have appeared since 1987, due to the killing of a shark by a local villager.)

The track south between Nathamaki and Tua Tua runs along a golden palm-fringed beach. There's a cooperative store at **Nangaindamu** where you can buy *yanggona* and supplies. Koro kava is Fiji's best. A 30-minute hike up a steep trail from the co-op brings you to a waterfall and idyllic swimming hole. Keep left if you're on your own (taking a guide would be preferable).

Koro has an unusual inclined **airstrip** on the east side of the island near Namathu village. You land uphill, take off downhill. Sunflower Airlines can bring you here from Suva three times a week (F$60), and several carriers meet the flights.

The weekly Patterson Brothers and Consort Shipping Line ships from Suva tie up to the wharf near Muanivanua Point. All the ferries plying between Suva and Savusavu/Taveuni call here. Consort's *Spirit of Free Enterprise* calls northbound on Wednesday afternoon and early Sunday morning; the southbound trips often pass Koro without stopping. The Patterson Brothers ferry *Princess Ashika* leaves Suva for Koro at midnight Monday (F$31), departs Koro for Savusavu at 1100 Tuesday, then leaves Savusavu again for Koro at 1700 Wednesday, departing Koro for Suva at 2030. This vessel can also be used to travel between Koro and Ngau.

There are no hotels on Koro or Ngau, so you'll have to stay with locals or ask permission to camp. On both islands your best bet is to wait till you meet someone from there, then ask them to write you a letter of introduction to their relatives back home on the island. It's always best to know someone before you arrive. Make it clear you're willing to pay your own way, then don't neglect to do so.

Ngau

Ngau is the fifth-largest island in Fiji, with 16 villages and 13 settlements. There's a barrier reef on the west coast, but only a fringing reef on the east. A hot-spring swimming pool is close to the P.W.D. depot at **Waikama.** From Waikama, hike along the beach and over the hills to **Somosomo** village. If you lose the way, look for the creek at the head of the bay and work your way up it until you encounter the trail. There's a bathing pool in Somosomo with emerald green water.

A road runs from Somosomo to **Sawaieke** village, where the Takalaingau, high chief of Ngau, resides. The remnants of one of the only surviving pagan temples *(mbure kalou)* in Fiji

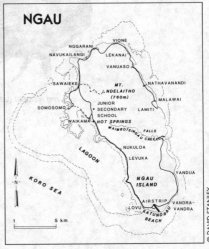

NGAU

is beside the road at the junction in Sawaieke. The high stone mound is still impressive.

It's possible to climb **Mt. Ndelaitho** (760 meters), highest on the island, from Sawaieke in three or four hours. The first hour is the hardest. From the summit there is a sweeping view. MacGillivray's Fiji petrel, a rare seabird of the albatross family, lays its eggs underground on Ngau's jungle-clad peaks. Only two specimens have ever been taken: one by the survey ship *Herald* in 1855, and a second by local writer Dick Watling in 1984.

The co-op and government station (hospital, post office, etc.) are at **Nggarani** at the north end of Ngau. Two ships a week arrive here from Suva on an irregular schedule, but there is no wharf so they anchor offshore. The wharf at **Waikama** is used only for government boats.

There are a number of waterfalls on the east coast, the best known behind **Lekanai** and up

Waimboteingau Creek, both an hour's walk off the main road. The "weather stone" is on the beach, a five-minute walk south of **Yandua** village. Bad weather is certain if you step on it or hit it with another stone.

There are no guesthouses on Ngau, but the driver of the carrier serving the airstrip may be willing to arrange village accommodations. Have your *sevusevu* ready and also contribute F$10 pp a day, at least. The airstrip is on Katundrau Beach at the south end of Ngau. Flights to/from Suva on Sunflower Airlines are F$42 each way.

The Patterson Brothers ferry *Princess Ashika* departs Suva for Ngau Monday at midnight, leaving Ngau for Savusavu Tuesday at 0600. Southbound, the same ship departs Savusavu for Ngau Wednesday at 1700, leaving Ngau for Suva Thursday at 0700 (F$29). The same vessel also calls at Koro and Taveuni.

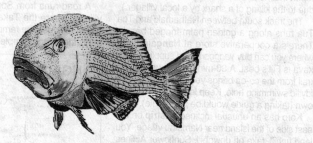

red snapper (Lutjanus blackfordi)

VANUA LEVU

Though only half as big as Viti Levu, 5,556-square-km Vanua Levu ("Great Land") has much to offer. The transport is good, the scenery varied, the people warm and hospitable, and far fewer visitors reach this part of Fiji than heavily promoted Nandi/Singatoka/Suva. Fijian villages are numerous all the way around the island—here you'll be able to experience real Fijian life, so it's well worth making the effort to visit Fiji's second-largest island.

The drier northwest side of Vanua Levu features sugarcane fields and pine forests, while on the damper southeast side copra plantations predominate, with a little cocoa around Natewa Bay. Toward the southeast the scenery is more a bucolic beauty of coconut groves dipping down toward the sea. Majestic bays cut into the island's south side, and one of the world's longest barrier reefs flanks the north coast. There are some superb locations here just waiting to be discovered, both above and below the waterline.

Fiji Indians live in the large market town of Lambasa and the surrounding cane-growing area; most of the rest of Vanua Levu is Fijian. Together Vanua Levu, Taveuni, and adjacent islands form Fiji's Northern Division (often called simply "the north"), which is subdivided into three provinces: the west end of Vanua Levu is Mbua Province; most of the north side of Vanua Levu is Mathuata Province; and the southeast side of Vanua Levu and Taveuni make up Thakaundrove Province. You won't regret touring this area.

Nambouwalu

The ferry from Viti Levu ties up to the wharf at this friendly little government station (the headquarters of Mbua Province), near the southern tip of Vanua Levu. The view from the wharf is picturesque, with Seseleka (421 meters) and, in good weather, Yandua Island visible to the northwest. From here it's 137 km by bus to Lambasa, or 141 km to Savusavu.

There are no hotels at Nambouwalu, but the lovely **Government Rest House**, up on the hillside above Nambouwalu, has two rooms with shared cooking facilities at F$5.50 pp. Try to make advance reservations with the district officer, Mbua, in Nambouwalu (tel. 84-010, ext. 60). Upon arrival, you could inquire at the Administrative Offices next to the post office, up on the hill above the wharf. If they say the Rest House is fully booked, ask at the **YWCA** in the village below, which sometimes has a room for rent. In a pinch, they'll probably allow you to camp. **Mr. Gaya Prasad** runs a very basic *dharamshala* (guesthouse) with cooking facilities just behind the store with the petrol pumps near the wharf. Present him with a monetary *sevusevu* upon departure.

The **Seaside Restaurant,** next to the store at the end of the wharf, is there mostly for the benefit of truck drivers waiting for the ferry, and it's usually closed at night. Local food is sold at the small market opposite this restaurant and there's sometimes a barbecue outside. Four small stores nearby sell groceries.

The large Patterson Brothers car ferry sails from Natovi on Viti Levu to Nambouwalu Tuesday to Saturday around 0600 (four hours, F$27). The same boat departs Nambouwalu for Natovi Tuesday to Saturday at 1030. At Natovi there are immediate ferry connections to/from Ovalau Island and buses to Suva. On Tuesday, Thursday, and Saturday at 1130 there's a direct Patterson Brothers ferry from Nambouwalu to Ellington Wharf near Rakiraki (F$26.40), where there are connections to Nananu-i-Ra Island and Lautoka. Patterson Brothers runs an express bus between Nambouwalu and Lambasa (four hours, F$7) for ferry passengers. This bus is quicker than the four regular buses to Lambasa (six hours), which make numerous detours and stops. All Patterson Brothers bus connections should be booked well ahead in conjunction with a ferry ticket, otherwise you may not be allowed aboard.

There's now a road along the south coast of Vanua Levu from Nambouwalu to Savusavu, but eastbound buses only reach as far as Ndaria, westbound buses as far as Nandivakarua. The 20-km gap is covered by carrier trucks. At Thongea, five km north of Ndaria, are

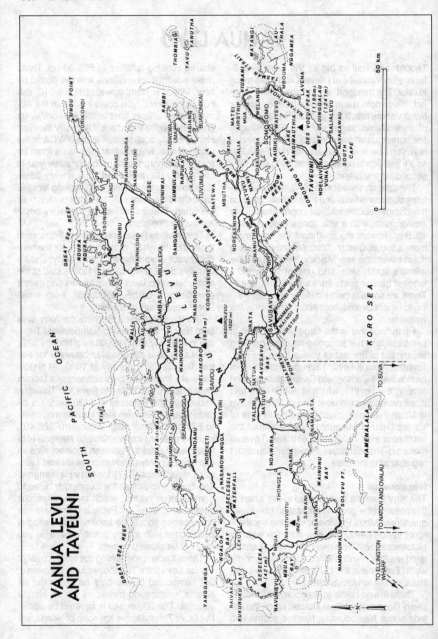

VANUA LEVU AND TAVEUNI

some small hot springs the local people use for bathing. Gold mining was carried out at Mt. Kasi near Ndawara from 1932 to 1943, and a study is underway to determine whether the mine can be recommissioned. Bauxite was mined in this area during the 1970s.

The Road to Lambasa

This twisting, tiring bus ride takes you past Fijian villages, rice paddies, and cane fields. The early sandalwood traders put in at **Mbua Bay.** At Mbua village on Mbua Bay is a large suspension bridge and the dry open countryside west of Mbua stretches out to Seseleka (421 meters).

About 13 km west of Lekutu, at Ngaloa Bay on the north side of the narrow neck of land that joins the Naivaka Peninsula to the main island, is **Dillon's Rock.** In September 1813 a party of Europeans took refuge here after being ambushed during a raid on a nearby village. After witnessing Swedish mercenary Charles Savage being killed and eaten by enraged Fijian warriors after he descended to negotiate a truce, Peter Dillon of the *Hunter* and two others managed to escape to their boat by holding muskets to the head of an important chief and walking between the assembled cannibals. (In 1826 Dillon earned his place in Pacific history by discovering relics from the La Pérouse expedition on Vanikoro Island in the Solomons, finally solving the mystery of the disappearance in 1788 of that famous French contemporary of Captain Cook.)

About five km north of Lekutu Secondary School, one km off the main road (bus drivers know the place), is Fiji's most accessible yet least known waterfall, the **Naselesele Falls.** This is a perfect place to picnic between bus rides, with a nice grassy area where you could camp. The falls are most impressive during the rainy season, but the greater flow means muddy water, so swimming is best in the dry season. There's a large basalt pool below the falls, and since nobody lives in the immediate vicinity, you'll probably have the place to yourself. Much of this part of the island has been reforested with pine.

Farther east the road passes a major rice-growing area and runs along the **Ndreketi River,** Vanua Levu's largest. A rice mill at Ndreketi and citrus project at Mbatiri are features of this area. The pavement begins near the junction with the road from Savusavu. In the Seanggangga settlement area between Mbatiri and Lambasa, about 60 square km of native land were cleared and planted with sugarcane and pine during the 1970s.

LAMBASA

Lambasa is a busy Indian market town, which services Vanua Levu's major cane-growing area. It's Fiji's third-largest city, with 18,000 inhabitants, four banks, and the Northern Division and Mathuata Province headquarters. Lambasa was built on a delta where the shallow Lambasa and Oawa rivers enter the sea; maritime transport is limited to small boats. Large ships must anchor off Malau, 11 km north. Lambasa's lack of an adequate port has hindered development.

Other than providing a good base from which to explore the surrounding countryside and a place to spend the night, Lambasa has little to interest the average tourist. That's its main attraction: since few visitors come, there's adventure in the air, good food in the restaurants, and fun places to drink for males (a little rowdy for females). It's not beautiful but it is real, and the bus ride that brings you here is great.

Sights

Lambasa has an attractive riverside setting with one long main street lined with shops and restaurants. The park along the riverside near the Lambasa Club is quite pleasant.

The **Lambasa Sugar Mill,** beside the Oawa River two km east of town, opened in 1894. At the height of the crushing season from May to December there's usually a long line of trucks, tractors, and trains waiting to unload cane at the mill—a most picturesque sight. From the road here you get a view of **Three Sisters Hill** to the right.

Anyone with an interest in archaeology should take the two-km ride on the Nakoroutari bus to **Wasavula** on the southern outskirts of Lambasa. Parallel stone platforms bearing one large monolith and several smaller ones are found among the coconut trees to the east of the road. This site (Fiji's first "national monument") is not well known, so just take the bus to Wasavula, get off, and ask.

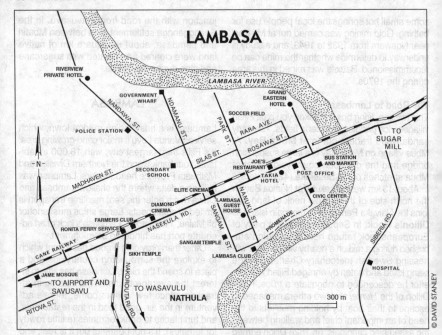

LAMBASA

© DAVID STANLEY

Around Lambasa

Other curiosities easily accessible by local bus include the suspension footbridge at **Mbulileka,** six km east (take the yellow and blue bus); the Firewalkers Temple at **Vunivau,** five km northeast, where Indian firewalking takes place twice a year between June and October; the Fiji Forests plant at **Malau,** 11 km north, where Lambasa's sugar harvest is loaded; the Snake Temple (Naag Mandir) at **Nangingi,** 12 km northeast, which contains a rock which Hindu devotees swear is growing; and the **Wainggele hot springs** (no bathing), 10 km southwest beyond the airport. Farther afield is the Floating Island at **Kurukuru,** between Nakelikoso and Numbu, 44 km northeast of Lambasa.

You can get a view of much of Vanua Levu from the telecommunications tower atop **Nde-laikoro** (941 meters), 25 km south of Lambasa, farther down the same road past the airport. Only a 4WD vehicle can make it to the top.

If you're a surfer, ask about hiring a boat out to the **Great Sea Reef** north of Kia Island, 40 km northwest of Lambasa.

Accommodations

The budget traveler's first choice should be the **Lambasa Guest House** (Box 259, Lambasa; tel. 812-155) on Nanuku Street, which has 10 rooms at F$10/11 single/double. Communal cooking facilities are provided but the Hindu hosts don't allow guests to cook beef on the premises, and previous visitors seem to have walked off with all the cutlery.

The seven-room **Riverview Private Hotel** (Box 129, Lambasa; tel. 811-367), on Namara Street beyond the police station, charges F$17/22 single/double for a room with shared bath in a quiet two-story concrete building. No cooking is allowed but the terrace overlooking the river is nice. This is a good second choice if the Lambasa Guest House is full.

The two-story **Grand Eastern Hotel** (Box 641, Lambasa; tel. 811-022, fax 814-011) on Gibson Street, just a few minutes' walk from the bus station, is a grand old colonial hotel overlooking the river. The 26 rooms in the rather run-down main building are F$14/20 single/double with shared bath, F$6 extra with bath, F$12 extra for a/c. The new wing by the river is much more expensive at F$53/60 single/double with a/c. Unfortunately the rooms in the old section are grubby and overpriced, and unless you're planning on going upmarket in the new wing, you'll do better elsewhere. No communal cooking facilities are provided but the meals in the atmospheric dining room are good.

The **Lambasa Club** (tel. 811-304) on Nanuku Street beside the river has two dark and dingy rooms at F$11/15 single/double. Also try the **Farmers Club** (tel. 811-633) on the main street with three rooms at F$10 single or double. You must arrive during regular business hours to get one (the same applies at the Lambasa Club).

Lambasa's most upmarket place to stay is the **Takia Hotel** (Box 7, Lambasa; tel. 811-655, fax 813-527), at 10 Nasekula Rd. above the shopping area right in the middle of town. The 32 rooms are F$55/65 single/double with fan, F$70/80 with a/c. If you have a business card, try asking for the commercial rate.

Offshore Resort

In 1992 the upmarket **Nukumbati Island Resort** (Box 1928, Lambasa; tel. 813-901, fax 813-914) opened on remote Nukumbati Island, 40 km west of Lambasa. The four spacious bungalows are F$660 double including meals (emphasis on seafood) and activities, with a seven-night minimum stay. Children are not allowed, and alcoholic drinks are extra. It's F$550 a day to hire the resort's game-fishing boat; land safaris are F$300. Access is by speedboat or 4WD vehicle from Lambasa (free for guests), or by chartered seaplane direct from Nandi (F$600).

Food

Simple Fijian, Chinese, and Indian meals are available for under F$3 at many places along Nasekula Road, including the **Moon Restaurant** (tel. 813-215), next to Elite Cinema, and the **Wun Wuh Cafe** (tel. 811-653), across from the bus station. For Indian food try the **Isalei Restaurant** (tel. 811-490), on Sangam Avenue, or the **Hare Krishna Vegetarian Restaurant** next to Sunflower Airlines on Nasekula Road.

Joe's Restaurant (tel. 811-766), upstairs in a building on Nasekula Road, has an inexpensive fast-food area with Formica tables, and an upmarket "wine and dine" section that wouldn't be out of place in Las Vegas. Despite the jarring decor, both are very popular, and the Chinese food served here puts Lambasa's ubiquitous chow mein houses to shame. Ask about the linen-tablecloth, low-light back room reserved for couples.

Entertainment

There are two movie houses in Lambasa. **Elite Cinema** has films in English and there's an evening show, while the **Diamond Cinema** is closed at night. Occasionally Diamond is the venue of live cultural programs, so check.

Calypso Nite Club (tel. 811-220), on Rara Avenue near the Grand Eastern Hotel, has music and dancing Friday and Saturday around 2200 (cover charge). You can dance, but it's sometimes a little rough. This is a predominantly Indian town so most of the nightlife is male oriented.

The **Lambasa Club** and the **Farmers Club** both serve cheap beer in a congenial male-oriented atmosphere. Couples will feel more comfortable at the Lambasa Club than at the Farmers, and there's a nice terrace out back facing the river. The pub upstairs in the **Takia Hotel** is a safe, fun place to drink, even though the bartenders are enclosed in a cage! There's also a disco at the Takia.

Services

The ANZ Bank is opposite the bus station, and the Westpac Bank is farther west on Nasekula Road.

There's a **public library** (weekdays 0900-1300/1400-1700, Saturday 0900-1200) in the Civic Center near Lambasa Bus Station. Public toilets are adjacent to the library.

Transportation

Air Fiji (tel. 811-188) has service three or four times a day from Lambasa to Suva (F$73). **Sunflower Airlines** (tel. 811-454) flies direct to Nandi (F$96) and Suva (F$72) twice daily, and to Taveuni (F$45) three times a week. **Vanua Air** (tel. 814-400) also arrives twice daily from Suva (F$66). To get to the airport, 10 km southwest of Lambasa, take the green and yellow Wainggele bus.

Patterson Brothers (tel. 812-444, fax 813-460) has an office in the arcade beside the Takia Hotel where you can book your bus/ferry/bus ticket through to Suva via Nambouwalu and Natovi (11.5 hours, F$38). This bus leaves Lambasa at 0530 daily except Sunday and Monday, and passengers arrive in Suva at 1700. There's also a direct bus/boat/bus connection from Lambasa to Lautoka via Ellington Wharf (near Nananu-i-Ra Island), and another service straight through to Levuka. Ask about the through bus/boat service from Lambasa to Taveuni, departing Lambasa Wednesday to Saturday at 0630 (six hours, F$22).

Ronita Ferry Services (Box 361, Lambasa; tel. 811-361), opposite the Mobil service station on Nasekula Road, sells tickets for a combined bus/boat service from Lambasa to Taveuni, departing Lambasa on Monday, Wednesday, and Friday at 0730.

To be dropped off on Kia Island, negotiate with the fishing boats tied up near the Lambasa Club. Village boats from Kia sometimes unload at the Government Wharf at the north end of Ndamanu Street on the other side of town. The **Consort Shipping Line** (tel. 811-144) has an office at the Government Wharf.

There are four regular buses a day (at 0630, 1030, 1315, and 1430) to Nambouwalu (F$6), a dusty, tiring six-hour trip. Another four buses a day run from Lambasa to Savusavu (2.5 hours, F$4), a very beautiful ride on an excellent paved highway over the Waisali Saddle between the Korotini and Valili mountains and along the palm-studded coast. The 0700 Lambasa-Savusavu bus connects with the bus/ferry service to Taveuni, making it possible to go straight through from Lambasa to Taveuni in a day. Other buses to Savusavu leave Lambasa at 0900, 1200, and 1500, but take the early bus before clouds obscure the views.

If your time is very limited but you want to see a lot, catch a morning flight from Suva or Nandi to Lambasa, then take an afternoon bus on to Savusavu, the best part of the trip. Otherwise stay in Savusavu and see Lambasa on a long day-trip.

Getting to outlying areas around Lambasa by bus can be confusing as there are several different bus companies and to get departure times you just have to keep asking. Otherwise, take pot luck: when you see a bus headed for one of the places mentioned under "Around Lambasa" above, just jump on and go for the ride.

Rental cars are available from **Budget Rent A Car** (tel. 811-199) on Ndongo Road west of town. Obtaining gasoline outside the two main towns is difficult, so tank up.

SAVUSAVU

Savusavu is a picturesque small town opposite Nawi Island on Savusavu Bay. The view from here across to the mountains of southwestern Vanua Levu and down the coast toward Nambouwalu is superlatively lovely. In the 1860s Europeans arrived to establish coconut plantations. They mixed with the Fijians and, although business went bust in the 1930s, their descendants and Fijian villagers still supply copra to the small coconut oil mill, eight km west of Savusavu, giving this side of Vanua Levu a pleasant agricultural air.

Savusavu is Vanua Levu's main port, and cruising yachts often rock at anchor offshore. The surrounding mountains and reefs make Savusavu a well-protected hurricane refuge. The diving possibilities of this area have been recognized by Jean-Michel Cousteau, who has used Savusavu as the base for his Ocean Search Project since 1990. Savusavu is also the administrative center of Thakaundrove Province and has three banks. In the past few years tourism has taken off around Savusavu, with new resorts springing up all the time, though the town is far from being spoiled.

Sights

The one main street through Savusavu consists of a motley collection of Indian and Chinese shops, parked taxis, loitering locals, and the odd tourist. Visit the small **hot springs** boiling out among fractured coral below the Hot Springs Hotel. Residents use the springs to cook native vegetables; bathing is not possible. Hopefully these quaint springs will never be developed for tourists and spoiled.

For a good circle trip, take a taxi from Savusavu past the airport to **Nukumbalavu** village (six km, F$5), at the end of road along the south side of the peninsula. From here you can walk west along the beach to the Cousteau Fiji Islands Resort on **Lesiatheva Point** in about an hour at low tide. Try to avoid cutting through the resort at the end of the hike as the Cousteau

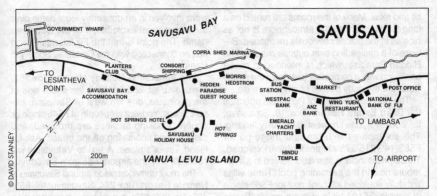

management disapproves. From Lesiatheva it's six km by road back to Savusavu.

Sports and Recreation

Eco Divers (Box 264, Savusavu; tel. 850-122, fax 850-344) at the Copra Shed Marina offers scuba diving, snorkeling, dinghy hire, windsurfing, sailing, village visits, waterfall tours, and guided hiking.

Fiji by Kayak (Box 43, Savusavu; tel. 850-372, fax 850-344) offers trips to Natewa Bay with kayaking, snorkeling, hiking, and a *lovo* lunch on a secluded sandy beach at F$99 pp, transfers from Savusavu included. It's a wonderful introduction to ocean kayaking and a great day out. Bookings can be made through Sea Fiji Travel (tel. 850-345) at the Copra Shed Marina.

Accommodations in Savusavu Town

We've arranged this accommodation section beginning at Savusavu Bus Station and working west through town to Lesiatheva Point, then east along the coast.

Hari Chand's **Hidden Paradise Guest House** (Box 41, Savusavu; tel 850-106), behind Sun Sang Cafe just beyond Morris Hedstrom, has six fan-cooled rooms at F$11/17 single/double with shared bath, including a good breakfast. Cooking and washing facilities are provided, and it's clean and friendly—don't be put off by the plain exterior. The Indian restaurant here is very inexpensive, but pork, beef, and booze are banned. A member of the Chand family may offer to show you around the Hindu temple up on the hill, if you ask. Recommended.

The **Hot Springs Hotel** (Box 208, Savusavu; tel. 850-430, fax 300-500), on the hillside overlooking Savusavu Bay, is named for the nearby thermal springs and steam vents. The 48 rooms, all with balconies offering splendid views, begin at F$44/55 single/double with fan, F$50/68 with a/c. (Sometimes special reduced rates are in effect—ask.) There's no beach nearby, but the swimming pool terrace is very pleasant. This former Travelodge is slightly run-down but still a convenient, medium-priced choice, and the hotel bar is open daily including Sunday. Catch the sunset here at happy hour. The Saturday night buffet is worth the F$11, even if they do put corned beef in the *palusami*.

David Manohar Lal's six-room **Savusavu Holiday House** (Box 65, Savusavu; tel. 850-216), also known as "David's Place," is just below the Hot Springs Hotel. Bed and a Fijian breakfast are F$13/19/24 single/double/triple (shared bath), F$10 pp dorm, or F$6 per tent to camp. There's a well-equipped kitchen. David's a delightful character to meet and also a strict Seventh-Day Adventist, so no alcoholic beverages are allowed on the premises. A cacophony of dogs, roosters, and the neighbor's kids will bid you good morning.

Savusavu Bay Accommodation (Lal Chand and Suresh Chand, Box 290, Savusavu; tel. 850-100), above Sea Breeze Restaurant on the main street, has seven standard rooms at F$11/17 single/double, and four a/c rooms at F$22 single or double. Cooking facilities are provided, and on the roof is a terrace where travelers can wash and dry their clothes or just sit and relax. Many of the rooms are rented on a long-term basis, and the atmosphere is not as nice as in the places previously mentioned. Beware of a misleading sign outside reading The Hidden Paradise, which is intended to cause confusion with a competitor just down the street. Such are the petty politics of small town life.

The Anglican Diocese of Polynesia operates the **Daku Estate Resort** (Box 18, Savusavu; tel. 850-046), one km west of the ferry landing. The six *mbures* with fan and fridge go for F$83/149/215/275 single/double/triple/quad. These prices include all meals, served in a large *mbure* next to the swimming pool. Three villas with fully equipped kitchens rent for F$66 single or double, F$104 triple, without meals. Profits from the resort are used to send gifted children from remote areas to boarding school, so you'll be contributing to a worthy cause. Daku faces a beach with some snorkeling possibilities.

Accommodations around Savusavu

On Lesiatheva Point six km southwest of Savusavu is the **Cousteau Fiji Islands Resort** (Private Bag, Savusavu; tel. 850-188, fax 850-340), which opened in mid-1987. In 1994 the resort was purchased by world-renowned oceanographer Jean-Michel Cousteau, and millions of dollars went into renovations prior to the reopening in April 1995. The original name Na Koro means "The Village," and that's what it re-creates, with 20 authentic thatched Fijian *mbures* (from F$374/442 double/triple including breakfast). The rooms have fans but no a/c, telephones, or cooking facilities. The restaurant is built like a towering pagan temple and executive chef Kathy Hoare can tell you anything you want to know about Fiji (as well as prepare healthy meals). Free activities include sailing, kayaking, fishing, and snorkeling. In addition, scuba diving, scuba instruction, underwater photography courses, and yacht charters with diving are offered by Gary Alford's on-site dive operation, "L'Aventure Cousteau." Also on the staff is marine biologist Jennifer Caselle, who arranges cultural and environmental tours. There's good snorkeling off the beach, though the resort's large Private Property signs warn nonguests to keep out. A taxi from Savusavu will run F$5. Bring insect repellent. (At last report, father and son, Jacques and Jean-Michel,

were involved in an unseemly legal battle over the commercial exploitation of the Cousteau name. The point is that the Fiji Islands Resort has no connection with the Cousteau Society in Paris.)

The **Vatukaluvi Holiday House** (Box 262, Savusavu; tel. 850-561), on the south side of the peninsula, one km west of Savusavu airport, accommodates six people at F$45 single or double. Cooking facilities are provided, and there's good snorkeling off the beach. Ask for Geoff Taylor's place. A taxi to Vatukaluvi will cost F$2 from the airport, F$5 from Savusavu.

The most upmarket place around Savusavu is **Namale Resort** (Box 244, Savusavu; tel. 850-435, fax 850-400), a working copra plantation founded in 1874, on a white-sand beach nine km east of Savusavu. The superb food and homey atmosphere amid exotic landscapes and refreshing white beaches make this one of Fiji's most exclusive resorts. The nine thatched *mbures* are F$575 double per night including gourmet meals and drinks (no cooking facilities and no singles). The mosquito nets over the beds, ceiling fans, and louvered windows give the units a rustic charm. Airport transfers and all activities other than scuba diving are free. Namale caters only to in-house guests—there's no provision for sightseers who'd like to stop in for lunch.

Kontiki Resort (Private Mail Bag, Savusavu; tel. 850-262, fax 850-355), also known as "Matani Kavika," on the Hibiscus Highway 15 km east of Savusavu, has 16 small thatched bungalows from F$105/165/180 single/double/triple, including airport transfers. The restaurant offers a good selection of international, Fijian, and Indian dishes, with main courses averaging F$15. No groceries are sold in the resort shop, only souvenirs and suncream. Set in a well-kept coconut grove, Matani Kavika has nearby many interesting caves, pools, trails, falls, ponds, and lakes to explore. Matani Kavika means "land of the wild plum tree," and such trees still exist on the grounds. Scuba diving (F$80 for two tanks) is available and a dive site known as Dream House is right at Kontiki's front door. The snorkeling is fine as well. There's also a swimming pool, nine-hole golf course, tennis courts, a marina, and many other activities, but the nearest beach is a kilometer away.

A more affordable choice would be **Mumu Resort** (Box 240, Savusavu; tel. 850-416), also east of Savusavu, about three km beyond Kontiki. The site is the spiritual home of Radini Mumu, a legendary queen of Fiji. In 1970 owner Gordon Edris, an ex-world traveler, did what many of us dream of doing: he retired to the South Seas and, together with his wife Rosie, slowly created a small retreat from their own resources without making the fatal mistake of taking a bank loan. Today the couple obviously enjoy sharing their wonderful little world with 15 fortunate guests. Rooms are F$25/35 single/double, the five-person "dream house" F$50 double, and there's also a F$12 dorm (often full). Campers are always most welcome (F$4/7 single/double). Communal cooking facilities are available, and Mumu's kitchen serves tasty Fijian and European dishes at budget prices. Mumu is surrounded by the Koro Sea on three sides, and two small uninhabited islands nearby are easily accessible. The snorkeling and scenery are good, the staff friendly, and there's scuba diving nearby at Kontiki. Paths wind endlessly through the property to clifftop lookouts with benches, through natural rock arches, and through tunnels right along the water's edge. A natural swimming hole is surrounded by a concrete terrace. A taxi here from Savusavu should be around F$12, a bus around F$1. Gordon and Rosie promise you'll get the most for your money at Mumu, but unless you've got a tent, call ahead to make sure there's a room for you. This unique place merits our highest recommendation in the low-budget category.

Offshore Island
Moody's Namenalala Island Resort (Private Mail Bag, Savusavu; tel. 813-764, fax 812-366), on a narrow high island southwest of Savusavu in the Koro Sea, is one of Fiji's top hideaways. Hosts Tom and Joan Moody ran a similar operation in Panama's San Blas Islands for 15 years until June 1981, when they were attacked by Cuna Indians who shot Tom in the leg and tried to burn the resort. The media reported at the time that the Indians had been scandalized by hotel guests who smoked marijuana and cavorted naked on the beach, but Joan claims it was all part of a ploy to evict foreigners from San Blas to cover up drug-running activities.

In 1984, after a long search for a replacement, the couple leased Namenalala from the Fiji government, which needed a caretaker to protect the uninhabited island from poachers. Their present resort occupies less than 10% of Namenalala's 45 hectares, leaving the rest as a nesting ground to great flocks of red-footed boobies, banded rails, and Polynesian starlings. Giant clams proliferate in the surrounding waters within the 24-km Namena Barrier Reef, and from November to March sea turtles haul themselves up onto the island's golden sands to lay their eggs.

Each of the Moody's five bamboo and wood hexagonal-shaped *mbures* are well tucked away in the lush vegetation to ensure maximum privacy. Illuminated by romantic gas lighting, each features a private hardwood terrace with 270° views. Alternative energy is used as much as possible to maintain the atmosphere (though there is a secret diesel generator used to do the laundry and recharge batteries).

The cost to stay here is F$214 single or double, plus F$80 pp extra for the meal plan. The food is excellent, thanks to Joan's firm hand in the kitchen and Tom's island-grown produce. The ice water on the tables and in the *mbures* is a nice touch, and they don't push liquor sales the way some other resorts do.

This resort is perfect for birdwatching, fishing, and snorkeling, and scuba diving is available at F$60 per tank. If you want a holiday that combines unspoiled nature with interesting characters and a certain elegance, you won't go wrong here. Daily except Sunday, Beachcomber Cruises' high-speed catamaran *Ndrondrolangi* can whisk you from Lautoka to Namenalala in three hours at a cost of F$105 pp, or from Savusavu in less than 40 minutes at F$84 pp. A chartered seaplane from Nandi will run F$975. Moody's closes from 1 March to 1 May every year.

Food and Entertainment
The **Captain's Table** (tel. 850-511; open Monday to Thursday 0830-2030, Friday and Saturday 0830-2100, Sunday 1500-2100) at the Copra Shed Marina is a yachtie hangout claiming to offer "the best pizza on Vanua Levu," which isn't saying a lot when you think about it. Drop by even if you're not hungry to peruse the notice board, which bears photos of all the

yachts that have called at Savasavu recently. Most of Savusavu's hip young locals show up here eventually and in the evening the outdoor seating on the wharf is nice.

Several simple places around town offer basic meals of varying quality. The surly-staffed **Wing Yuen Restaurant,** next to the National Bank, increases the prices of their plates in response to unusual requests, such as leaving the meat out. Beware of the F$2.50 charge for a tiny pot of tea here. In contrast, the **New Ping Ho Cafe** (tel. 850-300), opposite the municipal market, accommodates vegetarians and everyone else with substantial portions of good food at decent prices. All the local expats eat here—no wonder the Wing Yuen's owner is so sour.

The **Vika Vuai's Cafe,** behind the town council next to the market, prepares good Fijian food. The **A1 Restaurant** near the bus station also has Indian curries.

The cook at the **Sea Breeze Restaurant** (tel. 850-100) below Savusavu Bay Accommodation can prepare a special Saturday evening dinner, provided you let him know the day before. The regular menu contains mostly Chinese dishes, and the portions are large. It's open Sunday for lunch and dinner. It's slightly cheaper than the New Ping Ho Cafe, but not as pleasant.

Drinkers can repair to the **Planters Club** (tel. 850-233) toward the wharf—the place is never out of Fiji Bitter. The weekend dances at the club are local events. Despite the Members Only sign outside, visitors are welcome. It's a vintage colonial club even without the colonists.

Services and Information

The ANZ Bank, National Bank, and Westpac Bank all have branches at Savusavu.

The **Copra Shed Marina** (Box 3, Savusavu; tel. 850-518) near the bus station houses the **Savusavu Yacht Club,** and visiting yachts can moor alongside for F$44 a week; offshore hurricane moorings are F$165 a month. There's a handy public card phone in the marina, and you can have your laundry done at the Copra Shed for F$5.

The **Bula Bookshop** at the Copra Shed Marina sells nautical charts as well as books.

Sea Fiji Travel (tel. 850-345, fax 880-344), in the Copra Shed Marina, is a full-service travel agency specializing in scuba diving and yacht charters.

Transportation

Air Fiji (tel. 850-538), next to the post office, flies into Savusavu twice daily from Suva (F$68) and three times a week from Taveuni. Ask Air Fiji about the flights from Savusavu to Levuka four times a week. **Sunflower Airlines** (tel. 850-141), around the corner from the ANZ Bank, has flights to Savusavu twice daily from Nandi (F$96) and daily from Taveuni (F$45). **Vanua Air** arrives twice daily from Suva (F$67) and Taveuni (F$44). The airstrip is beside the main highway, three km east of town, and you *will* pay for excess baggage here. Local buses to Savusavu pass the airport about once an hour, or take a taxi for F$2.

Beachcomber Cruises' high-speed catamaran *Ndrondrolangi* departs Savusavu for Natovi at 0945 (two hours, F$34) and Lautoka at 1400 (three hours, F$55) daily except Sunday. A bus connection to Suva (F$5) is available at Natovi. The **Consort Shipping Line Ltd.** (tel. 850-279) runs the large car ferry *Spirit of Free Enterprise* from Suva to Savusavu (12 hours, F$30 deck, F$55 cabin). The ferry leaves Suva northbound Wednesday and Saturday, and leaves Savusavu southbound Monday and Thursday around 1700. Northbound the ship continues to Taveuni, and between Savusavu and Suva it calls at Koro.

Patterson Brothers Shipping (tel. 850-161) at the Copra Shed Marina operates the car ferries *Ovalau II* and *Princess Ashika,* which depart Suva for Savusavu Monday at midnight via Ngau and Koro (14.5 hours, F$31). The return journey departs Savusavu Wednesday at 1700. Ask Patterson Brothers about the bus/boat connection to Taveuni, which should depart Savusavu Wednesday to Saturday at 0915 (four hours, F$20). All of the above schedules change frequently, so check.

Four buses a day go from Savusavu to Lambasa (92 km, F$4). The 1030 bus from Savusavu to Napuka connects at Mbutha Bay with the daily ferry *Grace* to Taveuni (F$5), which departs Natuvu around 1300. It's a beautiful boat trip but it can be rough if the wind is up. The five-hour bus/boat connection goes straight through from Savusavu to Taveuni, so use a toilet before leaving as there are none along the way, and bring a snack. Westbound the connection is poor, involving a wait of several hours at Mbutha Bay. About nine local buses a day run to Lesiatheva Point (45 cents), a favorite snorkeling spot.

Numerous taxis congregate at Savusavu market; they're quite affordable for short trips in the vicinity.

Avis Rent A Car (tel. 850-184) has an office next to the Shell service station in Savusavu. **Budget Rent A Car** (tel. 850-700) is next to the post office, while **Thrifty Car Rental** (tel. 850-232) is near the Hot Bread Kitchen.

MBUTHA BAY

Along the Hibiscus Highway

This lovely coastal highway runs 77 km east from Savusavu to Natuvu, then up the east side of Vanua Levu to the old Catholic mission station of **Napuka** at the end of the peninsula. Old frame mansions from the heyday of the 19th-century planters can be spotted among the palms. **Mbutha Bay** is a recognized "hurricane hole," where ships can find shelter during storms. Coupmaster Sitiveni Rabuka hails from **Ndrekeniwai** village on Natewa Bay, one of the largest bays in the South Pacific.

The **Mbutha Bay Resort and Yacht Club** (Natuvu, Mbutha Bay; tel. 880-370, fax 880-510), also known as Natuvu Plantation, next to the ferry wharf at Natuvu, has rooms with shared bath at F$39 double, with private bath F$50, and a five-room dorm at F$11 pp (campers F$6 pp). Managing director Sylvia Dobry hopes to eventually establish a writers' colony here and plans six medium-priced *mbures* for the coconut grove along the beach. The Reef Terrace Restaurant on the waterfront side of the plantation house serves meals upon request (check out the bakery items), and there are cooking facilities in the dorm. Yachties are welcome to anchor off the resort and use the facilities. Activities in this area include a hike to Tangithi Peak, birdwatching (the rare orange flame dove inhabits the upper forest), and the three-hour afternoon bus ride to Napuka and back (at 1300).

Buses to Savusavu leave Mbutha Bay at 0600, 0830, and 1600 (three hours, F$3). In the other direction, you can leave Savusavu for Mbutha at 1030, 1430, and 1630 except on Sunday.

Kioa

The Taveuni ferry passes between Vanua Levu and Kioa, home of some 300 Polynesians from Vaitupu Island, Tuvalu (the former Ellice Islands). In 1853 Captain Owen of the ship *Packet* obtained Kioa from the Tui Cakau, and it has since operated as a coconut plantation. In 1946 it was purchased by the Ellice islanders, who were facing overpopulation on their home island.

The people live at **Salia** on the southeast side of Kioa. The women make baskets for sale to tourists, while the men go fishing alone in small outrigger canoes. If you visit, try the coconut toddy *(kaleve)* or more potent fermented toddy *(kamanging)*. Kioa and nearby Rambi are the only islands in Fiji where the government allows trees to be cut for toddy.

Rambi

In 1855, at the request of the Tui Cakau on Taveuni, a Tongan army conquered some Fijian rebels on Rambi. Upon the Tongans' departure a few years later, a local chief sold Rambi to Europeans to cover outstanding debts. Before WW II the Australian firm Lever Brothers ran a coconut plantation here. In 1940 the British government began searching for an island to purchase as a resettlement area for the Micronesian Banabans of Ocean Island (Banaba) in the Gilbert Islands (present Kiribati), whose home island was being ravaged by phosphate mining. At first Wakaya Island in the Lomaiviti Group was considered, but the outbreak of war and the occupation of Ocean Island by the Japanese intervened. Back in Fiji, British officials decided Rambi Island would be a better homeland for the Banabans than Wakaya, and in March 1942 they purchased Rambi from Lever Brothers using £25,000 of phosphate royalties deposited in the Banaban Provident Fund.

Meanwhile the Japanese had deported the Banabans to serve as laborers on Kusaie (Kosrae) in the Caroline Islands, and it was not until December 1945 that the survivors could be brought to Rambi, where their 4,500 descendants live today. Contemporary Banabans are citizens of Fiji and live among Lever's former coconut plantations at the northwest corner of the island. The eight-member Rambi Island Council administers the island.

The island reaches a height of 472 meters and is well wooded. The former Lever headquarters is at Tabwewa, while the airstrip is near Tabiang. Rambi's other two villages are Uma and Buakonikai. At Nuku between Uma and Tabwewa is a post office, clinic, and four-room guesthouse. This colonial-style structure is the former Lever Brothers manager's residence and is little changed since the 1940s except for the extension now housing the dining area and lounge. One of the rooms is reserved for island officials; the rest are used mostly by contract workers. Other guests pay F$40 pp a night, which includes three meals. The facilities are shared (no hot water) and the electric generator operates 1800-2100 only—just enough time to watch a video. The former doctor's residence on Rambi is also rented out occasionally.

Considering the limited accommodations and the remoteness of Rambi, it's a good idea to contact the office of the **Rambi Council of Leaders** (Box 329, Suva; tel. 303-653, fax 300-543), 1st Floor, Ramson House, Pratt Street, Suva, before setting out. Hopefully this office will be able to make your guesthouse bookings and provide other information. You could also try phoning the Rambi Island Council at tel. 84-020, ext. 33. Remember that Rambi is not a tourist resort and it's very good form to obtain prior approval before visiting the community. Otherwise you could create unnecessary problems for yourself and others, and you could even be turned away.

Rambi lives according to a different set of rules than the rest of Fiji; in fact, about all they have in common are their monetary, postal, and educational systems, kava drinking (a Fijian implant), and Methodism. The local language is Gilbertese and the social order is that of the Gilbert Islands. Most people live in hurricane-proof concrete-block houses devoid of furniture, with personal possessions kept in suitcases and trunks. The cooking is done outside in thatched huts. If you happen to visit a family, your local contact will go in first to announce your arrival. Only after the house has been fixed up and other interested parties have arrived will you be eagerly welcomed into the home.

Alcoholic beverages other than traditional coconut toddy are not allowed on Rambi, so take something else as gifts. On Friday nights the local *maneaba* in Tabwewa village rocks to a disco beat and dancing alternates with sitting around the omnipresent kava bowl, but on Sunday virtually everything grinds to a halt. Another charming feature: adultery is a legally punishable offense on Rambi.

To get there catch the daily Napuka bus at 1030 from Savusavu to Karoko. Otherwise, a taxi from Savusavu Airport to Karoko will run F$80. A chartered speedboat from Karoko to the wharf at Tabwewa on the northwest side of Rambi costs F$45 each way, less if people off the Napuka bus are going over anyway. Patterson Brothers was considering instituting a direct ferry service from Natuvu and Taveuni to Rambi, so check. On Rambi itself, motorized transport consists of one 4WD vehicle, a truck, and a few school buses which ply the single 23-km road from Tabwewa to Buakonikai.

TAVEUNI

Long, green, coconut-covered Taveuni is Fiji's third-largest island. It's 42 km long, 15 km wide, and 470 square km in area. Only eight km across the Somosomo Strait from Vanua Levu's southeast tip, Taveuni is known as the Garden Island of Fiji because of the abundance of its flora. Around 60% of the land is under tropical rainforest. Its surrounding reefs and those off nearby Vanua Levu are some of the world's top dive sites. The strong tidal currents in the strait nurture the corals, but can make diving a tricky business for the unprepared. Because Taveuni is free of the mongoose, there are many wild chickens, *kula* parrots, silktails, ferntails, and orange-breasted doves, making this a special place for birders.

The island's 16-km-long, 1,000-meter-high volcanic spine causes the prevailing trade winds to dump colossal amounts of rainfall on the island's southeast side, and considerable quantities on the northwest side. At 1,241 meters, Uluinggalau in southern Taveuni is the second-highest peak in Fiji, and Des Voeux Peak (1,195 meters) in central Taveuni is the highest point in the country accessible by road. The European discoverer of Fiji, Abel Tasman, sighted this ridge on the night of 5 February 1643. The almost inaccessible southeast coast features plummeting waterfalls, soaring cliffs, and crashing surf. The 12,000 inhabitants live on the island's gently sloping northwest side.

The deep, rich volcanic soil nurtures indigenous floral species such as *Medinilla spectabilis,* which hang in clusters like red sleigh bells, and the rare *tangimauthia (Medinilla waterousei),* a climbing plant with red-and-white flower clusters 30 cm long. *Tangimauthia* grows only around Taveuni's 900-meter-high crater lake and on Vanua Levu. It cannot be transplanted and blossoms only from October to December. The story goes that a young woman was fleeing from her father, who wanted to force her to marry a crotchety old man. As she lay crying beside the lake, her tears turned to flowers. Her father took pity on her when he heard this and allowed her to marry her young lover.

In the past decade Taveuni has become very popular as a destination for scuba divers and those in search of a more natural vacation area than the overcrowded Nandi/Coral Coast strips. Even the producers of the film *Return to the Blue Lagoon* chose Taveuni for their 1990 remake. Despite all this attention, Taveuni is still about the most beautiful, scenic, and friendly island in Fiji. It's a great place to hang out, so be sure to allow yourself enough time here.

SIGHTS

Central Taveuni

Taveuni's post office, police station, hospital, government offices, and Country Club are on a hilltop at **Waiyevo,** above the Garden Island Resort. On the coast below are the island's main banks and its biggest hotel.

To get to the **Waitavala Sliding Rocks,** walk north from the Garden Island Resort about four minutes on the main road, then turn right onto the signposted side road leading to Waitavala Estates. Take the first road to the right up the hill, and when you see a large metal building on top of a hill, turn left and go a short distance down a road through a coconut plantation to a clearing on the right. The trail up the river to the sliding rocks begins here. The water slide in the river is especially fast after heavy rains, yet the local kids go down standing up! Admission is free.

The **180th degree of longitude** passes through a point marked by a signboard one km south of Waiyevo. One early Taveuni trader overcame the objections of missionaries to his doing business on Sunday by claiming the international date line ran through his property. According to him, if it was Sunday at the front door, it was already Monday around back. Similarly, European planters got their native laborers to work seven days a week by having Sunday at one end of the plantation, and Monday at the other. An 1879 ordinance ended this by placing all of Fiji west of the date line, so you're no longer able to stand here with one foot in the past and the other in the present.

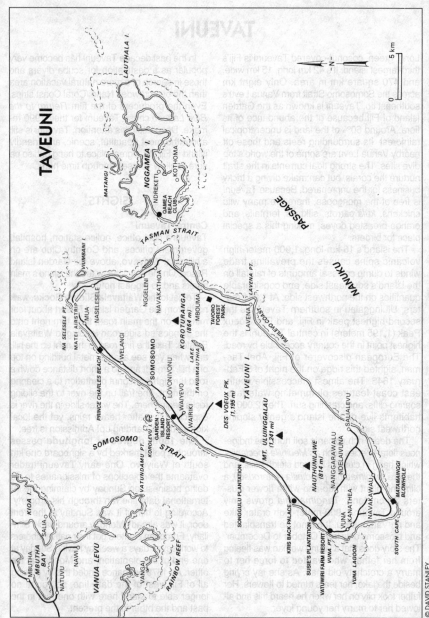

© DAVID STANLEY

At **Wairiki,** a kilometer south again, are a few stores and the picturesque Catholic mission, with a large stone church containing interesting sculptures and stained glass. There are no pews: the congregation sits on the floor Fijian style. From Wairiki Secondary School you can hike up a tractor track to the large **concrete cross** on a hill behind the mission in 30 minutes each way. You'll be rewarded with a sweeping view of much of western Taveuni and across Somosomo Strait. A famous 19th-century naval battle occurred here when Taveuni warriors turned back a large Tongan invasion force, with much of the fighting done from canoes. The defeated Tongans ended up in Fijian ovens and the French priest who gave valuable counsel to the Fijian chief was repaid with laborers to build his mission.

A jeep road from Wairiki climbs to the telecommunications station on **Des Voeux Peak.** This is an all-day trip on foot with a view of Lake Tangimauthia as a reward (clouds permitting). To hire a jeep to the viewpoint would cost F$60-80. The lake itself is not accessible from here.

One of the only stretches of paved road on Taveuni is at Songgulu Plantation or "Taveuni Estates" (tel. 880-044), about eight km south of Waiyevo. This ill-fated condo development features an attractive golf course by the sea, tennis courts, and a bowling green, plus street signs pointing nowhere, empty roads, sewers, and 30 unfinished condominiums built by an undercapitalized real estate speculator who badly miscalculated Taveuni's potential for Hawaii-style residential development.

Southern Taveuni

Transportation to the south end of Taveuni is difficult with only two buses a day from Somosomo (at 1215 and 1645). Since the 1645 bus spends the night at Vuna and doesn't return to Somosomo until the next morning, the only way to really see southern Taveuni is to also spend the night down there. If this isn't possible, the roundtrip bus ride leaving Somosomo around noon is still well worth doing.

The bus from Somosomo runs south along the coast to Susie's Plantation, where it turns inland to Ndelaivuna. There it turns around and returns to the coast, which it follows southeast to Navakawau via South Cape. On the way back it cuts directly across some hills to Kanathea and continues up the coast without going to Ndelaivuna again. Southeast of Kanathea there is very little traffic.

A hike around southern Taveuni provides an interesting day out for anyone staying at Susie's Plantation or one of the other nearby resorts. From Susie's a road climbs east over the island to **Ndelaivuna,** where the bus turns around at a gate. The large Private Property sign here is mainly intended to ward off miscreants who create problems for the plantation owners by leaving open cattle gates. Visitors with sense enough to close the gates behind themselves may proceed.

You hike one hour down through the coconut plantation to a junction with two gates, just before a small bridge over a (usually) dry stream. If you continue walking 30 minutes down the road straight ahead across the bridge you'll reach **Salialevu,** site of the Bilyard Sugar Mill (1874-96), one of Fiji's first. In the 1860s European planters tried growing cotton on Taveuni, turning to sugar when the cotton market collapsed. Later, copra was found to be more profitable. A tall chimney, boilers, and other equipment remain below the school at Salialevu.

After a look around, return to the two gates at the bridge and follow the other dirt road southwest for an hour through the coconut plantation to **Navakawau** village at the southeast end of the island. Some of Fiji's only Australian magpies (large black-and-white birds) inhabit this plantation.

Just east of South Cape as you come from Navakawau is the **Matamainggi Blowhole,** where trade wind-driven waves crash into the unprotected black volcanic rocks, sending geysers of sea spray soaring skyward, especially on a southern swell. The viewpoint is just off the main road.

At **Vuna** the lava flows have formed pools beside the ocean, which fill up with fresh water at low tide and are used for washing and bathing.

Northern Taveuni

Somosomo is the chiefly village of Thakaundrove and the seat of the Tui Cakau, Taveuni's "king"; the late Ratu Sir Penaia Ganilau, first president of Fiji, hailed from here. There are two distinct parts of the village, divided by a small stream where women wash their clothes. The southern portion is the island's commercial center with several large Indian stores and a couple of places to stay. Pacific Transport has its bus terminus here.

The northern part of Somosomo is the chiefly quarter with the personal residence of the Tui Cakau on the hill directly above the bridge (no entry). Beside the main road below is the large hall built for the 1986 meeting of the Great Council of Chiefs. Missionary William Cross, one of the creators of today's system of written Fijian, who died at Somosomo in 1843, is buried in the attractive new church next to the meeting hall. There's even electric street lighting in this part of town!

The challenging trail up to lovely **Lake Tangimauthia,** 823 meters high in the mountainous interior, begins behind the Mormon church at Somosomo. The first half is the hardest. You'll need a full day to do a roundtrip, and a guide (F$40) will be necessary as there are many trails to choose from. You must wade for half an hour through knee-deep mud in the crater to reach the lake's edge. Much of the lake's surface is covered with floating vegetation, and the water is only five meters deep.

Eastern Taveuni

There are three lovely waterfalls in **Tavoro Forest Park and Reserve** (admission F$5), just south of Mbouma on the northeast side of Taveuni. From the information kiosk on the main road it's an easy 10-minute walk up a broad path along the river's right bank to the lower falls, which plunge 20 meters into a deep pool. You can swim here, and change rooms, toilets, picnic tables, and a barbecue are provided. A well-constructed trail leads up to a second falls in about 30 minutes, passing a spectacular viewpoint overlooking Nggamea Island and Taveuni's northeast coast. You must cross the river once, but a rope is provided for balance. Anyone in good physical shape can reach this second falls with ease, and there's also a pool for swimming. The muddy, slippery trail up to the third and highest falls involves two river crossings with nothing to hold onto, and it would be unpleasant in the rain. This trail does cut through the most beautiful portion of the rainforest, and these

upper falls are perhaps the most impressive of the three, as the river plunges over a black basalt cliff, which you can climb and use as a diving platform into the deep pool. The water here is very sweet.

Tavoro Forest Park was developed with well-spent New Zealand aid money at the request of the villagers themselves, and all income goes to local community projects. In 1990 an agreement was signed putting the area in trust for 99 years and the forest park was established a year later. There are plans to eventually cut a trail from Tavoro right up to Lake Tangimauthia, but this awaits the creation of suitable overnight accommodations at Mbouma and additional outside funding. For the time being visitors are allowed to sleep on mats in the park information kiosk at F$5 per head; otherwise it might be possible to camp or stay with the locals.

Mbouma is easily accessible by public bus daily except Sunday. If you depart Waiyevo or Somosomo on the 0830 bus, you'll have about three and a half hours to see the falls and have a swim before catching the 1400 bus back to Waiyevo. This second bus does a roundtrip to Lavena, six km south (the 0830 bus finishes at Mbouma), and it's worth jumping on for the ride even if you don't intend to get off at Lavena.

At Lavena the New Zealand government has financed the **Lavena Coastal Walk,** which opened in May 1993. The information kiosk where you pay the F$5 admission fee is right at the end of the road at Lavena and, when space is available, it's possible to sleep on one of the four mattresses on the floor upstairs in the kiosk at F$5 pp. There's no store here but the villagers will prepare meals for you at F$3 each. Otherwise, bring groceries and cook your own behind the kiosk—protect the food from mice. Lighting is by kerosene lamp, and mosquito coils are essential. Additional accommodation may be available by the time you get there, and this is urgently required as it's not possible to visit Lavena as a day-trip by public bus (taxis charge F$80 return to bring you here). Buses depart Lavena for Somosomo Monday to Saturday at 0600 and 1400, Sunday at 0800. The beach at Lavena is one of Fiji's most spectacular beaches (be careful with the currents if you snorkel). The film *Return to the Blue Lagoon* was filmed here.

From the information kiosk at Lavena you can hike the five km down the Ravilevo Coast to stunning **Wainimbau Falls** in about an hour and a half. The last 30 minutes is a scramble up a creek bed, and during the rainy season you may have to wade or swim. There are two falls here that plunge into the same deep pool and diving off either is excellent fun (allow four hours there and back from Lavena with plenty of stops). It's also possible to visit the falls by motorboat, which can be arranged at the kiosk. A boat to Wainimbau Falls and Wainivakau Falls is F$50 for up to three persons or F$15 pp for groups of four to six. If you also want to see **Savuleveyavonu Falls**, which plummets off a cliff directly into the sea, you must pay F$75 for up to three people or F$25 pp for up to six. Intrepid ocean kayakers sometimes paddle the 20 km down the back side of Taveuni, past countless cliffs and waterfalls. It's well worth spending a few days in this attractive area if you possibly can.

Sports and Recreation

Taveuni and surrounding waters have become known as one of Fiji's top diving areas. The fabulous 31-km Rainbow Reef off the south coast of eastern Vanua Levu abounds in turtles, fish, overhangs, crevices, and soft corals, all in five to 10 meters of water. Favorite dive sites here include White Sandy Gulley, Jack's Place, Cabbage Patch, Pot Luck, Blue Ribbon Eel Reef, the Ledge, Jerry's Jelly, Coral Garden, and especially the Great White Wall. Beware of strong currents in the Somosomo Strait.

Way back in 1976, Ric and Do Cammick's **Dive Taveuni** (Postal Agency, Matei, Taveuni; tel. 880-441, fax 880-466) pioneered scuba diving in this area and they're still one of Fiji's most reliable operators. They charge F$105 for two tanks including lunch (hire gear not available), but their clients are mostly groups that have prebooked from abroad.

Walk-in divers are catered to by **Rainbow Reef Divers** (tel. 880-286) at the Garden Island Resort. The daily two-tank dives are F$99 (no one-tank dives), and PADI scuba certification costs F$440. You'll find cheaper dive shops but Rainbow's facilities are first rate.

Budget-minded divers should check out **The Dive Center** (Box 69, Taveuni; tel. 880-125, fax 880-202) at Susie's Plantation, which offers boat dives on the Rainbow Reef at F$44/77 for one/two tanks (plus F$15 extra for gear). Night diving is F$55; shore dives F$22. The Center's four-day NAUI scuba certification courses are F$415 if you're the only student, or F$363 pp for two or more students (group instruction usually begins on Monday). There's a five percent surcharge on credit card payments. Susie's makes a perfect base for these activities.

Offshore dive resorts such as Matangi Island and Qamea Beach Club receive mostly upscale divers who have booked from outside Fiji, and accommodations there are much more expensive than those on Taveuni.

The dive shop at the Garden Island Resort rents ocean kayaks at F$22 a half day, F$33 a full day.

Little Dolphin Sports (tel. 880-130), opposite the Matei Postal Agency Supermarket, near the east end of the airstrip, rents sailboards (F$15 a day), mountain bikes (F$15 a day), paddle boats (F$15 a day), and snorkeling gear (F$5 a day). It's run by an Australian named Scott who is a mine of information.

For something special, consider a day cruise on the luxury yacht *Seax of Legra,* operating on Wednesday and Saturday (Warwick and Dianne Baine, tel./fax 880-141). You sail for two hours to one of the islands off northern Taveuni, spend three hours there swimming, snorkeling, and having lunch on board, then sail another two hours back. Reservations must be made by 1600 the day before (F$70 pp including a buffet lunch aboard, four-person minimum). In good weather it's sure to be an unforgettable experience.

ACCOMMODATIONS

Accommodations in Northern Taveuni

For convenience, the accommodations listings that follow are arranged from top to bottom down the west side of Taveuni. Expensive and budget properties are mixed, so scan the entire list before choosing your place to stay. **Tuvununu Paradise Garden Inn** (c/o Postal Agency, Matei, Taveuni; tel. 880-465), just east of Naselesele village, offers rooms in a large wooden building overlooking Viubani Island at F$39/61 single/double, or F$14 pp in the dorm. The tidal flat in front of the inn is beautiful but not ideal for swimming, and at last report the Tuvununu was closed.

Several residents of the airport area have built nice little bungalows next to their homes or fixed up rooms in their personal residences, which they rent to tourists. For instance, **Little Dolphin Sports** (tel. 880-130), less than a kilometer east of the airport, has a bungalow at F$45 a night or F$300 a week. Audrey of **Audrey's Cafe** (tel. 880-039), a bit closer to the airport, has a cottage at F$55. An old steam tractor stands rusting under a coconut tree across the street. A couple of hundred meters west, Mrs. Dolores Porter (tel. 880-299) of **Lomalangi Beachfront Home** has a four-bed apartment at F$65. Two houses west is the **Coconut Grove Cafe** (tel. 880-328, fax 880-050), where Ronna Goldstein rents a fan-cooled beachfront cottage for F$55/66 single/double. Cooking facilities are provided at all of these places (and a supermarket is nearby), but it's important to call ahead to check availability as the rooms are often full. Use the card phone at the airport for this purpose (Air Fiji sells phone cards).

Quiet, friendly **Niranjan's Budget Accommodation** (c/o Postal Agency, Matei, Taveuni; tel. 880-406), also known as Airport Motel, is just a five-minute walk east of the airport. The four clean rooms in the main building, each with two beds, fridge, fan, and cooking facilities, go for F$22/33/44 single/double/triple. These rooms are excellent value and Niranjan's also has an annex called Airport Motel two doors away, with four cheaper rooms with shared bath at F$22 double. The electric generator is on 1800-2200. The manager serves one of the best curry dinners you'll taste in these parts for F$10 pp. This is one of the best places to stay in this area—recommended.

Directly opposite the airport terminal is the absurdly expensive **Garden of Eden Villa** which costs F$1250 a night (minimum stay one week). If you can afford those bucks you can also afford to call the manager, Peter Madden (tel. 880-252), long distance from anywhere in the world and question him about what he's offering. Who knows, he may even throw in the yacht!

Bibi's Hideaway (Box 80, Waiyevo, Taveuni; tel. 880-443), about 500 meters south of the airport, has something of the gracious atmosphere of the neighboring resorts without the sky-high prices. One room in a two-room cottage is F$30 single or double, while a larger family unit is F$70/80 double/triple. The film crew from *Return to the Blue Lagoon* stayed here, and with the extra income the owners built a deluxe *mbure,* which is F$50 single or double. All three units have access to cooking facilities. Bibi's is located on lush, spacious grounds, and James, Victor, and Agnes Bibi will make you feel right at home. It's an excellent medium-priced choice if you don't mind being a bit away from the beach.

A hundred meters south are two of Taveuni's most exclusive properties. **Maravu Plantation Resort** (c/o Matei Postal Agency, Taveuni; tel. 880-555, fax 880-600) is a village-style resort in a real 20-hectare copra-making plantation, a kilometer south of the airport. It has 10 comfortable *mbures* with ceiling fans at F$167/198/227 single/double/triple. The meal plan at the resort restaurant is F$68 pp extra. There's also a bar and swimming pool on the landscaped grounds. Nonguests must make reservations to eat here (the food is good, but count on F$35 pp for dinner). Airport transfers are F$6.

Almost across the street from Maravu Plantation is the upmarket **Dive Taveuni Resort** (Ric and Do Cammick, Postal Agency, Matei, Taveuni; tel. 880-441, fax 880-466), which is patronized mostly by scuba divers who arrive on prepaid packages. This place doesn't really cater to people who stroll in unannounced looking for a place to stay (and they're closed in February and March). The eight very pleasant *mbures* accommodate 10 guests at F$178 pp, including three meals and transfers. The property is on a cliff overlooking the ocean, with great views from the open terrace dining area. No alcohol is sold, so bring your own.

Down the hill from these and just north of Prince Charles Beach, just over one km south of the airport, are two of Taveuni's two best-established campgrounds. **Beverly Campground** (tel. 880-381), run by Bill Madden, is a shady place, nice if you value your privacy. It's F$5 pp in your own tent, F$6 pp in Bill's tent, or F$11 pp in a *mbure.* Cooking facilities (one-time charge of F$2 for gas) are available in a nearby *mbure,* but bring food. Bill can supply fresh fruit and vegetables, and he even serves a good dinner for F$7. It's right on the beach but the whole place could use a cleaning up and the snorkeling is poor.

A few hundred meters south is another good place just across the road from a white-sand beach. **Lisi's Campground** (Vathala Estate, Postal Agency Matei; tel. 880-194), in a small village a kilometer southwest of Beverly, is F$5 pp to camp, or F$10 pp in a small *mbure.* If you don't have a tent, they may be able to rent you one. A separate shower/toilet block is reserved for guests. Cooking facilities are available in a *mbure* (fresh fruit provided every morning), and hosts Mary and Lote Tuisago serve excellent Fijian meals at reasonable prices. Horseback riding is possible, and you're welcome to help with the "work," collecting fruit or making copra, if you want. You get to meet local people here as everyone joins the afternoon volleyball game, and in the evening there's kava drinking, often with music.

British yachties Warwick and Dianne Baine (Box 89, Waiyevo, Taveuni; tel./fax 880-141) rent a self-catering apartment in their lovely two-story home adjacent to Lisi's Campground at F$105 for up to four persons (two single and one double bed).

Accommodations in Western Taveuni

The original budget hotel on Taveuni was **Kaba's Motel & Guest House** (Box 4, Taveuni; tel. 880-233, fax 880-202) at Somosomo, which charges F$15/25/35 single/double/triple in one of four double rooms with shared facilities in the guesthouse. The cooking facilities are very good. The newer motel section is F$30/38/48 for one of the six larger units with kitchenette, fridge, fan, phone, and private bath—good value. The water is solar-heated, so cold showers are de rigueur in overcast weather (ask for a discount in that case). Kaba's Supermarket up the street has a huge selection of videos you can rent to play on the guesthouse VCR.

A friendly Indian family runs **Kool's Accommodation** (Box 10, Waiyevo, Taveuni; tel. 880-395), just south of Kaba's at Somosomo. The six rooms in two long blocks facing the eating area are F$9/14 single/double, and cooking facilities are provided. As the price may suggest, it's

more basic than Kaba's and only for those on the lowest of budgets.

Sunset Accommodation (Box 15, Taveuni; tel. 880-229), on a dusty corner near the wharf at Lovonivonu, has two basic rooms behind a small store at F$8/12 single/double. Again, this is only a low-budget place to crash.

The **Garden Island Resort** (Box 1, Waiyevo, Taveuni; tel. 880-286, fax 880-288), by the sea at Waiyevo, three km south of Somosomo, has 28 a/c rooms in an attractive two-story building at F$55/77/88 single/double/triple, or F$18 in the four-bed dorm. If your air conditioner isn't operating, the ceiling fan should suffice. The buffet breakfast and dinner plan is F$32 pp, and eating by the pool is fun. Formerly known as the Castaway, this was Taveuni's premier (and only) hotel when it was built by the Travelodge chain in the 1960s. Several changes of ownership later, the Garden Island has been eclipsed by the offshore resorts. There's no beach, but the Garden Island offers a restaurant, bar (happy hour 1700-1800), evening entertainment, swimming pool, excursions, and water sports. Snorkeling trips are arranged three times a day to Korolevu Island (F$11). It's a nice medium-priced place in which to hang out if you like large hotels.

Accommodations in Southern Taveuni

Kris Back Palace (Box 22, Taveuni; tel. 880-246), between Songgulu Plantation and Susie's Plantation, is still being developed but their beautiful stretch of rocky coastline and crystal clear snorkeling waters have always existed. For now, you can only count on a good place to pitch your tent (F$8 pp), or perhaps a bed in a thatched two-bed *mbure* (F$12 pp). The friendly managers will allow you to pick fruit at no cost in their plantation, and scuba diving can be arranged.

Susie's Plantation (Box 69, Waiyevo, Taveuni; tel. 880-125, fax 880-202), just north of Vuna Point at the south end of Taveuni, offers peace and quiet amid picturesque rustic surroundings, at the right price. Rates begin at F$35 double for a room with shared bath in the plantation house, or F$45 double for a simple seaside *mbure.* The dorm costs F$1250 pp; camping F$10 per tent (tolerated but not encouraged). You can cook your own food (a well-stocked grocery store is at Vatuwiri Farm, a 10-minute walk south). Otherwise pay F$30 pp extra for three meals in the restaurant, housed in the oldest missionary building on the island (nonguests welcome). Electricity exists only during the dinner hours. This atmospheric resort right on the ocean has its own resident diving instructor, who leads daily trips to the Great White Wall and Rainbow Reef. The PADI scuba certification course offers a great opportunity to learn how to dive, but even if you're not a diver, you'll enjoy the superb snorkeling right off their rocky beach or at nearby Namoli Beach (best at low tide, as the current picks up appreciably when the tide comes in). Horseback riding can be arranged. Susie is a real character and some people stay here for months. Recommended.

The **Vatuwiri Farm Resort** (c/o Postal Agency, Vuna, Taveuni; tel. 880-316) at Vuna Point, a kilometer south of Susie's, offers the possibility of staying on an authentic working farm established in 1871 by James Valentine Tarte. The Tartes now produce beef, vanilla, and copra, and rent several small cottages to tourists for F$70 a night. A long workers' dormitory block has been renovated, and beds in the six double rooms are F$20 each. Three good meals are F$35 pp extra. The rocky coast here is fine for snorkeling, and horseback riding is available. The Tarte family is congenial and this is perhaps your best chance to stay on a real working farm in Fiji.

Paul Masirewa owns land on lovely Namoli Beach, a 10-minute walk off the main road from Vuna village, a kilometer south of Vatuwiri Farm. He'll probably grant permission to camp if he likes you, and he's available as a guide for explorations of the surrounding area.

OTHER PRACTICALITIES

Food
Each of the three accommodation areas mentioned above has grocery shopping possibilities. Those staying on the northern part of the island will appreciate the well-stocked supermarket at the Matei Postal Agency between the airport and Naselesele village. Their generous ice cream cones are almost worth a special trip. The variety of goods available at Kaba's Su-permarket in Somosomo is surprising and a cluster of other small shops is adjacent. Small grocery stores also exist at Wairiki and Waiyevo. The only well-stocked grocery store in southern Taveuni is at Vatuwiri Farm, a kilometer south of Susie's Plantation.

The only nonhotel eatery on the island is the **Wathi-Po-Ee Restaurant** (open weekdays 0730-1700, Saturday 0730-1500) next to the Westpac Bank in Waiyevo. They serve reasonable Chinese and local meals, although prices are somewhat inflated by the nearby Garden Island Resort (which also has a restaurant).

Several of the one-unit accommodation places near the airport serve meals, including Ronna Goldstein's **Coconut Grove Cafe** (tel. 880-328). A bacon-and-cheese sandwich and coffee for lunch will run F$8, and at dinner you can get fresh fish of the day for F$13 or lobster for F$25, both with a choice of sauces, garlic bread, stir-fried vegetables, and rice. A F$8 "backpacker menu" is also available. Reservations are required for dinner but not at lunchtime. It's a bit of a splurge, but you dine on their veranda overlooking the sea, Mareta's cooking is excellent, and Ronna can tell you anything you want to know about Taveuni. A similar scene revolves around **Audrey's Cafe,** run by an American woman at Matei, a bit east of the airport. Audrey offers afternoon tea to guests who also enjoy the great view from her terrace, and she has various homemade goodies to take away.

Entertainment
The **180 Meridian Cinema** at Wairiki shows mainly violence and horror films.

There isn't any tourist-oriented nightlife on Taveuni beyond what's offered at the **Garden Island Resort,** which stages a *meke* and *lovo* Wednesday at 1830 (F$20 pp).

The **Taveuni Country Club** (tel. 880-133), next to the police station up the hill at Waiyevo, is a safe, local drinking place. It's open Thursday to Saturday only.

Services
Traveler's checks can be changed at the Westpac Bank (tel. 880-035) and National Bank branches, both near the Garden City Resort at Waiyevo (Monday to Thursday 0930-1500, Friday 0930-1600).

A haircut from the barber next to Kaba's Motel in Somosomo is F$2/3 for men/women.

Getting There

Matei Airstrip at the north tip of Taveuni is serviced twice daily by **Air Fiji** (tel. 880-062) from Suva (F$87), and **Sunflower Airlines** (tel. 880-461) from Nandi (F$116) and Savusavu (F$45). Sunflower also arrives from Lambasa (F$45) three times a week. **Vanua Air** flies here twice daily from Suva (F$87) and Savusavu (F$44). Flights to/from Taveuni are often heavily booked. You get superb views of Taveuni from the plane: sit on the right side going up, the left side coming back. Krishna Brothers in Somosomo is the agent for Air Fiji; the agent of Vanua Air (tel. 880-291) is next to the Hot Bread Kitchen in Somosomo.

Patterson Brothers has the ferries *Princess Ashika* and *Ovalau II* from Suva to Taveuni via Ngau, Koro, and Savusavu (22 hours, F$36) every Monday at midnight, departing Taveuni for the return trip Wednesday at 1000. The Patterson agent is Lesuma Holdings (tel. 880-036) in the back of the store between the Westpac and National banks. **Consort Shipping** operates the weekly *Spirit of Free Enterprise* service from Suva to Taveuni via Koro and Savusavu (24 hours, F$34). This ferry departs Suva northbound Wednesday at 0500 and leaves Taveuni southbound Thursday at 1300. The Consort agent (tel. 880-261) is at the fish market opposite the Garden Island Resort.

Patterson Brothers also operates the barge *Yaumbula* between Taveuni and Natuvu at Mbutha Bay on Vanua Levu, leaving Taveuni Wednesday to Saturday at 0800 (two hours, F$10), leaving Natuvu at 1300. They also carry cars and vans for F$50. Through tickets are available to Savusavu (four hours, F$20) and Lambasa (six hours, F$22), but the bus connection at Natuvu doesn't work every day, so check.

The small passenger boat *Grace* (tel. 880-134), also known as the *Ronita,* departs Taveuni for Natuvu Monday to Friday at 0830 (two hours, F$5), with connections to Savusavu and Lambasa (F$22) on Monday, Wednesday, and Friday only. Ask about combined boat/bus tickets on both the *Yaumbula* and the *Grace,* and be

aware that without such a prearranged connection, you might have to wait around at Mbutha Bay a couple of hours before the bus to Savusavu (F$3) shows up (there are only public buses from Natuvu to Savusavu in the early morning and at 1600). If no bus is around, you may be able to find a carrier, but expect a rough trip. Eastbound the bus/boat connection at Mbutha Bay is immediate.

If you arrive by boat at Taveuni, you could disembark at any one of three places. Some small boats from Vanua Levu transfer their passengers to the beach at Waiyevo by outboard. The *Spirit of Free Enterprise* and most of the other large ferries tie up at a wharf a kilometer north of Waiyevo. There's a third wharf at Lovonivonu village, a km north again, midway between Waiyevo and Somosomo, and this is often used by the Vanua Levu boats and other smaller cargo boats.

Getting Around

Pacific Transport (tel. 880-278) buses leave Waiyevo and Somosomo northbound to Mbouma (F$2) at 0830, 1215, and 1645; southbound to Vuna (F$2) they leave at 1215 and 1645, Saturday at 0830, 1215, and 1645. The northbound 0830 bus turns around at Mbouma, but the 1215 and 1645 buses carry on to Lavena (F$2). Sunday service is very infrequent, although there are sometimes buses to Mbouma and Vuna at 1600. Check the current schedule carefully as soon as you arrive. The buses begin their journeys at the Pacific Transport garage at Somosomo, but they all head first south to Waiyevo hospital to pick up passengers.

One of Taveuni's biggest drawbacks is the extremely dusty road up the northwest coast, which makes it very unpleasant to walk anywhere between Wairiki and the airport when there's a lot of fast traffic passing. This combined with rather expensive taxi fares and sporadic buses can make getting around rather inconvenient. Taveuni's minibus taxis only operate on a charter basis and don't run along set routes picking up passengers at fixed rates. The taxi fare from the wharf to Somosomo is F$2; from the airport to Somosomo it will be F$10.

Kaba's Supermarket (tel. 880-058) in Somosomo rents cars at F$77 a day with unlimited mileage (minimum two days), or F$44 a day plus 30 cents per km, insurance included. Fast-moving vehicles on the gravel roads throw up small stones which can smash your front window (and you'll have to pay the damages). As you pass approaching cars, hold your hand against the windshield just in case. It may be cheaper to hire a minibus taxi and driver for the day than to rent a car. Write out a list of everything you want to see, then negotiate a price with a driver. Otherwise, save money by using the buses for long rides and taxis for shorter hops.

OFFSHORE ISLANDS

Nggamea Island

Nggamea (Qamea) Island, just three km east of Taveuni, is the 12th-largest island in Fiji. It's 10 km long with lots of lovely bays, lush green hills, and secluded white-sand beaches. Land crabs *(lairo)* are gathered in abundance during their migration to the sea here in late November or early December. The birdlife is also rich, due to the absence of the mongoose. Outboards from villages on Nggamea land near Navakathoa village on the northeast side of Taveuni. Best time to try for a ride over is Thursday or Friday afternoons. Vatusongosongo village on Nggamea is inhabited by descendants of blackbirded Solomon islanders.

The **Qamea Beach Club Resort** (Postal Agency, Matei, Taveuni; tel. 880-220, fax 880-092) opened on the west side of Nggamea in 1984. The 11 thatched *mbures* with fans and fridges go for F$270/315/345 single/double/triple (no children under 12 allowed), and the meal plan is another F$75 pp a day (no cooking facilities). Meals are taken in a central dining room and lounge designed like a *mburekalau* (temple). The boat transfer from Taveuni airport is F$60 pp return. Activities such as windsurfing, snorkeling, sailing, outrigger canoeing, and hiking are included in the basic price, but scuba diving and fishing are extra. Some of the best dive sites in the world are close at hand and the snorkeling off the fine white-sand beach is superb. Reader Steve McCarthy of Portland, Oregon, had this comment:

Something is wrong here. This place is fairly expensive but it has gone downhill seriously. The food was mediocre, mbure *maintenance poor, and the staff, especially the men, surly. There was pressure to dive, buy drinks at the bar, etc. The pool was filthy and never cleaned in spite of vigorous requests.*

Matangi Island

Matangi is a tiny volcanic island just north of Nggamea, its sunken crater forming a lovely palm-fringed bay. The island is privately owned by the Douglas family, which has been producing copra on Matangi for five generations and still does. In 1988 they diversified into the hotel business.

Matangi Island Resort (Box 83, Waiyevo, Taveuni; tel. 880-260, fax 880-274), 10 km northeast of Taveuni, makes no bones about serving as a base for scuba divers. They also cater to families and couples looking for a quiet holiday, and the deluxe treehouse *mbure*, perched 10 meters up in an almond tree, is popular among honeymooners (F$310 pp). Other guests are accommodated in 10 neat thatched *mbures* costing F$188/255/290 single/double/triple, well spaced among the coconut palms below Matangi's high jungly interior. To the above, add another F$86 pp for the compulsory meal package (no cooking facilities), and boat transfers from Taveuni are F$63 pp return (reduced rates available for children). Diving costs F$118 for two tanks, and the live-aboard dive boat MV *Matangi Princess II* is based here costing from F$415 pp a day double occupancy including diving.

Lauthala Island

Lauthala Island, which shares a barrier reef with Nggamea, was depopulated and sold to Europeans in the mid-19th century by the chief of Taveuni, after the inhabitants sided with Tongan chief Enele Ma'afu in a local war. Today it's owned by the estate of the late multimillionaire businessman and New York publisher Malcolm Forbes, who is buried on the island. In 1972 Forbes bought 12-square-km Lauthala from the Australian company Morris Hedstrom for US$1 million. He then spent additional millions on an airstrip, wharf, and roads, and on replacing the thatched *mbures* of the 225 Fijian inhabitants with red-roofed cement-block boxes. Forbes's former private residence stands atop a hill overlooking the native village, the inhabitants of which make copra.

Prior to his death in 1990, Forbes opened his island to affluent tourists who now stay in seven *mbures,* each with living room, bar, and kitchen. The housekeeper prepares guests'

breakfasts in their cottages; other meals can be taken in the plantation house, in Forbes's house, at the beachside barbecue area, or as a picnic anywhere on the island. The price is F$425 pp per night (three-night minimum stay), including all meals, "a reasonable supply" of liquor, sports, scuba diving, and deep-sea fishing. The resident general manager of **Fiji Forbes Inc.** (Box 41, Waiyevo, Taveuni; tel. 880-077, fax 880-099) is the only chief on Lauthala.

THE LAU GROUP

Lau is by far the most remote part of Fiji, its 57 islands scattered over a vast area of ocean between Viti Levu and Tonga. Roughly half of them are inhabited. Though all are relatively small, they vary from volcanic islands to uplifted atolls to some combination of the two. Tongan influence has always been strong in Lau, and due to Polynesian mixing the people have a somewhat lighter skin color than other Fijians. Historically the chiefs of Lau have always had a political influence on Fiji far out of proportion to their economic or geographical importance.

Vanua Mbalavu (52 square km) and Lakemba (54 square km) are the largest and most important islands of the group. These are also the only islands with organized accommodations, and Vanua Mbalavu is the more rewarding of the two. Similarly, Moala is a large mountainous island with much to offer, while there is little for the average visitor on Thithia.

Once accessible only after a long sea voyage on infrequent copra-collecting ships, four islands in Lau—Lakemba, Vanua Mbalavu, Moala, and Thithia—now have regular air service from Suva. Occasional private ships also circulate through Lau, usually calling at five or six islands on a single trip, but they usually only offer deck passage (see "Transportation" in the "Suva" section for details). As none of these islands is prepared for tourism, the reception you may receive varies. Sometimes you'll be welcomed as a guest, other times they'll only want to know when you're leaving. No banks are to be found in Lau.

NORTHERN LAU

Vanua Mbalavu
The name means the "long land." The southern portion of this unusual, seahorse-shaped island is mostly volcanic, while the north is uplifted coral. An unspoiled environment of palm-fringed beaches backed by long grassy hillsides

VANUA MBALAVU

NAMBAVATU
BAY OF ISLANDS
VUTUNA
AVEA
ANDAVATHI I.
DAKUIRASIA
TOTA
MATAVURA
MASOMO BAY
MAVANA
YANUTHALOA
NDALITHONI
MALAKA
NARUARUA
AIRPORT
MUALEVU
MUAMUA
BOITATHE
VANUA MBALAVU ISLAND
LEVUKANA
URUONE
NDAKUROLOMALOMA
LOMALOMA
YANUYANU
NAROTHIVO
LAGOON
NAKAMA
RAVIRAVI LAGOON
NAMALATA
MALATA
SUSUI
SUSUI
URONA
MUNIA

0   4 km

© DAVID STANLEY

FIELD MUSEUM OF NATURAL HISTORY, CHICAGO

Necklaces of whale's teeth were a badge of chiefly authority. At night men would use wooden headrests to preserve their carefully coiffured hairdos.

and sheer limestone cliffs, this is a wonderful area to explore. There are varied vistas and scenic views on all sides. To the east is a barrier reef enclosing a lagoon 37 by 16 km. The Bay of Islands at the northwest end of Vanua Mbalavu is a recognized hurricane shelter. The villages of Vanua Mbalavu are impeccably clean, the grass cut and manicured. Large mats are made on the island and strips of pandanus can be seen drying before many of the houses.

In 1840 Commodore Wilkes of the U.S. Exploring Expedition named Vanua Mbalavu and its adjacent islands enclosed by the same barrier reef the Exploring Isles. In the days of sail, Lomaloma, the largest settlement, was an important Pacific town. The early trading company Hennings Brothers had its headquarters here. The great Tongan warlord Enele Ma'afu conquered northern Lau from the chiefs of Vanua Levu in 1855 and made Lomaloma the base for

his bid to dominate Fiji. A small monument flanked by two cannons on the waterfront near the wharf recalls the event. Fiji's first public botanical garden was laid out here over a century ago, but nothing remains of it. History has passed Lomaloma by. Today it's only a big sleepy village with a hospital and a couple of general stores. Some 400 Tongans live in Sawana, the south portion of Lomaloma village, and many of the houses have the round ends characteristic of Lau. Fiji's current president, Ratu Sir Kamisese Mara, was born in Sawana.

Sights

Copra is the main export and there's a small coconut oil mill at **Lomaloma.** A road runs inland from Lomaloma up and across the island to **Ndakuilomaloma.** From the small communications station on a grassy hilltop midway there's an excellent view.

Follow the road south from Lomaloma three km to **Narothivo** village, then continue two km beyond to the narrow passage separating Vanua Mbalavu and Malata islands. At low tide you can easily wade across to **Namalata** village. Alternatively, work your way around to the west side of Vanua Mbalavu, where there are isolated tropical beaches. There's good snorkeling in this passage.

There are **hot springs** and **burial caves** among the high limestone outcrops between Narothivo and Namalata, but you'll need a guide to find them. This can be easily arranged at Nakama, the tiny collection of houses closest to the cliffs, upon payment of a nominal fee. Small bats inhabit some of the caves.

Rent a boat to take you over to the **Raviravi Lagoon** on Susui Island, the favorite picnic spot near Lomaloma for the locals. The beach and snorkeling are good, and there's even a cave if you're interested. **Munia Island** is a privately owned coconut plantation where paying guests are accommodated in two *mbures*.

Events

A most unusual event occurs annually at Masomo Bay, west of **Mavana** village, usually around Christmas. For a couple of days the Mavana villagers, clad only in skirts of *ndrauninggai* leaves, enter the waters and stir up the muddy bottom by swimming around clutching logs. No one understands exactly why, and magic is thought to be involved, but this activity stuns the *yawa,* or mullet fish, that inhabit the bay, rendering them easy prey for waiting spears. Peni, the *mbete* (priest) of Mavana, controls the ritual. No photos are allowed. A Fijian legend tells how the *yawa* were originally brought to Masomo by a Tongan princess.

Accommodations
Mr. Poasa Delailomaloma and his brother Laveti operate a charming traditional-style rest house in the middle of Lomaloma village. A bed and all meals cost F$25 pp. It makes a great base from which to see the island, and you get a feel for village life while retaining a degree of privacy. Recommended.

The **Lomaloma Resort** (Box 55, Lomaloma; tel. 880-446, fax 880-303), on tadpole-sized Yanuyanu Island just off Lomaloma, is the creation of Ratu Sir Kamisese Mara, paramount chief of the Lau Group. Ratu Mara strongly opposed tourist development in Lau during his long tenure as Fiji's prime minister, so this is a rather ironic retirement project. He's also a part owner of Vanua Air. The seven round-ended *mbures* (or *fales*) furnished in the traditional style rent for F$275/450 single/double, including meals, drinks, nonmotorized activities, and airport transfers. Children under 12 are not accommodated. Less expensive shared accommodation in the "Dive Village" on the back side of the island may also be available, and scuba diving is possible with Dan Grenier's Lomaloma Crystal Divers. Book direct or through Sun Tours Ltd. (Box 9403, Nandi Airport; tel. 722-666, fax 790-075).

Getting There
Vanua Air flies to Vanua Mbalavu twice a week from Suva (F$98 one-way) and Thithia (F$22). The flights are heavily booked, so reserve your return journey before leaving Suva. A bus runs from the airstrip to Lomaloma. After checking in at the airstrip for departure you'll probably have time to scramble up the nearby hill for a good view of the island. Boat service from Suva is only every couple of weeks.

Several carriers a day run from Lomaloma north to Mualevu, and some carry on to Mavana.

Other Islands of Northern Lau
After setting himself up at Lomaloma on Vanua Mbalavu in 1855, Chief Ma'afu encouraged the establishment of European copra and cotton plantations, and several islands are freehold land to this day. **Kanathea,** to the west of Vanua Mbalavu, was sold to a European by the Tui Cakau in 1863, and the Kanathea people now reside on Taveuni. **Mango Island,** a copra estate formerly owned by English planter Jim Barron, was purchased by the Tokyu Corporation of Japan in 1985 for F$6 million.

In 1983 **Naitamba Island** was purchased from TV star Raymond Burr by the California spiritual group Johannine Daist Communion for US$2.1 million. Johannine Daist (45 Lovoni Rd., Samambula, Suva; tel. 381-466, fax 370-196) holds four-to-eight-week meditation retreats on Naitamba for longtime members of the communion. The communion's founder and teacher, Baba Da Free John, the former Franklin Albert Jones (tel. 880-188), who attained enlightenment in Hollywood in 1970, resides on the island.

There's a single Fijian village and a gorgeous white-sand beach on **Yathata Island.** Right next to Yathata and sharing the same lagoon is 260-hectare **Kaimbu Island,** which was owned by the Rosa family from 1872 to 1969, when it was purchased by fiberglass millionaires Margie and Jay Johnson. In 1987 the Johnsons opened **Kaimbu Island Resort** (Kaimbu Island Postal Agency; tel. 880-333, fax 880-334), which consists of only three spacious octagonal guest cottages renting at F$1550 per couple per day (minimum stay six nights—children not accommodated). The price includes gourmet meals, drinks, snorkeling, sailing, windsurfing, sportfishing, scuba diving, and just about anything else you desire, plus a chartered flight from Suva or Taveuni to Kaimbu's central airstrip. Bookings are handled by Kaimbu Island Associates (Box 10392, Newport Beach, CA 92658, U.S.A.; tel. 800/473-0332, fax 714/644-5773). At last report, a 50% interest in the resort was available for US$2.5 million (contact René Boehm in Hamburg, Germany, at fax 49-40/340-568).

Vatu Vara to the south, with its soaring interior plateau, golden beaches, and azure lagoon, is privately owned and unoccupied much of the time. The circular, 314-meter-high central limestone terrace, which makes the island look like a hat when viewed from the sea, gives it its other name, Hat Island. There is reputed to be buried treasure on Vatu Vara.

Katafanga to the southeast of Vanua Mbalavu was at one time owned by Harold Gatty, the famous Australian aviator who founded Fiji Airways (later Air Pacific) in 1951.

Thithia, between Northern and Southern Lau, receives Vanua Air flights from Suva (F$95) twice a week. Several Fijian villages are found on Thithia, and land is leased to European companies for copra planting. Fiji's only black-and-white Australian magpies have been introduced to Thithia and Taveuni.

Wailangi Lala, northernmost of the Lau Group, is a coral atoll bearing a lighthouse, which beckons to ships entering Nanuku Passage, the northwest gateway to Fiji.

LAKEMBA

Lakemba is a rounded volcanic island reaching 215 meters. The fertile red soils of the rolling interior hills have been planted with pine, but the low coastal plain, with eight villages and all the people, is covered with coconuts. To the east is a wide lagoon enclosed by a barrier reef.

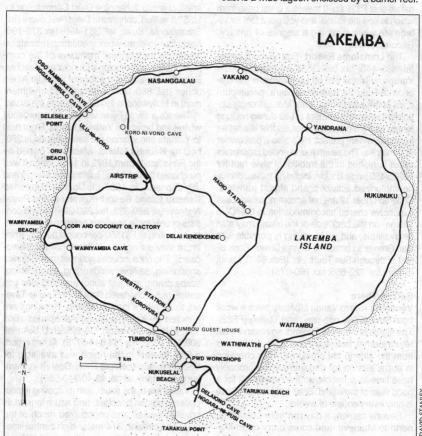

LAKEMBA

© DAVID STANLEY

In the olden days, the population lived on Delai Kendekende, an interior hilltop well suited for defense.

The original capital of Lakemba was Nasanggalau on the north coast, and the present inhabitants of Nasanggalau retain strong Tongan influence. When the Nayau clan conquered the island, their paramount chief, the Tui Nayau, became ruler of all of Southern Lau from his seat at Tumbou. During the 1970s and 1980s Ratu Sir Kamisese Mara, the present Tui Nayau, served as prime minister of Fiji.

Sights

A 29-km road runs all the way around Lakemba. From the Catholic church you get a good view of **Tumbou,** an attractive village and one of the largest in Fiji, with a hospital, wharf, several stores, and the Lau provincial headquarters. Tumbou was originally situated at Korovusa just inland, where the foundations of former houses can still be seen. Farther inland on the same road is the forestry station and a nursery.

The Tongan chief Enele Ma'afu (died 1881) is buried on a stepped platform behind the Provincial Office near Tumbou's wharf. In 1869 Ma'afu united the group into the Lau Confederation and took the title Tui Lau. Two years later he accepted the supremacy of Cakobau's Kingdom of Fiji, and in 1874 he signed the cession to Britain. Alongside Ma'afu is the grave of Ratu Sir Lala Sukuna (1888-1958), an important figure in the development of indigenous Fijian self-government. David Cargill and William Cross, the first Methodist missionaries to arrive in Fiji, landed on the beach just opposite the burial place on 12 October 1835. Here they invented the present system of written Fijian.

Coconut Factory

Four km west of Tumbou is the coir (husk fiber) and coconut oil factory of the **Lakemba Cooperative Association** at Wainiyambia. Truckloads of coconuts are brought in and dehusked by hand. The meat is then removed and sent to the copra driers. Coconut oil is pressed from the resulting copra and exported in drums. The dry pulp remaining after the extraction is bagged and sold locally as feed for pigs. The husks are flattened and soaked, then fed through machinery that separates the fiber. This is then made into twine, rope, brushes, and doormats, or it is bundled to be used as mattress fiber. Nothing is wasted. Behind the factory is Wainiyambia Beach, one of the most scenic on Lakemba.

Nasanggalau and Vicinity

The best limestone caves on the island are near the coast on the northwest side of Lakemba, 2.5 km southwest of Nasanggalau. **Oso Nambukete** is the largest; the entrance is behind a raised limestone terrace. You walk through two chambers before reaching a small, circular opening about one meter in diameter, which leads into a third chamber. The story goes that women attempting to hide during pregnancy are unable to pass through this opening, thus giving the cave its name, the "Tight Fit to the Pregnant" Cave.

Nearby is a smaller cave, **Nggara Mbulo** ("Hidden Cave"), which one must crawl into. Warriors used it as a refuge and hiding place in former times. The old village of Nasanggalau was located on top of the high cliffs behind the caves at Ulu-ni-koro. The whole area is owned by the Nautonggumu clan of Nasanggalau, and they will arrange for a guide to show you around for a fee. Take a flashlight and some newspapers to spread over the openings to protect your clothing.

Each October or November the Nasanggalau people perform a shark-calling ritual. A month before the ritual, a priest *(mbete)* plants a post with a piece of tapa tied to it in the reef. He then keeps watch to ensure that no one comes near the area, while performing a daily kava ceremony. When the appointed day arrives, the caller wades out up to his neck and repeats a chant. Not long after, a large school of sharks led by a white shark arrives and circles the caller. He leads them to shallow water, where all but the white shark are formally killed and eaten.

East of Tumbou

Two less impressive caves can be found at Tarakua, southeast of Tumbou. **Nggara-ni-pusi** has a small entrance, but opens up once you get inside. **Delaiono Cave** is just below a huge banyan tree; this one is easier to enter and smaller inside.

The best beach near Tumbou is **Nukuselal,** which you can reach by walking east along the coastal road as far as the P.W.D. workshops. Turn right onto the track, which runs along the west side of the compound to Nukuselal Beach.

Into the Interior
Many forestry roads have been built throughout the interior of Lakemba. You can walk across the island from Tumbou to Yandrana in a couple of hours, enjoying excellent views along the way. A radio station operates on solar energy near the center of the island. **Aiwa Island,** which can be seen to the southeast, is owned by the Tui Nayau and is inhabited only by flocks of wild goats.

Accommodations
The **Tumbou Guest House** (Lau Provincial Office, Tumbou, Lakemba; tel. 42-090, ext. 35) has four simple rooms with shared bath at F$16 pp bed/breakfast, plus F$3 each for lunch and dinner. It's a nice way to get off the beaten track, but be sure to call ahead for reservations as persons on official business have priority and there's nowhere else to stay. The locals at Tumbou concoct a potent homebrew *(umburu)* from cassava.

Getting There
Both **Air Fiji** and **Vanua Air** fly to Lakemba twice a week from Suva (F$98). Vanua Air also arrives twice weekly from Moala (F$39). A bus connects the airstrip to Tumbou, and buses run around the island four times weekdays, three times daily weekends.

OTHER ISLANDS OF SOUTHERN LAU

Aside from Lakemba, other islands of Central Lau include Nayau, Vanua Vatu, Aiwa, and Oneata. **Oneata** is famous for its mosquitoes and tapa cloth. In 1830 two Tahitian teachers from the London Missionary Society arrived on Oneata and were adopted by a local chief who had previously visited Tonga and Tahiti. The men spent the rest of their lives on the island, and there's a monument to them at Ndakuloa village.

In a pool on **Vanua Vatu** are red prawns similar to those of Vatulele and Vanua Levu. Here the locals can summon the prawns with a certain chant.

Mothe is known for its tapa cloth, which is also made on Namuka, Vatoa, and Ono-i-Lau. **Komo** is known for its beautiful girls and dances *(meke),* which are performed whenever a ship arrives. Mothe, Komo, and Olorua are unique in that they are volcanic islands without uplifted limestone terraces.

The **Yangasa Cluster** is owned by the people of Mothe, who visit it occasionally to make copra. Fiji's best *tanoa* are carved from *vesi* (ironwood) at **Kambara,** the largest island in southern Lau. The surfing is also said to be good at Kambara, if you can get there.

Fulanga is known for its woodcarving; large outrigger canoes are still built on Fulanga, as well as on **Ongea.** Over 100 tiny islands in the Fulanga lagoon have been undercut into incredible mushroom shapes. The water around them is tinged with striking colors by the dissolved limestone, and there are numerous magnificent beaches. Yachts can enter this lagoon through a narrow pass.

Ono-i-Lau, far to the south, is closer to Tonga than to the main islands of Fiji. It consists of three small volcanic islands, remnants of a single crater, in an oval lagoon. A few tiny coral islets sit on the barrier reef. The people of Ono-i-Lau make the best *mangi mangi* (sennit rope) and *tambu kaisi* mats in the country. Only high chiefs may sit on these mats. Ono-i-Lau formerly had air service from Suva, but this has been suspended.

The Moala Group
Structurally, geographically, and historically, the high volcanic islands of Moala, Totoya, and Matuku have more to do with Viti Levu than with the rest of Lau. In the mid-19th century they were conquered by the Tongan warlord Enele Ma'afu, and today they're still administered as part of the Lau Group. All three islands have varied scenery, with dark green rainforests above grassy slopes, good anchorage, many villages, and abundant food. Their unexplored nature yet relative proximity to Suva by boat make them an ideal escape for adventurers. No tourist facilities of any kind exist in the Moala Group.

Triangular **Moala** is an intriguing 68-square-km island, the ninth largest in Fiji. Two small crater lakes on the summit of Delai Moala (467 meters) are covered with matted sedges, which will support a person's weight. Though the main island is volcanic, an extensive system of reefs flanks the shores. Ships call at the small government station of Naroi, also the site of an airstrip that receives Sunflower Airlines flights from Suva three times a week (F$77). **Vanua Air** lands on Moala twice a week from Suva (F$73) and Lakemba (F$39).

Totoya is a horseshoe-shaped high island enclosing a deep bay on the south. The bay, actually the island's sunken crater, can only be entered through a narrow channel known as the Gullet, and the southeast trades send high waves across the reefs at the mouth of the bay, making this a dangerous place. Better anchorage is found off the southwest arm of the island. Five Fijian villages are found on Totoya, while neighboring **Matuku** has seven. The anchorage in a submerged crater on the west side of Matuku is one of the best in Fiji.

ROTUMA

This isolated six-by-14-km volcanic island, 600 km north of Viti Levu, is surrounded on all sides by more than 322 km of open sea. There's a saying in Fiji that if you can find Rotuma on a map it's a fairly good map. The climate is damp.

In the beginning Raho, the Samoan folk hero, dumped two basketfuls of earth here to create the twin islands, joined by the Motusa Isthmus, and installed Sauiftonga as king. Tongans from Niuafo'ou conquered Rotuma in the 17th century and ruled from Noa'tau until they were overthrown.

The first recorded European visit was by Captain Edwards of HMS *Pandora* in 1791, while he was searching for the *Bounty* mutineers. Christianity was introduced in 1842 by Tongan

Wesleyan missionaries, followed in 1847 by Marist Roman Catholics. Their followers fought pitched battles in the religious wars of 1871 and 1878, with the Wesleyans emerging victorious. Escaped convicts and beachcombers also flooded in but mostly succeeded in killing each other off. Tiring of strife, the chiefs asked Britain to annex the island in 1881, and it has been part of Fiji ever since. European planters ran the copra trade from their settlement at Motusa until local cooperatives took over.

Rotuma is run like a colony of Fiji, with the administration in the hands of a district officer responsible to the district commissioner at Levuka. Decisions of the 15-member Rotuma island council are subject to veto by the national gov-

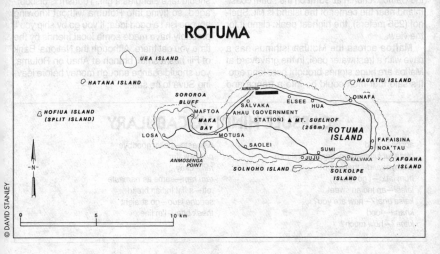

ernment. The island wasn't directly represented in the old house of representatives, being lumped into the Lau Group constituencies, although it did have an appointed senator. In early 1988 Rotuma attempted to secede from Fiji, citing human rights violations by the military-backed republican regime. The Fijian district officer on the island promptly demonstrated his disgust by blasting the flag of the new Republic of Rotuma with a shotgun. Soon after, a "peace-keeping force" of 13 Rotuman soldiers arrived.

Some 2,800 Rotumans presently inhabit the island, and another 4,600 of their number live in Suva. The light-skinned Polynesian Rotumans are easily distinguished from Fijians. The women weave fine white mats. Fiji's best oranges are grown here and Rotuma kava is noted for its strength.

Sights

Ships arrive at a wharf on the edge of the reef, connected to Oinafa Point by a 200-meter coral causeway, which acts as a breakwater. There's a lovely white beach at **Oinafa.** The airstrip is to the west, between Oinafa and Ahau, the government station. At **Noa'tau** southeast of Oinafa is a co-op store; nearby, at **Sililo,** visit a hill with large stone slabs and old cannons scattered about, marking the burial place of the kings of yore. Look for the fine stained-glass windows in the Catholic church at **Sumi** on the south coast. Inland near the center of the island is Mt. Suelhof (256 meters), the highest peak; climb it for the view.

Maftoa across the Motusa Isthmus has a cave with a freshwater pool. In the graveyard at Maftoa are huge stones brought here long ago. It's said four men could go into a trance and

carry the stones with their fingers. **Sororoa Bluff** (218 meters) above Maftoa should also be climbed for the view. Deserted **Vovoe Beach** on the west side of Sororoa is one of the finest in the Pacific. A kilometer southwest of Sororoa is **Solmea Hill** (165 meters), with an inactive crater on its north slope. On the coast at the northwest corner of Rotuma is a natural **stone bridge** over the water.

Hatana, a tiny islet off the west end of Rotuma, is said to be the final resting place of Raho, the demigod who created Rotuma. A pair of volcanic rocks before a stone altar surrounded by a coral ring are said to be the King and Queen stones. Today Hatana is a refuge for seabirds. **Hofiua** or Split Island looks like it was cut in two with a knife; a circular boulder bridges the gap.

Getting There

Both **Sunflower Airlines** and **Vanua Air** fly to Rotuma from Suva twice weekly (F$250). The monthly government boats carry mixed cargo out, copra back. Unless you really want to spend a month on Rotuma, book your return flight before leaving Suva.

As yet there are no organized accommodations on Rotuma. Many Rotumans live in Suva, however, and if you have a Rotuman friend he/she may be willing to send word to his/her family to expect you. Ask your friend what you should take along as a gift. Tourism is discouraged, so flying into Rotuma without knowing anyone isn't a good idea; if you go by ship you'll probably have made some local friends by the time you get there. Although the National Bank of Fiji has a small branch at Ahau on Rotuma, you should change enough money before leaving Suva to be safe.

CAPSULE HINDI VOCABULARY

accha—good
bhaahut julum—very beautiful (slang)
dhanyabaad—thank you
hum jauo—I go (slang)
jalebi—an Indian sweet
kaise bhai?—how are you?
khana—food
kitna?—how much?

namaste—hello, goodbye
pani—water
rait—okay
ram ram—same as *namaste*
roti—a flat Indian bread
seedhe jauo—go straight
theek bhai—I'm fine

CAPSULE FIJIAN VOCABULARY

Although most people in Fiji speak English fluently, mother tongues include Fijian, Hindi, and other Pacific languages. Knowledge of a few words of Fijian, especially slang words, will make your stay more exciting and enriching. Fijian has no pure *b, c,* or *d* sounds as they are known in English. When the first missionaries arrived, they invented a system of spelling, with one letter for each Fijian sound. To avoid confusion, all Fijian words and place-names in this book are rendered phonetically, but the reader should be aware that, locally, "mb" is written *b,* "nd" is *d,* "ng" is *g,* "ngg" is *q,* and "th" is *c.*

Au lako mai Kenada.—I come from Canada.
au la o—Vanua Levu version of *mbarewa*
au lili—affirmative response to *au la o* (also *la o mai*)
Au ni lako mai vei?—Where do you come from?
Au sa lako ki vei?—Where are you going?

dua tale—once more
dua oo—said by males when they meet a chief or enter a Fijian *mbure*

e rewa—a positive response to *mbarewa*

io—yes

kana—eat
kauta mai—bring
kauta tani—take away
kaivalangi—foreigner
koro—village
Kothei na yathamu?—What's your name?

lailai—small
lako mai—come
lako tani—go
levu—big, much
lima—five
loloma yani—please pass along my regards

maleka—delicious
mangiti—feast
marama—madam
matanggali—a clan lineage
mbarewa—a provocative greeting for the opposite sex
mbula—a Fijian greeting
mothe—goodbye

Na thava onggo?—What is this?
Ndaru lako!—Let's go!
ndua—one
ndua tale—one more

nggara—cave
Nice mbola—You're looking good.
Ni sa mbula—Hello, how are you? (can also say *sa mbula* or *mbula vinaka;* the answer is *an sa mbula vinaka*)
ni sa mothe—good night
ni sa yandra—good morning

phufter—a gay male (a disrespectful term)

rewa sese—an affirmative response to *mbarewa*
rua—two

sa vinaka—it's okay
senga—no, none
senga na lengga—you're welcome
sota tale—see you again

talatala—reverend
tambu rewa—a negative response to *mbarewa*
tolu—three
tulou—excuse me
turanga—sir, Mr.

va—four
vaka lailai—a little, small
vaka levu—a lot, great
vaka malua—slowly
vaka totolo—fast
vale—house
vale lailai—toilet
vanua—land, custom, people
vinaka—thank you
vinaka vaka levu—thank you very much
vu—an ancestral spirit

wai—water

yalo vinaka—please
yandra—good morning
yanggona—kava, grog

GORDON OHLIGER

NEW CALEDONIA

INTRODUCTION

New Caledonia (Kanaky) is unique. In Nouméa, the capital, the fine French restaurants, exclusive boutiques, and cosmopolitan crowds all remind you that this is the Paris of the Pacific. Yet on the east coast of the main island and on all of the outliers, the Kanaks (from *kanaka,* the Hawaiian word for "human") and *la Coutume* (native custom) have survived almost a century and a half of brutal repression.

New Caledonia is a contradiction and an anachronism, the last surviving stronghold of white colonialism in Melanesia. Here the clash of the irresistible force of Kanak nationalism against the immovable mass of entrenched French settlers has catapulted the territory into world headlines more than once. Yet things have grown quieter since 1988, when a 10-year truce was signed in preparation for a promised vote on independence in 1998.

Very few tourists stray beyond Nouméa, but to really see New Caledonia you must cross the Chaîne Centrale to Grande Terre's exotic east coast or travel by sea or air to the charming outer islands. Despite the recent political prob-

lems, the whole of New Caledonia is safe to visit and you'll be received with warmth and interest, especially when they hear you speaking English. This big French colony just north of the tropic of Capricorn, midway between Fiji and Australia, is quite unlike its neighbors and will surprise you in every respect.

The Land

New Caledonia consists of a cigar-shaped mainland (Grande Terre), the Isle of Pines, the Loyalty Group, and the small uninhabited dependencies of Walpole Island (125 hectares), the d'Entrecasteaux Reefs (64 hectares), and the more distant Chesterfield Islands (101 hectares). The d'Entrecasteaux Reefs consist of two separate lagoons centered on tiny Huon and Surprise Islands, with a deep strait 10 km wide between. The territory's 18,576 square km are divided into three provinces: North Province (9583 square km), South Province (7012 square km), and Loyalty Islands Province (1981 square km).

Grande Terre is part of the great fold in the earth's surface that runs from the central highlands of Papua New Guinea to the northern peninsula of New Zealand. The geology is complex, with metamorphic, sedimentary, and volcanic rock present. Don't underestimate its size: Grande Terre is 400 km long and 50 km wide, the sixth-largest island in the South Pacific (after New Guinea, the two islands of New Zealand, Tasmania, and New Britain). It's slowly sinking as the Australian Plate pushes under the Pa-

cific Plate to the east; the winding, indented coastline is a result of this submergence. Ten km off both coasts is the second-longest barrier reef in the world, which marks how big the island once was.

Locals refer to Grande Terre as "Le Caillou" or "Le Roché" (The Rock). The interior is made up of row upon row of craggy mountains throughout its length, such as Mt. Panie (1,639 meters) in

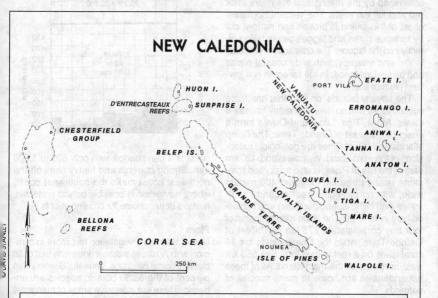

NEW CALEDONIA

PORT VILA — EFATE I.

HUON I.

D'ENTRECASTEAUX REEFS — SURPRISE I.

CHESTERFIELD GROUP

BELEP IS.

VANUATU
NEW CALEDONIA

ERROMANGO I.

ANIWA I.

TANNA I.

ANATOM I.

BELLONA REEFS

GRANDE TERRE

OUVEA I.
LIFOU I.
TIGA I.
MARE I.

LOYALTY ISLANDS

CORAL SEA

NOUMEA
ISLE OF PINES

WALPOLE I.

-N-

0   250 km

NEW CALEDONIA AT A GLANCE

	AREA (SQUARE KM)	HIGHEST POINT (M)	POPULATION (1989)	PERCENTAGE KANAK
Grande Terre	16,192	1,639	144,051	37
Isle of Pines	152	262	1,465	94
Mare	642	138	5,646	99
Lifou	1,196	90	8,726	98
Ouvea	132	39	3,540	98
Isles Belep	70	283	745	99
Total	**18,576 ***		**164,173**	**45**

* includes other dependencies

the north and Mt. Humboldt (1,634 meters) in the south, and it contains 40% of the world's reserves of nickel (enough to last another 200 years at the present rate of extraction), as well as profitable deposits of other minerals such as tungsten, cobalt, copper, gold, manganese, iron, and chromium. The landscape, you'll notice, is wounded in many locales by huge open-pit mines—the Great Red Menace. Bulldozer tracks and drill holes leave ugly scars, and sediments unleashed by the mining turn the rivers thick red and kill the reefs. The verdant northeast coast of this island is broken and narrow, cut by tortuous rivers and jagged peaks falling directly into the lagoon. The drier southwest coast is low and swampy, with wide coastal plains and alluvial lowlands. In the far south is a lowland plain of lakes.

The Loyalty Islands, on the other hand, are uplifted atolls with no rivers but many limestone caves. Maré, Tiga, Lifou, and Ouvéa form a chain 100 km east of Grande Terre. The Belep Islands and Isle of Pines are geological extensions of the main island. Walpole Island, 130 km east of the Isle of Pines, is also an uplifted limestone island three km long and 400 meters wide, with no protective reef around its 70-meter-high cliffs. Guano (fertilizer) was exploited here in 1910-36. The Huon Islands consist of four tiny coral islands 275 km northwest of Grande Terre, while the Chesterfields are 11 coral islets on a reef in the Coral Sea 550 km west-northwest of the main island. All of these dependencies are home to many species of seabirds.

Climate

New Caledonia is farther south than most other South Pacific islands; this, combined with the refreshing southeast trade winds, accounts for its sunny, moderate climate, similar to that of the south of France. It can even be cool and windy from June to September, and campers will need sleeping bags. The ocean is warm enough for bathing year-round.

December to March is warm and rainy; it's also the cyclone season. The cyclonic depressions can bring heavy downpours and cause serious flooding. The windward northeast coast of Grande Terre catches the prevailing winds and experiences as much as 3,000 mm of precipitation a year, while the leeward southwest

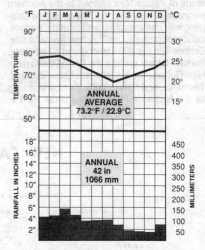

NOUMÉA'S CLIMATE

ANNUAL AVERAGE
73.2°F / 22.9°C

ANNUAL
42 in
1066 mm

coast is a rain shadow with only 800 to 1,200 mm. Strong currents and heavy seas off the northeast coast make the southwest coast, where navigation is possible behind protective reefs, a better choice for cruising yachts.

Flora

New Caledonia's vegetation has more in common with Australia's than it does with that of its closer tropical neighbor, Vanuatu. Seventy-five percent of the 3,250 botanic species are endemic. There are extensive areas of mangrove swamp and savanna grassland along the west coast. The only sizable forests are in the mountains.

The territory's most distinctive tree is a pine known as the *Araucaria columnaris,* which towers 30-45 meters high, with branches only two meters long. It's common along the more forested east coast and in the south, standing on low hills along the rockier shorelines and on the offshore islands. Often confused with the better-known Norfolk pine, the *Araucaria columnaris* or "candelabra" pine has a cylindrical profile whereas the Norfolk pine is conical. They're the most prominent floral features of these neighboring islands when viewed from the sea, and European mariners from Captain Cook onwards have been suitably impressed.

The most characteristic tree of the savannas of the northern and western of Grande Terre is the *niaouli,* a relative of the eucalyptus. This tree has a white, almost completely fireproof bark, which peels off in papery layers and is used as an excellent medicinal oil, somewhat like eucalyptus oil. Through its ability to survive bush fires, the *niaouli* plays an important environmental role in this mountainous country by maintaining the continuity of the vegetation.

Fauna

The only native mammals are the flying fox (a bat) and the rat. The pig was unknown to the indigenous people prior to European contact. The deer that inhabit the savannas of Grande Terre are descended from two pairs introduced in 1862. Some of the butterflies possess a rare beauty. Eighty-eight species of birds are found in New Caledonia, 18 of them endemic. Only a few hundred specimens of the Ouvéa parakeet still exist.

The national bird is the flightless *cagou (Rhynochetos jubatus),* or Kagu, about the size of a small rooster. This bird has lovely soft gray plumage, contrasted by striped brown-and-white wings. The *cagou's* crest rises when the bird is angered, and its cry is like the bark of a dog. It eats insects, worms, and snails. As it hatches only one egg a year and is slow on the ground, the *cagou* is approaching extinction: real dogs often outrun and kill it. A few hundred survive in Rivière Bleue Territorial Park at the west end of Yaté Lake and elsewhere.

The extreme richness of life on the reefs compensates for the lack of variety on land. New Caledonia's 1,600 km of barrier reefs are home to 350 species of coral, 1,500 species of fish, and 20,000 species of invertebrates. The territory's protected lagoons total 23,000 square km, with an average depth of 20 meters—the largest lagoon complex in the world.

HISTORY

Prehistory

It's not certain when the Papuan peoples reached New Caledonia. Some 300 earth mounds dating from 6000 B.C. discovered on the Isle of Pines were once thought to prove habitation for at least 8,000 years, but the mounds are now accepted as having been constructed by extinct giant birds. What is known for sure is that Austronesian-speakers have been here for over 3,000 years. *Lapita* sites have been found near Koné and on the Isle of Pines, the pottery carbon-dated at earlier than 1000 B.C. Prehistoric rock carvings are found throughout the territory. Back migrations of Polynesians reached the Loyalty Islands just a few hundred years before the Europeans.

The Kanak clans lived in small villages of 50 people and farmed their own land, using sophisticated irrigation systems and terraced taro gardens. Kanak culture has been called the "yam civilization," because of the importance of this tuber as a staple and in ceremonial exchanges. Land was owned collectively but controlled by the oldest son of the first clan to settle in the place.

The center of the village was the *grande case,* a large conical-roofed house where the chief

Masks such as these represented water spirits and were produced only in the north part of Grande Terre. The headdress and beard were made of human hair; the lower portion of the costume shrouded the body of the dancer in a net of feathers.

lived and ceremonies were performed. Religion was animistic. Of the many spirits loose in the land, the most powerful were the clan ancestors. Society was based around a relationship between the living and their ancestors, both of whom the chief represented, in a sense.

A number of clans formed an autonomous tribe. There was little contact between local tribes, and many languages evolved; most people lived in the interior, and language groups extended across the main island, rather than down the coasts. When Captain Cook, the first European, arrived in September 1774, there were over 70,000 Kanaks living in these islands.

Contact and Conquest

Cook landed at Balade, on the northeast coast of Grande Terre, and gave New Caledonia its name—the mountainous island reminded him of the Scottish Highlands (Caledonia was the Romans' name for Scotland). After more navigators (d'Entrecasteaux and Huon de Kermadec), traders arrived looking for sandalwood and bêche-de-mer. The first missionaries were Protestants from the London Missionary Society, who established themselves on Maré (1841) and Lifou (1842) islands. French Catholic missionaries arrived at Balade in 1843, but Kanak hostility and British protests caused them to withdraw four years later.

At this time France was watching enviously the establishment of successful British colonies in Australia and New Zealand. So in 1853, with the idea of creating a penal colony similar to that in New South Wales, Emperor Napoléon III ordered the annexation of New Caledonia. The Loyalties were claimed in 1866. Île Nou, an island in Nouméa Bay, never attained the notoriety of its contemporary, Devil's Island off South America, but between 1864 and 1897 some 20,000 French convicts were transported there, although no more than 8,000 were present at any one time. They were used for public works and construction projects in the early days.

Some 3,900 political prisoners from the Paris Commune were held on the Isle of Pines during 1871-79. Unlike the common criminals who had preceded them, many of the *communards* were cultured individuals. For example, Louise Michel, the "red virgin," taught Kanak children in Nouméa and took an active interest in the indigenous way of life. In her memoirs, Michel compared the freedom struggle of the Kanaks to that of Paris in 1871.

Colonialism and War

In 1864 Jules Garnier, a French mining engineer, discovered nickel on the banks of the Diahot River. Copper was found at Balade in 1872, cobalt in 1875. In 1876 the Société le Nickel (SLN) was established and mining began in earnest. That year the French government established a series of "indigenous reservations" for the confinement of the natives in areas the French miners and settlers didn't want, opening the rest of Grande Terre to mining and stock raising.

This sparked a violent reaction in 1878, as High Chief Atai of La Foa managed to unite many of the central tribes and launched a guerrilla war that cost 200 Frenchmen and 1,200 Kanaks their lives. Eventually Atai was betrayed by a rival tribe and assassinated. His head was sent to a Paris museum for exhibit, but has since been stolen. In the repression that followed, many clans were forced off their own lands onto that of other clans, leading to further rivalry and disruption. The abandoned taro terraces can still be seen. Most of the French political prisoners on the island (Louise Michel was an exception), who had fought for their own freedom just a few years previously, assisted the colonial regime in repressing the "savages."

The French government assumed title to two-thirds of Grande Terre, another quarter was eventually given or sold to white settlers, and only 10% of the main island (in scattered, hilly areas) was left to the original inhabitants. Title to even these crowded holdings was uncertain. The *colons* (settlers) brought in cattle and sheep and occupied the river valleys and coastal plains. Tribes were relocated in 150 villages under puppet chiefs and were easily controlled by French *gendarmes*. To obtain cheap labor, the French imposed a heavy poll tax on the Kanaks, effectively forcing them to work for the *colons* in order to obtain the money to pay. With their traditional way of life disrupted, the Kanak population declined from around 60,000 in 1878 to 42,500 in 1887, and 27,100 in 1921. Only during the 1930s did their numbers again increase.

In 1917, the forced recruitment of Kanaks into the French army led High Chief Noel to appeal to his people to fight the French at home as well as Kanak soldiers had fought the Germans abroad (1,000 Kanaks were killed in WW I). Although not as widespread as the 1878 revolt, the fighting lasted two months in north and northwest Grande Terre, and 11 Europeans and 200 Kanaks died. Further land alienations followed. The depression of the 1930s wiped out many small French farmers, and land was concentrated in the hands of a few, as it is today.

In June 1940, after the fall of France, the Conseil Général of New Caledonia voted unanimously to support the Free French government, and in September the pro-Vichy governor was forced to leave for Indochina. The territory became an important Allied base in March 1942, and the fleet that turned back the Japanese navy in the Battle of the Coral Sea (May 1942) was based at Nouméa. Hundreds of thousands of American troops and a lesser number of New Zealand troops passed this way; in the Pacific, only San Francisco handled more wartime cargo. Several Nouméa neighborhoods still bear names like "Receiving" and "Motor Pool" bestowed at this time. Kanaks employed by the Americans received much better treatment than they had come to expect from the French.

Political Development

After WW II, France had a fairly progressive colonial policy. In 1946, New Caledonia became an Overseas Territory, and partly due to a shortage of labor in the nickel industry, the Kanaks were finally given French citizenship and allowed to leave their reservations without police permission. In 1951, the French parliament gave the right to vote to a large number of indigenous people throughout the French Union, and Maurice Lenormand of the multiracial Union Calédonienne was elected to the French National Assembly. Lenormand's lobbying won an elected territorial assembly with the power to make laws, and by 1957, New Caledonia seemed on the road to independence.

Then came an armed uprising by French settlers on 18 June 1958 and the rise to power in France of Général de Gaulle, who dissolved the territorial assembly and appointed a repressive new governor. All French governments since de Gaulle have worked against independence. In 1963 Lenormand was jailed for a year and deprived of his civil liberties by the French government for five years in a frame-up involving the bombing of the Territorial Assembly. The same

year, the French National Assembly scrapped New Caledonia's limited autonomy and returned full control to the governor.

Lenormand's successor, Roch Pidjot, Kanak chief of the La Conception tribe near Nouméa, represented the Union Calédonienne in the French National Assembly for two decades until his retirement in 1986. His many proposals for self-government were never considered. A 1977 gerrymander created a second National Assembly seat for Nouméa and the west coast of Grande Terre, and this was taken a year later by businessman Jacques Lafleur, the wealthiest person in New Caledonia. In 1979 the Union Calédonienne united with four other pro-independence parties to form the Front Indépendantiste, which took 14 of the 36 seats in the Territorial Assembly.

On 19 September 1981, Pierre Declercq, secretary-general of the Union Calédonienne, was shot through a window of his Mont Dore home. No one has ever been brought to trial for this crime. Declercq's murder further united the independence movement, and in the 1982 elections, the Front Indépendantiste gained a majority in the territorial assembly. Jean-Marie Tjibaou (pronounced "tee-bow"), a former Catholic priest, became vice-president of the government council.

Crisis

Prior to the May 1981 election of François Mitterrand, the French left had assured the Kanaks that their right to self-determination would be respected. Once in power, the Socialists' promises proved empty. Thus disillusioned Kanak activists reorganized their movement into the Front de Libération Nationale Kanake et Socialiste (FLNKS) and decided to actively boycott the territorial assembly elections of 18 November 1984. Their demand was immediate independence.

Roadblocks were set up and ballot boxes destroyed. Though thousands of transient French cast ballots, voter turnout dropped from 75% in the 1979 elections to under 50% in 1984. By default, the anti-independence Rassemblement pour la Calédonie dans la République (RPCR) won 34 of the 42 seats. On 1 December 1984 the FLNKS proclaimed a Provisional Government of Kanaky and tightened its roadblocks throughout the territory. President Mitterrand's personal envoy Edgard Pisani arrived on 3 December

1984 and declared that he would work out a plan for self-government within two months.

Two nights later, on 5 December 1984, a gang of French *colons* armed with automatic weapons, dynamite, dogs, and searchlights ambushed a group of 17 unarmed FLNKS militants as they drove home in the mountains near Hienghène. Stopped by a felled tree and caught in a crossfire, the Kanaks tried to escape across a river. For half an hour the killers hunted them down like animals, finishing off the wounded until the river ran red with blood. In the end 10 Kanaks died, including two brothers of Jean-Marie Tjibaou, head of the provisional government. French *gendarmes* stationed five km away didn't bother to visit the scene for 16 hours, although they were called shortly after the incident. A week later seven of the killers, including members of third- and fourth-generation settler families, gave themselves up and were jailed.

Appalled by this atrocity, Pisani sought a solution that would bring the two sides together in a semi-independent state freely associated with France. On 7 January 1985, Pisani announced a plan calling for a referendum on independence on 1 July 1985 and self-government in association with France from 1 January 1986. France would control defense and foreign affairs, and French citizens would have special status. Then on 12 January 1985, police sharpshooters shot and killed schoolteacher Éloi Machoro, minister of the interior in the provisional government, and Marcel Noraro, an

aide, as they stood outside their rural headquarters near La Foa. (It's believed the same French secret service elements that later planned the *Rainbow Warrior* bombing in July 1985 were responsible for this and other provocations in New Caledonia.) In retaliation, the giant French-owned Thio and Kouaoua nickel mines were blown up by the Kanaks as whites rioted against independence in Nouméa. The FLNKS rejected Pisani's "neocolonial" plan.

In March 1985 an undaunted Pisani submitted his plan to Mitterrand, and in April French Prime Minister Laurent Fabius announced a new decentralization program featuring greater autonomy, land reform, and a say for the Kanaks in the territory's affairs. The territorial assembly elected in November 1984 was to be abolished, and a 43-seat territorial congress created to represent four regions, northern and central Grande Terre, the Loyalty Islands, and Nouméa. Nouméa would have 18 seats elected by universal suffrage, the other three regions (with Kanak majorities), 25 seats. The congress was to decide on independence before the end of 1987.

After protests that the French population was not properly represented, the number of Nouméa seats was increased to 21 in a 46-seat body. In August 1985 President Mitterrand recalled the French National Assembly from holidays to enact the legislation. Territorial elections took place on 29 September 1985. The pro-independence FLNKS won the three rural regions, while the anti-independence RPCR took Nouméa (over 80% of Kanaks voted for the FLNKS). After this election, the political situation quieted down. Thirty-two people, Kanaks and French, died during the 1984-1985 confrontations.

Reaction

In March 1986 conservatives under Prime Minister Jacques Chirac took over the French national assembly from the Socialists. Chirac immediately adopted a hard, anti-independence line: the concessions granted under the Socialists were to be undone. Chirac's Minister of Overseas Territories, Bernard Pons, recentralized power in the high commissioner by transferring the funds intended for regional development away from the regional councils. The economic agency created to promote development in Kanak areas through soft loans and outright grants was abolished, and land purchased under the Socialists for redistribution to Kanak tribes was turned over to extremist French settlers. French elite troops were stationed at mobile camps next to Kanak villages, the same "nomadization" tactics the French army had used in Algeria and Chad to study and intimidate potential opponents.

These backward steps convinced the South Pacific Forum, meeting at Suva in August 1986, to vote unanimously to ask the United Nations to reinscribe New Caledonia on its list of non-self-governing territories (the territory had previously been on the list until 1947). On 2 December 1986 the U.N. General Assembly voted 89-24 to reinscribe New Caledonia on the decolonization list—a major diplomatic defeat for France. The situation in the territory was to be reviewed annually by the U.N. Committee of 24, focusing international attention on the situation.

Responding to international criticism, the French government held a referendum on independence in the territory on 13 September 1987. The Socialists had proposed a referendum giving voters the option of independence in association with France. Under Chirac the choice was simply complete independence or remaining part of France. The FLNKS insisted that only those with one parent born in the territory (be they Kanak or French settler) be allowed to vote. (Though Kanaks themselves couldn't vote at all until 1953, the 25,000 immigrants who had entered the country between 1969 and 1974 were now to decide its fate.) Chirac insisted that everyone who had been there longer than three years must be allowed to vote. So, with the outnumbered Kanaks boycotting the vote, the result was 98% in favor of France.

In October 1987 Pons announced a plan that would redefine the council boundaries to ensure that Kanaks and settlers each controlled two regions, a net loss to the Kanaks of one. Henceforth the regional councils would only be responsible for municipal affairs, road maintenance, agriculture, and folklore. Authority was to be centralized in a 10-member executive council that would replace the territorial congress, overturning Fabius reforms granting the Kanaks limited autonomy in the regions outside Nou-

méa. Pons's plan denationalized the Kanaks by claiming that only French citizens existed in New Caledonia; the existing native reserves were to be considered freehold land available for sale to anyone. Kanak claims to land rights and independence were to be considered totally irrelevant. In January 1988 the French National Assembly voted 289-283 to adopt the Pons Statute. After this the Chirac regime simply refused to negotiate with the Kanaks.

The Ouvéa Massacre

In September 1986 a French examining magistrate named Semur ordered the release of seven self-confessed killers of the 10 Kanaks murdered at Hienghène in December 1984 because they had acted in "self defense." This provoked an international furor, and on 20 November an appeal court ruled that the seven men had to stand trial. This took place in Nouméa in October 1987 and a jury of eight whites and one Indonesian deliberated over dinner for two hours before acquitting the defendants in a major travesty of justice. Jean-Marie Tjibaou said this was "proof that the murder of Kanaks is encouraged by the French judicial system." Soon after, he issued a statement that read: "The shooting season for Kanaks has begun . . . whitemen have permits authorizing hunting and thus to massacre Kanaks. Kanaks must be fully aware of this state of affairs and recognize that no one will come to their help." Yeiwéné Yeiwéné, the Loyalty Islands regional president, called on Kanaks to arm themselves in self-defense.

From its founding in 1984 the FLNKS had preached nonviolence. This policy seemed to have failed, so just prior to the 24 April 1988 elections for the four redistributed regions the FLNKS declared a "muscular mobilization" to accompany their election boycott. Throughout the territory, Kanaks erected roadblocks and fired on police who attempted to remove them. A general uprising was planned, but at dawn on 22 April a commando of 40 Kanaks acted prematurely and captured the *gendarmerie* at Fayaoué on Ouvéa in the Loyalty Islands, killing four police and capturing another 27. Sixteen of the prisoners were taken to a cave near the north end of the island and held hostage. Forewarned, every other *gendarmerie* in the territory went on alert.

Kanaks are forced to serve in the French armed forces for 11 months. There's about one well-armed French soldier for every four adult Kanaks.

DAVID ROBIE

On 4 May 1988, just three days prior to the French presidential elections, "Rambo" Chirac ordered an assault on the cave to garner right-wing support for his election campaign against Mitterrand. During "Operation Victor" at 0600 the next morning, 300 elite counterinsurgency troops attacked the cave, massacring 19 Kanaks and freeing the hostages unharmed, for a loss of two of the assaulting force. Kidnap leader, Alfonse Dianoud, a former student priest, was beaten to death by the troops as he lay wounded on a stretcher, and six other Kanaks were executed by the French troops after they surrendered. There were no Kanak survivors—their bullet-ridden bodies were unrecognizable. Other Ouvéa residents were tortured by the French secret service agents, and 33 prisoners were deported to France. The French soldiers who carried out these atrocities have never been brought to justice.

The Matignon Accords

The policies of Chirac and Pons had propelled New Caledonia to the brink of civil war, costing another 25 people their lives. Yet the Kanak blood spilled at Ouvéa didn't rally sufficient support for Chirac to win the French presidency, and Mitterrand was reelected. A month later, parliamentary elections were held in France, and the Socialists returned to power. The renewed violence had chastened everyone, so on 26 June 1988 the FLNKS leader Jean-Marie

Tjibaou and the RPCR chief Jacques Lafleur met in Paris under the auspices of Socialist Prime Minister Michel Rocard to work out a compromise. The settlers were worried the Socialists would be sympathetic to independence, while the Kanaks wanted back the economic powers they had enjoyed briefly under the Fabius plan.

Under the peace accords signed at the Matignon Palace in Paris by the French government, the RPCR, and the FLNKS on 20 August 1988, all sides agreed to direct rule from Paris for one year, followed by a federal system for nine. The Pons Statute was to be scrapped and the territory divided into three self-governing provinces, North Province, South Province, and Loyalty Islands Province, with provincial elections in June 1989. There was to be balanced economic development based on decentralization and new training programs for Kanaks. Three-quarters of A$55 million in development funds were to be channeled into the Kanak regions. A new referendum on independence was to take place in 1998, with voting restricted to those eligible to vote in 1988 and children of voting age. Amnesty was to be granted to 200 Kanak militants and to settlers charged with crimes against Kanaks. What the accords didn't do is significantly increase territorial autonomy, nor did it guarantee a more equal division of the territory's wealth, most of which is concentrated in the settler-controlled South Province. The Kanak leaders who signed the accords failed to

(top) kava session, Toni's Guest House, Nuku'alofa, Tonga (photo by M.E. de Vos);
(bottom) Tongan wedding party, Tongatapu, Tonga (photo by Robert Kennington)

(top) Pola Island, American Samoa (photo by Gerald M. Ludwig, U.S. Fish and Wildlife Service);
(bottom left) Yasur volcano, Tanna, Vanuatu; (bottom right) taro (photos by David Stanley)

consult their followers to seek approval or to demand an inquiry into the Ouvéa Massacre.

On 6 November 1988 a referendum was held in France, and 80% of voters approved the plan. This meant that the agreement couldn't be altered by a simple act of parliament should the government in Paris change—a major Kanak demand. Yet FLNKS hardliners such as Yann Celene Uregei strongly opposed the accords as a sellout that didn't guarantee independence. They argued that the FLNKS should refuse to cooperate with continued colonial rule and mount a last-ditch, all-or-nothing independence struggle. The split deepened as several FLNKS factions refused to participate in the June 1989 elections. The Ouvéa people felt totally betrayed, especially after an unfortunate photo of Tjibaou shaking hands with Jacques Lafleur was widely published—Lafleur, who was thought to have engineered the acquittal of the murderers of Tjibaou's brothers and instigated the Ouvéa Massacre.

Then, on 4 May 1989, at a commemorative service on Ouvéa for the massacre victims, the final act: the moderate FLNKS leaders Jean-Marie Tjibaou, 53, and Yeiwéné Yeiwéné, 44, were shot and killed at point-blank range by Djoubelly Wea, whose father had died from electric shocks inflicted by uniformed French thugs a year before. Wea himself, who acted alone, was immediately slain by Tjibaou's bodyguard. As Jean Guiart, director of the Museum of Man in Paris, wrote in the French journal *Réalités du Pacifique:*

It was like a death in a Greek tragedy, the destiny of a man born from the blood of the dead of the 1917 insurrection, who dies for the blood spilled by other French soldiers in 1988.

Recent Events

In June 1989, elections were held for the three provincial assemblies created under the Matignon Accords. The FLNKS gained comfortable majorities in North and Loyalty Islands provinces, while the settler-based RPCR won in South Province. The RPCR's large majority in Nouméa also gave it enough seats to control the Territorial Congress.

The 1995 elections largely duplicated these results, although a new party called "Une Nouvelle Caledonie pour tous" led by Didier Leroux won seven of the 32 seats in South Province. Leroux claims his party is non-independence rather than anti-independence and its appearance reflects dissatisfaction at the continuing domination of political and economic life by Lafleur's RPCR. In Nouméa the neo-fascist National Front won two seats. In North Province the 15 seats were split between two independence parties, the FLNKS (six seats) and Palika (five seats). Leroux has tended to align his party with the pro-independence camp, tilting the balance of power away from the RPCR.

The situation in New Caledonia remains volatile, as the old split between French loyalists and supporters of independence is replaced by a new division of those for or against the accords. Many young Kanaks are dissatisfied with a settlement that has given their leaders comfortable jobs but themselves much less. In fact, the issue may already have been decided, as it's estimated that only 43.6% of the 1998 electorate will be Kanak, not nearly enough to win the referendum without considerable Wallisian and European support. The French government is throwing large sums of money at the Kanaks to soften the blow and make the territory more economically dependent than ever.

Whatever the outcome of the 1998 vote it's highly unlikely the French government will ever allow true self-determination for the Kanak people, especially with an opportunistic rightist like Jacques Chirac occupying the French presidency. By threatening to withdraw aid, the government in Paris will be able to dictate the referendum result without lifting a finger. France is determined to keep New Caledonia for its mineral riches, both on land and undersea, and the role it plays in projecting French military power around the world. Millions of deaths were needed to convince France it had to give up Algeria and Indochina, and French policy in New Caledonia remains the same: to hold on as long as feasible, whatever the cost.

GOVERNMENT

New Caledonia is a French overseas territory run by a high commissioner appointed by the president of France. The high commissioner controls international relations, foreign investment, immigration, navigation and air traffic, trade, finance, the Exclusive Economic Zone, communications, justice, defense, and the police.

Each of three provinces has a regional assembly in charge of planning, economic development, social welfare, and culture within its area. The 32 members of the South Province Assembly, 15 members of the North Province Assembly, and seven members of the Loyalty Islands Province Assembly are elected by proportional representation every six years.

Together the members of the provincial assemblies make up the 54-member Territorial Congress, which controls public health, social services, primary education, public transport, highways, electricity, sports and culture, taxation, and the territorial budget. As executive head of the Territorial Congress, the high commissioner can intervene in its actions at any time and govern by decree. The president and one of the two vice-presidents of the congress and each of the assemblies sit on the nine-member Consultative Committee with the high commissioner.

Local government is organized into 32 communes, each with an elected mayor and municipal council. The communes are grouped into four administrative subdivisions, with headquarters at La Foa, Koné, Poindimié, and Wé (Lifou). Nouméa has a separate municipal government.

Everyone born in New Caledonia is legally a French citizen and can vote in French presidential elections. Two deputies are elected to the French National Assembly, one from the east coast of Grande Terre and outer islands, one from the west coast and Nouméa. A senator, elected by the municipal and provincial councils, is also sent to Paris.

ECONOMY

New Caledonia has a classic colonial economy, being primarily a source of raw materials for France and a market for finished French products. France supplies 46% of the territory's imports, other European Union countries 17%, Australia 10%, the U.S. seven percent, and Japan six percent. New Caledonia's mineral exports are sent to Japan (30%), France (28%), and other European Union countries (21%). Despite exports averaging half a billion Australian dollars a year, imports exceed a billion dollars and the territory has the second largest trade deficit in the South Pacific (after Tahiti-Polynesia).

Economic power is centered in Greater Nouméa, with 70% of the retail trading space, all of the industry except mining, and most tourism and government services. The French state provides 30% of the territorial budget and spends around US$250 million a year on the salaries of civil servants seconded from metropolitan France. Since the signing of the Matignon Accords in 1988, per capita aid to New Caledonia has doubled. A high portion of development aid ends up as profits for French companies, which carry out government contracts.

The territory's taxation system is based on high indirect taxes on imports and exports (thereby inflating the cost of living), while direct company and income taxes (which would fall most heavily on Europeans) remain extremely low. The minimum monthly wage in New Caledonia is CFP 70,000 (compared to just Vt8000 in Vanuatu), but the income of the average Kanak family is only a third that of a Caledonian French family. The old *Caldoche* families—Ballande, Barrau, Lafleur, Frogier, Daly, de Rouvray, and Pentecost—control the local economy and politics. They profit most from colonial rule and are firmly committed to continuing it.

Mining

New Caledonia ranks third in world nickel production (after Canada and Russia), and nickel accounts for 90% of territorial exports. A third of the nickel by value is exported as raw ore, two-thirds partly refined. The nickel ore is high grade, being free of arsenic, although the presence of asbestos has been linked to a high lung cancer rate among miners.

Nickel is required for the manufacture of high-tensile metals used in the nuclear industry and armaments production. (France is the world's largest arms exporter, with sales to 56 countries.) Because of this, the French government considers nickel a "strategic" metal, and all mining permits must be approved by the Minister for Industrial Development in Paris. This, and the requirement that there be 50% French participation in any foreign investment in the territory, restricts the exploitation of nickel to French companies. Société le Nickel, which owns the smelter at Nouméa, was part of the Rothschild international mining conglomerate until its nationalization in 1982. Today it is part of the government-controlled Eramet conglomerate.

There are large nickel mines at Thio, Poro, and Népoui. In 1990 Kanak-controlled North Province purchased an 85% interest in Jacques Lafleur's Société Minière de Pacifique Sud in a French-financed move to ensure a steady supply of ore. Chrome and iron ore were formerly exported, but these operations have closed due to market conditions.

While half the population enjoys the benefits of nickel mining, the other half suffers its effects. The industry has led to the importation of foreign labor, making the Kanaks a minority in their own land, while that very land has been expropriated from beneath their feet. New Caledonia has the world's highest incidence of asthma-related deaths due to nickel dust thrown up by the mining and smelting. The World Health Organization has ruled that nickel dust is such a toxic cancer-causing agent that there is no safe level of human exposure.

Tourism

After nickel, tourism is the most important industry, with Japan, Australia, France, and New Zealand providing the most visitors. New Caledonia is the only South Pacific country where Japan supplies the largest number of tourists—nearly a third of the 80,753 arrivals in 1993 were Japanese, a result of nonstop flights from Tokyo. The number of North American visitors is negligible. Current plans to market New Caledonia as

an ecotourism destination are at odds with the widespread environmental devastation wrought by nickel mining.

Recently the Kanak-controlled North Province has moved into tourism in a big way with a new Club Med at Hienghène, a major resort between Koumac and Poum, and direct investments in existing Nouméa hotels such as the Ibis and Surf. In partnership with the French Accor hotel chain, North Province has tried to break the stranglehold on tourism previously held by local French businessmen. French-controlled South Province responded by limiting the opening hours of Nouméa's Casino Royal (which North Province had bought) and granting a casino license to the newly built Hôtel Le Méridien.

In the tribal areas, the Kanaks have resisted the efforts of French businessmen to set up hotels and the few French resorts that did appear on the outer islands were later burned. Instead, a system of Melanesian-owned *gîtes* provides accommodations in rural areas. Thus, as guests of Kanak people, visitors to remote areas are not viewed as intruders.

Agriculture

Agriculture supports 38% of the population of New Caledonia but represents only 1.8% of the gross domestic product. Only four percent of Europeans work in agriculture, compared to 60% of the Kanaks, yet two-thirds of the arable land is controlled by 1,000 French settlers. The

Cité Pierre Lenquette, a low-cost housing project for Kanaks directly downwind of Nouméa's nickel smelter

DAVID STANLEY

greater part of this alienated land is concentrated in large estates over 15 square km in size, owned by a total of only 37 individuals. One French farm alone covers 367 square km; another is 149 square km.

Land remains the basic issue behind the political unrest in New Caledonia, and a Melanesian land-*using* culture continues to find itself confronted by a European land-*owning* culture. The French Socialists attempted to buy tracts of land from the *colons* and give them back to the original owners. The government agency in charge of this program was bombed by right-wing terrorists twice in 1985, and the next year Jacques Chirac's hardline conservative government simply abolished it.

Yams are the main subsistence crop, followed by taro, manioc, and sweet potatoes. From 1865 to 1890, the cultivation of sugarcane was attempted; it failed due to labor costs and milling problems. Cotton was grown from 1860 right up until the 1930s, when drought, disease, and the world depression brought it to an end. Coffee, introduced in the first days of French colonization, is still grown today, mostly the *robusta* type. Kanaks participate in coffee growing, but the processing and marketing is in the hands of large French companies such as Ballande.

By far, beef cattle raising has always been the most important monetary agricultural activity, mostly large herds kept by Europeans on the west coast. Due to high demand, meat still has to be imported, however. Pig and shrimp farming are well developed. Yet on an island that could feed a population many times its size, food still accounts for nearly a fifth of New Caledonia's imports by value.

THE PEOPLE

Of the 164,000 inhabitants of New Caledonia, 45% are Melanesian, 34% European, nine percent Wallisian, three percent Tahitian, three percent Indonesian, and two percent Vietnamese. Other Asians, ni-Vanuatu, West Indians, and Arabs make up the remaining four percent. About 60% of the Europeans were born in New Caledonia. Most of the other 40% are French civil servants and their families temporarily present in the territory, or refugees from the former French colonies in Algeria, Vietnam, and Vanuatu. The Vietnamese and Indonesians were brought in to work in the mines early this century; by 1921 some 4,000 of them were present.

Nearly 60% of the population lives in Nouméa and vicinity, including 80% of the Europeans, 85% of the Asians, and 90% of the Polynesians. The capital is growing fast as regional centers like La Foa, Bourail, Koumac, and Poindimié stagnate, with populations around the 1,000 mark. With 70% of the total population living in cities and towns, New Caledonia is the most heavily urbanized entity in the South Pacific.

During the nickel boom of 1969-73, the European population increased in size by a third, and the number of Polynesians doubled. In the late 1990s jumbo jets from Paris continue to unload dozens of new European immigrants each week. At the 1989 census, 22% of the total population was listed as born outside the region and this percentage is believed to be much higher today. These migrations were and are directly encouraged by the French government specifically to make the Kanaks a minority, thus ensuring continued French rule.

Of the 21,630 convicts transported to New Caledonia from 1864 to 1897, just over a thousand stayed on as settlers *(colons)* on land granted them when they were freed. These and other early French arrivals are called *Caldoches,* while the present transients who come only to make money to take back to France are referred to as *métros* or *zoreilles* (the ears). French expatriates holding government jobs in New Caledonia are notoriously overpaid. French shopkeepers and small ranchers in the interior are known as *broussards,* while the 2,500 French who migrated to the territory from Algeria are the *pieds noir* (black feet).

The Kanaks are also known as Ti-Va-Ouere, the Brothers of the Earth. They own all of the smaller islands surrounding Grande Terre and their reservations on the main island. There is a striking contrast between the affluent French community around Nouméa and the poverty of Kanak villages on the northeast coast of Grande Terre and on the outer islands.

About 67% of the total population is Catholic, 21% Evangelical, and four percent Muslim, but religion is polarized, with 90% of French settlers Catholic, and Kanaks constituting 90% of the membership of the two branches of the Église Évangélique.

La Coutume

In essence, the present conflict in New Caledonia is a clash of cultures. For over a century, the Kanaks have been obliged to adopt a foreign way of life that styled itself as superior to their own. Despite the Kanaks' acceptance of a foreign language, religion, dress, and money economy, indigenous custom *(la Coutume)* continues to maintain a surprising strength just beneath the surface. Today the Kanak people struggle not only to regain their lands but also to reassert their own culture over another, which they both embrace and reject.

Language

There are some 30 indigenous languages, all Austronesian, which can be broadly organized into eight related areas: five on Grande Terre and one on each of the Loyalties. The Kanak languages all developed from a single mother tongue but are today mutually incomprehensible (thus it is incorrect and denigrating to call them "dialects"). Lifou is the language with the most speakers: about 8,000 on Lifou itself, plus a few thousand in Nouméa. French is the common language understood by most (although 14.3% of the Kanak population cannot speak French). Very few people in New Caledonia understand English.

Language Courses

In 1987 the **Université Française du Pacifique** was created, with campuses in New Caledonia and Tahiti-Polynesia. The Centre Universitaire de Nouvelle-Calédonie (B.P. 4477, Nouméa; tel. 25-49-55, fax 25-48-29) near Magenta Air-

port and at Nouville offers courses in the arts, social sciences, languages, law, and science. The academic year for CUNC's 1,200 students runs from February to September, with examinations continuing into October. Foreign students are welcome, but application must be made through the cultural adviser at the French consulate or embassy in the country of residence, and pre-enrollment formalities must be complete by December. Annual tuition fees are reasonable at CFP 22,000, and the university hostel is just CFP 15,000 a month for students arriving under an exchange program, but there are only 35 rooms. Lectures are in French, so foreigners may have to take a refresher course, and there are other academic requirements. If you're interested, write for information.

French language and civilization courses specially designed for English speakers are offered by the **Centre de Rencontres et d'Echanges Internationaux du Pacifique** (B.P. 3755, Nouméa; tel. 25-41-24, fax 25-40-58). CREIPAC is based in the old chapel at Nouville, just outside Nouméa; most of the students are in university groups from Australia and New Zealand and come to round out their French studies. Individuals are also welcome, and the usual programs last two or three weeks, with 15 hours of classes a week. It's not cheap: instruction alone runs CFP 3500 an hour for one person, CFP 2500 pp for two, CFP 2000 pp for three, CFP 1500 pp for four, with a 15-hour minimum. The instructors are professionals trained in teaching French as a foreign language, and advanced students qualify for diplomas. All-inclusive packages covering lessons, accommodations, some meals, airport transfers, and sightseeing excursions are available with prices substantially reduced for groups of 15 or more.

ON THE ROAD

Highlights

New Caledonia's greatest attractions are undoubtedly its capital, the northeast coast of the main island, and the neighbor islands. Nouméa combines the ambience of a French provincial town with the excitement of a Côte d'Azure resort. Hienghène on Grande Terre's east coast is a place of remarkable beauty, with high mountains dropping dramatically to the sea. The Isle of Pines's Kuto/Kanuméra area is postcard perfect with exquisite white beaches backed by towering pines. New Caledonia's finest beach runs right up one side of Ouvéa, also a scene of martyrdom in the struggle of the Kanak people against the scourge of French colonialism.

Sports and Recreation

Organized sporting activities are most easily arranged at Nouméa or on the Isle of Pines. The "Yacht Charters" section under "Nouméa" lists several bareboat and crewed yacht charter opportunities, and the sheltered waters from Nouméa to Prony Bay and the Isle of Pines are a prime cruising area. Windsurfers ply the waters off Nouméa's Anse Vata and the Isle of Pines's Kuto Bay.

Two companies offer scuba diving from Nouméa, but it's also possible to rent tanks and head off on your own. As yet, the only other places where scuba diving is offered are on the Isle of Pines and at the Malabou Beach Hôtel north of Koumac. Nouméa has two 18-hole golf courses, and another 18-hole course is near Bouloupari. The Poé Beach Resort near Bourail has a nine-hole course. There are numerous hiking opportunities around these large islands. The best-known long-distance hike is across the mountains from Hienghène to Voh.

Terra Incognita (B.P. 18, Dumbea; tel. 41-61-19) offers weekend canoeing and kayaking trips to wild rivers, tranquil lakes, and scenic bays throughout the territory. This is a great way to see some of New Caledonia's beauty spots at their best while enjoying an exhilarating sport with local pros. They also rent canoes and kayaks.

Music

Traditional Kanak musical culture is divided into household music (lullabies, vocal games, healing and religious songs, flute tunes) and that of public ceremonies (rhythmical speeches, mimic dances, male songs, Protestant hymns). The ceremonial music is performed during funerals or mourning, at the feast of the first yam, during Christian religious services, and at modern cultural events. Despite the linguistic diversity, Kanak music and dance are remarkably uniform across Grande Terre, though there are differences with the Loyalty Islands.

The closing ceremony of the yearlong period of mourning for an important chief involves a great ceremonial exchange between members of the paternal and maternal lines. A male orator standing on a wooden platform delivers a rhythmical speech as men around him utter hushing sounds and the gifts are exchanged. In the Loyalties such speakers stand on the ground, and rhythm is not employed.

The climax of many ceremonies is a round dance, which lasts an entire night. A dozen musicians pounding bamboo tubes on the ground, shaking and scraping beaters, urge on two male singers as the dancers circulate counterclockwise around the group stamping their feet. The relays of singers relate historical events and claim magical inspiration. Hundreds of people may participate in a round dance at a major ceremony, and there must be no pause in the music or dancing until dawn.

Mimic dance tells a story through gestures and often imitates nature, such as the hopping or strutting of birds. The dancers stand in two lines, with lead dancers weaving between them as bamboo tubes are pounded or struck. On Grande Terre male mimic dancers, dressed in coconut leaves or grass, their bodies painted black, act out legends, history, or important cycles such as yam growing. Only in the Loyalties are such dances accompanied by a mixed choir. Mimic dancers in the Loyalties wear coconut rattle garters and strike bundles of hand-held leaves as they perform mimic dances of events such as the hauling of a canoe onto a beach.

Polyphony (music with several independent but harmonious melodic parts) comes naturally to most Pacific peoples, and the four-part mixed choirs of New Caledonia demonstrate how strongly Kanak vocal music has been influenced by 19th-century Protestant hymns.

The compact disc *Kanak Songs: Feasts and Lullabies* (LDX 274 909), in the Le Chant du Monde series, released in 1990 by the Musée de l'Homme, Paris, provides an excellent introduction to the folk music of the Kanaks. For contemporary urban Kanaks, reggae is all the rage.

Public Holidays and Festivals

Public holidays include New Year's Day (1 January), Easter Monday (March/April), Labor Day (1 May), 1945 Victory Day (8 May), Ascension Day (a Thursday in May), Pentecost (a Monday in May), Bastille Day (14 July), Assumption Day (15 August), New Caledonia Day (24 September), All Saints' Day (1 November), Armistice Day (11 November), and Christmas Day (25 December). The school holidays run from 15 December till the end of February.

Bastille Day (14 July) features a military parade and aerial show at Anse Vata in Nouméa. The parade on New Caledonia Day (24 September) recalls the day in 1853 when Admiral Despointes took possession of New Caledonia for France. The Agricultural Fair at Bourail in August features rodeos and other colorful activities. Don't miss it. If you're in Nouméa around the second Saturday in October, ask about *Braderie,* a popular street fair for which the whole population turns out. Stores in Nouméa hold a sale called Bravo l'Été at this time.

There's a triathlon the third Sunday in April, an international marathon the third Sunday in July, a bicycle race around Grande Terre in August or September, and a car race about the end of November.

Accommodations

Prices at the hotels are manageable for two, but high for one. Hotel rooms are subject to the three percent general sales tax (TGPS), and this tax is usually not included in the quoted prices and is added later. Some of the top-end hotels raise their rates during high seasons: in May, 15 August to 15 September, and 15 De-

cember to 31 January. Others only have two seasons: high October to March, and low April to September. In this book we quote the high season prices. A small French country hotel is called a *relais,* while an *auberge de jeunesse* is a youth hostel.

New Caledonia's well-developed system of *gîtes* is unique in the Pacific. Basically a *gîte* offers simple Melanesian-style accommodations in thatched cottages, usually near a beach. Toilet facilities may be private or shared, and electricity may or may not be installed. Since the *gîtes* are run by the Kanaks themselves, you'll be readily accepted in the community if you're staying there. Though some are poorly run, the best *gîtes* are excellent value. The main flaw in the system is that Air Calédonie and the territorial tourism authorities require the *gîte* owners to charge unreasonably high prices to prevent them from being too competitive with the French-owned hotels in Nouméa (and to allow them to pay off their government loans). Bargaining isn't possible and about the only way to get around an absurdly high official tariff is to ask to camp on the premises, which in most cases the Kanak owners will happily allow you to do for a reasonable fee. Shared cooking facilities are often provided and meals (CFP 1500-3500) are served. Seafood is a specialty, but here too the *gîtes* are required to charge about the same as Nouméa restaurants, so check what other people are having before ordering as the price may not correspond to what you get. The *gîtes* are concentrated on the Loyalty Islands and Isle of Pines, but some are also found around Grande Terre. To reserve a cottage at any of the *gîtes* go to **Air Calédonie** (B.P. 212, Nouméa; tel. 28-65-64, fax 28-13-40), 39 rue de Verdun, Nouméa. If you only want to camp at a *gîte* you can just show up.

Women should keep in mind that while monokini sunbathing is okay in Nouméa, it could lead to serious problems anywhere else in the territory. *Never* swim topless or naked in front of a Kanak village. There are lots of isolated beaches where you can do it, and if you want to be seen, there's always Nouméa.

Camping

New Caledonia is one of the few places in the South Pacific where camping is widely understood, practiced, and accepted. French soldiers on leave from Nouméa do it all the time, and bourgeois French locals consider it a legitimate way to spend a weekend. There are many organized campgrounds on Grande Terre. On the outer islands camp at a *gîte*.

Almost anyone you ask will readily give you permission to pitch your tent, but do ask. Otherwise you might be violating custom and could cause yourself a needless problem. Take care with your gear around Poindimié, where rip-offs have occurred. Otherwise it's hassle-free.

Food

New Caledonian's restaurants are good but very expensive. The easiest way to keep your bill down is to stick to one main plate *(plat de résistance)* and eschew appetizers, salads, alcohol, coffee, and dessert. The bread and water on the table are free and tipping is unnecessary. Also watch for the *plat du jour*, a reasonably priced businessperson's lunch of two courses, bread, and dessert. Outside Nouméa most hotel restaurants offer a *prix fixe* dinner, though it's usually cheaper to order one plate à la carte if you can. At restaurants and bars, draft beer *(bière à la pression)* is slightly cheaper than bottled or tinned beer, and table wine *(vin ordinaire)* in a carafe is less expensive than bottled wine.

In Nouméa pizza is one of the less expensive things to have, and there are many Vietnamese restaurants. If you've never tried Vietnamese food, you'll find it's like Chinese food,

stocking up with baguettes at a Nouméa bakery

only spicier. Curries are good value, as is *porc au sucre* (sweet pork), which comes with "sour" (vinegary) vegetables to maintain the Oriental *yin-yang* balance. French *coq au vin* and North African couscous are other dishes to try.

A *bougna* is a Kanak food parcel consisting of sliced root vegetables such as taro, manioc, and yams soaked in coconut milk, wrapped in banana leaves with pork, chicken, or seafood, and cooked over hot stones in an earthen oven for a couple of hours. If you attend a Kanak feast you'll see dozens of *bougna* packages consumed by countless relatives. At some *gîtes* you can order a *bougna* capable of feeding four persons for about CFP 3500.

Since New Caledonia is associated with the European Union, the foods available in the supermarkets are totally different from those offered in most other South Pacific countries. Buy long crusty *baguettes* and flaky *croissants* to complement the pâté, wine, and cheese. Together these are the makings of a memorable picnic. Note that grocery stores are not allowed to sell beer or wine from Saturday at 1200 to Monday at 0600. Note, too, how little local produce is available in the stores.

Visas and Officialdom

Citizens of the European Union, Canada, the U.S., Japan, and New Zealand do not require a visa. Others should check with their airline a few weeks ahead—Australians must apply for a visa (free) in advance. For details, call the French consulate in Canberra (tel. 02/6270-5111), Sydney (tel. 02/9261-5779), or Melbourne (tel. 03/9820-0921).

Visitors from the U.S., Japan, Switzerland, and most Commonwealth countries are allowed to stay one month. Citizens of European Union countries get three months and French are admitted for an unlimited stay. Everyone (French included) must have an onward ticket. This requirement is strictly enforced and there's no chance of slipping through without one. Visa extensions are handled by the Police de l'Air et des Frontières (tel. 27-28-22), either at La Tontouta Airport or at Nouméa Port.

Nouméa is the only port of entry for cruising yachts. Arriving yachts should contact the port authorities over channel 67, who will send Customs and Immigration to meet them at the new

DESTINATION NEW CALEDONIA

wharf on Moselle Bay. The formalities are simpler than those in Tahiti-Polynesia and no bond is required. The Club Nautique Caledonien (tel. 26-27-27) is at Baie des Pêcheurs.

Money

The currency is the French Pacific franc or CFP (pronounced "say eff pay"). There are banknotes of 500, 1000, 5000, and 10,000 and coins of one, two, five, 10, 20, 50, and 100. The CFP is linked to the French franc: CFP 100 equals 5.5 French francs. You can determine the current value of the CFP by finding out how many French francs you receive for your dollar/pound, then multiplying by 18.18. As an approximate rule of thumb, US$1 = CFP 87. New Caledonia and Tahiti-Polynesia use the same currency, and although the notes may bear Nouméa or Papeete mint marks, the two are freely interchangeable.

Banks are open weekdays 0730-1530. All banks charge CFP 500 commission for each foreign currency transaction, whether buying or selling, and usually give the same rate for cash or traveler's checks. However French francs are converted back and forth at a fixed rate without commission, so that's the best currency to bring by far. It's difficult or impossible to change foreign currency in rural areas—do it before you leave Nouméa. Credit cards are only useful in Nouméa.

New Caledonia's form of taxation—high import and export duties—and the elevated salaries paid to local French officials make this the South Pacific's most expensive country to visit by far. In addition, there's a three percent sales tax, which also applies to hotel rooms. You'll be hard pressed to find a cup of coffee for under CFP 200 or the simplest *plat du jour* meal for even CFP 1500. Camera film is also much cheaper in Fiji, Vanuatu, and Australia, so bring a good supply. Backpackers can easily survive because hitchhiking is easy, camping is accepted, and the supermarkets sell excellent picnic fare, but the cost of living will wallop you if you want to travel in relative comfort. If you're planning to rent a car and stay in regular hotels, try to link up with another like-minded couple as the price for four is only slightly more than what one or two will spend. On the positive side, tipping isn't usually done in New Caledonia and is sometimes even considered offensive. Notice how the locals never tip in restaurants.

Post and Telecommunications

Faxes *(télécopies)* can be sent from any post office (CFP 900 a page to Australia or New Zealand). Most businesses receive their mail through their post office box or *boîte postale* (B.P.).

The cheapest way to make international calls is by using a telephone card *(télécarte),* available at any post office in denominations of CFP 1000 (25 units), CFP 3000 (80 units), and CFP 5000 (140 units). Not only do calls placed with telephone cards have no three-minute minimum, but they're charged at a rate 25% lower than if the call were placed manually through an operator. This savings is significant in an area where the basic charges are high (CFP 285 a minute to Australia or New Zealand, CFP 569 a minute to Canada or the U.S., CFP 640 a minute to Britain or Germany, all using a card). To place an international call with a card, dial the international access code 00, the country code, the area code, and the number. International calls placed from hotel rooms are charged double.

Telephone cards can also be used for local calls, which cost CFP 32 for six minutes 0600-2000, CFP 32 for 12 minutes 2000-0600. Interprovincial calls within New Caledonia are CFP 32 a minute 0800-1600, CFP 32 for 90 seconds 0600-0800 and 1600-2000, and CFP 32 for two minutes 2000-0600. For the local operator, dial 10; for the international operator, dial 19; for information, dial 12.

New Caledonia's telephone code is 687.

Business Hours and Time

Business hours are weekdays 0730-1100 and 1400-1800 and Saturday 0730-1100, though large supermarkets in Nouméa remain open Monday to Saturday 0700-2000 and Sunday 0730-1130 and 1500-1900. Banking hours are weekdays 0730-1530. Main post offices are open weekdays 0745-1115 and 1215-1500, Saturday 0730-1100. Smaller branch post offices around Nouméa are closed on Saturday.

New Caledonia follows the same hour as Vanuatu, an hour before Sydney and an hour behind Auckland and Fiji.

Media

Radio and television in the colony are dominated by the government-owned "Radiodiffusion Television Française pour l'Outre-Mer" (RFO), and 90% of the programming originates in France. The rest is mostly sports.

The only daily paper in the territory is *Les Nouvelles Calédoniennes* (B.P. 179, Nouméa; tel. 27-25-84, fax 28-16-27), owned since 1987 by French press baron Robert Hersant, owner of the Paris daily *Le Figaro*. Several weekly papers are published, including *Les Nouvelles Hebdo* (B.P. 3577, Nouméa; tel. 28-62-33).

Health

The government health service is run by the army, and most of the doctors are military officers recruited in France. Tourists are usually referred to private doctors. A yellow fever vaccination is required, but only if you've been in an infected area (South America or Africa) within the previous six days. Recommended vaccinations include poliomyelitis, immune globulin or hepatitis A, and typhoid fever, though only for those traveling outside Nouméa. By mid-1994 HIV antibodies had been detected in 115 people and there were 37 confirmed cases of AIDS, one of the highest per capita incidences in the South Pacific. New Caledonia's tap water contains high levels of heavy metals resulting from mining, but it's unlikely to cause problems on a short visit. On the brighter side, there's no malaria.

TRANSPORTATION

Getting There

Air France (tel. 28-88-11) is the main international carrier connecting New Caledonia to Europe and North America with direct flights to Nouméa twice a week along a Paris-Singapore-Jakarta-Sydney-Nouméa routing. Their weekly Nouméa-Papeete flight connects in Tahiti with flights to/from Los Angeles and Paris, making it possible to go right around the world on Air France. Twice a week Air France flies nonstop between Nouméa and Tokyo. All flights are heavily booked, so don't forget to reconfirm your onward reservations, otherwise they'll be canceled automatically. (Air France has gone to a lot of trouble to hire the most surly, unhelpful staff for their reservations office in Nouméa, so just smile and console yourself that we've already sent them our compliments here.)

AOM French Airlines (tel. 24-12-12, fax 24-12-13) flies from Paris (Orly) to Nouméa via Bangkok weekly. Their round-the-world ticket Paris-Los Angeles-Papeete-Nouméa-Bangkok-Paris is several hundred dollars cheaper than any comparable fare on Air France. AOM's low season for Nouméa flights is mid-September to mid-June. For more information on AOM and Air France see "Getting There" in this book's main introduction.

Air Calédonie International (B.P. 3736, Nouméa; tel. 27-61-62, fax 27-27-72), a local carrier based in New Caledonia, connects the territory to Auckland, Brisbane, Melbourne, Nandi, Papeete, Port Vila, Sydney, and Wallis Island. Their weekly flight to Wallis and Papeete is operated jointly with Air France. The most direct access to New Caledonia from North America is via Air Calédonie International's weekly flight to/from Nandi, Fiji, although connections through Australia are much more frequent.

The national airlines of several neighboring countries also fly straight to Nouméa: **Air New Zealand** (tel. 28-34-39) from Auckland weekly; **Air Vanuatu** from Port Vila daily; and **Qantas** (tel. 28-65-46) from Brisbane, Melbourne, and Sydney. All of the above flights operate out of La Tontouta Airport (NOU).

Getting Around by Air

Air Calédonie (B.P. 212, Nouméa; tel. 25-21-77, fax 25-03-26), the domestic commuter airline, uses Magenta Airport (GEA) near Nouméa. Several times a day their 46-passenger ATR 42s and 19-passenger Dornier 228s fly to the Loyalty Islands (Maré, Lifou, and Ouvéa), CFP 7490 one-way. The interisland link between the three larger Loyalties and Tiga costs CFP 2840 to CFP 5540 per sector. Ask Air Calédonie about special package tickets that allow a visit to all four Loyalty Islands from Nouméa for one price with accommodations included. There are two flights a day to the Isle of Pines, CFP 5030 one-way. Twice a week you can fly from Koumac to remote Belep off the northwest coast of Grande Terre, CFP 5630 one-way.

On all these flights, the baggage allowance is 10 kg pp, and there's a CFP 1000 penalty if you change or cancel a reservation less than 48 hours in advance. Reconfirm your return reservation immediately upon arrival at an outer island. It's usually easy to get a seat to the Loyalty Islands, but the flights to the Isle of Pines are often fully booked by Japanese day-trippers, so inquire well ahead. If you're told the plane is full, take the ship to the Isle of Pines and fly back. Also check the daily French tabloid newspaper for special deals on weekend trips from Nouméa.

Getting Around by Other Means

Grande Terre has good bus service and the fares are reasonable (turn to the Nouméa section for information on buses and local boat services). Cheapest are the buses marked *subventionne,* subsidized mail runs; inquire about these at local post offices. All around the island *beware of buses leaving 15 minutes early!* Hitchhiking is easy and you'll have some very interesting conversations, if you speak French.

For information on interisland boat service, turn to "Transportation" in the "Nouméa" section.

AIRPORTS

International Airport

La Tontouta Airport (NOU) is 53 km northwest of Nouméa and 112 km southeast of Bourail. As your plane is taxiing up to the terminal, glance across the runway at the French air force hangars to see if their counterinsurgency helicopters or Neptune bombers are in. It's also fun to pick out the sandbagged machine gun posts around the airport perimeter.

The S.C.E.A. airport bus charges a stiff CFP 1800 for the ride to Nouméa; private minibuses charge about the same. The Nouméa Youth Hostel has an arrangement with S.C.E.A. whereby you get your first night in the dormitory free if you take that bus, and when you want to return to La Tontouta, the hostel sells S.C.E.A. tickets for only CFP 500. Although foreign tourists are routinely herded toward the S.C.E.A. bus, you can also wait for the blue interurban bus (CFP 400), to the left as you leave the terminal. They run hourly from Monday to Saturday, but only until 1800 (every other hour on Saturday afternoon). On Sunday the blue bus runs every two hours. The blue bus follows the old road through picturesque towns and carries colorful local passengers, while the tourist bus zips along the toll road nonstop. Airport-bound, don't plan a tight connection if you travel this way. A taxi to Nouméa will be an absurd CFP 8000, or you can rent a car from Avis (tel. 35-11-74) or Hertz (tel. 35-12-77) at the airport. You could also walk one km out to the main highway and hitch.

The airport bank is open for most arrivals, but not all departures, offering about the same rate you'll get in town. If it's closed, there's another bank on the main highway near the airport. If you think you may later want to store excess luggage at the airport, ask about it at the information desk upon arrival. There's no airport tax.

Domestic Airport

Magenta Airport (GEA) is five km northeast of downtown Nouméa. City bus no. 7 will drop you right at the door (every 15 minutes 0515-1845, CFP 100). A taxi from the Place des Cocotiers costs about CFP 800. There are no coin lockers, so leave excess baggage elsewhere. Air Calédonie has a reservations office (open weekdays 0730-1115 and 1400-1730, Saturday 0730-1115) at the airport.

NOUMÉA

Nouméa was founded in 1854 by Tardy de Montravel, who called it Port de France, and in 1860 the French moved their capital from Balade to Nouméa. A French governor arrived two years later and convicts condemned to the penal colony on Île Nou followed in 1864. Robert Louis Stevenson, who visited in 1890, remarked that Nouméa was "built from vermouth cases." The town remained a backwater until 1942, when American military forces arrived to transform this landlocked port into a bastion for the war against Japan. Admiral "Bull" Halsey directed the Solomon Islands campaign from his headquarters on Anse Vata.

Today this thriving maritime center near the south end of the New Caledonian mainland is a busy, crowded, cosmopolitan city made rich mostly by nickel. Over half the population of the territory resides here, almost 100,000 people if residents of nearby Mont Dore, Dumbéa, and

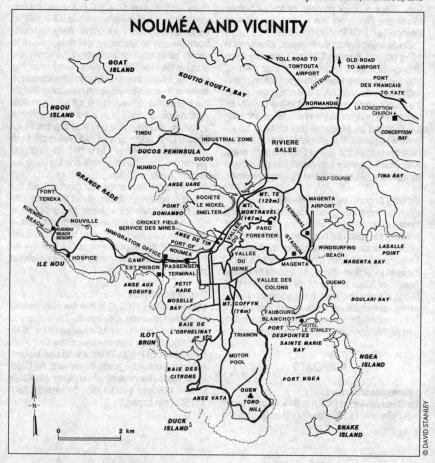

NOUMÉA AND VICINITY

© DAVID STANLEY

Païta are included. The city is predominantly French, the only South Pacific town with a white majority. Kanak women in their Mother Hubbard dresses add color to the market area, and bathing beauties bask at Nouméa's swank Anse Vata beach, where most of the luxury hotels are found. Windsurfers and sailboaters hover offshore, and it's clear that this is a moneyed tourist's paradise. The city is especially beautiful from November to January, when the flame trees (poincianas) bloom red. This is Paris *sans hauteur*.

Since it's only a couple of hours by jet from Australia or New Zealand, most tourists limit their visit to Nouméa, but New Caledonia has much more to offer than just its capital city. Leave Nouméa and you're back in Melanesia, among the island's original Kanak inhabitants, for whom land and custom are worth more than money. From European consumers to third-world tribes it's quite a contrast, and you can't claim to have seen the territory until you get across to the northeast coast or out to one of the islands.

When planning your day, remember that on weekdays nearly everything in Nouméa closes for the 1100-1400 siesta—a three-hour break! So get an early start.

SIGHTS

Historic Nouméa

The **Place des Cocotiers,** with its statues, fountains, and *pétanque* players is the ideal place to begin your tour. In December the poincianas (flame trees) set this wonderful central square alight in hues of red and orange. Points of interest include the **old town hall** (1880) on the north side of the square, the Monumental Fountain (1892), point zero for all mileages in the territory, in the middle, and the graffiti-covered statue of Admiral Olry, governor 1878-1880, at the west end.

Walk north on rue du Général Mangin past rue de l'Alma (Nouméa's trendy shopping street) to the **old military hospital,** built by convict laborers in the 1880s and still the main medical facility in the city. Turn right on avenue Paul Doumer and you'll come to **Government House,** the residence of the French High Commissioner. The quaint colonial police with round

caps guarding the building are French *gendarmes*. Go right, then left up rue de la République two blocks, to the **Territorial Congress** on the right.

Walk south on boulevard Vauban to the **Protestant Church** (1893) at the head of rue de l'Alma. Continue south on Vauban to **St. Joseph's Catholic Cathedral** (1894), which was built by convict labor. Enter this fine old building overlooking the city through the side doors to see the stained-glass windows. Continue east from the cathedral along rue Frédéric Surleau to the **French army barracks** *(caserne)* on Place Bir Hakeim. The barracks have changed very little since their construction in 1869. The war memorial in front of the barracks lists on three sides the full names of the European servicemen from New Caledonia who died in WW I but only the places of origin of the 372 Kanaks who died.

Return west along avenue de la Victoire to 41 avenue du Maréchal Foch and the **Bernheim Library** (tel. 27-23-43; open Tuesday and Thursday 1330-1830, Wednesday and Friday 0900-1100 and 1330-1900, Saturday 0900-1100 and 1330-1730). In 1901 Louis Bernheim, a miner who made his fortune in the territory, donated the money for its first library (the only time a local mining mogul has ever given away anything). What had been the New Caledonian pavilion at the Paris Universal Exposition of 1900 was used to house the collection, and the original building still stands alongside the present reading room. To this day it's the only real public library in the territory.

New Caledonia Museum

This outstanding museum (B.P. 2393, Nouméa; tel. 27-41-79), 45 avenue du Maréchal Foch, two blocks south of the Bernheim Library, was founded in 1971. There's a great deal of material on Kanak culture: woodcarvings, masks, daily implements, canoe and house designs, petroglyphs, and *Lapita* pottery. In the courtyard is an unusual botanical collection, and behind the museum a traditional full-sized *grande case* (big house) from Canala. The main shortcoming is that all of the labels are in French only. It's open daily except Tuesday and holidays 0900-1115 and 1215-1630; admission is free—don't miss it.

If you'd like to clear your head after the museum, climb **Mont Coffyn** for the sweeping view; there's a ceramic map at the top for orientation. Go south on avenue du Maréchal Foch to rue Duquesne, turn left and go up two blocks to rue Guynemer, where you turn right, then left, and go up the hill. Use the map in this book. As you stand beside the immense two-armed Cross of Lorraine, you'll be able to pick out Amédée Lighthouse.

Nearby Beaches

Baie des Citrons and Anse Vata, Nouméa's finest beaches, are near the southern end of Nouméa's scalloped peninsula. Very attractive and easily accessible by bus, they're also cluttered with hotels and tend to be crowded; elsewhere in New Caledonia you can usually have a beach all to yourself. Topless sunbathing is fine for men and women at Anse Vata and Baie des Citrons.

The **Nouméa Aquarium** (B.P. 395, Nouméa; tel. 26-27-31; open Tuesday to Friday 0930-1130 and 1330-1645, Saturday and Sunday 1330-1645, admission CFP 600, students CFP 200, children CFP 100), located between Baie des Citrons and Anse Vata, has a good collection of reef fish, sponges, cuttlefish, nautilus, sea snakes, sea slugs, and fluorescent corals. It tends to be a little overrated, however, and the small size and jewelrylike displays are drawbacks. Go early on a fine afternoon, as there's no artificial lighting.

On Anse Vata east of the Aquarium is the new headquarters of the **South Pacific Commission** (tel. 26-20-00), which opened in 1995. A description of this regional organization is provided in this book's main introduction under the heading "Government." Next door is ORSTOM, a major French scientific research agency.

A road to the left just beyond the municipal swimming pool leads up to **Ouen Toro Hill** and a fine panorama (a 15-minute walk). Two six-inch cannons were set up here in 1940 by the Australian army to cover the reef passage in the vicinity of Amédée Lighthouse, visible to the south. Promenade Pierre Vernier along Baie Sainte Marie east of Ouen Toro is an attractive place to stroll between the rows of palms, and there's a training track complete with pull-up bars, balance logs, etc.

Nouville

This former island, **Île Nou,** jutting west of Nouméa, is now connected to the city by a land-reclamation project using waste from the nickel smelter. English seaman John Paddon had a trading post here as early as 1845. After 1864, Île Nou became notorious when the French converted it into a penal colony housing more than 3,000 prisoners at a time. **Camp Est Prison** on Île Nou is still a major prison where Kanak freedom fighters are held.

Bus no. 13 will take you directly to the chapel, workshops, and buildings of the original 19th-century prison, until recently occupied by the **Mental Institution** (hospice). A school teaching French as a foreign language is now here (see "Language Courses" in the chapter introduction). There are quiet beaches to the west of the hospice, and you can walk the dirt road right around the end of Île Nou in about an hour.

An evocative sight is **Fort Tereka** (1878), perched on a hilltop at the far west end of Île Nou. This spot offers one of the finest scenic viewpoints in the South Pacific, with the entire central chain of Grande Terre in full view. Four big 138-mm cannon mounted on wheels were set up here in 1894-96 to defend the harbor. Two more, placed opposite to create a crossfire, are now in front of the New Caledonia Museum.

Get to the fort by walking from the hospice to the Kuendu Beach Resort. Go past the resort on the inland side, then up around to the left. At the top of the rise, you'll see the shell of an old colonial building on the left; the road to the guns is the one that goes uphill due north on the right. There are shortcuts to come back, and a swim at **Kuendu Beach** (topless) would certainly be in order. This is where Nouméa's European residents come on weekends to get away from the tourists at Anse Vata.

Société Le Nickel

The northern section of Nouméa is not as attractive as the southern; here, on Pointe Doniambo, is the giant metallurgical factory, Société le Nickel. Established in 1910 and expanded to its present size in 1958 and 1992, the smelter has about 1,700 employees (only 17% of them Kanaks). It processes much of New Caledonia's nickel ore, and the rest is exported to Japan in its natural state. Toxic discharges of sulfur dioxide and nickel compounds have caused serious health problems among Kanaks living in the Cité Pierre Lenquette low-cost housing area directly east of the smelter (company regulations prohibit emissions when the wind is blowing south toward central Nouméa and Anse Vata).

Ore for the smelter is collected from a number of giant, open-cut mines around Grande Terre by the ore carriers *Nickel I* and *Nickel II,* leaving terrible scars in their wake, particularly on the northeast coast of the island. Two distinct products are smelted: ferronickel and matte. The former, sold to a variety of industrialized countries, is 75% iron and 25% nickel, used in the manufacture of stainless steel. Matte, sent to the company's Le Havre (France) plant, is 80% nickel and cobalt, used in the making of high-quality steel products.

If you're really interested, the Service des Mines (tel. 27-39-44), located between the smelter and downtown, has a small collection of rocks on display weekdays 0730-1130 and 1215-1600 (free).

Parc Forestier

Visit this botanical garden and zoo five km northeast of downtown to see the flightless and rapidly disappearing *cagou (Rhynochetos jubatus),* New Caledonia's official territorial bird. The excellent ornithological collection also includes the rare Ouvéa parakeet. There are a few mammals, of which the flying foxes stand out. The botanical collection continues to be disappointing, but it is growing.

You can get to the Parc Forestier by taking bus no. 12 to the Cité Pierre Lenquette low-cost housing complex at Montravel, then walking one and a half km uphill. The garden (tel. 27-89-51) is open Monday to Saturday 1330-1700, Sunday and holidays 1100-1700, admission CFP 300 (children 12 and under CFP 100).

Otherwise it's a 45-minute walk from the Nouméa Youth Hostel. Follow the radio towers north and turn left up the signposted gravel road past the three towers of the Centre Récepteur Radioelectrique. There are many excellent scenic views along the way, the best from the summit of **Montravel** (167 meters), accessible up a 400-meter stairway before you reach the Parc. Amédée Lighthouse is visible once again on the horizon south of the summit, just to the left of Ouen Toro. To the northeast the twin peaks of Mt. Koghi (1,061 meters) dominate the

Only a few hundred specimens of the Ouvea parakeet (Eunymphicus cornutus uveansis) *still exist in the world.*

horizon, while due east the oval profile of Mont Dore (772 meters) stands alone. You also get a good view of the dismal apartment blocks of Cité Pierre Lenquette where thousands of Kanaks live in unhealthy conditions directly downwind of toxic emissions from the nickel smelter. The French planners who designed this subsidized housing to provide an inexhaustible pool of cheap labor have been remarkably successful in effacing the Kanak's cultural identity while poisoning their bodies.

The Barrier Reef

Amédée Lighthouse, on a tiny island 18 km south of Nouméa, was prefabricated in Paris and set up here in 1865 to guide ships through Grande Terre's barrier reef. At 56 meters high, it's still the tallest metal lighthouse in the world, and you can mount the 231 steps. Several companies offer day-trips to Amédée for around CFP 7000 pp including Polynesian music and a buffet lunch. Among the boats doing this trip are the 30-meter cruiser *Mary D* (B.P. 233, Nouméa; tel. 26-31-31, fax 26-39-79), and the high-speed catamaran *Starship Genesis* (B.P. 2419, Nouméa; tel. 26-24-40, fax 26-23-40), 101 route de l'Anse Vata. Both leave from the Club Med wharf daily around 0845 and are back by 1700.

A cheaper way to get to Amédée Lighthouse is on the Amédée Diving Club's catamaran *Spanish Dancer* (see "Sports and Recreation," below). This departs the Club Med wharf daily except Tuesday at 0745 and costs only CFP 3000 pp without lunch (children 12 and under

CFP 1500). The Club serves a good lunch on Amédée for CFP 1500 extra, otherwise take along your own food and drink. The capacity is limited, so book a day or two ahead.

The floating aluminum **Seahorse Pontoon** (tel. 26-24-40) is anchored on the barrier reef 23 km west of Nouméa. Here you can see coral and fish through glass panels or go snorkeling. A full-day visit is CFP 8700 (children CFP 5200), including a 50-minute ride on the fast catamaran *Manta* from Baie de la Moselle, snorkeling gear, a glass-bottom boat ride, and a barbecue lunch (CFP 4950 for a half day without lunch).

Sports and Recreation

Scuba diving is offered by the **Amédée Diving Club** (Bernard Andreani, B.P. 2675, Nouméa; tel. 26-40-29, fax 28-57-55), 138 route de l'Anse Vata (near Hôtel Le Lagon). Morning and afternoon dives take place on a choice of 11 sites around Amédée Lighthouse. Two-tank dives are CFP 10,350 weekdays, CFP 11,000 weekends, plus CFP 3000 for equipment (if required). Snorkelers can go along for CFP 3000 (mask and snorkel rental CFP 1000 extra). Every Wednesday there's night diving.

Scuba diving is also offered by **Nouméa Diving** (tel. 25-16-88, fax 43-59-68), 12 rue Auguste Brun, in the Latin Quarter.

If you only want to rent equipment for shore diving, try **Marine Corail** (B.P. 848, Nouméa; tel. 27-58-48, fax 27-68-43), 26 rue du Général Mangin.

The attractive **municipal swimming pool** (tel. 26-18-43), just beyond Club Med at the far end of Anse Vata, is open weekdays 1000-1700,

Saturday 1300-1700, Sunday 0930-1200 and 1300-1615, admission CFP 150. The adjacent **municipal tennis courts** are lighted at night.

An 18-hole **municipal golf course** (tel. 41-80-00) is at Dumbéa, 15 km northwest of Nouméa on the old road. In 1995 the 18-hole **Tina Sur Mer Golf Course** opened on Tina Bay just beyond Magenta Airport.

Have a workout at the **Squash Club** (tel. 26-22-18), 21 route Jules Garnier opposite the marina on Baie de l'Orphelinat. Rackets are available and there's an inexpensive bar on the premises (a hangout for English-speaking yachties).

Most afternoons in Place des Cocotiers and next to the beach at Anse Vata you'll see men playing *pétanque,* a French bowling game in which metal balls the size of baseballs are thrown, not rolled, at other balls.

Saturday and Sunday afternoons from March to November is the time for **cricket**—jolly good show! Both Kanak men and women play on the gravelly surface just beyond the town center toward the nickel smelter, and at the Terrain de Cricket off route de l'Anse Vata. Two people stand at each crease, one to hit and the other to run. There are no overs, and bowler and wicket keeper swap roles as needs arise. They play two innings in three hours (international cricketers take five days). The ball is bouncy, and the dress is informal, with Mother Hubbard dresses as good as jeans, football gear, or Indonesian-style sarongs. The whole spectacle would horrify cricket purists, but it's great fun to watch—and you can get some good photos if you're brave enough to stand up close.

Melanesian women playing cricket

AIR NEW ZEALAND

ACCOMMODATIONS

Youth Hostel and Camping

The budget traveler's best headquarters is the A-frame **Nouméa Youth Hostel** (B.P. 767, Nouméa; tel. 27-58-79, fax 27-48-17), or *auberge de jeunesse,* on Colline de Semaphore (fantastic sunsets from here). Four-bed dormitory accommodation costs CFP 1000 pp, otherwise it's CFP 2600 double for a twin room. If you don't have an up-to-date Y.H.A. card you'll be charged CFP 100 pp extra. The hostel does fill up at times but in emergencies you'll probably be allowed to crash in the ping-pong room. Unlike hostels in many other countries, it's open all day, there's no age limit, and you can stay as many nights as you like. Everyone must do a daily housekeeping chore.

One of its biggest advantages is the excellent cooking facilities, which will save you a lot of money on food, and alcohol in moderation is allowed. Not only is this 88-person capacity hostel an inexpensive place to stay, but it's a center for exchanging information with other travelers. The hostel will store excess luggage for you when you go to the outer islands and will also exchange foreign banknotes without commission. Some stairs below the hostel provide a shortcut to town, but there have been muggings here at night, so it's best to walk up winding rue Olry after dark. Wardens Jacky Sorin and Andrea Schaefer run a tight little ship—the best and only *real* youth hostel in the South Pacific.

There's no obvious place to pitch a tent in Nouméa itself, though you could always try Île Nou (stay out of sight on the road and well away from the prison and satellite communications installation). In a pinch you could camp free in the park by the river at Dumbéa, just north of Nouméa; the Dumbéa, Païta, and La Tontouta buses all pass here. A regular campground is on Ongoué Beach, several kilometers off the main highway from Païta (transportation required). The owner of the **Restaurant le Relais des Ailes** (tel. 35-11-76) at the turnoff to La Tontouta Airport may allow you to pitch a tent out back if your flight arrives/departs at an inconvenient time.

Budget Hotels

You can't beat the location of the 26-room **Hôtel Caledonia** (B.P. 2168, Nouméa; tel. 27-38-21, fax 27-81-45), 10 rue Auguste Brun, in the Latin Quarter behind the museum. It's cheerful, but noisy from traffic: CFP 4000 single or double with shared bath, CFP 4500 with private bath, CFP 5000 with kitchen. The large full-color photos of atmospheric nuclear testing at Moruroa above the reception desk help explain why the owners are a little gruff if you don't speak French, but it's still good value.

The **Hôtel San Francisco** (B.P. 4804, Nouméa; tel. 28-26-25), 55 rue de Sébastopol, caters mostly to long-term residents who pay by the month. The hotel bar looks like something out of a Clint Eastwood flick.

The 18 rooms at **Hôtel La Pérouse** (B.P. 189, Nouméa; tel. 27-22-51, fax 27-11-87), 33 rue de Sébastopol, are CFP 4100/4600 single/double with shared bath, CFP 5700/6050 with private bath. There are no cooking facilities.

Next door to the Hôtel Ibis on Baie des Citrons is **Hôtel de la Baie** (B.P. 2515, Nouméa; tel. 26-21-33), 5 promenade Roger Laroque, which usually rents by the week or month, though you can sometimes get a double with kitchenette for CFP 4000, if you're lucky. Inquire at Pizza Pino downstairs.

There are two reasonably priced motels in Val Plaisance near Anse Vata Beach, but both often full. The three-story, 22-unit **Motel Anse Vata** (B.P. 4453, Nouméa; tel. 26-26-12, fax 25-90-60), 19 rue Gabriel Laroque, is only a 10-minute walk from Anse Vata beach: CFP 5000/5340 single/double (or CFP 100,000 a month). The two-story, 16-unit **Motel Le Bambou** (tel. 26-12-90, fax 26-30-58) is at 44 rue Spahr, a 10-minute walk farther inland: CFP 5000 single or double. The rooms at both motels have private bath, fridge, cooking facilities, and mosquitoes, but air-conditioning is extra. Monthly rates are available.

Medium-Priced Hotels

The **Hôtel Le Paris** (B.P. 2226, Nouméa; tel. 28-17-00, fax 27-60-80), just below the Catholic cathedral at 45 rue de Sébastol, has 48 a/c rooms at CFP 5820/6400 single/double (or CFP 29,200/32,500 a week), tax included. This might be your place if you're interested in the local French social scene, though noise from the cafe downstairs is a drawback.

The **Paradise Park Motel** (B.P. 9, Nouméa; tel. 27-25-41, fax 27-61-31) is at 34 rue du P.R.

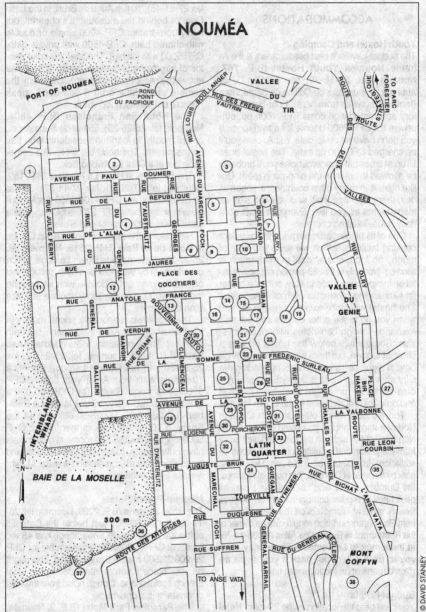

NOUMÉA

PORT OF NOUMEA

ROND POINT DU PACIFIQUE

VALLEE DU TIR

RUE LOUIS BOULANGER

RUE DES FRERES VAUTRIN

ROUTE DES DEUX VALLEES

TO PARC FORESTIER

ROUTE STRATEGIQUE

AVENUE PAUL DOUMER

AVENUE DU MARECHAL FOCH

RUE DE LA REPUBLIQUE

RUE GEORGES

RUE D'AUSTERLITZ

RUE DE L'ALMA

RUE DU GENERAL JEAN

RUE JULES FERRY

RUE DE

RUE

JAURES

PLACE DES COCOTIERS

FRANCE

RUE ANATOLE

GOUVERNEUR SAUTOT

VERDUN

RUE DRIANT

RUE MANGIN

RUE DE

RUE

GALLIENI

RUE

BOULEVARD

RUE OLRY

RUE OLRY

VALLEE DU GENIE

RUE VAUBAN

DE

SOMME

LA CLEMENCEAU

DE

SEBASTOPOL

AVENUE

AVENUE DU MARECHAL BRUN

RUE EUGENE

RUE D'AUSTERLITZ

PORCHERON

LATIN QUARTER

RUE FREDERIC SURLEAU

RUE DU DOCTEUR

VICTOIRE

RUE DU DOCTEUR LE SCOUR

RUE CHARLES DE VERNEILH

PLACE BIR HAKEIM

LA VALBONNE

ROUTE DE L'ANSE VATA

RUE LEON COURSIN

GUEGAN

TOURVILLE

RUE GUYNEMER

RUE BICHAT

RUE DUQUESNE

RUE FOCH

RUE SUFFREN

RUE DU GENERAL SARRAIL

RUE DU GENERAL LECLERC

MONT COFFYN

INTERISLAND WHARF

BAIE DE LA MOSELLE

—N—

300 m

ROUTE DES ARTIFICES

TO ANSE VATA

(1) (2) (3) (4) (5) (6) (7) (8) (9) (10) (11) (12) (13) (14) (15) (16) (17) (18) (19) (20) (21) (22) (23) (24) (25) (26) (27) (28) (29) (30) (31) (32) (33) (34) (35) (36) (37) (38)

© DAVID STANLEY

NOUMÉA

1. Old Marine Terminal
2. General Hospital "Gaston Bourret"
3. Government House
4. Ballade Supermarket
5. Marine Corail
6. Territorial Congress
7. Protestant Church
8. Old Town Hall
9. Australian Consulate
10. La Palette Restaurant
11. New Marine Terminal
12. City Hall
13. Nouméa Tourist Office
14. Brasserie Le St. Hubert
15. Hôtel La Pérouse
16. Center Voyages/American Express
17. Destination New Caledonia/Air Calédonie
18. Youth Hostel
19. Cultural Center
20. Restaurant Hameau II
21. Air France
22. St. Joseph's Cathedral
23. Café de Paris/Hôtel Le Paris
24. Bus Terminal
25. Bernheim Library
26. Rex Cinema
27. Army Barracks
28. Market
29. Police Station
30. Post Office
31. Restaurant Quan Hue
32. New Caledonia Museum
33. Relais de la Poste
34. Hôtel Caledonia
35. Courthouse
36. South Province Headquarters
37. Nouméa Yacht Charters
38. Mont Coffyn Viewpoint

Roman in Vallée des Colons, east of downtown on the way to Magenta Airport. The 62 a/c studios with cooking facilities begin at CFP 6400/7000 single/double, but it's often fully booked with French contract workers who pay by the month.

The lively **Hôtel Ibis Nouméa** (B.P. 819, Nouméa; tel. 26-20-55, fax 26-20-44), 9 promenade Roger Laroque, is right on Baie des Citrons. The 60 a/c rooms with fridge and TV in this neat four-story building begin at CFP

9500/10,600 single/double, tax included (CFP 1000 extra if you want a view of the sea). You're likely to meet a mix of off-duty French military personnel and Aussie tourists if you stay here.

The **Mocambo Hôtel** (B.P. 678, Nouméa; tel. 26-27-01, fax 26-38-77), 49 rue Jules Garnier, a four-story building just off Baie des Citrons, has 38 drab a/c rooms with TV and fridge beginning at CFP 8000 single or double.

Just around the corner from the Mocambo is the **Marina Beach Hotel** (B.P. 4622, Nouméa; tel. 28-76-33, fax 26-28-81), 4 rue Auguste Page, which opened in 1995. The 20 self-contained apartments at CFP 6600/6900 single/double (CFP 1000 extra for a/c).

The four-story **Lantana Beach Hôtel** (B.P. 4075, Nouméa; tel. 26-22-12, fax 26-16-12), 113 promenade Roger Laroque, faces onto Anse Vata. A small shopping arcade is downstairs. The 37 a/c rooms are CFP 7000/8000 single/double. Stay here if you want to sleep in the belly of the tourist strip.

Upmarket Hotels

Le Surf Novotel (B.P. 4230, Nouméa; tel. 28-66-88, fax 28-52-23), 55 promenade Roger Laroque, on the point separating Anse Vata from Baie des Citrons, has 235 a/c rooms in several connected high-rise buildings beginning at CFP 12,600 single or double garden view, CFP 14,900 sea view. Happy hour at the hotel bar is Monday 1800-1900 (two drinks for the price of one). Rows of slot machines and the swank Casino Royal are right on the premises (shorts, jeans, thongs, and persons under 21 prohibited). Le Surf is always worth a visit even if you don't intend to spend any money.

Le Lagon Nouméa (B.P. 440, Nouméa; tel. 26-12-55, fax 26-12-44), 143 route de l'Anse Vata, is a six-story high-rise just inland from the beach. The 59 tastefully decorated a/c apartments with kitchenette, fridge, and TV begin at CFP 10,000 for a studio, CFP 12,000 for a one-bedroom, CFP 15,000 for a two-bedroom (weekly rates available). Specify whether you want a double or twin beds. It's popular with Japanese groups.

Hôtel Isle de France (B.P. 1604, Nouméa; tel. 26-24-22, fax 26-17-20), 20 rue Boulari, is one block back from Anse Vata. All of its 103 a/c apartments in a five-story edifice and a circular 15-story tower have cooking facilities and TV. Prices begin at CFP 16,800 for a two-person studio, CFP 19,000 for a four-person one-bedroom, CFP 24,000 for a six-person two-bedroom. Some nautical activites are included and weekly rates are available.

The 101-room **Nouvàta Parkroyal** (B.P. 137, Nouméa; tel. 26-22-00, fax 26-17-77), 123 promenade Roger Laroque, is right across from the beach at Anse Vata. The 71 a/c rooms in the recently renovated four-story main building are CFP 17,000 single or double garden view, CFP 21,000 ocean view, while behind the hotel are 28 rooms in seven four-room villas at CFP 15,500. The two suites are CFP 44,000.

Nouméa's **Club Méditerranée** (B.P. 515, Nouméa; tel. 26-12-00, fax 26-20-71) is directly below Ouen Toro at the southeast end of Anse Vata. The 280 simple a/c rooms are always filled by people on cheap package tours from Japan or Australia—you can't just walk in and ask for a room. In fact, you don't walk in at all: there are guards at the gate. Bookings must be made

through Agence Club Med (tel. 27-43-39, fax 26-33-87), 41-43 rue de Sébastopol. Most of the rooms have twin beds, with meals and activities included in the package tariff (CFP 13,000 pp double occupancy a day, plus the Club Med membership fee). This seven-story building (formerly the Château Royale) is the only Anse Vata hotel without a road between it and the beach.

Next door to Club Med is Nouméa's top hotel, the 253-room **Le Méridien** (B.P. 1915, Nouméa Cedex 98846; tel. 26-50-00, fax 26-51-00), which opened in February 1995. Rooms are CFP 21,000 single or double standard, CFP 23,000 deluxe, plus tax. Two of the hotel's curving high-rise wings enclose a large swimming pool and the third is six stories high. The hotel has direct access to the beach and a full range of sporting facilities are available. Nouméa's second gambling casino, a 400-seat conference center, and four restaurants are also here.

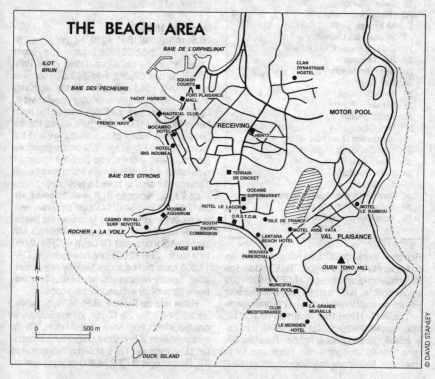

THE BEACH AREA

© DAVID STANLEY

Hotels around Nouméa

The **Kuendu Beach Resort** (B.P. 404, Nouméa; tel. 27-89-89, fax 27-60-33) is on Kuendu Beach near the west end of the Île Nou peninsula. The 20 thatched bungalows with cooking and laundry facilities, each capable of accommodating up to five persons, are CFP 12,000/14,000 garden/beach daily, or CFP 75,000/88,000 weekly. On Sunday there's a buffet lunch here with folksy entertainment. It's good if you're looking for more natural surroundings than are found in the city. Four times a day bus no. 13 comes this far (most buses on this route turn around at the hospice).

Hôtel Le Stanley (B.P. 1617, Nouméa; tel. 26-32-77, fax 25-26-56) is on Sainte Marie Bay at Ouémo, beyond Magenta Airport. The 58 a/c studios and suites with kitchenette, balcony, TV, and fridge begin at CFP 12,000 single or double. Their swimming pool is wedged between the main four-story building and a rocky shore. A free shuttle bus runs to town twice daily, and bus no. 7 also goes there.

Escapade Island Resort (B.P. 4918, Nouméa; tel./fax 28-53-20) is on Maître, a reef islet surrounded by a white sandy beach just southwest of Nouméa. This Japanese-operated resort caters mostly to Japanese packaged tourists. The 44 rooms with fan are clustered in 11 blocks of four rooms each (CFP 15,900 single or double). Cooking facilities aren't provided, and restaurant meals add up. The transfer to the island by catamaran departs Nouméa's Baie de la Moselle daily at 0830.

If you're bumped from a flight due to overbooking, the airline may put you up at the **Tontoutel** (B.P. 8, La Tontouta; tel. 35-11-11, fax 35-13-48), near La Tontouta International Airport, 45 km from Nouméa. The 43 a/c motel rooms (CFP 6500/8000 single/double) are in long single-story blocks. Hopefully the swimming pool, bar, and TV will keep you entertained.

FOOD

Budget Places to Eat

Nouméa's ubiquitous snack bars will prepare a filling sandwich *(le sandwich)* for CFP 200 and up. This consists of a generous length of *baguette*-style bread with your favorite filling,

plus lettuce and tomatoes. It's a meal in itself. One place serving this is the Vietnamese-run **Snack le Vilbar** (tel. 28-48-48), 55 rue de Sébastopol.

Snack Kim-Ly (tel. 27-45-55), 33 rue de Verdun at rue de Sébastopol, has omelettes and good inexpensive bowls of Chinese soup until 2200. Also try the *nems* (Vietnamese spring rolls) here. The Vietnamese-operated **Restaurant Hameau II** (tel. 28-48-32; closed Sunday), 32 rue de Verdun, serves filling dishes like steak and *frites* at reasonable prices. It's one of the few low-budget places open for dinner.

For breakfast try **La Palette Chez Angele** (tel. 28-28-78), 51 rue Jean Jaurès, or have their *plat du jour* lunch. Places offering a *plat du jour* lunch weekdays include **Self Foch** (tel. 28-37-77), 8 avenue du Maréchal Foch; **Café Le Flore** (tel. 28-12-47), 39 rue de Sébastopol; and **Café Moustache** (tel. 28-42-21; closed Sunday), 37 rue de Verdun. All these are closed in the evening. Most establishments catering mainly to locals stop serving lunch at 1300 and dinner at 1900.

Better Restaurants

Nouméa has over 130 restaurants serving dishes like *coq au vin* (chicken in wine sauce) and *champignons provençales* (mushrooms seasoned with garlic and parsley). The cuisine is *très bon;* indeed, given the prices, it has to be! Many have a special set menu for a complete meal, varying anywhere from CFP 1500 to CFP 2500. The restaurants start serving lunch around 1100, and by 1200 the *plats du jour* could be gone, so arrive early. The more expensive dishes on the regular menu will be available till around 1330. Dinner is usually 1800-2200.

Brasserie le St. Hubert (tel. 27-21-42; closed Sunday), 44 rue Anatole France on Place des Cocotiers, is popular among the local *pieds noir* who order dishes like couscous, fried fish, or steak and *frites,* which they wash down with carafes of red Algerian wine. This is *the* place for cold draft beer and local atmosphere—just don't voice any pro-Kanak sympathies, if you know what's good for you.

Sample Vietnamese cooking at **Restaurant Tan Viet** (tel. 28-30-76), 15 rue de Sébastopol, or **Restaurant Quan Hue** (tel. 28-56-72), 5 rue du Docteur Guegan. El Cordobés (tel. 27-47-68), 1 rue Bichat in the Latin Quarter, is one of

Nouméa's finest French restaurants despite the Spanish name.

Restaurants at the Beach

As you'd expect, the places out at Anse Vata are high priced, although snack bars such as **Snack Bambino Vata** (tel. 26-11-77), 119 promenade Roger Laroque, and **Jullius** (tel. 26-13-38), 117 promenade Roger Laroque, have things like hamburgers, *croques monsieurs* (grilled ham-and-cheese sandwiches), and French waffles to keep you going.

Pizzeria San Rémo (tel. 26-18-02), 119 promenade Roger Laroque, right next to the Nouvàta Parkroyal, has some of the best pizza in the Southern Hemisphere (CFP 1350 and up for one person). A more exotic choice would be **Restaurant Annapurna** (tel. 26-10-35; closed Sunday), 153 route de l'Anse Vata near Hôtel Le Lagon, with non-vegetarian Indian dishes at lower-than-average prices. The Cantonese food at **La Grande Muraille** (tel. 26-13-28; closed Sunday and Monday), beyond the municipal swimming pool, is more expensive but good value. Try the Imperial duck.

Restaurant La Concha (tel. 26-44-67), 7 promenade Roger Laroque below the Hôtel Ibis at Baie des Citrons, is run by Basques—good food at average prices. Occasionally there's entertainment. The lively bar attached to this restaurant is a bit of a hangout for visiting yachties, and the Vietnamese snack bar next door to La Concha serves full meals for CFP 600 and up.

Groceries

The **public market** (open daily 0500-1000), beside Baie de la Moselle, is the place to buy fresh fruit and vegetables. The fish stalls are almost as good as the aquarium. Daily 1700-2300 a row of food vans parked along rue Georges Clemenceau next to the market dish out inexpensive takeaway curries in a colorful night market.

Nouméa has over a half dozen large supermarkets and department stores, including **Ballande** (tel. 27-20-31; open weekdays 0730-1800, Saturday 0730-1730 for groceries only), 21 rue de l'Alma. It's one of the few places open at lunchtime and has a good coffee bar. **Océanie** on route de l'Anse Vata near Hôtel Le Lagon is open weekdays 0600-1930, weekends 0600-1230/1500-2000. Enjoy a memorable picnic in the Place des Cocotiers or on Anse Vata Beach with a *baguette,* Camembert cheese, and French table wine from one of these.

ENTERTAINMENT

Nouméa cinemas include the **Rex** (tel. 27-24-83), on avenue de la Victoire, the **Plaza** (tel. 28-66-60), 65 rue de Sébastopol, the **Hickson City** (tel. 28-30-82), 6 rue Frédéric Surleau, and the **Hickson Liberty** (tel. 28-30-35), 18 rue de la Somme. All foreign films shown are dubbed into French, with no subtitles (screenings at 1400 and 2000, admission CFP 700). The Plaza is probably you best bet and they charge half price on Tuesday.

For such a cosmopolitan city, the nightlife in Nouméa is disappointing and trends change fast—ask around for the current "in" place. The daily newspaper and posters around town announce which restaurants have live music and even stand-up comedians. You don't pay any more to eat at one of these places, nor are they necessarily the most expensive. Many places are private clubs, but properly dressed visitors can get in easily by paying a membership fee at the door. One such place is **Club Privé le Joker** (tel. 27-17-77; opens at 2100 daily), 41 rue de Sébastopol, and several more are at Anse Vata. **New Orleans** (tel. 27-80-05), 12 rue du Général Mangin, has live jazz on Thursday nights.

The crowd at the **Relais de la Poste** (tel. 28-37-87), corner of Eugène Porcheron and Docteur Guegan in the Latin Quarter, is pleasantly bohemian, and you'll even see Kanaks in there. The manager at **Café de Paris** (tel. 28-20-00), 47 rue de Sébastopol, speaks English and is a bit of a character, but the café au lait is lousy. It's fun to sit and watch the off-duty French soldiers posing.

At Anse Vata **Charle's Bar Américain** (tel. 26-11-47), 119 promenade Roger Laroque next to the Nouvàta Parkroyal, is a popular and noisy late-night hangout on weekends.

High rollers frequent the **Casino Royal** (tel. 26-16-90) at the Surf Novotel on Anse Vata. The female casino staff wear evening gowns, the male croupiers black tie, and punters are also required to dress smartly to enter the gaming salon (no shorts, jeans, thongs, or running shoes). You must show your passport at the door—locals and persons under 21 aren't admitted. The CFP 400 admission fee includes CFP 1000 in "free" gambling chips to get you started (free admission for hotel guests). Dress requirements and the admission fee don't apply at the casino's slot machine section. The slots are operating from 1300 daily, the gambling salon from 2000.

Less pretentious than the casino are the bingo games held daily from 1400 onwards at 7 rue Jules Ferry (CFP 100 a card). Of course, you'll need to know French (or find a helper).

Cultural Shows for Visitors
Polynesian dancing may be seen at Le Grill in **Le Surf Novotel** (tel. 28-66-88) one or two evenings a week (ask about it); just enter the bar to enjoy it and the attempts of Japanese tourists to join in. On Sunday afternoons Polynesian dancing comes with the seafood buffet (CFP 3000) at the **Kuendu Beach Resort** (tel. 27-89-89). Also ask about Polynesian dancing at **Hôtel Isle de France** (tel. 26-24-22) on rue Boulari, Anse Vata.

Amac Tours (tel. 26-38-38), Galerie Palm Beach, offers a Melanesian feast on Friday nights at CFP 6700 pp, including dinner, singing, dancing, a display of handicrafts, and hotel transfers.

Shopping
Rue de l'Alma, with its numerous boutiques and specialty shops, is Nouméa's most exclusive shopping street. Watch for the *soldes* sign, which indicates a sale. Among the many places selling locally made handicrafts is **Curios du Pacifique** (tel. 26-97-52), 23 rue Jean Jaurès, and the **Maison de Lifou** (tel. 27-47-81), 48 rue Anatole France. One shop, in a basement below **Le Coin du Cuir** (tel. 28-26-58), 23 rue Anatole France, sells authentic-looking Kanak war clubs made on the premises.

Nouméa has several new shopping malls with many visitor-oriented shops, restaurants and activities offices. The largest of these are the **Galerie Palm Beach**, 127 promenade Roger Laroque next to the Nouvàta Parkroyal on Anse Vata, and the **Port Plaisance Mall**, 10 rue

ceremonial jade mace, a symbol of chieftanship

James Garnier, Baie des Pècheurs (bus no. 6).

Colorful stamps and first-day covers are available at the **Philatelic Bureau** (tel. 27-48-81; weekdays 0745-1115 and 1200-1430) in the main post office. They also sell the stamps of Tahiti-Polynesia and Wallis and Futuna.

Buy camping and snorkeling gear at **R. Deschamps** (tel. 27-39-61), 34 rue de la Somme, or rent a tent from **Messageries Calédoniennes** (tel. 27-36-03), 46/48 rue Georges Clémenceau. They also sell used tents.

SERVICES AND INFORMATION

Money
There are several banks along avenue de la Victoire that will change money for CFP 500 commission (no commission on French francs). In past the numerous branches of the Westpac Bank have changed traveler's checks without commission when the amount was under CFP 10,000, but this may already have changed.

You can change American Express traveler's checks without paying a commission at **Center Voyages** (B.P. 50, Nouméa; tel. 28-40-40, fax 27-26-36; weekdays 0730-1100/1330-1730, Saturday 0800-1100), 4th Floor, 27 bis, avenue du Maréchal Foch. They'll hold clients' mail.

Post
The main post office's hours are weekdays 0745-1115 and 1215-1530, Saturday 0730-1100. Poste restante at the main post office holds mail two weeks only, before returning to sender, but you can pay a fee to have them forward mail. There's a CFP 50 fee per letter to pick up mail.

Consulates
The **Australian Consulate General** (tel. 27-24-14; open Monday to Friday 0800-1130/1330-1630), 8th Floor, 19 avenue du Maréchal Foch, opposite the old town hall, issues free tourist visas.

Other countries with diplomatic offices in Nouméa are Belgium (tel. 28-46-46), Indonesia (tel. 28-25-74), Italy (tel. 27-33-47), Japan (tel. 25-37-29), the Netherlands (tel. 28-57-20), New Zealand (tel. 27-25-43), Switzerland (tel. 26-11-59), and Vanuatu (tel. 27-17-77).

Information

Tourist information on Nouméa is available at the **Office du Tourisme de Nouméa** (B.P. 2828, Nouméa; tel. 28-75-80, fax 28-75-85), 24 rue Anatole France (Place des Cocotiers), whereas **Destination New Caledonia** (B.P. 688, Nouméa; tel. 27-26-32, fax 27-46-23), 39 rue de Verdun, has information on the whole territory. Both dole out free brochures and can answer questions (preferably in French).

For information on the Loyalty Islands try the **Maison des Îles Loyauté** (tel. 28-93-60, fax 28-91-21), 113 avenue Roger Laroque (in front of the Lantana Hôtel), the **Maison de Lifou** (tel. 27-47-81), 48 rue Anatole France, or **Air Calédonie** (tel. 28-65-64, fax 28-13-40), 39 rue de Verdun. **North Province** has an information office (tel. 27-78-05, fax 27-48-87) at 39-41 rue de Verdun.

The territory's equivalent of the Sierra Club is the **Association pour la Sauvegarde de la Nature Néo-Calédonienne** (B.P. 1772, Nouméa; tel./fax 28-32-75), 37 rue Georges Clémenceau. Ask about their monthly excursions.

The **Institut Territorial de la Statistique** (B.P. 823, Nouméa; tel. 28-31-56, fax 28-81-48), 2nd Floor, 5 rue Gallieni, has specialized statistical publications.

Librairie Pentecost (tel. 25-72-50, fax 28-54-24), 34 rue de l'Alma, and **Librairie Montaigne** (tel. 27-34-88), 23 rue de Sébastopol, sell colored I.G.N. topographical maps of New Caledonia and Vanuatu (and English newspapers and magazines). Most Nouméa bookstores carry the excellent I.G.N. 1:500,000 "Carte Touristique" of New Caledonia.

The **Agence de Developpement de la Culture Kanak** (tel. 28-32-90, fax 28-21-78), 100 avenue James Cook, Nouville, sells books, magazines, videos, and music cassettes on Kanak culture.

Reconfirm your international flight reservations at **Air Calédonie International** (tel. 27-61-62), 8 rue Frédéric Surleau, **Air France** (tel. 28-88-11), 41 rue de Sébastopol, **Air New Zealand** (tel. 28-34-39), 14 rue Georges Clémenceau, **AOM French Airlines** (tel. 24-12-12), 1 rue d'Ypres, **Air Vanuatu** (tel. 28-66-77),

20 rue du Général Mangin, or **Qantas** (tel. 28-65-46), 35 avenue du Maréchal Foch.

Health

The **Hôpital "Gaston Bourret"** (tel. 27-21-21), avenue Paul Doumer, accepts only emergency cases, so if you have a non-life-threatening medical problem go to the **Clinique Magnin** (tel. 27-27-84), 1 rue du R.P. Roman, Vallée des Colons (just east of downtown), the **Clinique de la Baie des Citrons** (tel. 26-18-66), 5 rue Fernand Legras, or the **Polyclinique de l'Anse Vata** (tel. 26-14-22), 180 route de l'Anse Vata, all privately operated. The AIDS hotline (tel. 28-88-28) is staffed Wednesday 1600-2100, otherwise try the STD clinic at the hospital. To call a doctor in emergencies, dial 15, or contact **Ambulances S.O.S.** (tel. 28-66-00).

TRANSPORTATION

For information on domestic flights from Nouméa to other parts of New Caledonia, see "Transportation" in the chapter introduction.

By Ship

Ballande Maritime (B.P. 97, Nouméa; tel. 28-33-84, fax 28-73-88), 22 avenue James Cook, Nouville, will be able to tell you when the monthly Banks Line freighter service to Port Vila will arrive in Nouméa, then you must check with the captain to see if they'll take you.

Amacal Agence Maritime Caledonienne (tel. 28-72-22), 5 rue d'Austerlitz, represents the **Compagnie Wallisienne de Navigation,** whose ship, the *Moana II,* makes the Nouméa-Futuna-Wallis-Nouméa trip monthly. Occasionally it calls at Suva, Fiji.

Interisland Ferry

The **Société Maritime des Îles Loyauté** (Gare Maritime des Îles, 3 rue Jules Ferry; tel. 28-93-18) operates the 249-passenger ferry *Président Yeiwéné* to the islands. The vessel departs Nouméa at 1500 every other Monday for Ouvéa and Lifou, at 1700 every other Monday for Lifou and Maré, at 1800 on Wednesday for Maré and Lifou, and at 1900 on Friday for the Isle of Pines. Fares from Nouméa are CFP 4000/4900 economy/first class to the Loyalty Islands, CFP

3000/3500 to the Isle of Pines. These prices include a couchette on the overnight trips. Inter-island fares with a seat only are CFP 1950 between Ouvéa and Lifou, or CFP 2900 between Lifou and Maré. A seat on the afternoon trip from the Isle of Pines back to Nouméa is CFP 1500. Add three percent tax to all fares. Not only does the ferry save you one night's hotel bill on the overnight trips, but it lands right in the towns so you're also spared airport transfer charges. During holiday periods the ferry is fully booked and advance reservations are recommended at all times.

Interurban Buses

Most long-distance buses leave from the Gare Routière (tel. 27-82-32) on rue d'Austerlitz near the market. The times quoted below could change and there may only be one or two buses a day to the place you want to go, so always check the posted schedules a day or two ahead. Friday is a bad day to set out on a long trip as many buses are timed to take office workers home for the weekend, leaving Nouméa around 1745 and arriving at outlying towns very late. The buses do fill up, so arrive at the station early.

The bus to La Tontouta Airport (one hour, CFP 400) departs from the bus station hourly 0530-1730 Monday to Saturday, every two hours on Sunday. There's also the S.C.E.A. airport bus (tel. 28-61-00; CFP 2000), which will pick you up at your hotel or hostel (discount for YHA members).

The bus to Yaté (two hours, CFP 600) leaves at 1145 daily except Sunday. To Thio (two hours, CFP 800) the bus leaves at 1145 Monday to Saturday, at 1800 Sunday. Buses to Canala and Kouaoua via La Foa run daily.

The west coast is well served, with buses to Bourail (three hours, CFP 900) at 1230 Monday to Thursday, at 1730 Friday, at 1145 Saturday; to Koné (four hours, CFP 1100) at 0930 Monday to Saturday, at 1300 Sunday; to Koumac (5.5 hours, CFP 1450) at 1130 Monday to Saturday, at 1000 Sunday; to Poum (seven hours, CFP 1650) at 1000 Monday to Thursday, at 1800 Friday, at 1130 Sunday; and to Pouébo (seven hours, CFP 1650) via Koumac at 0800 Wednesday and at 1745 Friday.

To the east coast, there are buses to Houaïlou (four hours, CFP 1050) at 1200 daily; to Poin-

dimié (five hours, CFP 1250) at 1030 Monday to Friday, at 1130 Saturday and Sunday; and to Hienghène (six hours, CFP 1450) via Houaïlou at 0545 and 0800 Monday to Saturday, at 1000 Sunday.

In addition to the regular buses mentioned above, there are cheaper mail buses *(subventionné)* to Yaté at 0530 (CFP 290) and to Hienghène at 0545 (CFP 960). Carefully check on these.

City Buses

Nouméa's city bus system *(transport en commun)* is excellent; a flat fare of CFP 100 is charged (pay the driver). There are 12 different routes, serving such places as Anse Vata (nos. 3 and 6), Baie des Citrons (no. 6), Magenta Airport (no. 7), and Nouville (no. 13). The buses run every 10-30 minutes 0530-1845 daily. Catch them at the bus terminal downtown or at marked bus stops along the routes. You must flag the bus down, but drivers won't stop if every seat is full.

Taxis and Hitching

The main Nouméa taxi stand is in the Place des Cocotiers. All taxis have meters (CFP 250 flag fall plus CFP 100 a km) with a surcharge at night and on weekends. If you speak French you can call a radio taxi 24 hours a day by dialing 28-35-12. An extra CFP 100 is charged in this case.

To hitch take city bus no. 8 (Pont des Français) to Normandie at the junction of RT 1 to Bourail and RT 2 to Yaté. For the toll road north, take bus no. 9 to Rivière-Salée. Unless saving a few hundred francs is crucial it's better to take the La Tontouta bus to the airport to get well out on the road to Bourail, or the Robinson, St. Louis, or Plum buses for the road to Yaté. Hitching up the southwest coast is easy, but it's difficult elsewhere due to lack of traffic. Also, very few drivers speak English.

Vehicle Rentals

Car rental rates begin around CFP 2800 a day, plus CFP 29 a kilometer. Those kilometers can add up, so inquire about unlimited mileage rates (often with a two-day minimum rental). Full collision insurance is an extra CFP 1100 a day and up. Expect to pay around CFP 100 a liter (or US$4 per American gallon) for gasoline, and in remote areas tank up every chance you get. Any driver's license will do, but Avis, Hertz, Mencar, and some of the others only rent to those 25 and older. Driving is on the right and the use of seat belts is compulsory. If two cars meet at an unmarked town intersection, the car on the right has priority.

Some of the least expensive cars are available from **AB Rent-A-Car** (B.P. 3417, Nouméa; tel. 28-12-12, fax 27-71-55), 36 avenue du Maréchal Foch, and **Pacific Car** (tel. 27-60-60, fax 28-45-40), 9 rue de Soissons, Faubourg Blanchot. AB has unlimited-kilometer rentals and they'll rent to anyone aged 21 and over. **Nouméa Car** (tel./fax 27-56-36), 9 rue Bichat, offers motorcycles (CFP 5000 daily, plus CFP 29 a km), 4WD vehicles, and boats. **Hertz** (B.P. 335, Nouméa; tel. 26-18-22, fax 27-81-14), 113 route de l'Anse Vata, has 4WD jeeps at CFP 10,500 a day plus insurance with unlimited mileage (minimum two days). **Mencar** (tel. 27-61-25, fax 28-17-59), 8 rue Jean Jaurès, rents Isuzu jeeps at CFP 62,000 a week, 700 kilometers included. **Avis** (B.P. 155, Nouméa; tel. 27-54-84, fax 28-62-90), Rond Point du Pacifique, offers 4WD Ferozza vehicles with unlimited mileage and insurance included at CFP 30,000 for three days, CFP 66,000 a week, or CFP 112,900 a fortnight. **Europcar/Visa** (tel. 26-24-44, fax 28-61-17), 8 rue Auguste Brun, offers the same at CFP 59,000 a week, CFP 95,000 a fortnight, or CFP 120,000 for three weeks, and their minimum age is 21. Also try **Auto Centrale Location** (tel. 28-46-44, fax 28-46-72), 6 rue Auguste Brun, and **Budget** (tel. 26-20-09, fax 27-52-72), 3 rue de la République.

Car rentals on the Loyalty Islands can be reserved through **Tour des Îles** (B.P. 9149, Nouméa; tel. 26-41-42, fax 26-29-28), 17 rue Colnett, Motor Pool.

Bicycles can be rented from **Curios** (tel. 26-23-78), 27 promenade Roger Laroque, Baie des Citrons (CFP 1600/4500 per day/week, CFP 20,000 deposit). Shops on Anse Vata and in the new maritime passenger terminal also rent bicycles and mopeds.

Yacht Charters

Nouméa Yacht Charters (B.P. 1068, Nouméa; tel. 28-66-66, fax 28-74-82), 1 route des Artifices, Baie de la Moselle, offers bareboat or skippered charters out of Nouméa. The usual trip is to sail to the Isle of Pines and back in five to seven days. Luxurious six-berth, 11-meter Beneteau yachts are used. The yacht charter companies listed in the "Getting There" section of this book's introduction handle advance bookings. **Pacific Charter** (tel. 26-10-55, fax 28-57-55), 138 route de l'Anse Vata, is similar.

Pacific Sun Sail (B.P. 14311, Nouméa; tel./fax 25-92-87), Baie de la Moselle, rents smaller, simpler yachts. A four-berth First 210 yacht is CFP 18,000/34,000/45,000 for one/two/three days, a five-berth First 285 CFP 24,000 a day. These easy-to-manage boats are perfect for exploring the lagoon around Nouméa.

Many other crewed charter boats work out of Nouméa, including the ketch *Viking,* the racing yacht *Pepsi,* the catamaran sailboat *Privilege,* the yacht *Rehutaï IV,* and the yacht *Alcyon* (at Isle of Pines). The actual fleet changes all the time as boats come and go, so check with Destination New Caledonia for current information.

Tours

Amac Tours (B.P. A3, Nouméa Cédex; tel. 26-38-38, fax 26-16-62), Galerie Palm Beach, can handle most travel arrangements around New Caledonia. Amac's organized sightseeing tours from Nouméa include half-day trips to Mont Dore and Mt. Koghi, and full-day trips to Rivière Bleue Territorial Park (CFP 7000 pp), Yaté, Bourail, and Thio (CFP 8500 pp). Don't book a one-day package to Ouvéa or the Isle of Pines, however, as these are rushed, overpriced, and superficial and will only appeal to those who enjoy being herded by a Japanese-speaking guide.

Pacific Raids (tel. 28-23-25), 9 cité Bellevue, Haut Magenta, offers safaris around Grande Terre in four-wheel-drive landcruisers and sightseeing by helicopter. **Aventure Pulsion** (B.P. 9131, Nouméa; tel. 26-27-48, fax 25-35-11), 20 rue Jean Jaurés, specializes in kayaking, trekking, and horseback riding tours, and there are special programs for young people aged 12-18.

On weekends once or twice a month, three-day package tours to Norfolk Island are offered by the domestic airline **Air Calédonie** (tel. 28-78-88, fax 28-76-20), 39 rue de Verdun. For information about Norfolk, turn to this book's "Pitcairn Islands" chapter. If you happen to coincide, you'll find it a most interesting trip.

GRANDE TERRE

YATÉ AND THE SOUTH

Mont Dore

Some 30 km east of Nouméa across Boulari Bay is the Commune of Mont Dore, a favorite weekend destination for city dwellers. Buses to Plum (one hour, CFP 350) depart Nouméa weekdays hourly until 1800, Saturday every two hours, and four times on Sunday. Other buses turn around at Saint Louis (CFP 220). These excellent services make Mont Dore an easy and inexpensive day-trip from Nouméa.

La Conception Church (1874), south of the highway just a few kilometers outside Nouméa, contains many *ex votos* left to thank the Virgin Mary for favors and miracles. In the graveyard beside the road leading to the church is the tomb of the former secretary-general of the Union Calédonienne, Pierre Declercq, murdered on 19 September 1981 by persons unknown. His tombstone reads: *assassiné dans le combat pour la libération de peuple Kanak.* Roch Pidjot, co-founder of the Union Calédonienne, is also buried here.

East again is picturesque St. Louis Mission, founded in 1859, with New Caledonia's oldest church. A road just beyond the mission leads seven km inland to Parc de la Thy, where you'll find six hiking trails, a stream with waterfalls and pools, and thatched picnic pavilions. Camping is allowed here. Also in this area is Ranch de la Coulée (tel. 43-36-94), with horseback riding.

Mont Dore and Plum are favorite beaches for Nouméans though the water is rather murky and during the week it's dead. A popular day hike from here is to the summit of Mont Dore (772 meters) for the view. Near Plum is a small wooden chapel built by American troops stationed here during WW II (French troops are still here).

Two places to stay are just southeast of Plum. Nukuhiva (tel. 42-41-41) at Plage 1000 has seven self-catering bungalows at CFP 6000. About one and a half km beyond is La Nouvelle Siesta (B.P. 83, Mont Dore; tel. 43-39-10, fax 43-44-04) with nine thatched bungalows at CFP 3800 single or double (no cooking). Camping is CFP 500 pp. Both have a restaurant and swimming pool.

A new place in this area is Le Vallon Dore (B.P. 113, Mont Dore; tel. 43-32-08, fax 43-66-66) with four bungalows without kitchens at CFP 3500 and seven with kitchens at CFP 6000. A swimming pool and restaurant are on the premises.

Yaté

Yaté, 81 km east of Nouméa, is a good place for a weekend out of the city. The bus goes as far as Touaourou Mission, and sometimes to Unia and Goro. The journey is through grandiose, empty country with good views. To the north is Parc Provincial de la Riviére Bleue, 18 km off the main road, and to the south the Plaine des Lacs, with its amazing variety of plantlife. The road winds along the shore of Yaté Lake (48 square km) for quite a distance before descending to the northeast coast.

The access road to the giant hydroelectric dam, or *barrage* (erected 1959), is to the left just before the final pass. It's two km north to the dam, which produces about 270 million kilowatt-hours a year (a quarter of the territorial requirements). A narrow old road continues past the dam seven km down to the powerhouse, passing a beautiful, high waterfall on the way. From Yaté Generating Station, it's only one and a half km east to the Unia ferry *(bac),* then another two km around to the bridge at the junction of the Nouméa, Yaté, and Goro roads.

The coastal plain is narrow here, and the alternate views of inlets, mountains, and sea are fine. At the south tip of Grande Terre, about 23 km from Yaté bridge, is Goro village, with Wadiana Falls a kilometer beyond. Climb to the top of the falls for a view across to the Isle of Pines and all the intermediate reefs, but beware of loose rocks. Two km beyond the falls are a pair of giant rusting cantilever loaders, which once fed iron and chrome ore from conveyors directly into waiting ships. The scenery is superb.

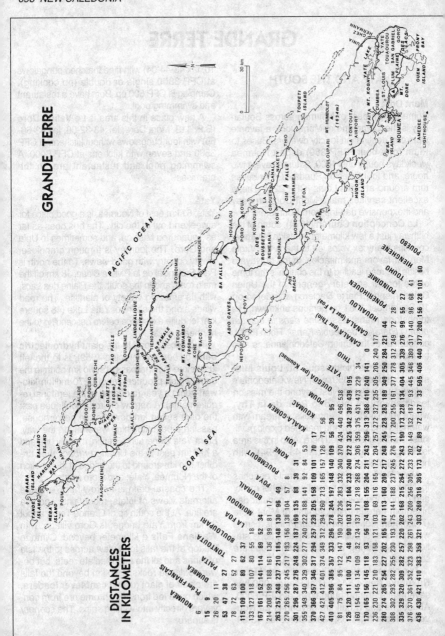

If you're traveling by public transport, you'll have to spend the night here. The bus back to Nouméa leaves Touaourou Mission Monday to Saturday at 0600 (two hours, CFP 600). Owners of the gîtes south of Touaourou help their guests connect with this bus. Hitching is easiest on the weekend.

Accommodations at Yaté

A kilometer north of Touaourou Mission is **Gîte Iya** (Paul Vouti, tel. 46-42-23), with three bungalows at CFP 5000, plus camping for CFP 1000 per tent.

Budget travelers will do no better than **Gîte San Gabriel** (Mr. Abel Atti, tel. 46-42-77), four km beyond Touaourou Mission. The five basic thatched bungalows with toilet are CFP 4000 single or double, and camping is CFP 1000 per tent. If you're driving around and want to stop for a picnic here, it's CFP 500 per car. Set in a coconut grove right on a lovely beach, San Gabriel is charming, with a friendly Melanesian staff. Meals are available (including lobster), or cook your own over an open fire (bring food). At low tide, explore the pools and crevices in the raised reef just one km northwest of San Gabriel along the beach. One deep pool full of eels appears to extend back into a submerged cave. The snorkeling is only so-so.

The **Gîte Wadiana** (Mr. Charles Attiti, B.P. 34, Yaté; tel. 46-41-90), beyond Goro, is CFP 2800 double with shared facilities, CFP 3500 with private bath. Camping is CFP 800 (small tent) or CFP 1000 (large tent). There's a relaxing sitting room and a beach (murky water). The restaurant here is popular among Nouméa residents, who often spend Sunday afternoon here (dinner CFP 3200). You can also order a *bougna* capable of feeding five for CFP 3500 (24 hours notice required).

Ouen and Casy Islands

Barren Ouen Island is separated from the southern tip of Grande Terre by Woodin Strait. The **Turtle Club** (B.P. 121, Nouméa; tel. 28-53-62) on the west side of Ouen has 20 duplex units at CFP 6500/7500/8500 single/double/triple. Meals in the restaurant are expensive and there are no cooking facilities. Yachties are welcome here. Boat transfers from Nouméa (61 km) are CFP 3250 pp return. Just across the grass-covered

Visitors to Yaté are accommodated in these thatched cottages at San Gabriel Camping.

DAVID STANLEY

airstrip from the Club is **Gîte Wokoue** (B.P. 598, Mont Dore; tel. 28-57-67) with three bungalows at CFP 5000, camping CFP 1000.

In 1994 the Colonial-style **Hôtel Casy** (B.P. 717, Mont Dore; tel./fax 26-47-77) opened on Casy Island in Prony Bay. The 20 fan-cooled rooms with bath in two main buildings are CFP 6500/7000/8000 single/double/triple, plus CFP 500 for a sea view, then there's a CFP 3500 pp charge for return boat transfers from Nouméa.

THE CENTER

Bouloupari

About 20 km northwest of La Tontouta Airport is **Les Paillottes de la Ouenghi** (B.P. 56, Nouméa; tel. 35-17-35, fax 35-17-44), a small resort by the Ouenghi River with 15 thatched bungalows at CFP 6500 single or double. There's a restaurant/bar, swimming pool, tennis court, 18-hole golf course, kayaking, and horseback riding. Eight km beyond is Bouloupari, a small village at the foot of Mt. Ouitchambo, 78 km northwest of Nouméa. Here a road forks 47 km northeast to Thio.

Thio

Since 1889, Thio has been the most important mining center in New Caledonia. On arriving from Bouloupari, turn right to Thio Mission, Bota Méré Hill, and the beach. The Marist church here dates from 1868. From the beach you can see the nickel workings on the plateau to the northwest and the port to the southeast. The ore is brought down in buckets suspended from a moving cable and then loaded into ships bound for Nouméa and Japan for processing. You could camp on the beach.

Thio village is two and a half km northwest of here, at the foot of the plateau beside the Thio River. It's a rather dismal little town, with a post office in an old colonial building, two banks, a *gendarmerie,* and a clinic. The **Musée de la Mine SLN** mining museum (tel. 44-51-77), a block from the bridge, is open Wednesday 0830-1200 and weekends 0900-1200 (free). The **Restaurant Escapade** (tel. 44-53-10; closed weekends) near the Mairie offers basic accommodations. The bus to Nouméa (CFP 800) departs Thio Post Office Monday to Saturday at 0500 and Sunday at 1515.

The **Gîte d'Ouroué** (Mr. A. Chamoinri, tel. 44-51-63), on Ouroué Beach, five km north of Thio just off the road to Canala, has four bungalows (CFP 3000) and a camping area (CFP 500 per tent). All guests share a common kitchen.

Thio leapt into international prominence late in 1984, when 200 FLNKS militants under Éloi Machoro captured the *gendarmerie* and town and held them for almost two months in a standoff against the French army. Seven roadblocks were set up, but when the FLNKS began house-to-house searches for arms and ammunition, the French sent in snipers to eliminate Machoro. Unfortunately, the police helicopter landed in the wrong place, and the marksmen were captured by the Kanaks. In January 1985 the French decided to take no chances and sent 300 *gendarmes* to surround an isolated farmhouse near La Foa where Machoro and some others were meeting. Other marksmen arrived and murdered Machoro and a second man in

cold blood as they stood outside the building. In retaliation, Kanaks blew up the French mines at Thio, causing US$3 million in damages.

From Thio, a one-way road with a timetable *(horaire)* for traveling in each direction leads 35 km northwest over the Col de Petchécara to Canala. Independence martyr Éloi Machoro is buried in Nakéty village, 10 km before Canala. There's no bus from Thio to Nakéty, and buses from Nakéty to Nouméa via Canala and La Foa leave before dawn. If you don't have a car you'll almost certainly have to hitch.

Around Canala

Canala Bay is the best hurricane refuge for shipping on the northeast coast, and during the days of sail in the late 19th century this feature and mining activity made Canala an important center. Today it's Kanak country. The turnoff for **Ciu Falls** is two km southeast of Canala, then it's another four km in to the falls themselves. **Hôtel Chez Jeannette** (B.P. 7, Canala; tel. 42-30-13) at the north entrance to Canala offers food and 13 rooms (CFP 1500 per room) in a run-down colonial home, and you may camp. Buses leave Canala for Nouméa (CFP 1000) around dawn.

At La Crouen, 14 km east of Canala, are **thermal hot springs,** where you can bathe for half an hour in a 42° C sulfur pool for CFP 300 (tel. 42-31-35; daily 0730-2200). It's especially good for anyone suffering from arthritis, asthma, or rheumatism. Camping at the springs is CFP 300. Farther east is the turnoff to the mining center of Kouaoua, 45 km northwest of Canala. From this junction, the main highway cuts south across the mountains to La Foa, passing tons of cascading water from several fantastic waterfalls along the way.

At Sarraméa, about 15 km before La Foa, is *Caldoche*-operated **Evasion 130** (B.P. 56, La Foa; tel. 42-32-35), a couple of kilometers off the main road to Canala from Petit Couli village, with 19 bungalows without cooking facilities at CFP 4000/4500 single/double. It's surrounded by verdant hills with trails to hike and streams in which to swim.

La Foa

La Foa, 65 km northwest of La Tontouta Airport, is an alternative place to spend the night before catching a flight. It's an orderly *Caldoche* town surrounded by lush fields, acacia trees, and stately *Araucaria columnaris* pines. People from the surrounding farms and villages come to shop at La Foa's Ballande supermarket, and there are two banks. Fairly frequent buses up the west coast stop in front of the post office.

At the south entrance to La Foa is a small metal bridge erected in 1909 by two students of Gustave Eiffel. The adjacent larger bridge over the La Foa River was built during WW II. Just outside La Foa on the road to Bourail is the workshop of **Rémy Weiss, Sculpteur** (tel. 42-11-26), who does woodcarving in the traditional Melanesian fashion. He usually has a few works for sale in the front room of his home.

Hôtel Banu (B.P. 57, La Foa; tel. 42-11-19, fax 44-35-50), opposite the post office in the center of town, is an old colonial-style building with 11 pleasant rooms at CFP 3200/4000 single/double without bath, CFP 4200/5000 with bath. The seafood restaurant (closed Sunday night) at the hotel has a reasonable *plat du jour* lunch, but dinner is expensive. Avoid making any pro-Kanak comments in the hotel bar.

If you have a car you can camp free at Ouano Beach, 12 km off the main highway between Bouloupari and La Foa. Toilets and showers are provided.

Bourail

Although this town, 167 km northwest of Nouméa, is the second largest in the territory, it's a disappointing little place after Nouméa. Along the one main street are the church, post office, banks, *gendarmerie,* town hall, and school, six essential facilities you'll find in most New Caledonian towns. Use Bourail as a stopover on a trip around the island or as a base for visiting the surrounding area. In August an agricultural fair is held here—the best time to come. The French army has two companies of infantry stationed near here.

There's not a lot to see in Bourail, although you could hike up to the cross on the hillside just east of town for the view. A market is held at the west end of Bourail on Tuesday and Saturday mornings. Worth a visit is the **Bourail Museum** (tel. 44-16-66) on the main street, in a storehouse remaining from the penitentiary set up here in 1867. The museum displays the history of the region, in particular the life of early French settlers, a few Kanak artifacts, seashells, and photos from WW II. It's open Wednesday, Saturday, and Sunday 0800-1100 and 1300-1700; admission free.

Plenty of buses pass through Bourail, and the times are posted on a board at the stop, but the drivers will only let you on if there's an empty seat. This can be a problem on Sunday and with buses headed for the east coast, which arrive full from Nouméa. Thus it's probably best to visit Bourail on your way back to Nouméa rather than getting out here on your way north.

Vicinity of Bourail

Bourail was an important New Zealand training base during WW II and there's a **N.Z. military cemetery** nine km southeast of town, right beside the main highway from Nouméa. About two km south is an **Arab cemetery** where convicts sent to New Caledonia after the Berber insurrection in Algeria in 1871 and their descendents (who still live in nearby Nessadiou village) are buried.

One recommended trip from Bourail takes in **Pierced Rock** (Roche Percée), on a side road eight km west. A tunnel cuts through an eroded quartz cliff here and at low tide you can get through to the other side. Don't attempt this at high tide, however, as there's rough sea there. Nearby is a very good beach for swimming, snorkeling, and freelance camping.

One km farther along the main road is the track up to **Belvédère Viewpoint,** with a fine view of Néra River, the coast, and Turtle Bay. **Turtle Bay** (Baie des Tortues) is just up the coast from Pierced Rock, accessible from the road to the viewpoint. Be there early in the morning between November and March to see nesting turtles (extremely rare). Camping is possible here, but it's open to the sea and wind.

Nine km past Pierced Rock along the same road is **Poé Beach,** the longest beach on Grande Terre. A camping ground and small resort share 18 km of unbroken sands.

Accommodations at Bourail

At the two-story **Monitel de Bourail** (B.P. 499, Bourail; tel. 44-17-77, fax 44-16-33), opposite the market at the north end of town, the 20 a/c rooms with bath and TV are CFP 5500/6000 single/double. The hotel restaurant has a good *plat du jour* lunch weekdays.

Hôtel La Néra (tel. 44-16-44, fax 44-18-31), beside the Néra River just southeast of Bourail, has eight a/c rooms with bath in a long sterile block at CFP 4800/5600 single/double.

Hôtel El Kantara (B.P. 244, Bourail; tel. 44-13-22, fax 44-20-33), by the Néra River near the Pierced Rock, eight km west of Bourail, has 20 rooms with bath at CFP 4500 single or double, CFP 5000 triple, swimming pool, and tennis court. The *pied noir* owner has endowed his hotel with an Algerian air. It's your best bet if you're driving.

At the beginning of Poé Beach, 16 km from Bourail, is a well-managed **campsite** (tel. 44-14-10) offering plenty of sand, banyan trees, fresh water, showers, toilets, and excellent surfing (CFP 400 per tent, plus CFP 100 per car).

The **Poé Beach Resort** (B.P. 481, Bourail; tel. 44-18-50, fax 44-10-70), about a kilometer farther up the same beach, has 24 fan-cooled rooms with fridge and TV at CFP 6600 single or double, CFP 7200 triple, plus six a/c bungalows at CFP 8500 single or double, CFP 9100 triple (no cooking facilities). The resort, which opened in 1991, has a restaurant, bar, pool, tennis courts, nine-hole golf course, horseback riding, and many other activities.

THE NORTHEAST COAST

Vicinity of Houaïlou
The winding road from Bourail follows sparkling rivers and crosses the **Col de Roussettes** (381 meters), a pass named for the big red fruit bats of the region. There are good views, especially of the abandoned Kanak taro terraces.

A kilometer off the main highway, four hours from Nouméa by bus, is the riverside town of Houaïlou, a Kanak stronghold. *Araucaria columnaris* pines are common here. Accommodation is provided by Mrs. Druminy (tel. 42-51-03), who has six rooms at CFP 1500/2000/2500 single/double/triple. Call ahead, as the rooms are often occupied on a long-term basis. A restaurant is nearby.

You could also camp on the wild, deserted beach adjacent to Houaïlou airstrip. The access

road is three km north of the bridge, then another two km to the beach (go around the south end of the airstrip). There's plenty of driftwood for campfires here, and you can get water from a tap at the airstrip, but this site is very exposed to the wind and sea.

Up the Coast
As you continue up the coast, your first stop will be spectacular **Bâ Falls,** 15 km northwest of Houaïlou bridge and on the mountain side only one and a half km upstream from the highway. There's a large swimming area at the base of the falls. After a swim, climb to the top for the view. (There have been reports of break-ins to the parked cars of visitors to the falls.)

Ponérihouen, 44 km northwest of Houaïlou, is a picturesque little town by the river of the same name. Coffee is the main cash crop in this area, and there's an experimental station in town. The long steel bridge just beyond Ponérihouen dates from WW II. Mr. Michel Blancher (tel. 42-85-14) allows camping opposite his store in Ponérihouen at CFP 1000 per tent.

Poindimié
This inviting small town, 308 km from Nouméa, was founded during WW II, as several Quonset huts attest, and today it's the administrative center of the northeast coast. Stock up at the Ballande supermarket in the center of town or change money at one of the banks. Buses to Hienghène leave at 1150 and 1310 Monday to Saturday, at 1510 on Sunday. Most buses to Nouméa (CFP 1250) leave Poindimié in the morning Monday to Saturday and around noon on Sunday.

Koyaboa Hill offers a fine overlook from its 390-meter summit. There's a jeep track from beyond Hôtel Le Tapoundari to the radio towers on top. The **public swimming pool** (CFP 200 admission, hours variable) near the hotel features a 1961 mosaic by Victor Vasarely, the famous Hungarian creator of op-art. The scuba diving in this area is good because there isn't any mine-produced erosion killing the reefs with sediment.

Accommodations at Poindimié
Hôtel Le Tapoundari (tel. 42-71-11), opposite Poindimié's WW II vintage bridge, has five standard rooms with private bath for CFP 3100/

(top left) scuba diver (photo by Ed Meili); (top right) acropora, Rose Island, American Samoa;
(bottom left) leaffish, Rose Island, American Samoa (preceding two photos by Gerald M. Ludwig,
U.S. Fish and Wildlife Service); (bottom right) fish and coral (Tahiti Tourisme)

(top) Children's Day procession, Tanna, Vanuatu
(bottom) rust in peace, American gun, Blunt's Point, Tutuila, American Samoa (photos by David Stanley)

3400/4200 single/double/triple, and six a/c rooms with cooking facilities at CFP 4500/4800/5600. Meals in the hotel restaurant are excellent.

The **Hôtel de la Plage** (B.P. 97, Poindimié; tel. 42-71-28, fax 42-70-44) is next to a grocery store near Tiéti Beach on the north edge of Poindimié. It charges CFP 5000 single or double for one of the 16 fan-cooled rooms, plus CFP 800 extra for one of the four with a/c. The hotel restaurant serves a good continental breakfast, including an ample pot of local coffee.

Poindimié's most upmarket place to stay is the **Monitel de Tiéti** (B.P. 154, Poindimié; tel. 42-72-73, fax 42-72-24), also at Tiéti Beach, with five a/c rooms at CFP 6500/7500 single/double and four rectangular bungalows at CFP 7500/8500. There's a swimming pool.

There's also a free **municipal camping area** at Tiéti Beach. It's a nice, grassy spot, but don't go off and leave your things unattended, as there have been rip-offs here.

Gîte Napoémien (tel. 42-74-77), in the lovely Napoémien Valley four km inland from Poindimié, has two bungalows with cooking facilities at CFP 1500 pp. Camping is CFP 1000 per tent (toilets and showers provided). Upon request, the managers will prepare a *bougna* picnic lunch sufficient for four people at CFP 3000 with chicken or CFP 3500 with prawns.

Touho

This small settlement on a bay, 27 km northwest of Poindimié, has a mission church (1889) typical of many on the island, plus mandarin orchards, coffee plantations, and tall pines. A few local fishing boats are based here, and Touho is a pleasant place to hang out for a few days.

Camping Aménagé Lévéque (B.P. 3, Touho; tel. 42-88-19), next to the grocery store in Touho, charges campers CFP 300 per tent, and there are basic bungalows with beds but no bedding in which you can roll out your sleeping bag for CFP 1000 pp.

Relais Alison (Madam Pisniak, B.P. 52, Touho; tel. 42-88-12), opposite Camping Lévéque, offers five a/c rooms with private bath at CFP 4500/5300 single/double. Meals are very expensive here.

Camping Gastaldi (tel. 42-88-24) is three km from town. Take the Hienghène road over the hill to a turnoff to the right, then it's one and a half km farther in toward the beach. This free camping ground rates among the nicest and most peaceful on the island.

Gîte de Mangalia (tel. 42-87-60) on the beach at Patouane, 13 km northwest of Touho, has eight duplex bungalows at CFP 4000 single or double. Cooking facilities are not provided and meals are expensive here.

HIENGHÈNE AND THE NORTH

The scenery around the small town of Hienghène (pronounced "yang-GAIN"), 376 km from Nouméa, is unquestionably the finest in New Caledonia. A hundred years ago Kanaks under Bouarate struggled against French colonialists here; in December 1984, 10 unarmed Kanaks on their way home from a political meeting were ambushed and murdered by French settlers just up the river.

Several km before Hienghène on the road from Touho, you see high **limestone cliffs** on the right with a salt lake at their base. A road leading to huge **Lindéralique Cave** *(grotte)* on the far side of these cliffs is three km before Hienghène (CFP 200 admission to the cave). There's a free campsite with running water on the beach a little before the *grotte*.

A bit closer to Hienghène at the top of the pass is a turnoff to the viewpoint *(point de vue)*—one of the most beautiful spots on the island. From here, you'll see huge isolated rocks named **Sphinx** (150 meters high) and **Brooding Hen** (60 meters high) guarding the mouth of Hienghène Bay. The town itself is on a rocky spur at the mouth of the river. Across the bay are nestled the tiny white buildings of **Ouaré Mission,** with the high coastal mountains behind. Several fine coral islets are seen offshore. From town the Brooding Hen looks more like the **Towers of Notre Dame,** its other name.

As you come into Hienghène, look between the viewpoint and the bridge is the **Centre Cultural Association Doohuny** (B.P. 72, Hienghène; tel. 42-81-50), which should be visited for its mixture of modern and traditional architecture. The exhibition room is open weekdays during office hours.

Araucaria columnaris
*pines before Hienghène's
Brooding Hen*

ARCHIVES NATIONALES SECTION OUTREMER, FRANCE

Tiendanite

Hike across the mountains from Hienghène to Voh along the "Chemin des Arabes" in a couple of days. The trail begins at Tiendanite up the valley and a rough road to Voh. Mr. Léopold Raguet (tel. 35-57-49) at Voh has four rooms for rent at CFP 1500 pp.

Tiendanite, the home village of former FLNKS leader Jean-Marie Tjibaou, has a special place in the history of New Caledonia. Fourteen Kanaks from this village were killed in a 1914 uprising against the French. During the 1917 uprising, the village was burnt to the ground, the men sent to prison in Nouméa, the women to work as servants for the *colons.* Later, Tjibaou's grandfather assembled some people to rebuild the village. In 1984, 10 men from this village of 120 people were brutally murdered by French *colons,* who were eventually set free by a French jury. No other village in the South Pacific has suffered more 20th-century colonial exploitation and genocide than Tiendanite. You can visit the graves of Tjibaou and the 10 killed in 1984.

Accommodations around Hienghène

Unfortunately there's nowhere to stay right in Hienghène itself. You can camp at the Base Nautique (tel. 42-81-51), on the beach below the football field (CFP 350 per tent to use the toilet and shower). Otherwise, you may be able to camp free at the Cultural Center.

The Ouenpouès tribe, between Hienghène and Ouaième, about seven km northwest of Hienghène, runs the **Gîte Wéouth** (Alice, tel. 42-81-19), with four bungalows at CFP 1500 pp. Camping is CFP 750 per tent.

In late 1992 the **Koulnoué Village Club Méditerranée** (B.P. 63, Hienghène; tel. 42-81-66, fax 42-81-75) opened 10 km south of Hienghène. The 50 thatched a/c bungalows are CFP 9500 single or double, meals not included. Activities include tennis, swimming pool, and other standard Club Med features. Hienghène airstrip is nearby. Bookings are handled by Agence Club Med (tel. 27-43-39, fax 26-33-87), 41-43 rue de Sébastopol, Nouméa. The local Kanak villagers received a 10% interest in the resort plus 40 hotel jobs in exchange for providing the land.

From Hienghène

Buses to Nouméa leave Hienghène in the early morning. A mail bus leaves Hienghène for Pouébo Monday, Tuesday, and Thursday at 1400, Friday at 1800, connecting in Pouébo with a bus to Koumac on Monday and Thursday only. Hitchhikers will find that very little traffic comes this way.

The coastline northwest from Hienghène features towering mountains with slopes falling right to the sea, empty beaches with fine coral just offshore, numerous high waterfalls clearly visible from the road, and deep green-blue rivers full of small fish such as you've never seen before.

This is also the most traditional area on Grande Terre, with the greatest number of *cases*.

There's a free ferry at Ouaième. A local legend explains that a bridge can never be built here because of a giant who lives up the river. The giant is part shark, and such a structure would block its route to the sea. What's known for sure is that the river is shark-infested, and it's unlikely you'll see any locals swimming here.

It's possible to climb to the top of **Mt. Panié** (1,639 meters), New Caledonia's highest peak, from near Tao waterfall; there are several shelters on the mountain for hikers.

Gîte de Galarino (Léon Foord, tel. 35-64-38), between the Ouaième ferry and Pouébo, has two self-contained bungalows at CFP 3000 and a beachside camping area at CFP 700 per tent. Parking is CFP 500 per car. It's an idyllic, end-of-the-world type of place.

Pouébo

The first Catholic missionaries arrived at Pouébo in 1847 but were soon driven off by the Kanak inhabitants. The persistent fathers returned in 1852 for a more successful second try to establish a mission. A gold rush here in the 1860s led to much French land grabbing and a Kanak revolt. The present mission church was completed in 1875. You can camp on St. Mathieu Beach, two km northeast of Pouébo.

Buses leave Pouébo for Koumac Monday and Thursday at 1600, Wednesday and Friday at 0825; for Nouméa via Koumac Monday to Thursday at 0600 and Sunday at 1015; for Nouméa via Hienghène Sunday at 1100; and for Hienghène Tuesday at 1130 and Thursday at 0900. This haphazard schedule calls for careful planning unless you have a car or are prepared to hitch.

Balade to Ouégoa

Balade, 17 km northwest of Pouébo, also has a notable place in New Caledonian history, as this is where Captain Cook landed in 1774. Later, Rear Admiral Despointes annexed New Caledonia for France at a ceremony near Balade in 1853, as a bronze monument (1913) by the highway loudly proclaims.

Just before the monument is the short access road to lovely Mahamate Beach, where Cook's men observed an eclipse of the sun on 6

September 1774. Today you may camp on these deserted sands. **Camping Col d'Amos** (Mr. Dubois) on the way to Ouégoa charges CFP 1000 per tent.

The Diahot River draining into Harcourt Bay in the far north of Grande Terre is navigable for 32 km. After the Diahot River Bridge near Ouégoa, traffic along the road increases. **Le Normandon** (tel. 35-68-28) near the bridge at Ouégoa has five basic rooms with bath at CFP 2000 pp. Camping is free if you take the expensive dinner (CFP 2000) at the restaurant.

THE NORTHWEST COAST

Koumac

This town, 370 km northwest of Nouméa, has little to offer the traveler other than a place to spend the night. Have a look at the Melanesian-style woodcarvings in the **Catholic church,** though. The church building itself was originally an aircraft hangar! The road inland beside the church leads seven km to some rather exciting **limestone caves.** The longest stretches three km underground, but hikers should keep in mind that there's no water in the vicinity. **Club Hippique La Crinière** (B.P. 319, Koumac; tel. 47-50-01; closed Monday), two km east of Koumac off the road to the caves, offers horseback riding.

A bus to Nouméa leaves Koumac daily at 1145 (5.5 hours, CFP 1450). Buses to Poum leave Koumac Monday to Thursday at 1540, Wednesday at 1315, Friday at 1615, and Sunday at 1710.

Accommodations at Koumac

Hôtel Le Grand Cerf (B.P. 58, Koumac; tel. 35-61-31, fax 35-60-16), on the traffic circle in the center of Koumac, has nine a/c bungalows with private facilities from CFP 5000/5500 single/double. The restaurant is good and there's a swimming pool. The Air Calédonie agent is here.

Cheaper, but not as nice, is **Hôtel Le Passiflore** (tel. 35-62-10), opposite Ballande supermarket 500 meters up the road to the caves. The six rooms with shared bath are CFP 3500 single or double; the five with private bath cost CFP 4500. **Snack la Panthère Rose** (tel. 35-63-47) near Le Passiflore is a good place for lunch or a beer.

Koumac's most upmarket place is **Monitel de Koumac** (B.P. 75, Koumac; tel. 35-66-66, fax 35-62-85), a few hundred meters down the road to Nouméa, with 13 bungalows and 16 a/c rooms starting at CFP 6500/7500 single/double. The weekday *plat du jour* lunch here is good value.

A campsite called **Camping de Pandop** (Monsieur Frouin, tel. 35-62-46) is windy but beautifully situated by the sea, only two km from Koumac (take the road opposite the church at the traffic circle and keep left). Camping is CFP 1000 per tent.

North of Koumac

The coastal highway runs 56 km northwest of Koumac to the town of Poum on Banaré Bay, with good views along the way. Tanle Bay, southeast of Poum, is a recognized hurricane shelter for shipping. From the village, you can climb Mt. Poum (413 meters) in about an hour. **Chez Madame Frouin Restaurant** (tel. 35-64-70), near the beach at Poum, has three self-catering rooms for CFP 4500, but it's often full. Watch your gear if you camp freelance on the beach at Poum.

Facing the white sands of Néhoué Bay, 15 km southeast of Poum, is the **Malabou Beach Hôtel** (B.P. 4, Poum; tel. 35-60-60, fax 35-60-70), part of the Accor/Novotel hotel chain. Opened in October 1991, the hotel has 37 spacious a/c bungalows beginning at CFP 9300 double. Add CFP 5650 pp for three meals (no cooking facilities). Tennis courts, freshwater swimming pool, and full sporting facilities are offered. The **Pacific Diving Center** is based here. An 850-meter airstrip has been built next to the property.

Some 31 km north of Poum, near Boat-Pass, the northernmost tip of Grande Terre, is the **Gîte de Poingam** (Henry Fairbank, tel. 88-24-20), with seven bungalows accommodating up to four persons at CFP 5000/5600/6200 single/double/triple. Camping is CFP 500 per tent, plus CFP 200 pp. The seafood served in the restaurant is excellent. You'll need your own transport to get here.

Belep Islands

Twice a week, there's an Air Calédonie flight from Koumac to the Belep Islands (CFP 5630 one-way), some 50 km north of Grande Terre's northern tip. The flight lands near Wala on Art Island. This trip is worth taking if you want to get well off the beaten track, but book ahead in Nouméa and be prepared to camp. Occasional boats ply the waters between Wala and Poum.

From 1892 to 1898, these islands were used as a leper colony, and the French forcibly exiled all the inhabitants to Balade. There's still a bit of resentment over this, but once the locals know you're not French, they're more friendly.

Koné

The 100-km road southeast from Koumac to Koné offers only occasional gum trees to break the monotony—this is cattle country. Koné is the capital of the North Province and a growing administrative center; several banks are here. As part of the development of this area, a new road is being built from Koné to Poindimié with French aid money. Although Koné has some appeal, the main reasons for stopping are the horseback expeditions organized by two local companies. Both offer weeklong excursions across the mountains from Koné to Hienghène and back, or shorter three-day rides into the Pamalé Valley.

Koné Rodeo (Patrick Ardimanni, tel. 35-51-51) does a seven-day Hienghène ride and three-day mountain rides (CFP 22,000 pp). The price is all-inclusive (typical French Caledonian food, lodging, evening campfires, horses, etc.). A minimum of eight persons is required to do a trip, but they do as many as 30 a year and individuals can join one of them, so call well ahead. Patrick has 40 horses and speaks good English.

The other horseback company is **Randonnée Equestre** (Eric Tikarso, tel. 35-53-68), based in the Kanak village of Ateou. Eric lives beside the cemetery in Koné. Randonnée requires five participants, and you'll need to know a little French. These rides must be arranged in advance either by phoning or through Center Voyages/American Express (B.P. 50, Nouméa; tel. 28-40-40, fax 27-26-36). If you're looking to join a group, weekends are best. This is a great opportunity if you can spare the cash.

The ultraenergetic can hike to **Foué Beach** (six km one-way), where camping is possible, or climb **Koné Peak** (236 meters) via Baco village (four km one-way).

Southbound buses to Nouméa (CFP 1100) leave Koné daily at 1310, Monday to Saturday at 0805, and Sunday at 1215. Northbound, you can catch a bus to Koumac Monday to Saturday at 1540 and Sunday at 1410; to Poum Monday to Thursday at 1410 and Sunday at 1540; and to Pouébo Wednesday at 1210.

Accommodations at Koné

Budget travelers usually stay at 15-room **L'Escale de Koné** (Madame Yoshida, B.P. 25, Koné; tel. 35-51-09), right at the bus stop in Koné, where a room without bath is CFP 3000/3500 single/double, with bath CFP 3500/4000. Meals are served.

Relais Madiana (Madam Vincon, B.P. 339, Koné; tel. 35-50-09, fax 35-50-03), a block away in the center of town, has four a/c rooms at CFP 3200/4300/5500 single/double/triple. At last report the Madiana was closed for renovations, so these prices may have changed.

The 20-room **Monitel l'Hibiscus** (B.P. 45, Koné; tel. 35-52-61, fax 35-55-35), a few blocks away at the town's south entrance, is CFP 5000/6500 single/double and up.

The **Hôtel Koniambo** (Yannick Girard, B.P. 35, Koné; tel. 35-51-86, fax 35-53-03), directly opposite the airstrip three km west of Koné, charges CFP 5500/6000 for one of the 13 self-catering rooms with bath or the 12 a/c bungalows without cooking facilities (plus CFP 500 if you use the a/c). Ask about their special weekend rate. The Koniambo allows camping free of charge for those taking dinner (CFP 1800 including wine) at their restaurant. They have a swimming pool.

Inland from Koné, the **Gîte de Atéou** (tel. 35-56-13) near the Pamalé Valley has one Kanak *case* at CFP 1500; camping is also possible.

South of Koné

The **Hôtel Le Bougainville** (B.P. 78, Pouembout; tel. 35-52-55, fax 35-59-84) at Pouembout, nine km south of Koné, has six bungalows and seven a/c rooms at CFP 5800 single or double, CFP 6300 triple. The hotel's restaurant and reception area share a mock Kanak *grande case*.

If you have your own transportation you could also go to **Gîte Le Tamaon** (B.P. 46, Pouembout; tel./fax 35-57-26), on a cattle station 13 km from Pouembout. The two rooms with shared bath are CFP 1000 pp, a bungalow CFP 3000/4000 with kitchenette. Horseback riding is arranged.

Between Pouembout and Poya is the old nickel port of Népoui, now being redeveloped as an alternative port to Nouméa for North Province. Large open-cut nickel mines are here. The **Adio Caves** at Poya are 14 km off the main highway; there's little traffic, so forget it unless you have your own transportation.

unicornfish (Naso unicornus)

ISLE OF PINES

Across a strait of shoals and coral banks, 70 km southeast of Grande Terre, is the stunningly beautiful Isle of Pines, famous for its former French penal colony. In 1774 Captain Cook named the 17-by-14-km island for its extraordinary 60-meter-high *columnaris,* but the Kanak name is Kwenyii (Kunié). The chiefs of this enticing isle arrived from Aneityum in present Vanuatu centuries ago, and the Kwenyii people were great traders, sailing far and wide in their big outrigger canoes.

British Protestant missionaries landed in 1841 but were killed a year later when they became involved in a dispute between sandalwood traders and the Kwenyii islanders. More recently, missionaries of a different kind tried to build a 600-bed Club Med on the island, but the locals torpedoed the project when they learned that it would have meant converting the entire Kanuméra/Kuto area into an out-of-bounds pleasure resort for affluent foreigners. Their foresight means these fantastic cocaine-white beaches are largely untouched—a tropical paradise of the first order. During the **Festival of the Yams,** which coincides with the yam harvest in March or April, you'll see *pilou* dancing and formal presentations of yams.

Orientation

Because the French government has not tried to deprive the Kwenyii people of their island, they remained aloof during the political upheavals of the 1980s, which had little affect on tourism here. Thus you needn't fear that you are walking into a tense situation, because you aren't. The locals welcome visitors and a few simple courtesies will ensure that you remain on their good side. Be aware, for example, that nude or topless sunbathing is not allowed on the Isle of Pines, and that walking around villages or along the road in a bathing suit is also bad form. Windsurfing is allowed in Kuto and Kanuméra bays, but not elsewhere, and those interested in fishing or freelance camping should ask permission of a local adult. Discretion in the use of alcohol is also wise.

SIGHTS

Kanuméra/Kuto

Kanuméra/Kuto is one of the gems of the Pacific: Kuto with its long rolling surf, Kanuméra with its gentle turquoise waters. The talcum-soft beaches curve around a narrow neck of sand, which joins the **Kuto Peninsula** to the rest of the island. Towering pines contrast with curving palms, casuarinas, gum trees, ferns, wild orchids, and other flowers to create an environment of exotic richness, separated from the sea by a wide strip of snowy white sand. Kanuméra is a photographer's dream, although the snorkeling is second-rate.

Follow the footpath from the main wharf right around the Kuto Peninsula for a series of scenic views. Another good walk is to the northwest

ISLE OF PINES

(map showing: GADJI PASS, GIE ISLAND, OUPERE GROTTO, BAY OF CRABS, UPE PASS, MONEORO ISLAND, GADJI, ISLE OF PINES, OUATOMO ISLAND, WAPAN, AIRPORT, OUMAGNE CAVES, OUAMEO BAY, OUATCHIA CAVE, PARADISE CAVE, KOUMO ISLAND, IRON PLATEAU, ORO PENINSULA, OUPI BAY, OURO BAY, DEPORTEE'S CEMETERY, KUTEMA BEACH, OURO BAKERY, MORO ISLAND, KUTO BAY, WHARF, PIC NGA (262 m), ST. JOSEPH BEACH, KOUTOMO ISLAND, BAYONNAISE ISLAND, VAO, ADVENTURE ISLAND, VAO BAY, GU BAY, BROSSE ISLAND, KANUMERA BAY, 5 km, N)

Big dugout sailing canoes line St. Joseph's Beach on the Isle of Pines.

around Kuto Bay, then across the rocky headland on the trail to wild **Kutema Bay.**

For a sweeping panorama of the entire island and a profile of Grande Terre on the horizon, climb to the cross atop **Pic Nga** (262 meters) in an hour (easy). The trailhead is midway on the Kanuméra/Kuto cutoff, but it's poorly marked; look carefully to the southeast of the house with several pine trees in the front yard. You'll know you're going the right way when you start seeing red paint splashed on the trees.

Farther Afield

During 1871-1879, around 3,900 political prisoners from the Paris Commune were held on the Isle of Pines. After an amnesty in 1880 the *communards* were allowed to return to France and the island continued as a regular prison colony until 1912. Pigs now forage in the old prison yard and the narrow, cheerless brick cells— snuffling scavengers in the gloomy and forbidding atmosphere. Some of the ruins are visible behind the **bakery** at Ouro, but the baker's vicious dogs deter visitors. One building can be reached via the track inland on the other side of the highway.

To get to the **Deportees' Cemetery,** continue one km north on the airport road and take the first turn on the right. The cemetery where some 260 deportees are buried is to the left, about 500 meters inland. To the right is a track right across the island.

The administrative center and largest village on the island is Vao, seven km east of Kanuméra. French Catholic missionaries arrived at Vao in 1848, and the present church dates from 1860. Unfortunately, its interior has been ruined by a heavy-handed restoration. Climb up to the chapel above the church for the view. The chief's house *(chefferie)* at Vao is surrounded by a driftwood palisade.

Two km due east of the church is **St. Joseph Beach,** with as fine a collection of large dugout sailing canoes *(pirogues)* as you'll find anywhere in the Pacific. Oupi Bay is dotted with their sails. Daily at 0930 and 1330 the glass-bottom boat *Douetikorail* (tel. 46-10-10) does 90-minute scenic cruises around Oupi Bay from St. Joseph.

Speleology

The Isle of Pines boasts three important caves, each one different from the others. Using the map, **Paradise Cave** is very easy to find: take the obvious path to the right at the end of the access road. Much of the cave is flooded, and there are refreshing pools where you can take a dip, but only experienced scuba divers with lamps and a guide should enter the dark areas.

The **Oumagne Caves** are a 30-minute walk from the airport, and these can also be done on your own—this is a cave for everyone. The cave floor is relatively level, and a large opening at the far end provides lighting. A fast-flowing stream disappears into the cave as swarms of swallows circle overhead. During tribal fighting in

Thick stalactites hang in the Oumagne Caves, a few kilometers from the Isle of Pines's airport.

1855-56, Hortense, daughter of Grand Chief Vendegou, took refuge in this cave for several months. Later she became Queen Hortense and a close collaborator with Marist missionaries on the island.

The unmarked trail to **Ouatchia Cave** begins about a 40-minute walk southeast of the Oumagne Caves. Watch for a cross on a hilltop to the right (the second cross you'll see) and a low ridge off to the left. The trail begins behind some houses a few hundred meters north, where there are pine trees on both sides of the road. You'll probably have to find someone to ask, and getting a guide to lead you through the cave would be a very good idea. Give him a pack of cigarettes for his trouble. With a good flashlight, you can go along the narrow passage quite a distance underground past some sparkling white formations. Ouatchia Cave is by far the most difficult of these three caves, but it's also the best.

Scuba Diving

New Caledonia's top scuba diving operator is **Nauticlub** (B.P. 18, Vao, Isle of Pines; tel. 46-11-22, fax 46-12-27), also known as the Kunié Scuba Center, based at the Relais de Kodjeue and on the Kuto Peninsula. The charge is CFP 6000

(one tank), CFP 8000 (two tanks), plus CFP 1000 for gear (if required). There's a CFP 5000 surcharge if less than four divers are present. If you'd like to learn to dive, their four-day PADI open-water course is CFP 42,000 (medical statement required). Swiss diving instructor Tony Klotz has been on the island over 20 years and knows around 40 dive sites. Ask him about the poisonous sea snakes sometimes encountered here.

The best reef diving is at **Gadji Pass** off the north end of the island, especially the **Gie Island Drop-off** and fantastic **Oupere Grotto.** The strong tidal flow means abundant marinelife and spectacular coral and sponge coloration, which can be appreciated through rents in the reef. Nauticlub also offers freshwater diving into **Paradise Cave,** with its huge stalactites and stalagmites—truly a unique experience.

PRACTICALITIES

Accommodations

Gîte Ouré (Christine Kouathe, B.P. 28, Isle of Pines; tel. 46-11-20) at the east end of beautiful Kanuméra Bay is a perfect place to camp (CFP 1000 per tent). For those without a tent, there are eight small beach bungalows in a gardenlike setting. The charge is CFP 1500/2000 single/double in bungalows with shared facilities, and CFP 3000/3700 single/double in bungalows with private facilities capable of accommodating up to three or four (beware of mice in all units).

Gîte Nataiwatch (Guillaume et Eulalie Kouathe, B.P. 26, Isle of Pines; tel. 46-11-13, fax 46-12-29) is in the same area as Gîte Ouré but farther inland away from the beach. The four older thatched bungalows with a fridge, cooking facilities, and shared bath and the eight newer units with private bath but no kitchens are all CFP 4900/5500/6100 single/double/triple. Camping is in a separate area with a shelter and amenities block (CFP 900/1200 single/double). The restaurant (closed,Sunday) at the Nataiwatch is pleasant; nonguests are welcome to wander in and order a meal or a drink, one of the few places on the island where you can do this. You're probably better off splurging on the snails (CFP 2500) or lobster (CFP 3200) here; just let them know ahead.

The Isle of Pines' newest property is the **Hôtel Koubugny** (Gustave Petersen, B.P. 1, Isle of Pines; tel./fax 46-12-23), which opened in early 1995 just across the road from Kuto Bay. The 12 a/c bungalows are overpriced at CFP 12,000 for a triple unit, CFP 14,000 for a five-person family unit (no camping). The hotel restaurant caters mostly to Japanese day-trippers who have lunch here, but they'll prepare you an excellent seafood meal (CFP 3500 complete) upon request.

Just inland from Kuto Bay and behind the restaurant of the same name is **Gîte Kuberka** (Caroline Vendegou, B.P. 4, Isle of Pines; tel. 46-11-18, fax 46-11-58), with three bungalows and eight rooms at CFP 4800/5400/6000 single/double/triple, all with private bath, TV, and fridge (no cooking facilities). Camping is CFP 800/1000 single/double.

At the far end of Kuto Bay is **Gîte La Reine Hortense** (Eugène et Suzanne Apikaoua, B.P. 38, Isle of Pines; tel. 46-11-19), which charges about the same as Gîte Nataiwatch but tends to get a lot of wind off the open sea. Cooking facilities are provided, and you can camp. At last report this place was closed.

Scuba divers often stay at the **Relais de Kodjeue** (Jojo et Agnès Lepers, B.P. 75, Isle of Pines; tel./fax 46-11-42) on an excellent beach at Ouaméo Bay. The nine bungalows with private bath (six of them also with cooking facilities) are CFP 5800 single or double. Six newer bungalows without kitchens are CFP 6500. A six-unit block without cooking facilities costs CFP 4100 per room. There's no camping. The Relais de Kodjeue has a swimming pool, tennis court, and sailboats for rent. It's also one of the only places on the islands where you can rent a car or motor scooter, but check them carefully before you ride off. The food in the restaurant is excellent, and you can even buy groceries here if you want to cook your own.

Gîte Manamaky (Arlette Vakoume, B.P. 24, Isle of Pines; tel. 46-11-31) is on lovely St. Joseph Beach, two km east of Vao. The seven thatched bungalows with bath are CFP 4800/5300/5800 single/double/triple (no cooking facilities). Camping is possible. If you'd like to tour the island by *pirogue* (CFP 3500 pp), ask here. Credit cards are not accepted.

Food

All of the gîtes serve meals but eating at them twice a day quickly becomes expensive. Luckily there are four grocery stores at Vao, open Monday to Saturday 0700-1200 and 1500-1900, Sunday 1000-1200. The bakery at Ouro opens Monday to Saturday 0630-1000 and 1630-1800 only. Early Saturday morning a small market materializes at Vao; another at Kuto is open Wednesday and Saturday mornings 0645-0800. If you're a drinker, bring your own supply from Nouméa.

Restaurant Kuberka (tel. 46-11-18), just inland from Kuto, specializes in upscale seafoods, like small sweet lobster, marinated squid, and fried fish, served at trestle tables beneath a thatched roof. You must order ahead. Nearby is a French military vacation camp (tel. 46-11-14) with a well-stocked bar, but you're not welcome.

Services

The post office and clinic are in Vao, while the *gendarmerie* is at Kuto. There's no bank on the island, so change enough money before leaving Nouméa.

Transportation

Air Calédonie flies to the Isle of Pines twice a day (CFP 5030) with additional flights on weekends. Japanese day-trippers often pack the planes, so book well ahead. The isle's wartime airport sits on an 81-meter-high plateau at the center of the island, nine km from Kanuméra. There's a bus from the airport to the *gîtes* (CFP 1500 roundtrip), but it's only there if someone has reserved a room at a *gîte*. Air Calédonie has an office (tel. 46-11-08) at Kuto open weekdays 0730-0800, 0930-1115, and 1400-1600. At other times, read the blackboard outside.

The interisland ferry *Président Yeiwéné* ties up to the wharf on Kuto Bay. The vessel departs Nouméa for the Isle of Pines every Friday at 1900, charging CFP 3000/3500 economy/first class for the 11-hour overnight trip. It spends Saturday night at Kuto, departing for the return Sunday at 1500 (CFP 1500 for a seat on this seven-hour trip). A special weekend return package is available at CFP 11,500/15,000 economy/first class, accommodations included. Book well ahead.

The *gîtes* or Nauticlub can arrange car rentals at CFP 5000 a day, plus CFP 50 per km. Bicycles rent for CFP 1200 a half day, CFP 1700 a full day. A cash deposit is required.

Traffic is thin around the island, but most people will give you a lift, and if you don't mind doing a lot of walking, you should be able to complete the 40-km loop around the island in one day. The *gîtes* can arrange a three-hour island minibus tour for around CFP 1500.

THE LOYALTY ISLANDS

This coralline group, 100 km east of Grande Terre, consists of the low-lying islands of Ouvéa, Lifou, Tiga, and Maré, each about 50 km apart, plus several islets. Though Captain Cook never saw them, the Loyalties are visible from the tops of New Caledonia's mountains. The people are mostly Kanak, although Ouvéa was colonized by Polynesians from Wallis Island hundreds of years ago. In 1899, the French government declared the Loyalties an indigenous reserve, thus they were spared the worst features of colonialism, and almost 99% of the population is Kanak.

The lifestyle here is unhurried, and many people grow their own yams, taro, and sweet potatoes in bush gardens. If you're here for the sand and sun, the Loyalties have some of the finest beaches in the world. The locals are pleasant and friendly, the camping is fine, and tourism is undeveloped. Be aware, however, that almost nobody speaks English (though you'll get by).

The Protestant missionaries who arrived on Maré in 1841 and Lifou in 1842 had already converted most of the inhabitants by the time the French colony was declared in 1853. French Catholics arrived at Maré in 1866, and a period of religious strife ensued. After a battle on Maré in 1871, some 900 Catholicized islanders were exiled with their French missionaries to the Isle of Pines.

Today these islands are a stronghold of the independence movement, and Ouvéa in particular has suffered terribly from events described elsewhere in this chapter. Fortunately, most locals can distinguish between French officials and legitimate visitors, but it's always a good idea to make it very clear to everyone that you're not French.

OUVÉA

Ouvéa (Iaai) is everything you'd expect in a South Pacific island. Twenty-five km of unbroken white sands border the lagoon on the west side of the island and extend far out from shore, giving the water a turquoise hue. The wide western lagoon, protected by a necklace of coral islands and a barrier reef, is the only one of its kind in the Loyalties. Croissant-shaped Ouvéa is tilted, with rocky cliffs pounded by surf on the eastern ocean side of the island, but fine beaches may be found even here. At one point on this narrow atoll, only 45 meters separates the two coasts.

Traditional circular houses with pointed thatched roofs are still common in the villages, and the compound of each village chief on Ouvéa is surrounded by a high palisade of driftwood logs. Two of the best of these are at St. Joseph. Due to a Polynesian invasion in the 18th century, the inhabitants of the far ends of the island (St. Joseph, Lékine, Mouli) speak the Wallisian language (Ua), while those in the cen-

OUVÉA

ter speak Iaai, the original Kanak tongue. All 3,500 Ouvéa islanders speak French as well. Until the recent troubles, Ouvéa produced 80% of the territory's copra.

On 4 May 1988, this enchanted island was the scene of the Ouvéa Massacre when 300 French police stormed a cave near Gossana to rescue 16 *gendarmes* held hostage there after being captured on 22 April by pro-independence Kanak commandos. Nineteen Kanaks died in the assault, including several who suffered extrajudicial execution at the hands of the French police after being wounded and taken prisoner. None of the hostages had been harmed. Thus Ouvéa is a symbol of martyrdom and the heroic resistance of the Kanak people to the savage repression of French colonialism.

Northern Ouvéa

A paved highway extends south from St. Joseph to Fayaoué (23 km), the administrative center, then on to Mouli (another 19 km). St. Joseph is a friendly village strung along the lagoon, with several general stores and a large Catholic mission (1912). Near the mission is the low stockade of the local chief's *case*. This chief also runs the adjoining store, and he may give you permission to camp on the beach. The beach curves northwest away from St. Joseph.

Also, there are several fine protected beaches at Ognat, eight km east of St. Joseph on the ocean side. To reach the large natural **sinkhole** *(trou d'eau)* near the coast, several km southeast of St. Joseph, take the Ognat road east and turn right at Weneki just after a curve. Keep straight ahead past an abandoned quarry. At the fork a kilometer beyond this, go left. The sinkhole is near some coconut trees and a large garden at the end of the road. The Grand Chief of Weneki keeps turtles in the brackish water of the hole until they are required for his table, but never mind, you can swim. No one has ever found the bottom of this deep, dark hole. There's another sinkhole, the **Trou d'Anawa,** at Casse-Cou between St. Joseph and Wadrilla.

At Wadrilla, visit the graves of the 19 Kanaks murdered by French troops in 1988. During a commemorative ceremony for these men exactly one year after the event, FLNKS leaders Jean-Marie Tjibaou and Yeiwéné Yeiwéné were assassinated here by a Kanak activist who felt they had sold out the independence cause by making a deal with the French government. Ironically, the death of the two leaders froze that agreement into a sort of holy writ, which no one has dared to tamper with since. Whether it will ever lead to independence as Tjibaou and Yeiwéné wished remains to be seen.

Southern Ouvéa

Beyond the east end of the airstrip, near the center of the island, is a road leading straight to a high limestone cliff thick with stalactites and stalagmites. The entrance to **Ouloup Cave** is just opposite, a small opening at the back of the pit. Bones from old burials may be seen. The guide to the caves lives in the house at the end of the airstrip, and if he's around, ask his permission before proceeding. Midway between the house and the cliff is a banyan tree on the right; a deep hole under the tree contains water. It's thought that the roots of this banyan and those of another at Canala on Grande Terre connect through this "way of the spirits." Notice a water-filled cave farther along on the right.

At Fayaoué, strung along the lagoon near the middle of the atoll, are the post office, clinic, and two small stores. Farther south, many tropical fish are visible from the bridge connecting Mouli to the rest of Ouvéa, and the swimming here is good (but beware of currents). The famous cliffs of Lékine are also clearly visible from this bridge. Approach them by following the beach around. Long ago, before the island was uplifted, wave action undercut these towering walls of limestone. Massive stalactites tell of the great caverns for which this area is noted. On this island of superb beaches, the best is at Mouli.

Accommodations

There are a number of *gîtes* opposite the beach at Fayaoué. **Gîte Beautemps-Beaupré** (Suzanne Oine, B.P. 52, Ouvéa; tel. 45-71-32) is at Banout, just north of the junction of the airport and lagoonside roads. The three rooms with shared bath are CFP 3500 single or double, the three thatched bungalows CFP 5000. Good food is served here, and they rent cars and bicycles. **Gîte Hwatau** (Chez Suzanne Apopa; tel. 45-72-59) and **Gîte Fleury** (Fleury Trondgnajo, tel. 45-71-36) are to the left of the junction, both around CFP 3500 double. Ask Fleury about cheaper *case* accommodations. In 1995 the 20-bungalow **Ouvéa Beach Resort** opened at Fayaoué. A camping ground is at Lékine. Ouvéa has a water shortage, so use it sparingly.

Transportation

Air Calédonie (tel. 45-71-42) lands at Ouloup Airstrip, six km from Fayaoué, several times a day (CFP 7490 from Nouméa, CFP 3620 from Lifou). A bus meets most of the flights from Nouméa (except on Sunday) for the ride to Fayaoué post office, or all the way to St. Joseph, where the driver lives.

The interisland ferry *Président Yeiwéné* (tel. 45-52-50) ties up to a wharf on the lagoon side between Fayaoué and St. Joseph. The ferry leaves Nouméa for Ouvéa every other Monday afternoon and continues to Lifou and Nouméa early Tuesday morning. There are no voyages from Lifou to Ouvéa.

LIFOU

Lifou (Drehu), the largest and most populous of the Loyalties, is *the* place for the adventurer to get very lost for a while. It's a bigger island than Tahiti or Western Samoa's Upolu. Like Maré, Lifou is a raised atoll, and the cliffs and terraces of the various periods of geologic emergence are clearly visible from the air.

Some 8,500 people live on Lifou, and Drehu, the local language, is the most widely spoken of the Kanak languages. Wé, the main town, is the administrative center of the Loyalty Islands, but the three grand chiefs of Lifou reside at Nathalo, Dueulu, and Mou. British Protestant missionaries arrived at Mou in 1842 and converted the local chief. When the Catholics landed after the French takeover in 1853, a rival chief in northern Lifou welcomed them, and a period of religious strife began that was finally settled when a French military expedition conquered Lifou in 1864.

Traditional round houses resembling beehives with conical roofs are still common on Lifou. During the cool season, the locals light a fire in the stone hearth of their *case* and sleep there on woven mats. The rest of the year people move back into their houses and the *cases* are vacant. You may be invited to occupy one—you'll find it hard to repay their kindness.

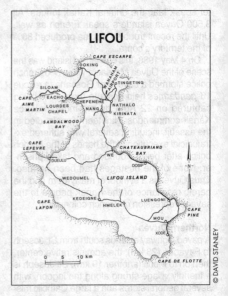

Around Lifou

Wé is situated on Châteaubriand Bay at the south end of a truly magnificent white beach. Wé's Catholic church with its round towers looks like it was transported here from Mexico. Nearby is the grave of Fao, a Polynesian Protestant missionary who arrived in 1842 to found a mission. Just a five-minute walk from Gîte Luécilla near Wé is a **cave** with a clear freshwater pool where you can swim. To get there, take the Nathalo road and look for a path near some wrecked cars on the left.

The good modern highway from Wé to Mou and Xodé follows the coast beside a cliff thick with stalagmites and passes a superb protected beach with talcum sand at Luengöni. A large cave with an underground pool is found between Mou and Xodé, along with another fine beach on the coast here.

The *case* of the grand chief of Nathalo, near the airport, is the largest of its kind in New Caledonia. A low palisade surrounds this imposing structure held aloft by great tree trunks set in a circle. Ask permission to go inside. Even more massive is **Nathalo Church** (1883), a monument to the zeal of early French Catholicism. The interior retains the original decoration.

About 15 km northwest of Nathalo is Doking village, the houses of which are perched above the coastal cliffs. The snorkeling here is good.

There's another cave and underground pool near the highway on the east side of Chépénéhe—in fact, you'll find these everywhere on Lifou if you ask. One of the most picturesque spots on the island is the **Chapel of Our Lady of Lourdes** (1898), perched atop a peninsula above Sandalwood Bay, five km east of Chépénéhe. To get there, take a bus or hitch five km west to Eacho, then follow a poorly marked track after the last house (ask). The view from the chapel is breathtaking, and there's a fair beach nearby (on any other island it would be considered excellent). Between the chapel and Chépénéhe is a new wharf where your ship might decide to drop you.

Accommodations

The **Relais des Cocotiers** (Pierre Pilgrim, B.P. 75, Wé; tel. 45-11-36) is near the stadium at Wé, 15 km south of the airport. It's only a short walk from the administrative center but far from the beach. The six thatched bungalows with private bath are CFP 4000/4500/5000 single/double/triple. The Relais has a popular restaurant/bar that's well worth seeking out, even if you're not staying here.

The village you see across Châteaubriand Bay from the wharf at Wé is Luécilla. On the fine white beach near the village is **Motel Chez Rachelle** (Rachel Peteisi, B.P. 95, Wé; tel. 45-12-43), also known as the Gîte de Luécilla..The eight thatched bungalows with private bath and TV are CFP 6500/7000/7500 single/double/triple, while the three rooms are CFP 6000/6500/7500. Cooking facilities are provided in all of these. Otherwise you can camp at CFP 500 pp.

Lifou's most upmarket accommodation is the **Hôtel Lifou Plaisance** (B.P. 63, Wé; tel. 45-14-44, fax 45-13-33), on the beach at Dosip, a small village seven km southeast of Wé. There are three large four-room bungalows; the 12 rooms each cost CFP 5500/8000/9600 single/double/triple, and there's a restaurant, swimming pool, tennis court, sauna, gymnasium, etc. Rental cars and bicycles are available.

Gîte Neibash (B.P. 308, Wé; tel. 45-15-68) at Luengöni has three bungalows at CFP 6000/

6500 single/double, and one traditional Kanak *case* at CFP 2500 pp. Camping is CFP 1000 and bicycles are for rent.

Gîte Hnaxulu (B.P. 21, Wé; tel. 45-16-42) at Wédoumel has five bungalows at CFP 3500 triple and *case* accommodation at CFP 1500 pp. **Gîte Dueulu** (tel. 45-14-32) at Dueulu provides *case* space at CFP 1500. **Faré Falaise** (Georges Kahlemu, tel. 45-16-48) at Doking is similar.

It's easy to find a place to camp elsewhere, just ask permission first.

Other Practicalities

All clustered together at Wé you'll find the post office, two banks, town hall, clinic (tel. 45-12-12), Air Calédonie office (tel. 45-11-11), and *gendarmerie* (tel. 45-12-17). A grocery store is also at Wé.

Saturday morning there's a market in the hall in front of Wanaham Airport, two km from Nathalo village, and near the airport terminal is a small store where you can get hot tea and coffee.

The *gîtes* will pick up guests with reservations at the airport for CFP 1800 roundtrip. Buses from Wé, Eacho, and other parts of the island connect with the afternoon flight to/from Nouméa, which makes this the best time to arrive.

The interisland ferry *Président Yeiwéné* (tel. 45-19-59) departs from the new wharf at Wé for Maré and Nouméa every other Tuesday morning, direct to Nouméa every other Tuesday afternoon and every Thursday afternoon. There are no departures for Ouvéa. Occasionally another wharf at Chépénéhe is used, so check and book ahead.

Garage Avenod (tel. 45-11-42) at Luécilla near Wé rents cars at about CFP 8000 a day, but make sure there's adequate fuel; Lifou often experiences shortages. The hitching on Lifou is much better than on Maré or Ouvéa, as there are many more cars and everyone stops.

TIGA

The Air Calédonie flight between Lifou and Maré stops on this two-by-six-km island twice a week (CFP 3570 from Lifou, CFP 2840 from Maré). Legend tells how a rat once tried to hitch a ride from Lifou to Maré on the back of a passing turtle. The turtle eventually tired of this and threw the rat off its back, forming the tiny island of Tiga.

The one 350-inhabitant village, near the airstrip in the northwest corner of the island, has a small store and a good beach. A north-south track approaches the cliffs at the south end of Tiga. You'll have to camp or sleep in the airport if you stop over.

MARÉ

Maré (Nengone) is an uplifted atoll, its elevated plateau flanked by dramatic cliffs and punctuated with caves. The island's 6,000 inhabitants speak a language known as Nengone, and there are divisions between Protestants and Catholics. Oranges were once common on Maré (harvested in May and June), but the orchards have not been replanted. It's a friendly, welcoming island.

Around Maré

Maré Airport is only two km from a large Catholic mission at La Roche. Massive stone walls enclose the mission compounds, and a tall, white Gothic church towers above the settlement, itself dominated by a high limestone cliff topped by a cross. You'll need sturdy shoes to climb up to the

cross on a path departing from the north side of the church; there's a sweeping view of the pine-studded island. In time of war, the Maré people have always sought refuge on this cliff, and it's called "La Roche qui Pleure" (the rock that weeps). Religious fighting took place here in 1869, 1880, and 1890. A road leads north from La Roche Mission a kilometer and a half to the picturesque cliffs on the coast (no beach). The location is lovely, and there's plenty of space to pitch a tent.

Just beyond Wakoné, seven km east of La Roche, is a deep abyss in the coastal cliffs, which ancient warriors would leap across to prove their bravery, giving the place its name, **Le Saut du Guerrier** (Warrior's Leap). The scenery around here is superb.

The island's administrative center is at Tadine, where the ship from Nouméa calls. A monument at the wharf recalls the 126 persons who perished in the disappearance of the interisland trader *Monique* in 1953. No trace of the ship was ever found. The assassinated Kanak leader Yeiwéné Yeiwéné is buried in this, his hometown.

At Netche, eight km north of Tadine, is the residence of Nidoish Naisseline, grand chief of Maré and a leader of Liberation Kanak Socialiste (LKS). Chief Naisseline has withdrawn his party's support from the Matignon Accords process, which he feels has diverted the Kanak political movement from its true objective of independence, yet in 1995 he was elected president of Loyalty Islands Province. Several monuments near Chief Naisseline's house across from the adjacent church commemorate early Protestant missionaries.

Ceigeïté Beach, eight km south of Tadine, is Maré's finest, its palm-fringed white sands and clear waters inviting the swimmer and snorkeler. At Medu village, southeast of Wabao, is a deep karst cave. The 138-meter-high coastal cliffs south of Medu are the highest point on the Loyalty Islands.

Practicalities

The **Hnala Village** (B.P. 40, Tadine; tel. 45-43-96, fax 45-43-87), next to Tadine post office, has five rooms in a long block at CFP 4000/5000 single/double. A restaurant and car rental service are available.

Gîte Si-Hmed (B.P. 150, Tadine; tel. 45-41-51) is on Ceigeïté Beach just west of Wabao, 20 km southwest of the airport. The seven thatched bungalows with private bath are CFP 4000/4500/5000 single/double/triple, three rooms CFP 2500, and camping (CFP 1000 per tent) is possible. Gîte Si-Hmed serves ample meals (seafood or local dishes), but you must order a few hours before. Airport transfers are CFP 2400 roundtrip.

Gîte La Fourmi (B.P. 124, Tadine; tel. 45-42-96) at Netche offers two bungalows with shared facilities (CFP 3000/4000 single/double), and camping is CFP 500 per tent.

There's a post office, bank, *gendarmerie,* and clinic at Tadine. A market functions in the hall adjoining La Roche Airport on Wednesday and Saturday mornings. A co-op store with a limited selection is at Tadine.

Transportation

Air Calédonie flights are CFP 7490 from Nouméa, CFP 5540 from Lifou. Public transport doesn't exist on Maré, but the gîte owners pick up guests at the airport if they've been forewarned. The gîtes rent cars, but if you rent one, make sure the fuel tank is full; Maré has been known to run out of gasoline. Renting a bicycle at a gîte is a much cheaper, better option on flat Maré, and hitching is also possible, so long as you're prepared to walk if no cars pass.

The interisland ferry *Président Yeiwéné* (tel. 45-40-69) calls at Tadine on its way to Lifou and Nouméa every Thursday morning, direct to Nouméa every other Tuesday afternoon. Book ahead.

kauri pine cone

CAPSULE FRENCH VOCABULARY

À quelle heure?—At what time?
auberge de jeunesse—youth hostel

aujourd'hui—today
bonjour—good day
bon marché—cheap
bonsoir—good evening

café très chaud—hot coffee
cascade—waterfall
casse-croûte—snack
C'est loin d'ici?—Is it far from here?
cher—expensive
Combien ça fait?—How much does it cost?
  Combien ça coûte?
  Combien? Quel prix?
conserves—canned foods

demain—tomorrow
Devrais-je demander la permission?—Should I ask permission?

Est-ce que je peux camper ici?—May I camp here?

fruits de mer—seafood

gendarmerie—police station
grottes—caves

hier—yesterday
horaire—timetable

Il fait mauvais temps.—It's bad weather.

J'aime . . .—I like . . .
Je désire, je voudrais . . .—I want . . .
Je fais de l'autostop.—I am hitchhiking.
Je ne comprends pas.—I don't understand.
Je t'aime.—I love you.
Je vais à . . .—I am going to . . .
Je voudrais camper.—I wish to camp.
Jusqu'où allez-vous?—How far are you going?

la chômage, les chômeurs—unemployment, the unemployed
la clef—the key
la falaise—the cliff
la plage—the beach
la route, la piste—the road
l'eau—water
le lait—milk
le pain—bread
le terrain de camping—campsite
le vin—wine

merci—thank you
merde—shit

Où allez-vous?—Where are you going?
Où habitez-vous?—Where do you live?
oui—yes
Où se trouve . . .?—Where is . . .?

plat du jour—set meal

Quel travail faites-vous?—What work do you do?

salut—hello
s'il vous plaît—please

une boutique, un magasin—a store
une chambre—a room

Vous êtes très gentil.—You are very kind.

NUMBERS

un—1
deux—2
trois—3
quatre—4
cinq—5
six—6
sept—7
huit—8
neuf—9
dix—10
onze—11
douze—12
treize—13
quatorze—14
quinze—15
seize—16
dix-sept—17
dix-huit—18
dix-neuf—19
vingt—20
vingt et un—21
vingt-deux—22
vingt-trois—23
trente—30
quarante—40
cinquante—50
soixante—60
soixante-dix—70
quatre-vingts—80
quatre-vingt-dix—90
cent—100
mille—1,000
dix mille—10,000
million—1,000,000

GORDON OHLIGER

VANUATU
INTRODUCTION

This string of lush green islands, 2,250 km northeast of Sydney, received worldwide attention in 1980 when the ponderous Anglo-French New Hebrides Condominium blossomed into the Ripablik Blong Vanuatu. Since then, the country has expressed its independence by developing a new national identity based on Melanesian *kastom*.

It's a colorful land of many cultures, full of fascinating surprises. Make discoveries for yourself by asking any ni-Vanuatu (indigenous inhabitant) for the nearest cave, waterfall, swimming hole, hot spring, blowhole, cliff, or old burial place. The general beauty and relaxed way of life are its biggest attractions.

No other South Pacific country harbors as many local variations. The glamorous duty-free shops and gourmet restaurants of the cosmopolitan capital, Port Vila, contrast sharply with unchanging, traditional villages just over the horizon. You'll be moved and touched by the friendliness, warmth, and sincerity of the ni-Vanuatu, certainly Vanuatu's biggest attraction.

Away from the packaged day tours and commercial resorts, this unpolished jewel of the South Pacific is still a land of adventure.

The Land

The 82 islands of Vanuatu (the name means "Land Eternal") stretch north-south 1,300 km from the Torres Islands near Santa Cruz in the Solomons to minuscule Matthew and Hunter islands (also claimed by France) east of New Caledonia. This neat geographical unit is divided into three groups: the Torres and Banks islands in the north, the Y-shaped central group from Espiritu Santo and Maewo to Efate, and the Tafea islands (Tanna, Aniwa, Futuna, Erromango, and Aneityum) in the south. Together they total 12,189 square km, of which the 12 largest islands account for 93%. Espiritu Santo and Malekula alone comprise nearly half of Vanuatu's land area.

Vanuatu is comprised of ash and coral: volcanic extrusion first built the islands, then limestone plateaus were added to them through tec-

VANUATU

TORRES IS.

HIU
METOMA
TEGUA
LINUA
LOH
OTOGA

VOT
TANDE

UREPARAPARA

MOTA LAVA

VANUA LAVA
PORT PATTESON
SOLA
MOTA

BANKS IS.

GAUA
TARASAG
ONTAR
MERIG

MERE LAVA

CAPE
CUMBERLAND

BIG
BAY
SAKAO
PORT OLRY
NAONE

ESPIRITU
SANTO
LUGANVILLE
AMBAE
LONGANA
MAEWO

WUSI
PALIKULO
WALAHA
PATTESON PASSAGE

TUTUBA
SARA

ARAKI
AORE
MELSISI

TAMAMBO
PENTECOST

VAO
ATCHIN
RANO
WALI
LONORORE

AMOKH
NORSUP
OLAL
BUNLAP

BOUGAINVILLE STRAIT
CRAIG
COVE
SELWIN STRAIT

PORT STANLEY
ULEI
AMBRYM

MALEKULA
LAMAP
PAAMA

SOUTH WEST BAY
LAMEN BAY
LOPEVI

EPI
VALESDIR

TONGOA

EMAE
TONGARIKI

MAKURA
SHEPHERD IS.

MATASO

NGUNA

MOSO
EMAO

ERETOKA

PORT VILA
EFATE

SOUTH PACIFIC OCEAN

CORAL SEA

0   100km

N

DILLON'S BAY
ERROMANGO
IPOTA

A Melanesian custom: It's a practice on these
islands to breed pigs, mostly for their tusks. The
lower incisors are first knocked out so the upper
tusks will grow inward, sometimes even penetrating
the cheek. This upper pair, which would normally
grind against the teeth in the lower jaw, thus curve
into an almost spiral ring. The pigs are highly valued
by their owners, and the meat and tusks are prized
at initiation rites and funeral feasts.

ANIWA

TANNA
LENAKEL
WHITESANDS

FUTUNA

TAFEA ISLANDS

ANELGHOWHAT
ANEITYUM

VANUATU AT A GLANCE

ISLAND	AREA (SQUARE KM)	HIGHEST POINT (M)	POPULATION (1989)	POPULATION DENSITY
Espiritu Santo	4,010	1,879	1,117	5.3
Malekula	2,024	863	15,085	7.5
Efate	887	647	27,455	31.0
Erromango	887	886	1,254	1.4
Ambrym	666	1,270	7,189	10.8
Tanna	561	1,084	19,825	35.3
Pentecost	499	946	11,336	22.7
Epi	444	833	3,236	7.3
Ambae	399	1,496	8,583	21.5
Vanua Lava	343	946	1,343	3.9
Gaua	315	797	1,285	4.1
Maewo	300	811	2,362	7.9

tonic uplift. The islands form part of a chain of volcanic activity stretching from New Zealand up through Vanuatu and the Solomons to the islands off New Guinea. Besides Yasur Volcano on Tanna, there are active volcanoes on Lopevi, Ambrym, and Gaua, plus a submarine volcano near Tongoa. Lopevi has a classic cone 1,413 meters high, with a five-km base; when it last erupted in the early 1970s, Lopevi's population was permanently relocated to nearby Epi.

Vanuatu sits on the west edge of the Pacific Plate next to the 8,000-meter-deep New Hebrides Trench. This marks the point where the Indo-Australian Plate slips under the Pacific Plate in a classic demonstration of plate tectonics. Its islands are pushed laterally 10 centimeters a year in a northwest direction, accompanied by earthquakes and volcanic eruptions. In the past three million years Vanuatu has also been uplifted 700 meters, or approximately two millimeters a year. Although Vanuatu is relatively young geologically, this uplifting has created the series of stepped limestone plateaus you'll see on many of the islands.

Climate

Vanuatu has a hot, rainy climate—tropical in the north and subtropical in the south. The rainy season is November to April, but sudden tropical showers can occur anytime. May to July are the best months for hiking—cooler and drier, and from June to September, evenings on the southern islands can even be brisk. The southeast trade winds blow steadily year-round, though they're stronger and more reliable from April to October. During the wet season, winds from the north or west occur under the influence of hurricanes and tropical lows.

Vanuatu is the most hurricane-prone country in the South Pacific. Between 1970 and 1985 no fewer than 29 hurricanes struck Vanuatu; on average, any given locality can expect to be hit by a hurricane every other year (usually between January and April). As in other parts of the South Pacific, hurricanes have become more frequent and stronger in recent years (this may somehow be related to the greenhouse effect). The southernmost islands are less vulnerable to hurricanes and get less rain than the hotter islands north of Efate.

For a weather report dial 22932.

Flora and Fauna

The eastern, or windward, sides of the islands are equatorial, with thick rainforests. The leeward sides, which get less rain, are often open tropical woodlands or savanna, especially in the south. Higher up on the mountains is a humid zone of shrub forest. About 75% of the natural forest cover remains, although pressure from logging and agricultural clearing is increasing.

A principal botanical curiosity of Vanuatu is giant banyan trees *(nabangas),* which often dominate village meeting or dancing places

PORT VILA'S CLIMATE

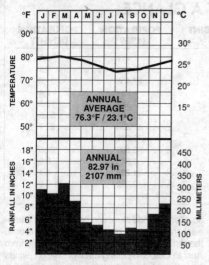

ANNUAL
AVERAGE
76.3°F / 23.1°C

ANNUAL
82.97 in
2107 mm

(nasaras), especially on Tanna. The multirooted banyan begins by growing around another tree, which it eventually strangles out of existence. These massive twisting mazes of trunks and vines are among the earth's largest living organisms. Also unique is a prehistoric giant tree fern called namwele, which has great cultural significance and is used in many of the large carvings sold in Port Vila.

The indigenous fauna includes flying foxes, lizards, spiders, and butterflies. Of Vanuatu's two snakes, the Pacific boa and flowerpot snake, only the latter is poisonous, though innocuous and rare. Three species of banded sea snakes are found in Vanuatu (of 52 species worldwide). The snakes crawl up on shore and hide among the rocks at night. Although poisonous, they're timid and no threat to snorkelers or scuba divers (though it would be foolish to try to handle them). Occasionally people wading through murky water will step on one, and they sometimes get caught in fishing nets, but even then bites are seldom fatal, as the snakes inject only a small amount of poison.

Vanuatu's colorful reefs hold its greatest store of life, including potentially dangerous tiger sharks in some areas (especially the corridor between Ambrym and eastern Malekula). In

Vanuatu sharks are associated with a particular type of magic that involves certain individuals who can either become sharks or control sharks.

Though introduced by man, the pig is now considered indigenous. Ni-Vanuatu in the central and northern islands knock out the male animal's upper canine teeth so its lower tusks have nothing to grind against, and in six or seven years the tusks grow into a full circle. Culturally even more valuable than tusker pigs are the rare hermaphrodite pigs (narave), usually found on northern islands such as Espiritu Santo, Malo, Ambae, Maewo, and northern Pentecost, where the world's highest ratio of intersexual pigs per generation is found. In 1993 Florida reader James K. McIntyre identified a large number of hermaphrodite pigs at Avunatari village on Malo. Nowhere else in the world are pigs of this type found in such numbers.

Birdlife is rich; 54 native species include honey eaters, fantails, finches, goshawks, kingfishers, parrots, peregrine falcons, pigeons, robins, swiftlets, thrushes, trillers, and warblers. Espiritu Santo has the greatest variety of birds, from great flocks of tiny red cardinals by the roadside to the chestnut-bellied kingfisher and the rare Santo mountain starling unique to the island's highest peaks.

HISTORY AND GOVERNMENT

Taem Blong Bifoa

Vanuatu may have been populated since before 3000 B.C., though little is known for certain as the early habitation sites are probably now below sea level. Lapita pottery found on Malo near Espiritu Santo dates from 1300-1100 B.C., on Efate from 350 B.C. Around 700 B.C., new arrivals from the Solomons brought a second type of pottery called Mangaasi, with incised and applied relief designs, which they carried on to Fiji and New Caledonia. Fresh immigrants under the legendary Chief Roy Mata occupied the central islands circa A.D. 1200. Excavations conducted by French archaeologist Jose Garanger on Eretoka Island off western Efate in 1967 uncovered a burial involving the sacrifice of 40 members of this chief's entourage, dating to 1265—a remarkable confirmation of oral tradition by modern science.

As today, the first inhabitants probably lived in small villages and had a greater variety of languages and customs than the whole of Europe. Each clan was autonomous; relations between groups were often based on ceremonial gift-giving, while individuals related to one another through arranged marriages. Wives, considered property, were exchanged between villages to create links. Spirits were controlled by magic. To work one's way up through the graded societies and become a "big man," an individual had to amass wealth in pigs to purchase his rank. This *nimanke* system was more widespread in the north than in the center and south, where descent was usually hereditary. The borrowing and loaning of pigs between men created a complex system of bonds and obligations, which strengthened the group and relationships between groups (still a common practice). Only the most able men could rise in this system. Clans raided one another and the victim's bodies were eaten to capture the power of their spirits; these cannibal raids being reciprocal, one never wandered far from his home village. One was relatively free from the danger of attack along traditional trade routes and within the area of traditional ritual links.

European Contact

The first European to arrive was the Hispanic explorer Pedro Fernandez de Quirós, who pulled into Espiritu Santo's Big Bay on 29 April 1606,

believing he had found the "lost" southern continent. When he and his men landed, pious, God-fearing Quirós knelt and kissed the sand, naming the island Terra Austrialis del Espiritu Santo, after the Holy Ghost. He claimed possession of it and everything to the south as far as the South Pole in the name of the king of Spain and the Catholic Church. Quirós planned to build a model Christian settlement on the site, but his treatment of the inhabitants soon led to open hostility which, together with sickness and dissent among his own men, drove this visionary mystic away after only three weeks.

White men did not return for 162 years, when Bougainville sailed between Espiritu Santo and Malekula in 1768, disproving Quirós's theory that they were part of a southern continent. Bougainville named the northern islands the Great Cyclades. In 1774, Captain Cook became the first European to really explore and chart the entire group, naming it New Hebrides, after the Scottish islands.

Christianity and Depopulation

The sandalwood traders operated in the islands from 1825 to 1865. Their methods created deep resentment among the islanders, so when the first white members of the London Missionary Society landed on Erromango (Martyr Island) in 1839, they were clubbed and eaten. Samoan missionaries were sent next, but many were also killed or died from malaria. Worse still, they

view of Tanna Island

M.G.L. DOMENY DE RIENZI

introduced diseases such as measles, influenza, and dysentery, which devastated whole populations. Well-wishers in Australia and elsewhere sent secondhand garments to clothe the naked savages. Regrettably, these were also impregnated with disease, and some sandalwood traders deliberately distributed clothes they knew to be infected with smallpox to wipe out the inhabitants of the areas they wished to exploit.

Since converts—who had the closest contact with missionaries—were the most affected by these epidemics, the newcomers were thought to be evil sorcerers, and the ni-Vanuatu resisted any way they could. From a precontact population of about half a million, the number of ni-Vanuatu dropped to 40,000 in 1920. Islands like Erromango remain relatively unpopulated today, and only after 1920 did Vanuatu's population begin to rise. Some ni-Vanuatu still refuse to accept Christianity and regard all white men with suspicion. Although a majority had been "converted" by 1900, their understanding of doctrine was shallow, and mass defections from the church have occurred since WW II, especially on Tanna. About 16% of the population continues to follow *kastom*.

The Melanesian Mission (Anglican) and the Presbyterians divided the group into spheres of influence, with the Anglicans in the northeast and the Presbyterians in the center and south. Rather than risk establishing a mission in the islands, Anglican Bishop George Selwyn took young ni-Vanuatu to New Zealand and Norfolk Island for training. Catholicism became established in the central islands after 1887, but little headway was made on Malekula and Espiritu Santo until recently. The missionaries managed to stop village warfare and cannibalism, facilitating the entry of the next two groups—the labor recruiters and European settlers.

The Blackbirders
From 1863 to 1904 some 40,000 ni-Vanuatu were recruited to work in the canefields of Queensland, Australia, and another 10,000 went to Fiji and New Caledonia. As much as half the adult male population of some islands went abroad. Though many young men welcomed the chance for adventure and escape from the restrictions of village life, conditions were hard. The blackbirders sometimes resorted to kid-

napping the islanders, or herding them together by brute force. Outriggers were sunk and the survivors "rescued"; others were bought outright from chiefs for beads, tobacco, mirrors, and muskets. Returnees often brought with them diseases and alcohol, which decimated the home population.

In the end, most of the laborers were deported from Australia in 1906 when the White Australia Policy took effect, but a large percentage died abroad. Some of the returnees to Tanna were so irate about being evicted from Australia that they drove all whites off the island. One of the most lasting legacies of the labor trade was the evolution of a pidgin tongue called Bislama, the national language.

Planters and Land
The first impetus for establishing European plantations in Vanuatu was the high price of cotton during the American Civil War. When cotton collapsed, the planters switched to bananas, cacao, coffee, and copra. The first plantations were on Tanna and Efate, followed later by Espiritu Santo. Though British subjects from Australia arrived first, in 1882 the Compagnie Calédonienne des Nouvelles Hébrides began acquiring large tracts of native land. The Australian-based trading company Burns Philp followed in 1895, but by 1900 French colonists outnumbered British two to one.

Though the first traders and missionaries had been mostly English, the French recognized the agricultural potential of the islands and wanted another colony to strengthen their position in New Caledonia. This alarmed the Australians, who thought one French colony on their doorstep was enough. In 1878 the British and French governments agreed not to annex Vanuatu without consulting one another. To protect the planters' interests and regulate the labor trade, the two nations established a Joint Naval Commission in 1887 with jurisdiction over the islands. It could only intervene in the event of war; during the hurricane season, when the Naval Commission vessels had to be withdrawn, there was no law other than the musket.

During this period, 12% of Vanuatu's land, including the best tracts, was permanently alienated, 10% by French companies and two percent by Australian. Traditionally, land could not be sold in Vanuatu, only the *use* of the land temporarily assigned. Many sales were instigated by a few individuals and not agreed upon by consensus as custom required. The ni-Vanuatu had little understanding of the alienation taking place; when they tried to resist, British and French warships were sent to bombard coastal villages.

The Colonial Period
In 1902 the Germans began to show an interest in these "unclaimed" islands, so the British and French quickly appointed resident commissioners. In 1906, three years after an auspicious visit to Paris by the francophile English King Edward VII, the Anglo-French New Hebrides Condominium was established. The arrangement was formalized in the Protocol of 1914, then proclaimed in 1923.

The Condominium system of government resulted in an expensive duplication of services and administration, as each colonial power implemented its own judiciary, police force, hospitals, schools, etc. Each power had jurisdiction over its own citizens and the natives, but the ni-Vanuatu were not permitted to claim either British or French nationality, and in effect became stateless. A Joint Court was set up, and land titles registered before 1896 could not be challenged. This institutionalized the large European plantations. In addition, the ni-Vanuatu didn't have the right of appeal from native courts to the Joint Court. Actually, this combination of administrations had little impact on the ni-Vanuatu, other than freezing an unjust social structure, and they could simply ignore the Condominium pandemonium if they wished. Education remained in the hands of the missionaries right into the 1960s, and nearly half of the population is still illiterate. Although a teachers' college opened in 1960, there wasn't a British secondary school (Malapoa College) until 1966, a French secondary school (the lycée) until 1968. In 1989, 44% of ni-Vanuatu children aged five to 19 were still not attending school.

Despite the fact that the budget of the French Residency was twice that of the British, the latter were more effective, due to a long-standing policy of localization and advanced training for Melanesians. France wasted much of its money on a large staff of expatriates, failing to train a

French-speaking native elite capable of assuming power. In the early 1970s the French began a crash program to build a French-speaking majority, but of course it was too late.

During WW II, major American bases on Espiritu Santo and Efate were used as staging areas for the Solomons campaign. These islands didn't suffer as the Solomons and New Guinea did. The Japanese bombed Espiritu Santo once, but only managed to kill a cow. (A San Diego reader, Gordon De Mara, sent us a photo he took in 1944 of the animal's grave marker. It read: "Here lies Bossy. Tojo got her September 15, 1943, because she was walking around during a blackout.") On Tanna the apparent wealth of the U.S. soldiers gave fresh impetus to the Jon Frum cargo cult, which already existed before the war. In turn, the romance of these islands inspired novelist James A. Michener to write *Tales of the South Pacific*, his first book, with Ambae starring as "Bali Hai." In May 1942, over 100,000 Americans arrived on Espiritu Santo to construct an instant Quonset city, complete with telephones, radio station, movie houses, hospitals, crushed-coral roads, bridges, airfields, and wharves, so by the end of the war a whole infrastructure had been installed.

The Road to Independence
The independence of Vanuatu was not generously granted, as it had been elsewhere in the South Pacific, but had to be won through a long, bitter struggle against bungling colonial administrators, entrenched settlers, and opportunists. In 1971, the New Hebrides Cultural Association emerged to resist large land purchases and subdivisions by an American businessman, one Eugene Peacock. Three months later, the Association became the New Hebrides National Party, headed by Father Walter Lini of Pentecost (an Anglican priest). The party soon won grassroots support throughout the islands, mostly among English-speaking Protestants, by calling for a return of all alienated land to its customary owners. Several French-oriented parties (the "moderates") were also created; they favored prolonged collaboration with the British and French governments.

These factions forced the ruling powers to establish a Representative Assembly in 1975, but it was dissolved in 1977 following a boycott

Flashback to 1980: From left to right are Jimmy Stevens, the rebel leader; General Ted Diro, P.N.G. Defense Force commander at the time; Sir Julius Chan, former prime minister of P.N.G.; and Father Walter Lini, former prime minister of Vanuatu.

HIRI, PAPUA NEW GUINEA

by the Vanua'aku Party (formerly the National Party), which demanded the elimination of appointed members, as well as immediate independence. The crisis was resolved in 1978, with the creation of a Government of National Unity temporarily uniting the two factions. A constitution was signed in October 1979, and in elections a month later the Vanua'aku Party won a two-thirds majority. Understandably, little of this was popular with the French! Most of the plantations were owned by French nationals, who outnumbered British subjects three to one. Their influence was especially strong on Espiritu Santo. The French administration adopted a disruptive policy of encouraging local divisions and disturbances as a means of wringing concessions from the Vanuatu government. The British, who just wanted to get out as soon as possible, were unable to interfere with their partner because all Condominium decisions had to be bilateral and the French just stonewalled.

The Republic of Vemarana

The key figure in the independence disruptions was Jimmy Stevens, a charismatic Tongan/Scottish half-caste with a large following on Espiritu Santo and some of the central islands. Basically he was a nonconformist, suspicious of the Vanua'aku Party leadership, which was composed mainly of ni-Vanuatu British civil servants and Protestant clergy. They in turn regarded Jimmy as a dangerous cargo cultist. His Nagri-

amel Party began as an agricultural reform movement centered at Tanafo village in the bush 20 km north of Luganville. Nagriamel represented a turning away from European influence and a return to native ways. In 1971 Nagriamel petitioned the United Nations to halt further sales of land on Espiritu Santo to American interests for development as hotel and investment properties.

Ironically, by May 1980 Stevens had come full circle, after accepting US$250,000 in aid, arms, and radio transmitting equipment from the Phoenix Foundation, an American right-wing organization run by millionaire businessman Michael Oliver. In 1972, Oliver and associates had attempted to declare a tax-free Republic of Minerva on Tonga's Minerva Reef, until the king gave them the boot. Later Phoenix attempted to engineer the secession of Abaco Island in the Bahamas. When this failed, Oliver turned his attention to Espiritu Santo, which was to become a capitalist's paradise, free of government controls. Already four areas on the island had been subdivided into 5,000 lots, of which 2,000 had been sold to individual Americans. Aore Island, off Espiritu Santo, was to have become a health resort and casino. Stevens, who now styled himself "President Moli Stevens," declared Espiritu Santo the independent "Republic of Vemarana," and Vanua'aku Party supporters were driven off the island. The Coconut War had begun.

Escalation

During it all, French police stood by and took no action. Stevens had visited Paris and received encouragement from French President Giscard d'Estaing prior to the rebellion. The French apparently intended to have Espiritu Santo continue as a French colony, as had occurred with Mayotte when Comoros in the Indian Ocean achieved independence from France in 1975. Chief Minister Walter Lini responded by imposing an economic boycott on Espiritu Santo, but he was unable to prod the British and French authorities into putting down the revolt, as no unilateral action was permitted under Condominium laws. A simultaneous disorder on Tanna dwindled when Alexis Yolou, its "moderate" leader, was shot dead.

There was talk of delaying the independence scheduled for 30 July 1980, but Father Lini announced that he would declare Vanuatu's independence unilaterally if Britain and France reneged on their promises. Additionally, neighboring countries such as Australia, New Zealand, and Papua New Guinea indicated that they would recognize such independence (Western Samoa was the first to actually do so). Thus, the colonial powers were forced to adhere to their original timetable, and Vanuatu became an independent republic on the scheduled day. To prevent bloodshed, the British and French sent military forces to Espiritu Santo to disarm Stevens's followers just a week before independence. Forced to leave afterward, the French ripped out telephones, air-conditioners, and anything else they could move from their offices to make things as difficult as possible for the new government. Had the British not been involved, the French would never have agreed to independence.

The Outcome

In August 1980, Papua New Guinea troops (the Kumul force) replaced the British/French forces on Espiritu Santo and arrested Jimmy Stevens, who was sent to Port Vila for trial. Stevens's son Eddie was killed by a grenade when he tried to run a roadblock. This was the first military intervention by the forces of one Pacific country in the territory of another since the 19th century, and it fostered a wave of Melanesian solidarity that led to the creation of the Melanesian Spearhead regional grouping in 1988.

Jimmy Stevens was sentenced to 14.5 years imprisonment for his part in the rebellion, during which Luganville was looted and burned. Most of the 70 ni-Vanuatu arrested along with Stevens were released within a year, but over the next two months 260 French residents who had sided with the rebellion were rounded up and deported to New Caledonia. Documents captured at the rebel headquarters at Tanafo implicated aides to French Resident Commissioner Jean-Jacques Robert (who himself had come to New Hebrides from Comoros) as direct accomplices in the secession.

After Independence

The first years of independence were uneventful, with the Vanua'aku Party government employing anti-colonial, anti-nuclear rhetoric to forge a regional identity while quietly pursuing the capitalistic domestic policies established during the Condominium. The tax haven created in 1971 was left in place, and confiscated land could be leased back for up to 75 years at low rates. In short, little changed and fears of "Melanesian socialism" proved unfounded. Development and power became centralized in Port Vila with an indigenous political elite working in tandem with expatriate business interests.

In 1982, Vanuatu closed its ports to American warships that refused to confirm or deny whether they were carrying nuclear weapons—the first Pacific country to do so. In 1983, legislation was passed that made Vanuatu the first totally nuclear-free nation in the Pacific: nuclear weapons, ships, power plants, and waste-dumping are all prohibited. Vanuatu was the first South Pacific country to acquire full membership in the Non-Aligned Movement. These positions proved useful in playing different groups of foreigners off against one another, and Vanuatu has been able to garner support from both right-wing libertarians and left-wing internationalists as a result.

The Barak Sope Affair

In November 1987, the Vanua'aku Party was reelected, with a reduced majority in parliament. A month earlier, Vanuatu had expelled the French ambassador on grounds that he was financing the opposition parties. After the election, a fierce leadership struggle erupted between Prime Minister Walter Lini, who had suffered a cerebral hemorrhage while visiting Washington, D.C., in February 1987, and party secretary-general Barak Sope, Father Lini's closest advisor since 1976. In 1986 Sope created an international furor by sending ni-Vanuatu to Libya for training. On their return, the trainees became Sope's "bodyguards." Though Father Lini held onto his position, declining health and Sope's personal ambition seemed to have weakened his grip.

On 10 May 1988 the government seized the Vila Urban Land Corporation (VULCAN), holder of property leases in the city on behalf of customary landowners in Erakor, Ifira, and Pango. VULCAN, of which Sope was chairman, was supposed to return income from the leases to the villages; instead, money was being reinvested in other commercial enterprises, and there were allegations that millions of dollars had "disappeared." The government failed to explain to the landowners what was happening, and when Sope (from Ifira) made an inflammatory radio broadcast about land rights, concerned villagers took to the streets to denounce Father Lini (from rural Pentecost). What began as a peaceful demonstration turned into a drunken antigovernment riot when free alcohol was distributed to sympathizers by Sope militants. Sope was present during the march and seemed to be the instigator of the events, which inflicted over a million dollars of damage on the capital.

Father Lini charged that VULCAN was indeed corrupt: 98% of its income went to administration in 1987, including huge salaries and advances to Sope and friends. Sope was sacked from the cabinet and stripped of his party post. When Sope and four supporters (the "Gang of Five") boycotted parliament, they were expelled from both party and parliament. They formed a Melanesian Progressive Party (MPP) and in desperation turned to the pro-French opposition for support. A few days later, Maxime Carlot Korman, leader of the Union of Moderate Parties (UMP), and 17 opposition members were also expelled for boycotting parliament. A rump parliament then called for by-elections to replace the expelled members. Sope's MPP and the UMP boycotted these by-elections in December 1988.

At this point the largely ceremonial head of state, President Ati George Sokomanu (Sope's uncle), greatly exceeded his authority by attempting to dissolve parliament and form an interim government with Sope as prime minister. Sokomanu accused Father Lini of trying to create a one-party state, while Father Lini charged Sope with coercion, opportunism, and corruption. Within hours Sope, Sokomanu, and the interim government were arrested by the Vanuatu Mobile Force and charged with sedition. In February 1989 Presbyterian pastor Fred Timakata replaced Sokomanu as president, and in March, Sokomanu was sentenced to six years in prison for attempting to overthrow the elected government, while Sope and Carlot Korman each got five years. A month later, a court of appeal overturned these convictions and set the men free.

Recent Events

By 1991 Father Lini's declining health and increasingly erratic, nonconsultative style of leadership had brought government business almost to a standstill, with mass sackings of government ministers and public servants suspected of disloyalty. At the Vanua'aku Party congress in April 1991, Father Lini managed to have the election of a new party leadership postponed, but he suffered a mild heart attack soon after. In August, the party held a special leadership congress at Mele village and elected ex-foreign minister Donald Kalpokas to replace Father Lini (who boycotted the congress) as party president. Despite a vote of no confidence by the congress, Father Lini refused to resign as prime minister, but in September he was defeated in a parliamentary vote of no confidence and replaced by Donald Kalpokas as prime minister.

To mark the 20th anniversary of the founding of the Vanua'aku Party in August 1991, Jimmy Stevens was finally freed, after serving 11 years of his sentence at Port Vila's jail. His followers throughout the archipelago assembled 20 pigs with fully circled tusks to present to the government as an act of atonement (the pigs were later returned to their owners). Stevens had been under hospital treatment for high blood pressure for some time, and his release, just weeks before Father Lini himself was voted out of office, culminated an era in the country's history. In February 1994, Jimmy Stevens died at Tanafo.

After losing his post, Father Lini rallied his supporters and formed the National United Party (NUP) to contest the elections scheduled for December 1991. With the Vanua'aku Party thus divided, Maxime Carlot Korman's UMP won 19 of the 46 seats while polling only 30.6% of the popular vote (down from the 39.9% it had won in 1987). Carlot Korman formed a coalition with the NUP, which had obtained 10 seats; a shift away from Vanuatu's former anti-French foreign policy soon followed. In mid-1995 Carlot Korman was the only Pacific leader who refused to condemn French nuclear testing, and he even ordered Radio Vanuatu not to report the testing at all.

Prior to 1991, the Lini government had expelled three successive French ambassadors for supporting the francophone opposition. An indication of how much had changed was Carlot Korman's 1992 expulsion of the acting Australian high commissioner after he protested an amendment giving the Minister of Finance draconian powers to arbitrarily cancel business licenses (the Supreme Court later judged the amendment unconstitutional). Soon after, Vanuatu announced it was opening a consulate in Nouméa as close ties with France were resumed. In March 1994 Jean-Marie Leye was elected president, and two weeks later Jimmy Stevens's son, Frankie Stevens, was appointed leader of government business in Parliament.

The November 1995 election resulted in a new coalition between the UMP and the NUP, with Serge Vohor as prime minister.

Government

Vanuatu has a parliamentary system of government and the prime minister is the leader of the majority party in Parliament. Parliament's 46 members are elected for four-year terms, and the prime minister appoints his cabinet from among these members. A National Council of Chiefs (Malvatumauri) advises on matters relating to custom. Parliament and the heads of the provincial governments elect a president, who serves a five-year term as ceremonial head of state.

In 1994 the 11 local government councils were replaced by six provinces: Torba (Torres and Banks), Sama (Santo and Malo), Penama (Pentecost, Ambrym, and Malekula), Shefa (Shepherds, Epi, and Efate), and Tafea (Tanna, Anatom, Futuna, Erromango, and Aniwa). The government

presented this as a decentralization of authority away from Port Vila, whereas the opposition viewed it as a gerrymander to increase the government's reelection possibilities. At last report, seven political parties were represented in Parliament: the Union of Moderate Parties, the Vanua'aku Pati, the Melanesian Progressive Party, the National United Party, the People's Democratic Party, Tan Union, and Nagriamel.

Vanuatu's cultural, political, and economic diversity is mirrored in the nation's politics. The 1993 split of Walter Lini's National United Party into two factions in a squabble over ministerial appointments and the subsequent realignment of the governing coalition is typical of the Machiavellian mentality of the political elite. Close political allies can become foes overnight, and former bitter adversaries have no compunctions about forming alliances. Call it democracy or simply the Melanesian tradition of shifting alliances, much time and effort which should be going into solving the country's social and economic problems is devoted to politicking for personal gain. Before retiring in 1994, President Timakata warned that corruption at the highest levels of government is on the increase, which is worrisome since society's standard watchdog, a free press, is not present in Vanuatu.

ECONOMY

Agriculture and Land

Roughly 75% of the population lives by subsistence agriculture. Root crops such as yams, taro, manioc, and sweet potatoes are grown, with copra produced for cash sale. The Commodity Marketing Board subsidizes copra prices to ensure a regular income for the village producers who account for 80% of Vanuatu's copra.

The constitution specifies that land can only be owned by indigenous ni-Vanuatu. At independence, all alienated land was returned to its customary owners; former landlords were given five years to go into partnership, lease the land, or otherwise dispose of it. Leases of up to 75 years are now available. A problem has arisen in determining just who owns what land, as many ni-Vanuatu claim the same areas.

The government is attempting to implement a system for deciding on the claims and registering titles, but there have been many complications. Although about 40% of the land is arable, only 17% is presently utilized, mostly in coastal areas. Cattle bred with light-colored French Charolais and Limousin stock roam under the coconuts to provide beef for canning and export.

Trade

Vanuatu imports four times as much as it exports and has a huge trade imbalance with its largest trading partner Australia, which sells Vanuatu 16 times more than it buys. New Zealand buys almost nothing from Vanuatu but is its second largest supplier. Copra is the largest export, accounting for a third of total exports by value, shipped mostly from Luganville to Holland. Exports such as frozen beef (sold to Japan), cacao (sold to France, Holland, and Germany), clothing (sold to Australia), and sawn timber (sold to Australia and New Caledonia) are also significant. The export of unprocessed logs was halted in June 1994 after it became clear that logging already underway would have stripped the country bare in five years.

Frozen fish was eliminated as an export item in 1986, when the U.S. stopped such imports (to Hawaii and Puerto Rico) from Vanuatu. As a result, the Japanese company that had operated the freezer plant at Palikulo on Espiritu Santo for 19 years turned the facility over to the government, which has kept it going on a reduced scale. Some 400 ni-Vanuatu serve as crew on Taiwanese fishing boats, on which they are reportedly overworked and otherwise exploited.

The import economy is dominated by large European trading companies. In rural areas, cooperatives once collected agricultural exports and handled marketing, but individually owned stores are now becoming more common. In 1990 a Swedish company launched National Breweries Ltd. as a joint venture with the government to produce Tusker beer and Pripps Lager. A new industrial park is being created on Espiritu Santo, and there's a government plan to allow some 3,000 Asian migrants to settle on Espiritu Santo to increase tax revenues by stimulating economic development in that area.

Taxation and Evasion

Although Vanuatu has occasionally pursued a confrontational left/center foreign policy, its domestic policies (inherited from the Condominium) are ultra-right. There are no company taxes, personal income taxes, estate duties, capital gains taxes, or exchange controls. Instead, government revenue is obtained from customs duties, export taxes, company registration fees, licensing fees, property taxes (Port Vila and Espiritu Santo only), the 10% tourist taxes, fishing licenses, and outside aid (from Australia, Japan, and Britain). Import duties account for 70% of government income and are a major cause of the high cost of living. In January 1995 a four percent turnover tax was imposed leading to an inflationary jump in prices.

Vanuatu offers excellent facilities to foreigners wishing to evade their own country's taxation, public auditing, and secrecy laws. In 1971, the British Companies Regulation was enacted, giving tax-free status to companies registered in what was then New Hebrides. Today some 1,400 foreign companies and 80 dummy banks participate in the tax-haven scheme, providing about 400 jobs and contributing 12% of the gross domestic product. Several dozen accounting, banking, legal, and investment services help Asian and European corporations avoid taxation. In 1991 the Australian and New Zealand governments passed legislation greatly restricting the use of tax havens by their citizens after televised revelations that some large corporations were paying only one percent tax by laundering their profits through these facilities.

In 1981, Vanuatu also established a shipping registry or flag-of-convenience law modeled on Liberia's, which allows foreign shipping companies to duck taxation, safety regulations, union labor, and government controls. With the political chaos in Vanuatu's main competitors, Liberia and Panama, the annual number of ships registered has jumped from 76 in 1985 to about 500 in recent years with the main users American, Japanese, and Hong Kong ship owners. The New York company that administers the registry retains a 30% cut, and the rest goes to the Vanuatu government. Vanuatu's neutrality as a member of the Non-Aligned Movement is sometimes useful to vessels caught up in international conflicts, while its willingness to stand up to countries like Australia, France, and the U.S.

politically is gratifying to tax haven clients concerned about the secrecy of their financial arrangements.

Tourism

Tourism focuses on the resorts of Port Vila, with Tanna serving as a day-trip destination. For many years Espiritu Santo was played down as a tourist destination due to political fallout from the independence disturbances, and only since the change of government in 1991 has tourism to Santo been actively promoted. Luganville's Pekoa Airport is now being expanded, and there are rumors that it will soon receive international flights (probably from Nouméa). Cruise ships call frequently at Port Vila, "Mystery Island" (Aneityum), and Champagne Beach (Santo), unloading about 60,000 one-day visitors a year. In fact, Vanuatu receives more cruise ship visitors than any other South Pacific country. Over half of the 40,000 regular tourists are Australians, a sixth New Zealanders, a tenth New Caledonians.

From 1981 to 1987, tourism was controlled by Ansett Airlines, which provided the country's air link to Australia. Then Ansett pulled out after the government refused to contribute to marketing costs and imposed a royalty fee for the right to fly the country's colors. This forced the government to form Air Vanuatu and to begin spending large sums of its own money on promotion. In 1989, the government also took over Australian-owned Air Melanesiae, which had run the domestic air service for a quarter of a century, and set up Vanair, which has since sharply increased its fares. Port Vila International Airport was extended to receive Boeing 767 aircraft in 1990 (with Australian aid) and got a shiny new terminal building in 1991 (with Japanese aid). The relative importance of tourism has increased from 14% of the gross domestic product in 1983 to 38% in 1990.

Vanuatu's two-tier neocolonial economy is strikingly obvious in tourism. In the top tier are the overwhelming majority of tourist hotels and resorts, owned and operated by foreign companies or resident expatriates. These tend to charge Australian prices, making Vanuatu an expensive destination by South Pacific standards. Recently the Rural Business Development branch of the Department of Cooperatives has begun assisting ni-Vanuatu villagers in creating simple, low-cost guesthouses in rural areas to provide an alternative to the foreign-owned hotels. Examples of this are the Port Resolution Nipikinamu Yacht Club on Tanna and Wala Island Resort off Malekula. Interestingly, during their 11 years in office, the pro-indigenous Lini government did nothing to promote ni-Vanuatu participation in tourism; this shift only took place after a francophone-dominated government was elected in 1991.

THE PEOPLE

Sixty-seven of Vanuatu's 82 islands are populated, but most of the country's 150,000 people live on 16 main islands. At 12 persons per square km, the population density is low. After a century of depopulation due to warfare, blackbirding, and introduced diseases, Vanuatu now has one of the highest birthrates in the Pacific, and 44% of the population is under the age of 15. It also has the highest infant mortality rate in the South Pacific with 45 deaths per thousand. Ni-Vanuatu continue to migrate to Port Vila from rural areas in search of jobs, excitement, and better services. One in eight now lives in the capital, with people from the same outer islands congregating in their own suburban communities.

Just over a third of the population is Presbyterian, with Anglicans, Roman Catholics, and followers of the Jon Frum Cargo Cult making up a sixth each. Smaller groups include the Seventh-Day Adventists, Church of Christ, and Assemblies of God. About 10,000 people still follow traditional Pacific religions.

Although 98% of the population is Melanesian (ni-Vanuatu), there are also Europeans, Chinese, and Vietnamese. Thousands of indentured Vietnamese laborers were imported earlier this century to work on the French plantations, but most were repatriated by 1963. The number of non-ni-Vanuatu has declined from 6,880 in 1979 to 3,469 in 1989, over half of them in Port Vila.

Although the Melanesians arrived in Vanuatu from the northwest thousands of years ago, a back migration of Polynesians from the east occurred less than a thousand years ago. Polynesian languages are still spoken on Futuna, Emae, and Ambae islands, and in Ifira and Mele villages on Efate. A Polynesian hierarchy of chiefs is still evident in much of central and southern Vanuatu. In physical appearance the Polynesians have been almost totally assimilated by the surrounding Melanesian peoples, largely due to a custom requiring a young man to take his bride from a neighboring clan.

Traditional Culture

The ni-Vanuatu possess an amazing variety of cultures, from the "land-diving" clansmen of South Pentecost to the festival-rich society of the inhabitants of volcanic Tanna. Customs differ from island to island and remain strong despite generations of missionary influence. In the interiors of the two largest islands, Malekula and Espiritu Santo, are some of the most traditional peoples in the Pacific. Penis wrappers *(nambas)* are still worn by men in remote regions of Malekula, North Ambrym, South Pentecost, and Tanna. Traditional magic is still practiced throughout Vanuatu, with that of Maewo, Ambrym, and Epi reputed to be the strongest.

FIELD MUSEUM OF NATURAL HISTORY, CHICAGO

An Ambrym man poses beside an image he carved.

Traditional culture revolves around the pig, of which each clan or leader tries to acquire the greatest number. Almost any social offense can be compensated for with the payment of pigs. On the islands north of the Shepherds, the pigs are killed ritually when the tusks, used for body decoration, reach their greatest length. This ritual killing raises the social status of the individual in the village hierarchy *(nimangki)*. In the south, during the *nekowiar,* a clan alliance ritual, one clan gives gifts to another in the form of dances, songs, kava, yams, and taro, and these will eventually have to be given back in yet another *nekowiar.*

Even today, traditional art objects are often associated with public rituals or male secret societies, and a man has to accumulate considerable wealth to advance through the graded levels. Large carved figures, masks, and slit drums often still have to be provided for the advancement ceremony, in addition to payments of pigs. In some areas, different helmet masks are made for each level; these masks become temporary homes for ancestral or other types of spirits. In southern Malekula, curved pig's tusks ornamented them and are kept after pig sacrifices as evidence of wealth.

Women

Women are more equal to men in the northern matrilineal islands; on islands like Ambrym, Malekula, south Pentecost, and Tanna, where descent is patrilineal, males dominate society. In times past, women on the central and northern islands belonged to secret societies, but always of lower grade than those of the men. Though men and women work together in the villages, the women are responsible for chores considered less prestigious, such as cooking and caring for gardens and pigs. The burdens of a subsistence economy usually fall more heavily on the women. Too often, the men in Port Vila spend much of their time drinking kava and gossiping with friends, while the women keep the families going.

A woman cannot become a "big man" by accumulating wealth—in fact, she herself is considered part of her husband's wealth. The payment of bride-price is still common throughout Vanuatu, and some young girls have even been called "Toyotas," an indication of their market value as potential wives. To control inflation the Malvatumauri, Vanuatu's National Council of Chiefs, has placed a Vt300,000 ceiling on bride-prices (a Toyota costs over Vt1.5 million). Being viewed as tradable objects is a heavy burden for ni-Vanuatu women; girls are often deprived of educational opportunities by their own families, which consider them primarily child-bearers for the clan of their future husband. Some educated women refuse to marry, as it would mean forfeiting all rights to the family's property.

Most women treated for injuries at hospitals are victims of domestic violence, and the police only take action in the most extreme cases. Desertion of families by men is also a big problem. Interestingly enough, maltreatment of women is often more common in missionized communities and the towns than in traditional areas where customary law prevails. A husband in a "kastom area" will try to avoid beating his wife ("without cause") as she might run away ("with just cause"), back to her original family, and the husband would thus lose the bride-price he paid.

Since independence, things have begun to change. There are now 50:50 quotas for both sexes in forms one to four, to give girls an equal chance to attend secondary school. In December 1987, Hilda Lini (Walter Lini's younger sister) became the first ni-Vanuatu woman elected to parliament and, in December 1991, Ms. Lini was appointed Minister of Health in the UMP/NUP coalition government. The **National Council of Women** (Box 975, Port Vila; tel. 23108) has 13 island councils and 75 smaller area councils around the country.

More ni-Vanuatu women wear Mother Hubbard dresses than women in any other Pacific country—they're common even in Port Vila. It's another manifestation of the enduring strength of Melanesian *kastom,* something you'll encounter often as you travel around this country.

Language

With 105 indigenous languages, most having several dialects, Vanuatu boasts the world's highest density of languages per capita. All of these tongues (none with over 5,000 speakers) belong to the Austronesian family of languages spoken from Madagascar to Easter Island. Many ni-Vanuatu are fluent in five or six languages: a few in local languages, Bislama, English, and French.

Although English and French are also official languages, Bislama is the national language. It developed as a traders' tongue in the 19th century and took hold among the indentured native laborers in Queensland. The name derives from bêche-de-mer, an edible sea slug sought by early traders. This dialect of Pidgin English is now spoken by around 60% of ni-Vanuatu and is the main communication medium between persons from different language groups, though they speak their mother tongues at home. Most parliamentary debates are conducted in Bislama, but education is still conducted in either English or French.

Bislama verbs have no tenses: finished and unfinished actions are defined by adverbs. Nouns are often descriptions of use. *Blong* indicates possession, while *long* takes the place of most other prepositions. Vowels are pronounced as in Spanish. English speakers usually can't distinguish between *b* and *p, d* and *t, f* and *v,* and *g* and *k.* The letter *b* is preceded by an "m" sound, *d* by an "n" sound.

Bislama can sound deceptively simple to the untrained ear, but the meaning is not always what one would expect from a literal translation into English. Over the years it has developed into a complex language by adopting indigenous linguistic structures. The ability to speak Bislama properly is only attained through careful study (there are several dictionaries) and practice. The University of the South Pacific has a university-level Bislama course.

ON THE ROAD

Highlights

The overwhelming majority of tourists visit only Efate, Espiritu Santo, and Tanna, and indeed these three islands contain Vanuatu's best-known sights, including the country's only towns, Port Vila and Luganville. Tanna is acclaimed for Yasur Volcano and the Jon Frum Cargo Cult, Efate has an interesting road around its coast, and Espiritu Santo boasts some of the South Pacific's finest beaches. Ambrym is less known but outstanding for its active volcanoes. Virtually all of the islands are worth visiting by those willing to slow down and enjoy the unspoiled local environment and friendly people. It's easy to get lost and found in Vanuatu.

Sports and Recreation

Scuba diving is well developed with two active dive shops in Port Vila and another two at Santo. Diving is also possible from charter vessels off the north side of Efate. Game fishing is available at Port Vila. Other active sports to pursue are windsurfing in Vila's Erakor Lagoon, horseback riding at one of the two ranches on opposite sides of Port Vila, and yachting on a charter vessel based at Port Vila or Luganville.

Golf is big here, with two major 18-hole golf courses on Efate and smaller resort courses at two Port Vila hotels. There's also a golf course at Santo.

All of the above is the domain of tourists, expatriates, and affluent locals; hiking is the sport most commonly practiced by the vast majority of the population, although they'd hardly think of it as such. Well-used trails exist on all the outer islands, with Tanna especially accessible in this regard. It's quite possible to hike right across islands like Tanna and Erromango. Hiking around Espiritu Santo is a much bigger undertaking with local guides required.

Mountain climbers should consider the active volcanoes of Ambrym: Benbow and Marum in the south and Vetlam in the north. All are quite accessible to those willing to hire local guides and pay occasional custom fees to local chiefs. Ambae also has a central peak worth a climb. There are many other possibilities.

If surfing is Polynesia's finest gift to the world of sport, Melanesia's greatest contribution is perhaps bungee jumping, which A.J. Hackett saw on Pentecost Island in 1979 and later introduced to New Zealand. Hackett replaced the islanders' vines with expandable rubber lines, and today thousands of people a year prove something to themselves and others by taking the jump, just as the Pentecost men have been doing for hundreds of years.

Public Holidays and Festivals

Public holidays include New Year's Day (1 January), National Chiefs Day (5 March), Good Friday, Easter Monday (March/April), Ascension Day (April/May), Labor Day (1 May), Independence Day (30 July), Assumption Day (15 August), Constitution Day (5 October), All Saints' Day (1 November), National Unity Day (29 November), Christmas Day (25 December), and Family Day (26 December). The Monday before Independence Day is Children's Day.

Important annual events include the Jon Frum Festival at Sulphur Bay, Tanna, on 15 February, and the Pentecost Land Dive weekly in April and May. Independence Day sees a parade, food and kava stalls, sporting events, and custom dancing in Port Vila. Expect all of the events to begin an hour late.

ACCOMMODATIONS AND FOOD

Accommodations

The 10% hotel tax is not included in some of the prices listed in this book. Hotels often quote the basic price and add the tax to your bill later. Meals at licensed restaurants serving alcohol are also taxed 10%, but unlicensed snack bars are tax-free.

The only commercial accommodations are on Efate, Tanna, and Espiritu Santo. Camping is possible and safe elsewhere, but always get permission from the landowner or chief. Some churches, provincial councils, and women's groups have basic rest houses in rural areas and you can obtain advance information by calling the local government headquarters on the numbers provided in this book.

Often people will invite you into their own homes if they think you're in a jam, and in such cases it doesn't hurt to offer payment (gifts or money). Always give back as much as you receive, be considerate and polite, and make sure you don't overstay your welcome.

Food

Lap lap is the national dish. Bananas and root vegetables such as yams, taro, and manioc are grated, then kneaded to a paste, to which coconut cream and aromatic leaves are added. Pork or seafood can be included. The mixture is then wrapped in the leaves of a plant resembling the banana tree and cooked using hot stones in an earth oven. The best *lap lap* is made in remote villages, though a plain variety is sold at the Port Vila market. In the northern islands breadfruit is pounded in a wooden bowl to make a food called *nalot.*

Other local specialties include mangrove oysters (served cold) and freshwater prawns (steamed with young bamboo stalks and mayonnaise). If you see "poulet" on a restaurant menu, don't assume it's chicken, as the local deep-water red snapper goes by that name. Coconut crab is often served at tourist restaurants, with the result that the slow-growing creatures are rapidly becoming an endangered species. Vanuatu's five species of flying foxes are also occasionally sacrificed for tourists' plates, a black mark against Vanuatu.

Kava

Kava is consumed in many Pacific countries, but that of Vanuatu is the strongest, bearing little resemblance to weak Fijian kava. It's especially potent because the roots are not dried as they are in Fiji, but are diced while still green, then mashed and mixed with water (not strained as in Fiji). Prior to independence, kava drinking in the towns was discouraged by missionaries and government officials, but today it's become a cultural icon, the indigenous alternative to Western alcohol. Traditionally, kava is a ritual *kastom* drink, but in Port Vila it's now entirely social, with the many kava saloons called kava bars or *nakamals* doing brisk business from 1800 onward.

Genetic and chemical analysis has demonstrated that kava has been cultivated in northern Vanuatu for at least 3,000 years, and from here its use may have spread to other areas. More varieties exist here than anywhere else, with Tanna and northern Pentecost especially famous for their kava. Its medicinal use as a natural tranquilizer is well recognized by the European pharmacological industry. A relaxing kava tea is also made in Vanuatu.

Kava is narcotic, rather than alcoholic. One coconut shell full is enough; after several shells you won't be able to lift your arms or walk, and your mouth will feel as if the dentist had just given you novocaine. Don't eat anything before drinking kava or mix alcohol with it. Although it looks and tastes like dishwater, kava is pure relaxation, leaves no hangover, and never prompts aggression (unlike beer). The mind remains clear, and there are no hallucinations. It's not exactly hygienic though, because in central and southern Vanuatu, children chew the roots (at least on the outer islands). Most urban *nakamals* now use meat grinders to crush the roots.

SERVICES AND INFORMATION

Visas and Officialdom

Most nationalities don't require a visa for a stay of one month or less, although onward tickets are required. The immigration officer may ask at which hotel you intend to stay, but just name any of those listed in this book. Three extensions, one month at a time, are possible. The only immigration offices are in Port Vila and Luganville. Elsewhere, take your passport to a police station; they'll send it to Port Vila for the extension. Visa extensions are free but companies requiring work permits for expatriate staff must pay Vt50,000 per overseas employee.

It's possible to obtain a residence permit by investing over US$50,000 in a local business, and retirement here is also possible. Be aware, however, that expatriates who upset the authorities in any way are subject to deportation orders with no explanation given, whatever their legal or business standing in Vanuatu.

Both Port Vila and Luganville are ports of entry for cruising yachts. There are heavy fines for calling at outer islands before checking in (especially Tanna), and special permission is required to call at an outer island after checking out. At Port Vila the protected anchorage behind Iririki Island is good but deep. A Vt3000 port fee is payable upon departure.

Doing any sort of research in Vanuatu involves getting clearance from the Vanuatu Cultural Center (Box 184, Port Vila; tel. 22129, fax 26589). In 1985 the Vanuatu Government placed a moratorium on research in Vanuatu by expatriates working in the social sciences (anthropology, archaeology, linguistics, etc.). Only two research permits in anthropology have been granted since then, and both these were at the request of Vanuatu. The idea is to wait until ni-Vanuatu are able to do the work in their own way and to keep sacred knowledge hidden. Considering this, one should take care not to appear to be conducting research, or problems could arise. Cinematographers and others doing documentaries also require advance approval from the Cultural Center.

Money

The vatu is the unit of currency in Vanuatu; US$1 = Vt111 approximately (the word *vatu* means "stone"). There are notes of 500, 1000, and 5000, coins of one, two, five, 10, 20, 50, and 100. Though linked to special drawing rights (SDR) in the International Monetary Fund, the vatu is not well known abroad and can be hard to get rid of, so change your excess into the currency of the next country on your itinerary.

The main banks serving Vanuatu are the ANZ Bank, the Bank of Hawaii, and the Westpac Bank, with branches at Port Vila and Luganville. The National Bank also has branches at Lakatoro (Malekula) and Lenakel (Tanna), and although these do change foreign currency, before leaving for an outer island it's a good idea to make sure you have enough vatu to see you through. Rates of exchange differ slightly from bank to bank, so check around before changing large amounts. At last report there was no American Express representative in Vanuatu, although the Westpac Bank gives cash advances on American Express, MasterCard, and Visa credit cards.

Be aware that Vanuatu is an expensive country, with a cost of living noticeably higher than neighboring Fiji or Solomon Islands but about the same as New Caledonia. There aren't many ways to spend money out in the bush, but most of the facilities associated with modern life come dear (largely as a result of high customs duties). As in most of the Pacific, there's no tipping in Vanuatu.

Telecommunications

Post offices sell telephone cards in denominations of 30 units (Vt560), 60 units (Vt1120), and 120 units (Vt2240). By using a phone card for international calls you avoid three-minute minimum charges; card phones have been installed on Efate, Espiritu Santo, Tanna, and Malekula. To call abroad, dial the international code 00, the country code, the area code (if any), and the number. To get the local operator dial 90, directory assistance 91.

Domestic calls within Vanuatu are much cheaper weekdays 1800-0600 and all day on weekends and holidays. At this time you can call anywhere in the country at a rate of one unit (Vt17) for six minutes. For international calls, a slightly reduced rate is available on calls to Australia, Fiji, New Caledonia, New Zealand, and Solomon Islands only 2000-0600 Monday to Saturday and all day Sunday and holidays. Calls to North America are Vt523 a minute at all times (Vt413 a minute to Europe).

Vanuatu's telephone code is 678.

Business Hours and Electricity

Business hours are weekdays 0730-1130 and 1400-1700, Saturday 0730-1130. Post offices are usually open 0730-1530. Banking hours are generally weekdays 0830-1500. Most bureaucratic offices are closed for lunch 1130-1330, although shops, banks, and travel agencies remain open all day.

The electric voltage is 220-240 volts, 50 cycles, with two- or three-pronged plugs.

Media

The dour *Vanuatu Weekly* (Private Mail Bag 049, Port Vila; tel. 22999) is published in Bislama, French, and English by the government's Department of Media Services (Vt70). Both the *Weekly* and Radio Vanuatu have long been subject to government interference as the party in power seeks to deny a platform to its opponents. Television broadcasting began in 1991 with 50-50 programming in English and French.

The *Trading Post and Weekly Nius* (Box 1292, Port Vila; tel. 26535, fax 23343) is a lot more fun to read and costs only Vt20. Their "happenings and events" page keeps you up to date on what Vila's expat community is doing. The *Trading Post's* Australian publisher Mark Neil-Jones has to tread softly to avoid antagonizing powerful government officials, so try to read between the lines. The same company publishes Vanuatu's only Bislama newspaper, *Vanuatu Wantok Niuspepa,* and the tourist magazine, *Hapi Tumas Long Vanuatu,* both free.

Health

Vanuatu is in the Melanesian malaria belt, which continues up through the Solomon Islands into Papua New Guinea; there's none in New Caledonia and Fiji. Although malaria is mostly a problem on the islands north of Port Vila during summer (November to May), prophylactic pills should always be taken, as the disease has been reported everywhere year-round. Begin taking pills a week before you arrive and continue for four weeks after you leave.

Officially you're supposed to have a prescription to buy malaria pills in Vanuatu but the pharmacies in Port Vila usually sell the pills to tourists without bothering about prescriptions. Chloroquine-resistant *Plasmodium falciparum* malaria accounts for 73% of infections here, so turn to "Malaria" under "Health" in the Solomon Islands chapter introduction and follow that advice. The malarial mosquito here is *Anopheles*

farauti, which feeds at night or on overcast days and rests outdoors.

Dengue fever and hepatitis B are also present in Vanuatu, so read about them in the main introduction. Recommended (but not compulsory) vaccinations are immune globulin or Havrix vaccine (for viral hepatitis A) and the one against typhoid fever. All minor cuts should be treated seriously: a little iodine at the right time can save you a lot of trouble later. The tap water in Port Vila and Luganville is safe to drink, but elsewhere one should take precautions.

TRANSPORTATION

Getting There

The country's flag carrier, **Air Vanuatu** (Box 148, Port Vila; tel. 23848, fax 26591), flies to Port Vila from Sydney three times a week, from Auckland, Brisbane, and Nandi twice a week, and from Melbourne via Sydney weekly. Air Vanuatu and **Air Calédonie International** (tel. 22895) have a joint service from Nouméa four times a week. All Air Vanuatu flights are non-smoking. In the U.S. you can obtain information about Air Vanuatu by calling 800/677-4277.

Solomon Airlines (tel. 23848) flies between Honiara and Port Vila three times a week. **Air Pacific** (tel. 22836) also flies from Nandi to Port Vila three times a week with connections twice a week to/from Tokyo. The most direct route from North America is via Air Pacific's nonstop Los Angeles-Nandi service, connecting in Fiji for Vanuatu.

Vanuatu is included in Air Pacific's Pacific Air Pass (US$449) and in the Solomon Airlines Discover Pacific Pass (US$399-599), both providing easy access from Fiji. These 30-day passes are described in the main introduction to this book, under the heading "Getting Around."

Getting Around

Government-owned **Vanair** (Private Mail Bag 069, Port Vila; tel. 22753, fax 23910) offers over a hundred weekly services to 29 airstrips, with 20-passenger Twin Otters based at Port Vila and Espiritu Santo. You can fly from Port Vila to Espiritu Santo (Vt9800) four times a day, once or twice daily via Norsup. Flights from Port Vila to Tanna (Vt8700) run twice daily, via Ipota or Dillon's Bay once or twice weekly. Vanair also operates reduced Sunday service to Espiritu Santo, Norsup, and Tanna. Details of Vanair's many local services appear throughout this chapter.

In recent years, fares on Vanair (which has a monopoly on internal air service) have skyrocketed, making getting around Vanuatu a very expensive proposition. No stopovers are allowed—the fare from Port Vila to Espiritu Santo is Vt9800 direct, or Vt11,600 with a stopover at Norsup on the way. Roundtrip fares are double the one-way fare. A tax of Vt250 is added to each leg of your ticket (included in the ticket price). The 25% student discount isn't usually available to foreigners, but you can always try to get one. Because airfares are so high the planes are seldom fully booked. The baggage allowance is only 10 kilograms, but you can take excess luggage at Vt100 a kilo. Folding kayaks up to four meters long can be carried on the Twin Otters.

Reservation changes must be made one day in advance and "no shows" forfeit the full value of their ticket. Reconfirm your onward reservations immediately *upon arrival* at an outer island. Sometimes a plane can be diverted to make an unscheduled stop at an airstrip along the way if there are passengers to pick up or drop off. This can also work in reverse: they can forget to land where you're supposed to get on or off even though you've booked. On some flights if you ask nicely you'll usually be allowed to sit up front with the pilot and perhaps even fly a more scenic route (such as over Ambrym's volcano).

It's less expensive to travel interisland by local trading boat; some of these are described under "Port Vila," following. There are no set schedules and conditions are basic—your savings on the flight are soon eaten up if you have to wait around. This type of travel is more for the adventure than for the transportation, as you get to see the coastlines of many remote islands at stops along the way. Fishing boats and outboards can be hired to take you between nearby islands north of Efate, but it's only cheaper than flying if there are two or three of you. Rental cars and taxis are only available on Efate and Espiritu Santo. Elsewhere you can hitch rides in trucks, but traffic is sparse and you're expected to pay the driver.

To be really independent, take a small folding sea kayak and see delightful islands, bays, lagoons, beaches, and reefs on your own. The west coasts are better sheltered from the southeast trades, but avoid the hurricane season. Between the islands are big rollers and strong currents, so don't risk going interisland this way.

Airport

Port Vila International Airport (VLI) is six km north of Port Vila. This wartime airstrip is popularly known as Bauerfield, for Lt. Col. Harold M. Bauer, USMC, who was shot down over Guadalcanal in 1942. Bauer himself supervised construction of the airstrip in just 30 days in May 1942. There are separate terminals for domestic and international flights. The domestic terminal is the old international terminal; the new international terminal was built with Japanese aid money in 1990.

The Tour Vanuatu airport bus costs Vt400 pp. Otherwise walk a hundred meters to the exit where the main road leaves the airport parking lot and wait for a regular public bus, which will take you into town for Vt100. These buses aren't allowed to compete by picking up passengers right in front of the terminal, but there's no problem using them once you get past the taxis. If you need to stretch your legs after a tiring flight, you could begin walking the one and a half km to Tagabe and flag down any public bus you see. Taxis can run anywhere from Vt800-1200 for the trip into town, depending on the destination.

The tourist information counter at the airport can give you a list of every hotel in Vanuatu with current prices, then you can use the pay telephone near the departure check-in counters to call them up to verify availability and rates. The Westpac Bank has a window (tel. 23174) also near the check-in counters, which opens for all international flights. They change traveler's checks without commission but their rate is not so hot, so only change enough money to tide you over for a day or two. You lose about 10% when you change vatu back into dollars here.

There's a duty-free shop, but it's a poor place to unload leftover vatu as it's inside the departure lounge—should you decide not to buy anything you'll be stuck with the vatu. The goods are overpriced and the selection is poor.

A departure tax of Vt2000 in local currency is payable on international flights, one of the highest airport taxes in the South Pacific (wasn't this supposed to be a tax haven?). Everyone passing customs and immigration controls must pay this tax, even if they leave again the same day on another aircraft (only transit passengers continuing on the same flight are exempt). On domestic flights the tax is Vt250 but you pay it when you buy your ticket.

EFATE

Port Vila (pop. 20,000) is the commercial, administrative, touristic, and strategic heart of Vanuatu, the crossroads of the islands to the north and south. A cosmopolitan, attractive town, with many yachts anchored in the harbor, Port Vila snuggles around a picturesque bay, well protected from the southeast trades by a jutting peninsula. A narrow neck of land separates the harbor from the plush resorts on L-shaped Erakor Lagoon. Settle in for a week till you get your bearings.

Havannah Harbor, on the north side of 42-by-23-km Efate (Vate) Island, was the first European settlement, but in the late 1870s, drought and malaria forced the settlers to shift 31 km to the site of Port Vila. Plantations were created, and a few traders set up shop, but only after establishment of the Condominium in 1906 did a town form. Commercial activities occupied the waterfront; the colonial administration settled into the hills above. The town expanded quickly during WW II and again during the New Caledonian nickel boom of the early 1970s as the French reinvested their profits.

Today Port Vila is a modern capital city with excellent facilities, scenic beauty, and a relaxed atmosphere. Add the French *joie de vivre,* which pervades the town, to the varied shopping, easy transport, and many things to see and do, and you'll have one of the most exciting cities in the Pacific. Don't spend all your time in Port Vila, however, as Tanna, Espiritu Santo, Ambrym, and the other islands also have much to offer.

Be aware too that Port Vila is small enough for a cruise-ship load of tourists to have an overwhelming impact. Thus it's best to drop into South Pacific Shipping (tel. 22836) opposite Better Price Supermarket early in your stay to ascertain the dates of impending cruise ship dockings, then make a point of avoiding the Australian carnival hordes by being elsewhere those days. Even if you don't mind crowds, it's important to know when they'll be there beforehand because all organized tour and sporting activities will be monopolized by boat passengers that day. On the brighter side, visitors arriving from the South Pacific Bible Belt will be relieved to hear that the restaurants and shops of Port Vila are open on Sunday. Just keep in mind the peculiar hours kept by the local bureaucracy, who usually start work around 0730, then knock off for a long siesta 1130-1400. Attend to any official business first thing in the morning.

SIGHTS OF PORT VILA

Downtown
Begin with a visit to the **Vanuatu Cultural Center** (Box 184, Port Vila; tel. 22129, fax 26589; open weekdays 0900-1130 and 1400-1730, Saturday 0900-1130, Vt200 admission). Housed in the first major building to be erected after the hurricane of 1959, the center opened in 1961 and consists of a public library, a research collection, a handicraft center, and a museum of stuffed birds, insects, and shells. Don't miss the native artifacts room, with a superb collection of articles from Malekula. Upon request, they'll screen videotapes about local customs, the independence celebrations, etc. Some 45 ni-Vanuatu field workers collaborate with the museum, documenting traditional culture for future generations. On the lawn outside is a large metal pot used on Aneityum Island a century ago to cook whale blubber. (In April 1993 a devastating hurricane did serious damage to the Cultural Center, and both library and museum were still closed in 1995.)

One of Vanuatu's best-known contemporary artists is **Aloi Pilioko,** a Wallisian who created the reliefs on Pilioko House opposite the Bank of Hawaii. Aloi's associate, **Nicolai Michou-touchkine,** runs an exquisite dress shop (tel..

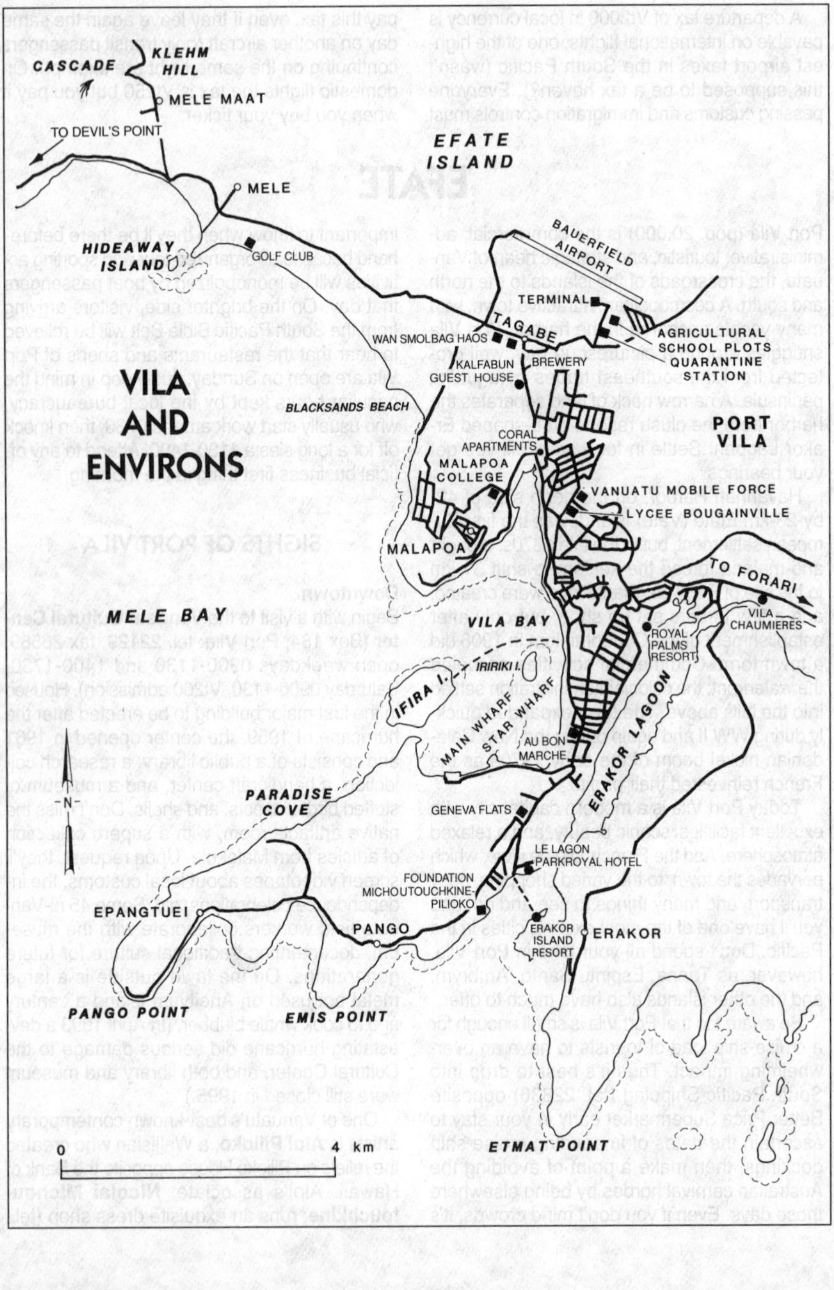

CASCADE

KLEHM HILL

MELE MAAT

TO DEVIL'S POINT

MELE

EFATE ISLAND

BAUERFIELD AIRPORT

HIDEAWAY ISLAND

GOLF CLUB

TERMINAL

TAGABE

WAN SMOLBAG HAOS

KALFABUN GUEST HOUSE

BREWERY

AGRICULTURAL SCHOOL PLOTS QUARANTINE STATION

VILA AND ENVIRONS

BLACKSANDS BEACH

CORAL APARTMENTS

MALAPOA COLLEGE

VANUATU MOBILE FORCE

LYCEE BOUGAINVILLE

PORT VILA

MALAPOA

MELE BAY

VILA BAY

TO FORARI

VILA CHAUMIERES

IFIRA I.

IRIRIKI I.

MAIN WHARF

STAR WHARF

ROYAL PALMS RESORT

PARADISE COVE

AU BON MARCHE

GENEVA FLATS

ERAKOR LAGOON

EPANGTUEI

PANGO

FOUNDATION MICHOUTOUCHKINE-PILIOKO

LE LAGON PARKROYAL HOTEL

PANGO POINT

EMIS POINT

ERAKOR ISLAND RESORT

ERAKOR

N

0   4 km

ETMAT POINT

© DAVID STANLEY

23367) in Pilioko House. Have a look upstairs at Nicolai's brilliant line of hand-printed clothing created in the Oceanic tradition of usable art. You'll often find him at work in his shop and this could be a unique opportunity to obtain a garment custom designed for you by a world-renowned artist in the astrological colors of your star sign.

The road beside Pilioko House leads up to the **French war memorial** (1914-1918), from which you'll get an excellent view of Port Vila and Vila Bay. The island you see nearest town is Iririki, once the British commissioner's residence and now a major resort. Farther out is Ifira Island, where the customary landowners of much of the Port Vila townsite live (the name Vila is a European corruption of Ifira). The **prime minister's office,** the large building with the Vanuatu flag flying in front on the same hill as the war memorial, is the former French Residency (no entry). Up the hill from here is the colonial-style **Supreme Court,** called the Joint Court during the Condominium days. During WW II the building served as a U.S. military headquarters.

Retrace your steps halfway back down the hill, then turn left at the town hall and follow Avenue General de Gaulle and Avenue Winston Churchill around to **Independence Park,** the former British Paddock. Overlooking the park is the **Ministry of Home Affairs,** the old British Residency. Under the Condominium, the British community lived in this vicinity, while the more numerous French were on the plateau behind the French Residency and in a quarter northeast of the Catholic cathedral.

Back down on the main street are two more colorful murals by Aloi Pilioko, one on the front of the **post office,** another on the side wall of the building across the street facing Café La Tentation. In July 1994 a new covered **market** opened at the south end of the pleasant Sea Front Promenade. The small pavilion across from the market is the former House of Parliament with an attractive mural (1980) by students of the French *lycée.* Behind this is the **Constitution Building,** once the headquarters of the Condominium bureaucracy and still government offices.

A free ferry shuttles frequently from a wharf near Better Price Supermarket to **Iririki Island,** site of one of Port Vila's largest tourist resorts. There's a footpath right around the island and good snorkeling at Snorkeler's Cove on the opposite side of Iririki from town (bring reef shoes if you have them). Where else can you go snorkeling in the main harbor of a country's capital? Many lovely trees grow only on Iririki, and it's definitely worth a visit.

Another launch (Vt50 one-way) from the same wharf leaves for **Ifira Island** every hour or so. The tombs of a few missionaries and the first Christian chief of Ifira, Kalsakau I, are behind the large Presbyterian church just above the landing on Ifira. Local politician Barak Sope has a large house on the island. Ifira is not promoted as a tourist attraction and, as in all ni-Vanuatu villages, you ought to ask permission before wandering around. Smile and be sociable with the other passengers on the launch and someone will take you under their wing.

South of Town

From both the Iririki and Ifira boats you can see the large red-roofed **Parliament building,** erected with Chinese aid in 1992, overlooking the harbor to the south. There's an interesting socialist-style monument in front of the main entrance to Parliament, and across the field opposite the monument is the **Chief's National Nakamal,** a traditional-style building where cultural programs are presented to tourists. A new National Museum is to be constructed between Parliament and the Chief's Nakamal.

The beauty spot of Port Vila is undoubtedly the Erakor Lagoon. Take a bus to the Erakor Island landing next to Le Lagon Hotel, then catch the free ferry (24-hour service) across to **Erakor Island,** another perfect place to sunbathe, swim, and snorkel. You're not allowed to bring your own food or drinks for a picnic, but lunch at the resort is fairly reasonable (Vt750 and up). Until a cyclone in 1959, Erakor village (now on the lagoon's east side) was on this island. Samoan teachers from the London Missionary Society arrived here as early as 1845, and after 1872, Presbyterian missionaries Rev. and Mrs. J.W. Mackenzie were based on Erakor. The tombstones of Mrs. Mackenzie, three of her children, and some early Polynesian missionaries can still be seen on the island.

ALOI PILIOKO

When you return to the mainland, walk left along the beach as far as the point. New construction has made this harder to do, and you may be forced to pick up a stone to ward off the occasional dog, but persevere. You'll eventually reach a colorful gate marked Restaurant And Museum, which will admit you to the Chez Gilles et Brigitte Restaurant (tel. 26000, closed Sunday). Walk past the restaurant to the **Foundation Nicolai Michoutouchkine et Aloi Pilioko** (Box 224, Port Vila; tel. 23367, fax 24224) where these well-known artists have studios. The foundation's art gallery (open daily 0900-1700, admission free) contains many tastefully arrayed South Pacific artifacts and works of art. Don't miss this. (If you decide against trying to get there via the beach, walk back up to the main road, turn left and follow the Pango road southwest just less than two km until you see the sign. A city bus might also agree to take you there.)

After visiting the Foundation, continue along the beach or road a kilometer to **Pango village.** Notice the large stake-and-net fish traps offshore. Surfers will find possibilities in this area. You must pay a custom fee to use the beach at Pango Point, six km from Le Lagon Parkroyal Hotel.

University Complex
Port Vila's **University of the South Pacific Complex** (Box 12, Port Vila; tel. 22748, fax 22633), east of downtown at the beginning of the Forari highway, was erected with New Zealand aid in 1989 to house the USP's Pacific Languages Unit and Law Department. The Pacific Languages Unit was established in 1984 to elevate the status of the Pacific vernaculars and protect them from foreign influence. Outstanding, inexpensive books on the Pacific written by the island people themselves are sold in the university administrative office (weekdays 0800-1130 and 1330-1600). The USP library here is open Monday, Wednesday, and Friday 0800-1130 and 1330-1700, Tuesday and Thursday 0800-1130 and 1230-1900. If you're academically inclined, it's worth dropping in.

North of Town
Frequent buses run to Tagabe on the airport highway where **National Breweries Ltd.** (tel. 22435) welcomes visitors to witness the brewing of the famous Tusker beer weekdays at 1000 and 1400. Take another bus west past the Port Vila Golf and Country Club (where U.S. troops came ashore on 2 March 1942) to **Mele** village, the largest village in Vanuatu. The big Presbyterian church reflects the British influence here.

The tourist resort on nearby **Hideaway Island** is popular among scuba divers. A launch (Vt500 roundtrip) ferries tourists to the island (good snorkeling), but don't come on a cruise ship day as endless boatloads of passengers are shuttled over to the island. Bringing your own food and drink onto Hideaway Island isn't allowed.

A road leads 12 km west from Mele to **Devil's Point.** In the days of sail, ships had a hard time rounding this point against the prevailing southeast trades, and often had to wait in Tukutuku Bay for the winds to slacken. The tidal rip here is strong. There are some lovely coves beyond the point and it's a good place to snorkel but you'll need your own transportation.

The road around Efate turns inland to **Mele Maat,** just northwest of Mele, where people from Ambrym were resettled after a big eruption on their home island in 1913. Just beyond Mele Maat there's a signposted **cascade** (admission Vt500), accessible from the bridge at the foot of

Klehm Hill. Wade up the river to a waterfall that tumbles down from the plateau into the beautiful jungle green setting like a miniature Iguazu. Many lovely pools are near this upper falls.

SIGHTS AROUND EFATE

A 132-km road runs around Efate's 887 square km; the American servicemen who built it during WW II dubbed the road U.S. Route No. 1. In 1991 the U.S. government offered to pave the road as a gift to mark the 10th anniversary of Vanuatu's independence. The trick was that work had to be done by U.S. Navy Seabees who would arrive in their own ship, and when the navy refused to confirm or deny whether the

vessel would be carrying nuclear weapons, nuclear-free Vanuatu was forced to turn down the American "gift." Today the road is steep and rough from Mele Maat to Emua, then much flatter and smoother from Emua all the way back to Port Vila.

Vast coconut plantations with herds of grazing Charolais cattle characterize much of Efate's coastal plain, while the interior is impenetrable rainforest. There's no bus service beyond Port Vila and vicinity, but you could try hitching around the island (difficult), take a circle-island bus tour (Vt3800-4500), or rent a car. If there are a few of you, it should be possible to charter one of the Port Vila city buses for a full-day ride around the island at Vt10,000 or so. A taxi around the island will run Vt8000 for the car.

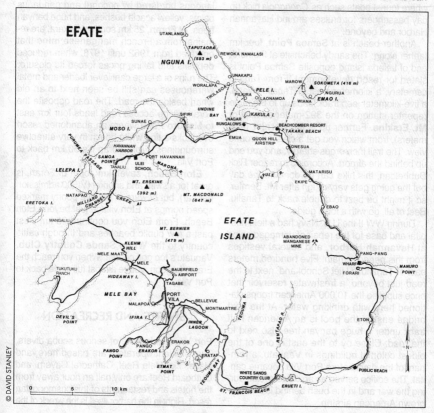

EFATE

UTANLANGI

TAPUTAORA (593 m)

REWOKA NAMALASI

NGUNA I.

UNAKAPU

WORALAPA

MAROW

SOKOMETA (416 m)

PELE I.

TIKILASOA

PILURA

LAONAMOA

NGURUA

EMAO I.

SIFIRI

UNDINE BAY

NAGAR

KAKULA I.

WIANA

SUNAE

MOSO I.

BUNGALOWS

BEACHCOMBER RESORT

HAVANNAH HARBOR

EMUA

TAKARA BEACH

SAMOA POINT

TANALIU

PORT HAVANNAH

MARONA R.

QUOIN HILL AIRSTRIP

ONESUA

LELEPA I.

ULEI SCHOOL

MT. ERSKINE (392 m)

MATARISU

EPULE R.

ERETOKA I.

NATAPAO

HILLIARD CHANNEL

CREEK AI

MT. MACDONALD (647 m)

EKIPE

EBAO

MANGALIU

MT. BERNIER (479 m)

EFATE ISLAND

ABANDONED MANGANESE MINE

KLEHM HILL

PANG-PANG

WHARF

MANURO POINT

MELE MAAT

MELE

FORARI

TUKUTUKU RANCH

BAUERFIELD AIRPORT

HIDEAWAY I.

TAGABE

MELE BAY

MALAPOA

PORT VILA

BELLEVUE

MONTMARTRE

DEVIL'S POINT

IFIRA I.

TEOUMA R.

ETON

PANGO POINT

INNER LAGOON

ERAKOR

PANGO

ERAKOR

RENTABAO R.

ERATAP

ETMAT POINT

TEOUMA BAY

N

WHITE SANDS COUNTRY CLUB

ST. FRANCOIS BEACH

ERUETI I.

PUBLIC BEACH

0   5   10 km

© DAVID STANLEY

Be aware that the far side of Efate is much less developed than the Port Vila side, so take enough to eat and drink as shops may be few and far between. You may be asked to pay custom fees to use village beaches.

The highway climbs steeply from Mele Maat to the top of **Klehm Hill,** which has an excellent view. The road then crosses a plateau and descends to the beach at **Creek Ai,** 24 km from Port Vila. If you want to go across to Lelepa Island ring the gong and they'll come pick you up at Vt500 per boatload each way. For Vt2000 return per group some of the water taxi boatmen will take you across and show you a large cave beyond the village. You could even stay in the village, but in this case you should bring a few gifts. Nearby is the Naguswai Mooring Base where tourist boats such as *Coongoola* pick up day passengers for cruises around Havannah Harbor and beyond.

Another beach is at **Samoa Point,** four km farther along. The sandy beachsite at the north end of Lelepa Island opposite Samoa Point is slated for resort development. From Tanaliu cemetery, a kilometer west of Tanaliu village, a five-kilometer jeep track leads up to the radio repeater station on the 392-meter summit of **Mt. Erskine.** Farther up is **Mt. Bernier** (479 meters), from which you get a clear all-around view. The trail then drops sharply, and you end up behind the airport. According to reader Rick Dubbeldan, this hike can be done in one day but the going gets very rough after Mt. Bernier, so it might be best to double back to Tanaliu. Best of all, go with a local guide.

During WW II the U.S. Navy had a field hospital and base for the repair of damaged ships at **Havannah Harbor,** and several vestiges from this period remain. Five hundred meters east of Tanaliu is Ulei School and, next to the road just beyond, a freshwater reservoir that once supplied the 10,000 American troops stationed here with drinking water. At the next bridge east of the pool is an American half track under a huge banyan tree also next to the road. Close by to the east is one of the oldest colonial buildings in Vanuatu, a remnant of the days before Port Vila became capital. The edifice served as an officers' club during the war and in the bush behind is an overgrown American airstrip.

At the entrance to **Siviri** village, a couple of kilometers off the main road, is a cave (Vt100 admission) used locally as a source of drinking water. Villagers commute to the large islands of Nguna and Pele from the wartime wharf at **Emua** on the north coast of Efate, 44 km from Port Vila. Village outboards to Emao Island leave from **Takara Beach,** 10 km farther east. The U.S.-built Quoin Hill fighter airstrip near here is kept usable. A couple of small resorts in this area offer bungalow accommodations and restaurants (see "Accommodations" and "Food," below). The large traditional building next to the road at **Ekipe** is used for cultural presentations to tourists on circle-island bus tours.

The broad, gravel road down the east side of Efate passes white sandy beaches and green lagoons bordered by coconut and pandanus palms, yellow acacia bushes, and huge banyan trees. At **Forari,** 25 km south of Takara, are remains from a French **manganese mine** that operated from 1962 until 1978, when reduced deposits and falling prices forced its closure. The ruins of a large cantilever loader and metal warehouses can still be seen next to an old wharf beside the road. The road opposite the Forari village access road leads four km east to **Manuro Point** where an abandoned resort overlooks a fine white beach in very attractive surroundings. From Forari it's 50 km back to Port Vila.

Eton Beach, seven km south of Forari, is great for a swim and snorkel (Vt500 admission per car), but beware of the five poorly marked speed bumps at Eton village just beyond Eton Beach. From Eton you continue 25 km west past a few public beaches and through cattle country to the **White Sands Country Club,** Vanuatu's top golf course. When you reach the Erakor Lagoon, you're almost full circle back to Port Vila.

SPORTS AND RECREATION

Port Vila is a favorite of serious scuba divers. Two efficient operators are based here, and places like Mele Reef, Cathedral Cavern, and Outboard Reef are only half an hour away from the hotels and restaurants of this cosmopolitan resort. Right in the harbor itself is the wreck of the

Star of Russia, a fully rigged clipper ship that sank near the main wharf in 1950. Fresh-nutrient seawater constantly cleans and feeds the sealife, and the visibility is excellent. You'll see lava tubes, huge table corals, coral columns, clown fish, and feather starfish—the underwater photographer will go octopus here. Only sharks are rare.

Nautilus Scuba (Box 78, Port Vila; tel. 22398, fax 25255), next to the Waterfront Bar and Grill, offers morning and afternoon scuba trips on one of their four boats at Vt3500 without gear (reductions on six- and 10-dive packages available). Snorkelers are welcome to go along for Vt1000 (bring your own mask and snorkel). This professional diving center offers complete PADI openwater certification courses for Vt30,000 including all equipment. They also sell scuba gear.

Scuba Action (Box 1110, Port Vila; tel. 22749, fax 23663), also known as Scuba Holidays, Club Marine, and Club Nautica, beside Scooters Bar near the Iririki Island jetty, offers scuba diving off Hideaway Island at Vt3500 pp if three or more divers go, Vt4500 pp for two divers, or Vt6500 for one diver. A day-trip to Hideaway for snorkelers is Vt3000 including hotel transfers and lunch.

Sailboats and other nautical gear can be hired at the water sports hut, to the left along the beach as you get off the Iririki Island Resort ferry.

Game fishing charters are offered on the powerboat *Calli Amanda* (Box 333, Port Vila; tel. 23490, 23096), based at the Waterfront Bar and Grill. The Vt8000-per-hour cost can be split between four anglers. These operators know their waters and the catches are impressive (retained by the captain).

The 18-hole championship golf course at the **White Sands Country Club** (Box 906, Port Vila; tel./fax 22090), 18 km east of Port Vila, is the venue of the Vanuatu Golf Open in July or August. Green fees here are Vt2500, plus Vt800 for a half set of clubs and a buggy. Call them up for information on their free shuttle bus from Port Vila. The 18-hole **Port Vila Golf and Country Club** (Box 358, Port Vila; tel. 22564) at Mele is less expensive at Vt1500 green fees and Vt500 for clubs and a buggy; it's open daily. Both the Royal Palms Resort and Hotel Le Lagon have smaller golf courses for guests.

Ranch de la Colle (Box 233, Port Vila; tel. 22071), just east of the Mele golf course, offers horseback riding Tuesday to Sunday afternoons from 1330. The **Club Hippique** (Box 1206, Port Vila; tel. 23347), east of Port Vila, also offers horseback riding. The Adventure Center (tel. 22743) in the Olympic Hotel courtyard runs half-day bus tours to the ranches with riding included at Vt2800 pp.

See soccer from the bleachers at the stadium every Saturday afternoon. Cricket is played in Independence Park on Saturday. Squash courts are available at Club Vanuatu (Vt200 for 30 minutes).

ACCOMMODATIONS

Budget Accommodations

The **Kalfabun Guest House** (Box 494, Port Vila; tel. 24484), on the main road into town, two km from the airport, accommodates young budget travelers at Vt1500 pp in one of three small bungalows (singles must share or pay for both beds). Camping is half price but they only allow it when all of the rooms are occupied. You can cook light meals in the main building where Bob Kalfabun and his family reside. Bob gives a 10% discount if you pay a week in advance, but charges a Vt100 surcharge if you stay only one night. He takes his guests to a village feast on Friday night and admission for them is half price. There's a lot of traffic noise but it's still the only low-budget guesthouse in town.

In 1989, local politician Barak Sope opened the pleasant three-story **Talimoru Hotel** (Box 110, Port Vila; tel. 23740, fax 25369) on Cornwell Street, Seaside. The 42 small fan-cooled rooms (18 singles and 24 doubles) are Vt2500/3685 single/double without balcony, Vt2750/3850 with balcony, a light breakfast included. The toilet and shower are down the hall but they're kept very clean, with hibiscus flowers decorating the washbasins. A valid student ID card should get you a 10% discount. Aside from the restaurant and bar, the Talimoru has Port Vila's only hotel *nakamal* (kava bar) right on the premises and poker machines in the lobby.

Several of the missions in Port Vila provide accommodations. **Sutherland House,** on Gloucester Street opposite Vila East Primary

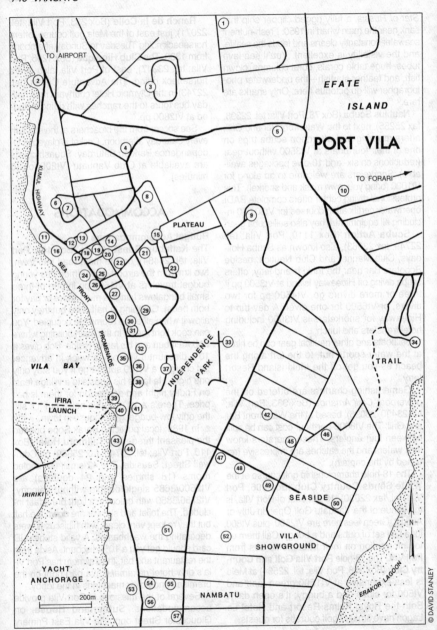

PORT VILA

EFATE ISLAND

TO AIRPORT

KUMUL HIGHWAY

SEA FRONT

PROMENADE

PLATEAU

INDEPENDENCE PARK

TO FORARI

TRAIL

VILA BAY

IFIRA LAUNCH

IRIRIKI

YACHT ANCHORAGE

SEASIDE

VILA SHOWGROUND

NAMBATU

ERAKOR LAGOON

0   200m

N

© DAVID STANLEY

PORT VILA

1. Vietnamese Cemetery
2. Trader Vic's
3. Stadium
4. Georges Pompidou Building/Survey Dept.
5. Club Imperial
6. Radio Vanuatu
7. Lunchtime Food Market
8. Catholic Cathedral
9. Supreme Court
10. University of the South Pacific
11. Coongoola Cruises
12. Hotel Olympic
13. Le Kiosque Bookstore
14. British/Australian high commissions
15. French War Memorial (1914-1918)
16. Rossi Restaurant
17. Vanuatu Cultural Center
18. National Tourism Office

19. Natapoa Takeaway
20. Chinatown
21. Town Hall
22. Police Station
23. Prime Minister's Office
24. Stop Press
25. French Embassy
26. Immigration Office/Bank of Hawaii
27. Center Point Supermarket
28. Le Flamingo Night Club
29. Club Vanuatu
30. Lolam House/Vanair
31. Post Office
32. Frank King Tours
33. Ministry of Home Affairs
34. Royal Palms Resort
35. Market
36. Constitution Building
37. Presbyterian Church Office
38. Better Price Supermarket
39. BP Wharf

40. Scooters Bar
41. Ballande Center
42. Sutherland House
43. Waterfront Bar and Grill/Nautilus Scuba
44. Marina Motel
45. Sarabetu Transit House
46. Central Hospital
47. Tropical Market (taxi stand)
48. Ah Tong Motel
49. Talimoru Hotel
50. Red Laet Nakamal
51. Parliament
52. Chiefs National Nakamal
53. Le Rendez-Vous Restaurant
54. Cine Hickson
55. Windsor International Hotel
56. Kaiviti Village Motel
57. Man Wah Chinese Restauran

School near the hospital, offers six beds (and cooking facilities) at Vt1750/2500 single/double. Check in at the Presbyterian Church office (Box 150, Port Vila; tel. 22722) on Independence Park weekdays 0800-1130 and 1330-1600; at other times go directly to the house. If you phone they'll say they're full, so go in person. The Church of Christ **Sarabetu Transit House** (Box 638, Port Vila; tel. 22469), closer to the hospital, is Vt1500/2000 single/double, and communal cooking facilities are provided.

The **University of the South Pacific** (Box 12, Port Vila; tel. 22748, fax 22633) rents eight rooms in four bungalows overlooking an intersection below the campus. Prices are Vt1500 pp, but you must arrive weekdays 0800-1130 and 1330-1600 when the main office is open. The rooms are often occupied by students or university guests, so it's best to call ahead.

Medium-Priced Hotels

The three-story **Coral Motel Apartments** (Box 1054, Port Vila; tel./fax 23569) is at the head of Vila Bay on the main road between the airport and Port Vila. The 10 modern studios with cooking facilities and TV are Vt5000/5500/6000 single/

double/triple, with price reductions for stays of three nights or more and monthly rates. Bus service from here to town is good.

The three-story **Hotel Olympic** (Box 230, Port Vila; tel. 22464, fax 22953), also known as "Iririki Centre Ville," is nearly opposite the ANZ Bank in central Port Vila. The 20 a/c rooms are overpriced at Vt9500/10,500 single/double. Self-contained apartments are Vt13,500. The functional Olympic caters to businesspeople with direct-dial telephones, telex, and secretarial services.

Just south of downtown Port Vila opposite Nautilus Scuba is the **Marina Motel** (Box 681, Port Vila; tel./fax 22566). The 10 a/c apartments in the main two-story building are Vt6500/7200 single/double. Fridge and cooking facilities are in each room, and there's a pool (usually empty).

The three-story **Windsor International Hotel** (Box 810, Port Vila; tel. 22150, fax 22678) combines a resort atmosphere (swimming pool) with businesslike convenience to Port Vila. The 20 studios are Vt7300 single or double, the 11 one-bedroom suites Vt10,500 single or double. There are also two two-bedroom apartments with washing machines at

Vt11,000. All of the older rooms in the two-story blocks have kitchens, but avoid the 54 higher-priced "orchid rooms" in the new three-story blocks, which lack cooking facilities. All units have fridge, fan, and private bath. The hotel restaurant is reasonable.

The three-story **Kaiviti Village Motel** (Box 152, Port Vila; tel. 24684, fax 24685), next to the Windsor International, has nine two-bedroom apartments and 28 studio apartments with cooking facilities at Vt7500 single or double, Vt10,000 for four people, Vt11,000 for five, Vt12,000 for six. Only the downstairs units have a/c, but those upstairs have balconies. The motel also features a swimming pool and laundry facilities, and Au Bon Marché Supermarket is conveniently nearby.

The **Ah Tong Motel** (Box 80, Port Vila; tel. 23218) near the Talimoru Hotel is intended for long stays and is usually fully booked. When available, the 10 units with cooking facilities are Vt6800 a day or Vt80,000 a month.

Pacific Lagoon Apartments (Box 827, Port Vila; tel. 23860, fax 24377), on the Erakor Lagoon a few hundred meters southwest of Le Lagon Hotel toward Pango, has 10 two-bedroom units with fan, accommodating up to four people at Vt42,000 a week for the unit. Each has a fully equipped kitchen. Rentals of less than a week are not available, but prorating is possible for longer stays.

Just to the east of Port Vila on the road to Forari is friendly **Vila Chaumières** (Box 400, Port Vila, tel. 22866, fax 24238), on the narrow passage between the Erakor and Inner lagoons. The lagoon waters here are too murky for swimming. The four hexagonal cottages (Vt8500 single or double, Vt10,000 triple) have cooking facilities, but children are not accommodated. The units lack privacy, as they're right on the walkway to the restaurant. On the other hand, the restaurant is excellent, for both the food and ambience, so it might be worth dropping by for a meal (restaurant open daily 1130-1400 and 1800-2300). It's enjoyable to eat on the terrace overlooking the lagoon. A variety of seafood is served at prices no higher than you'd pay at the other tourist restaurants around town. At lunchtime the city buses will drop you here, but for dinner you'll probably have to call a taxi to get home (unless you have a car).

Hideaway Island Resort (Box 1110, Port Vila; tel. 22963, fax 23867) on Mele Island, nine km northwest of Port Vila, has an office next to Scooters Bar just up from the Iririki ferry wharf. Rebuilt after a hurricane in 1992, Hideaway has 10 bungalows at Vt8500/12,000 single/double, six double rooms with shared bath at Vt5500/7000, and a 24-bed dormitory at Vt2250 pp. Cooking facilities are not provided and the full meal plan is Vt3200 pp. Airport transfers are Vt850 pp return. Hideaway is promoted as a scuba camp for packaged-tour Australians; diving costs Vt3500 per dive, plus Vt1500 for equipment. Scuba certification (Vt32,000) is available if three people sign up. This tiny coral island can get crowded, and on cruise ship days it's literally flooded with day-tripping people.

Upmarket Hotels

Iririki Island Resort (Box 230, Port Vila; tel. 23388, fax 23880), on an island in Vila Bay directly opposite downtown Port Vila, opened in 1986. The 70 a/c bungalows are priced according to whether they face the harbor from above (Vt17,000 single or double) or are right down on the water (Vt19,000). Each has one queen-size and one single bed, fridge, video, and furnished balcony. Included in the complex are an open-plan restaurant with an elevated terrace overlooking the pool and harbor. Non-motorized water sports are free, but the beach isn't as good as those on the Erakor Lagoon. The snorkeling, on the other hand, is far better. A convenient free ferry to town operates round-the-clock (guests only after 1830).

Several resort hotels face the Erakor Lagoon. The four-star **Royal Palms Resort** (Box 215, Port Vila; tel. 22040, fax 23340), formerly the Intercontinental Hotel, is a high-rise hotel block with 156 a/c rooms (most with balcony) beginning at Vt15,000 single or double. Vanuatu's only genuine gambling casino is located at this hotel, and there's a six-hole golf course. Nonmotorized sporting activities such as windsurfing, paddle boating, snorkeling, surf skiing, catamaran boating, outrigger canoeing, golf, and tennis are free to guests, but nautical gear must stay within sight of the hotel. Nicolai Michoutouchkine stages a fashion show at the Royal Palms every Wednesday at 1900. The waters here aren't as clear as those near Le Lagon Hotel, and Iririki Island Resort is more convenient to town, but the Royal Palms is by far the more easygoing of the three. Backed by rainforest, surrounded by gardens, and facing a bright, sandy beach, it's a pleasant place to stay. In 1995 France's Méridien hotel chain was in the process of taking over management of the property with plans to add another 100 rooms, and hopefully they won't alter its character.

Le Lagon Parkroyal Hotel (Box 86, Port Vila; tel. 22313, fax 23817) is near the mouth of the Erakor Lagoon, three km from Port Vila. Aside from 109 a/c hotel rooms (from Vt14,000 single or double) in seven two-story buildings, Le Lagon has 27 bungalows (from Vt18,500). All rooms are fridge-equipped, and a few have a jacuzzi (ask). As usual, a lagoon view costs more than a garden view. Le Lagon has a swimming pool, tennis courts, a twelve-hole golf course, and nautical activities. The original thatched Le Lagon Hotel was badly damaged by a hurricane in 1987 and then rebuilt in concrete, losing much of its character in the process. A stone seawall separates an area of raked sand from the water and the formerly luxuriant vegetation has been cleared. In January 1995 management of Le Lagon was taken over by a Japanese company, the South Pacific Hotel Corporation.

Though a third cheaper than Le Lagon Parkroyal just across the water, **Erakor Island Resort** (Box 24, Port Vila; tel./fax 22983) has a far better beach and is a lot more relaxed. The nine well-appointed, fan-cooled bungalows on a long sandy lagoon island are Vt9500/10,500/12,000 single/double/triple, and in addition there are four two-story bungalows accommodating up to five persons for a flat Vt13,500. There are no cooking facilities, so you must eat at their restaurant. Even if you're staying elsewhere, Erakor Island makes a nice destination for lunch (Vt750 and up) and an afternoon of lounging on their white-sand beach. The bungalows are well away from the public beach in front of the restaurant, however, so resort guests aren't bothered by day-trippers. Access to Port Vila is quick and easy via their free ferry and public buses. We recommend Erakor Island Resort as your best choice in this category.

Hotels around Efate
Nagar Beach Bungalows (Box 939, Port Vila; tel. 23221, fax 23442) is at Paonangisu on the north side of Efate, 50 km from Port Vila clockwise on a rough, steep road, or 80 km counterclockwise on a wide, flat road. It's one of the only resorts on the island owned and operated by ni-Vanuatu. Fanny and Henry Cyrel have two new two-bedroom bungalows accommodating up to six persons at Vt7000, and four older double bungalows with shared bath at Vt2000 pp plus tax. Camping on the grounds costs Vt500 pp. The units are attractive, each with a veranda and chairs. There are no cooking facilities but a bowl of tropical fruit and a flask of hot water are provided free. The Cyrels' restaurant is open 0700-0900 and 1100-1530 and 1800-2200—try the steak sandwich (Vt480). Their beach is poor but for Vt2000 return per group they'll drop you on the white sands of Kakula (Rabbit) Island. Nagar is an ideal place to break a trip around the island but be prepared for large groups on circle-island bus tours that often take lunch here.

The **Beachcomber Resort** (Box 947, Port Vila; tel. 23576, fax 26458), formerly called Takara Resort, three km east of Nagar, is another convenient stop on your way around the island. It's slightly more upmarket than Nagar, but it has the advantage of a unique circular thermal hot-spring pool for the exclusive use of house guests and restaurant patrons. The six self-contained duplex units cost Vt4000 for up to four persons, Vt5000 for up to eight, tax additional. There's hot water in the showers but no fridge or coffee-making facilities in the rooms. Meals in the restaurant are pricey. Some car rental agencies in Port Vila offer a free night at Beachcomber for those taking a car for two days, so ask around. Beachcomber is in the process of being upgraded and expanded, so you may find a much larger resort here with higher prices.

The **White Sands Country Club** (Box 906, Port Vila; tel./fax 22090), 18 km east of Port Vila, charges Vt7000 single or double for each of the nine thatched bungalows with fan (no cooking facilities). In addition to an 18-hole golf course, the Club has a white-sand beach, swimming pool, tennis courts, and restaurant. Beware of the undertow if you swim here. There's a free shuttle bus to/from Port Vila four times a day (call for information).

FOOD

Budget Places to Eat

The 10% tourist tax only applies to licensed restaurants serving alcoholic beverages, so you'll save money twice over by dining at one of the gastronomic tax havens mentioned below. Around lunchtime weekdays, buy good, inexpensive home-cooked food at the stands in the open area on the hill in front of Radio Vanuatu. It's about Vt200 for a plate of chicken or fish and rice straight from the pot. Come early—by 1300 everything will be gone. It's also a good place to get a Vt20 cup of coffee throughout the day.

Some of the best budget food in town is dished out at **Natapoa Takeaway and Snack** (tel. 26377) in Chinatown, inland one block from the Cultural Center and to the right. A heaping plate of curry chicken and rice is Vt300, with free cold water to wash it down. Most of the dishes are based on chicken or beef but a surprising variety of vegetables comes with the meals. It's open for lunch and dinner daily except Sunday—recommended.

The **Café de Paris** (tel. 26664), next door to Natapoa Takeaway, also serves good lunch specials listed on a blackboard (about Vt500 a plate).

Club Vanuatu (tel. 22615), next to the Unelco electric generating plant on the backstreet behind the post office, moved into this flashy new building in 1994. It's a private club but tourists are allowed to sign the visitor's book at the door (persons without shoes or a shirt not admitted). The street-level dining room serves reasonably priced hot meals, and the club's other facilities include a video room, lending library, snooker, billiards, darts, squash courts, slot machines, and a bar. Watch CNN on a huge screen. They're open Monday to Thursday 1000-midnight, Friday and Saturday 1000-0200, Sunday 1000-2100.

One of the cheapest places in Port Vila to get an inexpensive breakfast or lunch is the self-service cafeteria in **Au Bon Marché Supermarket** (tel. 22945; daily 0630-1830) on the main road just south of town. Away from meal times, it's a nice relaxed place to sit and write postcards over a cup of coffee.

Nearly all the Chinese restaurants around Port Vila also have takeaways—a good way of saving money if you can get the food back to your room or to a picnic spot before it gets cold. The **Man Wah Restaurant** (tel. 23091), behind the Windsor International Hotel is the best of these. They're open for lunch Tuesday to Saturday 1100-1330, daily from 1800 for dinner.

Upmarket Restaurants

Expect to pay 10% tax at all of the following restaurants (none of which allow you to bring your own drinks). The garden terrace overlooking the harbor at the **Rossi Restaurant** (tel. 22528; closed Sunday and Monday) in the center of town is a nice place for a leisurely lunch. If you come for dinner, don't arrive too late and miss the sunset. Vanuatu's oldest hotel was on this site until recently.

Ma Barker's (tel. 22399) opposite the Cultural Center is very touristy but okay if you're dying for an Aussie-style steak. The thatched **Waterfront Bar and Grill** (tel. 23490; closed Sunday) serves better steaks (local beef) and seafood and has a salad bar and coconut pie. The bar here is a yachtie hangout.

Trader Vic's (tel. 24940) on Kumul Highway at the north end of town is okay for pizza and beer. The more upscale **Pisces Restaurant** attached has Italian-style seafood.

Le Rendez-Vous (tel. 23045; closed Sunday), across from Cine Hickson, is simply Port Vila's finest French restaurant. You'll get a great sunset view as you dine on roast duck with apples or deep-fried prawns in this elegant thatched building.

L'Houstalet (tel. 22303; daily from 1800), just past Au Bon Marché Supermarket and on the opposite side of the road, has 16 varieties of oven-baked pizza, which is also available takeaway. This quaint establishment is a rallying point for the local French community.

Chez Gilles et Brigitte (tel. 26000; closed at lunch Saturday and all day Sunday), next to beach at the Foundation Michotouchkine-Pilioko on the way to Pango, features yet more fine French cuisine with a choice of sauces and great salads. To have lunch or dinner in this unique artistic environment next to the sea is something special.

Also remember the outstanding seafood restaurant at **Vila Chaumières** (tel. 22866), mentioned previously under "Accommodations."

Cafes

El Gecko (tel. 25597; closed Sunday), in the courtyard beside Goodies near the Cultural Center, is a nice place for a coffee.

Café La Tentation Pâtisserie (tel. 22261; open weekdays 0700-1900, weekends 0700-1300), opposite the post office, has Port Vila's best coffee and French pastries, and it's also good for breakfast.

La Terrasse (tel. 22428), across the street from the French embassy in the center of town, is Port Vila's most authentic French cafe.

Groceries

Port Vila's picturesque **market** opposite the post office operates Tuesday to Saturday. In addition to fresh fruit and vegetables, a few handicrafts are sold. No one will hassle you to buy anything, so look around as you please, just don't bargain—the prices are low enough to begin with. Get there early for the best selection of produce.

For other groceries try the large supermarkets, Au Bon Marché, Better Price, and Center Point. **Center Point** (tel. 22631; weekdays 0700-1900, Saturday 0700-1300, Sunday 0700-1200 and 1600-1900) is especially well stocked and has a good grocery section with fresh croissants and *pain au chocolat.* Excellent ice cream is dispensed from a cart in front of Center Point. The stores in Chinatown sometimes have cheaper canned goods.

Ah Pow Bakery (tel. 22215), on Dauphin Street just behind Houstalet Restaurant near Au Bon Marché, sells cheap croissants and other pastries (this bakery delivers bread all around Efate every night). French baguettes are a great buy at Vt40.

ENTERTAINMENT

Cine Hickson (tel. 22431) shows films in French nightly except Thursday at 2000 and 2200 (admission Vt300).

Le Flamingo Night Club (tel. 25788), opposite Center Point Market Place near the post office, is a sharp, modern disco that is supposed to open nightly at 1700, though they often remain closed until 2000 when the Vt500 cover charge comes into effect. Tuesday is "price busters" night, with half-price drinks all evening and no cover charge. Dress regulations apply.

Club Imperial (tel. 26541), between the university and the jail, is more of a local place, and on Friday and Saturday nights it really gets lively.

L'Houstalet Restaurant (tel. 22303), mentioned above, functions as a nightclub after 2230 daily, and on Friday and Saturday nights it's packed. There's a Vt300 cover charge but you only have to pay it on weekends. It's a good place to mix with francophone locals. **Club Vanuatu** (tel. 22615) has dances Friday and Saturday nights.

The **Palms Casino** (Box 1111, Port Vila; tel. 24308, fax 22394) at the Royal Palms Resort features blackjack, baccarat, roulette, and slots. Dress regulations are more relaxed than at the Casino Royal in Nouméa (neat, casual attire okay, but you must wear shoes). That's logical as their clientele is more likely to consist of laid-back Aussies and Kiwis instead of the high-rolling Japanese and French tourists you see around Nouméa. It's open daily from 1130 until the last customer leaves (passport required, admission free). Unfortunately many ni-Vanuatu are addicted to the gambling machines both here and at the Talimoru and Windsor International hotels, and entire weekly pay packets are often swallowed by the monsters, leading to real hardship for local families.

Kava *Nakamals*

Around sunset the local expat community gathers for happy hour at the **Red Laet** near the Talimoru Hotel, one of about a hundred *nakamals* or kava bars in Port Vila serving that strong Vanuatu kava at Vt50-100 a shell. Most are patronized primarily by people from a particular outer island and function like social clubs. You'll be welcome if you enter with respect, keep your voice down, and don't make abrupt movements. In the villages, local women aren't allowed to frequent the *nakamals,* but in Port Vila it's usually no problem; kava drinkers are generally pretty mellow, but these are predominantly male enclaves. Locations change, so just ask for a kava bar near your hotel.

Cultural Shows for Visitors

If you're at all interested in live theater, you won't want to miss a performance by the **Wan Smolbag Theater,** a local troupe that brings contemporary social issues to the stage with unexpected professionalism and talent. **The Vanuatu Show** is a two-hour combination of historical skits, storytelling, custom dancing, kava sampling, etc. *Down Paradise Street* is a musical with 13 original songs revealing what lies behind the Pacific smile. You're allowed to take photos of the performances freely, and during the intermission *lap lap* is served in the foyer for a nominal fee. The kava after the show is on the house. At last report performances were Thursday at 1900 in Wan Smolbag Haos, around the corner from National Breweries at Tagabe, 50 meters up the road to Mele. Check posters around town for the current venue, or ask at the Adventure Center (tel. 22743) in the Olympic Hotel courtyard. The Adventure Center sells tickets (Vt800-1000 pp), or you can buy one at the door. We give this show a full 10 out of 10. (If you're very lucky, you may encounter Wan Smolbag in some remote village staging a performance in Bislama with a theme such as "building your own toilet," "family planning," or "violence against women," courtesy of some overseas aid donor. Impressive!)

Foot-stompin' **custom dancing** accompanies the weekly barbecues and feasts at the major hotels, usually on Wednesday at Iririki Island Resort (tel. 23388), on Saturday at both the Royal Palms Resort (tel. 22040) and Le Lagon Hotel (tel. 22313). If you're not that hungry, a drink at the bar should get you in. Call ahead to verify the show times.

Village feasts are held at Mele, Pango, and Erakor villages several nights a week (often Wednesday and Friday) with string band music, custom dancing, kava drinking, and island food served buffet style. Admission including transportation is usually Vt2500 for adults or Vt1250 for children. **Solo's Feast** at Mele village is every Friday night 1900-2200. **Frank King Tours** (tel. 22808) takes visitors to a different feast at Pango village. Unlike the tourist shows mentioned above, attending one of these is sort of like being invited to a private village party.

SHOPPING

You can buy one of those colorful Mother Hubbard dresses in the Chinese stores on the street running inland from Ma Barker's. The **Center Point Market Place,** across the parking lot from Center Point Supermarket, also has authentic Mother Hubbards. These dresses are highly recommended for women thinking of visiting remote areas, and they make great party attire at home.

In quite another category are the designer clothes available at many sharp boutiques around Port Vila. Beware of fake products bearing counterfeit brand names, or much better, stick to the autographed apparel available at **Michoutouchkine Creations** (tel. 23367) in Pilioko House, previously mentioned.

The **Second Hand Shop** on BP Wharf in town sells used books, as well as cheap secondhand clothes. **The Beer Essentials** (tel. 26190) near the ANZ Bank on Kumul Highway has Tusker beer T-shirts.

Some of Port Vila's finest shops are on Bougainville Street, which runs inland from Hotel Olympic to the Catholic cathedral. Madame Bastion's **L'Atelier Galerie d'Art** (tel. 23654), opposite Hotel Olympic, has a good selection of local paintings and handicrafts.

Vila Duty Free Gifts (tel. 23443) opposite the post office has cheap postcards, film, and souvenirs. The **Philatelic Bureau** (tel. 22000) on the left inside the post office has some very colorful stamps. Avoid buying anything on a cruise ship day, as some prices are jacked up 15%.

Crafts

A good place to pick up authentic crafts is the **Handikraf Blong Vanuatu** boutique (Box 962, Port Vila; tel. 23228) adjoining the Cultural Center, a nonprofit outlet that opened in 1982. They sell stone- and woodcarvings, fern figures, slit gongs both large and small, bowls, war clubs, pig killing clubs, spears, bows and arrows, fish traps, model canoes, canoe prows, masks, rattles, panpipes, combs, shell necklaces, grass skirts, shoulder bags, mats, native pottery, and curved boar tusks. The best articles come from Ambrym. Also notice the Pentecost money mats with batik designs. The large iron anchor embedded in cement in the courtyard was recovered in 1958 from the *Astrolabe,* one of the ships of French explorer La Pérouse, lost at Vanikolo in the Solomons in 1788.

The Department of Agriculture's Quarantine Station (tel. 23130) near the airport fumigates plants and plant products (fern carvings, grass skirts, etc.) and issues a phytosanitary certificate (about Vt400) for their export.

SERVICES

Money
The Westpac Bank near the post office, the ANZ Bank opposite Hotel Olympic, and the Bank of Hawaii change traveler's checks without commission. All banks close at 1500 weekdays and exchange rates vary—check around.

You can also change money at **Goodies** (tel. 23445; open weekdays 0800-1730, weekends 0830-1200), opposite the Cultural Center, and their rates are better than the bank's!

Post and Telecommunications
The post office opens weekdays 0730-1630. Port Vila is a fairly safe place from which to mail parcels, even by surface mail. Small surface mail packets up to two kilograms benefit from a reduced rate (Vt530 maximum). Poste restante mail is held two months.

Place long-distance telephone calls and send faxes at **Vanitel** (tel. 22185; weekdays 0730-2000, Saturday 0730-1200) adjacent to the main post office. Card telephones are available at the post office, Ballande Center, Talimoru Hotel, hospital, university, and airport, the easiest way to call by far.

Immigration Office
The **Immigration** office (tel. 22354) above the French Pharmacy in central Port Vila gives free visa extensions (return air ticket required).

Consulates
The countries with diplomatic missions in Port Vila are Australia (tel. 22777), Britain (tel. 23100), China (tel. 23598), France (tel. 22353), New Zealand (tel. 22933), and Sweden (tel. 22944). If you need a P.N.G. visa, the honorary consul of Papua New Guinea (tel. 22439) is upstairs in Bougainville House opposite Le Kiosque Bookstore.

Laundromats and Public Toilets
Pacific Wash and Dry (tel. 26416; daily 0700-1800) in the Ballande Center near Better Price is a genuine coin-operated laundromat costing Vt300 to wash or dry.

EZY Wash (tel. 24386), below the Olympic Hotel, is a self-service laundromat open weekdays 0730-1830, Saturday 0730-1630, Sunday 0800-1130 (also Vt300 to wash or dry). Both are expensive due to high electricity rates.

Free public toilets are found in the Ballande Center opposite the Iririki Island wharf.

Yachting Facilities
Yachting World (tel. 23273) next to the Waterfront Bar and Grill charges visiting yachts Vt4000 a week for seawall moorings, Vt3000 a week for harbor moorings.

The **Vanuatu Cruising Yacht Club** (Box 525, Port Vila; tel. 24634) at the Waterfront Bar and Grill offers a book swap, mail forwarding, local information, and free cruising guides to Vanuatu.

Health
The **Central Hospital** (tel. 22100) accepts outpatient consultations weekdays 0700-0930 (Vt3000 for tourists). On weekends and holidays only emergency cases are accepted. Fill prescriptions at the hospital dispensary.

Actually, it's cheaper, faster, and more efficient to see a private doctor, such as Dr. Jean-Luc Bador (tel. 23065), opposite Le Kiosque Bookstore (consultations Vt2800). Dr. Bador speaks good English and he's very helpful to travelers. His specialty is acupuncture.

Dr. Hervé Collard (tel. 22306) has a private dental surgery practice in the Oceania Building on rue de Paris.

INFORMATION

The **National Tourism Office** (Box 209, Port Vila; tel. 22685, fax 23889; weekdays 0730-1130 and 1330-1630, Saturday 0800-1100), above the Nissan showroom opposite the Cultural Center, supplies useful maps and information sheets. Ask for free copies of *Hapi Tumas Long Vanuatu* and *Pacific Paradise.*

Visit **Frank King's Visitors Club** (Box 635, Port Vila; tel. 22808, fax 22885), across from the market, to pick up their yellow-colored *Comprehensive Tour Guide,* which provides information not found in the tourism office publications. Luggage can be left for the day at Frank King's.

Jack Keitadi, curator at the **Vanuatu Cultural Center** (Box 184, Port Vila; tel. 22129), can often provide information on really remote areas.

The **Statistics Office** (Private Mail Bag 019, Port Vila; tel. 22110, fax 24583), behind the prime minister's office, sells informative reports on the economy. Ask for a copy of their free publication *Vanuatu Facts and Figures.*

The **Lands Survey Department** (Private Mail Bag 024, Port Vila; tel. 22427, fax 25973; weekdays 0730-1130 and 1300-1600), below the Ministry of Health in the Georges Pompidou Building, sells excellent topographical maps of all the islands of Vanuatu at Vt600 each. Though very useful, the maps are not 100% reliable, as they've never been ground checked. Local navigational charts are also sold here.

The **Alliance Française** (Box 219, Port Vila; tel. 22947, fax 26700), just behind the French Embassy but in the same compound, has a library with the latest French newspapers and magazines, and they organize interesting activities such as movie nights, concerts, exhibitions, dancing classes, and even group hikes. The Alliance offers French language courses with two two-hour classes a week.

Bookstores

Port Vila has several good bookstores. **Stop Press** (Box 557, Port Vila; tel. 22232, fax 23252) opposite the French Embassy carries a variety of topographical maps of Vanuatu and a few books on the Pacific. **Le Kiosque** (Box 814, Port Vila; tel. 22044) on Bougainville Street sells a handy French-Bislama phrasebook called *Apprenons le Bichlamar* (Vt300). **Chew Store** (tel. 24298) across the street from Le Kiosque also sells books. **Snoopy's Stationery** (Box 357, Port Vila; tel. 22328, fax 24604) opposite the market is also worth checking.

Airline Offices

Reconfirm your international flight at **Air Vanuatu** (tel. 23848) next to the post office. The **Air Calédonie International** office (tel. 22739) is below Hotel Olympic.

TRANSPORTATION

By Air

Vanair (tel. 22753), next to the post office, has southbound flights from Port Vila to Tanna (Vt8700) twice daily, to Tanna via Dillon's Bay twice weekly, and to Tanna via Ipota and Aniwa weekly. Twice a week the Tanna flights continue to Aneityum and Futuna. Northbound there are four flights a day to Espiritu Santo (Vt9800), at least one a day to Espiritu Santo via Norsup and a few also via Lamap or Southwest Bay. Three times a week the Port Vila-Espiritu Santo service goes via Lonorore, Sara, Longana, and Walaha. Other routes from Port Vila are to Emae (Vt3700), Tongoa (Vt4800), Craig Cove (Vt6700), and Ulei (Vt6300) two or three times a week. For more information on internal flights, see "Transportation" in the Vanuatu chapter introduction.

Ships to Other Countries

There are no regular passenger-carrying freighter services to any adjacent country. **South Pacific Shipping** (tel. 22387) puts out a monthly mimeographed sheet, *Shipping Movements,* which lists when all large cargo boats will be in and where they're going. To arrange passage, you must deal directly with the captain of the ship concerned. The Banks Line has a monthly trip to Honiara, and South Pacific Shipping will know the dates (the fare will probably be more than a plane ticket).

Local Shipping

Passenger-carrying cargo boats depart Port Vila for Luganville once or twice a week, with stops at Malekula, Epi, Paama, Ambrym, Pentecost, Maewo, and Ambae. The through trip takes two or three days, depending on ports of call, and the deck fare sometimes includes meals. Cabins are not always available. Take along some food, as the journey's length varies according to cargo and the weather. Some boats with Seventh-Day Adventist crews stop running on Saturday (ask). Don't expect any luxuries on these ships—they're extremely basic.

Ifira Shipping (Box 68, Port Vila; tel. 24445, fax 25934) at the BP Wharf runs the barge MV *Saraika* from Port Vila north to Epi, Paama, Ambrym, Pentecost, Ambae, and Espiritu Santo

(Vt5000 one-way), and south to Erromango, Tanna (Vt4000 one-way), Aneityum, Futuna, and Aniwa on a regular basis. This is probably your best bet if you want a cabin.

Toara Coastal Shipping (Box 437, Port Vila; tel. 22370, 24807), at Cook Corner, Nambatu (near Au Bon Marché), operates the MV *Marata* (20 passengers) and the larger MV *Aloara* (106 passengers) from Port Vila to Emae, Tongoa, Epi, Paama, Ambrym, Pentecost, and Santo. A dorm bed on the ship from Port Vila costs Vt3400 to South Ambrym, Vt4000 to Pentecost, Vt6000 to Santo, meals included.

If you're really serious about going by ship, ask around the wharves opposite Better Price on the main street. Smaller boats like the *El Shaddai* also do the three-day Vila-Santo run (Vt5000 one-way, food included). The barge *Roena* and other interisland boats are often found at the Star Wharf, which is the second wharf to check. The Harbormaster at the main wharf may have information on government boats (Marine Department). Shipping news is given on Radio Vanuatu in Bislama at 1030 and 1730, sometimes in English after the news at 2030. A two-week cruise on one of the interisland trading ships would be a real adventure, taking you to places few tourists ever see.

By Bus and Taxi

Although no regular public buses travel right around Efate, bus service is fairly frequent within Port Vila itself. The minibuses are all privately owned by the drivers, and there aren't any set routes. You just flag down a bus headed in the right direction and tell the driver where you want to go. If it harmonizes with the previously requested destinations of the other passengers, he'll take you anywhere in the town area between Le Lagon Hotel, Port Vila, and the airport for a flat fare of Vt100. To Mele or Pango the fare is a bit more. The public buses are mostly the smaller 11-seat minibuses; the bigger 22-seat (usually white) buses are for package tours. Taxi drivers prevent the buses from picking up right at the airport door; so if you're there, walk down the road a short distance and flag down a bus. Service is frequent, but the last bus to Tagabe leaves at 2100.

Taxis have a red letter T in the license number while public buses have a red letter B. The taxis

have meters, but some are strangely cheaper than others. It's always possible to ask the fare before setting out and get a fixed rate, without using the meter. If you call for a taxi (tel. 22979, 22870, or 25135), you must pay for the driver's journey from the depot at Tropical Market Store near Parliament, in addition to your trip. Fares average Vt100 a kilometer, so from the airport it's about Vt700 from the center of town, Vt800 to the Royal Palms Resort, or Vt900 to Le Lagon Hotel. After dark there's a Vt200 supplement.

You may be able to arrange a ride in the back of a truck to North Efate by asking the women at the market if they know of any vehicles headed that way. These usually leave after 1500 and cost Vt300 pp, if they like you. Any truck headed for Emua wharf could drop you at Nagar Bungalows, where camping is possible.

Car Rentals

Foreign driver's licenses are accepted, but most of the companies won't rent to persons under 25 years of age (21 years at Avis). Most rentals come with unlimited kilometers, and there are discounts for rentals of more than two days. All companies take Vt1100 a day for compulsory insurance (Hertz Vt1300 a day), but even with insurance you're still responsible for the first Vt100,000 in damage to the car. Add 7.5% tax to all charges. On cruise ship days all vehicles will be taken, another reason to find out when the next love boat is due in so you can beat the fun-loving masses to the booking office and be gone when they arrive.

Gasoline is hard to come by outside Port Vila, so fill up before you set out around the island. The only gas station on the north side of Efate is next to the store at Emua. Driving is on the right. Speed limits are 40 kph in town, 60 kph elsewhere; in roundabouts, the vehicle entering from the right has the right of way. Cattle grids and speed bumps across the road are a real hazard for those driving around Efate and must be crossed slowly. Check the spare tire as you take delivery of the car—you never know.

Discount Rentals (Box 537, Port Vila; tel. 23242, fax 23898), at the Adventure Center in the Olympic Hotel courtyard and at the BP service station a bit south of Au Bon Marché Supermarket, rents cars with 200 km free mileage at Vt4400 a day, plus Vt1100 insurance, plus 7.5% tax. If you rent for two days you get a free night at the Beachcomber Resort on the north coast. On three-day rentals the fourth day is free.

Budget Rent a Car (Box 349, Port Vila; tel. 23170, fax 24693) in the Olympic Hotel courtyard charges identical rates beginning at Vt4400 a day, but with unlimited kilometers (it's unlikely you'd do over 200 km anyway). Budget sometimes unloads old wrecks on unsuspecting tourists, so protest if they try to give you what appears to be Uncle Eddie's second car. Their brochure promises a "discount voucher pack," but only believe it if you see it.

Thrifty (Box 128, Port Vila; tel. 22244, fax 23685) is cheaper at Vt3800 a day including 160 km (extra km Vt25). Book their cars at Handikraf Blong Vanuatu next to the Cultural Center, at Le Lagon Hotel, or at their head office next to National Breweries in Tagabe.

Avis (Box 1297, Port Vila; tel. 24816, fax 24968) has a car rental office at the Royal Palms Resort. They also have an office at the airport (tel. 22570) but it's well hidden in a kiosk outside the international terminal (look around the corner to the left as you come out, or ask). Their rates are similar to those at Thrifty.

Hertz (Box 341, Port Vila; tel. 25700, fax 25511), next to Club Imperial near the University of the South Pacific, is the most expensive at Vt5100.

Scooter and Bicycle Rentals

I.S. Moped Rentals (Box 286, Port Vila; tel. 22470, fax 24362), opposite La Cabane Chez Felix Restaurant near the start of the road to the Main Wharf, has Honda 50cc mopeds for Vt2200 daily, Vt9200 weekly. A security deposit of Vt3000 is required. The mopeds aren't very effective on rough roads and steep slopes. Helmets (provided) must be worn.

You can rent a larger motorbike at **Scooters Beer and Burger Bar** near the Iririki Island ferry wharf for Vt2200 for three hours, insurance included.

Sportz Power (tel. 26326), in the row of shops opposite Rossi Restaurant, rents tandem bicycles at Vt1600 a day, regular bicycles at Vt1300 a day.

Local Tours

Frank King Tours (Box 635, Port Vila; tel. 22808, fax 22885), across the main road from the market, offers a wide variety of trips, friendly service, and expert commentary. The full-day around-the-island bus tours (Vt4500) and half-day 4WD treks up Mt. Erskine (Vt3500) are worthwhile. Horseback riding, scuba diving, fishing, guided hikes, and even overnight trips to Tanna can be arranged.

Aliat Wi Tours (Box 678, Port Vila; tel. 25225, fax 25684), upstairs in the building opposite Le Kiosque Bookstore, offers circle-island tours Tuesday, Thursday, and Saturday (Vt3800 including lunch). Bookings for this, and most other tours, cruises, and activities can be made at the **Adventure Center** (tel. 22743) inside the Olympic Hotel.

Helicopters Vanuatu (Box 366, Port Vila; tel. 24424, fax 24693), also at the Olympic Hotel, offers joy rides around southern Efate for Vt4000 pp, or they'll drop you for the day on a deserted island or beach, or by a jungle river, for Vt7500 pp.

Day Cruises

The "Coral Appreciation Cruise" on the glass-bottom boat *L'Espadon 2* (Vt4500 including lunch) offered by **Frank King Tours** (tel. 22808) is one of the best of its kind in Port Vila. There are several opportunities to snorkel (gear provided), and the commentary on coral and marinelife is interesting. The glass-bottom boat *Neptune II* (tel. 22272) offers half-day snorkeling trips at Vt2850.

Several companies run day cruises along the north side of Efate from Havannah Harbor. For example, the 23-meter sailing ketch *Coongoola* (Box 991, Port Vila; tel. 25020, fax 22979), built at Brisbane in 1949, operates daily except Monday. The Vt6200 pp price includes bus transfers from Port Vila, snorkeling gear, and a barbecue lunch. Scuba diving is available twice a week at Vt3900 extra, gear included.

The 13-meter trimaran *Golden Wing* of **Sailaway Cruises** (Box 611, Port Vila; tel. 25155, fax 24452) does both north and south Efate snorkeling cruises. Those prone to seasickness will be happy to know that the seven-meter-wide *Golden Dragon* doesn't lean over when it's sailing. Book through the Adventure Center in the Olympic Hotel courtyard. If you can spare the cash, the Havannah Harbor trips are a great day out and a perfect way to see the other side of the island at its best.

ERROMANGO

Although rugged and untouristed, Erromango is easily accessible as a stopover between Port Vila and Tanna. Better yet, Vanair flights between Port Vila and Tanna call at Dillon's Bay twice a week, at Ipota weekly. This makes it possible to arrive at one, hike across the island, and leave from the other. It's not easy, though, and you'll need a guide part of the way. A minimum of three (preferably four) days is required to do this. There are lots of ups and downs, so pack light. A tent is essential—you can't always count on staying with the locals. Water is available at villages, but bring your own food, plus stick tobacco for gifts. Take a compass, good boots, and a reliable companion.

Erromango has only two roads, one from Dillon's Bay airstrip to Unpongkor village and a logging road across the island to Port Narvin. Maps show a network of logging roads spreading out from Ipota, but these are mostly overgrown and difficult to follow, even on foot. Besides, there are no motor vehicles at Ipota, and only three at Dillon's Bay. The locals travel around the island by outboard speedboat (expensive) or on trails through the bush.

ERROMANGO

If you want to hike, begin from the Dillon's Bay side, going to Ipota via Happy Land. You should be able to do the first half of the walk on your own and find a guide to take you across the island at Happy Land. Offer about Vt2000 for this service. Tim Thorpe, a volunteer who spent two years on Erromango, offers this advice:

Be warned of three things: first, not all guides know the tracks as well as they claim; second, the Erromangan can go all day on a spoonful of water, no food, and little rest; and third, klosup *to an Erromangan generally translates as* longwe *to a non-Erromangan.*

Dillon's Bay

A truck sometimes meets the flights at Dillon's Bay airstrip and carries passengers the eight km to Unpongkor village for about Vt300 pp. The road drops sharply into the Williams River Valley to the village, beautifully situated at the river mouth. As the sun sets across the Coral Sea, you know you've reached one of the farthest ends of the earth.

In 1825, Irish trader Peter Dillon discovered vast stands of sandalwood here. Dillon managed to obtain very little of the precious wood, and ships that followed soon clashed with the inhabitants. Plaques in the church at Unpongkor commemorate the martyrdom of John Williams and James Harris (1839), George and Ellen Gordon (1861), and George's brother, James Gordon (1872). On the other side of the river in the village cemetery are monuments to these well-meaning missionaries, killed by the Erromangans as a consequence of the methods used by the traders and the diseases introduced by the messengers of God themselves.

Later, many Erromangans were carried off to labor in the Australian cane fields, and those few who returned brought back further disease and discord. From 20,000 in the early 1800s, Erromango's population plummeted to 400 by 1930. There are only 1,250 inhabitants today. Old burial caves dot the cliffs along the west and south coasts.

Meteson's Guest House (William Mete, Box 409, Port Vila; tel. 22745, fax 23442) in the center of Unpongkor offers native-style accommodations with shared facilities at Vt4000 pp including basic meals. If you bring your own food and don't require the meals (a good idea), it's cheaper, but always make sure the price you're to pay is clearly understood before agreeing to stay there. Bargaining may be possible. If you're planning an early start the next day, forget breakfast or you'll waste half the morning waiting. There's a small co-op store nearby. You could also camp on the grass beside the river or just set out hiking and camp up on the plateau.

Dillon's Bay to Ponumbia

An experienced hiker should have little trouble going from Dillon's Bay to Ponumbia on his/her own. After a steep climb up a jeep track from Dillon's Bay, you travel south across an open plateau. After two hours, you come to an obvious fork in the road. The track to the left goes up to the telecommunications tower atop Mt. Fetmongkum (636 meters). Keep straight.

About 10 minutes beyond this junction is a straight, level stretch for about 200 meters, followed by a sharp right turn in the road, which descends to a lighthouse on the coast. The footpath to **Happy Land** is straight ahead at the curve. You go through an enchanted forest, and after about an hour, climb up to **Buniakup**, the first settlement. Beyond Tamsel, there's a steep descent to a hamlet at the mouth of the Pongkil River. Have a swim and a rest in preparation for the sharp climb back to the plateau.

The terrain levels out on top and you walk for a couple of hours through a string of traditional settlements, all the way to **Ponumbia.** Sunday is a good day to visit this area, as most people will be relaxing at home and happy to talk to you. There's a good view of the coast from the cow pasture at Potlusi.

Ponumbia to Ipota

Beyond Ponumbia, the trail to Ipota is much more difficult to follow; consider hiring a guide. The villagers in this area have to walk the whole route to Dillon's Bay to buy soap and kerosene, so it shouldn't be too hard to convince someone to go to the co-op at Ipota instead. It's a fairly strenuous 10-hour walk from Ponumbia to Ipota

with a guide, at least a day and a half without. Only go alone if you're very experienced—even then, at times you'll think you're lost.

After a moderately steep descent 40 minutes out of Ponumbia, you come to a dip in the trail. At the far top of the dip, just before the final descent to South River, look for the branch trail to Ipota leading up to the left. About five minutes along this trail, you come to a T-junction. Keep left and pass through a garden. After an hour an extremely steep descent leads you to a tributary of the South River (knee deep). The climb on the other side is less severe. About 15 minutes along the level trail on top there's a turnoff to the right to South River. Keep straight.

After another 10 minutes, you reach **Punmoungo,** the only settlement between Ponumbia and Ipota. Keep right after Punmoungo and follow a creek to a small river. If you think you've lost the way, go upstream 500 meters and keep looking on the right.

About an hour out of Punmoungo, you enter a logged-out area, stripped of kauri and *tamanu* by a French company between 1966 and 1973. Between here and Ipota, you're on and off several logging roads. Often you descend through the forest on shortcuts and must cross two small rivers. Precise instructions are hard to give, as they would be lengthy and perhaps confusing. Even the 1:100,000 survey map is of little use. A compass and a sense of direction are more helpful. If you feel you're lost, backtrack a little or work your way up and down the river till you find a trail in the right direction. When you reach a burned-off area that has been sloppily replanted in *cordia,* you're near Ipota.

Ipota to Dillon's Bay

The east side of Erromango gets more rain than the west, which accounts for the lush forests and huge banyans. Visit the wreck of a tugboat carried 500 meters up the river estuary during a hurricane, just south of Ipota airstrip, and find your way through the village to the coast for a good view of Urantop across Cooks Bay. A swimming hole has been blasted out of the raised reef here. At Ipota, camp on the grass beside the airstrip, right in the middle of the forestry settlement. Two poorly stocked stores are here. In a couple of hours you can do Ipota to death, so if you've got a day to kill before catching a flight out, hike south to **Ifo** village in three hours.

The hike north to **Port Narvin** takes a day or more. A guide will be required unless you're a *very* experienced hiker. There's one big river to cross at the northwest corner of Cooks Bay, and a canoe will be necessary (ask at the one-family settlement nearby). Beyond is the trail leading inland to Port Narvin, one of the nicest spots on the island with a pleasant beach and nearby waterfall. The **Souki Hunting Lodge** at Port Narvin accommodates visitors at Vt3000

pp including all meals. An excellent side-trip can be made to the top of **Urantop** (837 meters), though it's often cloud-covered. On a clear day, the view is superb. A logging road has been cut through the *tamanu*-dominated primary rainforest, or "dark bush," between Port Narvin and Dillon's Bay, a day's walk.

Many other possibilities present themselves for hiking on Erromango, such as Port Narvin to Rampunalvat (guide unnecessary), Rampunalvat to Elizabeth Bay (guide essential), and Antioch to Ifo, then on to Ipota (guide optional).

TANNA

Vanuatu's second-most visited island (after Efate), Tanna is renowned for its active volcano, potent kava, coffee plantations, custom villages, cargo cultists, exciting festivals, strong traditions, magnificent wild horses, long black beaches, gigantic banyan trees, two-meter-long yams, and day-tripping packaged tourists. Due to its southerly location it's cooler than Efate and there's no problem with malaria. The alternating black and white beaches, often separated only by a narrow headland, are unusual. The island is Vanuatu's most heavily populated, and well-used trails crisscross the landscape. Leave the roads and you'll enter a wonderland of charming, innocent people living as close to nature as their ancestors did before them. Here the real Tanna remains, almost untouched by a century and a half of traders, missionaries, officials, and other visitors. A second airstrip has recently been constructed near Port Resolution and hotel developments are planned, so don't wait too long to come.

Kava

Every village has its *nasara,* an open area surrounded by gigantic banyan trees, where the men gather nightly to drink kava at the *nakamal* (men's house). Tanna kava is strong and sudden. One cup will stone you; two cups will knock you out. The green roots of a pepper shrub *(Piper Methysticum)* are first chewed into a pulp, spit out on a leaf, then mixed with a little water and squeezed through a coconut frond into a cup to be drunk all at once.

If a man touches any part of the campfire during the ceremony, it's thought that his house

will burn down. After finishing the kava, speaking above a whisper is extremely bad manners. Women in the villages are still forbidden to take part in this gathering or even to see it. If they're caught trying, they have to pay a fine of one good kava root. Way back when, they would have been put to death.

Events

Custom dances are held on the occasion of marriages, circumcisions (many in July), etc. Ask around to find out where the next one will be held. The most important event of the year is the Nekowiar Festival, with its famous Toka Dance. This ritual may be held in August or around the end of the year. The Toka celebrates the circumcision of young boys and is accompanied by pig killing, feasting, and dancers with painted faces and grass skirts—the works.

It can take six or seven years to prepare for these massive ceremonial gift-giving sessions, which cement alliances between villages and clans. The festival lasts three to five days and on the eve of the last day, thousands of men from every village on the island participate in a wild dance, which continues through the night. The next morning, over a hundred pigs may be slaughtered. There's usually a Nekowiar on Tanna every year, and tourists pay a mere Vt5000 admission to attend this stirring event.

The Jon Frum Cargo Cult

The Tannese were declared converted to Presbyterianism in the early years of this century, yet just prior to WW II a movement to reestablish

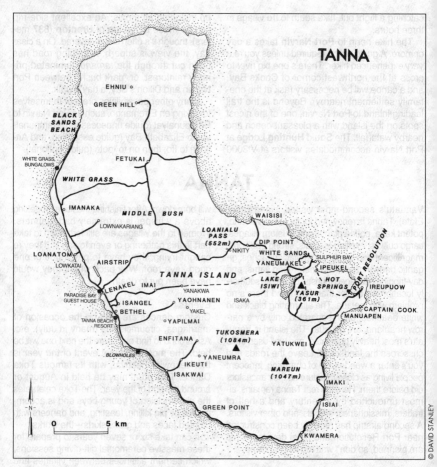

© DAVID STANLEY

traditional values emerged in southern Tanna when a spirit began appearing at Green Point around sunset. In 1942, 1,000 men from Tanna were recruited by the Americans to work at military bases on Efate, and the sight of huge quantities of war materiel and black soldiers gave this movement a new meaning.

A sort of cultural hero emerged who would come from across the sea bringing wealth in abundance, Jon "from" America. As the symbol of their newfound religion, the Tannese took the red cross seen on wartime ambulances on Efate, and today the villages north of Yasur Volcano

and elsewhere are dotted with little red crosses neatly surrounded by picket fences, bearing witness to this extraordinary chain of events.

The priests and prophets of these cargo cults are called "messengers," and they foretell the return of the ships laden with cargo for Man Tanna, escorted by Jon Frum, the reincarnation of an ancient deity. Towers with tin cans strung from wires, imitating radio stations, were erected so Jon Frum could speak to his people. The movement declares that money must be thrown away, pigs killed, and gardens left uncared for, since all material wealth will be provided in the end by Jon Frum.

Formerly it was felt that missionaries and government administrators had interfered with this Second Coming; thus the movement sometimes manifested itself in noncooperation with them. Beginning in 1940 the British authorities arrested cult leaders and held them without trial in Port Vila, but new devotees sprang up to take their places. There's also a Prince Philip cult among the custom people at Yaohnanen dating back to the prince's visit to what was then New Hebrides in 1974. Followers believe the prince originally came from Tanna in another form and will eventually return to rule over them.

SIGHTS

Yasur Volcano

Yasur Volcano (361 meters), the chief attraction of Tanna, is 30 km from Lenakel Airstrip in the eastern part of the island. It's one of the most accessible volcanoes of its kind in the world, and for the convenience of tour groups, a road goes almost to the summit on the mountain's south side. It's also possible to climb the path up the north slope, to the left between the vegetation and the ashfield (40 minutes). Either way, you'll pay an exorbitant Vt1600 pp "Volcano Landing Fee" to the "Volcano Committee" for each visit.

At 940° C, Yasur hisses, rumbles, and spits, constantly erupting in minor explosions, which emit small filaments of volcanic glass called Pele's Hair. Cargo cultists believe that Jon Frum lives beneath the fires of Yasur, where he commands an army of 5,000 souls. The slopes are scattered with boulders considered sacred by the Tannese, and black dust from the crater covers everything for kilometers. Some days are better for viewing than others, depending on smoke, wind, etc. At night it's an unforgettable fireworks display.

The best time to climb Yasur is around 1700, to see it and the surroundings in daylight, then stay for the sunset and to see the crater at night—the most spectacular time by far as molten lava shoots up into the sky every few minutes. Views down into the crater are quite spectacular—steam and masses of black ash seethe furiously, discharging cinders and rocks, while gas burns your throat. The sulfur fumes can be choking, the noise deafening. Restrictions on how close to the crater's edge visitors are permitted to go were imposed in early 1995, when two tourists and a local guide were killed by a projectile that hurled them eight meters.

A barren ash plain surrounds Yasur, with freshwater Lake Isiwi to the west. You could spend hours walking across the ash plain and around Lake Isiwi watching the ash crowds billow from Yasur's summit as the volcano roars. A road along the north side of Lake Isiwi leads up to **Isaka** village; a two-and-a-half-hour hike along a bush trail beyond Isaka is Vecel Falls.

Sulphur Bay

Just northeast of Yasur is Sulphur Bay village, stronghold of the Jon Frum movement, where American flags fly from tall bamboo poles. As you arrive you'll be shown the Headquarters where the flags are kept at night. A signboard on the wall lists the names of three chiefs imprisoned by the British for 17 years. In 1957 they were released and on 15 February that year the American flags were first raised, a date commemorated by a major feast here each year.

The grave of one of these chiefs, Tommy Nampus, an important Jon Frum leader, stands on the east (or ocean) side of the village common. At the far end of the common is the Jon Frum church with its red cross and other iconography. Ask to speak to prophet Elizabeth, a daughter of Nampus, who lives just behind the church. To the right of Sulphur Bay's beautiful black beach, steam from Yasur Volcano curls among the cliffs flanking the bay. You may be asked for a custom fee of Vt200 pp to visit Sulphur Bay village (have exact change).

On Friday nights Jon Frum supporters from most of East Tanna converge on Sulphur Bay for a ceremony, which begins around 2000. Various "teams" take turns singing and playing music while villagers in grass skirts dance outside the shelter. The ceremony goes on most of the night, and if you wish to stay late you'll be able to sleep in the Headquarters or on the floor of a hut just opposite that serves as a village guesthouse. If you attend the Friday night ceremony take along a pack of cigarettes or a few sticks of tobacco for the chiefs, who will be sitting under a large tree at one end of the square. You can purchase hibiscus-fiber grass skirts from the Sulphur Bay villagers, a beautiful and genuine buy.

Sulphur Bay villagers before a Jon Frum cross

On Saturday a similar Jon Frum ceremony takes place at **Imanaka,** near White Grass on the other side of the island. The Jon Frum Cult is also active at **Middle Bush,** although custom people are in the majority.

Port Resolution

It's a pleasant two-and-a-half-hour hike straight over the mountains on a well-trodden footpath from Sulphur Bay to Port Resolution. The trail is easy to find from the Sulphur Bay end. If beginning at Port Resolution, go to the hot springs at the northwest end of the beach near the cliffs and ask someone there to show you the way. The Port Resolution locals use the hot springs for washing and cooking. They can also call a 250-kg male dugong (sea cow) named Chief Kaufis from the sea nearby for Vt500. If the dugong appears, you're lucky; if not they keep your money anyway. Captain Cook sailed into this bay in 1774 and named it after his ship. The locals wouldn't allow him to visit Yasur Volcano. Today there's good anchorage in the bay for yachts.

Continue to **Ireupuow** village and have a look at the splendid high white beach. Several red Jon Frum crosses stand on Ireupuow's central square. A half hour from here is a point featuring a rock pyramid called **Captain Cook,** where the famous navigator made observations. A beautiful golden beach is next to the

point. The main road goes back to Sulphur Bay or White Sands between Lake Isiwi and Yasur. Immense banyan trees line the way.

Across the Island

Tanna's largest village and administrative center is **Lenakel** on the west coast. The market and a cluster of general stores are near a large concrete wharf built by the Japanese in 1988. Most government offices are at Isangel, on a hill about two km southeast. Coffee grown in northern Tanna is roasted in a factory at Lowkatai just north of Lenakel.

Village footpaths cross the island. One trail begins near the hospital, another next to the driveway into the Agriculture Station at Isangel (the "Melbourne" trail). A truck can drive six km up the latter route to Yanakwa, then it's another 10 km on foot through dense forest to Lake Isiwi. The path follows a ridge and from Isangel it's an easy uphill walk for about four hours, the first half through villages and the second through the jungle. The last two hours or so of the hike is downhill and across the ash plain to either White Sands or Sulphur Bay. These trails are well known, regularly used, and easy to learn about and follow. A good hiker could make it across in a day.

There are many more such hikes in south and north Tanna, and the 1:50,000 topographical map (obtainable at the Survey Office in Port Vila) is the only guide you need. Hiking on Tanna is safe and easy as there are no thorns on the trees, no dangerous lizards on the ground, and even the local dogs are mellow. You'll pass through some of the 92 villages where people still live in the traditional way (no Christians or Jon Frummers).

The Custom Villages

The road to the custom villages begins at the top of the incline a few hundred meters south of the Tanna Beach Resort. **Yapilmai Falls** are about midway between the main road and Yaohnanen, down the hill to the right. **Yaohnanen** is the center of the custom area where the men wear penis sheaths or *nambas,* and the women colorful grass skirts. They attended church until the 1940s, when they returned to their traditional religion. Only in the 1970s did they shed Western clothing. Packaged tourists are often brought to Yaohnanen to see custom dances, buy grass skirts, and tour the "primitive" village.

Chief Jack Naiva of Yaohnanen is very friendly to visitors who respect his customs, and he may allow you to stay in the village if he likes you (a pack of cigarettes helps). If you're willing to put on a *namba* or a grass skirt and perhaps do some gardening you'll be very welcome. They'll feed you on rats and cicadas—actually, rat tastes quite good, sort of like chicken. Chief Jack's son Jack Malia can arrange dancing at **Yakel** village, about 500 meters up the road past the Kustom Skul. Here you'll probably see a few men and boys with long hair bound in the traditional style.

Consider making a full day out of Yaohnanen and Yakel, walking there and back. When you enter the village *nasara*, sit down and wait for somebody. Ask if it's all right to look around and to visit the Prince Philip house, for which a custom gift of Vt1000 pp should be presented to the chief. After the evening kava you could walk back to the main road and try to catch a lift.

PRACTICALITIES

Accommodations in West Tanna

Paradise Bay Guest House (Box 9, Tanna; tel. 68695, fax 68625) is a European-style frame house directly behind the Tafea Cooperative Store at Lenakel, one km from the airstrip. The six rooms with shared bath are Vt2250/2500 single/double, which makes it expensive for singles but fine for couples. Three of the rooms are only separated from the rest of the house by thin partitions, so peace and quiet will depend on who your neighbors are. You'll probably be allowed to camp next to the guesthouse when all of the rooms are full. Good communal cooking facilities are provided. This is the former personal residence of island traders Bob and Russell Paul, who decided to return to Australia after independence. A nice common lounge faces the garden, and the guesthouse is in a pleasant location overlooking the coast—convenient, comfortable, and good value.

The **Tafea Council Guest House** (Box 28, Tanna; tel. 68638, fax 68689), behind the post office in Isangel, has five rooms at Vt2000 pp.

Check in at the local government offices during business hours. Although cooking facilities are provided and a store is nearby, it's overpriced, run-down, and not a very pleasant place to stay.

Also on the west coast are two clusters of overpriced tourist bungalows. The 11-unit **Tanna Beach Resort** (Box 27, Tanna; tel./fax 68610), on a narrow black sand beach near Lenakel, five km south of the airstrip, has dingy rooms in a long hut facing the restaurant at Vt7000/9000 single/double, and thatched bungalows facing the beach at Vt10,500 single or double. There's a swimming pool. Not only are you overcharged for your room but they really sock you with meal prices of Vt1000 for a sandwich or Vt3500 for a three-course dinner (without drinks). There are no coffee-making or cooking facilities in the rooms. Their organized sightseeing tours also cost the earth—carefully check all prices before heading down this way. If you stay here you won't be able to see any of the fabulous sights of East Tanna unless you fork over additional big bucks for the tours. This place is to be avoided.

White Grass Bungalows (Chief Tom Namake, Box 5, Tanna; tel. 68688) is in wild-horse country, 12 km north of Lenakel and far from everything. The five thatched bungalows with solar energy and leaky roofs are Vt6000/6900/7200 single/double/triple. Airport transfers are Vt1000 pp return and their tours are also a rip-off.

Accommodations at White Sands

Rather than putting up around Lenakel you're better off staying in East Tanna with **David and Alice Iou** (Box 16, Tanna; no phone), behind the Presbyterian church down the hill from the cooperative store at White Sands. Just ask for "Pastor David." David and Alice have been accommodating readers of this book for nearly 15 years, and they presently rent two basic rooms in a ramshackle European-style house at Vt1500/2000 single/double. You can camp here at Vt700 pp, just be prepared to get some ash on your tent if the wind starts blowing this way. Local meals are Vt200 for breakfast, Vt300 for a light lunch, and Vt500 for dinner. A few years ago David built three bungalows for visitors near Dip Point, but these were blown away by a hurricane in March 1994; guests now sleep in his own home, a better location anyway. He has plans to build a few bungalows at White Sands when he retires from his ministry in 1999, and it's possible he'll even get started earlier.

Provided you don't mind roughing it a bit, you'll like the family atmosphere at David and Alice's place, and because it's the closest accommodations to Yasur Volcano, it makes a good base for nocturnal visits. You can hear the roar of the volcano from your bed. This is one of the few places on the island where you're left alone to do your own thing, and most of the best sights of Tanna are within walking distance. The White Sands people are extremely friendly, so it's also a good way to experience village life. David will advise on such free activities as bush walks to local swimming holes and waterfalls, beach picnics, and the Friday night Jon Frum service at Sulphur Bay. A beautiful beach is just below their place, but you could only snorkel there on a very calm day and even then the currents might be dangerous. The local kids have fun jumping in and splashing around near shore. David's neighbor James has a pickup truck that doubles as a taxi for local trips. A pickup from the airport to White Sands will run Vt3000 for a special trip, otherwise get them for Vt300 pp, as explained under "Transportation," below.

Nikity Guest House (Box 913, Tanna; tel. 68616) is near Dip Point on the road from Lenakel to White Sands. There are four rooms in a European-style house at Vt2800 pp, and a grocery store is on the premises. The volcano tour costs Vt3600 pp, airport transfers Vt5000 return. It's far from the beach and a fair walk from the volcano too.

Accommodations at Port Resolution

Adjacent to Ireupuow village near the eastern tip of Tanna is the **Port Resolution Nipikinamu Yacht Club** or PRNYC (tel. 68606) with six thatched bungalows with shared bath at Vt2200 pp including breakfast and dinner. Lighting is by kerosene lamp. If you require alcohol you must bring it with you, but it's probably a better idea to stick to the kava served at the club *nakamal*. The location is splendid, atop a cliff overlooking Port Resolution, with several good beaches nearby. It does seem rather exposed to hurricanes, however, so it wouldn't hurt to check

beforehand at the Waterfront Bar and Grill in Port Vila—they'll know the current situation and may be able to make bookings. The Tour Vanuatu office (tel. 22733) in Port Vila may also have information. The PRNYC is run as a community development project with financial assistance from overseas donors.

So far the Nipikinamu has resisted the general Tanna tendency to gouge visitors for sightseeing tours, but check. Guests may snorkel with the local dugong at no additional charge, and the staff take guests out on interesting bush hikes to local hot springs, beaches, the Captain Cook rock, and gardens. They have their own taxi for island visits, and tours to Yasur Volcano are offered at fixed prices far lower than those charged by the Lenakel tourist bungalows. Airport transfers are Vt4000 each way per group (not pp). Yachts may anchor off the resort at no charge, and yachties are welcome at the Nipikinamu clubhouse and on the organized tours.

Food and Drink

A cluster of general stores is near the airstrip at Lenakel. The village women spread out their produce on the ground at various locations weekdays. The biggest market takes place beside the Tafea Cooperative Store in Lenakel on Monday and Friday. At Vt20 a bunch for almost anything, it's the best buy on the island. Bread is baked locally but it's often all sold out by noon. Take all your own food with you if you go walkabout on the east coast.

Just south of the wharf at Lenakel is the friendly **Silae Restaurant**, where you can get a filling local meal of meat and rice for Vt120 weekdays only. Everyone pays the same here! Nearby is John Louhman's **Uma Restaurant**, where similar fare is available at higher prices (be sure to ask first).

The **Rolling Sea Kava Bar** and several similar establishments are at the junction of the Isangel and circuminsular roads. These are male domains, although accompanied white women are allowed in. They're great places to socialize.

Services

The National Bank (tel. 68615) next to the Tafea Cooperative Store at Lenakel changes traveler's checks weekdays 0800-1100 and 1330-1500.

There's a card telephone at the co-op. The post office (tel. 68687) is at Isangel.

Transportation

Vanair has flights from Port Vila to Tanna (Vt8700 one-way) twice a day, twice weekly via Erromango. From Tanna's airport it's a pleasant 15-minute downhill walk to Lenakel. Minibus transfers to the west coast tourist bungalows are Vt890 pp roundtrip.

You can also come from Port Vila by ship. Lenakel receives a boat from Port Vila about twice a month, often the barges *Roena* and *Saraika*.

A couple of trucks and minibuses offer unscheduled service between Lenakel and White Sands (Vt300 pp) every weekday—be prepared to wait. It's essential to fix the price with the taxi-truck drivers before setting out, and even then they may ask for more when you arrive. Be polite with them, but firm. There's quite a bit of traffic between Lenakel and White Sands, so if you suspect trouble, just wait for the next one.

Both the west coast tourist bungalows offer expensive sightseeing tours, such as a six-hour trip to Yasur, Sulphur Bay, and the White Grass wild horses by 4WD jeep (Vt6000 pp plus the Vt1600 "Volcano Landing Fee"). A morning trip to Yaohnanen to see people wearing *nambas* is Vt4000 pp (kava included), while a night visit to the volcano costs Vt6000 pp plus the Vt1600 "Volcano Landing Fee." The above prices are valid assuming at least two people are going; if you're alone it's Vt1000-1500 extra.

OTHER TAFEA ISLANDS

Aniwa and Futuna

These two small islands east of Tanna, each with a population of around 400, are quite different. Aniwa (eight square km) is a low island covered with orange trees, the fruit of which is very sweet and juicy. The villages are near the airstrip and the people very friendly. A magnificent snorkeling spot is north of the airstrip, and there's good anchorage.

The people of 11-square-km Futuna are Polynesian. You could stay at one of the villages near the airstrip but there's not much to do other than climb the 643-meter extinct volcano. Getting

around is difficult, as the tracks go over ladders of bamboo, and in some cases you'll find yourself clinging to rocks 30 meters directly above the sea along the forbidding coast. Vanair flies to Futuna from Port Vila (Vt9500), Tanna (Vt4500), and Aneityum (Vt4700) weekly.

Aneityum

Aneityum (Anatom), southernmost inhabited island in Vanuatu, is somewhat cooler and drier than the rest of the country. Its 160 square km rise to 852 meters, but ample flat areas are available for cultivation. Totemic petroglyphs and kauri stands are found on Aneityum, and 80 species of orchid flourish here. In the 1840s whalers from far and wide were based at Inyeug, a sandy islet just off the southwest side of Aneityum where the airstrip is today.

The Rev. John Geddie, first Presbyterian missionary to establish himself in Vanuatu, arrived in 1848 and built a 1,000-seat stone church, the ruins of which can still be seen. His efforts were in vain, however, as introduced diseases such as measles and dysentery ravaged the population, which eventually fell from 3,500 to 800, only 350 of whom were Geddie's converts. Today, about 550 people live in two villages on the south coast. Every two weeks the cruise ship *Fairstar* drops as many as a thousand tourists at a time on this "Mystery Island."

Vanair flies to Aneityum from Port Vila (Vt11,300), Tanna (Vt4500), and Futuna (Vt4700) weekly. The launch transfer from Inyeug, the airstrip island, to Analgawat village on the main island is Vt50 pp. The three-room **Mystery Island Guest House** (tel. 68672) on Inyeug accommodates visitors in a single thatched building at Vt1000 pp. There's a communal kitchen but the toilet is outside.

Matthew and Hunter

These small, uninhabited islands are subjects of a territorial dispute between France and Vanuatu, one of the few such disputes in the South Pacific. The islands were discovered in the late 18th century but largely forgotten until 1962, when two New Hebrides expatriates tried to claim them by means of a legal action before the Joint Court in Port Vila. This attracted the interest of French Condominium officials, who tried to send a warship to Matthew to claim the island for

France. The party was unable to land, due to high seas, but later one of the expats managed to swim ashore and plant a coconut tree to validate his own claim.

In 1965, the French announced that the British government had agreed that the islands could be attached to New Caledonia, despite the fact that they had always appeared on the map of New Hebrides and been considered a part of that colony. In 1975, the French did manage to get ashore and erect plaques, but their claims were not recognized by the incoming Vanuatu government, which had the Vanuatu flag raised and sovereignty proclaimed shortly after Independence Day 1980. Both islands are still claimed by both countries, and though of little economic value in themselves, they would form an important addition to the Exclusive Economic Zone of either Vanuatu or New Caledonia. In

1985 the French sent troops to occupy Matthew as a precaution against colonization by Vanuatu. The South Pacific Forum Fisheries Agency recognizes Vanuatu's claim for fisheries licensing purposes.

Matthew, 350 km southeast of Aneityum and 450 km east of Grande Terre, is an actively volcanic island a little over a kilometer long. The two peaks are separated by a narrow isthmus of sand and ashes: the west peak is older and reaches 177 meters, while the younger east peak (142 meters) features smoking fumaroles in its rocky crater.

Hunter, 69 km east of Matthew, is an abrupt basalt block 297 meters high. No anchorage is possible, due to the great depths, and there are sulfur-colored cliffs on the west side. Seabirds are the only inhabitants of both Matthew and Hunter.

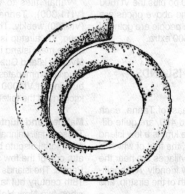

A curved boar's tusk has always been a symbol of authority.

MALEKULA

Shaped like a sitting dog, Malekula (Mallicollo) is a big 2,053-square-km island of 15,000 inhabitants speaking 30 different languages. The rugged interior of southern Malekula is inhabited by some of the most traditional clans on earth, while the island's east coast features the gentle beauty of continuous coconut plantations. In 1991, a Taiwanese company previously ac- cused of bribing Vanuatu government officials was granted a 40-year contract to log Malekula. When inept company employees bulldozed a village cemetery and water supply pool, there was such a furor that the agreements were can- celed and the loggers sent packing.

The once-feared Big Nambas formerly lived on the plateau at Amokh in the northwest of the

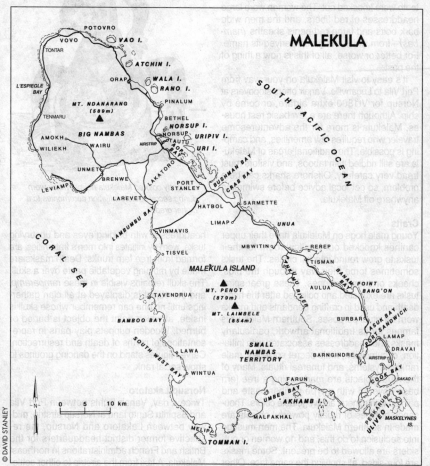

island, but since the death of Chief Virhambat in 1988, they've all moved down to the coast, and the deserted fortified village at Amokh is now taboo. Up until the 1930s, internecine tribal fighting was conducted almost constantly among the 2,000 clansmen, and cannibalism was frequently practiced by the powerful hereditary chiefs (the last recorded case was in 1969). The men would barter yams and pigs for women, and if a man valued his wife highly, he would do her honor by arranging an expensive, secret ritual, during which the woman's two front teeth were knocked out. The women wore large headdresses of red fibers, and the men wide bark belts and large red penis sheaths *(nambas)*—from which the group derived its name. For better or worse, all of this is now a thing of the past.

It's easy to visit Malekula on your way from Port Vila to Luganville. Vanair offers stopovers at Norsup for Vt1800 extra airfare, or come by ship. Although there are a few basic rest houses, Malekula is more for the adventuresome traveler who requires few amenities, and camping is possible. The traditional areas of Malekula are still riddled with taboos, and visitors must tread very carefully. Offshore sharks can be a problem, so get local advice before swimming anywhere off Malekula.

Crafts

Young male hogs on Malekula have their upper canines knocked out to allow room for their tusks to grow round into full circles. The tusks sometimes force their way through the pigs' cheeks or even jawbones. These great spiral tusks are extracted and polished after the hog's death and used in crafting pendants and masks worn for ritual purposes. Southern Malekula is famous for its traditional artwork, particularly masks and headdresses associated with initiation, circumcision, male secret societies, male ranking systems, and funereal rituals. Many of the ritual objects are made using a tree fern base covered with a type of fiber paste and painted with mineral and vegetable colors. Thousands of types of ritually powerful objects are made in southern Malekula. The men must go into seclusion to do this, and no women or outsiders are allowed to be present. Some masks are four-sided, all showing the same face. Other

LOUISE FOOTE

a brightly colored Malekula helmet mask worn during secret society initiation ceremonies to a higher grade

headdresses with bulging eyes and upcurving tusks, worn by initiates into men's fraternities, are formed from tree fern trunks. Death masks are made by molding vegetable paste over a skull. The skull remains visible in these *ramparamp*, and the object is displayed at all clan gatherings until no one can remember whose skull is inside, at which point the object is buried or burned. Wooden puppets play parts in representations of myths of death and resurrection. Carved figures stand on the dancing grounds to show social rank.

Norsup/Lakatoro

Twice a day, Vanair flights between Port Vila and Espiritu Santo land at Norsup airstrip, midway between Lakatoro and Norsup, the respective former district headquarters for the British and French administrations in northeast Malekula. A taxi from the airstrip to either settlement will be Vt300, but don't count on finding one waiting. A bus would cost Vt100. Grab any form of transport you see, or be prepared to walk the four km to Lakatoro.

The three-room Norsup Rest House is usually occupied by long-term tenants. A better bet is the basic five-room **Lakatoro Rest House,** seven km south of Norsup: Vt1000 pp and there are cooking facilities. To stay at either you must first contact the local government council office (Box 22, Lakatoro; tel. 48491, fax 48442) in Lakatoro. Call ahead from Port Vila or Luganville to find out what's available. A famous rat lives in the roof of the Lakatoro Rest House.

Near the government offices at Lakatoro is a traditional-style open-air **Cultural Center,** which opened in 1991 with Canadian aid. Ask here for Vianney Atbatun, who is very knowledgeable about the island and leads tours to otherwise inaccessible traditional areas. Other amenities of Lakatoro include the well-stocked Lakatoro Consumer Store with excellent chocolate ice cream cones, the Kalpen Restaurant nearby, and a branch of the National Bank (tel. 48400), where you can change money. A market materializes here on Wednesday morning, and dances are held at the Lakatoro Youth Center most Friday nights.

Norsup is the site of the largest coconut plantation in Vanuatu, built during the 1920s with Vietnamese labor. A hospital (tel. 48410) and post office (tel. 48452) are at Norsup, and market day here is Saturday morning. It's possible to walk along the shore from Norsup to **Tautu** village near the airport—beautiful white Aop Beach is right at the end of the airstrip. In the bush behind Tautu is the site of the old village, abandoned in 1918. You can still see the posts of the chief's house, an amphitheater of broken stone slabs for tribal meetings, a stone "bed" where the bodies of dead enemies were displayed before being consumed at dinner, stone boxes for holding skulls, and standing stones erected by men who had passed grading ceremonies. The place is now overgrown and ravaged by pigs.

A longer walk from Norsup is through the forest to the timber mill and cocoa project at **Larevet** (15 km one-way). A trail runs south along the coast from Larevet to Vinmavis, where a road cuts back across to the east coast. Many

convivial and picturesque red-and-green parrots are seen around here.

North of Norsup

Many French-speaking villages are strung along the coast north of Norsup and on small offshore islands. These islands are famous for their megalithic culture, especially the stone-lined dancing grounds and drums. Ships between Norsup and Luganville call at them several times a week, and a local minibus runs periodically from Norsup to Atchin and Vao (Vt200).

Take the minibus all the way north to **Vao,** and ask someone to paddle you across to Vao Island. Inquire where the woodcarver works. He has two rooms, one with raw or "ethnic" masks and canoe prows he's reluctant to sell, another full of polished airport art. Some very fine bowls go for Vt5000. Outside the Catholic church are two well-carved *tam tam* drums, and more are to be seen at the *natsaro* (dancing ground). The *nakamal* is also worth a visit. Return to the mainland and walk south to **Atchin** in an hour. After sleepy Vao, the contrast of Atchin—mecca of ni-Vanuatu capitalism and a big SDA village—is startling.

On Wala Island between Norsup and Vao is the locally operated **Wala Island Resort** (Box 55, Norsup, Northeast Malekula; no phone) with six thatched bungalows at Vt2000 pp including breakfast and dinner. All have a veranda overlooking a white-sand beach, but the toilets and showers are communal and there's no running water or electricity. It's on the site of a traditional dancing ground where wooden *tam tams* stand. Some old burials and magical stones around the resort may be taboo, so ask about that and the safety of swimming in these waters. Alick Nawinmal on nearby Rano Island also takes guests. Both Wala and Rano offer a unique village experience and tours to the mainland are arranged. Cruising yachts are welcome to anchor offshore. Information is available from the Waterfront Bar and Grill in Port Vila.

Lamap

Lamap, at the southeast corner of Malekula, adjoins Port Sandwich, where Captain Cook came ashore to a friendly welcome. Port Sandwich is the best harbor in Vanuatu, as it affords protection from all winds and has a good holding ground. Dinghies can be taken five km up the river at the head of the bay. The wharf, three km west of the police station, affords a lovely view of the area.

You'll probably arrive at the airstrip near Dravai village, five km south of the police station. Vanair calls here three times a week between Port Vila, Norsup, and Espiritu Santo. Camp on the grass beside the airstrip or proceed north to Lamap, where a small council rest house (Vt1000 pp) adjoins the police station. For advance information about staying here, call Lamap post office, tel. 48444. Bread and other supplies are available from local stores. Ambrym Island is just northeast of Lamap, but speedboats across are rare. Lopevi Island's volcanic cone looms exotically behind Paama Island in the distance.

The Small Nambas

The jungles of the interior of south Malekula are home to the Small Nambas. Because no missionaries penetrated here, the 400-500 clanspeople living in many scattered villages have retained their traditional customs right up to today. The men wear small *nambas* made of banana leaves and are famous for their gaudy face masks and body paint worn during funeral rites. No roads penetrate their territory, although the Small Nambas sometimes come to Mbwitin and South West Bay to trade. In the late 1980s Small Namba society disintegrated and the inhabitants spread to new settlements scattered around the southern part of the island. Many taboos govern this area; one established by the Vanuatu Government prohibits tourists from visiting the Small Nambas.

ESPIRITU SANTO

With 4,010 square km, Espiritu Santo is Vanuatu's largest island. Mt. Tabwemasana (1,879 meters), highest peak in the country, has never known a recorded climb, and it's believed that still-uncontacted "pygmy" peoples reside in the impassable interior jungles. Espiritu Santo has played a central role in the history of the country, from Quirós's 1606 settlement on Big Bay to the giant support base set up by the Americans during WW II, and the Coconut Rebellion of 1980.

Wusi on the isolated west coast (accessible only by boat) is the source of some of Vanuatu's only native pottery, made as part of a ceremony in May and June. The island possesses great economic potential, and most of Vanuatu's copra, cocoa, timber, and beef exports are shipped from Luganville, yet development has stagnated since independence. This beautiful island has much to offer the visitor, including untouched beaches, wild jungle hikes, friendly country villages, good communications, and an attractive, untouristed main town. A visit is recommended.

Apart from Port Vila, Luganville is the only other incorporated community in Vanuatu. It lies at the island's southeast corner on the Segond Channel, a 13-km-long waterway that offers anchorages sheltered enough for a ship to ride out a hurricane. Luganville is called Canal by

the locals because of this strait; to people in Port Vila, it's simply Santo. Coconut crabs scamper through the plantations to the west of town at dusk, and magic mushrooms abound in the cow pastures to the east. Watch for the white lime houses made of coral plaster, a peculiarity of this area.

Luganville is a mixture of French, Chinese, Vietnamese, and American influences, with a certain Wild West air. During WW II, 100,000 U.S. servicemen were stationed at the three bomber airfields and two fighter strips here, and a major dry dock functioned at Palikulo. Today, many of the buildings in Luganville are still vintage Quonset huts. With a population of 7,000, the town is an important economic center. Ninety percent of Vanuatu's copra, two-thirds of its frozen meat, and all its cacao pass through Luganville's docks. The 1980 independence disturbances seriously disrupted the local economy, however, and things have never really been the same.

SIGHTS OF SANTO

Sights around Town
Unity Park along Segond Channel near the mouth of the Sarakata River is the site of the

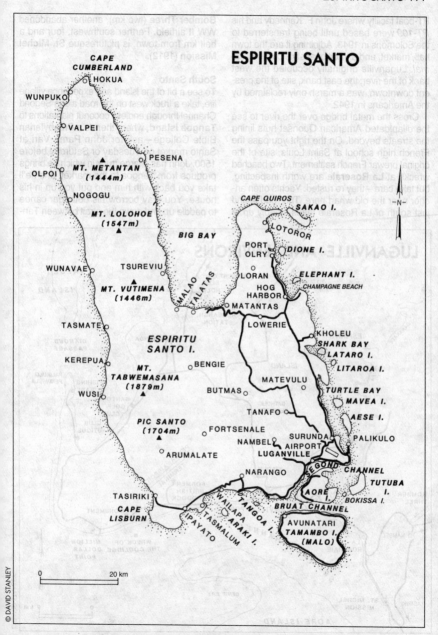

ESPIRITU SANTO

CAPE CUMBERLAND
HOKUA
WUNPUKO
VALPEI
PESENA
MT. METANTAN
(1444m)
OLPOI
NOGOGU
MT. LOLOHOE
(1547m)

SAKAO I.
CAPE QUIROS
LOTOROR
DIONE I.
PORT OLRY
BIG BAY
ELEPHANT I.
TSUREVIU
CHAMPAGNE BEACH
WUNAVAE
MT. VUTIMENA
(1446m)
LORAN
HOG HARBOR
MATANTAS
TASMATE
LOWERIE
KEREPUA
KHOLEU
SHARK BAY
MT. TABWEMASANA
(1879m)
BENGIE
LATARO I.
LITAROA I.
WUSI
BUTMAS
MATEVULU
TURTLE BAY
MAVEA I.
TANAFO
AESE I.
PIC SANTO
(1704m)
FORTSENALE
SURUNDA
PALIKULO
NAMBEL
AIRPORT
ARUMALATE
LUGANVILLE
NARANGO
SEGOND CHANNEL
TUTUBA I.
AORE I.
TASIRIKI
BOKISSA I.
CAPE LISBURN
TANGOA I.
BRUAT CHANNEL
WAILAPA
ARAKI I.
IPAYATO
TASMALUM
AVUNATARI
TAMAMBO I.
(MALO)

ESPIRITU SANTO I.

MALAO
TALATAS

0   20 km

© DAVID STANLEY

PT-boat facility where John F. Kennedy and his *PT-109* were based until being transferred to the Solomons in 1943. Adjoining it are the town hall, market, and a traditional-style chiefs *nakamal.* Luganville originally occupied the west bank of the river; the east bank, site of the present downtown, was a marsh only reclaimed by the Americans in 1942.

Cross the metal bridge over the river to see the dilapidated American Quonset huts lining the streets beyond. On the right you pass the French high school at Saint Louis, site of the original prewar French settlement. Two beached wrecks at **La Roseraie** are worth inspecting, but take care—they're rusted. Yachts often anchor near the old wharf here. The road inland just south of La Roseraie leads steeply up to

Bomber Three (two km), another abandoned WW II airfield. Farther southwest, four and a half km from town, is picturesque **St. Michel Mission** (1912).

South Santo

To see a bit of the island and experience village life, take a truck west on the road along Segond Channel through endless coconut plantations to **Tangoa Island,** where there's a Presbyterian Bible College—ask for John Pama Vari at Santo market on Tuesday or Saturday before 1500. John has a large truck in which he brings produce from Tangoa to the market, and he'll take you back with him and put you up in his house. You may borrow his outrigger canoe to paddle up and down the strait between Tan-

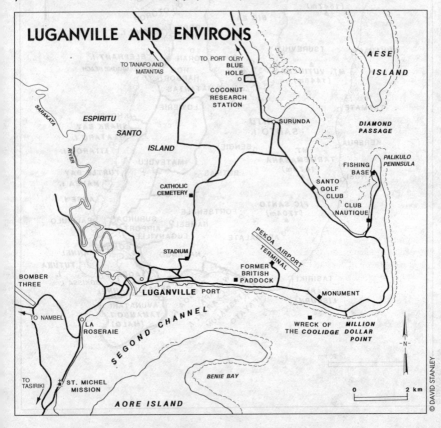

LUGANVILLE AND ENVIRONS

© DAVID STANLEY

Abandon ship! Troops are taken off the USAT President Coolidge, which hit a mine off Santo on 25 October 1942. The wreck is now a favorite of scuba divers.

NATIONAL ARCHIVES, WASHINGTON, D.C.

goa and the mainland (excellent anchorage for yachts here), but don't swim—too many sharks. Hike up to **Narango** for the view. This is an easy, rewarding trip. (The above appeared in previous editions of this book, and John has since written in asking us to send him *more* visitors!)

Palikulo Peninsula

The area east of Luganville as far as the Palikulo Peninsula is usually done as a day-trip. About a kilometer beyond the airport turnoff, near the monument to Captain Elwood J. Euart of the 103rd Field Artillery Battalion (1942), is a road to the shore of Segond Channel. The wreck of the USAT *President Coolidge,* a 22,000-ton prewar luxury liner converted into a troop ship, lies completely underwater on an angle at the edge of the reef here, the bow 21 meters underwater. The *Coolidge* sank on 26 October 1942, when it hit two mines in its haste to get into port without a pilot. Though 5,150 marines were on board at the time, it took two hours for the ship to sink, and most had time to get off. There were only two casualties, a fireman killed in the initial explosion and Captain Euart, who became trapped in the galley after courageously helping a group of soldiers escape. Today the 210-meter *Coolidge* is famous among the scuba set as the largest diveable wreck in the world.

One km farther along the coastal road is **Million Dollar Point,** where the U.S. forces dumped immense quantities of war materiel before their departure from Espiritu Santo. The local planters refused an American offer to sell them the equipment at a giveaway rate, thinking they'd get it all for free. But a ramp was built out into the water and all rolling stock driven off the end (anthropologist Kirk Huffman calls it "the greatest pig kill of all time"). Today, rusting metal and Coke bottles litter the coast for hundreds of meters in both directions. Million Dollar Point and the *Coolidge* were declared historical reserves in 1983, and it's illegal to take any souvenirs from this area.

After another four and a half km on the coastal road, take the turnoff to the right, which leads north a short distance to the **Club Nautique.** There's a beach, picnic area, toilet, and shower here, and you may be able to camp for a nominal fee. Since Palikulo Bay is better protected from the southeast trades than Segond Channel; cruising yachts often anchor off the Club Nautique and use the facilities. At the end of the road, two km north of the club, is the **South Pacific Fishing Company** (Box 237, Luganville; tel. 36319), a formerly Japanese-operated cannery that exported fish to the U.S. from 1957 to 1986. The government now uses the facility to freeze and transship tuna from Taiwanese longline boats.

East Santo

Just north of **Surunda** (nine km northeast of Luganville), at the back of the Coconut Research Station (IRHO), is a deep, spring-fed pool known as the Blue Hole, with transparent water—the perfect place to cool off. There's a good beach along the coast to the north of the station. Find a second 17-meter-deep Blue Hole near the abandoned American airstrip near **Matevulu College,** another nine km north of Surunda: at the west end of the airstrip, turn left on the road, then right and through two gates. This one has become rather green but it's still a refreshing place to swim.

A 50-km ride up the coastal highway, through coconut plantations crowded with cattle, brings you to friendly **Hog Harbor,** Espiritu Santo's second-largest village. An English-speaking village, Hog Harbor has a fine *nakamal* where you can while away the hours getting to know the inhabitants. An American base squatted here during WW II, and in the early 1970s, American developer Eugene Peacock attempted to subdivide and sell choice beachfront property near his Lokalee Beach Resort to American Vietnam war veterans. Peacock's land grab set in motion the movement toward independence. Some bitter fighting around Hog Harbor during the Coconut War still makes the locals uptight, so think twice about stopping if you're French!

Champagne Beach, one of the finest in the Pacific, is three km off the main road near Hog Harbor. This property is in dispute, so you may be asked to pay the Vt200 admission fee twice! Food is available at the nearby Lonnoc Bungalows. The talcum white sands curve around a turquoise lagoon, with picturesque Elephant Island offshore, a coconut plantation and high, jungle-clad slopes behind. Look for a freshwater spring on the east side of the beach at low tide. Cows often stop there for a sunset drink. Unfortunately, the cruise ship *Fairstar* has begun stopping at Champagne to unload 1,200 passengers at a go, so you might check before making the trip.

At the end of the road 13 km north of Hog Harbor is the French-speaking community of **Port Olry,** with its large Catholic mission. The site is idyllic, and two lakes are on nearby Dione Island, accessible on foot at low tide. Swim in a transparent, spring-fed pool, inland before the second gate on the track north from the village. Visit **Rennet wharf** for the view, or climb the bush track west of Port Olry for a panorama of the entire area.

Into the Interior

Tanafo (also known as Fanafo or Vanafo), 22 km north of Luganville, was the center of the 1980 Santo Rebellion. The Nagriamel Custom Movement met in the thatched meetinghouse, and Jimmy Stevens was captured as he sat under the immense banyan tree, drinking kava. Today, it's quieter, and tourists are even bused in to see traditional dances and similar activities. The villagers cling to custom as a political statement. A taxi from Luganville will run Vt3000-4000, and the sight of nearly naked men and tattooed topless women coming out of the misty bush to gather around your taxi could be something you'll never forget. Once you've been granted permission to visit the village, a welcome song will be sung, you'll shake hands with everyone and sign the visitors book, and then someone will show you around and answer questions.

Until early 1992 Tanafo didn't officially exist. Officials weren't allowed to visit, and no taxes were paid. Naturally, the people are still rather suspicious, and it's essential to get Chief Terry Bullock's permission to walk around or take photos. The Nagriamel office at the end of the road should be your first stop. The meetinghouse of the pre-1980 cargo cult is still in excellent shape, with fading political paintings and notices. Tanafo has one of Vanuatu's most striking *nakamals,* narrow and very long. A large waterfall is also near here. The interior village Butmas is a three-hour walk from Tanafo.

A bush road continues north from Tanafo toward **Big Bay,** but there's very little traffic. Just before the steep descent to Matantas, this road meets a road from the east coast near Hog Harbor through Lowerie. It was at Matantas on Big Bay that the Spanish conquistador Quirós established his "New Jerusalem" in 1606. A wall eight meters long with two gun openings, near the point where the Matantas River empties into the bay, is reputed to date from this time. In 1995 it was announced that 4,400 hectares of land in this area had been allocated to a new national park.

LUGANVILLE

1. Hospital
2. Prison
3. Church of Christ Transit House
4. Cine Hickson
5. Natapoa Motel
6. Catholic Church
7. Luganville College
8. Site of Wartime U.S. Camp
9. Market
10. Town Hall
11. Chinese Club
12. Hotel Santo
13. Santo Dive Tours
14. Vanair/Westpac Bank
15. Formosa Restaurant
16. Lands Survey Department
17. Asia Motel
18. Better Price Supermarket
19. New Look Hotel
20. Shell Service Station (FKC)
21. Art Blong Yumi
22. Police/Immigration
23. Post Office
24. Provincial Office

If one is *very* keen (and a bit crazy), it's possible to walk from Big Bay to Wailapa in South Santo in six hard days. It's damp and slippery, and you'll have to cross fast rivers up to your neck, but you'll see some of the most remote people in the Pacific. Don't go during the rainy season (January to April) if you're not into drowning. You can buy food from villagers along the way, but you'll need a strong stomach. Take plenty of stick tobacco to give them. A guide, of course, would be required. Ask for Chief Robert at **Talatas.** Longer, but less rigorous, is the walk along the coast to Cape Cumberland. In fact, it's possible to hike right around Espiritu Santo this way if you're experienced and well equipped. This is as far off the beaten track as you can get in the South Pacific.

Sports and Recreation

Allan Power's **Santo Dive Tours** (Box 233, Luganville; tel. 36822) offers scuba diving on the *President Coolidge,* or at Million Dollar Point (Vt3000 pp, or Vt2500 each if you book 12 dives). He'll rent tanks, weights, and belt alone if you're *very* persuasive, but he does require certification cards—no cowboy divers, please! Allan has been diving the *Coolidge* for 26 years and knows every nook and cranny. Unlike some dive shops that specialize in large groups from Australia, Allan caters mostly to individuals and most of his dives are shore dives. Ask for him at the Hotel Santo; he lives across the street.

Exploration Diving Ltd. (Box 164, Luganville; tel. 36638, fax 36101) charges Vt3500/6000 for one/two tank boat dives, and they also do PADI certification courses. While you're definitely better off sticking with Allan for the *Coolidge,* Exploration Diving's two dive boats can reach offshore wrecks and reefs he doesn't visit.

In February 1995 Kevin and Mayumi Green moved their dive shop from the Bokissa Island Resort to the Santo Sports Club in Luganville, and they now do business under the name

Aquamarine (Box 395, Luganville; tel./fax 36196). Diving from one of their two boats costs Vt3500/18,900/28,000 for one/six/10 dives, hotel pickups at 0800 or 1400 included. Night dives from their boats are Vt4000, shore diving at the *Coolidge* is Vt2500 (Vt3000 at night). Snorkelers are welcome on their boats at Vt1500 pp. You can rent equipment such as buoyancy compensators, regulators, wetsuits, snorkeling gear, and torch at their office. Aquamarine does introductory one-dive resort courses at Vt7900 for one person, Vt6650 pp for two or more, and an open water certification course costs Vt42,000 for one, Vt32,000 pp for two or more (medical certificate required). They also offer fishing trips beginning at Vt28,000 for four hours all inclusive (the catch stays with the boat). Surcharges are collected from anyone paying by credit card.

The rough can be very rough on the front nine holes at the **Santo Golf Club** (tel. 36623); watch for crocodiles near the seventh tee. Green fees are low and clubs are available, but you'll probably only find other golfers here on weekends.

PRACTICALITIES

Budget Accommodations

Eight-room **Asia Motel** (Box 78, Luganville; tel. 36323) opposite Better Price looks dirty, but at Vt1650/2400 single/double with private bath, it's not bad value. The rooms on the right (especially room no. 9) are quieter than those on the left. Communal cooking facilities are available. At last report the noisy disco next to the Asia had closed down as a result of frequent fistfights, but the locals still sit around playing mah-jongg all night. The Asia is not recommended for single women.

A better bet is the **New Look Hotel** (Box 228, Luganville; tel. 36440, fax 36095) nearby, with nine clean fan-cooled rooms at Vt2750/3850/4950 single/double/triple. The rooms with a/c and private bath are a bit extra. Cooking facilities are provided. Look for the manager behind the building if the store is closed.

The two-story **Unity Park Motel** (Box 85, Luganville; tel. 36052, fax 36025) overlooks Unity Park between the Chinese Club and Hotel Santo

in the center of town. The 13 clean rooms with communal cooking and bathing facilities are Vt1300/2000 single/double downstairs, Vt2750 double upstairs with a balcony.

The **Natapoa Motel** (Box 107, Luganville; tel. 36643), two blocks back behind Hotel Santo, has rooms with cooking facilities and private bath at Vt3000 single or double, with weekly rates available.

The **Church of Christ Transit House** (Box 86, Luganville; tel. 36633), at Sarakata just up from the market, offers dorm beds and communal cooking facilities at Vt800 pp.

Jaranmoli Bungalows (Joseph Maranda, Box 239, Luganville; tel./fax 36857) is on the site of the former British paddock, two km east of town on the way to the airport. You stay in one of nine simple bungalows with three beds, fan, toilet, and shower at Vt1260/2625 single/double; discounts are available for long stays. Cooking is possible in a kitchen shared by all guests. It's owned by the local government, and profits go toward rural development—a model for Vanuatu tourism!

The **Lobé Lobé Resort** (Box 175, Luganville; tel. 36309, fax 36497) offers two thatched bungalows on a beach outside Luganville at Vt2000.

Upmarket Accommodations

The only international-style hotel is **Hotel Santo** (Box 178, Luganville; tel. 36250, fax 36749), a flashy two-story building in the middle of town. Its 22 a/c rooms in the main building are overpriced at Vt8250/9350/10,450 single/double/triple. They cater especially to scuba divers and have eight unadvertised "budget" rooms in an annex set aside for them (Vt4290/5390 single/double). Facilities include a restaurant, bar, swimming pool, and tour desk.

The **Bougainville Resort** (Box 116, Luganville; tel. 36257, fax 36647) is on a white-sand beach five km west of town. One of the 18 a/c bungalows here will set you back Vt8500/9500/10,500 single/double/triple, including breakfast. Scuba divers with PADI certification cards sometimes get a discount. A restaurant with an attractive terrace and a swimming pool amid the bungalows round out this attractive French-owned resort. If your budget's flexible, it's worth dropping in for a meal even if you're staying elsewhere, but call ahead so they'll know you're coming. Airport transfers are Vt1000 pp each way.

Accommodations around Espiritu Santo

Oyster Island Resort (Gaetan Giovanni, Box 283, Luganville; tel./fax 36196), close to Matevulu College, 15 km north of Pekoa Airport, opened in 1992. It lies on a small island about 200 meters offshore, and visitors are picked up at a dock near the mouth of the river coming from the Matevulu Blue Hole. The two fancooled bungalows with bath are Vt5500/7000 double/triple, while the five with shared bath go for Vt4500/6000 with breakfast included in all rates. Their traditional-style restaurant right on the beach serves dishes like poulet fish (Vt1900), fresh oysters (Vt900), and pepper steak (Vt1300). Dugout canoes for paddling around the lagoon are provided, and skippered yacht charters and day-trips are available on the 18-meter sloop *Miz Mae*. Scuba diving can be arranged with Aquamarine. A taxi to the resort landing will cost about Vt1500, and there are two daily buses at Vt200 pp.

One km west of Champagne Beach, 55 km north of Luganville, is Kalmer Vocor's **Lonnoc Bungalows** (Box 190, Luganville; tel. 36850, fax 36347), alias Lonnoc Beach Resort or Lokalee Guest House. There are three units at Vt1200 pp, and the kerosene lighting and communal bucket showers add a romantic touch. Camping is possible. Communal cooking facilities are provided, and there's also a restaurant/bar. It's set slightly away from the beach and is meticulously maintained. You can't beat the swimming and snorkeling around here, and there are neighboring villages to visit. Kalmer is a former member of parliament and an excellent source of information on the area. Transport to/from Luganville is arranged every afternoon around 1500 for CFP 500 pp each way, so call them up. Highly recommended.

The **Bokissa Island Resort** (Box 261, Luganville; tel./fax 36855) is on a sandy coral cay between Aore and Tutuba, seven km from Luganville by boat (Vt3500 pp roundtrip). The 12 thatched bungalows with fan are Vt9600 single or double, Vt11,600 triple. There are no cooking facilities and meals cost extra. The reef diving around Bokissa is incredible and there are two wrecks, the destroyer USS *Tucker* and the coastal trader *Henry Bonneaud*, near the island. Call the resort as they sometimes do daytrips from Santo including lunch, which work out well. Bokissa closes down when no groups are present. At last report Bokissa's dive shop had moved to Luganville and the resort was for sale.

Food

The inexpensive **Formosa Restaurant** (tel. 36228), across the street from the Westpac Bank, has quite good fish soup, sweet and sour dishes, lobster, and gourmet crab. They're open daily (on Sunday dinner only) and will even give you *Newsweek* to read with dinner! Dining in their beer garden, with its distant sea view, is great—recommended.

Leslie Tonklin's **Natangora Café** (tel. 36753; closed Sunday), on the main street, has a cozy atmosphere, and aside from the tasty cakes, pies, burgers, and omelettes, they have the best milk shakes in the South Pacific. **Eat Cheap** near Vanitel serves full meals of steak, rice, taro, and *kumala*.

Madelines Restaurant (tel. 36148; closed Sunday) in the center of town serves reasonable steaks and seafood. **Carmels Restaurant and Bar** (closed Monday) has more upmarket Italian food; the local expat community congregates here after work on Friday.

The snack bar at **Better Price** (tel. 36126) offers meat pies, sandwiches, and cold drinks, but groceries are a better buy. The **Chinese stores** are cheaper than Better Price, however, and they stay open till sundown, even on weekends and holidays.

Get a large plate of beef, chicken, or fish and rice at the back of the **market** on market days (Tuesday, Thursday, and Saturday mornings) for Vt200.

Entertainment

Cine Hickson (tel. 36340) near the courthouse runs French films only.

The bar at the **Santo Sports Club** (tel. 36375) pretty well sums up Luganville's social scene. For kava there's **Wagonwheels Nakamal** near the Bougainville Resort.

Services

The ANZ Bank, Bank of Hawaii, National Bank, and Westpac Bank all have branches in Luganville. Card telephones are available at the airport, hospital, and Better Price.

The **Immigration office** (tel. 36724) is at Police Headquarters, near the post office. The **Lands Survey Department** (tel. 36330), opposite Better Price, sells topographical maps. The **Northern District Hospital** (tel. 36345) offers outpatient consultations weekdays 0700-1000.

Connie Wells's **Art Blong Yumi** (Box 59, Luganville; tel. 36830, fax 36025) on the main street is well worth browsing to get an idea of the type of handicrafts made on the island, including Wusi pottery, *tam tams,* and masks. Connie's also a talented artist and does portraits upon request. The inmates at the prison next to the hospital make some of the best carvings.

Yachting Facilities

Cruisers might like to know that one of the only slips in Vanuatu offering haul-out facilities (Vt20,000, plus a per diem) for yachts is at the Seventh-Day Adventist high school (tel. 36414) in Port Lautour on the south side of Aore Island. It can handle up to 40 tons, and a well-equipped workshop adjoins, but only boats drawing less than 1.9 meters can enter the lagoon here at high tide. The slip at Palikulo can haul out ships up to 100 tons.

TRANSPORTATION

By Air

Vanair (tel. 36421) flies from Espiritu Santo to Port Vila (Vt9800) four times a day, twice daily via Norsup. Another route from Espiritu Santo to Port Vila goes via Longana, Sara, and Lonorore three times a week, making stopovers on Malekula, Ambae, and Pentecost possible to and from Port Vila. Even if you don't plan to stop anywhere between Port Vila and Santo, ask to be booked on a flight that makes one or two stops for some free aerial sightseeing. Aircraft based at Espiritu Santo also fly to Maewo (Vt4800) three times a week, to Gaua (Vt6000), Sola (Vt6900), Mota Lava (Vt6900), and Torres (Vt8100) twice a week, and to Craig Cove (Vt6100) and Ulei (Vt5900) weekly. Many offbeat interisland flights operate between remote outer islands, so study their timetable.

By Ship

The shipping companies operating the Luganville-Port Vila passenger service don't maintain offices here, so you have to go onboard and deal directly with the captains. There are three departures a week, with the ships stopping at many smaller islands along the way. **South Pacific Shipping** (tel. 36235) beside the supermarket only handles cargo, but they'll be able to tell you when the various ships are due in port. You might get on a Chinese trading ship doing two-week trips out of Espiritu Santo collecting copra. Many other cargo ships tie up at the Simonsen Wharf, just east of Luganville, and one leaves almost every day. Just go down to the wharf and start asking.

By Road

The East Star Express bus service runs up the east coast to Hog Harbor. A taxi to the airport is Vt400, to Palikulo Vt800. The locals travel by trucks, which gather at Luganville market. Tuesday is market day for the South Santo people, so you can be sure of a ride to Tangoa Island (Vt350) that afternoon. The East Santo people come in on Thursday, so that day look for rides to Tanafo, Big Bay, Hog Harbor, and Port Olry (Vt350). On Saturday, both groups arrive simultaneously, so you might get a ride almost anywhere. Another good place to wait for rides is the benches in front of the Shell Service Station (Fung Kwan Chee, tel. 36352) in the center of town. Most trucks gas up here before leaving.

Car rentals are available from the **Formosa Restaurant** (Box 217, Luganville; tel. 36228), **Andersons Car Hire** (Box 344, Luganville; tel. 36300), and **Santo Car Hire** (Box 178, Luganville; tel. 36250, fax 36749) at Hotel Santo. **Exploration Diving** (Box 164, Luganville; tel. 36638, fax 36101) rents bicycles at Vt1000/5600 daily/weekly.

Tours

Tom Wells of **Espiritu Santo Tours** (Box 105, Luganville; tel. 36192, fax 36025) offers the usual day-trips, in addition to "jungle walking adventures" such as a climb up Mt. Tabwemasana in search of the rare mountain starling. Tom organizes hikes along the west coast, fishing trips, and Melanesian feasts. He offers reduced rates for groups of eight people or more.

Day-trips and overnight charters are offered on the four-stateroom, 18-meter sloop *Miz Mae,* based at Oyster Island Resort (tel./fax 36390). A seven-hour day cruise from the Palikulo Club Nautique is Vt5500 pp, the three-hour sunset cruise Vt3300 pp, and scuba diving from the boat is easily arranged through Aquamarine. This spacious yacht can be used to cruise northern Vanuatu at Vt59,900/75,000 per night for four/six persons including meals, airport transfers, and crew. A special weekend rate of Vt37,900 pp from Friday afternoon to Monday morning is also offered. This is an excellent way to get in some

sailing while seeing a bit of the country, and your German hosts Tom and Dorothy go out of their way for you. Advance reservations with a 25% deposit are required for overnight trips.

Airport
Pekoa Airport (SON), between Luganville and Palikulo, is five km east of town. Pekoa is a reconditioned WW II airstrip, one of five remaining in the area. Occasional buses (Vt100) and taxis (Vt400) connect the airport to town. If none are around, someone will offer you a lift—it's that kind of place.

OTHER ISLANDS

AMBRYM

Ambrym, like Tanna, is famous for its highly active volcanoes and native culture, yet it's much less impacted by tourism. Periodic eruptions have left a 12-km ash plain near the center of the island, lava valleys, and a rocky, broken coast. The black volcanic soil contrasts sharply with the deep green vegetation. Swimming off the black-sand beaches is not advisable due to the presence of sharks.

The 7,000 inhabitants live in the three corners of this triangular island, and their only links are by foot and sea. Two of these communities, Craig Cove in the west and Ulei in the east, have airstrips, with Vanair flights from Port Vila (Vt6700) two or three times a week, from Espiritu Santo (Vt5100) and Lamap (Vt2500) weekly. North Ambrym is accessible only by ship.

The Ambrym islanders are wary of art collectors who come trying to purchase their tribal heirlooms and have been known to direct an arrow or two their way. On the other hand, high-quality woodcarvings and tree fern figures continue to be produced in large quantities, and these they are eager to sell. As in most of northern Vanuatu, a powerful system of traditional copyright applies and only those with the traditional rights to make certain types of objects are allowed to do so.

Traditional Culture
Vanuatu's best known handicrafts come from North Ambrym, especially the tall slit drums

called *tam tams* in Bislama. Craftsmen slot and hollow two-meter breadfruit logs, then carve faces on them, and these are used as signal drums. Also characteristic are the black tree ferns carved for the *mhehe* graded rituals, and bamboo flutes up to a meter long with burnt-in geometric designs. Painted masks with hair of bleached banana fiber are worn in rites to increase the yield of yams.

Storytellers on Ambrym use intricate sand drawings to illustrate their tales. Up to 180 stylized patterns that the artist draws without removing his finger from the sand can convey a variety of messages. Ambrym sorcerers are famous throughout Vanuatu for their magic, often associated with the destructive power of the island's volcanoes. Masks worn by participants in Rom dances during the Ole ceremony represent certain spiritual aspects of power associated with yams.

South Ambrym
At the corrugated-metal Government Guest House (Vt1000 pp) in **Craig Cove,** they serve *lap lap* and rice in the evening, tea and bread in the morning, all for a nominal amount. Prior to arrival, call the Craig Cove Local Council (tel. 48499) for information on accommodations.

To hire a truck from Craig Cove to Lalinda is Vt2000. Otherwise, take a plane or ship to **Ulei** and hike west along the beach on the south coast between the end of the roads at Pawe and Bwele. The airstrip at Ulei ends at a cliff. Near the Catholic mission at **Sesivi** is a swimmable hot spring in the sea.

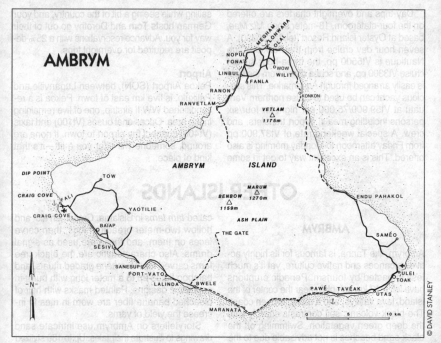

AMBRYM

NOPUL
FONA
LINBUL
RANON
RANVETLAM

MEGHAM
ONWARA
OLAL
WILIT
WOW
FANLA
KONKON

VETLAM
△
1175m

DIP POINT
TOW

CRAIG COVE
FALI

CRAIG COVE
YAOTILIE

BAIAP

SÉSIVI

SANESUP
PORT-VATO
LALINDA

AMBRYM   ISLAND

MARUM
△
1270m
BENBOW
△
1159m

ASH PLAIN

THE GATE

ENDU PAHAKOL

SAMÉO

ULEI
TOAK

BWELE

PAWÉ   TAVÉAK

UTAS

MARANATA

0   5   10 km

© DAVID STANLEY

A comfortable staging ground for volcano-bound visitors is the five-room **Milee Resthouse** (tel. 48412) at Sanesup, about 12 km from Craig Cove airstrip. For Vt3500 a day you get sleeping accommodations in a clean traditional-style house and three ample meals. Proprietor Enos Falau can provide a guide to climb the volcano at Vt1000 and will lend you a tent at no charge. Ask Enos about the art of sand drawing. A pick-up from Sanesup to Lalinda costs Vt800.

From near Lalinda, you can follow a creek bed up to the vast ash plain near the center of the island. The village chief collects a Vt500-1000 pp custom fee and can supply a guide for another Vt1000. Allow three hours' hard climbing to the Gate (750 meters). From here you can look across the vast ash plain to Benbow (1,159 meters) and Marum (1,270 meters). Clouds can roll in and cover you quite suddenly, and your guide may claim he doesn't know the way to Marum and refuse to take you to Benbow. It's strictly business for the locals, and you only get what you pay for.

North Ambrym

North Ambrym is one of the most traditional areas in Vanuatu. Paramount Chief Tofor resides at Fanla, less than an hour's walk from the SDA mission at Linbul. He'll show you an adze made from iron allegedly given to his ancestors by Captain Cook. Otherwise all there is to see at Fanla is a few slit drums on the dance platform and some statues. To take photos, stick tobacco and Vt1000 must be presented. You might be able to stay at the Catholic mission at Olal, but leave a donation. The northernmost villages are mostly French-speaking.

From Linbul it's a three-hour hike through gardens and bush to the top of Mt. Vetlam (1,175 meters), with good views in clear weather. Ask at Ranon about the possibilities of climbing Marum from this side. The two-room **Solomon Douglas Guest House** (Vt1000 pp, meals extra) at Ranon is *the* place to stay if you're into local art. Women may also be able to sleep in the Women's Club House at Ranon (ask for Sarah). From North Ambrym, you can hike south to Ulei in two days, but not south-west to Craig Cove, as the way is blocked by lava flows. A motorboat from Ranon to Craig Cove should cost around Vt5000, which can be shared among other passengers.

PENTECOST

South Pentecost is renowned for its land diving *(Nangol)*, a thrilling spectacle on this thickly forested island. Men tie liana vines to their ankles, then jump head-first from atop 30-meter man-made towers, jerking to a halt just centimeters from the ground. Slack in the lifeline vine eases the shock as it stretches to its limit, and the platforms are designed to sway, so the jumpers are rarely injured. During the two weeks it takes to build a tower, women are banned from the area, and guards are posted each night to protect it from the "poison man."

The story goes that custom originated when a woman trying to escape an angry husband lured him into a trap by climbing a banyan tree. As the fellow climbed after her she tied previously prepared liana vines to her ankles and jumped, followed by the man—he fell to his death while she was saved by the vines.

Today this daring feat forms part of festival of yams, and there's no stigma attached to any diver who "chickens out." Before jumping, a participant can make a speech refuting allegations against him or he can criticize anyone he likes, including the chief, on the assumption that if he lies the spirit of the tower will let him die. The jumping is optional and done for fun—many men and boys do so at every opportunity. Even eight-year-olds prove their courage by hurtling themselves from these giddy heights. Only speakers of the Sa language may perform the ritual.

When the plunging diver is about to smash to the ground, the vines stretch out fully. This slows, and finally stops, his fall just as his head brushes the spaded soil, symbolically refertilizing the earth for the next crop of yams. The diving takes place every Saturday in April and May, soon after the yam harvest. Today the diving has taken on a second function: paying spectators have become the main cash crop for these villagers. It's a rare opportunity to witness an event that has unexpectedly become a part of modern life in the form of bungee jumping.

In 1995 a dispute arose over the diving when the Department of Culture banned land diving that year on grounds that the original significance was being lost as the jumps were staged for tourists, and most of the entry fees were going to a few chiefs. Tour Vanuatu protested that it had commitments to overseas tour operators, so the first scheduled dive went ahead anyway at Wali village. As the tourists assembled it soon became clear that something was very wrong when one of the vines snapped and

A Pentecost land diver leaps from a tower, liana vines tied to his ankles.

a diver had to be flown to Port Vila with a broken hip bone. A similar dispute in 1974 resulted in the death of a diver before the eyes of Queen Elizabeth. Much soul searching over land diving is now going on in both Pentecost and Port Vila, and it's quite likely that regular dives timed to fit into tourist itineraries will become a thing of the past.

A series of waterfalls is behind Melsisi, a Catholic station halfway up the west coast. You can climb all but the last waterfall, and great swimming/jumping holes accompany them. Great snorkeling, too, on the reef off Melsisi with caves, canyons, and abundant fish. Climb the hill behind the village for the view. The people of Pentecost are divided into two matrilineal cross-marrying clans whose gardens and swimming areas are marked off by stones or trees. Ask someone to point these out to you.

Practicalities

Vanair has flights to Lonorore from Port Vila (Vt14,300), Espiritu Santo (Vt4900), Walaha (Vt3900), Longana (Vt3700), Redcliffe (Vt3500), and Sara (Vt3100) three times a week. Unfortunately there's no connection to Craig Cove and Ulei on Ambrym. Sara airstrip in north Pentecost is very short, rough, and subject to closure after rains.

In past, tour operators in Port Vila have run day-trips from Efate every Saturday in April and May to see the land diving on Pentecost for Vt40,000 pp. Included in the package were a flight over Ambrym's crater to peek at the bubbling lava inside, and lunch (unless someone forgot to bring it along). The jumps were originally held at **Bunlap** village, on the southeast side of Pentecost, but in recent years they've been held at Wali near Lonorore airstrip to spare tourists an exhausting four-hour hike across the island.

Although the tour companies will deny it, it's possible to stay with the locals and pay a custom fee of about Vt5000-7500 pp to see and photograph the jump. Any visitors who make it across to Bunlap or Ranwas are accommodated for Vt2000 pp including meals. Photography fees are another Vt2000, but after a bit of friendly *tok tok*, you may be able to take photos for nothing. Bunlap is picturesque, built in the tradition-

al style on a slope. This is a strong custom area, so inquire about taboo days, especially pertaining to women.

Several small local rest houses (Vt1000 pp) are available on Pentecost; for information call the local government council at Abwatuntora (tel. 38304) or Loltong (tel. 38394), both in North Pentecost, or Pangi (tel. 38301), South Pentecost.

AMBAE

Ambae (Aoba) resembles a capsized canoe, with Maewo and Pentecost the broken outriggers. During WW II, a U.S. serviceman named James Michener was stationed at Espiritu Santo, and the sight of Ambae on the horizon fascinated him so much that he called it "Bali Hai"—much better than the name "Leper Island," which Bougainville gave it in 1768 (there were no lepers on Ambae). The people's skin color is lighter than that of other ni-Vanuatu, possibly due to some Polynesian mixing. During the colonial period, women from Ambae were considered good potential wives by local planters, though no European plantations were ever set up on Ambae itself.

Ambae is noted for its massive volcanic peak (1,496 meters), which contains two warm-water lakes with sulfurous water in its dormant crater. The lakes are thought to be the eyes of the mountain. The god Tagaro took the fire from

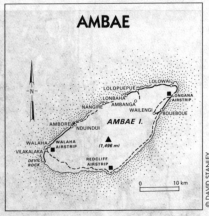

these craters and threw it across to neighboring Ambrym. There are seven islands in the lakes and a fumarole beside one. As you swim around, test the echo against the walls of the crater rim. The mountain can be climbed from **Ambanga** in four hours each way, but it's often socked in by fog, and there could be problems about taboos. A guide is required.

It's better to climb to the lakes from **Vilakala-ka,** near Walaha airstrip at the west end of the island. Unless you plan to camp on top, it will take a full day, so set out before 0700. A guide is essential, and Nicholas in Vilakalaka should be willing for Vt2000 per group. It's a difficult (but fantastic) hike, with bush knives chopping all the way. In March 1995 tremors were felt on Ambae, and the volcano began emitting thick black clouds of ash and smoke, raising fears that a major eruption was imminent.

From **Walaha,** you can hike 35 km along the north coast to Longana and fly out from there. The pretty village of **Lolopuepue** on the north coast is the former French headquarters, attested to by its Catholic church and stone buildings. The Church of Melanesia mission, hospital (tel. 38302), post office, and administrative center are at **Lolowai,** on the east end of the island, where a good harbor and Longana airstrip are found. For information on the two-room Tausala Guest House (Vt1000/1500 single/double) at Saratamata, near Longana airstrip, call the secretary of the Local Government Council (tel. 38348). Cooking facilities are provided. Another council rest house is at Ambore toward Walaha airstrip, and the secretary will also know about it. Charlie Bani runs a guesthouse at Nduindui.

A variety of Vanair flights service Ambae's three airstrips. Walaha receives flights from Espiritu Santo (Vt3100) six times a week; Lonorore (Vt3900), Sara (Vt3200), and Port Vila (Vt9700) three times a week; and Maewo (Vt3500) twice a week. Longana is served from Espiritu Santo (Vt4200) six times a week; and from Lonorore (Vt3700), Maewo (Vt2700), Port Vila (Vt11,300), and Sara (Vt2500) three times a week. Redcliff gets flights from Espiritu Santo (Vt3600), Lonorore (Vt3500), and Port Vila (Vt9300) three times a week. With careful planning you could fly into one airstrip and out from another.

THE BANKS AND TORRES ISLANDS

The out-of-the-way Banks Islands are noted for their handicrafts and traditional dancers. **Gaua** (Santa Maria) is a circular green island with many stone house foundations that recall the large prehistoric population ravaged by black-birding and disease. Gaua is interesting for its fumaroles and sulfur springs, and especially the deep crater lake drained by a waterfall at the center of the island. John Stevens and Alain Christopher both run simple guesthouses on Gaua at Vt1500 pp with meals. Gaua receives Vanair flights from Espiritu Santo (Vt6000), Sola (Vt2900), and Mota Lava (Vt3500) twice a week.

The main airstrip for the Banks is at Sola on **Vanua Lava,** 22 km north of Gaua. Vanair services arrive from Espiritu Santo (Vt6900), Gaua (Vt2900), Mota Lava (Vt2400), and Torres (Vt8100) once or twice a week. Near the airstrip is Port Patteson, a natural harbor with safe anchorage year-round. Jets of steam rise from the hot springs on the slopes of Mt. Sere'ama (921 meters), but otherwise there's not a lot to see. Call the local government council at Sola (tel. 38550) for information on places to stay. Waterfall Bay on the west side of Vanua Lava has good anchorage for yachts.

Mota and **Mere Lava** have beautiful symmetrical cones. Terraced villages stand on the steep slopes of Mere Lava. **Ureparapara Island** is a sunken volcano with a drowned crater that large ships can sail into.

An airstrip also exists at the east end of **Mota Lava,** with weekly Vanair flights from Torres (Vt5500), Sola (Vt2400), Gaua (Vt3500), and Espiritu Santo (Vt6900). Nearby is an interesting cave, one of the few accessible caves in the Banks. If you don't mind crawling, you'll get a spectacular view from the far end of the cave. To visit the cave, ask for Stander Haward of nearby Valuwa village. A local priest named Father Luke Dini runs the seven-bungalow **Harry Memorial Beach Resort** (no phone) facing a white-sand beach on the tiny island of Rah, 500 meters off the southwest end of Mota Lava (Vt1000 pp with shared bath). Meals are served in their restaurant. It's a real "do nothing but relax" type of place.

Surfers should go on to the **Torres Islands,** an outlying corner of the Pacific not explored until the mid-1800s. **Loh Island** has weekly Vanair service from Espiritu Santo (Vt10,300) and Sola (Vt8100).

A good way to see these remote islands is on a 10-day roundtrip from Espiritu Santo on a copra-collecting vessel. You'll often get the chance to get off and look around during loading. Very few travelers make it this far.

CAPSULE BISLAMA VOCABULARY

bilong baim—for sale

em ia haumas?—how much is it?
em i hat smol smol—it's warm
em i lait nau—it's late

go insait nating—admission fee
gut moning—good morning
gut naet—good night

i gut nomo—just fine

karim olsem yu laik—help yourself

lukim yu—see you later

me les lilbit—I feel a little tired
mi mus paiim long hau mas?—how much should I pay?
mi no harim—beg your pardon?
mi no save—I don't understand/know
mi tekem emia—I'll take this one

nam bilong mi . . .—my name is . . .

olgeta samting bilong mi hia—these are my things
ol men—men's
ol woman—women's

plis—please
pusim—push
puspus—intercourse

taim i ren—rainy season
tata—goodbye
tenk yu tumas—thank you very much
tumora—tomorrow

wanem nem bilong yu?—what's your name?
wanem taim?—what time is it?

yo no toktok—silence
yu orait?—how are you?
yu save?—do you understand/know?
yumi mit wea?—where can we meet?

GORDON OHLIGER

SOLOMON ISLANDS
INTRODUCTION

One of the last corners of the world to fall under European religious and political control, the Solomon Islands remain today the best-kept secret in the South Pacific. Like neighboring Vanuatu, it's a land of contrasts and adventure, with jungle-clad peaks, mighty volcanoes, uplifted atolls, crashing waterfalls, mist-enshrouded rainforests, dark lagoons, scattered islands, and brilliant coral reefs. It's all here: shark-callers, war wreckage, gold, and malaria; every Pacific race is present, from blue-black Papuans to chocolate-colored, blond Melanesians, bronze-skinned Micronesians, and fair-complexioned Polynesians. The variety of cultures and customs is striking, and the traditional ways are remarkably alive.

Unless you're on a tour, you'll find travel outside the capital, Honiara, an unstructured, make-your-own-arrangements affair. The number of visitors is negligible, and most of those who do come stay only for a few days, mainly in the capital. This gives slightly intrepid travelers an unparalleled opportunity to get well off the beaten track and have a genuine South Sea paradise all to themselves. So you're in for something totally original! Indeed, these are the Happy Isles.

The Land
With its 27,556-square-km area, the Solomons is the second-largest insular nation of the South Pacific (after Papua New Guinea). This thickly forested, mountainous country, 1,860 km northeast of Australia, is made up of six large islands in a double line (Choiseul, Isabel, Malaita, and New Georgia, Guadalcanal, Makira), about 20 medium-size ones, and numberless smaller islets and reefs—922 islands in all, 347 of them inhabited. The group stretches over 1,800 km from the Shortlands in the west to Tikopia and Anuta in the east, and nearly 900 km from Ontong Java atoll in the north to Rennell Island in the south.

The Solomons are on the edge of the Indo-Australian and Pacific plates, which accounts for volcanic activity, past and present. Tinakula, Savo, Simbo, and Vella Lavella are active parts

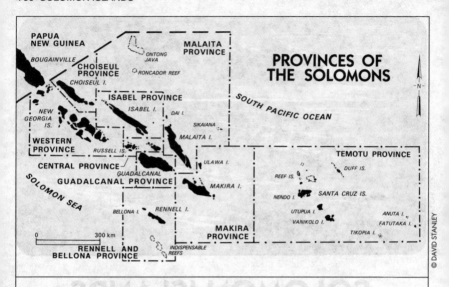

PROVINCES OF THE SOLOMONS

PAPUA NEW GUINEA

BOUGAINVILLE

CHOISEUL PROVINCE

CHOISEUL I.

ONTONG JAVA

RONCADOR REEF

MALAITA PROVINCE

ISABEL PROVINCE

ISABEL I.   DAI I.

SIKAIANA

MALAITA I.

SOUTH PACIFIC OCEAN

NEW GEORGIA IS.

WESTERN PROVINCE

RUSSELL IS.

CENTRAL PROVINCE

GUADALCANAL

ULAWA I.

GUADALCANAL PROVINCE

MAKIRA I.

TEMOTU PROVINCE

REEF IS.   DUFF IS.

NENDO I.   SANTA CRUZ IS.

UTUPUA I.   ANUTA I.

VANIKOLO I.   FATUTAKA I.

TIKOPIA I.

SOLOMON SEA

BELLONA I.   RENNELL I.

MAKIRA PROVINCE

0   300 km

RENNELL AND BELLONA PROVINCE

INDISPENSABLE REEFS

© DAVID STANLEY

THE SOLOMONS AT A GLANCE

PROVINCE	MAIN TOWN	POPULATION (1986)	AREA (SQUARE KM)	HIGHEST POINT (SQUARE KM)
Guadalcanal	Honiara	80,826	5,336	2,447
Malaita	Auki	80,183	4,243	1,303
Rennell & Bellona	Tingoa	1,802	276	220
Central	Tulagi	16,720	1,000	510
Western	Gizo	41,803	5,279	1,661
Choiseul	Taro	13,569	3,294	1,060
Isabel	Buala	14,564	4,014	1,392
Makira	Kirakira	21,646	3,188	1,250
Temotu	Lata	14,683	926	923
Solomon Islands	**Honiara**	**285,796**	**27,556**	**2,447**

of the circum-Pacific Ring of Fire, and there's a submarine volcano called Kavachi just south of the New Georgia Group. The New Britain Trench, southwest of the chain, marks the point where the Indo-Australian Plate is shoved under the Pacific Plate. This causes frequent earthquakes and uplifting; consequently, many of the Polynesian outliers are elevated atolls. Rennell is one of the best examples of a raised limestone atoll in Oceania.

The other islands are mostly high and volcanic, with luxuriant rainforest shrouding the rugged terrain. Under these conditions roadbuilding is difficult; only Malaita and Guadalcanal have fairly extensive networks. The wide coastal plain east of Honiara on Guadalcanal is the only area of its kind in the group. The soil ranges from extremely rich volcanic to relatively infertile limestone. The rivers are fast and straight, often flooding the coastal areas during storms. Geographically and culturally, the northwest islands of Bougainville and Buka belong to the Solomons, but are politically part of Papua New Guinea.

Climate

The Solomons are hot and humid year-round, but the heaviest rainfall comes in summer, December to March. Hurricanes build up at this time, but they move south and rarely do much damage here. Between November and April, winds are generally from the west or northwest *(komburu),* though occasionally from the southeast, with long periods of calm punctuated by squalls.

The southeast trade winds *(ara)* blow almost continually from the end of April to November (if the wind shifts to north or west at this time, it means a storm is on the way). The most pleasant time to visit is winter, July to September, when rainfall, humidity, and temperatures are at their lowest. On the high islands the southeast coasts, which face the winds, are far wetter than the more sheltered north coasts. Yet the cooling sea breezes temper the heat and humidity along all coasts year-round.

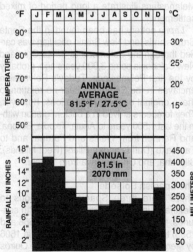

TULAGI'S CLIMATE

Flora and Fauna

Mangroves and coconut groves shelter the coastal strips, while the interiors of the high islands are swallowed by dense rainforest. The forest climbs through 24 belts, from towering lowland hardwoods to the mosses atop Guadalcanal's 2,300-meter peaks. Where the forests have been destroyed by slash-and-burn agriculture or logging, grasslands have taken hold. Crocodiles lurk in brackish mangrove swamps in the river deltas, while sago palms grow in freshwater swamps. More than 230 varieties of orchids and other tropical flowers brighten the landscape. Of the 4,500 species of plants recorded so far, 143 are known to have been utilized in traditional herbal medicine.

The endemic land mammals (opossum, bats, rats, and mice) are mostly nocturnal, so it's unlikely you'll see them. Birdlife, on the other hand, is rich and varied, with about 190 species including 16 species of white-eyes, fantails, rails, thrushes, and honeyeaters that occur only here. The most unusual is the megapode, or incubator, a bird that lays large eggs in the warm volcanic sands of the thermal areas. After about 40 days, the newly hatched megapodes dig themselves out and are able to fly short distances as soon as their wings dry. There are many species of colorful parrots and 130 species of butterflies, including several species of birdwings.

The 70 species of reptiles include crocodiles, frogs, lizards, skinks, snakes, toads, and marine turtles. The five species of sea turtles nest from November to February. Several of the 20 species of snake are poisonous, but fortunately they're not common and are no threat. Centipedes and scorpions are two other potentially dangerous but seldom-encountered jungle creatures. The isolated Santa Cruz Group has fewer indigenous species than the main island chain.

Sharks are common offshore, so ask local advice before swimming. These creatures earned a certain notoriety among sailors and airmen during WW II, but the problem seems to have receded. White-sand beaches are safer than black. No shark attacks have been reported in the Santa Cruz Islands in recent memory. Many islanders have a curious rapport with the shark and believe that the souls of their ancestors live on in them. Shark worship has made Malaita relatively free of shark attacks.

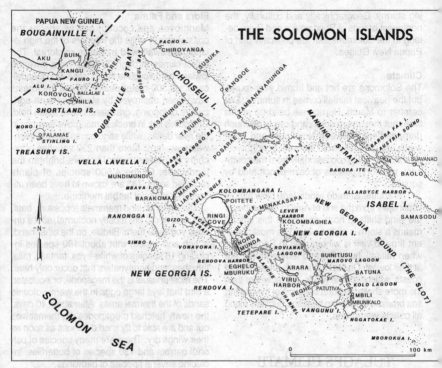

THE SOLOMON ISLANDS

PAPUA NEW GUINEA

BOUGAINVILLE I.

AKU
BUIN
KANGU
FAURO I.
ALU I.
KOROVOU
BALLALAE I.
ANILA

SHORTLAND IS.

MONO I.
FALAMAE
STIRLING I.

TREASURY IS.

VELLA LAVELLA I.
MUNDIMUNDI
MBAVA I.
BARAKOMA
RANONGGA I.
GIZO
SIMBO I.
VONAVONA I.
RENDOVA HARBOR
EGHELO
MBURUKU
NEW GEORGIA IS.
RENDOVA I.
TETEPARE I.

PACHO R.
CHIROVANGA
SUSUKA
PANGGOE
SASAMUNGGA
PAPARA
TASURE
PARASO
MANGGO BAY
POSARAE
ROB ROY I.
VAGHENA I.
KOLOMBANGARA I.
POITETE
VELLA GULF
LIAPARI
MARAVARI
MENAKASAPA
KULA GULF
RINGI
COVE
NORO
MUNDA
ROVIANA
LAGOON
BLANCHE
VIRU
HARBOR
SEGHE
PATUTIVA
VANGUNU I.
NGGATOKAE I.

ZAMBANAVARUNGGA
BARORA FAA I.
AUSTRIA SOUND
OKIA
SUAVANAO
BARORA ITE I.
BAOLO
ALLARDYCE HARBOR
ISABEL I.
SAMASODU
LEVER
HARBOR
KOLOMBAGHEA
NEW GEORGIA I.
BUINITUSU
MAROVO LAGOON
ARARA
BATUNA
KOLO LAGOON
MBILI
MBUNIKALO
MBOROKUA I.

CHOISEUL I.
CHOISEUL BAY
KAREKI
BOUGAINVILLE STRAIT
MANNING STRAIT
NEW GEORGIA SOUND (THE SLOT)
SOLOMON SEA
BLACKETT STRAIT

-N-

0   100 km

HISTORY AND GOVERNMENT

Prehistory

The first inhabitants were Papuan-speaking hunters and gatherers, who may have arrived as early as 30,000 years ago. Some 4,000 years ago, Austronesian-speaking agriculturists joined their predecessors. The earliest date of known human habitation, provided by the radiocarbon dating of remains from Vatuluma Posovi Cave (excavated by David Roe) near the Poha River, Guadalcanal, is 1300-1000 B.C. Stone tools found here date from 4000 B.C. Due to the nature of the objects discovered and the absence of pottery (the 19th-century inhabitants of the island still had no pottery), it's believed that the occupants of this quite sizable cave were the direct ancestors of the present-day people of Guadalcanal. On the other hand, the many different languages currently spoken by the Melanesians illustrate a long period of mixed settlement.

Lapita pottery has been found in the Santa Cruz Islands, and New Britain obsidian was carried through the Solomons to Santa Cruz and New Caledonia some 3,000 years ago, probably by the first Polynesians. Today's Polynesian enclaves in the Solomons bear no relation to these original eastward migrations, however. Their forebears arrived in a back-migration within the last 1,500 years to Anuta, Tikopia, Bellona, and Rennell from Wallis and Futuna, and to Taumako (Duff Islands), Pileni (Reef Islands), Sikaiana, and Ontong Java from Tuvalu.

The Spanish Episode

There were three Spanish expeditions to Melanesia in the late 16th and early 17th centuries: two by Alvaro de Mendaña (in 1568 and 1595) to the Solomon Islands, and one in 1606 by Mendaña's pilot Pedro Fernandez de Quirós to Vanuatu. Incan legends told of a rich land 600 leagues west of Peru, so the eager conquistadors prepared an expedition to find the elusive El Dorado.

Mendaña set out from Peru in November 1567 and arrived on 7 February 1568 at Estrella Bay, Isabel Island, to become the first European to "discover" the Solomons. Mendaña established a base on Isabel, where his men built a small, five-ton, undecked vessel to explore reefs that would have destroyed a bigger, clumsier ship. At the beginning of March, a fleet of war canoes paddled near the Spanish ship, presenting Mendaña with a quarter of baked boy, nicely garnished with taro roots. Mendaña sailed his brigantine among the islands, giving them the Spanish names still used today.

In retaliation for violence and treachery initiated earlier on Guadalcanal by a subordinate commander, the islanders massacred nine members of a watering party sent out by Mendaña. The Spaniards then burned every village within reach, and when they departed, Guadalcanal was left in ashes and death. Mendaña left Makira for Peru on the morning of 17 August 1568.

He returned in 1595, stopping en route to discover and name the Marquesas Islands in Polynesia. This time Mendaña landed on Nendo, in the Santa Cruz Group, where he hoped to found a Spanish colony. For this reason a number of women accompanied the expedition, including Mendaña's ambitious wife, Doña Isabel Barreto, who hoped to be queen of the wealthy Solomon Islands. Yet Mendaña himself and many others soon died of malaria. The three surviving Spanish ships left for the Philippines, though one became separated and probably sank off San

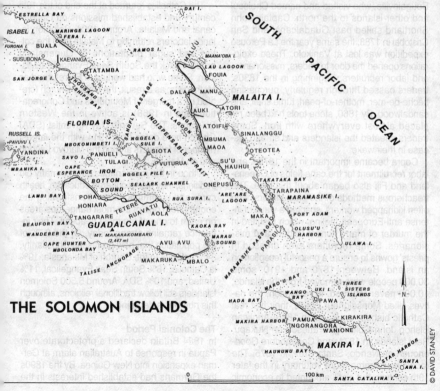

THE SOLOMON ISLANDS

© DAVID STANLEY

Cristobal (Makira). In 1606 Mendaña's pilot, Pedro Fernandez de Quirós, made another attempt at colonization on Espiritu Santo in Vanuatu before the Spanish gave up on the area.

Mendaña found no gold in the Solomons, but he gave the islands their exotic name, implying to his royal patrons that they were as rich as, or even the source of, King Solomon's treasure—an early example of a real estate salesman's trickery. The name soon appeared on maps and in formal reports, and was eventually adopted as official. Mendaña placed the Solomons far to the east of their actual location, and for the next 200 years they were lost to European explorers.

Recontact and Exploitation

In 1767, Captain Philip Carteret rediscovered Santa Cruz and Malaita, followed a year later by Bougainville, who visited and named Choiseul and other islands to the north. Captain John Shortland sailed past Guadalcanal and San Cristobal in 1788, the same year the La Pérouse expedition was lost at Vanikolo. These explorations opened the door to traders, missionaries, and labor recruiters. Beginning in the 1830s, traders passed through regularly, purchasing bêche-de-mer, mother-of-pearl, turtle shell, and sandalwood. By 1860, stone tools had been replaced almost everywhere with iron. Some traders cheated the islanders and spread disease in their wake.

Copra became important in the 1870s, and labor recruitment for the cane fields of Queensland and Fiji also began about this time. The treacherous methods of the blackbirders, who often kidnapped workers, sparked a wave of intense anti-European feeling, which resulted in the murder of many honest traders and missionaries. Some recruiters even dressed as priests' gowns to ensure a peaceful reception on an island. Between 1870 and 1910, some 30,000 people were removed from the islands; 10,000 never returned. In retaliation, the natives killed Monseigneur Epalle, their first real Catholic bishop, on Isabel in 1845; Anglican Bishop John Coleridge Patteson on Nukapu, Reef Islands, in 1871; and Commodore Goodenough on Nendo, Santa Cruz, in 1875. The recruiting became more voluntary in the later 19th century, but it still amounted to economic

slavery. This system died out in Queensland in 1904, when most blacks were expelled from Australia, and in Fiji in 1910.

The Missionaries

The earliest attempts to implant Christianity in the Solomons were by Catholics: first Mendaña in the 16th century, then the Society of Mary in the 1840s. Mendaña failed, and the Marists withdrew in 1848. A decade later, the Anglicans of New Zealand began to take an interest in the Solomons. Rather than sending white missionaries directly into the area, they used the more cautious technique of taking Solomon Islanders to a facility on Norfolk Island (between New Caledonia and New Zealand) for training. The Melanesian Mission of those days, covering both northern Vanuatu and the Solomons, has grown into today's Church of Melanesia (Anglican).

The Catholics returned at the end of the 19th century and established missions on Guadalcanal and Malaita. Around 1904, Solomon Islands laborers returning to Malaita from the cotton and sugar plantations of Queensland brought back the South Seas Evangelical Mission. Some who had worked in Fiji returned as Methodists; as a result, the United Church (created by a merger of Methodists and Congregationalists in 1968) is active in the Western Solomons. The Seventh-Day Adventist (SDA) Church here dates from 1914 with the largest number of followers around the Marovo Lagoon and on Malaita.

Although the missionaries effaced many old traditions, they also pioneered education, health care, and communications, transforming the country from one of the most dangerous areas on earth to one of the most peaceful. Their influence remains strong today. Of the 97% of the population that now professes Christianity, 34% belongs to the Church of Melanesia, 19% is Catholic, 18% South Seas Evangelical, 11% United, and 10% SDA. Around 5,500 Solomon Islanders still follow traditional religions, although this number is declining.

The Colonial Period

In 1884 Britain declared a protectorate over Papua in response to Australian alarm at German expansion into New Guinea. By the 1890s the Germans had established interests in the

The Pacific War

After Singapore fell in February 1942, the South Pacific was fully exposed to attack. Stung by the Doolittle raid on Tokyo in April, the Japanese moved south and occupied Tulagi, Florida Group, in May 1942. A Japanese invasion fleet sailed toward Port Moresby in Papua, but was turned back in the Battle of the Coral Sea. On 4 June another invasion fleet was stopped at the Battle of Midway, in which Japan lost four aircraft carriers.

In the Solomons, however, the war was just beginning, as the Japanese landed on Guadalcanal on 7 July. They quickly began constructing an air base on the site of today's Henderson Airport, from which they could strike at Australia and counter an American base already underway at Espiritu Santo, Vanuatu. A month later 10,000 U.S. Marines went ashore at Red Beach and quickly captured the partly completed airstrip and unarmed Korean construction workers, but the next day Japanese planes prevented U.S. transports from unloading supplies. That night, a Japanese task force of eight warships stole silently past a destroyer patrol near Savo Island and sent four Allied cruisers and two destroyers to the bottom of Iron Bottom Sound—one of the worst naval defeats ever suffered by the United States. These savage attacks forced Allied naval forces to withdraw.

The Japanese then began an intense campaign to push the 10,000 Marines into the sea. Supplies and troops were funneled down The Slot (a wide channel that divides the Solomons into two chains of islands) on the "Tokyo Express," and Japanese planes like "Washing Machine Charlie" and "Louie the Louse" bombed Guadalcanal from dusk to dawn. The Marines held out for six months against malaria, blood-curdling banzai charges, and bombardment by land and sea. By this time, however, American reinforcements and supplies were pouring in, so in February 1943, the Japanese secretly moved their 12,000 surviving troops to a newly built airfield on New Georgia, thereby shortening the communication distance to their headquarters in Rabaul. The Americans followed them to New Georgia in July, with major actions at Rendova and Munda, but a few diehard Japanese detachments held out on Choiseul and in the Shortlands until 1945.

Charles Woodford, a naturalist sent to the Solomons in 1885 to collect for the British Museum, created the first colonial administration almost singlehandedly.

North Solomons (Bougainville and Buka), so in 1893 the British also declared a protectorate over New Georgia, Guadalcanal, Makira, and Malaita to limit German advances, protect resident Europeans, and in response to pleas from missionaries, to control the labor trade.

In 1896 C.M. Woodford, the first resident commissioner, set up headquarters at Tulagi in the Florida Group, with orders to raise sufficient local revenue to cover his own expenses. The Santa Cruz Group, Rennell, and Bellona became part of the British Solomon Islands Protectorate in 1898 and 1899. In 1900 Germany ceded to Britain the Shortlands, Choiseul, Isabel, and Ontong Java in exchange for a free hand to annex Samoa.

The first decade of the 20th century saw the establishment of large coconut plantations by Levers (1905), Burns Philp (1906), and Fairymead (1909), as well as expansion of the missions, which retained full control of education. British control often didn't extend far beyond the coastal strip, and government officials seemed to appear in villages only to collect taxes and punish people. Life led a sleepy course until the Japanese seized the Solomons in 1942.

A B-17 bomber over the Solomons on 5 October 1942; in the background, smoke is rising from Gizo town.

NATIONAL ARCHIVES, WASHINGTON, D.C.

Guadalcanal is significant because it was the first U.S. victory against land-based Japanese forces during WW II.

Some 21,000 Japanese and 5,000 American soldiers were killed or wounded on Guadalcanal itself, plus many more in the surrounding sea and air. Official histories do not mention how many Solomon Islanders were killed. A Solomon Islands Defense Force was established in 1939, but at the time of the Japanese invasion it consisted of only seven Europeans, two Chinese, and 178 local police who were hurriedly evacuated from Tulagi. In December 1942 a Service Battalion was formed, with a base on Malaita where Solomon Islanders were trained to act as scouts for the U.S. Marines. The Americans called the battalion the "International Brigade," due to its mix of British, New Zealand, Fijian, and Solomons personnel, who only numbered a couple of hundred. The battalion was disbanded after the liberation of Guadalcanal in 1943.

In November 1942 the British Resident Commissioner formed the Solomon Islands Labor Corps, and by mid-1944 over 3,700 islanders were working for the Americans as porters, orderlies, and guides. Although the booklet *Among Those Present* published by the British Colonial Office in 1946 claimed that all were volunteers who were "reluctant to accept wages," the book *The Big Death,* published by the University of the South Pacific in 1988, contains testimonies from veterans who claimed they were pressed into service under dangerous conditions for low pay, that the British treated them as inferiors, and that gifts of food and clothing they had received from the Americans were confiscated and burned. Throughout the conflict villagers risked their lives to rescue downed airmen and seamen, and many American lives were saved, including that of President John F. Kennedy.

Also highly active was the coastwatching organization, which used radio transmitters to report on Japanese movements from behind enemy lines. Many of these coastwatchers were members of the British administration who knew the area well, but they were aided by militant churchmen, nuns, planters, mission nurses, and hundreds of loyal islanders.

The Aftermath
World War II left deep scars on the Solomons. The former capital, Tulagi, was devastated when the Americans recaptured it, so the returning British administration chose to establish a new capital at Honiara to take advantage of the infrastructure installed by the Americans during the war. A high percentage of the Solomons' roads and airstrips date from the war. Military dumps and scattered wreckage can still be found in the bush east of Henderson Airport, although time and souvenir-hunters are beginning to take their toll.

Perhaps the most unexpected outcome of the campaign was the rise of the Ma'asina Ruru (the Brotherhood) movement, dubbed "Marching Rule" by local expatriates. Thousands of islanders who'd been forced into the bush to avoid the fighting returned and found great American armies possessed of seemingly limitless wealth and power. This spectacle, coupled with dissatisfaction in a colonial system that treated natives like naughty children, gave birth to a widespread cargo cult on Malaita. Ma'asina Ruru attempted to reorganize society on the basis of "custom," but in 1948 the British administration decided that things were moving in an undesirable direction and used police to crush the movement. By 1949, some 2,000 islanders had been imprisoned for refusing to cooperate with the government.

This adversity united the Malaita people for the first time, and the British were forced to respond. The Malaita Council, formed as a compromise in 1953, was the beginning of the system of local government followed in the Solomons today. Unlike cargo cults in Vanuatu and New Guinea, little remains of the original "Marching Rule," although individual Americans are still popular. By 1964 the local government councils were handling all regional affairs. A nominated Legislative Council was created in 1960; some elected members were added in 1964. In 1974 this became an almost entirely elected Legislative Assembly. Internal self-government followed in 1976, and full independence on 7 July 1978. A 1977 ordinance converted all alienated land owned by foreigners into 75-year, fixed-term estates on lease from the government, a system which continues today.

In 1988 Solomon Islands joined Papua New Guinea and Vanuatu to form the Melanesian Spearhead Group to support the independence struggle in New Caledonia. In 1992, however, relations with P.N.G. worsened abruptly after incursions into the Shortlands by the P.N.G. Defense Force in pursuit of rebels from Bougainville Island. Solomon Islands accused Australia (which has huge mining interests on Bougainville) of backing P.N.G. and called on the United Nations to monitor its northwestern frontier. In April 1993 Solomon Islands sent additional field police to the area after two boatloads of P.N.G.

troops landed on Mono Island and exchanged fire with Solomons police. Both sides in the conflict have deployed patrol boats originally supplied by Australia for use in protecting their 200-mile fisheries zones. (For more information on this conflict, write Bougainville Freedom Movement, Box 134, Erskineville, NSW 2043, Australia.) In response to the crisis, Solomon Islands has created a new paramilitary force independent of its police. In typical third-world style, this force has been deployed mostly to protect Asian loggers against local villagers' resistance to their depredations.

Government

The head of state is an appointed governor-general who represents the British Crown. The 47-member National Parliament elects a prime minister from its ranks, while the 18-minister cabinet is chosen by the prime minister from among those members of parliament who supported him; opposition members routinely cross the floor after being tempted with ministerial appointments. Most members of parliament belong to one of several political parties based on personalities rather than issues; others are nominally independent and sell their votes to the highest bidder. There's a high turnover of members, and reelection possibilities usually depend on members procuring pork barrel allocations for their own ridings. This system means the most qualified people don't always get the top jobs, and it has led to uncontrolled deficit spending, almost bankrupting the country.

In 1981 seven provinces were created, each with an elected premier and provincial assembly. In 1991 Choiseul Province was separated from Western Province, and in 1993 Rennell and Bellona Province was created out of Central Province. Honiara is administered separately from Guadalcanal Province by the Honiara Town Council. Although many powers have been transferred from the national to the provincial governments, the latter are largely dependent on the former for financing. The provincial governments are supported by the head tax, a colonial levy originally intended to force the islanders to sell part of their produce or work for planters. Within each province are various area councils—each with a president—that deal with local or village matters. Not only is there an overabundance of elected officials, 32% of the total workforce is employed by the central government and another 5.6% by the provincial governments.

ECONOMY

The monetary economy is largely based on the exploitation of the country's rich natural resources by foreign corporations; expatriates control most business. Exports are reasonably diversified. Timber is the main export, followed by fish. Palm oil, cacao, and copra are a distant third, fourth, and fifth. Small quantities of shells and gold are also exported. Imports are primarily manufactured goods, fuels, and food. Australia profits greatly from trade with the Solomons, supplying 73% of its imports but taking less than six percent of its exports.

Solomon Islands has the weakest currency in the South Pacific, largely a result of the government's printing money to cover budget deficits. Between 1985 and 1993, the retail price index increased from 100 to 245.4, much higher than anywhere else (Tonga was second in the region with 172.7). In 1994 inflation was 12.8%. As the Solomon Islands dollar falls, pressure mounts from the growing foreign debt (US$157 million in 1993), dwindling reserves, and the large trade deficit.

The government itself owns a huge chunk of the economy through the Investment Corporation of Solomon Islands, a statutory authority under the Ministry of Finance and Economic Planning. The ICSI holds equity in Kolombangara Forest Products Ltd. (49%), Levers Solomons Ltd. (40%), Sasape Marina Ltd. (100%), Solomon Airlines (100%), Solomon Islands Plantations Ltd. (30%), Solomon Taiyo Ltd. (51%), and Solomon Telekom Ltd. (60%). Contrary to a stated official aim of privatization, several of the foreign partners in these enterprises, including Levers and Taiyo, have tried to sell their shares to the government. In 1995 the government's Commodities Export Marketing Authority took over Levers, which had announced it was technically bankrupt.

Solomon Islands receives about A$55 million in foreign aid a year, a low US$174 per capita (1990 figures). The main donors are Aus-

tralia, Japan, the Asian Development Bank, the European Union, and New Zealand, in that order. Most Japanese aid money is spent on infrastructure, such as bridges, airports, harbors, and roads to support Japanese business activities. Most American aid is spent on the construction of grandiose memorials to their own WW II victories.

As yet tourism has played only a small role in the economy, though government-financed airport improvements now allow the largest jets to land at Honiara. In 1990 the government founded Solomon Airlines, which made heavy losses trying to run a Boeing 737-400 on low-load east-west routes. In mid-1994 the airline was forced to swap this plane for a smaller Boeing 737-300 leased from Qantas, and service to Cairns was dropped. In 1991 Solomon Islands received only 11,105 tourists, a quarter the number that visited Vanuatu and only four percent as many as Fiji. A third of the tourists come from Australia, 14% from New Zealand, and less than 10% each from the U.S. and Japan. A surprisingly high percentage of the latter groups are WW II veterans, whereas many of the Australians and New Zealanders are scuba divers. Mass tourism is still undeveloped here, and there is strong local opposition to foreign hotel development outside Honiara. In December 1987 the Australian-owned Anuha Island Resort off the north side of Nggela Sule was burned down over a land dispute and no new resorts have appeared since.

Logging

Throughout the Solomons, some of the Pacific's last untouched rainforests are falling to the chainsaw in an irreparable exploitation by transnational timber companies that export raw logs to Japan (in 1991 only 10% of the exported wood was sawn timber, the rest was logs). Logging for export only began in 1961, but already about half the accessible lowland rainforest has been logged, and it's estimated that within eight years this resource will be totally depleted.

A recent United Nations report asserts that current logging licenses for three million cubic meters of logs a year are 11 times higher than the sustainable rate of 270,000 cubic meters a year. The report points out that reforestation will take 30-40 years in areas that have been carefully logged, or 45-200 years where environmental controls are disregarded (as is usually the case). Less than a tenth of the areas presently being logged are replanted, and the lack of reforestation has caused rapid erosion, fouling water supplies, and leaving the land infertile. Virtually all reforestation is with fast-growing exotic species.

In recent years the comparatively small South Pacific forests have attracted the attention of Malaysian corporations due to sharply increased prices for tropical hardwood on world markets caused by the phasing out of log exports from Sabah and Sarawak (Malaysia). In 1992 log production in Solomon Islands increased 80%, in 1993 another 20%, far beyond sustainable levels. There have been persistent allegations that government ministers, provincial premiers, civil servants, local officials, and village chiefs have been accepting bribes from the Asian logging companies to facilitate concessions and licenses. In July 1994 the managing director of Malaysia's Berjaya Group in Solomon Islands was deported after offering the government's forestry minister an envelope containing SI$10,000 in cash at an official meeting.

Local villagers have had to fight ongoing battles against these companies and their own government for control of their lands. If a tree brings in SI$500, SI$405 of it goes to the overseas company, SI$85 to the government, and only SI$10 to the landowner. The government is supposed to use almost half its share for reforestation, but it only replants its own land, not customary land. A sustainable alternative to this "robber economy" does exist in the form of portable or walkabout sawmills. Portable chainsaw milling by local people brings villagers 100 times the return of large-scale logging by foreign companies, and does far less harm to the environment. But with big royalties coming in, most government officials and international agencies are uninterested in options which bring in no royalties and few taxes.

The transnational Unilever pioneered logging on Gizo in 1963. By 1982 public patience had ended, and when Unilever began operations on New Georgia without local consent, outraged local residents attacked and destroyed the logging camp at Enoghae, causing SI$2 million in damages. In 1986, continuing local resistance forced Levers Pacific Timbers to wind up a quarter century of logging in Western Province; they lost SI$45 million when their equipment was auctioned off. In March 1994 eight bulldozers belonging to the Hong Kong logging company Golden Springs International were burned at Qerasi on New Georgia by customary landowners who claimed the company was not adhering to the conditions of their logging agreement.

In June 1993 Francis Billy Hilly replaced Solomon Mamaloni as prime minister, and an effort began to rein in the loggers. In July a ban was placed on the export of round logs with a declared value below market prices, followed in August 1994 by a moratorium on new logging licenses. Simultaneously the Australian government offered Solomon Islands A$2 million in aid on the condition that all logging leases for the proposed World Heritage Site in the Marovo Lagoon area be terminated. Hilly accepted at once and announced that the export of round logs was to be phased out by 1997. In October 1994 several members of parliament were enticed to cross over to the opposition, and the Hilly government lost its majority in parliament, bringing the pro-logger Mamaloni back into power. Hilly claimed that "external elements" had engineered his downfall because of his efforts to control the export of raw logs. One of Mamaloni's first acts was to cut the export duty on round logs 50%, and he has deployed paramilitary police to protect highly destructive Malaysian logging operations against resistance from local residents.

As the giant slow-growing native trees disappear, many rare endemic species of birds and butterflies face extinction due to the destruction of their habitat. Some companies routinely take food trees and protected species. Felled logs are often left to rot in the forest without being paid for—the aggressive Malaysian loggers use techniques that would never be permitted in Malaysia itself. Clearly, the Asian logging companies are the 20th-century equivalent of the 19th-century blackbirders, with the difference that trees instead of people are stolen. The current administration is squandering the country's natural resources for short-term political advantage.

Fishing

Commercial fishing is the Solomons' second-largest industry, with over SI$114 million worth of fish exported a year. In 1972, the Japanese firm Taiyo Fisheries and the government set up a jointly run cannery at Tulagi. In 1990, a second, much larger cannery opened at Noro, near Munda, with a current workforce of 550 women and 160 men. Taiyo has only reported a profit twice since 1972, allowing it to pay little or nothing in taxes. Taiyo freezes two-thirds of its tuna catch at Noro and ships it to Japan, Thailand, and Fiji for processing. Canned fish is exported to the European Union. The taking of bait fish from local reefs by Taiyo has reduced the subsistence catch of tuna by villagers.

Solomon Islanders employed by Taiyo are offered no chance for advancement into management due to "language barriers." The female cannery workers at Noro begin at 0600, with a break from 1130-1300, and their day can end anytime between 1830 and 2100, depending on the amount of fish available. They must work standing up and some claim they receive no overtime pay if they have to stay late, and that anyone who objects is fired. Most complain bitterly about the low pay, poor transportation, boring work, and deafening noise in the canning section. A 1993 report by Mari Sasabe to the Pacific Conference of Churches points out that most of the female workers at Noro are girls aged 16-20 who could not afford a secondary education. The report examines the social implications of a situation where most boys of the same age are unemployed and where the girls are willing to allow themselves to be exploited by the Japanese cannery management because the possibilities open to them in their home villages are even worse. The cannery operates seven days a week by employing Seventh-Day Adventist workers on Sunday.

In 1990 the government sold the country's second fishing fleet, National Fisheries Developments Ltd., to the Canadian company B.C. Packers, after NFD accumulated large debts. The Canadians have invested SI$5 million expanding the company's operation based at Tulagi. At the time of the sale, NFD owned 11 pole-and-line fishing boats and one purse seiner. In 1991 a Filipino company, Markirabelle, also began fishing operations in the Solomons from a base at Kirakira.

Solomons waters are among the richest tuna fishing grounds in the Western Pacific, and the Forum Fisheries Agency (FFA) is headquartered on a hill just east of Honiara. This body carries on the wartime tradition of coastwatching by attempting to police the 200-nautical-mile Exclusive Economic Zones of the 16 South Pacific Forum member states, and by negotiating licensing fees with overseas fishing interests. This task is not always easy.

In 1984, the U.S. purse seiner *Jeanette Diana* was caught poaching tuna deep inside the Solomons' 200-mile fisheries zone and ordered forfeit by a local court. The U.S. slapped an embargo on Solomons fish and threatened action against anyone purchasing the US$3.5 million ship and helicopter. In the end, the San Diego company that owned the ship paid a SI$72,000 fine and bought the ship back for SI$770,000, which the U.S. government reimbursed and deducted from their meager foreign aid to the Solomons—a good example of U.S. "fish imperialism."

The embargo cost Solomon Islands SI$10 million in lost sales to the U.S., and the resulting ill will is still simmering. For years the American Tunaboat Association resisted paying licensing fees to the Solomon Islands, secure in the knowledge that the U.S. government would back them up and bail them out should they

PACKED BY
SOLOMON TAIYO LTD.

Solomon Islands
Net Weight : 180gm
INGREDIENTS : skipjack tuna Flake
vegetable oil/salt added.

Solomon Blue BRAND

FRESH PACK

SKIPJACK BONITO WETEM OEL TAEM IU OPENEM TIN FINIS

ever be challenged, but in 1986 the U.S. finally agreed to pay the South Pacific nations for the right to fish in their waters. Since then there have been no problems. To date the Japanese government has consistently refused to sign a multilateral fishing agreement of this kind, preferring to use their economic muscle to twist a better deal out of the island governments one by one.

Mining

Since 1936, Solomon Islanders have collected alluvial gold by hand panning and sluicing along the Chovohio River at Guadalcanal's Gold Ridge. About 200 locals hold alluvial gold mining permits, selling around 30,000 grams of unrefined gold a year to 10 licensed traders. It's rumored that large quantities of gold are smuggled out of the country, creating a drain on the balance of payments and robbing customary landholders.

Several foreign companies have held tenders on a gold ore site at Gold Ridge, which is estimated to harbor reserves of 1.3 million metric tonnes valued at US$40 million, but as yet large-scale mining of the bedrock has not begun. In mid-1995 an Australian company, Saracen, announced that it hoped to be in production by 1997. Numerous foreign companies have held prospecting licenses in recent years, but unlike neighboring Papua New Guinea, where several mammoth mines exist, none have yet resulted in a producing mine. There are undeveloped bauxite deposits on Rennell and Vaghena, phosphates on Bellona, and nickel on San Jorge.

Plantations

Lever Brothers operates vast coconut plantations in the Russell Islands on tracts leased from the government as 75-year fixed-term estates, and in 1990 they opened a mill at Yandina to crush copra into coconut oil, the Solomons' first such mill. Village copra production still accounts for 75% of the country's total, however, and the government subsidizes this industry heavily to provide an income for rural inhabitants.

The palm oil plantations and modern oil mill on Guadalcanal are joint efforts of the government (which owns 40%), landowners (four percent), and the Commonwealth Development Corporation (56%). Most of the palm oil is exported to the European Union under preferential tariffs. In 1986 the rice industry on the plains of northern Guadalcanal was destroyed by Hurricane Namu, but after rehabilitation the Solomons began exporting rice again in 1990.

Social Issues

Some 84% of the population relies on subsistence agriculture. In 1990 only 26,000 people were in paid employment, and of this group (just eight percent of the total population), only 17% were women. Another 12,000 people work part-time. A third of all jobs are in the public sector, and almost 60% of all paid employment is found in and around Honiara. Some 65% of children between the ages of five and 19 are not attending school, the highest such proportion in the South Pacific (excluding Papua New Guinea, where it's 67%).

Some 6,000 young people leave school each year, but less than 10% find work, and the gap between the haves and have-nots is increasing. Many young men hang on in Honiara for years as *liu,* a word that means "wanderer" but that we would translate as "unemployed." In November 1989, ethnic strife hit Honiara, as 5,000 *masta liu* from Malaita rioted after a perceived insult by Polynesians from Rennell and Bellona, though the root cause of the riot was seen as a feeling of powerlessness by this underclass. Peace was restored when the government agreed to pay SI$200,000 compensation money to the Malaitans.

The influx of village people to Honiara has strained the traditional custom of providing hospitality to visiting relatives. Squatter settlements have sprung up on the ridges behind Honiara, and some of the suburbs are now dangerous after dark. The area between the market and Chinatown is potentially dangerous after dark. Alcoholism and crime, though still modest compared to Papua New Guinea, are growing problems, and one need only look at the "rascal" situation in Port Moresby to appreciate the threat.

Alternative Development Agendas

The most active nongovernment organization bringing villagers into the mainstream of the development process is the **Solomon Islands Development Trust** (SIDT). Since 1984, the SIDT's outreach program has sent mobile teams to hundreds of remote village groups to conduct workshops on natural resources, forestry, minerals, water supplies, health, and bait fish. Team members teach the villagers how to understand and prepare for disasters, both natural and man-made, while also covering themes such as balanced cash cropping, sanitation, and family planning.

SIDT teams have stymied rainforest destruction on some islands while assisting with the reforestation of customary land on others. The SIDT theater group SEI! enhances villagers' awareness by acting out environmental and nutrition skits for village audiences. A women's section stresses issues of particular interest to their village sisters. The programs center on improving village life as a way of beginning and sustaining grassroots development.

Most of the SIDT's funding comes from church or development groups abroad, plus the governments of Australia, Canada, New Zealand, and the U.K. The SIDT's magazine, Link, published six times a year, carries fascinating articles on subjects like gold mining, tourism, education, and youth, all seen from an authentic indigenous point of view. For an airmail subscription, send US$10 in cash to Solomon Islands Development Trust, Box 147, Honiara. In Honiara, pick up a copy for SI$1 at ACOR Stationer next to Solomon Airlines in the center of town, or at their office (tel. 21130) in New Chinatown (see the Honiara map).

THE PEOPLE

About 94% of the Solomon's 325,000 people are Melanesians. These islanders have an astounding variety of complexions—ranging from light tan to blue-black. Generally, the darker groups live in the west and north, the lighter in the southeast. Their features can be prognathous and heavy, or delicate and fine-boned. Bushy blond hair is often seen with chocolate-colored skin, especially on Malaita.

Another four percent of the population consists of Polynesians living on Rennell, Bellona, Sikaiana, Ontong Java, Anuta, and Tikopia— the so-called "Polynesian Fringe." To add to the variety, thousands of Micronesian Gilbertese were resettled near Honiara and Gizo in the early 1950s, where small European and Chi-

nese communities are also found. Solomon Islands is the only country in the world that has managed to recognize both Chinas, and the number of Chinese residents is growing. Chinese businessmen are said to own 85% of the prime real estate around Honiara.

Village Life

Eight out of 10 Solomon Islanders live on shifting, subsistence agriculture in small rural villages, operating much as they did before the white man arrived. Most villages are near the shore, so fresh fish play an important role in the diet, supplemented by wild pigs hunted with dogs and spears, plus the occasional chicken. On Malaita many people live in the interior and keep small herds of cattle for food. Everywhere native vegetables, including taro, yams, sweet potato, and cassava, are grown in small individual plots and provide the bulk of the diet.

The basic social unit is the extended family or clan, which may consist of about 200 "wantoks." Some clan members can recite a genealogy of ancestors going back 10 generations. Villagers work collectively on community projects, and

FIELD MUSEUM OF NATURAL HISTORY, CHICAGO

Australian photographer J. W. Beattie took this photo of a man of the Florida Islands in 1913.

there's much sharing among clans, yet individuals keep their own gardens and can readily tell you what land they own. Land may be passed on by the mother or father, depending on local custom. Customary land accounts for 87% of the Solomons, another nine percent is owned by the government, and the rest by individual Solomon Islanders. About two percent is leased to foreigners, though only people born in the Solomons may own land. Disputes over land and boundaries are common. In a 1994 issue, *Solomons Magazine* quoted Catholic aid worker Dr. John Roughan thus:

When I first got there, I thought the people were poor. In cash terms, they probably were. But when I asked "who owns that mountain over there?" they answered, "Mifela." "And who owns that one way over there?" "Oh, mifela, too." That broadened my horizons on the concept of wealth.

The achievements of individuals are evaluated by their value to the community as a whole, and a villager who shows too much initiative or ability in his own affairs is more likely to inspire jealousy and resentment rather than admiration. Social status among the Melanesians is based on land ownership, but an individual can also increase his standing in the community by displaying his wealth at a ritual feast. A successful feast-giver becomes a "big man" in this way—descent is less important. (In Polynesia chiefs are hereditary.) Throughout the Solomons, custom, or *kastom*, is used to justify any number of differing traditional social orders.

Education is neither compulsory nor free, and nearly half the population has no formal education whatever. Around 85% of Solomon Islanders are illiterate. There's strong opposition to family planning, and the birthrate is 3.7%. Each Solomon Islands woman has an average of 5.3 children, the highest fertility rate in the South Pacific. Some 45% of the inhabitants are under the age of 15, and the population doubles every 20 years.

Language
Approximately 65 distinct indigenous languages are presently in use in the Solomons, the most

widely spoken of which are Kwara'ae (25,000 speakers on Malaita), Lau (10,000 speakers on Malaita), Roviana (9,000 speakers around New Georgia), and Cheke Holo (8,000 speakers on Isabel). Most of these derive from the same parent tongue, Austronesian, and all of the Polynesian languages are also Austronesian. Smaller groups speaking 11 Papuan languages are scattered throughout the Solomons and are perhaps remnants of an earlier population largely replaced or absorbed by the Austronesians. The most-used Papuan language is Bilua (6,000 speakers on Vella Lavella).

Today, most Solomon Islanders understand Pijin, and it has become the everyday tongue of tens of thousands of outer islanders living in the Honiara melting pot. Pijin takes its vocabulary largely from English, though the grammar is Melanesian. Pijin was introduced by sandalwood traders in the early 19th century ("pijin" is the Chinese pronunciation of "business"). Today it's used mainly as a contact language between tribes.

Although the vocabulary may be limited, there's a richness and freshness to the grammatical constructions which always delights newcomers. Pijin has only two prepositions, *bilong*, which shows possession, and *long*, which covers all other prepositions. Solomon Islands Pijin varies considerably from the pidgins of New Guinea or Vanuatu. Trying to communicate in Pijin will add enjoyment to your visit.

CONDUCT AND CUSTOMS

Conduct
Though it's okay to walk through a village along a road, ask permission of whoever's there before leaving the road. All lagoon waters are considered village property, and permission must be obtained before fishing or sometimes even snorkeling. Some Solomon Islanders resent being "exploited" by tourists who earn big money selling their snapshots to magazines, so ask before you shoot.

Keep your body well covered if you want to be treated with respect. Women should take care when visiting isolated areas or hiking alone in the Solomons, as cases of physical and sexual abuse by aggressive local males have been reported. Local women are subject to myriad taboos, and foreign women visiting remote villages should always ask if it's allowed to do certain things, such as sitting in a place reserved for men.

Custom Fees

From time to time you'll encounter a situation whereby people ask you to pay money to visit an archaeological site, to see natural phenomena such as a hot spring or cave, or to enter a traditional village visited regularly by tourists. Often local villagers will paddle out to a yacht as soon as the anchor goes down and demand a fee to use their reef, even a reef far offshore. The way the villagers look at it, these things belong to them, so how can wealthy outsiders expect to be able to use them for nothing?

They may start off by asking a ridiculously high amount (SI$20 pp), but will usually (though not always) come down after negotiations. The operators of the live-aboard dive boats pay SI$3 pp to dive on village reefs, and SI$80 per group to visit the villages themselves. All custom fees we know about are mentioned in this book. Have small bills with you, and try to avoid paying more than SI$5 pp. Please help out by sending us precise details of other custom fees you encounter, so we can mention them herein, giving future visitors the opportunity to decide in advance whether it's still worth the trouble and expense to go to a certain place. Reader Robert Kennington (who is married to a Malaitan) sent us this:

The attitude of some people on Malaita is unfortunate because as soon as they see foreigners, they're out to get what they can by deceit. Everywhere we went on Malaita we were met somewhere along the way by at least one individual who would subsequently say that he was the landowner, etc., and that we were trespassing and therefore had to pay compensation. Each of these individuals was lying, and after a big show they always went away empty handed. In each case we had gone through the right channels first, and we always had one of the customary owners along with us. It just goes to show that on major expeditions into remote areas it's essential to have someone with you who knows the area and the people. Patience is also important.

Actually, the custom fees are not only aimed at tourists: villagers short of cash regularly demand "compensation" from each other for offenses such as speaking to a girl, walking under a clothesline, etc. Anyone unfortunate enough to have such a claim made against them should tread very lightly indeed.

sasalapa (Annona muricata)

ON THE ROAD

Highlights

Solomon Islands has many highlights, the most accessible of which are the war remains around Henderson Airport, the snorkeling or scuba diving on the two Bonegi wrecks northwest of Honiara, and the panpipe players who perform regularly at Honiara hotels. Another great experience is the boat trip from Honiara to Gizo, passing many romantic outer islands. Gizo itself is a delightful little town with adequate facilities, and the *Toa Maru*, which the American scuba newsletter *In Depth* calls "one of the top five wreck dives in the world." Once you've "done" these sights, you'll be ready for some real exploring.

Sports and Recreation

The biggest organized sport here is definitely scuba diving, with two professional dive shops in Honiara, two more in Gizo, and yet another in Munda. One of the Honiara shops has a branch at the Tambea Holiday Beach Resort; in Western Province, the Uepi Island Resort on the Marovo Lagoon caters almost exclusively to scuba divers. The Solomon's top diving facilities, however, are the live-aboard dive boats described in the "Transportation" section, which follows. When diving, keep in mind that the nearest recompression chamber is in Townsville, Australia, and emergency air evacuation will cost A$30,000.

Golfers have at their disposal a flat nine-hole course outside Honiara. It's a friendly, inexpensive course worth trying if you happen to be there, but at last report no club rentals were available.

There are unlimited possibilities for hikers in the Solomons. Good day hikes are from Honiara to Mataniko Falls, Auki to Riba Cave, and Gizo to Titiana. Several strenuous long-distance hikes exist on Guadalcanal, including the three-day trek across the island via Gold Ridge. A guide is required on these. The really adventurous hiker will find many hiking areas that seldom see a white face on outer islands such as Malaita, Isabel, and Makira.

Anglers are well catered for at the Zipolo Habu Resort on Lola Island near Munda. The resort boat is available from trolling in the lagoon or open sea at SI$50 an hour plus fuel (shared between two anglers), or SI$25 an hour for bottom fishing. Rods, reels, and lures are provided. Some of the Pacific's best fishing is in and around the Vonavona Lagoon, and manager Joe Entrikin is one of the Solomon's top fishermen.

The most popular spectator sports here are rugby and soccer, with baseball and volleyball also seen.

Music

The traditional music of the Solomons varies greatly between the different cultural regions. One of the most interesting instruments is the bundle panpipe, a bundle of about a dozen tubes of different sizes open at both ends or closed at the lower end. The open-ended panpipes sound an octave higher than the closed variety, thus the closed pipes are longer. The player moves his head to blow the different tubes—the bundle itself remains stationary. The panpipe players stand or sit in two rows facing one another while whistles or bamboo trumpets produce a continuous background drone. The songs often imitate sounds of nature, such as the calls of birds, and are related to the spirit world. The panpipe ensembles play at funeral cycles, which can last up to eight years, or at important public events. The most famous contemporary panpipe bands are from Malaita.

A distant relative of these is the characteristic bamboo bands of the Western Solomons, invented here in the 1920s. Some 15 to 24 horizontal pieces of bamboo of varying length are struck on their open ends with rubber thongs, to the accompaniment of guitar and ukulele. As yet little known to the world of music, bamboo rhythms will win you at once.

Vocal choirs often sing while sitting in two rows, each person shaking a hand-held rattle-stick. Men's narrative songs may be accompanied by clapping sticks. Both the instrumental and vocal music of the Solomons is polyphonic (made up of several independent but harmonious melodic parts).

A listing of a few compact discs of authentic Solomon Islands music is provided in the "Resources" section at the end of this book.

Public Holidays

National holidays include New Year's Day (1 January), Good Friday, Easter Monday (March/April), Whitmonday (May/June), the Queen's Birthday (the Friday closest to 14 June), Independence Day (7 July), and Christmas Days (25 and 26 December).

In addition, there are provincial holidays: Temotu (8 June), Central (29 June), Isabel (8 July), Guadalcanal (1 August), Makira (3 August), Malaita (15 August), and Western (7 December). These dates can vary a day or two either way. The Church of Melanesia prohibits all custom dancing during the 40 days before Easter (March/April).

Arts and Crafts

All traditional handicrafts are either ceremonial or functional. The woodcrafts generally range from small domestic items such as combs and bowls, through a variety of figures and heads to objects as large as whole canoes, complete with decorated hulls and figureheads. Nontraditional carvings of fish, birds, or humans, although often good, are made solely to sell to visitors. Some traditional items, such as war clubs, masks, and *nguzunguzu,* are now made in miniature to increase their desirability to tourists.

The fantastic cultural diversity of this country is reflected in its artwork. The most distinctive local carving is the *nguzunguzu* (pronounced "noozoo noozoo") of Western Province, depicted herein. The carved sharks and dolphins of the same area are made to European taste but are of exceptional workmanship. The shark is a popular figure because it's believed that the soul of a successful fisherman is reincarnated in a shark. Carving in the west is done in brown-streaked kerosene wood *(Corsia subcordata)* or black ebony, both hardwoods, which may be inlaid with nautilus shell or mother-of-pearl.

Another excellent purchase is the shell money of Malaita, made into beautiful necklaces. Handicrafts from Malaita are often useful items like combs, bamboo lime containers (for use with betelnut), rattles, flutes, panpipes, and fiber carrying bags. Watch too for traditional jewelry, such as headbands, earrings, nose and ear plugs, pendants, breastplates, and armbands, mostly made from shell. Bone and shell fishhooks make authentic souvenirs.

Guadalcanal people excel in weaving strong, sturdy bags, baskets, and trays from the *asa* vine *(Lygodium circinnatum).* These items are known collectively as Bukaware. The Polynesians of the Solomons make fine miniature canoes. The small woven pandanus bags of Bellona are commonly used by the people. Santa Ana and Santa Catalina in Makira Province are other sources of quality handicrafts, especially the striking black ceremonial pudding bowls inlaid with shell.

Solomon Islands handicrafts are of high quality. Bargaining is not prac-

NGUZUNGUZU

Figureheads such as the one pictured here were once attached to the prow of war canoes, just above the waterline, as they set out from the Western Solomons on headhunting expeditions. Depending on the type of expedition, the doglike spirit would have beneath its chin either two clenched fists (war) a head (headhunting), or a dove (peace). The mother-of-pearl shell inlay work is characteristic. A *nguzunguzu,* such as those sold at craft outlets in Honiara, makes an excellent souvenir.

ticed, but if you feel the cost is too high, hesitate a few moments, then ask the seller if he has a second price. Consider, however, the amount of time that went into making the object. Outside Honiara you can often trade cassettes, radios, watches, women's clothing, jeans, and sunglasses for handicrafts. The superb Melanesian-style decoration in some of the churches (especially Catholic) is worth noting. Remember that any handicrafts incorporating the body parts of sea turtles or marine mammals (e.g., dolphin or whale teeth) cannot be taken into the U.S., Australia, and many other countries.

ACCOMMODATIONS AND FOOD

The only large hotels are in Honiara, the capital. There are tourist lodges at Auki, Malu'u, Munda, and Gizo, cottages at Marau Sound and on Pigeon Island (Reef Islands), and beach resorts at Tambea, Vulelua (both near Honiara), Munda, and Uepi Island (Marovo Lagoon). Government rest houses (SI$15-20 pp) are found at Tulagi, Buala, Kirakira, and elsewhere, and these always have cooking facilities. A 10% hotel tax is charged, and most room prices quoted in this book are without tax. Only the main hotels in Honiara and Gizo accept credit cards—everywhere else you must pay cash. Some hotels and dive shops in the Solomons quote rates in Australian dollars to make them look lower.

Camping is still rare in the Solomons and should only be done in remote areas. Before pitching your tent, get permission from the customary landowner, often the village chief. This is almost invariably granted, although you'll probably first be asked to stay with them. If you insist on camping beside someone's house, it may appear that you consider their home unworthy of your presence. If you accept their hospitality, be it inside or outside the house, it's proper to reciprocate with gifts such as stick tobacco and matches, plastic bags of Spear coarse-cut tobacco, small kitchen knives, etc. Corned beef, tea, and sugar are also appreciated by village hosts and are a nice way of saying "thank you" for hospitality received.

Villagers often have little idea of the value of money and will expect large sums if you offer cash, so it's best to stick to gifts. Note, however,

that followers of the South Sea Evangelical Mission and Seventh-Day Adventists don't smoke, chew betel or tobacco, or drink alcohol, so be prudent with your gifts. Note too that stepping over a sitting or sleeping person is considered a serious insult.

You'll be given food in most villages you visit—including some you hadn't intended to eat in! Most coastal villages have small trade stores, so there's little need to carry much food with you unless you go "big bush" (inland). If you plan to stop on any isolated island for a period of time, be sure to take plenty of food with you, so as not to become a burden. Don't overstay your welcome.

SERVICES AND INFORMATION

Visas and Officialdom
Everyone needs a passport and an onward ticket. Commonwealth citizens, Americans, and most Western European nationals are given a passport stamp upon arrival allowing a stay up to the flight date on their plane ticket, to three months maximum. Almost everyone with a confirmed onward reservation within seven days is eligible for a transit visa upon arrival.

Extensions of stay (SI$25) for a further three months, to a total of six months maximum in any 12-month period, can be had at the Immigration Office (fax 22964) in Honiara. You must bring along your air ticket with a confirmed reservation; the extension will be to the date of your flight out. Don't bother claiming that you're doing some sort of research as a way of getting more time; this requires prior clearance and will only raise questions.

Permanent immigration to the Solomons is very difficult. If you marry a Solomon Islander you must apply for a permit to stay two years, after which it may be possible to obtain permanent residence. Citizenship is possible after 10 years, and you must renounce your former citizenship. To obtain a work permit, you must apply from outside the country, enclosing a letter from your prospective employer. All immigration regulations are strictly enforced, and a cooperative attitude on your part is essential.

There are regular immigration offices at Gizo, Honiara, Korovou, Lata (Graciosa Bay), and

Munda. In addition, cruising yachts can check in with customs at Tulagi and Yandina, provided they reach Honiara or Munda within two weeks. It's possible to check out from any of these ports. All visiting yachts must pay a SI$100 lighthouse fee (despite this fee, many navigational lights are out of order—beware). If your boat will be entering through an obscure port, try to bring some Solomon Islands currency with you, or be prepared for customs officials and locals who insist that American, Australian, and Solomon Islands dollars are all worth the same!

Money

The Solomon Islands dollar (SI$) is linked to a trade-related basket of currencies, and the rate is adjusted daily. Before independence in 1978 the Australian dollar was the currency used in Solomon Islands and the SI$ was originally introduced at a rate of one to one. Since then it has depreciated to about A$1 = SI$2.50, or US$1 = SI$2.99. There are banknotes of two, five, 10, 20, and 50 dollars, and coins of one, two, five, 10, 20, and 50 cents, plus a seven-sided SI$1 coin depicting a *nguzunguzu,* which makes an excellent souvenir.

Banking hours in Honiara are weekdays 0830-1500. Otherwise you can change money at the Mendaña Hotel at a 10% lower rate. The National Bank, Westpac Bank, and ANZ Bank have branches where traveler's checks may be changed in Auki, Gizo, Kirakira, Munda, and Noro. Elsewhere, you must have enough local currency to tide you over as the minor National Bank agencies don't handle foreign currency. None of the banks charge commission to change traveler's checks but the Westpac and ANZ banks generally give a better rate than the

National Bank (which is 51% owned by the Bank of Hawaii).

If you don't like carrying a lot of cash around with you, consider opening a SI$ passbook account at the National Bank, which will allow you to withdraw money at any of their 40 outer-island agencies, usually at post offices.

Before leaving, be sure to change all your leftover Solomon Islands dollars into the currency of the next country on your itinerary, as SI$ are hard to convert outside the country. It's prohibited to export over SI$250 in Solomon Islands banknotes in cash. Credit cards are accepted only in Honiara and Gizo, and the use of them can be expensive since the amount will first be converted into Australian dollars, then into your own currency. Obtaining cash advances is also expensive for the same reason, plus you'll have to pay interest. American Express is not represented. Sales tax rates are 10% on restaurant meals or hotel rooms, five percent on car rentals or professional services, and two and a half percent on telephone calls. There's no tipping.

Telecommunications

Operator-assisted calls are not available in Honiara, so to make a long-distance call you must purchase a telephone card, sold in denominations of SI$10, SI$20, and SI$50, plus two and a half percent tax. The cards are good for both domestic and international calls and can be used at card phones all around the Solomons. (According to one reader, Solomon Islands telephone cards are compatible with card telephones in New Zealand, so don't throw away an unfinished Solomons card if you're flying down to Auckland! This could change.)

The cost of calls per minute (using a card) is SI$1.68 to Auki or Gizo, SI$4.68 to Australia, SI$4.94 to Fiji or New Zealand, SI$5.99 to Vanuatu and most other South Pacific countries, and SI$9.58 to North America and Europe. International calls are charged in segments of one minute. Domestic direct-dial calls are much cheaper weekdays 1800-0800 and all day weekends and holidays. Internationally, cheaper rates are in effect after 1800 Saturday and all day Sunday.

The international access code for overseas calls is 00. To get the operator, dial 100/102 domestic/overseas. The information number is 101/112 domestic/overseas.

You can send or receive faxes via "public fax" at Solomon Telekom offices throughout the country. These offices will also deliver faxes to post office boxes or individuals within their local areas, so it's a good way to make contact if the numbers provided herein prove inadequate: Auki (fax 40220), Buala (fax 35056), Gizo (fax 60128), Honiara (fax 23110), Kirakira (fax 50145), Lata (fax 53036), Munda (fax 61150), Noro (fax 61075), Tulagi (fax 32180), Yandina (fax 21292). All of these places except Noro also have post offices.

Solomon Islands' telephone code is 677.

Media

The Solomon Islands Broadcasting Corporation (Box 654, Honiara; tel. 20051) transmits on MW 1035kz, 0600-2300 daily. They broadcast the Radio Australia news at 0800 and 1000, and the BBC World Service news at 1700. There's no local television as yet.

Among the local newspapers are the *Solomon Star* (Box 255, Honiara; tel. 22062, fax 21572), which appears on Wednesday and Friday; the *Solomon Voice* (Box 1235, Honiara; tel. 20116, fax 20090), published every Wednesday; the *Solomon Times* (Box 212, Honiara; tel. 25120), published every two or three weeks; and the Government Information Service's *Solomon Nius* (Box 718, Honiara; tel. 21300, fax 20401), published monthly. The *Solomon Star* is far and away the more independent and newsy of the four.

The Solomon Islands Development Trust's magazine *Link* (Box 147, Honiara; tel. 21130) is published every other month.

Solomon Airlines has an interesting in-flight magazine called *Solomons,* to which you can subscribe by sending US$30 to Box 23, Honiara.

Information

The **Solomon Islands Tourist Authority** (Box 321, Honiara; tel. 22442, fax 23986) puts out a number of useful brochures on the country.

Solomon Airlines offices and agents on the outer islands are good sources of information about accommodations, transport, diving, etc., in their area.

HEALTH

A yellow fever vaccination is required if you've been exploring the jungles of Africa or South America within the previous six days, otherwise there are no requirements. Suggested (but not obligatory) vaccinations include the hepatitis A vaccine or immune globulin, typhoid fever, tetanus, and cholera.

All tap water should be boiled before drinking. Take along insect repellent, sunscreen, and something to treat cuts. Even the smallest coral scratch can turn septic in no time at all if left untreated. There were 602 confirmed cases of sexually transmitted diseases in Honiara in 1990 (one reader recommended steering well clear of any person wearing makeup).

Malaria

Half of all cases of malaria reported in the Solomons are on Guadalcanal, with Malaita and Central Province also heavily affected. It's found everywhere in the country below 400 meters altitude, including Honiara, and the rainy season is the worst time. A full-scale eradication program began in 1970, with DDT house spraying, case detection, and treatment, and by 1975 malaria seemed to be on the way out. As a result, funding was cut, and from 1977 to 1983, the number of cases treated in the Solomons increased from 10,496 to 84,527 (a third of the population). In 1990 there were 86,820 cases, a third more were reported than in 1989 (in part due to better record keeping).

Today health officials no longer talk of eradication, only control, primarily by encouraging villagers to sleep under mosquito nets, cleaning up stagnant waters where mosquitoes breed, and introducing fish that eat the eggs. In this way it's hoped that the present rate of 350 cases per 1,000 inhabitants will be reduced to 30 per 1,000 by the end of the decade. Unbelievably, spraying is no longer considered effective because studies have shown that the mosquitoes learned not to land on sprayed areas! In any case, subsidizing net distribution is much cheaper than spraying and does no damage to the environment.

Malaria is a blood disease involving a parasite called *Plasmodium* that destroys red blood cells. A mosquito sucks in blood from a person or animal with malaria, then injects it into the next individual it bites. This is the only way malaria can be transmitted. The parasites multiply in the liver and only cause symptoms when they are periodically released back into the bloodstream, which is why bouts of malaria come and go. Symptoms begin 10 days to one year after the bite.

Avoid being bitten by wearing long pants and a long-sleeved shirt from dusk to dawn, using a good insect repellent, burning a mosquito coil at night, and sleeping under a mosquito net (check for gaps—mosquitoes are attracted by the carbon dioxide you exhale and will search for hours for an opening). Dark clothing, perfume, and aftershave lotion attract mosquitoes.

The two nocturnal malarial mosquitoes found in the Solomons, *Anopheles farauti* and *Anopheles punctulatus*, both rest outdoors, so by sleeping in screened quarters you're partly protected. The first feeds in- and outdoors at night or during overcast days, while the second feeds only outdoors. The prime biting time is 1800-1900, and 90% of bites are on the ankles.

Since 1980, chloroquine-resistant *Plasmodium falciparum* malaria has established itself in the Solomons and now accounts for 66% of cases. Fansidar and Maloprim are effective against this, though many doctors hesitate to prescribe them—there have been severe skin reactions and even fatalities following multiple doses of Fansidar in combination with chloroquine. Fansidar and Maloprim must not be taken by pregnant women or anyone allergic to sulpha drugs. Though chloroquine (sold under various brand names, including Nivaquine and Avloclor) may not prevent a *falciparum* malaria breakthrough, it will lessen the severity of an infection and prevent fatal malaria.

The U.S. Peace Corps in the Solomons instructs its volunteers to take two 100-mg Paludrine tablets a day, plus chloroquine twice a week. (The Paludrine kills parasites in the liver while chloroquine catches them in the bloodstream.) It's also useful to carry a presumptive

three-tablet treatment dose of Fansidar to be taken at the first signs of malaria (general malaise, headache, chills, and fever). Start taking 300 mg of chloroquine a week (after a meal) a week before you arrive, and more importantly, continue four weeks after you leave. The Pharmacy (tel. 22911) in central Honiara sells malaria pills across the counter without prescription at prices far lower than those charged in Australia or the States, and Maloprim seems to be the drug of choice (one Maloprim and two chloroquine tablets a week). Maloprim is not available in North America.

If you develop a fever, get a blood test as soon as possible. Later, if you become sick in another country (even *months* later), don't forget to tell the doctor you've been in the Solomons, because doctors often misdiagnose the symptoms as flu. Always assume it's malaria until the blood test proves otherwise. See "Health" in the main introduction to this book for more information. Don't let this situation prevent you from visiting the Solomons, but do take the precautions.

TRANSPORTATION

Getting There

The national carrier, **Solomon Airlines** (Box 23, Honiara; tel. 20031, fax 23992) flies its Boeing 737 to Honiara twice a week from Brisbane, Port Moresby, and Port Vila, and weekly from Auckland and Nandi. To avoid waste, several of these flights are joint services with Air Pacific, Air Niugini, and Qantas. In Brisbane, there are immediate connections to/from Melbourne and Sydney. To reach Honiara from Hong Kong or Singapore you'll probably transit Port Moresby. From North America, the easiest way to get there is via Fiji. From Europe, you have a choice of Fiji or Australia.

Air Pacific's nonstop Los Angeles-Nandi flight connects in Fiji for Honiara (two-night layover). Air New Zealand offers Los Angeles-Nandi-Honiara-Los Angeles for US$1228/1328/1528 low/shoulder/high season provided you begin on a Monday, Tuesday, or Wednesday (other days US$60 more). The low season is April to August. You must purchase the ticket 14 days in advance, pay US$75 to change flight dates, and pay a 35% cancellation penalty.

Solomon Airlines offers a 30-day Discover Pacific Pass, which allows you to fly Nandi-Honiara-Port Vila-Nandi for US$499. Similarly, **Air Pacific** (tel. 20516) has a Pacific Air Pass, which allows unlimited travel between Fiji, Vanuatu, Solomon Islands, Western Samoa, and Tonga during 30 days for US$599. This is good value, as the regular 28-day excursion fare from Nandi to Honiara is F$1015 (about US$700). Both of the above passes can only be purchased in North America or Europe, and full details are provided in this book's main introduction.

Air Nauru (tel. 22586) flies between Honiara and Nauru (A$183 one-way) weekly, with connections there for Tarawa, Fiji, Micronesia, and other points. Air Nauru's fare structure is lower than that of Solomon Airlines, so compare. See the main introduction for details.

Getting Around by Air

The government-owned **Solomon Airlines** (Box 23, Honiara; tel. 20031, fax 23992) offers convenient, punctual domestic air service, with more than 600 scheduled flights a month linking 23 airstrips in the Solomons. Their 20-passenger Twin Otters and 10-passenger Britten-Norman Islanders are fun to fly in. Island-hopping routes such as Honiara-Seghe-Munda-Gizo, Gizo-Ballalae-Choiseul-Gizo, Honiara-Bellona-Rennell-Honiara, and Honiara-Kirakira-Santa Cruz allow you see a number of islands without backtracking. They don't allow stopovers on through tickets, however, so you'll have to pay for each sector separately. The baggage allowance is 16 kilos on domestic flights, 20 kilos on international.

From Honiara there are flights to Auki (SI$83), Avu Avu (SI$60), Ballalae (SI$321), Bellona (SI$140), Choiseul Bay (SI$319), Fera/Buala (SI$111), Gizo (SI$236), Kirakira (SI$154), Marau (SI$79), Mbambanakira (SI$48), Mono (SI$326), Munda (SI$207), Parasi (SI$110), Rennell (SI$154), Ringi Cove (SI$221), Santa Ana (SI$197), Santa Cruz (SI$389), Seghe (SI$167), and Yandina (SI$79). These are the one-way fares, and a regular roundtrip is double.

Special 14- to 30-day excursion fares are about 30% lower. There's a 20% discount on domestic flights if you have an international ticket on Solomon Airlines. All domestic flights are heavily booked—reserve as far in advance as possible. Because airfares are relatively low, flights from Honiara to Munda and Gizo are often full, and it can be hard to organize a visit if you're staying two weeks or less in the Solomons. Thus you might consider booking from abroad in conjunction with your international ticket. On the brighter side, the service is fairly reliable and the flights are only canceled if a major hurricane is blowing.

North Americans and Europeans can purchase the Discover Solomon Pass, which allows four domestic flights within any 30-day period for US$199. This must be purchased prior to arrival, through Solomon Airlines offices in either Los Angeles (tel. 310/670-7302, fax 310/338-0708) or Frankfurt, Germany (tel. 49-69/172260, fax 49-69/729314).

Western Pacific Air Services (Box 411, Honiara; tel. 30533, fax 30476), next to the Pharmacy in central Honiara, flies to many small airstrips Solomon Airlines doesn't reach. This Seventh-Day Adventist church-operated airline has scheduled flights to Malaita, Yandina, Western Province, and Choiseul, and it's always worth comparing schedules (no service on weekends). Prices are the same on both airlines.

Getting Around by Boat

Interisland travel by ship is preferable to air, both for color and economy. Boat service from Honiara to Auki and Gizo is frequent and fairly regular, and virtually every other island in the country is accessible by boat. The government's **Marine Division** (Box G32, Honiara; tel. 21535) is the most reliable operator to the outer islands, while **Coral Seas Ltd.** (Box 9, Honiara; tel. 22811, fax 21975) and the **Malaita Shipping Company** (Box 584, Honiara; tel. 23502, fax 23503) are the largest private lines. A few hours checking around the shipping offices in Honiara will give you a good idea of what's available. The schedule is often up to the captain, so ask him when he's leaving before you go ashore at some remote port of call.

Fares are reasonable, with cabins costing only double the deck fare, so do try to get one if you'll be aboard more than one or two nights. You'll be expected to bring your own bedding. Buy food before boarding, as you may not have another chance to shop until the next day; on a long trip, take enough food to see you through. Hot water is supplied, but you'll need your own cooking and eating utensils. Purchase a grass mat to use for sleeping on deck or bring newspapers. Below deck, it may be hot and crowded. One of the main drawbacks on all the ships is the loud videos, which play well into the night and come back on before dawn. See "Transportation" under "Honiara" for details.

Scuba Tours

Ask any knowledgeable diver about Solomon Islands scuba diving and they'll probably mention the two live-aboard dive boats operated by **Bilikiki Cruises Ltd.** (Jane and Rick Belmare, Box 876, Honiara; tel. 20412, fax 23897). Their Honiara office is upstairs in a well-marked building near the Point Cruz Yacht Club. The original vessel was the 38-meter, 10-stateroom MV *Bilikiki,* based here since 1989. In 1992 a sister ship, the 13-cabin MV *Spirit of the Solomons,* joined the fleet. Groups on cruises of seven, 10, or 14 nights anchor right at the remote wrecks and reefs of the Florida, Russell, and New Georgia islands, most of them accessible only in this way. The ships have been specially adapted for scuba diving, with low platforms for easy entries and exits, and dive tenders are used.

In 1994 a new dive vessel, the 25-meter, five-cabin MV *Solomon Seas* appeared over the Solomons live-aboard horizon. It's operated by **Blue Lagoon Cruises Ltd.** (Frederick Douglas, Box 1022, Honiara; tel./fax 25300). The SI$825 pp per day price includes double-occupancy accommodations with all meals, airport transfers, tax, and unlimited diving (seven-night minimum). This is slightly cheaper than the *Bilikiki,* which costs SI$965 pp per day. Signing onto any of these ships locally would be pure luck, so buy an all-inclusive package through one of the scuba wholesalers mentioned in the main introduction

to this book. Two U.S. companies handling these trips are Tropical Adventures (tel. 800/247-3483) and Sea & Sea Travel Service (tel. 800/DIV-XPRT).

Airport

Henderson Airport (HIR) is 13 km east of Honiara. This historic airfield was begun by the Japanese and finished by the Americans in 1942. The original WW II control tower, a solitary steel-frame structure, still overlooks the runway. Outside the modern airport terminal are a couple of American war memorials and a Japanese AA gun.

The airport bus (if it's there) costs SI$10 right to your hotel, and if you haven't reserved a room they'll drive you around till you find one. The drivers are friendly and help with your luggage. Public minibuses marked "CDC 123" pass fairly frequently on the highway in front of the airport and charge only SI$2 to town. The taxi fare to town is SI$30. Avis and Budget both have counters at the airport.

There's no tourist information desk at the airport. The National Bank counter opens for international flights and gives a fair rate (SI$5 commission when changing back upon departure). A bar and duty-free shop are inside the departure lounge. (If you buy anything at one of the "duty-free" outlets in town, allow one week for goods to be delivered here.) For a treat, look for the man by the roadside in front of the Mobil Station across the street from the terminal. He sells cold coconuts from a white cooler (though he's not always there).

Customs checks are very thorough, in search of guns and video nasties on arrival, contraband gold, artifacts, and WW II munitions on departure. You'll probably have to open your bags (arrive a bit early to allow time for this). The departure tax is SI$30 on international flights only.

GUADALCANAL

Totaling 5,302 square km, Guadalcanal is the largest island in the Solomon Islands. The northern coastal plain contrasts with the Weather Coast in the south, where precipitous cliffs plunge into the sea. The interior is extremely rugged, rising to Mt. Makarakomburu (2,447 meters), the highest peak in the country.

Honiara, on Guadalcanal's north side, began as an army camp during WW II. After the war the British administration decided to utilize the abandoned American facilities here rather than return to their former capital, Tulagi, which had been devastated during the fighting. Honiara is also drier than Tulagi (it's protected from rains by high mountains to the south) and well placed to serve the North Guadalcanal plain. There are few safe anchorages on Guadalcanal and Honiara's harbor is also poor—only safe for yachts from April to October. Still, it's the major port of the group, and interisland ships bustle along the waterfront.

The name Honiara derives from the indigenous name for Point Cruz, *naho-ni-ara,* meaning "facing the east and southeast trade winds." Here in 1568, Mendaña, the European discoverer of the Solomons, raised a cross and claimed the island for Spain. Almost 400 years later in September 1942, the town area was the scene of heavy fighting, and the Mataniko River, which runs through the city, was the Japanese/American front line for several months. Quonset huts remain on the backstreets from the U.S. base established after the Japanese withdrawal.

Today Honiara is a booming minimetropolis of 40,000, where wide lawns, hibiscus, fig, frangipani, palm, and poinciana (flamboyant or flame) trees line the streets. Businesses and government offices crowd the narrow coastal strip behind Point Cruz, and residential areas cover the adjacent hillsides. Chinatown stretches along the right bank of the Mataniko River, while light industry and many schools are concentrated at Kukum, a suburb farther east.

Between 1976 and 1986 the city's population doubled, and 11% of the country's population now lives here, about 60% of them males.

Young men continue to be drawn to the bright lights, especially from Malaita and Western Province, and people with jobs are outnumbered by *masta liu,* the unemployed. This is still a safe city to wander through by day, but after dark you might wish to invest in a taxi, particularly if you have to pass the market area. Yet compared to Port Moresby, Honiara is a breeze, and this city is a lot less touristy that Port Vila.

Things to see and places to stay are abundant around Honiara. Most of the WW II battlefields east of Honiara can be seen on day-trips from the capital, while Lambi Bay is an overnight trip (or longer). The Marau Sound area is well worth a couple of days, and the adventuresome could continue west along the south coast. Many small hamlets in the interior, accessible only on foot, are reserved for the true explorer. Guadalcanal is *the* gateway to the Happy Isles.

SIGHTS

The Town Area

A good place to start is the **Solomon Islands National Museum** (Box 31, Honiara; tel. 22309; irregularly open weekdays 0900-1200 and 1300-1600, donation), opposite the Tourist Authority. The museum presents changing exhibits and gives a good introduction to the traditional life, crafts, and natural environment of the country. Videos of traditional dancing are shown upon request. Some booklets and handicrafts are available. The museum **Cultural Center** within the same compound has a collection of traditional buildings from eight of the Solomon's nine provinces constructed in 1991. When a cruise ship is in, there's often custom dancing here.

Between the museum and the police station is "Pistol Pete," a 155-mm Japanese howitzer that caused havoc by shelling Henderson Field during the Guadalcanal campaign. Inside the **Central Bank** on the other side of the police station are Rennellese woodcarvings, paintings, and a good collection of traditional currency. Across the street is **Government House,** residence of the governor-general (no entry). Farther

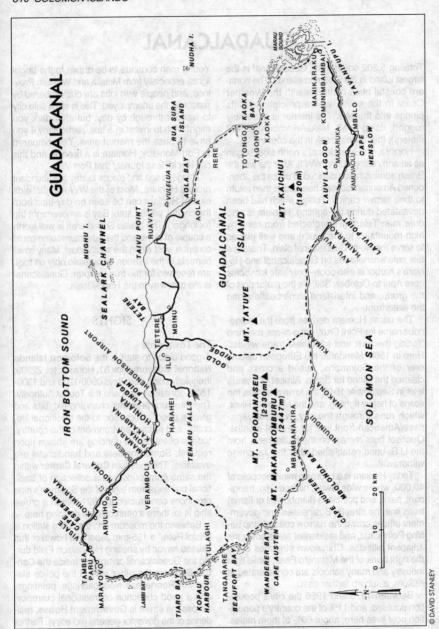

GUADALCANAL

© DAVID STANLEY

These big leaf houses in Watapamu village at the upper end of Honiara's Botanical Gardens are typical of many in the Solomons.

DAVID STANLEY

west, beyond the post office, is the **High Court Building** (1963-64).

Continue west past the Town Ground. Just before St. John's School, take the road inland past the prison checkpoint to the **Botanical Gardens,** where the grounds are always open (free). There's an herbarium and lily pond, plus many attractive paths through the rainforest adjoining the gardens. Upstream but still within the confines of the gardens is **Watapamu village** (named for the nearby water pump), fairly typical of rural villages in the Solomons and well worth visiting for those who will not be journeying outside Honiara.

Return to Mendaña Avenue from the gardens and walk west about 500 meters to **Rove Market,** where you can buy a fresh coconut to drink. Next to Police Headquarters across the street is the **Sergeant Major Jacob Vouza War Memorial** (1992) in memory of the country's most-decorated WW II hero. Captured and tortured by the Japanese, Vouza escaped to tell his story.

Back in the center of town, scramble up the hill behind the Mobil Service Station to visit the huge, conical **Parliament Building** (1993), which the United States government bankrolled to the tune of US$5 million in memory of the 450 U.S. soldiers and 1,200 marines who died on Guadalcanal. Ironically, the building was erected by a Japanese construction company. Enter the 600-seat public gallery if it's open.

Chinatown and Around

Take any bus east to **Central Hospital.** Locally known as Nambanaen, this American-built wartime hospital began life as the "Ninth Station." In 1993 the Taiwanese Government erected the modern extension on the west side of the hospital. Go through the hospital grounds to the beach and proceed west to the mouth of the **Mataniko River** (watch where you step as some locals use the beach as a toilet, converting it into a minefield). In shallow water just off this beach is the wreck of a Japanese tank cut to pieces by American artillery and small-arms fire on 23 October 1942.

The area behind the beach is **Lord Howe Settlement,** a large community of Polynesian people from Ontong Java. Beyond the settlement is **Chinatown,** an Oriental Wild West of photogenic high-porched wooden buildings adjacent to the riverside. Chinatown and the area around the old Mataniko bridge are among the prettiest parts of Honiara.

Walk through Chinatown, cross the old Mataniko River bridge, and proceed up **Skyline Drive** from the Catholic cathedral. Keep left and go up the ridge right to the top, a steep 15-minute climb, for a knockout view of the Mataniko Valley and the hills behind Honiara. You'll end up directly above a large squatter village of Malaita people. Notice the sago palms they use to roof their houses.

The main sight up this way, however, is the **U.S. War Memorial,** dedicated on 7 August 1992 to mark the 50th anniversary of the Red Beach landings. An interesting account of the campaign from the American point of view is inscribed on red marble tablets inside the monument compound (theoretically open daily 0900-

1600, but it's often closed). Even if you don't get in to read the inscriptions, it's still worth coming up for the excellent views of Chinatown, the grassy hills behind Honiara, and the WW II battle sites. If it's a hot day, seriously consider arriving by taxi (you can easily walk back). Skyline Drive, a WW II jeep track, meanders back into the boonies.

The Coastal Plain

Catch a minibus east along the Kukum Highway (known as "Highway 50" to American troops) past King George VI School. A kilometer east of the school is the turnoff to **Betikama Carvings** (Box 516, Honiara; tel. 30223, fax 30174), on the grounds of Adventist High School, one and a half km off the main road. There's a good display of woodcarvings made in SDA villages in the Marovo Lagoon area, a deteriorating collection of WW II relics including several plane parts, a small war museum, and a crocodile. The crafts sold here are high in both quality and price. It's open daily except Saturday 0800-1200 and 1300-1700; donation.

Return to the Kukum Highway and cross the Lungga River bridge, from which two tunnels are visible slightly to the right. The first was General Vandegrift's command post and later a communications center. The tunnel has many rooms on each side and goes under the hillock to the other side. An **underground wartime hospital** is farther to the right at a higher elevation and goes under the nearby hill with a

house on top. Both tunnels are accessible with a flashlight, though prominent signs warn that it could be dangerous to enter.

Bloody Ridge, perhaps the most meaningful WW II site in the Solomons, was the turning point of the ground war in the Pacific. If you'd like to visit, follow the dirt road around the west end of the airstrip and turn right at the T-junction. A white triangular memorial crowns Bloody Ridge, also known as "Edson's Ridge" for the American field commander. This is a hot 40-minute walk each way (no shade), but the views from the ridge are rewarding. A **Japanese War Memorial** is a kilometer farther along in the same direction. Over the past few years several villages have appeared around Bloody Ridge.

Henderson Field was the center of fighting during the first part of the Solomon Islands campaign. The initial Japanese counterattack came from the east on 21 August 1942, at Alligator Creek. This thrust was turned back, and on 8 September Edson's Raiders, who had arrived fresh from the capture of Tulagi, drove the Japanese positioned east of Henderson inland. On the nights of 13 and 14 September, these Japanese troops attacked the U.S. forces on Bloody Ridge, three km south of the airstrip. They were broken up, but five weeks later another Japanese army struggled along the Maruyama Trail from White River, passing behind Mt. Austin. On the nights of 23 and 24 October, they struck once more at Bloody Ridge but were again defeated, after suffering more than 2,000 casualties.

Return to the main road and catch another minibus to the Foxwood Sawmill, which adjoins **Red Beach.** The first U.S. Marine Division landed here on 7 August 1942 to begin its costly six-month struggle to capture Guadalcanal. One cannon still points out to sea, a silent, rusted sentinel.

Beyond the sawmill, you'll pass Levers copra/cacao estates and huge palm-oil plantations. Get off the bus at CDC2 market, within sight of the huge palm oil mill. Solomon Islands Plantations Ltd., in conjunction with the Commonwealth Development Corporation (CDC), has made Guadalcanal a major exporter of palm oil. (A hectare of oil palms produces three times more oil than a hectare of coconuts.) Rice was also once grown in this area.

A single gun guards Red Beach near Foxwood Timbers where the U.S. Marines landed on 7 August 1942.

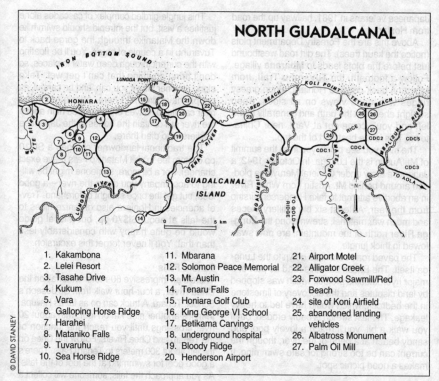

NORTH GUADALCANAL

1. Kakambona
2. Lelei Resort
3. Tasahe Drive
4. Kukum
5. Vara
6. Galloping Horse Ridge
7. Harahei
8. Mataniko Falls
9. Tuvaruhu
10. Sea Horse Ridge
11. Mbarana
12. Solomon Peace Memorial
13. Mt. Austin
14. Tenaru Falls
15. Honiara Golf Club
16. King George VI School
17. Betikama Carvings
18. underground hospital
19. Bloody Ridge
20. Henderson Airport
21. Airport Motel
22. Alligator Creek
23. Foxwood Sawmill/Red Beach
24. site of Koni Airfield
25. abandoned landing vehicles
26. Albatross Monument
27. Palm Oil Mill

© DAVID STANLEY

Walk two and a half km straight down the road that passes the palm oil mill to **Tetere Beach.** Follow the beach a few hundred meters to the right till you see the monument to five Austrian explorers from the *Albatross* expedition, murdered in 1896 by natives who wanted to prevent them from climbing sacred Mt. Tatuba (Tatuve) near Gold Ridge. Come back and follow the road along the beach to the west and turn inland on a track to see a large number of abandoned WW II **amphibious alligators** (LVT) lined up in hoary rustiness. As many as 27 of these are visible, and more are hidden from view in the bush (admission SI$5 pp).

The main road east from Honiara ends at **Aola** (60 km), the capital of Guadalcanal before WW II. Trucks leave Honiara market for Aola around 1500. Charles Woodward, the British naturalist who became resident commissioner in 1896, lived on Mbara Island just

off Aola in 1885 and 1886. For information on Vulelua Island Resort near Aola, see "Resorts," below. Hyundai Timber is logging this area.

Mount Austin
Walk, drive, or take a taxi up the excellent paved highway to the summit of Mt. Austin (410 meters) for a sweeping view of the north coastal plains. The Naha minibus will bring you to the start of this road. Most of the historic battlefields are visible from here. For five months in the latter part of 1942, Japanese troops held Mt. Austin and used it to direct artillery fire on the American marines around Henderson Field below. Even after the main mountain fell, surrounded Japanese held out another month on ridges such as Gifu, Sea Horse, and Galloping Horse, until starvation, suicide, or banzai assaults finally cut them down. This history explains the large white **Solomon Peace Memorial Park,** erected by

Japanese veterans in 1981, halfway up the road from Honiara.

Above this are the Forestry Department plots (notice the kauri trees). The dirt road westbound just before the plots leads to **Mbarana** village. Follow a footpath, the **Tuvaruhu Trail,** from Mbarana back down to Honiara, along grassy ridges with good views on all sides. Keep straight ahead on the path and generally to the left and you'll come out at Vara, near Chinatown. This is the best part of the trip.

The river you see below you from the summit of Mt. Austin is the Lungga. In October 1942, a Japanese army under General Maruyama plodded around behind Mt. Austin from White River in an abortive attempt to take Henderson airstrip from the rear. At least six big artillery pieces and much war materiel, strewn along the **Lungga River** north of the mountain, are now swallowed in thick jungle.

The paved road continues down to the Lungga itself. The British built this road as part of a major hydroelectric project, which was stopped by land disputes and the discovery of limestone in the bedrock, which would have led to heavy leakage. The last stretch is badly eroded, but if you walk a bit, you'll reach a lovely pool and sandy beach at a bend of the river, though the current can be too strong for safe swimming. It makes a good picnic spot.

Mataniko Falls

One of the most amazing waterfalls in the South Pacific is only a two-hour walk south of Honiara up the Mataniko River. Follow the road from Chinatown up the riverside to its end at Tuvaruhu. Galloping Horse Ridge, a major WW II battlefield, towers over Tuvaruhu to the west. Cross the river and follow a trail up over the grassy hillsides and down toward a forest. You pass to the left of a small coconut grove and Harahei village. The final descent to the falls is down a steep, slippery, forested incline.

There are many large pools for cooling off after this exhausting hike, but the main sight is a gigantic, swallow-infested, stalagmite-covered cave, with an arm of the river roaring right through. The river itself pours out of a crack in a limestone cliff just above and tumbles down into the cave through a crevice totally surrounded by white water.

This jungle-girdled complex of cascades alone justifies a visit, but the intrepid should swim/hike down the Mataniko through the gorge back to Tuvaruhu in a couple of hours. You'll be floating with the current through deep water in places, so don't bring anything that can't get wet. Take along an inner tube if you can, and be careful, as people have drowned here. After a storm the river can flood. Caves on the slopes high above the river still contain the bones of the Japanese soldiers who died there.

The traditional landowner charges a SI$10 pp custom fee to visit Mataniko Falls (have exact change). For a bit more, someone might be willing to accompany you down the river—a good idea, but get the price straight beforehand. Travel agencies in Honiara also organize hikes to the falls at about SI$70 pp, but a local guide would be quite happy with considerably less than that. You'll never forget this excursion.

Tenaru Falls

There's an impressive 60-meter waterfall on the **Chea River,** a four-hour walk from St. Joseph's School, Tenaru. A truck can go as far as Hailupa, then it's another nine km on foot, with about 20 river crossings until you reach the junction of the Tenaru and Chea Rivers. Follow the Chea on the left about 300 meters to Tenaru Falls. There's a good pool for swimming at the foot of the falls. As you approach the falls, someone will collect a SI$10 pp custom fee (try to give it to the right person and avoid paying twice).

West of Honiara

At **Poha,** nine km west of Honiara, is a Japanese war memorial and a wrecked U.S. floating crane just offshore. A footpath heads inland along the Poha River toward Tangarare on the southwest coast. Follow this upstream till you reach a cliff where there's a cave with carvings and drawings, one of the oldest inhabited sites yet excavated in the Solomons. You'll probably be charged a custom fee to visit. If you'd like to visit some villages and have a swim in the river, continue along this same way a while. The track soon becomes extremely difficult, however, so a hike across to Tangarare probably isn't possible.

At **Bonegi Beach,** five km west of Poha, are the wrecks of two Japanese freighters sunk offshore in November 1942; one is partly above water and the other only three meters down, so snorkeling is possible on both (SI$5 admission).

About 22 km west of Honiara is an experimental **giant clam farm** established by the International Center for Living Aquatic Resources Management (ICLARM) in 1988. This facility is intended to eventually supply baby clams to hundreds of private clam farmers around the Pacific; through farming, this largest of all clams, the *Tridacna gigas,* may be saved from extinction. Visitors are welcome.

A few kilometers beyond is **Fred Kona's War Museum** (admission SI$10 pp) at Vilu village. This attraction includes a run-down customary village and picnic area for tourists, as well as three or four wrecked planes, four Japanese field guns, and an assortment of scrap metal that has been dragged in. Don't go to a lot of trouble to see it.

Find outboard canoes to Savo Island in the village near **Cape Esperance Lighthouse** or at **Visale,** 38 km west of Honiara. Japanese submarine *I-123* is on the reef five meters down just offshore from Veuru, a kilometer west of Visale. Ask for Johnny Serverio, who paddles snorkelers out for a nominal custom fee. The **Tambea Holiday Beach Resort** (see "Resorts," below) is just beyond. It was from here that many Japanese troops made their final escape from Guadalcanal in February 1943.

The north coast highway terminates at **Lambi Bay,** 69 km west of Honiara. Dalsol Ltd. is the main commercial logger in this area. Village trucks leave Lambi Bay for Honiara nearly every morning.

A more adventurous way to get there is to take a Marine Division boat to **Tangarare,** then walk back to Lambi Bay in a day or more. There are two chest-deep crocodile creeks to cross. A good surfing spot (right-handers) is near the river mouth at Tangarare, and there's good diving along this beautiful coastline. A footpath travels the entire south coast from village to village.

Sports and Recreation

Honiara's oldest dive shop is **Island Dive Services** (John and Ingrid Carr, Box 414, Honiara; tel. 22103, fax 21493), operating since 1982. They offer two scuba/snorkeling trips daily at

0900 and 1400 from their base at the Kitano Mendaña Hotel (open daily 0800-1700). Snorkeling is SI$58, scuba diving SI$140 for one tank, gear included (certification mandatory). If you have your own equipment the prices come down to SI$32 for snorkeling, SI$90 for scuba diving (a second dive the same day is always SI$90). Island Dive Services offers night dives on the two Bonegi wrecks to see the rare "flashlight fish," and they have a seven-meter boat for dives on offshore sites (although most of the dives are shore dives). Their scuba certification course is SI$810 plus SI$150 for registration if you're alone, SI$690 pp for two, SI$590 pp for three, SI$490 pp for four. Certified divers can also rent tanks, backpacks, and weight belts here and organize their own shore diving from a rental car.

Scuba diving is also offered by **Dive Solomons** (Box 186, Honiara; tel. 20520, fax 23110) with dive shops next to the Guadalcanal Club, at the Honiara Hotel, and at the Tambea Holiday Beach Resort. Their prices are SI$63 for snorkeling (gear included) or SI$100 for scuba diving (SI$150 with all equipment). We've heard they're friendly, enthusiastic, and professional and compete very well with Island Dive Services—both companies are recommended.

The main sites visited are two wrecked Japanese transport ships at Bonegi northwest of Honiara (good for both snorkeling and diving), a sunken trading boat full of tame moray eels (scuba only), and Tasafaronga Reef. There's also a beach dive to a B-17 Flying Fortress bomber encrusted in soft corals 15 meters down off Ndoma. The Honiara dive shops offer mostly shore dives but some boat diving is also available.

The **Honiara Golf Club** (Box 195, Honiara; tel. 30181), across the road from King George VI High School between Honiara and the airport, charges green fees of SI$10 for the nine holes. No clubs are for hire, but there's a good bar here. The course is laid out on the old Kukum "Fighter Two" airstrip so it's dead flat, though the club's pleasant colonial atmosphere is fun. Visitors are welcome.

On Saturday afternoon catch a game of rugby (October to March) or soccer (April to August) at the **Lawson Tama Stadium** opposite Central Hospital. The action starts about 1400, and the entrance fee is cheap.

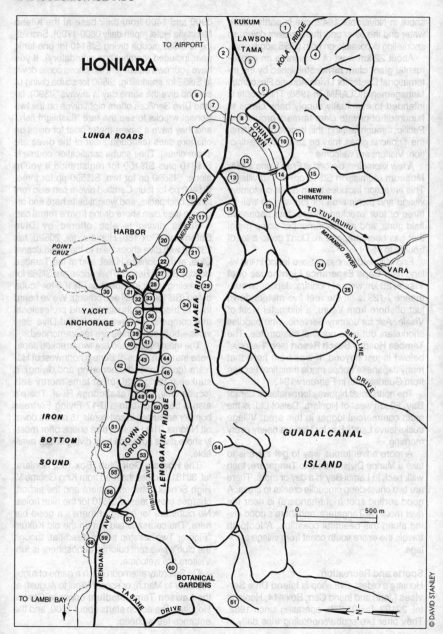

HONIARA

TO AIRPORT

KUKUM

LAWSON
TAMA

KOLA RIDGE

CHINA-
TOWN

LUNGA ROADS

NEW CHINATOWN

TO TUVARUHU

MATANIKO RIVER

VARA

HARBOR

MENDANA AVE.

POINT
CRUZ

VAVAEA RIDGE

YACHT
ANCHORAGE

SKYLINE DRIVE

IRON
BOTTOM
SOUND

TOWN
GROUND

LENGAKIKI RIDGE

GUADALCANAL
ISLAND

HIBISCUS AVE.

MENDANA AVE.

TO LAMBI BAY

TA SAHE DRIVE

BOTANICAL
GARDENS

0   500 m

© DAVID STANLEY

N

HONIARA

1. Forum Fisheries Agency
2. Central Hospital
3. University of the South Pacific
4. Tropicana Motel
5. Squash Courts
6. submerged Japanese tank
7. Lord Howe Settlement
8. Mandarin Restaurant/ Mataniko Saloon
9. Super Motel
10. Chan Wing Supermarket
11. Honiara Hotel
12. Public Library
13. Catholic Cathedral
14. Independence Arch
15. Solomon Islands Development Trust
16. Central Market
17. Quality Motel
18. Patty's Family Transit
19. Travelers Motel
20. Guadalcanal Provincial Offices

21. United Church Rest House
22. Church House
23. Church of Melanesia Transit House
24. Malaita village
25. U.S. War Memorial
26. Marine Division
27. Hot Bread Kitchen
28. Westpac Bank
29. South Seas Evangelical Church Transit House
30. Pasofi Snack Bar
31. Malaita Shipping Co./Quarantine Office
32. ANZ Bank
33. Lena Cinema
34. Parliament Building
35. Solomon Airlines
36. Kingsley's Fastfood Center
37. Point Cruz Yacht Club
38. NPF Plaza
39. Tourist Authority
40. Kitano Mendaña Hotel
41. Solomon Islands National Museum

42. Government House
43. Police Station
44. Hibiscus Hotel
45. Solomon Telekom
46. Post Office
47. Motel Tropics
48. High Court Building
49. Survey and Cartography Division
50. Hydrographic Office
51. Guadalcanal Club
52. La Pérouse Restaurant
53. YWCA
54. Testimony Guest House
55. Honimed Clinic/Minana Handicrafts
56. Iron Bottom Sound Hotel
57. Radio Happy Isles
58. Rove Market
59. Rove Police Headquarters
60. Herbarium
61. Watapamu village

ACCOMMODATIONS

Budget Accommodations

Just under a dozen rest houses and hostels around Honiara offer reasonable accommodations, usually with communal cooking facilities provided. A few charge *per bed* and singles can often get the per person rate, though some bargaining may be required. Houses available for long-term rentals are listed on a notice board inside Consumers Supermarket.

The basic seven-room **Church of Melanesia Transit House** is up the dusty road behind the Hot Bread Kitchen. Yelping dogs, dirty showers, and sagging beds can be a problem, but at SI$15 pp it's one of the cheapest places in town, and you only get what you pay for. To get in you must apply to the office, 2nd Floor, Church House (Box 19, Honiara; tel. 21892; weekdays 0730-1200/1330-1630). It's usually full up with locals.

A better choice would be the 10-room **United Church Rest House** (Box 18, Honiara; tel.

20028, fax 20453) nearby. Follow Cluck Street up from Mendaña Avenue and turn right at the top of the hill. The cost is SI$30 pp, and singles will be expected to share. Many travelers stay here because of the great location, good facilities, and moderate rates, and it can be rather noisy due to foreigners chatting away on the front porch late at night and locals up doing their housework in the early morning. Keep your room door firmly locked at all times (even if you're only out on the porch) as there are a few light-fingered guests.

One of the best places to stay is **Patty's Family Transit** (Box 279, Honiara; tel. 25078, fax 30806), conveniently located on spacious grounds just up the hill from the Catholic cathedral. Patty's has five triple rooms at SI$35 pp, with good cooking facilities and a large sitting room downstairs.

Up the hill from Patty's is the basic **South Seas Evangelical Church Transit House** (Box 16, Honiara; tel. 22800) on Vavaea Ridge. The three doubles and one four-bed bunkroom downstairs are SI$25/40 single/double. Full cooking facilities are provided, and smoking and drinking are not allowed (thank goodness!). The showers are solar-heated.

If none of these work out you could always try the **Kukum Transit House** (Box 878, Honiara; tel. 20473, fax 23110) near the Kukum Shopping Center, three km east of downtown (good bus service). The six rooms with bath are SI$33 pp and communal cooking facilities are provided. The locals around here are friendly and helpful.

The **YWCA** (Box 494, Honiara; tel. 22661), across the field from the Guadalcanal Club, offers accommodations for visiting women at SI$27/38 single/double. It's a good place for female travelers to meet local women, but it's often full.

Medium-Priced Accommodations

The **Travelers Motel** (Box 56, Honiara; tel. 25721, fax 25735) has a good location in the "Fijian Quarters" just up the road inland on the west side of the Mataniko Bridge near Chinatown. The 17 rooms with private baths in this two-story building go for SI$70 single or double downstairs, SI$80 upstairs, plus 10% tax—it's a bit overpriced. There are communal cooking facilities. The screened windows are not very soundproof, so you hear everything around you.

The **Quality Motel** (Box 521, Honiara; tel. 25150, fax 25277), on the hillside directly above the market, is at the top end of this category. The 17 rooms in this two-story building begin at SI$88/110 single/double with fan, fridge, and bath. The large family rooms are SI$200 without a/c, SI$230 with a/c, cooking facilities included.

While centrally located, the **Hibiscus Hotel** (Box 268, Honiara; tel. 21205 or 22269, fax 21771) on Hibiscus Avenue is a bit of a dive. The 10 fan-cooled rooms with private facilities and fridge are SI$93/121 single/double. Some rooms are rented to locals on a short-term basis (half hour) at cut rates. On Thursday, Friday, and Saturday there's a disco in the Pipeline Nightclub until 0200, and private parties are often held in the "Leaf Haus" next to the hotel, so you might check on all that if noise bothers you. The hotel's public bar is usually full of Japanese fishermen and various hangers-on, so beware of prowlers. Others stock up at the hotel bottle shop. Despite these features, tourists

often stay at the Hibiscus and some say it's okay. In mid-1995 Island Hotels Ltd. of Papua New Guinea bought the Hibiscus and unveiled plans to renovate and expand the property under the new name Hotel King Solomon. When complete, the new swimming pool and 46 additional rooms will make this one of Honiara's top medium-priced accommodations.

Nearby but a bit hard to find is **Motel Tropics** (Box 1296, Honiara; tel. 25048) on Lenggakiki Ridge, directly up a concrete stairway behind the Hydrographic Office on Hibiscus Avenue. The seven rooms with bath and good views are SI$77 single or double.

A lot of people rave about friendly, locally owned **Testimony Guest House** (Sam and Noel Ploso, Box 122, Honiara; tel. 21530, fax 21341), on Lenggakiki Ridge just above Honiara. The 12 rooms are SI$70 double with shared bath, or SI$80 double with private bath. If you're alone you can sometimes get one bed for SI$40, but you'll have to share if they fill up (unlikely). The rooms with private bath are excellent value: ask for room no. 3, which has a pleasant balcony. Communal cooking facilities are available, and cold drinks and a few basic groceries are sold at the reception. You may be able to use their washing machine. Testimony is on a quiet, airy hilltop—a good place to stay if you want to relax and recuperate, or are only waiting for transportation out of Honiara. Visiting Peace Corps volunteers often stay here. Take a taxi (SI$6) here the first time as it's hard to find, but once you're here the staff will run you into town free. There's a shortcut trail up from the Hibiscus Hotel.

A number of other medium-priced motels are in the hills above Chinatown and Kukum, including the **Honiara Tropicana Motel** (Box 241, Honiara; tel. 24104) on West Kola Ridge, **Fountain Family Inn** (Box 1196, Honiara; tel. 21552) on Kola Ridge, and **Pakoe Accommodation** (Box 679, Honiara; tel. 21336, fax 20308) on East Kola Ridge. All charge about the same as the places mentioned above, but are far less convenient and thus only worth checking out if everything closer to town happens to be full.

Upmarket Accommodations

The 66-room **Honiara Hotel** (Tommy Chan, Box 4, Honiara; tel. 21737, fax 20376) near

Chinatown is a pleasant place to stay if you want a regular hotel room with reasonable facilities. They have a few non-a/c "budget" rooms with shared bath in the old wing for SI$85/110 single/double, a/c rooms with private bath and fridge for SI$155/180/205 single/double/triple. Rooms in the new wing on an upper terrace begin at SI$230/260 single/double, plus 10% tax. An offbeat funicular elevator carries you up to the rooms. There's a swimming pool and a good bar, but skip the restaurant, as its Chinese-style food is poor value, especially at night. Even if you're not staying here, it's well worth dropping by on Wednesday and Friday evenings for the panpipe playing. The hotel bar is good.

Super Motel (Box 176, Honiara; tel. 22509, fax 22870), also known as "Super Accommodation," in Chinatown, has 12 a/c rooms with bath, video, and fridge at SI$100/120 single/double standard, SI$150/170 deluxe, plus tax. Unfortunately this large modern building is out of place in Chinatown, and it's hard to judge what sort of clientele they're after.

Since 1967 Honiara's premier (and most pretentious) hotel has been the 94-room **Kitano Mendaña** (Box 384, Honiara; tel. 20071, fax 23942). In 1990 the Japanese construction company Kitano purchased the hotel from the government and invested SI$10 million in a face-lift. The standard a/c rooms with fridge and private bath are SI$140/160 single/double, deluxe rooms SI$200/220, plus 10% tax. The three-story building doesn't have an elevator, so specify ground floor when booking if this poses a problem. Prices are low by international standards, but despite the renovations the rooms are rather worn. There's a freshwater swimming pool. The continental buffet breakfast (SI$24), Friday night barbecue (SI$38), and Sunday night Gilbertese dancing (free) are good. Don't change money here, as they give a rate 10% lower than the bank.

In 1995 the **Iron Bottom Sound Hotel** (Box 1892, Honiara; tel. 25833, fax 24123) opened near the access road to the Botanical Gardens. The 36 a/c rooms in a series of long single-story blocks next to the sea are SI$209/220 single/double including breakfast. Ask for a room with a sea view (there's no beach here). Their restaurant serves Cantonese food.

Two km west of Rove Market is the **Lelei Resort** (Jeff Olson, Box 235, Honiara; tel. 20720, fax 22970) with six rooms in a two-story building on a rocky shore with a nice view of Savo Island. Rooms are SI$240 plus tax and the resort's large restaurant is said to be good. Get there on the frequent White River minibus.

If you'll be renting a car to explore the battlefields east of Honiara, the **Airport Motel** (Box 251, Honiara; tel. 30446, fax 30411), makes a good base. The 19 a/c rooms with bath begin at SI$110/130 single/double, plus 10% tax. There's a restaurant and bar, but no cooking facilities to prepare your own meals. The beach is a kilometer away, and the owner plans to shift his operation down there over the next few years, so check. The present motel is only about 500 meters east of the airport terminal, so it's worth considering if you have to catch a very early flight.

Resorts

If you'd like to get away from it all and relax by a sheltered black beach, consider **Tambea Holiday Beach Resort** (Box 4, Honiara; tel. 23639, fax 20376), 45 km west of Honiara. There are 22 bungalows with fan, fridge, toilet, and shower (but no cooking facilities) at SI$140/160/180 single/double/triple, plus 10% tax. The meal package is SI$77 pp for three meals. Dive Solomons has a dive shop at the resort, with diving on nearby reefs, caves, and perhaps Japanese submarine *I-123* (if local villagers who "own" the sub allow). If you've never tried scuba diving, you can do a "resort course" here (SI$185) or a full PADI certification course (SI$875). Sand flies on the beach are a drawback, but there's a swimming pool, and many non-motorized nautical activities are free to guests. Visale village, with its large Catholic mission, is within walking distance. It's a good place to spend the weekend because there's a special feast and custom dancing on Saturday night; Sunday it's a barbecue under the stars. Transfers from the Honiara Hotel (which is under the same ownership) are SI$20 pp each way. Otherwise you can easily get to Tambea by passenger truck from Honiara market for SI$5.

A less expensive resort than Tambea is **Vulelua Island Resort** (Brendan O'Shea, Box 96, Honiara; tel./fax 29684), on a tiny island surrounded by a white beach a kilometer off the north shore of Guadalcanal, 68 km southeast of Honiara. The six thatched seaside bungalows with private bath are SI$220 pp, meals and nautical gear (masks, snorkels, and canoes) included (tax extra). Reductions are possible if you book locally. The Sunday seafood buffet is SI$35 pp extra but coffee and tea in the restaurant are free all day, and drink prices on the island are fair. Credit cards are not accepted, but traveler's checks are okay. The snorkeling is good (better than at Tambea), scuba diving can be arranged, and there's a tennis court. It's a great place to relax, but gets crowded when local expats arrive for the weekend. Yachties are welcome here. Transfers from Honiara to the landing at Ande-Ande cost SI$80 pp (two-person minimum), then a free motorized canoe carries you over to the island. If you come on your own, flash your headlights or a mirror to call the boat over.

FOOD

Budget Restaurants

Your possibilities for eating out in Honiara are not as good as in the other South Pacific capitals. Apart from a number of basic snack bars serving curry beef with rice for SI$8, there isn't a lot to choose from. Many of the budget eateries close at night, so if you have cooking facilities, plan on preparing your own dinner and having lunch on the run.

The cheapest places are at the Central Market. The **B-Kool Dairy Bar** (tel. 23234) here sells milk shakes and ice cream, while the adjacent **Honiara Fish Market** offers big servings of fried fish and chips—a complete meal.

In the center of town, inexpensive meals and ice cream can be obtained at the food court of the NPF Plaza opposite the National Museum. Farther back in the same plaza, you can get a good breakfast or just a cup of coffee at the Kofi Haus inside **Consumers Supermarket** (tel. 21798; weekdays 0830-1630, Saturday 0800-1230). A sandwich bar and bakery are adjacent. **Kingsley's Fastfood Center** (tel. 22936) nearby specializes in barbecued chicken, curried rice, hamburgers, and noodle soup. **Amy's Snack Bar** in front of Lena Cinema sells cold coconuts—cheaper than bottled drinks and much better.

A Thai-Chinese lady runs **Pasofi Snack Bar** (tel. 24022) on Point Cruz, with fried noodles, sweet-and-sour fish, and beef curries. There are seats outside, and it's open till around 1700 daily except Sunday—excellent.

The best supermarket in town is **Chan Wing Ltd.** (tel. 22414; weekdays 0800-1800, Saturday 0730-1300), near Super Motel in Chinatown. It puts Consumers Supermarket to shame. It pays to shop around, as grocery prices vary considerably.

Better Restaurants

Other than the filling pub lunches at the Point Cruz Yacht Club and the famous Friday night barbecue at the Kitano Mendaña Hotel (SI$38), the possibilities for eating out in Honiara are dismal. There are lots of pricey Chinese restaurants around town, none of them worth singling out. Unlike American or European Chinese restaurants where everyone orders an individual meal such as chop suey or chow mein, at the Honiara Chinese restaurants all of the dishes are meant to be consumed collectively by everyone at the table. In the true Chinese fashion, they're served one at a time, and the process tends to be long and drawn out in the hope of selling you more drinks (not listed on the menu and expensive). Thus the success of your meal is closely related to your ordering ability and previous experience doesn't count. If you decide to take a chance, you'll only find them open for lunch 1200-1400 and dinner 1900-2200. Expect prices to be higher at dinner and count on spending a minimum of SI$30 pp (double or triple what a comparable meal would cost in Fiji). Expect 10% tax to be added to all of the prices on the menu.

Of the hotel restaurants, the one at the Hibiscus Hotel (tel. 24138; closed Sunday) is the favorite, specializing in Thai cuisine and pizza. If you want your meal spicy, you must say so. The restaurant at the Kitano Mendaña has Japanese food, while the Honiara Hotel restaurant features Chinese dishes.

One of the only non-hotel, non-Chinese restaurants in town is **La Pérouse** (tel. 23720; Monday to Saturday 1200-1330/1900-2130), near the Guadalcanal Club. They specialize in French cuisine and seafood, plus 17 varieties of ice cream sundae. The lunch menu is less expensive than dinner. Some of the tables are set right down near the shore for romantic dining, and with its attractive island decor and affordable prices, it's the best restaurant in town.

ENTERTAINMENT

See four trashy action films daily at **Lena Cinema** (tel. 22255) in the center of town. No movies begin after 1700. Several other small cinemas around Honiara show video films. Of course, no royalties are paid to the movie companies, and what you see depends on what caught the projectionist's eye at the video rental shop the day before.

Honiara's expatriate community congregates at the **Point Cruz Yacht Club** (tel. 22500) weekdays after work. Friday afternoon the place is packed. Daily except Sunday you can get good-value meals to go with the cheap beer. There's video Tuesday night and the usual notice board if you're looking for a yacht/crew. Check for notices of organized hikes—perfect for women unwilling to risk going alone. The Yacht Club is open Monday to Thursday 0900-1400 and 1530-2230, Friday 0900-1400 and 1530-midnight, Saturday 0900-2230, Sunday 0900-2200. Have the doorman sign you in.

The "G Club" or **Guadalcanal Club** (tel. 22212) was once the reserve of British colonials but since independence it has fallen into a steady decline—the Yacht Club is now much more popular. At last report there were still tennis courts, billiards, dances (Friday), and a cheap bar (Tuesday happy hour) here, and foreign visitors are welcome. An impressive Japanese field gun stands sentinel over the adjacent dive shop.

There's a dance at the **Police Club** next to Rove Police Headquarters on Tuesday, Friday, and Saturday nights (SI$5 admission). Also try the **Pipeline Disco Nightclub** at the Hibiscus Hotel (tel. 22269), which pumps up Thursday, Friday, and Saturday 2100-0200 (dress regulations).

Honiara's most colorful nightlife unfolds in the bars of Chinatown. If you've got guts, step into the **Mataniko Saloon** next to the Mandarin Restaurant, Honiara's roughest Wild West bar. Wire grills protect the bartender dispensing cold cans of Foster's, and you better keep your hands on the table, partner. More of a threat to your wallet than your life are the various Chinese gambling establishments in the vicinity of Super Motel. After dark, you've got a fair chance of being mugged if you're caught wandering anywhere between here and the market, so take a taxi.

Cultural Shows for Visitors

The top events of the week are the **panpipe performances** on the large shell stage at the Honiara Hotel (tel. 21737), Wednesday and Friday at 1900. The best panpipe band appearing here is Narasirato from Are'are in South Malaita (internationally renowned since their tours to England in 1993 and Canada in 1994). Narasirato T-shirts and cassettes are sold at the performances. The Mao Dancers from Kwara'ae, Malaita, are also very good. Every other Friday during the school year, the boys of St. Martin's School play panpipes and perform custom dances at the **Kitano Mendaña Hotel** (tel. 20071)—another great show. If you have the chance, attend any performance by the Betikama Adventist bamboo band or St. Joseph's Tenaru panpipe group.

The panpipe musicians are often followed by **Gilbertese dancing,** but unfortunately some of the Gilbertese groups have begun performing mock Polynesian dances to recorded Tahitian music, which is hardly worth seeing. If you do like the show, it's customary to show your appreciation by contributing a banknote or two to the dancer who pleases you most *during* the dance. Watch how the locals do it. Beware if a dancer comes up and places a garland of flowers on your head. Next thing you know she'll have you dancing with her up on the stage! Gilbertese dancing is often seen at the Kitano Mendaña Hotel Sunday at 2000.

SHOPPING

The **Central Market** (open all day but best before 1030) is the place to buy fruit, vegetables, and shell money. Prices vary considerably from one stall to another, so shop around. Don't bargain, just keep looking.

Without question, Honiara's best buys are traditional handicrafts. Most evenings carvers peddle their wares outside the Kitano Mendaña Hotel, and whenever a cruise ship docks, dozens of people sell handicrafts in the field behind the National Museum. The handicraft shop in the museum itself is good, and in Room no. 40 in the NPF Plaza across the street you can buy items made by local women.

The **King Solomon Arts and Crafts Center** (tel. 21620) opposite Solomon Airlines has been recommended by readers as the least expensive place to buy handicrafts. **Melanesian Handicrafts** (tel. 22189), also on Mendaña Avenue, sells a variety of handicrafts.

Another place to try is **Minana Handicrafts** (tel. 22940), next to Honimed Clinic on the way to the Botanical Garden. Visit all of these and you'll soon become an expert.

The Quarantine Office (tel. 21430), in an unmarked building next to Mamara Estates Ltd., across the street from the Marine Division, will fumigate handicrafts made of grass, leaves, or other natural materials and issue a certificate required to import the items into other countries. At least one working day is required and there's a SI$12 fee.

Sturdy baskets of this kind are woven from the asa vine by Guadalcanal villagers. Because they were once traded at Buka in the North Solomons (P.N.G.), they are known as "Buka baskets."

LOUISE FOOTE

The **Philatelic Bureau** (Box G31, Honiara; tel. 21821, fax 21472) beside the post office sells beautiful stamps and first-day covers, which make excellent souvenirs. The **Central Bank** (tel. 21791) sells uncirculated commemorative coins, many of which are on display in the lobby.

SERVICES

Money
The Westpac Bank, the ANZ Bank, and the National Bank are all near one another in the center of town (weekdays 0830-1500). American Express is not represented.

Post and Telecommunications
The main post office is open weekdays 0800-1630, Saturday 0800-1100. Honiara post office is uncrowded, the staff are friendly and cooperative, and postal rates in the Solomons are low. Send all your parcels, postcards, and aerograms from here. Always use airmail, even for parcels, as sea mail to Europe or North America can take six months. Poste restante at the post office is usually reliable and they claim to hold letters six months, which makes this a good place to receive mail if you're on an open-ended itinerary.

Place long-distance calls using a card telephone at **Solomon Telekom** (tel. 21164, fax 24220; weekdays 0800-1800, weekends 0800-1200), next to the post office. Operator-assisted calls are not available. Other public phones are at the post office, at the Kitano Mendaña Hotel, and at the airport.

Immigration Office
The Immigration office (tel. 21440, fax 22964) in the Ministry of Commerce across Mendaña Avenue from the post office is open weekdays 0900-1100 and 1300-1500.

Consulates
Get free Australian visas in 24 hours at the **Australian High Commission** (tel. 21561; weekdays 0800-1200), behind the Central Bank.

Other countries with diplomatic offices in Honiara are European Union (tel. 22765), Japan (tel. 22953), New Zealand (tel. 21502), Papua New Guinea (tel. 20561), Taiwan (tel. 22590), and the U.K. (tel. 21705).

Public Toilets

Public toilets are available in the Kitano Mendaña Hotel, the Honiara Hotel, and at the Point Cruz Yacht Club. At last report, there were no laundromats in Honiara.

INFORMATION

The helpful **Tourist Authority** (tel. 22442, fax 23986; weekdays 0800-1200 and 1330-1600) across from the museum can supply a complete accommodations list with current prices, plus many useful brochures. This is one of the few tourist offices in the South Pacific which is only too happy to advise on ways of getting off the beaten track, staying with local people, arranging rides in outboard canoes, etc. If you're looking for real adventure, they'll have plenty of suggestions.

The **Survey and Cartography Division Map Sales Office** (tel. 21511; weekdays 0800-1130 and 1300-1600), Hibiscus Avenue and Koti Lane, has detailed topographical maps of the whole country.

The **Hydrographic Office** (tel. 20610), opposite the Survey and Cartography Division, sells locally produced charts and tide tables.

Bookstores and Libraries

An interesting assortment of local books is sold at **News Power Newsagent** (tel. 22069) in the Anthony Saru Building behind the NPF Plaza.

The **University of the South Pacific Center** (Box 460, Honiara; tel. 21307, fax 21287), behind the National Gymnasium east of Chinatown, carries books by Solomon Islanders (recommended titles include *The Confession* by Julian Maka'a and *The Alternative* by John Saunana).

The **Solomon Islands Development Trust** (tel. 21130) in new Chinatown has fascinating magazines on local social and environmental issues, Pijin comic books, and SIDT T-shirts. ACOR Stationer next to Solomon Airlines also sells their magazine *Link*.

The **Public Library** (tel. 23227), on Watts Road between the market and Chinatown, is open Monday, Tuesday, Thursday, Friday 1000-1300 and 1600-1800, Saturday 0900-1200, Sunday 1400-1700.

The **National Library** (tel. 21601; weekdays 0800-1200 and 1300-1630) is in the building directly behind the Public Library.

HEALTH

The **Central Hospital** (tel. 23600) is overcrowded, so if you need medical attention, consider visiting a private doctor rather than spending a long time waiting there. Any of the clinics mentioned below should be able to do a malaria slide check quickly and inexpensively.

Dr. Pimbo Ogatuti of the **Island Medical Center** (tel. 23277; weekdays 0800-1200/1300-1600, Saturday 0800-1200), on Cluck Street on the way up to the United Church Guest House, charges about SI$25 for consultations.

Nearby is Dr. Steve Sanga Aumanu's **Wantok Clinic** (tel. 21461; weekdays 0800-1200 and 1330-1600, Saturday 0900-1200) in the Guadalcanal Provincial Offices. Dr. Sanga Aumanu is the one to see for any problem related to scuba diving (coral cuts, etc.).

A third choice is Dr. H. Posala's **Honimed Clinic** (tel. 22029; Monday, Tuesday, and Thursday 0800-1200 and 1330-1600, Friday 0800-1200 and 1330-1500, Sunday 0900-1200), just down from La Pérouse Restaurant.

The **Honiara Dental Clinic** (tel. 22754; Monday to Thursday 0830-1200 and 1300-1630, Friday 0800-1200 and 1300-1500) is on Ashley Street next to Kingsley's Fastfood Center. There's also a Dental Clinic (tel. 23600) at Central Hospital.

TRANSPORTATION

For domestic air services from Honiara, see "Transportation" in the chapter introduction.

Travel around the Solomons by ship is not only easy, it's one of the main attractions of this country. There are many services, and fares are reasonable—plan on doing most of your interisland travel this way. You'll make numerous friends on board and really get to see the Solomons.

Orient yourself by looking over the ships in Honiara harbor; most of the shipping company offices are nearby. Some ships won't accept passengers for safety reasons, and you should pick the larger vessels if you doubt your ability as a sailor. Cabin fares (when available) are about double one-way deck fares, and meals aren't usually included. If you want a cabin, try to book a few days in advance. Forget attempting to catch a boat just before Christmas when schedules and routes change at a moment's notice and everything's full.

Ships to Western Province

The boat trip from Honiara to Gizo is one of the finest scenic cruises in the South Pacific. It's less rough westbound from Honiara to Gizo than eastbound from Gizo to Honiara because you go with the prevailing winds. Thus if you were going to fly one way anyway, it's a good plan to go out by boat and return to Honiara by plane. Book your return flights before leaving Honiara. However, you only get to see the Marovo Lagoon by day on the way back to Honiara.

In 1994 the Western Provincial Government bought the 30-meter MV *Western Queen,* which shuttles between Honiara and Gizo weekly, departing Honiara Wednesday at 1300 and arriving at Gizo Thursday around noon. Every second week this ship extends its journey to the Shortland Islands and Choiseul Bay. It's always a good ship to try if you want a cabin because there are 78 double cabins with toilet. Inquire at the **Western Development Corporation** in the NPF Plaza.

Otherwise, two major companies compete on Honiara-Gizo route. The *Ramos I* of the **Malaita Shipping Co.** (Box 584, Honiara; tel. 23502, fax 23503), just down toward the harbor from the ANZ Bank, departs Honiara for Gizo Saturday at 1900. This ship calls at Patutiva (SI$49 deck) Sunday morning and arrives at Gizo (SI$65 deck) late Sunday night.

Every Sunday at 1000 **Coral Seas Ltd.** (Box 9, Honiara; tel. 22811, fax 21975), on Hibiscus Avenue behind the Hot Bread Kitchen, sends the *Iuminao* to Patutiva (SI$56 deck), Munda (SI$64 deck), and Gizo (26 hours; SI$70 deck). First class costs about 50% more. The ship arrives in Gizo on Monday afternoon and starts back toward Honiara a few hours later, calling at the New Georgia and Marovo Lagoon pickup points on Tuesday and arriving in Honiara early Wednesday morning.

The *Iuminao* lies lower in the water than most other ships and is more stable. The *Ramos I* is shorter and higher than the *Iuminao* and in rough weather it tosses a lot, so the lower in the ship you can get the better. Although the *Iuminao* is an older ship than the *Ramos I,* the accommodation is much better with lots of wooden benches in economy. When it's not crowded, first class on the **Ramos I** is good, with long padded benches on which to stretch out, while first class on the *Iuminao* consists of individual reclining seats (better on crowded trips). On an overnight trip, first class or a cabin might be worth considering on the *Ramos I,* although there's a large protected room downstairs for economy passengers. Unfortunately, the *Ramos I* plays noisy videos in both the downstairs room and in the first class lounge (also a problem on the *Iuminao*). The crew on the *Iuminao* is more environmentally conscious than the one on the *Ramos I,* who dump their garbage into the open sea as soon as they're out of port. Signs on the *Iuminao* prohibit throwing trash overboard. On the way to Gizo, there will be markets of cooked food at some of the ports of call, but you have to be quick or you'll miss out. It's best to take your own food along.

Ships to Malaita

Coral Seas Ltd. (tel. 22811) runs the *Compass Rose II* to Auki Wednesday at 1830 (arrives at midnight) and Sunday at 2200 (an overnight trip). The same company has the larger *Iuminao* from Honiara to Auki Friday at 1830 (six hours; SI$25 deck, SI$44 first class). On both of these ships, first class costs a third to a half more, a cabin about double. It's not worth paying extra for first class on the *Compass Rose II,* as noisy videos prevent you from getting much sleep in the first class lounge and the roof leaks.

The **Malaita Shipping Co.** (tel. 23502) runs the *Ramos I* from Honiara to Auki Tuesday at 1800 (arriving 2330). In late 1994 a second vessel, the 32-meter MV *Ramos II,* entered service between Honiara and Auki.

The high-speed, 136-passenger *Ocean Express* departs Honiara for Auki Monday at 0700 (3.5 hours, SI$35). The office (Box 966, Honiara; tel. 24281; weekdays 0800-1200 and 1300-1600, Saturday 0800-1130) is upstairs in the M.P. Kwan Building on Mendaña Avenue.

Ships to Isabel

The high-speed vessel **Ocean Express** (tel. 24281) zips from Honiara to Buala Tuesday at 0800 (6.5 hours, SI$50). There's a stop at Tatamba en route.

The **Isabel Development Co.** (Box 92, Honiara; tel. 22126, fax 22009), in the aluminum warehouse directly behind the Marine Division office, runs the *Ligomo* to Buala (SI$38 deck) once a week, twice a month up the west coast of Isabel as far as Kia.

Ship to Makira

The **Ocean Express** (tel. 24281) leaves Honiara for Kirakira Thursday at 0800 (8.5 hours, SI$60), calling at Marau Sound (SI$40) on the way.

Ship to Tulagi

The **National Fisheries Developments Ltd.** (Box 717, Honiara; tel. 21506, fax 21459), opposite the Coral Seas office, runs the *Tulagi Express* from Honiara to Tulagi on Tuesday, Friday, and Saturday at 1400 (two hours; SI$20). The return trip back to Honiara leaves Tulagi at 0630 the same days.

Ships around Guadalcanal

Once a week the **Guadalcanal Provincial Government** (tel. 20041, ext. 30) has a ship right around Guadalcanal, traveling clockwise or counterclockwise on alternate weeks, a four-day trip. It's usually either the MV *Wango* or the MV *Kangava,* departing Honiara Tuesday at 0800. You could stop off at Marau Sound and fly back. Inquire at the Provincial Office on Mendaña Avenue.

Marine Division

The government-operated **Marine Division** (tel. 21535) offers regular service to the outer islands. A blackboard that lists departures is in the Marine Division office, where you also buy your ticket. There's a ship to Sikaiana and Ontong Java every three weeks, and a monthly trip to Rennell and Bellona. These voyages average five days.

The Marine Division does a monthly run to the eastern outer islands of Makira, Santa Cruz, Utupua, Duff, Vanikolo, Anuta, and Tikopia. The roundtrip voyage takes about 25 days, SI$56

deck one-way to the last stop. The ship makes an extra circle around the Santa Cruz Islands before calling at Vanikolo for the second time; thus, you could stop off for about 10 days on this remote island before reboarding the same ship to return to Honiara. Other stopovers are possible. Add to your journey by getting off at Kirakira (Makira) on the way back and visiting Star Harbor and Santa Ana from there.

Other Ships

Less well-known are the old Chinese trading boats, full of South Seas flavor, which run between Honiara and Gizo fortnightly. There are also mission ships to many points; ask the crews along the waterfront. Also check the MV *King Solomon* booking office in the row of shops west of the Westpac Bank.

Melanesia Holdings (tel. 23749, fax 23280), the economic branch of the Church of Melanesia, runs three mission ships, the *Charles Fox, Southern Cross,* and *Kopuria* to various destinations, including south Guadalcanal. Check at the church business office upstairs in Church House.

By Canoe

To reach Savo Island, ask at the landing beside the Point Cruz Yacht Club if any canoes are going back. Unless you insist on the "hitching" rate of SI$15 pp, you'll be expected to pay SI$120-200 for a special trip. The organized day-trip to Savo is SI$150 pp return, but it's a long, hard day. Try to do the four-hour canoe journey in the early morning before the wind wakes the sea up, and be prepared to get soaked even on an apparently calm day. You'll pass through schools of dolphins and flying fish. The Tourist Authority can advise on canoes to Savo (ask them to put you in touch with Alan Kemakezee).

However, it's cheaper and faster to look for a canoe to Savo from Visale, near the west end of Guadalcanal. Catch the afternoon truck that leaves Honiara market for Visale around 1500 (SI$5). This connects with a canoe to Savo (SI$8).

By Bus

The big red buses that once served Honiara and environs on an hourly basis have now been replaced by scores of private minibuses that cruise up and down the main road from Rove to KG6 (King George VI High School) every five minutes or so. Some buses go as far west as White River. Eastbound they reach CDC123 out beyond Tetere about every 15 minutes throughout the day. Buses marked Naha turn inland at Kukum before reaching KG6. Buses within the town area operate until 2100 daily. All buses have destination boards in the front window, and fares run SI$1 anywhere between Rove and KG6, SI$2 to the airport, SI$2.50 to Foxwood Timbers, SI$4 to CDC2, and SI$5 to CDC3. Baggage is free and the conductors are fairly honest, but it's best to have small bills.

By Truck

Passenger trucks depart Honiara market for Lambi Bay (SI$8) and Aola (SI$8), at opposite ends of the north coast highway, daily except Sunday at about 1500. Other trucks make more frequent, shorter trips. Vehicles bearing white license plates with black lettering are public vehicles that charge fares.

Taxis

Taxi drivers are fairly honest, but always ask the price beforehand, as they don't have meters, and expect prices to increase at night. Expect to pay about SI$3 a km, plus SI$2 per piece of large luggage (don't tip the driver). Single passengers sit in front. If you're in a small group, you could hire a taxi for the day to tour the battlefields around the airport for about the same as it would cost to rent a car. Make a list of the places you want to see, then get a flat rate, including waiting time, gas, and mileage.

Car Rentals

Budget/Solomon Motors (Box 20, Honiara; tel. 23205, fax 23593) has offices next to the Mobil Garage near the Mendaña, at the Honiara Hotel, and at the airport. Their cheapest unlimited-mileage Suzuki costs SI$110/660 daily/weekly, plus SI$30/180 collision insurance (SI$500 deductible), plus five percent tax. Ask about their reduced half-day rate (valid 0900-1500).

More expensive is **Avis/Pacific Car Rentals** (Box 87, Honiara; tel. 24180, fax 24181), at the airport and inside the Kitano Mendaña Hotel. Their cheapest Daihatsu is SI$150 a day with unlimited kilometers, plus SI$30 compulsory collision insurance. If you rent for seven days, you get one day free.

Driving is on the left. Take care with the tricky one-way street system in the center of Honiara and rough roads and narrow bridges elsewhere. Beware of minibuses stopping suddenly. At night watch out for people walking along the edge of the road and drunken drivers everywhere. Don't leave valuables unattended in a parked car. Rental cars are not available elsewhere in the Solomons.

Tours

If time is short, several companies offer guided sightseeing tours of Honiara and the WW II sites. **Guadalcanal Travel Service** (Box 114, Honiara; tel. 22586, fax 23887) offers the three-hour "eastern battlefields" tour (SI$45) three times a week. The five-hour "western battlefields" trip (SI$80) includes lunch at Tambea Resort, but it's long and dusty. On Thursday there's a five-hour trek to Tenaru Falls (SI$70, plus an additional SI$10 pp for a local guide—not mentioned in their brochure).

Tour Solomons (Box 337, Honiara; tel. 21630, fax 21637) does transfers to Vulelua Island Resort or Tambea Holiday Beach Resort at SI$80 pp (two-person minimum). Their East Guadalcanal Tour is SI$84 for one person (SI$70 pp for two to four persons); the West Guadalcanal Tour is SI$120 for one (SI$95 pp for two to four). Their office is near the market across the street from the Quality Motel.

SOUTHEAST GUADALCANAL

It's possible to hike right across the island from CDC1, east of Honiara, to Kuma on the south coast via **Gold Ridge.** This is a major undertaking, requiring a local guide and three days of hard slugging. Villages like Old Case and Tinomeat date from the 1936 gold rush, and the locals still earn pocket money from gold won from the streams. They're very wary of European gold prospectors, so don't do any panning, whatever you do! Earth Movers Pacific Timbers is in charge of logging this region.

There are provincial rest houses on the Weather Coast, near the airstrips at Avu Avu, Marau Sound, and Mbambanakira (with Solomon Airlines flights three times a week). The flight from Honiara to Avu Avu (61 km, SI$60) takes you across at low altitude, with wonderful views of the valleys.

A road built in 1978 and not maintained since links Avu Avu to Marau Sound (50 km), but the only vehicles on it are tractors, which pass every couple of weeks. It's a slightly boring two-day walk. The south coast is the rainiest part of the country, and during rainy season (July to September) the short, shallow rivers become impassable after big storms.

The Moro Cult

In 1953 a cargo cult led by visionary Chief Moro was founded at **Makaruka,** a village three km up the Alualu River between Avu Avu and Marau Sound. In 1957 Moro called for a return to the *kabilato* and grass skirts after a visit by a spirit who instructed him to lead his people in a return to the old ways. He taught people how to live in harmony with each other and nature. Today the Moro movement, known as the Gaenalu Association, has 5,000 followers scattered around Guadalcanal. Of the four associated villages, today only **Komuvaolu** is totally traditional, though the three custom house "banks" brimming with shell money and *tambu* objects are still well guarded at Makaruka.

To visit the Moro community, you must first ask permission, then adopt traditional dress, which means a small bark loincloth for men and grass skirts for women. Ask for the Principal Administration Officer at the Guadalcanal Provincial Office (tel. 20041) in Honiara. He will contact Chief Moro to make sure he doesn't mind seeing you. Otherwise, ask for Victor Totu at the Guadalcanal Cultural Center, also in the provincial offices. He'll put you on the right track. To get there you must either fly to Avu Avu and then charter an outboard canoe for the 20-km trip east, hike several days across the island from the end of the road below Gold Ridge, or try using the weekly provincial boat around Guadalcanal.

Marau Sound

Marau Sound at the east tip of Guadalcanal has an extensive system of barrier reefs, offshore islands, and secure anchorages for yachts. Giant clam shells are found in this area. Direct Solomon Airlines flights to Marau Sound are available several times a week from Honiara (103 km, SI$79) and Auki (SI$92). The high-speed vessel *Ocean Express* stops here between Honiara and Kirakira on Thursday.

Most people come to stay in one of the six tall thatched *vales* at the **Tavanipupu Island Resort** (Box 236, Honiara; no phone), set on the emerald lagoon flanked by fine white beaches. Three large traditional-style buildings serve as a lounge, dining room, and reception. Originally purchased for five rifles by Norwegian trader Oscar Svensen in 1890, the present owners, Dennis Bellote and Keith Peske, bought the place from the Humphrey family in 1986 and have created this exotic hideaway since then. At last report, the price for rooms was SI$100-250, but ask at the Western Pacific Air Services office in Honiara. Another option is one of the three rooms at the **Manikaraku Rest House,** on the mainland a 15-minute walk from the airstrip, SI$20 pp.

MALAITA PROVINCE

This hot, humid, thickly forested island is the second largest and most densely populated of the Solomons: its 80,000 inhabitants make up almost a third of the country's population. Malaita is one of the country's few islands where people reside in the jungle-clad interior. The bush people live in isolated hamlets of two or three houses, and as many as 10,000 still believe in ancestral spirits (though tenacious missionaries are working to change this).

Many Malaitans have tried to escape their island's limited economic opportunities by emigrating to other islands; there's a large community of them in Honiara. In blackbirding times, nearly 10,000 Malaitans labored in the cane fields of Queensland, Australia. Today, they work on plantations throughout the Solomons and are likely to be your fellow passengers on interisland ships. Copra production is one of the few ways most Malaitans have of making cash money, although there have been attempts to introduce cattle and cacao. Commercial logging is being carried out by Maving Brothers in the north and Goldenspring in the south.

Malaita has the most extensive road network in the Solomons, but most are in bad repair and can be closed by rains. The main town is Auki. There's little difficulty going inland, provided you have a guide. Malaita is wet, and the forest floor is permanently damp. The walking is slow, and good boots are essential.

The People

The Malaitans have a reputation of cantankerousness. During the 19th century, shipwrecked sailors were regularly cooked and eaten. The tribes conducted headhunting raids against Isabel Islanders and each other, forcing the people to live in fortified villages. When blackbirders kidnapped villagers, the Malaitans took revenge by attacking visiting European ships. As punitive raids followed the murder of missionaries, leading to new retaliatory attacks, the traditional conflict between the peoples of the coast and interior intensified with the introduction of firearms by returning workers.

In 1927 the British district officer and a police party were massacred during a campaign to collect head taxes and all outstanding rifles. The British responded by arresting 200 Kwaio tribesmen (of whom 30 died in captivity), hanging six, sending an Australian cruiser to shell coastal villages, poisoning Kwaio taro gardens, and turning native police from rival tribes loose on those responsible.

Even before WW II, Malaitan plantation workers were refusing to obey overseers who kept them in line with whips and dogs. When war came, many Malaitan men went to work for the Americans on Guadalcanal. The fair, generous treatment they received and the sight of black Americans dressed like whites and enjoying equal, though separate, rights had an impact. In hope of trading American rule for British, the Marching Rule cargo cult emerged in 1944. Villages were reorganized under new chiefs and surrounded by stockades with watchtowers, and huts were prepared to store the cargo soon to arrive from the United States.

By 1949 the British decided things were getting out of hand and suppressed the movement by arresting 2,000 of its followers. Though things calmed down in 1952, when local councils were established to represent the people, many Malaitans still distrust outsiders, and large numbers in the interior resist all forms of Western influence. They in turn are often resented by other Solomon Islanders, who see them forming communities on other islands and playing a disproportionately active role in today's cash economy.

Traditional Currency

The shell money of the Langa Langa Lagoon, on the northwest side of Malaita, is made by breaking shells into small pieces, boring them with a drill, and stringing them together. Patient rubbing of the shell pieces between two grooved stones gives them their circular shape. Thousands of minute discs go into a *tafuliae,* or string, which contains 10 strands of shells two to three meters long and bears a fixed rate of exchange to the official currency (presently SI$380). This auxiliary form of currency is used for quasi-ceremonial transactions, such as buying wives (10 strings), pigs, canoes, or land, and as settlement or compensation for injuries.

Shells vary in value according to the color and size of the shell parts used: pink is the most expensive, then orange, white, and lastly black. Generally, the smaller the size of the shell piece, the more expensive it is. Pink-lipped *spondylus* ("pink money") is made only from the lip of the shell and is the most valuable, worth four or five times as much as white.

Dolphin teeth are also used as custom money on Malaita (1,000 teeth for a wife, at 40 cents a tooth), and dolphin drives to obtain teeth are conducted at Mbita'ama Harbor (northwest Malaita), Port Adam (Maramasike Island), and Sulufou (Lau Lagoon). A sorcerer in a canoe taps magical stones together underwater to attract the dolphins, which are then led ashore by other villagers in canoes, butchered, and the meat divided. Flying-fox teeth and pigs are also exchanged on Malaita.

In the Western Solomons, ceremonial currency is in the form of large heavy rings, four centimeters thick and 24 centimeters in diameter, cut out of the shell of the giant clam. A ring with a small patch of yellow on the edge is worth more than a plain white one. In Santa Cruz, great rolls of red-feather money are used as bride price. The men who have the customary rights to make the coils pluck a few feathers from captured scarlet honeyeaters before releasing the birds.

AUKI

Auki (population 4,000), at the northern end of the Langa Langa Lagoon, has been the administrative center since 1909. It's a lazy, laid-back little town with frequent ferry service from Honiara (106 km). The setting is picturesque, and there are many interesting places to visit in the vicinity. A trip to Kwai Island off East Malaita is possible when the road to Atori is open, but the excursion to Malu'u is much easier. Auki is closer to the bush than Honiara, more colorful and relaxed, so it's a fast, easy escape from the dusty capital. For most visitors, Auki is Malaita's port of entry.

Lilisiana

For 18 generations the saltwater people of the Langa Langa Lagoon have lived on tiny artificial-reef islands, which offered protection from raids by the bush people of the interior and were free of mosquitoes. A perimeter was made in the lagoon from blocks of coral, filled with more coral and covered with earth to form an island. The inhabitants remained dependent on their mainland gardens and fresh water, but a unique culture evolved.

One such artificial island is Auki Island, within view of Auki wharf. The two families on this island still maintain a few traditional sites, but most inhabitants moved away after a hurricane devastated their homes. It's now possible to walk (20 minutes) to Lilisiana, the new village on the mainland—to the right as you look out to sea from Auki. Here you can observe shell money being manufactured in authentic surroundings. If you show an interest people will bring out shell money necklaces for sale. There are isolated stretches of sandy beach along the track to the right just before you reach Lilisiana.

Other Sights

Take the road inland just before the bridge, less than a kilometer south of Auki wharf, to cool off in the **Kwaibala River** near the pump house. The water is clear and the locals friendly. You could rent a dugout canoe at **Ambu** village near here.

Auki's strangest sight is **Riba Cave** near Dukwasi village, a strenuous one-hour hike up the road leading inland from Auki Lodge. It'll cost SI$10 to go through (they'll start off asking SI$20 or more, so bargain), and the cave is slippery, drippy, and muddy, so dress accordingly. Thousands of swallows inhabit the cave roof. From the entrance, the cave passage leads a short distance to an impressive sinkhole. Across the sinkhole at the entrance to the largest chamber is a giant stalagmite in the form of a man, named Louis. Once worshipped, it's been worn smooth by rubbing. The passage leads through a spectacular maze of caverns far underground, eventually merging with an underground knee-deep river, unswimmable.

· When you return from Riba Cave, the friendly Dukwasi villagers may have tea prepared for you. Take along some self-rising flour from Auki and give it to Martin before going to the cave. He makes great hot bread. This is a good rainy-day trip.

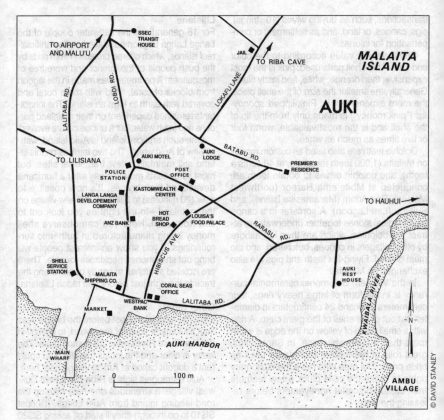

© DAVID STANLEY

Accommodations

The **Auki Rest House** (tel. 40250), operated by the Malaita Development Authority, has two 10-bed dormitories at SI$20 pp—high for what's offered: cooking, but filthy toilets and a basic appearance.

The spotless **South Seas Evangelical Church Transit House** (Box 14, Auki; tel. 40173, fax 40220), behind Auki Bookshop, has three rooms (eight beds) at SI$30 pp. There are cooking facilities and a sitting room. It's a clean, quiet place to stay (no smoking allowed).

The **Auki Motel** (Box 153, Auki; tel. 40014), above a store on the road to Malu'u, is SI$30 per bed in any of the five three-bed rooms. Their restaurant (open all day on weekdays, lunch only on Saturday) is reasonable and a good place for a coffee.

Most tourists stay at **Auki Lodge** (Box 170, Auki; tel. 40131, fax 40220), which has a veranda overlooking the landscaped grounds. The two fan-cooled rooms are SI$85/115 single/double, three standard a/c rooms are SI$150/180, and two deluxe a/c rooms are SI$180/210. There's a restaurant (expensive) and bar (reasonable) on the premises, and the entire complex was completely renovated for a Melanesian Spearhead summit in July 1994. This is the only place where you can get a room with private bath.

A local place called **Dave's Transit** (David Ganifiri, Box 197, Auki; tel. 40045) with four rooms at SI$30 pp is up Lokafu Lane from Auki Lodge, and there are several other unmarked places accommodating local travelers around here run by people like Owen Newman, Kenny

Leong, and John Bulu—ask around if you'd like to get away from the regular places to stay.

Food
Auki market functions from Monday to Saturday but is best early Wednesday and Saturday mornings. The butcher shop by the market is cheap.

Louisa's Food Palace near the post office serves breakfast (0730-1000), lunch (1030-1500), and dinner (1900-2130) daily, but on Sunday it's only dinner. The food is surprisingly good for such an unpretentious place.

Services
The ANZ, National, and Westpac banks have branches in Auki that will change foreign currency and traveler's checks. The post office is open weekdays 0800-1200 and 1300-1530, Saturday 0900-1100. Kilu'ufi Hospital (tel. 40272) is three km north of Auki.

Shopping
The **Kastomwealth Center** (Box 79, Auki; tel. 40177), opposite the post office, sells shell money and necklaces made from shell money at fixed prices. It's a good place to pick up a unique souvenir.

The **Langa Langa Development Company** sells bracelets and necklaces made from shell money.

Transportation
Gwaunaruu airstrip (AKS) is 11 km north of Auki; the airline minibus is SI$10. Solomon Airlines (tel. 40163) next to Auki Lodge has flights from Honiara (111 km, SI$83) daily, from Fera (SI$103) and Marau Sound (SI$92) twice a week, and from Parasi (SI$98) weekly.

Auki is also well serviced by passenger ships to Honiara (six hours, SI$25). The **Coral Seas Ltd.** office (tel. 40188) beside the Westpac Bank accepts bookings for the *Compass Rose* departing Auki for Honiara Monday and Thursday at 0900, and the *Iuminoa* to Honiara Saturday at 0900. The faster *Ocean Express* departs for Honiara Monday at 1230 (3.5 hours, SI$35).

The **Malaita Shipping Co.** opposite the wharf sells tickets to Honiara on the *Ramos I*, which leaves Wednesday at 0900.

The **Marine Office** (tel. 40143) behind the Malaita Shipping Co. sometimes has government boats from Auki to South Malaita, but it's much easier to get to South Malaita from Honiara.

There's no regular bus service on the island, so you travel by passenger truck (Malu'u SI$10, Fouia SI$14, Atori SI$12); they're usually in Auki on days when ships arrive. This is the easiest time to catch rides to anywhere.

LANGA LANGA LAGOON

The artificial islands in the Langa Langa Lagoon are home to some of the last of the shark callers. Many of these people still worship their ancestors, whose spirits are embodied in sharks that the high priest summons. Skeptics say the sharks come because they hear the gongs being beaten underwater, a conditioned reflex. Yet no one knows for sure why the sharks eat only the offerings and leave the people who swim among them alone.

A boy stands on a submerged rock and feeds the sharks pieces of cooked pig one by one as the priest calls each by the name of its human spirit. The largest piece is given last, to the oldest shark. Should a fisherman be capsized in the deep sea, he can summon a shark, using a special language the shark understands. After the shark has carried him ashore, the fisherman must offer a sacrificial pig, otherwise he will be eaten on his next fishing trip. (Note, however, that shark calling is not included in regular artificial island tours.)

Laulasi
On this small island, 13 km south of Auki, are large spirit houses with high pitched roofs, the names of famous priests inscribed on the gables. When a priest dies, his body is taken to neighboring Alite to rot. Later the skull is retrieved and placed in the House of Skulls. Offerings are presented at shark-calling ceremonies in the gap between the two islands. The pigs used for these offerings are held by the shore in pens big enough for a man—the offering in times past, before pigs were substituted.

Women and children are forbidden to enter the custom houses, and no one dressed in red or black will be permitted to land on the island. Tourists are shown how to make shell money

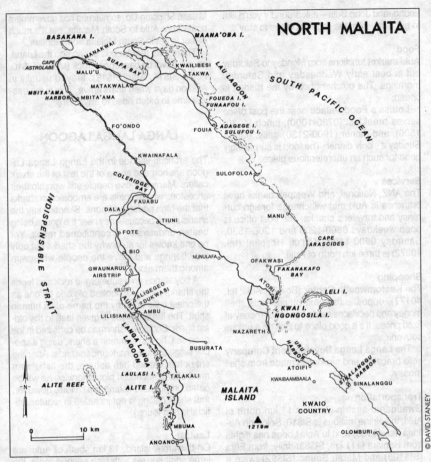

NORTH MALAITA

using manual drills; after they're gone, the diamond-headed drill bits come back out. The village on Alite is similar.

Getting There

Colin Bauwane at Auki Lodge organizes outboard tours to Laulasi or Alite islands (five hours). The SI$250 per group price includes custom dancing, a demonstration of shell money making, a tour of the custom places, and lunch. Book 24 hours in advance.

Sometimes you can hire a motorized canoe to Laulasi from near Auki Market for SI$100, then pay the islanders a SI$30 pp custom fee for the right to look around (no dances or lunch).

The road south from Auki reaches beyond Su'u Bay, and passenger trucks go as far as Hauhui. There's more frequent service to Talakali (14 km, SI$2), on the mainland opposite Laulasi. There you may be able to hire an outboard for SI$20 roundtrip (less if you paddle across the two km yourself in a dugout), but you'll still be charged the SI$30 pp fee to look around. A similar fee is collected at Alite. Talakali's population, incidentally, is Seventh-Day Adventist, so don't bother going on Saturday.

MALU'U

This pleasant little government station at the island's northern tip, halfway between Auki and Fouia, makes an excellent base from which to visit heavily populated North Malaita. The villagers are very friendly and warmly welcome visitors, and traffic to and from Auki is fairly frequent.

Sights

On the beach at Malu'u is a monument to the first missionary to land on Malaita (in 1894). From the market, walk east along the beach until you meet the main road again. There's a bathing beach here, and the reef protects you from most sharks. Go snorkeling on Diula, opposite the tiny offshore island. Out across the lagoon, good surf breaks at the west end of the reef. This left-hander works best at high tide in a one-and-a-half-meter swell (November to March only). Where the swells come from two directions the shifting peaks cause havoc. There's also good diving along the inside edge of the lagoon.

At **A'ama** village on the hilltop just above Malu'u, visit the *biu* (young men's house). At **Manakwai** village, a few kilometers west of Malu'u on the main road, is a small cascade, a mini-hydro station, and a good place to swim in the river. Ask the person in the electric generating station if you can follow the trail up the large water pipe.

To get to **Basakana Island**, take a truck to the beach opposite and light a smoky fire. Someone will come across from the village to fetch you. There's a cave to visit on Basakana, plus many fine beaches.

Accommodations and Tours

Bartholomew Wanefalea's **Malu'u Lodge** (no phone), above Tang's store facing the waterfront, has seven clean, functional double rooms with shared bath at SI$40 per bed. Communal cooking facilities are available, and there's a large sitting room. A two-hour snorkeling trip to the reef and to see the submerged Japanese plane costs SI$100 for the boat (up to seven people can go for that price). To rent the boat for a full day of surfing or sightseeing costs SI$200.

Guided visits to local villages (SI$200 a day) and panpipe concerts are also possible.

The **Baptist Church** at Keru village on the hill behind Malu'u has a two-room guesthouse with cooking facilities at rates much lower than those charged at Malu'u Lodge. Ask for Henrik Rilalo or his father Rubin Rilalo. They can supply guides for bush walks into the surrounding hills. It's a good choice if you want to stay in a village environment.

Groceries may be purchased at the three stores down by the harbor or from the market (open Monday, Wednesday, Thursday, and Saturday 0600-0900).

Matakwalao

Visit Matakwalao market (Wednesday and Saturday) by truck from Malu'u. Ask for John Risavo and hire him as a guide; you'll be in for a touch of real adventure. John is *nambawan* in the bush. If you don't meet him at the market, get someone to guide you to his jungle hamlet, a three-hour walk from Matakwalao. This will give you an idea of what you'll be in for. There may be problems in visiting the stones on Malaita Hill, but John knows other traditional places deep in the rainforest that you can visit with less effort.

LAU LAGOON

Over 60 artificial islands are found in the 36-km-long Lau Lagoon on the northeast side of Malaita. These are inhabited by the so-called island builders, who bring coral blocks, sand, and earth on log rafts to convert lagoon shallows into solid land. With the constant cool breezes, the air is incredibly fresh out on these man-made islands. On the mainland they grow taro, yams, potatoes, papaya, leafy vegetables, bananas, and sugarcane. The women travel back and forth from their island homes to the gardens, and the men fish most of the time. The large canoes for dolphin-hunting are made by sewing together long planks of wood and caulking the seams with a putty made from the nut of the *tita* tree *(Parinari glaberrima)*.

Though Christianity is increasing, some people on islands such as Foueda, Funaafou, and Adagege still practice the same custom religion as the people of Laulasi/Alite. Here you'll find a *beu* (men's house) where chiefs are buried in their canoes, plus heathen places of worship, with a sacrificial altar, cemetery, House of Skulls, etc. Entry to the *beu* is prohibited, but you can often see in from outside. There is no *beu* at Sulufou, which is now thoroughly Christianized. After childbirth women are sent to a *bisi* (women's house) for 30 days. Shark calling is also practiced here on special occasions, announced by the pagan priests.

Takwa

Takwa is only 12 km from the end of the road at Fouia. The final passage to Takwa wharf by boat passes many artificial islands, a fitting introduction to the Lau Lagoon. A market near the Catholic mission at Takwa sets up every Saturday with shell money and porpoise teeth circulating alongside Solomon Islands currency. Swim in the river at the landing where the dugout canoes of the saltwater people arrive. Kwailibesi airstrip is near Takwa.

Sulione

People from the traditional islands of Foueda and Funaafou come to the market at Sulione on the main road near Fouia every Monday and Thursday, and it might be possible to go back with them. In 1935, the Seventh-Day Adventist converts on Foueda were banished to nearby Ropa, now linked to Foueda by a wooden footbridge. Foueda is mostly Christian today. On Funaafou is a Cultural Center housing old artifacts and many *tambu* places.

Sulufou

The road and truck route from Auki ends at **Fouia** wharf (120 km), on the mainland opposite the artificial islands of Sulufou and Adagege. For a few dollars someone will paddle you the 500 meters over to Sulufou, largest and oldest of the artificial islands. The picturesque village is partly built on stilts over the lagoon. In front of the big Anglican church is a stone where fugitives from northern Malaita sat to obtain sanctuary and protection. You could be requested to contribute something to this church for the visit.

Unfortunately, there's no organized place to stay at Fouia or Sulufou, so you either have to

a clamshell ornament from Malaita incised with frigate bird designs

make it a day-trip from Malu'u or go native. You can sometimes catch a ship or outboard down the coast to Atori or Kwai.

SOUTHEAST MALAITA

East Malaita

Take a truck from Auki via Dala to **Atori**, provided the road hasn't been closed by rains. Midway at Nunulafa is a bridge over the Auluta Gorge. Some good **surfing beaches** are north of Atori. Fakanakafo Bay is the closest, accessible by canoe from Atori, but press on to Manu village for the good left-handers. A coastal trail runs north from Fakanakafo Bay to Fouia.

Kwai is a beautiful island with kind, friendly people. Village houses are densely packed here and on neighboring Ngongosila Island. There's a native rest house with cooking facilities at the edge of the island, where you can stay (ask for Paul Alafa or David Loke, the village baker). It's only three km from Atori to Kwai Island, but the outboard boys charge SI$20 roundtrip (the locals pay SI$2), so try to hitch a ride with someone off your truck. Outboard canoe rentals are totally unreasonable throughout this area.

In 1927, British District Officer William Bell, his cadet K.C. Lillies, and 13 native policemen were speared by Kwaio tribesmen at Kwaiambe (Gwee'abe) on Sinalanggu Harbor. Later, British officials looked the other way when north Malaita police murdered about 70

Kwaio prisoners, including women and children, in cold blood to avenge their slain comrades, and the Kwaio have never received compensation for the 200 tribespeople who died during the affair. The book *Lightning Meets the West Wind,* by Roger Keesing and Peter Corris (Melbourne: Oxford University Press, 1980), tells the story. To visit the graves of Bell and Lillies, wade across the sandbar from Kwai to Ngongosila at low tide.

A road is underway from Atori to Atoifi, presently as far as Nazareth. Atoifi on Uru Harbor is a center for those Kwaio who have accepted Christianity, and a large Seventh-Day Adventist hospital is here. There's an airstrip with Western Pacific Air flights from Honiara (SI$88) Monday to Friday, some of which also call at Auki. The pagan population lives in small, scattered hamlets on the upland plateaus. Kwaibaambaala, in the foothills between Atoifi and Sinalanggu, is one traditional village sometimes visited.

Trips deeper into the **Kwaio Country** above Sinalanggu to see the "Hidden People" can be arranged, but be prepared for high charges for transport and guides. Even today, the Kwaios in the hills follow the traditions and taboos of their ancestors, and visitors are rare. In 1965 a missionary from New Zealand was killed here. In his book *Conversations with the Cannibals* (see "Resources" at the end of this book), American writer Michael Krieger decries the way the Seventh-Day Adventist Church links desperately needed medical aid to conversions, and how the Solomon Island government collects taxes from these people but provides no services. New Zealand reader Robert Kennington sent us this:

We climbed up into the mountains of West Kwaio for seven hours, up and down ridges and into the virgin forest, until we came to a neat, clean village high in the mountains. By the time we got there the children from nearby gardens had run ahead and given advance warning, so when we appeared on the scene everyone from the youngest to the oldest was wearing clothing. One could see that the clothes had just been put on, *and under the dresses one could clearly note the bulge from the cane belt the women wear. It was especially amusing the way the kids had been forced to put on something, and at every opportunity off would come those pants! The people were shy at first but hospitable and a few could understand pijin if spoken slowly. To go to such places one really needs a guide.*

South Malaita

No road connects South Malaita to Auki, so either fly to Parasi (SI$98 one-way from Auki) or take a truck south to Hauhui, then a motorized canoe on south. The Wairaha River, south of Hauhui, is Solomon Island's largest.

Apio is at the southwest entrance to Maramasike Passage. Just 3.7 meters deep near the center, this passage is only open to vessels of light draft. A bush road now runs from Apio, opposite Maka on Malaita, to Olusu'u, near the southeast end of Maramasike, or Small Malaita. Few tourists come here.

THE POLYNESIAN OUTLIERS

Sikaiana

This tiny atoll, 177 km northeast of Malaita, is inhabited by the descendants of Tongans, as proved by a variety of filarial mosquito found on Sikaiana and Tonga but nowhere else in the world. Four reef islets mark the triangular Te Moana Lagoon. There's no anchorage, and access is by small boat through the surf. Less than 500 people live here.

Ontong Java

This 70-by-26-km boot-shaped atoll encloses 1,400 square km of lagoon, making it the second-largest atoll in the world (after 2,174-square-km Kwajalein in the Marshall Islands). Ontong Java's 122 islands total only 12 square km of dry land. This is the northernmost point in the Solomon Islands, and only 70 km separate Ontong Java from Nukumanu atoll in Papua New Guinea. The inhabitants are related and often travel in outboards between the two, trading in bêche-de-mer.

ONTONG JAVA

HENUAKAI

PELAU

—N—

ONTONG JAVA

LAGOON

KELOMA
LABAHA
KE ILA

LUANGIUA

KE AVAIKO
PASSAGE

0   10   20   30 km

© DAVID STANLEY

Ke Avaiko Passage, just south of Luangiua Island, leads directly to the lagoon anchorage off the village. The supply ship calls at Luangiua, Labaha, and Pelau, the only permanently inhabited islands, but the people reside part-time on many others, fishing and making copra. All the islets are planted with coconuts, and production is large; swamp taro is cultivated in deep pits in the interior of several islands.

Ontong Java was named by Tasman on 22 March 1643. Ontong was probably derived from the Malay *untung* (luck, fortune, destiny, fate); in other words, "Java Luck." Tasman's ships had been subjected to squalls for months on end, and he was most likely congratulating himself on the improved conditions. In 1791 Captain Hunter renamed it Lord Howe Island, but the previous name stuck. The local Polynesians believe they originated on Niue; Luangiua means literally "Niue number two" (Luaniue). In 1907, Ontong Java had 5,000 inhabitants, but epidemics reduced it to only 700 by 1927. Now it's back up to about 1,400 (1,000 in Luangiua and 400 in Pelau).

This atoll is one of the few places in the Solomons where houses are built directly on the ground (dirt floor—no stilts). The cemeteries here are striking for their large carved tombstones. Casual visitors are welcome to look around the villages, but the chiefs want to be sure you leave on the same ship. There have been problems with Westerners who just showed up and thought they could stay. You might be able to spend a night or two in Luangiua, however, as the ship visits the other settlements to pick up copra. Bring your own food, as little is available from the two stores.

RENNELL AND BELLONA PROVINCE

RENNELL

Two hundred km south of Guadalcanal are two Polynesian islands, Rennell and Bellona, about 25 km apart. Rennell, an 80-by-16-km raised atoll surrounded by sheer 100-meter cliffs, is by far the larger. In fact, at 692 square km it's the largest, and perhaps the finest, elevated atoll on earth. **Lake Te Nggano** (155 square km) on the southeast side of Rennell is the largest lake in the South Pacific, with about 200 small islands dotted around its edges. The saline water in the lake is at sea level but it's surrounded by high cliffs. The docile Rennell Island Krait (*Laticausa crockeri*)—or Tugihono as the Rennellese call it—a unique sea snake, lives only in this lake. Of the 50 species of birds on Rennell, 21 are endemic. Eighty percent of Rennell is forested. East Rennell has been nominated as a UNESCO World Heritage Site, something it well deserves.

Due to the murder of three Melanesian Seventh-Day Adventist missionaries in 1910, Rennell was closed to Europeans until 1934. Conversion to SDA Christianity took place in 1938, when a picture of Christ was seen to speak. Overnight the people gave up their traditional ways, such as tattooing, and adopted Western dress. The Rennellese still practice *hetakai*, traditional wrestling, at custom feasts. The object is to knock the opponent down. Among the many handicrafts are walking sticks, hardwood crocodile carvings, miniature weapons, woven bags, and mats. Other than a few tiny stores, no business of any kind exists on Rennell, and all 2,500 villagers live from their gardens. Though threatened by loggers and bauxite miners, Rennell is still well off the beaten track.

The airstrip (RNL) is at Tinggoa, at Rennell's west end. A road built in 1977 by the Japanese mining company Mitsui (the company did exploratory work, but pulled out when bauxite prices fell) leads through lush rainforest down to the small port, Lavanggu, where the monthly ship from Honiara calls. The ship also stops at Tuhungganggo. A canoe from Lavanggu to Tuhungganggo is SI$10 pp or SI$120 for a special trip (one hour), possible in good weather only. From Tuhungganggo a steep stairway known as "ten story" climbs over sharp limestone cliffs, then it's a four-km stroll to Te Nggano village, one of four on the lake. A new European Union-financed road runs from Lavanggu to Tebaitahe village right on Lake Te Nggano. This is by far the most magical part of Rennell. Plans are underway to build a new airstrip near the lake in east Rennell. For yachts, there's good anchorage on the south shore of Kanggava Bay with excellent snorkeling.

Getting around Rennell is a problem, as the tractor that's supposed to meet the boats and planes often breaks down, and the distances are large. To walk from Lavanggu to Tinggoa will take six hours if you go straight or eight with stops. Theoretically a tractor-trailer (50 cents pp) leaves the airstrip end of Rennell around 0630 and takes two hours to get to Lavanggu along a coral road, returning shortly after arrival at Lavanggu. To hire a tractor from the airstrip to Lavanggu is SI$20. You'll get soaked if it rains. Take heart: the beach at Lavanggu is great, and there's a splendid view of it from the village above.

RENNELL AND BELLONA

BELLONA I.

MANGGAUTU

TINGGOA AIRSTRIP

RENNELL I.

LAVANGGU

KANGGAVA BAY
SATAN'S POINT

TUHUNGGANGGO

LAKE TE NGGANO

-N-

0   20km

© DAVID STANLEY

In July 1989 Paul Tauniu opened the **Taha-matangi Guesthouse** (no phone), an airy European-style building on the shores of Lake Te Nggano. Up to five persons are accommodated in the one main building at SI$30 pp. Paul organizes bushwalking and lake tours to see the unique wildlife of the area. Locally produced meals of crab, fish, chicken, pineapple, papaya, banana, and taro are served (additional charge). The Tourist Authority in Honiara will have information. The local stores have little more than canned fish, corned beef, and stick tobacco, so bring food. Rennell is free of malaria.

BELLONA

Like Rennell, Bellona is a cliff-girdled uplifted atoll. Rich phosphate deposits exist here, but the islanders rightly fear that mining would devastate their homeland. Bellona is much easier to visit than Rennell, as it's smaller and nothing is

more than an hour's walk away. The handsome, intelligent people are a fun-loving bunch descended from the same stock as the Rennellese. Most live in the fertile interior.

The Polynesians first migrated to this island 25 generations ago and upon arrival wiped out the Hiti, Melanesian cave dwellers who previously inhabited the island. The Hiti caves still dot the cliffs and are fascinating to explore, though they're very cramped.

A man named Renbel has built the **Suani Resthouse** (Box 592, Honiara; tel. 23846) on Bellona. Accommodations in the main five-bed building are SI$26 pp. Also ask about **Aotaha Guest House.** There's no malaria on Bellona, but the mosquitoes are of a type that bite all night (not just at dusk), so bring plenty of repellent. If you have an underwater flashlight, ask someone to take you crayfishing at night. Solomon Airlines has flights from Honiara (SI$140) and Rennell (SI$47) twice a week.

CENTRAL PROVINCE

Tulagi

Tulagi, a small island about five km in circumference in the Florida Group, was the island capital of the Solomons from 1896 to 1942. Burns Philp had its head station on Makambo Island, nearby. The Japanese entered unopposed on 3 May 1942 after a hasty British evacuation, and Tulagi was badly damaged during the American invasion three months later. The Americans built a seaplane base on nearby Ghavutu Island, and a good concrete wharf from that time remains. Their PT-boat squadrons were also based at Tulagi. Another remnant of the old days on Tulagi is the marine base, where shipbuilding and repairs are still carried out.

The deep strait between Tulagi and Nggela forms a good harbor, well sheltered from the southeast trade winds. In 1973, the Japanese Taiyo Corporation took advantage of this by establishing a fish-freezing and canning plant here, but in 1990 this facility was shifted to Noro in Western Province. Today the Canadian-owned National Fisheries Development Ltd. fishing fleet is based here. There's a striking hand-hewn passage cut by prewar prisoner's between the

wharf and the rest house. The British resident commissioners lived at **Nambawan Haos,** on the hill above the cut. Follow a footpath (three hours) clockwise around the island for great views. Today Tulagi (population 1,750) is the headquarters of Central Province, an odd collection that includes the Florida Islands, Savo, and the Russell Islands.

The **Central Province Rest House** has six double rooms with shared cooking facilities at SI$20 pp. Check in at the Provincial Office (tel. 32100, ext. 4). Also try **Vanita Accommodation** (Annette Dennis, Box 376, Honiara; tel. 32157) near the wharf with two rooms at SI$55 double. Tulagi has a market and two Chinese stores. Buy frozen skipjack at the NFD cold storage for home cooking.

The Florida Islands

There are two large islands here, Nggela Sule and Nggela Pile, separated by narrow Utaha Passage. Tulagi is off the south coast of Nggela Sule. To get away for a week, take a walk around Nggela Pile for its scenic views, golden beaches, and village life. Catch a ship from Honiara to **Siota Mission,** then walk a couple of days along the coast to Vuturua village and have someone paddle you across to Peula. Three stalactite caves are along the way, but you'll need a guide to find them. Continue on the coast to Ndende and across to Dadala village on Utaha Passage. Finish your expedition with a canoe ride to Taroaniana shipyard, where you should be able to find a canoe to Tulagi or a ship back to Honiara. (Attention yachties: this Anglican Church-operated shipyard can handle major repairs! Contact them at tel. 23031 or fax 21486.)

Savo

Savo is a cone-shaped island on **Iron Bottom Sound,** named for the number of warships sunk in the vicinity during WW II. Savo's dormant volcano last erupted in 1840, but it's still considered potentially dangerous. Near the center of the island are two craters, one inside the other. A trip up to the steaming, 485-meter-high crater is worth trying—if you can find a guide and you're fit. Two boiling hot springs are on the crater's edge, and more on the volcano's sides are used for cooking. The chief of Kaonggele collects a SI$5 pp custom fee to use the village path to the crater.

Savo is also famous for its megapode bird (*Megapodius freycinet*) or *skrab dak*. This small dark bush turkey lays billiard-ball-sized eggs underground, then leaves them to hatch by heat from either the sun or the island's warm volcanic sands. Unfortunately, the number of megapodes is declining fast due to unrestrained harvesting of the eggs. See them in the early morning near **Panueli.**

A tractor track runs right around 31-square-km Savo's shark-infested shores, passing 14 villages. The inhabitants all speak a Papuan language, Savosavo, one of the few non-Austronesian languages of the Solomons. Traditionally Savo people fish by suspending a hook from a kite behind the canoe. There's a fissure just a short distance inland from **Siata** village where the locals cook their food. All drinking and washing water on Savo comes from wells, and the water in them is also often warm: boil it before drinking. A rural water supply project is gradually improving this situation but there's still no electricity.

The only regular place to stay is the **Legalau Nature Side Village** (Ben Duva, Box 922, Honiara), on the northwest side of Savo, with two three-bed cottages at SI$30 pp. Local meals are served and guides are provided for hikes to the megapode field or the volcano. Ask at the Solomon Islands Tourist Authority about this place. Also ask at **J & L Carriers** (tel. 24132) in Room no. 29, upstairs in the NPF Plaza Building in Honiara; J & L can book accommodations on Savo. A boat to Legalau often leaves from Point Cruz Yacht Club at 1300 (SI$20 pp).

It's also possible to stay with local villagers, such as Nathaniel Niuau of the Agriculture Division or John Tome at Kakalaka village. This is probably only worth pursuing if Legalau happens to be full the day you arrive.

Although most outboards (SI$8-15 pp) go to Visale or Honiara on Guadalcanal, it's sometimes possible to find a ship from Savo to Tulagi and vice versa.

The Russell Islands

The Russell Islands consist of two adjacent larger islands, Mbanika and Pavuvu, plus many smaller islets. Levers Solomons Ltd. has huge copra plantations on the islands, where tourism isn't promoted, though the expat plantation management is friendly once they know you. The Solomon's first coconut-oil mill opened here in 1989. Levers runs some 2,000 head of cattle across the islands, and wild water buffalo dwell in the swamps of Mbanika, descendants of escaped domestic stock. Wild donkeys are also seen in and around Yandina at night.

The U.S. took the Russells unopposed in February 1943 and built a pair of airstrips from which to launch attacks on New Georgia. The American Quonset huts facing Yandina wharf are now used for copra storage. Local children can show you a WW II military dump near Renard Airfield, featuring what's left of a U.S. fighter plane. If you befriend the Yandina police, they may take you out with them on patrol.

Weekdays two Levers barges (free) depart Yandina for outlying estates such as Pepesala and Saumata, both inhabited by Tikopia people. From Pepesala a free launch runs to West Bay on Pavuvu Island, the main U.S. camp in the Russells during WW II. From there it's only a half-hour walk to the Tikopian village of Nukufero. Farther on is Saumata, where you can pick up a barge back to Yandina. Aside from the Tikopians, there's a Bellonan settlement called Mukava. In addition, several small villages are inhabited by indigenous Russell Islanders, descendants of a Papuan-speaking people once decimated by headhunters from the Roviana Lagoon and Savo. In April 1995 the Mamaloni government deployed its paramilitary police on Pavuvu to protect loggers sent by the Malaysian company Maving Brothers, which had obtained a license to clearcut the island's pristine rainforests over the heated objections of local residents.

Ask the airline or Levers's Honiara office (tel. 22939, fax 23496) arrange your stay at Levers's company rest house (tel. 21779, fax 21785), behind the administration offices, 500 meters to the left from the wharf—unexpected arrivals are not appreciated. It's SI$35 pp a night with cooking facilities and a lovely seaside view. If you stay there, you'll be able to use the facilities of the nearby Mbanika Club, including swimming pool, tennis courts, library, and bar (the only place to get a beer).

Groceries are sold at two stores a block to the right of the post office and main wharf as you arrive. The butcher shop near the post office sells very cheap beef, but there's a four-kilogram-per-day limit on purchases. Yachties often share the money among others and stock up here. Ask the butcher when they'll be dumping the offal at Shark Point, as sharks appear from nowhere whenever this happens and go into a feeding frenzy, which is fun to watch from the cliff. Bring adequate mosquito repellent to the Russells.

Getting there is easy, as most ships between Honiara and Gizo call at Yandina on the east side of Mbanika (SI$34 deck from Honiara, SI$61 deck to Gizo one-way). Solomon Airlines flies to Renard Airfield (XYA) from Honiara (95 km, SI$79 one-way) three times a week and from Seghe (163 km, SI$112 one-way), Munda (SI$154), and Gizo (SI$182) weekly; the Solomon Airlines bus into nearby Yandina is free. To get back to the airport, check with the Solomon Airlines office (tel. 21779) in the Levers administration building. Western Pacific Air flies from Yandina to Batuna (SI$95) on the Marovo Lagoon.

Queen Victoria's Birdwing (Onithoptera victoriae) is found only in the Solomon Islands. As specimens are among the most highly prized of all butterflies, their export is government controlled.

WESTERN PROVINCE

Western Province with the New Georgia Group at its core is easily the most attractive and varied area in the country. High vegetation-shrouded volcanoes buttress the enticing lagoons of Marovo and Roviana, respectively off the eastern and southern coasts of New Georgia. These vast stretches of dazzling water are dotted with hundreds of little green islets, either covered in dense jungle or planted with coconuts. To the north, the remote Shortland and Treasury groups form Western's outback. Sadly, commercial logging is gradually decimating the great rainforests of New Georgia, Rendova, and Kolombangara.

The inhabitants have the darkest skin in the Solomons. Over a dozen different languages are spoken, but people in this province have long had contact with missionaries, and you'll find very eloquent, well-informed individuals in the most unlikely places. Here the women own the land, which is passed down through the oldest daughter. Headhunting once forced the inhabitants to build their homes on inaccessible interior ridges (where many custom places are now found), but with the demise of interisland raiding the people soon moved down to cooler coastal sites. In the 1950s and '60s thousands of Micronesian Gilbertese were resettled at Gizo, Shortland, and Vaghena, adding to the diversity.

Travel among the many islands of the New Georgia Group is almost totally by sea, which makes getting around easy, yet there are also feeder roads from the main centers of Munda, Noro, Ringi Cove, and Gizo, which help the hiker and hitcher. There are many villages, and the people are helpful and hospitable. They'll often volunteer to take you between islands in their big outboard canoes. Always offer to pay about SI$10 pp, whether they ask or not. To hire a canoe for sightseeing in this area will be SI$50 a day and up, plus gas. The exact amount will depend on who you know, how affluent you look, and how badly they think you want to go. The scheduled weekly passenger ship from Honiara to Gizo via Patutiva, Viru Harbor, Mburuku, Munda, and Ringi Cove offers an excellent introduction to the New Georgia Islands.

Arts and Crafts

The Westerners are skilled carvers, shaping *nguzunguzus,* masks, turtles, dolphins, sharks, and model canoes from kerosene wood or black ebony inlaid with mother of pearl. The *kapkap* or *dala* is a forehead ornament made from a circular clamshell disk but embossed with turtle shell, which makes it a prohibited import into many countries. Unfortunately, some carvers have begun working in a grotesque nontraditional style (the so-called "Spirit of the Solomons" series).

Village carvers around the Marovo Lagoon are famous for their workmanship. Cruising yachts are big customers for handicrafts, so the villagers use mirrors to flash a signal to passing boats that carvings are available. No sooner is the anchor dropped than the dugout canoes arrive. It's quite acceptable to barter radios, tools, sandpaper, bush knives, fish hocks, fishing line, batteries, medicine, bedsheets, plates, sewing machines, paint, perfume, tobacco, foodstuffs,

overmodeled human skull

RAUTENSTRAUCH-JOEST MUSEUM, COLOGNE, GERMANY

raincoats, women's clothing, jeans, T-shirts, shoes, and toys for crafts. Actually, you can buy Marovo carvings just as cheaply in Honiara, and the selection will be better.

The Marovo Lagoon

On the ship from Honiara, you travel first through the huge Marovo Lagoon, which James A. Michener called "one of the seven natural wonders of the world." A thin string of islands shelters this semicircular lagoon as it swings around Vangunu Island from Nggatokae to New Georgia. The best beaches are on the ocean-side coral islands; mangrove swamps are more common along the volcanic shorelines within. The Marovo Lagoon is one of two sites in the Solomons presently under consideration for UNESCO World Heritage Site status. A cruise through the lagoon makes for great scenic viewing, though some of the ships from Honiara pass at night.

You won't see any dancing anywhere around the Marovo Lagoon, as the Seventh-Day Adventist Church has banned it, and there are rumors that dancing causes pregnancy. The SDA devotees frown on all "heathen" customs, but will carve and market many a *nguzunguzu* for profit. The SDA sabbath runs from sundown on Friday to sundown on Saturday, and this is a bad time to arrive.

On Nggatokae Island, at the south end of the lagoon, ask for Robert Siloko who takes visitors. He knows lots of interesting spots to visit around **Mbili Passage** (where the boat stops). Billy Vinajama at Bagholae village does stonecarvings. Western Pacific Air flies to Nggatokae from Honiara (SI\$145).

There's a large Seventh-Day Adventist mission at **Batuna** with a post office, hospital, sawmill, agricultural school, shop, and a Thursday market. High quality handicrafts can be purchased at Batuna Vocational School. Ask for Philemon Pulekele, a teacher at the school, who can usually arrange paying-guest accommodation. Western Pacific Air flies directly here from Honiara (SI\$155), Yandina (SI\$95), and Munda (SI\$75), or take the *luminao* to Gasini, then a canoe.

Uepi Island

Uepi Island (Roco Ltd., Box 920, Honiara; tel. 26074, fax 26076—ask for Jeffrey Simbe), 12 km northeast of Patutiva, midway in the chain of islands forming the barrier of the Marovo Lagoon, is a secluded but well-organized resort near a white coral beach. The six bungalows with private bath, fridge, and coffee-making facilities go for SI\$183/256/337 single/double/triple. There are also two rooms with bath but no fridge and a three-room lodge with fridge but shared bath at SI\$126/188/247. The accommodations are not luxurious and there's no hot water but it's all quite adequate for such a remote location. A generator provides electricity. The compulsory meal add-on is SI\$100 pp per day. They give you a picnic basket lunch, and the three-course buffet dinner is served at two long communal tables, so you soon get to know everyone. The food is good (ample seafood and fresh fruit), but drinks at the bar are expensive. Guests are flown into Seghe, where the canoe to Uepi (pronounced "you-pee") will be waiting. Transfers from Seghe to the island are SI\$60 pp roundtrip. Reductions on all services are available for children 12 and under, but add 10% tax to everything.

At those prices Uepi caters mostly to packaged-tourist Australians who come to scuba dive around giant clams, four-meter gorgonian fan corals, sponge gardens, eels, barracuda, and gray whaler sharks. You're charged extra for everything you do here, except playing volleyball with the friendly staff or paddling a dugout canoe. A good six-hour tour to the custom village costs SI\$45. The tour up a river is SI\$40. Fishing in the lagoon costs SI\$30 an hour for the boat. Scuba diving is SI\$90 per dive (night dives SI\$100). Bring your own snorkeling gear with you, otherwise it's SI\$10 per day. There's good snorkeling right off their dock—lots of fish. Yachties are not welcome at Uepi Island. Uepi Island bookings must be confirmed by Tropical Paradise Ltd., Box 84 HP, Hermit Park, Queensland 4812, Australia (tel./fax 61-7-4775-1323).

Seghe Point

Seghe, on New Georgia Island at the southwest end of the lagoon, is the communications hub of Marovo. Solomon Airlines has almost daily flights from Munda (71 km, SI\$67), Gizo (122 km, SI\$92), Yandina (163 km, SI\$112), and Honiara (256 km, SI\$167) to the wartime airstrip (EGM) the Americans built in only 10 days. After heavy

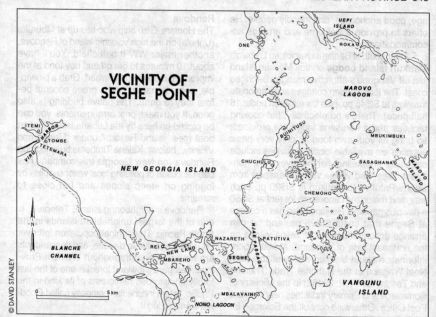

VICINITY OF SEGHE POINT

© DAVID STANLEY

rains the grassy airstrip is often flooded, though this doesn't interfere with flight schedules. All that spray may look dangerous, but the pilots do it all the time. There's a sunken P38 Lightning fighter in the water off the passage end of the airstrip. During WW II, coastwatcher Donald Kennedy and a small force of Solomon Islanders carried out many daring guerrilla raids against the Japanese near Seghe and supplied vital information on their movements.

The passenger ships all stop at **Patutiva** wharf on Vangunu Island, just across scenic Njae Passage from Seghe. Northbound from Honiara, if you plan to disembark here the *Ramos I* is more convenient as it calls here Sunday morning, whereas the *Iuminoa* passes in the middle of the night of Sunday/Monday. A good, cheap market materializes at Patutiva whenever the Honiara ship arrives—jump off and back on fast to buy oranges and bananas. Dugout canoes propelled by outboard, paddle, or sail carry people around the lagoon from Patutiva, and hitching a ride isn't too hard. However, even low-budget backpackers look rich to some, so agree on a price beforehand.

Backpackers often charter a speedboat (ask for Billy Sangaru) from Patutiva to **Buinitusu**, a button-sized island with 70 inhabitants. On the mainland opposite Buinitusu, Mr. Muven Kuve has built four leaf huts for visitors. Cooking is possible. The charge is reasonable (about SI$25 pp a day or SI$75 pp a week including all the tropical fruit you can eat; camping is half price). Muven has an outboard canoe that you can hire to get around the lagoon and up jungle rivers. Fish barbecues and village feasts are arranged if three or four people are present. He'll also loan you a dugout to paddle yourself or provide a guide for bush hikes. Over the years Muven has been very helpful to low-budget travelers, so don't hesitate to stop and visit him. We've heard that Muven has recently moved to Cheke village. In Gizo, Mr. Golden Ringi at the Provincial Government office will have information about Buinitusu.

Mr. Gillis Palmer of **Mbareho Island** in the Nono Lagoon has written us inviting yachties and other travelers to visit his island. According to Gillis, the attractions of Mbareho include taboo places, coral reefs, carvings, war wreckage, good anchorage, and friendly people. He offers to provide a welcome and arrange accommodations.

Farther south is Benjamin Kaniotoku Lomulo's **Matikuri Island Lodge** on tiny Matikuri Island just off Vangunu's attractive mangrove-fringed coast. The four wooden cottages accommodate travelers at SI$45 pp, plus tax (children under 16 half price). There's no electricity, but cooking facilities and a kerosene fridge are provided, so bring all your own food as only very basic supplies are available locally. Activities include canoeing, snorkeling, fishing, river trips, rainforest hikes, and village visits. Transport from Seghe/Patutiva to Matikuri is SI$20 pp each way, and motorized canoes are for rent at SI$50 a day plus gasoline. Benjamin also has a cottage at Seghe that costs SI$25 pp, and he can arrange accommodations at Telina village on the northeast side of Vangunu. At last report, information about Matikuri was available from Noel Wagapu at the National Trade Training and Testing Unit (tel. 22482) in the Ministry of Commerce and Primary Industries near Honiara Post Office. Otherwise consult the Solomon Islands Tourist Authority.

Viru Harbor

The ship next enters beautiful, landlocked Viru Harbor and calls briefly at Tetemara landing. As you come in between the high coral cliffs, look up above the white triangular navigational aid on the left to see the long barrel of a **Japanese gun**, still pointing skyward. Five stone fortresses, two on the north and three on the south, guarded the harbor entrance in ancient times.

Today Viru Harbor serves as a logging camp and is a stronghold of Seventh-Day Adventist fundamentalism. The offices of Kalena Timber are at Itemi, just a short distance farther up the harbor from Tetemara. A free ferry shuttles constantly (daily except Saturday 0500-1800) between Tetemara, Itemi, and Tombe (a wood-carving village). There's a Forestry Station at Arara, 10 km from Tetemara by road. Aside from the Honiara-Gizo ships, you can get out of Viru Harbor by taking a canoe to Seghe. Ask about the mail run. Western Pacific Air flies to Viru from Batuna (SI$60) and Honiara (277 km, SI$183).

Rendova

The Honiara-Gizo ship also ties up at Mburuku (Ughele) on the high volcanic island of Rendova, another major WW II battlefield. You'll have about 10 minutes to get off and buy food at the impromptu market on the wharf. Grab a pineapple, some bananas, and a green coconut before they're gone. The native pudding is also good. If you make prior arrangements, you can be picked up here by the Lubaria Island Resort boat (see "Island Resorts" under "Munda and Vicinity," below). Kalena Timber is busy logging Rendova (on New Georgia this company has been accused of polluting local water supplies by logging on steep slopes and too close to streams).

Rendova's neighboring island, Tetepare, is one of the largest uninhabited islands in the South Pacific. The original population left over 200 years ago due to disease, and descendants are now scattered throughout Western Province. Tetepare's lowland forest is one of the last totally undisturbed rainforests of its kind in the Pacific, yet an Indonesian company called Goodwill wants to log it.

MUNDA AND VICINITY

Munda, the metropolis of New Georgia, is little more than a string of villages centered on Lambete beside the Roviana Lagoon; the name "Munda" describes the whole area. The government wharf, administration offices, air terminal (MUA), and rest houses are all at **Lambete,** while the United Church maintains its Solomon Islands headquarters and runs Helena Goldie Hospital at **Kokenggolo** near an old wharf, two km west of Lambete. The United Church also operates **Goldie College** near the Diamond Narrows. A vast wartime airstrip stretching from Lambete to Kokenggolo still dominates Munda, a huge plain of crushed coral. The Americans built the fine coral roads here by dredging up limestone, crushing it with a steamroller, then pumping saltwater over the road to harden it like cement.

The dark-skinned people of Roviana Lagoon were once much-feared cannibals who raided far and wide in their long canoes. In 1892 a punitive raid by a British warship broke the power of the

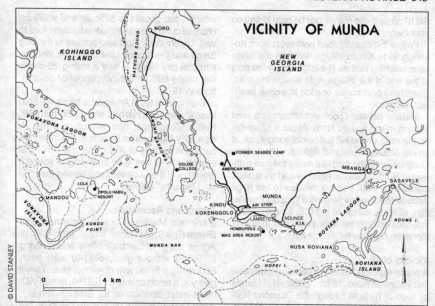

© DAVID STANLEY

VICINITY OF MUNDA

NORO
KOHINGGO ISLAND
HATHORN SOUND
NEW GEORGIA ISLAND
VONAVONA LAGOON
DIAMOND NARROWS
GOLDIE COLLEGE
FORMER SEABEE CAMP
AMERICAN WELL
MBANGA
SASAVELE
LOLA
ZIPOLU HABU RESORT
MANDOU
VONAVONA ISLAND
KUNDU POINT
KINDU
KOKENGGOLO
MUNDA
AIR STRIP
LAMBETE
NDUNDE KIA
HOMBUPEKA I.
MAQ AREA RESORT
ROVIANA LAGOON
NDUME I.
MUNDA BAR
NUSA ROVIANA
N
HOPEI I.
ROVIANA ISLAND

0   4 km

headhunters, and a few years later Methodist missionaries converted the survivors. Though the change from those days is striking, much remains the same around this lagoon. You might see old men netting fish, outriggers bringing in live turtles, and fish leaping through the sea.

In 1898 a 12-year-old Roviana islander named Alick Wickham introduced the world to the traditional swimming technique we now know as the crawl. Alick had gone to Sydney two years earlier with his Australian father, and when he easily beat all the Aussie kids at a local swimming carnival, an Australian coach sat up. The technique was perfected and became a sensation at the 1900 Olympics. Alick later worked as a stuntman in a circus, served with the coastwatchers during WW II, and died in Honiara at the ripe age of 81 in 1967.

Sights

Have a swim in the spring-fed freshwater pool near the canoe house at Lambete wharf. Next, follow the coastal road east from Lambete a kilometer to **Kia** village. In the bush just behind the houses of Kia is a large U.S. military dump with huge landing craft deliberately cut in half,

amphibious tanks, trucks, aircraft engines, guns, and even a small Japanese tank, all piled up where the Americans left them when they pulled out after the war. Many beautiful pink and blue orchids bloom in the bush beyond. Ask for Mr. John Collinson (nicknamed "Homelo"), the landowner, who will be happy to show you around for a SI$5 pp custom fee. Much more war materiel is sunken or dumped in the lagoon off Kia, and small copra driers along the waterfront still utilize wartime 44-gallon petrol drums.

Now head for **Kokenggolo.** The Japanese secretly built the gigantic airstrip that dominates this area. They camouflaged their work by suspending the tops of coconut trees on cables above the runway—surely one of the more remarkable accomplishments of the war. The Americans captured Munda on 5 August 1943 after heavy fighting. Avid snorkelers should visit the sunken aircraft in the lagoon just off the beach near Kokenggolo hospital: a single-engine Corsair fighter is beside a pole near shore, while a larger two-engine Nelly bomber in good condition is farther out in about seven meters of water. If there are a few of you, try hiring a motorized canoe at Lambete wharf for around

SI$10 pp as these planes can be hard to find on your own.

Follow the coastal road northwest from Kokenggolo to **Kindu** village. Women are often seen washing clothes in a large spring-fed pool at the end of the village, right beside the road. Swim here or continue one km to a clear freshwater stream.

Midway between pool and stream is a road leading inland toward Noro. About a kilometer up this road, on the left just before a slight rise, is an old American well and water supply system. Continue along the road till it meets the new highway to Noro. Cross the highway and go straight ahead on a bush trail five minutes to two large **Japanese AA guns** flanking a flagpole foundation, all that's left of the big U.S. Seabee Camp that once covered this area. Hitch back to Munda along the highway for a circle trip.

Vicinity of Munda

A copra-exporting facility is near the Japanese fish freezer at **Noro,** 16 km northwest of Munda by road or by boat through the Diamond Narrows. The Solomon Taiyo Ltd. cannery at Noro cans 20,000 tons of tuna a year, including the dark-meat "Solomons Blue" *tin pis* (canned fish). There are three wharfs at Noro: the government wharf where the Honiara-Gizo ship ties up, the Fisheries wharf, and the Taiyo wharf next to the cannery.

At **Enoghae Point,** east of Noro, four 140-mm Japanese coastal defense guns still lurk in the bush. Only one of the guns is still in good shape; the others have been pulled apart by scrap metal scavengers. There's a sunken Japanese freighter in shallow water at Mbaeroko Bay nearby. The Levers logging camp at Enoghae was burned in 1982 by villagers opposed to the operations. Now the logging is done by Golden Springs.

Roviana Island, just southeast of Munda across the lagoon, was the stronghold of the notorious headhunter Ingava, whose ferocity led to the sacking and burning of his ridgetop fortress by Commander David of the *Royalist* in 1892. The sacred **Dog Stone** is near the southeast end of this broken coral fortress.

There are a few other custom places near Munda, such as the **Island of Skulls** near Kundu Point, or the **Stones of Bau** deep in the interior, but access is difficult, and you'll be charged outlandish customary admission fees to visit. Unfortunately this also applies to the Dog Stone and the "Cave of the Giant." At Mbanga you can pay SI$20 to see a rotting 20-meter war canoe built for the independence celebrations in 1978.

During WW II the Americans had a PT-boat base at **Rendova Harbor,** and a local man, Mr. Kettily Zongahite, has set up a **John F. Kennedy Museum** on Lubaria Island facing the harbor, in memory of JFK's brief stay here. The easiest way to visit is by arranging to spend a few days at the Lubaria Island Resort (see "Island Resorts," below).

Sports and Recreation

Dave and Mariana Cooke's **Solomon Sea Divers** (Box 9, Munda; tel. 61224, fax 61225) at Agnes Lodge in Lambete offers scuba diving at SI$90 without gear, SI$140 with gear. Snorkeling is SI$50 with or without gear. They'll give you a resort course for SI$180, or full PADI open-water certification for SI$870. The Roviana Lagoon waters offer limited visibility but Solomon Sea Divers visits many sites beyond the reef.

Budget Accommodations

The **Somba Rest House** (Box 22, Munda; tel. 61083), just a five-minute walk from Munda Airport, is sometimes called "Sogabule's Lodge" after the owner, John Sogabule. The easiest way to find it is to ask for Mary Makini, the caretaker (there's no sign on the building). The three double rooms with fan are SI$25 pp and communal cooking facilities are provided—good value.

You could also stay with the villagers at **Ndunde** village, between Lambete and Kia. Mr. Robertson Bato has recently built a large eight-room rest house at Ndunde (the only two-story building in the village)—ask about it. Several of the houses nearby are owned by Mrs. Vera Lilo, who rents them out for long stays. Don't expect any electricity at Ndunde.

About 150 meters west of Lambete Police Station is **Sunflower House,** a large two-room leaf house with cooking facilities and electric lighting. It's SI$25 pp a night, and the friendly owners may offer you fresh fruit each morning.

Ask at **PX Merle Aqorau** store next to the Educational Division office, a five-minute walk from the airport.

Medium-Priced Accommodations

The **Munda Motel** (M.P. Kwan, Box 37, Munda; tel. 61143) is the only two-story building visible from the airport terminal. This motel just opened in 1995 and the rates were unknown at press time, but the six rooms do share cooking facilities.

Nearby is 11-room **Agnes Lodge** (David Kera, Box 9, Munda; tel. 61133, fax 61225), formerly the Munda Rest House, just a stone's throw from the air terminal and government wharf at Lambete. It's SI$75 for up to three persons in a room with shared bath in the old wing, SI$125 in a double room with bath in the new wing. A deluxe room is SI$200 for up to four persons. There's also a "backpackers' rate" of SI$25 per bed in shared rooms in the old wing. Add 10% tax to all rates, plus another 20% commission if you book through a travel agent in Australia. A meal and accommodation package is SI$150 pp (double occupancy). No cooking facilities are provided, so you must patronize their restaurant. Sandwiches are available, but a sign at the bar advises patrons that nonguests must order full meals after 1800. This is the only place in Munda to get a beer (check your change). Canoe rentals at Agnes Lodge are SI$30 an hour, petrol included (up to six persons). Half-day lagoon trips from the lodge are SI$100 pp.

Under the same ownership is **Noro Lodge** (Box 9, Munda; tel. 61238), about a five-minute walk from the government wharf at Noro. The four rooms without bath are SI$100 for one to four persons, while another four rooms with bath are SI$150 for one to three persons.

Island Resorts

The **Maqarea Resort** (Box 66, Munda; tel. 61164, fax 61165), pronounced "Mangaraya," on tiny Hombupeka Island just offshore from Lambete, has four thatched bungalows with private bath at SI$85/145 single/double. No cooking facilities are available, no choice of food is possible at meal times, and there's not a lot to do other than relax.

If you want to have an island to yourself, Agnes Lodge rents out a lovely part-leaf cottage on nearby **Hopei Island,** just offshore from Munda, complete with fridge, oven, and toilet. It's SI$400 a night for up to six persons, transfers included. You can bring your own food, otherwise full provisions can be ordered at SI$60 pp a day. It may seem remote, but be aware of theft.

Mr. Kettily Zongahite's **Lubaria Island Resort** (Box 27, Munda; tel. 61149) is on a small island facing Rendova Harbor, 10 km southwest of Munda. The three double rooms in the European-style guesthouse with shared cooking facilities are SI$30/50/80 single/double/triple, while a room in the three-room thatched family cottage is SI$100. Lighting is by gas lamp. You must bring all your own food with you, as there are no stores here, although fresh fruit, fish, and vegetables can occasionally be purchased from local villagers. If the guesthouse is full, you could camp on Lubaria. When enough guests are present, a cultural-exchange concert evening is arranged. Motorized canoe transfers are SI$60 from Munda or SI$80 from Mburuko roundtrip per group. A number of canoe tours around the area are offered at SI$80-100 pp (expensive due to the high customary entry fees built into the price). Add 10% tax to all costs. To assure an easy arrival at Lubaria, write to Kettily a week or two in advance, or ask for Kettily's sister, Rosie Zongahite, who works at Helena Goldie Hospital (tel. 61121) at Kokenggolo.

One of the nicest little hideaways in these parts is Joe & Liz Entrikin's **Zipolo Habu Resort** (Box 164, Munda; no phone, fax 61150) on Lola Island at the east entrance to the Vonavona Lagoon. Lola's a medium-size island with a white sandy beach from which one gets a lovely lagoon view. Set in a coconut grove, all buildings on the premises are built from local materials. The three two-bedroom cottages with fridge, gas stove, kerosene lamp, and mosquito nets are SI$50/70/90 single/double/triple, plus tax. Camping is SI$25 per tent. In past guests were encouraged to bring food and do their own cooking, but in 1994 a thatched restaurant was erected on the island, so ask if cooking is still possible when booking. A small shop at the resort sells basic groceries and rents snorkeling gear. It's a perfect place to get away from it all and relax. As you lie in bed the jungle sounds lull you to sleep. Thirty minutes from Munda by boat, this resort is a real favorite among anglers, and the resort canoe is available for fishing trips, sightseeing, and shopping excursions at fixed rates. Credit cards are not accepted here. Transfers cost SI$45 per cottage from Munda or Noro (free if you stay five nights or longer).

Food and Entertainment
There are four general stores at Lambete, including a Chinese store, **M.P. Kwan Trading** (tel. 61143). The **Hot Bread Kitchen** behind the police station near the airport bakes bread daily (arrive early on Sunday). Sporadic markets happen near Lambete wharf and Kokenggolo hospital.

There's custom dancing at Munda on 23 May, anniversary of the arrival of the first missionaries (in 1902), 7 July (Independence Day), Christmas, and New Year's Day. The singing and dancing show the influence of Tongan missionaries. Ask if any bamboo bands will be playing while you're there.

Services
The National Bank has a branch next to the airport terminal at Lambete and another at Noro, both changing traveler's checks.

Getting There
Solomon Airlines (tel. 61152) has flights several times a day to Gizo (SI$53) and Honiara (327 km, SI$207), several times a week to Seghe (71 km, SI$67), Yandina (SI$154), Ballalae (211 km, SI$157), and Choiseul Bay (217 km, SI$138), and weekly to Ringi Cove (29 km, SI$42).

Solomon Airlines office, the customs office, and the immigration office (tel. 61071) are all inside the airport terminal. The small coffee counter in the terminal opens at flight times. Western Pacific Air has an office at Mae General Trading store near the air terminal.

The *Ramos I* calls here Sunday at 1700 bound for Gizo, Monday at 0900 bound for Honiara. Boat fares from Munda are SI$64 deck to Honiara, SI$30 deck to Gizo.

Due to the lack of a main wharf at Munda, the ships from Honiara cannot tie up here and you must negotiate with a private canoe owner to take you to/from the small wharf next to Agnes Lodge at Lambete. The Munda-Honiara boat stops some distance offshore, and canoe operators will want SI$10 pp to take you there. One

way to avoid this is by disembarking at Noro, where there is a wharf, and hitching down to Munda (16 km). If arriving from Honiara during daylight you'll get the added bonus of seeing the Diamond Narrows (which are just after Munda).

Since the airfare from Munda to Gizo is relatively low, consider taking the boat from Honiara direct to Noro, hitching a ride down to Munda in the back of a truck, flying from Munda to Gizo, then either taking the boat or flying from Gizo back to Honiara. Try to book the Munda-Gizo leg before leaving Honiara.

Getting Around
Good roads connect Munda to Mbanga landing (near Sasavele) and Noro. The Port Authority truck (marked "SIPA") carries passengers from Noro to Munda sporadically at SI$2 pp. Otherwise you could simply hitch, although there isn't a lot of traffic. It's easier to go from Lambete to Noro. Weekdays just before 0800, you can usually get a ride from Lambete to Noro in the truck that brings children to school at Lambete. Ask around the night before.

KOLOMBANGARA

Kolombangara is a classic cone-shaped volcano 30 km across and almost circular in shape that soars to 1,770 meters. The native name of this island-volcano is Nduke. You can climb it from Iriri or Vanga villages, accessible by canoe from Gizo market, where the locals sell their products and shop. To go up and down in one day would be exhausting, so camp partway and reach the top early the next morning; by midday the summit is shrouded in clouds and you'd miss the view. But in the mist, the stunted, moss-covered forest on top will haunt you. The extinct crater is four km across and as much as 1,000 meters deep, with the Vila River, which passes Ringi, draining it on the southeast side.

A coastal road runs around the island's 678 square km, with old logging roads up most of the ridges. Ringi, two km from the wharf (where the Honiara ships stop), is the former headquarters of Levers Pacific Timbers, which pulled out of Kolombangara in 1986 after 20 years of logging, leaving behind dirty rivers, fewer materials for house-building, fewer animals and birds, fewer herbs for custom medications, massive erosion, confusion, and social problems. The Iriri villagers struggled long and hard against Levers for adequate compensation for the rape of their forests.

Ringi Cove and Vicinity

The wharf and airport are on opposite sides of Ringi Cove station, both a 15-minute walk away. There's a small market in Ringi. Vilu Plantation, on Blackett Strait just south of the cove airstrip, was an important Japanese base during WW II. Rusted Japanese guns molder in the bush near the airstrip. There are weekly Solomon Airlines flights from Ringi Cove to Munda (29 km, SI$42), Gizo (31 km, SI$43), and Honiara (356 km, SI$221). Find outboard canoes to Noro or Munda near the canoe shed at the Ringi Cove wharf.

The very comfortable **KFPL Rest House** (tel. 60230, fax 60020) is up toward the Forestry Department nursery, three km from the wharf or a 15-minute walk from the airstrip. It's the former private residence of the general manager of the logging company and the three a/c rooms are SI$50 pp with breakfast. No cooking facilities are provided but the staff prepare meals. There's 24-hour electricity.

GIZO

The administrative center of the Western Solomons since 1899, Gizo (4,500 inhabitants), on the island of the same name, is a pleasant little town, the second largest in the Solomons. It's quite a "modern" place, with electric street lights, a hospital, banks, and many Chinese stores. Downtown Gizo is like a second version of Honiara's Chinatown. You'll like the leisurely lifestyle and variety of things to see and do.

An important shipping and shopping center for the Western Solomons, Gizo lies 383 km northwest of Honiara. A large Gilbertese community has been resettled here. Gizo has a lovely setting with several small islands just offshore and a picturesque view across Blackett Strait as Kolombangara looms to the right.

After their PT boat was cut in half by a Japanese destroyer on 1 August 1943, John F.

© DAVID STANLEY

Kennedy and his 10 shipmates took shelter on Kasolo, or **Plum Pudding Island,** between Gizo and Kolombanga, from which he was rescued by a Solomon Islander. The ship from Honiara passes right beside Plum Pudding (anyone aboard could point it out).

Sights

Gizo Island is 11 km long, five km wide, and 180 meters high. For a great view of the harbor and surrounding islands, climb the hill behind town. During WW II the Japanese had a major barge-repair base here. Near the police station is a memorial stone to the local trader Captain Alexander Ferguson—"Killed by natives at Bougainville Island."

A good half-day trip from Gizo town involves taking a truck from Gizo market to the end of the line at the Gilbertese village of **Titiana,** then returning to town along the beach in a couple of hours. You may have to use the road from Titiana to New Manra village to avoid some mangroves, and the section from New Manra to Gizo jail is best done at low tide, but all in all, it's an easy scenic walk. If you can't find a truck to Titiana at the market, do the walk in reverse, following the road east out of town past the hospital and jail and along the beautiful beach, then return to Gizo by road directly from New Manra village.

A couple of kilometers outside Gizo on the road to New Manra is **Gizo Forest Park** (admission free), a jungly slope planted with exotic tropical trees in the early 1960s as part of an effort to acclimatize new species for the country's commercial forests. The Forestry Division still uses this arboretum for research, and many of the plots are labeled with the names of the trees and dates of planting. Unfortunately the trails through the park are overgrown, but with the free park map booklet available from the tourism office in Gizo you can still find your way around (without the booklet only botanists would get much out of the place). If the tourism office doesn't have any booklets, ask at the Forestry Division next to the Survey Department nearby. The entrance to the Forest Park is poorly marked. If you're coming from Gizo town, turn left on the first road after the power station and pass two "TABU Gizo Town Water Supply Catchment" signs until you see the Gizo Forest Park sign on the right. If you're coming from New Manra, turn right on first road after a small pump house.

A major all-day hike begins by crossing the island, then following the beach road past the Gilbertese villages of New Manra and Titiana to Pailongge, a Melanesian village. Continue along the beach road for a few more hours to **Sagheraghi**, where an overgrown lumber road along the hilltops leads back to town (branch tracks off the high road lead nowhere). This hike gives you the chance to see central Gizo, which Levers Pacific Timbers clearcut beginning in 1963, leading to the extinction of the unique Gizo white-eye. You'll still encounter some red-and-green coconut lorries and giant white cockatoos along the way. The snorkeling off Sagheraghi is superb, with a double reef and 25-meter drop-off between.

Sports and Recreation

Danny and Kerrie Kennedy's **Adventure Sports** (Box 21, Gizo; tel. 60253, fax 60297), or "Dive Gizo," opposite Diver's Lodge, offers scuba diving at SI$95 including tank, belt, and weights, SI$140 with all equipment (two dives SI$225). Snorkeling is SI$35 without equipment, SI$60 with equipment. Unlike Honiara, these are boat dives. If you've never done scuba before, you can take their "resort course" for SI$180 or a full NAUI scuba certification course for SI$850 all-inclusive. You won't find a more relaxed place

than Gizo in which to learn how to dive. Danny himself is something of a South Seas beachcomber, has been since 1985. You'll find his enthusiasm and good humor contagious.

Scuba diving is also offered by the **Gizo Dive Service** (Box 120, Gizo; tel. 60153, fax 60137), or "Dive Solomons," at the Gizo Hotel. Scuba diving is SI$100 without gear, SI$140 with gear; snorkeling SI$40 without gear, SI$65 with gear. They offer a resort course for SI$175 and open-water scuba certification for SI$875. In addition, they have trolling or bottom fishing trips at SI$100 an hour (up to four passengers). These companies compete, so prices tend to vary slightly.

Be sure to dive on the 140-meter Japanese transport ship *Toa Maru,* if nothing else. This enormous wreck 18 meters below in Kololuka Bay is still intact in eight to 35 meters of water, with saki bottles in the galley and two-man tanks in the hold. Grand Central Station, a sloping dropoff off the north end of Gizo, is the ultimate fish and coral dive. Other dive spots include the shallow reef at Nusatupe Island, Naru Wall, the Hellcat fighter near Q-Island in the Vonavona Lagoon, and a Zero aircraft in five meters of water just off Gizo's market—ideal to finish off a tank. According to Danny Kennedy, there have never been any problems with sharks in the waters he frequents off Gizo.

Accommodations

There's a real shortage of budget accommodation in Gizo, and it's not unusual to arrive to find everything other than the expensive Gizo Hotel fully booked. Thus you might want to call ahead.

One of the best places to stay is the new four-room **Naqua Rest House** (Box 127, Gizo; tel. 60274 or 60092), also known as the "KML Rest House," run by Meshach Ngodoro and family on the hill just above the wharf. There are great views of town and the lagoon from the balcony, and the communal cooking facilities are excellent, all at SI$30 pp. Alcohol is not allowed. Information is available at the hardware store next to the National Bank.

On a breezy slope a bit farther up the same way past Naqua is **Phoebe's Rest House** (Box 61, Gizo; tel. 60161, fax 61150) with four double rooms with shared bath at SI$35 pp including tax. There's a comfortably furnished lounge,

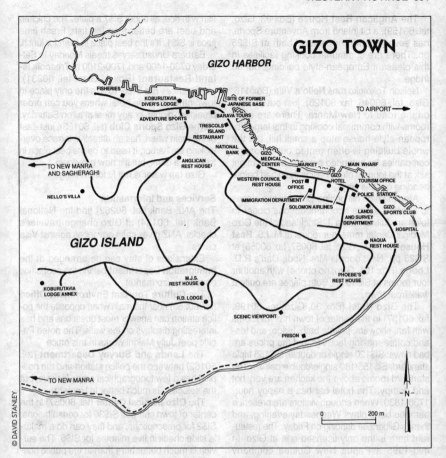

GIZO TOWN

GIZO HARBOR

GIZO ISLAND

FISHERIES
KOBURUTAVIA DIVER'S LODGE
SITE OF FORMER JAPANESE BASE
ADVENTURE SPORTS
BARAVA TOURS
TRESCOLS ISLAND RESTAURANT
NATIONAL BANK
ANGLICAN REST HOUSE
GIZO MEDICAL CENTER
MARKET
MAIN WHARF
WESTERN COUNCIL REST HOUSE
POST OFFICE
GIZO HOTEL
TOURISM OFFICE
IMMIGRATION DEPARTMENT
SOLOMON AIRLINES
POLICE STATION
LANDS AND SURVEY DEPARTMENT
GIZO SPORTS CLUB
NAQUA REST HOUSE
HOSPITAL
PHOEBE'S REST HOUSE
M.I.S. REST HOUSE
R.D. LODGE
SCENIC VIEWPOINT
PRISON

NELLO'S VILLA
KOBURUTAVIA LODGE ANNEX

TO NEW MANRA AND SAGHERAGHI
TO NEW MANRA
TO AIRPORT

© DAVID STANLEY

N
0   200 m

cooking facilities, and a veranda with one of the most panoramic views in the South Seas. You're treated like one of the family.

The very basic **Western Council Rest House** (no phone), formerly known as the Junior Rest House, opposite the market, has 10 four-bedded dormitory rooms at S1$3 per bunk (no mattress). Cooking facilities are provided, but it's extremely basic and noisy, and should be considered as a last resort only. There's a 2100 curfew, and no alcohol is allowed.

Koburutavia Diver's Lodge (Box 50, Gizo; tel. 60257, fax 60297) has two sections. The

seven-room waterfront lodge opposite Adventure Sports is often crowded with Australian scuba divers on short packaged holidays. Far up on the hill behind the town are three overflow rooms in a two-story house accommodating a total of eight persons. At either, the cost is S1$35 pp plus tax with shared bath. Cooking facilities are provided. If everything's full, the kind owners, Lawry and Regina Wickham, may allow you to camp at one of the lodges for S1$10 pp. The restaurant/bar behind the waterfront section of the lodge has a great view of Gizo harbor.

The **Anglican Rest House** (Box 93, Gizo; tel. 60159), a bit inland from Adventure Sports, has seven rooms with shared bath at SI$25 pp. There are communal cooking facilities in this pleasant European-style building, but no fridge.

Nelson Tokotoko runs **Nello's Villa** (Box 116, Gizo; tel. 60046, fax 60128), just out of town on the road to New Manra. There are eight rooms with communal cooking in this large European-style house atop a small hill, but the whole building is often rented out to foreign companies for extended periods, so you might ask at the tourism office beside the wharf before heading out this way.

Atop the high hill behind Gizo are two places to check if all the accommodations closer to town are full. Dr. Mata J. Strickland of the Gizo Medical Center rents four rooms at **M.J.S. Rest House** (Box 126, Gizo; tel. 60057, fax 60056) at SI$25 pp. Next door is Mrs. Node Dari's **R.D. Lodge** (Box 101, Gizo; no phone) with another four rooms at SI$40 pp. Both places are quite a walk from town.

The **Gizo Hotel** (Box 30, Gizo; tel. 60199, fax 60137) in the center of town has 15 rooms with fan, showers, private bath, fridge, and tea- and coffee-making facilities, but the prices are bad news: SI$120 single or double, SI$155 triple standard, SI$155/180 single/double deluxe. The standard rooms above the kitchen are very hot and dumpy. The hotel bar has a happy hour, 1730-1830. When enough visitors are present a bamboo band plays Wednesday evening, and there's Gilbertese dancing on Friday. The restaurant here is the only licensed one at Gizo. In mid-1995 a Papua New Guinea company bought the Gizo Hotel and redeveloped the property with another 30 rooms, a new restaurant, tavern, and airline office. Gizo is slowly being discovered.

Food and Entertainment

There's a market along the waterfront Monday to Saturday. You can often buy fresh fish at Fisheries, west of the center beyond Adventure Sports.

Marilyn Saepio's **Mini-T Snack Bar** (weekdays 1100-1500), next to REFA Gizo, down the alley opposite the Gizo Medical Center (no sign), serves well-prepared meals of chicken, meat, or fish with rice, all about SI$7 a plate. The chicken and beef are better than the fish. Fresh lime juice is SI$1. It's the best place in town for lunch.

Barbara Unusu serves meals Monday to Saturday 0730-1400 and 1700-2100 at **Trescols Island Restaurant** (Box 1, Gizo; tel. 60231). Lunch prices run SI$6-10. It's the only place in town other than the hotel where you can order breakfast, dinner, or any meal at all on Saturday.

The **Gizo Sports Club** (tel. 60163), just east of the main wharf, has an attractive terrace overlooking the harbor. It used to be the best place in town for a drink, but it's now run-down.

Gizo tap water is not fit for drinking.

Services and Information

The ANZ Bank (tel. 60262) and the National Bank (tel. 60134) at Gizo change traveler's checks. ANZ gives cash advances against Visa cards.

Extensions of stay can be arranged at the **Immigration Department** behind the post office opposite Gizo market.

The **Culture Tourism Environment Office** (tel. 60250) near the main wharf opposite the police station can answer most questions and has interesting displays on the walls. The noted Pacific poet Jully Makini works in this office.

The **Lands and Survey Department** (tel. 60162) between the police station and the hospital has a few topographical maps for sale, but the selection is much better in Honiara.

The **Gizo Medical Center** (tel. 60057) in the center of town charges SI$30 for consultations, SI$2 for prescriptions, and they can do a malaria slide check in five minutes for SI$6. The service is much better here than at the public hospital (tel. 60224).

Transportation

Solomon Airlines (tel. 60173), across the street from the police station, has daily service from Gizo to Munda (51 km, SI$53), Seghe (122 km, SI$92), and Honiara (377 km, SI$236), three flights a week to Choiseul Bay (166 km, SI$115) and Ballalae (159 km, SI$118), and weekly to Ringi Cove (31 km, SI$43) and Yandina (SI$182). Keep in touch with the airline office as schedules tend to change on short notice. Also check **Western Pacific Air** above the Gizo Medical Center. The airstrip (GZO) is on Nusatupe Island, a quick boat ride (SI$10 pp) from the wharf in front of the Gizo Hotel.

The Coral Seas ship *Iuminao* departs Gizo for Honiara Monday at 1500 (SI$70 deck, SI$94 first class, SI$130 cabin to Honiara, SI$30 deck to Munda). On the journey from Gizo to Honiara, the *Iuminao* sleeps anchored off Noro, calls at the New Georgia and Marovo Lagoon ports on Tuesday, and arrives in Honiara Wednesday at 0500. The *Ramos I* arrives in Gizo Sunday at 2030 and heads southbound to Honiara (SI$65 deck) again Monday at 0300, arriving Tuesday at 0700. Tickets for the Coral Seas boat can be purchased at the Gizo Hotel reception. Tickets for the *Ramos I* can only be purchased at the purser's office aboard ship after the boat arrives. The *Western Queen* departs Gizo for Honiara Sunday at 1000. Ask about roundtrips to the Shortland Islands and Choiseul Bay on this ship, an excellent way to see some remoter areas.

The Shipping Officer in the Provincial Office (tel. 60250) opposite the police station will know about government boats like the MV *Vele*, which sails from Gizo to the Shortland Islands monthly. The one four-bed cabin on the *Vele* costs SI$72 for the entire room for the three-day trip—an interesting minicruise, if you happen to connect. The MV *Betua* based at Choiseul Bay on Choiseul comes to Gizo monthly, and the Shipping Officer should know when.

Outboard canoes leave Gizo market for Vella Lavella, Kolombangara, Ranongga, and Simbo. Ask along the waterfront. You can hire an outboard canoe to go right around Gizo or elsewhere at SI$150 for a full day, petrol included. Ten people can go for that price.

A white truck provides passenger service between Gizo market and Titiana about five times a day (SI$1.20).

Tours

Ron Parkinson of **Barava Tours** (Box 137, Gizo; tel. 60221) offers four-wheel-drive land tours to Sagheraghi at SI$55 pp (six hours). There's time to snorkel on the reef, and Ron knows all there is to know about the local flora, fauna, and customs, so you'll find going with him a rewarding experience. Both Barava Tours and Adventure Sports sell handicrafts, but they're more expensive than in Honiara and not as good.

VELLA LAVELLA

This large island across the Gizo Strait is easily accessible by outboard canoe from Gizo (about SI$15 pp). Transport can be unreliable, however, so expect to stay a day or two longer than you might want. A wartime road runs right up the southeast side of the island, but all the bridges have long since been washed out. At Niarovai, a couple of hours' walk northeast of Maravari (with several big rivers to cross), is a **New Zealand War Memorial.** As recently as 1978 a Japanese straggler was found on Vella Lavella, and rumors of additional Japanese soldiers still holding out in the bush have long been circulated, in hope of attracting Japanese tourists to the island!

The most unusual attraction of Vella Lavella is the **thermal area,** an hour's walk inland from Paraso Bay on the northeast side of the island. There are megapode birds, hot springs, and bubbling mud in a desertlike area near the Ngokosole River (crocodiles). The only access to Paraso is by chartered canoe. Ask the driver to take you right around Vella Lavella, rather than coming back the same way. If you decide to snorkel off Vella Lavella, ask local residents if crocodiles pose any danger before you go in the water.

Mr. Walter Semepitu at **Maravari** village has erected a simply furnished leaf cottage (SI$20 pp, local food included). Here you'll experience typical village life, with at least a little privacy. There's a clear river nearby for swimming.

The Americans built an airstrip (VEV) on the beach at Barakoma, between Liapari and Maravari, and Solomon Airlines has flights to Gizo (27 km, SI$44), Munda (77 km, SI$69), Ballalae (SI$101), and Mono (SI$103). Hyundai Timber and Allardyce Lumber have logging concessions in this area.

SIMBO

Simbo, the westernmost island of the New Georgia Group, was once a base for 19th-century headhunting raids. Later in the 1880s northbound sea captains called at Simbo on their way from Sydney to Canton, and it became one of the first islands in the Solomons to accept Christian missionaries. The islanders still make

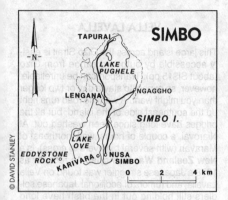

tapa, which they dye blue-green in one of the island's sulfurous hot springs.

Today this tiny island (12 square km), 40 km southwest of Gizo, is better known for its **thermal area,** one of only four in the Solomons (the other three are on Vella Lavella, Savo, and Tinakula). Smoking fumaroles and a sulfur-stained hillside are clearly visible from the sea at Ove, on the southwest side of Simbo. Sulfur-rich seepage points drain into a brackish lake, the habitat of megapodes. The hot springs are too hot to touch. Visitors must pay SI$20 pp to customary landowners to tour the thermal area; if a large group arrives, there's quite a ruckus over who's going to get all the money. The only access to Ove is by boat (not included in the SI$20 fee) or along a roundabout trail that crosses the mountain from Karivara.

Megapode rookeries at Nusa Simbo village opposite Karivara can be seen with permission of the chief, who also sells the eggs of the fast-disappearing birds. Don't let yourself be hustled here. The **hot springs** easiest to enjoy are near the bridge on the trail linking Nusa Simbo to Lengana, the main village. The hot water mixes with tidal water in the lagoon, and you can have a good swim.

There's good anchorage for yachts at Lengana, a freshwater shower on the wharf, and several general stores nearby. For accommodations at Lengana talk to Samson Eli or sleep in a classroom at the school. Every Monday and Friday there's an outboard canoe from Lengana to Gizo. A trail leads north from Lengana to Tapurai, where the two chiefs who own the thermal area reside. Negotiate with them for a visit.

THE SHORTLAND ISLANDS

The Shortland Islands are one of most isolated outposts in the Pacific. Though officially part of Solomon Islands' Western Province, the Shortlands are much closer geographically, culturally, and linguistically to North Solomons Province in Papua New Guinea. The modern partition of the area dates from 1899, when the Germans ceded the Shortlands to Britain but held onto Bougainville itself.

During WW II the Japanese fortified the islands to shield their large bases in southern Bougainville. Though the New Zealanders took the Treasury Islands just to the southwest in October 1943, the Japanese entrenched in the Shortlands themselves were bombed and bypassed by the Allies. In early 1992 fighting between the secessionist Bougainville Revolutionary Army and the Papua New Guinea Defense Force spilled over into the Shortlands when P.N.G. patrol boats and troops made incursions into Solomon Island territory in pursuit of BRA fighters and persons supplying contraband gasoline to the Bougainville rebels.

Alu Island

Alu, the largest and most visited island of the group, is just off the southern tip of Bougainville. Most ships call at the tiny government station of **Korovou** on Alu's southeast corner. Cruising yachts can clear the Solomons here, and the officials are quite friendly. There's a fairly good store at the Catholic mission station of Nila on Poporang Island, just across the water from Korovou. Also near Korovou is the Lofang camp of Allardyce Timber Co., where round logs are exported to Japan. As a result of the 1992 border incidents a detachment of paramilitary police is now stationed at Lofang. On the northwest side of Alu Island are the Gilbertese resettlement villages of Kamaleai and Harapa.

Japanese 140-mm coastal defense guns lurk in the bush on the hillside near Nila. Other relics of the Japanese occupation include an intact radar station, searchlights, an ammunition bunker, seaplanes, trucks, and motorcycles with their sidecars rusting away. Sunken seaplanes are at the bottom of the bay between Alu and

Poporang islands with one nearly intact Japanese bomber in eight meters of snorkeling water just east of Nila.

The only regular place to stay is run by a man named Sylvester on nearby Faisi Island. He charges SI$50 pp to stay in a two-room guesthouse with communal cooking and bathing facilities. Bring adequate food, toilet paper, and mosquito coils. There are several beaches on this attractive island and several wrecked WW II planes, which are little more than heaps of scrap metal now. For information radio the Administration Officer at Korovou. Sylvester can help with the necessary canoe hires, but make sure the price is well understood so you don't get ripped off. Expect to pay SI$60 a day plus gasoline, or SI$40 each way for a special trip to Ballalae Airstrip. This interesting area doesn't receive over a dozen individual visitors a year, so you'll be in for something totally original! At last report the Nila Guest House was closed.

Ballalae

The airstrip (BAS) serving the Shortlands is on uninhabited Ballalae Island, with access to and from Korovou in the airport canoe (30 minutes, SI$10 pp). Be prepared to get wet. There are weekly Solomon Airlines flights to Mono (64 km, SI$60), Choiseul Bay (66 km, SI$64), Barakoma (SI$101), Gizo (159 km, SI$118), Munda (211 km, SI$141), Seghe (282 km, SI$157), and Honiara (536 km, SI$321).

An almost perfectly preserved Japanese "Betty" bomber graces Ballalae airstrip, and there are other planes and war wreckage in the bush. Along Ballalae's coast are concrete bunkers sporting Japanese guns and overturned searchlights still in fair condition despite the years. The Japanese forced several hundred British civilian prisoners brought from Singapore to build the airstrip on Ballalae. None left the island alive. Bring insect repellent and be prepared for black stinging ants.

CHOISEUL, ISABEL, AND MAKIRA

The other three big islands of the Solomons—Choiseul, Isabel, and Makira—are seldom visited by outsiders. Communications are difficult and the roads short to nonexistent; the conveniences of modern life don't extend far beyond the narrow confines of the few small government and mission outposts. This, of course, is the very appeal of these islands, so buy a detailed map from the Survey and Cartography Division in Honiara and blaze your own trail. Please let us hear what you find!

CHOISEUL PROVINCE

Choiseul (pronounced Choysle), which separated from Western Province in 1991, is linked more to the Shortlands, Gizo, and Munda than to distant Honiara. The best way to "do" Choiseul is to take a weeklong trip around the island on a Marine Division supply ship. You might visit up to 45 villages this way, some only for a few minutes to drop off passengers, some others for a few hours. As almost all the villages are on the coast, you get good value for your money.

The new provincial capital, Taro, is on the tiny airport island in **Choiseul Bay,** at the northwest end of the island. Solomon Airlines flies direct to Choiseul Bay (CHY) from Ballalae (66

Massive clamshell plaques bearing dancing figures of this kind were once used on Choiseul to close the opening of a container bearing the skull of a dead chief.

km, SI$64), Mono (130 km, SI$93), and Gizo (166 km, SI$115).

Chirovanga, on the northeast side of Choiseul, is a Catholic mission station with an Australian priest and a church on a hill overlooking the sea. About 10 villages lay inland from the mission, and traditional pottery is still made in this area. Near Chirovanga you'll find the Pacho River cascades. Lots of footpaths cross Choiseul, for instance Sasamungga to Susuka. A guide would be essential. Eagon Resources Development Ltd. is hard at work logging Choiseul.

A large Gilbertese community has been resettled on **Vaghena** (Wagina) Island off the southeast end of Choiseul. The original Melanesian inhabitants of Vaghena were wiped out by headhunters from Choiseul. Vaghena's 78 square km of uplifted coral are thought to contain significant bauxite deposits. The Choiseul boat stops at Vaghena both north- and southbound, so a week's stay at one of the three villages would be possible.

ISABEL PROVINCE

Named for Alvaro de Mendaña's wife, Isabel's 240-km-long northwest-southeast landmass is the longest in the Solomons. The indigenous name for the island is Bughotu. The jungly interior is thick with towering vine-clad trunks and umbrella ferns, forming a habitat for monitor lizards and an array of birds. On small islands such as Leghahana near Sisiga Point off the northeast coast live flightless megapode birds. Commercial logging is carried out in western Isabel by the Eastern Development Co. and Axiom Forest Products.

Headhunters from Simbo and the Roviana Lagoon depopulated much of northern Isabel during the early 1800s. Today most of the inhabitants live in the southeast corner of the island, the point farthest away from New Georgia. As in Santa Cruz, most extended families on Isabel are matrilineal; descent and land pass through the mother. Some villages like Kia have quite an assortment of husbands from all around the Solomons! Almost the entire population of Isabel belongs to the Church of Melanesia. One of the Pacific's rarest varieties of tapa originates on Isabel: stained pale blue with a leaf dye.

If you visit keep in mind that tourists are unheard of on Isabel, one of the least developed islands in the Solomons. Village life is generally unchanged since time immemorial, so a lot of tact and an understanding of Melanesian custom are required. People tend to be very apprehensive about approaching visitors and often end up saying "yes" when they mean something else. A basic smattering of Pidgin will help, but modesty is even more essential. Be aware too that cowboy prospectors sometimes come sniffing for gold on Isabel—don't be mistaken for one.

Southeast Isabel

The administrative center is at **Buala** (population 2,000) on the Maringe Lagoon in southeast Isabel. The six-room **Mothers' Union Rest House** (tel. 35035) in Buala provides accommodations with cooking facilities at around SI$15 pp. This Church of Melanesia-operated place is super friendly, provided you don't drink. The four-room **Provincial Government Rest House** is SI$20 pp. A video center of sorts, post office, police station, and a good hospital (tel. 35016) complete the amenities of Buala.

An hour's walk southeast of Buala is **Tholana Falls,** where the Sana River falls straight into the sea. The river dries up during the dry season. Another hour or two inland from the falls is Hirotonga village, with a sweeping view of the entire Maringe Lagoon and even Malaita. You can also climb Mount Kubonitu or Marescott (1,392 meters), just southwest of Buala and the highest peak on Isabel.

Most rural villages on Isabel have a simple leaf house to accommodate visitors, but only southwest Isabel is laced with footpaths from village to village. The 22-km road across Isabel from Kolomola near Buala to **Kaevanga** wharf on Ortega Channel is the longest on Isabel. From Kaevanga you can hike northwest along the coast to Susubona and Kilokaka. Otherwise try to get a lift from Kaevanga to **San Jorge,** a really weird island where all the "spirits" of Isabel are supposed to be. Visit the vanishing lake, caves full of skulls, islands covered with snakes, etc. An elderly chief on San Jorge is able to call not only sharks but crocodiles as well. Sounds like fun, but it's actually very serious. There's a village on San Jorge, but it's uncertain how welcome visitors would be. Catholic Bishop Epalle was murdered here in 1845.

Southeast down the coast from Kaevanga is Vulavu. A pleasant trail crosses the hills to Kamaosi Secondary School in two hours and continues on to Tatamba, from where you should be able to catch a boat such as the *Ocean Express* to Buala or Honiara. This same path splits at one point with that branch, ending up in Sepi—handy for transport in either direction. Aside from the government boats quite a few fishing boats call at Sepi, and you might score a quick lift back to Honiara. Tatamba's a government station with a rest house and post office. It's an easy three-day hike along the coast from Tatamba to Buala past lots of villages.

Northwest Isabel

Kia, a large village (two stores, clinic) on Austria Sound at the northwest end of Isabel, is perhaps the most interesting on Isabel. The Kia people once worshipped the stars and sacrificed the bodies of slaves to protective sharks. Some of Kia's houses are built on the steep hills surrounding the bay, but most are on stilts over the lagoon. The people visit their gardens (and toilets) on other small islands in the lagoon by canoe. There are virtually no roads at the northwest corner of Isabel, and even trails are rare. Government boats sailing around Isabel often spend the night at Kia, and 12 hours is enough at a place where you can't walk far. There's no connection between Kia and Vaghena Island.

Transportation

Solomon Airlines (tel. 35015) has flights from Honiara (156 km, SI$111) three times a week to the airstrip (FRE) on Fera, a four-km-long offshore island from which motorized canoes cross to Buala (SI$5 pp).

Ships ply between Honiara and Buala about weekly, while government boats cover this route about once a month. The MV *Ocean Express* calls here on Tuesday. The Marine Division ships *Leili* or *Butai* go right around Isabel in four or five days every two weeks with stops at about 15 villages. One especially attractive stop is Furona Island halfway down the west coast. Only Buala, Kia, and Keavanga have wharves. Whenever possible, the government boat spends the weekend at Buala.

MAKIRA/ULAWA PROVINCE

Makira (San Cristobal) has some level land in the north, but the south coast falls precipitously to the sea. **Makira Harbor,** on the southwest coast, is the most secure anchorage in the Solomons, and **Star Harbor,** at the east end of the island, is also good. In 1595 the *Santa Isabel,* one of the four ships of Mendaña's ill-fated second expedition, became separated from the others at Santa Cruz. It sailed on to Makira, where passengers and crew camped on a hilltop at Pamua on the north coast, west of Kirakira. Their eventual fate is unknown.

Remote caves in Makira's inaccessible interior are inhabited by the **Kakamora,** a race of midgets a meter tall who have been called "the leprechauns of the Pacific." They go naked, have very small teeth, and their long straight hair comes down to their knees. Most are harmless, but some Kakamora have been known to attack other men. It's said that one Kakamora is as strong as three or four men. Unfortunately, however, the Kakamora are probably more myth than fact.

Local craft items include carved figures, black inlaid ceremonial food bowls from Santa Ana, and talking drums. There are more pigs on Makira than people.

Kirakira and Around

Ships between Honiara and Santa Cruz call at **Kirakira** (population 3,000), the administrative center of the province, on the middle north coast of Makira. The Filipino-owned fishing company Makirabelle Ltd. has a base here. Solomon Airlines (tel. 50198) also flies to Kirakira (IRA) from Honiara (237 km, SI$154) four times a week and from Santa Cruz (429 km, SI$262) twice weekly.

The nine-room **Kirakira Rest House** (tel. 50111) provides basic accommodations with shared bathing and cooking facilities at SI$20 pp. The friendly Fijian lady running it allows you to drink beer.

The only roads on Makira run along the north coast from Kirakira, nine km to the east and 56 km to the west (to Wango Bay). Much logging is done in the area by Star Harbor Timber. Ask about ships to Star Harbor, Santa Ana, and Santa Catalina, the most beautiful areas in the province.

The *Mako Mako* Dance

This burlesque or mime is performed on Santa Catalina, a small island off the southeast end of Makira. On the village green the males, their bodies smeared with reddish clay, don hideous makeup and high conical masks. These dancers play the "men of the trees"—primitive jungle folk. The dance is accented by the dull notes of a conch shell. Suddenly the "canoe people" arrive from across the waters, and the "men of the trees" run in panic. Then a very realistic mock battle takes place between these two levels of Pacific Island civilization.

Star Harbor

About 100 skilled carvers live in the Star Harbor area. The oldest and most expert bear the title *mwane manira,* and their work is avidly sought by museums and serious collectors. Visitors can buy directly from these craftspeople. Although full-sized canoes and house-posts are the most famous carvings, model canoes, decorated bowls, skull containers, human figures, and sharks are all crafted and sold.

Santa Ana

There's an excellent, reefless beach on Santa Ana where sea turtles come ashore. Traditional Natagera village is just behind; ask to see the war canoes and two custom houses rebuilt after a hurricane in 1971. Though only men are actually allowed inside the house, women get an adequate view through the open walls. Be sure to ask permission before taking photos of any custom items on this island. The local carvers make unique wooden fish floats. There are two freshwater lakes on Santa Ana, and safe, secure anchorage for yachts on the west side of the island. Solomon Airlines flies directly here from Honiara (312 km, SI$197) and Kirakira (76 km, SI$69) weekly.

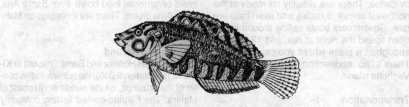

wrasse (Halichoeres nebulosus)

TEMOTU PROVINCE

The Santa Cruz Group, 665 km east of Honiara, is by far the most remote of the major island groupings of the Solomons. Included are 25-by-17-km Nendo, the Reef Islands, the Duff Islands, and the high islands of Utupua and Vanikolo. Tinakula, just north of Nendo, is a surpassingly graceful, almost symmetrical, active volcano. The Reef Islands are composed of low coral terraces and sandy cays, while the others are mostly volcanic, with steep jungle slopes. Hundreds of kilometers southeast are tiny Tikopia and Anuta.

The Melanesians settled on the larger islands, the Polynesians on the smaller, more isolated outliers. *Lapita* pottery has been found on both Nendo and the Reef Islands. Intriguingly, all of the non-Polynesian languages of Temotu are Papuan.

The first European to arrive was the Spaniard Mendaña, who attempted to establish a colony at the south end of Graciosa Bay on Nendo in 1595. Days later, when mutiny set in, Mendaña went ashore and executed his camp commander. After Mendaña himself died here on 18 October 1595, the settlement was abandoned. The crew, sick and dying, called Nendo "a corner of hell in the claws on the devil." Of Mendaña's 378 men, death claimed 47 within a month. The next to arrive was Carteret, on 12 August 1767. As he anchored off Nendo, he observed a "wild country and black, naked, woolly-haired natives."

Santa Cruz is famous for its feather money. Thousands of red feathers from the honey bird are stuck onto a coiled band as long as 10 meters. Ten belts of feather money is the traditional price of a bride (widows half price).

NENDO

Nendo is by far the largest of the Santa Cruz Group. Its densely wooded hills rise to a height of about 520 meters. The island has considerable reserves of bauxite. The mangrove-fringed south and east coasts contrast with the rocky northern shores, where fine beaches are often found. At Venga, on the sandy west shore of Nendo, people perform custom dances unchanged since time immemorial. Dancers at Banua village wear traditional shell and feather ornaments as they dance and sing around a

Uninhabited, 800-meter-high Tinakula Island in the Santa Cruz Group is the most active volcano in the Solomons. In 1595 one of Mendaña's ships sank near Tinakula, which was erupting at the time. This photo shows the island during the brief 1971 eruption.

SURVEY AND CARTOGRAPHY DIVISION, SOLOMON ISLANDS GOVERNMENT

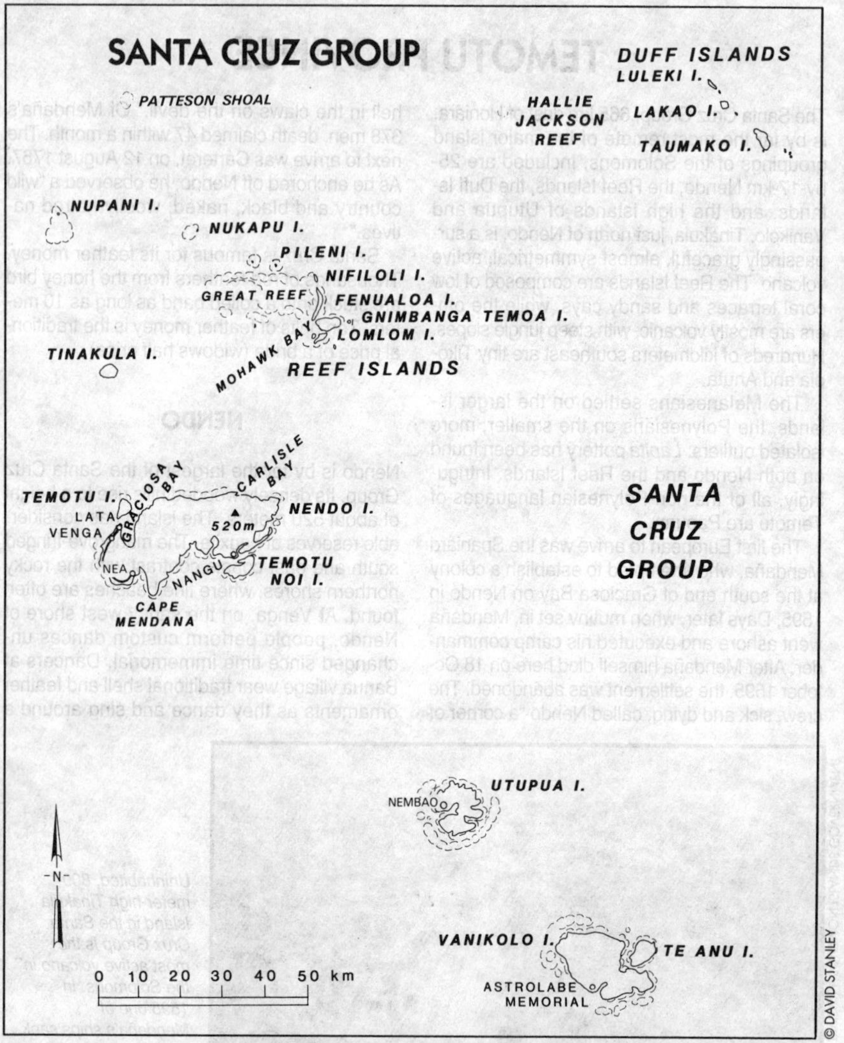

SANTA CRUZ GROUP

PATTESON SHOAL

DUFF ISLANDS
LULEKI I.
LAKAO I.
TAUMAKO I.

HALLIE
JACKSON
REEF

NUPANI I.

NUKAPU I.

PILENI I.

NIFILOLI I.

GREAT REEF

FENUALOA I.

GNIMBANGA TEMOA I.

LOMLOM I.

MOHAWK BAY

TINAKULA I.

REEF ISLANDS

CARLISLE
BAY

GRACIOSA
BAY

TEMOTU I.
LATA
VENGA

NENDO I.

520m

NEA

NANGU

TEMOTU
NOI I.

CAPE
MENDANA

**SANTA
CRUZ
GROUP**

UTUPUA I.

NEMBAO

VANIKOLO I.

TE ANU I.

ASTROLABE
MEMORIAL

0 10 20 30 40 50 km

-N-

© DAVID STANLEY

betel tree all night. August and September are the best months to see custom dancing on Nendo, but no dancing at all takes place in Temotu Province during Lent (the 40 days before Easter).

The administrative center of Temotu Province is at **Lata** (population 1,500) at the northwest corner of Nendo on the west side of Graciosa Bay. Temotu (Malo) Island partly closes this bay to the north. The airstrip (SCZ) and wharf are both within minutes of Lata. One of Mendaña's anchors is set in concrete by a jetty. The road south along the west side of Graciosa Bay passes many beautifully situated villages. Also take the road up past the radio towers at Lata and along the plateau. You pass many bush gardens and tracks leading down to isolated coastal settlements such as Nea (via Noipe). Bring a topographical map with you from Honiara.

Levers Pacific Timbers ships once loaded logs from Shaw Point on the opposite side of Graciosa Bay from Lata and also had a sawmill there. At the entrance to Carlisle Bay on the north shore of Nendo is an overgrown memorial to Commodore Goodenough, killed here in 1875. The scenic white beach and good yacht anchorage are Carlisle Bay's other attractions. Hike/canoe your way to Nangu on the south coast, where there's a wharf, store, radio operator, etc. Temotu Noi Island, just 15 minutes from Nangu by outboard, has a crocodile-infested freshwater lake.

Accommodations
The **Provincial Government Rest House** behind Radio Temotu has three rooms at SI$20 pp. Communal cooking and bathing facilities are provided. To get in, see the Personnel Officer, Provincial Office, tel. 53028, near the post office. It's often full.

At Freshwater Point near the wharf is **Paul Teai's Rest House**, charging SI$15 pp. It's very friendly and in a nice location, with gas cooking and electric lighting. John Melanoli also accepts guests in his leaf house near the wharf at Lata. George Pea has an iron-roofed leaf dwelling without electricity near the powerhouse.

For a longer stay ask for Brown Bolan, whose leaf house with a timber floor and nice sea view is available by the month. No electricity, but lantern and cooking facilities are available. If you stay in a village, consider giving a quality general-purpose knife instead of money.

The local shops are poorly stocked. About the only place to get fresh fruit and vegetables is every Wednesday and Saturday morning 0600-0900 when a produce market forms at the wharf between the Fisheries Department and the copra shed. You have to be there at dawn for a good selection. The Fisheries Department by the wharf sells very cheap fish.

Services
The National Bank has agencies at Lata and Mohawk Bay (Reef Islands), but don't count on

them accepting foreign currency. The Immigration office (tel. 53061) in Lata will give visa extensions, and yachts can check in and out here.

Transportation
Solomon Airlines (tel. 53057) arrives at Santa Cruz (SCZ) twice a week from Honiara (647 km, SI$389 one-way) and Kirakira (428 km, SI$262).

Shipping information is posted on the notice board by the Lata administration offices. A provincial boat, the MV *Leili,* makes roundtrips Lata-Mohawk Bay-Nangu-Utupua-Vanikolo-Lata fairly often. The Marine Division ship connects Honiara to Nendo monthly (SI$49 deck). Ask around the wharf for outboards to Nangu or the Reef Islands. Contribute for gas.

OTHER ISLANDS

The Reef Islands
These low coral islands, 70 km northeast of Graciosa Bay, have long sandy beaches and no malaria. The inhabitants are mostly Melanesians, excepting the Polynesians on tiny Nifiloli and Pileni, as well as Nupani Island to the northwest. Gnimbanga Temoa Island has a series of caverns containing freshwater pools. Anglican bishop J.C. Patteson was murdered on Nukapu in 1871 after a blackbirding ship spread ill will throughout the area.

One of the remotest outer island resorts in the South Pacific is the **Ngarando Faraway Resort** (no telephone; fax 53036) on Pigeon Island, Mohawk Bay. The accommodations on offer are Ngarando House, a European-style bungalow with two bedrooms at SI$125/200/275 single/double/triple; and Nanivo Cottage, a leaf house costing SI$100/175/250. Both units have shower, toilet, and cooking facilities. Meals with the host family cost SI$20/30 /55 for breakfast/lunch/dinner (add 10% tax to all charges). Cash payment only will be accepted. Videos are shown for SI$5, and the resort's satellite dish picks up TV stations from around the world. Snorkeling gear, canoes, and outboards are provided free (you pay only for the gas). There's excellent snorkeling, and scuba-diving gear is for rent (certification card required).

Ngarando is run by the Hepworth clan, including twin brothers Bressin and Ross and their parents Diana and Tom, a colorful bunch of genuine South Seas characters who've been here longer than anyone can remember. Their general store sells local vegetables, fresh fruit and fish, canned groceries, and other trade goods as if this were still the 19th century. The wild parrots add to Pigeon Island's veritable Robinson Crusoe air.

Transfers from Graciosa Bay to Pigeon Island are by motorized canoe, a three-hour, 100-km trip, costing SI$250/325/375 for two/three/four persons. Construction of an airstrip on adjacent Lomlom Island has been pending for years, and at last report the European Union was making serious noises about finally getting the job done, so access could become easier. Check with the Marine Division in Honiara for a government ship direct to Mohawk Bay (twice monthly, SI$86/172 deck/cabin).

The Duff Islands
The Duff Islands, 88 km northeast of the Reef Islands, consist of nine small volcanic islands in a line 27 km long. Taumako Island, the largest, is 366 meters high. The inhabitants are Polynesian.

Vanikolo
This Melanesian volcanic island (also called Vanikoro) was stripped of its kauri trees by an Australian firm earlier this century. Both ships of the La Pérouse expedition, the *Boussole* and the *Astrolabe,* were wrecked on the reef at Vanikolo during a terrible storm in 1788. Despite a search for La Pérouse by d'Entrecasteaux four years later, his fate was unknown to the world for four decades until Irish sea captain Peter Dillon happened upon the remains in 1826 and solved the mystery (Dillon was knighted by the French government and given a pension for his efforts). Two years later, Dumont d'Urville visited Vanikolo, recovered some cannon and anchors, and set up a memorial to La Pérouse on the south side of the island.

The two wrecked French frigates are about 500 meters apart on the northwest side of the island. From the wreckage, archaeologists have theorized that the *Boussole* dropped its anchors as it was driven toward the reef; the ship swung round and had its stern ripped apart. Evidently the *Astrolabe* tried to go through a false pass nearby in an attempt to rescue the crew of the first ship from behind, but was also wrecked. The Vanikolo people told Peter Dillon how the French survivors had built a small ship from the wreckage and sailed away. Their eventual fate has never been learned, but even today expeditions continue to visit Vanikolo in search of more relics of this dramatic episode in Pacific history.

the monument to French explorer La Pérouse on Vanikolo Island, Solomon Islands

M.G.L. DOMENY DE RIENZI

TIKOPIA AND ANUTA

Tikopia

This three-by-five-km dot in the ocean, 120 km southwest of the nearest other dot (Anuta), is an ancient volcano with a crater lake, Te Roto, rising to 366 meters. Pandanus trees surround the brackish lake waters, home to ducks and fish. The inhabitants of both Tikopia and Anuta are Polynesians who arrived in planned expeditions from Wallis Island some 14 generations ago. Wallis itself was colonized from Tonga, thus this is an outpost of the old Tongan culture. Anthropologist Raymond Firth did fieldwork here in 1928-29, and his book *We, The Tikopia* is still the classic on the island. Firth returned in 1952 and wrote *Social Change in Tikopia*.

Tikopia is ruled by four chiefs. Until recently these chiefs did not recognize the central government, but now the number-two chief, Ariki Tafua, has indicated his willingness to submit, much to the fury of the other three. The only thing preventing the Ministry of Police from establishing a post on Tikopia is the fact that the police commissioner in Honiara is himself a Tikopian! The British inserted a clause in the Solomon Islands constitution asserting that Tikopia and Anuta would be self-governing until the chiefs jointly decided to integrate with the rest of the country, and there will probably be a legal challenge if Honiara attempts to take control on the basis of only one "yes" vote.

There's no electricity, all the houses are traditional, and the ground is cultivated with sticks. As a precaution against famine, food is fermented in the ground for up to two years. The dead used to be buried inside the houses and provided with food, but missionaries have stopped that practice. Some of the teenage girls still use lime to bleach their hair blonde, and many of the men wear their hair, along with their beards, at maximum length. Many are tattooed and wear tapa loincloths. The women cut their hair very short. Most Tikopians go topless.

Tikopia and Anuta are the southern and eastern limits of betel chewing in the Pacific. Kava was last made on Tikopia in the 1950s in connection with the traditional religion. Now if someone arrives from Fiji with powdered kava, people will mix and drink it mainly out of curiosity. Kava plants are said to still grow on Tikopia, but nobody bothers to harvest them, probably because the church is against it and also out of respect for sacred sites and paraphernalia.

Now the church and government schools are educating the young in another culture, and Tikopia's traditional life is starting to die. Materialism is catching on, and the children don't feel comfortable with their parents. The chiefs tried to outlaw bras and long trousers, but those responsible for enforcing this decision were ineffectual, and the younger generation now wears western dress.

Yachties often visit Tikopia without clearing Solomon Islands Customs. They're allowed to stay if they present each of the four chiefs a nice gift, such as four-gallon drums of kerosene, lanterns, flashlights, bush knives, files, axes, spades, fishing nets, mosquito nets, spear guns and rubbers, or perfume.

Shops, government offices, and police don't exist on Tikopia, though there is a well-equipped clinic at Faea and a two-way radio. Visitors can usually stay at the nurse's house near the clinic for a small fee. The reef is the only toilet. Take care with the amiable chief of Faea District and his family, as they're out to get what they can—be it in the nicest way—and will give a distorted view of the place. Spend more time in Ravenga and Namo districts; the three chiefs of Ravenga are all very welcoming.

Very few people speak English; Pidgin or a Polynesian language are more useful. It's forbidden to purchase old artifacts from the people; if you do, the chiefs will confiscate the goodies. Bring mosquito repellent.

Anuta

Anuta is less than a kilometer across and 65 meters high. Both it and Tikopia are still governed by their traditional chiefs, and the influence of the Solomon Islands government is minimal. As at Tikopia, many people are still dressed in tapa, though some of the young now wear Western garb. Advance permission is required to stay on the island. Fatutaka Island (Mitre), 42 km southeast of Anuta, is uninhabited.

CAPSULE SOLOMON ISLANDS PIJIN VOCABULARY

aesboks—refrigerator
arakwao—white man

bagarap—broken down
basta yu man!—damn you!
bele ran—diarrhea
belo—noon
bia blong Solomon—betel nut
bulumakao—cattle

daedae—to be in love with

garem—to have
gudfala—nice

haomas?—how much?
hem i stap wea?—where is he (it)?

iu go baek!—go away!

kabilato—loincloth
kabis—edible greens
kago—luggage, goods
kaikai—food
kalabus—jail

kaliko—clothes
kasem—to reach
kastom kaliko—traditional dress
kastom mani—traditional currency
koko—penis
kokorako—chicken
klosap—near, close
kros—angry

liu—jobless
longwe—far
luksave—to recognize

mere—woman
mifala—us
mi no save—I don't understand
moabetta—better

naes bola!—hey good lookin!
nambaten—the worst
nambawan—the best
nating—no

pikinini—child

raosem—to clear out

saedgo—that side
saedkam—this side
samting nating—it doesn't matter
sapos—if
save—to know
save tumas—wise
smol rod—footpath
staka—plenty
susu—milk, breast

taem bifoa—the past
tanggio tumas—thank you very much

wanem—what did you say?
wantok—kinsperson
waswas—shower, swim
waswe—why
wetim—with

yumi—we

men of Tikopia, Solomon Islands

M.G.L. DOMENY DE RIENZI

APPENDIX

INFORMATION OFFICES

REGIONAL

Tourism Council of the South Pacific, GPO Box 13119, Suva, Fiji Islands (fax 679/301-995)

Tourism Council of the South Pacific, 475 Lake Blvd., Tahoe City, CA 96145, U.S.A. (fax 916/583-0154)

Tourism Council of the South Pacific, 375 Upper Richmond Road West, East Sheen, London SW14 7NX, England (fax 44-181/878-0998)

Tourism Council of the South Pacific, rue Americaine 27, 1050 Brussels, Belgium (fax 32-2/538-2885)

TAHITI-POLYNESIA

Tahiti Tourisme, B.P. 65, Papeete, Tahiti (fax 689/43-66-19)

Tahiti Tourisme, 300 North Continental Blvd., Suite 180, El Segundo, CA 90245, U.S.A. (fax 310/414-8490)

Tahiti Tourisme, 444 Madison Ave., 16th Floor, New York, NY 10020, U.S.A. (fax 212/838-7855)

Tahiti Tourisme, Level 1, Southpac Tower, 45 Queen St., Auckland, New Zealand (fax 64-9/373-2415)

Tahiti Tourisme, 620 St. Kilda Rd., Suite 301, Melbourne 3004, Victoria, Australia (fax 61-3/9521-3867)

Tahiti Tourisme, 2-5, 2-6 Angkasa Raya Building, Jalan Ampang, 50450 Kuala Lumpur, Malaysia (fax 60-3/242-1129)

Pacific Leisure, Tung Ming Building, Suite 902, 40 Des Voeux Road, Central, Hong Kong (tel. 852/525-3290)

Tahiti Tourisme, Sankyo Building (No. 20) Room 802, 3-11-5 Iidabashi, Chiyoda-Ku, Tokyo 102, Japan (fax 81-3/3265-0581)

Oficina de Turismo de Tahiti, Casilla 16057, Santiago 9, Chile (fax 56-2/251-2826)

Office du Tourisme de Tahiti, 28 Boulevard Saint-Germain, 75005 Paris, France (fax 33-16-1/4325-4165)

Fremdenverkehrsbüro von Tahiti, Haingasse 22, D-61348 Bad Homburg v.d.H, Germany (fax 49-617/269-0458)

EASTER ISLAND

Servicio Nacional de Turismo, Providencia 1550, Casilla 14082, Santiago de Chile, Chile (fax 56-2/236-1417)

COOK ISLANDS

Cook Islands Tourist Authority, P.O. Box 14, Rarotonga, Cook Islands (fax 682/21-435)

Cook Islands Tourist Authority, 6033 West Century Blvd., Suite 690, Los Angeles, CA 90045, U.S.A. (fax 310/216-2868)

Cook Islands Tourist Authority, 330 Parnell Road, P.O. Box 37391, Auckland, New Zealand (fax 64-9/309-1876)

Cook Islands Tourist Authority, 1/177 Pacific Highway, North Sydney, NSW 2060, Australia (fax 61-2/9955-0447)

Pacific Leisure, Tung Ming Building, 40 Des Voeux Road, Central, Box 2382, Hong Kong

NIUE

Niue Tourism Office, P.O. Box 42, Alofi, Niue (fax 683/4225)

Niue Tourism Office, P.O. Box 68-541, Newton, Auckland, New Zealand (fax 64-9/308-9720)

KINGDOM OF TONGA

Tonga Visitors Bureau, P.O. Box 37, Nuku'alofa, Kingdom of Tonga (fax 676/22-129)

Tonga Visitors Bureau, P.O. Box 18, Neiafu, Vava'u, Kingdom of Tonga (fax 676/70-630)

Tonga Visitors Bureau, 360 Post St., Suite 604, San Francisco, CA 94108, U.S.A. (fax 415/781-3964)

Tonga Visitors Bureau, 642 King St., Newtown, Sydney, NSW 2042, Australia (fax 61-2/9723-9074)

Tonga Visitors Bureau, Box 24-054, Royal Oak, Auckland, New Zealand (fax 64-9/636-8973)

Tongan High Commission, 36 Molyneux St., London W1H 6AB, England (fax 44-171/723-9074)

AMERICAN SAMOA

Office of Tourism, P.O. Box 1147, Pago Pago, American Samoa 96799, U.S.A. (fax 684/633-1094)

WESTERN SAMOA

Western Samoa Visitors Bureau, P.O. Box 2272, Apia, Western Samoa (fax 685/20-886)

Western Samoa Visitors Bureau, 50 King St., Sydney, NSW 2000, Australia (fax 61-2/9299-1119)

TOKELAU

Office for Tokelau Affairs, P.O. Box 865, Apia, Western Samoa (fax 685/21-761)

Administrator of Tokelau, Ministry of Foreign Affairs & Trade, Private Bag 18-901, Wellington, New Zealand (fax 64-4/472-9596)

WALLIS AND FUTUNA

Bureau des Wallis et Futuna, B.P. C5, Nouméa Cédex, New Caledonia (fax 687/28-42-83)

TUVALU

Tourism Officer, Ministry of Commerce, Trade, and Industries, Box 33, Vaiaku, Funafuti, Tuvalu (fax 688/20829)

Tuvalu Embassy, P.O. Box 14449, Suva, Fiji Islands (fax 679/301-023)

Tuvalu Consulate-General, Suite 307, 301 George St., Sydney, NSW 2000, Australia

FIJI ISLANDS

Fiji Visitors Bureau, G.P.O. P.O. Box 92, Suva, Fiji Islands (fax 679/300-970)

Fiji Visitors Bureau, P.O. Box 9217, Nandi Airport, Fiji Islands (fax 679/720-141)

Fiji Visitors Bureau, Suite 220, 5777 West Century Blvd., Los Angeles, CA 90045, U.S.A. (fax 310/670-2318)

Fiji Visitors Bureau, Level 12, St. Martin's Tower, 31 Market St., Sydney, NSW 2000, Australia (fax 61-2/9264-3060)

Fiji Visitors Bureau, Suite 204, 620 St. Kilda Rd., Melbourne 3000, Australia (fax 61-3/9510-3650)

Fiji Visitors Bureau, P.O. Box 1179, Auckland, New Zealand (fax 64-9/309-4720)

Fiji Visitors Bureau, 14th floor, NOA Bldg., 3-5, 2-Chome, Azabudai, Minato-ku, Tokyo 106, Japan (fax 81-3/3587-2563)

Fiji Embassy, 34 Hyde Park Gate, London SW7 5DN, England (fax 44-171/584-2838)

Representation Plus, 375 Upper Richmond Road West, London SW14 7NX, England (fax 44-181/392-1318)

Interface Int. GmbH, Dirksenstrasse 40, 1020 Berlin, Germany (fax 49-302/381-7641)

NEW CALEDONIA

Destination New Caledonia, B.P. 688, Nouméa 98800, New Caledonia (fax 687/27-46-23)

Office du tourisme de Nouméa, B.P. 2828, Nouméa, New Caledonia (fax 687/28-75-85)

Destination New Caledonia, 2nd Level, 30 Clarence St., Sydney, NSW 2000, Australia (fax 61-2/9290-2242)

Destination New Caledonia, 7th Floor, 84 William St., Melbourne, Victoria 3000, Australia (fax 61-3/9642-0953)

Destination New Caledonia, 8th Floor, 324 Queen St., Brisbane, Queensland 4000, Australia (fax 61-7/3221-4331)

Destination New Caledonia, 57 Fort St., 3rd Floor, P.O. Box 4300, Auckland, New Zealand (fax 64-9/379-2874)

Maison de la France, Landic No. 2, Akasaka Park Building, 2-10-9 Akasaka, Minato-ku, Tokyo 107, Japan (fax 81-3/3505-2873)

Maison de la Nouvelle-Calédonie, 7 rue du Général Bertrand, 75007 Paris, France (fax 33-1/4065-9600)

VANUATU

Vanuatu National Tourism Office, P.O. Box 209, Port Vila, Vanuatu (fax 678/23889)

SOLOMON ISLANDS

Solomon Islands Tourist Authority, P.O. Box 321, Honiara, Solomon Islands (fax 677/23986)

Government Information Service, P.O. Box G1, Honiara, Solomon Islands (fax 677/20401)

Solomon Islands Tourist Authority, Suite 20, 37 Alexander St., Crows Nest, Sydney, NSW 2065, Australia (fax 61-2/9438-5197)

RESOURCES

GUIDEBOOKS

Box, Ben, ed. *South American Handbook.* Trade & Travel Publications, 6 Riverside Court, Lower Bristol Road, Bath BA2 3DZ, England (fax 44-1225/469461). Highly recommended for anyone combining a trip to Latin America with the South Pacific via Easter Island.

Fisher, Jon. *Uninhabited Ocean Islands.* Loompanics Unlimited, Box 1197, Port Townsend, WA 98368, U.S.A. This unique book and Fisher's other work, *The Last Frontiers on Earth,* are essential reading for anyone considering relocating to the South Pacific. Write Loompanics for a free copy of "The Best Book Catalog in the World."

Hammick, Anne. *Ocean Cruising on a Budget.* Camden, Maine: International Marine Publishing. Hammick shows how to sail your own yacht safely and enjoyably over the seas while cutting costs. Study it beforehand if you're thinking of working as crew on a yacht.

Health Information For International Travel. An excellent reference published annually by the Centers for Disease Control, U.S. Public Health Service. Available from the Superintendent of Documents, U.S. Government Printing Office, Washington, DC 20402, U.S.A.

Hinz, Earl R. *Landfalls of Paradise: The Guide to Pacific Islands.* Honolulu: University of Hawaii Press. With 97 maps and 40 tables, this is the only genuine cruising guide to all 32 island groups of Oceania.

Ryan, Paddy. *The Snorkeler's Guide to the Coral Reef.* Honolulu, University of Hawaii Press, 1994. Covers everything from the Red Sea to the Pacific Ocean.

Schroeder, Dirk. *Staying Healthy in Asia, Africa, and Latin America.* Chico: Moon Publications, 1995. Order a copy of this book if you'd like to acquire a degree of expertise in tropical medicine.

Skinner, Gwen. *The Cuisine of the South Pacific.* Auckland: Hodder & Stoughton Ltd. Recipes for over 400 island delicacies.

Smith Elliot. *Cook Islands Companion.* Pacific Publishing Co., 735 San Carlos Ave., Albany, CA 94706, U.S.A. Worth ordering if you plan a long stay in the Cooks.

Stanley, David. *Micronesia Handbook.* Chico: Moon Publications. Covers the North Pacific countries of Nauru, Kiribati, the Marshall Islands, the Federated States of Micronesia, the Republic of Belau, Guam, and the Northern Marianas in the same manner as the book you're reading.

DESCRIPTION AND TRAVEL

Amadio, Nadine. *Pacifica: Myth, Magic, and Traditional Wisdom from the South Sea Islands.* New York: Harper Collins, 1993. Based on an Australian television series, this lavishly illustrated book deals with many of the classic themes and stories of the South Pacific. If your library has it, check it out.

Finney, Ben. *Voyage of Discovery: A Cultural Odyssey through Polynesia.* University of California Press, 1994. A complete account of the 1985 journey of the sailing canoe *Hokule'a* through Polynesia.

Frisbie, Robert Dean. *The Book of Pukapuka, A Lone Trader On A South Sea Atoll.* Honolulu: Mutual Publishing. A delightful depiction of daily life on one of the Northern Cook Islands in the interwar period.

Heyerdahl, Thor. *Kon Tiki.* Translated by F.H. Lyon. Chicago: Rand McNally, 1950. Convinced that the mysterious origin of the Polynesians lies in the equally mysterious disappearance of the pre-Incan Indians of Peru, the author finds that only by repeating their feat of sailing some 6,500 km across the Pacific in a balsa raft can he substantiate his theory.

Hinz, Earl R. *Pacific Wanderer.* Stamford, CT: Westcott Cove Publishing, 1991. Hinz has sailed the Pacific in his own yacht for over 20 years and in this collection of articles previously published in *Seas* and *Cruising World,* he shares his experiences.

Krieger, Michael. *Conversations with the Cannibals: The End of the Old South Pacific.* Hopewell, NJ: The Ecco Press, 1994. Krieger's encounters with a crooked preacher on Palmerston, former cannibals on Malekula, a sorcerer on Ambrym, cargo cultists on Tanna, tribal warriors on Malaita, and the dauntless missionaries of Batuna provide glimpses of passing ways of life in Cook Islands, Tuvalu, Vanuatu, and Solomon Islands. His account of the desecration of the Kwaio by fundamentalist missionaries and their own government is perhaps a sad last chapter in 200 years of European exploitation in this part of the world.

Kyselka, Will. *An Ocean in Mind.* Honolulu: University of Hawaii Press, 1987. Analyzes the learning techniques of Nainoa Thompson, who successfully navigated without the use of modern navigational equipment the re-created traditional Polynesian sailing vessel, *Hokule'a,* during its second roundtrip journey between Hawaii and Tahiti in 1980.

Lewis, David. *We: the Navigators.* Honolulu: University of Hawaii Press, 1994. A 2nd edition of the 1972 classic on the ancient art of landfinding in the Pacific.

London, Jack. *The Cruise of the Snark.* International Marine Publishing. A reprint of London's 1911 classic about his journey to the Solomon Islands aboard the 17-meter ketch *Snark.*

McCall, Grant. *Rapanui: Tradition and Survival on Easter Island.* Honolulu: University of Hawaii Press, 1994. Distributed in Australia by Allen and Unwin. A comprehensive summary of what is known about the island and its current inhabitants.

Murray, Spencer. *Pitcairn Island: The First 200 Years.* Bounty Sagas, Box 1302, La Canada, CA 91012-5303, USA. A comprehensive survey of all things related to Pitcairn, past and present.

Neal, Tom. *An Island to Myself.* New York: Holt, Rinehart, and Winston, 1966. Tom's tale of his six years alone on Suwarrow atoll in the Cooks.

Stevenson, Robert Louis. *In the South Seas.* New York: Scribner's, 1901. The author's account of his travels through the Marquesas, Tuamotus, and Gilberts by yacht in the years 1888-90.

Theroux, Paul. *The Happy Isles of Oceania.* London, Hamish Hamilton, 1992. The author of classic accounts of railway journeys sets out with kayak and tent to tour the Pacific. Theroux has caught the mood of paradise in a way that makes his book really satisfying to read.

Watson, Thomas F., Jr. *Pacific Passage.* Camden, ME: International Marine Publishing. The story of voyage through Polynesia under sail with extensive notes on navigation, yacht handling, trip planning, and natural history.

Winchester, Simon. *The Pacific.* London: Hutchinson, 1991. A wide-angle overview of the entire region.

Wright, Ronald. *On Fiji Islands.* New York: Penguin Books, 1986. Wright relates his travels to Fijian history and tradition in a most pleasing and informative way.

GEOGRAPHY

Crocombe, Ron. *The South Pacific, An Introduction.* Suva: Institute of Pacific Studies, 1989. A collection of lecture notes covering a wide range of topics.

Derrick, R.A. *The Fiji Islands: Geographical Handbook.* Suva: Government Printing Office, 1965.

Donnelly, Quanchi, and Kerr. *Fiji in the Pacific: A History and Geography of Fiji.* Jacaranda Wiley, Box 1226, Milton, QLD 4064, Australia. The updated 4th edition appeared in 1994.

Freeman, Otis W., ed. *Geography of the Pacific.* New York: John Wiley, 1951. Although dated, this book does provide a wealth of background information on the islands.

Oliver, Douglas L. *The Pacific Islands.* Honolulu: University of Hawaii Press, 1989. A new edition of the classic 1951 study of the history and economies of the entire Pacific area.

Ridgell, Reilly. *Pacific Nations and Territories.* Published by Bess Press, Box 22388, Honolulu, HI 96823, U.S.A. One of the few high school geography textbooks on the region.

NATURAL SCIENCE

Bahn, Paul, and John Flenley. *Easter Island, Easter Island.* London: Thames and Hudson, 1992. A well-illustrated study of man's impact on an isolated island environment, and how that led to his degradation. A message from our past for the future of our planet.

Crawford, Peter. *Nomads of the Wind.* London: BBC Books, 1993. A beautifully illustrated natural history of Polynesia that grew out of a five-part television series.

Hargreaves, Bob, and Dorothy Hargreaves. *Tropical Blossoms of the Pacific.* Ross-Hargreaves, Box 11897, Lahaina, HI 96761, U.S.A. A handy 64-page booklet with color photos to assist in identification; a matching volume is titled *Tropical Trees of the Pacific.*

Hinton, A.G. *Shells of New Guinea and the Central Indo-Pacific.* Australia: Jacaranda Press, 1972. A photo guide to identification.

Lebot, Vincent, Lamont Lindstrom, and Mark Marlin. *Kava—the Pacific Drug.* Yale University Press, 1993. A thorough examination of kava and its many uses.

Martini, Frederic. *Exploring Tropical Isles and Seas.* Englewood Cliffs, N.J.: Prentice-Hall, 1984. A fine introduction to the natural environment of the islands.

Mayr, Ernst. *Birds of the Southwest Pacific.* Rutland, VT: Charles E. Tuttle Co., 1978. Though poor on illustrations, this paperback reprint of the 1945 edition is still an essential reference list for birders.

Merrill, Elmer D. *Plant Life of the Pacific World.* Rutland, VT: Charles E. Tuttle Co., 1981. First published in 1945, this handy volume is a useful first reference.

Mitchell, Andrew W. *A Fragile Paradise: Man and Nature in the Pacific.* London: Fontana, 1990. Published in the U.S. by the University of Texas Press under the title *The Fragile South Pacific: An Ecological Odyssey.* Andrew Mitchell, an Earthwatch Europe deputy director, utters a heartfelt plea on behalf of all endangered Pacific wildlife in this brilliant book.

Muse, Corey, and Shirley Muse. *Birds and Birdlore of Samoa.* Seattle: University of Washington Press. Descriptions and illustrations of the 72 bird species inhabiting or visiting Samoa, 31 of which are found nowhere else.

Pratt, Douglas. *A Field Guide to the Birds of Hawaii and the Tropical Pacific.* Princeton, N.J.: Princeton University Press, 1986. The best in a poorly covered field.

Tinker, Spencer Wilkie. *Fishes of Hawaii: A Handbook of the Marine Fishes of Hawaii and the Central Pacific Ocean.* Hawaiian Service, Inc., Box 2835, Honolulu, HI 96803, U.S.A. A comprehensive, indexed reference work.

Watling, Dick. *Mai Veikau: Tales of Fijian Wildlife.* Suva: Fiji Times, 1986. A wealth of easily digested information on Fiji's flora and fauna. Copies are available in local bookstores.

Whistler, W. Arthur. *Polynesian Herbal Medicine.* Available at US$32.95 from Publications Office, National Tropical Botanical Garden, Box 340, Lawai, Kauai, HI 96765, U.S.A. This book discusses traditional and contemporary herbal medicinal practices in Polynesia. Whistler's *Flowers of the Pacific Islands Seashore* is distributed by the University of Hawaii Press.

HISTORY

Beaglehole, J.C. *The Life of Captain Cook.* Camden, ME: International Marine Publishing. A well-written account of Cook's achievements in the context of the era in which Cook lived. Beaglehole also edited Cook's three volumes of journals.

Bellwood, Peter. *Man's Conquest of the Pacific.* New York: Oxford University Press, 1979. One of the most extensive studies of the prehistory of Southeast Asia and Oceania ever published.

Bellwood, Peter. *The Polynesians: Prehistory of an Island People.* London: Thames and Hudson, 1987. A well-written account of the archaeology of Polynesian expansion.

Bennett, Judith A. *Wealth of the Solomons.* Honolulu: University of Hawaii Press, 1986. A general history of the Solomon Islands, 1800-1978.

Bennett, William, et al. *The Big Death.* Suva: University of the South Pacific, 1988. Most histories of the Pacific War focus exclusively on the activities of foreigners; in this unique book nine Solomon Islanders recall how it was for them.

Blanton, Casey, ed. *Picturing Paradise: Colonial Photography of Samoa, 1875 to 1925.* Southeast Museum of Photography, Box 2811, Daytona Beach, FL 32120, U.S.A. The essays included in this catalog contain much information on the history of culture contact in the islands.

Bonnemaison, Joël. *The Tree and the Canoe: History and Ethnogeography of Tanna.* Honolulu: University of Hawaii Press, 1994. The story of how the Tannese revived their original creation myths as a defense against outside influences.

Buck, Peter H. *Vikings of the Pacific.* Chicago: University of Chicago Press, 1959. A popular narrative of Polynesian migrations.

Connell, John. *New Caledonia or Kanaky? The Political History of a French Colony.* Pacific Research Monograph No. 16, National Centre for Development Studies, Australian National University, Canberra, Australia. First appearing in 1987, this major book explores the historic sources of the conflict in the divided French territory.

Davis Wallis, Mary. *Life in Feejee: Five Years Among the Cannibals.* First published in 1851, this book is the memoir of a New England sea captain's wife in Fiji. It's a charming if rather gruesome firsthand account of early European contact with Fiji and has some fascinating details of Fijian customs. You'll find ample mention of Cakobau, who hadn't yet converted to Christianity. Reprinted by the Fiji Museum, Suva, in 1983 and sold at the museum shop. A rare South Seas classic!

Field, Michael J. *Mau: Samoa's Struggle for Freedom.* Auckland: Pasifika Press, 1991. The story of a nonviolent freedom movement.

Fraser, Helen. *New Caledonia: Anti-Colonialism in a Pacific Territory.* Monograph No. 3, 1988, Peace Research Center, RSPAS, ANU, Canberra, ACT 0200, Australia.

Garrett, John. *To Live Among the Stars: Christian Origins in Oceania.* Suva: Institute of Pacific Studies, 1982. The first complete history of Christianity in the Pacific. A sequel, *Footsteps in the Sea: Christianity in Oceania to World War II,* appeared in 1992.

Henningham, Stephen. *France and the South Pacific: A Contemporary History.* Honolulu: University of Hawaii Press, 1992. This lucid book brings French policy in the South Pacific into clear focus.

Herda, Phyllis, Jennifer Terrell, and Neil Gunson, eds. *Tongan Culture and History.* Canberra: Australian National University, 1990. This collection of papers covers a wide range of interesting topics.

Howe, K.R. *Where the Waves Fall.* Honolulu: University of Hawaii Press, 1984. This history of the South Seas from first settlement to colonial rule maintains a steady and sympathetic focus on the islanders themselves.

Howe, K.R., Robert C. Kiste, and Brij V. Lal, eds. *Tides of History.* Honolulu: University of Hawaii Press, 1994. Distributed in Australia by Allen and Unwin. A collection of essays on the Pacific islands in the 20th century.

Langdon, Robert. *The Lost Caravel.* Sydney: Pacific Publications, 1975. The author proposes that Spanish castaways from Magellan's fleet gave a totally new direction to Polynesian culture, an audacious theory that has met with little approval among professional anthropologists and historians.

Langdon, Robert. *Tahiti: Island of Love.* Australia: Pacific Publications, 1979. A popular history of Tahiti since the European discovery in 1767.

Martin, John. *Tonga Islands: William Mariner's Account.* Nuku'alofa: Vava'u Press, 1981. Mariner, a survivor of the 1806 *Port au Prince* massacre at Ha'apai, became the adopted son of the warrior king Finau 'Ulukalala II and stayed in Tonga four years before returning to England.

Moorehead, Alan. *The Fatal Impact.* New York: Harper & Row, 1966. European impact on the South Pacific from 1767 to 1840, as illustrated in the cases of Tahiti, Australia, and Antarctica.

Oliver, Douglas L. *Return to Tahiti: Bligh's Second Breadfruit Voyage.* Honolulu: University of Hawaii Press, 1988. Offers insights on the inhabitants of Tahiti and their customs at the time of European contact.

Scarr, Deryck. *Fiji: A Short History.* Honolulu: University of Hawaii Press, 1984. A balanced look at Fijian history from first settlement to 1982.

Scott, Dick. *Years of the Pooh-Bah.* Auckland: Hodder & Stoughton, 1991. A history of the colonial era in the Cook Islands.

PACIFIC ISSUES

Crocombe, Ron, ed. *Land Tenure in the Pacific.* Suva: Institute of Pacific Studies, 1987. Twenty specialists contributed to this basic study of customs, equality, privilege, colonization, productivity, individualism, and reform.

Danielsson, Bengt, and Marie-Thérèse Danielsson. *Poisoned Reign: French Nuclear Colonialism in the Pacific.* Penguin Books, 1986. An updated version of *Moruroa Mon Amour,* first published in 1977.

Dé Ishtar, Zohl, ed. *Daughters of the Pacific.* Melbourne: Spinifex Press, 1994. A stirring collection of stories of survival, strength, determination, and compassion told by indigenous women of the Pacific. The stories relate their experiences, and the impact on them by nuclear testing, uranium mining, neo-colonialism, and nuclear waste dumping.

Ernst, Manfred. *Winds of Change.* Suva: Pacific Conference of Churches, 1994. A timely examination of rapidly growing religious groups in the Pacific islands and unequaled source of information on contemporary religion in the South Pacific.

Hamel-Green, Michael. *The South Pacific Nuclear Free Zone Treaty: A Critical Assessment.* Canberra: Peace Research Center, Australian National University, 1990. Hamel-Green demonstrates how Australia forced through a toothless treaty designed to appease regional antinuclear sentiment, then was humiliated when the U.S. refused to sign.

Hau'ofa, Epeli, et al. *A New Oceania: Rediscovering Our Sea of Islands.* Suva: University of the South Pacific, 1993. A collection of papers by 20 academics on the theme of islands and ocean as part of an undivided whole (in contrast to the usual perception of tiny islands lost in a boundless sea).

Robertson, Robert T., and Akosita Tamanisau. *Fiji—Shattered Coups.* Australia: Pluto Press, 1988. The first detailed analysis to emerge from Fiji of events which shook the South Pacific. Robertson, a history lecturer at the University of the South Pacific until expelled by Rabuka, and his wife Tamanisau, a reporter with the *Fiji Sun* until Rabuka closed the paper down, wrote the book secretly in Fiji and smuggled out the manuscript chapter by chapter. A military raid on their Suva home failed to uncover the book in preparation.

Robie, David. *Blood on their Banner*. London: Zed Books, 1989. Robie, a veteran New Zealand journalist specializing in the islands, examines the nationalist struggles in New Caledonia and other Pacific territories. In the U.S., it's available from Zed Books, 171 First Ave., Atlantic Heights, NJ 07716; in Britain from Zed Books, 57 Caledonian Rd., London N1 9BU; in Australia from Pluto Press, Box 199, Leichhardt, NSW 2040. Highly recommended.

Robie, David. *Eyes of Fire: The Last Voyage of the Rainbow Warrior*. Philadelphia: New Society Publishers, 1986. Robie was aboard the Greenpeace protest vessel sunk at Auckland by French terrorists. His photos and firsthand account tell the inside story.

Robie, David, ed. *Tu Galala: Social Change in the Pacific*. Wellington: Bridget Williams Books, 1992. Distributed in Australia by Pluto Press (address above). In this book, Robie has collected a series of essays examining the conflicting influences of tradition, democracy, and westernization, with special attention to environmental issues and human rights.

Weingartner, Erich. *The Pacific: Nuclear Testing And Minorities*. London: Minority Rights Group, 1991. A recent survey of the various environmental, political, and social issues facing the peoples of the Pacific. Available from Cultural Survival, 46 Brattle St., Cambridge, MA 02138, U.S.A.

SOCIAL SCIENCE

Calkins, Fay. *My Samoan Chief*. Honolulu: University of Hawaii Press, 1971. The life of a young American woman in her Samoan husband's native land. A delightful account of cross-cultural contact.

Cizeron, Marc, and Marianne Hienly. *Tahiti: Life on the Other Side*. Suva: Institute of Pacific Studies, 1983. Four lower-income urban Tahitians describe their experiences, and community leaders reflect on what must be done to help the Tahitian poor.

Danielsson, Bengt. *Love in the South Seas*. Honolulu: Mutual Publishing. Sex and family life of the Polynesians, based on early accounts as well as observations by the noted Swedish anthropologist.

Firth, Dr. Raymond. *We: the Tikopia*. London: Allen and Unwin, 1936. The classic study of a small, isolated Polynesian community.

Foerstel, Lenora, and Angela Gilliam, eds. *Confronting the Margaret Mead Legacy: Scholarship, Empire, and the South Pacific*. Philadelphia: Temple University Press, 1992. Mead's impact on western anthropology and her views of colonialism, imperialism, and business interests in the South Pacific.

Freeman, Derek. *Margaret Mead and Samoa: The Making and Unmaking of an Anthropological Myth*. Cambridge. Mass.: Harvard University Press, 1983. An Australian academic refutes Margaret Mead's theory of Samoan promiscuity and lack of aggression.

Howell, William. *The Pacific Islanders*. New York: Scribner's, 1973. An anthropological study of the origins of Pacific peoples.

Krämer, Dr. Augustin. *The Samoa Islands*. Auckland: Pasifika Press, 1994. A definitive, two-volume ethnological work translated from the German original.

Levy, Robert. *Tahitians: Mind and Experience in the Society Islands*. Chicago: University of Chicago Press, 1973. Levy's study, based on several years of field work on Tahiti and Huahine, includes an intriguing examination of the *mahu* (transvestite) phenomenon.

Mead, Margaret. *Letters from the Field*. Edited by Ruth Nanda. New York: Harper & Row, 1977. Describes Mead's experiences in American Samoa, Manus, the Sepik, and Bali. See also Mead's *Coming of Age in Samoa*.

Oliver, Douglas L. *Native Cultures of the Pacific Islands*. Honolulu: University of Hawaii Press, 1988. Intended primarily for college-level courses on precontact anthropology, history, economy, and politics of the entire region; an abridged version of Oliver's *Oceania,* listed below.

Oliver, Douglas L. *Oceania: The Native Cultures of Australia and the Pacific Islands.* Honolulu: University of Hawaii Press, 1989. A massive, two-volume, 1,275-page anthropological survey.

Roth, G. Kingsley. *Fijian Way of Life.* 2nd ed. Melbourne: Oxford University Press, 1973. A standard reference on Fijian culture.

Tangatapoto, Vainerere, et al. *Atiu, An Island Community.* Suva: Institute of Pacific Studies, 1984. Eight residents of Atiu write about life on their island, with many invaluable insights on the traditional culture of the Cooks.

LITERATURE

Bermann, Richard A. *Home from the Sea.* Honolulu: Mutual Publishing. A reprint of the 1939 narrative of Robert Louis Stevenson's final years in Samoa.

Burdick, Eugene. *The Blue of Capricorn.* Honolulu: Mutual Publishing. Stories and sketches about the Pacific by the coauthor of *The Ugly American.*

Davis, Tom. *Vaka: Saga of a Polynesian Canoe.* Suva: University of the South Pacific, 1992. This historical novel's protagonist is a legendary voyaging canoe that sails between the diverse isles of Oceania for 12 generations. The lore of three centuries of Polynesian migration, including legends, customs, navigational and sailing techniques, genealogies, tribal hierarchies, and titles, is encapsulated in this simple chronicle. Prosaic elements such as female offspring, commoners, the passage of time, illness, and failure receive scant attention from Davis.

Daws, A. Gavan. *A Dream of Islands: Voyages of Self-Discovery in the South Seas.* Honolulu: Mutual Publishing. A popular biography of John Williams, Herman Melville, Walter Murray Gibson, Robert Louis Stevenson, and Paul Gauguin.

Day, A. Grove. *Pacific Literature: One Hundred Basic Books.* Honolulu: University Press, 1971. Reviews of books on the Pacific by European writers.

Day, A. Grove, and Carl Stroven, eds. *Best South Sea Stories.* Honolulu: Mutual Publishing, 1964. Fifteen extracts from the writings of famous European authors.

Hall, James Norman. *The Forgotten One and Other True Tales of the South Seas.* Honolulu: Mutual Publishing. A book about expatriate writers and intellectuals who sought refuge on the out-of-the-world islands of the Pacific.

Hall, James Norman, and Charles Bernard Nordhoff. *The Bounty Trilogy.* New York: Grosset and Dunlap, 1945. Retells in fictional form the famous mutiny, Bligh's escape to Timor, and the mutineers' fate on Pitcairn.

Hau'ofa, Epeli. *Tales of the Tikongs.* Auckland: Longman Paul Ltd., 1983. Reprinted by Beake House (Fiji) in 1993 and the University of Hawaii Press in 1994. An amusingly ironic view of Tongan life: "Our people work so hard on Sunday it takes a six-day rest to recover." The development aid business, exotic religious sects, self-perpetuating bureaucracy, and similar themes provide a milieu for the tales of the Tikongs: in Tiko nothing is as it seems. A classic of Pacific literature.

Lay, Graeme. *Motu Tapu.* Auckland: Pasifika Press, 1990. Short stories of the South Pacific. Lay has also written a travelogue called *Passages—Journeys in Polynesia* (Auckland: Tandem Press, 1993).

Loti, Pierre. *The Marriage of Loti.* Honolulu: University of Hawaii Press, 1976. This tale of Loti's visits to Tahiti in 1872 helped foster the romantic myth of Polynesia in Europe.

Maka'a, Julian. *The Confession and Other Stories.* Suva: Institute of Pacific Studies, 1985. A collection of nine short stories about young Solomon Islanders attaining manhood. Though unpolished, the stories contrast the alienation of city life with social control of the village.

Malifa, Fata Sano. *Alms for Oblivion*. New York: Vantage Press, 1993. A rather pessimistic novel about hypocrisy and corruption in Samoan society by the founder of the *Samoa Observer*. As the protagonist Niko develops from nonconformist Bohemian to successful businessman and finally terminal alcoholic, the petty avarice of church, chiefs, and politicians is revealed in hyperbolic detail.

Maugham, W. Somerset. *The Trembling of a Leaf*. Honolulu: Mutual Publishing. The responses of a varied mix of white males—colonial administrator, trader, sea captain, bank manager, and missionary—to the peoples and environment of the South Pacific. Maugham is a masterful storyteller, and his journey to Samoa and Tahiti in 1916-1917 supplied him with poignant material.

Melville, Herman. *Typee, A Peep at Polynesian Life*. Evanston, Ill.: Northwestern University Press, 1968. In 1842 Melville deserted from an American whaler at Nuku Hiva, Marquesas Islands. This semifictional account of Melville's four months among the Typee people was followed by *Omoo* in which Melville gives his impressions of Tahiti at the time of the French takeover.

Michener, James A. *Return to Paradise*. New York: Random House, 1951. Essays and short stories. Michener's *Tales of the South Pacific*, the first of over 30 books, opened on Broadway in 1949 as the long-running musical *South Pacific*. This writer's ability to gloss over the complexities of life explains his tremendous popularity, and the predictable stereotypes in his one-dimensional South Seas tales perpetuate the illusory myth of the island paradise. Michener's portrayal of Fiji Indians in his story "The Mynah Birds" borders on outright racism.

Pillai, Raymond. *The Celebration*. Suva: South Pacific Creative Arts Society, 1980. A collection of short stories in which the heterogeneous nature of Fiji Indian society is presented by an accomplished narrator.

Pouesi, Daniel, and Michael Igoe. *The Stone Maiden and Other Samoan Fables*. KIN Publishers, 558 East Double St., Carson, CA 90745, U.S.A. A collection of 18 fables used to illustrate Samoan proverbs.

Saunana, John. *The Alternative*. Honiara: University of the South Pacific, 1980. The struggle of a young Solomon Islander to find his place in a world still dominated by the declining absurdities of colonial rule—a well-written vignette of the time.

Stead, C.K., ed. *Faber Book of Contemporary South Pacific Stories*. London: Faber and Faber, 1994. Over half the stories are from New Zealand and noted island writers such as Albert Wendt are not included.

Steubel, C., and Brother Herman. *Tala O Le Vavau: The Myths, Legends, and Customs of Old Samoa*. Auckland: Pasifika Press, 1987.

Subramani. *South Pacific Literature: From Myth to Fabulation*. Suva: Institute of Pacific Studies, 1992. This academic study of island writers up to 1985 provides a useful reference for students of Pacific literature. Unlike expatriates such as Hall, Maugham, Melville, and Michener who view the South Pacific through European eyes, Subramani's writers put the islanders at the center of their narratives. Subramani's book is only interesting when read in conjunction with the works themselves.

Wendt, Albert. *Flying Fox in a Freedom Tree*. Auckland: Longman Paul Ltd., 1974. A collection of short stories in which the men cannot show fear or emotion, while the women appear only as sex objects.

Wendt, Albert. *Leaves of the Banyan Tree*. Honolulu: University of Hawaii Press, 1994. A reprint of the 1980 Wendt classic. Wendt was the first South Pacific novelist of international stature and his semi-autobiographical writings are full of interest.

Wendt, Albert. *Pouliuli*. Auckland: Longman Paul Ltd., 1977. This is probably Wendt's finest novel, masterfully depicting the complex values and manipulative nature of Samoan society. No other book explains more about Samoa today.

Wendt, Albert. *Sons for the Return Home.* Auckland: Longman Paul Ltd., 1973. The story of a Samoan youth brought up amid discrimination in New Zealand, yet unable to readjust to the cultural values of his own country.

THE ARTS

Barrow, Terence. *The Art of Tahiti.* London: Thames and Hudson, 1979. A concise, well-illustrated survey of works of art from the Society, Austral, and Cook islands.

Brake, Brian, James McNeish, and David Simmons. *Art of the Pacific.* New York: Abrams, 1979. One of the finest, most sensitive books ever published on Oceanic art. Penetrating interviews with contemporary islanders are juxtaposed with stunning photos of the finest art objects from their past, now in the museums of New Zealand.

Danielsson, Bengt. *Gauguin in the South Seas.* New York: Doubleday, 1966. Danielsson's fascinating account of Gauguin's 10 years in Polynesia.

Gathercole, Peter, Adrienne L. Kaeppler, and Douglas Newton. *The Art of the Pacific Islanders.* Washington, D.C.: National Gallery of Art, 1979. The catalog of a wide-ranging exhibition of Oceanic art. The introduction is excellent.

Gauguin, Paul. *Noa Noa.* A Tahitian journal kept by this famous artist during his first two years in the islands.

Guiart, Jean. *The Arts of the South Pacific.* New York: Golden Press, 1963. A well-illustrated coffee-table art book, with the emphasis on the French-dominated portion of Oceania. Consideration is given to the cultures that produced the works.

Hanson, Louise, and F. Allan Hanson. *The Art of Oceania: A Bibliography.* Boston: G.K. Hall & Co., 1988.

Kaeppler, Adrienne L. *Polynesian Dance.* Honolulu: Bishop Museum Press, 1983. Describes the traditional dances of Hawaii, Tahiti, the Cook Islands, Tonga, and Niue.

Lee, Georgia. *The Rock Art of Easter Island: Symbols of Power, Prayers to the Gods.* Monumenta Archaeologica Vol. 17. UCLA Institute of Archaeology Publications, 405 Hilgard Ave., Los Angeles, CA 90024, U.S.A. A readable 1992 examination of a fascinating subject. Alan Drake's *The Ceremonial Center of Orongo* and Dr. William Liller's *The Ancient Solar Observatories of Rapanui* (both available from the Easter Island Foundation, 666 Dead Cat Alley, Woodland, CA 95695, U.S.A.) are also highly recommended for all Easter Island buffs.

Linkels, Ad. *Fa'a-Samoa: The Samoan Way.* Published in 1995 by Mundo Étnico, Sibeliusstraat 707, 5011 JR Tilburg, The Netherlands, this book is a complete survey of Samoan music from conch shell to disco.

Linton, Ralph, and Paul S. Wingert. *Arts of the South Seas.* New York: Museum of Modern Art, 1946. Although dated, this book provides a starting point for the study of the art of Polynesia.

Moyle, Richard. *Tongan Music.* Auckland: Auckland University Press, 1987. A look at one of the South Pacific's best-preserved musical systems, in which song and dance are living parts of the culture. Also see *Sounds of Change in Tonga* by Ad Linkels, available from the Friendly Islands Bookshop in Nuku'alofa.

Price, Christine. *Made in the South Pacific: Arts of the South Sea People.* London: The Bodley Head, 1979. A concise yet comprehensive examination of the handicrafts; well researched and written.

DISCOGRAPHY

Music lovers will be pleased to hear that authentic Pacific music is becoming more readily available on compact disc. In compiling this selection we've tried to list non-commercial recordings that are faithful to the traditional music of the islands as it exists today. Island music based on Western pop has been avoided. Most of the

CDs below can be ordered through specialized music shops; otherwise write directly to the publishers.

Bagès, Gérard, ed. *Chants de L'Ile de Pâques* (92553-2). Buda Musique, 188 boulevard Voltaire, 75011 Paris, France. Sixteen traditional songs from Easter Island, in the collection "Musique du Monde" (recording date not provided).

Coco's Temaeva (S 65808). Manuiti Productions, B.P. 755, Papeete, Tahiti (fax 689/43-27-24). Founded by Coco Hotahota in 1962, Temaeva has won more prizes at the annual Heiva i Tahiti festivals than any other professional dance troupe.

Fanshawe, David, ed. *Exotic Voices and Rhythms of the South Seas* (EUCD 1254). ARC Music, Box 11288, Oakland, CA 94611, U.S.A. Cook Islands drum dancing, a Fijian *tralala meke*, a Samoan *fiafia*, a Vanuatu string band, and Solomon Islands panpipes selected from the 1,200 hours of tapes in the Fanshawe Pacific Collection.

Fanshawe, David, ed. *Heiva i Tahiti: Festival of Love* (EUCD 1238). ARC Music. Fanshawe has captured the excitement of Tahiti's biggest festival in these pieces recorded live in Papeete in 1982 and 1986. Famous groups led by Coco Hotahota, Yves Roche, Irma Prince, and others are represented.

Fanshawe, David, ed. *Spirit of Polynesia* (CD-SDL 403). Saydisc Records, Chipping Manor, The Chipping, Wotton-U-Edge, Glos. GL12 7AD, England. An anthology of the music of 12 Pacific countries recorded between 1978 and 1988. Over half the pieces are from Tahiti-Polynesia and Cook Islands. A *Spirit of Melanesia* sequel is planned.

Linkels, Ad and Lucia Linkels, eds. *Fa'a-Samoa* (PAN 2066CD). PAN Records, Box 155, 2300 AD Leiden, The Netherlands (fax 31-71/522-6869). This 29-track recording made in 1982 contains everything from the blowing of a conch shell to traditional dance music, string bands, drumming, brass bands, church choirs, and

even unexpected village sounds, such as the calling of the pigs. This and the other PAN Records compact discs listed below form part of the series "Anthology of Pacific Music" and extensive booklets explaining the music come with the records. Music stores can order PAN compact discs through Arhoolie, 10341 San Pablo Ave., El Cerrito, CA 94530, U.S.A. (fax 510/525-1204), Festival Distribution, 1351 Grant St., Vancouver, BC V5L 2X7, Canada (fax 604/253-2634), and Tropic Records, 50 Stroud Green Road, London N4 3EF, England (fax 44-171/281-5671).

Linkels, Ad and Lucia Linkels, eds. *Fiafia* (PAN 150CD). The traditional dances of 11 Pacific countries recorded during six field trips between 1979 and 1992. Some songs and rhythms are provided in two versions: the original version and a new one, or two different original versions.

Linkels, Ad and Lucia Linkels, eds. *Faikava: The Tongan Kava Circle* (PAN 2022CD). Kava drinking songs by nine different ensembles recorded in 1986 and 1990.

Linkels, Ad and Lucia Linkels, eds. *Ifi Palasa: Tongan Brass* (PAN 2044CD). On this CD recorded in 1982, 1986, and 1990, brass bands mix with Polynesian conch shell blasts and traditional nose flutes.

Linkels, Ad and Lucia Linkels, eds. *Malie! Beautiful!* (PAN 2011CD). An outstanding survey of Tongan dance music recorded during important celebrations and competitions in 1982, 1986, and 1990.

Linkels, Ad and Lucia Linkels, eds. *Tuvalu: A Polynesian Atoll Society* (PAN 2055CD). Recorded in Tuvalu in 1990. Sung poetry forms the basis of the musical repertoire in Tuvalu with melody, harmony, rhythm, and dance used as vehicles to convey the lyrics.

Music of Marginal Polynesia (VICG 5276). In the series "World Sounds" produced by Victor Entertainment, Inc., Tokyo, Japan, and distributed in the U.S. by JVC Musical Industries, Inc., 3800 Barham Blvd., Ste. 305, Los Angeles, CA

90068, U.S.A. (tel. 213/878-0101, fax 213/878-0202). The music of Fiji, Wallis and Futuna, and Tuvalu, recorded 1977-85.

Music of Polynesia, Vol. II (VICG 5272). In the series "World Sounds." The music of the Tuamotu and Austral islands, recorded 1977-90.

Music of Polynesia, Vol. III (VICG 5273). In the series "World Sounds." The music of Easter Island and the Marquesas Islands, recorded 1977-85.

Music of Polynesia, Vol. IV (VICG 5274). In the series "World Sounds." The music of Samoa and Tonga, recorded 1977-85.

Nabet-Meyer, Pascal, ed. *The Tahitian Choir, Vol. I* (Triloka Records 7192-2). Triloka Inc., 7033 Sunset Blvd., Los Angeles, CA 90028, U.S.A. Recorded at Rapa Iti in 1991.

Nabet-Meyer, Pascal, ed. *The Tahitian Choir, Vol. II* (Shanachie 64055). Choral singing and chanting from Rapa Iti in the Austral Group (recording date not provided).

South Pacific Drums (PS 65066). Manuiti Productions, B.P. 755, Papeete, Tahiti (fax 689/43-27-24). A compilation of 39 of the best percussion recordings in Manuiti's archives—an excellent introduction to the traditional music of Polynesia.

Tumuenua Dance Group, *Cook Island Drums, Chants, and Songs* (CD VOY 1335). A 1991 release by Ode Record Company, Auckland, New Zealand. An outstanding selection of traditional Cook Island music. Distributed through the PAN network previously mentioned.

Zemp, Hugo, ed. *Musics & Musicians of the World: Solomon Islands* (D 8027). Paris: Unesco Collection Auvidis, 1990. A compact disc of Fataleka and Baegu music from Malaita, recorded in 1969 and 1970. Zemp also edited the CD *Polyphonies of the Solomon Islands (Guadalcanal and Savo)* (LDX 274 663) in the series "Le Chant du Monde" released by the Musée de l'Homme, Paris (recorded 1974). Both discs display the virtuosity of Solomon Island pan-

pipe players. In the same series is *Kanak Songs: Feasts and Lullabies* (LDX 274 909), recorded in New Caledonia during 1984-87.

Zemp, Hugo, ed. *Iles Salomon, Musique du Guadalcanal* (Acora Radio France C580 049). Female funeral chants, male singing, and panpipe playing recorded in 1970.

LANGUAGE

Allardice, R.W. *A Simplified Dictionary of Modern Samoan.* Auckland: Pasifika Press, 1985.

Churchward, C. Maxwell. *Tongan Grammar.* Nuku'alofa: Vava'u Press, 1985.

Hunkin, Galumalemana Afeleti L. *Gagana Samoa: A Samoan Language Coursebook.* Auckland: Pasifika Press, 1988. An accompanying cassette is available.

Murray, John J. *The Book of Pidgin English.* Australia: Robert Brown and Associates. The standard work on Neo-Melanesian.

Schultz, Dr. E. *Samoan Proverbial Expressions.* Auckland: Pasifika Press, 1980. Grouped according to subject, with English translations and explanations.

Schutz, A.J. *Say It In Fijian.* Sydney: Pacific Publications, 1979. An entertaining introduction to the language. Another text by Schutz, *The Fijian Language,* is published by the University of Hawaii Press.

Shumway, Eric B. *Intensive Course in Tongan.* A 130-lesson course available for US$16 from the Institute for Polynesian Studies, Brigham Young University, Box 1979, Laie, HI 96762, U.S.A. The accompanying set of 23 cassette tapes is US$80.

Tryon, Darrell T. *Say It In Tahitian.* Sydney: Pacific Publications, 1977. For lovers of the exotic, an instant introduction to spoken Tahitian.

REFERENCE BOOKS

Craig, Robert D. *Dictionary of Polynesian Mythology.* Westport, CT: Greenwood Press, 1989. Aside from hundreds of alphabetical entries listing the legends, stories, gods, goddesses, and heroes of the Polynesians, this book charts the evolution of 30 Polynesian languages.

Craig, Robert D. *Historical Dictionary of Polynesia.* Metuchen, NJ: Scarecrow Press, 1994. This handy volume contains alphabetical listings of individuals (past and present), places, and organizations, plus historical chronologies and bibliographies by island group. A similar work on Melanesia is in preparation.

Douglas, Ngaire and Norman Douglas, eds. *Pacific Islands Yearbook.* Australia: Angus & Robertson Publishers. Despite the title, a new edition of this authoritative sourcebook has come out about every four years since 1932. Although a rather dry read, it's still the one indispensable reference work for students of the Pacific islands.

The Far East and Australasia. London: Europa Publications. An annual survey and directory of Asia and the Pacific. Provides abundant and factual political and economic data; an excellent reference source.

Fry, Gerald W., and Rufino Mauricio. *Pacific Basin and Oceania.* Oxford: Clio Press, 1987. A selective, indexed Pacific bibliography, which actually describes the contents of the books, instead of merely listing them.

Jackson, Miles M., ed. *Pacific Island Studies: A Survey of the Literature.* Westport: Greenwood Press, 1986. In addition to comprehensive listings, there are extensive essays that put the most important works in perspective.

Motteler, Lee S. *Pacific Island Names.* Honolulu: Bishop Museum Press, 1986. A comprehensive gazetteer listing officially accepted island names, cross-referenced to all known variant names and spellings.

Oceania: A Regional Study. Washington, D.C.: U.S. Government Printing Office, 1985; extensive bibliography and index. This 572-page tome forms part of the area handbook series sponsored by the U.S. Army and intended to educate American officials. A comprehensive, uncritical source of background information.

Robie, David. *Nius Bilong Pasifik: Mass Media in the Pacific.* University of PNG Press, Box 320, Uni P.O., NCD, Papua New Guinea (fax 675/267-187). A comprehensive resource book on the South Pacific News media and social/cultural issues such as the environment, freedom of information, and human rights. It has an extensive section on each Pacific nation with social and political information, as well as news media details. Distributed in Australia by the Australian Center for Independent Journalism, Box 123, Broadway, NSW 2007 (fax 61-2/9281-2976).

Silveira de Braganza, Ronald, and Charlotte Oakes, eds. *The Hill Collection of Pacific Voyages.* San Diego: University Library, 1974. A descriptive catalog of antique books about the Pacific.

South Pacific Economies: Statistical Summary. Nouméa: South Pacific Commission. Trade patterns, price indices, aid flows, tourism, and population and social characteristics are covered in this useful publication issued every couple of years.

BOOKSELLERS AND PUBLISHERS

Some of the titles listed above are out of print and not available in regular bookstores. Major research libraries should have a few, otherwise write to the specialized antiquarian booksellers or regional publishers listed below for their printed lists of recycled or hard-to-find books on the Pacific. Sources of detailed topographical maps or navigational charts are provided in the following section.

Antipodean Books, Maps, and Prints. Antipodean Books, Box 189, Cold Spring, NY 10516, U.S.A. (tel. 914/424-3867, fax 914/424-3617). A complete catalog of out-of-print and rare items.

Australia and the Pacific. Peter Moore, Box 66, Cambridge, CB1 3PD, England. The European distributor of books from the Institute of Pacific Studies of the University of the South Pacific, Fiji. Moore's catalog also lists antiquarian and secondhand books.

Australia, the Pacific and South East Asia. Serendipity Books, Box 340, Nedlands, WA 6009, Australia (tel. 61-8/9382-2246, fax 61-8/9388-2728). The largest stocks of antiquarian, secondhand, and out-of-print books on the Pacific in Western Australia. Free catalogs are issued regularly.

Boating Books. International Marine Publishing Co., TAB Books, Blue Ridge Summit, PA 17294-0840, U.S.A. (tel. 800/822-8158, fax 717/794-5291). All the books you'll ever need to teach yourself how to sail.

Books from the Pacific Islands. Institute of Pacific Studies, University of the South Pacific, Box 1168, Suva, Fiji Islands. Their specialty is books about the islands written by the Pacific islanders themselves. Many are rather dry academic publications of interest only to specialists, so order with caution.

Books, Maps & Prints of the Pacific Islands. Colin Hinchcliffe, 12 Queens Staith Mews, York, YO1 1HH, England (tel. 44-1904/610679, fax 44-1904/641664). An excellent source of antiquarian or out-of-print books, maps, and engravings.

Books on Oceania, Africa, Archaeology & Anthropology, & Asia. Michael Graves-Johnston, Bookseller, Box 532, London SW9 0DR, England (fax 44-171/738-3747).

Books Pasifika Catalogues. Box 68-446, Newton, Auckland 1, New Zealand (fax 64-9/377-9528). A good starting point for New Zealanders.

Books & Series in Print. Bishop Museum Press, Box 19000-A, Honolulu, HI 96817-0916, U.S.A. An indexed list of books on the Pacific available from Hawaii's Bishop Museum. A separate list of "The Occasional Papers" lists specialized works.

Current Publications from the Pacific Islands. Pan Pacifica, 1511 Nuuanu Ave., PT 194, Honolulu, HI 96817, U.S.A. A source of recent official publications and research-level documents from museums and universities. Their primary clients are large research libraries.

Hawaii and Pacific Islands. The Book Bin, 228 S.W. Third St., Corvallis, OR 97333, U.S.A. (tel./fax 503/752-0045). An indexed mail-order catalog of hundreds of rare books on the Pacific. If there's a particular book about the Pacific you can't find anywhere, this is the place to try.

Hawaii: New Books. University of Hawaii Press, 2840 Kolowalu St., Honolulu, HI 96822, U.S.A. This catalog is well worth requesting if you're trying to build a Pacific library.

Moon Handbooks. Moon Publications Inc., Box 3040, Chico, CA 95927, U.S.A. Write for a copy of this free catalog of Moon travel handbooks or, in you live in the U.S., call 800/345-5473.

Pacificana. Messrs Berkelouw, "Bendooley," Old Hume Highway, Berrima, NSW 2577, Australia (tel. 61-2/4877-1370, fax 61-2/4877-1102). A detailed listing of thousands of rare Pacific titles. Payment of an annual subscription of A$25 entitles one to 25 catalogs a year. They also have stores in Sydney (19 Oxford St., Paddington, NSW 2021, Australia; tel. 61-2/9360-3200) and Los Angeles (830 North Highland Ave., Los Angeles, CA 90038, U.S.A.; tel. 213/466-3321).

Pacificana. Books of Yesteryear, Box 257, Newport, NSW 2106, Australia (fax 61-2/9918-0545). Another source of old, fine, and rare books on the Pacific.

Pacific and Southeast Asia—Old Books, Prints, Maps. Catalog No. 39. Bibliophile, 24 Glenmore Rd., Paddington, NSW 2021, Australia (tel. 61-2/9331-1411, fax 61-2/9361-3371).

Société des Océanistes Catalogue. Musée de l'Homme, 75116, Paris, France. Many scholarly works (in French) on Polynesia are available from this body.

Tales of the Pacific. Mutual Publishing Company, 1127 11th Ave., Mezzanine B, Honolulu, HI 96816, U.S.A. (tel. 808/732-1709, fax 808/734-4094). The classics of expatriate Pacific literature, available in cheap paperback editions.

Technical Publications. South Pacific Regional Environment Program, Box 240, Apia, Western Samoa (fax 685/20-231). A list of specialized publications on environmental concerns.

The 'Nesias' & Down Under: Some Recent Books. The Cellar Book Shop, 18090 Wyoming, Detroit, MI 48221, U.S.A. (tel./fax 313/861-1776). A wide range of in-print and out-of-print books on the Pacific.

MAP PUBLISHERS

Defense Mapping Agency Catalog of Maps, Charts, and Related Products: Part 2—Hydrographic Products, Volume VIII, Oceania. National Ocean Service, Distribution Branch, N/CG33, 6501 Lafayette Ave., Riverdale, MD 20737, U.S.A. A complete index and order form for nautical charts of the Pacific. The National Ocean Service also distributes nautical charts put out by the National Oceanic and Atmospheric Administration (NOAA).

Index to Topographic Maps of Hawaii, American Samoa, and Guam. Distribution Branch, U.S. Geological Survey, Box 25286, Denver Federal Center, Denver, CO 80225, U.S.A.

International Maps. Hema Maps Pty. Ltd., MLC Building, 239 George St., Brisbane, QLD 4001, Australia (fax 61-7/3211-3684). Maps of the Pacific, Solomon Islands, Vanuatu, and Western Samoa. They also distribute IGN maps of New Caledonia and Tahiti.

PERIODICALS

Asia & Pacific Viewpoint. Victoria University Press, Victoria University of Wellington, Box 600, Wellington, New Zealand. Twice a year; annual subscription NZ$60 worldwide. A scholarly journal encompassing a range of disciplines concerned with the systematic, regional, and theoretical aspects of economic growth and social change in the developed and developing countries.

Atoll Research Bulletin. Washington, D.C.: Smithsonian Institution. A specialized journal and inexhaustible source of fascinating information (and maps) on the most remote islands of the Pacific. Consult back issues at major libraries.

Banaba/Ocean Island News. Stacey M. King, Box 536, Mudgeeraba, QLD 4213, Australia (tel./fax 61-7/5530-5298). This lively newsletter covers virtually everything relating to the Banabans of Fiji and Kiribati.

The Centre for South Pacific Studies Newsletter. Centre for South Pacific Studies, The University of New South Wales, Kensington, NSW 2033, Australia. A useful bimonthly publication that catalogs scholarly conferences, events, activities, news, employment opportunities, courses, scholarships, and publications across the region.

Commodores' Bulletin. Seven Seas Cruising Assn., 1525 South Andrews Ave., Suite 217, Fort Lauderdale, FL 33316, U.S.A. (fax 305/463-7183; US$53 a year worldwide by airmail). This monthly bulletin is chock-full of useful information for anyone wishing to tour the Pacific by sailing boat. All Pacific yachties and friends should be Seven Seas members!

The Contemporary Pacific. University of Hawaii Press, 2840 Kolowalu St., Honolulu, HI 96822, U.S.A. (published twice a year, US$30 a year). Publishes a good mix of articles of interest to both scholars and general readers; the country-by-country "Political Review" in each number is a concise summary of events during the preceding year. The "Dialogue" section offers informed comment on the more controversial issues in the region, while recent publications on the islands are examined through book reviews. Those interested in current topics in Pacific island affairs should check recent volumes for background information. Recommended.

ENVIRONWatch. South Pacific Action Committee for Human Ecology and Environment, Box 1168, Suva, Fiji Islands (fax 679/302-548; US$10 a year). This quarterly newsletter from SPACHEE provides excellent background on environmental concerns in Fiji and throughout the region.

Environment Newsletter. The quarterly newsletter of the South Pacific Regional Environment Program, Box 240, Apia, Western Samoa (fax 685/20-231).

Europe-Pacific Solidarity Bulletin. Published monthly by the European Center for Studies Information and Education on Pacific Issues, Box 151, 3700 AD Zeist, The Netherlands (fax 31-3404/25614).

German Pacific Society Bulletin. Feichtmayr Strasse 25, D-80992 München, Germany. At DM 70 a year, Society membership is a good way for German speakers to keep in touch. News bulletins in English and German are published four times a year, and study tours to various Pacific destinations are organized annually.

Globe Newsletter. The Globetrotters Club, BCM/Roving, London WC1N 3XX, England. This informative travel newsletter, published six times a year, provides lots of practical information on how to tour the world "on the cheap." Club membership (US$18 plus a US$5 joining fee) includes a subscription to *Globe,* a globetrotter's handbook, a list of other members, etc. This is *the* club for world travelers.

In Depth. Box 90215, Austin, TX 78709, U.S.A. (tel. 512/891-9812). A consumer protection-oriented newsletter for serious diving scuba divers. Unlike virtually every other diving publication, *In Depth* accepts no advertising, which allows them to tell it as it is.

Insula. Division of Ecological Sciences, 1 rue Miollis, 75007 Paris, France (fax 33-1/4065-9897). This UNESCO-supported magazine carries technical articles on the environment, population, and sustainable development of islands worldwide, with frequent reference to the Pacific.

Islands Business Pacific. Box 12718, Suva, Fiji Islands (annual airmailed subscription US$45 to North America, US$55 to Europe, A$35 to Australia, NZ$55 to New Zealand). A monthly newsmagazine with the emphasis on political and economic trends in the Pacific. It's a bit more opinionated than *Pacific Islands Monthly* and even has a gossip section called "Whispers" that provides interesting insights.

Journal of Pacific History. Division of Pacific and Asian History, RSPAS, Australian National University, Canberra, ACT 0200, Australia. Since 1966 this publication has provided reliable scholarly information on the Pacific. Outstanding.

Journal of the Polynesian Society. Department of Maori Studies, University of Auckland, Private Bag 92019, Auckland, New Zealand. Established in 1892, this quarterly journal contains a wealth of material on Pacific cultures past and present written by scholars of Pacific anthropology, archaeology, language, and history.

Oceanic Linguistics. University of Hawaii Press, 2840 Kolowalu St., Honolulu, HI 96822, U.S.A. (published twice a year, US$19). The only journal devoted exclusively to the study of the Oceanic area.

Pacific Affairs. University of British Columbia, 2029 West Mall, Vancouver, B.C. V6T 1Z2, Canada (quarterly).

Pacific AIDS Alert. Published monthly by the South Pacific Commission, B.P. D5, 98848 Nouméa Cédex, New Caledonia. An informative news-oriented publication dedicated to limiting the spread of sexually transmitted diseases.

Pacific Arts. Pacific Arts Association, c/o Dr. Michael Gunn, PAA Secretary/Treasurer, c/o A.A.O.A., The Metropolitan Museum of Art, 1000 Fifth Ave., New York, NY 10028, U.S.A. (fax 212/570-3879). For US$40 PAA membership, one will receive their annual magazine "devoted to the study of all the arts of Oceania" and four issues of their newsletter.

Pacific Islands Monthly. G.P.O. Box 1167, Suva, Fiji Islands (annual subscription A$42 to Australia, US$45 to North America, and A$63 to Europe; fax 679/303-809). Founded in Sydney by R.W. Robson in 1930, *PIM* is the granddaddy of regional magazines. In June 1989 the magazine's editorial office moved from Sydney to Suva. Roman Grynberg's brilliant economic analyses and David North's political reports are alone worth the price of the magazine.

Pacific Journalism Review. South Pacific Center for Communication and Information in Development, University of PNG, Box 320, Uni P.O., NCD, Papua

New Guinea (fax 675/267-187). Co-edited by noted Pacific writer David Robie, the *Review* tackles the controversial side of Pacific news coverage and is essential reading for anyone interested in the state of the media today in the Pacific.

Pacific Magazine. Box 25488, Honolulu, HI 96825, U.S.A. (fax 808/373-3953; every other month; US$15 annual subscription). This business-oriented newsmagazine, published in Hawaii since 1976, will keep you up-to-date on what's happening in the South Pacific and Micronesia. Recommended.

Pacific News Bulletin. Pacific Concerns Resource Center, Box 803, Glebe, NSW 2037, Australia (A$12 a year in Australia, A$25 a year elsewhere). A 16-page monthly newsletter with up-to-date information on nuclear, independence, environmental, and political questions.

Pacific Research. Research School of Pacific and Asian Studies, Coombs Building, Australian National University, Canberra, ACT 0200, Australia (fax 61-2/6249-0174; A$25 a year). This monthly periodical of the Peace Research Center publishes informative articles on regional conflicts.

Pacific Studies. Box 1979, BYU-HC, Laie, HI 96762-1294, U.S.A. (quarterly, US$30 a year). Funded by the Polynesian Cultural Center and published by Hawaii's Brigham Young University.

Pacifica. Quarterly journal of the Pacific Islands Study Circle of Great Britain (John Ray, 24 Woodvale Ave., London SE25 4AE, United Kingdom). This philatelic journal is exclusively concerned with the postal history of the islands.

Rapa Nui Journal. Box 6774, Los Osos, CA 93412, U.S.A. (quarterly, US$25 a year in North America, US$35 elsewhere). An interesting mix of scholarly reports and local news of interest to Rapanuiphiles.

South Sea Digest. G.P.O. Box 4245, Sydney, NSW 2001, Australia (A$150 a year in Australia, A$175 overseas). A private newsletter on political and economic matters, published every other week. It's a good way of keeping abreast of developments in commerce and industry.

The South Pacific Review. Commonwealth Communications Ltd., 7-11 Kensington High St., London W8 5NP, England. A quality magazine focusing on business and development in the Asia-Pacific region.

The Surf Report. Box 1028, Dana Point, CA 92629, U.S.A. (fax 714/496-7849; $42 a year). A monthly summary of worldwide surfing conditions, with frequent feature articles on the islands.

Third World Resources. 464 19th St., Oakland, CA 94612, U.S.A. (two-year subscription US$35 to the U.S. and Canada, US$50 overseas). A quarterly review of books, articles, audiovisual materials, and organizations involved with development issues in the third world.

Tok Blong Pasifik. South Pacific Peoples Foundation of Canada, 1921 Fernwood Road, Victoria, BC V8T 2Y6, Canada (fax 604/388-5258; $25 a year). This quarterly of news and views focuses on regional environmental, development, human rights, and disarmament issues. Recommended.

Travel Matters. Moon Publications Inc., Box 3040, Chico, CA 95927, U.S.A. Residents of the U.S. can request a free subscription to this useful quarterly publication by calling 800/345-5473 or by writing. Others must send a credit card authorization for US$7 to cover postage.

The Washington Pacific Report. Pacific House, Suite 400, 1615 New Hampshire Ave. NW, Washington, D.C. 20009-2520, U.S.A. (published twice a month, $159 a year domestic, $184 outside U.S. postal zones). An insider's newsletter highlighting strategic, diplomatic, and political developments involving the insular Pacific.

AN IMPORTANT MESSAGE

Authors, editors, and publishers wishing to see their publications listed here should send review copies to:

David Stanley
c/o Moon Publications
P.O. Box 3040
Chico, CA 95927-3040, U.S.A.

GLOSSARY

aa **lava**—*see* pahoehoe

ahimaa—*see* umu

ahu—a Polynesian stone temple platform

AIDS—Acquired Immune Deficiency Syndrome

anse—cove (French)

ANZUS Treaty—a mutual-defense pact signed in 1951 between Australia, New Zealand, and the U.S.

aparima—a Tahitian hand dance

archipelago—a group of islands

ariki—a Polynesian high chief; the traditional head of a clan or tribe; in Tahitian, *ari'i*

Arioi—a pre-European religious society, which traveled among the Society Islands presenting ceremonies and entertainments

atoll—a low-lying, ring-shaped coral reef enclosing a lagoon

bareboat charter—chartering a yacht without crew or provisions

bark cloth—see *tapa*

barrier reef—a coral reef separated from the adjacent shore by a lagoon

bêche-de-mer—sea cucumber; an edible sea slug; in Tahitian, *rori;* in French, *trépang; see also* pidgin

betel nut—the seed of the fruit of the betel palm *(Areca catechu),* chewed in Melanesia with a little lime and leaves from the pepper plant

blackbirder—A 19th-century European recruiter of island labor, mostly ni-Vanuatu and Solomon Islanders taken to work on plantations in Queensland and Fiji.

breadfruit—a large, round fruit with starchy flesh grown on an *uru* tree *(Artocarpus altilis)*

BYO—Bring Your Own (an Australian term used to refer to restaurants that allow you to bring your own alcoholic beverages)

caldera—a wide crater formed through the collapse or explosion of a volcano

cargo cult—Melanesian religious movement or movements promising salvation through the return of ancestors who will bring European-introduced goods (cargo) to their descendants

cassava—manioc; the starchy edible root of the tapioca plant

CEP—Centre d'Expérimentation du Pacifique; the French nuclear-testing establishment in Tahiti-Polynesia

chain—an archaic unit of length equivalent to 20 meters

ciguatera—a form of fish poisoning caused by microscopic algae

CMAS—Confédération Mondiale des Activites Subaquatiques

coastwatchers—Allied intelligence agents who operated behind Japanese lines during WW II

coir—coconut husk sennit used to make rope, etc.

confirmation—A confirmed reservation exists when a supplier acknowledges, either orally or in writing, that a booking has been accepted.

copra—dried coconut meat used in the manufacture of coconut oil, cosmetics, soap, and margarine

coral—a hard, calcareous substance of various shapes composed of the skeletons of tiny marine animals called polyps

coral bank—a coral formation over 150 meters long

coral head—a coral formation a few meters across

coral patch—a coral formation up to 150 meters long

custom owner—traditional tribal or customary owner based on usage

cyclone—Also known as a hurricane (in the Caribbean) or typhoon (in Japan). A tropical storm that rotates around a center of low atmospheric pressure; it becomes a cyclone when its winds reach 64 knots. In the Northern Hemisphere, cyclones spin counterclockwise, while south of the equator they move clockwise. The winds of cyclonic storms are deflected toward a low-pressure area at the center, although the "eye" of the cyclone may be calm.

deck—Australian English for a terrace or porch

desiccated coconut—the shredded meat of dehydrated fresh coconut

DGSE—Direction Générale de la Sécurité Extérieure; the French CIA

direct flight—a through flight with one or more stops but no change of aircraft, as opposed to a nonstop flight

dugong—a large plant-eating marine mammal; called a manatee in the Caribbean

EEZ—Exclusive Economic Zone; a 200-nautical-mile offshore belt of an island nation or seacoast state that controls the mineral exploitation and fishing rights

endemic—native to a particular area and existing only there

ESCAP—Economic and Social Commission for Asia and the Pacific

expatriate—a person residing in a country other than his/her own; in the South Pacific such persons are also called "Europeans" if their skin is white, or simply "expats."

fa'afafine—the Samoan term for men who act and dress like women; called *mahu* in Tahiti-Polynesia, *fakaleiti* in Tonga

FAD—fish aggregation device

fafa—a "spinach" of cooked taro leaves

fale—Samoan house; in Tahitian *fare*

farani—French; *français*

fautau—the highest formal representative of the Samoan people

filaria—parasitic worms transmitted by biting insects to the blood or tissues of mammals. The obstruction of the lymphatic glands by the worms can cause an enlargement of the legs or other parts, a disease known as elephantiasis.

fissure—a narrow crack or chasm of some length and depth

FIT—foreign independent travel; a custom-designed, prepaid tour composed of many individualized arrangements

fringing reef—a reef along the shore of an island

gendarme—a French policeman on duty only in rural areas in France and French overseas territories

GPS—Global Positioning System, the space age successor of the sextant

guano—manure of seabirds, used as a fertilizer

guyot—a submerged atoll, the coral of which couldn't keep up with rising water levels

Havai'i—legendary homeland of the Polynesians

HIV—Human Immunodeficiency Virus, the cause of AIDS

jug—a cross between a ceramic kettle and a pitcher used to heat water for tea or coffee in Australian-style hotels

kanaka—a human being in both Polynesia and Melanesia; formerly used in the pejorative sense for "native"

kava—a Polynesian word for the drink known in the Fijian language as *yanggona*. This traditional beverage is made by squeezing a mixture of the grated root of the pepper shrub *(Piper methysticum)* and cold water through a strainer of hibiscus-bark fiber.

kumara—sweet potato *(Ipomoea batatas)*

lagoon—an expanse of water bounded by a reef

langi—a megalithic tomb for early Tonga kings, in the form of a stepped limestone pyramid

Lapita pottery—pottery made by the ancient Polynesians from 1600 to 500 B.C.

laplap—see pareu

lavalava—see pareu

lava tube—a conduit formed as molten rock continues to flow below a cooled surface during the growth of a lava field. When the eruption ends, a tunnel is left with a flat floor where the last lava hardened.

leeward—downwind; the shore (or side) sheltered from the wind; as opposed to windward

lei—a garland, often of fresh flowers, but sometimes of paper, shells, etc., hung about the neck of a person being welcomed or feted

le truck—a truck with seats in back, used for public transportation on Tahiti

live-aboard—a tour boat with cabin accommodation for scuba divers

LMS—London Missionary Society; a Protestant group that spread Christianity from Tahiti (1797) across the Pacific

maa Tahiti—Tahitian food

mahimahi—dorado, Pacific dolphinfish (no relation to the mammal)

mahu—a male Tahitian transvestite, sometimes also homosexual

makatea—an uplifted reef around the coast of an elevated atoll

mama ruau—actually "grandmother," but also used for the Mother Hubbard long dress introduced to Tahiti by missionaries

mana—authority, prestige, virtue, "face," psychic power, a positive force

manahune—a commoner or member of the lower class in pre-Christian Tahitian society

mangrove—a tropical shrub with branches that send down roots forming dense thickets along tidal shores

manioc—cassava, tapioca, a starchy root crop

maohi—a native of Tahiti-Polynesia

Maori—the Polynesians of New Zealand and the Cook Islands

marae—a Tahitian temple or open-air cult place, called *meae* in the Marquesas; a Samoan village green *(malae);* a Maori meeting place. The Fijian word is *rara.*

masi—see tapa

matrilineal—a system of tracing descent through the mother's familial line

mbalolo—in Fijian, a reef worm *(Eunice viridis)*, called *palolo* in Samoa

mbuli—Fijian administrative officer in charge of a *tikina;* subordinate of the Roko Tui

Melanesia—the high island groups of the western Pacific (Fiji, New Caledonia, Vanuatu, Solomon Islands, Papua New Guinea)

Micronesia—chains of high and low islands mostly north of the Equator (Carolines, Gilberts, Marianas, Marshalls)

moai—an Easter Island statue

monoi—perfumed coconut oil

motu—a flat reef islet

nakamal—in the villages of Vanuatu, an open area surrounded by gigantic banyan trees, where men gather nightly to drink kava

namba—a penis wrapper or sheath worn by the Big and Small Namba tribes of interior Malekula, Vanuatu

NAUI—National Association of Underwater Instructors

ndalo—see taro

NGO—nongovernmental organization

NFIP—Nuclear-Free and Independent Pacific movement

ni-Vanuatu—an indigenous inhabitant of Vanuatu

Oro—the Polynesian god of war

ORSTOM—Office de la Recherche Scientifique et Technique d'Outre-Mer

ote'a—a Tahitian ceremonial dance performed by men and women in two columns

overbooking—the practice of confirming more seats, cabins, or rooms than are actually available to ensure against no-shows

pa—ancient Polynesian stone fortress

Pacific rim—the continental landmasses and large countries around the fringe of the Pacific

PADI—Professional Association of Dive Instructors

pahoehoe lava—A smooth lava formation with wavy, ropelike ripples created when very hot, fluid lava continues to flow beneath a cooling surface. *Aa* lava, on the other hand, is slow-moving, thick, and turbulent, creating a rough, chunky surface.

palagi—a Polynesian word used throughout the region to refer to Europeans; also *papalagi;* in Tahitian *papa'a*

palolo—see mbalolo

palusami—a Samoan specialty of coconut cream wrapped in taro leaves and baked

pandanus—screw pine with slender stem and prop roots. The sword-shaped leaves are used for plaiting mats and hats. In Tahitian, *fara.*

parasailing—a sport in which participants are carried aloft by a parachute pulled behind a speedboat

pareu—a Tahitian saronglike wraparound skirt or loincloth; *lavalava* in Samoan, *sulu* in Fijian, *laplap* in Melanesia, *sarong* in Indonesian

pass—a channel through a barrier reef, usually with an outward flow of water

passage—an inside passage between an island and a barrier reef

patrilineal—a system of tracing descent through the fathers familial line

pawpaw—papaya

pelagic—relating to the open sea, away from land

peretane—Britain, British in Tahitian

pidgin—a form of speech with a limited vocabulary and simplified grammar used for communication between groups speaking different languages; also known as bêche-de-mer, Bislama, and Neo-Melanesian.

pirogue—outrigger canoe (French), in Tahitian *vaa*

poe—a sticky pudding made from bananas, papaya, pumpkin, or taro mixed with starch, baked in an oven, and served with coconut milk

poisson cru—raw fish marinated in lime (French), in Tahitian *ia ota;* in Fijian *kokonda;* in Japanese *sashimi*

Polynesia—divided into Western Polynesia (Tonga and Samoa) and Eastern Polynesia (Tahiti-Polynesia, Cook Islands, Hawaii, Easter Island, and New Zealand)

punt—a flat-bottomed boat

pupu—traditional Tahitian dance group

Quonset hut—a prefabricated, semicircular, metal shelter popular during WW II

raatira—Tahitian chief, dance leader

rain shadow—the dry side of a mountain, sheltered from the windward side

Ratu—a title for Fijian chiefs, prefixed to their names

reef—a coral ridge near the ocean surface

Roko Tui—senior Fijian administrative officer

sailing—the fine art of getting wet and becoming ill while slowly going nowhere at great expense

scuba—self-contained underwater breathing apparatus

self-contained—a room with private facilities (a toilet and shower not shared with other guests); as opposed to a "self-catering" unit with cooking facilities

sennit—braided coconut-fiber rope

shareboat charter—a yacht tour for individuals or couples who join a small group on a fixed itinerary

shifting cultivation—a method of farming involving the rotation of fields instead of crops

shoal—a shallow sandbar or mud bank

shoulder season—a travel period between high/peak and low/off-peak seasons

siapo—*see* tapa

SPARTECA—South Pacific Regional Trade and Economic Cooperation Agreement; an agreement that allows certain manufactured goods from Pacific countries duty-free entry to Australia and New Zealand

SPREP—South Pacific Regional Environment Program

subduction—the action of one tectonic plate wedging under another

subsidence—geological sinking or settling

sulu—*see* pareu

symbiosis—a mutually advantageous relationship between unlike organisms

tabu—also *tapu, kapu, tambu;* taboo, sacred, set apart, forbidden, a negative force

tahua—in the old days a skilled Tahitian artisan; today a sorcerer or healer

tamaaraa—a Tahitian feast

Tamaha—daughter of the *Tu'i Tonga Fefine* (queen of Tonga)

tamure—a new name for Ori Tahiti, a very fast erotic dance

tanoa—a special wide wooden bowl in which *yanggona* (kava) is mixed; used in ceremonies in Fiji, Tonga, and Samoa

ta'ovala—a mat worn in Tonga by both sexes over a kilt or skirt

tapa—a cloth made from the pounded bark of the paper mulberry tree *(Broussonetia papyrifera)*. It's soaked and beaten with a mallet to flatten and intertwine the fibers, then painted with geometric designs; called *siapo* in Samoan, *masi* in Fijian, *ahu* in old Tahitian.

tapu—*see* tabu

taro—a starchy elephant-eared tuber *(Colocasia esculenta)*, a staple food of the Pacific islanders; called *ndalo* in Fijian

tatau—the Tahitian original of the adopted English word tattoo

tavana—the elected mayor of a Tahitian commune (from the English "governor")

tifaifai—a Tahitian patchwork quilt based on either European or Polynesian motifs

tiki—a humanlike sculpture used in the old days for religious rites and sorcery

tikina—a group of Fijian villages administered by a *mbuli*

tinito—Tahitian for Chinese

TNC—transnational corporation (also referred to as a multinational corporation)

toddy—The spathe of a coconut tree is bent to a horizontal position and tightly bound before it begins to flower. The end of the spathe is then split, and the sap drips down a twig or leaf into a bottle. Fresh or fermented, toddy *(tuba)* makes an excellent drink.

to'ere—a hollow wooden drum hit with a stick

trade wind—a steady wind blowing toward the equator from either northeast or southeast

trench—the section at the bottom of the ocean where one tectonic plate wedges under another

tridacna clam—eaten everywhere in the Pacific, its size varies between 10 centimeters and one meter

tropical storm—a cyclonic storm with winds of 35 to 64 knots

tsunami—a fast-moving wave caused by an undersea earthquake

tu'i (Polynesian)—king, ruler

umara—see kumara

umu—an underground, earthen oven; called *ahimaa* in Tahitian, *lovo* in Fijian. After A.D. 500, the Polynesians had lost the art of making pottery, so they were compelled to bake their food, rather than boil it.

vigia—a mark on a nautical chart indicating a dangerous rock or shoal

volcanic bomb—lumps of lava blown out of a volcano, which take a bomblike shape as they cool in the air

wantok—a pidgin English term for a member of the same clan or tribe

windward—the point or side from which the wind blows, as opposed to leeward

yam—the starchy, tuberous root of a climbing plant

yanggona—*see* kava

zories—rubber shower sandals, thongs, flip-flops

INTERNATIONAL AIRPORT CODES

AKL—Auckland	IPC—Easter Island	SEA—Seattle
APW—Apia/Faleolo	IUE—Niue	SFO—San Francisco
BNE—Brisbane	LAX—Los Angeles	SIN—Singapore
CHC—Christchurch	MEL—Melbourne	SUV—Suva
CNS—Cairns	MNL—Manila	SYD—Sydney
DPS—Denpasar/Bali	NAN—Nandi	TBU—Tongatapu
FGI—Apia/Fagalii	NOU—Nouméa/La Tontouta	TRW—Tarawa
FUN—Funafuti	OSA—Osaka	TYO—Tokyo
GEA—Nouméa/Magenta	POM—Port Moresby	VLI—Port Vila
GUM—Guam	PPG—Pago Pago	WLG—Wellington
HIR—Honiara	PPT—Papeete	WLS—Wallis
HNL—Honolulu	RAR—Rarotonga	YVR—Vancouver
INU—Nauru	SCL—Santiago	YYZ—Toronto

ALTERNATIVE PLACE NAMES

Alu—Shortland
Ambae—Aoba
Anatom—Aneityum
Aneityum—Anatom
Aoba—Ambae
Ba—Mba
Bass Islands—Marotini Islands
Bau—Mbau
Bellingshausen—Motu One
Beqa—Mbengga
Buca—Mbutha
Bughotu—Isabel
Bukuya—Mbukuya
Choiseul—Lauru
Cicia—Thithia
Colo-i-Suva—Tholo-i-Suva
Danger—Pukapuka
Deuba—Deumba
Deumba—Deuba
Drehu—Lifou
Easter Island—Isla de Pascua
Easter Island—Rapa Nui
Efate—Vate
Ellice Islands—Tuvalu
Espiritu Santo—Santo
Falcon—Fonuafo'ou
Fonuafo'ou—Falcon
French Polynesia—Tahiti-
    Polynesia
Futuna—Hoorn
Galoa—Ngaloa
Gau—Ngau
Gaua—Santa Maria
Grande Terre—New Caledonia
Hervey—Manuae
Hoorn—Futuna
Hull—Maria
Iaai—Ouvéa
Isabel—Bughotu
Isabel—Santa Isabel
Isla de Pascua—Easter Island
Isle of Pines—Kwenyii
Kadavu—Kandavu
Kanaky—New Caledonia
Kandavu—Kadavu
Kolombangara—Nduke
Korotogo—Korotogo
Korotongo—Korotogo
Kwenyii—Isle of Pines
Labasa—Lambasa

Lakeba—Lakemba
Lakemba—Lakeba
Lambasa—Labasa
Laucala—Lauthala
Lauru—Choiseul
Lauthala—Laucala
Lifou—Drehu
Lord Howe—Ontong Java
Luangiua—Ontong Java
Luganville—Santo
Maiao—Tapuaemanu
Makira—San Cristobal
Malekula—Mallicollo
Mallicollo—Malekula
Mamanuca—Mamanutha
Mamanutha—Mamanuca
Manuae—Hervey
Manuae—Scilly
Maré—Nengone
Maria—Hull
Marotini Islands—Bass Islands
Maupihaa—Mopelia
Maupiti—Maurau
Maurau—Maupiti
Mba—Ba
Mbau—Bau
Mbengga—Beqa
Mbilua—Vella Lavella
Mbukuya—Bukuya
Mbutha—Buca
Mohotani—Motane
Mopelia—Maupihaa
Moruroa—Mururoa
Motane—Mohotani
Motu Iti—Tupai
Motu One—Bellingshausen
Mururoa—Moruroa
Nabouwalu—Nambouwalu
Nadarivatu—Nandarivatu
Nadi—Nandi
Nambouwalu—Nabouwalu
Nandarivatu—Nadarivatu
Nandi—Nadi
Natadola—Natandola
Natandola—Natadola
Nduke—Kolombangara
Nendo—Santa Cruz
Nengone—Maré
New Caledonia—Grande Terre
New Caledonia—Kanaky

New Hebrides—Vanuatu
Ngaloa—Galoa
Ngau—Gau
Niue—Savage
Olohega—Swains
Ontong Java—Lord Howe
Ontong Java—Luangiua
Ouvéa—Iaai
Penrhyn—Tongareva
Port Vila—Vila
Pukapuka—Danger
Qamea—Nggamea
Rabi—Rambi
Rambi—Rabi
Rapa Nui—Easter Island
San Cristobal—Makira
Santa Cruz—Nendo
Santa Isabel—Isabel
Santa Maria—Gaua
Santo—Espiritu Santo
Santo—Luganville
Savage—Niue
Scilly—Manuae
Shortland—Alu
Sigatoka—Singatoka
Singatoka—Sigatoka
Sikaiana—Stewart Island
Stewart Island—Sikaiana
Swains—Olohega
Tahiti-Polynesia—French
    Polynesia
Tapuaemanu—Maiao
Thithia—Cicia
Tholo-i-Suva—Colo-i-Suva
Toberua—Tomberua
Tokelau—Union Group
Tomberua—Toberua
Tongareva—Penrhyn
Tupai—Motu Iti
Tuvalu—Ellice Islands
Union Group—Tokelau
Uvéa—Wallis
Vanikolo—Vanikoro
Vanikoro—Vanikolo
Vanua Balavu—Vanua Mbalavu
Vanua Mbalavu—Vanua Balavu
Vanuatu—New Hebrides
Vate—Efate
Vella Lavella—Mbilua
Vila—Port Vila
Wallis—Uvéa

INDEX

Page numbers in **boldface** indicate the primary reference. *Italicized* page numbers indicate information in captions, charts, illustrations, maps, or special topics.

ABOUT THE AUTHOR

Three decades ago, David Stanley's right thumb carried him out of Toronto, Canada, onto a journey that has so far wound through 168 countries, including a three-year trip from Tokyo to Kabul. His travel guidebooks to the South Pacific, Micronesia, Alaska, and Eastern Europe opened those areas to budget travelers for the first time.

During the late 1960s, David got involved in Mexican culture by spending a year in several small towns near Guanajuato. Later he studied at the universities of Barcelona and Florence, before settling down to get an honors degree (with distinction) in Spanish literature from the University of Guelph, Canada.

David Stanley atop Tahiti's Mt. Aorai

In 1978 Stanley linked up with future publisher Bill Dalton, and together they wrote the first edition of South Pacific Handbook. Since then, Stanley has gone on to write additional definitive guides for Moon Publications, including Micronesia Handbook, Fiji Islands Handbook, Tahiti-Polynesia Handbook, and early editions of Alaska-Yukon Handbook. He wrote the first three editions of Lonely Planet's Eastern Europe on a Shoestring. His books have informed a generation of budget travelers.

Stanley makes frequent research trips to the areas covered in his guides, jammed between journeys to the 79 countries and territories worldwide he still hasn't visited. In travel writing David Stanley has found a perfect outlet for his restless wanderlust. His zodiac sign is Virgo.

MOON TRAVEL HANDBOOKS
THE IDEAL TRAVELING COMPANIONS

Moon Travel Handbooks provide focused, comprehensive coverage of distinct destinations all over the world. Our goal is to give travelers all the background and practical information they'll need for an extraordinary travel experience.

Every Handbook begins with an in-depth essay about the land, the people, their history, art, politics, and social concerns—an entire bookcase of cultural insight and introductory information in one portable volume. We also provide accurate, up-to-date coverage of all the practicalities: language, currency, transportation, accommodations, food, and entertainment. And Moon's maps are legendary, covering not only cities and highways, but parks and trails that are often difficult to find in other sources.

Below are highlights of Moon's Asia and Pacific Travel Handbook series. Our complete list of Handbooks covering North America and Hawaii, Mexico, Central America and the Caribbean, and Asia and the Pacific, are listed on the order form on the accompanying pages. To purchase Moon Travel Handbooks, please check your local bookstore or order by phone: (800) 345-5473 Monday-Friday 8 a.m.-5 p.m. PST.

MOON OVER ASIA
THE ASIA AND THE PACIFIC TRAVEL HANDBOOK SERIES

"Moon guides are wittily written and warmly personal; what's more, they present a vivid, often raw vision of Asia without promotional overtones. They also touch on such topics as official corruption and racism, none of which rate a mention in the bone-dry, air-brushed, dry-cleaned version of Asia written up in the big U.S. guidebooks."

—*Far Eastern Economic Review*

BALI HANDBOOK
by Bill Dalton, 428 pages, **$12.95**
"This book is for the in-depth traveler, interested in history and art, willing to experiment with language and food and become immersed in the culture of Bali."

— *Great Expeditions*

BANGKOK HANDBOOK
by Michael Buckley, 221 pages, **$13.95**
"Helps make sense of this beguiling paradox of a city . . . very entertaining reading."

—*The Vancouver Sun*

FIJI ISLANDS HANDBOOK
by David Stanley, 275 pages, **$13.95**
"If you want to encounter Fiji and not just ride through it, this book is for you."

—*Great Expeditions*

HONG KONG HANDBOOK
by Kerry Moran, 347 pages, **$15.95**
"One of the most honest glimpses into Hong Kong the Peoples Republic of China would like never to have seen."

—*TravelNews Asia*

INDONESIA HANDBOOK
by Bill Dalton, 1,351 pages, **$25.00**
"Looking for a fax machine in Palembang, a steak dinner on Ambon or the best place to photograph Bugis prahus in Sulawesi? Then buy this brick of a book, which contains a full kilogram of detailed directions and advice."

—*Asia, Inc. Magazine*

"The classic guidebook to the archipelago."

—*Condé Nast Traveler*

JAPAN HANDBOOK
by J.D. Bisignani, 952 pages, **$22.50**
Winner: Lowell Thomas Gold Award, Society of American Travel Writers
"The scope of this guide book is staggering, ranging from an introduction to Japanese history and culture through to the best spots for shopping for pottery in Mashie or silk pongee in Kagoshima."

—*Golden Wing*

"More travel information on Japan than any other guidebook."

—*The Japan Times*

MICRONESIA HANDBOOK
by David Stanley, 342 pages, **$11.95**
"Remarkably informative, fair-minded, sensible, and readable . . . Stanley's comments on the United States' 40-year administration are especially pungent and thought-provoking."

—*The Journal of the Polynesian Society*

NEPAL HANDBOOK
by Kerry Moran, 428 pages, **$18.95**
Winner: Lowell Thomas Gold Award, Society of American Travel Writers
"This is an excellent guidebook, exploring every aspect of the country the visitor is likely to want to know about with both wit and authority."

—*South China Morning Post*

NEW ZEALAND HANDBOOK
by Jane King, 544 pages, **$19.95**
"Far and away the best guide to New Zealand."

—*The Atlantic*

OUTBACK AUSTRALIA HANDBOOK
by Marael Johnson, 432 pages, **$18.95**
Winner: Lowell Thomas Silver Award, Society of American
Travel Writers
"Well designed, easy to read, and funny"

—*Buzzworm*

PAKISTAN HANDBOOK
by Isobel Shaw, 660 pages, **$22.50**
Pakistan Handbook guides travelers from the heights of the
Karakorams to the bazaars of Karachi, from sacred mosques in
Sind to the ceasefire line of Azad Kashmir. Includes a detailed
trekking guide with several itineraries for long and short treks
across the Hindu Kush, Karakorams, and Himalayas.

PHILIPPINES HANDBOOK
by Peter Harper and Laurie Fullerton, 638 pages, **$17.95**
"The most comprehensive travel guide done on the Philippines.
Excellent work."

—*Pacific Stars & Stripes*

SOUTHEAST ASIA HANDBOOK
by Carl Parkes, 1,103 pages, **$21.95**
Winner: Lowell Thomas Bronze Award, Society of American
Travel Writers
"Plenty of information on sights and entertainment, also provides
a political, environment and cultural context that will allow visitors
to begin to interpret what they see."

—*London Sunday Times*

SOUTH KOREA HANDBOOK
by Robert Nilsen, 590 pages, **$14.95**
"One of a small number of guidebooks that inform without being
pedantic, and are enthusiastic yet maintain a critical edge . . . the
maps are without parallel."

—*Far Eastern Economic Review*

SOUTH PACIFIC HANDBOOK
by David Stanley, 832 pages, **$22.95**
"Moon's tribute to the South Pacific, by David Stanley, is next to
none. "

—*Ubique*

TAHITI-POLYNESIA HANDBOOK
by David Stanley, 243 pages, **$13.95**

"If you can't find it in this book, it is something you don't need to know."

—*Rapa Nui Journal*

THAILAND HANDBOOK
by Carl Parkes, 800 pages, **$19.95**

"Carl Parkes is the savviest of all tourists to Southeast Asia."

—*Arthur Frommer*

TIBET HANDBOOK
by Victor Chan, 1,103 pages, **$30.00**

"Not since the original three volume Murray's Handbook to India, published over a century ago, has such a memorial to the hot, and perhaps uncontrollable passions of travel been published. . . . This is the most impressive travel handbook published in the 20th century."

—*Small Press Magazine*

"Shimmers with a fine madness."

—*Escape Magazine*

VIETNAM, CAMBODIA & LAOS HANDBOOK
by Michael Buckley, 650 pages, **$18.95**

The new definitive guide to Indochina from a travel writer who knows Asia like the back of his hand. Michael Buckley combines the most current practical travel information—much of it previously unavailable—with the perspective of a seasoned adventure traveler. Includes 75 maps.

STAYING HEALTHY IN ASIA, AFRICA, AND LATIN AMERICA
by Dirk G. Schroeder, ScD, MPH, 197 pages, **$11.95**

"Read this book if you want to stay healthy on any journeys or stays in Asia, Africa, and Latin America."

—*American Journal of Health Promotion*

MOONBELT

A new concept in moneybelts. Made of heavy-duty Cordura nylon, the Moonbelt offers maximum protection for your money and important papers. This pouch, designed for all-weather comfort, slips under your shirt or waistband, rendering it virtually undetectable and inaccessible to pickpockets. It

features a one-inch high-test quick-release buckle so there's no more fumbling around for the strap or repeated adjustments. This handy plastic buckle opens and closes with a touch, but won't come undone until you want it to. Moonbelts accommodate traveler's checks, passports, cash, photos, etc. Size 5 x 9 inches. Available in black only. **$8.95**

PERIPLUS TRAVEL MAPS

Periplus Travel Maps are a necessity for traveling in Southeast Asia. Each map is designed for maximum clarity and utility, combining several views and insets of the area. Transportation information, street indexes, and descriptions of major sites are included in each map. The result is a single map with all the vital information needed to get where you're going. No other maps come close to providing the detail or comprehensive coverage of Asian travel destinations. All maps are updated yearly and produced with digital technology using the latest survey information. **$7.95**

Periplus Travel Maps are available to the following areas:

Bali	Ko Samui/
Bandung/W. Java	Lombok
Bangkok/C. Thailand	S. Thailand
Batam/Bintan	Penang
Cambodia	Phuket/S. Thailand
Chiangmai/N. Thailand	Sabah
Hong Kong	Sarawak
Indonesia	Singapore
Jakarta	Vietnam
Java	Yogyakarta/C. Java
Kuala Lumpur	

VISIT MOON ONLINE

In 1994, Moon Publications created a World Wide Web (WWW) travel information center featuring current and back issues of Moon's quarterly newsletter, *Travel Matters,* and an extended excerpt from Moon's *Staying Healthy in Asia, Africa, and Latin America.* Special features of Moon's Web site include: a sophisticated multimedia adaptation of Moon's *Big Island of Hawaii Handbook,* by J.D. Bisignani, with point-and-click imagemaps and dozens of pictures, sound files, and hypertext links. Also included on the site is *Road Trip USA,* a travel guide to the "blue highways" that crisscross America between and beyond the interstates. The *Road Trip* exhibit includes a map with hundreds of original entries and links to local Internet sites. WWW explorers are encouraged to participate in the exhibit by contributing their own travel tips on small towns, roadside attractions, regional foods, and places to stay. Find our homepage at:

http://www.moon.com

MOON TRAVEL HANDBOOKS

NORTH AMERICA AND HAWAII

Alaska-Yukon Handbook (0161)	$14.95
Alberta and the Northwest Territories Handbook (0676)	$17.95
Arizona Traveler's Handbook (0536)	$16.95
Atlantic Canada Handbook (0072)	$17.95
Big Island of Hawaii Handbook (0064)	$13.95
British Columbia Handbook (0145)	$15.95
*Colorado Handbook (0447)	$18.95
Georgia Handbook (0390)	$17.95
Hawaii Handbook (0005)	$19.95
Honolulu-Waikiki Handbook (0587)	$14.95
Idaho Handbook (0617)	$14.95
Kauai Handbook (0013)	$13.95
Maui Handbook (0579)	$14.95
*Montana Handbook (0498)	$17.95
Nevada Handbook (0641)	$16.95
New Mexico Handbook (0153)	$14.95
Northern California Handbook (3840)	$19.95
Oregon Handbook (0102)	$16.95
*Road Trip USA (0366)	$22.50
Texas Handbook (0633)	$17.95
Utah Handbook (0684)	$16.95
*Washington Handbook (0455)	$18.95
Wyoming Handbook (3980)	$14.95

ASIA AND THE PACIFIC

Bali Handbook (3379)	$12.95
Bangkok Handbook (0595)	$13.95
Fiji Islands Handbook (0382)	$13.95
Hong Kong Handbook (0560)	$15.95
Indonesia Handbook (0625)	$25.00
Japan Handbook (3700)	$22.50
Micronesia Handbook (3808)	$11.95
*Nepal Handbook (0412)	$18.95
*New Zealand Handbook (0331)	$19.95
*Outback Australia Handbook (0471)	$18.95
*Pakistan Handbook (0692)	$22.50
Philippines Handbook (0048)	$17.95

Southeast Asia Handbook (0021)	$21.95
South Korea Handbook (3204)	$14.95
South Pacific Handbook (0404)	$22.95
Tahiti-Polynesia Handbook (0374)	$13.95
*Thailand Handbook (0420)	$19.95
Tibet Handbook (3905)	$30.00
*Vietnam, Cambodia & Laos Handbook (0293)	$18.95

MEXICO

Baja Handbook (0528)	$15.95
Cabo Handbook (0285)	$14.95
Cancún Handbook (0501)	$13.95
Central Mexico Handbook (0234)	$15.95
Mexico Handbook (0315)	$21.95
Northern Mexico Handbook (0226)	$16.95
Pacific Mexico Handbook (0323)	$16.95
Puerto Vallarta Handbook (0250)	$14.95
Yucatán Peninsula Handbook (0242)	$15.95

CENTRAL AMERICA AND THE CARIBBEAN

Belize Handbook (0307)	$15.95
Caribbean Handbook (0277)	$16.95
Costa Rica Handbook (0358)	$19.95
Jamaica Handbook (0129)	$14.95

INTERNATIONAL

Egypt Handbook (3891)	$18.95
Moon Handbook (0668)	$10.00
Moscow-St. Petersburg Handbook (3913)	$13.95
Staying Healthy in Asia, Africa, and Latin America (0269)	$11.95

* New title or edition, please call for availability

PERIPLUS TRAVEL MAPS

All maps $7.95 each

Bali	Indonesia	Penang
Bandung/W. Java	Jakarta	Phuket/S. Thailand
Bangkok/C. Thailand	Java	Sabah
Batam/Bintan	Kuala Lumpur	Sarawak
Cambodia	Ko Samui/	Singapore
Chiangmai/N. Thailand	Lombok	Vietnam
Hong Kong	S. Thailand	Yogyakarta/C. Java

WHERE TO BUY MOON TRAVEL HANDBOOKS

BOOKSTORES AND LIBRARIES: Moon Travel Handbooks are sold worldwide. Please contact our sales manager for a list of wholesalers and distributors in your area.

TRAVELERS: We would like to have Moon Travel Handbooks available throughout the world. Please ask your bookstore to write or call us for ordering information. If your bookstore will not order our guides for you, please contact us for a free title listing.

> **Moon Publications, Inc.**
> **P.O. Box 3040**
> **Chico, CA 95927-3040 U.S.A.**
> **tel.: (800) 345-5473**
> **fax: (916) 345-6751**
> **e-mail: travel@moon.com**

IMPORTANT ORDERING INFORMATION

PRICES: All prices are subject to change. We always ship the most current edition. We will let you know if there is a price increase on the book you order.

SHIPPING AND HANDLING OPTIONS: Domestic UPS or USPS first class (allow 10 working days for delivery): $3.50 for the first item, 50 cents for each additional item.

EXCEPTIONS: *Tibet Handbook* and *Indonesia Handbook* shipping $4.50; $1.00 for each additional *Tibet Handbook* or *Indonesia Handbook*.

Moonbelt shipping is $1.50 for one, 50 cents for each additional belt.

Add $2.00 for same-day handling.

UPS 2nd Day Air or Printed Airmail requires a special quote.

International Surface Bookrate 8-12 weeks delivery: $3.00 for the first item, $1.00 for each additional item. Note: Moon Publications cannot guarantee international surface bookrate shipping. Moon recommends sending international orders via air mail, which requires a special quote.

FOREIGN ORDERS: Orders that originate outside the U.S.A. must be paid for with either an international money order or a check in U.S. currency drawn on a major U.S. bank based in the U.S.A.

TELEPHONE ORDERS: We accept Visa or MasterCard payments. Minimum order is US$15.00. Call in your order: (800) 345-5473, 8 a.m.-5 p.m. Pacific standard time.